Artificial Higher Order Neural Networks for Computer Science and Engineering:
Trends for Emerging Applications

Ming Zhang
Christopher Newport University, USA

INFORMATION SCIENCE REFERENCE
Hershey · New York

Director of Editorial Content:	Kristin Klinger
Director of Book Publications:	Julia Mosemann
Acquisitions Editor:	Mike Killian
Development Editor:	Joel Gamon
Publishing Assistant:	Kurt Smith
Typesetter:	Devvin Earnest
Quality control:	Jamie Snavely
Cover Design:	Lisa Tosheff
Printed at:	Yurchak Printing Inc.

Published in the United States of America by
Information Science Reference (an imprint of IGI Global)
701 E. Chocolate Avenue
Hershey PA 17033
Tel: 717-533-8845
Fax: 717-533-8661
E-mail: cust@igi-global.com
Web site: http://www.igi-global.com/reference

Library of Congress Cataloging-in-Publication Data

Artificial higher order neural networks for computer science and engineering : trends for emerging applications / Ming Zhang, editor.
    p. cm.
  Includes bibliographical references and index.
  Summary: "This book introduces and explains Higher Order Neural Networks (HONNs) to people working in the fields of computer science and computer engineering, and how to use HONNS in these areas"--Provided by publisher.
  ISBN 978-1-61520-711-4 (hardcover) -- ISBN 978-1-61520-712-1 (ebook) 1. Neural networks (Computer science) 2. Computer science--Data processing. 3. Computer engineering--Data processing. I. Zhang, Ming, 1949 July 29-
  QA76.87.A698 2010
  006.3'2--dc22
                    2009050067

British Cataloguing in Publication Data
A Cataloguing in Publication record for this book is available from the British Library.

All work contributed to this book is new, previously-unpublished material. The views expressed in this book are those of the authors, but not necessarily of the publisher.

Dedication

To
my mother
Wenshao Zuo

and my father
Changdong Zhang

List of Reviewers

M. A. Christodoulou, *Technical University of Crete, Greece*
Satchidananda Dehuri, *Fakir Mohan University, India*
Noriyasu Homma, *Cyberscience Center Tohoku University, Japan*
Yannis L. Karnavas, *Supreme Technological Educational Institution of Crete, Greece*
Frank L. Lewis, *The University of Texas at Arlington, USA*
Zhao Lu, *Tuskegee University, USA*
Junichi Murata, *Kyushu University, Japan*
Siamak Najarian, *Amirkabir University of Technology, Iran*
Joao Pedro Neto, *Faculdade de Ciencias, Portugal*
Luis Ricalde, *Universidad Autonoma de Yucatan, Mexico*
Edgar Sanchez, *Unidad Guadalajara, CINVESTAV, Mexico*
David Selviah, *University College London, UK*
M. N. Vrahatis, *University of Patras, Greece*
Wen Yu, *CINVESTAV-IPN, Mexico*
Ming Zhang, *Christopher Newport University, USA*

Table of Contents

Section 1
Artificial Higher Order Neural Networks for Computer Science

Chapter 1

Ming Zhang, Christopher Newport University, USA

Chapter 2

João Pedro Neto, Faculdade de Ciências, Portugal

Chapter 3

M. G. Epitropakis, University of Patras, Greece
V. P. Plagianakos, University of Patras, Greece
M. N. Vrahatis, University of Patras, Greece

Chapter 4

Shuxiang Xu, University of Tasmania, Australia

Chapter 5

Wen Yu, Cinvestav-IPN, México

Chapter 6

Mohammed Sadiq Al-Rawi, University of Aveiro, Portugal
Kamal R. Al-Rawi, Petra University, Jordan

Detailed Table of Contents

Section 1
Artificial Higher Order Neural Networks for Computer Science

Section 1, Artificial Higher Order Neural Networks for Computer Science, includes chapter 1 to chapter 6. Higher Order Neural Network Group –based Adaptive Trees, Higher Order Neural Networks for Symbolic, Sub-symbolic and Chaotic Computations, Evolutionary algorithm Training of Higher Order Neural Networks, Adaptive Higher order Neural Network Models for Data Mining, Robust Adaptive Control Using Higher Order Neural Networks and Projection, and On the Equivalence between Ordinary Neural Networks and Higher Order Neural Networks are introduced.

Higher Order Neural Network Group-based Adaptive Tolerance Trees, presents the artificial Higher Order Neural Network Group-based Adaptive Tolerance (HONNGAT) Tree model for translation-invariant face recognition. Moreover, face perception classification, detection of front faces with glasses and/or beards, and face recognition results using HONNGAT Trees are presented. The artificial higher order neural network group-based adaptive tolerance tree model is an open box model and can be used to describe complex systems.

Higher Order Neural Networks for Symbolic, Sub-symbolic and Chaotic Computations deals with discrete and recurrent artificial neural networks with a homogenous type of neuron. With this architecture, this chapter shows how to perform symbolic computations by executing high-level programs within this network dynamics. Next, using higher order synaptic connections, it is possible to integrate common sub-symbolic learning algorithms into the previous architecture. Thirdly, taking advantage of the chaotic properties of dynamical systems, this chapter presents some uses of chaotic computations with the same neurons and synapses, and, thus, creating a hybrid system of three computation types.

Chapter 3

M. G. Epitropakis, University of Patras, Greece
V. P. Plagianakos, University of Patras, Greece
M. N. Vrahatis, University of Patras, Greece

Evolutionary Algorithm Training of Higher Order Neural Networks aims to further explore the capabilities of the Higher Order Neural Networks class and especially the Pi-Sigma Neural Networks. The performance of Pi-Sigma Networks is evaluated through several well known neural network training benchmarks. In the experiments reported here, Distributed Evolutionary Algorithms are implemented for Pi-Sigma neural networks training. More specifically, the distributed versions of the Differential Evolution and the Particle Swarm Optimization algorithms have been employed.

Chapter 4

Shuxiang Xu, University of Tasmania, Australia

This chapter addresses using Artificial Neural Networks (ANNs) for data mining because ANNs are a natural technology which may hold superior predictive capability, compared with other data mining approaches. The chapter proposes Adaptive HONN models which hold potential in effectively dealing with discontinuous data and business data with high order nonlinearity. The proposed adaptive models demonstrate advantages in handling several benchmark data mining problems.

Chapter 5

Wen Yu, Cinvestav-IPN, México

Robust Adaptive Control Using Higher Order Neural Networks and Projection, presents a novel robust adaptive approach for a class of unknown nonlinear systems. Firstly, the neural networks are designed to identify the nonlinear systems. Secondly, a linearization controller is proposed based on the neuro identifier. This chapter also proposes a robust neuro-observer, which has an extended Luenberger structure

Chapter 6

Mohammed Sadiq Al-Rawi, University of Aveiro, Portugal
Kamal R. Al-Rawi, Petra University, Jordan

On the Equivalence between Ordinary Neural Networks and Higher Order Neural Networks, studies the equivalence between multilayer feedforward neural networks referred as Ordinary Neural Networks (ONNs) that contain only summation (Sigma) as activation units, and multilayer feedforward Higher order Neural Networks (HONNs) that contains Sigma and product (Pi) activation units.

Section 2
Artificial Higher Order Neural Networks for Simulation and Modeling

Section 2, Artificial Higher Order Neural Networks for Simulation and Modeling, is from chapter 7 to chapter 11. Rainfall Estimation Using Neuron-Adaptive Artificial Higher Order Neural Networks, Analysis of Quantization Effects on Higher Order Function and Multilayer Feedforward Neural Networks, Improving Sparsity in Kernel Principal Component Analysis by Polynomial Kernel Higher Order Neural Networks, Analysis and Improvement of Function Approximation Capabilities of Pi-Sigma Higher Order Neural Networks, and Dynamic Ridge Polynomial Higher Order Neural Network are studied.

Chapter 7

Rainfall Estimation Using Neuron-Adaptive Higher Order Neural Networks, studies the rainfall estimation. Definitions of one-dimensional, two-dimensional, and n-dimensional NAHONN models are studied. Specialized NAHONN models are also described. These models are further shown to be capable of automatically finding not only the optimum model but also the appropriate order for high frequency, multi-polynomial, discontinuous data. This chapter further demonstrates that NAHONN models are capable of modeling satellite data.

Chapter 8

Analysis of Quantization Effects on Higher Order Function and Multilayer Feedforward Neural Networks, investigates the combined effects of quantization and clipping on Higher Order function neural networks (HOFNN) and multilayer feedforward neural networks (MLFNN). These chapters analyzes the performance degradation caused as a function of the number of fixed-point and floating-point quantization bits under the assumption of different probability distributions for the quantized variables, and then compare the training performance between situations with and without weight clipping, and derive in detail the effect of the quantization error on forward and backward propagation.

Chapter 9

Improving Sparsity in Kernelized Nonlinear Feature Extraction Algorithms by Polynomial Kernel Higher Order Neural Networks, studies the polynomial kernel higher order neural networks. This chapter focuses on the application of the newly developed polynomial kernel higher order neural networks in improving the sparsity and thereby obtaining a succinct representation for kernel-based nonlinear feature extraction algorithms. Particularly, the learning algorithm is based on linear programming support vector regression, which outperforms the conventional quadratic programming support vector regression in model sparsity and computational efficiency.

Chapter 10

Junichi Murata, Kyushu University, Japan

Analysis and Improvement of Function Approximation Capabilities of Pi-Sigma Higher Order Neural Networks, finds that A Pi-Sigma higher order neural network (Pi-Sigma HONN) is a type of higher order neural network, where, as its name implies, weighted sums of inputs are calculated first and then the sums are multiplied by each other to produce higher order terms that constitute the network outputs.

Chapter 11

Rozaida Ghazali, Universiti Tun Hussein Onn Malaysia, Malaysia
Abir Jaafar Hussain, Liverpool John Moores University, UK
Nazri Modh Nawi, Universiti Tun Hussein Onn Malaysia, Malaysia

Dynamic ridge Polynomial Higher Order Neural Network, proposes a novel Dynamic Ridge Polynomial Higher Order Neural Network (DRPHONN). The architecture of the new DRPHONN incorporates recurrent links into the structure of the ordinary Ridge Polynomial Higher Order Neural Network (RPHONN). RPHONN is a type of feedforward Higher Order Neural Network (HONN) (Giles & Maxwell, 1987) which implements a static mapping of the input vectors.

Section 3
Artificial Higher Order Neural Networks for Computer Engineering

Section 3, Artificial Higher Order Neural Networks for Computer Engineering, contains chapter 12 to chapter 16. Fifty Years of Electronic Hardware Implementations of First and Higher Order Neural Networks, Recurrent Higher Order Neural Network Control for Output Trajectory Tracking with Neural Observers and Constrained Inputs, Artificial Higher Order Neural Network Training on Limited Precision Processors, Recurrent Higher Order Neural Observers for Anaerobic Processes, and Electrical Machines Excitation Control via Higher Order Neural Networks are presented.

Chapter 12

David Selviah, University College London, UK
Janti Shawash, University College London, UK

Fifty Years of Electronic Hardware Implementations of First and Higher Order Neural Networks, celebrates 50 years of first and higher order neural network (HONN) implementations in terms of the physical layout and structure of electronic hardware, which offers high speed, low latency in compact, low cost, low power, mass produced systems. Low latency is essential for practical applications in real time control for which software implementations running on CPUs are too slow. The chapter traces the chronological development of electronic neural networks (ENN) discussing selected papers in detail from analog electronic hardware, through probabilistic RAM, generalizing RAM, custom silicon Very Large Scale Integrated (VLSI) circuit, Neuromorphic chips, pulse stream interconnected neurons to Application Specific Integrated circuits (ASICs) and Zero Instruction Set Chips (ZISCs).

    Luis J. Ricalde, Universidad Autonoma de Yucatan, Mexico
    Edgar N. Sanchez, CINVESTAV, Unidad Guadalajara, Mexico
    Alma Y. Alanis, CUCEI, Universidad de Guadalajara, Mexico

Recurrent Higher Order Neural Network Control for Output Trajectory Tracking with Neural Observers and Constrained Inputs, presents the design of an adaptive recurrent neural observer-controller scheme for nonlinear systems whose model is assumed to be unknown and with constrained inputs. The control scheme is composed of a neural observer based on Recurrent High Order Neural Networks which builds the state vector of the unknown plant dynamics and a learning adaptation law for the neural network weights for both the observer and identifier. These laws are obtained via control Lyapunov functions.

    Janti Shawash, University College London, UK
    David R. Selviah, University College London, UK

Artificial Higher Order Neural Network Training on Limited Precision Processors, investigates the training of networks using Back Propagation and Levenberg-Marquardt algorithms in limited precision achieving high overall calculation accuracy, using on-line training, a new type of HONN known as the Correlation HONN (CHONN), discrete XOR and continuous optical waveguide sidewall roughness datasets by simulation to find the precision at which the training and operation is feasible. The importance of this chapter findings is that they demonstrate the feasibility of on-line, real-time, low-latency training on limited precision electronic hardware.

    Edgar N. Sanchez, CINVESTAV, Unidad Guadalajara, Mexico
    Diana A. Urrego, CINVESTAV, Unidad Guadalajara, Mexico
    Alma Y. Alanis, Universidad de Guadalajara, Mexico
    Salvador Carlos-Hernandez, CINVESTAV, Unidad Saltillo, México

Recurrent Higher Order Neural Observers for Anaerobic Processes, proposes the design of a discrete-time neural observer which requires no prior knowledge of the model of an anaerobic process, for estimate biomass, substrate and inorganic carbon which are variables difficult to measure and very important for anaerobic process control in a completely stirred tank reactor (CSTR) with biomass filter; this observer is based on a recurrent higher order neural network, trained with an extended Kalman filter based algorithm.

Chapter 16

Electric Machines Excitation Control via Higher Order Neural Networks, is demonstrating a practical design of an intelligent type of controller using higher order neural network (HONN) concepts, for the excitation control of a practical power generating system. This type of controller is suitable for real time operation, and aims to improve the dynamic characteristics of the generating unit by acting properly on its original excitation system. The modeling of the power system under study consists of a synchronous generator connected via a transformer and a transmission line to an infinite bus.

Section 4
Artificial Higher Order Neural Network Models and Applications

Section 4, Artificial Higher Order Neural Network Models and Applications, consists of chapter 17 to chapter 22. Higher Order Neural Networks: Fundamental Theory and Applications, Identification of Nonlinear Systems Using a New Neuro-Fuzzy Dynamical System Definition Based on High Order Neural Network Function Approximators, Neuro – Fuzzy Control Schemes Based on High Order Neural Network Function Aproximators, Back-Stepping Control of Quadrotor: A Dynamically Tuned Higher Order Like Neural Network Approach, Artificial Tactile Sensing and Robotic Surgery Using Higher Order Neural Networks, and A Theoretical and Empirical Study of Functional Link Neural Networks (FLANNs) for Classification are provided.

Chapter 17

Higher Order Neural Networks: Fundamental Theory and Applications, provides fundamental principles of higher order neural units (HONUs) and higher order neural networks (HONNs). An essential core of HONNs can be found in higher order weighted combinations or correlations between the input variables. By using some typical examples, this chapter describes how and why higher order combinations or correlations can be effective.

    Y. S. Boutalis, Democritus University of Thrace, Greece
    M. A. Christodoulou, University of Crete, Greece
    D. C. Theodoridis, Democritus University of Thrace, Greece

Identification of Nonlinear Systems Using a New Neuro-Fuzzy Dynamical System Definition Based on High Order Neural Network Function Approximators, studies the nonlinear systems. A new definition of Adaptive Dynamic Fuzzy Systems (ADFS) is presented in this chapter for the identification of unknown nonlinear dynamical systems. The proposed scheme uses the concept of Adaptive Fuzzy Systems operating in conjunction with High Order Neural Network Functions (HONNFs). Weight updating laws, for the involved HONNFs, are provided, which guarantee that the identification error reaches zero exponentially fast. Simulations illustrate the potency of the method and comparisons on well known benchmarks are given.

    D. C. Theodoridis, Democritus University of Thrace, Greece
    M.A. Christodoulou, Technical University of Crete, Greece
    Y. S. Boutalis, Democritus University of Thrace, Greece

Neuro–Fuzzy Control Schemes Based on High Order Neural Network Function Approximators, studies the control schemes. The indirect or direct adaptive regulation of unknown nonlinear dynamical systems is considered in this chapter. Since the plant is considered unknown, this chapter first proposes its approximation by a special form of a fuzzy dynamical system (FDS) and in the sequel the fuzzy rules are approximated by appropriate HONNFs.

    Abhijit Das, The University of Texas at Arlington, USA
    Frank L. Lewis, The University of Texas at Arlington, USA
    Kamesh Subbarao, The University of Texas at Arlington, USA

A Dynamically Tuned Higher Order Like Neural Network Approach, Studies the control of quadrotor. The dynamics of a quadrotor is a simplified form of helicopter dynamics that exhibit the same basic problems of strong coupling, multi-input/multi-output design, and unknown nonlinearities. The Lagrangian model of a typical quadrotor that involves four inputs and six outputs results in an underactuated system. The stability of the control law is guaranteed by a Lyapunov proof. The control approach described in this chapter is robust since it explicitly deals with un-modeled state dependent disturbances without needing any prior knowledge of the same. A simulation study validates the results such as decoupling, tracking etc obtained in the paper.

Artificial Tactile Sensing and Robotic Surgery Using Higher Order Neural Networks, introduces a new medical instrument, namely, the Tactile Tumor Detector (TTD) able to simulate the sense of touch in clinical and surgical applications. All theoretical and experimental attempts for its construction are presented. Theoretical analyses are mostly based on finite element method (FEM), artificial neural networks (ANN), and higher order neural networks (HONN). The TTD is used for detecting abnormal masses in biological tissue, specifically for breast examinations. The results show that by having an HONN model of our nonlinear input-output mapping, there are many advantages compared with ANN model, including faster running for new data, lesser RMS error and better fitting properties.

A Theoretical and Empirical Study of Functional Link Neural Networks (FLNNs) for Classification, focus on theoretical and empirical study of functional link neural networks (FLNNs) for classification. We present a hybrid Chebyshev functional link neural network (cFLNN) without hidden layer with evolvable particle swarm optimization (ePSO) for classification. The hybrid cFLNN is a type of feed-forward neural networks, which have the ability to transform the non-linear input space into higher dimensional space where linear separability is possible. This chapter shows its effectiveness of classifying the unknown pattern using the datasets.

Preface

This is the first book which introduces Higher Order Neural Networks (HONNs) to people working in the fields of computer science and computer engineering, and presents to them that HONNs is an open box neural networks tool compare to traditional artificial neural networks. This is the first book which includes details of the most popular HONNs models and provides opportunities for millions of people working in the computer science and computer engineering areas to know what HONNs are, and how to use HONNs in computer science and computer engineering areas.

Artificial Neural Networks (ANNs) are known to excel in pattern recognition, pattern matching and mathematical function approximation. However they suffer from several well known limitations– they can often become stuck in local, rather than global minima, as well as taking unacceptably long times to converge in practice. Of particular concern, especially from the perspective of data simulation and predictions, is their inability to handle non-smooth, discontinuous training data, and complex mappings (associations). Another limitation of ANN is a 'black box' nature – meaning that explanations (reasons) for their decisions are not immediately obvious, unlike techniques such as Decision Trees. This then is the motivation for developing artificial Higher Order Neural Networks (HONNs), since HONNs are 'open-box' models and each neuron and weight are mapped to function variable and coefficient.

In recent years, researchers use HONNs for pattern recognition, nonlinear simulation, classification, and prediction in the computer science and computer engineering areas. The results show that HONNs are always faster, more accurate, and easier to explain. This is the second motivation for using HONNs in computer science and computer engineering areas, since HONNs can automatically select the initial coefficients, even automatically select the model for applications in computer science and computer engineering areas.

This book introduces the HONN group models and adaptive HONNs, and makes sure the people working in the computer science and computer engineering areas can understand HONN group models and adaptive HONN models, which can simulate not only nonlinear data, but also discontinuous and unsmooth nonlinear data. The HONNs knowledge from this book will be used in many different areas. This book explains why HONNs can approximate any nonlinear data to any degree of accuracy, and make sure people working in the computer science and computer engineering can understand why HONNs are much easier to use, and HONNs can have better nonlinear data simulation accuracy.

Let millions of people working in the computer science and computer engineering areas know that HONNs are much easier to use and can have better simulation results, and understand how to successfully use HONNs model and hardware designs for nonlinear data simulation and prediction. HONNs will challenge traditional artificial neural network products and change the research methodology that people are currently using in computer science and computer engineering areas for the pattern recognition, nonlinear simulation, classification, and prediction. Artificial neural network research is one of the new directions for new generation computers. Current research suggests that open box artificial HONNs play an important role in this new direction. Since HONNs are open box models, they can be easily accepted and used by the people working in the information science, information technology, management, economics, and business areas.

The book is organized into four sections and a total of twenty two chapters. Section 1, Artificial Higher Order Neural Networks for Computer Science, includes chapter 1 to chapter 6. Section 2, Artificial Higher Order Neural Networks for Simulation and Modeling, is from chapter 7 to chapter 11. Section 3, Artificial Higher Order Neural Networks for Computer Engineering, contains chapter 12 to chapter 16. Section 4, Artificial Higher Order Neural Network Models and Applications, consists of chapter 17 to chapter 22. The brief descriptions of each of the chapters are as follows:

Chapter 1, Higher Order Neural Network Group-based Adaptive Tolerance Trees, presents the artificial Higher Order Neural Network Group-based Adaptive Tolerance (HONNGAT) Tree model for translation-invariant face recognition. Moreover, face perception classification, detection of front faces with glasses and/or beards, and face recognition results using HONNGAT Trees are presented. When 10% random number noise is added, the accuracy of HONNGAT Tree for face recognition is 1% higher that artificial neural network Group-based Adaptive Tolerance (GAT) Tree, and is 6 % higher than a general tree. When the gamma value of the Gaussian Noise exceeds 0.3, the accuracy of HONNGAT Tree for face recognition is 2% higher than GAT Tree, and is about 9 % higher than that of a general tree. The artificial higher order neural network group-based adaptive tolerance tree model is an open box model and can be used to describe complex systems.

Chapter 2, Higher Order Neural Networks for Symbolic, Sub-symbolic and Chaotic Computations, deals with discrete and recurrent artificial neural networks with a homogenous type of neuron. With this architecture, this chapter shows how to perform symbolic computations by executing high-level programs within this network dynamics. Next, using higher order synaptic connections, it is possible to integrate common sub-symbolic learning algorithms into the previous architecture. Thirdly, taking advantage of the chaotic properties of dynamical systems, this chapter presents some uses of chaotic computations with the same neurons and synapses, and, thus, creating a hybrid system of three computation types.

Chapter 3, Evolutionary Algorithm Training of Higher Order Neural Networks, aims to further explore the capabilities of the Higher Order Neural Networks class and especially the Pi-Sigma Neural Networks. The performance of Pi-Sigma Networks is evaluated through several well known neural network training benchmarks. In the experiments reported here, Distributed Evolutionary Algorithms are implemented for Pi-Sigma neural networks training. More specifically, the distributed versions of the Differential Evolution and the Particle Swarm Optimization algorithms have been employed. Each processor of a distributed computing environment is assigned a subpopulation of potential solutions. The subpopulations are independently evolved in parallel and occasional migration is allowed to facilitate the cooperation between them. The novelty of the proposed approach is that it is applied to train Pi-Sigma networks using threshold activation functions, while the weights and biases were confined in a narrow band of integers (constrained in the range [-32, 32]). Thus, the trained Pi-Sigma neural networks can be represented by using only 6 bits. Such networks are better suited for hardware implementation than the real weight ones and this property is very important in real-life applications. Experimental results suggest that the proposed training process is fast, stable and reliable and the distributed trained Pi-Sigma networks exhibit good generalization capabilities.

Chapter 4, Adaptive Higher Order Neural Network Models for Data Mining, discusses the data mining. Data mining, the extraction of hidden patterns and valuable information from large databases, is a powerful technology with great potential to help companies survive competition. Data mining tools search databases for hidden patterns, finding predictive information that business experts may overlook because it lies outside their expectations. This chapter addresses using Artificial Neural Networks (ANNs) for data mining because ANNs are a natural technology which may hold superior predictive capability, compared with other data mining approaches. The chapter proposes Adaptive HONN models which hold potential in effectively dealing with discontinuous data and business data with high order nonlinearity. The proposed adaptive models demonstrate advantages in handling several benchmark data mining problems.

Chapter 5, Robust Adaptive Control Using Higher Order Neural Networks and Projection, presents a novel robust adaptive approach for a class of unknown nonlinear systems. Firstly, the neural networks are designed to identify the nonlinear systems. Dead-zone and projection techniques are applied to weights training, in order to avoid singular cases. Secondly, a linearization controller is proposed based on the neuro identifier. Since the approximation capability of the neural networks is limited, four types of compensators are addressed. This chapter also proposes a robust neuro-observer, which has an extended Luenberger structure. Its weights are learned on-line by a new adaptive gradient-like technique. The control scheme is based on the proposed neuro-observer. The final structure is composed by two parts: the neuro-observer and the tracking controller. The simulations of a two-link robot show the effectiveness of the proposed algorithm.

Chapter 6, On the Equivalence between Ordinary Neural Networks and Higher Order Neural Networks, studyiesthe equivalence between multilayer feedforward neural networks referred as Ordinary Neural Networks (ONNs) that contain only summation (Sigma) as activation units, and multilayer feedforward Higher order Neural Networks (HONNs) that contains Sigma and product (Pi) activation units. Since the time they were introduced by Giles and Maxwell (1987), HONNs have been used in many supervised classification and function approximation applications. Within the context discussed in this chapter, HONNs are given in a form that weights are adjustable real-valued numbers (on contrary to most of the previous works were HONN weights are non-negative integers). In doing that, HONNs have more expressive power and the possibility of being trapped in a local minim is reduced. This real-valued weights notion was not possible without introducing a proper normalization to the input data as well as proposing a modification to the neuron activation function. Using simple mathematics and by proposing a normalization to the input data, it is easy to show that HONNs are equivalent to ONNs. The converted ONN posses the features of the HONN and they have exactly the same functionality and output. The proposed conversion of HONN to ONN would permit using the huge amount of optimization algorithms to speed up the convergence of HONN and/or finding better topology. Recurrent HONNs and cascaded correlation HONNs can be simply defined via their equivalent ONNs and then trained with backpropagation, scaled conjugate gradient, Lavenberg-Marqudat algorithm, brain damage algorithms. Using the developed equivalency model, this chapter also gives an easy method to convert a HONN to its equivalent ONN. Results on XOR and function approximation problems showed that ONNs obtained from their corresponding HONNs converged well to a solution. Different optimization training algorithms have been tested on feedforward structure and cascade correlation where the later have shown excellent function approximation results.

Chapter 7, Rainfall Estimation Using Neuron-Adaptive Higher Order Neural Networks, studies the rainfall estimation. Real world data is often nonlinear, discontinuous and may comprise high frequency, multi-polynomial components. Not surprisingly, it is hard to find the best models for modeling such data. Classical neural network models are unable to automatically determine the optimum model and appropriate order for data approximation. In order to solve this problem, Neuron-Adaptive Higher

Order Neural Network (NAHONN) Models have been introduced. Definitions of one-dimensional, two-dimensional, and n-dimensional NAHONN models are studied. Specialized NAHONN models are also described. NAHONN models are shown to be "open box". These models are further shown to be capable of automatically finding not only the optimum model but also the appropriate order for high frequency, multi-polynomial, discontinuous data. Rainfall estimation experimental results confirm model convergence. This chapter further demonstrates that NAHONN models are capable of modeling satellite data. When the Xie and Scofield (1989) technique was used, the average error of the operator-computed IFFA rainfall estimates was 30.41%. For the Artificial Neural Network (ANN) reasoning network, the training error was 6.55% and the test error 16.91%, respectively. When the neural network group was used on these same fifteen cases, the average training error of rainfall estimation was 1.43%, and the average test error of rainfall estimation was 3.89%. When the neuron-adaptive artificial neural network group models was used on these same fifteen cases, the average training error of rainfall estimation was 1.31%, and the average test error of rainfall estimation was 3.40%. When the artificial neuron-adaptive higher order neural network model was used on these same fifteen cases, the average training error of rainfall estimation was 1.20%, and the average test error of rainfall estimation was 3.12%.

Chapter 8, Analysis of Quantization Effects on Higher Order Function and Multilayer Feedforward Neural Networks, investigates the combined effects of quantization and clipping on Higher Order function neural networks (HOFNN) and multilayer feedforward neural networks (MLFNN). Statistical models are used to analyze the effects of quantization in a digital implementation. This chapter analyzes the performance degradation caused as a function of the number of fixed-point and floating-point quantization bits under the assumption of different probability distributions for the quantized variables, and then compares the training performance between situations with and without weight clipping, and derive in detail the effect of the quantization error on forward and backward propagation. No matter what distribution the initial weights comply with, the weights distribution will approximate a normal distribution for the training of floating-point or high-precision fixed-point quantization. Only when the number of quantization bits is very low, the weights distribution may cluster to ±1 for the training with fixed-point quantization. This chapter establishes and analyzes the relationships for a true nonlinear neuron between inputs and outputs bit resolution, training and quantization methods, the number of network layers, network order and performance degradation, all based on statistical models, and for on-chip and off-chip training. The experimental simulation results verify the presented theoretical analysis.

Chapter 9, Improving Sparsity in Kernelized Nonlinear Feature Extraction Algorithms by Polynomial Kernel Higher Order Neural Networks, studies the polynomial kernel higher order neural networks. As a general framework to represent data, the kernel method can be used if the interactions between elements of the domain occur only through inner product. As a major stride towards the nonlinear feature extraction and dimension reduction, two important kernel-based feature extraction algorithms, kernel principal component analysis and kernel Fisher discriminant, have been proposed. They are both used to create a projection of multivariate data onto a space of lower dimensionality, while attempting to preserve as much of the structural nature of the data as possible. However, both methods suffer from the complete loss of sparsity and redundancy in the nonlinear feature representation. In an attempt to mitigate these drawbacks, this chapter focuses on the application of the newly developed polynomial kernel higher order neural networks in improving the sparsity and thereby obtaining a succinct representation for kernel-based nonlinear feature extraction algorithms. Particularly, the learning algorithm is based on linear programming support vector regression, which outperforms the conventional quadratic programming support vector regression in model sparsity and computational efficiency.

Chapter 10, Analysis and Improvement of Function Approximation Capabilities of Pi-Sigma Higher Order Neural Networks, finds that A Pi-Sigma higher order neural network (Pi-Sigma HONN) is a type of higher order neural network, where, as its name implies, weighted sums of inputs are calculated first and then the sums are multiplied by each other to produce higher order terms that constitute the network outputs. This type of higher order neural networks have good function approximation capabilities. In this chapter, the structural feature of Pi-Sigma HONNs is discussed in contrast to other types of neural networks. The reason for their good function approximation capabilities is given based on pseudo-theoretical analysis together with empirical illustrations. Then, based on the analysis, an improved version of Pi-Sigma HONNs is proposed which has yet better functions approximation capabilities.

Chapter 11, Dynamic Ridge Polynomial Higher Order Neural Network, proposes a novel Dynamic Ridge Polynomial Higher Order Neural Network (DRPHONN). The architecture of the new DRPHONN incorporates recurrent links into the structure of the ordinary Ridge Polynomial Higher Order Neural Network (RPHONN). RPHONN is a type of feedforward Higher Order Neural Network (HONN) (Giles & Maxwell, 1987) which implements a static mapping of the input vectors. In order to model dynamical functions of the brain, it is essential to utilize a system that is capable of storing internal states and can implement complex dynamic system. Neural networks with recurrent connections are dynamical systems with temporal state representations. The dynamic structure approach has been successfully used for solving varieties of problems, such as time series forecasting, approximating a dynamical system (Kimura & Nakano, 2000), forecasting a stream flow, and system control. Motivated by the ability of recurrent dynamic systems in real world applications, the proposed DRPHONN architecture is presented in this chapter.

Chapter 12, Fifty Years of Electronic Hardware Implementations of First and Higher Order Neural Networks, celebrates 50 years of first and higher order neural network (HONN) implementations in terms of the physical layout and structure of electronic hardware, which offers high speed, low latency in compact, low cost, low power, mass produced systems. Low latency is essential for practical applications in real time control for which software implementations running on CPUs are too slow. The chapter traces the chronological development of electronic neural networks (ENN) discussing selected papers in detail from analog electronic hardware, through probabilistic RAM, generalizing RAM, custom silicon Very Large Scale Integrated (VLSI) circuit, Neuromorphic chips, pulse stream interconnected neurons to Application Specific Integrated circuits (ASICs) and Zero Instruction Set Chips (ZISCs). Reconfigurable Field Programmable Gate Arrays (FPGAs) are given particular attention as the most recent generation incorporate Digital Signal Processing (DSP) units to provide full System on Chip (SoC) capability offering the possibility of real-time on-line and on-chip learning.

Chapter 13, Recurrent Higher Order Neural Network Control for Output Trajectory Tracking with Neural Observers and Constrained Inputs, presents the design of an adaptive recurrent neural observer-controller scheme for nonlinear systems whose model is assumed to be unknown and with constrained inputs. The control scheme is composed of a neural observer based on Recurrent High Order Neural Networks which builds the state vector of the unknown plant dynamics and a learning adaptation law for the neural network weights for both the observer and identifier. These laws are obtained via control Lyapunov functions. Then, a control law, which stabilizes the tracking error dynamics is developed using the Lyapunov and the inverse optimal control methodologies. Tracking error boundedness is established as a function of design parameters.

Chapter 14, Artificial Higher Order Neural Network Training on Limited Precision Processors, investigates the training of networks using Back Propagation and Levenberg-Marquardt algorithms in limited precision achieving high overall calculation accuracy, using on-line training, a new type of HONN known as the Correlation HONN (CHONN), discrete XOR and continuous optical waveguide sidewall roughness datasets by simulation to find the precision at which the training and operation is feasible. The BP algorithm converged to a precision beyond which the performance did not improve. The results support previous findings in literature for Artificial Neural Network operation that discrete datasets require lower precision than continuous datasets. The importance of this chapter findings is that they demonstrate the feasibility of on-line, real-time, low-latency training on limited precision electronic hardware.

Chapter 15, Recurrent Higher Order Neural Observers for Anaerobic Processes, proposes the design of a discrete-time neural observer which requires no prior knowledge of the model of an anaerobic process, for estimate biomass, substrate and inorganic carbon which are variables difficult to measure and very important for anaerobic process control in a completely stirred tank reactor (CSTR) with biomass filter; this observer is based on a recurrent higher order neural network, trained with an extended Kalman filter based algorithm.

Chapter 16, Electric Machines Excitation Control via Higher Order Neural Networks, is demonstrating a practical design of an intelligent type of controller using higher order neural network (HONN) concepts, for the excitation control of a practical power generating system. This type of controller is suitable for real time operation, and aims to improve the dynamic characteristics of the generating unit by acting properly on its original excitation system. The modeling of the power system under study consists of a synchronous generator connected via a transformer and a transmission line to an infinite bus. For comparison purposes and also for producing useful data in order for the demonstrating neural network controllers to be trained, digital simulations of the above system are performed using fuzzy logic control (FLC) techniques, which are based on previous work. Then, two neural network controllers are designed and applied by adopting the HONN architectures. The first one utilizes a single pi-sigma neural network (PSNN) and the significant advantages over the standard multi layered perceptron (MLP) are discussed. Secondly, an enhanced controller is designed, leading to a ridge polynomial neural network (RPNN) by combining multiple PSNNs if needed. Both controllers used, can be pre-trained rapidly from the corresponding FLC output signal and act as model dynamics capturers. The dynamic performances of the fuzzy logic controller (FLC) along with those of the two demonstrated controllers are presented by comparison using the well known integral square error criterion (ISE). The latter controllers, show excellent convergence properties and accuracy for function approximation. Typical transient responses of the system are shown for comparison in order to demonstrate the effectiveness of the designed controllers. The computer simulation results obtained show clearly that the performance of the developed controllers offers competitive damping effects on the synchronous generator's oscillations, with respect to the associated ones of the FLC, over a wider range of operating conditions, while their hardware implementation is apparently much easier and the computational time needed for real-time applications is drastically reduced.

Chapter 17, Higher Order Neural Networks: Fundamental Theory and Applications, provides fundamental principles of higher order neural units (HONUs) and higher order neural networks (HONNs). An essential core of HONNs can be found in higher order weighted combinations or correlations between the input variables. By using some typical examples, this chapter describes how and why higher order combinations or correlations can be effective.

Chapter 18, Identification of Nonlinear Systems Using a New Neuro-Fuzzy Dynamical System Definition Based on High Order Neural Network Function Approximators, studies the nonlinear systems. A new definition of Adaptive Dynamic Fuzzy Systems (ADFS) is presented in this chapter for the identification of unknown nonlinear dynamical systems. The proposed scheme uses the concept of Adaptive Fuzzy Systems operating in conjunction with High Order Neural Network Functions (HONNFs). Since the plant is considered unknown, this chapter first proposes its approximation by a special form of an adaptive fuzzy system and in the sequel the fuzzy rules are approximated by appropriate HONNFs. Thus the identification scheme leads up to a Recurrent High Order Neural Network, which however takes into account the fuzzy output partitions of the initial ADFS. Weight updating laws, for the involved HONNFs, are provided, which guarantee that the identification error reaches zero exponentially fast. Simulations illustrate the potency of the method and comparisons on well known benchmarks are given.

Chapter 19, Neuro–Fuzzy Control Schemes Based on High Order Neural Network Function Approximators, studies the control schemes. The indirect or direct adaptive regulation of unknown nonlinear dynamical systems is considered in this chapter. Since the plant is considered unknown, this chapter first proposes its approximation by a special form of a fuzzy dynamical system (FDS) and in the sequel the fuzzy rules are approximated by appropriate HONNFs. The system is regulated to zero adaptively by providing weight updating laws for the involved HONNFs, which guarantee that both the identification error and the system states reach zero exponentially fast. At the same time, all signals in the closed loop are kept bounded. The existence of the control signal is always assured by introducing a novel method of parameter hopping, which is incorporated in the weight updating laws. The indirect control scheme is developed for square systems (number of inputs equal to the number of states) as well as for systems in Brunovsky canonical form. The direct control scheme is developed for systems in square form. Simulations illustrate the potency of the method and comparisons with conventional approaches on benchmarking systems are given.

Chapter 20, Back-Stepping Control of Quadrotor: A Dynamically Tuned Higher Order Like Neural Network Approach, Studies the control of quadrotor. The dynamics of a quadrotor is a simplified form of helicopter dynamics that exhibit the same basic problems of strong coupling, multi-input/multi-output design, and unknown nonlinearities. The Lagrangian model of a typical quadrotor that involves four inputs and six outputs results in an underactuated system. There are several design techniques are available for nonlinear control of mechanical underactuated system. One of the most popular among them is backstepping. Backstepping is a well known recursive procedure where underactuation characteristic of the system is resolved by defining 'desired' virtual control and virtual state variables. Virtual control variables is determined in each recursive step assuming the corresponding subsystem is Lyapunov stable and virtual states are typically the errors of actual and desired virtual control variables. The application of the backstepping is even more interesting when a virtual control law is applied to a Lagrangian subsystem. The necessary information to select virtual control and state variables for these systems can be obtained through model identification methods. One of these methods includes Neural Network approximation to identify the unknown parameters of the system. The unknown parameters may include uncertain aerodynamic force and moment coefficients or unmodeled dynamics. These aerodynamic coefficients generally are the functions of higher order state polynomials. This chapter discusses how can implement linear in parameter first order neural network approximation methods to identify these unknown higher order state polynomials in every recursive step of the backstepping. Thus the first order neural network eventually estimates the higher order state polynomials which is in fact a higher order like neural net (HOLNN). Moreover, when these artificial Neural Networks are placed into a control loop, they become dynamic artificial Neural Network whose weights are tuned only. Due to the inherent characteristics of the quadrotor, the Lagrangian form for the position dynamics is bilinear in the controls, which is confronted using a bilinear inverse kinematics solution. The result is a controller of intuitively appealing structure having an outer kinematics loop for position control and an inner dynamics loop for attitude control. The stability of the control law is guaranteed by a Lyapunov proof. The control approach described in this chapter is robust since it explicitly deals with un-modeled state dependent disturbances without needing any prior knowledge of the same. A simulation study validates the results such as decoupling, tracking etc obtained in the paper.

Chapter 21, Artificial Tactile Sensing and Robotic Surgery Using Higher Order Neural Networks, introduces a new medical instrument, namely, the Tactile Tumor Detector (TTD) able to simulate the sense of touch in clinical and surgical applications. All theoretical and experimental attempts for its construction are presented. Theoretical analyses are mostly based on finite element method (FEM), artificial neural networks (ANN), and higher order neural networks (HONN). The TTD is used for detecting abnormal masses in biological tissue, specifically for breast examinations. This chapter presents a research work on ANN and HONN done on the theoretical results of the TTD to reduce the subjectivity of estimation in diagnosing tumor characteristics. This chapter uses HONN as a stronger open box intelligent unit than traditional black box neural networks (NN) for estimating the characteristics of tumor and tissue. The results show that by having an HONN model of our nonlinear input-output mapping, there are many advantages compared with ANN model, including faster running for new data, lesser RMS error and better fitting properties.

Chapter 22, A Theoretical and Empirical Study of Functional Link Neural Networks (FLNNs) for Classification, focus on theoretical and empirical study of functional link neural networks (FLNNs) for classification. We present a hybrid Chebyshev functional link neural network (cFLNN) without hidden layer with evolvable particle swarm optimization (ePSO) for classification. The resulted classifier is then used for assigning proper class label to an unknown sample. The hybrid cFLNN is a type of feed-forward neural networks, which have the ability to transform the non-linear input space into higher dimensional space where linear separability is possible. In particular, the proposed hybrid cFLNN combines the best attribute of evolvable particle swarm optimization (ePSO), back-propagation learning (BP-Learning), and Chebyshev functional link neural networks (CFLNN). This chapter shows its effectiveness of classifying the unknown pattern using the datasets. The computational results are then compared with other higher order neural networks (HONNs) like functional link neural network with a generic basis functions, Pi-Sigma neural network (PSNN), radial basis function neural network (RBFNN), and ridge polynomial neural network (RPNN).

Acknowledgment

The editor would like to acknowledge the help of all involved in the collation and the review process of the book, without whose support the project could not have been satisfactorily completed. Deep appreciation and gratitude are due to Prof. David Doughty, Dean of College of Natural and Behavioral Sciences, Prof. Douglas Gordon, former Dean of College of Liberal Arts and Sciences, and Prof. George Webb, former Dean of College of Sciences, Christopher Newport University, for giving me grants to support my research and the editing this book. Deep appreciation and gratitude are also due to Dr. Edward Brash, Chair of Department of Physics, Computer Science and Engineering, Professor. A. Martin Buoncristiani and Professor Randall Caton, former Chairs of Department of Physics, Computer Science and Engineering, Christopher Newport University, for providing research funding to support my research. My appreciations are also due to Dr. David Hibler, Professors of Department of Physics, Computer Science and Engineering, Christopher Newport University, for always strongly supporting my research. I would like thank my distinction supervisor, Dr. Rod Scofield, retired Senior Scientist of National Oceanic and Atmospheric Administration (NOAA), Washington DC, USA for supporting my artificial neural network research and awarding me as an USA National Research Council Postdoctoral Fellow (1991-1992) and a Senior USA National Research Council Research Associate (1999-2000). I would like to thank Dr. John Fulcher, Professor of University of Wollongong in Australia, for a long time of research cooperation in the artificial neural network area since 1992.

I wish to thank all of the authors for their insights and excellent contributions to this book. Most of the authors of chapters included in this book also served as referees for chapters written by other authors. Thanks go to all the reviewers who provided constructive and comprehensive reviews and suggestions.

Special thanks also go to the publishing team at IGI Global, whose contributions throughout the whole process from inception of the initial idea to final publication have been invaluable. In particular to Joel Gamon, and Rebecca Beistline, who continuously prodded via e-mail for keeping the project on schedule, and to Kristin M. Klinger and Jan Travers whose enthusiasm motivated me to initially accept this invitation for taking on this project.

Special thanks go to my family for their continuous support and encouragement, in particular, to my wife, Zhao Qing Zhang, for her unfailing support and encouragement during the years it took to give birth to this book.

Ming Zhang
Editor, PhD & Professor
Christopher Newport University, USA
July 29th, 2009

Section 1
Artificial Higher Order Neural Networks for Computer Science

Chapter 1
Higher Order Neural Network Group–Based Adaptive Tolerance Trees

Ming Zhang
Christopher Newport University, USA

ABSTRACT

Recent artificial higher order neural network research has focused on simple models, but such models have not been very successful in describing complex systems (such as face recognition). This chapter presents the artificial Higher Order Neural Network Group-based Adaptive Tolerance (HONNGAT) Tree model for translation-invariant face recognition. Moreover, face perception classification, detection of front faces with glasses and/or beards, and face recognition results using HONNGAT Trees are presented. When 10% random number noise is added, the accuracy of HONNGAT Tree for face recognition is 1% higher that artificial neural network Group-based Adaptive Tolerance (GAT) Tree, and is 6% higher than a general tree. When the gamma value of the Gaussian Noise exceeds 0.3, the accuracy of HONNGAT Tree for face recognition is 2% higher than GAT Tree, and is about 9% higher than that of a general tree. The artificial higher order neural network group-based adaptive tolerance tree model is an open box model and can be used to describe complex systems.

INTRODUCTION

Artificial higher order neural network models have been widely used for patten recognition with the benefit of HONNs being open box models (Bishop (1995); Park, Smith, & Mersereau (2000); Spirkovska, & Reid (1992, and1994); and Zhang, Xu, & Fulcher (2007)). Shin and Ghosh (1991) introduce a novel feedforward network called the pi-sigma network. This network utilizes product cells as the output units to indirectly incorporate the capabilities of higher order networks while using a fewer number of weights and processing units. The pi-sigma network is an efficient higher order neural network for

DOI: 10.4018/978-1-61520-711-4.ch001

pattern classification and function approximation. Linhart and Dorffner (1992) present a self-learning visual pattern explorer and recognizer using a higher order neural network, which could improve the efficiency of higher order neural networks, is built into a pattern recognition system that autonomously learns to categorize and recognize patterns independently of their position in an input image. Schmidt and Davis (1993) explore alternatives that reduce the number of network weights while pattern recognition properties of various feature spaces for higher order neural networks. Spirkovska and Reid (1993) describe coarse-coded higher order neural networks for PSRI object recognition. The authors describe a coarse coding technique and present simulation results illustrating its usefulness and its limitations. Simulations show that a third-order neural network can be trained to distinguish between two objects of 4096×4096 pixels. Wan and Sun (1996) show that the higher order neural networks (HONN) have numerous advantages over other translational rotational scaling invariant (TRSI) pattern recognition techniques for automatic target recognition. Morad and Yuan (1998) present a method for automatic model building from multiple images of an object to be recognized. The model contains knowledge which has been computed during the learning phase from large 2D images of an object for automatic model building and 3D object recognition. A neuro-based adaptive higher order neural network model has been developed by Zhang, Xu, and Fulcher (2002) for data model recognition. Voutriaridis, Boutalis, and Mertzios (2003) propose ridge polynomial networks in pattern recognition. Ridge polynomial networks (RPNs) are special class of high order neural networks with the ability of high order neural networks for perform shift and rotation. Development of new higher order neural network models for face recognition is the first motivation of the chapter.

Artificial higher order neural networks have very successfully been used for invariant pattern recognition (Artyomov and Yadid-Pecht (2005); He and Siyal (1999); Kaita, Tomita, & Yamanaka (2002); Kanaoka, Chellappa, Yoshitaka, & Tomita (1992), and Lisboa & Perantonis (1991)). Reid, Spirkovska, and Ochoa (1989) demonstrate a second-order neural network that has learned to distinguish between two objects, regardless of their size or translational position, after being trained on only one view of each object. Spirkovska and Reid (1990a) present the results of experiments comparing the performance of the symbolic learning algorithm with a higher order neural network in the distortion invariant object recognition domain. Spirkovska and Reid (1990b) study the connectivity strategies for non-fully connected higher order neural networks and shown that by using such strategies an input field of 128×128 pixels can be attained while still achieving in-plane rotation and invariant recognition. Spirkovska and Reid (1991) present a coarse-coding applied to HONNs, in which the invariances are built directly into the architecture of a HONN, for object recognition. It is noted that a higher order neural network (HONN) can be easily designed for position, scale, and rotation invariant (PSRI) object recognition. Zhou, Koch, & Roberts (1991) find that selective attention can be used to reduce the number of inputs for a high-order neural network and, by selecting appropriate scanning mechanism, invariance to translation can be developed for invariant object recognition. Perantonis and Lisboa (1992) discuss the recognition of two-dimensional patterns independently of their position, orientation, and size by using high-order networks. A method is introduced for reducing and controlling the number of weights of a third-order neural network. Wu and Chang (1993) explore the use of the higher order neural networks to implement an invariant pattern recognition system that is insensitive to translation, rotation, and scaling. Kroner (1995) uses adaptive averaging in higher order neural networks for invariant pattern recognition, and found that, for the task of position invariant, scale invariant, and rotation invariant pattern recognition, higher order neural networks have shown good separation results for different object classes. He and Siyal (1998) try to recognize transformed English letters with modified higher order neural networks.

The authors found that higher order neural networks (HONNs) are effective neural models for invariant pattern recognition. However, one of the main problems in HONNs is that they are sensitive to distortion of the input patterns. Wang, Sun, and Chen (2003) study the recognition of digital annotation with invariant HONN based on orthogonal Fourier-Mellin moments. A recently developed type of moments, Orthogonal Fourier-Mellin Moments (OFMMs) is applied to the specific problem of full scale and rotation invariant recognition of digital annotation. Zhang, Jing, and Li (2004) propose a new fast high-order neural network learning algorithm for invariant pattern recognition. The new learning algorithm uses some properties of trigonometry for reducing and controlling the number of weights of a third-order network used for invariant pattern recognition. The new models of HONN shold recognize the invirant face is the second motivation of the chapter.

Few Artificial Neural Network (ANN) research has concentrated on neural network group models. Naimark and Stern (1982) present a theory of group representations for face processing models. Matsuoka, Hamada, and Nakatsu[1989] studied the integrated neural network. Pentland and Turk [1989] provide holistic model. Tsao (1989) uses Lie group theory to the computer simulation of 3D rigid motion. Unlike the research previously described, Yang (1990) concerns himself with the activities of neuron *groups*. Willcox (1991) devises the neural network hierarchical model which consists of binary-state neurons grouped into clusters, and can be analysed using a Renormalization Group (RG) approach. Lumer (1992) proposes a new mechanism of selective attention among perceptual groups as part of his computational model of early vision. Hu (1992) proposes a level-by-level learning scheme for artificial neural groups. Zhang, Fulcher, and Scofield (1997) develop artificial neural network group for rainfall estimation. This work in addition to other studies in this field, can be used as the basis for higher order neural network group theory, which is the third motivation of this chapter.

Conventional ANN models are incapable of handling discontinuities in the input training data. ANNs do not always perform well because of the complexity of the patterns. Artificial neural networks function as "black boxes", and thus are unable to provide explanations for their behavior. The "black boxes" characteristic is seen as a disadvantage by users, who prefer to be presented with a rationale for the recognition being generated. In an effort to overcome these limitations, interest has recently been expressed in using Higher Order Neural Network (HONN) models for data simulation and pattern recognition. Such models are able to provide information concerning the basis of the data they are recognition, and hence can be considered as 'open box' rather than 'black box' models. Furthermore, HONN models are also capable of simulating higher frequency and higher order nonlinear data, thus producing superior data recognition, compared with those derived from ANN-based models. This is the motivation therefore for developing the Polynomial Higher Order Neural Network (PHONN) model for data simulation and recognition (Zhang, Murugesan, and Sadeghi, 1995). Zhang & Fulcher (1996b) extend this idea to group PHONN models for data simulation. Zhang, Zhang and Fulcher (2000) develop higher order neural network group models for data approximation. The problem we need to address is to devise a neural network structure that will not only act as an open box to simulate modeling and recognition functions, but which will also facilitate learning algorithm convergence. We would like to demonstrate how it is possible to simulate discontinuous functions, to any degree accuracy, using higher orderneural network group theory, even at points of discontinuity. This is the fourth motivation of the chapter.

Adaptive tree models have been widely studied. Armstrong and Gecsei (1979) develop an adaptation algorithm of binary tree networks for optical characters reconization, with each node of the tree performing the function *AND* or *OR*. Sanger (1991) proposes the Least Mean Square (LMS) tree, which is a new constructive neural network algorithm for image human face recognition. Zhang, Crowley, Dunstone, and

Fulcher (1993) develop a Neural network Adaptive Tolerance (NAT) Tree technique for face recognition, in which every node is a neural network in tolerance space. NAT Tree can be connected and grown in tolerance space as well. Sankar (1993) provides a new pattern classification method called Neural Tree Networks (NTN). The NTN uses a neural network at each tree node. The results show that the NTN compares favourably to both neural networks and decision trees. But when use NTN to recognise complex pattern, the tolerance and accuracy are still problems. Because single neural network as a node is not good enough for complex pattern recognition. The decision function for complex pattern is always noncontinuous and nonsmooth. Single neural network can not simulate noncontinuous and nonsmooth function very well. Zhang & Fulcher (1996a) develope an artificial neural network group-based adaptive tolerance (GAT) trees for translation-invariant face recognition, which can used to describe complex system. GAT trees are black box models and are hard to use formular when modelling whole systems. Higher order neural networks are open box models and have potential feature for pattern recognition. A Higher Order Neural Network Group-based Adaptive Tolerance (HONNGAT) tree, which is open box model, will be presented for solving complex pattern recognition problem with noncontinuous and nonsmooth function. This is the fifth motivation of the chapter.

This chapter gives the definitions of artificial higher order neural network sets, higher order neural network group, higher order neural group models, and higher order neural network group node of tree. The HONNGAT tree model and face recognition system are developed. By using HONNGAT tree, the experimental results of face perception recognition, recognition of front face with glasses and/or beards, and face recognition are provided. In the appendix, details of definitions of generalised artificial higher order neural network sets, proof of the inference, and HONNGAT tree definitions are described.

ARTIFICIAL HIGHER ORDER NEURAL NETWORK SETS

A *set* (Waerden, 1970) is defined as a collection of *elements* which possess the same properties. The symbol

$$a \in A$$

means:

A is a set, and a is an element of set A.

The *artificial higher order neural network set* is a set in which every element is an HONN. The symbol

$$honn \in \boldsymbol{HONNS} \text{ (where: } honn = f{:}\boldsymbol{R}^{n} \rightarrow \boldsymbol{R}^{m})$$

means:

HONNS is an HONN set, and *honn*, which is one kind of artificial higher order neural network, is an element of set **HONNS**. The domain of the artificial higher order neural network *honn* inputs is the n-dimensional real number $\boldsymbol{R}^{n}$. Likewise, the *honn* outputs belong to the m-dimensional real number $\boldsymbol{R}^{m}$.

Figure 1. The artificial higher order neural network set **HONNS** *and its subsets*

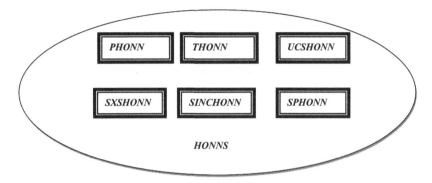

The neural network function *f* is a mapping from the inputs of *honn* to its outputs.

The set **PHONN** is a set whose elements are all artificial polynomial higher order neural networks. The set $PHONN^{1,9,13,3}$ is one in which every element is an artificial polynomial higher order neural network comprising one output neuron, two hidden layers (of 9 neurons and 13 neurons respectively), and 3 input neurons. Moreover, **PHONN** is a subset of the artificial higher order neural network set **HONNS**. We have:

$$PHONN^{1,9,13,3} \subset PHONN \subset HONNS$$

Many other kinds of artificial higher order neural networks exist apart from the artificial polynomial higher order neural network - PHONN, such as (Zhang, 2009a and 2009b2009b):

- Trigonomitrical Higher Orer Neural Netowrks (THONN);
- Ultra high frequency Cosine and Sine trigonometric Higher Order neural Network (UCSHONN);
- SINC and Sine Polynomial Higher Order Neural Netowrks (SXSPHONN);
- SINC Higher Order Neural Networks (SINCHONN);
- Sigmoid Polynomial Higher Order Neural Networks (SPHONN);

This list is not meant to be exhaustive; *new* HONN models continue to be reported in the literature on a regular basis.

We define the artificial higher order neural network set **HONNS** as the *union* of the **subsets** of **PHONN**, **THONN**, **UCSHONN**, **SXSPHONN**, **SINCHONN**, **SPHONN**, ... and so on (Figure 1). In formal notation, we write:

$$HONNS = PHONN \cup THONN \cup UCSHONN \cup SXSPHONN \cup SINCHONN \cup SPHONN \cup ....$$

We next introduce the concept of the *generalised* HONN *set*, prior to discussing higher order *neural network groups*. HONN Generalised Sets (**HONNGS)** are defined as the union of additive HONN sets (**HONN⁺**) and product HONN sets (**HONN***), as detailed in Appendix A, which we write as:

Figure 2. Relationship between sets **HONNS** *and sets* **HONNGS (= HONN***∪ **HONN⁺)**

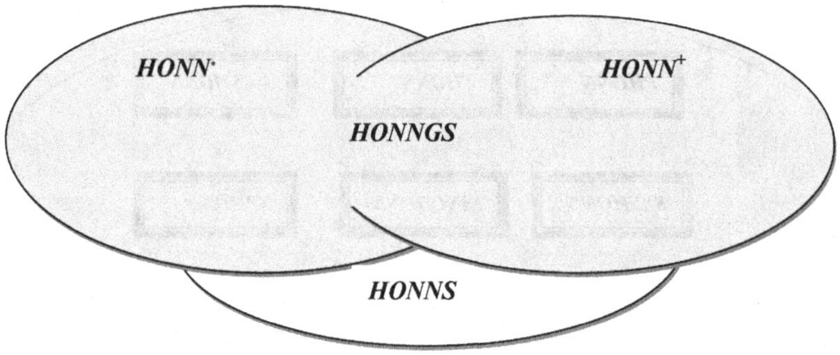

$HONNGS = HONN^* \cup HONN^+$

The elements of set **HONNS** are higher order neural networks; the elements of set **HONNGS**, by contrast, are higher order neural network *groups*. The difference between a higher order neural network and a higher order neural network group was illustrated previously in Figure 2, in which we see that higher order neural network generalised set **HONNGS** is a more generalised form of higher order neural network set **HONNS**. Accordingly, higher order neural network groups should hold more potential for characterising complex systems.

HIGHER ORDER NEURAL NETWORK GROUP

Following the group definitions by Inui (1978) and Naimark (1982), we have:

a nonempty set **HONNG** is called a *higher order neural network group*, if **HONNG** ⊂ **HONNGS**(the higher order neural network generalised set), and either the product $h_i h_j$ or the sum $h_i + h_j$ is defined for every two elements h_i, h_j ∈ **HONNG**.

Additive Notation of Higher Order Neural Network Groups

For a higher order neural network group defined in additive notation form, the following conditions must hold (associated law of composition):

(a) $h_i + h_j$ ∈ **HONNG**, ∀ h_i, h_j ∈ **HONNG**;
(b) $(h_i + h_j) + h_k = h_i + (h_j + h_k)$, ∀ h_i, h_j, h_k ∈ **HONNG**;
(c) ∃ a unique element h_0 in **HOONG** such that $h_0 + h = h + h_0 = h$ ∀ h ∈ **HONNG** (h_0 is called the identity element of the group **HONNG**);
(d) for every element h ∈ **HONN**, ∃ a unique element, designated -h, for which $h + (-h) = (-h) + h = h_0$(the element -$h$ is called the inverse of h); it is evident that h is the inverse of -h, so that -(- h) = h).

There are two examples as follows:

the additive generalised polynomial higher order neural network set **PHONN⁺** is a higher order neural network group if "addition" is taken to mean "plus". As another example, Boolean operator logical *OR* can be used as "addition". Then the additive generalised polynomial higher order neural network set **PHONN⁺** is a higher order neural network group as well.

Product Notation of Higher Order Neural Network Groups

For a higher order neural network group defined in product notation form, the following conditions must hold (associated law of composition):

(a) $h_i h_j \in$ **HONNG**, $\forall h_i, h_j \in$ **HONNG**;

(b) $(h_i h_j)h_k = h_i(h_j h_k)$, $\forall h_i, h_j, h_k \in$ **HONNG**;

(c) $\exists$ a unique element h_e in **N** such that $h_e h = hh_e = h \ \forall h \in$ **HONNG**; (h_e is called the identity element of the group **HONNG**);

(d) for every element $h \in$ **HONN**, $\exists$ a unique element - designated h^{-1} - for which $hh^{-1} = h^{-1}h = h_e$ (the element h^{-1} is called the inverse of h; it is obvious that h is the inverse of h^{-1}, so that $(h^{-1})^{-1} = h$).

Two examples are as follows:

Consider for example the product generalised polynomial higher order neural network set **PHONN***. This is a higher order neural network group if "product" is taken to mean "multiplication" of the higher order neural network outputs. As another example, Boolean operator logical AND can be used as "product". Then the product generalised polynomial higher order neural network set **PHONN*** is a hogher order neural network group as well.

Higher Order Neural Network Algebra Sum Groups

Higher Order Neural Network Algebra Sum Groups - HONNASGs - are higher order neural network groups in which each addition $h_i + h_j$ is defined as an *Algebraic Sum* of every two elements $h_i, h_j \in$ **HONNG**. Apart from Algebra Sum Groups, other higher order Neural Network Groups can be similarly defined, according to how each product $h_i h_j$ and/or addition $h_i + h_j$ is defined for every two elements $h_i, h_j \in$ **HONN** (such as Algebraic Product $[h_i h_j]$, Integral Operation, Differential Class, Boolean Algebraic, or Triangular Exponential, Logarithmic or Hyperbolic Functions, and so forth).

Higher Order Neural Network Piecewise Function Groups

We are particularly interested to the present the Higher Order Neurla Network Piecewise Function Groups (HONNPFGs). Higher Order Neural Network Piecewise Function Groups are defined as those in which each addition $h_i + h_j$ is a *Piecewise Function* for every two elements $h_i, h_j \in$ **HON**HHg**NG**:

$$h_i + h_j = h_j + h_i = \begin{cases} h_i, & A < I <= B \\ h_i, & B < I <= C \end{cases}$$

$$\left(h_{i}\right)+\left(h_{j}\right)+\left(h_{k}\right)$$
$$=\left(\left(h_{i}\right)+\left(h_{j}\right)\right)+\left(h_{k}\right)$$
$$=\left(h_{i}\right)+\left(\left(h_{j}\right)+\left(h_{k}\right)\right)$$
$$=\begin{cases} h_{i}, & A < I <= B \\ h_{j}, & B < I <= C \\ h_{k}, & C < I <= D \end{cases}$$

where: I input to the higher order neural networks; A, B, C, and D are constants

Such a piecewise function ensures that higher order neural networks satisfy the necessary conditions to be regarded as a higher order neural network group. Firstly, equation implies that piecewise function higher order neural networks satisfy condition (b). Furthermore, if we choose to build these higher order neural networks in the form of a *generalised* higher order neural network set, this automatically satisfies conditions (a), (c), and (d). Thus piecewise functions can be used to ensure that the higher order neural networks satisfy *all* of the necessary group conditions. The constants A, B, C, and D can be chose heuristically.

Inference of Higher Order Neural Network Piecewise Function Groups

Hornik (1991) proved the following general result: "Whenever the activation function is continuous, bounded and nonconstant, then for an arbitrary compact subset $X \subseteq R^{n}$, standard multilayer feedforward networks can approximate any continuous function on X arbitrarily well with respect to uniform distance, provided that sufficiently many hidden units are available".

A more general result was proved by Leshno (1993): "A standard multilayer feedforward network with a locally bounded piecewise continuous activation function can approximate *any* continuous function to *any* degree of accuracy if and only if the network's activation function is not a polynomial".

Zhang, Fulcher, & Scofield (1997) provided a general result for neural network group: "Consider a neural network Piecewise Function *Group*, in which each member is a standard multilayer feedforward neural network, and which has a locally bounded, piecewise continuous (rather than polynomial) activation function and threshold. Each such group can approximate *any* kind of piecewise continuous function, and to *any* degree of accuracy."

An inference is provided as follows and proved by Appendix B: "Consider a higher order neural network Piecewise Function *Group*, in which each member is a standard multilayer feedforward higher order neural network, and which has a locally bounded, piecewise continuous (rather than polynomial) activation function and threshold. Each such group can approximate *any* kind of piecewise continuous function, and to *any* degree of accuracy."

In the real world, if the function being analysed varies in a discontinuous and nonsmooth fashion with respect to input variables, then such functions cannot be effectively simulated by a higher order neural network. By contrast, if we use higher order neural network *groups* to simulate these functions, it *is* possible to simulate discontinuous functions to any degree accuracy, even at points of discontinuity

HIGHER ORDER NEURAL NETWORK GROUP MODELS

Higher Order Neural Network models use trigonometric, linear, multiply, power and other neuron functions based on the following form:

$$z = \sum_{k1,k2\ldots km=0}^{n} c\prod_{j=1}^{m} \left[f_1\left(c_1 x_1\right)\right]^{k1} \left[f_2\left(c_2 x_2\right)\right]^{k2} \left[f_1\left(c_j x_j\right)\right]^{kj} \quad \left[f_m\left(c_m x_m\right)\right]^{km}$$

Let m=2, c = c_{k1k2}, $c_1 = c_{k1k2}{}^x$, $c_2 = c_{k1k2}{}^y$, x_1=x, and x_2=y, we have:

$$z = \sum_{k1,k2=0}^{n} c_{k1k2}\left[f_1\left(c_{k1k2}{}^x x\right)\right]^{k1} \left[f_2\left(c_{k1k2}{}^y y\right)\right]^{k2}$$

$$= \sum_{k1,k2=0}^{n} \left(c_{k1k2}{}^o\right)\left\{c_{k1k2}{}^{hx}\left[f_1\left(c_{k1k2}{}^x x\right)\right]^{k1}\right\}\left\{c_{k1k2}{}^{hy}\left[f_2\left(c_{k1k2}{}^y y\right)\right]^{k2}\right\}$$

where: $c_{k1k2} = \left(c_{k1k2}{}^o\right)\left(c_{k1k2}{}^{hx}\right)\left(c_{k1k2}{}^{hy}\right)$

where: Output Layer Weights: $(c_{k1k2}{}^o)$
Second Hidden Layer Weights: $(c_{k1k2}{}^x)$ and $(c_{k1k2}{}^y)$
First Hidden Layer Weights: $(c_{k1k2}{}^{hx})$ and $(c_{k1k2}{}^{hy})$

Choosing a different function f_1 results in a different higher order neural network model.

Trigonometric Polynomial Higher Order Neural Network (THONN) Model

Let: $f_1(c_{k1k2}{}^x x) = sin(c_{k1k2}{}^x x)$; $f_2(c_{k1k2}{}^y y) = cos(c_{k1k2}{}^y y)]$

$$z = \sum_{k1,k2=0}^{n} c_{k1k2}\left[f_1\left(c_{k1k2}{}^x x\right)\right]^{k1} \left[f_2\left(c_{k1k2}{}^y y\right)\right]^{k2}$$
then

$$= \sum_{k1,k2=0}^{n} \left(c_{k1k2}{}^o\right)\left\{c_{k1k2}{}^{hx}\left[\sin\left(c_{k1k2}{}^x x\right)\right]^{k1}\right\}\left\{c_{k1k2}{}^{hy}\left[\cos\left(c_{k1k2}{}^y y\right)\right]^{k2}\right\}$$

Polynomial Higher Order Neural Network (PHONN) Model

Let: $f_1(c_{k1k2}{}^x x) = (c_{k1k2}{}^x x)$; and $f_2(c_{k1k2}{}^y y) = (c_{k1k2}{}^y y)$

then $O_2\left(H_{i,j}\right) = \begin{cases} 1, O\left(H_{i,j}\right) \in \xi_2\left(H_{i,j}\right) \\ 0, otherwise \end{cases}$

$$= \sum_{k1,k2=0}^{n} \left(c_{k1k2}{}^o\right)\left\{c_{k1k2}{}^{hx}\left(c_{k1k2}{}^x x\right)^{k1}\right\}\left\{c_{k1k2}{}^{hy}\left(c_{k1k2}{}^y y\right)^{k2}\right\}$$

Sigmoid Polynomial Higher Order Neural Network (SPHONN) Model

Let: $f_1(c_{k1k2}{}^x x)] = 1/(1+exp(-c_{k1k2}{}^x x))$; $f_2(c_{k1k2}{}^y y) = (1/1+exp(-c_{k1k2}{}^y y))]$

then $z = \displaystyle\sum_{k1,k2=0}^{n} c_{k1k2} \left[f_1 \left(c_{k1k2}{}^x x \right) \right]^{k1} \left[f_2 \left(c_{k1k2}{}^y y \right) \right]^{k2}$

$= \displaystyle\sum_{k1,k2=0}^{n} \left(c_{k1k2}{}^o \right) \left\{ c_{k1k2}{}^{hx} \left[1 / \left(1 + \exp\left(-c_{k1k2}{}^x x \right) \right) \right]^{k1} \right\} \left\{ c_{k1k2}{}^{hy} \left[\left(1 / 1 + \exp\left(-c_{k1k2}{}^y y \right) \right) \right]^{k2} \right\}$

Higher Order Neural network Group (***HONNG***) is one kind of neural network group, in which each element is a higher order neural network, such as PHONN, THONN, or SPHONN. We have:

HONNG $\subset$ ***Artificial Neural Network Group***

where: ***HONNG*** = { ***PHONN, THONN, SPHONN,* ......**}

PHONN, ***THONN***, and ***SPHONN*** are subsets

In the following section, this chapter describe three different ***HONNG*** models.

Polynomial Higher Order Neural Network Group (*PHONNG*) Model

The ***PHONNG*** model is a PHONN model *Group*. It is a piecewise function group of Polynomial Higher Order Neural Networks, and is defined as follows:

Z = { z_1, z_2, z_3, ..., z_i, z_{i+1}, z_{i+2}, ...}

where $z_i = ln [(z_i')/(1-z_i')]$

$z_i \in \mathbf{K}_i \subset \mathbf{R}^n, \mathbf{K}_i$ is a compact set

$z_i' = 1/(1+ e^{-zi})$

$z_i = \displaystyle\sum_{k1,k2=0}^{n} \left(c_{ik1k2}{}^o \right) \left[\left(c_{ik1k2}{}^x \right) x \right]^{k1} \left[\left(c_{ik1k2}{}^y \right) y \right]^{k2} = \displaystyle\sum_{k1,k2=0}^{n} c_{ik1k2} x^{k1} y^{k2}$

$c_{ik1k2} = (c_{ik1k2}{}^o)[(c_{ik1k2}{}^x)^{k1}][(c_{ik1k2}{}^y)^{k2}]$

In the ***PHONNG*** Model (Piecewise Function Group), group *addition* is defined as the *piecewise* function:

$$z = \begin{cases} z_1, & z_1 \ inputs \in K_1 \\ z_2, & z_2 \ inputs \in K_2 \\ z_i, & z_i \ inputs \in K_i \\ z_i + 1, & z_{i+1} \ inputs \in K_{i+1} \end{cases}$$

where: $z_i \ inputs \in K_i \subset R^n, K_i$ is a compact set

The **PHONNG** Model is an open and convergent model which can approximate any kind of piecewise continuous function *to any degree of accuracy*, even at discontinuous points (or regions).

Trigonometric Polynomial Higher Order Neural network Group (*THONNG*) Model

In order to handle discontinuities in the input training data, the Trigonometric Polynomial Higher Order Neural Network *Group* (**THONNG**) model has also been developed. This is a model in which every element is a *trigonometric* polynomial higher order neural network - THONN (Zhang & Fulcher, 1996b). The domain of the THONN inputs is the *n*-dimensional real number R^n. Likewise, the THONN outputs belong to the *m*-dimensional real number R^m. The higher order neural network function *f* constitutes a mapping from the inputs of THONN to its outputs.

THONN $\in$ **THONNG**

where: THONN $= f:R^n \rightarrow R^{m;THONNG}$is the group model

Based on the inference of Zhang, Fulcher & Scofield (1997), each such higher order neural network group can approximate any kind of piecewise continuous function, and to any degree of accuracy. Hence, **THONNG** is also able to simulate discontinuous data.

Sigmoid Polynomial Higher Order Neural network Group (*SPHONNG*) Model

In order to handle discontinuities in the input training data, the sigmoid polynomial higher order neural network *Group* (**SPHONNG**) model has also been developed. This is a model in which every element is a *sigmoid* polynomial higher order neural network (SPHONN). The domain of the SHONN inputs is the *n*-dimensional real number R^n. Likewise, the SHONN outputs belong to the *m*-dimensional real number R^m. The higher order neural network function *f* constitutes a mapping from the inputs of SHONN to its outputs.

SPHONN $\in$ **SPHONNG**

where: SPHONN $= f:R^n \rightarrow R^{m;SPHOONG}$is group model

Each such higher order neural network group can approximate any kind of piecewise continuous function, and to any degree of accuracy. Hence, **SPHONNG** is also able to simulate discontinuous data.

Based on the discussion above, we have that Higher Order Neural Network Group (**HONNG**) is one kind of neural network group, in which each element is a higher order neural network, or higher order neural network group:

HONNG ⊂ Artificial Neural Network Group

where:

HONNG = { *PHONN, THONN, SPHONN,... PHONNG, THONNG, SPHONNG, ...*}

PHONN, THONN, and *SPHONN* are subsets

PHONNG, THONNG, and SPHONNG are group models

HIGHER ORDER NEURAL NETWORK GROUP NODE OF TREE

Figure 3 shows the structure of a HONNGAT Tree node. The significant feature of this node is that it is neither an higher order artificial neuron nor an higher order artificial neural network, but rather a higher order neural network group (*HONN$_1$, HONN$_2$, ..., HONN$_k$*) in tolerance space. (Zeeman, 1962). The basic function of node is a classifier. Because the node is consisted of higher order neural network group. So higher order neural network group-based note is a complex pattern classifier. The basic function of node can be detail describes by a set of operator (See appendix C Artificial Higher order neural network Node Operator set):

HNO = { *HNO0, HNO1,HNG, HNO2* }

The brief discuss about neural network group-based node are as follows:

1. Inputs of node $I_f(H_{i,j})$ and $I_d(H_{i,j})$
    Let: $H_{i,j}$: HONN Group-Based (HONNGB) node, adaptive node and label node,
    where *i*: the level or deep of the HONNGAT Tree; *j*: the *jth* node *n* the *i* level
    The inputs of node are Fire Input-- $I_f(H_{i,j})$ and Data Input -- $I_d(H_{i,j})$. Fire Input has been connected to output of parent node. The Fire Input is a binary number (0 or 1). Data Input is the pattern data that is needed to be recognised or trained. For face recognition, Data Input is the face data matrix (we use 28*28 pixels matrix, each pixel has 256 grey level). In testing, Data Input -- $I_d(H_{i,j})$ is the *IMA(i,j)* pattern that we want to recognise. In the training, Input Data -- $I_d(H_{i,j})$ are translated training data *IMAu(i,j)* (see appendix C).
2. Higher order neural network Node Operator 0 --*HNO0*
    In the testing, when Fire Input equals 1, the node is fired and the Data Input can accepted by node. Otherwise, the Data Input can not be input into the node. In the training, Data input can always be input into the node. We use *HNO0* (HONN Node Operator 0) to describe this function (see appendix C) . So in the training or fired cases, Input Data (Face, for example) has been input into the node and higher order neural network group input -- $I(H_{i,j})$ equals Input Data -- $I_d(H_{i,j})$.
3. Higher order neural network Node Operator 1 -- HNO1
    All K higher order neural networks (a group of higher order neural networks) are used for training or testing using higher order neural network group input I(Hi,j). After training, the best weights

Figure 3. HONN group-based node of tree

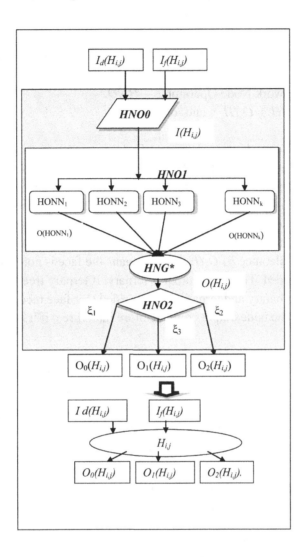

are found and fixed for each higher order neural network (we use THONN as basic higher order neural network). In the training, one higher order neural network has been trained to suit a special case. For example, higher order neural network 1 (HONN1) has been trained for recognising centre face of facial image IMA0(i,j), higher order neural network 2 (HONN2) for lower-left face of facial image IMA1(i,j), and so on. Therefore, after training, the K higher order neural networks can recognise not only centre face but also lower-left face and so on. This model can solve shifting invariant problem very well. The trained K higher order neural networks can be used for testing. We use HONN Node Operator 1 -- HNO1 describe this procedure. After HNO1, we got O(HONN1), O(HONN2), ... O(HONNk), the output of each K higher order neural networks.

4. Higherorder neural network Group Operator -- HNG

Then the K outputs of higher order neural networks, O(HONN1), O(HONN2), ... O(HONNk), are calculated by "*". "*" means AND or OR operation. We use Higher order neural network Group Operator -- HNG to represent this function. After HNG operate (see appendix C), higher order neural network group output O(Hi,j) has been generated. The reason we use higher order neural network group is not only a group of higher order neural networks have been used, but also when AND or OR is used as group product, the total conditions for group definition, based on the group theory, are held. The reason why we chose *AND* or *OR* as group product will be given in this section later on.

5.   Higher order neural network Node Operator 2 -- *HNO2*
      and outputs of node $O_0(H_{i,j})$, $O_1(H_{i,j})$, and /or $O_2(H_{i,j})$

The higher order neural network group output $O(H_{i,j})$ ranges from 0 to 1. In the testing, the $O(H_{i,j})$ could be any real number between 0 and 1. We use Zeeman (1962) Tolerance Space definition (Appendix C) to distinguish the test results. Because tolerance space has more general meaning than the thresholds (Chen, 1982). We use HONN Node Operator 2 (*HNO2*) to do distinguish. Finally the pattern could be classified several classes. We use $O_0(H_{i,j})$, $O_1(H_{i,j})$, and /or $O_2(H_{i,j})$ to represent the recognition results. For example, for front face recognition, if pattern is in tolerance ξ_1, $O_0(H_{i,j})=1$, it means the face is front face. If pattern is in tolerance ξ_2, $O_1(H_{i,j})=1$, it means the face is not front face. The node output is binary, if binary tree is needed. The node output is ternary, if ternary tree is needed. The node output is binary or ternary, if mixed binary and ternary tree is needed (for face recognition, this is good choice based on the experiments). The node output could be more than three, if it is needed for real world pattern recognition.

The features of "*OR*" and "*AND*" higher order neural network groups are that not only can they approximate any continuous function, and to any degree of accuracy, but that they are also able to approximate *any* kind of Multiple-Peak piecewise continuous function with nonsmooth and noncontinuous point(s), and again to *any* degree of accuracy. Moreover, they are able to approximate *any* kind of Sole-Peak piecewise continuous function with nonsmooth and noncontinuous point(s), to *any* degree of accuracy. Because of these features, higher order neural network groups render face recognition more accurate.

Two deductions follow directly from Leshno's result(1993) as the features of "*OR*" and "*AND*" higher order neural network groups are proved by the following:

Deduction 1:

Consider a higher order neural network "*OR*" Function *Group*, in which each member is a higher order neural network, with a locally bounded, piecewise continuous (rather than polynomial) activation function and threshold. Each such group can approximate *any* kind of Multiple-Peak piecewise continuous function with nonsmooth and non continuous point(s), and to *any* degree of accuracy.

Deduction 2:

Consider a higher order neural network "*AND*" Function *Group*, in which each member is a higher order neural network, with a locally bounded, piecewise continuous (rather than polynomial) activation function and threshold. Each such group can approximate *any* kind of Sole-Peak piecewise continuous function with nonsmooth and noncontinuous point(s), and to *any* degree of accuracy.

Figure 4 shows the features of higher order neural network groups in one dimension. Figure 4(a) is the "*OR*" group of higher order neural networks for approximating a multi-peak function with nonsmooth point (x1) and noncontinuous point (x2). Figure 4(b) is the "*AND*" group of higher order neural networks for approximating a sole-peak function with nonsmooth point (x1) and noncontinuous point (x2). A single higher order neural network cannot approximate the multiple-peak function with nonsmooth and noncontinuous points. Neither can a single higherorder neural network approximate a sole-peak function

Figure 4. The features of "OR" and "AND" higher order neural network groups

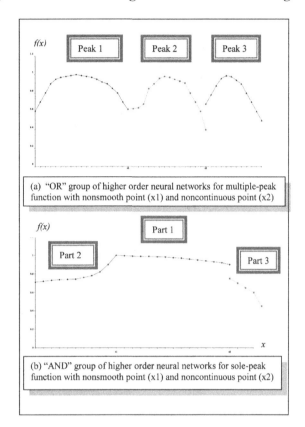

(a) "OR" group of higher order neural networks for multiple-peak function with nonsmooth point (x1) and noncontinuous point (x2)

(b) "AND" group of higher order neural networks for sole-peak function with nonsmooth point (x1) and noncontinuous point (x2)

with nonsmooth and noncontinuous points. This explains why higher order neural network groups have more features than a single higher order neural network.

For shifting invariant front face recognition, we use center front face as one training case and left shift and right shift as other two training cases. We shift center front face two pixels left as a left shift face and shift center front face two pixels right as a right shift face. The center, left and right front face as input data of higher order neural network. The output of higher order neural network is the recognition function of the front face. After training, we have three peaks represent each centre, left or right face. let us look at the Figure 4(a), peak 1 represents the recognition function of left front face, peak 2 for centre front face, and peak 3 for right front face. (In Figure 4, X is 1 dimension. In real world X is 256 dimensions. Here we just want to use Figure 4 to explanation why piecewise continuous functions with nonsmooth and noncontinuous point(s) are true and existed in real world). The joint point(s) between peaks is always nonsmooth and sometimes noncontinuous in the experiments. No one higher order neural network can approximate the function with 3 peaks and nonsmooth and noncontinuous points.

When we recognise target face, target face could be made up, with or without beards, and with or without glasses. The target face without glasses and beards, target face with glasses, and target face with beards are as inputs into the higher order neural network. The output of higher order neural network for target face is the function of the target face. We found, in the experiments, The function of target face is always is sole-peak function but with nonsmooth and noncontinuous point(s). Let us look at Figure 4 (b) (Here we still use 1 dimension to instate 256 dimensions, just for explanation why this case hap-

Figure 5. Higher order neural network group-based adaptive tolerance (HONNGAT) tree

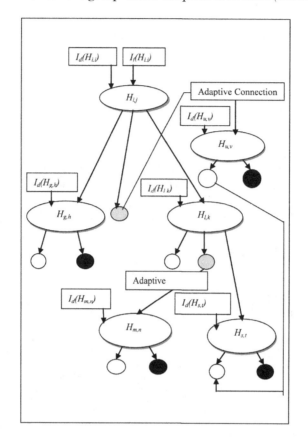

pened in real world). The part 1 is the function of target face without glasses and beards. The part 2 is the function of target face with glasses. The part 3 is the function of target face with beards. No one higher order neural network can approximate the sole-peak function with nonsmooth and noncontinuous points shown in Figure 4 (b).

For face recognition, especially in real world conditions, we need to be able to approximate multiple-peak or sole peak functions with nonsmooth and noncontinuous points. In experiments, for example, the output of higher order neural network for front face recognition is a multiple-peak function which may have nonsmooth and/or noncontinuous point(s). Thus if the "*OR*" higher order neural network group has been used to approximate the front face function, the front face classification accuracy will be much better than if we were to use a single higher order neural network. The output of higher order neural network for target face recognition is always a sole-peak one, which may have nonsmooth and/or noncontinuous point(s). In this case, if the "*AND*" higher order neural network has been used for approximation, the accuracy is better than what would be obtained with one higher order neural network.

In this chapter, "*OR*" and "*AND*" higher order neural network groups have been used as the nodes for HONNGAT Tree. This leads to more accurate and more efficient face recognition.

Figure 6. Translation-invariant face recognition system using HONNGAT trees

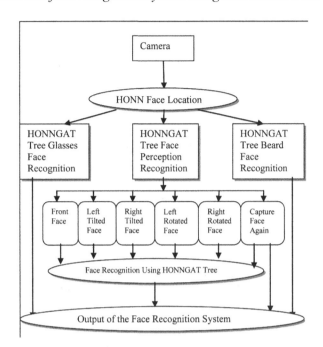

HONNGAT TREE MODEL

The basic HONNGAT Tree model is shown in Figure 5, and comprises both binary and ternary trees. Adaptive connections and adaptively growing trees, the nodes of which are still higher order neural networks, have been developed for translation-invariant face recognition. Adaptive connection and growth can be described in terms of tolerance space theory (Zeeman, 1962).

Figure 5 shows the adaptive growth of a HONNGAT Tree. We use Higher order neural network Adaptive Operator -- *HAO* to represent it. Because the output $O(H_{l,k})$ of node $H_{l,k}$ is within tolerance $\xi_3(H_{l,k})$, node *Nm,n* was added and fired. In such a manner the HONNGAT Tree has "grown" a node. The adaptively growing tree is therefore very useful for adding new faces which need to be recognised. Also shown in Figure 5 are adaptive connections within the HONNGAT Tree. Because output $O(H_{i,j})$ of node $H_{i,j}$ is within tolerance $\xi_3(H_{i,j})$, node *Nu,v* is added and connected to node $H_{i,j}$. One output of $H_{u,v}$ has been connected to an output of node $H_{s,t}$. Such an adaptively connected HONNGAT Tree is very efficient for recognising topologically deformed faces.

When a face is shifted or rotated, face recognition becomes considerably more difficult. To solve this, a translation-invariant face recognition technique has been developed. The basic idea of this chapter is to include all shifted and rotated faces in 2-dimensions as training examples for the neural network node (we use Higher order neural netwotk Translating OPerator -- *HTO* to represent it). Thus after training, the artificial higher order neural network group-based node is able to recognise shifted and rotated faces in 2-dimensions. Suppose facial image *IMA(i,j)* consists of 32*32 pixels.

Using Higher order neural netwotk Translating Operator -- *HTO*, the *IMAo(i,j)*, center face (28*28 pixels) can been got for the central part of facial image *IMA(i,j)*. The *IMA1(i,j)*, lower-left face (28*28 pixels), has been chosen by the upper-right part of facial image *IMA(i,j)*. Similarly, all the shifted faces in

Figure 7. Face perspective classfication using HONNGAT

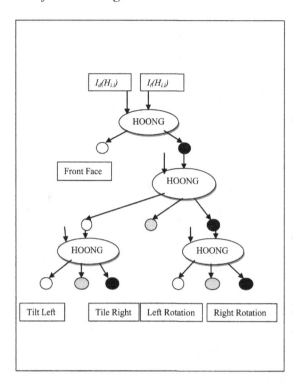

2-dimensions are chosen from facial image *IMA(i,j)*. The same technique can also be used for rotated face recognition. In 2-dimensions, rotated faces can easily be obtained by rotating facial image *IMA(i,j)*.

HONNGAT Tree model can be written as:

HONNGAT Tree operator set ***HONNGAT****: IMA(i,j)* → *LS*

where:

IMA(i,j): a 2-dimensional black and white image which represents a human face.
LS: a Label Set in which each label corresponds to a different human face (from *1* to *m*) or no one is recognised (∅);
LS= {∅, 1, 2, 3, ..., i, ..., m}.

HONNGAT: Higher Order Neural Network Groug-based Adaptive Tolerance tree model operator set;
HONNGAT = { ***HTO, HNO, HPO, HLO, HAO*** }
Where:
HTO: Higher order neural network Translating OPerator that can translate facial image *IMA(i,j)* into centre face, left face, right face and so on -- shift and rotate the face image in 2 dimension.
HNO: Higher order neural network Node Operator set that is a complex pattern classifier.
HPO: Higher order neural network Path Operator set which let parent node's output equals to input of son node in the tree.

HLO: Higher order neural network Label leaf Operator set which indicate the labelled person has been recognised.

HAO: Higher order neural network Adaptive node Operator set that adds adaptive connection and growing node(s) in the HONNGAT Tree if parent node output is within the tolerance.

It means after ***HONNGAT*** operator set be used on the face image *IMA(i,j)*, The Human face could be recognised by label set *LS*. Detailed description can be seen in Appendix C.

The procedure of the HONNGAT tree can be described by following algorithm:

1. Build a standard binary tree. The level (*M*) of tree dependents on the number (*N*) of target objectives. The node of tree is a higher order neural network group-based node. *THONN* and other higher order neural network can be chosen as basic higher order neural network. (For face recognition, we use $M = log_2 N + 2$ based on the experimental results and chose *THONN* as basic higher order neural network for group-based node.)

2. Collect the higher order neural network training samples as more as possible. (For face recognition, face images *IMA(i,j)* have been collected for training higher order neural networks.)

3. Using Higher order neural network Translating Operator set, ***HTO***, to translate the training samples to center, right, left position and so on for training higher order neural networks of group-base node. (For face recognition, face images *IMA(i,j)* have been translated into center face, right face, left face and so on (*IMAu(i,j)*) by ***HTO*** for training higher order neural networks of group-base node. For example, in 2 dimension, we move center face 2 pixels right to get right face.)

4. Training higher order neural networks of higher order neural network group-base note in the tree to find the bast weights for higher order neural networks. After training, all weights of higher order neural networks are fixed. Artificial Higher order neural network group Node Operator set -- ***HNO***

Figure 8. Front glasses and beard face classification using HONNGAT tree

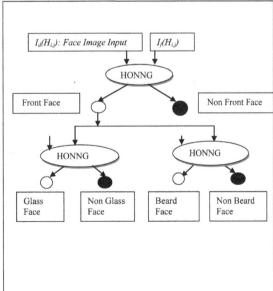

has been found. (For face recognition, The first level node has been trained for front face recognition. There are 9 *THONN* higher order neural networks in the node. Each higher order network has been trained for recognising one translated front face -- say *THONN$_1$* for center front face, *THONN$_2$* for right front face, *THONN$_3$* for left front face, and so on. After training, the first level node can classify front face and non-front face at 9 different positions. Then next level node has been trained to classify all target faces as class 1, other nontarget face as class 2. The following level node has been trained to divided all target face as two subclasses. One is class 1.1 and another is 1.2. This procedure continues until every lowest node of each branch in the tree represents one target face. After training, all weights are found and fixed. It means *HNO* has been found.)

5.   Confirm the paths of tree. Let Fire Input of node equals to the output of parent node and get Higher order neural network Path Operator set -- **HPO**.

6.   Chose label for each new target face and get Higher order neural network Label Operator -- **HLO**.

7.   Testing object (testing face) has been input into Data Input of each fired node. If the testing objective (testing face) is the trained objective (face), one lowest node will be fired, the output of node is 1, and one label will be choose for represent this test object. It means this testing object (testing face) has been recognised. If no label appear, it means this object is not the one of objects been trained.

Figure 9. HONNGAT tree for front face recognition

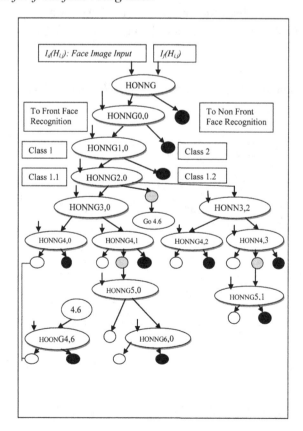

Figure 10. Noise versus face recognition accuracy

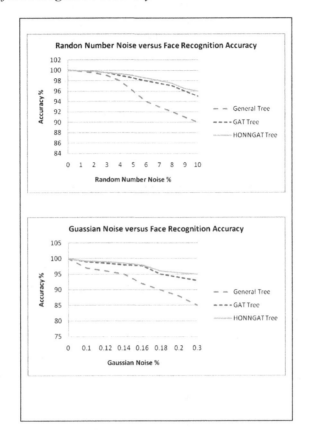

8. If no more training samples need to be added to the tree, Exit. If more training samples need to be added to the HONNGAT Tree, go to (9).

9. If new target objects (faces) needed to be recognised, using the Higher order neural network Adaptive node Operator -- *HAO* find the adaptive points in the tree. Then to grow tree and go to (3). If topologically deforming old target objects (faces) needed to be recognised, using the Higher order neural network Adaptive node Operator -- *HAO* find the adaptive points in the tree. Then build connection node and go to (3). If no new target objects (faces) needed to be recognised, go to (10).

10. Stop.

FACE RECOGNITION USING HONNGAT TREE MODELS

Face Recognition System

Machine face recognition system is difficult to build since a face is either deformed topologically, translated in 3-dimensions, or when the face environment and background is complicated. Figure 6 shows our face recognition system which organized as following components:

1. The camera captures images of people as they make their way to the check-in desk. Using higher order neural network techniques, faces are located within these captured images.
2. The face will be classified as a front face, tilted to the left, tilted right, rotated to the left, or rotated right.
3. At the same time, faces with glasses and/or beards will be classified using the HONNGAT Tree technique.
4. HONNGAT Trees are used for face recognition. Following successful classification, translation-invariant faces are recognised using adaptive connection and growth of HONNGAT Trees in tolerance space. Output of the system will show the face recognition result.

Face Perception Recognition Using HONNGAT Trees

28*28 pixels face image with 256 grey level are used and lighting condition is 60 *lux*. The experimental results for face perception recognition using HONNGAT trees are shown in Figure 7. There are 765 different faces in the system face database for face perception recognition. For copy right purpose, all the faces shown in the figures of this chapter are chosen from MS Office clip art samples, not the real faces used for the traing and test by HONNGAT Tree. For front face recognition, 85 different perspective faces were chosen as training exemplars. This leaves 680 faces for testing. HONNGAT Trees are then used for testing. Only one error case is forthcoming, resulting in an error rate of only 0.147%. After training, HONNGAT trees are able to recognise tilted and rotated faces with a similar level of confidence. 135 faces were chosen as training cases, 630 faces for testing. The observed error is 0.158% for tilted face recognition and 0.317% for rotated face recognition.

Recognition of Glasses and/or Beards Using HONNGAT Tree

HONNGAT Tree has been used for recognising front faces with glasses and beards. The 2-level HONN-GAT Tree structure is shown in Figure 8. In order to recognise front beard faces, 5 faces were chosen to train HONNGAT node. 60 faces are testing cases. The output of the HONNGAT Tree node converged after 1400 iterations. The network was then tested using faces it had not previously seen. The outputs of the Artificial Higher Order Neural Network group are all greater than 0.93 for the 6 front beard face test cases. For all other 54 people (not front beard faces), the outputs of the HONNGAT Tree node are all less than 0.43. In order to recognise front glasses faces, 6 faces were chosen for training HONNGAT nodes. 61 face are testing cases. The output of the HONNGAT Tree node began to converge after 1200 iterations. Once trained, the network was tested with faces it had not previously met. The outputs of the artificial higher order neural network group were all more than 0.86 for the 3 front glasses test faces. For all other 58 (non front glasses) persons, the outputs of the HONNGAT Tree node were all less than 0.28.

Front Face Recognition Using HONNGAT Tree

The Model of the HONNGAT Tree used for front face recognition is shown in Figure 9. One HONN-GAT Tree node is used for face perspective recognition, especially for picking up the front faces for next recognition procedure.

From Level 0 to Level 4, the basic HONNGAT Tree model is used to recognise the front face. Different faces will be recognised at the different label nodes. In order to recognize faces, each artificial neural network group based node needs to be trained prior to testing. Each node of the HONNGAT Tree is trigonometric higher order neural network group with the following configuration: input layer - 28*28 neurones; hidden layer; output layer - 1 neuron. The model of Figure 9 only describes the basic operation of the HONNGAT Tree. In order to recognise 1024 target faces, the basic HONNGAT Tree model only needs 12 Levels. This means that if a 12 level basic HONNGAT Tree model is chosen, recognising a specific person only takes about 2 seconds for recognise 1024 target face from million people by using the computer build in 2008.

In Figure 9, nodes *HONNG4,6* has been identified as the adaptive connection nodes from which the tree is to be connection. Such connection enables the system to recognize same people with deforming within the tolerance. Thus adaptive connection can also occur in a growing HONNGAT Tree.

In Figure 9, nodes *HONNG5,0* has been identified as the adaptive nodes from which the tree is to be grown. Such growth enables the system to recognise new people. Thus adaptive growth can also occur in a growing HONNGAT Tree.

Figure 10 shows the results obtained using HONNGAT Tree for face recognition. The total number of faces is 765. 20 faces have been chosen for training, 745 face are testing face, and eight faces designated as target faces. This simulation is similar to the real-world situation encountered at airports: a lot of people pass through Customs in airport, but only a very few of these are of interest. In order to recognise 8 people from 765 different faces, The HONNGAT Tree makes *no* mistakes under laboratory conditions.

In Figure 10, the effect of random noise on recognition accuracy is examined. The results are as follows: when 10% random number noise is added, the accuracy of HONNGAT Tree is 1% higher that GAT Tree, and is 6% higher than a general tree. The effect of Gaussian Noise on recognition accuracy is also demonstrated in Figure 10. The results can be summarised as follows: when the gamma value of the Gaussian Noise exceeds 0.3, the accuracy of HONNGAT Tree is 2% higher thanGAT Tree, and is about 9% higher than for a general tree. The results show that HONNGAT Tree is more tolerant.

CONCLUSION

This chapter presents the artificial higher order neural network group-based model - HONNGAT Tree for translation-invariant face recognition. The results of HONNGAT Tree for face perception classification, distinguishing between front glasses faces and faces with beards under laboratory conditions have been presented. Recognition occurs in real time. Addition of new target faces does not require retraining of the network. Moreover, the HONNGAT Tree model can be used for recognition with large sized face databases.

Recent artificial higher order neural network research has focused on simple models, but such models have not been very successful in describing complex systems (such as face recognition). HONNGAT Tree is one kind of higher order neural group-based model which not only offers a means whereby we can describe very complex systems, but also opens up an entirely new avenue for research into artificial higher order neural network models.

ACKNOWLEDGMENT

I would like to acknowledge the financial assistance of the following organizations in the development of Higher Order Neural Networks: Fujitsu Research Laboratories, Japan (1995-1996), Australian Research Council (1997-1998), the US National Research Council (1999-2000), and the Applied Research Centers and Dean's Office Grants of Christopher Newport University, VA, USA (2001-2008).

REFERENCES

Armstrong, W. W., & Gecsei, J. (1979). Adaptation Algorithms for Binary Tree Networks. *IEEE Transactions on Systems, Man, and Cybernetics, 9*(5), 276–285. doi:10.1109/TSMC.1979.4310196

Artyomov, E., & Yadid-Pecht, O. (2005). Modified high-order neural network for invariant pattern recognition. *Pattern Recognition Letters, 26*(6), 843–851. doi:10.1016/j.patrec.2004.09.029

Bishop, C. M. (1995). *Neural Networks for Pattern Recognition*. Oxford, UK: Oxford Univ. Press.

Chen, L. (1982). Topological Structure in Visual Perception. *Science, 218*, 699. doi:10.1126/science.7134969

Fukunaga, K. (1972). *Introduction to Statistical Pattern Recognition*. San Diego, CA: Academic Press.

He, Z., & Siyal, M. Y. (1998). Recognition of transformed English letters with modified higher-order neural networks. *Electronics Letters, 34*(25), 2415–2416. doi:10.1049/el:19981654

He, Z., & Siyal, M. Y. (1999, August). Improvement on higher-order neural networks for invariant object recognition. *Neural Processing Letters, 10*(1), 9–55. doi:10.1023/A:1018610829733

Hornik, K. (1991). Approximation capabilities of multilayer feedforward networks. *Neural Networks, 4*, 251–257. doi:10.1016/0893-6080(91)90009-T

Hu, Shengfa, & Yan, P. (1992). Level-by-Level learning for artificial neural groups. *ACTA Electronica SINICA, 20*(10), 39-43.

Inui, T., Tanabe, Y., & Onodera, Y. (1978). *Group Theory and Its Application in Physics*. Heidelberg, Germany:Springer-Verlag.

Kaita, T., Tomita, S., & Yamanaka, J. (2002, June). On a higher-order neural network for distortion invariant pattern recognition. *Pattern Recognition Letters, 23*(8), 977–984. doi:10.1016/S0167-8655(02)00028-4

Kanaoka, T., Chellappa, R., Yoshitaka, M., & Tomita, S. (1992). A Higher-order neural network for distortion unvariant pattern recognition. *Pattern Recognition Letters, 13*(12), 837–841. doi:10.1016/0167-8655(92)90082-B

Kroner, S. (1995). Adaptive averaging in higher order neural networks for invariant pattern recognition. In *Proceedings of the IEEE International Conference on Neural Networks* (Vol. Pp. 2438 - 24435)

Leshno, M, Lin, V., & Ya, P., A., & Schocken, S. (1993). Multilayer feedforward networks with a non-polynomial activation function can approximate any function. *Neural Networks, 6,* 861–867. doi:10.1016/S0893-6080(05)80131-5

Linhart, G., & Dorffner, G. (1992). A self-learning visual pattern explorer and recognizer using a higher order neural network. In . *Proceedings of International Joint Conference on Neural Networks, 3,* 705–710.

Lisboa, P., & Perantonis, S. (1991). Invariant Pattern Recognition Using Third-Order Networks and Zernlike Moments. In [).Singapore.]. *Proceedings of the IEEE International Joint Conference on Neural Networks, II,* 1421–1425. doi:10.1109/IJCNN.1991.170599

Lumer, E. D. (1992). Selective attention to perceptual groups: the phase tracking mechanism. *International Journal of Neural Systems, 3*(1), 1–17. doi:10.1142/S0129065792000024

Matsuoka, T., Hamada, H., & Nakatsu, R. (1989). Syllable Recognition Using Integrated Neural Networks In *Proceedings ofIntl. Joint Conf.* [Washington D.C.]. *Neural Networks,* 251–258.

Morad, A. H., & Yuan, B. Z. (1998, October 12-16). HONN approach for automatic model building and 3D object recognition. In *Proceedings of 1998 Fourth International Conference on Signal Processing* (vol.2, pp. 881 – 884).Naimark, M. A., & Stern, A. I. (1982). *Theory of Group Representations.* Berlin, Germany: Springer-Verlag.

Park, S., Smith, M. J. T., & Mersereau, R. M. (2000, October). Target Recognition Based on Directional Filter Banks and higher-order neural network. *Digital Signal Processing, 10*(4), 297–308. doi:10.1006/dspr.2000.0376

Pentland, A., & Turk, M. (1989). Face Processing: Models for Recognition, In *Proceedings of SPIE - Intelligent Robots and Computer Vision VIII: Algorithms and Technology* (pp 20-35).

Perantonis, S. J., & Lisboa, P. J. G. (1992). Translation, rotation, and scale invariant pattern recognition by high-order neural networks and moment classifiers. *IEEE Transactions on Neural Networks, 3*(2), 241–251. doi:10.1109/72.125865

Reid, M. B., Spirkovska, L., & Ochoa, E. (1989, June 18-22). Rapid training of higher-order neural networks for invariant pattern recognition. In . *Proceedings of International Joint Conference on Neural Networks, 1,* 689–692. doi:10.1109/IJCNN.1989.118653

Reid, M. B., Spirkovska, L., & Ochoa, E. (1989). Simultaneous position, scale, rotation invariant pattern classification using third-order neural networks. *International Journal on Neural Networks, 1,* 154–159.

Sanger, T. D. (1991). A Tree-Structured Adaptive Network for Function Approximation in High-Dimensional Spaces. *IEEE Transactions on Neural Networks, 2*(2), 285–293. doi:10.1109/72.80339

Sankar, A., & Mammone, R. J. (1993). Growing and pruning neural network tree network. *IEEE Transactions on Computers, 42*(3), 291–299. doi:10.1109/12.210172

Schmidt, W. A. C., & Davis, J. P. (1993). Pattern recognition properties of various feature spaces for higher order neural networks. *IEEE Transactions on Pattern Analysis and Machine Intelligence, 15*(8), 795–801. doi:10.1109/34.236250

Shin, Y., & Ghosh, J. (1991, July 8-14). The pi-sigma network: an efficient higher-order neural network for pattern classification and function approximation. In []. Seattle, USA.]. *Proceedings of the International Joint Conference on Neural Networks, 1,* 13–18.

Spirkovska, L., & Reid, M. B. (1990, Novermber 6-9). An empirical comparison of ID3 and HONNs for distortion invariant object recognition. In *Proceedings of the 2nd International IEEE Conference on Tools for Artificial Intelligence* (pp. 577 – 582).

Spirkovska, L., & Reid, M. B. (1990, June 17-21). Connectivity strategies for higher-order neural networks applied to pattern recognition. In . *Proceedings of International Joint Conference on Neural Networks, 1,* 21–26. doi:10.1109/IJCNN.1990.137538

Spirkovska, L., & Reid, M. B. (1991, July 8-14). Coarse-coding applied to HONNs for PSRI object recognition. In []. Seattle, USA.]. *Proceedings of the International Joint Conference on Neural Networks, 2,* 931.

Spirkovska, L., & Reid, M. B. (1992). Robust position, scale, and rotation invariant object recognition using higher-order neural networks . *Pattern Recognition, 25*(9), 975–985. doi:10.1016/0031-3203(92)90062-N

Spirkovska, L., & Reid, M. B. (1993). Coarse-coded higher-order neural networks for PSRI object recognition. *IEEE Transactions on Neural Networks, 4*(2), 276–283. doi:10.1109/72.207615

Spirkovska, L., & Reid, M. B. (1994). Higher-order neural networks applied to 2D and 3D object recognition. *Machine Learning, 15*(2), 169–199.

Tsao, T.-R. (1989, June 18-22). A group theory approach to neural network computing of 3D rigid motion. In *Proceedings ofIntl. Joint Conf. Neural Networks. 2,* 275-280. Washington D.C.

van der Waerden, B. L. (1970). *Algebra. New York:* Frederick Ungar Publishing Co.

Voutriaridis, C., Boutalis, Y. S., & Mertzios, B. G. (2003, July 2-5). Ridge polynomial networks in pattern recognition. In *Proceedings of 4th EURASIP Conference on Video/Image Processing and Multimedia Communications* (vol.2, pp.519 – 524).

Wan, L., & Sun, L. (1996, May 20-23). Automatic target recognition using higher order neural network. In *Proceedings of the IEEE 1996 National Aerospace and Electronics Conference* (Vol. 1, pp. 221 – 226).

Wang, J., Sun, Y., & Chen, Q. (2003, November 2-5). Recognition of digital annotation with invariant HONN based on orthogonal Fourier-Mellin moments. In *Proceedings of 2003 International Conference on Machine Learning and Cybernetics* (Vol. 4, pp.2261 – 2264).

Willcox, C. R. (1991). Understanding hierarchical neural network behaviour: a renormalization group approach. *Journal of Physics. A. Mathematical Nuclear and General, 24,* 2655–2644. doi:10.1088/0305-4470/24/11/030

Wu, J., & Chang, J. (1993, October 25-29). Invariant pattern recognition using higher-order neural networks. In [).Nagoya, Japan.]. *Proceedings of International Joint Conference on Neural Networks*, *2*, 1273–1276.

Yang, X. (1990). Detection and classification of neural signals and identification of neural networks (synaptic connectivity). *Dissertation Abstracts International - B, 50*(12), 5761.

Zeeman, E. C. (1962), The topology of the brain and visual perception. In M. K. Fork, Jr (eds.), *Topology of 3-manifolds and related Topics* (pp.240-256).Englewood Cliffs, NJ: Prentice-Hall, Inc.

Zhang, M. (2009a). Artificial Higher Order Neural Network Nonlinear Models: SAS NLIN or HONNs. In M. Zhang (Ed.), *Artificial Higher Order Neurla Networks for Economics and Business* (pp. 1-47). Hershey, PA: IGI Global

Zhang, M. (2009b).Ultra Higher Frequency Trigonometric Higher Order Neural Networks for Time Series Data Analysis. In M. Zhang (Ed.), *Artificial Higher Order Neurla Networks for Economics and Business* (pp. 133-163). Hershey, PA: IGI Global

Zhang, M., Crowley, J., Dunstone, E., & Fulcher, J. (1993, October 14). Face Recognition, *Australia Patent*, No.PM1828.

Zhang, M., & Fulcher, J. (1996). Face recognition using artificial neural network group-based adaptive tolerance (GAT) trees . *IEEE Transactions on Neural Networks*, *7*(3), 555–567. doi:10.1109/72.501715

Zhang, M., & Fulcher, J. (1996, September 15-18). Neural network group models for financial data simulation. In*Proceedings of World Congress On Neural Networks* (pp. 910-913). San Diego, CA.

Zhang, M., Fulcher, J., & Scofield, R. (1997). Rainfalll estimation using artificial neural network group . *International Journal of Neurlcomputing*, *16*(2), 97–115.

Zhang, M., Murugesan, S., & Sadeghi, M. (1995, October 30 - November 3). Polynomial higher order neural network for economic data simulation. In*Proceedings of International Conference On Neural Information Processing* (pp. 493-496). Beijing, China.

Zhang, M., Xu, S., & Fulcher, J. (2002, January). Neuron-Adaptive Higher Order Neural Network Models for Automated Financial Data Modeling. *IEEEE transactions on Neural Networks, 13*(1), 188-204.

Zhang, M., Xu, S., & Fulcher, J. (2007). ANSER: an Adaptive-Neuron artificial neural network System for Estimating Rainfall using satellite data. *International Journal of Computers and Applications*, *29*(3), 1–8. doi:10.2316/Journal.202.2007.3.202-1585

Zhang, M., Zhang, J. C., & Fulcher, J. (2000, April). Higher order neural network group models for data approximation . *International Journal of Neural Systems*, *10*(2), 123–142.

Zhang, S. J., Jing, Z. L., & Li, J. X. (2004). Fast learning high-order neural networks for pattern recognition. *Electronics Letters*, *40*(19), 1207–1208. doi:10.1049/el:20045550

Zhou, X., Koch, M. W., & Roberts, M. W. (1991, July 14). Selective attention of high-order neural networks for invariant object recognition. In []. Seattle, USA.]. *Proceedings of International Joint Conference on Neural Networks*, *2*, 9378.

APPENDIX

The following definitions are needed in order to describe the HONNGAT Tree model:

Appendix A: Generalised Artificial Higher Order Neural Network Sets

Generalised artificial higher order neural networks are defined as the union of product generalised and additive generalised artificial higher order neural network sets.

Additive Generalised Artificial Higher Order Neural Network Sets

An *additive generalisedHONN set - HONN⁺* - is a set in which element $honn^+_i$ is either an artificial higher order neural network or an additive generalized higher order neural network, for which the following conditions hold:

(a) $honn^+_i$ *HONNS*;

or

if an addition $honn^+_i + honn^+_j$ is defined every two elements $honn^+_i$, $honn^+_j$ *HONNS*,   then $honn^+_i + honn^+_j$ *HONN⁺*, $honn^+_i$, $honn^+_j$ *HONNS*;

or

if an addition $honn^+_i + honn^+_j$ is defined for every two elements

$honn^+_i$ *HONNS* and $honn^+_j$ *HONN⁺*,   then $honn^+_i + honn^+_j$ *HONN⁺*, $honn^+_i$ *HONNS* and $honn^+_j$ *HONN⁺*;

or

if an addition $honn^+_i + honn^+_j$ is defined every two elements $honn^+_i$, $honn^+_j$ *HONN⁺*,

then $honn^+_i + honn^+_j$ *HONN⁺*, $honn^+_i$, $honn^+_j$ *HONN⁺*;   (b) an element $honn^+_{i0}$ in *HONN⁺* such that

$honn^+_{i0} + honn^+_i = honn^+_i + honn^+_{i0} = honn^+_i$, $honn^+_i$ *HONN⁺*;

($honn^+_{i0}$ is called the *identity* element of the set *HONN⁺*);

(c) for every element $honn^+_i$ *HONN⁺*,

there exists a unique element, designated $honn^+_i$,

for which $honn^+_i + (-honn^+_i) = (-honn^+_i) + honn^+_i = honn^+_0$,

(the element $-honn^+_i$ is called the *inverse* of $honn^+_i$);

Product Generalised Artificial Higher Order Neural Network Sets

A *product generalisedHONN set - HONN** - is a set in which each element $honn^*_i$ is either an artificial higher order neural network or a product generalised higher order neural network, for which the following conditions hold:

(a) $honn^*_i$ *HONNS*;

or

if the product $honn^*_i honn^*_j$ is defined for every two elements $honn^*_i$, $honn^*_j$ *HONNS*,

then $honn^*_i honn^*_j$ *HONN**, $honn^*_i$, $honn^*_j$ *HONNS*

or

if a product $honn^*_i honn^*_j$ is defined for every two elements

$honn^*_i$ *HONNS* and $honn^*_j$ *HONN**,

then $honn^*_i honn^*_j$ *HONN**, $honn^*_i$ *HONNS* and $honn^*_j$ *HONN**;

or

a product $honn^*_i honn^*_j$ is defined for every two elements $honn^*_i$, $honn^*_j$ *HONN**,

then $honn^*_i honn^*_j$ *HONN**, $honn^*_i$, $honn^*_j$ *HONN**;   (b) an element $honn^*_{ie}$ in *HONN** such that

$honn^*_{ie} honn^*_i = honn^*_i honn^*_{ie} = honn^*_i$, $honn^*_i$ *HONN**

($honn^*_{ie}$ is called the *identity* element of the set *HONN**);

(c) For every element $honn^*_i$ *HONN**, a unique element, designated $honn^{*-1}_i$, for which $honn*_i honn*^{-1}_i = honn*^{-1}_i honn*_i = honn*_e$,

(the element $honn*^{-1}_i$ is called the *inverse of $honn*_i$*);

HONN Generalized Sets

The *artificial higher order neural network generalised set - HONNGS -* is the union of the product set **HONN*** and the additive set **HONN⁺**. Each element $honn_i$ is either an artificial higher order neural network or a generalised higher order neural network. We write:

HONNGS = HONN* HONN⁺

The first example, let's consider the derivation of the **THONN** generalised set:

THONN^{1,9,13,3} = THONN*^{1,9,13,3} THONN⁺^{1,9,13,3}

Now in order to define the unique $thonn*^{1,9,13,3}_i$ and $thonn^{+1,9,13,3}_i$ elements for the *inverse of $thonn^{1,9,13,3}_i$*, we assign the same structures and weights to them, except that the inverse element has outputs of opposite sign. This is consistent with Group Theory generally, since if an element n is a member of a group, then its inverse $1/n$ is also a member of the same group.

The second example, let's consider the derivation of the **PHONN** generalised set:

PHONN^{1,9,13,3} = PHONN*^{1,9,13,3} PHONN⁺^{1,9,13,3}

Now in order to define the unique $phonn*^{1,9,13,3}_i$ and $phonn^{+1,9,13,3}_i$ elements for the *inverse of $phonn^{1,9,13,3}_i$*, we assign the same structures and weights to them, except that the inverse element has outputs of opposite sign. This is consistent with Group Theory generally, since if an element n is a member of a group, then its inverse $1/n$ is also a member of the same group.

The third example, let's consider the derivation of the **SPHONN** generalised set:

SPHONN^{1,9,13,3} = SPHONN*^{1,9,13,3} SPHONN⁺^{1,9,13,3}

Now in order to define the unique $sphonn*^{1,9,13,3}_i$ and $sphonn^{+1,9,13,3}_i$ elements for the *inverse of $sphonn^{1,9,13,3}_i$*, we assign the same structures and weights to them, except that the inverse element has outputs of opposite sign. This is consistent with Group Theory generally, since if an element n is a member of a group, then its inverse $1/n$ is also a member of the same group.

The elements of set **HONNS** are higher order neural networks; the elements of set **HONNGS**, by contrast, are higher order neural network *groups*. The difference between a higher order neural network and a higher order neural network group was illustrated previously in Figure 2, in which we see that higher order neural network generalised set **HONNGS** is a more generalised form of higher order neural network set **HONNS**. Accordingly, higher order neural network groups should hold more potential for characterising complex systems.

Appendix B: Proof of the Inference

An inductive proof of this inference is provided as follows:

Inference:

"Consider a higher order neural network Piecewise Function *Group*, in which each member is a standard multilayer feedforward higher order neural network, and which has a locally bounded, piecewise continuous (rather than polynomial) activation function and threshold. Each such group can approximate *any* kind of piecewise continuous function, and to *any* degree of accuracy."

We use the following definitions in our proof:

H_w: the higher order neural network with n input units, characterised by w;

P: the compact set, $P \ R^n$;

$C(R^n)$: the family of "real world" functions one may wish to approximate with feedforward higher order neurl network architectures of the form H_w;

s: every continuous function, $s \ C(R^n)$;

G: the family of all functions implied by the network's architecture - namely the family when w runs over all possible values;

g: a good approximation to s on P, $g \ G$;

$L^\infty(P)$: essentially bounded on P in R^n with respect to Lebesgue measurement;

$L^\infty_{loc}(P)$: locally essentially bounded on P in R^n with respect to Lebesgue measurement;

HONNPFG (Higher Order Neural Network Neural Network Piecewise Function Group): the higher order neural network group in which each addition $h_i + h_j$ is defined as the *Piecewise Function* for every two elements $h_i, h_j \ HONNG$.

$$h_i + h_i = \begin{cases} h_i, I_i = \left(I \in P_1\right) \\ h_i, I_i = \left(I \in P_2\right) \end{cases}$$

where I_i, I_j, and I (inputs to the higher order neural networks)

Proof:

Step 1: $P_1 = P$

Based on the Leshno theorem (1993),

$$\lim_{j=\infty} ||s - f_i|| \, L\infty\left(P\right) = 0$$

So we have $\lim_{j=\infty} ||s - g_i|| \, L\infty\left(P_1\right) = 0$

Step 2: $P_1 \ P_2 = P$

$$s = \begin{cases} s_1 \; a \; continuous \; function \; on \; P_1 \\ s_2 \; a \; continuous \; function \; on \; P_2 \end{cases}$$

In $\boldsymbol{P}_1$, we have:

$$\lim_{j=\infty} ||\, s_1 - g_i^{(1)} \,|| \, L\infty \left(P_1 \right) = 0$$

There exists a function $g^{(1)}$ which is a good approximation to s_1 on $\boldsymbol{P}_1$.
In $\boldsymbol{P}_2$, we have:

$$\lim_{j=\infty} ||\, s_2 - g_i^{(2)} \,|| \, L\infty \left(P_2 \right) = 0$$

There exists a function $g^{(2)}$ which is a good approximation to s_2 on $\boldsymbol{P}_2$.
Based on the earlier definition of Neural Network Piecewise Function Groups,

$$h_1 + h_2 = \begin{cases} h_1 = g^{(1)}, & I_1 = \left(I \in P_1 \right) \\ h_2 = g^{(2)}, & I_2 = \left(I \in P_2 \right) \end{cases}$$

where I_1, I_2, and I (inputs to the higher order neural networks)
Step 3: $\boldsymbol{P}_1 \; \boldsymbol{P}_2 \; ...... \; \boldsymbol{P}_m = \boldsymbol{P}$,
m is an any integer and m $\rightarrow \infty$.

$$s = \begin{cases} s_1, \; a \; continuous \; function \; on \; P_1 \\ s_2, \; a \; continuous \; function \; on \; P_2 \\ s_m, \; a \; continuous \; function \; on \; P_m \end{cases}$$

Based on the definition of Neural Network Piecewise Function Group, we have:

$$h_1 + h_2 + ... + h_m = \begin{cases} h_1 = g^{(1)}, & I \in P_1 \\ h_2 = g^{(2)}, & I \in P_2 \\ h_m = g^{(m)}, & I \in P_m \end{cases}$$

Step 4: $\boldsymbol{P}_1 \; \boldsymbol{P}_2 \; ...... \; \boldsymbol{P}_m \; \boldsymbol{P}_{m+1} = \boldsymbol{P}$

$$s = \begin{cases} s_1 \ a \ continuous \ function \ on \ P_1 \\ s_2 \ a \ continuous \ function \ on \ P_2 \\ s_m \ a \ continuous \ function \ on \ P_m \\ s_{m+1} \ a \ continous \ function \ on \ P_{m+1} \end{cases}$$

In $\boldsymbol{P}_{m+1}$, based on Leshno's Theorem (1993), we have:

$$\lim_{j=\infty} || s_{m+1} - g_i^{(m+1)} || \ L\infty\left(P_{m+1}\right) = 0$$

There exists a function $g^{(m+1)}$ which is a good approximation to s_{m+1} on $\boldsymbol{P}_{m+1}$. Based on step 3, we have:

$$h_1 + h_2 + ...+ h_m + h_{m+1} = \begin{cases} h_1 = g^{(1)}, & I \in P_1 \\ h_2 = g^{(2)}, & I \in P_2 \\ h_m = g^{(m)}, & I \in P_m \\ h_{m+1} = g^{(m+1)}, & I \in P_{m+1} \end{cases}$$

In the real world, if the function being analysed varies in a discontinuous and nonsmooth fashion with respect to input variables, then such functions cannot be effectively simulated by a higher order neural network. By contrast, if we use higher order eural network *groups* to simulate these functions, it *is* possible to simulate discontinuous functions to any degree accuracy, even at points of discontinuity

Appendix C: HONNGAT Tree Definitions

(1) <u>Image Definitions:</u>
    Row index set: $Sr = \{1,2, ..., Nr\}$
    Column index set: $Sc = \{1,2, ..., Nc\}$
    Space field: $Sr \times Sc$
    Grey set: N_i
    $E_1, E_2 ..., E_k$ Euclidean space: $EE = \{E_1, E_2, ... E_i, ..., E_k\}$
    Image Operator $\boldsymbol{IMAO}$: $Sr \times Sc \to EE$
    Let:
    $E_i = \{1, 2, 3, ... N_i\}$
    $N_i = 256, (i = 1,2,3)$
    $EE = \{E_1, E_2, E_3\}$
    then
    $\boldsymbol{IMAO}(i, j)$ is the colour image which can be described as a colour human face.
    Let:
        $i \quad = 1$ for Ei and
    $EE = E_1$

Digital Image Operator $\boldsymbol{IMA}$: $Sr \times Sc$

then

$IMA(i, j)$ is a black-and-white image which can be used to represent a human face.

Let:

Label Set: $LS = \{1, 2, ..., M\}$,

each label corresponds to a different human face

(2) Tolerance Space Definitions:

The definitions for tolerance space are as follows (details, please see Zeeman, 1962):

Given the Set: $\boldsymbol{X}, \boldsymbol{Y}, \boldsymbol{Z}$,

then tolerance ξ is a type of relation in the set $\boldsymbol{X}$ or $\boldsymbol{Y}$ or $\boldsymbol{Z}$

We define Tolerance Space $(\boldsymbol{X}, \xi)$ as follows:

Let:

If x $\boldsymbol{X} \rightarrow (x, x)$ ξ

If x $\boldsymbol{X}, y$ $\boldsymbol{Y}$, and (x, y) ξ

then (y, x) ξ.

If x $\boldsymbol{X}, y$ $\boldsymbol{Y}, z$ $\boldsymbol{Z}$ and (x, y) ξ, (y, z) ξ

then (x, z) ξ or $(x, z) \notin \xi$.

(3) Higher Order Neural Network Definitions:

$H_{i,j}$: Higher Order Neural Network Group-Based (HONNGB) node, adaptive node and label node, where i: the level or deep of the HONNGAT Tree

j: the *jth* node n the i level

$I_f(H_{i,j})$: The fire input of the node $H_{i,j}$

if $I_f(H_{i,j}) = 1$, the node has been fired

$I_d(H_{i,j})$: The data input of the node $H_{i,j}$

if $I_f(H_{i,j}) = 1$, $I_d(H_{i,j})$ can be input to node $H_{i,j}$

$I(H_{i,j})$: The input to HONNGB node $H_{i,j}$

$O(HONN_k)$: The output of higher order neural network $HONN_k$

$O(H_{i,j})$: The output from HONNGB node $H_{i,j}$

$O_0(H_{i,j})$, $O_1(H_{i,j})$, $O_2(H_{i,j})$: Outputs of node $H_{i,j}$

binary outputs are: $O_0(H_{i,j})$ and $O_2(H_{i,j})$

ternary outputs are: $O_0(H_{i,j})$, $O_1(H_{i,j})$, and $O_2(H_{i,j})$

$P(H_{i,j}, H_{l,k})$: Path of the HONNGAT Tree between nodes $H_{i,j}$ and $H_{l,k}$

(4) Higher Order Neural Network Group-based Adaptive Tolerance Tree operator $\boldsymbol{HONNGAT}$

Considering the above definitions, the Higher Order Neural Network Group-based Adaptive Tolerance Tree model can be written as:

Higher Order Neural Network Group-based Adaptive Tolerance Tree operator

$\boldsymbol{HONNGAT}$: $IMA(i, j) \rightarrow LS$

This means that after $IMA(i, j)$ has been operated upon by the $\boldsymbol{HONNGAT}$ operator -which incorporates an adaptive function and uses the translation invariant face recognition technique - an object (human face) can be recognised by label set LS.

The Higher Order Neural Network Groug-based Adaptive Tolerance tree operator $\boldsymbol{HONNGAT}$ is the operator set:

$\boldsymbol{HONNGAT} = \{ \boldsymbol{HTO, HNO, HPO, HLO, HAO} \}$

Each operator or operator set belongs to one of the following four types:

(4.1) Higher Order Neural Network Translating Operator - **HTO**

Higher order neural network Translating Operator -- **HTO** uses the translation invariant face recognition technique and is defined as:

HTO$(IMA(i,j))$: $IMA(i,j) \rightarrow IMA_u(i,j)$, $u=0,1.2, ...N_u$

where:

$IMA_0(i,j)$: centre face of facial image $IMA(i,j)$

$IMA_1(i,j)$: lower-left face of facial image $IMA(i,j)$

$IMA_2(i,j)$: lower face of facial image $IMA(i,j)$

$IMA_3(i,j)$: lower-right face of image $IMA(i,j)$

$IMA_4(i,j)$: right face of facial image $IMA(i,j)$

$IMA_5(i,j)$: upper-right face of facial image $IMA(i,j)$

$IMA_6(i,j)$: up face of facial image $IMA(i,j)$

$IMA_7(i,j)$: upper-left face of facial image $IMA(i,j)$

$IMA_8(i,j)$: left face of facial image $IMA(i,j)$

....

(4.2) Higher Order Neural Network Node Operator Set - **HNO**

The Higher order neural network Node Operator **HNO**$(H_{i,j})$, which has the adaptive function within tolerance space is the set of operators:

HNO$(H_{i,j}) =$

{ **HNO0**$(I_f(H_{i,j}), I_d(H_{i,j}))$, **HNO1**$(H_{i,j}, IMA(i,j))$, **HNG**, **HNO2**$(O(H_{i,j}))$}

where:

$$HNO0\left(I_f\left(H_{i,j}\right), I_d\left(H_{i,j}\right)\right): \begin{cases} I\left(H_{i,j}\right) = I_d\left(H_{i,j}\right) = IMA\left(i,j\right), \text{ if } I_f\left(H_{i,j}\right) = 1 \text{ for testing} \\ I\left(H_{i,j}\right) = \varnothing, \qquad\qquad\qquad \text{ if } I_f\left(H_{i,j}\right) = 0 \text{ for testing} \\ I\left(H_{i,j}\right) = I_d\left(H_{i,j}\right) = IMA\left(i,j\right), \text{ for training} \end{cases}$$

$$u = 1, 2, 3, ..., Nu$$

HNO1$(H_{i,j}, I_d(H_{i,j}))$: $I(H_{i,j}) \rightarrow O(HONN_k)$ $k=1,2 ..., k$

Where **HNO1** is one kind of higher order neural network operator

(for example **THONN**).

Higher Order Neural Netowrk Group operator -- **HNG** is used for all higher order neural networks in the group:

HNG: $O(H_{i,j}) = O(HONN_1) * O(HONN_2) * O(HONN_3)* ......* O(HONN_k)$

Where: * means *AND* or *OR*.

For the binary case:

HNO2$(O(H_{i,j}))$: $(H_{i,j}) \rightarrow \{ O_0(H_{i,j}), O_2(H_{i,j}) \}$

The binary output is:

$$O_0\left(H_{i,j}\right) = \begin{cases} 1, O\left(H_{i,j}\right) \in \xi_1\left(H_{i,j}\right) \\ 0, otherwise \end{cases}$$

$$O_1\left(H_{i,j}\right) = \begin{cases} 1, O\left(H_{i,j}\right) \in \xi_2\left(H_{i,j}\right) \\ 0, otherwise \end{cases}$$

For the ternary case:

$HNO2(O(H_{i,j})):O(H_{i,j}) \rightarrow \{ O_0(H_{i,j}), O_1(H_{i,j}), O_2(H_{i,j}) \}$

The ternary output is:

$$O_0\left(H_{i,j}\right) = \begin{cases} 1, O\left(H_{i,j}\right) \in \xi_1\left(H_{i,j}\right) \\ 0, \textit{otherwise} \end{cases}$$

$$O_1\left(H_{i,j}\right) = \begin{cases} 1, O\left(H_{i,j}\right) \in \xi_3\left(H_{i,j}\right) \\ 0, \textit{otherwise} \end{cases}$$

$$O_2\left(H_{i,j}\right) = \begin{cases} 1, O\left(H_{i,j}\right) \in \xi_2\left(H_{i,j}\right) \\ 0, \textit{otherwise} \end{cases}$$

where $\xi_1(H_{i,j})$, $\xi_2(H_{i,j})$, and $\xi_3(H_{i,j})$ are tolerance values for node $H_{i,j}$.

Now let:

Higher order neural network Node Operator set $HNO=\{ HNO(H_{i,j}) \}$

$i=1,2,...,Nr; j=1,2,...,Nc$

$H_{i,j}$ is the artificial higher order neural network node

(4.3) <u>Higher Order Neural Network Path Operator set - **HPO**</u>

Higher order neural network Path Operator $HPO(H_{i,j}, H_{l,k})$:

$I_f(H_{l,k}) = O_m(H_{i,j})$, m = 0, or 1, or 2

Now let:

Operator set $HPO=\{ HPO(H_{i,j}, H_{l,k}) \}$ $i=1,2,...,Nr; j=1,2,...,Nc$

$l=1,2,...,Nr; k=1,2,...,Nc$

(4.4) <u>Higher Order Neural Netowrk Label Operator - **HLO**</u>

Higher order neural network Label Operator $HLO(H_{i,j})$:

if lowest level node in different branch $Om(H_{i,j}) = 1$,

m = 0, or 1, or 2

Now let:

$HLO(H_{i,j})$: $LS \rightarrow i, i = 1,2,3, ..., m$

else

$HLO(H_{i,j})$: $LS \rightarrow \varnothing$

Now let:

Higher order neural network Node Operator Operator set

$HLO=\{ HLO(H_{i,j}) \}$ $i=1,2,...,Nr; j=1,2,...,Nc$

$H_{i,j}$ is label node of artificial higher order neural network

(4.5) <u>Higher Order Neural Network Adaptive node Operator set - **HAO**</u>

Higher order neural network Adaptive node Operator $HAO(H_{i,j})$ means:

If $O(H_{l,k})$ $\xi_m(H_{l,k})$ and $O_m(H_{l,k}) = 1$ (m = 0, 1, or 2)

Add node $H_{i,j}$ that be connected to $O_m(H_{p,k})$ if needed,

and $O_m(H_{i,j}) = I_j(H_{i,j}) = 1$ (m = 0, 1, or 2)

The function of $HAO(H_{i,j})$ means that if the adaptive node is fired, its output will be 1.

Now Let:

Higher order neural network Node Operator set $HAO=\{ HAO(H_{i,j}) \}$

$i=1,2,...,Nr; j=1,2,...,Nc$, $H_{i,j}$ is an adaptive node

Chapter 2
Higher Order Neural Networks for Symbolic, Sub-Symbolic and Chaotic Computations

João Pedro Neto
Faculdade de Ciências, Portugal

ABSTRACT

This chapter deals with discrete and recurrent artificial neural networks with a homogenous type of neuron. With this architecture we will see how to perform symbolic computations by executing high-level programs within this network dynamics. Next, using higher order synaptic connections, it is possible to integrate common sub-symbolic learning algorithms into the previous architecture. Thirdly, taking advantage of the chaotic properties of dynamical systems, we present some uses of chaotic computations with the same neurons and synapses, and, thus, creating a hybrid system of three computation types.

INTRODUCTION

This chapter presents a method to merge symbolic, sub-symbolic and chaotic computation into a single neural network architecture using **higher order neural networks**. First, we introduce a high-level programming language to hard-wire the neural net model. In this language we can handle **symbolic computation** (meaning that the information flow of a given synapse has a fixed semantic content, like a value of a certain data type or a synchronization signal). Using higher order neurons – corresponding to special constructs called neuron-synapse connections – we show how to include learning processes and **sub-symbolic computation** (where content is spread in several data units). The end result is a neural net partially *hard*-wired and partially *soft*-wired by a suitable learning algorithm with modules performing programming tasks and modules supporting sub-symbolic tasks. The last main section shows uses of chaotic properties inscribed in these complex dynamical systems, namely, a mechanism of blind search and a random number generator.

DOI: 10.4018/978-1-61520-711-4.ch002

BACKGROUND

Despite the first paper by McCulloch & Pitts (1943) which introduced neural networks as logic computing devices, symbolic computation is not a common thread in neural networks scientific works. However, there are some articles and books in the literature that focus on symbolic capabilities, (Gruau, 1995; Siegelmann, 1996; Carnell, 2007).

The JANNeT system (see Gruau (1995) for details) introduces a dialect of Pascal with some parallel constructs. This algorithmic description is translated, using several automated steps (first on a tree-like data structure and then on a low-level code, named *cellular code*), to produce a non-homogenous neural network (there are four different neuron types) able to perform the required computations. In JANNeT, every neuron is activated only when all its synapses had transferred their values. Since this may not occur at the same instant, the global dynamics is not synchronous. A special attention is given to design automation of the final neural network architecture.

The neural language project NIL, outlined in Siegelmann (1993) and Siegelmann (1996), is also able to perform symbolic computations by using certain sets of constructions that are compiled into an appropriate neural net (using the same homogeneous neural architecture presented herein). It has a complex set of data types, from boolean and scalar types, to lists, stacks or sets that are kept inside a single neuron, using fractal coding.

Symbolic computation, within the typical and well-studied sub-symbolic features of neural networks, provides opportunities to create **hybrid systems** able to use both types of computations. The significance of systems which integrate symbolic and sub-symbolic computing techniques has been already consolidated; see Wilson & Hendler (1993) for an analysis of these types of hybrid systems. Motivation for this structural hybridization can be found both in biology (persons are able to process high level symbolic concepts supported by the neural biochemistry of the brain) and in engineering (intelligent control design tends to incorporate symbolic and sub-symbolic processing, in order to achieve better performances). There are several different ways to accomplish this hybridization. Some models separate completely the two computation methodologies, using the output of the sub-symbolic structure as an input to the classical AI control schemata (Hendler & Dickens, 1991). Others use symbolic and sub-symbolic information in the same data structure (as we do in this chapter), blurring the distinctions among them, like in Lange *et al.* (1989). Others still encapsulate subsystems of both kinds, and interface them through supervisors that control and hide different computing demands and resources of the subsystems (Wilson & Hendler, 1993). Also hybrid systems are useful in many areas, like vision and object recognition (Buker, 1998), machine learning and rule extraction (McMillan, 1992; Osório & Amy, 1999; Sentiono, 2000) or sorting algorithms (Chen & Honavar, 1999).

This integration is achieved using **higher order nets** (i.e., networks having neurons with higher order transfer functions). These types of nets have been used before. Most of the previous work on higher order neural nets study the superior computational power achieved by these types of transfer function, that can possibly multiply activations, and not only take a linear function of them. Pollack (1987) built a finite higher order neural network model with universal properties. Sun *et al.* (1991) shows another Turing computational equivalence of second-order nets. Goudreau *et al.* (1994) deals with networks with the Heavyside (step) activation function. They show that single layer second order nets are strictly more powerful than single layer first order networks. An application to learn finite state automata using second order neural nets is described in Giles *et al.* (1992).

Finally, the idea of using chaos for computing purposes has also been around in the last years (Sinha & Ditto, 1998; Guoguang *et al.*, 2001; Munakata *et al.*, 2002; Lourenço, 2004). We particularly address the use of simulated chaos in neural networks as alternative and potentially more useful method of solution to the problems of blind search and random number generation.

SYMBOLIC COMPUTATION

Computability analysis of the analog neural net model is due to Hava Siegelmann and Eduardo Sontag (Siegelmann & Sontag, 1994, 1995). They used a quite simple model to establish lower bounds on the computational power of analog recurrent neural nets (Siegelmann, 1999). These systems satisfy the classical constraints of computation theory, namely, (a) input is discrete and finite, (b) output is discrete, and (c) the system is itself finite (i.e., control is finite). The functions computable by such a model depend on the type of the weights. With integer type, the neural network has the power of finite automata, like the McCulloch and Pitts neural net model (McCulloch & Pitts, 1943; Minsky, 1967). Rational weights give Turing power to neural nets and with real weights we can compute non recursive functions. See Siegelmann (1999) for a systematic approach.

Herein, the analog recurrent neural net is a discrete time dynamic system, $\mathbf{x}(t+1) = \varphi(\mathbf{x}(t), \mathbf{u}(t))$, with initial state $\mathbf{x}(0) = \mathbf{x}_0$, where t denotes time, $x_i(t)$ denotes the activity (firing frequency) of neuron i at time t, within a population of N interconnected neurons, and $u_k(t)$ denotes the value of input channel k at time t, within a set of M input channels. The application map φ is taken as a composition of an affine map with a piecewise linear map of the interval [0,1], known as the piecewise linear function σ:

$$\sigma = \begin{cases} 1 & , x \geq 1 \\ x & , 0 < x < 1 \\ 0 & , x \leq 0 \end{cases}$$

The dynamic system becomes,

$$x_j(t+1) = \sigma(\sum_{i=1}^{N} a_{ji} x_i(t) + \sigma = \begin{cases} 1 & , x \geq 1 \\ x & , 0 < x < 1 \\ 0 & , x \leq 0 \end{cases} c_j)$$

where a_{ji}, b_{jk} and c_j are rational weights. Figure 1 displays a graphical representation of a single equation, used throughout this chapter. When a_{ji} (or b_{jk} or a_{jj}) takes value 1, it is not displayed in the graph.

Figure 1. Graphical notation for neurons, input channels and their interconnections

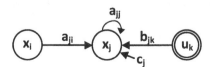

Figure 2. Graphical notation for neurons, input channels and their interconnections (modules are denoted by squares)

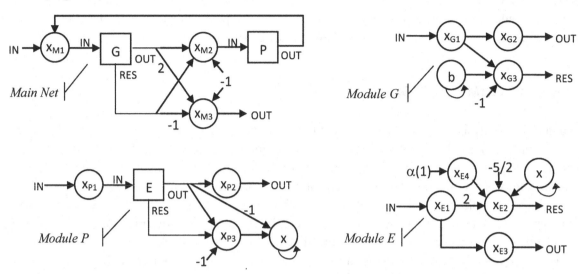

How to perform arbitrarily computations over these networks? One way is to specify algorithms to use a high-level programming language to write algorithms that can be automatically translated into the proper low-level description readable for a specific hardware. Herein, the hardware is the neural networks and the programming language is called NETDEF.

NETDEF is a high-level parallel programming language able to describe arbitrarily complex algorithms. It is an imperative language, with syntax and semantic very close to those of Occam. Its main concepts are processes and channels. A program can be described as a collection of processes executing concurrently, and communicating with each other through channels or shared memory. The language has assignment, conditional and loop control structures, it supports several data types, variable and function declarations, and several other processes. It uses a **modular** synchronization mechanism based on handshaking for process ordering. More detailed descriptions may be found in Neto & Costa (1999) and Neto *et al.* (2003).

Let's consider a simple example of how NETDEF programs are transformed into neural networks. For instance, to translate while b do x:= x+1 (i.e., while boolean variable b is true, increment integer variable 'x' by 1), the compiler will create nets schemas, or modules, for each atomic concept present in the instruction (namely, a main module to execute the cycle, a module for the increment, another for reading the value of variable 'b', and another to assign the new value into 'x').

In the main module synapse IN sends value 1 (from some previous neuron) into x_{M1} neuron thus starting the computation. Module G computes the value of boolean variable 'b' and sends the 0/1 result through synapse RES. This result is synchronized with an output of 1 through synapse OUT. The next two neurons decide between stopping the process ('b' is false) or executing module P ('b' is true), iterating again. The dynamic system is described by the following equations:

$$x_{M1}(t+1) = \sigma(x_{IN}(t) + x_{P2}(t))$$

$$x_{M2}(t+1) = \sigma(x_{G2}(t) + x_{G3}(t) - 1.0)$$

$$x_{M3}(t+1) = \sigma(2.x_{G2}(t) - x_{G3}(t) - 1.0)$$

Module G just accesses the value 'b' and outputs it through neuron x_{G3}. This is achieved because x_{G3} bias -1.0 is compensated by value 1 sent by x_{G1}, allowing value 'b' to be the activation of x_{G3}. This module is defined by:

$$x_{G1}(t+1) = \sigma(x_{M1}(t))$$

$$x_{G2}(t+1) = \sigma(x_{G1}(t))$$

$$x_{G3}(t+1) = \sigma(x_{G1}(t) + b(t) - 1.0)$$

Module P makes an assignment to the real variable 'x' with the value computed by module E. Before neuron x receives the activation value of x_{P3}, the module uses the output signal of E to erase its previous value.

$$x_{P1}(t+1) = \sigma(x_{M2}(t))$$

$$x_{P2}(t+1) = \sigma(x_{E3}(t))$$

$$x_{P3}(t+1) = \sigma(x_{E2}(t) + x_{E3}(t) - 1.0)$$

In module E the increment of 'x' is computed (using $\alpha(1)$ for the code of real 1). The extra $-1/2$ bias of neuron x_{E2} is necessary due to the internal coding:

$$x_{E1}(t+1) = \sigma(x_{P1}(t))$$

$$x_{E2}(t+1) = \sigma(2.x_{E1}(t) - x_{E4}(t) + x(t) - 5/2)$$

$$x_{E3}(t+1) = \sigma(x_{E1}(t))$$

$$x_{E4}(t+1) = \sigma(\alpha(1))$$

The dynamics of neuron x is given by:

$$x(t+1) = \sigma(x(t) + x_{P3}(t) - x_{E3}(t))$$

However, if neuron x is used in other modules, the compiler will add more synaptic links to its equation.

There are two types of information flowing through the synaptic connections, values from data types (booleans, integers…) and synchronization signals defining when a certain module starts and signals when its computation ends.

Figure 3. Net structure for x + y

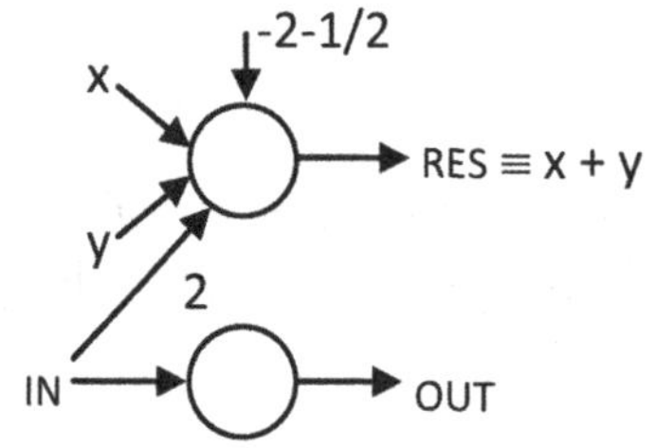

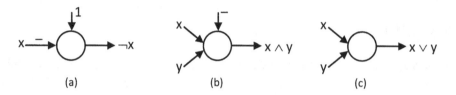

Figure 4. Boolean operators: (a) NOT X, (b) X AND Y, (c) X OR Y

Data Flow

To take into consideration the lower and upper saturation limits of the activation function σ, every value x of a given basic type is encoded into some value of $[0,1]$. For each type T, there is an injective encoding map $\alpha_T : T \rightarrow [0,1]$ mapping a value $x \in T$ onto its specific code. Basic types include *boolean, integer* and *real*.

If resources are bounded, then there exists a limit to the precision of every value (reals are bounded rationals). Considering a maximum precision of P digits, the minimum distance between any two values is 10^{-P}. Let us denote 10^P by M.

- For booleans, T is B = {TRUE, FALSE}, the encoding map is $\alpha_B(x) =$
- For integers, T is Z = { - , ..., } and $\alpha_Z(x) =$
- For reals within $[a, b]$ the coding is $\alpha_{[a,b]}(x) =$

Each data type has several operators. An arbitrary set of operators (with constants, variables and input data) forms an expression that after evaluation returns a result of some type. The net for each expression starts its execution when it receives signal IN (more details below). After evaluation, it returns the final result through output RES and at the same time outputs signal OUT. We present an example of this structure for the binary integer sum, that is easily adapted to the other operators.

The extra -2 in the bias of the upper neuron stops the signals from variables x and y, until an input signal arrives (which overrides the extra -2 in order to compute the sum).

These are the typical McCulloch-Pitts Boolean operators (McCulloch & Pitts, 1943).

There are arithmetical and relational operators for integers. Recall that M is the maximum rational number possible to represent with the limited resources available.

A similar reasoning is used to produce the real operators, including multiplication by a constant, but not binary multiplication (which appears in the next section).

Figure 5. Integer operators: (a) –x, (b) x + y, (c) x – y, (d) x < y, (e) x > y

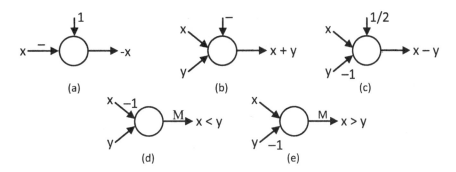

Synchronization Flow

Neural networks are models of massive parallelism. In this model, at each instant, *all* neurons are updated, possibly with new values. This means that a network step with *n* neurons is a parallel execution of *n* assignments. Since programs (even parallel programs) have a sequence of well-defined steps, there must be a way to control it. This is done, in our case, by a handshaking synchronization mechanism. There are two main options: sequential and parallel execution of modules. To provide with these mechanisms, each NETDEF process has a specific and modular subnet binding its execution and its synchronization part. Each subnet is activated when the value 1 is received through a special input validation line IN. The computation of a subnet terminates when the validation output neuron OUT sends value 1.

There is another type of synchronization: the use of channels for inter-module communication. The process SEND sends a value through a channel, blocking if the channel is full, and process RECEIVE receives a value through the channel, blocking if the channel is empty.

So, each channel is denoted by two neurons, one to keep the processed value and another neuron to keep a boolean flag (with value 1 if the channel is empty, or 0 otherwise).

Figure 6. Block processes: (a) sequential execution, (b) parallel execution. All subnets are denoted by squares

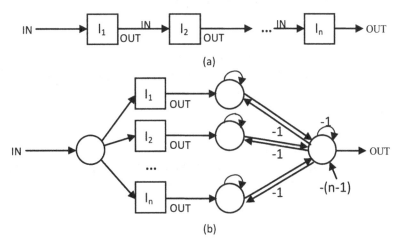

Figure 7. Channel instructions: (a) VAR C: CHANNEL, (b) SEND X INTO C (c) RECEIVE Y FROM C

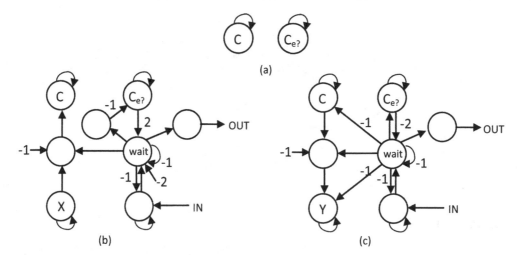

Yet another way to synchronize is to use shared global variables. Processes can communicate through global variables. In principle, each neuron could access every other neuron in the net. The variable scope is an *a priori* restriction made by the compilation process.

SUB-SYMBOLIC COMPUTATION

The next step is to integrate learning mechanisms into the computation tools already developed, merging these two standard computation methodologies (symbolic and sub-symbolic) in one single neural architecture. A further extension of the current conceptual schema, called NETDEF+ was devised to be:

- *Simple* – the neural net model should remain as close as possible to its initial formulation.
- *Expressive* – the neural net model should be expressive enough to model new tools and new mechanisms.
- *Modular* – in NETDEF we had a specific concern about **modularity**; modularity must be preserved in the extension.

To accomplish these requirements, Neto *et al.* (2000) included neuron-synaptic connections into the neural network model. Although we are not concerned with biological plausibility, the existence of neuron-synaptic connections in the brain is known to exist in the complex dendritic trees of genuine neural nets (see Shepherd (1994) for details). Their main task is to convey values and use them to update and change other synaptic weights.

In this new **higher order model**, each neuron can compute a rational polynomial of its inputs, i.e., $\mathbf{x}(t+1) = \phi(\mathbf{x}(t), \mathbf{u}(t))$, with initial state $\mathbf{x}(0) = \mathbf{x}_0$, where the application map ϕ is the composition of a polynomial with rational coefficients with the piecewise sigmoid σ. The new dynamic system becomes,

$$x_j(t+1) = \sigma(P_j(x_1(t), ..., xn(t), u_1(t), ..., um(t)))$$

Figure 8. Obtaining a netdef neural network. (a) The schematics of an algorithm, (b) A netdef program, (c) The neural network description. The netdef compiler automates step (b) to (c)

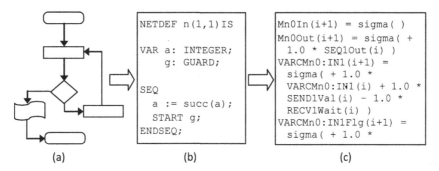

(a)   (b)   (c)

Figure 9 displays a diagram of a neuron-synaptic connection, linking neuron x to the connection between neurons y and z. Synapse of weight w_{zy} receives the previous activation value of x. The dynamics of neuron z is defined by the higher order dynamic rule[1]:

$$z(t+1) = \sigma(2a.x(t).y(t) - a(x(t) + y(t)) + 0.5a + 0.5) \qquad (1)$$

Is it worthwhile to include higher order equations? In out model, there is no increase of computational power, since NETDEF is already Turing equivalent (with bounded resources). However, there are some pertinent advantages that justify the extension. The next sections will illustrate these benefits.

Dynamic Structures

Features associated with neuron-synapse connections (of second order neurons) are deletion and insertion of connections at execution time. If a synapse receives a zero weight, it can be seen as being removed from the architecture. Likewise, a zero weight synapse receiving a non-zero value will be added to the net. This feature implies a self-modifiable neural network. In order to allow NETDEF+ to perform deletions and insertions, we introduce a new process named LINK. A LINK process changes the synaptic weight of a pair of neurons. Its syntax is,

LINK (*<input-neuron>, <new-weight-value>, <output-neuron>*)

In the next figure, neuron w_{yx} keeps the synaptic weight until an input signal comes through channel IN. At that moment, the neuron w_{yx} resets its activation to zero. At the same time the incoming signal

Figure 9. Graphical notation for the neuron-synapse connection in equation (1)

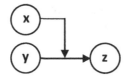

Figure 10. Neural net schema for LINK *(x, w, y) process*

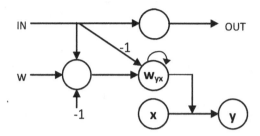

through IN cancels the bias of the left data neuron, and the new value 'w' is inserted in the next step of computation as the new activation of neuron w_{yx}. The synaptic weight is changed at runtime. The diagram of the compiled net follows:

By using a LINK(x, 0, y) process, the synapse between neurons x and y is virtually deleted. Inputting a non-zero value reinserts the synapse. Deleting all inputs/outputs of a neuron separates it from its network. This feature adds an architectural self-modifying mechanism through high order synaptic connections.

Learning

A system that undergoes changes stimulated by the environment is capable of learning. A learning algorithm is a well-defined procedure that specifies how the system changes according to outside information. In this way, learning can be seen as the execution in run time of some hard-wiring algorithm, running under the inputs from the environment. Many neural learning algorithms, like backpropagation, receive inputs and adapt the synaptic weights, pulling the network wiring towards the solution of the problem. Each algorithm uses some appropriate procedures to update the network weights, inspired by means of pure mathematical reasoning (e.g., the Least Mean Squares rule) or by biological inspiration (e.g., the Hebb rule).

The NETDEF+ model makes possible the change of synaptic weights at runtime, so that it should also be conceivable to implement learning algorithms with it. The *control structure* (or *control network*) given by the NETDEF language can be used to regulate learning processes, since it is flexible enough to handle arbitrary algorithms. Usually, neural learning algorithms consist of several weight calculations and they define how the entire module should change in order to respond in a new way to the environment (see Haykin (1999) for a description of several learning algorithms). The *learning structure* (or *learning network*) consists of a set of neurons, arranged in an appropriate architecture (in layers, in a bidimensional grid), keeping the knowledge acquired during the learning procedure.

The learning module embodies the control structure and the learning structure. This module is activated by outside requests, like processing the information presented by a new learning sample, or resetting the weight values. Control and learning are implemented in the same homogeneous framework, and they are joined together homogeneously. The integration of the learning process combines symbolic and sub-symbolic computations using modular higher order (second-order) neural nets which are able implement learning and adaptable neural networks. The next section presents an example of learning modules using high order nets.

Figure 11. The learning net

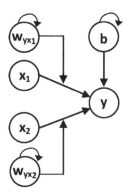

The Hebb Rule Revisited

In this section, we discuss Hebb's learning rule built on top of NETDEF+. This is a simple, classic learning rule that is straightforward to understand and implement, and it serves as a good example to present how this type of networks can execute learning algorithms. We choose the classical problem of learning binary Boolean operators. The input vector **x** has two dimensions and the output vector **y** has one dimension.

The Hebb rule, one of the first learning rules presented in the literature, had a biological inspiration. Succinctly, it says that if two connected neurons are simultaneously active, their synaptic interconnection should be selectively strengthened. Hebb rule states that for each sample $<x_1, x_2; y>$, synapse w_{yxi} should be strengthened if and only if $x_i = y$. The sample values are bipolar (in this case, we use the codes for -1 and $+1$), introducing a compensation mechanism to avoid synapse saturation presented in the original Hebb rule. The common interpretation is that the synaptic connection is updated by $\Delta w_{yxi} = \eta.x_i.y$ (the learning coefficient η is taken to be 1 for simplicity).

As said before, the Hebb module is divided into two parts, the *learning net* and the *control net*.

Learning net. The learning structure with two layers (input and output) is outlined in the next figure. Each synapse has a neuron that keeps its current weight. There is also a neuron keeping the current bias. In general, the learning net reflects the topology of the network data structure needed to implement the learning algorithm.

Control net. This network controls the learning and classification tasks over the knowledge kept in the learning net. It is divided into the following components:

- The data structure. In this example, it consists of input (the **x** vector), and desired output (the **y** vector) that needs to be kept. This is done using a set of neurons, one for each vector component, as in figure 12 (even if it not strictly necessary to compute the Hebb rule, it will be needed to execute iterative learning algorithms).

Figure 12. The input and output vectors

- The synaptic updating structure, where the synaptic change formula is evaluated accordingly. For the Hebb learning algorithm, the actual formula is $w_{yxi}(t+1) = w_{yxi}(t) + x_i(t).y(t)$ (the bias update formula is simpler, $b(t+1) = b(t) + y(t)$ and the corresponding net is not displayed). The subnet which performs this computation is automatically built by the compiler, and it is showed in figure 13 (the actual compiled subnet is more complex, but we have simplified it for the clarity of exposition).

- The interface structure, where all communications with the remaining network are made. To achieve maximum transparency between symbolic and sub-symbolic computations, each learning module is seen from the outside as a function. These *learning functions* can be used as any other function except that they need training before being called. This interface structure is autonomous relative to learning, so learning processes and classification processes are independent and can, whenever needed, run in parallel. We will not present it due to space limitations, since its configuration is more complex.

Compilation

The compiler takes a NETDEF+ program and translates it into a text description defining the neural network. Given a neural hardware, this text description would provide the necessary information for the algorithm execution. This is done by stating, for each neuron, all the input synapses and the respective weights (a number if it is a first-order connection, and another neuron for a high-order connection).

This neural network is homogenous (all neurons have the same activation function) and the system is composed only by first-order neurons. The final network is also an independent module, which can be used in some other context. Regarding time and space complexity, the compiled nets are proportional to the respective algorithm complexity. The language and its compiler show a practical example of how to automatically create neural networks that specify arbitrary complex algorithms.

COMPUTATION WITH CHAOS

Does chaos provide new perspectives to computing? Moore (1990) showed that some very simple dynamical systems (with as few as three degrees of freedom) are equivalent to Turing machines. He used a variant of shift maps (which commonly exemplify chaos in the literature) to establish the connection

Figure 13. Updating synapse w_{yxi}

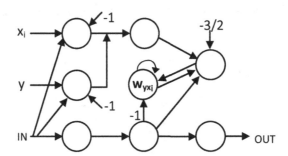

Figure 14. The network that computes $F_4(x) = 4x(1-x)$

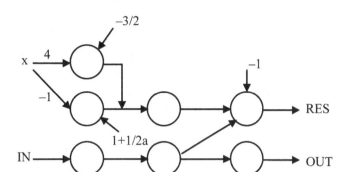

between these two areas. The chaotic feature in dynamical systems thus raises the problem of computing within the 'sensitivity to initial conditions' effect, which implies that those systems may produce totally different outputs due to very small changes in input. However, the most relevant point noted by Moore is that there is another structural dilemma: if a dynamical system is universal (i.e., is equivalent to a Turing machine), it inherits all properties of universal systems, namely their undecidability problems. The most famous is the halting-problem: given a machine with an initial input, will it stop? These problems do not have a solution! A property about Turing machines can be represented as the set of all Turing machines (e.g., encoded as strings) that satisfy that property. Rice's theorem states that any nontrivial property (a trivial property is always true or false) about the language recognized by a Turing machine is undecidable. The implication is that even if the input is known with absolute precision, there is a plethora of general questions that cannot be answered. As an example, the halting-problem for a dynamical system could be stated as: given f and x_0, will the orbit reach a hyperbolic type of attractor (fixed point or limit cycle), or will the attractor be of chaotic nature ('strange attractor')? This cannot be answered in general, meaning that the basin of attraction (the set of all points whose orbit converges to an attracting fixed point) is undecidable. Even the question if a given point x is periodic is undecidable.

Despite the unanswerable theoretical questions, there has been real progress on the more practical issue of performing computations using chaos. Sinha & Ditto (1998) and Munakata *et al.* (2002) showed that a sequence of coupled chaotic elements can perform simple computations, such as the emulation of logic gates, the encoding of integers, and arithmetic operations, obtained by fine tuning a very few number of parameters of the chaotic dynamical system. A different approach to computing over chaos, using neural networks, is presented in this chapter. Such networks are dynamical systems models that can exhibit chaotic behavior, as a consequence of its many degrees of freedom, nonlinearity and dissipation (Haykin, 1999). It might, thus, be rewarding to experiment with the properties of their associated attractors as computational objects. A computation problem in the context of dynamical chaotic behavior modeling may be described as, following Siegelmann (1999): the input is the initial condition in the state space, while the evolution of the state, or trajectory, is the process of computation, which evolves to an attractor, viewed as the output. The unpredictability of the output may be explored in computational situations where a possible extra complexity (increased by the feature of learning) over Turing machines is desirable, such as in the following two application examples developed at Neto *et al.* (2006).

Blind Search

Sometimes we deal with processes of which we know nothing about their internal structure (black boxes). For such processes, finding an input given the required output or result (within a certain tolerance interval) constitutes a problem of uninformed or blind search. In other terms, given y = f(x) and y, we wish to find x to a given precision. Considering the [0,1] domain, one possible solution is to check all decimal values (0.1, 0.2 ... 0.9) as inputs to the process. Then, all centesimal values (0.01, 0.02...), increasing the precision until a match is found.

A chaotic function f is topologically transitive. This means that if we choose any number N inside the domain of f, there is a dense orbit that will pass arbitrarily close to N. If we start at a point in this orbit and execute f, this orbit will pass close enough to the required result. This inspires a probing method: blind search using a dense orbit.

Devaney (1989) showed that the logistic function $F_4(x) = 4x(1-x)$ is chaotic in [0,1]. We can build a neural network that computes F_4. First, the function is split into two terms, $f(x) = 4x$ and $g(x) = (1-x)$, which are then multiplied. Our coding for reals is given by $\alpha_R(x) = (x-a)/(b-a)$, where [a,b] is the interval which is represented inside the network. Then, functions f and g are expressed by the compositions

$\alpha_R(f(\alpha_R^{-1}(x)))$ and $\alpha_R(g(\alpha_R^{-1}(x)))$.

$\alpha_R(f(\alpha_R^{-1}(x))) = 4x - 3/2$

$\alpha_R(g(\alpha_R^{-1}(x))) = -x + (1 + 1/2a)$

The following network multiplies both terms:
Function F_4 is then used to define the discrete time dynamic system:

$s(0) = x_0$

$s(t) = F_4^t(x_0)$

The trajectory of s, starting on a proper value, passes thru all values of [0,1] within any arbitrary small tolerance $\delta > 0$. Notice that this method is not efficient when something is known about the (not-so-)black box structure. However, when nothing is known, this method provides a simple solution described by the following neural structures.

Figure 15. Process SEED(*s*, x_0)

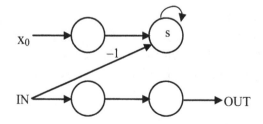

Two main processes are introduced: SEED and NEXT. Process SEED inserts a new value on the search module (the seed). Process NEXT produces the next iteration of system s, returning a new value between [0,1], as represented in the next figure:

The neural network computing F4 is embedded with the behavior of the discrete dynamic system:

Several experiments with 200,000 points in the interval [0,1] were implemented. Each point (inside a neighborhood of 2.5×10^{-6}) was visited at least once during 1 million steps. The average delay was 119 thousand iterations long before the point was visited again. Using the partition method (checking neighborhoods of size 10^{-1}, 10^{-2}...) results in an average of 111 thousand iterations, i.e., a 7% difference between both methods. Blind search is much simpler since it can be implemented by a discrete dynamic system using chaos (a feature that most dynamic systems have).

Random Numbers

The logistic function F_4 also provides a simple procedure to obtain random numbers with uniform deviation, by means of an interesting use of the internal complexity of a dense orbit within a chaotic function. This idea, however, is not new. Ulam & von Neumann (1947) discussed the iteration of F_4 to produce statistical distributions, and von Neumann (1951) pointed out that when iterating a shift map over a chaotic function, floating-point precision limits amplify the random properties of round-off errors and so rapidly obfuscate the chaotic function properties. Despite that, Wagner(1993) uses a matrix of inter-connected F_4 functions in standard computing to produce a random number generator, with good statistical properties and very large period. On the other hand, our new and simpler scheme also produced good results.

Most standard methods for obtaining sequences of random numbers with uniform deviation are based on the linear congruential generator. They work by iterating a function like s(t+1) = a.s(t)+c (modulo m). The value of m gives the maximum number of the sequence before it repeats itself. The triplet (a, c, m) = (75, 0, $2^{31}-1$) was proposed by Lewis, Goodman & Miller (1969), as a minimal quality standard against which other generators should be judged. With some care they produce good random sequences, but repeat after a maximum number of iterations. This obviously depends on the memory given to the primitive type used to compute the next random number (e.g., the primitive Java type "long" has 64 bits, and it is able to represent 264 different numbers at its finest). So, when choosing the best numbers

Figure 16. Function NEXT(s)

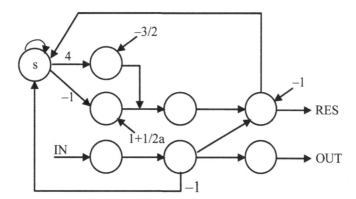

Figure 17. Neural random generator

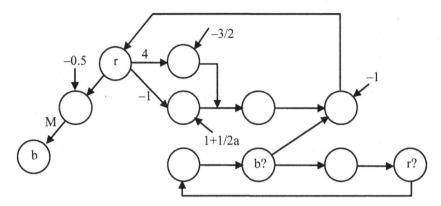

for the iteration method, it is relevant to know the bit size of the type we are using. Doubling its size (e.g., from 64 to 128 bits) means changing the parameters of the method to improve performance. A dense orbit has infinite period, but since we continue to be restricted by a fixed number of bits, the same problem of repetition occurs. Yet, now, the doubling of the type size does not imply a change in the iteration method or in any parameter.

The next module produces a pair of random numbers (a rational and a boolean) which are accessible at neurons r and b, when neurons $r?$ and $b?$ output value 1 (it takes four units of time to produce a new value).

Since all these neurons are computing new values on each instant, two access modules (called RANDR and RANDB) are required to control the output information flow (see next diagrams). Notice that this also gives another random source: the delay to ask for a next value affects that next value. The value produced at time t is different from the one produced at time t+1. This net has the asynchronous feature that it does not wait for a specific input to perform the next calculation, while the previous tool (blind search) is synchronous, because the net only outputs the next value after the IN channel receives value 1.

This random number generator is simple and good for explanatory purposes. However, as presented, it falls short of quality for practical use, mainly because it does not have a random behavior when its orbit is near 0 or 1. Combining at least two of these generators with different initial seeds can produce much better results, as shown in Neto *et al.* (2006), passing statistical tests that the linear congruential generator method could not.

CONCLUSION

The use of finite neural networks as deterministic machines to implement arbitrarily complex algorithms is possible by the automation of compilers like the one presented in this article for NETDEF. If neural net hardware becomes as easy to build as von Neumann hardware – the advances of computing processing power and size are getting us closer to the human brain processing capabilities; this fact combined with recent efforts like IBM & DARPA's SyNAPSE project working on neural oriented computers make this assumption more and more feasible –, then our approach will be able to insert algorithms into the massive parallel architecture of artificial neural nets.

Figure 18. Random processes: (a) RANDR and (b) RANDB

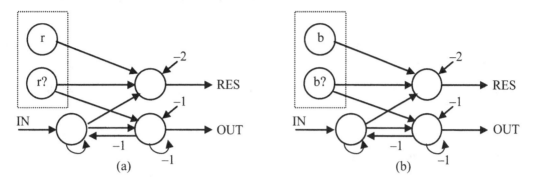

Also, since neural networks are dynamical systems – an algorithm execution is seen as a trajectory over a complex state space – they provide a powerful bridge for the mathematical areas of Computation Theory and Dynamical Systems.

ACKNOWLEDGMENT

I wish to thank those that contributed, over the last years, to the elaboration of these results. First to my former PhD supervisor, Professor José Felix Costa, whose help and guidance were crucial to this work. I wish to extend my thanks to Professors Ademar Costa and Helder Coelho for their timely support. Also, to the Informatics Dept. of the Faculty of Sciences of the University of Lisbon for the sabbatical period that eased the writing of this chapter.

REFERENCES

Büker, U., & Nixdorf, N. (1998). Hybrid Object Models: Combining Symbolic and Subsymbolic Object Recognition Strategies In *Proceedings of SCI'98 / ISAS'98* (pp. 444-451).

Carnell, A., & Richardson, D. (2007). Parallel computation in spiking neural nets. *Theoretical Computer Science, 386*(1-2), 57–72. doi:10.1016/j.tcs.2007.06.017

Chen, C., & Honavar, V. (1999). A Neural Network Architecture for Syntax Analysis . *IEEE Transactions on Neural Networks, 10*(1), 94–114. doi:10.1109/72.737497

Giles, C., Miller, C., Chen, D., Chen, H., Sun, G., & Lee, Y. (1992). Learning and extracting finite state automata with second-order recurrent neural networks. *Neural Computation, 4*(3), 393–405. doi:10.1162/neco.1992.4.3.393

Goudreau, M., Giles, C., Chakradhar, S., & Chen, D. (1994). First-Order Versus Second-Order Single-Layer Recurrent Neural Networks. *IEEE Transactions on Neural Networks, 5*(3), 511–513. doi:10.1109/72.286928

Gruau, F., Ratajszczak, J., & Wiber, G. (1995). A Neural Compiler. *Theoretical Computer Science, 141*(1-2), 1–52. doi:10.1016/0304-3975(94)00200-3

Guoguang, H., Cao, Z., Zhu, P., & Ogura, H. (2003). Controlling chaos in a chaotic neural network. *Neural Networks, 16*(8), 1195–1200. doi:10.1016/S0893-6080(03)00055-8

Haykin, S. (1999). *Neural Networks – A Comprehensive Foundation, 2ⁿᵈ ed*. Upper Saddle River, NJ: Prentice Hall.

Hendler, J., & Dickens, L. (1991). Integrating Neural and Expert Reasoning: An Example. In *Proceedings of AISB-91,* Leeds. Cited in Wilson, 93.

Lange, T., Hodges, J., Fuenmayor, M., & Belyaev, L. (1989). Descartes: Development Environment for Simulating Hybrid Connectionism Architectures, In *Proceedings of the 11ᵗʰ Annual Conference of the Cognitive Science Society,* Ann Arbor, MI. Cited in Wilson, 93.

Lewis, P., Goodman, O., & Miller, J. (1969). A pseudo-random number generator for the System 360. *IBM Systems Journal, 8*(2), 136–145.

Lourenço, C. (2004). Attention-locked computation with chaotic neural nets . *International Journal of Bifurcation and Chaos in Applied Sciences and Engineering, 14*(2), 737–760. doi:10.1142/S0218127404009442

McCulloch, W., & Pitts, W. (1943). A Logical Calculus of the Ideas Immanent in Nervous Activity. *The Bulletin of Mathematical Biophysics, 5,* 115–133. doi:10.1007/BF02478259

Mcmillan, C., Mozer, M., & Smolensky, P. (1992). Rule induction through integrated symbolic and subsymbolic processing. *Advances in Neural Information Processing Systems, 4,* 969–976.

Minsky, M. (1967). *Computation: Finite and Infinite Machines*. Upper Saddle River, NJ: Prentice Hall.

Moore, C. (1990). Unpredictability and Undecidability in Dynamical Systems. *Physical Review Letters, 64*(20), 2354–2357. doi:10.1103/PhysRevLett.64.2354

Munakata, T., Sinha, S., & Ditto, W. (2002). Chaos Computing: Implementations of Fundamental Logical Gates by Chaotic Elements. *IEEE Transactions on Circuits and Systems, 49*(11), 1629–1633. doi:10.1109/TCSI.2002.804551

Neto, J., & Costa, J. F. (1999). *Building Neural Net Software* (Tech. Rep. DI-99-05), Computer Science Department, University of Lisbon.

Neto, J., Costa, J. F., & Ferreira, A. (2000). Merging Sub-symbolic and Symbolic Computation, In H. Bothe and R. Rojas (eds). In*Proceedings of the Second International ICSC Symposium on Neural Computation* (pp.329-335).

Neto, J., Ferreira, A., & Coelho, H. (2006). On Computation over Chaos using Neural Networks Application to Blind Search and Random Number Generation. *Journal of Bifurcation and Chaos in Applied Sciences and Engineering, 16*(1), 59–66. doi:10.1142/S0218127406014587

Neto, J., Siegelmann, H., & Costa, J. F. (2003). Symbolic Processing in Neural Networks. *Journal of the Brazilian Computer Society, 8*(3), 58–70. doi:10.1590/S0104-65002003000100005

Osório, F., & Amy, B. (1999). INSS: A hybrid system for constructive machine learning . *Neurocomputing, 28*, 191–205. doi:10.1016/S0925-2312(98)00124-6

Pollack, J. (1987). *On Connectionism Models of Natural Language Processing* (Ph.D. thesis), Computer Science Dept., Univ. of Illinois, Urbana.

Setiono, R. (2000). Extracting M-of-N Rules from Trained Neural Networks. *IEEE Transactions on Neural Networks, 11*(2), 512–519. doi:10.1109/72.839020

Shepherd, G. (1994). *Neurobiology, 3ʳᵈ ed*. Oxford, UK:Oxford University Press.

Siegelmann, H. (1993). *Foundations of Recurrent Neural Networks* (Tech. Rep. DCS-TR-306), Department of Computer Science, Laboratory for Computer Science Research, The State University of New Jersey Rutgers.

Siegelmann, H. (1996). On NIL: The Software Constructor of Neural Networks. *Parallel Processing Letters, 6*(4), 575–582. doi:10.1142/S0129626496000510

Siegelmann, H. (1999). *Neural Networks and Analog Computation: Beyond the Turing Limit*, Birkhäuser.

Siegelmann, H., & Sontag, E. (1994). Analog Computation via Neural Networks. *Theoretical Computer Science, 131*, 331–360. doi:10.1016/0304-3975(94)90178-3

Siegelmann, H., & Sontag, E. (1995). On the Computational Power of Neural Nets. *Journal of Computer and System Sciences, 50*(1), 132–150. doi:10.1006/jcss.1995.1013

Sinha, S., & Ditto, W. (1998). Computing with distributed chaos. *Physical Review E: Statistical Physics, Plasmas, Fluids, and Related Interdisciplinary Topics, 60*(1), 363–377. doi:10.1103/PhysRevE.60.363

Sun, G., Chen, H., Lee, Y., & Giles, C. (1991). Turing equivalence of neural networks with second-order connections weights. In*Proceedings of International Joint Conference on Neural Networks*.

Ulam, S., & von Neumann, J. (1947). On combination of stochastic and deterministic processes [abstract]. *Bulletin of the American Mathematical Society, 53*, 1120.

von Neumann, J. (1951). Various techniques used in connection with random digits, In *von Neumann Collected Works* (pp. 768-770), Pergamon Press, Oxford.

Wagner, N. (1993). The logistic equation in random number generation. In*Proc. 13ᵗʰ Allerton Conference on Communications, Control, and Computing* (pp. 922-931). University of Illinois.

Wilson, A., & Hendler, J. (1993). *Linking Symbolic and Subsymbolic Computing* (Tech. Rep.), Dept. of Computer Science, University of Maryland.

ENDNOTE

[1]   The expression is the result of $\alpha(\alpha^{-1}(x(t))*\alpha^{-1}(y(t)))$. This calculation is necessary because the data flow values are encoded through the coding function α. The first argument refers to the neuron-synapse connection and the second to the input neuron.

Chapter 3
Evolutionary Algorithm Training of Higher Order Neural Networks

M. G. Epitropakis
University of Patras, Greece

V. P. Plagianakos
University of Patras, Greece

M. N. Vrahatis
University of Patras, Greece

ABSTRACT

This chapter aims to further explore the capabilities of the Higher Order Neural Networks class and especially the Pi-Sigma Neural Networks. The performance of Pi-Sigma Networks is evaluated through several well known neural network training benchmarks. In the experiments reported here, Distributed Evolutionary Algorithms are implemented for Pi-Sigma neural networks training. More specifically, the distributed versions of the Differential Evolution and the Particle Swarm Optimization algorithms have been employed. To this end, each processor of a distributed computing environment is assigned a subpopulation of potential solutions. The subpopulations are independently evolved in parallel and occasional migration is allowed to facilitate the cooperation between them. The novelty of the proposed approach is that it is applied to train Pi-Sigma networks using threshold activation functions, while the weights and biases were confined in a narrow band of integers (constrained in the range [-32, 32]). Thus, the trained Pi-Sigma neural networks can be represented by using only 6 bits. Such networks are better suited for hardware implementation than the real weight ones and this property is very important in real-life applications. Experimental results suggest that the proposed training process is fast, stable and reliable and the distributed trained Pi-Sigma networks exhibit good generalization capabilities.

DOI: 10.4018/978-1-61520-711-4.ch003

INTRODUCTION

Evolutionary Algorithms (EAs) are nature inspired methods solving optimization problems, which employ computational models of evolutionary processes. Various evolutionary algorithms have been proposed in the literature. The most important ones are: Genetic Algorithms (Goldberg, 1989; Holland, 1975), Evolutionary Programming (Fogel, 1996; Fogel et al., 1966), Evolution Strategies (Hansen & Ostermeier, 2001; Rechenberg, 1994), Genetic Programming (Koza 1992), Particle Swarm Optimization (Kennedy & Eberhart, 1995) and Differential Evolution algorithms (Storn & Price, 1997). The algorithms mentioned above share the common conceptual base of simulating the evolution of a population of individuals using a predefined set of operators. Generally, the operators utilized belong to one of the following categories: the *selection* and the *search* operators. The most commonly used search operators are the *mutation* and the *recombination*.

In general, EA's are parallel and distributed implementations and they are inspired by niche formation. Niche formation is a common biological phenomenon (Baeck et al., 1997). Niches could aid the differentiation of the species by imposing reproduction restrictions. Many natural environments can lead to niche formation. For example, remote islands, high mountains and isolated valleys, restrict the species and therefore the evolution process. Although diversity tends to be low in each subpopulation, overall population diversity is maintained through isolation. However, occasionally an individual escapes and reaches nearby niches, further increasing the diversity of their populations (Baeck et al., 1997).

In this chapter, we study the class of Higher Order Neural Networks (HONNs) and in particular Pi-Sigma Networks (PSNs), which were introduced by Shin and Ghosh (1991a). Although, in general, PSNs employ fewer weights and processing units than HONNs, and manage to indirectly incorporate many of HONNs' capabilities and strengths. PSNs have effectively addressed several difficult tasks, where traditional Feedforward Neural Networks (FNNs) are having difficulties, such as zeroing polynomials (Huang et al., 2005) and polynomial factorization (Perantonis et al., 1998). Here, we study PSN's performance on several well known neural network training problems.

The novelty of the proposed approach is that the PSNs were trained with small integer weights and threshold activation functions, utilizing distributed Evolutionary Algorithms. More specifically, modified distributed versions of the Differential Evolution (DE) (Plagianakos & Vrahatis, 2002; Storn & Price 1997) and the Particle Swarm Optimization (PSO) (Clerck, 2006; Kennedy, & Eberhart, 1995) algorithms have been used. DE and PSO have proved to be effective and efficient optimization methods on numerous hard real-life problems (see for example Branke, 1995; Clerc, 2006; Jagadeesan et al., 2005; Magoulas et al., 2004; Parsopoulos & Vrahatis, 2004, 2002; Plagianakos et al., 2005, 1998; Plagianakos & Vrahatis, 1999, 2002; Storn, 1999; Tasoulis et al., 2004, 2005). The distributed EAs has been designed keeping in mind that the resulting integer weights and biases require less bits to be stored and the digital arithmetic operations between them are easier to be implemented in hardware. An additional advantage of the proposed approach is that no gradient information is required; thus (in contrast to classical methods) no backward passes were performed.

Hardware implemented PSNs, with integer weights and threshold activation functions, can continue training if the input data are changing (on-chip training) (Plagianakos et al., 2005; Plagianakos & Vrahatis, 2002). Another advantage of neural networks with integer weights and threshold activation functions is that the trained neural network is to some extend immune to noise in the training data. Such networks only capture the main feature of the training data. Low amplitude noise that possibly contaminates the

Figure 1. Parallel and distributed evolutionary algorithms: a) single-population master-slave algorithms, b) single-population fine-grained algorithms, c) multiple-population coarse-grained algorithms, and d) hybrid approaches

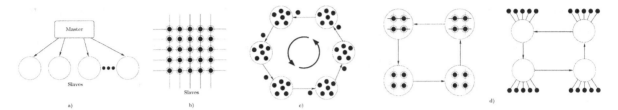

training set cannot perturb the discrete weights, because those networks require relatively large variations to "jump" from one integer weight value to another (Plagianakos & Vrahatis, 2002).

If the network is trained in a constrained weight space, smaller weights are found and less memory is required. On the other hand, the network training procedure can be more effective and efficient when larger integer weights are allowed. Thus, for a given application a trade off between effectiveness and memory consumption has to be considered.

The remaining of this chapter is organized as follows. The first Section reviews various parallel Evolutionary Algorithm implementations, while the next section briefly describes the mathematical model of HONNs and PSNs. The next section is devoted to the presentation of the distributed DE and PSO optimization algorithms. Finally, this chapter ends with extensive experimental results in well-known and widely used benchmark problems, followed by discussion and concluding remarks.

BACKGROUND

Parallel And Distributed Evolutionary Algorithms

Following the biological niche formation many parallel and distributed Evolutionary Algorithm implementations exist (Alba & Tomassini, 2002; Cantu-Paz, 1998, 2000; Gorges-Schleuter, 1991; Gustafson & Burke, 2006; Sprave, 1999). The most widely known are (Alba & Tomassini, 2002; Cantu-Paz, 1998; Sprave, 1999):

1. single-population (global) master-slave algorithms
2. single-population fine-grained algorithms
3. multiple-population coarse-grained algorithms
4. hierarchical parallel algorithms (hybrid approach)

In EA literature *single-population fine-grained algorithms* are also called *cellular EAs* (cEAs). The *multiple-population coarse-grained algorithms* are also known as *island models* or *distributed EAs* (dEAs). These two approaches are most popular among EA researchers and seem to provide a better sampling of the search space. Additionally, they improve the numerical and runtime behavior of the basic algorithm (Alba & Tomassini, 2002; Baeck et al., 1997;Cantu-Paz, 1998; Sprave, 1999).

In a *master-slave* implementation there exists a single panmictic population (selection takes place globally and any individual can potentially mate with any other), but the evaluation of the fitness of each individual is performed in parallel among many processors. This approach does not affect the behavior of the EA algorithm; the execution is identical to a basic sequential EA, but performed much faster (depending on the number of available processors).

According to the cEA approach each individual is assigned to a single processor and the selection and reproduction operators are limited to a small local neighborhood. Neighborhood overlap is permitting some interaction among all the individuals and allows a smooth diffusion of good solutions across the population.

We must note that one could use a uniprocessor machine to run cEAs and dEAs and still get better results than with sequential panmictic EAs. The main difference between cEAs and dEAs is the separation of individuals into distinct subpopulations (islands). In biological terms, dEAs resembles distinct semi-isolated populations in which evolution takes place independently. dEAs are more sophisticated as they occasionally exchange individuals between subpopulations, utilizing the migration operator. The migration operator defines the topology, the migration rate, the migration interval, and the migration policy (Cantu-Paz, 1998, 2000; Skolicki, 2005; Skolicki & De Jong, 2005).

The migration topology determines island interconnections. The migration rate is the number of individuals exchanged during the migration. The migration interval is the number of generations between two consecutive calls of the operator, while the migration policy defines the exchanged individuals and their integration within the target subpopulations. The migration rate and migration interval are the two most important parameters, controlling the quantitative aspects of migration (Alba & Tomassini, 2002; Cantu-Paz, 1998). In the case where the genetic material, as well as the selection and recombination operators, is the same for all the individuals and all subpopulations, we call these algorithms *uniform* dEA. On the other hand, when different subpopulations evolve with different parameters and/or with different individual representations, the resulting algorithm is called *nonuniform* dEA (Alba, 2002; Tanese, 1987). For the rest of the chapter we focus on uniform dEAs.

Hierarchical parallel algorithms combine at least two different methods of EA parallelization to form a hybrid algorithm. At the higher level, there exists a multiple-population EA algorithm, while at the lower levels any kind of parallel EA implementation can be utilized.

To conclude, the use of parallel and distributed EA implementation has many advantages (Alba, 2002), such as:

1. finding alternative solutions to the same problem
2. parallel search from multiple points in the space
3. easy parallelization
4. more efficient search, even without parallel hardware
5. higher efficiency than sequential EAs
6. speedup due to the use of multiple CPUs

For more information regarding parallel EA implementations, software tools, and theory advances the interested reader could refer to the following review papers and books (Alba, 2002; Alba & Troya, 1999; Cantu-Paz, 1998, 2000; Zomaya, 1996).

HIGHER ORDER NEURAL NETWORKS AND PI-SIGMA NETWORKS

In this section we will briefly review the Higher order Neural Networks. HONNs expand the capabilities of standard Feedforward Neural Networks by including input nodes that provide the network with a more complete understanding of the input patterns and their relations. Basically, the inputs are transformed so that the network does not have to learn some basic mathematical functions, such as squares, cubes, or sines. The inclusion of these functions enhances the network's understanding of a given problem and has been shown to accelerate training on some applications. However, typically only second order networks are considered in practice.

Moreover, higher order terms in HONNs can increase the information capacity of neural networks in comparison to neural networks that utilize summation units only. The larger capacity means that the same function or problem can be solved by a network having fewer units. As a result, the representational power of higher order terms can help solving complex problems with construction of significantly smaller networks, while maintaining fast learning capabilities (Leerink et al., 1995).

Several neural network models have been developed to gain an advantage in using higher order terms (Gurney, 1992; Leerink et al., 1995; Redding et al., 1993). Examples of these higher order neural networks are: product unit neural networks (Ismail, 2000), Pi-Sigma network (Ghosh & Shin, 1992; Shin & Ghosh, 1991a,b), Sigma-Pi networks (Lee Giles, 1987), second-order neural networks (Milenkovic, 1996) and functional link neural networks (Ghosh et al., 1992; Hussain et al., 1997; Zurada, 1992). The main disadvantage of the majority of the HONNs is that the required number of weights increases exponentially with the dimensionality of the input patterns.

On the other hand, the PSNs were developed to maintain the fast learning property and powerful mapping capability of single layer HONNs, whilst avoiding the combinatorial explosion in the number of free parameters when the input dimension is increased. In contrast to a single layer HONNs, the number of free parameters in PSNs increases linearly to the order of the network. For that reason, PSNs can overcome the problem of weight explosion that occurs in single layer HONNs and rises exponentially to the number of inputs.

Specifically, PSN is a multilayer feedforward network that outputs products of sums of the input components. It consists of an input layer, a single "hidden" (or middle) layer of summing units, and an output layer of product units. The weights connecting the input neurons to the neurons of the middle layer are adapted during the learning process by the training algorithm, while those connecting the neurons of the middle layer to the product units of the output layer are fixed. For this reason the middle layer is not actually hidden and the training process is significantly simplified and accelerated (Ghosh & Shin, 1992; Shin & Ghosh, 1991a,b).

Let the input $x = (1, x_1, x_2, ..., x_N)^T$, be an *(N+1)*-dimensional vector, where 1 is the input of the bias unit and $x_k, k = 1, 2, ..., N$ denotes the *k*-th component of the input vector. Each neuron in the middle layer computes the sum of the products of each input with the corresponding weight. Thus, the output of the *j*-th neuron in the middle layer is given by the sum:

$$h_j = w_j^T x = \sum_{k=1}^{N} w_{kj} x_k + w_{0j},$$

where $j = 1, 2, ..., K$ and w_{oj} denotes a bias term. Output neurons compute the product of the aforementioned sums and apply an activation function on this product. An output neuron returns:

$$y = \sigma\left(\prod_{j=1}^{K} h_j\right),$$

Where $\sigma(\cdot)$ denotes the activation function. The number of neurons in the middle layer defines the order of the PSN. This type of networks are based on the idea that the input of a K-th order processing unit can be represented by a product of K linear combinations of the input components. Assuming that *(N+1)* weights are associated with each summing unit, there is a total of *(N+1)K* weights and biases for each output unit. If multiple outputs are required (for example, in a classification problem), an independent summing layer is required for each one. Thus, for an M-dimensional output vector y, a total of $\sum_{i=1}^{M} (N+1)K_i$ adjustable weight connections are needed, where K_i is the number of summing units for the i-th output. This allows great flexibility as the output layer indirectly incorporates some of the capabilities of HONNs utilizing a smaller number of weights and processing units. Furthermore, the network can be either regular or can be easily incrementally expandable, since the order of the network can be increased by adding another summing unit in the middle layer without disturbing the already established connections.

A further advantage of PSNs is that we do not have to pre-compute the higher order terms and incorporate them into the network, as is necessary for a single layer HONN. PSNs are able to learn in a stable manner even with fairly large learning rates (Ghosh & Shin, 1992; Shin & Ghosh, 1991a,b). The use of linear summing units makes the convergence analysis of the learning rules for PSN more accurate and tractable. The price to be paid is that the PSNs are not universal approximators. Despite that, PSNs demonstrated competent ability to solve many scientific and engineering problems, such image compression (Hussain & Liatsis, 2002), pattern recognition (Shin et al., 1992), and financial time series prediction (Ming Zhang, 2006). Figure 2, exhibits the architecture of a K-th order Pi-Sigma network having N input components and M output product units.

The Training Algorithm of the PSNs

The PSNs can be trained using the gradient descent learning algorithm (in the neural network literature also known as the BackPropagation learning algorithm) on the estimated sum of the squared error. Thus, the training process can be realized by minimizing the error function E, defined as:

$$E = \frac{1}{2}\sum_{p=1}^{P}\sum_{j=1}^{M}\left(y_{j,p} - t_{j,p}\right)^2,$$

where p is an index over the training input-output pairs, P is the number of these pairs, M is the number of neurons in the output layer and $\left(y_{j,p} - t_{j,p}\right)^2$ is the squared difference between the output $y_{j,p}$ of the j-th neuron in the output layer, for pattern p, and the corresponding target value $t_{j,p}$. Each pass through the entire training set is called an epoch. Notice that, the error function is the objective (fitness) function.

Figure 2. Pi-Sigma network with multiple outputs

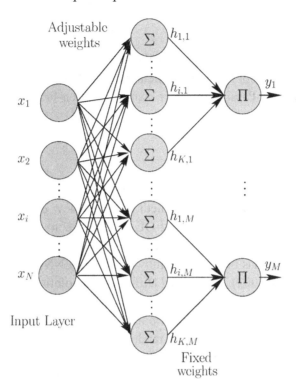

The weights of a PSN are updated according to the following equation:

$$\Delta w_{ij} = \eta(t_{j,p} - y_{j,p})\sigma'(\prod_{L=1}^{K} h_L)\prod_{L \neq i} h_L x_j,$$

where η is the learning rate, σ' is the derivative of the activation function, h_L is the output of the *L*-th neuron in the middle layer, and x_j is the *j*-th component of the current input pattern. Appropriate learning rate values help to avoid convergence to a saddle point or a maximum. In practice, a small constant learning rate is chosen (*0 <η< 1*) to secure the convergence of the BackPropagation training algorithm and avoid oscillations in a steep direction of the error surface. However, it is well known that this approach tends to be inefficient. The interested reader may refer to (Ghosh & Shin, 1992; Shin & Ghosh, 1991a,b).

Although FNNs and HONNs can be simulated in software, hardware implementation is sometimes required in real life applications, where high speed of execution is necessary. Thus, the natural implementation of FNNs or HONNs (because of their modularity) is a distributed (or parallel) one (Plagianakos & Vrahatis, 2002). In the next section we present the distributed EAs used in this study.

NEURAL NETWORK TRAINING USING DISTRIBUTED EVOLUTIONARY ALGORITHMS

For completeness purposes let us briefly present the Distributed Differential Evolution and Particle Swarm Optimization algorithms for higher order neural network training. Our distributed implementations are based on the Message Passing Interface standard, which facilitates the execution of parallel applications.

The Distributed DE Algorithm

Differential Evolution (DE) is an optimization method, capable of handling non-differentiable, discontinuous and multimodal objective functions. The method requires few, easily chosen, control parameters. Extensive experimental results have shown that DE has good convergence properties and in many cases outperforms other well known evolutionary algorithms. The original DE algorithm, as well as its distributed implementation, has been successfully applied to FNN training (Magoulas et al., 2004; Plagianakos & Vrahatis, 1999, 2002). Distributed Differential Evolution (DDE) for Pi-Sigma networks training is presented here.

The modified DDE maintains a population of potential integer solutions, *individuals*, to probe the search space. The population of individuals is randomly initialized in the optimization domain. At each iteration, called *generation*, new individuals are generated through the combination of randomly chosen individuals of the current population. Starting with a population of NP integer weight vectors, $w_g^i, i = 1, 2, ..., NP$, where g denotes the current generation, each weight vector undergoes mutation to yield a mutant vector, u_{g+1}^i. The mutant vector that is considered here (for alternatives see (Chakraborty, 2008; Price et al., 2005; Storn & Price, 1997)), is obtained through one of the following equations:

$$u_{g+1}^i = w_g^{\text{best}} + F \cdot \left(w_g^{r_1} - w_g^{r_2} \right), \tag{1}$$

$$u_{g+1}^i = w_g^{r_1} + F \cdot \left(w_g^{r_2} - w_g^{r_3} \right), \tag{2}$$

where w_g^{best} denotes the best member of the current generation and $F > 0$ is a real parameter, called *mutation constant* that controls the amplification of the difference between the two weight vectors. Moreover, $r_1, r_2, r_3 \in \left\{ 1, 2, ..., i-1, i+1, ..., NP \right\}$ are random integers mutually different and different from the running index i. Obviously, the mutation operator results in a real weight vector. As our aim is to maintain an integer weight population at each generation, each component of the mutant weight vector is rounded to the nearest integer. Additionally, if the mutant vector is not in the hypercube $[-32, 32]^D$, we calculate u_{g+1}^i using the following formula:

$$u_{g+1}^i = \text{sign}\left(u_{g+1}^i \right) \times \left(\left| u_{g+1}^i \right| \text{mod} 32 \right), \tag{3}$$

where sign is the well known three valued signum function. During recombination, for each component j of the integer mutant vector, u_{g+1}^i, a random real number, r, in the interval $[0,1]$ is obtained and compared with the *crossover constant, CR*. If $r \leq CR$ we select as the *j*-th component of the trial vector, v_{g+1}^i, the corresponding component of the mutant vector, u_{g+1}^i. Otherwise, we choose the *j*-th component of the target vector, w_g^i. It must be noted that the result of this operation is also a 6-bit integer vector. Next, we briefly describe the distributed PSO algorithm utilized in this study.

The Distributed PSO Algorithm

The Particle Swarm Optimization (PSO) algorithm is an Evolutionary Computation technique, which belongs to the general category of Swarm Intelligence methods. It was introduced by Eberhart and Kennedy (1995), PSO is inspired by the social behavior of bird flocking and fish schooling, and is based on a social-psychological model of social influence and social learning. The fundamental hypothesis to the development of PSO is that an evolutionary advantage is gained through the social sharing of information among members of the same species. Furthermore, the behavior of the individuals of a flock corresponds to fundamental rules, such as nearest-neighbor velocity matching and acceleration by distance (Eberhart et al., 1996; Kennedy & Eberhart, 1995). Like DE, PSO is capable of handling non-differentiable, discontinuous and multimodal objective functions and has shown great promise in several real-world applications (Clerc, 2006; Parsopoulos & Vrahatis, 2004, 2002).

More specifically, PSO is a population-based stochastic algorithm that exploits a population of individuals, to effectively probe promising regions of the search space. Thus, each individual (particle) of the population (swarm) moves with an adaptable velocity within the search space and retains in its memory the best position it ever encountered. There are two variants of PSO, namely the *global* and the *local*. In the *global* variant, the best position ever attained by all individuals of the swarm is communicated to all the particles, while in the *local* variant, for each particle it is assigned a neighborhood consisting of a pre-specified number of particles and the best position ever attained by the particles in their neighborhood is communicated among them (Eberhart et al., 1996).

More specifically, each particle is a *D*-dimensional integer vector, and the swarm consists of *NP* individuals (particles). Thus, the position the *i*-th particle of the swarm can be represented as: $X_i = \left(x_{i1}, x_{i2}, ..., x_{iD} \right)$. The velocity of each particle is also an *D*-dimensional vector, and for the *i*-th particle is denoted as: $V_i = \left(u_{i1}, u_{i2}, ..., u_{iD} \right)$. The best previous position of the *i*-th particle can be recorded as: $P_i = \left(p_{i1}, p_{i2}, ..., p_{iD} \right)$, and the best particle in the swarm, the particle with the smallest fitness function value, is indicated by the index *g*. Furthermore, the neighborhood of each particle is usually defined through the particles' indices. The most common topology is the *ring* topology, where the neighborhood of each particle consists of particles with neighboring indices (Mendes et al., 2004).

Clerc and Kennedy (2002), proposed a version of PSO which incorporates a new parameter χ, known as the *constriction factor*. The main role of the constriction factor is to control the magnitude of the velocities and alleviate the ``swarm explosion'' effect that prevented the convergence of the original PSO algorithm (Angeline, 1998). According to Clerc & Kennedy, (2002), the dynamic behavior of the particles in the swarm is manipulated using the following equations:

$$V_i(t+1) = \chi \left(V_i(t) + c_1 r_1 \left(P_i(t) - X_1(t) \right) + c_2 r_2 \left(P_g(t) - X_1(t) \right) \right), \tag{4}$$

$$X_i(t+1) = X_i(t) + V_i(t+1), \tag{5}$$

where $i = 1, 2, ..., NP$, c_1 and c_2 are positive constants referred to as *cognitive* and *social* parameters respectively, and r_1 and r_2 are randomly chosen numbers uniformly distributed in [0,1].

In a stability analysis provided in Clerc & Kennedy, (2002) it was implied that the constriction factor is typically calculated according to the formula:

$$\chi = \frac{2k}{\left|2 - \phi - \sqrt{\phi^2 - 4\phi}\right|}, \tag{6}$$

for $\phi > 4$, where $\phi = c_1 + c_2$, and $k = 1$.

The resulting position of the *i*-th particle $\left(X_i(t+1)\right)$ is a real weight vector. To this end, similarly to the DDE implementation, we round $\left(X_i(t+1)\right)$ to the nearest integer and subsequently utilize equation (3) to constrain it in the range [-32, 32]. Next, we briefly describe the operator controlling the migration of the best individuals.

The Migration Operator

The distributed versions of the DE and PSO algorithms have been employed according to the dEA paradigm. To this end, each processor is assigned a subpopulation of potential solutions. The subpopulations are independently evolved in parallel and occasional migration is employed to allow cooperation between them. The migration of the best individuals is controlled by the migration constant ϕ. A good choice for the migration constant is one that allows each subpopulation to evolve independently for some iterations, before the migration phase actually occur. There is a critical migration constant value below which the DDE and DPSO performance is hindered by the isolation of the subpopulations, and above which the subpopulations are able to locate solutions of the same quality as the panmictic implementations. Detailed description of the DDE algorithm and experimental results on difficult optimization problems can be found in (Plagianakos & Vrahatis, 2002; Tasoulis et al., 2004). A parallel implementation of the PSO algorithm can be found in (Nedjah et al., 2006).

Tools for Implementing a Parallel Evolutionary Algorithm

There are several communications tools or libraries for implementing a Parallel Evolutionary Algorithm. The majority of these toolkits are based on the message passing model of communication, since it allows to take advantage of the current hardware technology i.e. multi core computers having shared or distributed memory. In the message passing model, processes in the same or on physically different processors communicate by sending messages to each other through a communication medium, such as a standard or specialized network connection.

Among the most well-known and widely used tools for implementing parallel or distributed computations are: Sockets (Comer & Stevens, 1996), OpenMP[1], the Parallel Virtual Machine (PVM) (Sunderam, 1990), the Message Passing Interface (MPI) (MPI Forum, 1994), Java Remote Method Invocation (Sun), and the Globus toolkit for grid computing (Foster & Kesselman, 1997). Here, the implementation of the parallel Evolutionary Algorithms is based on the Message Passing Interface, which is briefly described in the next section.

The Message Passing Interface

The Message Passing Interface (MPI) is a portable message-passing standard that facilitates the development of parallel applications and libraries. MPI is the specification resulting from the MPI-Forum (1994), which involved several organizations designing a portable system which can allow programs to work on a heterogeneous network. MPI implementations for executing parallel applications run on both tightly-coupled massively-parallel machines and on networks of distributed workstations with separate memory. With this system, each executing process will communicate and share its data with others by sending and receiving messages. The MPI functions support process-to-process communication, group communication, setting up and managing communication groups, and interacting with the environment. Thus, MPI can be incorporated for dEA and/or cEA implementation.

A large number of MPI implementations are currently available, each of which emphasizes different aspects of high-performance computing or is intended to solve a specific research problem. In this study, the OpenMPI implementation of the MPI standard has been utilized. OpenMPI is open source, peer-reviewed, production-quality complete MPI implementation, which provides extremely high performance (Gabriel et al., 2004).

EXPERIMENTAL RESULTS

In this study, the sequential, as well as the distributed versions of the DE and PSO algorithms are applied to train PSNs with integer weights and threshold activation functions. Here, we report results from the following well known and widely used neural network training problems:

1. *N*-bit Parity check problems (Hohil et al., 1999; Rumelhart et al., 1987)
2. the Iris classification problem (Iris) (Asuncion & Newman, 2007)
3. the numeric font classification problem (NumFont) (Magoulas et al., 1997)
4. the MONK's classification problems (MONK1, MONK2, and MONK3) (Thrun et al., 1991)
5. the handwritten digits classification problem (PenDigits) (Asuncion & Newman, 2007)
6. the rock vs. mine sonar problem (Sonar) (Gorman & Sejnowski, 1988)
7. the Breast Cancer Wisconsin Diagnostic problem (BCWD) (Asuncion & Newman, 2007)

For all the training problems, we have used the fixed values of $F = 0.5$ and $CR = 0.7$ as the DE mutation and crossover constants respectively. Similarly, for the PSO algorithm, fixed values for the cognitive and social parameters $c_1 = c_2 = 2.05$ have been used, and the constriction factor $\chi = 0.729$ has been calculated using Eq. (6).

Regarding the number of hidden neurons, we tried to minimize the degrees of freedom of the PSN. Thus, the simpler network topology, which is capable to solve each problem, has been chosen. Below we exhibit the experimental results from the sequential and the distributed DE and PSO implementations. For all the experiments reported below, unless clearly stated, we utilize threshold activation functions and 6-bit integer weights.

Table 1. Simulation results (epochs) for the N-bit parity check problem

N	Topology	Algorithm	Generations			
			Min	*Mean*	*Max*	*St.D.*
2	2-2-1	DE_1	1	1.70	5	1.36
2	2-2-1	DE_2	1	5.04	12	4.92
2	2-2-1	PSO_1	1	1.92	10	1.26
2	2-2-1	PSO_2	1	2.07	13	1.71
3	3-3-1	DE_1	1	13.93	50	10.16
3	3-3-1	DE_2	1	17.98	77	13.95
3	3-3-1	PSO_1	1	23.21	177	21.91
3	3-3-1	PSO_2	1	29.06	281	35.28
4	4-4-1	DE_1	1	9.09	47	8.29
4	4-4-1	DE_2	1	9.66	34	8.55
4	4-4-1	PSO_1	1	2.02	10	1.42
4	4-4-1	PSO_2	1	2.20	17	1.74
5	5-5-1	DE_1	1	36.14	100	21.21
5	5-5-1	DE_2	1	35.98	100	21.76
5	5-5-1	PSO_1	1	27.01	200	28.51
5	5-5-1	PSO_2	1	28.53	210	29.74

Sequential DE and PSO Implementation

Here, we exhibit experimental results from the sequential DE and PSO algorithms. We call DE_1 and DE_2 the DE algorithms that use the mutation operators defined in equations (1) and (2), respectively. We call PSO_1 and PSO_2 the local and the global PSO variant, respectively. The neighborhood of each particle had a radius of one, i.e. the neighborhood of the i-th particle consists of the $(i-1)$-th and the $(i+1)$-th particles. Notice that the software used in this section does not contain calls to the MPI library. To this end, this implementation is marginally faster than the distributed implementation executed in just one computer node.

The first set of experiments consists of the N-bit parity check problems. These problems are well known and widely used benchmarks and are suitable for testing the non-linear mapping and "memorization" capabilities of neural networks. Although these problems are easily defined they are hard to solve, because of their sensitivity to initial weights and their multitude of local minima. Each N-bit problem has 2^N patterns with N attributes in each pattern. All patterns have been used for training and testing. For each N-bit problem we have used an N degree Pi-Sigma network (resulting N neurons in the middle layer). Here, we report results for N=2, 3, 4, and 5.

For each problem and each algorithm, we have used 10 individuals in each population and have conducted 1000 independent simulations. The termination criterion applied to the learning algorithm was the mean square training error (*MSE*) and it was different for each N-bit parity problem (0.05, 0.025, 0.125, and 0.125, respectively), following the experimental setup of (Ghosh & Shin, 1992). Notice that the PSNs trained here have threshold activation functions.

Table 1 shows the experimental results for the parity check problems. The reported parameters for the simulations that have reached solution are: *Min* the minimum number, *Mean* the mean value, *Max*

Figure 3. Average generalization results for training several PSNs with different order by BP, RProp, DE_1, DE_2, PSO_1 and PSO_2 algorithms (Sonar problem)

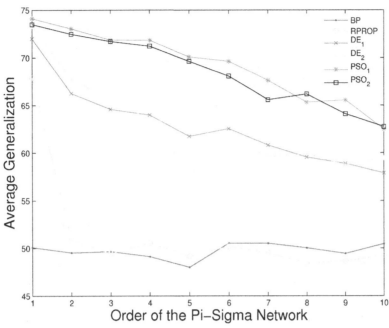

the maximum number, and *St.D.* the standard deviation of the number of training generations. All trained networks gave perfect classification capabilities for all problems. The results of PSNs having threshold activation functions reported below are equivalent or better than the results of PSNs trained using the classical back-propagation algorithm (Ghosh & Shin, 1992). An additional advantage of the proposed approach is that no gradient information is required, thus no backward passes were performed.

Furthermore, for comparison reasons with the classical Pi-Sigma training methods, 100 PSNs of various architectures were trained for the Sonar problem (see description below), using the classical BackPropgation (BP) method, the RProp method (Riedmiller & Braun, 1994), and the DE_1, DE_2, PSO_1

Table 2. Generalization results for the Iris classification problem

Network Topology	Mutation Strategy	Generalization (%)			
		Min	*Mean*	*Max*	*St.D.*
4-2-1	DE_1	50	93.5	100	6.639
4-2-1	DE_2	80	95.4	100	3.115
4-2-1	PSO_1	78	95.1	100	3.163
4-2-1	PSO_2	82	95.3	100	3.013
4-3-1	DE_1	80	94.9	100	3.115
4-3-1	DE_2	80	95.1	100	3.224
4-3-1	PSO_1	82	95.1	100	3.067
4-3-1	PSO_2	80	95.2	100	3.062

Table 3. Generalization results for the NumFont problem

Network Topology	Mutation Strategy	Generalization (%)			
		Min	*Mean*	*Max*	*St.D.*
64-1-1	DE_1	80	99.4	100	2.50
64-1-1	DE_2	100	100	100	0.00
64-1-1	PSO_1	80	95.9	100	5.70
64-1-1	PSO_2	90	99.8	100	1.21

and PSO_2 algorithms. For fair comparison, real value weights and logistic activation functions have been used. All network weights have been initialized in the range [-32, 32] with real values. The learning rate for the BP algorithm has been set to 0.01, while default parameters values have been employed for the RPROP algorithm (Riedmiller & Braun, 1994). Additionally, the termination criterion applied to all learning algorithms was the mean square training error to reach the fixed value of 0.05. The average classification accuracy of the trained PSNs is illustrated in Figure 3.

Firstly, we must note that the generalization capabilities of the algorithms decrease as the dimension of the weight space increases. It is evident that both BP and RPROP have not achieved satisfactory generalization. On the other hand, the evolutionary approaches have obtained good generalization results for all training networks and it was always superior comparing against the BP and RProp algorithms. Additionally, the BP and the RProp algorithms occasionally converged to the predefined error goal and most of the times they converged to an undesired local minimum. As a result the trained PSNs exhibited bad classification accuracy.

The performance for all versions of DE and PSO algorithms was more reliable, stable and in the examined cases, always converged to the desired training error goal. The PSO_1 and PSO_2 trained PSNs exhibited classification accuracy comparable to the accuracy of DE_1, and DE_2 trained PSNs for the first architecture, while for the remaining architectures PSO trained PSNs were clearly better. The incorporation of global

Table 4. Generalization results for the MONK's problems

Problem	Topology	Algorithm	Generalization (%)			
			Min	*Mean*	*Max*	*St.D.*
MONK1	17-2-1	DE_1	86	96.68	100	2.43
MONK1	17-2-1	DE_2	86	96.74	100	2.38
MONK1	17-2-1	PSO_1	80	95.16	100	3.30
MONK1	17-2-1	PSO_2	83	96.02	100	2.66
MONK2	17-2-1	DE_1	79	97.36	100	2.38
MONK2	17-2-1	DE_2	91	97.66	100	1.45
MONK2	17-2-1	PSO_1	90	96.86	100	1.69
MONK2	17-2-1	PSO_2	91	97.31	100	1.64
MONK3	17-2-1	DE_1	82	91.57	97	2.37
MONK3	17-2-1	DE_2	81	90.77	97	3.10
MONK3	17-2-1	PSO_1	80	92.02	99	2.97
MONK3	17-2-1	PSO_2	81	93.14	99	2.46

Table 5. Generalization results for the PenDigits problem

Network	Mutation	Generalization (%)			
Topology	Strategy	*Min*	*Mean*	*Max*	*St.D.*
16-2-1	DE_1	83.91	86.20	88.74	1.08
16-2-1	DE_2	81.53	84.60	87.71	1.16
16-2-1	PSO_1	82.38	84.76	87.19	1.20
16-2-1	PSO_2	82.59	85.16	87.70	1.17

optimization methods (such as EAs) instead of classical local optimization methods (such as BP and RProp) is recommended. Global optimization methods incorporate efficient and effective searching mechanisms that avoid the convergence to local minima and thus enhance the neural network training procedure, as well as the classification accuracy of the trained networks.

Below we report experimental results from the sequential DE and PSO implementations on (a) the numeric font, (b) the MONK's, (c) the handwritten digits, (d) the rock vs. mine sonar, and (e) the Breast Cancer Wisconsin Diagnostic classification problems. To present the generalization results the following notation is used in the following Tables: *Min* indicates the minimum generalization capability of the trained PSNs; *Max* is the maximum generalization capability; *Mean* is the average generalization capability; and *St.D.* is the standard deviation of the generalization capability. In all cases, average performance presented was validated using the well known test for statistical hypotheses, named *t-test* (see for example (Law & Kelton, 2000)), using the SPSS 15 statistical software package.

It must be noted that PSNs trained for the MONK1, MONK2, MONK3, the Sonar, and the Breast Wisconsin Cancer Diagnostic training problems have only one output unit, since all the samples of those datasets belong to one of the two available classes. On the other hand, the networks trained for the Num-Font and the PenDigits classification problems have ten output units (one for each digit), while for the Iris classification problem the network has three output units. To implement a PSN having multiple output units is equivalent to constructing PSNs having common input units and different middle layer units (thus, different sets of weights), each having one output unit. Thus, a PSN should be trained to discriminate samples from each problem class.

The Iris Classification Problem

The Iris classification problem is perhaps the best known problem to be found in the pattern recognition literature. The data set contains three classes of 50 instances each, where each class refers to a type of an

Table 6. Generalization results for the Sonar problem

Network	Mutation	Generalization (%)			
Topology	Strategy	*Min*	*Mean*	*Max*	*St.D.*
60-1-1	DE_1	58	73.81	87	4.24
60-1-1	DE_2	57	73.35	87	4.34
60-1-1	PSO_1	64	73.89	85	3.92
60-1-1	PSO_2	61	74.44	90	3.85

Table 7. Generalization results for the Breast Cancer Wisconsin Diagnostic problem

Network	Mutation	Generalization (%)			
Topology	Strategy	*Min*	*Mean*	*Max*	*St.D.*
30-1-1	DE_1	91	95.8	100	1.293
30-1-1	DE_2	90	95.7	100	1.272
30-1-1	PSO_1	91	95.6	99	1.250
30-1-1	PSO_2	91	95.7	99	1.289

iris plant. One class is linearly separable from the other two, while the latter are not linearly separable from each other.

For the Iris classification problem the aim is to train a PSN to predict the class of an iris plant (Asuncion & Newman, 2007). We trained three distinct PSNs, one for each iris plant class, each one having 4 input units and one output unit. We have conducted 1000 independent simulations for each network. The termination criterion applied to the learning algorithm was either a training error less than 0.001 or 2000 iterations. After being trained, each PSN was tested for its average generalization performance, using the *max* rule. The experimental results are presented in Table 2. The training procedure was very

Table 8. Generalization results for the MONK1 and MONK2 benchmark problems

Computer	Mutation	MONK1 Generalization (%)				MONK2 Generalization (%)			
Nodes	Strategy	*Min*	*Mean*	*Max*	*St.D.*	*Min*	*Mean*	*Max*	*St.D.*
1	DDE_1	90	97.26	100	2.18	93	98.00	100	1.42
1	DDE_2	89	97.44	100	2.06	94	98.12	100	1.39
1	$DPSO_1$	85	96.16	100	2.54	91	97.14	100	1.62
1	$DPSO_2$	91	97.59	100	1.71	93	98.19	100	1.23
2	DDE_1	90	97.81	100	2.18	94	97.88	100	1.36
2	DDE_2	89	97.84	100	1.73	93	97.74	100	1.56
2	$DPSO_1$	88	96.75	100	2.47	93	97.59	100	1.50
2	$DPSO_2$	90	97.59	100	1.92	96	98.35	100	1.19
4	DDE_1	93	98.13	100	1.79	93	98.12	100	1.14
4	DDE_2	91	97.90	100	1.93	93	98.00	100	1.46
4	$DPSO_1$	93	97.27	100	1.88	93	97.90	100	1.46
4	$DPSO_2$	93	97.87	100	1.49	95	98.21	100	1.12
6	DDE_1	91	97.86	100	1.91	94	98.12	100	1.25
6	DDE_2	92	97.73	100	1.85	94	97.79	100	1.28
6	$DPSO_1$	92	96.78	100	1.69	93	97.61	100	1.49
6	$DPSO_2$	92	97.80	100	1.68	95	98.18	100	1.22
8	DDE_1	92	98.22	100	1.59	95	97.96	100	1.33
8	DDE_2	93	97.77	100	1.59	95	98.24	100	1.15
8	$DPSO_1$	90	97.05	100	2.03	92	97.48	100	1.71
8	$DPSO_2$	94	97.91	100	1.26	95	98.19	100	1.08

fast and robust, while all trained PSNs exhibited high generalization accuracy for all classes of the Iris classification problem.

The Numeric Font Classification Problem

For the numeric font classification problem the aim is to train a PSN to recognize 8x8 pixel machine printed numerals from zero to nine in standard Helvetica font. After being trained, the PSN was tested for its generalization capability using Helvetica italic font (Magoulas et al., 1997). Note that the test patterns in the italic font have 6 to 14 bits reversed from the training patterns. To evaluate the average generalization performance the *max* rule was employed.

For the NumFont problem we trained 10 distinct PSNs, each one having 16 input units and one output unit. Thus, one PSN for each digit has been trained and we have conducted 1000 independent simulations for each network. The termination criterion applied to the learning algorithm was either a training error less than 0.001 or 1000 iterations. The experimental results are presented in Table 3. All algorithms exhibited high generalization accuracy. DE_1 in particular achieved 100% generalization success, followed closely by PSO_2. This indicates that the global variants exhibited better results for this problem.

Table 9. Generalization results for the MONK3 and SONAR benchmark problems

Computer	Mutation	MONK3 Generalization (%)				SONAR Generalization (%)			
Nodes	Strategy	Min	Mean	Max	St.D.	Min	Mean	Max	St.D.
1	DDE_1	83	92.69	97	2.19	61	76.62	88	5.87
1	DDE_2	81	91.06	97	2.98	60	76.49	90	6.08
1	$DPSO_1$	84	92.16	97	2.79	62	76.37	91	5.81
1	$DPSO_2$	86	92.90	98	2.42	60	77.16	90	5.46
2	DDE_1	87	92.49	97	2.14	54	76.22	90	5.87
2	DDE_2	82	90.99	96	2.62	62	76.40	90	5.63
2	$DPSO_1$	82	91.55	96	2.61	64	76.97	88	5.25
2	$DPSO_2$	83	91.99	98	3.04	62	77.55	90	5.82
4	DDE_1	83	92.37	97	2.47	61	75.90	90	6.23
4	DDE_2	82	90.40	97	3.14	64	76.05	88	5.32
4	$DPSO_1$	83	90.91	97	3.00	58	76.77	91	6.42
4	$DPSO_2$	85	92.80	98	2.48	62	76.90	88	5.54
6	DDE_1	84	92.71	96	2.11	58	76.59	87	5.92
6	DDE_2	83	90.45	96	3.22	58	75.89	87	6.20
6	$DPSO_1$	84	91.27	96	2.85	58	76.47	90	6.04
6	$DPSO_2$	82	91.67	98	3.33	61	75.48	90	5.66
8	DDE_1	85	92.34	96	1.93	61	76.53	87	5.60
8	DDE_2	82	90.64	95	2.66	60	76.06	91	5.83
8	$DPSO_1$	84	90.94	96	2.79	61	77.00	90	5.83
8	$DPSO_2$	80	92.51	97	2.67	60	77.16	90	6.26

Table 10. Generalization results for the Breast Cancer Wisconsin Diagnostic benchmark problem

Computer	Mutation	BCWD Generalization (%)			
Nodes	Strategy	*Min*	*Mean*	*Max*	*St.D.*
1	DDE_1	92	95.43	98	1.38
1	DDE_2	91	95.54	98	1.23
1	$DPSO_1$	93	95.83	98	1.16
1	$DPSO_2$	92	95.86	99	1.26
2	DDE_1	92	95.32	98	1.27
2	DDE_2	91	95.47	98	1.38
2	$DPSO_1$	92	95.68	99	1.35
2	$DPSO_2$	92	95.76	99	1.29
4	DDE_1	90	95.35	98	1.44
4	DDE_2	91	95.52	98	1.29
4	$DPSO_1$	91	95.67	99	1.38
4	$DPSO_2$	92	95.66	99	1.31
6	DDE_1	92	95.50	98	1.28
6	DDE_2	92	95.53	98	1.20
6	$DPSO_1$	92	95.82	98	1.25
6	$DPSO_2$	92	95.65	99	1.40
8	DDE_1	92	95.35	98	1.33
8	DDE_2	91	95.46	98	1.41
8	$DPSO_1$	92	95.55	98	1.27
8	$DPSO_2$	91	95.64	99	1.40

The MONK's Classification Problems

The MONK's classification problems are three binary classification tasks, which have been used for comparing the generalization performance of learning algorithms (Thrun et al., 1991). These problems rely on the artificial robot domain, in which robots are described by six different attributes. Each one of the six attributes can have one of 3, 3, 2, 3, 4, and 2 values, respectively, which results in 432 possible combinations that constitute the total data set (see (Thrun et al., 1991), for details). Each possible value for every attribute is assigned a single bipolar input, resulting 17 inputs.

For the MONK's problems we have tested PSNs having two units in the middle layer (i.e. 17-2-1 PSN architecture). Table 4 illustrates the average generalization results (1000 runs were performed). The termination criterion applied to the learning algorithm was either a training error less than 0.01 or 5000 iterations. Once again the DE and PSO trained PSNs exhibited high classification success rates. Notice that it has been theoretically proved that PSNs are capable to learn perfectly any Boolean Conjunctive Normal Form (CNF) expression (Shin & Ghosh, 1991b) and that the MONK's problems can be described in CNF.

Figure 4. Average elapsed wall-clock times for training PSNs by DDE$_1$, DDE$_2$, DPSO$_1$ and DPSO$_2$, for the MONK's and the Sonar problems

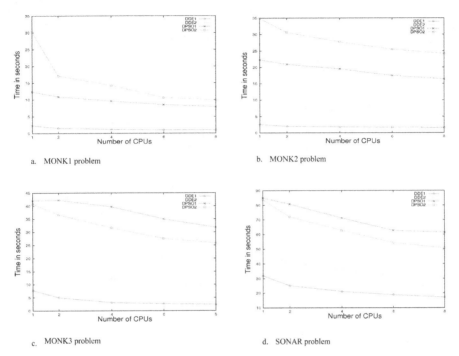

a. MONK1 problem

b. MONK2 problem

c. MONK3 problem

d. SONAR problem

The Handwritten Digits Classification Problem

The PenDigits problem is part of the UCI Repository of Machine Learning Databases (Asuncion & Newman, 2007) and is characterized by a real-valued training set of approximately 7500 patterns. In this experiment, a digit database has been assembled by collecting 250 samples from 44 independent writers. The samples written by 30 writers are used for training, and the rest are used for testing. The training set consists of 7494 real valued samples and the test set of 3498 samples.

For the PenDigits problem we trained 10 different PSNs, one PSN for each digit. We have conducted 100 independent simulations for each network and the termination criterion applied to the learning algorithm was either a training error less than 0.001 or 1000 iterations. Table 5 exhibits the average generalization results. The average classification accuracy of the trained PSNs for the PenDigits problem is about 85% for all algorithms.

The Sonar Problem

For the Sonar problem the task is to train a PSN to discriminate between sonar signals bounced off a metal cylinder (mine) and those bounced off a roughly cylindrical rock. In this experiment the dataset contains 208 samples obtained by bouncing sonar signals off a metal cylinder and a rock at various angles and under various conditions (Gorman & Sejnowski, 1988). There exist 111 samples obtained from mines and 97 samples obtained from rocks. Each pattern consists of 60 real numbers in the range [0, 1]. Each number represents the energy within a particular frequency band, integrated over a certain period of time. The trained PSNs have one unit in the middle layer (i.e. 60-1-1 PSN architecture).

Figure 5. Speedup of training PSNs by DDE$_1$, DDE$_2$, DPSO$_1$ and DPSO$_2$, for the MONK's and the Sonar problems

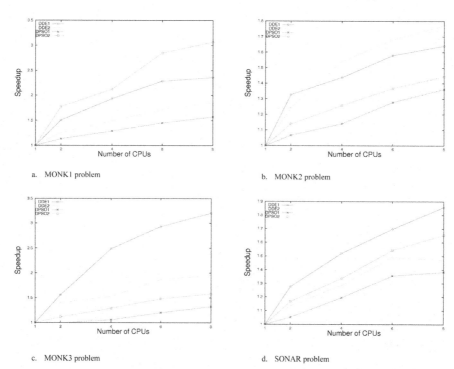

a. MONK1 problem

b. MONK2 problem

c. MONK3 problem

d. SONAR problem

The classification accuracy of the trained PSNs is exhibited in Table 6. The average classification accuracy obtained by the EA trained PSNs is comparable to the classification accuracy of FNNs.

The Breast Cancer Wisconsin Diagnostic Problem

For the Breast Cancer Wisconsin Diagnostic (BCWD) problem the task is to train a PSN to classify breast images into two classes: malignant and benign. The dataset contains 569 samples. The features of each pattern were computed from a digitized image of a fine needle aspirate (FNA) of a breast mass and they describe characteristics of the cell nuclei present in the image (Asuncion & Newman, 2007). There exist 357 samples in the benign and 212 malignant class, each one consisting of 30 real numbers. In this set of simulations it has been used a trained PSNs with one unit in the middle layer (i.e. 30-1-1 PSN architecture), while the termination criterion applied to the learning algorithm was either a training error less than 0.005 or 2000 iterations.

The classification accuracy of the trained PSNs is exhibited in Table 7. Once again the learning process was robust, fast and reliable, and the DE and PSO trained PSNs exhibited high classification success rates.

Figure 6. Average elapsed wall-clock and speedup times for training PSNs by DDE₁, DDE₂, DPSO₁ and DPSO₂, for the Breast Cancer Wisconsin Diagnostic problem

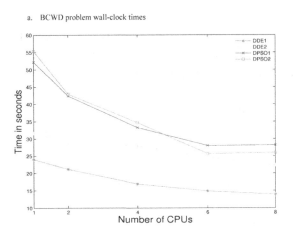

a. BCWD problem wall-clock times

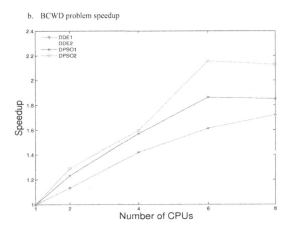

b. BCWD problem speedup

Distributed DE and PSO Implementations

In this section the DDE and the DPSO algorithms are applied to train PSNs with integer weights and threshold activation functions. Here, we report results on the MONK's (Thrun et al., 1991), on the Sonar (Gorman & Sejnowski, 1988), as well as on the Breast Cancer Wisconsin Diagnostic (Asuncion & Newman, 2007) benchmark problems.

For this set of experiments, we have conducted 1000 independent simulations for each algorithm, using a distributed computation environment consisting of 1, 2, 4, 6, and 8 nodes. For the DDE and DPSO algorithms, we have used the same values for the algorithms' parameters. The migration constant was $\varphi = 0.1$. The termination criterion applied to the learning algorithm was either a training error less than 0.01 or 5000 iterations.

As for the choice of the communication topology, islands with many neighbors are more effective than sparsely connected ones. However, this brings forth a tradeoff between computation and communication cost. The estimation of the optimal degree of the topology that minimizes the total computational cost is expensive and difficult. For the DDE and the DPSO implementation we have used the ring topology (each node communicates only with the next node on a ring).

In the distributed implementation, each processor evolves a subpopulation of potential solutions. To allow cooperation between the subpopulations, migration is employed. When a higher number of CPUs is utilized (i.e. higher number of subpopulations) the average generalization accuracy is slightly improved. This is probably due to the island model for the migration of the best individuals (Plagianakos & Vrahatis, 2002; Tasoulis et al., 2004).

The experimental generalization results of problems MONK1 and MONK2 are exhibited in Table 8, while the results of problems MONK3 and SONAR are presented in Table 9. Table 10 illustrates the generalization results for the Breast Cancer Wisconsin Diagnostic problem.

Overall, the results indicate that the training of PSNs with integer weights and thresholds, using the modified DDE and DPSO algorithms is efficient and promising. The learning process was robust, fast and reliable, and the performance of the distributed algorithms stable. Additionally, the trained PSNs utilizing DDE and DPSO exhibited good generalization capabilities.

The four methods considered here, exhibit similar performance. To better compare them, we have performed ANOVA tests and post hoc analysis (Tukey). For the 8 computer node case, the statistical results indicate that in the MONK problems the four methods exhibit different behavior, while they are equivalent in the SONAR and BCWD problems. More specifically, in the MONK1 problem the two PSO variants are equivalent, while in the MONK2 the global methods (i.e. DDE_2 and $DPSO_2$) are equivalent.

In addition to the generalization accuracy tests, we have also compared the four methods by means of the time needed to train the PSNs.

Distributed DE and PSO Algorithms: Time and Speedup Measurements

To better understand the efficiency of the proposed methods we have measured the time needed to converge to a solution. Figure 4 and Figure 6a illustrates average elapsed wall-clock times. For every experiment, the MPI timer (MPI Wtime) was used. This procedure is a high-resolution timer, which calculates the elapsed wall-clock time between two successive function calls. From the results, it is evident that the DDE algorithms are faster and trained the PSNs efficiently. Among the DDE algorithms DDE_1 is marginally better, while $DPSO_1$ and $DPSO_2$ seem equivalent.

Notice that DDE_1 mutation operator uses the best individual of the current generation for computation the mutant vector. On the other hand, DDE_2 computes the mutant vector from randomly chosen individuals. To this end, DDE_1 converges faster to a single minimum, while DDE_2 better explores the search space. Similarly, $DPSO_1$ is the local version of PSO, while $DPSO_2$ is the global version. Thus, to train a HONN for a new application, where the balance between exploration and exploitation is unknown, both local and global algorithms can be tried. Furthermore, one can start the training process using the DDE_2 or the $DPSO_2$ for better exploration and consequently switch to DDE_1 or $DPSO_1$ for faster convergence (Tasoulis et al., 2005). If only one algorithm must be utilized, in the case of an unknown problem, we recommend the use of the DDE_1 algorithm.

In addition to time measurements, we also calculated the speedup achieved by assigning each subpopulation to a different processor relative to assigning all subpopulations to a single processor. The speedup is illustrated in Figure 5 and in Figure 6b. In the literature various speedup measurement methods have been proposed. However, to perform fair comparison between the sequential and the parallel (or distributed) code, the following conditions must be met (Alba, 2002; Punch, 1998):

1) average and not absolute times must be used,
2) the uni- and multi-processor implementations should be exactly the same, and
3) the parallel (or distributed) code must be run until a solution for the problem is found.

To obtain the plotted values, we conducted 1000 independent simulations for 1, 2, 4, 6, 8 computer nodes and the average speedup is shown. For every simulation the training error goal was met and the migration constant was equal to 0.1.

Several factors can influence the speedup, such as the local area network load and the CPU load due to system or other users' tasks (Alba, 2002; He & Yao, 2006; Hidalgo et al., 2007). Nevertheless, the speedup results indicate that the combined processing power overbalances the overhead due to process communication and speedup is achievable. It must be noted that the DDE_1 and $DPSO_2$ generally exhibit higher speedup results, with DDE_1 being the most efficiently parallelized algorithm. Overall, the best speedup was achieved by DDE_1 on the MONK3 problem, when 8 computer nodes were utilized (approximately 3.2 times faster than the simulation utilizing one computer node). Once again the use of DDE_1 is recommended for large distributed systems.

CONCLUSION

In this chapter, we study the Pi-Sigma Networks and propose the utilization of the sequential as well as the parallel (or distributed) Evolutionary Algorithms for PSN training. For the proposed distributed DE and PSO training algorithms each processor of a distributed computing environment is assigned a subpopulation of potential solutions. The subpopulations are independently evolved in parallel and occasional migration of the best individuals is employed to allow subpopulation cooperation. Furthermore, the trained PSNs have threshold activation functions and small integer weights. Thus, their hardware implementation is significantly simplified.

The performance of PSNs is evaluated through well known neural network training problems and the experimental results suggest that the proposed training approach using DE or PSO is robust, reliable, and efficient. By assigning each subpopulation to a different processor significant training speedup was achieved. The PSNs were able to effectively address several difficult classification tasks. Moreover, the EA trained PSNs exhibited good generalization capabilities, comparable with the best generalization capability of PSNs trained using other well-known batch training algorithms, such as the BP and the RProp (Epitropakis et al., 2006).

The EA-trained PSNs exhibited high classification accuracy. However the local variant of the DE algorithm (DDE_1) was clearly the fastest one. Thus, the use of DDE_1, in an unknown optimization task, is recommended.

In a future communication we intend to rigorously compare the classification capability of PSNs against other soft computing approaches. Additionally, we will give experimental results of PSNs trained using hierarchical parallel Evolutionary Algorithms.

ACKNOWLEDGMENT

This work was partially supported by an "Empirikion Foundation" award that helped the acquisition and the setup of the distributed computer cluster.

REFERENCES

Alba, E. (2002). Parallel evolutionary algorithms can achieve super-linear performance. *Information Processing Letters*, *82*(1), 7–13. doi:10.1016/S0020-0190(01)00281-2

Alba, E., & Tomassini, M. (2002). Parallelism and evolutionary algorithms. *IEEE Transactions on Evolutionary Computation*, *6*(5), 443–462. doi:10.1109/TEVC.2002.800880

Alba, E., & Troya, J. M. (1999). A survey of parallel distributed genetic algorithms. *Complex.*, *4*(4), 31–52. doi:10.1002/(SICI)1099-0526(199903/04)4:4<31::AID-CPLX5>3.0.CO;2-4

Angeline, P. J. (1998). Evolutionary optimization versus particle swarm optimization: Philosophy and performance differences. In *EP '98: Proceedings of the 7th International Conference on Evolutionary Programming VII*, (pp. 601-610). London, UK: Springer-Verlag.

Asuncion, A., & Newman, D. (2007). UCI machine learning repository.

Baeck, T., Fogel, D. B., & Michalewicz, Z. (Eds.). (1997). *Handbook of Evolutionary Computation*. Oxford, UK: Oxford University Press.

Branke, J. (1995). Evolutionary Algorithms for Neural Network Design and Training. In *Proceedings of the First Nordic Workshop on Genetic Algorithms and its Applications*, (pp. 145-163).

Cantù-Paz, E. (1998). A survey of parallel genetic algorithms. *Calculateurs Paralèlèles . Réseaux et Systèmes Répartis*, *10*(2), 141–171.

Cantù-Paz, E. (2000). *Efficient and Accurate Parallel Genetic Algorithms*. Norwell, MA: Kluwer Academic Publishers

Chakraborty, U. K. (2008). *Advances in Differential Evolution*. Springer Publishing.

Clerc, M. (2006). *Particle Swarm Optimization*. ISTE Publishing Company.

Clerc, M., & Kennedy, J. (2002). The particle swarm - explosion, stability, and convergence in a multi-dimensional complex space. *Evolutionary Computation . IEEE Transactions on*, *6*(1), 58–73.

Comer, D. E., & Stevens, D. L. (1996). *Internetworking with TCP/IP vol III (2nd ed.): client-server programming and applications BSD socket version}*. Upper Saddle River, NJ: Prentice-Hall.

Eberhart, R., Simpson, P., & Dobbins, R. (1996). *Computational intelligence PC tools*.San Diego, CA: Academic Press Professional

Eberhart, R. C., & Kennedy, J. (1995). A new optimizer using particle swarm theory. In *Proceedings of 6th Symposium on Micro Machine and Human Science*, (pp. 39-43). Nagoya, Japan.

Epitropakis, M. G., Plagianakos, V. P., & Vrahatis, M. N. (2006). Higher-order neural networks training using differential evolution. In *International Conference of Numerical Analysis and Applied Mathematics*, (pp. 376-379). Crete, Greece: Wiley-VCH.

Fogel, D. (1996). *Evolutionary Computation: Towards a New Philosophy of Machine Intelligence*. Piscataway, NJ: IEEE Press

Fogel, L. J., Owens, A. J., & Walsh, M. J. (1966). *Artificial intelligence through simulated evolution*. West Sussex, Uk: Wiley.

Forum, M. P. I. (1994). MPI: A message-passing interface standard. (Technical Report UT-CS-94-230).

Foster, I., & Kesselman, C. (1997). Globus: A metacomputing infrastructure toolkit. *The International Journal of Supercomputer Applications*, *11*, 115–128. doi:10.1177/109434209701100205

Gabriel, E., Fagg, G. E., Bosilca, G., Angskun, T., Dongarra, J. J., Squyres, J. M., et al. (2004). Open MPI: Goals, concept, and design of a next generation MPI implementation. In *Proceedings, 11th European PVM/MPI Users' Group Meeting*, (pp. 97-104). Budapest, Hungary.

Ghosh, J., & Shin, Y. (1992). Efficient higher-order neural networks for classification and function approximation. *International Journal of Neural Systems*, *3*, 323–350. doi:10.1142/S0129065792000255

Goldberg, D. (1989). *Genetic Algorithms in Search, Optimization, and Machine Learning*. Reading, MA: Addison Wesley

Gorges-Schleuter, M. (1991). Explicit parallelism of genetic algorithms through population structures. In *PPSN I: Proceedings of the 1st Workshop on Parallel Problem Solving from Nature*, (pp 150-159). London: Springer-Verlag.

Gorman, R. P., & Sejnowski, T. J. (1988). Analysis of hidden units in a layered network trained to classify sonar targets. *Neural Networks*, *1*, 75–89. doi:10.1016/0893-6080(88)90023-8

Gurney, K. N. (1992). Training Nets of Hardware Realizable Sigma-Pi Units . *Neural Networks*, *5*(2), 289–303. doi:10.1016/S0893-6080(05)80027-9

Gustafson, S., & Burke, E. K. (2006). The speciating island model: an alternative parallel evolutionary algorithm. *Journal of Parallel and Distributed Computing*, *66*(8), 1025–1036. doi:10.1016/j.jpdc.2006.04.017

Hansen, N., & Ostermeier, A. (2001). Completely derandomized self-adaptation in evolution strategies. *Evolutionary Computation*, *9*(2), 159–195. doi:10.1162/106365601750190398

He, J., & Yao, X. (2006). Analysis of scalable parallel evolutionary algorithms. In *CEC 2006: IEEE Congress on Evolutionary Computation*, (pp 120-127).

Hidalgo, J. I., Lanchares, J., de Vega, F. F., & Lombraina, D. (2007). Is the island model fault tolerant? In *GECCO '07: Proceedings of the 2007 GECCO conference companion on Genetic and evolutionary computation*, (pp. 2737-2744), New York: ACM.

Hohil, M. E., Liu, D., & Smith, S. H. (1999). Solving the n-bit parity problem using neural networks. *Neural Networks, 12*(9), 1321–1323. doi:10.1016/S0893-6080(99)00069-6

Holland, J. H. (1975). *Adaptation in natural and artificial system*. Ann Arbor, MI:University of Michigan Press.

Huang, D. S., Ip, H. H. S., Law, K. C. K., & Chi, Z. (2005). Zeroing polynomials using modified constrained neural network approach. *IEEE Transactions on Neural Networks, 16*(3), 721–732. doi:10.1109/TNN.2005.844912

Hussain, A. J., & Liatsis, P. (2002). Recurrent pi-sigma networks for DPCM image coding. *Neurocomputing, 55*, 363–382. doi:10.1016/S0925-2312(02)00629-X

Hussain, A. J., Soraghan, J. J., & Durbani, T. S. (1997). A New Neural Network for Nonlinear Time-Series Modelling. *Neurovest Journal*, 16-26.

Ismail, A., & Engelbrecht, A. P. (2000). Global optimization algorithms for training product unit neuralnetworks. *In IJCNN 2000 . Proceedings of the IEEE-INNS-ENNS International Joint Conference on, 1*(2), 132–137.

Jagadeesan, A., Maxwell, G., & Macleod, C. (2005). Evolutionary algorithms for real-time artificial neural network training. *Lecture Notes in Computer Science, 3697*, 73–78.

Kennedy, J., & Eberhart, R. C. (1995). Particle swarm optimization. In *Proceedings IEEE International Conference on Neural Networks, IV*, (pp 1942-1948). Piscataway, NJ: IEEE Service Center.

Koza, J. R. (1992). *Genetic Programming: On the Programming of Computers by Means of Natural Selection*. Cambridge, MA: MIT Press

Law, A. M., & Kelton, W. D. (2000). *Simulation Modeling and Analysis*. New York: McGraw-Hill

Lee Giles, C. (1987). Learning, Invariance and Generalization in Higher-Order Neural Networks . *Applied Optics, 26*(23), 4972–4978. doi:10.1364/AO.26.004972

Leerink, L. R., Giles, C. L., Horne, B. G., & Jabri, M. A. (1995). Learning with product units. In G. Tesaro, D. Touretzky, & T. Leen (Eds.), *Advances in Neural Information Processing Systems 7*, (pp 537-544). Cambridge, MA: MIT Press.

Magoulas, G. D., Plagianakos, V. P., & Vrahatis, M. N. (2004). Neural network-based colonoscopic diagnosis using on-line learning and differential evolution. *Applied Soft Computing, 4*, 369–379. doi:10.1016/j.asoc.2004.01.005

Magoulas, G. D., Vrahatis, M. N., & Androulakis, G. S. (1997). Effective backpropagation training with variable stepsize. *Neural Networks, 10*(1), 69–82. doi:10.1016/S0893-6080(96)00052-4

Mendes, R., Kennedy, J., & Neves, J. (2004). The fully informed particle swarm: simpler, maybe better. *Evolutionary Computation . IEEE Transactions on, 8*(3), 204–210.

Milenkovic, S., Obradovic, Z., & Litovski, V. (1996). Annealing Based Dynamic Learning in Second-Order Neural Networks, (Technical Report), Department of Electronic Engineering, University of Nis, Yugoslavia.

Ming Zhang. (2008), *Artificial Higher Order Neural Networks for Economics and Business*, Christopher Newport University, USA.

Nedjah, N., Alba, E., & de Macedo Mourelle, L. (2006). *Parallel Evolutionary Computations (Studies in Computational Intelligence)*. New York, &Secaucus, NJ. Springer-Verlag

Parsopoulos, K. E., & Vrahatis, M. N. (2002). Recent approaches to global optimization problems through particle swarm optimization. *Natural Computing: an international journal, 1*(2-3), 235-306.

Parsopoulos, K. E., & Vrahatis, M. N. (2004). On the computation of all global minimizers through particle swarm optimization. *IEEE Transactions on Evolutionary Computation, 8*(3), 211–224. doi:10.1109/TEVC.2004.826076

Perantonis, S., Ampazis, N., Varoufakis, S., & Antoniou, G. (1998). Constrained learning in neural networks: Application to stable factorization of 2-d polynomials. *Neural Processing Letters, 7*(1), 5–14. doi:10.1023/A:1009655902122

Plagianakos, V. P., Magoulas, G. D., & Vrahatis, M. N. (2005). Evolutionary training of hardware realizable multilayer perceptrons. *Neural Computing & Applications, 15*, 33–40. doi:10.1007/s00521-005-0005-y

Plagianakos, V. P., Sotiropoulos, D. G., & Vrahatis, M. N. (1998). Evolutionary algorithms for integer weight neural network training (Technical Report No.TR98-04). University of Patras,Greece.

Plagianakos, V. P., & Vrahatis, M. N. (1999). Neural network training with constrained integer weights. In Angeline, P., Michalewicz, Z., Schoenauer, M., Yao, X., & Zalzala, A., (eds.), *Congress of Evolutionary Computation (CEC '99)*, (pp 2007-2013). Washington DC: IEEE Press.

Plagianakos, V. P., & Vrahatis, M. N. (2002). Parallel evolutionary training algorithms for `hardware-friendly' neural networks. *Natural Computing, 1*, 307–322. doi:10.1023/A:1016545907026

Price, K., Storn, R. M., & Lampinen, J. A. (2005). *Differential Evolution: A Practical Approach to Global Optimization (Natural Computing Series)*}. New York: Springer-Verlag

Punch, W. (1998). How effective are multiple populations in genetic programming. In Koza, J. e. a., editor, *Proceedings of the Third Annual Conference on Genetic Programming* (pp 308-313). Madison, WI: Morgan Kaufmann.

Rechenberg, I. (1994). Evolution strategy. In Zurada, J., Marks II, R., & Robinson, C., (eds). *Computational Intelligence: Imitating Life*. Piscataway, NJ: IEEE Press.

Redding, N. J., Kowalczyk, A., & Downs, T. (1993). Constructive Higher-Order Network Algorithm that is Polynomial in Time . *Neural Networks, 6*, 997–1010. doi:10.1016/S0893-6080(09)80009-9

Riedmiller, M., & Braun, H. (1994). RPROP -- *Description and Implementation Details* (Technical Report). Universitat Karlsruhe.

Rumelhart, D. E., McClelland, J. L., & the PDP Research Group, editors (1987). *Parallel Distributed Processing - Vol. 1*. Cambridge, MA: The MIT Press.

Shin, Y., & Ghosh, J. (1991a). The pi-sigma network: An efficient higher-order neural network for pattern classification and function approximation. In *International Joint Conference on Neural Networks.*

Shin, Y., & Ghosh, J. (1991b). Realization of boolean functions using binary pi-sigma networks. In Dagli, C. H., Kumara, S. R. T., & Shin, Y. C., (eds.), *Intelligent Engineering Systems through Artificial Neural Networks,* (pp 205-210). New York: ASME Press.

Shin, Y., Ghosh, J., & Samani, D. (1992). Computationally efficient invariant pattern classification with higher-order pi-sigma networks. In Burke and Shin, (Eds.), *Intelligent engineering systems through artificial neural networks-II,* (379-384). New York: ASME Press.

Skolicki, Z. (2005). An analysis of island models in evolutionary computation. In *GECCO '05:* In *Proceedings of the 2005 workshops on Genetic and evolutionary computation,* (386-389). New York: ACM.

Skolicki, Z., & Jong, K. D. (2005). The influence of migration sizes and intervals on island models. In *GECCO '05: Proceedings of the 2005 conference on Genetic and evolutionary computation,* (pp 1295-1302). New York: ACM.

Sprave, J. (1999). A unified model of non-panmictic population structures in evolutionary algorithms. In Angeline, P. J., Michalewicz, Z., Schoenauer, M., Yao, X., & Zalzala, A., (eds.), *Proceedings of the Congress on Evolutionary Computation, 2,* (pp 1384-1391). IEEE Press.

Storn, R. (1999). System design by constraint adaptation and differential evolution. *IEEE Transactions on Evolutionary Computation, 3,* 22–34. doi:10.1109/4235.752918

Storn, R., & Price, K. (1997). Differential evolution - a simple and efficient adaptive scheme for global optimization over continuous spaces. *Journal of Global Optimization, 11,* 341–359. doi:10.1023/A:1008202821328

Sunderam, V. S. (1990). PVM: a framework for parallel distributed computing. *Concurrency: Pract. Exper., 2*(4), 315–339. doi:10.1002/cpe.4330020404

Tanese, R. (1987). Parallel genetic algorithms for a hypercube. In *Proceedings of the Second International Conference on Genetic Algorithms on Genetic algorithms and their application,* (pp 177-183). Mahwah, NJ: Lawrence Erlbaum Associates.

Tasoulis, D. K., Pavlidis, N. G., Plagianakos, V. P., & Vrahatis, M. N. (2004). Parallel differential evolution. In *IEEE Congress on Evolutionary Computation (CEC 2004). 2,* (pp 2023-2029).

Tasoulis, D. K., Plagianakos, V. P., & Vrahatis, M. N. (2005). Clustering in evolutionary algorithms to efficiently compute simultaneously local and global minima. In *IEEE Congress on Evolutionary Computation (CEC 2005), 2,* (pp. 1847-1854).

Thrun, S. B. et.al. (1991). The MONK's problems: A performance comparison of different learning algorithms (Technical Report CS-91-197), Pittsburgh, PA.

Zomaya, A. Y. H. (1996). *Parallel and Distributed Computing Handbook.* New York: McGraw-Hill

Zurada, J. M. (1992). *Introduction to Artificial Neural Systems.* St. Paul MN:West Publishing Company.

ENDNOTE

[1]   The OpenMP API specification for parallel programming: http://openmp.org/

Chapter 4
Adaptive Higher Order Neural Network Models for Data Mining

Shuxiang Xu
University of Tasmania, Australia

ABSTRACT

Data mining, the extraction of hidden patterns and valuable information from large databases, is a powerful technology with great potential to help companies survive competition. Data mining tools search databases for hidden patterns, finding predictive information that business experts may overlook because it lies outside their expectations. This chapter addresses using ANNs for data mining because ANNs are a natural technology which may hold superior predictive capability, compared with other data mining approaches. The chapter proposes Adaptive HONN models which hold potential in effectively dealing with discontinuous data, and business data with high order nonlinearity. The proposed adaptive models demonstrate advantages in handling several benchmark data mining problems.

INTRODUCTION

Data mining, the extraction of hidden patterns and valuable information from large databases, is a powerful technology with great potential to help companies survive competition (Cios et al 2007, Han et al 2006). Traditionally, analysts have manually performed the task of extracting useful information from recorded data, however, the increasing volume of data in modern business calls for computer-based approaches. As data sets have grown in both size and complexity, there has been an inevitable shift away from direct hands-on data analysis towards automatic data analysis using more complex and sophisticated computational tools. The modern technologies of computers together with computer networks have made data collection and organization an easy task. However, the captured data needs to be converted into useful information and knowledge. Data mining refers to the entire process of applying

DOI: 10.4018/978-1-61520-711-4.ch004

computer-based methodology, including new techniques for knowledge discovery, from collected data (Masseglia et al 2007, Witten et al 2005).

Data mining tools can answer many business questions that traditionally were too time-consuming to resolve. They search databases for hidden patterns, finding predictive information that business experts may overlook because it lies outside their expectations. An example of pattern discovery is the analysis of retail sales data to identify seemingly unrelated products that are often purchased together. Another pattern discovery example is detecting fraudulent credit card transactions from collected data (Witten et al 2005). Data mining techniques can be implemented rapidly on existing software and hardware platforms to enhance the value of existing information resources. When implemented on high performance client/server or parallel processing systems, data mining tools can analyze massive databases to deliver answers to questions such as, "Which customers are most likely to buy this new product, and why?" (Masseglia et al 2007, Bigus 1996)

Data Mining, the idea of finding valuable information from large databases, is not new. What is new is the large-scale computerization of business transactions and the resulting flood of business data. What is new is the distributed computational power and the storage capabilities, which allow terabytes of business data to remain online, available for processing by client/server data mining systems. What is new are new neural network models with advanced algorithms for pattern recognition and prediction. When combined, these new technologies offer the promise of bringing huge benefit to businesses, and more importantly, preventing businesses from drowning in a sea of their own data (Masseglia et al 2007, Bramer 2007).

Looking for new ways to survive tense competition and to beef up sales, Australian retailers have been preparing customer loyalty and data mining systems to give them an insightful view of customer shopping habits. In 2006, Coles spent nearly $60 million on data mining systems for storing and analyzing customer data, and David Jones and Myer were conducting detailed data mining of customer information down to individual product sales (Woodhead 2006). Myer is now moving to adopt data mining techniques used by global giants Wal-Mart and Tesco as it works on making use of its information mountain collected through its loyalty and credit card schemes. Myer IT director Timothy Clark said that the company would deploy powerful new data mining tools in the near future as it introduces online shopping and data warehousing platforms in an $88 million investment program. However, Australian retailers lag well behind UK and US companies in mining consumer information (Woodhead 2007).

BACKGROUND

Data mining is usually supported by the following technologies: massive data collection, powerful multiprocessor computers, and data mining algorithms.

Whilst data collection is a relatively easy task and powerful computers as well as distributed systems are readily available, commonly used data mining algorithms include Artificial Neural Networks (ANNs), Decision Trees, Support Vector Machines, and Rule Induction (Bramer 2007, Han et al 2006). There are also several traditional approaches such as Nearest Neighbor Classification and Cluster Analysis (Witten et al 2005, Bigus 1996). Data mining is often applied to two separate processes: knowledge discovery and prediction. Knowledge discovery provides explicit information that has a readable form and can be understood by users. Forecasting, or predictive modeling provides predictions of future events and may be transparent and readable in some approaches (e.g. Rule Induction), but opaque in others such as

ANNs. However, several recent research findings have shown that it's possible to retrieve transparent rules from certain ANNs (Malone et al 2006).

A decision tree is a predictive model that can be viewed as a tree, which represents sets of decisions. A decision tree divides a large collection of data records into successively smaller sets of records by applying a sequence of simple decision rules, for classification and prediction. Decision trees use a graphical mechanism to compare competing alternatives and find values for those alternatives by combining uncertainties, costs, etc into specific numerical values. More descriptive names for decision tree models are classification trees or regression trees. A classification tree is used when the predicted outcome is the class to which the data belongs. On a classification tree, leaves represent classifications and branches represent combination of features that lead to those classifications. A regression tree is used when the predicted outcome can be considered a real number (e.g. the price of a car). It is also possible to use both a classification tree and a regression tree to tackle certain problems. In data mining, trees can be considered as the combination of mathematical and computing techniques to aid the description, categorisation, and generalisation of a given set of data. Decision Trees are easy to understand and are a white-box modelling approach. One drawback of Decision Trees is that simple decision rules can severely limit the type of classification boundaries which can be induced, while complex decision rules can make a tree hard to comprehend (Bramer 2007, Fayyad et al 1996).

Support vector machines (SVMs) are a set of related supervised learning methods used for classifications. Input data are considered as sets of vectors in an n-dimensional space, and an SVM constructs separating hyperplanes in that space, with each hyperplane maximizing the margin between two data sets. To calculate the margins, parallel hyperplanes are constructed, with one on each side of a separating hyperplane. Apparently, a good separation can be achieved by the hyperplane that has the largest distance to the neighboring datapoints of both classes, because, in general the larger the margin, the smaller the generalization error of the classifier.

The idea of using hyperplanes to separate the feature vectors groups works well when there are only two target categories, but how can SVM handle the case where the target variable has more than two categories? Several approaches have been suggested, but the most popular ones are: (1) The one-against-many approach where each category is split out and all of the other categories are merged; and, (2) The one-against-one approach where $k(k-1)/2$ models are constructed where k is the number of categories. SVM models are closely related to ANNs. In fact, a SVM model using a sigmoid kernel function is equivalent to a perceptron ANN with two layers. Using a kernel function, SVMs are an alternative training method for Radial Basis Function (RBF) and multi-layer perceptron ANN classifiers, in which the weights of the network are obtained by solving a quadratic programming problem with linear constraints, rather than by solving an unconstrained minimization problem as in standard ANN training. One drawback of SVMs is that, given complicated classification problems, it's not always easy to establish hyperplanes to clearly separate datasets (Sankar et al 2004).

Rule Induction is the extraction of useful if-then rules from databases based on statistical significance. The rules are extracted from a set of observations and may represent a full scientific model of the data, or merely represent local patterns in the data. Rule induction is a form of knowledge discovery in unsupervised learning systems. One disadvantage of Rule Induction is that the restriction to a particular rule representation restricts the classification and prediction power of the model (Fayyad et al 1996).

Cluster Analysis and Nearest Neighbour are among the oldest techniques used in data mining. Cluster Analysis groups together like records in a dataset, or more precisely, Cluster Analysis partitions a dataset into subsets (clusters), so that the data in each subset share some common trait - often proximity according to some defined distance metric. The Nearest Neighbour method uses representative examples of a dataset to approximate a model so that prediction on new examples can be derived from the attributes of similar examples in the model. The Nearest Neighbour algorithm is basically a refinement of Cluster Analysis in the sense that they both use some distance metric in some feature space to create either structure in the data or predictions. One difficulty with Cluster Analysis or the Nearest Neighbour approach is that a well-defined distance metric for determining the distance between data points is required but it's not always easy to do so (Witten et al 2005).

ANNS FOR DATA MINING

This chapter addresses using ANNs for data mining, for the following reasons. First, although usually considered a black-box approach, ANNs are a natural technology for data mining. ANNs are non-linear models that resemble biological neural networks in structure and learn through training. ANNs present a model based on the massive parallelism and the pattern recognition and prediction abilities of the human brain. ANNs learn from examples in a way similar to how the human brain learns. Then ANNs take complex and noisy data as input and make educated guesses based on what they have learned from the past, like what the human brain does. Given the requirements of data mining within large databases of historical data, ANNs are a natural technology for this application (McCue et al 2007). Next, ANNs (especially higher order ANNs) are able to handle incomplete or noisy data (Peng et al 2007, Wang 2003). Databases usually contain noise in the form of inaccuracies and inconsistencies. Lack of data validation procedures may allow a user to enter incorrect data. Data can also become corrupt during migration from one system to another. Missing data is a common problem especially when data is collected from many different sources. Finally, ANNs may hold superior predictive capability, compared with other data mining approaches (Xu 2007, Zhang et al 2007, Fulcher et al 2006, Browne et al 2004, Kohonen et al 2000). The predictive accuracy of a data mining approach strongly influences its effectiveness and popularity. Higher predictive accuracy with real data is an obviously desirable feature.

Many of the important data mining functions performed by ANNs are mirrored by those of the human brain. These include classification, clustering, associative memory, modeling, time-series forecasting, and constraint satisfaction (Cios et al 2007, Bigus 1996). These tasks, which are important for human survival as a species, involve simultaneous processing of large amounts of data, where fast and accurate pattern recognition and responses are required.

Classification refers to making distinctions between items, the most basic function performed by the human brain. We are able to analyse objects using the finest features to assess their similarities and differences. In the business environment there is also a need for making classifications. Examples are: should a loan application for a new house be approved? Should an application for extending a line of credit to a growing business be approved? Should the new catalog of a company be mailed to this set of customers or to another set? All of these decisions are made based on classification. Clustering refers to the ability to group like things together. The business applications of clustering are mainly in the marketing arena. By clustering customers into groups based on similar attributes such as which products they buy or demographics they share we can understand the markets in finer detail. Such information can be used to target specific groups of customers with products that many of them have previously purchased, or add-on services which might appeal to the groups. Associative memory refers to associating two or more items. In business, many products are closely related to each other so when a customer purchases one of them he is likely to also buy the others. ANNs such as Bidirectional Associative Memories and Hopfield networks have been shown to be of such capabilities (Han et al 2006). Modeling refers to learning to predict outcomes based on existing examples. An experienced stock trader watches the changes of leading economic indicators to know when to buy or sell. With learning algorithms, ANNs are able to learn the existing examples and then, given new inputs, make predictions. Such ability to generalize on novel cases is one of the greatest strength of ANNs. An important variation of modeling is time-series forecasting, which looks at what has happened for some period back through time and predicts for some point in the future, a more difficult but more rewarding task. Finally, constraint satisfaction refers to solving complex problems that involve multiple simultaneous constraints. Having multiple conflicting goals is a natural part of life. ANNs with their weighted connections between neurons have proven themselves extremely adept at solving constraint satisfaction and optimization problems.

Recent international progress in the field of ANNs for data mining include the following. A self-organising map (SOM) ANN model is designed in (Peng et al 2007) in an attempt to handle incomplete datasets for data mining. In (Malone et al 2006) a technique which can be used to extract propositional if-then type rules from an ANN model has been presented. Browne (2004) designs ANN algorithms to mine bioinformatics datasets, including the prediction of splice site junctions in Human DNA sequences. Wang (2003) proposes a SOM-based ANN model for data mining with incomplete data sets. Hansen et al (2002) report an extension of ANN methods for planning and budgeting in the State of Utah in the USA. Kohonen et al (2000) have demonstrated the utility of a huge SOM with more than one million nodes to partition a little less than seven million patent abstracts where the documents are represented by 500-dimensional feature vectors. Kim et al (1997) report an integrated ANN system for forecasting interest rates for corporate bonds and treasury bills. Brachman et al (1996) use an ANN-based approach to identify suspicious credit card transactions.

While conventional ANN models have been able to bring huge profits to many businesses, they suffer from several drawbacks. First, conventional ANN models do not perform well on handling incomplete or noisy data (Dong et al 2007, Peng et al 2007, Wang 2003). Next, conventional ANNs can not deal with discontinuities (which contrasts with smoothness: small changes in inputs produce small changes in outputs) in the input training data set (Xu 2007, Fulcher et al 2006, Zhang et al 2002). Finally, conventional ANNs lack capabilities in handling complicated business data with high order nonlinearity (Cios et al 2007, Fulcher 2006, Zhang et al 2002). These are the main reasons for the proposal of using Higher Order Neural Networks (HONNs) for data mining.

HONNS FOR DATA MINING

HONNs (Lee et al 1986) are ANNs in which the net input to a computational neuron is a weighted sum of products of its inputs (instead of just a weighted sum of its inputs, as with conventional ANNs). In (Xu 2007) HONN models have been used in several business applications. The results demonstrate significant advantages of HONNs over conventional ANNs such as much reduced network size, faster training, as well as improved forecasting errors. In (Ramanathan et al 2007) HONNs are used for data clustering which offer significant improvement when compared to the results obtained from using self-organising maps. In (Ho et al 2006) global exponential stability and exponential convergence issues of HONNs are studied. In (Fulcher et al 2006), HONNs have been used for dealing with non-linear and discontinuous financial time-series data, and are able to offer roughly twice the performance of conven-

Figure 1. (Giles 1987). Left, MLP (multi-layer perceptron) with three inputs and two hidden nodes; Right, second order HONN with three inputs

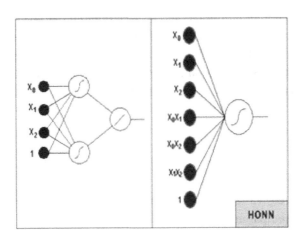

tional ANNs on financial time-series prediction. Zhang et al (2002) employ HONNs for financial data auto-modeling. Their algorithms are further shown to be capable of automatically finding an optimum model, given a specific application. In (Abdelbar 1998) a HONN model is applied to the classification into age-groups of abalone shellfish, a difficult benchmark to which previous researchers have tried to handle using different ANN architectures.

Adaptive HONNs are HONNs with adaptive neuron activation functions. The idea of setting a few free parameters in the neuron activation function (or transfer function) of an ANN is relatively new. Such activation functions are adaptive because the free parameters can be adjusted (in the same way as connection weights) to adapt to different applications. ANNs with adaptive activation function provide better fitting properties than classical architectures with fixed activation functions (such as sigmoid function). Zhang et al (2007) propose using an adaptive ANN for estimating rainfall by mining satellite data, which reduces the average errors of rainfall estimates for the total precipitation event to less than 10 per cent. Mishra (2006) uses an adaptive radial basis function neural network as a control scheme for a unified power flow controller to improve the transient stability performance of a multi-machine power system. Fiori (2003) presents adaptive ANNs and adjusts the free parameters in their activation functions in an unsupervised way by information-theoretic adapting rules. Zhang et al (2002) uses adaptive HONNs for automated financial data mining.

It has been demonstrated that Adaptive HONN models hold potential in effectively dealing with noisy and incomplete data, discontinuous data, and business data with high order nonlinearity (Xu 2007, Fulcher et al 2006, Peng et al 2007, Wang 2003, Zhang et al 2002). This chapter aims at developing novel data mining system, targeting some of these problems.

ADAPTIVE HONNS

HONNs were first introduced by (Giles 1987). The network structure of a three input second order HONN is shown below:

Adaptive HONNs are HONNs with adaptive activation functions. The network structure of an adaptive HONN is the same as that of a multi-layer ANN. That is, it consists of an input layer with some input units, an output layer with some output units, and at least one hidden layer consisting of intermediate processing units (see next section on the number of hidden units). We will only use one hidden layer as it has been mathematically proved that ANNs with one hidden layer is a universal approximator (Leshno 1993). Usually there is no activation function for neurons in the input layer and the output neurons are summing units (linear activation), the activation function in the hidden units is an adaptive one. Our adaptive activation function has been defined as the following:

$$\Psi\left(x\right) = A1 \cdot \sin\left(B1 \cdot x\right) + A2 \cdot e^{-B2 \cdot x^2} \tag{1}$$

where A1, B1, A2, B2, are real variables which will be adjusted (as well as weights) during training. Justification of the use of free parameters in the neuron activation function (1) can be found in (Xu 2008, Chen et al 1996, Xu 2000).

In our EXPERIMENTS section we use an HONN learning algorithm that is based on an improved steepest descent rule (Xu 2008) to adjust the free parameters in the above adaptive activation function (as well as connection weights between neurons). We will see that such approach provides more flexibility and better data mining ability compared with more traditional approaches.

OPTIMIZING THE NUMBER OF HIDDEN UNITS FOR HONNS

Optimizing the number of hidden layer neurons for an ANN to solve a practical problem remains one of the unsolved tasks in this research area. Setting too few hidden units causes high training errors and high generalization errors due to under-fitting, while too many hidden units results in low training errors but still high generalization errors due to over-fitting. It is argued that the best number of hidden units depends in a complex way on: the numbers of input and output units, the number of training cases, the amount of noise in the targets, the type of hidden unit activation function, the training algorithm, etc (Haykin 1999). A dynamic node creation algorithm for ANNs is proposed in (Ash 1989). Hirose (1991) proposes an approach which is similar to (Ash 1989) but removes nodes when small error values are reached. In (Rivals 2000) an algorithm is developed to optimize the number of hidden nodes by minimizing the mean-squared errors over noisy training data.

In this chapter we propose an approach for determining the best number of hidden nodes based on (Barron 1994), which reports that, using ANNs for function approximation, the rooted mean squared (RMS) error between the well-trained neural network and a target function f is shown to be bounded by

$$O\left(\frac{C_f^2}{n}\right) + O\left(\frac{nd}{N}\log N\right) \tag{2}$$

where n is the number of hidden nodes, d is the input dimension of the target function f, N is the number of training pairs, and C_f is the first absolute moment of the Fourier magnitude distribution of the target function f. The two important points of (2) are the approximation error and the estimation error between the well-trained neural network and the target function. For this research we are interested in the approximation error which refers to the distance between the target function and the closest neural network function of a given architecture (which represents the simulated function). To this point, Barron (1994) mathematically proves that, with $n \sim C_f (N/(d \log N))^{1/2}$ nodes, the order of the bound on the RMS error is optimized to be $O(C_f ((d/N) \log N)^{1/2})$.

Based on the above result, we can conclude that if the target function f is known then the best number of hidden layer nodes (which leads to a minimum RMS error) is

$$n = C_f (N/(d \log N))^{1/2} \tag{3}$$

Note that the above equation is based on a known target function f.

However, in most practical cases the target function f is not known, instead, we are usually given a series of training input-output pairs. In these cases, Barron (1994) suggests that the number of hidden nodes may be optimized from the observed data (training pairs) by the use of a complexity regularization or minimum description length criterion (Barron 1991). This is a criterion which reflects the trade-off between residual error and model complexity and determines the most probable model (in this research, the HONN with the best number of hidden nodes). Based on this, when f is unknown we use a complexity regularization approach to determine the constant C in the following

$$n = C (N/(d \log N))^{1/2} \tag{4}$$

The approach is to try an increasing sequence of C to obtain different number of hidden nodes, train an ANN for each number of hidden nodes, and then observe the n which generates the smallest RMS error (and note the value of the C). The maximum of n has been proved to be N/d (Barron 1991). Please note the difference between the equation (3) and the equation (4): in (3), C_f depends on a known target function f, which is usually unknown (so (3) is only a theoretical approach), whereas in our approach as shown in (4), C is a constant which does not depend on any function.

Based on our experiments conducted so far we have found that for a small or medium-sized dataset (with less than 10000 training pairs), when N/d is less than or close to 30, the optimal n most frequently occurs on its maximum, however, when N/d is greater than 30, the optimal n is close to the value of $(N/(d \log N))^{1/2}$.

ADAPTIVE HONN EXPERIMENTS

The first experiment has been conducted to process the German Credit dataset from the UCI Machine Learning Repository. This dataset classifies customers described by a set of 20 attributes as good customer or bad customer based on their credit risks. Examples of the customer attributes are: credit history, purpose of loan, credit amount, employment status, property status, age, etc. There are a total of 1000 instances in this dataset. There are no missing values in the set. Based on the previous section, the optimal number of hidden layer neurons for this experiment is $n = 4$.

For this exercise, the data set is divided into a training set made of 70% of the original set, a test set made of 15% of the original set, and a validation set made of 15% of the original set. After the adaptive HONN (with 4 hidden layer units) has been well trained over the training data pairs, it is tested on the test set, and then validated on the validation set. On the validation set, the correctness rate reaches 95.7%. To verify that for this example the optimal number of hidden layer neuron is 4, the same procedure has been executed by setting the number of hidden layer neurons to 3, 5, and 8, which results in correctness rates of 83.2%, 89.2%, and 81.3% on the validation set, respectively.

To verify the advantages of the adaptive HONN model, a conventional ANN with the sigmoid activation function (and one hidden layer) has been established for the same experiments. With 4 hidden neurons and the same training set, the conventional ANN reaches a correctness rate of only 79.1% on the validation set. After we change the number of hidden neurons to 3, 5, and 8, the correctness rates obtained are 73.5%, 74.7%, and 65.2%, respectively. These results seem to suggest that the adaptive HONN model holds better generalization capability than conventional ANNs. However, given the number of training pairs and the increased number of input neurons of adaptive HONNs, the conventional ANN models take less time to finish learning.

The second experiment has been conducted to process the Car Evaluation dataset from the UCI Machine Learning Repository. This dataset utilizes 6 attributes of cars to determine car quality (very bad, bad, good, or very good). The 6 attributes are: buying price, maintenance price, number of doors, capacity in terms of persons to carry, size of luggage boot, and estimated safety of car. There are a total of 1728 instances in this dataset. There are no missing values in the set. Based on the previous section, the optimal number of hidden layer neurons for this experiment is $n = 9$.

For this exercise, the data set has been divided into a training set made of 70% of the original set, a test set made of 20% of the original set, and a validation set made of 10% of the original set. After the adaptive HONN (with 9 hidden layer units) has been well trained over the training data pairs, it is tested on the test set, and then validated on the validation set. The correctness rate on the validation set reaches 96.3%. To verify that for this example the optimal number of hidden layer neuron is 9, the same procedure has been executed by setting the number of hidden layer neurons to 8, 10, and 14, which results in correctness rates of 84.7%, 88.9%, and 80.4% on the validation set, respectively.

An approach has been used to establish a conventional ANN with the sigmoid activation function (and one hidden layer) for the same experiments. With 9 hidden neurons and the same training set, the conventional ANN reaches a correctness rate of only 77.5% on the validation set. After we change the number of hidden neurons to 8, 10, and 14, the correctness rates obtained are 71.6%, 72.3%, and 66.9%, respectively. Again these results suggest that the adaptive HONN model holds better generalization capability than conventional ANNs.

The third experiment has been conducted to process the Insurance Company Benchmark dataset from the UCI Machine Learning Repository. In this dataset, customer attributes are represented by 86 variables. The dataset includes product usage data and socio-demographic data derived from areas which are represented by postal codes. The data has been supplied by the Dutch data mining company Sentient Machine Research and is retrieved from a real world business problem. The training set contains over 5000 descriptions of customers, including the information of whether or not they have a caravan insurance policy. A test set contains 4000 customers of whom only the organizers know if they have a caravan insurance policy. There are no missing values in the set. The task is to create an adaptive HONN model to learn the training set and then use it to predict on the test set.

Based on the previous section, the optimal number of hidden layer neurons for the adaptive HONN is $n = 5$. For this exercise, the set of 5000 instances has been divided into a training set made of 90% of the original set and a test set made of 10% of the original set. After the adaptive HONN (with 5 hidden layer units) has been well trained over the training data pairs, it is tested on the test set, and then applied on the set of 4000 instances. The correctness rate on the 4000 instances reaches 86.7%. To verify that for this example the optimal number of hidden layer neuron is 5, the same procedure has been executed by setting the number of hidden layer neurons to 4, 6, and 9, which results in correctness rates of 71.7%, 78.9%, and 81.4.4%, respectively. Similarly,

an approach has been used to establish a conventional ANN with the sigmoid activation function (and one hidden layer) for the same experiments. With 5 hidden neurons and the same training set and test set, the conventional ANN reaches a correctness rate of only 66.4.5%. After we change the number of hidden neurons to 4, 6, and 9, the correctness rates obtained are 61.2%, 62.2%, and 56.5%, respectively.

CONCLUSION

In this chapter novel Adaptive HONN models have been proposed and applied in handling several benchmark data mining tasks from the UCI Machine Learning Repository. Such models offer significant advantages over conventional ANNs such as more accurate predictions. A new approach for determining the best number of hidden nodes has been proposed. For future work, it would be a good idea to extend the research to involve large applications which contain training datasets of over 10000 input-out pairs. The abilities of the proposed models in handling noisy or incomplete datasets should also be investigated. Further comparison studies between our Adaptive HONN models and other ANN approaches should be conducted to demonstrate the advantages and disadvantages of each method.

REFERENCES

Abdelbar, A. M. (1998). Achieving superior generalisation with a high order neural network . *Neural Computing & Applications*, *7*(2), 141–146. doi:10.1007/BF01414166

Ash, T. (1989). Dynamic node creation in backpropagation networks. *Connection Science*, *1*(4), 365–375. doi:10.1080/09540098908915647

Barron, A. R. (1994). Approximation and Estimation Bounds for Artificial Neural Networks . *Machine Learning*, *14*, 115–133.

Barron, A. R., & Cover, T. M. (1991). Minimum complexity density estimation. *IEEE Transactions on Information Theory*, *37*, 1034–1054. doi:10.1109/18.86996

Bigus, J. P. (1996). *Data Mining with Neural Networks*. New York: McGraw-Hill.

Brachman, R. J., Khabaza, T., Kloesgen, W., Piatetsky-Shapiro, E., & Simoudis, E. (1996). Mining business databases . *Communications of the ACM*, *39*(11), 42–48. doi:10.1145/240455.240468

Bramer, M. (2007). *Principles of Data Mining*. New York: Springer.

Browne, A., Hudson, B. D., Whitley, D. C., Ford, M. G., & Picton, P. (2004). Biological data mining with neural networks: implementation and application of a flexible decision tree extraction algorithm to genomic problem domains . *Neurocomputing*, *57*, 275–293. doi:10.1016/j.neucom.2003.10.007

Chen, C. T., & Chang, W. D. (1996). A feedforward neural network with function shape autotuning . *Neural Networks*, *9*(4), 627–641. doi:10.1016/0893-6080(96)00006-8

Cios, K. J., Pedrycz, W., Swiniarski, R. W., & Kurgan, L. A. (2007). *Data Mining: A Knowledge Discovery Approach*. New York: Springer.

Dong, G., & Pei, J. (2007). *Sequence Data Mining (Advances in Database Systems)*. New York: Springer.

Fayyad, U. M., Piatetsky-Shapiro, G., Smyth, P., & Uthurusamy, R. (1996). *Advances in Knowledge Discovery and Data Mining*. Cambridge, MA:AAAI Press/The MIT Press.

Fiori, S. (2003). Closed-form expressions of some stochastic adapting equations for nonlinear adaptive activation function neurons . *Neural Computation*, *15*(12), 2909–2929. doi:10.1162/089976603322518795

Fulcher, J., Zhang, M., & Xu, S. (2006).Chapter V. Application of Higher-Order Neural Networks to Financial Time-Series Prediction, *Artificial Neural Networks in Finance and Manufacturing*, edited by Joarder Kamruzzaman, Rezaul Begg, and Ruhul Sarker. Hershey, PA: IGI Global.

Giles, L., & Maxwell, T. (1987). Learning Invariance and Generalization in High-Order Neural Networks. *Applied Optics*, *26*(23), 4972–4978. doi:10.1364/AO.26.004972

Han, J., & Kamber, M. (2006). *Data Mining: concepts and techniques*, Amsterdam; Boston: Elsevier.

Hansen, J. V., & Nelson, R. D. (2002). Data mining of time series using stacked generalizers. *Neurocomputing*, *43*, 173–184. doi:10.1016/S0925-2312(00)00364-7

Haykin, S. (1999). *Neural networks: a comprehensive foundation*.Upper Saddle River, N.J.: Prentice Hall.

Hirose, Y., Yamashita, I. C., & Hijiya, S. (1991). Back-propagation algorithm which varies the number of hidden units. *Neural Networks*, 4.

Ho, D. W. C., Liang, J. L., & Lam, J. (2006). Global exponential stability of impulsive high-order BAM neural networks with time-varying delays. *Neural Networks*, *19*(10), 1581–1590. doi:10.1016/j.neunet.2006.02.006

Kim, S. H., & Noh, H. J. (1997). Predictability of interest rates using data mining tools: a comparative analysis of Korea and the US . *Expert Systems with Applications*, *13*(2), 85–95. doi:10.1016/S0957-4174(97)00010-9

Kohonen, T., Kaski, S., Lagus, K., Salojarvi, J., Honkela, J., Paatero, V., & Saarela, A. (2000). Self organization of a massive document collection . *IEEE Transactions on Neural Networks*, *11*, 574–585. doi:10.1109/72.846729

Lee, Y. C., Doolen, G., Chen, H., Sun, G., Maxwell, T., Lee, H., & Giles, C. L. (1986). Machine learning using a higher order correlation network. *Physica D. Nonlinear Phenomena*, *22*, 276–306.

Leshno, M., Lin, V. Y., Pinkus, A., & Schocken, S. (1993). Multilayer feedforward networks with a nonpolynomial activation function can approximate any function. *Neural Networks*, *6*, 861–867. doi:10.1016/S0893-6080(05)80131-5

Malone, J., McGarry, K., Wermter, S., & Bowerman, C. (2006). Data mining using rule extraction from Kohonen self-organising maps. *Neural Computing & Applications, 15*(1), 9–17. doi:10.1007/s00521-005-0002-1

Masseglia, F., Poncelet, P., & Teisseire, M. (2007). Successes and New Directions in Data Mining. *Information Science Reference*. Hershey, PA: IGI Global.

McCue, C. (2007). *Data Mining and Predictive Analysis: Intelligence Gathering and Crime Analysis*. Oxford, UK: Butterworth-Heinemann.

Mishra, S. (2006). Neural-network-based adaptive UPFC for improving transient stability performance of power system . *IEEE Transactions on Neural Networks, 17*(2), 461–470. doi:10.1109/TNN.2006.871706

Mjalli, F. S., Al-Asheh, S., & Alfadala, H. E. (2007). Use of artificial neural network black-box modeling for the prediction of wastewater treatment plants performance. *Journal of Environmental Management, 83*(3), 329–338. doi:10.1016/j.jenvman.2006.03.004

Peng, H., & Zhu, S. (2007). Handling of incomplete data sets using ICA and SOM in data mining. *Neural Computing & Applications, 16*(2), 167–172. doi:10.1007/s00521-006-0058-6

Ramanathan, K., & Guan, S. U. (2007). Multiorder neurons for evolutionary higher-order clustering and growth . *Neural Computation, 19*(12), 3369–3391. doi:10.1162/neco.2007.19.12.3369

Rivals, I., & Personnaz, L. (2000, May 23-26). *A statistical procedure for determining the optimal number of hidden neurons of a neural model*, Second International Symposium on Neural Computation (NC'2000), Berlin, Germany. Pal, S. K., & Mitra, P. (2004),*Pattern recognition algorithms for data mining: scalability, knowledge discovery, and soft granular computing*, Boca Raton, FL: Chapman & Hall/CRC. UCI Machine Learning Repository. (n.d.). Retrieved January 21, 2009, from, http://archive.ics.uci.edu/ml/index.html

Wang, S. H. (2003). Application of self-organising maps for data mining with incomplete data sets. *Neural Computing & Applications, 12*(1), 42–48. doi:10.1007/s00521-003-0372-1

Witten, I. H., & Frank, E. (2005). *Data mining: practical machine learning tools and techniques*. Amsterdam The Netherlands: Elsevier/Morgan Kaufman.

Woodhead, B. (2006, October 10). *Retailers Scour Loyalty Data*.Retrieved January 6, 2008, from, http://www.australianit.news.com.au/story/0,24897,20551538-15306,00.html

Woodhead, B. (2007). *Myer Plans Data Slice and Dice*. Retrieved October 2, 2007, from http://www.theaustralian.com.au/australian-it/myer-plans-data-slice-and-dice/story-e6frgamo-1111114546456

Xu, S. (2008). Chapter XIV: Adaptive Higher Order Neural Network Models and Their Applications in Business. In Zhang M (ed), *Artificial Higher Order Neural Networks for Economics and Business*. Hershey, PAIGI Global.

Xu, S., & Zhang, M. (2000, July). Justification of a Neuron-Adaptive Activation Function, In *Proceeding of IJCNN'2000 (CD-ROM), paper NN0162*. Como, Italy

Yu, D. L., & Gomm, J. B. (2002). Enhanced neural network modelling for a real multivariable chemical process. *Neural Computing & Applications*, *10*(4), 289–299. doi:10.1007/s005210200001

Zhang, M., & Xu, S., 7 Fulcher, J. (2007). ANSER: an Adaptive-Neuron Artificial Neural Network System for Estimating Rainfall Using Satellite Data. *International Journal of Computers and Applications*, *29*(3), 215–222. doi:10.2316/Journal.202.2007.3.202-1585

Zhang, M., Xu, S., & Fulcher, J. (2002). Neuron-adaptive higher order neural-network models for automated financial data modeling. *IEEE Transactions on Neural Networks*, *13*(1), 188–204. doi:10.1109/72.977302

Chapter 5
Robust Adaptive Control Using Higher Order Neural Networks and Projection

Wen Yu
Cinvestav-IPN, México

ABSTRACT

By using dynamic higher order neural networks, we present a novel robust adaptive approach for a class of unknown nonlinear systems. Firstly, the neural networks are designed to identify the nonlinear systems. Dead-zone and projection techniques are applied to weights training, in order to avoid singular cases. Secondly, a linearization controller is proposed based on the neuro identifier. Since the approximation capability of the neural networks is limited, four types of compensators are addressed. We also proposed a robust neuro-observer, which has an extended Luenberger structure. Its weights are learned on-line by a new adaptive gradient-like technique. The control scheme is based on the proposed neuro-observer. The final structure is composed by two parts: the neuro-observer and the tracking controller. The simulations of a two-link robot show the effectiveness of the proposed algorithm.

1 INTRODUCTION

Feedback control of the nonlinear systems is a big challenge for engineer, especially when we have no complete model information. A reasonable solution is to identify the nonlinear, then a adaptive feedback controller can be designed based on the identifier. Neural network technique seems to be a very effective tool to identify complex nonlinear systems when we have no complete model information or, even, consider controlled plants as "black box".

Neuro identifier could be classified as static (feedforward) or as dynamic (recurrent) ones (Narendra & Parthasarathy, 1990). Most of publications in nonlinear system identification use static networks, for example Multilayer Perceptrons, which are implemented for the approximation of nonlinear function

DOI: 10.4018/978-1-61520-711-4.ch005

in the right side-hand of dynamic model equations (Jagannathan & Lewis, 1996). The main drawback of these networks is that the weight updating utilize information on the local data structures (local optima) and the function approximation is sensitive to the training dates (Haykin, 1994). Dynamic neural networks can successfully overcome this disadvantage as well as present adequate behavior in presence of unmodeled dynamics, because their structure incorporate feedback (Kosmatopoulos, Polycarpou, Christodoulou, & Ioannou, 1995; Rovithakis & Christodoulou, 1994; Yu &Li, 2001).

Neurocontrol seems to be a very useful tool for unknown systems, because it is model-free control, *i.e.*, this controller is not depend on the plant. Many kinds of neurocontrol were proposed in recent years, for example, Supervised Neuro Control (Hunt & Sbarbaro, 1991) is able to clone the human actions. The neural network inputs correspond to sensory information perceived by the human, and the outputs correspond to the human control actions. Direct Inverse Control (Grant & Zhang, 1989) uses an inverse model of the plant cascaded with the plant, so the composed system results in an identity map between the desired response and the plant one, but the absence of feedback dismisses its robustness; Internal Model Neuro Control (Narendra & Parthasarathy, 1990) used forward and inverse model are within the feedback loop. Adaptive Neuro Control has two kinds of structure: indirect and direct adaptive control. Direct neuro adaptive may realize the neurocontrol by neural network directly (Hunt & Sbarbaro, 1991). The indirect method is the combination of the neural network identifier and adaptive control, the controller is derived from the on-line identification (Narendra & Parthasarathy, 1990). Resent results show that discrete-time neural networks are also convenient for real applications (Jagannathan, 2006; Alanis, Sanchez & Loukianov, 2007; Yang, Ge, Chai, & Lee, 2008).

In this chapter we extend our previous results (Poznyak, Yu, Sanchez & Perez, 1999; Yu & Poznyak, 1999). The neuro control was derived by gradient principal, so the neural control is local optimal (Poznyak, Yu, Sanchez & Perez, 1999). No any restrictions of weights are needed, because the controller did not include the inverse of the weights. We assume the inverse of the weights exist, so the learning law was normal (Yu & Poznyak, 1999). The main contributions of this chapter are: 1) A special weights updating law for the higher order neural networks is proposed to assure the existence of neurocontrol. 2) Four different robust compensators are proposed. By means of a Lyapunov-like analysis we derive stability conditions for the neuro identifier and the adaptive controller. We show that the neuro identifier-based adaptive control is effective for a large classes of unknown nonlinear systems.

2 NEURO IDENTIFIER

The controlled nonlinear plant is given as:

$$\dot{x}_t = f(x_t, u_t, t), \quad x_t \in \Re^n, \, u_t \in \Re^n \tag{1}$$

where $f(x_t)$ is unknown vector function. In order to realize indirect neural control, a parallel neural identifier is used (Poznyak, Yu, Sanchez & Perez, 1999; Yu & Poznyak, 1999):

$$\frac{d}{dt}\hat{x}_t = A\hat{x}_t + W_{1,t}\sigma(\hat{x}_t) + W_{2,t}\varphi(\hat{x}_t)\gamma(u_t) \tag{2}$$

Figure 1. Parallel dynamic neural networks

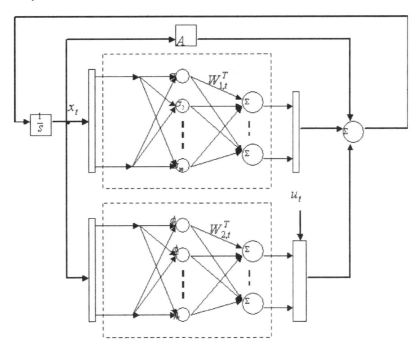

where $\hat{x}_t \in \Re^n$ is the state of the neural network, $W_{1,t}, W_{2,t} \in \Re^{n \times n}$ are the weight matrices, $A \in \Re^{n \times n}$ is a stable matrix. The vector functions $\sigma(\cdot) \in \Re^n$, $\varphi(\cdot) \in \Re^{n \times n}$ is a diagonal matrix. Function $\gamma(\cdot)$ is selected as $\|\gamma(u_t)\|^2 \le \bar{u}.$, for example $\gamma(\cdot)$ may be linear saturation function, $\gamma(u_t) = \begin{cases} u_t & \text{if } |u_t| < b \\ \bar{u} & \text{if } |u_t| \ge b \end{cases}.$

The elements of $\sigma(\hat{x}_t)$ and $\varphi(\hat{x}_t)$ are selected as the structure of higher order neural networks (Kosmatopoulos, Polycarpou, Christodoulou, & Ioannou, 1995)

$$\sigma_i(\hat{x}_t) = \prod_j^{l_i} z(\hat{x}_j), \quad \varphi_i(\hat{x}_t) = \prod_j^{h_i} z(\hat{x}_j) \quad i = 1 \cdots n$$

where $z(\hat{x}_j)$ is a typical sigmoid function

$$z(\hat{x}_j) = \frac{a_j}{1 + e^{-b_j \hat{x}_j}} + c_j \tag{3}$$

where $a_j, b_j, c_j > 0$, this can avoid $\varphi_i(\hat{x}_t) = 0$. The structure of this dynamic system is shown in Figure 1.

Remark 1 *The dynamic neural network (2) has been discussed by many authors (Kosmatopoulos, Polycarpou, Christodoulou, & Ioannou, 1995; Rovithakis & Christodoulou, 1994; Yu &Li, 2001). It can be seen that Hopfield model is the special case of this networks with* $A = diag\{a_i\}$, $a_i := -1 / R_i C_i$, $R_i > 0$ *and* $C_i > 0$. R_i *and* C_i *are the resistance and capacitance at the* i *th node of the network respectively.*

Let us define identification error as

$$\Delta_t = \hat{x}_t - x_t$$

Generally, dynamic neural network (2) cannot follow the nonlinear system (1) exactly. The nonlinear system may be written as

$$\dot{x}_t = Ax_t + W_1^0 \sigma(x_t) + W_2^0 \varphi(x_t)\gamma(u_t) - \tilde{f}_t \tag{4}$$

where W_1^0 and W_2^0 are initial matrices of $W_{1,t}$ and $W_{2,t}$

$$W_1^0 \Lambda_1^{-1} W_1^{0T} \leq \bar{W}_1, \quad W_2^0 \Lambda_2^{-1} W_2^{0T} \leq \bar{W}_2 \tag{5}$$

$\bar{W}_1$ and $\bar{W}_2$ are prior known matrices, vector function $\tilde{f}_t$ can be regarded as modelling error and disturbances. Because $\sigma(\cdot)$ and $\varphi(\cdot)$ are chosen as sigmoid functions, clearly they satisfy the following *Lipshitz* property

$$\tilde{\sigma}^T \Lambda_1 \tilde{\sigma} \leq \Delta_t^T D_\sigma \Delta_t, \quad \left(\tilde{\varphi}_t \gamma(u_t)\right)^T \Lambda_2 \left(\tilde{\varphi}_t \gamma(u_t)\right) \leq \bar{u} \Delta_t^T D_\varphi \Delta_t \tag{6}$$

where $\tilde{\sigma} = \sigma(\hat{x}_t) - \sigma(x_t)$, $\tilde{\varphi} = \varphi(\hat{x}_t) - \varphi(x_t)$, Λ_1, Λ_2, D_σ and D_φ are known positive constants matrices. The error dynamic is obtained from (2) and (4)

$$\dot{\Delta}_t = A\Delta_t + \tilde{W}_{1,t}\sigma(\hat{x}_t) + \tilde{W}_{2,t}\varphi(\hat{x}_t)\gamma(u_t) + W_1^0\tilde{\sigma} + W_2^0\tilde{\varphi}\gamma(u_t) + \tilde{f}_t \tag{7}$$

where $\tilde{W}_{1,t} = W_{1,t} - W_1^0$, $\tilde{W}_{2,t} = W_{2,t} - W_2^0$. We assume modeling error is bounded (Kosmatopoulos, Polycarpou, Christodoulou, & Ioannou, 1995; Rovithakis & Christodoulou, 1994; Yu &Li, 2001).

A1: The unmodeled dynamic $\tilde{f}$ satisfies

$$\tilde{f}_t^T \Lambda_f^{-1} \tilde{f}_t \leq \bar{\eta}$$

where Λ_f is a known positive constants matrix.
If we define

$$R = \bar{W}_1 + \bar{W}_2 + \Lambda_f, \quad Q = D_\sigma + \bar{u}D_\varphi + Q_0 \tag{8}$$

and the matrices A and Q_0 are selected to fulfill the following conditions:

1. the pair $(A, R^{1/2})$ is controllable, the pair $(Q^{1/2}, A)$ is observable,
2. local frequency condition (Willems, 1971) satisfies frequency condition

$$A^T R^{-1} A - Q \geq \frac{1}{4}\left[A^T R^{-1} - R^{-1}A\right]R\left[A^T R^{-1} - R^{-1}A\right]^T \tag{9}$$

then the following assumption can be established.

A2: There exist a stable matrix A and a strictly positive definite matrix Q_0 such that the matrix Riccati equation

$$A^T P + PA + PRP + Q = 0 \tag{10}$$

has a positive solution $P = P^T > 0$.

This condition is easily fulfilled if we select A as stable diagonal matrix. Next Theorem states the learning procedure of neuro identifier.

Theorem 1 *Subject to assumptions A1 and A2 being satisfied, if the weights* $W_{1,t}$ *and* $W_{2,t}$ *are* updated as

$$\dot{W}_{1,t} = s_t \left[-K_1 P \Delta_t \sigma^T(\hat{x}_t) \right]$$
$$\dot{W}_{2,t} = s_t \Pr \left[-K_2 P \varphi(\hat{x}_t) \gamma(u_t) \Delta_t^T \right] \tag{11}$$

where K_1, $K_2 > 0$, P *is the solution of Riccati equation* (10), $\Pr_i \left[\omega \right] \left(i = 1, 2 \right)$ *are projection functions* which are defined as $\omega = K_2 P \varphi(\hat{x}_t) \gamma(u_t) \Delta_t^T$

$$\Pr \left[-\omega \right] = \begin{cases} -\omega & \text{if } \left\| \tilde{W}_{2,t} \right\| < r \text{ or } \left\| \tilde{W}_{2,t} \right\| = r \text{ and } tr\left(-\omega \tilde{W}_{2,t} \right) \le 0 \\ -\omega + \frac{\left| \tilde{W}_{2,t} \right|^2}{tr\left(\tilde{W}_{2,t}^T (K_2 P) \tilde{W}_{2,t} \right)} \omega & \text{otherwise} \end{cases} \tag{12}$$

where $r < \left\| W_2^0 \right\|$ *is a positive constant.* s_t *is a dead-zone function*

$$s_t = \begin{cases} 1 & \text{if } \left\| \Delta_t \right\|^2 > \lambda_{\min}^{-1}(Q_0) \bar{\eta} \\ 0 & \text{otherwise} \end{cases} \tag{13}$$

then the weight matrices and identification error remain bounded, i.e.,

$$\Delta_t \in L_\infty, \quad W_{1,t} \in L_\infty, \quad W_{2,t} \in L_\infty \tag{14}$$

for any $T > 0$ the identification error fulfills the following tracking performance

$$\frac{1}{T} \int_0^T \left\| \Delta_t \right\|_{Q_0}^2 dt \le \kappa \bar{\eta} + \frac{\Delta_0^T P \Delta_0}{T} \tag{15}$$

where κ *is the condition number of* Q_0 *defined as* $\kappa = \frac{\lambda_{\max}(Q_0)}{\lambda_{\min}(Q_0)}$

Proof Select a Lyapunov function as

$$V_t = \Delta_t^T P \Delta_t + tr\left\{ \tilde{W}_{1,t}^T K_1^{-1} \tilde{W}_{1,t} \right\} + tr\left\{ \tilde{W}_{2,t}^T K_2^{-1} \tilde{W}_{2,t} \right\} \tag{16}$$

where $P \in \Re^{n \times n}$ is positive definite matrix. According to (7), the derivative is

$$\dot{V}_t = \Delta_t^T \left(PA + A^T P \right) \Delta_t + 2\Delta_t^T P \tilde{W}_{1,t} \sigma(\hat{x}_t) + 2\Delta_t^T P \tilde{W}_{2,t} \varphi(\hat{x}_t) \gamma(u_t) + 2\Delta_t^T P \tilde{f}_t$$
$$+ 2\Delta_t^T P \left[W_1^* \tilde{\sigma} + W_1^* \tilde{\varphi} \gamma(u_t) \right] + 2tr \left\{ \dot{\tilde{W}}_{1,t}^T K_1^{-1} \tilde{W}_{1,t} \right\} + 2tr \left\{ \dot{\tilde{W}}_{2,t}^T K_2^{-1} \tilde{W}_{2,t} \right\}$$

Since $\Delta_t^T P W_1^* \tilde{\sigma}_t$ is scalar, using (6) and matrix inequality

$$X^T Y + \left(X^T Y \right)^T \leq X^T \Lambda^{-1} X + Y^T \Lambda Y \tag{17}$$

where $X, Y, \Lambda \in \Re^{n \times k}$ are any matrices, Λ is any positive definite matrix, we obtain

$$2\Delta_t^T P W_1^* \tilde{\sigma}_t \leq \Delta_t^T P W_1^* \Lambda_1^{-1} W_1^{*T} P \Delta_t + \tilde{\sigma}_t^T \Lambda_1 \tilde{\sigma}_t \leq \Delta_t^T \left(P \bar{W}_1 P + D_\sigma \right) \Delta_t$$
$$2\Delta_t^T P W_2^* \tilde{\varphi}_t \gamma(u_t) \leq \Delta_t^T \left(P \bar{W}_2 P + \bar{u} D_\varphi \right) \Delta_t \tag{18}$$

In view of the matrix inequality (17) and **A1**,

$$2\Delta_t^T P \tilde{f}_t \leq \Delta_t^T P \Lambda_f P \Delta_t + \bar{\eta}$$

So we have

$$\dot{V}_t \leq \Delta_t^T \left[PA + A^T P + P \left(\bar{W}_1 + \bar{W}_2 + \Lambda_f \right) P + \left(D_\sigma + \bar{u} D_\varphi + Q_0 \right) \right] \Delta_t$$
$$+ 2tr \left\{ \dot{\tilde{W}}_{1,t}^T K_1^{-1} \tilde{W}_{1,t} \right\} + 2\Delta_t^T P \tilde{W}_{1,t} \sigma(\hat{x}_t) + \bar{\eta} - \Delta_t^T Q_0 \Delta_t$$
$$+ 2tr \left\{ \dot{\tilde{W}}_{2,t}^T K_2^{-1} \tilde{W}_{2,t} \right\} + 2\Delta_t^T P \tilde{W}_{2,t} \varphi(\hat{x}_t) \gamma(u_t) \tag{19}$$

Since $\dot{W} = \dot{W}_{1,t}$ and $\dot{W} = \dot{W}_{2,t}$, if we use **A2**, we have

$$\dot{V}_t \leq 2tr \left\{ \left[K_1^{-1} \dot{W}_{1,t}^T + K_1 P \Delta_t \sigma^T(\hat{x}_t) \right] \tilde{W}_{1,t} \right\} + \bar{\eta} - \Delta_t^T Q_0 \Delta_t$$
$$+ 2tr \left\{ \left[K_2^{-1} \dot{W}_{2,t} + P \varphi(\hat{x}_t) \gamma(u_t) \Delta_t^T \right] \tilde{W}_{2,t} \right\} \tag{20}$$

(I) if $\left\| \Delta_t \right\|^2 > \lambda_{\min}^{-1} \left(Q_0 \right) \bar{\eta}$, using the updating law as (up) we can conclude that:

$$\dot{V}_t \leq 2tr \left\{ \left[\Pr \left[P \varphi(\hat{x}_t) \gamma(u_t) \Delta_t^T \right] + P \varphi(\hat{x}_t) \gamma(u_t) \Delta_t^T \right] \tilde{W}_{2,t} \right\} - \Delta_t^T Q_0 \Delta_t + \bar{\eta} \tag{21}$$

    a. if $\left\| \tilde{W}_{2,t} \right\| < r$ or $\left[\left\| \tilde{W}_{2,t} \right\| = r$ and $tr \left(-\omega \tilde{W}_{2,t} \right) \leq 0 \right]$

$$\dot{V}_t \leq -\lambda_{\min} \left(Q_0 \right) \left\| \Delta_t \right\|^2 + \bar{\eta} < 0$$

    b. if $\left\| \tilde{W}_{2,t} \right\| = r$ and $tr \left(-\omega \tilde{W}_{2,t} \right) > 0$

$$\dot{V}_t \leq 2tr \left\{ K_2 P \frac{\left\| \tilde{W}_{2,t} \right\|^2}{tr \left(\tilde{W}_{2,t}^T \left(K_2 P \right) \tilde{W}_{2,t} \right)} \omega \tilde{W}_{2,t} \right\} - \Delta_t^T Q_0 \Delta_t + \bar{\eta}$$
$$\leq -\Delta_t^T Q_0 \Delta_t + \bar{\eta} < 0$$

V_t is bounded. Integrating (21) from 0 up to T yields

$$V_T - V_0 \leq -\int_0^T \Delta_t^T Q_0 \Delta_t dt + \bar{\eta} T$$

Because $\kappa \geq 1$, we have

$$\int_0^T \Delta_t^T Q_0 \Delta_t dt \leq V_0 - V_T + \int_0^T \Delta_t^T Q_0 \Delta_t dt \leq V_0 + \bar{\eta} T \leq V_0 + \kappa \bar{\eta} T \tag{22}$$

where κ is condition number of Q_0

(II) If $\left\| \Delta_t \right\|^2 \leq \lambda_{\min}^{-1}(Q_0) \bar{\eta}$, the weights become constants, V_t remains bounded. And

$$\int_0^T \Delta_t^T Q_0 \Delta_t dt \leq \int_0^T \lambda_{\max}(Q_0) \left\| \Delta_t \right\|^2 dt \leq \frac{\lambda_{\max}(Q_0)}{\lambda_{\min}(Q_0)} \bar{\eta} T \leq V_0 + \kappa \bar{\eta} T \tag{23}$$

From (I) and (II), V_t is bounded, (14) is realized. From (16) and $\tilde{W}_{1,t} = W_{1,t} - W_1^0$, $\tilde{W}_{2,t} = W_{2,t} - W_2^0$ we know $V_0 = \Delta_0^T P \Delta_0$. Using (22) and (23), (15) is obtained. The theorem is proved.

Remark 2 *The weight update law (11) uses two techniques. The dead-zone s_t is applied to overcome* the robust problem caused by unmodeled dynamic $\tilde{f}_t$. In presence of disturbance or unmodeled dynamics, adaptive procedures may easily go unstable. The lack of robustness of parameters identification was demonstrated (Egardt, 1979) and became a hot issue in 1980s. Dead-zone method is one of simple and effective tool. The second technique is projection approach which may guarantees that the parameters remain within a constrained region and does not alter the properties of the adaptive law established without projection (Ioannou & Sun, 1996). The projection approach proposed in this chapter is explain in Figure 2. We hope to force $W_{2,t}$ inside the ball of center W_2^0 and radius r. If $\left\| \tilde{W}_{2,t} \right\| < r$, we use the normal gradient algorithm. When $W_{2,t} - W_2^0$ is on the ball and the vector $W_{2,t}$ points either inside or along the ball i.e., $\frac{d}{dt} \left\| \tilde{W}_{2,t} \right\|^2 = 2tr\left(-\omega \tilde{W}_{2,t} \right) \leq 0$, we also keep this algorithm. If $tr\left(-\omega \tilde{W}_{2,t} \right) > 0$,

$tr\left[\left(-\omega + \frac{\left\| \tilde{W}_{2,t} \right\|^2}{tr\left(\tilde{W}_{2,t}^T \left(K_2 P \right) \tilde{W}_{2,t} \right)} \omega \right) \tilde{W}_{2,t} \right] < 0$, so $\frac{d}{dt} \left\| \tilde{W}_{2,t} \right\|^2 < 0$, $W_{2,t}$ are directed toward the inside or the ball,

i.e. $W_{2,t}$ will never leave the ball. Since $r < \left\| W_2^0 \right\|$, $W_{2,t} \neq 0$.

Remark 3 *Figure 2 and (4) show that the initial conditions of the weights and r will influence* identification accuracy. The algorithm proposed in this chapter cannot guarantee the convergence to optimal value (W_1^* and W_2^*), but we may make them closer to the optimal weights by selecting better initial weights. We design an off-line method to find these initial values. If we star from any weights W_1^0 and W_2^0, the algorithm (11) can make the identification error smaller, *i.e.*, $W_{1,k}$ and $W_{2,k}$ is better than W_1^0 and W_2^0. We use following steps to find the initial weights.

1. *Start from any initial value for $W_1^0 = W_{1,0}$, $W_2^0 = W_{2,0}$.*
2. *Do identification with these $W_{1,0}$, $W_{2,0}$ until T_0.*
3. *If the $\left\| \Delta\left(T_0\right) \right\| < \left\| \Delta\left(0\right) \right\|$, let $W_{1,T}$, $W_{2,T}$ as a new W_1^0 and W_2^0, go to 2 to repeat the identification process.*

Figure 2. Projection algorithm

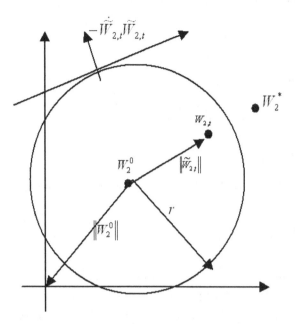

4.   *If the* $\left\| \Delta \left(T_0 \right) \right\| < \left\| \Delta \left(0 \right) \right\|$, stop this off-line identification, now $W_{1,T}$, $W_{2,T}$ are the final values for W_1^0 and W_2^0.

Remark 4 *Since the updating rate is* $K_i P$ ($i = 1, 2$), *and* K_i *can be selected as any positive matrix, the* learning process of the dynamic neural network (11) is free of the solution of Riccati equation (10).

Remark 5. *Let us notice that the upper bound (15) turns out to be sharp, i.e., in the case of no* *any uncertainties (exactly matching case:* $\tilde{f} = 0$) *we obtain* $\bar{\eta} = 0$ *and, hence,*

$$\limsup_{T \to \infty} \frac{1}{T} \int_0^T \left\| \Delta_t \right\|_{Q_0}^2 dt = 0$$

from which, for this special situation, the asymptotic stability property ($\left\| \Delta_t \right\| \underset{t \to \infty}{\to} 0$) *follows.* In general, only the asymptotic stability in average is guaranteed, because the dead zone parameter $\bar{\eta}$ can be never set zero.

3 ROBUST ADAPTIVE CONTROLLER BASED ON NEURO IDENTIFIER

From (4) we know that the nonlinear system (1) may be modeled as

$$\begin{aligned}
x_t &= A x_t + W_1^* \sigma(x_t) + W_2^* \varphi(x_t) \gamma(u_t) + \tilde{f} \\
&= A x_t + W_{1,t} \sigma(\hat{x}_t) + W_{2,t} \varphi(x_t) \gamma(u_t) + \\
\tilde{f} &+ \tilde{W}_{1,t} \sigma(\hat{x}_t) + \tilde{W}_{2,t} \varphi(x_t) \gamma(u_t) + W_{1,t}^* \tilde{\sigma}_t + W_1^* \tilde{\varphi} \gamma(u_t)
\end{aligned} \tag{24}$$

(24) can be rewritten as

$$\dot{x} = A x_t + W_{1,t}\sigma(\hat{x}_t) + W_{2,t}\varphi(x_t)\gamma(u_t) + d_t \tag{25}$$

where

$$d_t = \tilde{f} + \tilde{W}_{1,t}\sigma(\hat{x}_t) + \tilde{W}_{2,t}\varphi(x_t)\gamma(u_t) + W_{1,t}^*\tilde{\sigma}_t + W_1^*\tilde{\varphi}\gamma(u_t) \tag{26}$$

If updated law of $W_{1,t}$ and $W_{2,t}$ is (11), $W_{1,t}$ and $W_{2,t}$ are bounded. Using the assumption **A1,** d_t is bounded as $\bar{d} = \sup_t \|d_t\|$.

The object of adaptive control is to force the nonlinear system (1) following a optimal trajectory $x_t^* \in \Re^r$ which is assumed to be smooth enough. This trajectory is regarded as a solution of a nonlinear reference model:

$$\dot{x}_t^* = \phi\left(x_t^*, t\right) \tag{27}$$

with a fixed initial condition. If the trajectory has points of discontinuity in some fixed moments, we can use any approximating trajectory which is smooth. In the case of regulation problem $\phi\left(x_t^*, t\right) = 0$, $x^*(0) = c$, c is constant. Let us define the sate trajectory error as:

$$\Delta_t^* = x_t - x_t^*. \tag{28}$$

From (25) and (27) we have

$$\dot{\Delta}_t^* = A x_t + W_{1,t}\sigma(\hat{x}_t) + W_{2,t}\varphi(x_t)\gamma(u_t) + d_t - \phi\left(x_t^*, t\right). \tag{29}$$

Let us select the control action $\gamma\left(u_t\right)$ as linear form

$$\gamma\left(u_t\right) = U_{1,t} + \left[W_{2,t}\varphi\left(\hat{x}_t\right)\right]^+ U_{2,t} \tag{30}$$

where $U_{1,t} \in \Re^n$ is direct control part and $U_{2,t} \in \Re^n$ is a compensation of unmodeled dynamic d_t. As $\phi\left(x_t^*, t\right)$, x_t^*, $W_{1,t}\sigma(\hat{x}_t)$ and $W_{2,t}\varphi\left(\hat{x}_t\right)$ are available, we can select $U_{1,t}$ as

$$U_{1,t} = \left[W_{2,t}\varphi\left(\hat{x}_t\right)\right]^+ \left[\phi\left(x_t^*, t\right) - A x_t^* - W_{1,t}\sigma(\hat{x}_t)\right]. \tag{31}$$

where $\left[\bullet\right]^+$ stands for the pseudoinverse matrix in Moor-Penrose sense (Albert, 1972). Because $\varphi\left(\hat{x}_t\right)$ in (2) is different from zero, and $W_{2,t} \neq 0$ by the projection approach in *Theorem 1*. So

$$\left[W_{2,t}\varphi\left(\hat{x}_t\right)\right]^+ = \frac{\left[W_{2,t}\varphi\left(\hat{x}_t\right)\right]^T}{\left\|W_{2,t}\varphi\left(\hat{x}_t\right)\right\|^2} \tag{32}$$

Substitute (30), (31) and (32) into (29), we have So the error equation is

$$\dot{\Delta}_t^* = A\Delta_t^* + U_{2,t} + d_t \tag{33}$$

Four robust algorithms may be applied to compensate d_t.
(A) **Exactly Compensation**. From (25) and (2) we have

$$d_t = \left(\dot{x}_t - \frac{d}{dt}\hat{x}_t\right) - A\left(x_t - \hat{x}_t\right)$$

If x_t is available, we can select $U_{2,t}$ as $U_{2,t}^a = -d_t$, i.e.

$$U_{2,t}^a = A\left(x_t - \hat{x}_t\right) - \left(\dot{x}_t - \frac{d}{dt}\hat{x}_t\right) \tag{34}$$

So, the ODE which describes the state trajectory error is

$$\dot{\Delta}_t^* = A\Delta_t^* \tag{35}$$

Because A is stable, Δ_t^* is globally asymptotically stable.

$$\lim_{t\to\infty}\Delta_t^* = 0.$$

(B) **Approximate Compensation.** If x_t is not available, a approximate method may be used as

$$\dot{x}_t = \frac{x_t - x_{t-\tau}}{\tau} + \delta_t \tag{36}$$

where $\delta_t > 0$, is the differential approximation error. Let us select the compensator as

$$U_{2,t}^b = A\left(x_t - \hat{x}_t\right) - \left(\frac{x_t - x_{t-\tau}}{\tau} - \frac{d}{dt}\hat{x}_t\right) \tag{37}$$

So $U_{2,t}^b = U_{2,t}^a + \delta_t$, (35) become

$$\dot{\Delta}_t^* = A\Delta_t^* + \delta_t$$

Define Lyapunov-like function as

$$V_t = \Delta_t^{*T} P_2 \Delta_t^*, \quad P_2 = P_2^T > 0$$

The time derivative of (38) is

$$\dot{V}_t = \Delta_t^* \left(A^T P_2 + P_2 A \right) \Delta_t^* + 2\Delta_t^{*T} P_2 \delta_t$$

$2\Delta_t^T P_2 \delta_t$ can be estimated as

$$2\Delta_t^{*T} P_2 \delta_t \leq \Delta_t^{*T} P_2 \Lambda P_2 \Delta_t^* + \delta_t^T \Lambda^{-1} \delta_t$$

where Λ is any positive define matrix. So (39) becomes

$$\dot{V}_t \leq \Delta_t^* \left(A^T P_2 + P_2 A + P_2 \Lambda P_2 + Q_2 \right) \Delta_t^* + \delta_t^T \Lambda^{-1} \delta_t - \Delta_t^{*T} Q_2 \Delta_t^*$$

where Q is any positive define matrix. Because A is stable, there exit Λ and Q_2 such that the matrix Riccati equation

$$A^T P_2 + P_2 A + P_2 \Lambda^{-1} P_2 + Q_2 = 0 \tag{40}$$

has positive solution $P = P^T > 0$. Defining the following semi-norms:

$$\left\| \Delta_t^* \right\|_{Q_2}^2 = \limsup_{T \to \infty} \frac{1}{T} \int_0^T \Delta_t^* Q_2 \Delta_t^* dt$$

where $Q_2 = Q_2 > 0$ is the given weighting matrix, the state trajectory tracking can be formulated as the following optimization problem:

$$J_{\min} = \min_{u_t} J, \quad J = \left\| x_t - x_t^* \right\|_{Q_2}^2 \tag{41}$$

Note that

$$\limsup_{T \to \infty} \frac{1}{T} \left(\Delta_0^{*T} P_2 \Delta_0^* \right) = 0$$

based on the dynamic neural network (2), the control law (37) and (30) can make the trajectory tracking error satisfy the following property:

$$\left\| \Delta_t^* \right\|_{Q_2}^2 \leq \left\| \delta_t \right\|_{\Lambda^{-1}}^2$$

A suitable selection of Λ and Q_2 can make the Riccati equation (40) has positive solution and make $\left\|\Delta_t^*\right\|_{Q_2}^2$ small enough if τ is small enough.

(C) **Sliding Mode Compensation.** If x_t is not available, the sliding mode technique may be applied. Let us define Lyapunov-like function as

$$V_t = \Delta_t^{*T} P_3 \Delta_t^*$$

where P_3 is a solution of the Lyapunov equation

$$A^T P_3 + P_3 A = -I \tag{42}$$

Using (33) whose time derivative is

$$\dot{V}_t = \Delta_t^* \left(A^T P_3 + P_3 A\right) \Delta_t^* + 2\Delta_t^{*T} P_3 U_{2,t} + 2\Delta_t^{*T} P_3 d_t \tag{43}$$

According to sliding mode technique, we may select $u_{2,t}$ as

$$U_{2,t}^c = -k P_3^{-1} \operatorname{sgn}(\Delta_t^*), \quad k > 0 \tag{44}$$

where k is positive constant,

$$\operatorname{sgn}(\Delta_t^*) = \left[\operatorname{sgn}(\Delta_{1,t}^*), \cdots \operatorname{sgn}(\Delta_{n,t}^*)\right]^T \in \Re^n$$

Substitute (42) and (44) into (43)

$$\begin{aligned}
\dot{V}_t &= -\left\|\Delta_t^*\right\|^2 - 2k\left\|\Delta_t^*\right\| + 2\Delta_t^{*T} P d_t \\
&\leq -\left\|\Delta_t^*\right\|^2 - 2k\left\|\Delta_t^*\right\| + 2\lambda_{\max}\left(P\right)\left\|\Delta_t^*\right\|\left\|d_t\right\| \\
&= -\left\|\Delta_t^*\right\|^2 - 2\left\|\Delta_t^*\right\|\left(k - \lambda_{\max}\left(P\right)\left\|d_t\right\|\right)
\end{aligned}$$

If we select

$$k > \lambda_{\max}\left(P_3\right)\overline{d} \tag{45}$$

where $\overline{d}$ is define as (26), then $\dot{V}_t < 0$. So

$$\lim_{t \to \infty} \Delta_t^* = 0.$$

(D) **Local Optimal Control**. If x_t is not available and x_t is not approximated as (B). In order to analyze the tracking error stability, we introduce the following Lyapunov function:

$$V_t\left(\Delta_t^*\right) = \Delta_t^* P_4 \Delta_t^*, \quad P_4 = P_4^T > 0$$

Using (33), whose time derivative is:

$$\dot{V}_t = 2\Delta_t^{*T} P_4 \Delta_t^* = \Delta_t^*\left(A^T P_4 + P_4 A\right)\Delta_t^* + 2\Delta_t^{*T} P_4 U_{2,t} + 2\Delta_t^{*T} P_4 d_t \tag{46}$$

$2\Delta_t^{*T} P_4 d_t$ can be estimated as

$$2\Delta_t^{*T} P_4 d_t \leq \Delta_t^* P_4 \Lambda_4^{-1} P_4 \Delta_t^* + d_t^T \Lambda_4 d_t \tag{47}$$

Substituting (47) in (46), adding and subtracting the term $\Delta_t^{*T} Q_4 \Delta_t^*$ and $U_{2,t}^{dT} R_4 U_{2,t}^d$ with $Q_4 = Q_4^T > 0$ and $R_4 = R_4^T > 0$, we formulate:

$$\dot{V}_t \leq \Delta_t^*\left(A^T P_4 + P_4 A + P_4 \Lambda_4 P_4 + Q_4\right)\Delta_t^*$$
$$+2\Delta_t^{*T} P_4 U_{2,t}^d + U_{2,t}^{dT} R_4 U_{2,t}^d + d_t^T \Lambda_4^{-1} d_t - \Delta_t^* Q \Delta_t^* - U_{2,t}^{dT} R_4 U_{2,t}^d \tag{48}$$

Because A is stable, there exit Λ_4 and Q_4 such that the matrix Riccati equation

$$A^T P_4 + P_4 A + P_4 \Lambda_4 P_4 + Q_4 = 0. \tag{49}$$

So (48) is

$$\dot{V}_t \leq -\left(\left\|\Delta_t^*\right\|_{Q_4}^2 + \left\|U_{2,t}^d\right\|_{R_4}^2\right) + \Psi\left(U_{2,t}^d\right) + d_t^T \Lambda_4^{-1} d_t \tag{50}$$

where

$$\Psi\left(U_{2,t}^d\right) = 2\Delta_t^{*T} P_4 U_{2,t}^d + U_{2,t}^{dT} R_4 U_{2,t}^d$$

We reformulate (50) as:

$$\left\|\Delta_t^*\right\|_{Q_4}^2 + \left\|U_{2,t}^d\right\|_{R_4}^2 \leq \Psi\left(U_{2,t}^d\right) + d_t^T \Lambda_4^{-1} d_t - \dot{V}_t.$$

Then, integrating each term from 0 to τ, dividing each term by τ, and taking the limit, for $\tau \to \infty$ of these integrals' supreme, we obtain:

$$\limsup_{T\to\infty} \tfrac{1}{T} \int_0^T \Delta_t^{*T} Q_4 \Delta_t^* dt + \limsup_{T\to\infty} \tfrac{1}{T} \int_0^T U_{2,t}^{dT} R_4 U_{2,t}^d dt$$
$$\leq \limsup_{T\to\infty} \tfrac{1}{T} \int_0^T d_t^T \Lambda_4^{-1} d_t dt + \limsup_{T\to\infty} \tfrac{1}{T} \int_0^T \Psi\left(U_{2,t}^d\right) dt + \limsup_{T\to\infty} \tfrac{1}{T} \int_0^T \left[-\dot{V}_t\right] dt$$

In the view of definitions of the semi-norms (41), we have

$$\left\|\Delta_t^*\right\|_{Q_4}^2 + \left\|U_{2,t}^d\right\|_{R_4}^2 \leq \left\|d_t\right\|_{\Lambda_4^{-1}}^2 + \limsup_{T\to\infty} \frac{1}{T} \int_0^T \Psi\left(U_{2,t}^d\right) dt$$

It fixes a *tolerance level* for the trajectory tracking error. So, the control goal now is to minimize $\Psi\left(U_{2,t}^d\right)$ and $\left\|d_t\right\|_{\Lambda_4^{-1}}^2$. To minimize $\left\|d_t\right\|_{\Lambda_4^{-1}}^2$, we should minimize Λ_4^{-1}. From (5ARA), if select Q_4 to make (5ri) have solution, we can choose the minimal Λ_4^{-1} as

$$\Lambda_4^{-1} = A^{-T}Q_4 A^{-1}$$

To minimizing $\Psi\left(U_{2,t}^d\right)$, we assume that, at the given t (positive), $x^*\left(t\right)$ and $\hat{x}\left(t\right)$ are already realized and do not depend on $U_{2,t}^d$. We name the $U_{2,t}^{d*}\left(t\right)$ as *the locally optimal* control, because it is calculated based only on local information. The solution of this optimization problem is given by

$$\begin{cases} \Psi\left(u_{2,t}^d\right) = 2\Delta_t^{*T}P_4 u_{2,t}^d + U_{2,t}^{dT}R_4 U_{2,t}^d \\ \text{subject: } A_0(U_{1,t} + U_{2,t}^d) \leq B_0 \end{cases}$$

It is typical quadratic programming problem. Without restriction U^* is selected according to the linear squares optimal control law

$$u_{2,t}^d = -2R_4^{-1}P_4\Delta_t^* \tag{51}$$

Remark 6 *Approaches A and C are exactly compensations of d_t,* Approach A need the information

of x_t. Because Approach C uses the sliding mode control $U_{2,t}^c$ is inserted in the closed-loop system, chattering occur in the control input which may excite unmodeled high-frequency dynamics. To eliminate chattering, the boundary layer compensator can be used, it offers a continuous approximation to the discontinuous sliding mode control law inside the boundary layer and guarantees the output tracking error within any neighborhood of the origin (Corless & Leitmann, 1981).

Finally we give following design steps for the robust neuro controllers proposed in this chapter.

- According to the dimension of the plant (1), design a neural networks identifier (2) which has the same dimension as the plant. In (2), A can be selected a stable matrix. A will influence the dynamic response of the neural network. The bigger eigenvalues of A will make the neural network slower. The initial conditions for $W_{1,t}$ and $W_{2,t}$ are obtained as in Remark 3.
- Do on-line identification. The learning algorithm is (11) with the dead-zone in Theorem 1. We assume we know the upper bound of modeling error, we can give a value for $\bar{\eta}$. Q_0 is chosen such that Riccati equation (10) has positive defined solution, R can be selected as any positive defined matrix because Λ_1^{-1} is arbitrary positive defined matrix. The updating rate in the learning algorithm (11) is $K_1 P$, and K_1 can be selected as any positive defined matrix, so the learning process is free of the solution P of the Riccati equations (10). The larger $K_1 P$ is selected, the faster convergence the neuro identifier has.
- Use robust control (30) and one of compensation of (34), (37), (44) and (51).

Remark 7 *Although theory analysis is complex, but the above algorithms are very simple. They are fast enough for control objectives.*

4 NEURO OBSERVERS

When some states in (1) are not available, in order to construct a state-based control, we firstly need an observer. We consider the class of nonlinear systems given by

$$\dot{x} = f(x_t, u_t, t) + \xi_{1,t},$$
$$y_t = C^T x_t + \xi_{2,t}$$

(52)

where

$x_t \in \Re^n$ is the state vector of the system at time $t \in R^+ := \left\{ t : t \geq 0 \right\};$

$u_t \in \Re^q$ is a given control action;

$y_t \in \Re^m$ is the output vector, which is measurable at each time t ;

$f(\cdot) : \Re^n \to \Re^n$ is an unknown vector valued nonlinear function describing the system dynamics;

$C \in \Re^{n \times m}$ is the unknown output matrix;

$\xi_{1,t}$, $\xi_{2,t}$ are vector-functions representing external perturbations, which satisfy the assumption about ``bounded power(A3)'':

A3: $\limsup_{T \to \infty} \frac{1}{T} \int_0^T \left\| \xi_{i,t} \right\|_{\Lambda_{\xi_i}}^2 dt = \Upsilon_i < \infty, \ 0 < \Lambda_{\xi_i} = \Lambda_{\xi_i}^T, \ i = 1, 2.$ The matrices Λ_{ξ_i} are assumed to be a priori given.

A4: C has the following structure:

$$C = C_0 + \Delta C$$

where C_0 is known. For ΔC we assume that it satisfies a kind of the '*strip bounded condition*' (Poznyak & Sanchez, 1995).

$$\Delta C \Lambda_{\Delta C} \Delta C^T \leq C_{\Delta C}, \ \forall t \in R^+.$$

Let us select the recurrent neural networks (Rovithakis & Christodoulou, 1994) in order to construct the Luenberger-like observer (Kim, Lewis & Abdallah, 1996) as:

$$\frac{d}{dt} \hat{x}_t = A \hat{x}_t + W_{1,t} \sigma(\hat{x}_t) + W_{2,t} \varphi(\hat{x}_t) \gamma(u_t) + K_t \left[y_t - \hat{y}_t \right],$$
$$\hat{y}_t = C_0^T \hat{x}_t$$

(53)

where $A \in \Re^{n \times n}$ is a Hurtwitz matrix, $W_{1,t} \in \Re^{n \times n}$ is the weights matrix for nonlinear state feedback, $W_{2,t} \in \Re^{n \times n}$ is the input weights matrix, $K_t \in \Re^{n \times m}$ is the observer gain matrix, $\hat{x}_t$ is the state of the neural network. The matrix function $\varphi(\cdot)$ is assumed to be $\Re^{n \times n}$ diagonal. The vector functions $\sigma(\cdot)$ and $\gamma(.)$ are assumed to be $n-$ dimensional with the elements that increase monotonically.

The elements $\sigma_i(\cdot)$ and $\varphi_i(\cdot)$ are selected as the structure of higher order neural networks (Kosmato-poulos, Polycarpou, Christodoulou, & Ioannou, 1995)

$$\sigma_i(\hat{x}_t) = \prod_j^{l_i} z(\hat{x}_j), \quad \varphi_i(\hat{x}_t) = \prod_j^{h_i} z(\hat{x}_j) \quad i = 1 \cdots n$$

where $z(\hat{x}_j)$ is a typical sigmoid function.

The initial conditions $\hat{x}_0$ is assumed to be fixed. We name the proposed scheme as a neuro-observer (53). The estimation error is defined as:

$$\Delta_t := x_t - \hat{x}_t.$$

A5: The function $f(x_t, u_t, t)$ in (52) can be modeled exactly by the dynamic neural network (observer), with W_1^* and W_2^*, plus a modeling error (Kim, Lewis & Abdallah, 1996) $f(x_t, u_t, t) = Ax_t + W_1^* \sigma(x_t) + W_2^* \varphi(x_t) \gamma(u_t) + \Delta f(x_t, u_t, t)$ where Δf is the modeling error reflecting the effect of unmodelled dynamics. We assume that W_1^* and W_2^* are bounded as follows

$$W_1^* \Lambda_\sigma^{-1} W_1^{*T} \le \bar{W}_1, \quad W_2^* \Lambda_\varphi^{-1} W_2^{*T} \le \bar{W}$$

with a priory known matrices $\Lambda_\sigma^{-1}, \Lambda_\varphi^{-1}, \bar{W}_1$ and $\overline{W}_2$.

A6: The modeling error term Δf satisfies:

$$\Delta f^T(x_t, u_t, t) \Lambda_{\Delta f} \Delta f(x_t, u_t, t) \le C_{\Delta f} + x_t^T D_{\Delta f} x_t, \quad \forall u \in \Re^q, t \in R^+$$

where

$$0 < \Lambda_{\Delta f}^T = \Lambda_{\Delta f} \in \Re^{n \times n}, \ 0 < D_{\Delta f}^T = D_{\Delta f} \in \Re^{n \times n}$$

are known constant matrices, and $C_{\Delta f}$ and $D_{\Delta f}$ are known positive constants.

As for the sigmoid function $\sigma(\cdot), \gamma(\cdot)$ and $\varphi(\cdot)$, we assume that the following inequalities are fulfilled:

$$\sigma^T(x_t) Z_1 \sigma(x_t) \le x_t^T \Lambda_1 x_t + \Pi_1,$$
$$\varphi^T(x_t) Z_2 \varphi(x_t) \le x_t^T \Lambda_2 x_t + \Pi_2,$$
$$\gamma^T(x_t) Z_3 \gamma(x_t) \le x_t^T \Lambda_3 x_t + \Pi_3,$$

$$\tilde{\sigma}_t^T \Lambda_\sigma \tilde{\sigma}_t \le C_\sigma + \Delta_t^T D_\sigma \Delta_t,$$
$$\tilde{\varphi}_t^T \Lambda_\varphi \tilde{\varphi}_t \le C_\varphi + \Delta_t^T D_\varphi \Delta_t$$

where

$$\tilde{\sigma}_t := \sigma(x_t) - \sigma(\hat{x}_t), \ \tilde{\varphi}_t := \varphi(x_t) - \varphi(\hat{x}_t).$$

All matrices in (ru) are assumed to be known.

Throughout this chapter we will denote the class of nonlinear systems satisfying the assumptions **A3-A6** by H .

For each nonlinear system (52) and neuro-observer (53), we associate the performance index

$$J = J(\{K_t\}_{t\geq 0}, \{W_{1,t}\}_{t\geq 0}, \{W_{2,t}\}_{t\geq 0}) := \sup_{H} \limsup_{T\to\infty} \frac{1}{T} \int_0^T \Delta_t^T Q \Delta_t \, dt$$

which characterizes the quality of the state estimation process (53) for the class H of nonlinear systems (52). The constant strictly positive matrix Q normalizes the components of the error vector Δ_t, which could have different physical meanings. This performance index depends on the matrix $\{K_t\}_{t\geq 0}$ and on the weights $\{W_{1,t}\}_{t\geq 0}, \{W_{2,t}\}_{t\geq 0}$ which must be selected to provide a good quality of the estimation process for a given class H .

The formal statement of the robust filtering is as follows.

Statement of the problem: *For a given class* H *of nonlinear systems, for any given gain matrix function* $\{K_t\}_{t\geq 0}$ *and for any weight matrices* $\{W_{1,t}\}_{t\geq 0}, \{W_{2,t}\}_{t\geq 0}$, *obtain an upper bound*

$$J^+ = J^+(\{K_t\}_{t\geq 0}, \{W_{1,t}\}_{t\geq 0}, \{W_{2,t}\}_{t\geq 0})$$

on the performance index J *(* $J \leq J^+$ *) and minimize this bound estimate with respect to matrices* $\{K_t\}_{t\geq 0}$ *and* $\{W_{1,t}\}_{t\geq 0}, \{W_{2,t}\}_{t\geq 0}$, *i.e. realize*

$$\inf_{\{K_t\}_{t\geq 0}, \{W_{1,t}\}_{t\geq 0}, \{W_{2,t}\}_{t\geq 0}} J^+. \tag{54}$$

Remark 8 According to the definition given above, if

$$J^+(\{K_t^*\}_{t\geq 0}, \{W_{1,t}^*\}_{t\geq 0}, \{W_{2,t}^*\}_{t\geq 0}) < \infty$$

then the neuro-observer described by (53), with fixed matrices $\{K_t^*\}_{t\geq 0}, \{W_{1,t}^*\}_{t\geq 0}, \{W_{2,t}^*\}_{t\geq 0}$, guarantees also the property of stability to the error trajectories in an "*average sense*", which corresponds to the bounded seminorm used in (54). Later we will show that in presence of no disturbances and unmodelled dynamics (complete model matching), this neuro-observer grantees the asymptotic stability "in average" of the error vector.

Neuro-Observer Analysis and Synthesis

The theorems presented below constitute our main results on robust neuro-observer analysis and synthesis.

Let suppose that, additionally to **A3-A6,** the following assumption is fulfilled:

A7: There exist a strictly positive defined matrix Q , a stable matrix A and a positive constant δ such that the differential matrix Riccati equation

$$-\dot{P}_t = P_t A + A^T P_t + P_t R_0 P_t + Q_t \tag{55}$$

for any $t \in R^+$ has a strictly positive solution $P_t = P_t^T > 0$.

The matrices R_0, Q_t are defined as follows:

$$R_0 := \bar{W}_1 + \bar{W}_2 + \Lambda_{\xi_1}^{-1} + \Lambda_{\xi_2}^{-1} + \Lambda_{\Delta f}^{-1},$$

$$Q_t := D_\sigma + \left\| \gamma(u_t) \right\|^2 D_\varphi + Q + 2\delta, \delta > 0.$$

Remark 9 Notice that the differential Riccati equation (55) has a positive solution $P_t = P_t^T > 0$ if and only if the pair $(A, R_0^{1/2})$ is controllable and the pair $(Q_t^{1/2}, A)$ is observable and, additionally, for any $t \in R^+$ a special local frequency condition is fulfilled (Willems, 1971):

$$I - \left(R_0^{1/2}\right)\left[-i\omega I + A\right]^{-1} Q_t \left[i\omega I + A\right] R_0^{1/2} > 0 \quad \forall \omega\left(-\infty, \infty\right).$$

To satisfy this frequency condition it is sufficient to guarantee the validity of the following matrix inequality (Osorio & Poznyak, 1997)

$$A^T R_0^{-1} A > Q_t$$

at each time $t \geq 0$. This condition states a balance between the boundaries to admissable uncertainties ($\Lambda_{\xi_1}^{-1} + \Lambda_{\xi_2}^{-1} + \Lambda_{\Delta f}^{-1}$) in the description of unmodelled dynamics as well as external perturbation with the stability properties of a selected NN (matrix A) and with nonlinear properties of a given model to be controlled (matrix Q_t). Indeed, if the nonliniarities in NN belong to a more wide *conic-class* (D_σ and D_φ are big enough), it leads to a bigger value of the matrix Q_t and, as a result, for a fixed matrix A we have to demand less values of the matrix R_0. It means that admissable noises ($\Lambda_{\xi_1} + \Lambda_{\xi_2}$), unmodelled dynamic ($\Lambda_{\Delta f}$) and weight variation bounds ($\bar{W}_1, \bar{W}_2$) should be smaller such a manner to satisfy the constraint (55). For a selected dynamic NN all of these conditions can be easy fulfilled selecting the matrices A and Q adequately.

Let define

$$\tilde{y}_t := y_t - C_0^T \hat{x}_t, \quad N := \left(C_0 C_0^+ + \delta I\right)^{-1}.$$

At this stage we establish two theorems.

Lemma 1 *For any matrices* $X \in \Re^{n \times k}$ $Y \in \Re^{n \times k}$ *and any positive defined matrix* $\Lambda = \Lambda^T > 0$, $\Lambda \in \Re^{n \times n}$ *the following matrix inequality hold:*

$$X^T Y + Y^T X \leq X^T \Lambda X + Y^T \Lambda^{-1} Y,$$
$$\left(X + Y\right)^T \left(X + Y\right) \leq X^T \left(I + \Lambda\right) X + Y^T \left(I + \Lambda^{-1}\right) Y. \tag{56}$$

Proof Define

$$H := X^T \Lambda X + Y^T \Lambda^{-1} Y - X^T Y - Y^T X.$$

Then for any vector v we can introduce the vectors

$$v_1 := \Lambda^{1/2} X v \text{ and } v_2 := \Lambda^{-1/2} Y v.$$

Based on this notations we derive:

$$v^T H v = v_1^T v_1 + v_2^T v_2 - v_1^T v_2 - v_2^T v_1 = \left\| v_1 - v_2 \right\|^2 \geq 0 \tag{57}$$

or, in matrix form:

$$H \geq 0,$$

that is equivalent to (57). The inequality (57) is direct consequence of (56).

Theorem 2 *Under assumptions A1-A5, for a given class* H *of nonlinear systems described by (plant), and for any matrix sequences* $\left\{ K_t \right\}_{t \geq 0}, \left\{ W_{1,t} \right\}_{t \geq 0}, \left\{ W_{2,t} \right\}_{t \geq 0}$, *the following upper bound for the performance index (index) of the neuro-observer holds:*

$$J \leq J^+ = \overline{C} + D + \Upsilon_1 + \Upsilon_2 + \phi \left(\left\{ K_t \right\}_{t \geq 0} \right) + \psi \left(\left\{ W_{1,t} \right\}_{t \geq 0}, \left\{ W_{2,t} \right\}_{t \geq 0} \right)$$

where the constants Υ_1, Υ_2 *and*

$$\overline{C} := C_{\Delta f} + C_o + C_{\Delta c} + C_\varphi \sup_{\mathrm{H}} \limsup_{T \to \infty} \frac{1}{T} \int_0^T \left\| \gamma(u_t) \right\|^2 dt,$$

$$D := \sup_{\mathrm{H}} \limsup_{T \to \infty} \frac{1}{T} \int_0^T x_t^T \left[D_{\Delta f} + 2C_{\Delta C} \right] x_t dt,$$

$$0 \leq \phi \left(\left\{ K_t \right\}_{t \geq 0} \right) := \sup_{\mathrm{H}} \limsup_{T \to \infty} \frac{1}{T} \int_0^T \Delta_t^T \left(P_t K_t - \Omega^{-\frac{1}{2}} C_0^T \right) \left(P_t K_t - \Omega^{-\frac{1}{2}} C_0^T \right) \Delta_t dt.$$

where

$$\Omega := \Lambda_{\Delta C}^{-1} + \Lambda_{\xi_2}^{-1}$$

and

$$\psi \left(\left\{ W_{1,t} \right\}_{t \geq 0}, \left\{ W_{2,t} \right\}_{t \geq 0} \right) := \sup_{\mathrm{H}} \limsup_{T \to \infty} \frac{1}{T} \int_0^T \left\| tr \left(\tilde{W}_{1,t} L_{w1,t} + \tilde{W}_{2,t} L_{w1,t} \right) \right\| dt$$

with the weight estimation errors

$$\tilde{W}_{1,t} = W_1^* - W_{1,t}, \quad \tilde{W}_{2,t} = W_2^* - W_{2,t}$$

117

with matrix functions $L_{w1,t}, L_{w1,t}$ defined by

$$L_{w1,t} = 2\dot{\tilde{W}}_{1,t} + M_{1,t}\tilde{W}_{1,t}^T + 2P_t\sigma(\hat{x}_t)\tilde{y}_t C_0^+ N,$$

$$L_{w2,t} = 2\dot{\tilde{W}}_{2,t} + \left\|\gamma(u_t)\right\|^2 M_{2,t}\tilde{W}_{2,t}^T + 2P_t\varphi(\hat{x}_t)\gamma(u_t)\tilde{y}_t C_0^+ N.$$

Proof We initiate the proof deriving the error vector differential equation. Taking in account (52), (53) we obtain:

$$\dot{\Delta}_t = \dot{x}_t - \dot{\hat{x}}_t = f(x_t, u_t, t) + \xi_{1,t} - A\hat{x}_t - W_{1,t}\sigma(\hat{x}_t) - W_{2,t}\varphi(\hat{x}_t)\gamma(u_t) - K_t[y_t - C_0\hat{x}_t].$$

Calculating the derivative of the Lyapunov function

$$V_t := \Delta_t^T P_t \Delta_t + tr\left[\tilde{W}_{1,t}\tilde{W}_{1,t}^T\right] + tr\left[\tilde{W}_{2,t}\tilde{W}_{2,t}^T\right], \qquad P_t^T = P_t > 0$$

along the trajectories of the differential equation we derive:

$$\frac{dV_t}{dt} = \frac{\partial V_t}{\partial t} + \left(\frac{\partial V_t}{\partial \Delta_t}, \dot{\Delta}_t\right)$$

$$= \Delta_t^T \dot{P}_t \Delta_t + 2\Delta_t^T P_t \dot{\Delta}_t + 2tr\left[\tilde{W}_{1,t}^T \dot{\tilde{W}}_{1,t}\right] + 2tr\left[\tilde{W}_{2,t}^T \dot{\tilde{W}}_{2,t}\right].$$

Then we obtain

$$2\Delta_t^T P_t \dot{\Delta}_t = 2\Delta_t^T P_t\left[(A - K_t C_0)\Delta_t + W_1^*\tilde{\sigma}_t + W_2^*\tilde{\varphi}_t\gamma(u_t) + \tilde{W}_{1,t}\sigma(\hat{x}_t) + \tilde{W}_{2,t}\varphi(\hat{x}_t)\gamma(u_t)\right]$$
$$+ 2\Delta_t^T P_t\left[\Delta f - K_t\Delta C + \xi_{1,t} - K_t\xi_{2,t}\right].$$

Based on the assumptions **A3-A6** and applying Lemma 1, we get the inequalities:

$$2\Delta_t^T P_t W_1^*\tilde{\sigma}_t \leq \Delta_t^T\left(P_t W_1^*\Lambda_\sigma^{-1}W_1^{*T}P_t + D_\sigma\right)\Delta_t + C_\sigma,$$
$$\leq \Delta_t^T\left(P_t\bar{W}_1 P_t + D_\sigma\right)\Delta_t + C_\sigma,$$
$$\Delta_t^T P_t W_2^*\tilde{\varphi}_t\gamma(u_t) \leq \Delta_t^T\left(P_t W_2^*\Lambda_\varphi^{-1}W_2^{*T}P_t + \left\|\gamma(u_t)\right\|^2 D_\varphi\right)\Delta_t + \left\|\gamma(u_t)\right\|^2 C_\varphi,$$
$$\leq \Delta_t^T\left(P_t\bar{W}_2 P_t + \left\|\gamma(u_t)\right\|^2 D_\varphi\right)\Delta_t + \left\|\gamma(u_t)\right\|^2 C_\varphi,$$
$$2\Delta_t^T P_t\Delta f \leq \Delta_t^T P_t\Lambda_{\Delta f}^{-1}P_t\Delta_t + C_{\Delta f} + x_t^T D_{\Delta f}x_t,$$
$$-2\Delta_t^T P_t K_t\Delta C \leq \Delta_t^T P_t K_t\Lambda_{\Delta C}^{-1}K_t^T P_t\Delta_t + C_{\Delta C},$$
$$2\Delta_t^T P_t\xi_{1,t} \leq \Delta_t^T P_t\Lambda_{\xi_1}^{-1}P_t\Delta_t + \xi_{1,t}^T\Lambda_{\xi_1}\xi_{1,t},$$
$$-2\Delta_t^T P_t K_t\xi_{2,t} \leq \Delta_t^T P_t K_t\Lambda_{\xi_2}^{-1}K_t^T P_t\Delta_t + \xi_{2,t}^T\Lambda_{\xi_2}\xi_{2,t}.$$

From (52) we conclude:

$$C_0^T\Delta = y_t - C_0^T\hat{x}_t + \Delta C^T x_t + \xi_{2,t},$$
$$\Delta^T C_0 = \left(y_t - C_0^T\hat{x}_t\right)^T + \left(\Delta C^T x_t + \xi_{2,t}\right)^T.$$

Because $\Delta_t^T P_t\tilde{W}_{1,t}\sigma(\hat{x})$ is a scalar, then:

$$2\Delta_t^T P_t \tilde{W}_{1,t}\sigma(\hat{x}_t) = 2tr\left(\Delta_t^T P_t \tilde{W}_{1,t}\sigma(\hat{x}_t)\right) = 2tr\left(\tilde{W}_{1,t}P_t\sigma(\hat{x}_t)\Delta_t^T\right)$$

$$= 2tr\left[\tilde{W}_{1,t}P_t\sigma(\hat{x}_t)\Delta_t^T\left(C_0C_0^+ + \delta I\right)\left(C_0C_0^+ + \delta I\right)^{-1}\right]$$

$$= 2tr\left[\tilde{W}_{1,t}P_t\sigma(\hat{x}_t)\tilde{y}_t^T C_0^+ N\right] + 2\left(\Delta C^T x_t + \xi_{2,t}\right)^T \tilde{W}_{1,t}P_t C_0^+ N\sigma(\hat{x}_t)$$

$$+ 2\delta\Delta_t^T \tilde{W}_{1,t}P_t N\sigma(\hat{x}_t)$$

where

$$N := \left(C_0 C_0^+ + \delta I\right)^{-1}.$$

We derive:

$$2\left(\Delta C^T x_t + \xi_{2,t}\right)^T \tilde{W}_{1,t}P_t C_0^+ N\sigma(\hat{x}_t)$$

$$\leq \sigma(\hat{x}_t)^T N^T C_0^{+T} P_t \tilde{W}_{1,t}^T \left[\Lambda_{\Delta c}^{-1} + \Lambda_{\xi_2}^{-1}\right]\tilde{W}_{1,t}P_t C_0^+ N\sigma(\hat{x}_t) + \xi_{2,t}^T \Lambda_{\xi_2}\xi_{2,t} + x_t^T C_{\Delta c}x_t,$$

$$2\delta\Delta_t^T \tilde{W}_{1,t}P_t N\sigma(\hat{x}_t) \leq \delta\sigma(\hat{x})^T N^T P_t \tilde{W}_{1,t}^T \tilde{W}_{1,t}P_t N\sigma(\hat{x}_t) + \delta\Delta_t^T \Delta_t.$$

The same relationship can be obtained for

$$2\Delta_t^T P_t \tilde{W}_{2,t}\varphi(\hat{x})\gamma(u_t) = 2tr\left[\tilde{W}_{2,t}P_t\varphi(\hat{x}_t)\gamma(u_t)\tilde{y}_t^T C_0^+ N\right]$$

$$+ 2\left(\Delta C^T x_t + \xi_{2,t}\right)^T \tilde{W}_{2,t}P_t C_0^+ N\varphi(\hat{x}_t)\gamma(u_t) + 2\delta\Delta_t^T \tilde{W}_{2,t}P_t N\varphi(\hat{x}_t)\gamma(u_t)$$

$$\leq 2tr\left[\tilde{W}_{2,t}P_t\varphi(\hat{x}_t)\gamma(u_t)\tilde{y}_t^T C_0^+ N\right]$$

$$+ \left\|\gamma(u_t)\right\|^2 \varphi(\hat{x}_t)^T N^T C_0^{+T} P_t \tilde{W}_{2,t}^T \left[\Lambda_{\Delta c}^{-1} + \Lambda_{\xi_2}^{-1}\right]\tilde{W}_{2,t}P_t C_0^+ N\varphi(\hat{x}_t)$$

$$+ \xi_{2,t}^T \Lambda_{\xi_2}\xi_{2,t} + x_t^T C_{\Delta c}x_t$$

$$+ \delta\left\|\gamma(u_t)\right\|^2 \varphi(\hat{x}_t)^T N^T P_t \tilde{W}_{2,t}^T \tilde{W}_{2,t}P_t N\varphi(\hat{x}_t) + \delta\Delta_t^T \Delta_t.$$

Using the identity

$$2\Delta_t^T A_t \Delta_t = \Delta_t^T A_t \Delta_t + \Delta_t^T A_t^T \Delta_t,$$

and adding and substraction the term $\Delta_t^T Q\Delta_t\left(Q = Q^T > 0\right)$ in the right side hand, we obtain:

$$\frac{dV_t}{dt} \leq \Delta_t^T L_t \Delta_t + tr\left[\tilde{W}_{1,t}^T L_{w1}\right] + tr\left[\tilde{W}_{2,t}^T L_{w2}\right] + \left(C_t + \Upsilon_t + D_t - \Delta_t^T Q\Delta_t\right)$$

$$+ \Delta_t^T \left[P_t K_t\left(\Lambda_{\Delta C}^{-1} + \Lambda_{\xi_2}^{-1}\right)K_t^T P_t - PK_t C_0 - C_0^T K_t^T P\right]\Delta_t$$

where

$$C_t := C_{\Delta f} + C_\sigma + C_{\Delta c} + C_\varphi\left\|\gamma(u_t)\right\|^2,$$
$$D_t := x_t^T \left[D_{\Delta f} + 2C_{\Delta C}\right]x_t.$$

We denote

$$L_t := \dot{P}_t + P_t A + A^T P_t + P_t\left(\bar{W}_1 + \bar{W}_2 + \Lambda_{\xi_1}^{-1} + \Lambda_{\xi_2}^{-1} + \Lambda_{\Delta f}^{-1}\right)P_t +$$
$$+ \left(D_\sigma + \left\|\gamma(u_t)\right\|^2 D_\varphi + Q + 2\delta\right).$$

The differential equations) can be solved for initial conditions $\tilde{W}_{1,0} = 0$ and $\tilde{W}_{2,0} = 0$. If we use

(58) as the updating law, we obtain:

$$L_{w1,t} = 0, \ L_{w2,t} = 0.$$

Let denote

$$G_t := P_t K_t \Omega K_t^T P_t - P K_t C_0 - C_0^T K_t^T P$$
$$= \left(P_t K_t - \Omega^{-\frac{1}{2}} C_0^T \right) \left(P_t K_t - \Omega^{-\frac{1}{2}} C_0^T \right) - C_0^T \Omega^{-1} C_0$$
$$\leq \left(P_t K_t - \Omega^{-\frac{1}{2}} C_0^T \right) \left(P_t K_t - \Omega^{-\frac{1}{2}} C_0^T \right)$$

Then

$$\frac{dV_t}{dt} \leq C_t + \Delta_t^T G_t \Delta_t + \Upsilon_t + D_t - \Delta_t^T Q \Delta_t + \Delta_t^T G_t \Delta_t.$$

Integrating above, for the interval $t \in \left[0, T \right]$, and dividing both sides by T, we obtain:

$$\frac{1}{T} \int_0^T \Delta_t^T Q \Delta_t dt \leq \frac{1}{T} \int_0^T \Delta_t^T G_t \Delta_t dt + \frac{1}{T} \int_0^T \Upsilon_t dt + \frac{1}{T} \int_0^T \left(C_t + D_t \right) dt - \frac{1}{T} \left(V_T - V_0 \right)$$

$$\leq \frac{1}{T} \int_0^T \Delta_t^T G_t \Delta_t + \frac{1}{T} \int_0^T \Upsilon_t dt + \frac{1}{T} \int_0^T \left(C_t + D_t \right) dt - \frac{1}{T} V_0.$$

Taking limit for $T \to \infty$ and using upper limits for both sides, we finally obtain it.

Theorem 3 *The neuro-observer is described by (53), with gain matrix K_t given as*

$$K_t = P_t^{-1} \Omega^{-\frac{1}{2}} C_0^T$$

and with the following updating law (for any fixed initial conditions):

$$\dot{W}_{1,t} = M_{1,t} \tilde{W}_{1,t} + 2 P_t \sigma(\hat{x}_t) \tilde{y}_t^T C_0^+ N,$$

$$\dot{W}_{2,t} = \left\| u_t \right\|^2 M_{2,t} \tilde{W}_{2,t} + 2 P_t \varphi(\hat{x}_t) u_t \tilde{y}_t^T C_0^+ N. \tag{58}$$

where

$$M_{1,t} = P_t N \sigma(\hat{x}_t) \left(C_0^+ \left(\Lambda_{\Delta c}^{-1} + \Lambda_{\xi_2}^{-1} \right) C_0^{+T} + \delta \right) \sigma(\hat{x}_t)^T N^T P_t,$$

$$M_{2,t} = P_t N \varphi(\hat{x}_t) \left(C_0^+ \left(\Lambda_{\Delta c}^{-1} + \Lambda_{\xi_2}^{-1} \right) C_0^{+T} + \delta \right) \varphi(\hat{x}_t)^T N^T P_t$$

and matrices $\tilde{W}_{1,t}$, $\tilde{W}t_{2,t}$ *are the solutions of the following differential equations (with zero initial conditions):*

$$-2 \dot{\tilde{W}}_{1,t} = M_{1,t} \tilde{W}_{1,t}^T + 2 P_t \sigma(\hat{x}_t) \tilde{y}_t C_0^+ N,$$

$$-2\dot{\tilde{W}}_{2,t} = \left\| \gamma(u_t) \right\|^2 M_{2,t} \tilde{W}_{2,t}^T + 2P_t \varphi(\hat{x}_t)\gamma(u_t)\tilde{y}_t C_0^+ N$$

(C_0^+ is the pseudoinverse matrix in Moor-Penrose sense).

Proof If K_t is chosen and $W_{1,t}$, $W_{2,t}$ are chosen as (58), this theorem and its corollaries are proved.

Corollary 1 *The neuro-observer guarantees the properties*

$$\phi\left(\left\{K_t\right\}_{t\geq 0}\right) = 0$$

and

$$\psi\left(\left\{W_{1,t}\right\}_{t\geq 0}, \left\{W_{2,t}\right\}_{t\geq 0}\right) = 0.$$

Corollary 2 $W_{1,t}^*, W_{2,t}^*$ satisfy the updating, which guarantees the upper bound with

$$J^+ = \overline{C} + D + \Upsilon_1 + \Upsilon_2.$$

Remark 10:
Equation (56) implements the new learning law for the dynamic neural network weights.
Remark 11

- The term $\overline{C}$ in (54) is related to assumptions **A4** and **A6,** and is equal to 0 if the unmodelled dynamics is obtained:

$$\Delta f(0, u, t) = 0, \ \Delta C = 0.$$

- The term D in (54) is also related to assumptions **A2** and **A4,** and is equal to zero if we deal with bounded unmodelled dynamics, which corresponds to the case:

$$D_{\Delta f} = D_{\Delta C} = 0.$$

- If $D \neq 0$, to guarantee that right side hand of (54) would be bounded, we must additionally assume that the class $\mathbb{H}$ contains only nonlinear systems which are *"stable in average"*, i.e.

$$\sup_{\mathbb{H}} \limsup_{T \to \infty} \frac{1}{T} \int_0^T \left\| x_t \right\|^2 dt < \infty.$$

- In the case of no unmodelled dynamics we have

$$\overline{C} = D = 0.$$

- If we deal with a system without any unmodelled dynamics, *i.e.*, neural network matches the plant exactly $\left(\overline{C} = D = 0 \right)$ and without any external disturbances $\left(\Upsilon_1 = \Upsilon_2 = 0 \right)$ the neuro-observer (observer), with the matrix gain given by (KT), guarantees *"the stability in average"*, i.e.

$$\sup_{\mathrm{H}} \limsup_{T \to \infty} \frac{1}{T} \int_0^T \Delta_t^T Q \Delta_t \, dt = 0,$$

that, because the integrand is a quadratic term $\left(Q = Q^T > 0 \right)$, is equivalent to the fact of $\Delta_t \underset{t \to \infty}{\to} 0$.

5 NEURO OBSERVERS-BASED TACKING

In this section we will show that the observer described above can be successfully employed in trajectory tracking control when the state of the plant is not completely measurable. The control goal is to force the system states to track a signal generated by a nonlinear reference model as:

$$\dot{x}_t^* = \lambda(x_t^*, t).$$

Defining the following semi-norms:

$$\left\| x_t \right\|_{Q_c} = \limsup_{T \to \infty} \frac{1}{T} \int_0^T x_t^T Q_c \, x_t \, dt, \quad \left\| u_t \right\|_{R_c} = \limsup_{T \to \infty} \frac{1}{T} \int_0^T u_t^T R_c \, u_t \, dt$$

where $Q_c^T = Q_c > 0, R_c^T = R_c > 0$, the state trajectory tracking can be formulated as:

$$J_{\min} = \min J_t, \quad J_t = \left\| x_t - x_t^* \right\|_{Q_c} + \left\| u_t \right\|_{R_c} .$$

So, for any $\eta > 0$,

$$J_t \leq \left(1 + \eta \right) \left\| x_t - \hat{x}_t \right\|_{Q_c} + \left(1 + \eta^{-1} \right) \left\| \hat{x}_t - x_t^* \right\|_{Q_c} + \left\| u_t \right\|_{R_c} .$$

Remark 12 The problem of minimization of the term $\left\| x_t - \hat{x}_t \right\|_{Q_c}$ has already been solved in the previous paragraph for the neuro-observer analysis. So, the control goal is to minimize

$$\hat{J}_t = \left\| \hat{x}_t - x_t^* \right\|_{Q_c} + \left\| u_t \right\|_{R_c} .$$

The parameters $\eta > 0$ represents a weight of importance of state estimation with respect to tracking: if η is smaller we are paying more attention to a good tracking.

We define the state trajectory error as:

$$\Delta_t^* = \hat{x}_t - x_t^*.$$

So, the ODE which describes the state trajectory error is:

$$\dot{\Delta}_t^* = A\Delta_t^* + W_{1,t}\sigma(\Delta_t^* + x_t^*) + W_{2,t}\varphi(\Delta_t^* + x_t^*)\gamma(u_t) + \mu_t^*,$$
$$\mu_t^* = K_t\left[y_t - \hat{y}_t\right] + Ax_t^* - \lambda(x_t^*, t).$$

In order to analyze the tracking error stability, we introduce the following Lyapunov function:

$$V_t^* = \Delta_t^{*T}P_t^*\Delta_t^*, \quad P_t^{*T} = P_t^* > 0.$$

The time derivative is:

$$\frac{dV_t^*}{dt} = \Delta_t^{*T}P_t^*\dot{\Delta}_t^* + 2\Delta_t^{*T}P_t^*\dot{\Delta}_t^*$$
$$= 2\Delta_t^{*T}P_t^*\left(A\Delta_t^* + W_{1,t}\sigma(\Delta_t^* + x_t^*) + W_{2,t}\varphi(\Delta_t^* + x_t^*)\gamma(u_t) + \mu_t^*\right) + \Delta_t^{*T}\dot{P}_t\Delta_t^*.$$

Using Lemma 1 and **A8,** we may conclude that

$$2\left(\Delta_t^{*T}P_t^*W_{1,t}\right)\sigma(\Delta_t^* + x_t^*)$$
$$\leq \Delta_t^{*T}P_t^*\left(W_{1,t}Z_1^{-1}W_{1,t}^T\right)P_t^*\Delta_t^* + 2\Delta_t^{*T}\Lambda_1\Delta_t^* + 2x_t^{*T}\Lambda_1 x_t^* + \Upsilon_1,$$

$$2\left(\Delta_t^{*T}P_t^*\right)\mu_t^* \leq \Delta_t^{*T}P_t^*Z_3^{-1}P_t^*\Delta_t^* + \mu_t^{*T}Z_3\mu_t^*.$$

Taking into account that the following identity

$$2\left(\Delta_t^{*T}P_t^*W_{2,t}\right)\varphi(\Delta_t^* + x_t^*)\gamma(u_t)$$
$$= \left\|W_{2,t}^T P_t^*\Delta_t^{*T} + \varphi(\hat{x}_t)\gamma(u_t)\right\|^2 - \Delta_t^{*T}P_t^*W_{2,t}W_{2,t}^T P_t^*\Delta_t^* - \left\|\varphi(\hat{x}_t)\gamma(u_t)\right\|^2.$$

Adding and subtracting $\Delta_t^{*T}Q_c\Delta_t^*$ and $u_t^T R_c u_t$, we formulate:

$$\frac{dV_t^*}{dt} \leq \Delta_t^{*T}\left(\dot{P}_t + P_t^*A + A^T P_t^* + P_t^* R_t^* P_t^* + Q^*\right)\Delta_t^* + 2x_t^{*T}\Lambda_1 x_t^*$$
$$+\Psi_t(u_t) + \mu_t^{*T}Z_3\mu_t^* + \Upsilon_1 - \Delta_t^{*T}Q_c\Delta_t^* - u_t^T R_c u_t$$

where

$$Q^* := 2\Lambda_1 + Q_C,$$
$$R_t^* := W_{1,t}Z_1^{-1}W_{1,t}^T - W_{2,t}W_{2,t}^T + Z_3^{-1},$$
$$\Psi_t(u_t) := \left\|W_{2,t}^T P_t^*\Delta_t^{*T} + \varphi(\hat{x}_t)\gamma(u_t)\right\|^2 - \left\|\varphi(\hat{x}_t)\gamma(u_t)\right\|^2 + u_t^T R_c u_t.$$

According to Theorems 2 and 3 the weights of neural network $W_{i,t}$ $(i = 1, 2)$ are bounded

$$\left\|W_{i,t}\right\| \leq \bar{W}_i, \forall t \geq 0, \quad i = 1, 2.$$

So, the terms $W_{i,t}Z_i^{-1}W_{i,t}^T$ are also bounded

$$W_{i,t}Z_i^{-1}W_{i,t}^T \leq \lambda_{\max}\left(Z_i^{-1}\right)\bar{W}_i^2.$$

Using the estimate

$$R_t^* \le R^* := \lambda_{\max}\left(Z_1^{-1}\right)\bar{W}_1^2 + Z_3^{-1}$$

and selecting P_t^* as the positive solution of the differential matrix Riccati equation

$$P_t^* A + A^T P_t^* + P_t^* R_t^* P_t^* + Q_t^* = -\dot{P}_t^*$$

with constant parameters, we make zero the fix term in the right hand side of (54). Starting with an initial condition ($P_0^* = P_0^{*T} > 0$) close to the equilibrium point of this differential Riccati equation with a constant solutions, we can conclude that under conditions (Willems, 1971) the original one has a solution $P_t^* = P_t^{*T} > 0$. Then the time derivative of the Lyapunov function fulfills the inequality:

$$\frac{dV_t^*}{dt} \le 2x_t^{*T}\Lambda_1 x_t^* + \Psi_t(u_t) + \mu_t^{*T}Z_3\mu_t^* + \Pi_1 - \Delta_t^{*T}Q_c\Delta_t^* - u_t^T R_c u_t.$$

In order to calculate the control action, which minimizes the tracking error, let start by minimizing $\Psi_t(u_t)$, so $\frac{d\Psi_t(u_t)}{du_t}$ has to be equal to zero. To perform this minimization, we assume that, at the given t (positive), x_t^* and $\hat{x}_t$ are known and do not depend on u_t.

Remark 13 We name the signal u_t^*, minimizing $\Psi_t(u_t)$, *a locally optimal control*, because it is calculated based only on local information ($W_{2,t}$, Δ_t^* and $\hat{x}_t$).

To solve this optimization problem, let us consider the following recursive gradient scheme:

$$u_k(t) = u_{k-1}(t) - \tau_k\frac{d\Psi_t(u_{k-1}(t))}{du_t}, \quad u_0 = 0.$$

where the gradient $\frac{d\Psi_t(u_t)}{du_t}$ is calculated, and the sequence of the scalar parameter τ_t satisfies

$$\tau_k > 0, \quad \sum_{k=0}^{\infty}\tau_k = \infty, \quad \tau_k \to \infty$$

For example, we can select

$$\tau_k = \frac{1}{(1+k)^\varepsilon}, \quad \varepsilon \in (0,1]$$

Concerning u_t^*, we state the following lemma.

Lemma 2 The control u_t^* can be calculated as the limit of the sequence $\{u_k(t)\}$, i.e.,

$$u_k(t) \underset{k\to\infty}{\to} u_t^*$$

Proof It directly follows from the properties of the gradient method,

Figure 3. Neuro-observer and Trajectory Tracking Scheme

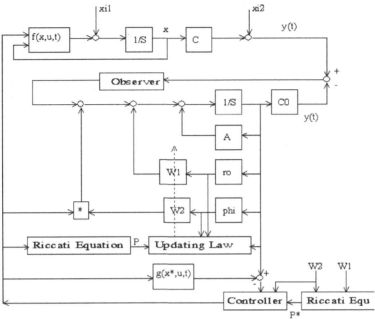

Corollary 3 If the input function to the neural network (53) depends linearly on u_t, we can select $\frac{d\gamma(u_t)}{du_t} = \Gamma$, and we can compensate the measurable signal μ_t^* by the modified control law:

$$u_t = u_t^c + u_t^*$$

where u_t^c satisfies the relation:

$$\hat{W}_{2,t}\varphi(\hat{x}_t)u_t^c + \mu_t^* = 0$$

and u_t^* is selected according to the linear squares optimal control law

$$u_t^* = -R_c^{-1}\Gamma\varphi(\hat{x}_t)\hat{W}_{2,t}^T P_t^* \Delta_t^{*T}. \tag{59}$$

Theorem 4 *For the system (52), the neuro-observer (53), and the control law (59), the following property holds:*

$$\left\| \Delta_t^* \right\|_{Q_c}^2 + \left\| u_t^* \right\|_{R_c}^2$$
$$\leq 2\left\| x_t^* \right\|_{\Lambda_1} + \limsup_{T\to\infty}\tfrac{1}{T}\int_0^T \Psi_t(u_t^*)dt + \limsup_{T\to\infty}\tfrac{1}{T}\int_0^T \mu_t^{*T}Z_3\mu_t^*dt + \Upsilon_1$$

where $\Upsilon_1 = \Upsilon_1^T > 0$).
Proof: After knowing the minimum $\Psi_t(u_t^*)$,

Figure 4. Identification of θ_1

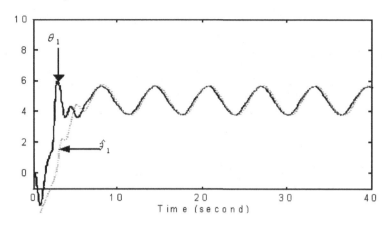

Figure 5. Identification of θ_2

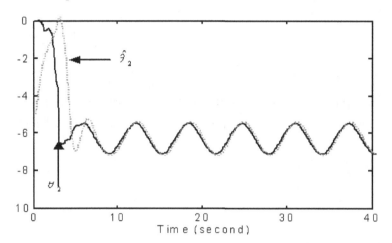

$$\overset{*}{V}_t \leq 2x_t^{*T}\Lambda_1 x_t^* + \Psi_t(u_t^*) + \mu_t^{*T}Z_3\mu_t^* + \Pi_1 - \Delta_t^{*T}Q_c\Delta_t^*V_t^* - u_t^{*T}R_cu_t^*.$$

We reformulate it as

$$\Delta_t^{*T}Q_c\Delta_t^*V_t^* + u_t^{*T}R_cu_t^* \leq 2x_t^{*T}\Lambda_1 x_t^* + \Psi_t(u_t^*) + \mu_t^{*T}Z_3\mu_t^* + \Pi_1 - \overset{*}{V}_t.$$

Then, integrating each term from 0 to T, dividing each term by T, and taking the limit (for $T \to \infty$) of these integrals' supreme, and considering

$$\limsup_{T\to\infty}\left(-\frac{1}{T}\int_0^T \overset{*}{V}_t\, dt\right) = \limsup_{T\to\infty}\left[-V_T^* + V_0^*\right] \leq \limsup_{T\to\infty}V_0^* = 0.$$

we conclude the theorem

The final structure of the neural network observer and the tracking controller is shown in Figure 3.

Figure 6. Tracking control of θ_1 (method A)

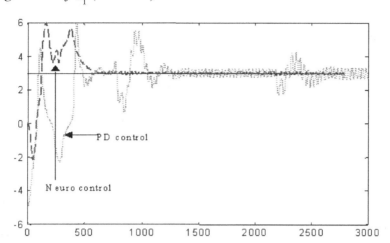

6 SIMULATIONS

In this section a two-links robot manipulator is used to illustrate the proposed approach. Its dynamics of can be expressed as follows (Lewis, Yesildirek & Liu, 1996):

$$M\left(\theta\right)\ddot{\theta} + V\left(\theta,\dot{\theta}\right)\dot{\theta} + G\left(\theta\right) + F_d\left(\dot{\theta}\right) = \tau \tag{52}$$

where $\theta \in \Re^2$ consists of the joint variables, $\dot{\theta} \in \Re^2$ denotes the links velocity, τ is the generalized forces, $M\left(\theta\right)$ is the intertie matrix, $V\left(\theta,\dot{\theta}\right)$ is centripetal-Coriolis matrix, $G\left(\theta\right)$ is gravity vector, $F_d\left(\dot{\theta}\right)$ is the friction vector. $M\left(\theta\right)$ represents the positive defined inertia matrix. If we define $x_1 = \theta = \left[\theta_1, \theta_2\right]$ is joint position, $x_2 = \dot{\theta}$ is joint velocity of the link, $x_t = \left[x_1, x_2\right]^T$, (52) can be rewritten as state space form (Nicosia & Tornambe, 1989) $\dot{x}_1 = x_2$ $\dot{x}_2 = H(x_t, u_t)$ (53) where $u_t = \tau$ is control input,

Figure 7. Tracking control of θ_2 (method A)

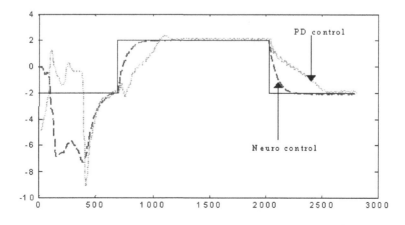

$$H(x_t, u_t) = -M(x_1)^{-1}\left[C(x_1, x_2)\dot{x}_1 + G(x_1) + F\dot{x}_1 + u_t\right]$$

(53) can also be rewritten as

$$\dot{x}_1 = \int_0^t H(x_\tau, u_\tau)d\tau + H(x_0, u_0)$$

(54)

So the dynamic of the two-links robot (52) is in form of (1) with

$$f(x_t, u_t, t) = \int_0^t H(x_\tau, u_\tau)d\tau + H(x_0, u_0)$$

The values of the parameters are listed below: $m_1 = m_2 = 1.53kg$, $l_1 = l_2 = 0.365m$, $r1 = r2 = 0.1$, $v1 = v2 = 0.4$, $k1 = k2 = 0.8$. Let define $\hat{x} = \left[\hat{\theta}_1, \hat{\theta}_2\right]^T$, $u = \left[\tau_1, \tau_2\right]^T$, the neural network for control is represented as

$$\frac{d}{dt}\hat{x} = A\hat{x} + W_{1,t}\sigma(\hat{x}_t) + W_{2,t}\varphi(\hat{x})u$$

(55)

We select $A = \begin{bmatrix} -1.5 & 0 \\ 0 & -1 \end{bmatrix}$, $\varphi(\hat{x}_t) = \text{diag}\left(\varphi_1(\hat{x}_1), \varphi_2(\hat{x}_2)\right)$, $\sigma(\hat{x}_t) = \left[\sigma_2(\hat{x}_2), \sigma_2(\hat{x}_2)\right]^T$

$$\sigma_i(\hat{x}_i) = \frac{2}{(1+e^{-2\hat{x}_i})} - \frac{1}{2}, \quad \varphi_i(\hat{x}_i) = \frac{2}{(1+e^{-2\hat{x}_i})} + \frac{1}{2}, \quad i = 1,2$$

We used *Remark 3* to obtain a suitable W_1^0 and W_2^0, start from random values, $T_0 = 100$. After 2 loops, $\left\|\Delta\left(T_0\right)\right\|$ does not decrease, we let the $W_{1,300}$ and $W_{2,300}$ as the new $W_1^0 = \begin{bmatrix} 0.51 & 3.8 \\ -2.3 & 1.51 \end{bmatrix}$ and $W_2^0 = \begin{bmatrix} 3.12 & -2.78 \\ 5.52 & -4.021 \end{bmatrix}$. For the update laws (11), we select $\bar{\eta} = 0.1$, $r = 5$, $K_1P = K_1P = \begin{bmatrix} 5 & 0 \\ 0 & 2 \end{bmatrix}$ If we select the generalized forces as

Figure 8. Tracking control of θ_1 (method B)

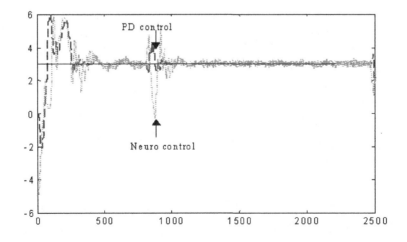

Figure 9. Tracking control of θ_2 (method B)

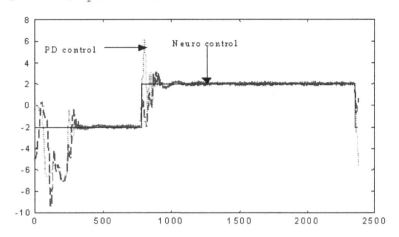

$$\tau_1 = 7\sin t, \quad \tau_2 = 0 \tag{56}$$

The identification results for θ are shown in Figure 4 and Figure 5. The identification errors are exit because we use signal layer neural network to model the dynamic of two links robot, there are unmodeled dynamics.

Now we check the neuro control. We assume the robot is changed at $t = 480$, after that $m_1 = m_2 = 3.5kg$, $l_1 = l_2 = 0.5m$, and the friction becomes disturbance as $D\sin\left(\frac{\pi}{3}t\right)$, D is a positive constant. We compare neuro control with a PD control as

$$\tau_{PD} = -10\left(\theta - \theta^*\right) - 5\left(\dot{\theta} - \dot{\theta}^*\right) \tag{57}$$

where $\theta_1^* = 3$; θ_2^* is square wave. So $\phi\left(\theta^*\right) = \dot{\theta}^* = 0$

The neuro control is (30)

$$\tau_{neuro} = \left[W_{2,t}\varphi\left(\hat{x}\right)\right]^{+}\left[\phi\left(x_t^*, t\right) - Ax_t^* - W_{1,t}\sigma(\hat{x})\right] + \left[W_{2,t}\varphi\left(\hat{x}\right)\right]^{+} U_{2,t}$$

$U_{2,t}$ is selected to compensate the unmodeled dynamics.

(A) $D = 1$. The link velocity $\dot{\theta}$ is measurable, as in (5u21), The results are shown in Figure 6 and Figure 7

(B) $D = 0.3$. θ is not available, the sliding mode technique may be applied, we select $u_{2,t}$ as (44)

$$u_{2,t} = -10 \times \text{sgn}(\theta - \theta^*)$$

The results are shown in Figure 8 and Figure 9.

(C) $D = 3$. We select $Q = \frac{1}{2}$, $R = \frac{1}{20}$, $\Lambda = 4.5$, the solution of following Riccati equation

$$A^T P + PA + P\Lambda P_t + Q = -\dot{P}$$

Figure 10. Tracking control of θ_1 *(method C)*

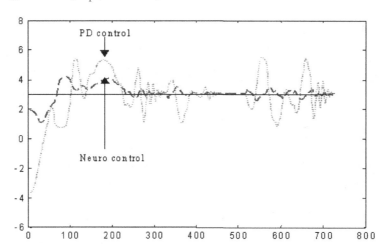

is $P = \begin{bmatrix} 0.33 & 0 \\ 0 & 0.33 \end{bmatrix}$. If without restriction τ , the linear squares optimal control law

$$u_{2,t} = -2R^{-1}P\left(\theta - \theta^*\right) = \begin{bmatrix} -20 & 0 \\ 0 & -20 \end{bmatrix}\left(\theta - \theta^*\right).$$

The results of local optimal compensation are shown in Figure 10 and Figure 11.

We may find that the neuro control is robust and effective when the robot is changed.

Remark 8 *From the above simulations, we can obtain the following conclusions: 1) model accuracy: it is well known that neural networks are universal estimators, they can approximate any nonlinear function to any prescribed accuracy, provided that sufficient hidden neurons and fuzzy rules are available. For this example, the HONN (55) can achieve good accuracy as MLP with reduced memory space, less computation time, less training parameters. 2) Training time versus memory: the major computational*

Figure 11. racking control of θ_2 *(method C)*

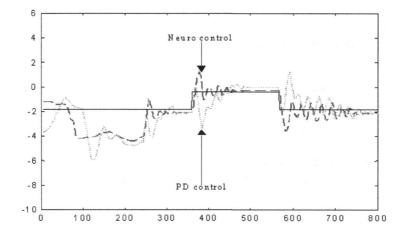

cost comes from weights training, the cost of memory access is very small although the memory space is big for HONN compared with MLP. 3).Parameters versus accuracy: model complexity is important in the context of system identification, which is corresponded to the hidden nodes of the neuro model.

According to the formula (53), we can construct the following neuro-observer:

$$\begin{bmatrix} \frac{d\hat{x}_1}{dt} \\ \frac{d\hat{x}_2}{dt} \end{bmatrix} = \begin{bmatrix} -\hat{a}_1 x_1 \\ -\hat{a}_2 x_2 \end{bmatrix} + W_1 \begin{bmatrix} \sigma(\hat{x}_1) \\ \sigma(\hat{x}_2) \end{bmatrix}$$
$$+ W_2 \begin{bmatrix} \varphi(\hat{x}_1) & 0 \\ 0 & \varphi(\hat{x}_2) \end{bmatrix} \begin{bmatrix} u_1 \\ u_2 \end{bmatrix} + K_t \left(y_t - \hat{y}_t \right),$$
$$\hat{y}_t = \hat{x}_1 + \hat{x}_2$$

We select

$$a_1 = \hat{a}_1 = 5, \quad \beta_1 = 3, \quad d_1 = 1, \quad x_1(0) = 10, \quad \hat{x}_1(0) = -1$$
$$a_2 = \hat{a}_2 = 10, \quad \beta_2 = 5, \quad d_2 = 1, \quad x_2(0) = -10, \quad \hat{x}_2(0) = -2$$

The gain matrix K_t is calculated as

$$K_t = P_t \begin{bmatrix} 10 & 0 \\ 0 & 10 \end{bmatrix} \begin{bmatrix} 1 \\ 1 \end{bmatrix}$$

where P_t is the solution of the differential matrix Riccati equation

$$-\dot{P}_t = P_t A + A^T P_t + P_t R_0 P_t + Q_t$$

Figure 12. Neuro-observer results for x_1

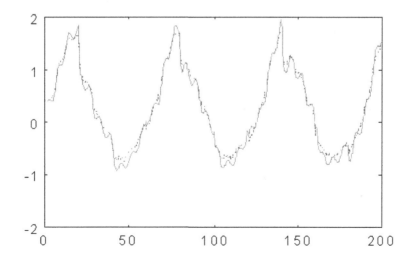

Figure 13. Neuro-observer results for x_2

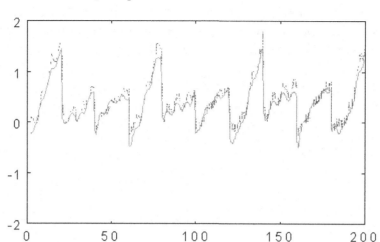

We select $Q = \begin{bmatrix} 0.2 & 0 \\ 0 & 0.2 \end{bmatrix}$, $Q_t = Q + 0.1 + 0.15\left(u_1^2 + u_2^2\right) + 0.01$,

$R_0 = \begin{bmatrix} 0.2 & 0 \\ 0 & 0.2 \end{bmatrix}$ and obtain the solution starting from initial conditions $P_0 = \begin{bmatrix} 5 & 0.03 \\ 0.03 & 3 \end{bmatrix}$, which

corresponds to the solution of the algebraic matrix Riccati equation when the left side hand of this

equation equal to zero. The initial weight matrix of the neural network is equal to $W_{1,0} = \begin{bmatrix} 0.1 & 2 \\ 5 & 0.2 \end{bmatrix}$.

$W_{2,0} = \begin{bmatrix} 0.1 & 0 \\ 0 & 0.1 \end{bmatrix}$. The nonliniarities σ_i and φ_i are chosen as sigmoidal:

$$\sigma_i(x_i) = \frac{2}{1 + e^{-2x_i}} - 0.5, \quad i = 1, 2.$$

To adapt on-line the neuro-observer weights, we use the learning algorithm (54):

$$\dot{W}_{1,t} = M_{1,t}\tilde{W}_{1,t} + \tfrac{\tilde{y}_t}{4}P_t \begin{bmatrix} \sigma(\hat{x}_1) & \sigma(\hat{x}_1) \\ \sigma(\hat{x}_2) & \sigma(\hat{x}_1) \end{bmatrix}$$

$$\dot{W}_{2,t} = u_t^2 M_{2,t}\tilde{W}_{2,t} + \tfrac{\tilde{y}_t}{4}P_t \begin{bmatrix} \varphi(\hat{x}_1)u_1 & \varphi(\hat{x}_1)u_1 \\ \varphi(\hat{x}_2)u_2 & \varphi(\hat{x}_2)u_2 \end{bmatrix}$$

where

$$M_{1,t} = \left(\sigma(\hat{x}_1) + \sigma(\hat{x}_2)\right)^2 P_t \begin{bmatrix} 0.13 & 0.02 \\ 0.02 & 0.13 \end{bmatrix} P_t,$$

$$M_{2,t} = \tfrac{0.13}{4}P_t \begin{bmatrix} \varphi(\hat{x}_1) & \varphi(\hat{x}_2) \\ \varphi(\hat{x}_1) & \varphi(\hat{x}_2) \end{bmatrix} P_t$$

Figure 14. Trajectory tracking for x_1

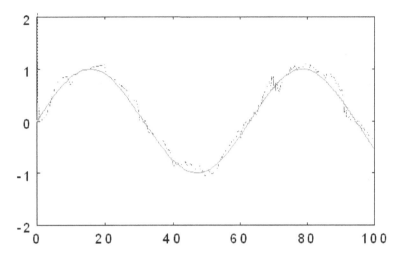

and matrices $\tilde{W}_{1,t}$, $\tilde{W}t_{2,t}$ are solutions of the following differential equations (with zero initial conditions):

$$-2\frac{d\tilde{W}_{1,t}}{dt} = M_{1,t}\tilde{W}_{1,t}^{T} + \frac{\tilde{y}_t}{4}P_t\begin{bmatrix}\sigma(\hat{x}_1) & \sigma(\hat{x}_1)\\ \sigma(\hat{x}_2) & \sigma(\hat{x}_2)\end{bmatrix},$$

$$-2\frac{d\tilde{W}_{2,t}}{dt} = \left(u_1^2 + u_2^2\right)M_{2,t}\tilde{W}_{2,t}^{T} + \frac{\tilde{y}_t}{4}P_t\begin{bmatrix}\varphi(\hat{x}_1)u_1 & \varphi(\hat{x}_1)u_1\\ \varphi(\hat{x}_2)u_2 & \varphi(\hat{x}_2)u_2\end{bmatrix}$$

The input signals u_1 and u_2 are chosen as *sine wave* and *saw-tooth* function. The corresponding results are shown as Figure 12 and Figure 13. The solid lines correspond to nonlinear system state responses, and the dashed line to neuro-observer. The abscissa values correspond to the number of iterations. It can be seen that the neural network state time evolution follows the given nonlinear system.

Figure 15. Trajectory tracking for x_2

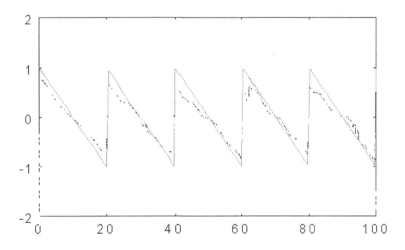

Figure 16. Time evolution of W_1

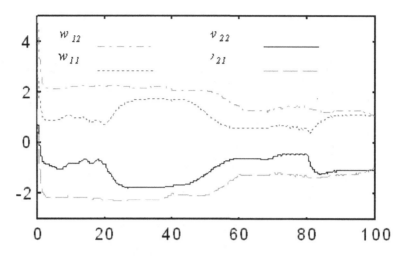

Trajectory Tracking Based on the Neuro-Observer

We implement the control law, which constitutes a feedback control with an on-line adaptive gain. Figure 14 and Figure 15 present the respective response, where the solid lines correspond to reference singles x_t^*, u_t^* and the dashed lines are the nonlinear system responses x_t .

The time evolution for the weight of the selected neural network is shown in Figure 16.

The time evolution of two performance indexes

$$J_\tau^\Delta := \frac{1}{\tau}\int_0^\tau \Delta^{*T}Q_c\Delta^{*T}dt, \ J_\tau^u := \frac{1}{\tau}\int_0^\tau u^{*T}R_c u^*dt$$

can be seen in Figure 17 and Figure 18.

Figure 17. Performance indexes of tracking error J_τ^Δ

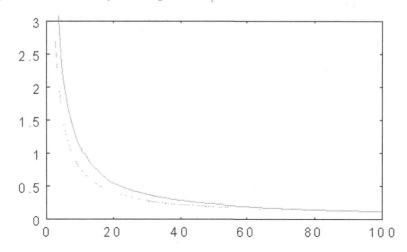

Figure 18. Performance indexes of tracking error J_{τ}^{u}

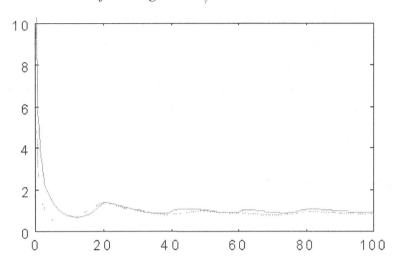

7 CONCLUSION

In this chapter, a new higher order neural controller for a class of unknown nonlinear systems is proposed. The main contributions are: 1) A new learning algorithm for neural networks approximation is proposed, which uses dead-zone and projection techniques. The dead-zone assures that the identification error is bounded, the projection approach avoids any singularity in the control law. 2) By means of Lyapunov analysis, we establish bounds for both the identifier and adaptive controller. 3) We give four different compensation method for unmodeled dynamics and establish a bound for the tracking error of the new neuro controller. Both the controller and the identifier work on-line. The simulation results show that the controllers proposed in this chapter is effective.

Apart from stability and high accuracy with regards to standard neural control, our HONN controller have some other advantages, such as less training time, greater convergence speed, less parameters, simpler structure, etc. Our future work will be on including real-time applications.

REFERENCES

Albert, A. (1972). *Regression and the Moore-Penrose Pseudoinverse*. New York: Academic Press.

Alanis, A. Y., Sanchez, E. N., & Loukianov, A. G. (2007). Discrete-Time Adaptive Backstepping Nonlinear Control via High-Order Neural Networks. *IEEE Transactions on Neural Networks*, *18*(4), 1185–1195. doi:10.1109/TNN.2007.899170

Corless, M. J., & Leitmann, G. (1981). Countinuous State Feedback Guaranteeing Uniform Ultimate Boundness for Uncertain Dynamic Systems. *IEEE Transactions on Automatic Control*, *26*(7), 1139–1144. doi:10.1109/TAC.1981.1102785

Egardt, P. (1979). *Stability of Adaptive Controllers*, Lecture Notes in Control and Information Sciences. Berlin, Germany: Springer-Verlag.

Grant, E., & Zhang, B. (1989). A neural net approach to supervised learning of pole placement. In *Proc. of 1989 IEEE Symposium on Intelligent Control.*

Haykin, S. (1994). *Neural Networks- A comprehensive Foundation.* New York: Macmillan College Publ. Co.

Hunt, K. J., & Sbarbaro, D. (1991). Neural Networks for Nonlinear Internal Model Control. *IEE Proceedings. Control Theory and Applications, 38,* 431–438.

Ioannou, P. A., & Sun, J. (1996). *Robust Adaptive Control.* Upper Saddle River, NJ: Prentice-Hall, Inc.

Jagannathan, S., & Lewis, F. L. (1996). Identification of nonlinear dynamical systems using multilayered neural networks. *Automatica, 32*(12), 1707–1712. doi:10.1016/S0005-1098(96)80007-0

Jagannathan, S. (2006). *Neural Network Control of Nonlinear Discrete-Time Systems.* New York: CRC Press.

Kim, Y. H., Lewis, F. L., & Abdallah, C. T. (1996). Nonlinear observer design using dynamic recurrent neural networks. *35th Conf. Decision Contr.*

Kosmatopoulos, E. B., Polycarpou, M. M., Christodoulou, M. A., & Ioannou, P. A. (1995). High-Order Neural Network Structures for Identification of Dynamical Systems. *IEEE Transactions on Neural Networks, 6*(2), 442–431. doi:10.1109/72.363477

Lewis, F. L., Yesildirek, A., & Liu, K. (1996). Multilayer Neural-Net Robot Controller with Guaranteed Tracking Performance. *IEEE Transactions on Neural Networks, 7*(2), 388–399. doi:10.1109/72.485674

Li, X., & Yu, W. (2004). Robust Adaptive Control Using Neural Networks and Projection, *Advances in Neural Networks -ISNN 2004, Srpinger-Verlgag . Lecture Notes in Computer Science, 3174,* 77–82.

Narendra, K. S., & Parthasarathy, K. (1990). Identification and control for dynamic systems using neural networks. *IEEE Transactions on Neural Networks, 1*(1), 4–27. doi:10.1109/72.80202

Nicosia, S., & Tornambe, A. (1989). High-Gain Observers in the State and Parameter Estimation of Robots Having Elastic Joins . *Systems & Control Letters, 13*(2), 331–337. doi:10.1016/0167-6911(89)90121-7

Osorio, A., & Poznyak, A. S. (1997). Robust Determistic Filtering for Linear Uncertain Time Varing Systems, *America Control Conference.*

Poznyak, A. S., Yu, W., Sanchez, E. N., & Perez, J. P. (1999). Nonlinear Adaptive Trajectory Tracking Using Dynamic Neural Networks. *IEEE Transactions on Neural Networks, 10*(5), 1402–1411. doi:10.1109/72.809085

Poznyak, A. S., & Sanchez, E. N. (1995). Nonlinear system approximation by neural networks: error stability analysis. *Intelligent Automation and Soft Computing, 1*(2), 247–258.

Rovithakis, G. A., & Christodoulou, M. A. (1994). Adaptive control of unknown plants using dynamical neural networks. *IEEE Transactions on Systems, Man, and Cybernetics, 24*(3), 400–412. doi:10.1109/21.278990

Willems, J. C. (1971). Least squares optimal control and algebraic Riccati equations. *IEEE Transactions on Automatic Control, 16*(6), 621–634. doi:10.1109/TAC.1971.1099831

Yang, C., Ge, S. S., Chai, T., & Lee, T. H. (2008). Output Feedback NN Control for Two Classes of Discrete-Time Systems With Unknown Control Directions in a Unified Approach. *IEEE Transactions on Neural Networks, 19*(11), 1873–1886. doi:10.1109/TNN.2008.2003290

Yu, W., & Poznyak, A. S. (1999). Indirect Adaptive Control via Parallel Dynamic Neural Networks. *IEE Proceedings. Control Theory and Applications, 146*(1), 25–30. doi:10.1049/ip-cta:19990368

Yu, W., & Li, X. (2001). Some New Results on System Identification with Dynamic Neural Networks. *IEEE Transactions on Neural Networks, 12*(2), 412–417. doi:10.1109/72.914535

Chapter 6
On the Equivalence Between Ordinary Neural Networks and Higher Order Neural Networks

Mohammed Sadiq Al-Rawi
University of Aveiro, Portugal

Kamal R. Al-Rawi
Petra University, Jordan

ABSTRACT

In this chapter, we study the equivalence between multilayer feedforward neural networks referred as Ordinary Neural Networks (ONNs) that contain only summation (Sigma) as activation units, and multilayer feedforward Higher order Neural Networks (HONNs) that contains Sigma and product (PI) activation units. Since the time they were introduced by Giles and Maxwell (1987), HONNs have been used in many supervised classification and function approximation. Up to the date of writing this chapter, the most cited HONN article by ISI Thomson Web of Knowledge is the work of Kosmatopoulos et al., (1995) by which they introduced a recurrent HONN modeling. A simple comparison with ONNs is usually performed in order to demonstrate the performance of some newly introduced HONN architecture. Is it true that HONNs outperform ONNs, how much do they differ? And how much do they commute? Does equivalence exists between a HONN and an ONN? Is it possible to convert a HONN to an equivalent ONN? And how neural network equivalence is defined? This chapter tries to answer most of these questions. Due to the existence of huge neural networks architectures in the literature, the authors of this work are concerned and think that equivalence studies are necessary to give abstract definitions and unified approaches which might help in better understanding of HONNs performance and their

DOI: 10.4018/978-1-61520-711-4.ch006

respective design. On contrary to most of the previous works were HONN weights are non-negative integers, HONNs are given in this chapter in a form such that weights are adjustable real-valued numbers. In doing that, HONNs might have more expressive power and there is an increase probability of having complex valued neuron outputs. To enable the use of the real-valued weights that may result in a complex valued neuron output we introduce normalization to the input data as well as a modification to neuron activation functions. Using simple mathematics and the proposed normalization to input data, we showed that HONNs are equivalent to ONNs. The converted equivalent ONN posses the features of HONN and they have exactly the same functionality and output. The proposed conversion of HONN to ONN would permit using the huge amount of optimization algorithms to speed up the convergence of HONN and/ or finding better topology. Recurrent HONNs, cascaded correlation HONNs, or any other complicated HONN can be simply defined via their equivalent ONNs and then trained with backpropagation, scaled conjugate gradient, Lavenberg-Marqudat algorithm, brain damage algorithms (Duda et al., 2000), etc. Using the developed equivalency model, this chapter also gives an easy bottom-up approach to convert a HONN to its equivalent ONN. Results on XOR and function approximation problems showed that ONNs obtained from their corresponding HONNs converged well to a solution. Different optimization training algorithms have been tested equivalent ONNs having feedforward structure and/or cascade correlation where the later have shown outstanding function approximation results.

1. INTRODUCTION

In our daily life we face several classification problems that are considered nonlinear, i.e., one cannot separate two categories using simply a line for two dimensional patterns, a plane for three dimensional patters, or a hyper plane as in multi-dimensional patters. Inspired by the biological neuronal system, computational intelligent based classification systems were developed in the past few decades and are widely known as computational neural networks. These computational networks possess powerful nonlinear classification ability and they are also known in the literature with other proximate names, such as artificial neural networks, and statistical neural networks. In this work, we choose to call multi-layer feedforward neural networks as Ordinary Neural Networks (ONNs) in order to distinguish them from Higher Order Neural Networks (HONNs). The reason is that both HONNs and ONNs are artificial, computational, multi-layer feedforward neural networks. Nonetheless, other terminologies of ONNs might exist such as first order neural networks (Giles, et al., 1988), or multi-layer perceptrons (Minsky and Papert 1969),

In order to solve nonlinear classification problems, an ONN with one or more hidden layers can be employed. Determining the proper number of hidden layers and the number of units in each hidden layer is accomplished by trial and error, dynamic adaptive algorithms e.g. surgeon brain damage algorithms (Duda et al., 2000). Several studies have used HONNs rather than ONNs in order to obtain better performance (Thimm, 1998; Thimm & Fiesler, 1997; Spirkovska & Reid, 1993; Rovithakis et al., 2004). To what degree we can rely on these outperformance results? When we investigate the literature we see that ONNs have only Sigma (summation) activation units, for example, the output of a $d-2-1$ ONN is given by:

$$z_k = f\left(w_{20} + w_{21}f\left(\sum_{i=0}^{d} w_i x_i \right) + w_{22}f\left(\sum_{i=0}^{d} w_i x_i \right) \right) \tag{1}$$

where $w's$ are the weights that connect different layers of ONN, x_i is the value of the i_{th} input taken from the input pattern $\mathbf{x} = [x_1, x_2, ..., x_d]$. In contrast, a HONN must have at least one PI (product unit) as was shown by Giles & Maxwell, (1987), hence, the output of an up to the second order HONN is given by:

$$z_k = f\left(w_0 + \sum_{i=0}^{d} w_i x_i + \sum_{i_1=0}^{d} \sum_{i_2=0}^{d} w_{i_1, i_2} x_{i_1} x_{i_2} \right) \tag{2}$$

Thus, the major difference between HONNs and ONNs is the way the activation is calculated, i.e., only sigma units are used to construct ONNs, while Sigma and PI units or just PI units are used to construct HONNs. Does this matter? In computer architecture, a multiplication operation can be implemented via an algorithm implementing several addition operations (Knuth, 1997; Kulisch, 2002). In fact, multiplications are defined for the whole numbers in terms of repeated addition and even multiplications of real numbers could be defined by a systematic generalization of this basic idea. With this in mind, HONNs could be converted to a very complex, large size, constrained ONNs. The hypothetical large sized ONN that equiv a HONN might justify the power of a moderate size HONN. Nonetheless, it is unfair to compare the computational cost of some HONN to another ONN that has the same number of units and synaptic connections. More than that, it is also unfair to compare the expressive power of a HONN to an ONN when they have the same number of units and synaptic connections. The reason is that the computational architecture and computational complexity of a HONN is much higher than that of an ONN. To overcome this dilemma it is necessary to develop a mathematical model for converting a HONN to its equivalent ONN and further studies can be performed later to answer questions about the expressive power and the computational complexity of both architectures.

In this chapter, neural networks equivalence is defined as follows; "Two neural networks are equivalent if they satisfy the following; randomly initialized to the same initial weights, pass through the same error values per epoch, their corresponding weights are exactly the same at each corresponding iteration and at the end of training, give exactly the same output for the same input, but their synaptic connections, synaptic activation, and their topology might differ". Lower terms or more constrained terms for equivalence definition might be defined without any problem. To explore this neural equivalence we will show using simple mathematical analyses that it is possible to convert a HONN to a nearly similar size equivalent ONN. Experimental tests will be conducted on the converted ONNs to show their ability to converge and classify typical classification problems.

BACKGROUND

In their article, Giles and Maxwell (1987) stated that higher-order weights capture higher-order correlations in data. Their first HONN work was introduced to solve a challenging computer vision problem known as invariance. After that, several other HONN works emerged: Hughen and Hollon (1991) stated that higher order networks have the advantage of ease training over multilayer perceptrons and showed better classification for Radar data than a Gaussian classifier. A HONN with a prior knowledge of the binary training patterns reduces computation time and memory when applied to 100x100 Pixels images (Artyomov & Yadid-Pecht, 2005). Rovithakis et al., (2004) presented an algorithm to determine the structure of HONNs applied to function approximation. Clark, (1995) employed HONNs for tracking, code recognition and memory management. Rovithakis, (1999) employed HONNs in control. Foltynie-wicz, (1995) developed a PI-Sigma-PI network structure for effective recognition of human faces in gray scale irrespective to their position, orientation and scale, and he claimed that it had small number of adjustable weights, rapid learning convergence, and excellent generalization properties. Abdelbar, (1998) showed that Sigma-PI HONNs perform better than ONNs in classification age-groups of abalone shellfish bench-mark. Kosmatopoulos et al., (1995) showed that if enough higher order connections are allowed to recurrent HONN then it is capable of approximating arbitrary dynamical systems. Their explanation is that the dynamic components are distributed throughout the network in the form of dynamic neurons. A HONN that learns the recognition of affine transformed images without any prior knowledge of the imaging geometry was proposed in (Al-Rawi, 2006). As most neural networks software is devoted for ONNs, Al-Rawi & Bisher, (2005) developed a software tool that can be used interactively to build HONNs. Still, the software cannot cope with the many optimization algorithms available for ONNs and only gradient descent with momentum had been considered. Therefore, if any HONN is equivalent to an ONN, then lots of HONN complicated optimization modeling efforts can be saved.

Despite the fact that many ideas have been proposed to apply HONNs for different problems and compare their classification accuracies to ONNs, there were no theoretical studies showing how they are related to each other. Different modifications to HONNs are heuristic, and/or model based inspired. As in any scientific research strategy, a proposed HONN is supported by experimental results to show its superiority upon other HONNs and ONNs. Therefore, we think that HONN importance is vague and its discriminatory power has not been fully exploited. Anyone can notice from the large literature and other scientific web resources that HONNs were not considered as one of the major artificial neural networks categories. Major artificial neural networks categories only include feedforward (ONNs), self organizing maps (Kohonen, 2000), recurrent neural networks (Elman, 1990), Hopfield networks, radial bases functions networks, stochastic neural networks, Boltzmann machine, Neuro-fuzzy networks, pprobabilistic neural networks, see (Duda et al., 2000) for details. Using methodologies similar to what we are going to discuss throughout this chapter, equivalence studies are very important in order to associate and equiv different artificial neural networks categories, this however is out of the scope of this chapter.

2. CONVERSION OF HIGHER ORDER NEURAL NETWORKS TO ITS EQUIVALENT ORDINARY NEURAL NETWORKS

We shall use simple mathematical analysis to show that HONNs are equivalent to ONNs. Without loosing generality, the analysis shown below does not assume a mix of PI and Sigma units at the same layer. Nonetheless, this mix of unites will be resolved later in this chapter. Let us start by defining the activation of neural units and then discuss and state their equivalence.

2.1 The Activation of a Summation Unit (Sigma Unit)

Suppose that $\mathbf{x} = [x_1, x_2, ..., x_d]$ is the input vector to a neuron unit, in the case we are discussing here, each Sigma unit has the following activation:

$$net_j = \sum_{i=1}^{d} w_{ji} x_i \, , \tag{3}$$

where $j = 1, 2, ..., n$, for a total of n Sigma units at this layer, $w_{ji} \in R$ is the synaptic weight at the connection between the i_{th} input (or the previous) unit and the j_{th} Sigma unit, and R is the set of real numbers.

2.2 The Activation of a Product Unit (PI Unit)

Many forms of HONNs are proposed in the literature, they are all based on PI and Sigma units' structure, and the way their synaptic weights are represented as fixed or adjustable, real-valued or positive integer valued. To discuss the general case, PI units with adaptive real-valued exponent weights is considered in this work. For input $\mathbf{x}$, each PI unit has the following activation:

$$net_j = \Pi_{i=1}^{d} \, x_i^{w_{ji}} \, , \tag{4}$$

where $j = 1, 2, ..., n$, for a total of n PI units at this layer, $w_{ji} \in R$ is the synaptic weight at the connection between the i_{th} input (or previous) unit and the j_{th} PI unit and R is the set of real numbers. Theoretically, a PI unit may be placed at any layer and its related weights can be calculated in the training phase using backpropagation of error and/or other optimization algorithms.

2.3 Equivalence of PI units with Sigma Units.

The purpose of this section is to find the relation between PI units and Sigma units. By using $\ln(\exp())$, equation (4) can be rewritten as:

$$net_j = \exp\left(\ln(\Pi_{i=1}^{d} \quad x_i^{w_{ji}})\right), \tag{5}$$

which can be rewritten as:

$$net_j = \exp\left(\sum_{i=1}^{d} \, \ln x_i^{w_{ji}}\right), \tag{6}$$

and using the notation $X_i = \ln x_i$, we may write (6) as

$$net_j = \exp\left(\sum_{i=1}^{d} w_{ji} X_i\right). \tag{7}$$

Equation (7) states that the activation of a PI unit is the same as the activation of a Sigma unit with two major differences; taking $\ln(\cdot)$ function to the inputs, and taking $\exp(\cdot)$ function to the result of the summation. Thus, converting a PI unit to a Sigma unit is possible using the form shown in (7) after taking care of $\exp(\cdot)$ and $\ln(\cdot)$ functions. How does this affects a HONN when a mix of Sigma and PI layers is used? i.e., does a HONN equivalent to an ONN in this case? This we shall discuss later.

2.4 Conversion of HONNs to ONNs

In this section, the equivalence of PI interconnections to Sigma interconnections is given. This concept can be used later to convert any HONN to its equivalent ONN. Let us consider a HONN with various PI and Sigma units, in this case, four different interconnections are possible between each pair of units: either Sigma-Sigma, PI-Sigma, Sigma-PI, or PI-PI (and the later three types are called PI interconnections). According to this vision, ONNs have only Sigma-Sigma interconnections having the following output at the current Sigma unit:

$$y_j = f_j\left(\sum_{i=1}^{d} w_{ji} x_i\right),$$

(8)

and the next Sigma unit fires the following output:

$$z_k = f_k\left(\sum_{j=1}^{n} w_{kj} y_j\right).$$

(9)

Thus, any HONN can be converted to an ONN if and only if we can reduce its possible PI interconnections to Sigma-Sigma interconnections with outputs as those shown in (8) and (9) and this constitutes the core idea of this work. Since Sigma-Sigma interconnections need no conversion, only the other three interconnections need conversion methodology. Without losing generality, let each layer either contains PI units or Sigma units, nonetheless, this restriction will be resolved later. In practice, the following interconnections might occur:

1. PI-Sigma Interconnection

The first case we shall discuss is a connection from a PI unit to a Sigma unit. In this case, the input vector **x** that feeds to the current PI unit comes from the previous layer, and the output of the current PI unit is given by:

$$y_j = f_j(net_j),$$

(10)

where $f_j(\cdot)$ is the activation function acting at the current PI unit, and net_j is PI's activation which has the form shown in (4) or the more progressive one shown in (7). Now, substituting (7) into (10) we get:

$$y_j = f_j\left(\exp\left(\sum_{i=1}^{d} w_{ji} X_i\right)\right),$$

(11)

where $X_i = \ln x_i$. By defining the composite function $\psi_j = f_j(\exp(\cdot))$, it is possible to write (11) as follows:

$$y_j = \psi_j\left(\sum_{i=1}^{d} w_{ji} X_i\right).$$

(12)

The PI output which is y_j that is shown in (12) is then feedforward to the next Sigma unit that has the following output:

$$z_k = f_k\left(\sum_{j=1}^{n} w_{kj} y_j\right)$$

(13)

where $f_k(\cdot)$ is the activation function acting at the Sigma unit. Equation (12) shows that the activation of each PI unit can be expressed as Sigma activation $\sum^{d} w_{ji} X_i$ similar to (3), but with an acting activation function given by $\psi_j(\cdot)$. It is clear from (12) and (13) that a PI-Sigma interconnection is equivalent to a Sigma-Sigma interconnection after taking $\ln(\cdot)$ to the inputs of the PI unit and using $\psi_j(\cdot)$ as activation function at the PI unit, see Figure1-a for illustration.

2. Sigma-PI Interconnection

Here we are discussing a connection from a Sigma unit to a PI unit. The output of the current Sigma unit is given by:

$$y_j = f_j\left(\sum_{i=1}^{d} w_{ji} x_i\right),$$

(14)

and similar to the treatment shown in (4) to (7), the output of the next PI unit is given by:

$$z_k = f_k\left(\exp\left[\sum_{j=1}^{n} w_{kj} \ln(y_j)\right]\right).$$

(15)

Substituting (14) into (15) yields:

$$z_k = \psi_k\left(\sum_{j=1}^{n} w_{kj} Y_j\right),$$

(16)

with

$$Y_j = \varphi_j\left(\sum_{i=1}^{d} w_{ji} x_i\right),$$

(17)

where $\varphi_j = \ln(f_j(\cdot))$ is the activation function resulted from the composition of $\ln(\cdot)$ and $f_j(\cdot)$, and the other composite activation function acting at the next unit is given by $\psi_k = f_k(\exp(\cdot))$. It is obvious from (16) and (17) that a Sigma-PI interconnection is reducible and equivalent to a Sigma-Sigma interconnection, see Figure1-b for illustration.

Figure 1. Conversion of possible HONN interconnections, a) PI-Sigma to a Sigma-Sigma interconnection, b) Sigma-PI to a Sigma-Sigma interconnection and, c) PI-PI to a Sigma-Sigma interconnection

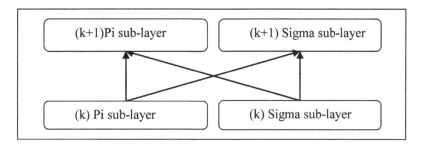

3. PI-PI Interconnection

Herewith, we have a connection from a PI unit to another PI unit. Analog to PI-Sigma and Sigma-PI interconnections, a PI-PI interconnection can be given as follows:

$$Y_j = \zeta_j \left(\sum_{i=1}^{d} w_{ji} X_i \right), \tag{18}$$

$$z_k = \psi_k \left(\sum_{j=1}^{n} w_{kj} Y_j \right), \tag{19}$$

where $\zeta_j = \ln(f_j(\exp(\cdot)))$, and $\psi_k = f_k(\exp(\cdot))$ Y_j is the output of the current PI unit, and z_k is the output of the next PI unit. Again, a PI-PI interconnection is reducible a Sigma-Sigma interconnection, see Figure 1-c for illustration.

As shown above, all PI interconnections can be converted to Sigma-Sigma interconnections and to perform the conversion one only needs to deal with (or find) the activation functions of the equivalent ONN.

3. A SIMPLE METHOD TO CONVERT A HONN TO ITS EQUIVALENT ONN

The previous section shows that any PI interconnection can be directly converted to a Sigma-Sigma interconnection by putting the activation function of each Sigma unit as a composition of $\ln(\cdot)$ and $\exp(\cdot)$, and the original activation function form of the unit. To make life easier in converting a HONN to an equivalent ONN, the following method is proposed:

Define an ONN with the same number of layers and units as that of the HONN you need to convert. Let γ_k be the activation function acting at each unit at the k_{th} layer of the newly defined ONN, and $f_k(\cdot)$ be the original activation function acting at each unit of the k_{th} layer of HONN that we are converting to ONN. Our major target is finding γ_k as a function of $f_k(\cdot)$. Using the equations presented in the previous section, the activation function at each Sigma unit in the newly defined equivalent ONN can be chosen according to the following criteria:

Case 1: Current unit at the k_{th} layer is Sigma and the next unit at the $(k+1)_{th}$ layer is PI yields:

$$\gamma_k = \ln(f_k(\cdot)) \tag{20}$$

Case 2: Current unit at the k_{th} layer is PI, and the next unit at the $(k+1)_{\text{th}}$ layer is Sigma yields:

$$\gamma_k = f_k(\exp(\cdot)). \tag{21}$$

Case 3: Current unit at the k_{th} layer is PI, and the next unit at the $(k+1)_{\text{th}}$ layer is PI yields:

$$\gamma_k = \ln(f_k(\exp(\cdot))) \tag{22}$$

Note: $\ln(\cdot)$ should be taken to the inputs whenever they are connected to a PI unit that lies at the first hidden layer.

Using the above conversion criteria, any HONN no matter how complicated can be converted to its equivalent ONN. Since the exponents and multiplications of HONN have been converted to additions in the equivalent ONN that might yield high numerical ranges which needs truncation and rounding, the equivalent ONN have more numerical stability than the original HONN. Using this simple conversion method, we may design very complicated HONNs like recurrent HONNs, cascade correlation HONNs, etc., see (Elman, 1990; Duda et al., 2000; Fahlman & Lebiere C, 1990) then we deal with the equivalent ONNs. Moreover, a bias might be treated as a unit with a fixed input and the generalization of the method to HONNs with bias units is straightforward.

In backpropagation of error one needs the first derivatives of the above activation functions, they are as shown below:

Case 1:

$$\gamma_k = \ln(f_k(\cdot)) \Rightarrow \gamma_k = \ln(f_k(\cdot)) \; \gamma_k' = [1/f_k(\cdot)]f_k'(\cdot) \Rightarrow \gamma_k' = [1/f_k(\cdot)]f_k'(\cdot) \tag{23}$$

Case 2:

$$\gamma_k = f_k(\exp(\cdot)) \Rightarrow \gamma_k = f_k(\exp(\cdot)) \; \gamma_k' = [f_k'(\exp(\cdot))]\exp(\cdot) \Rightarrow \gamma_k' = [f_k'(\exp(\cdot))]\exp(\cdot) \tag{24}$$

Case 3:

$$\gamma_k = \ln(f_k(\exp(\cdot))) \quad \Rightarrow \quad \gamma_k = \ln(f_k(\exp(\cdot))) \; \gamma_k' = [1/f_k(\exp(\cdot))][f_k'(\exp(\cdot))]\exp(\cdot) \quad \Rightarrow$$
$$\gamma_k' = [1/f_k(\exp(\cdot))][f_k'(\exp(\cdot))]\exp(\cdot) \tag{25}$$

A final important word in this section is that the conversion should be performed consecutively starting from the input layer, the first hidden, and so on until the output layer (current to next) and not the converse, i.e., using a bottom-up approach. Furthermore, having few Sigma to Sigma interconnections at any HONN requires no change in the activation functions at those connections.

4. HAVING SIGMA AND PI UNITS AT THE SAME LAYER

Generally speaking, any HONN may have both PI and Sigma units at the same layer. It is also possible to convert such kind of Mixed-Sigma-PI-Layer HONNs (MSPL-HONN) topology to equivalent ONNs by just manipulating activation functions at the equivalent ONN. As we have shown before, the activation function of each unit in the equivalent ONN depends on the corresponding current unit and the next unit of the original HONN. One can use the same conversion method described previously but the problem that we might face is the possibility of having two activation functions acting at the current unit, i.e., one goes to the next Sigma unit and another to the next PI unit. To solve this problem we suggest a new form of activation function called the dual activation function which acts at one Sigma unit, i.e., a Sigma units with two outputs. Converting a HONN of type MSPL-HONN topology yields this kind of dual activation function at the resultant equivalent ONN, see Figure 2-a that depicts a clear illustration of this case. Adopting this dual activation functionality at a Sigma unit, however, is not so hard to accomplish since each layer can be considered as consisted of two sub layers, a Sigma-sub layer and a PI-sub layer, as depicted in Figure 2-b.

The conversion of the above MSPL-HONN to an equivalent ONN is performed at each sub-layer and one has to find all the activation functions for the equivalent ONN as described in Section 4. Apparently, what we describe here will lead to a new concept in artificial neural networks which is dual activation function neuron, or multi output neuron. The following steps show how to convert MSPL-HONN to its equivalent ONN:

1. Define an ONN structure with the same number of layers and units as that of the MSPL-HONN.
2. Using the bottom up approach previously described, find the activation functions of the equivalent ONN. Each unit may have two activation functions depending on the current unit and the next unit and how PI and Sigma units are distributed.

Which fulfills the proof that even a HONN with mixed Sigma and PI units is equivalent to an ONN.

5. ENSURING EQUIVALENCE IN SOFTWARE IMPLEMENTATIONS

Several issues should be considered in order to directly use previous software originally designed for ONN implementation to handle an ONN equivalent to a HONN. The most important issue here is eliminating the possibility of having complex neuron output. The complex neuron output occurs when the input to a PI unit is negative and the synaptic weight of that PI unit has a fractional value.

It is a common practice in neural networks to use sigmoid squash shaped activation functions. This is necessary to make sure that the lower and upper bound of the neuron output are saturated, bounded and to approximate the McCulloch-Pits neuron that employs the step (hard limited) activation function. Since an ONN that is equivalent to some HONN contains $\ln()$ functions, it is important to choose the activation function(s) of that ONN carefully. This is because $\ln()$ functions yield complex values at $x<0$, and their limit approaches $-\infty$ at $x=0$ which may cause unhandled exception as well as unexpected result. This problem can be easily resolved by making all signals passing into PI units to have positive non zero values, therefore, the output of any unit should be shifted to only positive non-zero values as

Figure 2. HONN with mixed PI and Sigma units at each layer. a) Shows dual activation function that results from conversion, b) Each layer can be divided into two sub-layers

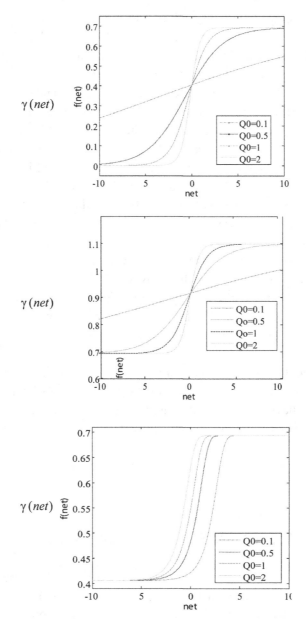

well as input data and this remarkable solution can be done by adapting the activation function of the original HONN.

Is it possible to do this shifting and/or normalization? Duda et al., (2000) in their pattern classification book noted "In any particular problem, we can always scale the input region to lie in a hypercube, and this condition is not limiting." As an example of how to shift the unit outputs to positive values let us consider the logistic activation function, we just have to add a tolerance value that makes it greater than zero, the following describes the case:

Figure 3. a) The activation function that result of converting a Sigma-PI interconnection to a Sigma-Sigma interconnection is given by $\gamma(net) = \ln\left[1 / \left(1 + \exp(-Q_0 net)\right) + \varepsilon\right]$ using $\varepsilon = 1$. b) The same activation function of (a) with $\varepsilon = 2$. c) The activation function that result from converting a PI-Sigma interconnection to a Sigma-Sigma interconnection is $\gamma(net) = \ln\left[1 / \left(1 + \exp(-Q_0 \exp(net))\right) + \varepsilon\right]$ using $\varepsilon = 1$ (using $\varepsilon = 2$ yields the same shape but shifted in the y-axis direction with nearly 0.3)

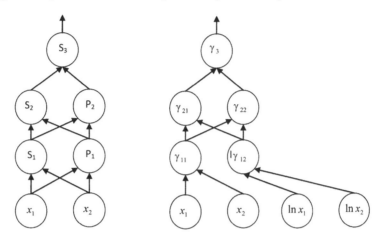

$$f(net) = \frac{1}{1 + \exp(-Q_0 net)} + \varepsilon, \tag{26}$$

where Q_0 is the temperature of the neuron, and $\varepsilon > 1$ is a value that is used to keep the range of the function above 0. Since a PI unit could be placed at the first hidden layer, it is also important to normalize inputs to lie within the unit hypercube I^n where $(I = [0,1])$. Moreover, we might need to remove the effect of $\ln(0) \to -\infty$, and $\ln(1) \to 0$ at the input layer therefore it is also necessary to normalize the input using ($I = [1 + \tau, 2]$) such that $\tau > 0$, i.e., $I = (1,2]$. As a matter of a fact, it is necessary to do this normalization of the input data even in the direct application of HONNs as a precaution of not setting the activation of some PI units to zero.

If one uses the form shown in (26), the equivalent ONN of some HONN may have at some of its units the following activation function $\gamma(net) = \ln\left[1 / (1 + \exp(-Q_0 net)) + \varepsilon\right]$, and the behavior of this function for different Q_0 and ε values is illustrated in Figure 3. One can see from Figure 3 that the activation function keeps its S-shape for $\varepsilon = 1$. It must be noted that the range of the activation function depicted in Figure 3 does not lie within [-1, 1] as the sigmoid does, however, this will not pose a problem since this shift will be compensated in the synaptic weights of the network during training. Moreover, the upper part of Figure 3-b is smoother than the lower part, and Figure 3-c shows an asymmetric squash function, see how the upper part saturates faster than the lower part. This really gives an idea of how HONNs behave if they were converted to ONN. Finally, $\varepsilon = 2$ is also a good choice since its lower saturation bound is above zero.

Figure 4.

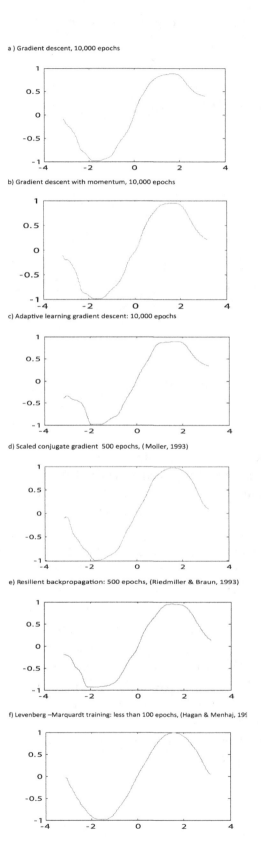

6. EXAMPLES

Example 1: Suppose that a HONN is consisted of 3 inputs, first hidden layer with 5 PI units with activation function f_1 and an output layer with 3 Sigma units with activation function f_2. The equivalent ONN can be found as follows:

Construct an ONN with three inputs, first hidden layer with 5 sigma units, and an output layer with 3 sigma units. Now using the method described in the Sec. 3, we can find the activation functions of the first hidden layer γ_1 and the output layer γ_2, they are given as follows:

$$\gamma_1() = \ln\left(f_1()\right) \tag{27}$$

$$\gamma_2() = f_2(\exp()) \tag{28}$$

Example 2: Suppose a HONN with 2 inputs, a PI unit with activation function P_1 and a Sigma unit with activation function S_1 at the first hidden layer, connected to another hidden layer with a PI and a Sigma units having P_2 and S_2 as activation functions respectively, then, the second hidden layer is connected to one Sigma unit output layer with activation function S_3. The equivalent HONN is as follows:

Using the method described in Sections 3 & 5, the activation functions of the equivalent ONN are as given below:

$$\begin{aligned}
\gamma_{31} &= S_3 \\
\gamma_{21} &= S_2, \\
\gamma_{22} &= P_2(\exp())
\end{aligned} \tag{29}$$

$$\gamma_{11} = \begin{cases} S_1 & \text{for connection between } S_1 \text{ and } S_2 \\ \ln\left(S_1()\right) & \text{for connection between } S_1 \text{ and } P_2 \end{cases}$$

$$\gamma_{12} = \begin{cases} P_1(\exp()) & \text{for connection between } P_1 \text{ and } S_2 \\ \ln(P_1(\exp())) & \text{for connection between } P_1 \text{ and } P_2 \end{cases} \tag{30}$$

While Figure 4-a contains mixed PI and Sigma units, all units of the graph shown in Figure 4-b are Sigma.

7. EXPERIMENTAL RESULTS

According to the conversion methods discussed in the previous sections, any software designed to simulate ONNs can be used directly to emulate HONNs. This can be done by just changing the activation function at the defined equivalent ONN. In this section, we shall use a neural network toolbox designed for neural networks and all what is needed is writing the source code for the activation functions between different units as that results from HONN conversion as was described in Sections 3 & 5. If one needs to consider HONNs with mixed units at each layer, then, the methods described in section 4 should be taking into account too.

The first problem discussed in this work is the typical nonlinear classification problem, the 2-bit parity problem also known as XOR problem. A PI-Sigma HONN will be used to solve this problem. The input/output data are as shown Table 1:

Since the first hidden layer is a PI layer, each input data is normalized by taking the ln(x+1), thus, 1's at the input layer are replaced by 1.0986 and a very simple PI-Sigma feed forward neural network with bias will be used. According to section 3 & 5, the activation function of the hidden PI units is f(net) = 1/ [1 + exp(-2*net)] + 1, and the activation function of the output Sigma unit is f(net) = 2/[1 + exp(-2*net)] -1. After converting this HONN to its equivalent ONN, it is trained using backpropagation of error, and the network converged well and gave the desired outputs.

In another experiment, a PI-Sigma HONN is used to approximate the Sine function. The input is x = {-π, 0.01- π, ..., π } which is then normalized using x_{norm} =ln[x+ min(x)+1] and the output (target) is y=sin(x_{norm}), therefore, this network has one input and one output units. Furthermore, ten PI hidden units are used in each of the experiments and the transfer function acting at each PI unit is f(net) = 1/[1 + exp(-2*net)] + 1. Each HONN is converted to an equivalent ONN by changing the activation function as discussed previously. Results of the above mentioned function approximation experiment are shown in Figures. 5 & 6. Various training and/or optimization methods are used to train feedforward and cascade correlation (equivalent) ONNs derived from HONNs.

As shown in Figures. 5 & 6, the best function approximation results are obtained using feedforward trained using Levenberg–Marquardt training as shown in Figure 5-f, and may be the best of all is cascade correlation trained with Levenberg–Marquardt as shown in Figure 6.

8. CONCLUSION

HONNs are equivalent to ONNs! This is the major conclusion of this chapter that may open a new research era in artificial neural networks. The equivalence proof shade new ideas on neural networks mechanism and topological issues, such as, a new discovery that a neuron may have dual activation function depending on HONN topology, so, why not using this phenomena in ONN topology design too? In fact, one might generalize this idea on new triple or quadruple activation function modes and study a new form of artificial neural networks. Other important issues we thrived through this chapter is that one can design any HONN, then, a neural networks software converts it to its equivalent ONN and thus may makes use of all the available neural networks modifications, optimizations, and learning strategies that already exist for ONNs. This means saving lots of time and efforts that one needs to spend in modeling those issues for HONNs from scratch. Due to HONNs complexity, the success of HONNs optimization and training modeling might not be straightforward in getting results and/or convergence of a solution, but, using equivalent ONNs more options are available with flexibility too.

One might look at the equivalence philosophy discussed in this work as a justification of how HONNs performance is related to ONNs and judging whether they are superior or not. After simple normalization of inputs, a HONN and its equivalent ONN have the same number of units and synaptic connections and they only differ by the activation functions acting at each unit. Still they differs with respect to arithmetic operations architecture point of view (multiplications are more complicated than additions) and equivalent ONNs has more complicated activation functions which means more research needs to be done to give a conclusive answer to this issue.

Table 1. XOR data

x_1	x_2	output
0	0	-1
0	1	1
1	0	1
1	1	-1

9. PROBLEMS: *SOME OF THE BELOW PROBLEMS MAY SERVE AS SUGGESTIONS FOR FUTURE RESEARCHES*

P1 Convert the HONN that Giles & Maxwell (1987) used to solve the XOR classification into its equivalent ONN.

P2 Given a fully connected HONN with a bias unit with the following topology: 3 inputs, 11 units (first) hidden layer of which 3 are PI units and 8 are Sigma units, 7 units at the second hidden layer of which 2 are Sigma units and 5 are PI units, and an output layer with on Sigma unit. Assume using S() as Sigma units activation function and P() as PI units activation function, find the equivalent ONN.

P3 This chapter showed that HONNs can be converted to ONNs, about the converse? Show that it is possible to convert an ONN to an equivalent HONN. Hint: use the activation of one Sigma unit and complete the proof.

P4 Assume using software that implement multi-layer neural network (ONN) that can be used for training, testing, cross validation, using different optimization methods. State what features should that software posse in order to be implemented on an ONN that was a HONN before conversion?

P5 Consider ONN with a dual activation function at each unit and an ONN with one activation function at each unit, is there a difference in terms of expressive power and training time? Hint: Perform a training task using some dataset to see the difference.

P6 In the discussion appeared previously in this chapter, the exp(ln(.)) have been used to convert

Figure 5. Approximation of Sin function by using a feedforward PI-Sigma HONN implementing exponent weights, results showed the solution found using the equivalent ONN. One can map the final ONN to the corresponding HONN

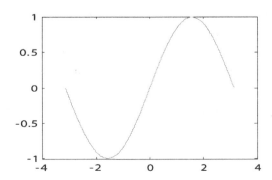

Figure 6. Approximation of sin function by using a cascade correlation PI-Sigma HONN after converting it to an equivalent ONN using cascade correlation (Fahlman & Lebiere C, 1990) implementing Levenberg–Marquardt as optimized training algorithm, less than 100 epochs are needed

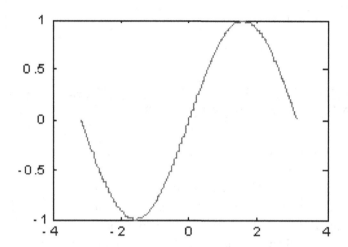

the PI unit into a Sigma unit. Is it possible to propose another methodology? If the answer is yes please specify that methodology.

P7   (a) Calculate the computational complexity of a HONN with d inputs, n hidden PI units, and c output Sigma units. (b) Calculate the computational complexity of the equivalent ONN and compare it with (a). Hint: to complete your discussion of this problem you are urged to read on the complexity of one multiplication and one addition operation (see for instance: The art of computer programming).

P8   Calculate the computational complexity of an L layers mixed PI Sigma layer HONN, assume that the number of PI and Sigma units in each layer is L_p and L_s respectively. Calculate the computational complexity of the equivalent ONN.

P9   Give the delta rule (the weight update rule used to train an ONN with backpropagation of error) to find Δw of a PI-PI interconnection layers that is converted to its ONN equivalent interconnection.

P10 Please specify why is it that the weight of a PI unit appears as an exponent rather than a coefficient.

P11 Is it possible that a HONN possess more expressive power (see Duda et al., 2000) and have too many local minima than an ONN with the same features. Hint: To be able to discuss this issue, suppose that an ONN_1 is defined with the same topology of some HONN, then covert the HONN to its equivalent ONN call it ONN_h. Compare the features of the two networks to reach a conclusion.

P12 Let the activation of a PI unit be given by $net_j = \beta \prod_{i=1}^{d} x_i^{w_{ji}}$ where β is some coefficient that may be fixed or adapted using some training algorithm. Does a HONN with this β coefficient equivalent to an ONN? Justify your answer.

P13 The Taylor expansion of the trigonometric sin function gives the following

$$\sin(x) = \sum_{j=0}^{\infty} (-1)^j x^{2j+1} / (2j+1)! \, .$$

  a.   Construct a HONN to approximate this function.
  b.   Find the equivalent ONN call it ONN_h.
  c.   Use a software tool to train the ONN_h that you designed in (a).
  d.   Compare your results with the following ONN, multi-layer feedforward with the following topology: one input, 10 hidden Sigma units with tanh() activation function, one output Sigma unit with a linear activation function.

Hint: to generate the training set calculate 15 values of sin from $-\pi$ to π, in other words the training set is

$T_R = \{(x,y): x = -\pi, -\pi + \pi / 7,..., \pi; y = \sin(x)\}$ Of course, x is the input and y is the target used in training. You may also generate the testing set $\{T_s\}$ as you did in with the training keeping in mind that $T_R \cap Ts = \varphi$ and size(T_R) <size(Ts).

P14 Show that a HONN that has d inputs implementing the translated multiplicative neuron (Iyoda et al, 2003) with its output given by:

$$z_k = f\left(b_k \prod_{j=1}^{n_h} (y_j - w_{kj})\right)$$

$$y_j = f\left(\sum_{i=1}^{d} (w_{ji} x_j - w_{0i})\right)$$

is equivalent to an ONN.

Hint: The above translated multiplicative NN has Sigma units at the first hidden layer, and PI units at the output layer. Assume that $k=1,2,..,c$ and n_h is the number of output PI units. More precisely, show that the equivalent ONN has the topology: d inputs, n_h fully connected Sigma units at the first hidden layer, n_h (two synapse connections) Sigma units at the second hidden layer, and c fully connected Sigma units at the output layer.

P15 The Higher order Functional Neural Networks HOFNNs (Giles & Maxwell, 1987) is used as a one layer neural network, a multiplication of the inputs that are connected to output units. The output of a neuron of a second order HOFNN is given by:

$$z_k = f\left(w_0 + \sum_{i=1}^{d} w_i x_i + \sum_{i1=1}^{d} \sum_{i2=1}^{d} w_{i1,i2} x_{i1} x_{i2}\right)$$

  a.   Show that the above HOFNN can be represented with the HONN of this chapter that has an activation as shown in Eq. (19) of this work. Therefore, this HOFNN is also equivalent to an ONN.
  b.   Use mathematical induction to show that HOFNN of any order is equivalent to ONN.
  c.   Propose a method to construct multi layer HOFNN, then a conversion to their equivalent ONN to be trained with backpropagation of error.

P16: Given a HONN with d inputs, n_h PI units and c output Sigma units. Find the total number of Sigma units in the equivalent ONN. Does this justify the outperformance of HONN to ONN saying that it needs less size?

P17: Give the delta rule used to train the backpropagation of error algorithms for the equivalent ONN shown in Figure4 (b).

REFERENCES

Al-Rawi, M. (2006). *Learning affine invariant pattern recognition using high-order Neural Networks*. International Conference on Artificial Intelligence and Machine Learning, (24-29.) Sharm El Sheikh, Egypt.

Al-Rawi, M., & Bisher, A. (2005). *An improved neural network builder that includes graphical networks and PI nodes. Human Computer Interaction*. (229-237), International Conference on Human Computer Interaction, Al-Zaytoona University, Amman, Jordan.

Abdelbar, A. (1998). Achieving superior generalization with a high order neural network. *Neural Computing & Applications, 7*(2), 141-146.

Artyomov, E., & Yadid-Pecht, O. (2005). Modified high-order neural network for invariant pattern recognition. *Pattern Recognition Letters, 26*(6), 843–851.

Clark, J. (1995). Tracking, code recognition, and memory management with high-order neural networks. *Applications and Science of Artificial Neural Networks*, SPIE *2492*, 964-973.

Duda, R., Hart, P., & Strok, D. (2000). *Pattern classification*. 2nd Ed., New York: Wiley-Interscience.

Elman, J. (1990). Finding structure in time. *Cognitive Science, 14*, 179-211

Fahlman, S., & Lebiere, C. (1990). The cascade-correlation learning architecture. In*Advances in Neural Information Processing Systems, 2*, 524-532, San Mateo, CA: Morgan Kaufmann.

Foltyniewicz, R. (1995). Efficient high order neural network for rotation, translation and distance invariant recognition of gray scale images. Computer Analysis of Images and Patterns. *Lecture Notes in Computer Science, 970*, 424-431.

Fukushima, K., & Wake, N. (1991). Handwritten alphanumeric character recognition by the Neocognition. *IEEE Transactions on Neural Networks, 2*(3), 355-365.

Ghosh, J., & Shin, T. (1992). Efficient higher-order neural networks for classification and function approximation. *International Journal of Neural Systems, 3*(4), 323-350.

Giles, C., Griffin, R., & Maxwell, T. (1988). Encoding geometric invariant in higher-order neural networks. In Anderson D (ed), *Neural Information Processing Systems* (pp.301-309), Proceedings of American Institute of Physics Conference..

Giles, C., & Maxwell, T. (1987). Learning invariance and generalization in high-order neural networks. *Applied Optics, 26*, 4972-4978.

Hagan, M., & Menhaj, M. (1994). Training feed forward network with the Marquardt algorithm. *IEEE Transactions on Neural Networks, 5*(6), 989-993.

He, Z, & Siyal, M. (1999). Improvement on higher-order neural networks for invariant object recognition. *International Journal of Computer Vision, 10*(1), 49-55.

Hughen, J., & Hollon, K. (1991). Millimeter wave radar stationary-target classification using a high-order neural network, *SPIE, 1469*, 341-350.

Iyoda, E., Nobuhara, H., & Hirota, K. (2003). A solution for the N-bit parity problem using a single translated multiplicative neuron. *Neural Processing Letters*, *18*(3), 213-218.

Knuth, D. (1997). *Fundamental Algorithms*. 3rd Ed. Reading, MA: Addison-Wesley.

Kohonen, T. (2000). *Self organizing networks*: 3rd edition. New York: Springer series in information sciences.

Kosmatopoulos, E., Polycarpou, M., Christodoulou, M., & Ioannou, P. (1995). High-Order Neural Network Structures for Identification of Dynamical Systems. *IEEE Transactions on Neural Networks*, *2* (6), 422-431.

Kulisch, U. (2002). *Advanced Arithmetic for the Digital Computer*. 1st Ed. New York: Springer;

Moller, M. (1993). A scaled conjugate gradient algorithm for fast supervised learning. Neural Networks, *6*(4), 525-533.

Minsky, M., & Papert, S. (1969). *Perceptrons.*Cambridge, MA, MIT Press.

Perantonis, S., & Lisboa, P. (1992). Translation, rotation, and scale invariant pattern recognition by high order neural networks and moment classifiers. *IEEE Transactions on Neural Networks*, *3*(2), 241-251.

Riedmiller, M., & Braun, H. (1993). A direct adaptive method for faster backpropagation learning: the Rprop algorithm. In *Proceedings of the International Conference on Neural Networks*, San Francisco.

Rovithakis, G. (1999). Robustifying nonlinear systems using high-order neural network controllers. *IEEE Transactions on Automatic Control, 44*(1), 102-108.

Rovithakis, G., Chalkiadakis, I., & Zervakis, M. (2004). High-order neural network structure selection for function approximation applications using genetic algorithms. *IEEE Transactions Systems Man Cybernetics (B)*, *34*(1), 150-158.

Rumelhart, D., Hinton, G., & Williams, R. (1986). Learning internal representations by error propagation. In Rumelhart D, McClelland J (eds) *Parallel Data Processing* (pp 318-362). Cambridge, MA: The MIT Press.

Spirkovska, L., & Reid, M. (1993). Coarse-coded higher-order neural networks for PSRI object recognition. *IEEE Trans on Neural Networks*, *4*(2), 276 – 283.

Thimm, G. (1998). *Optimization of high order perceptrons*. A PhD dissertation, Signal processing laboratory of the Swiss federal institute of technology.

Thimm, G., & Fiesler, E. (1997). High-order and multilayer perceptron initialization. *IEEE Transactions on Neural Networks*, *8*(2), 249-259.

Section 2
Artificial Higher Order Neural Networks for Simulation and Modeling

Chapter 7
Rainfall Estimation Using Neuron–Adaptive Higher Order Neural Networks

Ming Zhang
Christopher Newport University, USA

ABSTRACT

Real world data is often nonlinear, discontinuous and may comprise high frequency, multi-polynomial components. Not surprisingly, it is hard to find the best models for modeling such data. Classical neural network models are unable to automatically determine the optimum model and appropriate order for data approximation. In order to solve this problem, Neuron-Adaptive Higher Order Neural Network (NAHONN) Models have been introduced. Definitions of one-dimensional, two-dimensional, and n-dimensional NAHONN models are studied. Specialized NAHONN models are also described. NAHONN models are shown to be "open box". These models are further shown to be capable of automatically finding not only the optimum model but also the appropriate order for high frequency, multi-polynomial, discontinuous data. Rainfall estimation experimental results confirm model convergence. We further demonstrate that NAHONN models are capable of modeling satellite data. When the Xie and Scofield (1989) technique was used, the average error of the operator-computed IFFA rainfall estimates was 30.41%. For the Artificial Neural Network (ANN) reasoning network, the training error was 6.55% and the test error 16.91%, respectively. When the neural network group was used on these same fifteen cases, the average training error of rainfall estimation was 1.43%, and the average test error of rainfall estimation was 3.89%. When the neuron-adaptive artificial neural network group models was used on these same fifteen cases, the average training error of rainfall estimation was 1.31%, and the average test error of rainfall estimation was 3.40%. When the artificial neuron-adaptive higher order neural network model was used on these same fifteen cases, the average training error of rainfall estimation was 1.20%, and the average test error of rainfall estimation was 3.12%.

DOI: 10.4018/978-1-61520-711-4.ch007

1 INTRODUCTION

Artificial Higher Order Neural Network (HONN) models are the trends for emerging applications in the computer science and engineering areas. An, Mniszewski, Lee, Papcun, and Doolen (1988A and 1988B) test a learning procedure (HIERtalker), based on a default hierarchy of high order neural networks, which exhibited an enhanced capability of generalization and a good efficiency to learn to read English aloud. HIERtalker learns the 'building blocks' or clusters of symbols in a stream that appear repeatedly. Salem and Young (1991) study the interpreting line drawings with higher order neural networks. A higher order neural network solution to line labeling is presented. Line labeling constraints in trihedral scenes are designed into a Hopfield-type network. The labeling constraints require a higher order of interaction than that of Hopfield-type network. Liou and Azimi-Sadjadi (1993) present a dim target detection using high order correlation method. This work presents a method for clutter rejection and dim target track detection from infrared (IR) satellite data using neural networks. A high-order correlation method which recursively computes the spatio-temporal cross-correlations is used. Liatsis, Wellstead, Zarrop, and Prendergast (1994) propose a versatile visual inspection tool for the manufacturing process. The dynamically changing nature and the complex behavior of processes in manufacturing cells dictate the need for lean, agile and flexible manufacturing systems. Tseng and Wu (1994) post Constant-time neural decoders for some BCH codes. High order neural networks are shown to decode some BCH codes in constant-time with very low hardware complexity. HONN is a direct extension of the linear percep-tron: it uses a polynomial consisting of a set of product terms as its discriminant. Zardoshti-Kermani and Afshordi (1995) try classification of chromosomes by using higher-order neural networks. In this chapter, the application of a higher-order neural network for the classification of human chromosomes is described. The higher order neural network's inputs are 30 dimensional feature space extracted from chromosome images. Starke, Kubota, and Fukuda (1995) research combinatorial optimization with higher order neural networks-cost oriented competing processes in flexible manufacturing systems. Higher order neural networks are applied to handle combinatorial optimization problems by using cost oriented competing processes (COCP). This method has a high adaptability to complicated problems. Miyajima, Yatsuki, and Kubota (1995) study the dynamical properties of neural networks with product connections. Higher order neural networks with product connections which hold the weighted sum of products of input variables have been proposed as a new concept. In some applications, it is shown that they are more superior in ability than traditional neural networks. Wang (1996) researches the suppressing chaos with hysteresis in a higher order neural network. Artificial higher order neural networks attempt to mimic various features of a most powerful computational system-the human brain. Randolph and Smith (2000) have a new approach to object classification in binary images. In this chapter, Randolph and Smith address the problem of classifying binary objects using a cascade of a binary directional filter bank (DFB) and a higher order neural network (HONN). Rovithakis, Maniadakis, and Zervakis (2000) present a genetically optimized artificial neural network structure for feature extraction and classifica-tion of vascular tissue fluorescence spectrums. The optimization of artificial neural network structures for feature extraction and classification by employing Genetic Algorithms is addressed here. More precisely, a non-linear filter based on High Order Neural Networks whose weights are updated is used. Zhang, Liu, Li, Liu, and Ouyang (2002) discuss the problems of the translation and rotation invariance of a physiological signal in long-term clinical custody. This chapter presents a solution using high order neural networks with the advantage of large sample size. Rovithakis, Chalkiadakis, and Zervakis (2004) design a high order neural network structure for function approximation applications with using genetic algorithms, which entails both parametric (weights determination) and structural learning (structure selection). Siddiqi (2005) proposed direct encoding method to design higher order neural networks, since there are two major ways of encoding a higher order neural network into a chromosome, as required in design of a genetic algorithm (GA). These are explicit (direct) and implicit (indirect) encoding methods. The first motivation of this chapter is to use artificial HONN models for applications in the computer science and engineering areas.

HONN models have been widely researched. Jeffries (1989) presents a specific high order neural network design that can store, using n neutrons, any of the binomial n-strings. Machado (1989) gives a description of the combinatorial high order neural network model which is suitable for classification tasks. The model is based on fuzzy set theory, neural sciences studies, and expert knowledge analysis, which can handle knowledge in high order neural networks. Kosmatopoulos, Ioannou, and Christodoulou (1992) present the identification of nonlinear systems using new dynamic higher order neural network structures. The authors study the stability and convergence properties of recurrent higher order neural networks (RHONNs) as models of nonlinear dynamical systems. The overall structure of the RHONN consists of dynamical elements distributed throughout the higher order neural network. Kosmatopoulos, Polycarpou, Christodoulou, and Ioannou (1995) design the high order neural network structures for identification of dynamical systems. Several continuous-time and discrete-time recurrent higher order neural network models have been developed and applied to various engineering problems. Kariniotakis, Stavrakakis, and Nogaret (1996) try the wind power forecasting using advanced higher order neural networks models. In this chapter, an advanced model, based on recurrent high order neural networks, is developed for the prediction of the power output profile of a wind park. This model outperforms simple methods like persistence, as well as classical methods. Rovithakis, Gaganis, Perrakis, and Christodoulou (1996) design a recurrent higher order neural network model to describe manufacturing cell dynamics. A recurrent higher order neural network structure (RHONN) is employed to identify cell dynamics, which is supposed to be unknown. Brucoli, Carnimeo, and Grassi (1997) provide a design method for associative memories using a new model of discrete-time second-order higher order neural networks which includes local interconnections among neurons. Zhang, Zhang, and Fulcher (1997) present a financial simulation system using a higher order trigonometric polynomial neural network group model. *The model of* trigonometric polynomial high order neural network (THONN) is presented. The financial system was written in C, incorporates a user-friendly graphical user interface (GUI), and runs under X-Windows on a Sun workstation. Burshtein (1998) believes that recent results on the memory storage capacity of higher order neural networks indicate a significant improvement compared to the limited capacity of the Hopfield model. However, such results have so far been obtained. Zhang and Lu (2001) simulate financial data by using Multi-Polynomial Higher Order Neural Network (M-PHONN) model. A new model, called (M-PHONN), has been developed. Using Sun workstation, C++, and Motif, a M-PHONN simulator has been built as well. Qi and Zhang (2001) estimate rainfall using M-PHONN model. The M-PHONN model for estimating heavy convective rainfall from satellite data was tested. The M-PHONN model has 5% to 15% more accuracy than other existing higher order neural models. Campos, Loukianov, and Sanchez (2003) use recurrent high order neural networks to control motor synchronously. A nonlinear complete order model of a synchronous motor is identified using a dynamic higher order neural network. Based on this model a sliding mode controller is derived. This neural network identifier and the proposed control law allow rejecting external load. Kuroe (2004) presents higher order neural network models for learning and identifying deterministic finite state automata (FSA). The proposed models are a class of high order recurrent neural networks. The models are capable of representing FSA with the network size. Christodoulou, and Iliopoulos (2006) study higher order neural network models for prediction of steady-state and dynamic behavior, A three molecule module present, which has a wide range of functions in signal transduction, such as stress-response, cell-cycle-control, and cell-wall-construction. The second motivation of this chapter is to present new artificial HONN models for applications in the computer science and engineering areas.

A lot of design issues of artificial higher order neural network structures, algorithms and models have been studied recently. Jeffries (1989) presents a specific high order neural network design which can store, using n neurons, any number of any of the binomial n-strings. Yang and Guest (1990) design the high order neural networks with reduced numbers of interconnection weights. A multilayered network with the first layer consisting of parabolic neurons (constrained second-order neurons) is proposed. Each parabolic neuron requires only N+2 interconnections (where N is the number of inputs). Chang and Cheung (1992) study backpropagation algorithm in higher order neural network. By restructuring the basic HONN architecture, the traditional backpropagation algorithm can be extended to the supervised backpropagation learning scheme, which is used to develop a training algorithm for multilayer higher order neural networks. Chang, Lin, and Cheung (1993) provide polynomial and standard higher order neural network. The generalized back propagation algorithm is extended to multi-layer higher order neural networks. Two basic structures, the standard form and the polynomial form, are discussed. Heywood and Noakes (1993) contribute a simple addition to back-propagation learning for dynamic weight pruning, sparse higher order network extraction and faster learning. The enhancement to the backpropagation algorithm presented results from the need to extract sparsely connected networks from networks employing product terms. Young and Downs (1993) generalize the higher order neural networks. The theory of pac-learning has provided statements about the generalization capability of linear threshold networks. The authors present an extension of this work to higher order threshold neural networks and shows that the generalization ability of the higher order neural network. Cooper (1995) investigates higher order neural networks for combinatorial optimization improving the scaling properties of the Hopfield network. The dynamics of the Hopfield network are investigated too to determine why the network does not scale well to large problem sizes. It is seen that the Hopfield network encourages the formation of locally optimal segments, resulting in multiple seed points. Villalobos and Merat (1995) present a technique for evaluating the learning capability and optimizing the feature space of a class of higher-order neural networks. It is shown that supervised learning can be posed as an optimization problem in which inequality constraints. Yatsuki and Miyajima (1997) show associative ability of higher order neural networks. Higher order neural networks have been proposed as new systems. The authors also show some theoretical results on the associative ability of HONNs. Abdelbar and Tagliarini (1998) present a method that combines Bayesian learning, a statistical technique, a high order neural network with the property that the mapping embodied by the network can always be described by a polynomial-like equation. Li, Wang, Li, Zhang, and Li (1998) introduce the fully-connected higher order neuron and sparselized higher-order neuron. The mapping capabilities of the fully-connected higher order neural networks are investigated by authors. Gulez, Mutoh, Harashima, Ohnishi, and Pastaci (2000) design a high order neural network for the performance increasing of an induction motor under changeable load. Motor drives are traditionally designed with relatively inexpensive analog components. The weaknesses of analog systems are their susceptibility to temperature variations and the component aging. A higher order neural network has benefit to balance the load. Yamashita, Hirasawa, Hu, and Murata (2002) study multi-branch structure of layered higher order neural networks to make their size compact. The multi-branch structure has shown improved performance against conventional neural networks. Li, Hirasawa, and Hu (2003) research a new strategy for constructing higher order neural networks with multiplication units. The proposed method provides a flexible mechanism for incremental higher order neural network growth where higher order terms can be naturally generated. Wang, Wu, and Chang (2004) present a novel approach, called scale equalization (SE), to implement higher-order neural networks. SE is particularly useful in eliminating the scale divergence problem commonly encountered in higher order networks. Lin, Wu, and Wang (2005) also show that, by using scale equalization (SE) technique, scale equalized higher order neural network (SEHNN) is particularly useful in alleviating the scale divergence problem that plagues higher order neural network. The third motivation of this chapter is to provide new design of artificial HONN for applications in the computer science and engineering areas.

Recurrent higher order neural networks are researched a lot in the recent years. Baldi and Venkatesh (1993) examine the recurrent higher order neural networks of polynomial threshold elements with random symmetric interactions. Precise asymptotic estimates are derived for the expected number of fixed points as a function of the margin of stability. Kosmatopoulos and Christodoulou (1994) study the capabilities of recurrent high order neural networks (RHONNs), whose synapses are adjusted according to the learning law. Kosmatopoulos and Christodoulou (1995) investigate the structural properties of Recurrent High Order Neural Networks (RHONN) whose weights are restricted to satisfy the symmetry property. Tanaka and Kumazawa (1996) use recurrent higher order neural networks to learn regular languages. Kuroe, Ikeda, and Mori (1997) study a method for identification of nonlinear dynamical systems by recurrent high order neural networks. Rovithakis, Malamos, Varvarigon, and Christodoulou (1998) employ recurrent high order neural networks (RHONNs) to determine the unknown values of media characteristics that lead to user satisfaction without violating network limitations. Rovithakis (2000) discusses the tracking problem in the presence of additive and multiplicative external disturbances, for affine in the control nonlinear dynamical systems, whose nonlinearities are assumed unknown. A robustness of a neural controller in the presence of additive and multiplicative external perturbations based on recurrent high order neural networks has been provided. Christodoulou and Zarkogianni (2006) use recurrent High Order Neural Networks for identification of the Epidermal Growth Factor Receptor (EGFR) Signaling Pathway. The present work deals with a specific signaling pathway called EGFR PATHWAY which is composed of twenty three proteins and their interactions. The fourth motivation of this chapter is to provide new HONN for applications in the computer science and engineering areas.

Artificial higher order neural networks are good at simulating nonlinear models. Estevez and Okabe (1991) introduce a piecewise linear-high order neural network through error back propagation, which has a structure consisting of two layers of modifiable weights. The hidden units implement a piecewise linear function in the augmented input space, which includes high-order terms. Lee, Lee, and Park (1992) develop a neural controller of nonlinear dynamic systems using higher order neural networks. Higher order multilayer neural networks are used for identification and control of nonlinear dynamic systems, and their performance is compared with the performance of conventional linear multilayer neural networks. Vidyasagar studies the convergence of higher order neural networks with modified updating. The problem of maximizing a general objective function over the hypercube $\{-1, 1\}^n$ is formulated as that of maximizing a multi-linear polynomial over $\{-1, 1\}^n$. Kosmatopoulos and Christodoulou (1997) use higher order neural networks for the learning of robot contact surface shape. The problem of learning the shape parameters of unknown surfaces that are in contact with a robot end-effector can be formulated as a nonlinear parameter estimation problem. Rovithakis (1998) reinforces robustness using higher order neural network controllers for affine in the control nonlinear dynamical systems. A correction control signal is added to a nominal controller to guarantee a desired performance for the corresponding nominal system. Bouzerdoum (1999) present a new class of higher order neural networks with nonlinear decision boundaries.

This new class of HONN called shunting inhibitory artificial neural networks (SIANNs) for classification and function approximation tasks. In these networks, the basic synaptic interaction is of the shunting inhibitory type. Rovithakis (1999) tries robustifying nonlinear systems using higher order neural network controllers. A robust control methodology for affine control of nonlinear dynamical systems is developed. A correction control signal is added to a nominal controller to guarantee a desired performance for the corresponding nominal system. Zhang, Peng, and Rovithakis (2000) indicates that Rovithakis (1999) overlooked some essential assumptions regarding "robustifying nonlinear systems using high-order neural network controllers" (Rovithakis 1999). The authors consider a nonlinear dynamical system in their study. Rovithakis, Maniadakis, and Zervakis (2000) study artificial neural networks for feature extraction and classification of vascular tissue fluorescence spectrums. The use of neural network structures for feature extraction and classification is addressed here. More precisely, a nonlinear filter based on higher order neural networks (HONN) whose weights are updated by stable learning laws is used to extract the features. More than 10 chapters in Zhang (2009A) looks at nonlinear data simulations and predictions. Zhang (2009B) finds HONN nonlinear models can simulate nonlinear data better than SAS nonlinear method. Zhang (2009C) develops ultra high frequency trigonometric higher order neural networks. The author finds the error to simulate economics and business data by using ultra high frequency trigonometric HONN can be close to zero. The fifth motivation of this chapter is to provide new HONN for nonlinear model simulation in the computer science and engineering areas.

Adaptive higher order neural network models have been rigorously studied. Rovithakis, Kosmatopoulos, and Christodoulou (1993) use recurrent high order neural networks for robust adaptive control of unknown plants to mechanical systems. The proposed algorithm employs a recurrent higher order neural network (RHONN) identifier. Yu and Liang (1995) propose a higher order new neural network approach for eigenstructure extraction. It is based on the constraint optimal problem. It can be used to estimate the largest eigenvector of the covariance matrix adaptively and efficiently. Rovithakis, Gaganis, Perrakis, and Christodoulou (1998) use higher order neural networks to control manufacturing systems. Authors evaluate a neuron adaptive scheduling methodology by comparing its performance with conventional schedulers. Zhang, Xu, and Lu (1999) develop neuron-adaptive higher order neural network group models with neuron-adaptive activation functions. A learning algorithm is derived to adjust free parameters in the neuron-adaptive activation function as well as coefficients of the higher order neural networks. Rovithakis (2000) perform a neural adaptive tracking controller for multi-input nonlinear dynamical systems in the presence of additive and multiplicative external disturbances. Author discusses the tracking problem in the presence of additive and multiplicative external disturbances, for affine in the control nonlinear dynamical systems, whose nonlinearities are assumed unknown based on a recurrent higher order neural networks. Zhang (2001) presents a new model, called Adaptive Multi-Polynomial Higher Order Neural Network (A-PHONN). Using Sun workstation, C++, and Motif, an A-PHONN simulator has been built as well. Real world financial data simulations are presented by using A-PHONN model.

Zhang and Scofield (2001) test the A-PHONN model for estimating heavy convective rainfall from satellite data. The A-PHONN model has 6% to 16% more accuracy than the polynomial HONN and Trigonometric HONN. Zhang, Xu, and Fulcher (2002) point out that real-world financial data is often nonlinear, comprises high-frequency multipolynomial components, and is discontinuous (piecewise continuous). Not surprisingly, it is hard to model such data. Classical neural networks are unable to automatically model these data. The authors design neuron-adaptive higher order neural network models for automated financial data modeling. Xu and Zhang (2002) study adaptive higher order neural networks (AHONN) and its approximation capabilities. Authors also study the approximation capabilities of an adaptive higher-order neural network (AHONN) with a neuron-adaptive activation function (NAF) to any nonlinear continuous functional and any nonlinear continuous operator. Ge, Zhang, and Lee (2004) investigate adaptive higher order neural network control for a class of nonlinear systems with disturbances in discrete-time. Ricalde and Sanchez (2005) present the design of an adaptive recurrent neural observer for nonlinear systems which model is assumed to be unknown. The neural observer is composed of a recurrent higher order neural network which builds an online model. Zhang, Ge, and Lee (2005) study adaptive higher order neural network control for a class of discrete-time multi-input-multi-output (MIMO) nonlinear systems with triangular form inputs. Each subsystem of the MIMO system is in strict feedback form. Alanis, Sanchez, and Loukianov (2006) study discrete-time recurrent neural induction motor control using Kalman learning. This chapter deals with the adaptive tracking problem for discrete-time induction motor model in presence of bounded disturbances. In this chapter, a high order neural network structure is used to identify the plant model. Butt and Shafiq (2006) present a higher order neural network based root-solving controller for adaptive tracking of stable nonlinear plants. The use of intelligent control schemes in Nonlinear Model Based Control (NMBC) has gained widespread popularity. The higher order neural networks, in particular, have been used extensively to model the dynamics of nonlinear plants. The sixth motivation of this chapter is to provide adaptive HONN for applications in the computer science and engineering areas.

In this chapter, Neuron-Adaptive Higher Order Neural Network (*NAHONN*) Models with neuron-adaptive activation functions are introduced. How to use NAHONN to estimating rainfall will be discussed. Experimental results obtained by using NAHONNs for rainfall estimating are presented in this chapter.

2 NEURON-ADAPTIVE HIGHER ORDER NEURAL NETWORK (*NAHONN*)

Based on Zhang, Xu, and Fulcher (2002), followings are the definitions for neuron-adaptive higher order neural networks (NAHONNs).

Let:

h: the hth term in the *NAF* (Neural network Activation Function)

i: the ith neuron in layer-k

k: the kth layer of the neural network (k will be used later in the learning algorithm proof)

w: the maximum number of terms in the *NAF*

x: first neural network input

y: second neural network input

Z_1 one output of neuron for one, two, ... m-dimensional NAHONNs

$net_{i,k}$:   the input or internal state
of the i h neuron in the kth layer

$a_{i,j,k}$:   the weight that connects the jth neuron in
layer $k-1$ with the ith neuron in layer kwj ill
be used in the two-dimensional NAHONN formula

$o_{i,k}$:   the value of the output from the ith neuron in layer-k

For one-dimensional Neuron-Adaptive Higher Order Neural Networks:

$$net_{i,k} = a_{i,x,k} \cdot x$$

For two-dimensional Neuron-adaptive higher order neural networks:

$net_{i,x,k}$: the input of the x neuron in the input layer

$net_{i,y,k}$: the input of the y neuron in the input layer

$$net_{i,x,k} = a_{i,x,k} \cdot x$$
$$net_{i,y,k} = a_{i,y,k} \cdot y$$

For m-dimensional Neuron-Adaptive Higher Order Neural Networks:

$$net_{i,1,k} = a_{i,1,k} \cdot x_1$$
$$net_{i,2,k} = a_{i,2,k} \cdot x_2$$
$$\ldots\ldots$$
$$net_{i,m,k} = a_{i,m,k} \cdot x_m$$

For multi m-dimensional Neuron-Adaptive Higher Order Neural Networks:

z: The zth output neuron in the output layer

Z_z: The zth output of the multi m-dimensional *NAHONN*.

2.1 *Multi* m-Dimensional *NAHONN* Definition

The multi m-dimensional Neuron-adaptive higher order neural network Activation Function (*NAF*) is:

$$\Phi_{i,k}\left(net_{i,1,k}, net_{i,2,k}, \ldots\ldots net_{i,m,k}\right)$$
$$= \sum_{h=1}^{w} f_{i,k,h}(net_{i,1,k}, net_{i,2,k}, \ldots\ldots, net_{i,m,k})$$

The *multi* m-dimensional NAHONN is defined as follows:

$$Z_z = \sum_{i=0}^{n} a_{z,i,k+1} \cdot \Phi_{i,k}\left(net_{i,1,k}, net_{i,2,k}, \ldots\ldots, net_{i,m,k}\right)$$
$$= \sum_{i=0}^{n} a_{z,i,k+1} \cdot \sum_{h=1}^{w} f_{i,k,h}(net_{i,1,k}, net_{i,2,k}, \ldots\ldots, net_{i,m,k})$$
$$= \sum_{i=0}^{n} a_{z,i,k+1} \cdot \sum_{h=1}^{w} f_{i,k,h}(a_{i,1,k} \cdot x_1, a_{i,2,k} \cdot x_2 \ldots\ldots, a_{i,m,k} \cdot x_m)$$

The structure of the multi m-dimensional *NAHONN* is shown in Figure 1.

Figure 1. Multi m–dimensional NAHONN structure

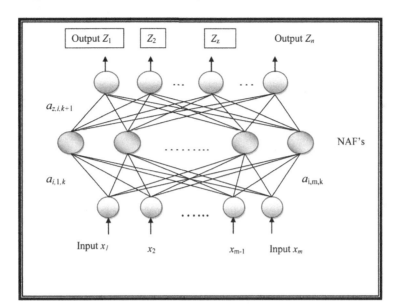

2.2 m-Dimensional *NAHONN* Definition

The m-dimensional Neuron-adaptive higher order neural network Activation Function (*NAF*) is:

$$\Phi_{i,k}\left(net_{i,1,k}, net_{i,2,k}, \ldots\ldots net_{i,m,k}\right)$$
$$= \sum_{h=1}^{w} f_{i,k,h}\left(net_{i,1,k}, net_{i,2,k}, \ldots\ldots, net_{i,m,k}\right)$$

The m-dimensional Neuron-Adaptive Higher Order Neural Network is defined as:

NAHONN (m-Dimensional):

$$Z_1 = \sum_{i=0}^{n} a_{1,i,k+1} \cdot \Phi_{i,k}\left(net_{i,1,k}, net_{i,2,k}, \ldots\ldots, net_{i,m,k}\right)$$
$$= \sum_{i=0}^{n} a_{1,i,k+1} \cdot \sum_{h=1}^{w} f_{i,k,h}\left(a_{i,1,k} \cdot x_1, a_{i,2,k} \cdot x_2 \ldots\ldots, a_{i,m,k} \cdot x_m\right)$$

The network structure of an m-dimensional *NAHONN* is the same as that of a multi-layer *FNN*. That is, it consists of an input layer with *m* input-units, an output layer with one output-unit, and one hidden layer consisting of intermediate processing units. A typical two-dimensional *NAHONN* architecture is depicted in Figure 1. Again, while there is no activation function in the input layer and the output neuron is a summing unit (linear activation), the activation function for the hidden units is the m-dimensional neuron-adaptive higher order neural network NAF.

Figure 2. m–dimensional NAHONN structure

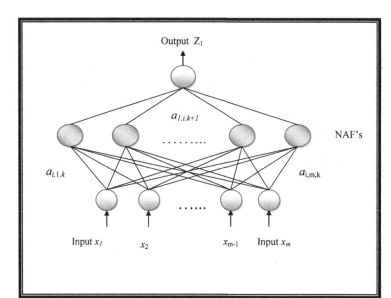

2.3 Two-Dimensional *NAHONN* Definition

The two-dimensional Neuron-adaptive higher order neural network Activation Function (*NAF*) is defined as:

NAF:

$$\Phi_{i,k}\left(net_{i,x,k}, net_{i,y,k}\right) = O_{i,k}\left(net_{i,x,k}, net_{i,y,k}\right)$$
$$= \sum_{h=1}^{w} f_{i,k,h}(net_{i,x,k}, net_{i,y,k})$$

Suppose:

$w = 5$

$f_{i,k,1}(net_{i,x,k}, net_{i,y,k}) = a1_{i,k} \cdot \sin^{c1_{i,k}}\left(b1_{i,k} \cdot (net_{i,x,k})\right) \cdot \sin^{e1_{i,k}}\left(d1_{i,k} \cdot (net_{i,y,k})\right)$

$f_{i,k,2}(net_{i,x,k}, net_{i,y,k}) = a2_{i,k} \cdot e^{-b2_{i,k} \cdot (net_{i,x,k})} \cdot e^{-d2_{i,k} \cdot (net_{i,x,k})}$

$f_{i,k,3}(net_{i,x,k}, net_{i,y,k}) = a3_{i,k} \cdot \dfrac{1}{1 + e^{-b3_{i,k} \cdot (net_{i,x,k})}} \cdot \dfrac{1}{1 + e^{-d3_{i,k} \cdot (net_{i,y,k})}}$

$f_{i,k,4}(net_{i,x,k}, net_{i,y,k}) = a4_{i,k} \cdot (net_{i,x,k})^{b4_{i,k}} \cdot (net_{i,y,k})^{d4_{i,k}}$

$f_{i,k,5}(net_{i,x,k}, net_{i,y,k}) = a5_{i,k} \cdot \sin c(b5_{i,k} \cdot net_{i,x,k}) \cdot \sin c(d5_{i,k} \cdot net_{i,y,k})$

The 2-dimensional Neuron-adaptive higher order neural network Activation Function then becomes:

$$\Phi_{i,k}\left(net_{i,k}\right) = \sum_{h=1}^{5} f_{i,k,h}(net_{i,x,k}, net_{i,y,k})$$

$$= a1_{i,k} \cdot \sin^{c1_{i,k}}\left(b1_{i,k} \cdot (net_{i,x,k})\right) \cdot \sin^{e1_{i,k}}\left(d1_{i,k} \cdot (net_{i,y,k})\right)$$

$$+ a2_{i,k} \cdot e^{-b2_{i,k} \cdot (net_{i,x,k})} \cdot e^{-d2_{i,k} \cdot (net_{i,y,k})}$$

$$+ a3_{i,k} \cdot \frac{1}{1 + e^{-b3_{i,k} \cdot (net_{i,x,k})}} \cdot \frac{1}{1 + e^{-d3_{i,k} \cdot (net_{i,y,k})}}$$

$$+ a4_{i,k} \cdot (net_{i,x,k})^{b4_{i,k}} \cdot (net_{i,y,k})^{d4_{i,k}}$$

$$+ a5_{i,k} \cdot \sin c(b5_{i,k} \cdot net_{i,x,k}) \cdot \sin c(d5 \cdot net_{i,y,k})$$

where:

$$a1_{i,k}, \quad b1_{i,k}, \quad c1_{i,k}, \quad d1_{i,k}, e1_{i,k}, a2_{i,k}, \quad b2_{i,k}, d2_{i,k},$$

$$a3_{i,k}, \quad b3_{i,k}, d3_{i,k}, a4_{i,k}, b4_{i,k}, d4_{i,k}, a5_{i,k}, b5_{i,k}, d5_{i,k}$$

are free parameters which can be adjusted (as well as weights) during training.

The two-dimensional Neuron-Adaptive Higher Order Neural Network is defined as:

$$NAHONN \quad (2-\dim ensional):$$

$$Z_1 = \sum_{i=0}^{n} a_{1,i,k+1} \cdot \Phi_{i,k}\left(net_{i,x,k}, net_{i,y,k}\right) = \sum_{i=0}^{n} a_{1,i,k+1} \cdot \sum_{h=1}^{w} f_{i,k,h}(a_{i,x,k} \cdot x, a_{i,y,k} \cdot y)$$

$$Let \quad w = 5, \quad NAHONN \quad (2-\dim ensional):$$

$$Z_1 = \sum_{i=0}^{n} a_{1,i,k+1} \cdot \Phi_{i,k}\left(net_{i,x,k}, net_{i,y,k}\right)$$

$$= \sum_{i=0}^{n} a_{1,i,k+1} \sum_{h=1}^{5} f_{i,k,h}(a_{i,x,k} \cdot x, a_{i,y,k} \cdot y)$$

$$= \sum_{i=0}^{n} a_{1,i,k+1} \cdot \left((a1_{i,k} \cdot \sin^{c1_{i,k}}\left(b1_{i,k} \cdot (a_{i,x,k} \cdot x)\right) \cdot \sin^{e1_{i,k}}\left(d1_{i,k} \cdot (a_{i,y,k} \cdot y)\right) \right.$$

$$+ a2_{i,k} \cdot e^{-b2_{i,k} \cdot (a_{i,x,k} \cdot x)} \cdot e^{-d2_{i,k} \cdot (a_{i,y,k} \cdot y)} + a3_{i,k} \cdot \frac{1}{1 + e^{-b3_{i,k} \cdot (a_{i,x,k} \cdot x)}} \cdot \frac{1}{1 + e^{-d3_{i,k} \cdot (a_{i,y,k} \cdot y)}})$$

$$\left. + a4_{i,k} \cdot (a_{i,x,k} \cdot x)^{b4_{i,k}} \cdot (a_{i,y,k} \cdot y)^{d4_{i,k}} + a5_{i,k} \cdot \sin c(a_{i,x,k} \cdot x) \cdot \sin c(a_{i,y,k} \cdot y) \quad \right)$$

where

$$a1_{i,k}, \quad b1_{i,k}, \quad c1_{i,k}, \quad d1_{i,k}, e1_{i,k}, a2_{i,k}, \quad b2_{i,k}, d2_{i,k},$$

$$a3_{i,k}, \quad b3_{i,k}, d3_{i,k}, a4_{i,k}, b4_{i,k}, d4_{i,k}, a5_{i,k}, b5_{i,k}, d5_{i,k}$$

are free parameters which can be adjusted (as well as weights) during training.

The network structure of the two-dimensional *NAHONN* is the same as that of a multi-layer *FNN*. That is, it consists of an input layer with *two* input-units, an output layer with one output-unit, and one hidden layer consisting of intermediate processing units. A typical two-dimensional *NAHONN* architecture is depicted in Figure 3. Again, while there is no activation function in the input layer and the output neuron is a summing unit (linear activation), the activation function for the hidden units is the two-dimensional neuron-adaptive higher order neural network NAF. ·

2.4 One-Dimensional *NAHONN* Definition

The one-dimension Neuron-adaptive higher order neural network Activation Function (*NAF*) is defined as:

$$NAF: \Phi_{i,k}\left(net_{i,k}\right) = O_{i,k}\left(net_{i,k}\right) = \sum_{h=1}^{w} f_{i,k,h}\left(net_{i,k}\right)$$

Figure 3. 2–dimensional NAHONN structure

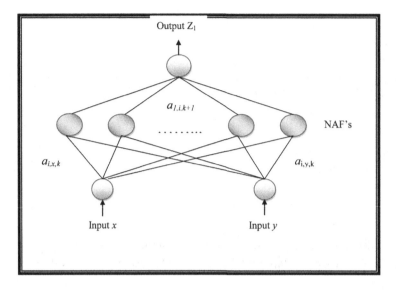

Suppose:

$$w = 5$$

$$f_{i,k,1}(net_{i,k}) = a1_{i,k} \cdot \sin^{c1_{i,k}}\left(b1_{i,k} \cdot (net_{i,k})\right)$$

$$f_{i,k,2}(net_{i,k}) = a2_{i,k} \cdot e^{-b2_{i,k} \cdot (net_{i,k})}$$

$$f_{i,k,3}(net_{i,k}) = a3_{i,k} \cdot \frac{1}{1 + e^{-b3_{i,k} \cdot (net_{i,k})}}$$

$$f_{i,k,4}(net_{i,k}) = a4_{i,k} \cdot (net_{i,k})^{b4_{i,k}}$$

$$f_{i,k,5}(net_{i,k}) = a5_{i,k} \cdot \sin c(b5_{i,k} \cdot net_{i,k})$$

The one-dimensional Neuron-adaptive higher order neural network Activation Function (*NAF*) then becomes:

$$\Phi_{i,k}(net_{i,k}) = \sum_{h=1}^{5} f_{i,k,h}(net_{i,k})$$
$$= a1_{i,k} \cdot \sin^{c1_{i,k}}\left(b1_{i,k} \cdot (net_{i,k})\right) + a2_{i,k} \cdot e^{-b2_{i,k} \cdot (net_{i,k})} + a3_{i,k} \cdot \frac{1}{1 + e^{-b3_{i,k} \cdot (net_{i,k})}}$$
$$+ a4_{i,k} \cdot (net_{i,k})^{b4_{i,k}} + a5_{i,k} \cdot \sin c(b5_{i,k} \cdot net_{i,k})$$

where:

$$a1_{i,k}, \; b1_{i,k}, \; c1_{i,k}, \; a2_{i,k}, \; b2_{i,k},$$
$$a3_{i,k}, \; b3_{i,k}, a4_{i,k}, b4_{i,k}, a5_{i,k}, b5_{i,k}$$

are free parameters which can be adjusted (as well as weights) during training.

The one-dimensional Neuron-Adaptive Higher Order Neural Network is defined as:

$NAHONN(1 - \dim ensional)$

$$Z_1 = \sum_{i=0}^{n} a_{1,i,k+1} \cdot \Phi_{i,k}\left(net_{i,k}\right) = \sum_{i=0}^{n} a_{1,i,k+1} \cdot \sum_{h=1}^{w} f_{i,k,h}(a_{i,x,k} \cdot x)$$

$Let \quad w = 5, \quad NAHONN(1 - \dim ensional)$

$$Z_1 = \sum_{i=0}^{n} a_{1,i,k+1} \cdot \Phi_{i,k}\left(net_{i,k}\right) = \sum_{i=0}^{n} a_{1,i,k+1} \cdot \sum_{h=1}^{5} f_{i,k,h}(a_{i,x,k} \cdot x)$$

$$= \sum_{i=0}^{n} a_{1,i,k+1} \left\{ a1_{i,k} \cdot \sin^{c1_{i,k}}\left(b1_{i,k} \cdot (a_{i,x,k} \cdot x)\right) + a2_{i,k} \cdot e^{-b2_{i,k} \cdot (a_{i,x,k} \cdot x)} \right.$$

$$\left. + a3_{i,k} \cdot \frac{1}{1 + e^{-b3_{i,k} \cdot (a_{i,x,k} \cdot x)}} + a4_{i,k} \cdot (a_{i,x,k} \cdot x)^{b4_{i,k}} + a5_{i,k} \cdot \sin c(b5_{i,k} \cdot a_{i,x,k} \cdot x) \right)$$

where:

$$a1_{i,k}, \quad b1_{i,k}, \quad c1_{i,k}, \quad a2_{i,k}, \quad b2_{i,k},$$
$$a3_{i,k}, \quad b3_{i,k}, a4_{i,k}, b4_{i,k}, a5_{i,k}, b5_{i,k}$$

are free parameters which can be adjusted (as well as weights) during training.

The network structure of a one-dimensional *NAHONN* is the same as that of a multi-layer Feedforward Neural Network (*FNN*). That is, it consists of an input layer with *one* input-unit, an output layer with one output-unit, and one hidden layer consisting of intermediate processing units. A typical one-dimensional *NAHONN* architecture is depicted in Figure 1. Now while there is no activation function in the input layer and the output neuron is a summing unit only (linear activation), the activation function in the hidden units is the one-dimensional neuron-adaptive higher order neural network NAF defined by equation 2.4. The one-dimensional *NANONN* is described by equation 2.4.

2.5 Learning Algorithm and Universal Approximation Capability of NAHONN

NAHONN learning algorithm is based on the steepest descent gradient rule (Zhang, Xu, and Fulcher, 2002). However, as the variables in the hidden layer activation function are able to be adjusted, NAHONN provides more flexibility and more accurate approximation than traditional higher order (and indeed NAHONN includes traditional higher order FNN (fixed activation function) FNNs as a special case).

A NAHONN with a neuron-adaptive activation function can approximate any piecewise continuous function with infinite (countable) discontinuous points to any degree of accuracy (Zhang, Xu, and Fulcher, 2002)

3. HEAVY RAINFALL ESTIMATION USING NAHONN MODELS

So far, no model can work well if the weather forecasting has to use non-continuous and unsmooth data as input. A challenge in this area is to build a new model for weather forecasting that uses non-continuous and unsmooth data is. An artificial neuron-Adaptive higher order Neural network expert System for Estimating Rainfall using satellite data (ANSER) has been developed for estimating rainfall within NOAA (the National Oceanic and Atmospheric Administration, US Department of Commerce). Artificial neuron-adaptive higher order neural network (NAHONN) models were used in this ANSER system.

Figure 4. 1–dimensional NAHONN structure

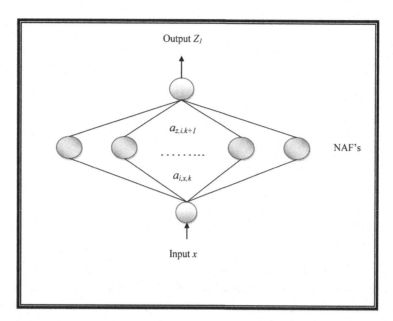

Rainfall estimation systems are complex. The fixed-neuron ANN models or HONN models are not sufficiently powerful to characterize such complex systems. Using neuron-adaptive NAHONN models enabled us to build a very powerful rainfall estimation system. In the ANSER system, cloud features and nonlinear functions vary in a discontinuous and unsmooth fashion with respect to input variables. Such features and functions cannot be effectively simulated using fixed-neuron ANNs or HONNs, since accuracy will be necessarily limited. Neuron-adaptive NAHONN models were instead used in the ANSER system to determine cloud features and nonlinear functions, for subsequent use in rainfall estimation. Rainfall estimation is a complicated, nonlinear, discontinuous process. Even using parallel and ANN-based reasoning networks leads to poor results. In other words, feed-forward neural networks with fixed activation function neural models could not provide correct reasoning in ANSER. Artificial neuron-adaptive higher order neural network models, on the other hand, can successfully perform this task.

3.1 ANSER Architecture

The architecture of the ANSER system can be seen in Figure 5. Output of ANSER is displayed in following Figure 6. ANSER system uses satellite data as input. Satellite data have been pre-processed and then ANSER uses all image processing methods and pattern recognition techniques to extract the feature, rule, model, and knowledge of rainfall. Seven features are extracted from the satellite data. They are cloud top temperature (CT), cloud top growth factor (CG), rainburst factor (RB), overshooting top factor (OS), cloud merger factor (M), saturated environment factor (SE), and storm speed factor(S). The cloud top temperature (CT) and cloud top growth factor (CG) are used as input for half an hour rainfall factor (G) predication using NAHONN model. Then half an hour rainfall factor (G), with rainburst factor (RB), overshooting top factor (OS), cloud merger factor (M), saturated environment factor (SE), storm speed factor (S), and moisture correction data (MC) are used as input for Neuron–Adaptive Higher Order

Figure 5. ANSER Structure with using neuron-adaptive higher order neural networks

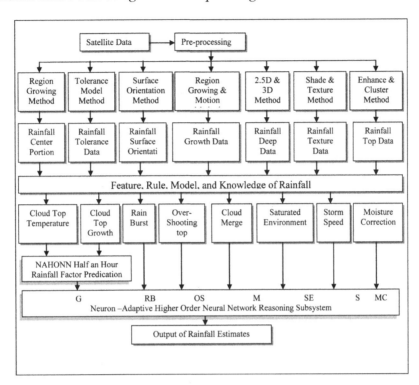

Neural Network Reasoning Subsystem. The output of Neuron–Adaptive Higher Order Neural Network Reasoning Subsystem is the rainfall estimation.

3.2 The Structures of NAHONNs for ANSER System

The two-dimensional Neuron-Adaptive Higher Order Neural Network is used for rainfall estimate factor G. Details are:

Let: $Z_1 = G$ (Rainfall estimate factor)

$\quad$ x $\quad$ = cloud top temperature

$\quad$ y $\quad$ = cloud growth

$$G = \sum_{i=0}^{3} a_{1,i,k+1} \cdot \Phi_{i,k}\left(net_{i,x,k}, net_{i,y,k}\right)$$

$$= \sum_{i=0}^{3} a_{1,i,k+1} \cdot \sum_{h=1,3} f_{i,k,h}\left(a_{i,x,k} \cdot x, a_{i,y,k} \cdot y\right)$$

$$= \sum_{i=0}^{3} a_{1,i,k+1} \cdot \big(\ (a1_{i,k} \cdot \sin^{c1_{i,k}}\left(b1_{i,k} \cdot (a_{i,x,k} \cdot x)\right) \cdot \sin^{e1_{i,k}}\left(d1_{i,k} \cdot (a_{i,y,k} \cdot y)\right)$$
$$+ a3_{i,k} \cdot \frac{1}{1+e^{-b3_{i,k} \cdot (a_{i,x,k} \cdot x)}} \cdot \frac{1}{1+e^{-d3_{i,k} \cdot (a_{i,y,k} \cdot y)}}))$$

Figure 6.

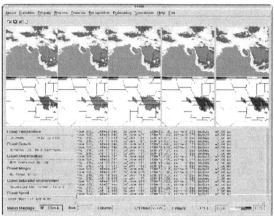

A   The Interface of the ANSER System

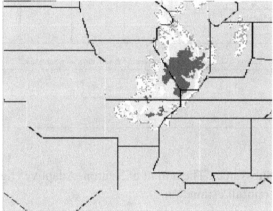

B   Output of Rainfall Estimate

Day: May 9th 2000		Time: 18Z
	Min	Max
LAT	37.032	38.765
LAN	87.906	88.480
NAVY	Rainfall 2.00mm	Rainfall 6.0 mm
ANSER	Rainfall 1.47mm	Rainfall 6.37mm

where

$$a1_{i,k}, \; b1_{i,k}, \; c1_{i,k}, \; d1_{i,k}, e1_{i,k}, a3_{i,k}, \; b3_{i,k}, d3_{i,k}$$

are free parameters which can be adjusted (as well as weights) during training.

The network structure of the two-dimensional *NAHONN* is in Figure 7. It consists of an input layer with *two* input-units, an output layer with one output-unit, and one hidden layer consisting of 3 neuron-adaptive neurons. The structures of neuron-adaptive neurons ($\Phi_{i,k}$) in NAHONN for Rainfall Estimate Factor G is depicted in Figure 8.

Figure 7. NAHONN for rainfall estimate factor

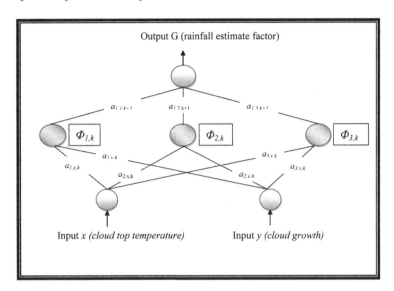

3.3 Results of NAHONN for Rainfall Estimate Factor

The results of comparative analysis experiments using *NAN, ANN, and NNG* are also presented, paying particular attention to error accuracy. The aim of this comparative analysis is to compare the features of NAHONN with NAN, ANN, and NNG models. Standard practice with comparison experiments is to ensure the same environmental conditions throughout. Accordingly, the same groups of testing data and same parameters were used for all three models (namely learning rate, number of hidden layers and so forth). In order to test rainfall simulations, we used expert knowledge to train NAHONN model. For example, when the cloud top temperature is between -58°C and -60°C, and the cloud growth is more than 2/3 latitude, the half hour rainfall estimate is 0.94 inch, according to experts from the Scofield (1987) of NOAA. Details of this expert knowledge are listed in the Table 1. The values in the table are ground truth based on the Scofield (1987) of NOAA. Table 1 presents the rainfall data estimation results using *ANN*(Artificial Neural Network), *NNG*(artificial Neural Network Group), *NAN*(artificial Neuron-Adaptive Neural network), and NAHONN(artificial Neuron-Adaptive Higher Order Neural Network) models. The average errors of *ANN, NNG, NAN,* and NAHONN are 6.32%, 5.42%, 5.32%, and 4.41% respectively. This means the *NAHONNN* model is about 17.1% better than the *NAN* model when using the rainfall estimate experimental database of Table 7.1; likewise *NAHONN* is around 18.6% better than NNG and 30.6% better than ANN model.

3.4 NAHONN Reasoning Network Structure

The basic architecture of the reasoning network for half-hourly satellite-derived rainfall estimation is a 3-layer 7-dimensional NAHONN model, comprising 7 input neurons, 5 adaptive neurons and 1 output neuron. The structure of the NAHONN mode for reasoning is shown in Figure 9. The structures of neuron-adaptive neurons ($\Phi_{i,k}$) in NAHONN for Rainfall Estimate is depicted in Figure 10.

Figure 8. NAHONN $\Phi_{i,k}$ Structure for rainfall estimate Factor G

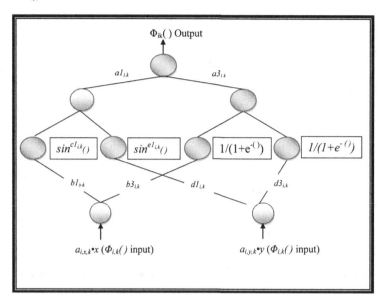

Let: Z_l = Half Hour Rainfall Estimates (inches)

x_1: G; x_2: RB; x_3: OS; x_4: M; x_5: MC; x_6: SE; x_7: S

$$
\begin{aligned}
G &= \sum_{i=0}^{5} a_{1,i,k+1} \cdot \Phi_{i,k}\left(net_{i,1,k}, net_{i,2,k}, net_{i,3,k}, net_{i,4,k}, net_{i,5,k}, net_{i,6,k}, net_{i,7,k}\right) \\
&= \sum_{i=0}^{5} a_{1,i,k+1} \cdot \sum_{h=1,3} f_{i,k,h}\left(a_{i,1,k} \cdot x_1, a_{i,2,k} \cdot x_2, a_{i,3,k} \cdot x_3, a_{i,4,k} \cdot x_4, a_{i,5,k} \cdot x_5, a_{i,6,k} \cdot x_6, a_{i,7,k} \cdot x_7\right)
\end{aligned}
$$

$$
= \sum_{i=0}^{5} a_{1,i,k+1} \cdot \left(\; (a1_{i,k} \cdot \prod_{m=1}^{7} \; \sin^{c1_{m,i,k}}\left(b1_{m,i,k} \cdot (a_{i,m,k} \cdot x_m)\right) \right.
$$

$$
\left. + \; a3_{i,k} \cdot \prod_{m=1}^{7} \; (\frac{1}{1+e^{-b3_{m,i,k} \cdot (a_{i,m,k} \cdot x_m)}}) \right)
$$

Figure 9. NAHONN for rainfall estimate

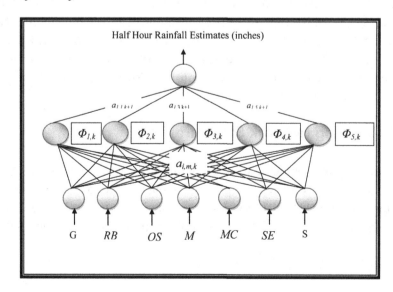

Table 1. Rainfall data simulation using ANN, NNG, NAN, and NAHONN models

Cloud Top Temperature	Cloud Growth Latitude Degree	Half Hour Rainfall inches	ANN |Error|%	NNG |Error| %	NAN |Error|%	NAHONN |Error|%
> -32° C	2/3	0.05	3.22	8.78	7.89	4.69
-36° C	2/3	0.20	9.92	6.52	6.97	5.34
-46° C	2/3	0.48	25.19	22.58	21.43	9.65
-55° C	2/3	0.79	14.63	14.21	15.32	8.32
-60° C	2/3	0.94	3.66	0.12	1.13	2.53
> - 32° C	1/3	0.05	10.47	8.03	7.56	6.34
- 36° C	1/3	0.13	3.50	4.18	4.09	5.63
- 46° C	1/3	0.24	3.52	4.24	4.21	5.12
- 55° C	1/3	0.43	0.22	1.89	1.84	3.21
- 60° C	1/3	0.65	3.21	0.65	0.75	2.14
- 70° C	1/3	0.85	9.01	5.12	4.56	3.24
< - 80° C	1/3	0.95	3.89	1.32	1.24	2.21
> -32° C	0	0.03	9.81	7.24	6.54	5.84
- 36° C	0	0.06	2.98	3.25	3.45	4.25
- 46° C	0	0.11	5.69	5.67	5.76	5.23
- 55° C	0	0.22	5.28	4.03	4.21	5.22
- 60° C	0	0.36	3.32	1.43	1.26	2.17
-70° C	0	0.49	0.77	2.78	1.76	1.52
< -80° C	0	0.55	2.50	1.12	1.08	1.23
Average			6.36	5.42	5.32	4.41

where

$a1_{i,k}$, $b1_{m,i,k}$, $c1_{mi,k}$, $a3_{i,k}$, $b3_{m,i,k}$ are weights of NAHOOH.

The inputs to and outputs from this reasoning network are as follows:

Inputs: G, RB, OS, M, MC, SE, S
Output: half-hourly satellite-derived rainfall estimates

Once the input data become available, they are *simultaneously* fed into the reasoning network. The reasoning network has been trained using the inputs from the above 7 factors and desired output data from the observation grand data. After training the reasoning rules, models, and knowledge (Now we can use the weighs and activation functions to describe the relationship between input and output) are stored in the weights of the (massively-parallel) NAHONN higher order neural network, so the reasoning network is capable of estimating rainfall using all rules and models simultaneously. This results in fast operation, especially when the rules, models, knowledge and factors are complex, nonlinear and discontinuous. Therefore, by using a massively parallel NAHONN reasoning network, rainfall estimates can be obtained quicker and more accurately. Using these weights, an NAHONN model and the SUN

Figure 10. NAHONN $\Phi_{i,k}$ Structure for Half Hour Rainfall Estimates

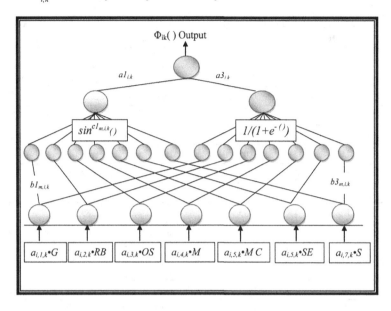

workstation, estimation of the total aerial rainfall took only several seconds, once all the input data were fed into the reasoning network.

3.5 Rainfall Estimation Results Using NAHONN Model

A comparison of the results of statistics method (Xie and Scofield, 1989), an ANN reasoning network (Zhang and Scofield, 1994), a neural network group (Zhang, Fulcher, and Scofield, 1997), the NAN model Zhang, Xu, and Fulcher, 2007), and the NAHONN model of the present study is presented in Table 2. When the Xie & Scofield technique was used, the average error of the operator-computed IFFA rainfall estimates was 30.41%. For the ANN reasoning network, the training error was 6.55% and the test error 16.91%, respectively. When the neural network group was used on these same fifteen cases, the average training error of rainfall estimation was 1.43%, and the average test error of rainfall estimation was 3.89%. When the neuron-adaptive artificial neural network group models was used on these same fifteen cases, the average training error of rainfall estimation was 1.31%, and the average test error of rainfall estimation was 3.40%.

When the artificial neuron-adaptive higher order neural network model was used on these same fifteen cases, the average training error of rainfall estimation was 1.20%, and the average test error of rainfall estimation was 3.12%.

Let us now consider a specific example (case 08 of Table 3): the rainfall estimation error resulting from Xie & Scofield's study is +96.21%, which falls to 18.2% with the ANN reasoning network. When the neural network group is used, the rainfall estimation test error is only -0.74%. However, when the NAN model is used, the rainfall estimation test error falls to -0.72%. When NAHONN model is used, the rainfall estimation test error is -0.67%. The *largest* observed error using the ANSER technique (incorporating a neuron-adaptive HONN model) is only +7.33% (case 10 of Table 2). By contrast, the largest error reported by Xie & Scofield was 96.21% (case 8 of Table 2).

Table 2. Satellite-derived precipitation estimates

No.	Date	Location	Observation (Inch)	X/S Error %	ANN Error %	NNG Error %	NAN Error %	NAHONN Error %
1 #	07/19/85	NY	6.0	+0.83	+14.0	+6.28	+4.36	3.56
2 *	05/16/86	IL/ MO	7.0	+10.0	-5.52	-3.37	-2.57	-2.32
3 *	08/04/82	WI	5.3	+62.08	-8.30	-1.64	-1.72	-1.83
4 *	05/03/87	MO	7.0	+47.86	-10.39	-0.94	-1.12	-0.93
5 *	05/26/87	IA	5.8	-18.62	-7.08	-1.64	-1.38	-1.27
6 #	08/13/87	KS	12.2	+16.62	+15.25	+1.59	+1.61	1.89
7 #	08/12/87	KS	8.7	-30.57	-21.0	-1.92	-1.74	-1.83
8 #	07/19/85	IA	9.5	+96.21	+18.2	-0.74	-0.72	-0.67
9 #	08/22/85	KS	4.2	-22.86	-13.3	+4.12	+3.83	+3.42
10 #	07/02/83	IL	5.2	+13.65	+18.1	+8.71	+7.65	+7.33
11 *	05/01/83	MO	6.0	-31.17	+4.0	+0.72	+0.65	+0.45
12 #	05/27/85	MO	4.2	+2.62	+18.5	-3.88	-3.84	-3.82
13 *	09/05/85	KS	6.2	-5.16	-1.90	-0.90	-0.87	-0.76
14 *	07/15/84	IA	5.0	+78.4	+8.80	+1.20	+1.18	+1.21
15 *	07/16/84	TN	4.2	+19.52	+6.43	-1.00	-0.98	-0.81
			Average |Error| %	30.41	6.55 * 16.91 #	1.43 * 3.89 #	1.31* 3.40 #	1.20* 3.12 #

X/S: Xie/Scofield's study

ANN: Artificial Neural Network multi layer perceptron as basic reasoning network

NNG: Neural Network Group used as reasoning network

NAN: Neuron-Adaptive artificial neural network as reasoning network in ANSER

NAHONN: artificial Neuron-Adaptive Higher Order Neural Network as reasoning network

*: Training cases for training neural network(s)

#: Test cases

4 CONCLUSION

In this chapter, we have presented *NAHONN* models with neuron-adaptive activation functions to automatically model any continuous function. Experiments with rainfall estimate data simulation indicate that the proposed *NAHONN* models offer significant advantages over traditional neural networks, which including much reduced network size, faster learning, and smaller simulation error.

Definitions of one-dimensional, two-dimensional, n-dimensional, and multi n-dimensional *NAHONN* models are studied. Specialized NAHONN models are also described. *NAHONN* models are shown to be "open box". These models are further shown to be capable of automatically finding not only the optimum model but also the appropriate order for high frequency, multi-polynomial, discontinuous data. Rainfall estimation experimental results confirm model convergence. We further demonstrate that *NAHONN* models are capable of modeling satellite data. When the Xie and Scofield (1989) technique was used, the average error of the operator-computed IFFA rainfall estimates was 30.41%. For the Artificial Neural Network (ANN) reasoning network, the training error was 6.55% and the test error 16.91%, respectively. When the neural network group was used on these same fifteen cases, the average training error of rainfall estimation was 1.43%, and the average test error of rainfall estimation was 3.89%. When the neuron-adaptive artificial neural network group models was used on these same fifteen cases, the average training error of rainfall estimation was 1.31%, and the average test error of rainfall estimation was 3.40%. When the artificial neuron-adaptive higher order neural network model was used on these same fifteen cases, the average training error of rainfall estimation was 1.20%, and the average test error of rainfall estimation was 3.12%. Neuron-adaptive higher order neural network models hold considerable promise for both the understanding and development of complex systems. Neuron-adaptive higher order neural network research remains open-ended, and holds considerable potential for developing complex systems.

ACKNOWLEDGMENT

Initial funding for this work was from Fujitsu Research Laboratories, Japan. It received subsequent support in the form of grants from both the University of Western Sydney and the Australia National Research Council. The theoretical work contained herein was performed while Dr. Ming Zhang was the recipient of a USA National Research Council Senior Research Associateship at the National Environmental Satellite Data and Information Service of NOAA. Dr. Ming Zhang would also like to thank the support from the Christopher Newport University.

REFERENCES

Abdelbar, A. M., & Tagliarini, G. A. (1998, May 4-9). A hybrid Bayesian neural learning strategy applied to CONNECT-4. In *Proceeding of the IEEE World Congress on Computational Intelligence* (vol.1, pp.402 – 407).

Alanis, A. Y., Sanchez, E. N., & Loukianov, A. G. (2006, July 16-21). Discrete- Time Recurrent Neural Induction Motor Control using Kalman Learning. In *Proceedings of International Joint Conference on Neural Networks* (pp.1993 – 2000).

An, Z. G., Mniszewski, S. M., Lee, Y. C., Papcun, G., & Doolen, G. D. (1988, March 14-18). HIERtalker: a default hierarchy of high order neural networks that learns to read English aloud. In *Proceedings of the Fourth Conference on Artificial Intelligence Applications* (pp.388).

An, Z. G., Mniszewski, S. M., Lee, Y. C., Papcun, G., & Doolen, G. D. (1988, July 24-27). HIERtalker: a default hierarchy of high order neural networks that learns to read English aloud. In . *Proceedings of IEEE International Conference on Neural Networks, 2,* 221–228. doi:10.1109/ICNN.1988.23932

Baldi, P., & Venkatesh, S. S. (1993). Random interactions in higher order neural networks. *IEEE Transactions on Information Theory, 39*(1), 274–283. doi:10.1109/18.179374

Bouzerdoum, A. (1999, November 16-20). A new class of high-order neural networks with nonlinear decision boundaries. In . *Proceedings of International Conference on Neural Information Processing, 3,* 1004–1009.

Brucoli, M., Carnimeo, L., & Grassi, G. (1997). Associative memory design using discrete-time second-order neural networks with local interconnections. *IEEE Transactions on Circuits and Systems. I, Fundamental Theory and Applications*, *44*(2), 153–158. doi:10.1109/81.554334

Burshtein, D. (1998). Long-term attraction in higher order neural networks. *IEEE Transactions on Neural Networks*, *9*(1), 42–50. doi:10.1109/72.655028

Butt, N. R., & Shafiq, M. (2006, April 22-23). Higher-Order Neural Network Based Root-Solving Controller for Adaptive Tracking of Stable Nonlinear Plants. In *Proceedings of IEEE International Conference on Engineering of Intelligent Systems* (pp.1 – 6).

Campos, J., Loukianov, A. G., & Sanchez, E. N. (2003, December 9-12). Synchronous motor VSS control using recurrent high order neural networks. In *Proceedings of 42nd IEEE Conference on Decision and Control* (vol. 4, pp.3894 – 3899)

Chang, C., & Cheung, J. Y. (1992, June 7-11). Backpropagation algorithm in higher order neural network. In . *Proceedings of International Joint Conference on Neural Networks*, *3*, 511–516.

Chang, C.-H., Lin, J.-L., & Cheung, J.-Y. (1993, March 28). Polynomial and standard higher order neural network. In . *Proceedings of IEEE International Conference on Neural Networks*, *2*, 989–994. doi:10.1109/ICNN.1993.298692

Christodoulou, M., & Zarkogianni, D. (2006, June). Recurrent High Order Neural Networks for Identification of the EGFR Signaling Pathway. In *Proceedings of 2006. MED '06. 14th Mediterranean Conference on Control and Automation* (pp.1 – 6).

Christodoulou, M. A., & Iliopoulos, T. N. (2006, June). Neural Network Models for Prediction of Steady-State and Dynamic Behavior of MAPK Cascade. In *Proceedings of 14th Mediterranean Conference on Control and Automation* (pp.1 – 9).

Cooper, B. S. (1995, November 27). Higher order neural networks for combinatorial optimisation improving the scaling properties of the Hopfield network. In . *Proceedings of IEEE International Conference on Neural Networks*, *4*, 1855–1860. doi:10.1109/ICNN.1995.488904

Estevez, P. A., & Okabe, Y. (1991, November 18-21). Training the piecewise linear-high order neural network through error back propagation. In [).Seattle, USA.]. *Proceedings of IEEE International Joint Conference on Neural Networks*, *1*, 711–716. doi:10.1109/IJCNN.1991.170483

Ge, S. S., Zhang, J., & Lee, T. H. (2004). Adaptive neural network control for a class of MIMO nonlinear systems with disturbances in discrete-time. *IEEE Transactions on Systems, Man and Cybernetics . Part B*, *34*(4), 1630–1645.

Gulez, K., Mutoh, N., Harashima, F., Ohnishi, K., & Pastaci, H. (2000, October 22-28). Design of a HONN (high order neural network) by using a DSP based system for the performance increasing of an induction motor under changeable load. In *Proceedings of 26th Annual Conference of the IEEE on Industrial Electronics Society* (Vol. 4, pp. 2315 – 2320).

Heywood, M., & Noakes, P. (1993, March 28). Simple addition to back-propagation learning for dynamic weight pruning, sparse network extraction and faster learning. In . *Proceedings of the IEEE International Conference on Neural Networks, 2,* 620–625. doi:10.1109/ICNN.1993.298546

Jeffries, C. (1989, March 26-28). Dense memory with high order neural networks. In *Proceedings of Twenty-First Southeastern Symposium on System Theory* (pp.436 – 439).

Jeffries, C. (1989, June 18-22). High order neural networks. In . *Proceedings of International Joint Conference on Neural Networks, 2,* 594. doi:10.1109/IJCNN.1989.118384

Kariniotakis, G. N., Stavrakakis, G. S., & Nogaret, E. F. (1996). Wind power forecasting using advanced neural networks models. *IEEE Transactions on Energy Conversion, 11*(4), 762–767. doi:10.1109/60.556376

Kosmatopoulos, E. B., & Christodoulou, M. A. (1994). Filtering, prediction, and learning properties of ECE neural networks. *IEEE Transactions on Systems, Man, and Cybernetics, 24*(7), 971–981. doi:10.1109/21.297787

Kosmatopoulos, E. B., & Christodoulou, M. A. (1995). Structural properties of gradient recurrent high-order neural networks. *IEEE Transactions on Circuits and Systems II: Analog and Digital Signal Processing, 42*(9), 592–603. doi:10.1109/82.466645

Kosmatopoulos, E. B., & Christodoulou, M. A. (1997). High-order neural networks for the learning of robot contact surface shape. *IEEE Transactions on Robotics and Automation, 13*(3), 451–455. doi:10.1109/70.585906

Kosmatopoulos, E. B., Ioannou, P. A., & Christodoulou, M. A. (1992, December 16-18). Identification of nonlinear systems using new dynamic neural network structures. In *Proceedings of the 31st IEEE Conference on Decision and Control* (vol.1, pp. 20 – 25).

Kosmatopoulos, E. B., Polycarpou, M. M., Christodoulou, M. A., & Ioannou, P. A. (1995). High-order neural network structures for identification of dynamical systems. *IEEE Transactions on Neural Networks, 6*(2), 422–431. doi:10.1109/72.363477

Kuroe, Y. (2004, August 4-6). Learning and identifying finite state automata with recurrent high-order neural networks.In *Proceedings of SICE 2004 Annual Conference* (vol. 3, pp.2241 – 2246).

Kuroe, Y., Ikeda, H., & Mori, T. (1997, October 12-15). Identification of nonlinear dynamical systems by recurrent high-order neural networks. In . *Proceedings of IEEE International Conference on Systems, Man, and Cybernetics, 1,* 70–75.

Lee, M., Lee, S. Y., & Park, C. H. (1992). Neural controller of nonlinear dynamic systems using higher order neural networks. *Electronics Letters, 28*(3), 276–277. doi:10.1049/el:19920170

Li, D., Hirasawa, K., & Hu, J. (2003, August 4-6). A new strategy for constructing higher order neural networks with multiplication units. In *Proceedings of SICE 2003 Annual Conference* (Vol. 3, pp. 2342 – 2347).

Li, W., Wang, Y., Li, W., Zhang, J., & Li, J. (1998, May 4-9). Sparselized higher-order neural network and its pruning algorithm. In *Proceedings of 1998 IEEE World Congress on Computational Intelligence* (Vol. 1, pp. 359 – 362).

Liatsis, P., Wellstead, P. E., Zarrop, M. B., & Prendergast, T. (1994, August 24-26). A versatile visual inspection tool for the manufacturing process. In *Proceedings of the Third IEEE Conference onControl Applications* (vol.3, pp. 1505 – 1510).

Lin, C., Wu, K., & Wang, J. (2005, October 10-12). Scale equalized higher-order neural networks. In *Proceedings of IEEE International Conference on Systems, Man and Cybernetics* (Vol. 1, pp. 816 – 821).

Liou, R.-J., & Azimi-Sadjadi, M. R. (1993). Dim target detection using high order correlation method. *IEEE Transactions on Aerospace and Electronic Systems, 29*(3), 841–856. doi:10.1109/7.220935

Machado, R. J. (1989, June 18-22). Handling knowledge in high order neural networks: the combinatorial neural model. In . *Proceedings of the International Joint Conference on Neural Networks, 2*, 582. doi:10.1109/IJCNN.1989.118339

Miyajima, H., Yatsuki, S., & Kubota, J. (1995. November 27-December 1). Dynamical properties of neural networks with product connections. In *Proceedingsof the IEEE International Conference on Neural Networks* (vol.6, pp. 3198 – 3203).

Qi, H., & Zhang, M. (2001, July 15-19). Rainfall estimation using M-PHONN model. In *Proceedings of International Joint Conference on Neural Networks* (Vol., pp.1620 – 1624).

Randolph, T. R., & Smith, M. J. T. (2000, December 17-20). A new approach to object classification in binary images. In *Proceeding of the 7th IEEE International Conference on Electronics, Circuits and Systems* (vol.1, pp.307 – 310).

Ricalde, L. J., & Sanchez, E. N. (2005, July 31). Inverse optimal nonlinear recurrent high order neural observer. In . *Proceedings of IEEE International Joint Conference on Neural Networks, 1*, 361–365. doi:10.1109/IJCNN.2005.1555857

Rovithakis, G., Gaganis, V., Perrakis, S., & Christodoulou, M. (1996, December 11-13). A recurrent neural network model to describe manufacturing cell dynamics. In *Proc. of the 35th IEEE Conf.on Decision and Control* (vol.2, pp.1728 – 1733).

Rovithakis, G., Maniadakis, M., & Zervakis, M. (2000, September 11-13). A genetically optimized artificial neural network structure for feature extraction and classification of vascular tissue fluorescence spectrums. In *Proceedings ofFifth IEEE International Workshop on Computer Architectures for Machine Perception* (pp.107 – 111).

Rovithakis, G. A. (1998, December 16-18). Reinforcing robustness using high order neural network controllers. In *Proceedings of the 37th IEEE Conference on Decision and Control* (vol.1, pp.1052 – 1057).

Rovithakis, G. A. (1999). Robustifying nonlinear systems using high-order neural network controllers. *IEEE Transactions on Automatic Control, 44*(1), 102–108. doi:10.1109/9.739082

Rovithakis, G. A. (2000). Performance of a neural adaptive tracking controller for multi-input nonlinear dynamical systems in the presence of additive and multiplicative external disturbances. *IEEE Transactions on Systems, Man and Cybernetics . Part A, 30*(6), 720–730.

Rovithakis, G. A. (2000, July 17-19). Robustness of a neural controller in the presence of additive and multiplicative external perturbations. In *Proceedings of the 2000 IEEE International Symposium on Intelligent Control* (pp. 7 – 12).

Rovithakis, G. A., Chalkiadakis, I., & Zervakis, M. E. (2004). High-order neural network structure selection for function approximation applications using genetic algorithms. *IEEE Transactions on Systems, Man and Cybernetics . Part B, 34*(1), 150–158.

Rovithakis, G. A., Gaganis, V. I., Perrakis, S. E., & Christodoulou, M. A. (1998, December 16-18). High order neural networks to control manufacturing systems-a comparison study. *Proceedings of the 37th IEEE Conference on Decision and Control* (vol.3, pp.2736 – 2737).

Rovithakis, G. A., Kosmatopoulos, E. B., & Christodoulou, M. A. (1993, October 17-20). Robust adaptive control of unknown plants using recurrent high order neural networks-application to mechanical systems. In *Proceedings of International Conference on Systems, Man and Cybernetics* (vol.4, pp. 57 – 62).

Rovithakis, G. A., Malamos, A. G., Varvarigon, T., & Christodoulou, M. A. (1998, December 16-18). Quality assurance in networks-a high order neural net approach. In *Proceedings of the 37th IEEE Conference on Decision and Control* (vol.2, pp.1599 – 1604).

Rovithakis, G. A., Maniadakis, M., & Zervakis, M. (2000, June 5-9). Artificial neural networks for feature extraction and classification of vascular tissue fluorescence spectrums. In *Proceedings. 2000 IEEE International Conference on Acoustics, Speech, and Signal Processing* (vol.6, pp.3454 – 3457).

Salem, G. J., & Young, T. Y. (1991, July 8-14). Interpreting line drawings with higher order neural networks. In []. Seattle, USA.]. *Proceedings of the International Joint Conference on Neural Networks, 1*, 713–721.

Scofield, R. A. (1987). The NESDIS operational convective precipitation estimation technique. *Monthly Weather Review, 115*, 1773–1792. doi:10.1175/1520-0493(1987)115<1773:TNOCPE>2.0.CO;2

Siddiqi, A. A. (2005, August 16-18). Genetically evolving higher order neural networks by direct encoding method. In *Proceedings of Sixth International Conference on Computational Intelligence and Multimedia Applications* (pp. 62 – 67).

Starke, J., Kubota, N., & Fukuda, T. (1995, November 27). Combinatorial optimization with higher order neural networks-cost oriented competing processes in flexible manufacturing systems. In . *Proceedings of IEEE International Conference on Neural Networks, 5*, 2658–2663. doi:10.1109/ICNN.1995.487830

Tanaka, K., & Kumazawa, I. (1996, June 3-6). Learning regular languages via recurrent higher-order neural networks. In . *Proceedings of IEEE International Conference on Neural Networks, 2*, 1378–1383.

Tseng, Y.-H., & Wu, J.-L. (1994, June 27-July1). Constant-time neural decoders for some BCH codes. In *Proceedings of IEEE International Symposium on Information Theory* (pp.343).

Vidyasagar, M. (1993, March 28). Convergence of higher-order neural networks with modified updating. In . *Proceedings of the IEEE International Conference on Neural Networks, 3*, 1379–1384. doi:10.1109/ICNN.1993.298758

Villalobos, L., & Merat, F. L. (1995). Learning capability assessment and feature space optimization for higher-order neural networks. *IEEE Transactions on Neural Networks, 6*(1), 267–272. doi:10.1109/72.363427

Wang, J., Wu, K., & Chang, F. (2004, November 8-10). Scale equalization higher-order neural networks. In *Proceedings of the 2004 IEEE International Conference on Information Reuse and Integration* (612 – 617).

Wang, L. (1996). Suppressing chaos with hysteresis in a higher order neural network. *IEEE Transactions on Circuits and Systems II: Analog and Digital Signal Processing, 43*(12), 845–846. doi:10.1109/82.553405

Xie, J., & Scofield, R. A. (1989). Satellite-derived rainfall estimates and propagation characteristics associated with mesoscal convective system (MCSs). *NAOO Technical Memorandum NESDIS, 25*, 1–49.

Xu, S., & Zhang, M. (2002, November 18-22). An adaptive higher-order neural networks (AHONN) and its approximation capabilities. In *Proceedings of the 9th International Conference on Neural Information Processing* (Vol. 2, pp. 848 – 852).

Yamashita, T., Hirasawa, K., Hu, J., & Murata, J. (2002, November 18-22). Multi-branch structure of layered neural networks. In *Proceedings of the 9th International Conference on Neural Information Processing* (vol.1, pp.243 – 247).

Yang, H., & Guest, C. C. (1990, June 17-21). High order neural networks with reduced numbers of interconnection weights. In . *Proceedings of the International Joint Conference on Neural Networks, 3*, 281–286. doi:10.1109/IJCNN.1990.137857

Yatsuki, S., & Miyajima, H. (1997, June 9-12). Associative ability of higher order neural networks. In *Proceedings of International Conference on Neural Networks, 2*, 1299–1304.

Young, S., & Downs, T. (1993). Generalisation in higher order neural networks. *Electronics Letters, 29*(16), 1491–1493. doi:10.1049/el:19930996

Yu, S. J., & Liang, D. N. (1995, May 22-26). Neural network based approach for eigenstructure extraction. In *Proceedings of the IEEE 1995 National Aerospace and Electronics Conference* (vol.1, pp. 102 – 105).

Zardoshti-Kermani, M., & Afshordi, A. (1995, November 27). Classification of chromosomes using higher-order neural networks. In . *Proceedings of IEEE International Conference on Neural Networks, 5*, 2587–2591. doi:10.1109/ICNN.1995.487816

Zhang, J., Ge, S. S., & Lee, T. H. (2005). Output feedback control of a class of discrete MIMO nonlinear systems with triangular form inputs. *IEEE Transactions on Neural Networks, 16*(6), 1491–1503. doi:10.1109/TNN.2005.852242

Zhang, J. C., Zhang, M., & Fulcher, J. (1997, March 24-25). Financial simulation system using a higher order trigonometric polynomial neural network group model. In *Proceedings of the IEEE/IAFE 1997 Computational Intelligence for Financial Engineering (CIFEr)* (pp.189 – 194).

Zhang, M. Xu. S., Lu, B. (1999, July 10-16). Neuron-adaptive higher order neural network group models. In *Proceedings of International Joint Conference on Neural Networks* (Vol. 1, pp. 333 - 336).

Zhang, M. (2001, July 15-19). Financial data simulation using A-PHONN model. *In Proceedings of International Joint Conference on Neural Networks* (Volume 3, pp.1823 – 1827).

Zhang, M., & Bo Lu (2001, July 15-19). Financial data simulation using M-PHONN model. In *Proceedings of IJCNN '01. International Joint Conference on Neural Networks* (vol.3, pp.1828 – 1832).

Zhang, M. (2009A). *Artificial Higher Order Neural Networks for Economics and Business*. Hershey, PA: IGI-Global.

Zhang, M. (2009B). Artificial Higher Order Neural Network Nonlinear Models: SAS NLIN or HONNs? In Book chapter in Ming Zhang (Editor), *Artificial Higher Order Neural Networks for Economics and Business* (pp. 1-47), Hershey PA: IGI-Global.

Zhang, M. (2009C). Ultra High Frequency Trigonometric Higher Order Neural Networks, Book chapter in Ming Zhang (Editor), *Artificial Higher Order Neural Networks for Economics and Business* (pp. 133-163), Hershey, PA:IGI-Global.

Zhang, M., Fulcher, J., & Scofield, R. (1997). Rainfall estimation using artificial neural network group. *Neurocomputing, 16*(2), 97–115. doi:10.1016/S0925-2312(96)00022-7

Zhang, M., & Scofield, R. A. (1994). Artificial neural network techniques for estimating heavy convective rainfall and recognition cloud mergers from satellite data. *International Journal of Remote Sensing, 15*(16), 3241–3262. doi:10.1080/01431169408954324

Zhang, M., & Scofield, R. A. (2001, July 15-19). Rainfall estimation using A-PHONN model. In . *Proceedings of International Joint Conference on Neural Networks, 3*, 1583–1587.

Zhang, M., Xu, S., & Fulcher, J. (2002). Neuron-adaptive higher order neural-network models for automated financial data modeling. *IEEE Transactions on Neural Networks, 13*(1), 188–204. doi:10.1109/72.977302

Zhang, M., Xu, S., & Fulcher, J. (2007). ANSER: adaptive neuron artificial neural network system for estimating rainfall. *International Journal of Computers and Applications, 29*(3), 215–222. doi:10.2316/Journal.202.2007.3.202-1585

Zhang, Y., Liu, W. F., Li, Y., Liu, X. L., & Ouyang, K. (2002). Translation and rotation invariance of physiological signal in long-term custody. In *Proceedings of 24th Annual Conference and the Annual Fall Meeting of the Biomedical Engineering Society* (vol.1, pp. 250 – 251).

Zhang, Y., Peng, P. Y., & Rovithakis, G. A. (2000). Comments on "Robustifying nonlinear systems using high-order neural network controllers". *IEEE Transactions on Automatic Control, 45*(5), 1033–1036. doi:10.1109/9.855579

Chapter 8
Analysis of Quantization Effects on Higher Order Function and Multilayer Feedforward Neural Networks

Minghu Jiang
Tsinghua University, China

Georges Gielen
Katholieke Universiteit Leuven, Belgium

Lin Wang
Beijing University of Posts and Telecom, China

ABSTRACT

In this chapter we investigate the combined effects of quantization and clipping on Higher Order function neural networks (HOFNN) and multilayer feedforward neural networks (MLFNN). Statistical models are used to analyze the effects of quantization in a digital implementation. We analyze the performance degradation caused as a function of the number of fixed-point and floating-point quantization bits under the assumption of different probability distributions for the quantized variables, and then compare the training performance between situations with and without weight clipping, and derive in detail the effect of the quantization error on forward and backward propagation. No matter what distribution the initial weights comply with, the weights distribution will approximate a normal distribution for the training of floating-point or high-precision fixed-point quantization. Only when the number of quantization bits is very low, the weights distribution may cluster to ±1 for the training with fixed-point quantization. We establish and analyze the relationships for a true nonlinear neuron between inputs and outputs bit resolution, training and quantization methods, the number of network layers, network order and performance degradation, all based on statistical models, and for on-chip and off-chip training. Our experimental simulation results verify the presented theoretical analysis.

DOI: 10.4018/978-1-61520-711-4.ch008

1. INTRODUCTION

Reducing the number of quantization bits in digitally implemented neural networks affects their circuit size or response time, and can diversify their applicability to areas such as pattern recognition or function approximation. This may lead to an increased interest in task-specific hardware implementation of neural networks (Kashefi, 1999; Hollis & Paulos, 1990; Lont & Guggenbuhl, 1992). Generally, a smaller number of quantization bits reduces VLSI surface area, while a larger number of quantization bits enables higher accuracy but increases the required complexity, the cost of the hardware and the response time of the neural networks. Hardware implementations of neural networks are characterized by low numerical precision. However, most of the standard algorithms for training of neural networks are not suitable for networks with quantization because they are based on gradient descent and require a high accuracy of the network parameters (Sakaue, Kohda & Yamamoto, et al. 1993). As a rule, designers must balance implementation accuracy and performance reliability. Several weight-quantization techniques have been developed to further reduce the required accuracy without deterioration of the network performance (Montalvo, Gyurcsik & Paulos, 1997). These algorithms offer hardware-friendly learning rules in case of limited accuracy and further improve the performance of neural networks.

The purpose of this work is to analyze in detail the impact of quantization on the performance of HOFNN and MLFNN for different probability distributions. The main contents of this chapter are the following. We investigate the combined effects of quantization and clipping on HOFNN and MLFNN performance towards more reliable and simple hardware implementations, and analyze the performance degradation caused by fixed-point and floating-point quantizations. We investigate how to make the effects of quantization as small as possible; how many bits are needed for backpropagation (BP) training and recall, and what HOFNN order and what MLFNN layer are necessary to represent physical states, parameters and variables to ensure a certain level of training and nonlinear mapping ability within given requirements. We adopt uniform probability distribution and normal probability distribution statistical models, and use a realistic sigmoid or hyperbolic tangent function as quantization error analysis for a true nonlinear neuron. We compare the training performances with and without weight clipping, and analyze the tendencies of the weights distribution in training with floating-point and fixed-point quantizations.

We derive in detail the effect of the quantization error on forward and backward propagation, and our method is less limited and based on more in-depth mathematical analysis. We establish and analyze the relationships for a true nonlinear neuron between inputs and outputs bit resolution, as well as the order, number of network layers and performance degradation, based on statistical models of on-chip and off-chip training.

This chapter is organized as follows. Section II demonstrates the theoretical analysis of quantization and its effects in the HOFNN and MLFNN. From statistical models, we establish the relationships among inputs and outputs bit resolution, network order number, number of layers and performance degradation for both fixed-point and floating-point quantizations. In Section III, experimental results are presented. The simulation results verify and confirm the theoretical analysis. Section IV summarizes the conclusions of this chapter. Finally, the mathematical proofs are contained in the appendices.

2. QUANTIZATION ANALYSIS OF HOFNN AND MLFNN

In order to increase the reliability of the analysis results and to more accurately predict the quantization error and the properties of the network, the true function of a nonlinear neuron (i.e., a realistic hyperbolic tangent function as activation function) is used with two different probability distributions.

2.1 Mathematical principle of HOFNN

Assuming that an N-dimensional pattern is nonlinearly expanded to N_w dimensions, the output of the HOFNN for node i can be written as:

$$\tilde{y}_i^{H-th} = f(y_i^{H-th}) = \tanh(\lambda y_i^{H-th} / N_w)$$

$$= \tanh(\lambda(\sum_{p_1=1}^{N} \sum_{p_2=p_1}^{N} \cdots \sum_{p_H=p_{H-1}}^{N} w_{i,p_1 p_2 \cdots p_H} x_{p_1} x_{p_2} \cdots x_{p_H} + \cdots$$

$$+ \sum_{p_1=1}^{N} \sum_{p_2=p_1}^{N} w_{i,p_1 p_2} x_{p_1} x_{p_2} + \sum_{p_1=1}^{N} w_{i,p_1} x_{p_1} + w_{i,N_w}) / N_w) \tag{1}$$

where $p_1, p_2, \cdots, p_H = 1, 2, \cdots, N$; $i = 1, 2, \cdots, s$ $N_w = C_{N+H}^H = \dfrac{(H+N)!}{H!N!}$; $x_{N_w} = 1$ and $w_{i,N_w} = \theta_{i,N_w}$

(denote the neuron's bias and threshold respectively); N is the dimension of the pattern, H is the order of the network, and s is the number of output nodes. λ is an amplifying factor decided by experiment; λ / N_w is a normalized factor which renders the input scale of internal activation in each neuron independent of the fan-in number and can decrease the chances that the network's output falls into a false saturated state. Moreover, it increases the ability of escaping from a false saturated output state or of breaking away from local minima (Reyner & Filippi, 1991).

2.2 Quantization and Clipping

For fixed-point quantization, assuming that signal x is quantised with M bits, a quantized function $Q(x)$ with a combination of quantization and clipping is as follows:

$$Q(x) = \begin{cases} q \cdot 2^{M-1}, & if & x > q \cdot 2^{M-1} = x_{max} \\ m \cdot q, & if\, m < 2^{M-1}\, \& & (m-1/2) \cdot q \leq x \leq (m+1/2) \cdot q \\ -q \cdot 2^{M-1}, & if & x < -q \cdot 2^{M-1} = -x_{max} \end{cases}, \tag{2}$$

where m is an integer, $x_{max} = 2^{M-1} q$ is the signal's maximal absolute value, and q is the quantization width. The performance of finite precision depends on the computational method, with the performance of floating-point quantization being higher than fixed-point quantization under the same word length. The dynamic range of the former is larger than the latter, although the implementation of the latter is simpler and its price lower. For the fixed-point quantization (Oppenheim & Schaffer, 1975), assuming that the quantization error of inputs and weights (independent of each other) is distributed uniformly in a certain range $[-q/2, q/2]$ and is a stationary random process of white noise, then its mean is zero and its variance is $\sigma_\Delta^2 = q^2 / 12$ For floating-point quantization (Oppenheim & Schaffer, 1975), the numbers are represented as: $(-1)^S * 2^{c} * T$, where mantissa T within $[1/2,1]$ is a pure binary fraction, S is the sign bit, and c represents the exponent bits of a non-negative integer. As the dynamic range of floating-point quantization is very large, overflow does not easily occur. After the floating-point quantization, the weight or the signal x becomes $Q[x] = x(1+\varepsilon) = x + e$, where $-q < \varepsilon < q$ is a relative error, with zero mean and variance $\sigma_\varepsilon^2 = q^2 / 3$.

2.3 The Fixed-Point Quantization Analysis of the 1ˢᵗ-Order Function Neural Network (FNN)

The internal activation of output node i for the 1ˢᵗ–order FNN is:

$$y_i^{1-st} = \sum_{p_1=1}^{N+1} w_{i,p_1} x_{p_1} . \tag{3}$$

After quantization, y_i^{1-st} becomes:

$$Q[y_i^{1-st}] = \sum_{p_1}^{N+1} (w_{i,p_1} + \Delta w_{i,p_1})(x_{p_1} + \Delta x_{p_1}) = y_i^{1-st} + \Delta y_i^{1-st}$$

where Δy_i^{1-st} is the quantization error of y_i^{1-st}. This quantization error is equal to:

$$\Delta y_i^{1-st} = \sum_{p_1}^{N+1} (\Delta w_{i,p_1} x_{p_1} + w_{i,p_1} \Delta x_{p_1}) , \tag{4}$$

where $p_1 = 1,2,\cdots,N+1; i = 1,2,\cdots,s$, and the second-order terms are omitted.

Combining Eqs. (3) with (4), we obtain the variance of y_i^{1-st}:

$$\sigma_{y_i^{1-st}}^2 = \sum_{p_1=1}^{N+1} E\{w_{i,p_1}^2 x_{p_1}^2\} = (N+1)\sigma_x^2\sigma_w^2 , \tag{5}$$

and the variance of Δy_i^{1-st}:

$$\sigma_{\Delta y_i^{1-st}}^2 = \sum_{p_1=1}^{N+1}\{E\{w_{i,p_1}^2\}\sigma_{\Delta x}^2 + E\{x_{p_1}^2\}\sigma_{\Delta w}^2\} = (N+1)[\sigma_w^2\sigma_{\Delta x}^2 + \sigma_x^2\sigma_{\Delta w}^2] . \tag{6}$$

Combining Eqs. (5) with (6), we obtain the noise-to-signal ratio (NSR) of the 1ˢᵗ–order FNN before the signal passes through a nonlinear activation function for the neuron i as:

$$NSR_{y_i^{1-st}} = \frac{\sigma_{\Delta y_i^{1-st}}^2}{\sigma_{y_i^{1-st}}^2} = \frac{\sigma_{\Delta x}^2}{\sigma_x^2} + \frac{\sigma_{\Delta w}^2}{\sigma_w^2} = \frac{2}{2^{2M_{in}^{1-st}}} , \tag{7}$$

where M_{in}^{1-st} is the number of quantization bits of the 1st–order FNN before the signal passes through a nonlinear activation function. Here we use the NSR as a measure of the system performance because it leads to an easier and simpler recursive expression of the quantization errors (Jiang & Gielen, 2003). For the sake of simplicity, we use uniform and normal probability distribution models to derive the effects of quantization error.

2.4 The Fixed-Point Quantization Analysis of the 2nd-Order FNN

We assume that the internal activation of the 2nd-order FNN for output node i can be written as:

$$y_i^{2-nd} = \sum_{p_1=1}^{N} \sum_{p_2=p_1}^{N} w_{i,p_1 p_2} x_{p_1} x_{p_2} + y_i^{1-st},$$

(8)

where $p_1, p_2 = 1, 2, \cdots, N; i = 1, 2, \cdots, s$. Further assuming that the error terms of higher order are negligible, then after quantization y_i^{2-nd} becomes:

$$Q[y_i^{2-nd}] = \sum_{p_1=1}^{N} \sum_{p_2=p_1}^{N} (w_{i,p_1 p_2} + \Delta w_{i,p_1 p_2})(x_{p_1} + \Delta x_{p_1})(x_{p_2} + \Delta x_{p_2}) + Q[y_i^{1-st}] \approx \sum_{p_1=1}^{N} \sum_{p_2=p_1}^{N} w_{i,p_1 p_2} x_{p_1} x_{p_2} + y_i^{1-st} + \Delta y_i^{2-nd},$$

where

$$\Delta y_i^{2-nd} = \sum_{p_1=1}^{N} \sum_{p_2=p_1}^{N} (w_{i,p_1 p_2} x_{p_1} \Delta x_{p_2} + w_{i,p_1 p_2} x_{p_2} \Delta x_{p_1} + x_{p_1} x_{p_2} \Delta w_{i,p_1 p_2}) + \Delta y_i^{1-st}$$

(9)

Δy_i^{2-nd} is the quantization error of y_i^{2-nd}. According to Appendix 1, we deduce the NSR of y_i^{2-nd} as

$$NSR_{y_i^{2-nd}} = \frac{\sigma_{\Delta y_i^{2-nd}}^2}{\sigma_{y_i^{2-nd}}^2} = \xi^{2-nd} \frac{2\sigma_\Delta^2}{\sigma_x^2} > \frac{2\sigma_\Delta^2}{\sigma_x^2} = NSR_{y_i^{1-st}},$$

(10)

where

$$\xi^{2-nd} = \frac{(15N+23)N\sigma_x^2 + 20(N+1)}{(10N+26)N\sigma_x^2 + 20(N+1)} > 1$$

(11)

2.5 The Fixed-Point Quantization Analysis of the 3rd-Order FNN

The internal activation of the 3rd-order FNN for output node i can be written as:

$$y_i^{3-rd} = \sum_{p_1=1}^{N} \sum_{p_2=p_1}^{N} \sum_{p_3=p_2}^{N} w_{i,p_1 p_2 p_3} x_{p_1} x_{p_2} x_{p_3} + y_i^{2-nd}$$

(12)

where $p_1, p_2, p_3 = 1, 2, \cdots, N; i = 1, 2, \cdots, s$. Further assuming that the error terms of higher order can be neglected, then after quantization y_i^{3-rd} becomes:

$$Q[y_i^{3-rd}] = \sum_{p_1=1}^{N} \sum_{p_2=p_1}^{N} \sum_{p_3=p_2}^{N} (w_{i,p_1p_2p_3} + \Delta w_{i,p_1p_2p_3})(x_{p_1} + \Delta x_{p_1})(x_{p_2} + \Delta x_{p_2})(x_{p_3} + \Delta x_{p_3}) + Q[y_i^{2-nd}]$$

$$\approx \sum_{p_1=1}^{N} \sum_{p_2=p_1}^{N} \sum_{p_3=p_2}^{N} w_{i,p_1p_2p_3} x_{p_1} x_{p_2} x_{p_3} + y_i^{2-nd} + \Delta y_i^{3-rd} ,$$

where Δy_i^{3-rd} is the quantization error of y_i^{3-rd}. This quantization error is equal to:

$$\Delta y_i^{3-rd} = \sum_{p_1=1}^{N} \sum_{p_2=p_1}^{N} \sum_{p_3=p_2}^{N} (w_{i,p_1p_2p_3} x_{p_1} x_{p_2} \Delta x_{p_3} + w_{i,p_1p_2p_3} x_{p_1} x_{p_3} \Delta x_{p_2} + w_{i,p_1p_2p_3} x_{p_2} x_{p_3} \Delta x_{p_1} + x_{p_1} x_{p_2} x_{p_3} \Delta w_{i,p_1p_2p_3}) + \Delta y_i^{2-nd} .$$

(13)

Based on the findings in Appendix 2, we deduce the NSR of y_i^{3-rd} as:

$$NSR_{y_i^{3-rd}} = \frac{\sigma^2_{\Delta y_i^{3-rd}}}{\sigma^2_{y_i^{3-rd}}} = \xi^{3-rd} \frac{2\sigma^2_\Delta}{\sigma^2_x} > \xi^{2-nd} \frac{2\sigma^2_\Delta}{\sigma^2_x} = \frac{\sigma^2_{\Delta y_i^{2-nd}}}{\sigma^2_{y_i^{2-nd}}} = NSR_{y_i^{2-nd}}$$

(14)

where

$$\xi^{3-rd} = \frac{\frac{70N^2 + 147N + 860}{210} N\sigma_x^4 + \frac{15N+23}{20} N\sigma_x^2 + (N+1)}{\frac{(35N^2 - 273N + 1258)}{210} N\sigma_x^4 + \frac{10N+26}{20} N\sigma_x^2 + (N+1)} > \xi^{2-nd} > 1$$

(15)

2.6 The Fixed-Point Quantization Analysis of the Hth-Order FNN

By doing a similar expansion of Eq. (12), we have the internal activation of the Hth-order FNN for output node i as follows:

$$y_i^{H-th} = \{\sum_{p_1=1}^{n} \sum_{p_2=p_1}^{n} \cdots \sum_{p_H=p_{H-1}}^{n} w_{i,p_1p_2\cdots p_H} x_{p_1} x_{p_2} \cdots x_{p_H}\} + y_i^{(H-1)-th}$$

(16)

where $p_1, p_2, \cdots p_H = 1, 2, \cdots, N; i = 1, 2, \cdots, s$ and $y_i^{(H-1)-th}$ is the internal activation of the $(H-1)^{th}$-order FNN for output node i. Further assuming that the error terms of higher order can be neglected, then after quantization y_i^{H-th} is expressed as:

$$Q[y_i^{H-th}] = \{\sum_{p_1=1}^{N} \sum_{p_2=p_1}^{N} \cdots \sum_{p_H=p_{H-1}}^{N} w_{i,p_1p_2\cdots p_H} x_{p_1} x_{p_2} \cdots x_{p_H}\} + y_i^{(H-1)-th} + \Delta y_i^{H-th}$$

where Δy_i^{H-th} is the quantization error of y_i^{H-th}. This quantization error is equal to:

$$\Delta y_i^{H-th} = \sum_{p_1=1}^{N} \sum_{p_2=p_1}^{N} \cdots \sum_{p_H=p_{H-1}}^{N} [w_{i,p_1p_2\cdots p_H} (x_{p_2} x_{p_3} \cdots x_{p_H} + x_{p_1} x_{p_3} \cdots x_{p_H} + \cdots + x_{p_1} x_{p_2} \cdots x_{p_{H-1}}) \Delta x_{p_H} + x_{p_1} x_{p_2} \cdots x_{p_H} \Delta w_{i,p_1p_2p_H}] + \sigma^2_{\Delta y_i^{(H-1)-th}}$$

(17)

Combining Eqs. (16) with (17) yields the variance of y_i^{H-th} :

$$\sigma_{y_i^{H-th}}^2 = \sum_{p_1=1}^{N} \sum_{p_2=p_1}^{N} \cdots \sum_{p_H=p_{H-1}}^{N} E\{w_{i,p_1 p_2 \cdots p_H}^2\} E\{x_{p_1} x_{p_2} \cdots x_{p_H}\}^2 + \sigma_{y_i^{(H-1)-th}}^2 \tag{18}$$

and the variance of Δy_i^{H-th} can be written as:

$$\sigma_{\Delta y_i^{H-th}}^2 = \sum_{p_1=1}^{N} \sum_{p_2=p_1}^{N} \cdots \sum_{p_H=p_{H-1}}^{N} \{E\{w_{i,p_1 p_2 \cdots p_H}^2\}(E\{x_{p_1} x_{p_2} \cdots x_{p_H}\}^2 + E\{x_{p_1} x_{p_2} \cdots x_{p_H}\}^2 + \cdots + E\{x_{p_1} x_{p_2} \cdots x_{p_H}\}^2) + E\{x_{p_1} x_{p_2} \cdots x_{p_H}\}^2\} \rho_\Delta^2 + \sigma_{\Delta y_i^{(H-1)-th}}^2 \tag{19}$$

Combining Eqs.(16) and (17) with (19), we express y_i^{H-th} into a general form (Jiang & Gielen 2001):

$$NSR_{y_i^{H-th}} = \frac{\sigma_{\Delta y_i^{H-th}}^2}{\sigma_{y_i^{H-th}}^2} = \xi^{H-th} \frac{\sigma_{\Delta y_i^{1-th}}^2}{\sigma_{y_i^{1-th}}^2}, \tag{20}$$

where $\xi^{H-th} > \xi^{(H-1)-th} > \cdots > \xi^{2-nd} > \xi^{1-st} = 1$ which is unrelated to the quantization error.

A neural network of sufficiently higher order can produce any arbitrary nonlinear function within a certain accuracy range (Pao, 1989). The number of elements in the network grows quite rapidly as a function of the parameters H and N. Even when the dimension N of the non-expanded pattern X is low, when H is high, the expanded dimension N_w may be very large and increases at a geometrical power, while the NSR and chip size increase dramatically as H increases. Increasing the order can improve the nonlinear function mapping ability of the network to some extent. Therefore, balance must be taken between the NSR and the order: the higher the order is, the more powerful its nonlinear ability is, but also the chip size and the NSR of the network will increase. In addition, the network's performance is not proportional to the order H when using finite-precision computations.

After quantization, the output of the Hth–order FNN for node i can be written as:

$$Q[\tilde{y}_i^{H-th}] = Q[f(Q[y_i^{H-th}])] = \tilde{y}_i^{H-th} + \Delta\tilde{y}_i^{H-th}.$$

2.7 The Fixed-Point Quantization Analysis of Output Function

The quantization error after the signal passes through a nonlinear activation function for output node i is approximately expressed by a first-order Taylor expansion of the activation function, giving:

$$\Delta\tilde{y}_i \approx \frac{\partial \tilde{y}_i}{\partial y_i} \Delta y_i = \lambda(1 - \tilde{y}_i^2)\Delta y_i / (N+1) \leq \lambda \Delta y_i / (N+1) \tag{21}$$

Here we explicitly state that the analysis is valid only if the higher-order terms of the Taylor expansion are negligible, i.e., when the number of quantization states is large enough to allow for small quantization errors. In this case, we obtain the variance of $\Delta\tilde{y}_i^{H-th}$ as

$$\sigma^2_{\Delta \tilde{y}_i^{H-th}} = (\frac{\partial \tilde{y}_i^{H-th}}{\partial y_i^{H-th}})^2 \sigma^2_{\Delta y_i^{H-th}} = \lambda^2 (1 - (\tilde{y}_i^{H-th})^2)^2 \sigma^2_{\Delta y_i^{H-th}} / (N+1)^2 = \lambda^2 (1 - (\tilde{y}_i^{H-th})^2)^2 (\sigma_w^2 \sigma_{\Delta x}^2 + \sigma_x^2 \sigma_{\Delta w}^2) / (N+1)$$

(22)

Eq. (22) is different from (Xie & Jabri, 1992)'s linear analysis and (Dundar & Rose, 1995)'s nonlinear analysis. These previous publications about the sensitivity and quantization error analysis of neural networks used only linear neurons with uniform probability distribution or simple nonlinear neurons, hence their ability to analyze accurately was limited. In our chapter we derive in detail the effects of the quantization error on forward and backward propagation. Our method is less restricted and is based on more in-depth mathematical analysis. We know that the closer the neuron output is to its saturation state, the more compressed its quantization error will be. Almost no quantization noise will occur when the activation function is over-saturated. Eq. (22) shows that the variance of the output error depends on the derivative of the neuron's output (i.e., the depth of saturation) and the variance of Δy_i^{H-th}.

If y_i^{H-th} is assumed to be a uniform distribution, then according to Appendix 3 the NSR of the Hth–order FNN for output node i before and after the signal passes through a nonlinear activation function obeys the following relationship:

$$NSR_{\tilde{y}_i^{H-th}} = \frac{\sigma^2_{\Delta \tilde{y}_i^{H-th}}}{\sigma^2_{\tilde{y}_i^{H-th}}} = \beta^{H-th} \frac{\sigma^2_{\Delta y_i^{H-th}}}{\sigma^2_{y_i^{H-th}}} \geq \frac{\sigma^2_{\Delta y_i^{H-th}}}{\sigma^2_{y_i^{H-th}}}$$

(23)

where

$$\beta^{H-th} = \frac{1}{1 - \frac{6\lambda^2 \sigma^2_{y_i^{H-th}}}{5 N_w^2} + \cdots} > 1$$

(24)

Eq.(24) is a monotonically increasing function of $\lambda \sigma_{y_i^{H-th}} / N_w$ within a limited range, and is unrelated to the quantization error. Its maximum and minimum value are equal to:

$$\lim_{\lambda \sigma_{y_i^{H-th}} / N_w \to 0} \beta^{H-th} \to 1 \text{ and } \lim_{\lambda \sigma_{y_i^{H-th}} / N_w \to \frac{\pi}{2\sqrt{3}}} \beta^{H-th} \to 1.976501 \text{ respectively.}$$

(25)

In the above theoretical analysis, signals, weights and the internal activation of the output nodes are all assumed to be uniformly distributed, but in fact this is not always the case. It has been concluded in (Tang & Kwan, 1993; Marco & Marco, 1996) that the weight distribution in a neural network resembles a normal distribution when the word width is long enough. If the fan-in number is large enough ($N_w > 30$), then according to the central limit theorem, the weighted sum can be seen as having N_w independent random input variables, and the probability density function of their weighted sum can then be considered to be a normal distribution. Under this assumption and according to the analysis in Appendix 4, the NSR of the Hth–order FNN for output node i before and after the signal passes through a nonlinear activation function obeys the following relationship:

$$NSR_{\tilde{y}_i^{H-th}} = \frac{\sigma_{\Delta \tilde{y}_i^{H-th}}^2}{\sigma_{\tilde{y}_i^{H-th}}^2} = \rho_i^{H-th} \frac{\sigma_{\Delta y_i^{H-th}}^2}{\sigma_{y_i^{H-th}}^2} \geq \frac{\sigma_{\Delta y_i^{H-th}}^2}{\sigma_{y_i^{H-th}}^2} \qquad (26)$$

where

$$\rho_i^{H-th} = \frac{\dfrac{\lambda^2}{N_w^2} \sigma_{y_i^{H-th}}^2 \displaystyle\int_{-\infty}^{\infty} \dfrac{4\exp(-s^2/2)}{(1+\cosh(\dfrac{2\lambda}{N_w}\sigma_{y_i^{H-th}}s))^2} ds}{\displaystyle\int_{-\infty}^{\infty} \tanh^2(\dfrac{\lambda}{N_w}\sigma_{y_i^{H-th}}s)\exp(-s^2/2)ds} > 1 \qquad (27)$$

Eq. (27) is a monotonically increasing function of $\lambda\sigma_{y_i^{H-th}}/N_w$ within a limited range, and is unrelated to the quantization error. Its maximum and minimum value are equal to:

$$\lim_{\frac{\lambda}{N_w}\sigma_{y_i^{H-th}}\to 0} \rho_i^{H-th} = 1 \text{ and } \lim_{\frac{\lambda}{N_w}\sigma_{y_i^{H-th}}\to\infty} \rho_i^{H-th} = 4 \text{ respectively.} \qquad (28)$$

From Eqs. (7) and (23), we know that the $NSR_{y_i^{H-th}}$ before the signal passes through a nonlinear activation function is related to the order H and the number of input bits and is unrelated to the quantization width. The larger the order H, the larger $NSR_{y_i^{H-th}}$ becomes. Regardless of which distribution the internal activation complies with, the NSR is always increased after the signal passes through a nonlinear activation function. The smaller $\lambda\sigma_{y_i^{H-th}}/N_w$ is, the smaller β^{H-th} or ρ_i^{H-th} becomes, and the less the NSR is increased after the signal passes through a nonlinear activation function. In contrast, the larger $X = \{x_1, x_2, \cdots, x_N\} \in R^N$ is, the larger β^{H-th} or ρ_i^{H-th} becomes, the more the NSR is increased after the signal passes through a nonlinear activation function. Because the compression factor λ/N_w of internal activation reduces the output NSR, it cancels the effect of the fan-in number. Usually $\lambda/N_w \ll 1$, thus $\lambda\sigma_{y_i^{H-th}}/N_w$ is decreased greatly following the reduction of β_i^{H-th} or ρ_i^{H-th}, and the NSR is effectively reduced. If we need to reduce the NSR after the signal passes through a nonlinear activation function, several measures can be taken, including reducing the input error, decreasing the order H, or reducing β^{H-th} or ρ^{H-th}, i.e., reducing $\lambda\sigma_{y_i^{H-th}}/N_w$. Because $\sigma_{y_i^{H-th}}^2$ is proportional to σ_x^2 and σ_w^2, when σ_x^2, σ_w^2 or λ/N_w is reduced, β^{H-th} or ρ^{H-th} can effectively be reduced.

We further assume that the number of quantization bits before and after the signal passes through a nonlinear activation function in the Hth-order FNN is denoted as M_{in}^{H-th} and M_{out}^{H-th} respectively. The input error is propagated feed-forward, and the NSR increases when the signal passes through a nonlinear neuron. If the density of internal activation is assumed to be a uniform distribution, then combining Eqs. (20) with (23) gives the following relationship:

$$NSR_{\tilde{y}_i^{H-th}} = \frac{\sigma_{\Delta \tilde{y}_i^{H-th}}^2}{\sigma_{\Delta \tilde{y}_i^{H-th}}^2} = \beta^{H-th} \frac{\sigma_{\Delta y_i^{H-th}}^2}{\sigma_{y_i^{H-th}}^2} = \beta^{H-th} \frac{1}{2^{2M_{out}^{H-th}}} = \beta^{H-th} \frac{2\xi^{H-th}}{2^{2M_{in}^{H-th}}},$$

from which we can easily derive:

$$M_{out}^{H-th} = M_{in}^{H-th} - (1/2)\log_2 2\xi^{H-th}\beta^{H-th}.$$

According to Eq. (25), if we select $\beta_{\max}^{H-th} = 2$, then

$$M_{out}^{H-th} = M_{in}^{H-th} - 1 - (1/2)\log_2 \xi^{H-th} \text{ (bits).} \tag{29}$$

Using the same reasoning, if the internal activation approximately complies with a normal distribution, then according to Eq. (28), if we select $\rho_{\max}^{H-th} = 4$ we have:

$$M_{out}^{H-th} = M_{in}^{H-th} - 3/2 - (1/2)\log_2 \xi^{H-th} \text{ (bits).} \tag{30}$$

The larger the internal activation and nonlinear compression are, the fewer bits M_{out}^{H-th} required. Comparing M_{out}^{H-th} with M_{in}^{H-th} in Eqs. (29) and (30), we know that M_{out}^{H-th} can decrease $(1 + (1/2)\log_2 \xi^{H-th})$ to $(3/2 + (1/2)\log_2 \xi^{H-th})$ bits depending on the distribution of internal activation. If we keep the NSR constant before and after the signal passes through a nonlinear activation function, i.e., if M_{out}^{H-th} is kept constant, then the precision of quantization must increase by $(1 + (1/2)\log_2 \xi^{H-th})$ to $(3/2 + (1/2)\log_2 \xi^{H-th})$ bits.

2.8 The Fixed-Point Quantization Analysis of MLFNN

Assuming that $X^{(l)}$ ($l = 1, 2, \cdots, L-1$) expresses the state vector of nodes in layer l with in total N_l nodes, $X^{(1)}$ is the input vector, $X^{(L)}$ and t are respectively the actual and target output vectors which are desired to be binary (-1 and 1). The activation function is a hyperbolic tangent. $w_{j,i}^{(l)}$ is the synaptic weight connecting the i-th node of layer l-1 to the j-th node of layer l in the L layers of the MLFNN. There are P training sample sets. $x_{N_l+1}^{(l)} = 1$ and $w_{j,N_l+1}^{(l+1)} = \theta_{j,N_l+1}^{(l+1)}$ denote a neuron's bias and threshold, respectively. The number of quantization bits after and before a neuron in layer l is further denoted by $M_{out}^{(l)}$ and $M_{in}^{(l)}$, respectively. q is the quantization width, Δx and Δw are the quantization noises, and are independent of each other and of all inputs and outputs.

By combining the inputs to a neuron, the output of node i of layer l can be written as:

$$x_i^{(l)} = f(y_i^{(l)}) = f(\sum_j w_{i,j}^{(l)} x_j^{(l-1)}) = \tanh(\lambda \sum_j w_{i,j}^{(l)} x_j^{(l-1)} / (N_{l-1} + 1)) \tag{31}$$

where $2 < l \le L$; $j = 1, 2, \cdots N_l$; $i = 1, 2, \cdots, (N_{l-1} + 1)$; λ is a constant decided by experiment.

Eq. (31) shows that when the neuron's fan-in is very large, the internal activation $y_i^{(l)}$ may be very large, which may cause saturation of analog circuits and numerical overflow in digital systems. The normalization by the compression factor $\lambda / (N_{l-1} + 1)$ makes $y_i^{(l)}$ unrelated to the fan-in number and can decrease the chance that the network's output falls into a false saturated state. Moreover, it increases the ability of escaping from a false saturated output state or of breaking away from local minima (Bayraktaroglu, Ogrenci & Dundar, et al., 1999). After quantization $y_i^{(l)}$ is as follows:

$$Q[y_i^{(l)}] = \sum_{j}^{N_{l-1}+1} (w_{i,j} + \Delta w_{i,j})(x_j + \Delta x_j) = \sum_{j=1}^{N_{l-1}+1} w_{i,j}^{(l)} x_j^{(l-1)} + \Delta y_i^{(l)} = y_i^{(l)} + \Delta y_i^{(l)}$$

where $\Delta y_i^{(l)}$ is the quantization error of $y_i^{(l)}$. This quantization error is equal to:

$$\Delta y_i^{(l)} = \sum_{j}^{N_{l-1}+1} (\Delta w_{i,j} x_j + w_{i,j} \Delta x_j) \tag{32}$$

where $j = 1, 2, \cdots, N_{l-1} + 1; i = 1, 2, \cdots, N_l$, and the 2nd-order items are omitted.

Combining Eqs. (31) and (32), we obtain the variance of $y_i^{(l)}$:

$$\sigma_{y_i^{(l)}}^2 = \sum_{j=1}^{N_{l-1}+1} E\{w_{i,j}^2 x_j^2\} = (N_{l-1} + 1)\sigma_{x^{(l-1)}}^2 \sigma_{w^{(l)}}^2 \tag{33}$$

and the variance of $\Delta y_i^{(l)}$:

$$\sigma_{\Delta y_i^{(l)}}^2 = \sum_{j=1}^{N_l+1} \{E\{w_{i,j}^2\}\sigma_{\Delta x^{(l-1)}}^2 + E\{x_j^2\}\sigma_{\Delta w^{(l)}}^2\} = 2(N_{l-1}+1)(\sigma_{x^{(l-1)}}^2 + \sigma_{w^{(l)}}^2)\sigma_{\Delta w^{(l)}}^2 \tag{34}$$

Combining Eqs. (33) and (34), we obtain the noise-to-signal ratio (NSR) of $y_i^{(l)}$ as:

$$NSR_{y_i^{(l)}} = \frac{\sigma_{\Delta y_i^{(l)}}^2}{\sigma_{y_i^{(l)}}^2}$$
$$= \frac{(N_{l-1}+1)[\sigma_{x^{(l-1)}}^2 \sigma_{\Delta w^{(l)}}^2 + \sigma_{w^{(l)}}^2 \sigma_{\Delta x^{(l-1)}}^2]}{(N_{l-1}+1)\sigma_{x^{(l-1)}}^2 \sigma_{w^{(l)}}^2} \tag{35}$$
$$= \frac{\sigma_{\Delta x^{(l-1)}}^2}{\sigma_{x^{(l-1)}}^2} + \frac{\sigma_{\Delta w^{(l)}}^2}{\sigma_{w^{(l)}}^2} = \frac{2}{2^{2M^{(l)}}}$$

The quantization error $\Delta x_i^{(l)}$ after the neuron for output node i of layer l of the FNN is approximately expressed by a first-order Taylor expansion of the activation function, giving:

$$\Delta x_i^{(l)} \approx \frac{\partial x_i^{(l)}}{\partial y_i^{(l)}} \Delta y_i^{(l)}$$
$$= \lambda(1 - (x_i^{(l)})^2)\Delta y_i^{(l)} / (N_{l-1} + 1) \le \lambda \Delta y_i^{(l)} / (N_{l-1} + 1) \tag{36}$$

Therefore, we obtain the variance of $\Delta x_i^{(l)}$ as:

$$\sigma_{\Delta x_i^{(l)}}^2 = (\frac{\partial x_i^{(l)}}{\partial y_i^{(l)}})^2 \sigma_{\Delta y_i^{(l)}}^2 = \lambda^2 (1 - (x_i^{(l)})^2)^2 \sigma_{\Delta y_i^{(l)}}^2 / (N_{l-1} + 1)^2$$
$$= \lambda^2 (1 - (x_i^{(l)})^2)^2 (\sigma_{w^{(l)}}^2 \sigma_{\Delta x^{(l-1)}}^2 + \sigma_{x^{(l-1)}}^2 \sigma_{\Delta w^{(l)}}^2) / (N_{l-1} + 1) \tag{37}$$

The variance of the output error depends on the derivative of the neuron's output (i.e. the deepness of saturation) and the variance of $\Delta y_i^{(l)}$.

If the internal activation $y_i^{(l)}$ complies with a uniform distribution, then according to same as the proof of Appendix 4, the NSR of output node i of layer l of the FNN after and before the neuron obeys the following relation:

$$NSR_{x_i^{(l)}}^{\max} = \beta_i^{(l)} NSR_{y_i^{(l)}} > \frac{\sigma_{\Delta x}^2}{\sigma_x^2} + \frac{\sigma_{\Delta w}^2}{\sigma_w^2} = NSR_{y_i^{(l)}} \tag{38}$$

where
$$\beta_i^{(l)} = \frac{1}{1 - \dfrac{6\lambda^2 \sigma_{y_i^{(l)}}^2}{5(N_{l-1}+1)^2} + \cdots} \tag{39}$$

It is a monotonically increasing function of $\dfrac{\lambda \sigma_{y_i^{(l)}}}{N_{l-1}+1}$ within the limited range, and it is also unrelated to the quantization error. Its maximum and minimum are respectively equal to:

$$\beta^{(l)}\bigg|_{\frac{\lambda \sigma_{y_i^{(l)}}}{N_{l-1}+1} \to 0} \to 1 \quad \text{and} \quad \beta^{(l)}\bigg|_{\frac{\lambda \sigma_{y_i^{(l)}}}{N_{l-1}+1} \to \frac{\pi}{2\sqrt{3}}} \to 1.976501 \tag{40}$$

According to the analysis in Appendix 5, the NSRs of output node i of layer l of the FNN after and before the neuron obeys the following relationship:

$$NSR_{x_i^{(l)}} = \frac{\sigma_{\Delta x_i^{(l)}}^2}{\sigma_{x_i^{(l)}}^2} = \rho_i^{(l)} \frac{\sigma_{\Delta y_i^{(l)}}^2}{\sigma_{y_i^{(l)}}^2} \geq \frac{\sigma_{\Delta y_i^{(l)}}^2}{\sigma_{y_i^{1l)}}^2} = NSR_{y_i^{(l)}} \tag{41}$$

where

$$\rho_i^{(l)} = \frac{\dfrac{\lambda^2}{(N_{l-1}+1)^2}\sigma_{y_i^{(l)}}^2 \displaystyle\int_{-\infty}^{\infty} \dfrac{4\exp(-s^2/2)}{(1+\cosh(\frac{2\lambda}{N_{l-1}+1}\sigma_{y_i^{(l)}}s))^2}\,ds}{\displaystyle\int_{-\infty}^{\infty} \tanh^2(\frac{\lambda}{N_{l-1}+1}\sigma_{y_i^{(l)}}s)\exp(-s^2/2)\,ds} \tag{42}$$

It is a monotonically increasing function of $\dfrac{\lambda \sigma_{y_i^{(l)}}}{N_{l-1}+1}$ within the limited range, and is also unrelated to the quantization error. Its maximum and minimum are respectively equal to:

$$\lim_{\frac{\lambda}{N_{l-1}+1}\sigma_{y_i^{(l)}} \to 0} \rho_i^{(l)} = 1 \text{ and } \lim_{\frac{\lambda}{N_{l-1}+1}\sigma_{y_i^{(l)}} \to \infty} \rho_i^{(l)} = 4 \tag{43}$$

2.9 The Effect of the Quantization Error on the Forward Propagation of MLFNN

For the fixed-point quantization, when N_{l-1} is small, the probability density function of the random variable $y_j^{(l)}$ is approximately a uniform distribution. Considering Eq. (38), the maximal NSR of $x_i^{(l)}$ is characterized by the following recursive formula:

$$NSR_{x_i^{(l)}}^{max} = \frac{\sigma_{\Delta x_i^{(l)}}^2}{\sigma_{x_i^{(l)}}^2}\Bigg|_{max} = \beta^{(l)}\left(\frac{\sigma_{\Delta w^{(l)}}^2}{\sigma_{w^{(l)}}^2} + \frac{\sigma_{\Delta x^{(l-1)}}^2}{\sigma_{x^{(l-1)}}^2}\right) = \beta^{(l)}\left(NSR_{x_i^{(l-1)}} + \frac{\sigma_{\Delta w^{(l)}}^2}{\sigma_{w^{(l)}}^2}\right) = \beta^{(l)}\left[\beta^{(l-1)}\left(NSR_{x_i^{(l-2)}} + \frac{\sigma_{\Delta w^{(l-1)}}^2}{\sigma_{w^{(l-1)}}^2}\right) + \frac{\sigma_{\Delta w^{(l)}}^2}{\sigma_{w^{(l)}}^2}\right]$$

$$= \beta^{(l)}[\beta^{(l-1)}\cdots\beta^{(3)}[\beta^{(2)}(\frac{\sigma_{\Delta x^{(1)}}^2}{\sigma_{x^{(1)}}^2} + \frac{\sigma_{\Delta w^{(2)}}^2}{\sigma_{w^{(2)}}^2}) + \frac{\sigma_{\Delta w^{(3)}}^2}{\sigma_{w^{(3)}}^2}] + \cdots + \frac{\sigma_{\Delta w^{(l-1)}}^2}{\sigma_{w^{(l-1)}}^2}] + \frac{\sigma_{\Delta w^{(l)}}^2}{\sigma_{w^{(l)}}^2}] \tag{44}$$

On the other hand, when N_{l-1} is large enough, then according to the central limit theorem the probability density function of $y_j^{(l)}$ approaches a normal distribution. Considering Eq. (41), the NSR of $x_i^{(l)}$ is then characterized by the following recursive formula:

$$NSR_{x_i^{(l)}} = \frac{\sigma_{\Delta x^{(l)}}^2}{\sigma_{x^{(l)}}^2} = = \rho^{(l)}\left(\frac{\sigma_{\Delta x^{(l-1)}}^2}{\sigma_{x^{(l-1)}}^2} + \frac{\sigma_{\Delta w^{(l)}}^2}{\sigma_{w^{(l)}}^2}\right) = \rho^{(l)}\left(NSR_{x_i^{(l-1)}} + \frac{\sigma_{\Delta w^{(l)}}^2}{\sigma_{w^{(l)}}^2}\right) = \rho^{(l)}\left[\rho^{(l-1)}\left(NSR_{x_i^{(l-2)}} + \frac{\sigma_{\Delta w^{(l-1)}}^2}{\sigma_{w^{(l-1)}}^2}\right) + \frac{\sigma_{\Delta w^{(l)}}^2}{\sigma_{w^{(l)}}^2}\right]$$

$$= \rho^{(l)}[\rho^{(l-1)}\cdots\rho^{(3)}[\rho^{(2)}(\frac{\sigma_{\Delta x^{(1)}}^2}{\sigma_{x^{(1)}}^2} + \frac{\sigma_{\Delta w^{(2)}}^2}{\sigma_{w^{(2)}}^2}) + \frac{\sigma_{\Delta w^{(3)}}^2}{\sigma_{w^{(3)}}^2}] + \cdots + \frac{\sigma_{\Delta w^{(l-1)}}^2}{\sigma_{w^{(l-1)}}^2}] + \frac{\sigma_{\Delta w^{(l)}}^2}{\sigma_{w^{(l)}}^2}] \tag{45}$$

The input errors are propagated feedforward from input layer to output layer. The NSR is enlarged layer after layer. If the internal activation complies with a uniform distribution, then according to Eq. (44), we have

$$NSR_{x_i^{(l)}} = \frac{\sigma_{\Delta x^{(l)}}^2}{\sigma_{x^{(l)}}^2} = \beta^{(l)}\left(NSR_{x_i^{(l-1)}} + \frac{\sigma_{\Delta w^{(l)}}^2}{\sigma_{w^{(l)}}^2}\right) = \beta^{(l)}\left(\frac{\sigma_{\Delta x^{(l-1)}}^2}{\sigma_{x^{(l-1)}}^2} + \frac{\sigma_{\Delta w^{(l)}}^2}{\sigma_{w^{(l)}}^2}\right) = \frac{1}{2^{2M^{(l)}}} \tag{46}$$

Taking into consideration the constraint Eq. (46), it can easily be found:

$$\frac{1}{2^{2M^{(l)}}} = \beta^{(l)}\frac{2}{2^{2M^{(l-1)}}}$$

giving

$$M^{(l)} = M^{(l-1)} - (1/2)\log_2\beta^{(l)} - 1/2$$

According to Eq. (40), if we select $\beta_{max}^{(l)} = 2$, then

$$M^{(l)} = M^{(l-1)} - 1 \text{ (bits)} \tag{47}$$

In the same reasoning, if $y_j^{(l)}$ complies with a normal distribution, then according to Eq. (43), if we select $\rho_{\max}^{(l)} = 4$, then

$$M^{(l)} = M^{(l-1)} - 3/2 \ \text{(bits)} \tag{48}$$

Because $1 \le \rho^{(l)}$ and $1 \le \beta^{(l)}$ always hold, we always have the following relationship:

$$M^{(L)} \le M^{(L-1)} \le \cdots \le M^{(1)}$$

The larger the internal activation and the larger the nonlinear compression are, the smaller the number of bits $M^{(l)}$ are needed. Combining Eqs. (47) and (48), we know that $M^{(l)}$ can decrease 1~1.5 bits per layer depending on the distribution of $y_j^{(l)}$. If we keep the NSR constant from input layer to output layer, i.e. $M^{(l)}$ is kept constant, then whenever a layer is added to the network, the precision of quantization must increase by 1~1.5 bits. The accuracy of the network on which the quantization error of the output has less effect depends mainly on that of input and hidden layers. As $1 \le \rho^{(l)}$ and $1 \le \beta^{(l)}$ are unrelated to the quantization error and enlarged layer by layer, then if we need to reduce the NSR of the output layer, one measure is to reduce the input error; another measure is to decrease the number of layers L; the third measure is to depress $\beta^{(l)}$ and $\rho^{(l)}$ (i.e. depress $\dfrac{\lambda}{N_{l-1}+1}\sigma_{y^{(l)}}$).

From the above analysis, we know that, no matter what distribution the internal activation of the neuron output complies with, the NSR after the nonlinear neuron is always enlarged. As the NSR increases with the number of layers, more bits are needed to keep the NSR constant. The necessary number of bits can be reduced from layer to layer if the neurons have an effective nonlinear compression; increasing the bits results in an improvement of the NSR which is independent of the fan-in number. If we change the fan-in number, and keep the number of layers constant, then the output NSR remains the same.

It was shown (Shima, Kimura, & Kamatani, et al., 1992; Dolenko & Card, 1995) that a MLFNN with a single hidden layer with nonlinear sigmoidal neurons and one output layer with linear neurons can uniformly approximate any continuous function to an arbitrary degree of exactness provided that the hidden layer contains a sufficient number of nodes. Concerning the numbers of neurons and weights in the fully connected MLFNN, the weight number is proportional to the square of the number of neurons. For a MLFNN with L layers, its number of neurons and weights are $\sum_{l=2}^{L} N_l$ and $\sum_{l=2}^{L} (N_{l-1}+1)N_l$ respectively.

Because the NSR increases with the layer number at a fixed number of quantization bits, and the ratio is independent of the number of input nodes, increasing the number of layers can improve the nonlinear ability of the network to some extent. The nonlinear ability of a MLFNN with a single hidden layer is enhanced by increasing the number of hidden nodes (Jiang, Gielen & Zhang, et al., 2003). Therefore, if the balance must be made between the NSR and the number of neurons, weights and layers, we think that a network with a single hidden layer is a better choice in the reality of finite precision.

2.10 The Floating-Point Quantization Analysis of HOFNN and MLFNN

For the 1st–order FNN, we assume that after floating-point quantization the internal activation y_i^{1-st} becomes $Q[y_i^{1-st}] = y_i^{1-st}(1+\varepsilon) = y_i^{1-st} + e_i^{1-st}$ For MLFNN, we assume that after floating-point quantization the internal activation $y_i^{(l)}$ of output node i of layer l of the FNN is $Q[y_i^{(l)}] = y_i^{(l)}(1+\varepsilon) = y_i^{(l)} + e_i^{(l)}$. Quantization errors are classified as additive errors and multiplicative errors, and their variance can be written as $\sigma_e^2 = \sigma_{e(*)}^2 + \sigma_{e(+)}^2$. The variance of multiplicative error for HOFNN is equal to:

$$\sigma_{e_i^{1-th}(*)}^2 = \sum_{p_1=1}^{N+1} \sigma_\varepsilon^2 \sigma_x^2 \sigma_{w_i}^2 = (N+1)\sigma_\varepsilon^2 \sigma_x^2 \sigma_{w_i}^2 . \tag{49}$$

Eq. (49) would be the variance of multiplicative error for MLFNN, when e_i^{1-th} is replaced into $e_i^{(l)}$, N is replaced into N_{l-1}.

The variance of additive error for HOFNN is equal to:

$$\sigma_{e_i^{1-st}(+)}^2 = \sum_{j=2}^{N+1} j\sigma_\varepsilon^2 \sigma_x^2 \sigma_{w_i}^2 = \frac{N(N+3)}{2}\sigma_\varepsilon^2 \sigma_x^2 \sigma_{w_i}^2 . \tag{50}$$

where N is the dimension of the pattern and q is the quantization width.

Eq. (50) would be the variance of additive error for MLFNN, when e_i^{1-th} is replaced into $e_i^{(l)}$, N is replaced into N_{l-1}.

Combining Eqs. (5) and (49) with (50), we obtain the NSR of the floating-point quantization y_i^{1-st} for HOFNN as:

$$NSR_{y_i^{1-st}}^{floit} = \frac{\sigma_{e_i^{1-st}}^2}{\sigma_{y_i^{1-st}}^2} = \frac{N^2+5N+2}{2(N+1)}\sigma_\varepsilon^2 = \frac{N^2+5N+2}{2(N+1)}\frac{q^2}{3} . \tag{51}$$

Eq. (51) would be the NSR of $y_i^{(l)}$ for MLFNN, when y_i^{1-th} is replaced into $y_i^{(l)}$, e_i^{1-th} is replaced into $e_i^{(l)}$, N is replaced into N_{l-1}.

For the case of floating-point quantization, from Eq. (51) it can be seen that the NSR before the signal passes through a nonlinear activation function is unrelated to the input signals and is a monotonically increasing function of the number of input nodes. As the number of input nodes increases, the number of additive and multiplicative items increases, and the additive and multiplicative errors become larger.

For the HOFNN with the floating-point quantization and because the NSR of a FIR filter is unrelated to the input signals (Oppenheim & Schaffer, 1975), we can think of the internal activation (the weighted sum of all inputs) as a FIR filter in which the NSR can be expressed as:

$$NSR_{y_i^{H-th}}^{floit} = \frac{\sigma_{e_i^{H-th}}^2}{\sigma_{y_i^{H-th}}^2} = F(N_w)\sigma_\varepsilon^2 , \tag{52}$$

where $F(N_w)$ is a monotonically increasing function of the number of input nodes. As the order increases, input nodes, additive and multiplicative terms increase, and the additive and multiplicative errors become larger. Eqs. (51) and (52) are valid only when the dynamic range or the number of exponent bits of the floating-point representation is large enough, therefore no clipping occurs in the computations and only the error of the limited mantissa remains to be considered. However, in practice the number of exponent bits of the floating-point representation is also limited, and therefore clipping and overflow always exist. When the exponent $c(=1)$ of floating point is very low, overflow easily occurs. In this case, the floating-point quantization is similar to fixed-point quantization, and the dynamic range of the former is larger than that of the latter at the same number of bits. If the exponent c increases with 1 bit, then the dynamic range of the floating-point representation will double and will be larger than that of the fixed-point representation. Here the NSR after the signal passes through a nonlinear activation function is also increased by a factor β_i^{H-th} or ρ_i^{H-th} as in the fixed-point computation.

Similar above analysis that the NSR before the neuron for the case of floating-point quantization is unrelated to the input signals of every layer but it is a monotonically increasing function of the number of input nodes of this layer. The more the number of input nodes, the more the number of additive and multiplicative items, and the larger the additive error and the multiplicative error. The NSR after the neuron is the same as that in the case of fixed-point quantization, but enlarged by a factor $\beta_i^{(l)}$ or $\rho_i^{(l)}$. The NSR of the output layer is also unrelated to the number of layers.

2.11 The Effects of Quantization Error on Backpropagation for HOFNN

The HOFNN uses a backpropagation (BP) gradient-descent algorithm to find the set of weights which corresponds to a global minimum of the error energy function, or at least the weights which give an error lower than the tolerable limit. There are two alternative approaches to weight quantization and clipping in the presence of finite precision: on-chip training (quantization and clipping at each iteration) and off-chip training (the training process is first performed on a high-precision computer; the weights are then quantified and downloaded to the chip and the recall is performed for the forward propagation). The on-chip updates are constrained by a finite-precision range which departs to some extent from the true gradient descent. This is not just an approximation of the gradient descent, but most of the time exhibits significantly different behavior, particularly when the learning rate is not small enough with respect to the number of training patterns (Dolenko & Card, 1995), and learning appears slower when more weights reach the limits of the clipping function. During training other clipping methods were studied (Holt & Hwang, 1993; Rumelhart, Hinton & Williams, 1986), for example on-chip training was first performed without quantization to get an initial estimate of the weights, then training was completed on a quantized network. In another approach, neural networks were trained off-chip and then weights were clipped for recall. This approach created some potential problems such as an increase in the probability of getting stuck into local minima (because new local minima may appear on the border of the allowed region in the weight space). But sometimes the network can leap over the local minima due to quantization. This can help convergence in some cases, however the procedure will not always guarantee convergence (Dundar & Rose, 1995).

A feasible approach to finding good weights is on-chip training which repeats the weight clipping at each iteration of the gradient method. Clipping during training results in neural networks with significantly better performances for recall, as this kind of training is shown to be more robust in performance for training and testing data. Because most computations are required in the training phase, the effects of quantization are more significant in this phase. In order to adapt the network to learn new patterns quickly, all computations must be attempted to be implemented on-chip (Shima, Kimura & Kamatani, et al., 1992)

For the sake of simplicity, we analyze two kinds of pattern classifications with only an output node under the condition of off-chip training. Assuming that a set of patterns in N-dimensional space $X = \{x_1, x_2, \cdots, x_N\} \in R^N$ is not linearly separable, and the pattern set of extended N_w dimensions is expressed as $Z = \{z_1, z_2, \cdots, z_{N_w}\} \in R^{N_w}$ which is linearly separable. The output weights are constrained within the range $\{-W_{max}, +W_{max}\}$, then the error energy function of the HOFNN is shown to be:

$$E = \frac{1}{2}\sum_p (e^{(p)})^2 = \frac{1}{2}\sum_p (t^{(p)} - (\tilde{y}^{H-th})^{(p)})^2 , \tag{53}$$

with p representing the number of training samples. The weights are updated according to gradient descent as:

$$W(k+1) - W(k) = \eta(k)\frac{\partial E[k]}{\partial W} = \frac{\eta\lambda}{N_w}(t - \tilde{y}^{H-th})\frac{\partial f}{\partial y^{H-th}} Z \tag{54}$$

where η is the learning rate, and k is the iteration number. We sum up to iteration number k and obtain:

$$W(k+1) = W(k) + \frac{\eta\lambda}{N_w}(t - \tilde{y}^{H-th})\frac{\partial f}{\partial y^{H-th}} Z = W(0) + \sum_{m=0}^{k}\frac{\eta\lambda}{N_w}(t - \tilde{y}^{H-th})\frac{\partial f}{\partial y^{H-th}} Z . \tag{55}$$

Due to the triangular inequality, we have

$$\left\|W(k+1)\right\|^2 \le \left\|W(0)\right\|^2 + \sum_{m=0}^{k}[\frac{\eta\lambda}{N_w}(t - \tilde{y}^{H-th})\frac{\partial f}{\partial y^{H-th}}]^2 \left\|Z\right\|^2 \le \left\|W(0)\right\|^2 + 4[\frac{\eta\lambda}{N_w}]^2 \left\|Z\right\|^2 (k+1) ,$$

i.e., the following inequality holds

$$\left\|W(k+1)\right\| \le \sqrt{\left\|W(0)\right\|^2 + 4[\frac{\eta\lambda}{N_w}]^2 \left\|Z\right\|^2 (k+1)} \tag{56}$$

Because a set of patterns in the expanded pattern space Z of the HOFNN is linearly separable, there exists a separating vector $C \in R^{N_w}$, and $\left\|C\right\| = 1$. In this case the following formulas hold:

$$C^T Z > 0 \text{ and } t - \tilde{y}^{H-th} > 0, \text{ if } C^T Z > 0 \; t - \tilde{y}^{H-th} > 0 \; Z \in class(+) \text{ and } t - \tilde{y}^{H-th} > 0 \text{ if } \tag{57}$$

$$C^T Z < 0 \text{ and } t - \tilde{y}^{H-th} < 0, \text{ if } C^T Z < 0 \; t - \tilde{y}^{H-th} < 0 \; Z \in class(-) \text{ and } t - \tilde{y}^{H-th} < 0, \text{ if } \tag{58}$$

Combining Eqs. (57) with (58), we know $(t - \tilde{y}^{H-th})C^T Z > 0$ always holds no matter whether $Z \in class(+)$ or $class(-)$. By multiplying vector C along two sides of Eq. (55), we obtain:

$$C^T W(k+1) = C^T W(0) + \sum_{m=0}^{k} \frac{\eta\lambda}{N_w}(t - \tilde{y}^{H-th}) \frac{\partial f}{\partial y^{H-th}} C^T Z = C^T W(0) + \sum_{m=0}^{k} \frac{\eta\lambda}{N_w} \left| C^T Z \right| \frac{\partial f}{\partial y^{H-th}} \left| t - \tilde{y}^{H-th} \right|$$

(59)

where $\dfrac{\partial f}{\partial y^{H-th}} > 0$ always holds.

Combining Eqs.(56) with (59) yields the following inequalities:

$$1 \geq \frac{C^T W(k+1)}{\left\| W(k+1) \right\|} \geq \frac{C^T W(0) + \sum_{m=0}^{k} \frac{\eta\lambda}{N_w} \left| C^T Z \right| \frac{\partial f}{\partial y_i^{H-th}} \left| t - \tilde{y}^{H-th} \right|}{\sqrt{\left\| W(0) \right\|^2 + 4[\frac{\eta\lambda}{N_w}]^2 \left\| Z \right\|^2 (k+1)}} .$$

(60)

When $k \to \infty$, the denominator of the right inequality approaches $O(\sqrt{k})$, and the following condition must be valid: $\dfrac{\eta\lambda}{N_w} \left| C^T Z \right| \dfrac{\partial f}{\partial y^{H-th}} \left| t - \tilde{y}^{H-th} \right| \to 0$; otherwise $\sum_{m=0}^{k} \dfrac{\eta\lambda}{N_w} \left| C^T Z \right| \dfrac{\partial f}{\partial y^{H-th}} \left| t - \tilde{y}^{H-th} \right|$ would grow infinitely as $O(k)$, then the ratio

$$\frac{C^T W(0) + \sum_{m=0}^{k} \frac{\eta\lambda}{N_w} \left| C^T Z \right| \frac{\partial f}{\partial y_i^{H-th}} \left| t - \tilde{y}^{H-th} \right|}{\sqrt{\left\| W(0) \right\|^2 + 4[\frac{\eta\lambda}{N_w}]^2 \left\| Z \right\|^2 (k+1)}}$$

will become infinity and conflict with Eq. (60). Therefore, for $\forall m > k$:

$$\frac{\eta\lambda}{N_w} \left| C^T Z \right| \frac{\partial f}{\partial y^{H-th}} \left| t - \tilde{y}^{H-th} \right| < \alpha$$

(61)

holds. For the output of a HOFNN, the following relation is satisfied:

$$\tilde{y}^{H-th} = f(y^{H-th})$$
$$= \tanh(\frac{\lambda}{N_w} \sum_{j=1}^{N_w} w_j z_j) < f(y_{max}^{H-th})$$
$$= \tanh(\lambda w_{max} z_{max}) < |t|$$

(62)

Taking the partial derivative of both sides of Eq. (62) for internal activation, we have

$$\frac{\partial f(y^{H-th})}{\partial y^{H-th}} > \frac{\partial f(y_{max}^{H-th})}{\partial y^{H-th}} = \theta .$$

(63)

Combining Eqs. (61) with (63), we have

$$\left| t - \tilde{y}^{H-th} \right| < \varepsilon = \frac{\alpha N_w}{\eta \lambda \left| C^T Z \right| \theta}.$$ (64)

Our aim is to try and find a set of weights which minimizes the error energy function inside the hypercube formed in the weight space. Assuming that the weight vector of node i is expressed by $W_i = [w_{i,1}, w_{i,2}, \cdots, w_{i,N_w}]$, $w_{i,j}$ is the weight which connects input node j to output node i, which are statistically independent of each other. If we use on-chip training, the weights are updated according to the gradient-descent algorithm (Rumelhart, Hinton & Williams, 1986) as:

$$Q[w_{i,j}(k+1) - w_{i,j}(k)] = Q[\eta Q[\delta_i] z_j],$$ (65)

where

$$Q[\delta_i] = Q[\lambda Q[(t_i - \tilde{y}_i^{H-th})(1 - (\tilde{y}_i^{H-th})^2)] / N_w]$$ (66)

and $j = 1, 2, \cdots, N_w; i = 1, 2, \cdots, s$; t_i and $\tilde{y}_i^{H-th}$ are the expected output and the real output of node i, respectively. From Eqs. (65) and (66), we see that because the internal activation is normalized in forward propagation, a compression factor

$$1 \geq \frac{C^T W(k+1)}{\left\| W(k+1) \right\|} \geq \frac{C^T W(0) + \sum_{m=0}^{k} \frac{\eta \lambda}{N_w} \left| C^T Z \right| \frac{\partial f}{\partial y_i^{H-th}} \left| t - \tilde{y}^{H-th} \right|}{\sqrt{\left\| W(0) \right\|^2 + 4[\frac{\eta \lambda}{N_w}]^2 \left\| Z \right\|^2 (k+1)}}$$

$/N_w$ will be generated by the derivative of activation in gradient descent during the BP process. The range of weight updates is compressed by λ / N_w. Although there are many methods to select the learning rate for fast training algorithms in high-precision computations (Karayiannis & Venetsanopoulos, 1992; Jiang, Gielen & Zhang, et al., 2003; Jiang, Gielen & Xing, et al., 2002), these methods are too complex for hardware implementations. In order to cancel these kinds of effects and improve the training performance, $k \to \infty$ is selected to be inversely proportional to λ / N_w. We further assume that $x_i \big|_{\max} = 1$, $i = 1, 2, \cdots, N$ meaning $z_j \big|_{\max} = 1$, $j = 1, 2, \cdots, N_w$. Then according to Eqs. (65) and (66) and the above analysis, when the value of the weight updates is smaller than the quantization width:

$$\left| w_{i,j}(k+1) - w_{i,j}(k) \right|$$
$$= \left| \eta \delta_i z_j \right| < \left| \eta \delta_i z_{\max} \right| = \left| \eta \delta_i \right| < q / 2$$ (67)

the network training will cease, where

$$\eta \delta_i = \frac{\eta \lambda \left| t_i - \tilde{y}_i^{H-th} \right| (1 - (\tilde{y}_i^{H-th})^2)}{N_w} = \frac{\eta \lambda F(W_i)}{N_w}$$ (68)

The random value $F(W_i)$ in Eq. (68) can be obtained by using Anand's method (Anand, Mehrotra & Mohan et al., 1995) to our quantization analysis, the conditional expectation $E_w\{\ \}$ in the first few iterations of BP after some simple derivations is:

$$E_w\{|t_i - \tilde{y}_i^{H-th}|(1-(\tilde{y}_i^{H-th})^2)\} = [1 - \sum_{r=1}^{N_w} \frac{q^2 2^{2M}}{12}(\frac{\lambda z_r}{N_w})^2] \qquad (69)$$

where the expected value of Eq. (69) is less than 1. Further, only when the conditional expectation $E_w\{\ \}$ of Eq.(67):

$$E_w\{|w_{i,j}(k+1) - w_{i,j}(k)|\} < E_w\{|\eta\delta_i|\}$$

$$= E_w\{\left|\frac{\eta\lambda F(W_i)}{N_w}\right|\} < E_w\{\left|\frac{\eta\lambda}{N_w}\right|\} < q/2 \qquad (70)$$

is satisfied, i.e., $\frac{\eta\lambda}{N_w} < q/2$, which prevents the weight from changing, the network training ceases. It implies that if there is only quantization and no clipping (the weights do not hit the upper and lower boundaries), then when the inequation $\frac{\eta\lambda}{N_w} > q/2$ holds, the iteration can be performed. In this case, according to Eq. (64), for all p training sample sets, the error is $|t - \tilde{y}^{H-th}| < \varepsilon$ and the HOFNN will converge to minima after limited weight updates. As the effect of the gradient descent on training with finite-precision computations (especially in clipping analysis) is difficult to measure, the statistical evaluation of the weight updates does not effectively determine the property of a network to learn (Moerland & Fiesler, 1997). Therefore, for weight clipping we just follow a qualitative analysis. During on-chip training, due to quantization and weight clipping all the contributions of a single iteration are summed in a nonlinear fashion. If the value of $O(\sqrt{k})$ is too small or Eq. (67) holds, then the rate of the weight updates will be too slow. If the value of η is too large, the value of the weight updates also increases, and the weights are quantized and clipped at each iteration. In addition, the weight updates may depart from the true gradient descent, especially due to nonlinear clipping at the upper and lower boundaries. During the training process, when the weights reach the border of $[-W_{max}, W_{max}]$, and the gradient is directed out of $[-W_{max}, W_{max}]$, the weights are updated along the projection of the gradient onto the borderline of $[-W_{max}, W_{max}]$ instead of along the gradient itself (Gori & Maggini, 1996). In this case, because both quantization and clipping errors exist, the weights are unlikely to be updated towards the direction of gradient optimization. Therefore, during the finite-precision training process, the BP algorithm is highly sensitive to weights. The training failure may be weight clipping or an insufficient weight resolution (Wessels & Barnard, 1992).

As the size of the network increases, the value of the weight updates decreases. When this value is smaller than the quantization width, the weights cannot change and the training fails. Insufficient weight accuracy is the main restriction on large-scale HOFNN hardware implementation. As the number of quantization bits decreases, the weights become more quantized and the NSR increases, adversely affecting network performance.

2.12 The Effect of the Quantization Error on Backpropagation for MLFNN

Feedforward networks use mostly the backpropagation (BP) algorithm of gradient descent for training. The goal of the training is to find the set of weights which corresponds to a global minimum of the error energy function, or at least the weights which give an error lower than some tolerable limit. There are mainly three kinds of training manners in the presence of finite precision:

1. On-chip training means quantization and clipping of the weights at each iteration.
2. Chip-in-the-loop learning: the neural network hardware is only used in the forward propagation of the training; the calculation of the new weights is done off-chip on a computer, which downloads the updated weights onto the chip after each training iteration.
3. Off-chip training means that its training process is performed on a high-precision computer; then the weights are quantified and downloaded on the chip, the recall is performed for the forward propagation.

Because most computations are required in the training phase, the effects of quantization are more significant in this phase. In order to adapt the learning of new patterns very quickly, all computations must be attempted to be implemented on-chip. The on-chip updates are constrained by a finite precision range which departs to some extent from the true gradient descent. This is not just an approximation of the gradient descent, but most of the time has a significantly different behavior, particularly when the learning rate is not small enough with respect to the number of training patterns (Gori & Maggini, 1996). The experimental results showed that slower learning appeared when more weights reached the limits of the clipping function. The performance with clipping during training is lower than that without clipping. As the effect of the gradient descent on training in computations with finite precision will be difficult to measure, the statistical evaluation of the weight updates do not effectively determine a propensity of the network to learn (Wessels & Barnard, 1992).

If we adopt on-chip training, then the weights of the output layer are updated according to the gradient descent algorithm as:

$$Q[w_{j,i}^{(L)}(k+1) - w_{j,i}^{(L)}(k)] = Q[\eta^{(L)} Q[\delta_j^{(L)}] x_i^{(L-1)}] \tag{71}$$

where

$$Q[\delta_j^{(L)}] = Q[\lambda Q[(t_j - x_j^{(L)})(1 - (x_j^{(L)})^2)] / (N_{L-1} + 1)] \tag{72}$$

and $j = 1, 2, \cdots, N_L$, $i = 1, 2, \cdots, N_{L-1} + 1$. η is the learning rate and k is the iteration number. The weights of the remaining layers are updated as:

$$Q[w_{j,i}^{(l)}(k+1) - w_{j,i}^{(l)}(k)] = Q[\eta^{(l)} Q[\delta_j^{(l)}] x_i^{(l-1)}] \tag{73}$$

where

$$Q[\delta_j^{(l)}] = Q[\lambda Q[(1 - (x_j^{(l)})^2)]$$

$$\cdot Q[\sum_{r=1}^{N_{l+1}} w_{r,j}^{(l+1)} Q[\delta_r^{(l+1)}]] / (N_{l-1} + 1)]$$

(74)

and $2 < l \le L - 1$, $j = 1, 2, \cdots, N_l$, $r = 1, 2, \cdots, N_{l+1}$, $i = 1, 2, \cdots, N_{l-1} + 1$.

Assuming that $x_i^{(l-1)}\big|_{\max} = 1$, for the output layer, combining Eqs. (71) with (72), we have that, if and only if

$$Q[\frac{\eta^{(L)} \lambda \big| t_j - x_j^{(L)} \big| (1 - (x_j^{(L)})^2)}{N_{L-1} + 1}] > q / 2$$

(75)

holds at each iteration, the weight updates can be performed. The random value $\big| t_j - x_j^{(L)} \big| (1 - (x_j^{(L)})^2)$ in Eq. (75) can be obtained by using Anand's method (Anand, Mehrotra & Mohan, et al., 1995) in our quantization analysis. The conditional expectation in the first few iterations of backpropagation after some simple derivations is:

$$E_{w^{(L)}} \{ \big| t_j - x_j^{(L)} \big| (1 - (x_j^{(L)})^2) \}$$

$$= [1 - \sum_{r=1}^{N_{L-1}} \frac{q^2 2^{2M}}{12} (\frac{\lambda x_r^{(L-1)}}{N_{L-1} + 1})^2] < 1$$

(76)

Combining Eq. (75) with (76), at least when $Q[\frac{\eta^{(L)} \lambda}{N_{L-1} + 1}] > q / 2$ is satisfied, the iteration can be performed.

For the L-1 layer, combining Eqs. (73) with (74), we have that, if and only if

$$Q[\frac{\eta^{(L-1)} \lambda^2 (1 - (x_j^{(L-1)})^2) x_i^{(L-2)}}{(N_{L-1} + 1)(N_{L-2} + 1)}$$

$$\sum_{r=1}^{N_L} w_{r,j}^{(L)} (t_r - x_r^{(L)})(1 - (x_r^{(L)})^2)] > q / 2$$

(77)

holds at each iteration, the weight updates can be performed. For the same reason, the conditional expectation of the random variable $\sum_{r=1}^{N_L} w_{r,j}^{(L)} (t_r - x_r^{(L)})(1 - (x_r^{(L)})^2)$ in the first few iterations of back-propagation satisfies:

$$E_{w^{(L)}} \{ \sum_{r=1}^{N_L} w_{r,j}^{(L)} (t_r - x_r^{(L)})(1 - (x_r^{(L)})^2) \} = \frac{N_L \lambda x_j^{(L-1)}}{(N_{L-1} + 1)} \frac{q^2 2^{2M}}{12}$$

(78)

Substituting Eq. (78) into (77), we have

Table 1. Comparison of misclassification (%) of different floating-point quantization bits (mantissa/exponent)

Architecture/bits	4/6 bits	6/5 bits	8/4 bits	Infinite precision
The 2nd order FNN	9.33	6.67	2.33	2.0
The 3rd order FNN	15.33	8.0	2.67	2.0
4-(17+1)-3	3.33	4.0	3.33	2.0
4-(7+1)-(6+1)-3	8.0	6.0	4.0	2.0

$$Q[\frac{\eta^{(L-1)}\lambda^3 N_L(1-(x_j^{(L-1)})^2)x_j^{(L-1)}x_i^{(L-2)}}{(N_{L-1}+1)^2(N_{L-2}+1)}\frac{q^2 2^{2M}}{12}] > q/2 \tag{79}$$

Due to the normalized internal activation in forward propagation, a compress factor $\lambda/(N_{l-1}+1)$ will be generated by the derivative of activation in a gradient descent during the BP process. By comparing Eq. (75) with (79), we find that the decrease of the weight updates by the compress factor will have an influence for the output and the other layers. From Eqs. (72) and (74), we know that the delta's decrease of the output layer is caused by the derivative of the internal activation in the layer, and the delta in the remaining layers is related to the derivative of the activation in this layer and the following layers. Therefore, the range of the weight updates is cumulatively decreased by the factor from the output to input layer. In order to cancel these kinds of effect and improve the training performance, $\eta^{(l)}$ is selected to be inversely proportional to the factor. If $\eta^{(l)}$ is selected too large, the weight updates are very large, then the weights are quantized and clipped at each iteration. If $\eta^{(l)}$ on the other hand is selected too small, then the rate of the weight updates is too slow (perhaps because the weight updates are less than the quantization width), and the network training paralyses. When the training fails to converge, then the weight updates are smaller than the quantization width, which prevents the weights from changing, further, there may be weight clipping or insufficient weight resolution.

During the training process with finite precision, the BP algorithm is highly sensitive to weights and training fails when the weight accuracy is worsened. The weight updates are very small for a large size of network. When they are smaller than the quantization width, this prevents the weights from changing and thus the network paralyses. It is a main reason to restrict the implementation of large-scale neural networks in the presence of limited accuracy.

3. EXPERIMENTS

We carried out several simulation experiments to evaluate and confirm the above theoretical results. The research results are directed to improved chip design, and are useful in creating simpler and more reliable hardware implementations. In the following experiments, two different performance measurements have been used: the first one is the minimal RMS error for an approximation problem, and the second one is the misclassification of patterns for a classification problem.

A. Classification for Fisher's Iris Data

We compare the performance of different quantization bits based on Fisher's Iris data. The classifiers use the 2nd– and the 3rd–order FNNs, the 2-layer FNN (the structure of the network is (4+1)-(17+1)-3)) and the 3-layer FNN (the structure of the network is (4+1)-(7+1)-(6+1)-3)), respectively. Fisher's Iris data set contains 150 samples belonging to three classes, for each of which there are 50 samples, and each input is a four-dimensional real vector. The original samples were translated and scaled such that each component of the input vector lies within the range [-1.0, +1.0]. 30 samples from each class were used for training, and all 50 samples from each class were used for testing. Training was stopped when the value of misclassification was unchanged or after 1000 epochs (for HOFNN), after 2000 epochs (for MLFNN). The weight matrices were initialized with random values uniformly distributed in the range $W=\{-1.0\sim+1.0\}$. The learning rate η was set within $\{0.0075N_w, 0.045N_w\}$ for HOFNN, $\eta^{(l)}$ was set within $\{0.05N_{l-1}\sim0.2N_{l-1}\}$ for the 2-layer FNN and $\{0.01N_{l-1}\sim0.08N_{l-1}\}$ for the 3-layer FNN. Where the highest learning rate was permitted convergence (i.e., did not lead to oscillations), $\lambda = 1.0$. The training parameters were made as large as possible to cause the weight updates to increase.

Assuming that the initial weights were uniformly distributed in the range $\{-1.0, +1.0\}$. Our experimental result shows that even if the initial weights comply with a uniform distribution and the maximal fan-in number of the 2nd–order FNN is equal to 15 (i.e., is not too large), the trained weights which are mainly distributed within the range $\{-4, +4\}$, appear to have a normal distribution using infinite precision. When the weight distribution of the floating-point quantization in which the mantissa is 19 bits and the exponent is 1 bit after on-chip training, it is observed that many weights are distributed within the range $\{-2, +2\}$, approaching a normal distribution, while some weights are distributed at +2 and –2 due to weight clipping. When the weight distribution with 20 bits fixed-point quantization after on-chip training, and shows that many weights are distributed near +1 or –1 due to clipping.

Even when the initial weights comply with a uniform distribution and the maximal fan-in number is equal to 17+1 for the 2-layer FNN, the trained weights, which are mainly distributed in the range $\{-2.5, +2.5\}$, can be approximately looked as a normal distribution when using infinite precision. When the weight distribution after on-chip training in the case of 20 bits fixed-point quantization, in which it is observed that most weights are distributed near +1 or –1 due to clipping. Even if the initial weights comply with a uniform distribution and the maximal fan-in number was equal to 15 (i.e. is not too large) for the 2-layer FNN, our experimental result shows that the trained weights which are mainly distributed within the range $\{-10, +10\}$ can be seen to have approximately a normal distribution using infinite precision. When the weight distribution with 16 bits fixed-point quantization in which, after on-chip training, it is observed that many weights are distributed near +1 or –1 due to clipping, showing that the dynamic range of the floating-point quantization is wider than that of the fixed-point quantization. The weight distribution of the floating-point quantization approaches approximately a normal distribution.

We conclude that no matter what distribution the initial weights comply with, the weights distribution will approximate a normal distribution for the training with floating-point or high-precision fixed-point quantization. Only when the number of quantization bits is very low, the weights distribution may cluster to ±1 in the case of training with fixed-point quantization. The above simulations of the distributions roughly match the theoretical analysis in section II, verifying that the dynamic range of the floating-point quantization is larger than that of the fixed-point quantization. The exponent increases with 1 bit, and consequently the dynamic range of the floating-point quantization doubles. When the mantissa and

Table 2. Mean vectors and covariance matrices for noisy XOR problem, 4 clusters and 500 samples per cluster

	Class 1		Class 2	
Mean Vector	Cov. Matrix		Mean Vector	Cov. Matrix
-0.9891 1.0257	0.4048 -0.0145 -0.0145 0.5684		-1.0191 -0.9249	0.4894 -0.0173 -0.0173 0.6554
0.9436 -1.0234	0.6690 0.0277 0.0277 0.4022		1.0216 0.9658	0.6228 0.0493 0.0493 0.3963

the exponent are large enough, the weight distribution of the floating-point quantization approaches a normal distribution.

Our experimental results show that the percentage of misclassification of the fixed-point quantization decreases dramatically when going from 8 to 10 bits, to around 10% at 10 bits. When going from 10 to 32 bits, the value of misclassification further decreases slowly, to around 7% at 32 bits. The percentage of misclassification of the floating-point quantization (exponent equal to 1 bit) decreases dramatically when going from 7 to 11 bits, to around 6% at 11 bits. When further going from 11 to 31 bits, the percentage of misclassification decreases slowly, to around 2.3% at 31 bits. Comparing these two kinds of quantizations, when the exponent $c(=1)$ of the floating-point quantization is very low, overflow easily occurs. In such a case, while the floating-point quantization has features similar to the fixed-point quantization, the dynamic range of the former is larger than that of the latter, and the performance of the former is improved 3-4% on average at the same number of bits compared with that of the latter. When there are fewer quantization bits, the 2nd–order FNN performs better than the 3rd–order FNN (because of the higher NSR of the 3rd–order FNN). When the number of quantization bits is increased, the percentage of misclassification of the 3rd–order FNN will be improved and even less than that of the 2nd–order FNN. At higher precisions, the higher-order FNN exhibits a greater nonlinear mapping ability. Table I shows the results of different numbers of floating-point quantization bits in the exponent, noting that increasing the value of the exponent can increase the dynamic range of computation, resulting in a smaller mantissa and better performance. The simulations and Table I reflect the analytical results derived above in this chapter.

For the MLFNN on-chip training, our experimental results show that the misclassification percentage of the fixed-point quantization decreases dramatically from 10 to 12 bits, and reaches around 10% at 12 bits; from 12 to 32 bits, the misclassification decreases slowly, and reaches around 8% at 32 bits. Below 28 bits the 2-layer FNN has a lower misclassification percentage than the 3-layer FNN, because in this case the NSR of the 3-layer FNN is higher. Above 24 bits both networks have almost the same misclassification error. The floating-point quantization has a better performance than the fixed-point quantization. The performance of the floating-point quantization (exponent is equal to 1 bit) on average is 5% improved compared to that of the fixed-point quantization with the same number of bits. Some results of the floating-point quantization for larger exponents (mantissa bits/exponent bits) were shown in Table II. It is observed that an increasing number of exponent bits can enlarge the dynamic range of computation, resulting in a lower number of mantissa bits and a better performance.

B. Noisy XOR Problem

For the noisy XOR data we used 2000 training patterns generated from 4 normal distributions (with mean vectors and covariance matrices as shown in Table II and corresponding to 2 classes and 4 clusters which consist of 500 random sample sets. 250 sample sets were trained by the 2nd–order, the 3rd–order FNNs, a 2-layer FNN (one single hidden layer, the structure of the network is (2+1)-(15+1)-1, here +1 denotes the bias node) and by a 3-layer FNN (two hidden layers, the structure of the network is (2+1)-(8+1)-(6+1)-1)) into 2 classes, and the remaining 250 sample sets were used to classify. Weight matrices were initialized with random values, uniformly distributed in the range W={-1.0~+1.0}. The learning rate $\eta^{(l)}$ was set within {$0.01N_{l-1}$~$0.25N_{l-1}$} for the 2-layer FNN and {$0.008N_{l-1}$~$0.15N_{l-1}$} for the 3-layer FNN, which was proportional to the fan-in number of the layer and the highest learning rate that permitted convergence (i.e. did not lead to oscillations), $\lambda = 1$. The training parameters were made as large as possible so that the weight updates would get larger. Training was stopped when the misclassification for the training set was unchanged or after 10000 epochs.

For the HOFNN, our experimental results show that the percentage of misclassification for on-chip training decreases dramatically when going from 4 to 10 bits, to around 16% at 10 bits. When going further from 10 to 20 bits, the percentage of misclassification decreases slowly, to around 15% at 20 bits. For off-chip training, the value of misclassification decreases dramatically when going from 4 to 8 bits, to around 19% at 8 bits. When going further from 8 to 20 bits, the percentage of misclassification decreases slowly, to around 17-19% at 20 bits. Above 8 bits, on-chip training performs better than off-chip training, and the 3rd–order FNN performs better than the 2nd–order FNN. Below 8 bits, the HOFNN has no hidden-layer nodes and the local-minimum problem does not occur easily. The performance of on-chip training is worse than off-chip training with low number of quantization bits (which differs from the multilayer feedforward neural networks; because local minima are present, the on-chip training could jump out of the local minimum, in which case performance could improve to some extent (Cybenco, 1989)) and the 2nd–order FNN performs better than the 3rd–order FNN, and has a lower NSR.

Our experimental results show that floating-point quantization (the exponent is equal to 1 bit) performs better than fixed-point quantization with fewer quantization bits, and the former allows to decrease the number of quantization bits to reach the same performance. On-chip training performs better than off-chip training when the quantization is larger than 9 bits. These experiments show that with fewer quantization bits, the change in order of the HOFNN become more sensitive. From the above experiments and analysis, we see that the system will not work if the number of quantization states is reduced to the extreme, such as the case in which the synaptic weights can only hold a few different values (1-2bits).

For MLFNN, the misclassification of the test set as a function of the number of bits for the floating-point quantization (the exponent is equal to 1 bit), the experimental results show that the misclassification percentage of the 2-layer FNN for on-chip training or chip-in-the-loop training decreases dramatically when going from 5 to 11 bits, and reaches around 17~19% at 11 bits. The misclassification percentage of the 3-layer FNN for on-chip training or chip-in-the-loop training decreases dramatically when going from 7 to 13 bits, and reaches around 14~15% at 13 bits. Above 15 bits, the misclassification of all training manners decreases slowly, and reaches around 14~18% at 23 bits. For off-chip training, the range of change of the misclassification percentage is less than that of on-chip training. Below 8 bits the 2-layer FNN has a lower misclassification than the 3-layer FNN. Above 13 bits the two kinds of on-chip training have a lower misclassification than off-chip training.

For MLFNN of the misclassification with different number of bits of the fixed-point quantization, our experimental results show that with fewer bits of quantization the 2-layer FNN has a better performance than the 3-layer FNN, because of the higher NSR of the 3-layer FNN. When the number of quantization bits is increased, the misclassification of the 3-layer FNN improves, and above 16 bits the misclassification of the 3-layer FNN is a little better than that of the 2-layer FNN. Because the exponent c (=1) of the floating-point quantization is very low, overflow easily occurs. In this case, while the floating-point quantization has similar features as the fixed-point quantization, the dynamic range of the former is wider than that of the latter, and the former has a better performance than the latter, especially for lower numbers of quantization bits.

C. Function Approximation

To verify the theoretical evaluation of BP learning with the finite-precision computations presented in this chapter, we used a function-mapping problem. The input to the network was a random number in the interval $[-1, +1]$ and the target was the mapping to the $0.7*\tanh(Cx)$ curve ($C=1.5$ for HOFNN and $C=2$ for MLFNN). The 2nd–order and the 3rd–order FNNs, 2-layer and 3-layer network structures $(1+1)$-$(10+1)$-1 and $(1+1)$-$(6+1)$-$(5+1)$-1 were used to simulate the approximation of the function. Training data consisted of 25 pairs of uniformly distributed data within the interval range $[-1, +1]$, and the testing data consisted of 25 pairs of randomly selected data which differed from the training data. The weight matrices were initialized with random values uniformly distributed in the range $W=\{-1.0, +1.0\}$. The training stopped when the minimal RMS error for each network output was reduced to $RMS_{min}=0.0027$ or after 3000 epochs. The learning rate $\eta^{(l)}$ was set within $\{0.1N_{l-1}$~$0.3N_{l-1}\}$ for the 2-layer FNN and $\{0.05N_{l-1}$~$0.1N_{l-1}\}$ for the 3-layer FNN, $\lambda = 1$. For the function approximation problem of the 2nd–order and the 3rd–order FNNs when using different numbers of bits for fixed-point quantization, our experimental results show that the minimal RMS error decreases dramatically when going from 4 to 8 bits, to around 4-5% at 8 bits. When going further from 8 to 28 bits, the minimal RMS error decreases slowly. The 2nd–order FNN has a lower minimal RMS error than the 3rd–order FNN below 8 bits, but when the quantization is above 16 bits, the 2nd–order FNN has a higher minimal RMS error than the 3rd–order FNN, because the 3rd–order FNN has a higher nonlinear function mapping ability. The minimal RMS error of the 3rd-order FNN can effectively be decreased using more quantization bits. In this case, on-chip training has a lower minimal RMS error than off-chip training, resulting in neural networks with significantly better performance for recall. Because on-chip training with more quantization bits creates weights better suited to training and testing, network performance is improved. The simulations reflect the analytical predictions from section II. When using different floating-point quantization bits for the 2nd–order and the 3rd–order FNNs, the fixed-point quantization has a performance trend similar to floating-point quantization, and that the minimal RMS error of floating-point quantization is only slightly lower than that of fixed-point quantization.

When using different bits of fixed-point quantization, on-chip training has similar performance as chip-in-the-loop training. The 2-layer FNN on-chip training has a lower minimal RMS error than the 3-layer FNN below 12 bits. But when the number of quantization bits is above 12, the 3-layer FNN has a lower minimal RMS error than the 2-layer FNN, because the 3-layer FNN has a higher nonlinear ability. The minimal RMS error can effectively be decreased using a higher number of quantization bits. For off-chip training the minimal RMS error is not sensitive to changing the number of quantization bits. Above 16 bits the minimal RMS error for on-chip training is lower than that of off-chip training. For the function approximation problem when using a different number of floating-point quantization bits, our experimental results show that on-chip training has similar performance as chip-in-the-loop training. The 2-layer FNN on-chip training has a lower minimal RMS error than the 3-layer FNN below 16 bits. But when the number of quantization bits is above 24, them the 3-layer FNN has a lower minimal RMS error than the 2-layers FNN. For off-chip training, the minimal RMS error is not too sensitive to changing the number of quantization bits. It can be concluded that the performance of off-chip training at low number of bits is better than that of on-chip training. Because quantization and clipping are performed at each iteration of on-chip training, the performance of training is poor at lower numbers of bits. But at high numbers of bits on-chip training enables weights better suited to training and testing, thus improving the performance of the network.

4. CONCLUSION

The noise-to-signal ratio (NSR) increases with the order of a HOFNN, or with the number of layers of the multilayer feedforward neural network (MLFNN) indicating that when the order or a layer is increased, more bits are needed to keep performance constant. A decrease in NSR follows an increase in the number of bits. No matter what distribution the internal activation of the outputs complies with, after the signal passes through a nonlinear neuron, the NSR is increased. Although the nonlinear neuron plays a role in the compression of signal and noise, the signal is compressed more than the quantization noise. The larger the internal activation and the nonlinear compression are, the fewer the number of bits required after the signal passes through a nonlinear activation function. The quantization error of the output has less effect on the network's accuracy than that of the input. If we need to reduce the NSR after the signal passes through a nonlinear activation function, we can reduce the input error, decrease the order H, or use

fewer β^{H-th} or ρ^{H-th}, i.e., less β_i^{H-th} ($\sigma_{y_i^{H-th}}^2$ is proportional to σ_x^2 and $NSR_{y_i^{H-th}}^{floit} = \dfrac{\sigma_{e_i^{H-th}}^2}{\sigma_{y_i^{H-th}}^2} = F(N_w)\sigma_\varepsilon^2$).

On-chip training results in a HOFNN with significantly better performance than off-chip training at a high number of bits, and enables weights better suited for training and testing, thus improving the performance and robustness of the network. Comparing the performance between floating-point and fixed-point quantizations, it is evident that the former has a larger dynamic range and better performance than the latter (with the same number of bits). When there are fewer quantization bits, the 2nd–order FNN has a lower NSR and performs better than the 3rd–order FNN. When the number of quantization bits is increased, the performance of the 3rd–order FNN is improved and is better than the 2nd–order FNN (because the higher-order FNN has a more powerful nonlinear function mapping ability). The experiments reveal that changing the order enables greater performance sensitivity with lower-bit quantization. The necessary number of bits can be reduced from layer to layer if the neurons have an effective nonlinear compression. Increasing the number of bits results in an improvement of the NSR, and the ratio is independent of the fan-in number. If we need to reduce the NSR after a neuron, one measure is to reduce the input error; another measure is to decrease the number of layers L; the third measure is to use less σ_x^2 and σ_w^2, or less $\lambda / (N_{l-1} + 1)$, which can effectively reduce the output NSR. The dynamic range of the floating-point quantization is wider than that of the fixed-point quantization, and it has a better performance especially for lower numbers of quantization bits. For a lower number of quantization bits, the 2-layer FNN has less misclassifications than the 3-layer FNN, because of the higher NSR of the 3-layer FNN. No matter what distribution the initial weights comply with, the weights distribution will approximate a normal distribution for the training with floating-point or high-precision fixed-point quantization. Only when the number of quantization bits is very low, the weights distribution may cluster to ±1 in the case of training with fixed-point quantization. The MLFNN is more sensitive to changing the number of layers for lower numbers of quantization bits. When the number of quantization bits is high, the performance of the 3-layer FNN is almost always better than that of the 2-layer FNN. The performance of off-chip training at low numbers of bits is better than that of on-chip training, because quantization and clipping are performed at each iteration by on-chip training. The performance of on-chip training is poor at lower numbers of bits. However, at higher numbers of bits on-chip training enables weights better suited for training and testing, thus improving the performance and robustness of network.

ACKNOWLEDGMENT

This work was supported by Postdoctoral Fellowship, Catholic University of Leuven, Belgium; National Natural Science Foundation (No. 60673109 and No.60871100) and the Teaching and Scientific Research Foundation for the Returned Overseas Chinese Scholars, State Education Ministry. State Key Lab of Pattern Recognition Open Foundation, Chinese Academy of Sciences.

REFERENCES

Anand, R., Mehrotra, K., & Mohan, C. K. (1995). Efficient classification for multiclass problems using modular neural networks. *IEEE Transactions on Neural Networks*, 6, 117–123. doi:10.1109/72.363444

Bayraktaroglu, I., Ogrenci, A. S., & Dundar, G. (1999). ANNSyS: an analog neural network synthesis system. *Neural Networks*, 12, 325–338. doi:10.1016/S0893-6080(98)00122-1

Cybenco, G. (1989). Approximations by supperpositions of a sigmoid function. *Mathematics of Control, Signals, and Systems*, 2, 303–314. doi:10.1007/BF02551274

Dolenko, B. K., & Card, H. C. (1995). Tolerance to analog hardware of onchip learning in backpropagation networks. *IEEE Transactions on Neural Networks*, 6, 1045–1052. doi:10.1109/72.410349

Dundar, G., & Rose, K. (1995). The effects of quantization on multilayer neural networks. *IEEE Transactions on Neural Networks*, 6, 1446–1451. doi:10.1109/72.471364

Gori, M., & Maggini, M. (1996). Optimal convergence of on-Line backpropagation. *IEEE Transactions on Neural Networks*, 7, 251–254. doi:10.1109/72.478415

Hollis, P. W., & Paulos, J. J. (1990). Artificial neural networks using MOS analog multipliers. *IEEE Journal of Solid State Circuits*, 25, 849–855. doi:10.1109/4.102684

Holt, J. L., & Hwang, J.-N. (1993). Finite error precision analysis of neural network hardware implementations. *IEEE Transactions on Computers*, 42, 1380–1389.

Lont, J. B., & Guggenbuhl, W. (1992). Analog CMOS implementation of a multiplayer perceptron with nonlinear synapses. *IEEE Transactions on Neural Networks, 3*, 457–465. doi:10.1109/72.129418

Jiang, M., & Gielen, G. (2001). The effect of quantization on the Higher Order function neural networks. In *Proceedings of IEEE International Workshop on Neural Networks for Signal Processing* (pp.143-152). New York: IEEE Press.

Jiang, M., & Gielen, G. (2003). The Effects of Quantization on Multilayer Feedforward Neural Networks. *International Journal of Pattern Recognition and Artificial Intelligence, 17*, 637–661. doi:10.1142/S0218001403002514

Jiang, M., & Gielen, G. (2004). Backpropagation Analysis of the Limited Precision on Higher Order Function Neural Networks. In J. Wang, (Ed.), *Advances in Neural Networks - ISNN 2004: Part I, Lecture Notes in Computer Science: Vol. 3173*, (pp. 305-310). Heidelberg, Germany: Springer-Verlag.

Jiang, M., Gielen, G., & Xing, B. (2002). A Fast Learning Algorithms of Time-Delay Neural Networks. *Information Sciences, 148*, 27–39. doi:10.1016/S0020-0255(02)00273-6

Jiang, M., Gielen, G., & Zhang, B. (2003). Fast learning algorithms for feedforward neural networks. *Applied Intelligence, 18*, 37–54. doi:10.1023/A:1020922701312

Karayiannis, N. B., & Venetsanopoulos, A. N. (1992). Fast learning algorithms for neural networks. *IEEE Transactions on Circuits and Systems-II: Analog and Digital Signal Processing, 39*, 453–474. doi:10.1109/82.160170

Kashefi, F. (1999). *Rapidly Training Device for Fiber Optic Neural Network.* Unpublished doctoral dissertation, University of Texas at Dallas.

Marco, G., & Marco, M. (1996). Optimal convergence of on-line backpropagation. *IEEE Transactions on Neural Networks, 7*, 251–254. doi:10.1109/72.478415

Moerland, P., & Fiesler, E. (1997). Neural network adaptations to hardware implementations. In E. Fiesler & R. Beale (Eds), *Handbook of Neural Computation* (pp.1-13). Cambridge, MA: Institute of Physics publishing and Oxford University Publishing.

Montalvo, A. J., Gyurcsik, R. S., & Paulos, J. J. (1997). Toward a general purpose analog VLSI neural network with on-chip learning. *IEEE Transactions on Neural Networks, 8*, 413–423. doi:10.1109/72.557695

Oppenheim, A. V., & Schaffer, R. W. (1975). *Digital signal processing.* Englewood Cliffs, NJ: Prentice-Hall, Inc.

Pao, Y. H. (1989). *Adaptive pattern recognition and neural networks.* Reading, MA: Addison-Wesley Publishing Company Inc.

Reyner, L. M., & Filippi, E. (1991). An analysis of the performance of silicon implementations of back-propagation algorithms for artificial neural networks. *IEEE Transactions on Computers, 40*, 1380–1389. doi:10.1109/12.106223

Rumelhart, D. E., Hinton, G. E., & Williams, R. J. (1986). Learning representations by back-propagation errors. *Nature, 323*, 533–536. doi:10.1038/323533a0

APPENDIX 1: PROOF OF EQS. (10) AND (11)

$$E\{x_i^2\} = E\{w_{l,j}^2\} = \sigma_x^2 = \sigma_w^2 = \int_{-q \cdot 2^{M-1}}^{q \cdot 2^{M-1}} \frac{x^2}{2q \cdot 2^{M-1}} dx = \frac{q^2 2^{2M}}{12} \,, \tag{A.01}$$

$$E\{x_i^4\} = \int_{-q \cdot 2^{M-1}}^{q \cdot 2^{M-1}} \frac{x^4}{q \cdot 2^M} dx = \frac{q^4 2^{4M}}{80} = (9/5)\sigma_x^4 \,, \tag{A.02}$$

$$\text{and } E\{x_i^6\} = \int_{-q \cdot 2^{M-1}}^{q \cdot 2^{M-1}} \frac{x^6}{q \cdot 2^M} dx = \frac{q^6 2^{6M}}{448} = (27/7)\sigma_x^6 \,, \tag{A.03}$$

According to Eqs. (9) and (A2), the variance of Δy_i^{2-nd} can easily be obtained:

$$\sigma_{\Delta y_i^{2-nd}}^2 = \sum_{p_1=1}^{N} \sum_{p_2=p_1}^{N} \{E\{(w_{i,p_1p_2} x_{p_1})^2\} + E\{(w_{i,p_1p_2} x_{p_2})^2\} + E\{(x_{p_1} x_{p_2})^2\}\}\sigma_\Delta^2 + \sigma_{\Delta y_i^{1-st}}^2$$

$$= \{\sum_{p_1=1}^{N} \sum_{p_2=p_1}^{N} \{E\{w_{i,p_1p_2}^2\}E\{x_{p_1}^2\} + E\{w_{i,p_1p_2}^2\}E\{x_{p_2}^2\}\} + \sum_{p_1=1}^{N} \sum_{p_2>p_1}^{N} E\{x_{p_1}^2\}E\{x_{p_2}^2\} + NE\{x_{p_1}^4\}\}\sigma_\Delta^2 + \sigma_{\Delta y_i^{1-st}}^2$$

$$= \frac{15N+23}{10} N\sigma_x^4\sigma_\Delta^2 + 2(N+1)\sigma_x^2\sigma_\Delta^2 \,. \tag{A.04}$$

Combining Eqs. (8) and (A1) with (A2) yields the variance of y_i^{2-nd} :

$$\sigma_{y_i^{2-nd}}^2 = \sum_{p_1=1}^{N} \sum_{p_2=p_1}^{N} E\{(w_{i,p_1p_2} x_{p_1} x_{p_2})^2\} + \sigma_{y_i^{1-st}}^2$$

$$= \sum_{p_1=1}^{N} \sum_{p_2>p_1}^{N} E\{w_{i,p_1p_2}^2\}E\{x_{p_1}^2\}E\{x_{p_2}^2\} + NE\{w_{i,p_1p_1}^2\}E\{x_{p_1}^4\} + (N+1)\sigma_x^2\sigma_w^2$$

$$= \frac{5N+13}{10} N\sigma_w^2\sigma_x^4 + (N+1)\sigma_x^2\sigma_w^2 \,. \tag{A.05}$$

Combining Eqs. (A4) with (A5), we deduce the NSR of y_i^{2-nd} as:

$$NSR_{y_i^{2-nd}} = \frac{\sigma_{\Delta y_i^{2-nd}}^2}{\sigma_{y_i^{2-nd}}^2} = \frac{\dfrac{15N+23}{10} N\sigma_x^4\sigma_\Delta^2 + 2(N+1)\sigma_x^2\sigma_\Delta^2}{\dfrac{5N+13}{10} N\sigma_w^2\sigma_x^4 + (N+1)\sigma_x^2\sigma_w^2}$$

$$= \frac{(15N+23)N\sigma_x^2 + 20(N+1)}{(10N+26)N\sigma_x^2 + 20(N+1)} \frac{2\sigma_\Delta^2}{\sigma_x^2} = \xi^{2-nd} \frac{2\sigma_\Delta^2}{\sigma_x^2} > \frac{2\sigma_\Delta^2}{\sigma_x^2} = NSR_{y_i^{1-st}} \,. \tag{A.06}$$

Eq. (A6) yields the desired result.

APPENDIX 2: PROOF OF EQS. (14) AND (15)

Combining Eqs. (13) and (A2) with (A3), we deduce the variance of Δy_i^{3-rd} as:

$$\sigma^2_{\Delta y_i^{3-rd}} = \sum_{p_1=1}^{N} \sum_{p_2=p_1}^{N} \sum_{p_3=p_2}^{N} \{\sigma_w^2[E\{(x_{p_1} x_{p_2})^2\} + E\{(x_{p_2} x_{p_3})^2\} + E\{(x_{p_1} x_{p_3})^2\}] + E\{(x_{p_1} x_{p_2} x_{p_3})^2\}\}\sigma_\Delta^2$$

$$+\sigma^2_{\Delta y_i^{2-nd}} = \{\frac{70N^2 + 147N + 860}{105} N\sigma_x^6 + \frac{15N+23}{10} N\sigma_x^4 + 2(N+1)\sigma_x^2\}\sigma_\Delta^2. \tag{A.07}$$

According to Eq. (12), the variance of y_i^{3-rd} can be written as:

$$\sigma^2_{y_i^{3-rd}} = \sum_{p_1=1}^{N} \sum_{p_2=p_1}^{N} \sum_{p_3=p_2}^{N} E\{(w_{i,p_1p_2p_3} x_{p_1} x_{p_2} x_{p_3})^2\} + \sigma^2_{y_i^{2-nd}}$$

$$= \frac{(35N^2 - 273N + 1258)}{210} N\sigma_w^2\sigma_x^6 + \frac{5N+13}{10} N\sigma_w^2\sigma_x^4 + (N+1)\sigma_x^2\sigma_w^2. \tag{A.08}$$

In order to yield the desired results, we introduce the Basal inequation into our proof.

$$\frac{a}{b} < \frac{a+c}{b+d} < \frac{c}{d} \tag{A.09}$$

If $N \geq 1$ and the signal inputs are limited within the range [-1, +1], then we have

$$\frac{\dfrac{70N^2 + 147N + 860}{210} N\sigma_x^4}{\dfrac{(35N^2 - 273N + 1258)}{210} N\sigma_x^4} > \frac{\dfrac{15N + 23}{20} N\sigma_x^2 + (N+1)}{\dfrac{10N + 26}{20} N\sigma_x^2 + (N+1)}.$$

According to the Basal inequation Eq. (A9), we have the following inequation:

$$\frac{\dfrac{70N^2 + 147N + 860}{210} N\sigma_x^4 + \dfrac{15N + 23}{20} N\sigma_x^2 + (N+1)}{\dfrac{(35N^2 - 273N + 1258)}{210} N\sigma_x^4 + \dfrac{10N + 26}{20} N\sigma_x^2 + (N+1)} > \frac{\dfrac{15N + 23}{20} N\sigma_x^2 + (N+1)}{\dfrac{10N + 26}{20} N\sigma_x^2 + (N+1)} \tag{A.10}$$

Combining Eqs. (A4), (A5), (A7) (A8) and (A10), we deduce the NSR of y_i^{3-rd} as:

$$NSR_{y_i^{3-rd}} = \frac{\sigma^2_{\Delta y_i^{3-rd}}}{\sigma^2_{y_i^{3-rd}}} = \frac{\dfrac{70N^2 + 147N + 860}{105} N\sigma^2_\Delta \sigma^6_x + \sigma^2_{\Delta y_i^{2-nd}}}{\dfrac{(35N^2 - 273N + 1258)}{210} N\sigma^2_w \sigma^6_x + \sigma^2_{y_i^{2-nd}}}$$

$$= \frac{\dfrac{70N^2 + 147N + 860}{210} N\sigma^4_x + \dfrac{15N + 23}{20} N\sigma^2_x + (N+1)}{\dfrac{(35N^2 - 273N + 1258)}{210} N\sigma^4_x + \dfrac{10N + 26}{20} N\sigma^2_x + (N+1)} \cdot \frac{2\sigma^2_\Delta}{\sigma^2_x}$$

$$= \xi^{3-rd} \frac{2\sigma^2_\Delta}{\sigma^2_x} > \xi^{2-nd} \frac{2\sigma^2_\Delta}{\sigma^2_x} = \frac{\sigma^2_{\Delta y_i^{2-nd}}}{\sigma^2_{y_i^{2-nd}}} = NSR_{y_i^{2-nd}} . \tag{A.11}$$

Eq. (A11) yields the desired result.

APPENDIX 3: PROOF OF EQS. (23) AND (24)

The parameters can be estimated after the signal passes through a nonlinear activation function. If $\tilde{y}_i^{H-th} = f(y_i^{H-th}) = \tanh(\lambda y_i^{H-th} / N_w)$, defining $\max\left|y_i^{H-th}\right| = A = \sqrt{3\sigma^2_{y_i^{H-th}}}$, when the probability $p_{y_i^{H-th}}$ of $\left|y_i^{H-th}\right| > A$ is very low and approaches a uniform distribution over the interval (-A, A), we have the mean of output node *i*:

$$E\{\tilde{y}_i^{H-th}\} = \frac{1}{2A} \int_{-A}^{A} \tanh(\lambda y_i^{H-th} / N_w) dy_i^{H-th} = 0 . \tag{A.12}$$

The variance of output node *i* is:

$$\sigma^2_{\tilde{y}_i^{H-th}} = \frac{1}{2A} \int_{-A}^{A} \tanh^2(\lambda y_i^{H-th} / N_w) dy_i^{H-th} = 1 - \frac{N+1}{\lambda A} \tanh(\lambda A / N_w) . \tag{A.13}$$

Combining Eqs. (A2), (A3), (22) and (A13) in finite precision (and when the fan-in number is small and hence the output of the neuron approaches a uniform distribution), we deduce the NSR of $\tilde{y}_i^{H-th}$ as:

$$NSR_{\tilde{y}_i^{H-th}} = \frac{\sigma^2_{\Delta \tilde{y}_i^{H-th}}}{\sigma^2_{\tilde{y}_i^{H-th}}} = \frac{\lambda^2 (1 - (\tilde{y}_i^{H-th})^2)^2 \sigma^2_{\Delta y_i^{H-th}} / N_w^2}{1 - \dfrac{N_w}{\lambda A} \tanh(\lambda A / N_w)} \leq NSR^{\max}_{\tilde{y}_i^{H-th}} = \frac{\lambda^2 \sigma^2_{\Delta y_i^{H-th}} / N_w^2}{1 - \dfrac{N_w}{\lambda A} \tanh(\lambda A / N_w)} \tag{A.14}$$

$$\tanh(x) = x - x^3 / 3 + 2x^5 / 15 - 17x^7 / 315 + 62x^9 / 2835 - \cdots + (-)^{n+1} 2^{2n}(2^{2n} - 1)B_n x^{2n-1} / (2n)! + \cdots$$

$$NSR^{\max}_{\tilde{y}^{H-th}_i} = \frac{\lambda^2 \sigma^2_{\Delta y^{H-th}_i} / N^2_w}{1 - \frac{N_w}{\lambda A}\tanh(\lambda A / N_w)} = \frac{\lambda^2 \sigma^2_{\Delta y^{H-th}_i} / N^2_w}{\frac{\lambda^2 A^2}{3N^2_w} - \frac{2\lambda^4 A^4}{15N^4_w} + \cdots}$$

$$= \frac{\sigma^2_{\Delta y^{H-th}_i} / \sigma^2_{y^{H-th}_i}}{1 - \frac{6\lambda^2 \sigma^2_{y^{H-th}_i}}{5N^2_w} + \cdots} = \beta^{H-th}\frac{\sigma^2_{\Delta y^{H-th}_i}}{\sigma^2_{y^{H-th}_i}} > \frac{\sigma^2_{\Delta y^{H-th}_i}}{\sigma^2_{y^{H-th}_i}} = NSR_{y^{H-th}_i} . \qquad (A.15)$$

Eq. (A15) yields the desired result.

APPENDIX 4: PROOF OF EQS. (26) AND (27)

If the fan-in number N_w is very large, then assuming that $u = y^{H-th}_i / \sigma_{y^{H-th}_i}$ approaches a normal distribution, according to Eq. (16), we have that $E[y^{H-th}_i] = 0$, $\sigma^2_u = 1$ and $E[u] = 0$ hold.

The variance of $\tilde{y}^{H-th}_i$ can be expressed as:

$$\sigma^2_{\tilde{y}^{H-th}_i} = \int_{-\infty}^{\infty} \tanh^2(\lambda y^{H-th}_i / N_w)\frac{1}{\sqrt{2\pi}\sigma_{y^{H-th}_i}}\exp(-\frac{(y^{H-th}_i)^2}{2\sigma^2_{y^{H-th}_i}})dy^{H-th}_i$$

$$= \int_{-\infty}^{\infty} \tanh^2(\lambda \sigma_{y^{H-th}_i} u / N_w)\frac{1}{\sqrt{2\pi}}\exp(-u^2 / 2)du . \qquad (A.16)$$

Assuming that the variance of Δy^{H-th}_i is $\sigma^2_{\Delta y^{H-th}_i}$, let $v = \dfrac{\Delta y^{H-th}_i}{\sigma_{\Delta y^{H-th}_i}} = \dfrac{\Delta y^{H-th}_i}{\sigma_{y^{H-th}_i}\sqrt{NSR_{y^{H-th}_i}}}$, where

$NSR_{y^{H-th}_i} = \dfrac{\sigma^2_{\Delta y^{H-th}_i}}{\sigma^2_{y^{H-th}_i}}$ is the NSR of y^{H-th}_i. Thus we have that $E[v] = 0$ and $\sigma^2_v = 1$ hold. The quantization error of $\tilde{y}^{H-th}_i$ is equal to:

$$\Delta \tilde{y}^{H-th}_i = \tanh[\frac{\lambda}{N_w}(y^{H-th}_i + \Delta y^{H-th}_i)] - \tanh[\frac{\lambda}{N_w}y^{H-th}_i]$$

$$= \tanh[\frac{\lambda}{N_w}\sigma_{y^{H-th}_i}(u + \sqrt{NSR_{y^{H-th}_i}}v)] - \tanh[\frac{\lambda}{N_w}\sigma_{y^{H-th}_i}u].$$

The variance of $\Delta \tilde{y}^{H-th}_i$ can be given as:

$$\sigma^2_{\Delta \tilde{y}_i^{H-th}} = \int_{-\infty}^{\infty} \int_{-\infty}^{\infty} (\tanh[\frac{\lambda}{N_w}\sigma_{y_i^{H-th}}(u + \sqrt{NSR_{y_i^{H-th}}}v)] - \tanh[\frac{\lambda}{N_w}\sigma_{y_i^{H-th}}u])^2 \frac{1}{\sqrt{2\pi}}\exp(-\frac{u^2+v^2}{2})dudv$$

$$(A.17)$$

Assuming that $\frac{\lambda}{N_w}\sigma_{y_i^{H-th}}\sqrt{NSR_{y_i^{H-th}}} << 1$ holds, then due to Eq. (A17), the variance of $\Delta \tilde{y}_i^{H-th}$ can be obtained:

$$\sigma^2_{\Delta \tilde{y}_i^{H-th}} = \frac{\lambda^2}{N_w^2}\sigma^2_{y_i^{H-th}}NSR_{y_i^{H-th}}\int_{-\infty}^{\infty}\frac{4\exp(-s^2/2)}{\sqrt{2\pi}(1+\cosh(\frac{2\lambda}{N_w}\sigma_{y_i^{H-th}}s))^2}ds \ .$$

$$NSR_{\tilde{y}_i^{H-th}} = \frac{\sigma^2_{\Delta \tilde{y}_i^{H-th}}}{\sigma^2_{\tilde{y}_i^{H-th}}} = \frac{\dfrac{\lambda^2}{N_w^2}\sigma^2_{y_i^{H-th}}\displaystyle\int_{-\infty}^{\infty}\dfrac{4\exp(-s^2/2)}{\sqrt{2\pi}(1+\cosh(\dfrac{2\lambda}{N_w}\sigma_{y_i^{H-th}}s))^2}ds}{\displaystyle\int_{-\infty}^{\infty}\tanh^2(\dfrac{\lambda}{N_w}\sigma_{y_i^{H-th}}s)\dfrac{\exp(-s^2/2)}{\sqrt{2\pi}}ds}NSR_{y_i^{H-th}} = \rho_i^{H-th}NSR_{y_i^{H-th}}$$

$$(A.18)$$

Proof of Eqs. (38) and (39) are same as Appendix 4.

APPENDIX 5: PROOF OF EQS. (41) AND (42)

$$E\{x_i^2\} = E\{w_{l,j}^2\} = \sigma_x^2 = \sigma_w^2 = \int_{-q \cdot 2^{M-1}}^{q \cdot 2^{M-1}}\frac{x^2}{2q \cdot 2^{M-1}}dx = \frac{q^2 2^{2M}}{12}$$

$$(A.19)$$

The parameters can be estimated after the nonlinear neuron, if $x_i^{(l)} = f(y_i^{(l)}) = \tanh(\lambda y_i^{(l)}/(N_{l-1}+1))$ Defining $\max|y_i^{(l)}| = A = \sqrt{3\sigma_{y_i^{(l)}}^2}$ which probability ($p_{y_i^{(l)}}$) of $|y_i^{(l)}| > A$ is very low and which is approximately a uniform distribution over the interval (-A, A), we have the mean of $x_i^{(l)}$:

$$E\{x_i^{(l)}\} = \frac{1}{2A}\int_{-A}^{A}\tanh(\lambda y_i^{(l)}/(N_{l-1}+1))dy_i^{(l)} = 0$$

$$(A.20)$$

The variance of $x_i^{(l)}$ is:

$$\sigma_{x_i^{(l)}}^2 = \frac{1}{2A}\int_{-A}^{A}\tanh^2(\lambda y_i^{(l)}/(N_{l-1}+1))dy_i^{(l)} = 1 - \frac{N_{l-1}+1}{\lambda A}\tanh(\lambda A/(N_{l-1}+1))$$

$$(A.21)$$

$$NSR_{x_i^{(l)}} = \frac{\sigma^2_{\Delta x_i^{(l)}}}{\sigma^2_{x_i^{(l)}}} = \frac{\lambda^2(1-(x_i^{(l)})^2)^2 \sigma^2_{\Delta y_i^{(l)}} / (N_{l-1}+1)^2}{1 - \frac{N_{l-1}+1}{\lambda A}\tanh(\lambda A / (N_{l-1}+1))}$$

$$= \frac{\lambda^2(1-(x_i^{(l)})^2)^2 \sigma^2_{y_i^{(l)}}}{(N_{l-1}+1)^2(1 - \frac{N_{l-1}+1}{\lambda A}\tanh(\lambda A / (N_{l-1}+1)))}(\frac{\sigma^2_{\Delta w^{(l)}}}{\sigma^2_{w^{(l)}}} + \frac{\sigma^2_{\Delta x^{(l-1)}}}{\sigma^2_{x^{(l-1)}}})$$

$$< \frac{\lambda^2 \sigma^2_{y_i^{(l)}}}{(N_{l-1}+1)^2(1 - \frac{N_{l-1}+1}{\lambda A}\tanh(\lambda A / (N_{l-1}+1)))}(\frac{\sigma^2_{\Delta w^{(l)}}}{\sigma^2_{w^{(l)}}} + \frac{\sigma^2_{\Delta x^{(l-1)}}}{\sigma^2_{x^{(l-1)}}}) = NSR^{\max}_{x_i^{(l)}} \qquad (A.22)$$

$$\beta^{(l)} = \frac{\lambda^2 \sigma^2_{y_i^{(l)}}}{(N_{l-1}+1)^2(1 - \frac{N_{l-1}+1}{\lambda A}\tanh(\lambda A / (N_{l-1}+1)))} \qquad (A.23)$$

$$\tanh(x) = x - x^3 / 3 + 2x^5 / 15 - 17x^7 / 315 + 62x^9 / 2835 - \cdots + (-)^{n+1}2^{2n}(2^{2n}-1)B_n x^{2n-1} / (2n)! + \cdots$$

$$\beta^{(l)} = \frac{\lambda^2 \sigma^2_{y_i^{(l)}}}{(N_{l-1}+1)^2[\frac{\lambda^2 3\sigma^2_{y_i^{(l)}}}{3(N_{l-1}+1)^2} - \frac{18\lambda^4 \sigma^4_{y_i^{(l)}}}{15(N_{l-1}+1)^4} + \cdots]} \qquad (A.24)$$

Eqs. (A22) and (A24) yield the desired result.

Chapter 9

Improving Sparsity in Kernelized Nonlinear Feature Extraction Algorithms by Polynomial Kernel Higher Order Neural Networks

Zhao Lu
Tuskegee University, USA

Gangbing Song
University of Houston, USA

Leang-San Shieh
University of Houston, USA

ABSTRACT

As a general framework to represent data, the kernel method can be used if the interactions between elements of the domain occur only through inner product. As a major stride towards the nonlinear feature extraction and dimension reduction, two important kernel-based feature extraction algorithms, kernel principal component analysis and kernel Fisher discriminant, have been proposed. They are both used to create a projection of multivariate data onto a space of lower dimensionality, while attempting to preserve as much of the structural nature of the data as possible. However, both methods suffer from the complete loss of sparsity and redundancy in the nonlinear feature representation. In an attempt to mitigate these drawbacks, this article focuses on the application of the newly developed polynomial kernel higher order neural networks in improving the sparsity and thereby obtaining a succinct representation for kernel-based nonlinear feature extraction algorithms. Particularly, the learning algorithm is based on linear programming support vector regression, which outperforms the conventional quadratic programming support vector regression in model sparsity and computational efficiency.

DOI: 10.4018/978-1-61520-711-4.ch009

1. INTRODUCTION

For the purpose of performing pattern recognition in high-dimensional spaces, the pre-processing procedures of mapping the data into a space of lower dimensionality is usually necessary and vital to achieve higher recognition accuracy. In general, a reduction in the dimensionality of the input space will be accompanied by a loss of some of the information which discriminates between different classes. Hence, the objective in dimensionality reduction is to preserve as much of the relevant information as possible. The well-known Principal component analysis (PCA) and Fisher discriminant analysis (FDA) are two important methods in this direction, and they have been used widely in the field of pattern recognition for their great practical significance.

By calculating the eigenvectors of the covariance matrix of the original inputs, principal component analysis (PCA) linearly transforms a high-dimensional input vector into a low-dimensional one whose components are uncorrelated (Diamantaras and Kung, 1996). The new coordinate values by which we represent the data are called principal components. It is often the case that a small number of principal components are sufficient to account for most of the structure in the data. PCA has been successfully used in the realms of face recognition (Kirby and Sirovich, 1990), radar target recognition (Lee and Ou, 2007) and faulty diagnosis (Yoon and MacGregor, 2004), and so on. Essentially PCA is an orthogonal linear transformation into a lower-dimensional coordinate system that preserves maximum variance in the data, thus minimizing mean-square error, computed as a subset of the Karhunen-Loève rotation.

Although PCA is useful in obtaining a lower dimensional representation of the data, as an unsupervised feature extraction algorithm, the directions that are discarded by PCA might be exactly the directions that are needed for distinguishing between classes. Contrary to the unsupervised PCA for feature extraction, by taking the label information of the data into account, Fisher discriminant analysis is a technique to find a direction w that separate the class means well (when projected onto the found direction) while achieving a small variance around these means. The quantity measuring the difference between the means is called *between class variance* and the quantity measuring the variance around these class means is called *within class variance*, respectively. Hence, the objective is to find a direction that maximizes the between class variance while minimizing the within class variance at the same time. The Fisher discriminant analysis also bears strong connections to least squares and Bayes classification.

On the other hand, PCA and FDA both seek to find a linear transformation to represent the data. The features extracted by them are therefore limited to linear combinations of input features, which results in their incapability in capturing more complex nonlinear-correlations and overestimate of the true dimensionality of the data (Bishop, 2006); for instance, PCA's linear model is suboptimal for image data (Mekuz, Bauckhagea & Tsotsos, 2009). In an attempt to surmount these restrictions, the kernel principal component analysis (KPCA) and kernel Fisher discriminant (KFD) were proposed as the nonlinear generalizations of PCA and FDA (Schölkopf, Burge & Smola, 1998; Mika et al, 1999). In KPCA, the original inputs were nonlinearly mapped into a high-dimensional feature space where the linear PCA was calculated, which is equivalent to nonlinear PCA in the original input space. Incorporating the kernel method into the conventional PCA, KPCA is very powerful in extracting nonlinear features by taking into account the high order information of the original inputs implicitly, and eventually leading to the excellent generalization performance for learning (Rosipal et al., 2001; Cao et al., 2003). Similar to that in KPCA, the idea of the KFD is to solve the problem of Fisher linear discriminant in a kernel feature space, thereby yielding a nonlinear discriminant in the input space. Particularly, for classification problems, a crucial advantage of the Fisher discriminant algorithm over standard support vector learning is that the outputs of the former can easily be transformed into conditional probabilities of the classes; in other words, numbers that state not only whether a given test pattern belongs to a certain class, but also the probability of this event. Being able to estimate the conditional probabilities can be very useful, for instance, in applications where the output of a classifier need to be merged with further sources of information (Schölkopf and Smola, 2002).

However, distinguished from the support vector learning with kernel where the dual problem reveal the kernelized problem naturally, the extracted nonlinear features are expressed as a kernel expansion on every data point in KPCA and KFD, which results in the complete loss of sparsity in model representation. Although the algorithm of kernel feature analysis (KFA) has been put forward as an effort to obtain a sparse feature extractor by using a modified setting of KPCA (Smola, Mangasarian & Schölkopf, 1999), it has been shown that KFA is plagued with the problem of grandmother representation in that it identifies a single data point as most important (Garcia-Osorio and Fyfe, 2005).

In this article, in an attempt to obtain a succinct representation for the nonlinear features obtained from KPCA and KFD, the polynomial kernel higher order neural network was employed to improve the sparsity and reduce the redundancy in the kernel expansion. The idea is to use the algorithm of linear programming support vector regression (LP-SVR) to determine the weights and structure of the polynomial kernel higher order neural network for the purpose of approximating the functional representation of the obtained nonlinear features. In LP-SVR, the nonlinear regression problem is treated as a linear one in the kernel space and the ℓ_1 norm of the coefficient vector of the kernel expansion was used as a regularizer. Due to the distinct mechanism used for selecting the support vectors, the LP-SVR is advantageous over the conventional quadratic programming support vector regression (QP-SVR) in flexibility to use more general kernel functions and fast learning based on linear programming. Particularly, it has been demonstrated that the model sparsity can be improved dramatically by using LP-SVR compared to that from QP-SVR (Lu & Sun, 2008; Lu & Sun, 2009). As an innovational machine learning technique, LP-SVR has been successful applied in estimating probability density function and solving linear operator equation (Weston et al., 1999), engine modeling (Bloch et al., 2008), nonlinear dynamical systems identification (Lu, Sun & Butts, 2009), image compression (Hadzic and Kecman, 2000), and so on. Herein, the remarkable sparsity inherited in LP-SVR was utilized to remove the redundancy and thereby get a concise representation for the nonlinear features obtained from KPCA and KFD.

The rest of this chapter is organized as follows. In the next two sections, the algorithms of KPCA and KFD are reviewed for the completeness of this article, respectively. The polynomial kernel higher order neural network is introduced in Section 4. In Section 5, the soft-constrained LP-SVR algorithm, including its application in polynomial kernel higher order neural networks for improving model sparsity in the kernel expansion of the nonlinear features derived from KPCA and KFD is elucidated. For solving the linear programming problem raised in LP-SVR, the primal-dual interior-point method is capitalized on for implementation in Section 6. Conclusion and future works are outlined in Section 7.

The following generic notations will be used throughout this chapter: lower case symbols such as $x, y, \alpha, \cdots$ refer to scalar valued objects, lower case boldface symbols such as $\boldsymbol{x}, \boldsymbol{y}, \boldsymbol{\beta}, \cdots$ refer to vector valued objects, and finally capital boldface symbols will be used for matrices.

2. KERNEL PRINCIPAL COMPONENT ANALYSIS FOR NONLINEAR FEATURE EXTRACTION

By combining inputs together to make a (generally smaller) set of features, Principal Component Analysis (PCA) searches for directions in the data that have largest variance and subsequently project the data onto it. Given a set of centered $m-$dimensional input vectors x_j, $j = 1, \cdots, \ell$ i.e., $\sum_{j=1}^{\ell} x_j = 0$, PCA linearly transforms each input feature vector x_j into a new feature vector $y_j = [y_{j1}, y_{j2}, \cdots, y_{jm}]^T$ by

$$y_j = W^T x_j \tag{1}$$

where $W = \left[w_1, w_2, \cdots, w_m\right]$ is the $m \times m$ orthogonal matrix whose ith column w_i is the ith eigenvector of the sample covariance matrix $U = \frac{1}{\ell} \sum_{j=1}^{\ell} x_j x_j^T$. In other words, PCA firstly solves the eigenvalue problem

$$\lambda_i w_i = U w_i, \quad i = 1, 2, \cdots, m, \tag{2}$$

where λ_i are the eigenvalues of U, and w_i are the corresponding eigenvectors forming a set of orthogonal directions. Based on the estimated orthogonal project direction vector w_i, the components of y_k are then calculated by projecting x_k onto the orthogonal direction w_j:

$$y_{ki} = \langle x_k, w_i \rangle = w_i^T x_k, \quad i = 1, 2, \cdots, m. \tag{3}$$

The new components y_{ki} are called principal components, which apparently are linear combinations of the components of x_k. By using the first several eigenvectors sorted in descending order of the eigenvalues, the number of principal components in y_k can be reduced. By rewriting the equation (2) as

$$w_i = \frac{1}{\lambda_i \ell} \sum_{j=1}^{\ell} \langle x_j, w_i \rangle x_j, \quad i = 1, 2, \cdots, m \tag{4}$$

it is obvious that the projection vector w_i lies in the subspace spanned by input data x_j, $j = 1, \cdots, \ell$.

Since PCA is a linear algorithm per se it is clearly beyond its capabilities to extract nonlinear structures in the data. KPCA is one approach of generalizing linear PCA into nonlinear case using the kernel method. The idea of KPCA is to firstly map the original input vectors x_j into a high-dimensional feature space by nonlinear mapping $\phi(x_j)$ and then to perform the linear PCA in feature space. The orthogonal project directions v_i are then computed by solving the following eigenvalue problem

$$\lambda_i v_i = \bar{U} v_i, \tag{5}$$

which is equivalent to a nonlinear PCA in the original input vector space. In light of the equation (4), the eigenvector v_i can be expressed as a linear combination of $\phi(x_j)$, $j = 1, \cdots, \ell$,

$$\boldsymbol{v}_i = \sum_{j=1}^{\ell} \alpha_{ij} \phi(\boldsymbol{x}_j) \tag{6}$$

i.e., $\boldsymbol{v}_i \in span\left\{\phi(\boldsymbol{x}_1), \phi(\boldsymbol{x}_2), \cdots, \phi(\boldsymbol{x}_\ell)\right\}$. From equation (5) and (6), it can be arrived that the expansion coefficients α_{ij} can be obtained by solving the following eigenvalue problem

$$\tilde{\lambda}_j \boldsymbol{\alpha}_j = \boldsymbol{K}\boldsymbol{\alpha}_j , \tag{7}$$

where $\boldsymbol{K}$ is the $\ell \times \ell$ kernel matrix, $\boldsymbol{\alpha}_j = \left[\alpha_{1j}, \alpha_{2j}, \cdots, \alpha_{\ell j}\right]^T$ and $\tilde{\lambda}_i = \ell\lambda_i$. The value of each element of $\boldsymbol{K}$ is defined as the inner product of $\phi(\boldsymbol{x}_i)$ and $\phi(\boldsymbol{x}_j)$, i.e., $\boldsymbol{K}_{ij} = k(\boldsymbol{x}_i, \boldsymbol{x}_j) = \langle \phi(\boldsymbol{x}_i), \phi(\boldsymbol{x}_j) \rangle$. The nonlinear principal component of $\boldsymbol{x}_k$ can be calculated by projecting the mapped pattern $\phi(\boldsymbol{x}_k)$ onto $\boldsymbol{v}_i$

$$y_{ki} = \langle \boldsymbol{v}_i, \phi(\boldsymbol{x}_k) \rangle = \sum_{j=1}^{\ell} \alpha_{ij}\langle \phi(\boldsymbol{x}_j), \phi(\boldsymbol{x}_k) \rangle = \sum_{j=1}^{\ell} \alpha_{ij}k(\boldsymbol{x}_j, \boldsymbol{x}_k), \tag{8}$$

which allows us to extract nonlinear features up to the number of data points ℓ. In the algorithm of KPCA, the kernel function provides an elegant way of working in the feature space, thereby avoiding all the troubles and difficulties inherent in high dimensions. This method is applicable whenever an algorithm can be cast in terms of dot product.

3. KERNEL FISHER DISCRIMINANT FOR NONLINEAR FEATURE EXTRACTION

Fisher discriminant analysis (FDA) aims at finding a linear projection such that the classes are well separated, and the separability can be measured by the between-class scatter and the within-class scatter.

Given a set of m − dimensional input vectors $\boldsymbol{x}_j$, $j = 1, \cdots, \ell$, ℓ_1 in the subset D_1 labeled ω_1 and ℓ_2 in the subset D_2 labeled ω_2. By projecting $\boldsymbol{x}_j$ onto the one-dimensional subspace in the direction of $\boldsymbol{w}$, a corresponding set of samples $y_j = \boldsymbol{w}^T\boldsymbol{x}_j$, $j = 1, \cdots, \ell$ divided into the subsets Υ_1 and Υ_2 can be obtained. Define $\boldsymbol{m}_1$ and $\boldsymbol{m}_2$ to be the empirical class means, i.e.

$$\boldsymbol{m}_i = \frac{1}{\ell_i} \sum_{\boldsymbol{x}_j \in D_i} \boldsymbol{x}_j . \tag{9}$$

Similarly, the means of the data projected onto the direction of $\boldsymbol{w}$ can be computed as

$$\mu_i = \frac{1}{\ell_i} \sum_{y_j \in \Upsilon_i} y_j = \frac{1}{\ell_i} \sum_{\boldsymbol{x}_j \in D_i} \boldsymbol{w}^T\boldsymbol{x}_j = \boldsymbol{w}^T\boldsymbol{m}_i \tag{10}$$

i.e. the means μ_i of the projections are the projected means $\boldsymbol{m}_i$. The variances σ_1, σ_2 of the projected data can be expressed as

$$\sigma_i = \sum_{x_j \in D_i} (w^T x_j - \mu_i)^T .$$ (11)

Then maximizing the between class variance and minimizing the within class variance can be achieved by maximizing

$$J(w) = \frac{(\mu_1 - \mu_2)^2}{\sigma_1 + \sigma_2}$$ (12)

which will yield a direction w such that the ratio of between-class variance and within-class variance is maximal. Substituting the equations (10) for the means and (11) for the variances into (12) yields

$$J(w) = \frac{w^T S_B w}{w^T S_W w}$$ (13)

where the between class scatter matrix S_B and within class scatter matrix S_W are defined as

$$S_B = (m_2 - m_1)(m_2 - m_1)^T$$ (14)

$$S_W = \sum_{i=1}^{2} \sum_{x_j \in D_i} (x_j - m_i)(x_j - m_i)^T .$$ (15)

The quantity in equation (13) is often referred to as Rayleigh coefficient or generalized Rayleigh quotient. It is well-known that the w maximizing Rayleigh is the leading eigenvector of the generalized eigenproblem

$$S_B w = \lambda S_W w$$ (16)

Similar to that in KPCA, to generalize the Fisher discriminant analysis into nonlinear features extraction, we map the original input vectors x_j into a high-dimensional feature space by nonlinear mapping $\phi(x_j)$ and then reformulate the problem in the feature space. Firstly, we rewrite S_W as

$$S_W = \sum_{i=1}^{2} \sum_{x_j \in D_i} (x_j x_j^T - m_i m_i^T)$$ (17)

and make the key assumption that

$$w = \sum_{j=1}^{\ell} \gamma_j \phi(x_j).$$ (18)

Rewriting the numerator in the generalized Rayleigh quotient (13) as

$$w^T S_B w = (w^T m_2 - w^T m_1)^2$$ (19)

where

$$w^T m_i = \sum_{r=1}^{\ell} \gamma_r \varphi^T(x_r) \frac{1}{\ell_i} \sum_{x_j \in D_i} \varphi(x_j)$$

$$= \sum_{r=1}^{\ell} \gamma_r \sum_{x_j \in D_i} \frac{\varphi^T(x_r)\varphi(x_j)}{\ell_i} = \sum_{r=1}^{\ell} \gamma_r \sum_{x_j \in D_i} \frac{k(x_r, x_j)}{\ell_i} \tag{20}$$

By defining the r-th component of the ℓ-dimensional column vector ϑ_i as $\left(\vartheta_i\right)_r = \sum_{x_j \in D_i} \frac{k(x_r, x_j)}{\ell_i}$

it can be followed from equation (20) that

$$w^T m_i = \gamma^T \vartheta_i \tag{21}$$

and then substituting (21) into (19) yields

$$w^T S_B w = \gamma^T (\vartheta_2 - \vartheta_1)(\vartheta_2 - \vartheta_1)^T \gamma = \gamma^T N \gamma , \tag{22}$$

where $N = (\vartheta_2 - \vartheta_1)(\vartheta_2 - \vartheta_1)^T$. On the other hand, it follows from

$$w^T \phi(x_j) = \sum_{r=1}^{\ell} \gamma_r \phi^T(x_r)\phi(x_j) = \sum_{r=1}^{\ell} \gamma_r k(x_r, x_j) \tag{23}$$

and equation (21) that

$$\begin{aligned} w^T S_W w &= \sum_{i=1}^{2} \sum_{x_j \in D_i} w^T \left[\phi(x_j)\phi^T(x_j) - m_i m_i^T \right] w \\ &= \sum_{i=1}^{2} \sum_{x_j \in D_i} \left[w^T \phi(x_j)\phi^T(x_j)w - w^T m_i m_i^T w \right] \\ &= \sum_{i=1}^{2} \sum_{x_j \in D_i} \left[\sum_{r=1}^{\ell} \gamma_r k(x_r, x_j) \sum_{s=1}^{\ell} \gamma_s k(x_s, x_j) - \gamma^T \vartheta_i \vartheta_i^T \gamma \right] \\ &= \sum_{i=1}^{2} \gamma^T \left[K_i K_i^T - \ell_i \vartheta_i \vartheta_i^T \right] \gamma \\ &= \gamma^T M \gamma \end{aligned} \tag{24}$$

where $\left(K_i\right)_{rj} = k(x_r, x_j)$ and $M = \sum_{i=1}^{2} \left[K_i K_i^T - \ell_i \vartheta_i \vartheta_i^T \right]$, $x_j \in D_i$. Substituting equations (22) & (24) back into the generalized Rayleigh quotient (13) yields

$$J(\gamma) = \frac{\gamma^T N \gamma}{\gamma^T M \gamma} \tag{25}$$

Hence, maximizing the Rayleigh coefficient (13) relative to w in the nonlinear feature space is equivalent to maximize $J(\gamma)$ in equation (25) with respect to γ, and the projections y_j of the mapped data $\phi(x_j)$ in the nonlinear feature space onto the single dimensional direction w can be calculated by using the equation (23) as follows

$$y_j = w^T \phi(x_j) = \sum_{r=1}^{\ell} \gamma_r k(x_r, x_j).$$

4. POLYNOMIAL KERNEL HIGHER ORDER NEURAL NETWORKS

Higher order neural networks (HONN) is a fully interconnected network, containing high-order connections of sigmoid functions in its neurons (Kosmatopoulos et al., 1995). Defining by x, y its input and output, respectively, with $x \in R^n$ and $y \in R$, the input-output representation of the HONN is ruled by

$$y = w^T \Psi(x) \tag{26}$$

where w is an L – dimensional vector of the adjustable synaptic weights and $\Psi(x)$ is an L – dimensional vector with elements $\Psi_i(x)$, $i = 1, 2, \cdots, L$, of the form

$$\Psi_i(x) = \prod_{j \in I_i} \left[s(x_j) \right]^{d_j(i)} \tag{27}$$

where I_i, $i = 1, 2, \cdots, L$, are collections of L unordered subsets of $\{1, 2, \cdots, n\}$ and $d_j(i)$ are non-negative integers. In equation (27), $s(x_j)$ is a monotone increasing smooth function, which is usually represented by sigmoidals of the form

$$s(x_j) = \frac{\mu}{1 + e^{-l(x_j - c)}} + \lambda, \ j = 1, 2, \cdots, n \tag{28}$$

In equation (28), the parameters μ, l represent the bound and the maximum slope of the sigmoidal curvature and λ, c, the vertical and horizontal shifts, respectively.

For the HONN model described above, it is known (Kosmatopoulos et al., 1995) that there exist integers L, $d_j(i)$ and optimal weight values w^*, such that for any smooth unknown function $f(x)$ and for any given $\varepsilon > 0$, one has $\left| f(x) - w^{*T} \Psi(x) \right| \le \varepsilon$, $\forall x \in \mathbb{Z}$, where $\mathbb{Z} \subset R^n$ is a known compact region. In other words, for sufficiently high-order terms, there exist weight values w^* such that the HONN structure $w^{*T} \Psi(x)$ can approximate $f(x)$ to any degree of accuracy over a compact domain.

As a kernel-based network architecture equivalent to HONN, the polynomial kernel higher order neural networks proposed very recently (Lu, Shieh & Chen, 2008) are capable to induce the feature map equivalent to equation (27) by defining the kernel function as

$$k(x, x_i) = k_{ploy2}(s(x), s(x_i)) = \left(\langle s(x), s(x_i) \rangle + 1 \right)^d \tag{29}$$

which can be viewed as a variation of the inhomogeneous polynomial kernel:

The following theorem guarantees the positive definiteness of the kernel shown in (29).

Theorem. (Schölkopf and Smola, 2002) If $\sigma : X \to X$ is a bijection mapping (a transformation which is one-to-one and onto), and if $k(x, x_i)$ is a kernel, then $k(\sigma(x), \sigma(x_i))$ is also a kernel.

Obviously, the sigmoid function given by equation (28) is a bijection mapping; therefore, the $k(x, x_i)$ in equation (29) is a kernel and the feature map induced by kernel (29) corresponds to the scaled high-order connections of sigmoid functions. Hence, a new three-layer network topology equivalent to HONN, called the polynomial kernel higher order neural network, can be defined as follows:

Input-layer: $net^1 = s(x)$, where x is the input vector;

Hidden-layer: $net_j^2 = (1 + s(x_j)^T net^1)^d$, where $s(x_j)$ is the weights vector connecting the j th node in the hidden layer to the input-layer, and x_j is the selected training point; $\left[s(x_1), \cdots, s(x_h)\right]^T$ is the interconnection matrix, where h is the number of hidden nodes;

Output-layer: $y = \beta^T net^2 = \sum_{i=1}^{h} \beta_i net_i^2$ where $net^2 = \left[net_1^2, \cdots, net_h^2\right]^T$ and $\beta = \left[\beta_1, \cdots, \beta_h\right]^T$ is the weight vector of the output layer.

In summary, the mathematical representation of a polynomial kernel network is

$$y = \sum_{i=1}^{h} \beta_i (1 + s(x_j)^T s(x))^d = \sum_{i=1}^{h} \beta_i k_{ploy2}(s(x), s(x_j)) \tag{30}$$

The main advantage of this polynomial kernel higher order neural network over HONN lies in the availability of systematic learning methods for determining its optimal topological structure and weights using structural risk minimization. The conventional support vector regression algorithm can be used for training the polynomial kernel higher order neural networks, where the learning procedure amounts to a quadratic programming problem.

5. SOFT-CONSTRAINED LINEAR PROGRAMMING SVR

Conceptually there are some similarities between the LP-SVR and QP-SVR. Both algorithms adopt the ε-insensitive loss function, and use kernel functions in model representation. In the LP formulation, only symmetry of the kernel is required. It is not necessary for the kernel to satisfy Mercer's conditions (or positive semi-definiteness) as in the original QP form of the SVR problem.

Consider regression problem given by equation (8) for nonlinear principal components

$$y_i = f_i(x) = \langle \upsilon_i, \varphi(x) \rangle =$$
$$\sum_{j=1}^{\ell} \alpha_{ij} \langle \varphi(x_j), \varphi(x) \rangle = \sum_{j=1}^{\ell} \alpha_{ij} k(x_j, x) \tag{31}$$

where i is the index for the nonlinear principal components obtained from KPCA. For KPCA, several commonly-used kernel functions in literatures are:

- Gaussian radial basis function (GRBF) kernel:

$$k(\boldsymbol{x}, \boldsymbol{x}') = exp\left(\frac{-\left\|\boldsymbol{x} - \boldsymbol{x}'\right\|^2}{2\sigma^2}\right) \tag{32}$$

- Polynomial kernel:

$$k(\boldsymbol{x}, \boldsymbol{x}') = (1 + \langle \boldsymbol{x}, \boldsymbol{x}' \rangle)^q \tag{33}$$

- Sigmoid kernel:

$$k(\boldsymbol{x}, \boldsymbol{x}') = tanh(\alpha\langle \boldsymbol{x}, \boldsymbol{x}' \rangle + \gamma) \tag{34}$$

- Thin plate spline kernel:

$$k(\boldsymbol{x}, \boldsymbol{x}') = \left\|\boldsymbol{x} - \boldsymbol{y}\right\|^2 \ln\left\|\boldsymbol{x} - \boldsymbol{y}\right\| \tag{35}$$

where σ, q, α, γ are adjustable parameters of the kernel functions. The GRBF kernel (32) and thin plate spline kernel (35) are in the class of translation-invariant kernels, and the polynomial kernel (33) and sigmoid kernel (34) are examples of rotation invariant kernels.

In an attempt to improve the sparsity in the nonlinear principal component representation (31), the kernel function (29) was used in the framework of $\varepsilon - $ SV regression. In this way, the nonlinear principal component can be represented in the form of polynomial kernel higher order neural networks, i.e.,

$$y_i = f_i(\boldsymbol{x}) = \sum_{j=1}^{\ell} \beta_{ij} k(\boldsymbol{x}_j, \boldsymbol{x}) \tag{36}$$

In $\varepsilon - $ SV regression, the goal is to find a function $f(\boldsymbol{x})$ that has at most ε deviation from the actually obtained targets y_i for all the training data, and at the same time, is as smooth as possible. To this end, the following regularization problem was considered,

$$minimize \; R_{reg}[f] = \sum_{i=1}^{\ell} L(y_i - f(\boldsymbol{x}_i)) + \lambda\left\|\boldsymbol{\beta}\right\|_1 \tag{37}$$

where $L(\cdot)$ is defined as the following $\varepsilon - $ insensitivity loss function,

$$L(y_i - f(\boldsymbol{x}_i)) = \begin{cases} 0, & if \; \left|y_i - f(\boldsymbol{x}_i)\right| \leq \varepsilon \\ \left|y_i - f(\boldsymbol{x}_i)\right| - \varepsilon, & otherwise \end{cases} \tag{38}$$

and $f(\boldsymbol{x})$ is in the form of (36) and $\left\|\boldsymbol{\beta}\right\|_1$ denotes the ℓ_1 norm in coefficient space. This regularization problem is equivalent to the following constrained optimization problem

$$minimize \quad \frac{1}{2}\|\boldsymbol{\beta}\|_1 + C\sum_{i=1}^{\ell}(\xi_i + \xi_i^*),$$

$$subject \;\; to \;\; \begin{cases} y_i - \sum_{j=1}^{\ell}\beta_j k(\boldsymbol{x}_j, \boldsymbol{x_i}) \leq \varepsilon + \xi_i, \\ \sum_{j=1}^{\ell}\beta_j k(\boldsymbol{x}_j, \boldsymbol{x_i}) - y_i \leq \varepsilon + \xi_i^*, \\ \qquad \xi_i, \;\; \xi_i^* \geq 0. \end{cases} \tag{39}$$

where the ξ_i and ξ_i^* are the slack variables, corresponding to the size of the excess positive and negative deviation respectively. This is a optimization problem with inequality constraints, and the optimization criterion penalizes data points whose y − values differ from $f(\boldsymbol{x})$ by more than ε. The constant $C > 0$ determines the trade-off between the flatness of f and the amount up to which deviations larger than ε are tolerated. From the geometric perspective, it can be followed that $\xi_i \xi_i^* = 0$ in SV regression. Therefore, it is sufficient to just introduce slack variable ξ_i in the constrained optimization problem (39). Thus, we arrive at the following formulation of SV regression with fewer slack variables

$$minimize \quad \frac{1}{2}\|\boldsymbol{\beta}\|_1 + 2C\sum_{i=1}^{\ell}\xi_i,$$

$$subject \;\; to \;\; \begin{cases} y_i - \sum_{j=1}^{\ell}\beta_j k(\boldsymbol{x}_j, \boldsymbol{x_i}) \leq \varepsilon + \xi_i, \\ \sum_{j=1}^{\ell}\beta_j k(\boldsymbol{x}_j, \boldsymbol{x_i}) - y_i \leq \varepsilon + \xi_i, \\ \qquad \xi_i \geq 0. \end{cases} \tag{40}$$

In an attempt to convert the optimization problem above into a linear programming problem, we decompose β_i and $|\beta_i|$ as follows

$$\beta_i = \alpha_i^+ - \alpha_i^-, \; |\beta_i| = \alpha_i^+ + \alpha_i^- \tag{41}$$

where $\alpha_i^+, \alpha_i^- \geq 0$. It is worth noting that the decompositions in (41) are unique, i.e., for a given β_i there is only one pair (α_i^+, α_i^-) which fulfills both equations. Furthermore, both variables cannot be larger than zero at the same time, i.e., $\alpha_i^+ \cdot \alpha_i^- = 0$. In this way, the ℓ_1 norm of β can be written as

$$\|\boldsymbol{\beta}\|_1 = \left(\underbrace{1, \; 1, \; \cdots, 1,}_{\ell} \; \underbrace{1, \; 1, \; \cdots, 1}_{\ell}\right)\begin{pmatrix}\boldsymbol{\alpha}^+ \\ \boldsymbol{\alpha}^-\end{pmatrix} \tag{42}$$

where $\boldsymbol{\alpha}^+ = (\alpha_1^+, \; \alpha_2^+, \; \cdots, \; \alpha_\ell^+)^T$ and $\boldsymbol{\alpha}^- = (\alpha_1^-, \; \alpha_2^-, \; \cdots, \; \alpha_\ell^-)^T$. Furthermore, the constraints in the formulation (40) can also be written in the following vector form

$$\begin{pmatrix} K & -K & -I \\ -K & K & -I \end{pmatrix} \cdot \begin{pmatrix} \alpha^+ \\ \alpha^- \\ \xi \end{pmatrix} \leq \begin{pmatrix} y + \varepsilon \\ \varepsilon - y \end{pmatrix} \tag{43}$$

where $K_{ij} = k(x_i, x_j)$, $\xi = (\xi_1, \xi_2, \cdots, \xi_\ell)^T$ and I is $\ell \times \ell$ identity matrix. Thus, the constrained optimization problem (40) can be implemented by the following linear programming problem

$$minimize \quad c^T \begin{pmatrix} \alpha^+ \\ \alpha^- \\ \xi \end{pmatrix},$$

$$subject \quad to \quad \begin{cases} \begin{pmatrix} K & -K & -I \\ -K & K & -I \end{pmatrix} \cdot \begin{pmatrix} \alpha^+ \\ \alpha^- \\ \xi \end{pmatrix} \leq \begin{pmatrix} y + \varepsilon \\ \varepsilon - y \end{pmatrix} \\ \alpha^+, \alpha^- \geq 0, \ \xi \geq 0 \end{cases} \tag{44}$$

where $c = \left(\underbrace{1, 1, \cdots, 1}_{\ell}, \underbrace{1, 1, \cdots, 1}_{\ell}, \underbrace{2C, 2C, \cdots, 2C}_{\ell} \right)^T$

In the QP-SVR case, the set of points not inside the tube coincides with the set of SVs. While, in the LP context, this is no longer true—although the solution is still sparse, any point could be an SV, even if it is inside the tube (Smola, Schölkopf & Ratsch, 1999). Actually, the sparse solution can still be obtained in LP-SVR even though the size of the insensitive tube is set to zero (Drezet and Harrison, 2001), due to the usage of soft constraints; however, usually sparser solution can be obtained by using non-zero ε.

6. PRIMAL-DUAL INTERIOR-POINT METHOD FOR LP-SVR

In the realm of linear programming, for the purpose of overcoming the potential weakness in the simplex methods, the interior-point method (IPM) was proposed in 1984, in which the iterative procedure moves through the interior of the feasible region rather than around the edges. As the elegant and powerful class of interior-point methods, the fundamental ideas of primal-dual interior-point methods (PD-IPM) were developed between 1987 and 1991.

Interior point methods are intimately linked with duality theory. Treat the linear programming problem (44) as the primal problem, the corresponding dual problem in symmetric form can be written as

$$minimize \quad \left((y + \varepsilon)^T, \ (\varepsilon - y)^T \right) z$$

$$subject \quad to \quad \begin{cases} \begin{pmatrix} K & -K \\ -K & K \\ -I & -I \end{pmatrix} \cdot z \geq -c \\ z \geq 0 \end{cases} \tag{45}$$

where $z = (z_1, z_2, \cdots, z_{2\ell})^T$ is the variable for the dual problem. Introducing the slack variables $p = (p_1, p_2, \cdots, p_{2\ell})^T \geq 0$ and $g = (g_1, g_2, \cdots, g_{3\ell})^T \geq 0$, and we can rewrite the primal problem (44) and the dual problem (45) in the standard form:

primal problem:

$$
\begin{aligned}
minimize \quad & c^T \begin{pmatrix} \alpha^+ \\ \alpha^- \\ \xi \end{pmatrix} \\
subject\ to \quad & \left\{ \begin{array}{c} \begin{pmatrix} K & -K & -I \\ -K & K & -I \end{pmatrix} \cdot \begin{pmatrix} \alpha^+ \\ \alpha^- \\ \xi \end{pmatrix} + p = \begin{pmatrix} y + \varepsilon \\ \varepsilon - y \end{pmatrix} \\ \alpha^+, \alpha^- \geq 0, \ \xi, p \geq 0 \end{array} \right.
\end{aligned}
\tag{46}
$$

Dual problem:

$$
\begin{aligned}
minimize \quad & \left((y + \varepsilon)^T, \ (\varepsilon - y)^T \right) z \\
subject\ to \quad & \left\{ \begin{array}{c} \begin{pmatrix} K & -K \\ -K & K \\ -I & -I \end{pmatrix} \cdot z - g = -c \\ z, g \geq 0 \end{array} \right.
\end{aligned}
\tag{47}
$$

For the dual pairs (46) & (47), the corresponding perturbed KKT equation can be written as

$$
\left\{ \begin{array}{c} \begin{pmatrix} K & -K & -I \\ -K & K & -I \end{pmatrix} \cdot \begin{pmatrix} \alpha^+ \\ \alpha^- \\ \xi \end{pmatrix} + p = \begin{pmatrix} y + \varepsilon \\ \varepsilon - y \end{pmatrix} \\ \begin{pmatrix} K & -K \\ -K & K \\ -I & -I \end{pmatrix} \cdot z - g = -c \\ D \cdot Ge = \mu e \\ Z \cdot Pe = \mu e \end{array} \right.
\tag{48}
$$

where $D = diag(\alpha_1^+, \alpha_2^+, \cdots, \alpha_\ell^+, \alpha_1^-, \alpha_2^-, \cdots, \alpha_\ell^-, \xi_1, \xi_2, \cdots, \xi_\ell)$ $G = diag(g_1, g_2, \cdots, g_{3\ell})$ $P = diag(p_1, p_2, \cdots, p_{2\ell})$, $Z = diag(z_1, z_2, \cdots, z_{2\ell})$ and e denote the vector of all ones. By using the Newton's method for solving the nonlinear system (48) consisting of 10ℓ algebraic equations, the step directions $\Delta\alpha^+$ $\Delta\alpha^-$, $\Delta\xi$, Δp, Δz, Δg can be computed by solving the following linear system of algebraic equations

$$
\left|
\begin{array}{l}
\begin{pmatrix} K & -K & -I \\ -K & K & -I \end{pmatrix} \cdot \begin{pmatrix} \Delta \boldsymbol{\alpha}^+ \\ \Delta \boldsymbol{\alpha}^- \\ \Delta \boldsymbol{\xi} \end{pmatrix} + \Delta p = \begin{pmatrix} y + \varepsilon \\ \varepsilon - y \end{pmatrix} - \begin{pmatrix} K & -K & -I \\ -K & K & -I \end{pmatrix} \cdot \begin{pmatrix} \boldsymbol{\alpha}^+ \\ \boldsymbol{\alpha}^- \\ \boldsymbol{\xi} \end{pmatrix} - p \\[20pt]
\qquad \begin{pmatrix} K & -K \\ -K & K \\ -I & -I \end{pmatrix} \cdot \Delta z - \Delta g = -c - \begin{pmatrix} K & -K \\ -K & K \\ -I & -I \end{pmatrix} z + g \\[20pt]
\qquad\quad G \begin{pmatrix} \Delta \boldsymbol{\alpha}^+ \\ \Delta \boldsymbol{\alpha}^- \\ \Delta \boldsymbol{\xi} \end{pmatrix} + D\Delta g = \mu e \text{ - } DGe \\[16pt]
\qquad\qquad P\Delta z + Z\Delta p = \mu e \text{ - } ZPe
\end{array}
\right. \tag{49}
$$

w h e r e $\quad \Delta \boldsymbol{\alpha}^+ = (\Delta \alpha_1^+, \ \Delta \alpha_2^+, \ \cdots, \ \Delta \alpha_\ell^+)^T \qquad \Delta \boldsymbol{\alpha}^- = (\Delta \alpha_1^-, \ \Delta \alpha_2^-, \ \cdots, \ \Delta \alpha_\ell^-)^T$

$\Delta \boldsymbol{\xi} = (\Delta \xi_1, \ \Delta \xi_2, \ \cdots, \Delta \xi_\ell)^T \qquad \Delta \boldsymbol{p} = (\Delta p_1, \Delta p_2, \cdots, \Delta p_{2\ell})^T \qquad \Delta \boldsymbol{z} = (\Delta z_1, \Delta z_2, \cdots, \Delta z_{2\ell})^T$,

$\Delta \boldsymbol{g} = (\Delta g_1, \Delta g_2, \cdots, \Delta g_{3\ell})^T$. The primal-dual interior point method works simultaneously on primal and dual linear programming problems and generates a sequence of pairs of their interior feasible solutions. Along the sequence generated, the duality gap converges to zero.

7. CONCLUSION

Since PCA and FDA are linear algorithms it is clearly beyond their capabilities to extract nonlinear structures from the data. It is where the KPCA and KFD algorithm set in the scenario of unsupervised and supervised learning. In this chapter, for the purpose of removing the redundancy and improving the sparsity in the representation of nonlinear features obtained by KPCA and KFD, the newly developed polynomial kernel higher order neural networks was utilized to approximate the functional relationship between the nonlinear features extracted and data points to obtain a succinct representation. The learning algorithm was based on LP-SVR and primal-dual interior-point method was employed to solve the linear programming problem efficiently.

REFERENCES

Bishop, M. C. (2006). *Pattern Recognition and Machine Learning*. New York:Springer.

Bloch, G., Lauer, F., Colin, G., & Chamaillard, Y. (2008). Support vector regression from simulation data and few experimental samples . *Information Sciences*, *178*(20), 3813–3827. doi:10.1016/j. ins.2008.05.016

Cao, L. J., Chua, K. S., Chong, W. K., Lee, H. P., & Gu, Q. M. (2003). A comparison of PCA, KPCA and ICA for dimensionality reduction in support vector machine . *Neurocomputing*, *55*, 321–336. doi:10.1016/S0925-2312(03)00433-8

Diamantaras, K. I., & Kung, S. Y. (1996). *Principal Component Neural Networks: Theory and Applications*. Hoboken, NJ: John Wiley & Sons.Drezet, P. M. L., & Harrison, R. F. (2001). A new method for sparsity control in support vector classification and regression. *Pattern Recognition*, *34*, 111–125.

Garcia-Osorio, C., & Fyfe, C. (2005). Regaining sparsity in kernel principal components. *Neurocomputing, 67*, 398–402. doi:10.1016/j.neucom.2004.10.115

Hadzic, I., & Kecman, V. (2000). Support vector machines trained by linear programming: theory and application in image compression and data classification. In *Prceedings of IEEE 5th Seminar on Neural Network Applications in Electrical Engineering*

Kirby, M., & Sirovich, L. (1990). Application of the Karhunen-Loève procedure for the characterization of human faces. *IEEE Transactions on Pattern Analysis and Machine Intelligence, 12*(1), 103–108. doi:10.1109/34.41390

Kosmatopoulos, E. B., Polycarpou, M. M., Christodoulou, M. A., & Ioannou, P. A. (1995). High-order neural network structures for identification of dynamical systems. *IEEE Transactions on Neural Networks, 6*, 422–431. doi:10.1109/72.363477

Lee, K. C., & Ou, J. S. (2007). Radar target recognition by using linear discriminant algorithm on angular-diversity RCS. *Journal of Electromagnetic Waves and Applications, 21*(14), 2033–2048. doi:10.1163/156939307783152902

Lu, Z., Shieh, L. S., & Chen, G. R. (2008). A new topology for artificial higher order neural networks: polynomial kernel networks, In M. Zhang (Ed.), *Artificial Higher Order Neural Networks for Economics and Business* (pp. 430–441). Information Science Reference Publishing.

Lu, Z., & Sun, J. (2008). Soft-constrained linear programming support vector regression for nonlinear black-box systems identification, In D. Vrakas and I. Vlahavas (Ed.), *Artificial Intelligence for Advanced Problem Solving Techniques* (pp. 137–146). Information Science Reference Publishing.

Lu, Z., & Sun, J. (2009). Non-Mercer Hybrid kernel for linear programming support vector regression in nonlinear systems identification . *Applied Soft Computing, 9*, 94–99. doi:10.1016/j.asoc.2008.03.007

Lu, Z., Sun, J., & Butts, K. R. (2009). Linear programming support vector regression with wavelet kernel: A new approach to nonlinear dynamical systems identification. *Mathematics and Computers in Simulation, 79*(7), 2051–2063. doi:10.1016/j.matcom.2008.10.011

Mekuz, N., Bauckhagea, C., & Tsotsos, J. K. (2009). Subspace manifold learning with sample weights. *Image and Vision Computing, 27*, 80–86. doi:10.1016/j.imavis.2006.10.007

Mika, S., Rätsch, G., Weston, J., Schölkopf, B., & Müller, K. R. (1999). Fisher discriminant analysis with kernel. In Y.H. Hu, J. Larsen, and S. Wilson, E. Douglas, (Eds.), *Neural Networks for Signal Processing*, (pp. 41–48). IEEE Press.

Rosipal, R., Girolami, M., Trejo, L. J., & Cichocki, A. (2001). Kernel PCA for Feature Extraction and De-Noising in Nonlinear Regression . *Neural Computing & Applications, 10*, 231–243. doi:10.1007/s521-001-8051-z

Schölkopf, B., Burges, C. J. C., & Smola, A. J. (1998). Nonlinear component analysis as a kernel eigenvalue problem, *Neural Computation, 10*, 1299–1319. Schölkopf, B., & Smola, A. J. (2002). *Learning with Kernels: Support Vector Machines, Regularization, Optimization, and Beyond*. Cambridge, MA: MIT Press.

Smola, A. J., Mangasarian, O. L., & Schölkopf, B. (1999) *Sparse kernel feature analysis* (Technical Report 99-04), University of Wiscosin, Data Mining Institute, Madison.Smola, A. J., Schölkopf, B., & Ratsch, G. (1999). *Linear programs for automatic accuracy control in regression.* InInternational Conference on Artificial Neural Networks, Berlin, Germany.

Weston, J., Gammerman, A., Stitson, M. O., Vapnik, V., Vovk, V., & Watkins, C. (1999). Support vector density estimation, In B. Schölkopf, C.J.C. Burges, A.J. Smola (Eds.), *Advances in Kernel Methods: Support Vector Learning*, (pp. 293–305). Cambridge, MA: MIT Press.

Yoon, S., & MacGregor, J. F. (2004). Principal-component analysis of multiscale data for process monitoring and fault diagnosis . *AIChE Journal. American Institute of Chemical Engineers*, *50*(11), 2891–2903. doi:10.1002/aic.10260

Chapter 10
Analysis and Improvement of Function Approximation Capabilities of Pi–Sigma Higher Order Neural Networks

Junichi Murata
Kyushu University, Japan

ABSTRACT

A Pi-Sigma higher order neural network (Pi-Sigma HONN) is a type of higher order neural network, where, as its name implies, weighted sums of inputs are calculated first and then the sums are multiplied by each other to produce higher order terms that constitute the network outputs. This type of higher order neural networks have good function approximation capabilities. In this chapter, the structural feature of Pi-Sigma HONNs is discussed in contrast to other types of neural networks. The reason for their good function approximation capabilities is given based on pseudo-theoretical analysis together with empirical illustrations. Then, based on the analysis, an improved version of Pi-Sigma HONNs is proposed which has yet better function approximation capabilities.

INTRODUCTION

A Pi-Sigma higher order neural network (Pi-Sigma HONN) or Pi-Sigma network is a type of higher order neural network originally proposed by Shin and Ghosh (1991). Pi-Sigma HONNs display good function approximation capabilities because of their higher order terms. In Pi-Sigma HONNs, their outputs are generated by products of sums, i.e., weighted sums of the input signals are calculated first (sigma-operations), and then these sums are multiplied by each other (pi-operations) to produce network outputs. This process of producing higher order terms, pi-sigma operation, is in contrast to sigma-pi operation used in another typical type of HONNs, Sigma-Pi HONNs, where higher order terms are first produced by multiplication of the input signals and then they are added together to form network outputs. The pi-sigma operations for producing higher order terms are considered to be efficient since they require a

DOI: 10.4018/978-1-61520-711-4.ch010

less number of parameters to yield the same number of higher order terms than the sigma-pi operations. And Pi-Sigma HONNs have better function approximation capabilities than Sigma-Pi HONNs with the same number of adjustable parameters (or weights). However, it has not been clarified why Pi-Sigma HONNs are better than Sigma-Pi HONNs. Finding this reason and improving Pi-Sigma HONNs based on the findings are the aim of this chapter. It should be worth mentioning here the main finding: it is not efficiency in higher order terms production but nonlinearity in terms of parameters that gives the Pi-Sigma HONNs better function approximation capabilities.

In the following sections, first, the background of this chapter is given, then Pi-Sigma HONNs are described in some more detail, and the numerical results are presented that illustrate the better function approximation capabilities of Pi-Sigma HONNs. To clarify its reason, a pseudo-theoretical analysis is made. The analysis also reveals a limitation of this type of networks, which gives the basis for an improved version of Pi-Sigma HONNs that will be proposed and evaluated later in this chapter.

BACKGROUND

There have been proposed a number of different kinds of higher order neural networks (HONNs). Most of them can be categorized into two groups based on how the higher order terms are produced in them. One group is the group of sigma-pi type higher order neural networks, and the other is the group of pi-sigma type higher order neural networks.

The first neural network named high-order neural network by Giles and Maxwell (1987) lies in the group of sigma-pi type HONNs. Each of its outputs is a weighted sum of higher order terms. In other words, higher order terms of the input signals are produced first (pi-operations), and then their weighted sums are calculated (sigma-operations). The group of sigma-pi type HONNs includes neural networks with Sigma Pi Units (Rumelhart, Hinton & McClelland, 1986) and neural networks with Product Units (Durbin & Rumelhart, 1989).

On the other hand, in a higher order neural network belonging to the pi-sigma group, the higher order terms are computed through sigma and pi operations but in reverse order: weighted sums of the input signals are calculated first, and then they are multiplied by each other. Pi-Sigma Networks and Ridge Polynomial Networks both proposed by Shin and Ghosh (1991; 1995) belong to this group. Moreover, if we focus on a distinctive feature of this group of HONNs which is not shared with the sigma-pi type HONNs, we can include the following networks in this group as well: Modular Networks (Jacobs & Jordan, 1993), Hierarchical Mixtures of Experts (HMEs) (Jordan, 1993), Neural Networks with Node Gates (Murata, Nakazono & Hirasawa, 1999; Myint, et al., 2000), Universal Learning Networks with Multiplication Neurons (Li, et al., 2001), Group Method of Data Handling (GMDH) (Farlow, 1984), and even Takagi-Sugeno type Fuzzy Models (Takagi & Hayashi, 1991).

HONNs are said to have better function approximation capabilities than the ordinary multi-layer perceptrons because of their higher order terms. Through numerical experiments, the author has confirmed that Pi-Sigma HONNs have better function approximation capabilities than ordinary multi-layer perceptrons and even Sigma-Pi HONNs. Although the researchers who proposed pi-sigma type networks asserted that pi-sigma type networks were more efficient than sigma-pi type networks, the discussions about the function approximation capabilities of Pi-Sigma HONNs have been focused mainly on whether they are universal function approximators or not (Shin & Ghosh, 1995). There is a question yet to be answered: why are Pi-Sigma HONNs better than Sigma-Pi HONNs? In the following, a pseudo-theoretical analysis

Figure 1. Architecture of typical Pi-Sigma HONN

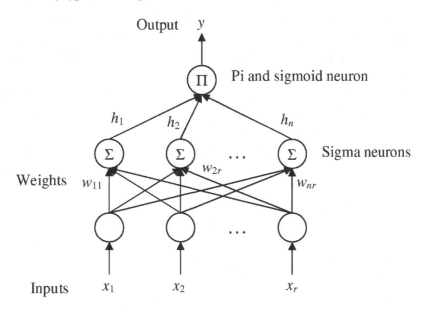

will be made to provide the answer to this question, and based on this analysis a simple but effective improvement on the Pi-Sigma HONNs will be proposed.

PI-SIGMA HIGHER ORDER NEURAL NETWORKS AND THEIR FUNCTION APPROXIMATION CAPABILITIES

Pi-Sigma HONNs and Their Features

The architecture of typical Pi-Sigma HONN is depicted in Fig.1. The figure shows a single-output network, but it can be easily extended to a multiple-output network. The network accepts inputs $x_1, ..., x_r$, and its output y is calculated according to the following equations:

$$y = s\left(\prod_{j=1}^{n} h_j\right),$$ (1a)

$$h_j = \sum_{i=1}^{r} w_{ji} x_i + \theta_j, \qquad j = 1,...n,$$ (1b)

where s stands for a sigmoid function, w_{ji} is a weight and θ_j is a bias parameter. Therefore, in Pi-Sigma HONNs, higher order terms are produced by sigma-operations (equation (1b)) and pi-operations (equation (1a)) in this order. This is where their name originates from. The pi-sigma operation is regarded as an efficient way to produce many higher order terms. For example, a product of two weighted sums $w_1x_1+w_2x_2+w_3x_3$ and $w_4x_4+w_5x_5+w_6x_6$ of signals $x_1, ..., x_6$ has six parameters $w_1, ..., w_6$ and yields nine second order terms $x_1x_4, ..., x_3x_6$ while a sigma-pi operation would require nine parameters $v_1, ..., v_9$ to produce the same nine terms in the form of $v_1x_1x_4 + v_2x_1x_5 + ... + v_9x_3x_6$. As this example shows, the pi-sigma operation introduces products of parameters w_iw_j in addition to products of signals x_ix_j. Therefore, the result of pi-sigma operation is nonlinear (product-nonlinear) in terms of not only their input signals but also their parameters. This is the main structural feature of Pi-Sigma HONNs that is not shared with Sigma-Pi HONNs.

The pi-sigma operation in the above example is in the form of multiplication of linear combinations of signals. However, we do not need to restrict ourselves to this particular type of operation. The category of Pi-Sigma HONNs can be extended to include such neural networks as Modular Networks, Hierarchical Mixtures of Experts (HMEs), Neural Networks with Node Gates, Universal Learning Networks with Multiplication Neurons, Group Method of Data Handling (GMDH) and even Takagi-Sugeno type Fuzzy Models. Some of these were originally developed taking localization or divide-and-conquer approach. The input domain is divided into several segments, and to each segment an indicator function is assigned which defines the segment. An indicator function typically takes the value 1 for the inputs within a segment and the value 0 for the inputs outside the segment. The indicator functions have parameters which are used to specify their corresponding segments. Then a simple sub-network with a number of parameters is constructed for each segment so that it gives a localized solution to a given problem. The problem can be function approximation or classification. The overall solution is produced as a sum of sub-networks each of which is multiplied by its corresponding indicator function. In this way, parameters contained in the sub-networks and those in the indicator functions are multiplied. So, the networks following localization or divide-and-conquer approach can be categorized as (generalized) Pi-Sigma HONNs. A typical architecture based on this concept is Takagi-Sugeno type fuzzy model, where the fuzzy set membership functions play the role of the indicator functions which are multiplied by simple local models to form the global model. In HME, the expert networks correspond to the localized solutions and the gating networks define the segments. In this way, all of these architectures include products of two or more formulae each of which consists of signals and parameters, and therefore, their outputs are product-nonlinear with respect to both inputs and parameters.

Numerical Illustrations of Function Approximation Capabilities of Pi-Sigma HONNs

Pi-Sigma HONNs have good function approximation capabilities given the number of parameters. Let us perform several numerical experiments to confirm this. Here we do not include the sigmoid function s that appeared in equation (1a) so that we can focus on the effects of sigma-operations and pi-operations only. Also, for simplicity, we consider the case where $n = 2$, in other words, our Pi-Sigma HONN output is a product of two linear combinations of input signals. The function approximation capabilities of the following three types of six-input single-output networks are compared:

$$y = (x_1 + w_2x_2 + w_3x_3)(w_4x_4 + w_5x_5 + w_6x_6), \tag{2}$$

$$y = v_1x_1x_2 + v_2x_2x_3 + v_3x_3x_4 + v_4x_4x_5 + v_5x_5x_6 + v_6x_6x_1, \tag{3}$$

$$y = u_1x_1 + u_2x_2 + u_3x_3 + u_4x_4 + u_5x_5 + u_6x_6. \tag{4}$$

Table 1. RMSEs of Pi-Sigma, Sigma-Pi and Sigma networks

Network	Average RMSE	Average of best RMSE
Pi-Sigma (eq. (2))	0.337	NA
Sigma-Pi (eq. (3))	0.372	0.371
Sigma (eq. (4))	0.371	0.370

Equation (2) represents a Pi-Sigma HONN, equation (3) expresses a Sigma-Pi HONN, and equation (4) is a linear or Sigma network. Note that the Pi-Sigma HONN has five weights whereas the Sigma-Pi and Sigma networks have six weights. In the numerical experiments, a term is dropped from equation (3) or (4) to keep the number of weights the same.

The networks are trained on training data sets consisting of ten tuples of input and desired output data $(x_1, \ldots, x_6; d)$. Each piece of data is a uniformly distributed random number over the interval $[-1, 1]$. The networks are trained so as to minimize the sum of squared errors between the actual outputs y and the desired outputs d. The Pi-Sigma HONN is trained by an algorithm similar to Asynchronous Learning Algorithm (Shin and Ghosh, 1995), and the other two networks are trained by the least squares method since they are linear in weights. In the below, the root mean square errors (RMSEs) on the training data sets after the training are shown. We perform 1000 runs with different pseudo random number sequences to generate the data sets. Note that the training data sets used here are randomly generated. Therefore, the data sets have no particular biases.

The average RMSEs on the training data sets over 1000 runs are listed in Table 1. In each single run, training of Sigma-Pi and Sigma networks (equations (3) and (4)) is performed six times in each of which one of their six terms is dropped in turn. As a result, we obtain six RMSEs, then the best RMSE is selected among these six values and their average RMSE is calculated. For these two networks, 'Averages of best RMSEs' in the table are averages of the best RMSEs over the 1000 runs, and 'Averages of RMSEs' are averages of average RMSEs.

As can be seen from the table, the average error of Pi-Sigma network is smaller than those of Sigma-Pi and Sigma networks. Other numerical experiments with different numbers of input variables, different network structure details and different data ranges also give the similar results. However it should be noted that the results shown in the table are average values over 1000 training data sets. Some data sets may be well approximated by a particular type of network, and some others may be by another type. Actually on some data sets, Pi-Sigma HONN shows poorer performance than Sigma-pi and/or Sigma networks. But, it performs better on the majority of the data sets. The generated data are uniformly distributed over the interval $[-1, 1]$, and there are no biases. Therefore, what is confirmed by these numerical examples is that, given unbiased sets of training data, Pi-Sigma HONNs have, on average, better function approximation capabilities than Sigma-Pi and Sigma type networks having the same number of weights.

FUNCTION APPROXIMATION CAPABILITIES OF PI-SIGMA HIGHER ORDER NEURAL NETWORKS

Analysis of Function Approximation Capabilities of Pi-Sigma HONNs

As the examples in the previous section illustrate, Pi-Sigma HONNs have better function approximation capabilities than Sigma-Pi and Sigma networks, given the number of weights. In this section, we investigate its reason and will show that this advantage comes primarily from not products of signals but products of parameters.

Let us begin the investigation with specifying the network and the training data set to be considered. We consider a single-output Pi-Sigma HONN with p parameters (weights and biases) which accepts r inputs $x_1, \ldots, x_r$ and produces an output y. Suppose that we have a set of N input data $x_1(1), \ldots, x_r(1); \ldots;$ $x_1(N), \ldots, x_r(N)$ together with their corresponding desired output data $d(1), \ldots, d(N)$. Here we assume $p < N$ since if the number of independent parameters p is equal to or larger than the number of data N then the data can be perfectly represented by the network.

Now we examine how well the Pi-Sigma HONN can represent and approximate the given data. For fixed values of parameters, the network produces N output values $y(1), \ldots, y(N)$ corresponding to the N input data. If these N output values are identical to our desired output data, then the desired output data are represented by the Pi-Sigma HONN without errors. The set of N output values $y(1), \ldots, y(N)$ can be viewed as a single point in an N-dimensional space. Let us call this space *output space*. When we vary the values of parameters in the network, the point that corresponds to the set of N output values moves in the N-dimensional output space, and its trajectory forms a region. If the point specified by the N desired output values is located in this region, then the network can represent it without any errors by properly adjusting its parameters. By changing the parameter values over the full extent of their domains, we obtain the largest of such regions, and we call it *zero-error region*. Dimensionality of a zero-error region is equal to the number of independent parameters contained in the network, p. Note that it does not depend on whether the network contains multiplication operations or not. If the network output is linear in terms of the parameters as is the case in Sigma-Pi and Sigma networks, the zero-error region becomes a p-dimensional linear subspace in the N-dimensional output space. For example, consider a Sigma-Pi HONN with p parameters whose input-output relationship is represented as

$$y = v_1 x_1 x_2 + v_2 x_2 x_3 + \ldots + v_p x_{r-1} x_r. \tag{5}$$

Then its N output values are expressed by the following equation:

$$\begin{bmatrix} y(1) \\ \vdots \\ y(N) \end{bmatrix} = v_1 \begin{bmatrix} x_1(1)x_2(1) \\ \vdots \\ x_1(N)x_2(N) \end{bmatrix} + \ldots + v_p \begin{bmatrix} x_{r-1}(1)x_r(1) \\ \vdots \\ x_{r-1}(N)x_r(N) \end{bmatrix} \tag{6}$$

Hence the vector $[y(1) \ldots y(N)]^T$ forms a p-dimensional linear subspace spanned by vectors $[x_1(1)x_2(1) \ldots x_1(N)x_2(N)]^T, \ldots, [x_{r-1}(1)x_r(1) \ldots x_{r-1}(N)x_r(N)]^T$. However, the output of Pi-Sigma HONN is nonlinear in its parameters because it includes the parameter multiplication operations, and therefore, the zero-error region is still p-dimensional but becomes a nonlinear manifold.

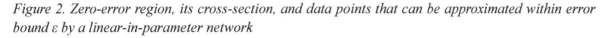

Figure 2. Zero-error region, its cross-section, and data points that can be approximated within error bound ε by a linear-in-parameter network

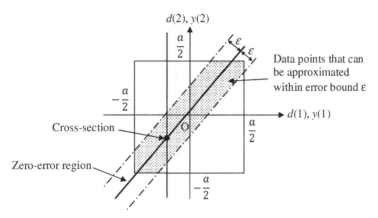

Dimensionality of the zero-error region is the same for Pi-Sigma, Sigma-Pi and Sigma type networks, if they have the same number of independent parameters. Of course the shapes of zero-error regions and their locations in the output space can be different. However, the regions all stretch infinitely. So, when we consider unbiased training data, in other words, data points located anywhere in the output space, we cannot tell which zero-error region covers larger area of data points. We can also look at this issue from a probability theory point of view. Any p-dimensional zero-error region in an N-dimensional output space, where $p < N$, has zero measure: the probability that any desired output data point falls in the p-dimensional zero-error region is zero. Therefore, we cannot distinguish the *precise representation* capabilities of these different types of networks.

Now we investigate the *approximation* capabilities of the networks rather than the precise representation capabilities. Let us assume that $N = 2$ for simplicity although this is not a realistic case. Then the output space is a two-dimensional space or a plane. In function approximation by neural networks, the input-output data to be approximated are bounded. So, imagine a square of the size $a \times a$ whose center is located at the origin of this plane as shown in Fig.2. We want to approximate data points located in this square by a single network. We assume that our approximation error tolerance is ε, i.e., we allow the distance between the desired output data point and the actual network output point equal to or less than ε but not more. Because we measure the distance in the output space, this tolerance corresponds to the upper bound on the root mean square errors.

For linear-in-parameter networks, namely, Sigma-Pi HONNs and Sigma networks, the zero-error region is a linear subspace in the output space. In the two-dimensional output space, it is a straight line. All the data points on the line segment clipped by the $a \times a$ square edges can be represented without errors. Also, the data points located within the distance ε from the line segment in this square (shaded area in Fig.2) can be approximated by the network within the allowable error bound. The maximum length of the line segment is $\sqrt{2}a$ (a diagonal of the square), and therefore the area of all the data points that can be approximated within the specified error bound ε is at most $\sqrt{2}a\varepsilon$ out of the a^2 square.

On the other hand, if the data are to be approximated by a Pi-Sigma HONN whose output is nonlinear in terms of parameters, zero-error region is a one-dimensional manifold or a curve. The curve can be winding or folded within the a^2 square as illustrated in Fig.3. Then its length in the square becomes

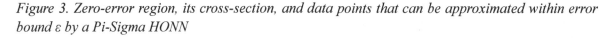

Figure 3. Zero-error region, its cross-section, and data points that can be approximated within error bound ε by a Pi-Sigma HONN

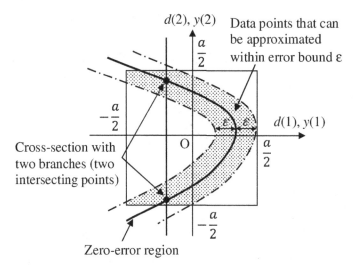

longer than $\sqrt{2a}$, and thus the area of all the data points that can be approximated within the specified error bound is larger than $\sqrt{2a}\varepsilon$.

The above is a simplified illustrative discussion where the output space is a two-dimensional space i.e., $N = 2$ and the number of parameters p is equal to 1. Note that a Pi-Sigma HONN with just one parameter does not actually exist because even the simplest form of pi-sigma operation requires three parameters. However, it can be concluded that for general N and p, given the desired data points distributed uniformly in a bounded region, a network whose output is nonlinear in its parameters forms a zero-error region that occupies a larger part of the bounded region and can approximate more data points within a specified error bound than any linear-in-parameter networks.

Illustrations of Function Approximation Capabilities of Pi-Sigma HONNs

Unfortunately, it is not easy to establish zero-error regions for Pi-Sigma HONNs because the regions are multi-dimensional nonlinear manifolds and they depend on the data vectors such as vector $[x_1(1)$ $x_2(1)\ \ldots x_1(N)x_2(N)]^T$ in equation (6). Thus we cannot prove theoretically rigorously that the regions where the data can be approximated by Pi-Sigma HONNs within the error bound are larger than those regions by linear-in-parameter networks. However, we can investigate whether this is the case or not with several examples.

To make it easy to understand the shape of zero-error regions, we look into the cross-sections of the regions obtained by fixing the values of several output data. Before inspecting the specific cross-sections, let us examine what a cross-section can tell us about a zero-error region using the examples shown in Figs.2 and 3. In these examples, if we fix $y(1)$ to a particular value, we will obtain a cross-section of the zero-error region cut by a vertical line. The cross-section for linear-in-parameter network consists of a single point as shown in Fig.2 since the zero-error region is a single line. On the other hand, for Pi-Sigma HONNs, it may be composed of two points as depicted in Fig.3 since the zero-error region is a curve. Therefore, if the cross-section has two or more branches, it implies that the zero-error region is a curved hyper-surface.

Now let us consider the following simplest single-output Pi-Sigma HONN with three weights:

$$y = (x_1 + w_2 x_2)(w_3 x_3 + w_4 x_4). \tag{7}$$

The zero-error region of this network is a three-dimensional manifold in N-dimensional output space. In other words, by changing the values of w_2, w_3 and w_4, the point corresponding to network output values $[y(1) \ldots y(N)]^{\mathrm{T}}$ moves in the output space and forms a three-dimensional region. We investigate the cross-section of zero-error regions formed by this Pi-Sigma HONN. Without loss of generality, we fix $y(1)$ and $y(2)$ to constants η_1 and η_2, respectively, as shown in the below:

$$y(1) = [x_1(1) + w_2 x_2(1)][w_3 x_3(1) + w_4 x_4(1)] = \eta_1, \tag{8a}$$

$$y(2) = [x_1(2) + w_2 x_2(2)][w_3 x_3(2) + w_4 x_4(2)] = \eta_2. \tag{8b}$$

By solving these equations, w_3 and w_4 can be expressed in terms of w_2. Then, on the cross-section of zero-error region, the other outputs $y(k)$, $k = 3, \ldots, N$ can be represented in terms of a single free parameter w_2 as,

$$
y(k) = A(k) \frac{x_1(k) + w_2 x_2(k)}{x_1(1) + w_2 x_2(1)}
$$
$$
+ B(k) \frac{x_1(k) + w_2 x_2(k)}{x_1(2) + w_2 x_2(2)}, \qquad k = 3, \ldots, N, \tag{9}
$$

where

$$
A(k) = \eta_1 \frac{x_4(2) x_3(k) - x_3(2) x_4(k)}{x_3(1) x_4(2) - x_3(2) x_4(1)},
$$
$$
B(k) = \eta_2 \frac{x_3(1) x_4(k) - x_4(1) x_3(k)}{x_3(1) x_4(2) - x_3(2) x_4(1)}
$$

Equation (9) is a parameterized expression of the cross-section with parameter w_2. Although it is one-dimensional, it is in an $(N-2)$-dimensional space. To understand its features clearly, let us consider its projection onto a plane having two axes of coordinates $y(k)$ and $y(k')$ with $k' \neq k$. Output $y(k')$ can be represented by equation (9) with k replaced with k',

$$
y(K') = A(k') \frac{x_1(k') + w_2 x_2(k')}{x_1(1) + w_2 x_2(1)}
$$
$$
+ B(k') \frac{x_1(k') + w_2 x_2(k')}{x_1(2) + w_2 x_2(2)} \tag{10}
$$

The projection is derived by eliminating w_2 from equations (9) and (10). Multiplying both sides of equation (9) by $[x_1(1) + w_2 x_2(1)][x_1(2) + w_2 x_2(2)]$, a quadratic equation in terms of w_2 is derived. This implies that, with $y(1)$, $y(2)$ and $y(k)$ being fixed, w_2 may have two possible values to take. By substitut-

Figure 4. Cross-sections of zero-error regions of Pi-Sigma HONNs

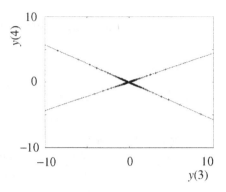

(a) Pi-Sigma HONN (7)

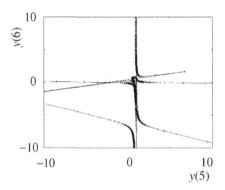

(b) Pi-Sigma HONN (12)

ing derived two values of w_2 into equation (10), we can obtain the projection of the cross-section which can have two branches and is, as can be seen from equation (9) or (10), nonlinear. This indicates that the cross-section itself is nonlinear and can have two branches and, in turn, that the zero-error region is a three-dimensional curved hyper-surface and is folded in the N-dimensional output space.

Next let us consider a case where $r = 6$ and $p = 5$. In this case we have the following alternative Pi-Sigma HONNs:

$$y = (x_1 + w_2 x_2)(w_3 x_3 + w_4 x_4 + w_5 x_5 + w_6 x_6), \tag{11}$$

$$y = (x_1 + w_2 x_2 + w_3 x_3)(w_4 x_4 + w_5 x_5 + w_6 x_6). \tag{12}$$

Similar calculations reveal that Pi-Sigma HONNs in the form of equation (11) have zero-error regions with at most four branches in their cross sections and that networks expressed in equation (12) have at most twelve branches.

To summarize the above discussions, the zero-error regions of such Pi-Sigma HONNs as expressed in equations (7), (11) and (12) are nonlinear, and their cross-sections may have multiple branches. The number of branches, or how many times the zero-error regions are folded, increases as the number of inputs and the number of parameters increase.

In order to confirm the above discussions, cross-sections of zero-error regions are drawn numerically for the Pi-Sigma HONNs expressed in equations (7) and (12). For the network in (7), N is chosen as 4 for ease of computation, and four data are randomly generated for each of input signals $x_1, \ldots, x_4$. To see the two-dimensional cross-section of zero-error region in the four-dimensional output space, values of $y(1)$ and $y(2)$ are fixed to 0.05, and the cross-section formed by the remaining $y(3)$ and $y(4)$ is drawn using equations (9) and (10) with w_2 ranging over $[-10, 10]$. Figure 4 (a) shows the cross-section, which actually consists of two branches. Also Fig.4 (b) shows the cross-section drawn for equations (12) with $N = 6$. Values of $y(1), \ldots, y(4)$ are fixed to produce the two-dimensional cross-section on $y(5)$-$y(6)$ plane. This cross-section has more number of branches than the cross-section in Fig.4 (a). Note that the cross-section for Sigma-Pi or Sigma network will be a single line with no branches on this plane. These results support the above discussions.

IMPROVEMENT OF PI-SIGMA HIGHER ORDER NEURAL NETWORKS

Curbing Excessive Nonlinearity

Pi-Sigma HONNs have better approximation capabilities than Sigma-Pi and Sigma networks on average over uniformly distributed and bounded desired output data. In the set of uniformly distributed data, data of various kinds and with various features are included: some may change sensitively depending on the input values; some may keep almost the same value regardless of the input values. If you do not know very well about the features of your desired output data, then Pi-Sigma HONNs will be the best choice. However, they might display poorer performance on some particular data sets. For example, if the desired input-output relationship is linear, it is predictable that a Sigma network will perform better than both Pi-Sigma and Sigma-Pi HONNs. Therefore it is hypothesized that the degree of variations of the desired output data in relation to the input data variations affects the function approximation errors.

Now, let us examine the results of another numerical experiment where Pi-Sigma, Sigma-Pi and Sigma networks are compared with each other on their function approximation capabilities on a smoothly varying data set. The experimental setup is the same as the previous one except that the training data are generated under the following restrictions on the first-order and the second-order differences of the signals:

$|\Delta x_i(k)| \leq 0.5, |\Delta d(k)| \leq 0.5, k = 2, \ldots, 10; i = 1, \ldots, 4,$

$|\Delta x_i(k) - \Delta x_i(k-1)| \leq 0.5, |\Delta d(k) - \Delta d(k-1)| \leq 0.5, k = 3, \ldots, 10; i = 1, \ldots, 4,$

where

$\Delta x_i(k) = x_i(k) - x_i(k-1), \Delta d(k) = d(k) - d(k-1).$

Table 2. RMSEs of Pi-Sigma, Sigma-Pi and Sigma networks on smoothly varying data

Network	Average RMSE	Average of best RMSE
Pi-Sigma (eq. (2))	0.245	NA
Sigma-Pi (eq. (3))	0.243	0.238
Sigma (eq. (4))	0.194	0.189

So the data do not vary much as the index k changes. In other words they are smooth with respect to the change in k. Since both the input and the desired output signals are smooth, their relationship is also smooth. The derived root mean square errors (RMSEs) are listed in Table 2. Unlike Table 1, Pi-Sigma HONN gives the worst errors. This indicates that the Pi-Sigma HONN is not the best network to approximate smoothly varying data. This poor performance is caused by the higher order terms in the Pi-Sigma HONN. The products of input signals make the network output vary more sensitively depending on the input values.

In order to remedy the above weak point of Pi-Sigma HONNs, a rather simple but effective improvement is proposed here. The idea underlying this improvement is to add a mechanism that can curb excessive nonlinearity introduced by the higher order terms. The output of Pi-Sigma HONN is inherently a higher order function of the inputs. If the relationship between the inputs and the desired output to be approximated is linear, for example, then this higher order feature is excessive. If we place an inverse function of the higher order function at the output of Pi-Sigma HONN, the higher order feature can be canceled out. It is not, however, appropriate to devise a complex and exotic function that can curb any kinds of excessive nonlinearity because it is not easy and it will damage the favorable features of Pi-Sigma HONNs originating from the nonlinearity. A simple function with some adaptivity is preferable. Here a sigmoid function is placed at the output of Pi-Sigma HONNs to curb the excessive nonlinearity. A sigmoid function has a convex part and a concave part. Also, it has a part that can approximately behave as a linear function when its parameters are chosen appropriately. So, it can either modify Pi-Sigma HONN output in one of two different (convex and concave) ways or do virtually nothing. The sigmoid function used here is expressed as follows:

$$\sigma(y) = \frac{a}{1 + e^{-b(y-c)}} + d, \tag{13}$$

where a, b, c and d are adjustable parameters. The output y from Pi-Sigma HONN is fed to the sigmoid function $\sigma(\cdot)$, then its value

$$z = \sigma(y) \tag{14}$$

is used as the final output of the network. The parameters regulate how the network output y is curbed or modified. Parameter c shifts the domain of sigmoid function, in other words, it shifts the graph of function horizontally. So, by adjusting it, we can choose the part of sigmoid function to be applied to the pi-sigma output y. Parameter b can control the curvature of the convex or concave part. Parameters a and d determine how the pi-sigma output y is modified. Moreover if b is positive and small and if c is adjusted so that $y - c$ stays around zero, then the sigmoid function is virtually a linear function, and it does essentially nothing to the pi-sigma output. Values of these parameters are determined together with the weights in the pi-sigma network so that the errors between the actual outputs and the desired outputs are minimized.

The performance of the improved Pi-Sigma HONN is evaluated and compared with other types of networks. In order to make fair comparisons, the same sigmoid function with four adjustable parameters is added to other types of networks as well. The specific input-output relationships of the networks are as follows:

$$\text{Pi-Sigma: } z = \sigma((x_1 + w_2 x_2 + w_3 x_3)(w_4 x_4 + w_5 x_5 + w_6 x_6)), \tag{15}$$

$$\text{Sigma-Pi: } z = \sigma(v_1 x_1 x_2 + v_2 x_2 x_3 + v_3 x_3 x_4 + v_4 x_4 x_5 + v_5 x_5 x_1), \tag{16}$$

$$\text{Sigma: } z = \sigma(u_1 x_1 + u_2 x_2 + u_3 x_3 + u_4 x_4 + u_5 x_5). \tag{17}$$

Here in equations (16) and (17) the input variable x_6 is dropped. As 'Average RMSE' column and 'Average of best RMSE' column in Table 1 or Table 2 indicate, it does not affect the results which particular one of the six terms in equations (3) and (4) is omitted. Therefore, the terms related to x_6 are dropped so that equations (15), (16) and (17) have exactly the same number of adjustable parameters. Equation (17) is nothing but a single neuron in multi-layer perceptrons. The networks are trained on data sets with four different restrictions:

Restriction 0: no restrictions on $|\Delta x_i(k)|$, $|\Delta d(k)|$, $|\Delta x_i(k) - \Delta x_i(k-1)|$ or $|\Delta d(k) - \Delta d(k-1)|$,
Restriction 1: $|\Delta x_i(k)| \leq 0.9$, $|\Delta d(k)| \leq 0.9$; $|\Delta x_i(k) - \Delta x_i(k-1)| \leq 0.8$, $|\Delta d(k) - \Delta d(k-1)| \leq 0.8$,
Restriction 2: $|\Delta x_i(k)| \leq 0.5$, $|\Delta d(k)| \leq 0.5$; $|\Delta x_i(k) - \Delta x_i(k-1)| \leq 0.4$, $|\Delta d(k) - \Delta d(k-1)| \leq 0.4$,
Restriction 3: $|\Delta x_i(k)| \leq 0.1$, $|\Delta d(k)| \leq 0.1$; $|\Delta x_i(k) - \Delta x_i(k-1)| \leq 0.05$, $|\Delta d(k) - \Delta d(k-1)| \leq 0.05$.

Restriction 3 is the tightest and gives the most smoothly varying data.

The obtained root mean square errors (RMSEs) listed in Table 3 show that the improved Pi-Sigma HONN exhibits the best approximation capability on all of four kinds of training data sets with different levels of smoothness. This confirms that the improvement works satisfactorily.

Combination of Improved Pi-Sigma HONNs

In equations (16) and (17), the terms related to x_6 are dropped so that the equations have exactly the same number of adjustable parameters as equation (15). But there are other options regarding which term is

Table 3. RMSEs of improved Pi-Sigma, Sigma-Pi and Sigma networks

Network	Average RMSE			
	Restriction 0	Restriction 1	Restriction 2	Restriction 3
Pi-Sigma (eq. (16))	0.201	0.218	0.124	0.037
Sigma-Pi (eq. (17))	0.289	0.278	0.244	0.153
Sigma (eq. (18))	0.254	0.228	0.191	0.154

dropped from the network. Also, Pi-Sigma HONN expressed in equation (15) is not the only possible one. For example, you can multiply a sum of x_1, x_3 and x_5 by a sum of x_2, x_4 and x_6 to generate another Pi-Sigma HONN. To compensate possible biases caused by picking up just one particular structure among a number of possible variations, it can be useful to combine those variations into a single network. Based on this idea, networks in the following form are derived,

$$z = \sum_{l=1}^{m} a_l z_l + \beta \tag{18}$$

where z is output of the combined network, α_l and β are parameters, and z_l is output from the lth variation or sub-network which is given as one of the following:

Here, $\left\{ i_1^l, i_2^l, ..., i_{p+1}^l \right\}$ is a permutation of $\{1, 2, ..., p, p+1\}$. Note that $r = p + 1$. Each sub-network z_l uses a different permutation. The combined Sigma network represented by equations (18) and (21) is the ordinary multi-layer perceptron with a linear function in its output neuron.

Performance of the combined networks is evaluated with $p = r - 1 = 5$ and $q = 3$. For Pi-Sigma network, there are $\binom{p+1}{q} / 2 = \binom{6}{3} / 2 = 10$ possible permutations, and therefore the number of sub-networks m in equation (18) can take a value up to 10. Therefore, the combined networks with different values of m ranging from 1 to 10 are trained on data sets containing randomly generated data with four different restrictions listed in Table 2, and their RMSEs are calculated. Because the number of parameters to be estimated is larger than that in the previous examples, we use data sets which contain 100 data each. The obtained RMSEs are tabulated in Table 4. The combined Pi-Sigma HONNs give the smallest errors for every restriction and every network complexity m. Since the RMSEs listed here are the errors on training data, they decrease as m increases and accordingly the number of adjustable parameters increases. The combined Sigma-Pi HONN gives the smallest average RMSE on unrestricted data sets (restriction

Table 4. RMSEs of layer combined Pi-Sigma, Sigma-Pi and Sigma networks

Restriction on data	Network	Number of sub-networks m									
		1	2	3	4	5	6	7	8	9	10
Restriction 0	Pi-Sigma	0.533	0.506	0.473	0.438	0.400	0.363	0.332	0.307	0.329	0.304
	Sigma-Pi	0.559	0.559	0.551	0.526	0.526	0.500	0.499	0.478	0.457	0.471
	Sigma	0.546	0.546	0.526	0.480	0.460	0.460	0.453	0.424	0.405	0.346
Restriction 1	Pi-Sigma	0.527	0.472	0.438	0.395	0.345	0.334	0.321	0.287	0.282	0.260
	Sigma-Pi	0.569	0.569	0.545	0.475	0.475	0.474	0.483	0.423	0.415	0.391
	Sigma	0.554	0.554	0.523	0.474	0.471	0.414	0.417	0.359	0.310	0.319
Restriction 2	Pi-Sigma	0.476	0.410	0.354	0.308	0.243	0.225	0.217	0.217	0.176	0.170
	Sigma-Pi	0.566	0.566	0.532	0.480	0.480	0.422	0.398	0.365	0.328	0.309
	Sigma	0.529	0.529	0.487	0.412	0.407	0.333	0.327	0.280	0.254	0.207
Restriction 3	Pi-Sigma	0.196	0.113	0.083	0.067	0.066	0.059	0.059	0.057	0.060	0.053
	Sigma-Pi	0.289	0.289	0.245	0.178	0.178	0.113	0.112	0.084	0.065	0.058
	Sigma	0.241	0.240	0.174	0.116	0.117	0.081	0.083	0.074	0.072	0.066

0) when $m = 9$. However the combined Pi-Sigma HONN attains the same level of small RMSE with less complexity $m = 4$. Similarly, the best result obtained by the combined Sigma network on this kind of data sets at $m = 10$ is achieved at $m = 7$ by the combined Pi-Sigma HONN. The RMSEs on the most smoothly varying data sets (restriction 3) exhibit similar results: the best RMSE obtained by the combined Sigma-Pi HONN with $m = 10$ is achieved at $m = 6$ by the combined Pi-Sigma HONN; the best RMSE by the combined Sigma network with $m = 10$ is attained at $m = 5$ by the combined Pi-Sigma HONN. These results indicate that the improved Pi-Sigma HONN can approximate data with different levels of smoothness with a fewer number of parameters than Sigma-Pi and Sigma networks.

CONCLUSION

In this chapter, the reason has been clarified why Pi-Sigma higher order neural networks display good function approximation capabilities, and an improved version of Pi-Sigma HONNs has been proposed that has yet better function approximation capabilities. The main structural feature that provides Pi-Sigma HONNs with their good capabilities is that their outputs are nonlinear in terms of their parameters. Because of this feature, the region consisting of desired output data that can be precisely represented by a Pi-Sigma HONN is a nonlinear manifold in the space composed of all possible data, and therefore the region that can be approximated within an error bound is larger than those by linear-in-parameter type neural networks. This gives small function approximation errors by Pi-Sigma HONNs on average over uniformly distributed data sets. To remedy the network's poor performance on smoothly varying data sets, a sigmoid function is placed to curb excessive nonlinearity of the network. The improved Pi-Sigma HONNs attain small errors on smoothly and non-smoothly varying data sets with a fewer number of parameters than other types of neural networks. The analysis on which the reasoning is based is not completely theoretical but several numerical results have been presented that support the analysis.

When the Pi-Sigma HONNs become more complicated and have more parameters, they will gain better function approximation capabilities. However, too complicated networks will cause difficulties in their training: the error minimizing problems will have many local minima. Also, such networks may have poor generalization capabilities. There will be an appropriate level of network complexity that gives the best balance among approximation capabilities, generalization capabilities and training easiness. As pointed out in the chapter, the main feature of Pi-Sigma HONNs is shared by other types of neural networks as well, i.e. their outputs contain products of their parameters. These networks are based on divide-and-conquer approach which is a natural approach that humans would take when they tackle complicated problems. This suggests that divide-and-conquer approach that can incorporate human knowledge would be very helpful to find well-balanced Pi-Sigma HONN architectures.

ACKNOWLEDGMENT

The author would like to thank Naoaki Yamamoto for his help in the numerical experiments.

REFERENCES

Durbin, R., & Rumelhart, D. E. (1989). Product Units: A Computationally Powerful and Biologically Plausible Extension to Backpropagation Networks. *Neural Computation, 1*, 133–142. doi:10.1162/neco.1989.1.1.133

Farlow, S. J. (1984). *Self-Organizing Methods in Modeling: GMDH Type Algorithms. New York*: Marcel Dekker.

Giles, C. L., & Maxwell, T. (1987). Learning, invariance, and generalization in high-order neural networks. *Applied Optics, 26*(23), 4972–4978. doi:10.1364/AO.26.004972

Jacobs, R. A., & Jordan, M. I. (1993). Learning piecewise control strategies in a modular neural network architecture. *IEEE Transactions on Systems, Man, and Cybernetics, 23*, 337–345. doi:10.1109/21.229447

Jordan, M. (1993). Hierarchical Mixtures of Experts and the EM Algorithm, In *Proc. 1993 Int. Joint Conf. Neural Networks* (pp. 1339-1344).

Li, D., Hirasawa, K., Hu, J., & Murata, J. (2001). Universal Learning Networks with Multiplication Neurons and its Representation Ability. In *Proc. Int. Joint Conf. Neural Networks* (pp. 150-155).

Murata, J., Nakazono, T., & Hirasawa, K. (1999). Neural Networks with Node Gates. In *Proc. 1999 Int. Conf. Electrical Engineering* (pp. 358-361).

Myint, H. M., Murata, J., Nakazono, T., & Hirasawa, K. (2000). Neural Networks with Node Gates. In *Proc. 9th IEEE Int. Workshop. Robot and Human Interface Communication* (pp. 253-257).

Rumelhart, D. E., Hinton, G. E., & McClelland, J. L. (1986). A General Framework for Parallel Distributed Processing. In *Parallel Distributed Processing, Vol.1: Foundations* (pp. 45-76). Cambridge, MA: MIT Press.

Shin, Y., & Ghosh, J. (1991). The Pi-sigma Network: An Efficient Higher-Order Neural Network for Pattern Classification and Function Approximation. In *Proc. Int. Joint Conf. Neural Networks* (pp. 13-18).

Shin, Y., & Ghosh, J. (1995). Ridge Polynomial Networks. *IEEE Transactions on Neural Networks, 6*(3), 610–622. doi:10.1109/72.377967

Takagi, H., & Hayashi, I. (1991). NN-driven fuzzy reasoning . *International Journal of Approximate Reasoning, 5*, 191–212. doi:10.1016/0888-613X(91)90008-A

Chapter 11
Dynamic Ridge Polynomial Higher Order Neural Network

Rozaida Ghazali
Universiti Tun Hussein Onn, Malaysia

Abir Jaafar Hussain
Liverpool John Moores University, UK

Nazri Mohd Nawi
Universiti Tun Hussein Onn, Malaysia

ABSTRACT

This chapter proposes a novel Dynamic Ridge Polynomial Higher Order Neural Network (DRPHONN). The architecture of the new DRPHONN incorporates recurrent links into the structure of the ordinary Ridge Polynomial Higher Order Neural Network (RPHONN) (Shin & Ghosh, 1995). RPHONN is a type of feedforward Higher Order Neural Network (HONN) (Giles & Maxwell, 1987) which implements a static mapping of the input vectors. In order to model dynamical functions of the brain, it is essential to utilize a system that is capable of storing internal **states** *and can implement complex* **dynamic** *system. Neural networks with* **recurrent connections** *are dynamical systems with temporal* **state** *representations. The* **dynamic** *structure approach has been successfully used for solving varieties of problems, such as time series forecasting (Zhang & Chan, 2000; Steil, 2006), approximating a dynamical system (Kimura & Nakano, 2000), forecasting a stream flow (Chang et al, 2004), and system control (Reyes et al, 2000). Motivated by the ability of recurrent* **dynamic** *systems in real world applications, the proposed DRPHONN architecture is presented in this chapter.*

INTRODUCTION

Functional Link Neural Network (FLNN) (Giles & Maxwell, 1987) is a type of HONN which naturally extends the family of theoretical feedforward network structure by introducing nonlinearities in input patterns enhancements. The network, however, suffers from the combinatorial explosion in the number of weights, when the order of the network becomes excessively high.

DOI: 10.4018/978-1-61520-711-4.ch011

A simple yet efficient alternative to FLNN is the Pi-Sigma Neural Network (PSNN) which was proposed by Shin and Ghosh (Shin & Ghosh, 1991). PSNN was introduced to overcome the problem of weight explosion in FLNN. The network has a regular structure and requires a smaller **number of free parameters**, when compared to other single layer HONNs. However, PSNN is not a universal approximator (Shin & Ghosh, 1995).

A generalization of PSNN is the Ridge Polynomial Higher Order Neural Network (RPHONN) (Shin & Ghosh, 1995). The network has a well regulated structure which is constructed by the addition of PSNNs of varying orders. Contrary to the FLNN, which utilizes multivariate polynomials, thus leading to an explosion in the **number of free parameters**, RPHONN uses univariate polynomials which are easy to handle. RPHONN is a universal approximator (Shin & Ghosh, 1995), and the network maintains the fast learning and powerful mapping properties of single layer HONNs and avoids the explosion of weights, as the number of inputs increases. Any multivariate polynomial can be represented in the form of a ridge polynomial and realized by RPHONN.

In this chapter, a new dynamically sized higher order recurrent neural network architecture is presented. The network will start with small basic structure, which will grow as the learning proceeds until the desired mapping task is carried out with the required degree of accuracy. The network is called the Dynamic Ridge Polynomial Higher Order Neural Network (DRPHONN).

THE PROPERTIES AND NETWORK STRUCTURE OF DRPHONN

In linear system, the use of past inputs values creates the Moving Average (MA) models. Meanwhile, the use of the past outputs values creates what is known as the Autoregressive (AR) models. Feedforward neural networks were shown to be a special case of Nonlinear Autoregressive (NAR) models, on the other hand Recurrent Neural Networks (RNNs) were shown to be a special case of Nonlinear ARMA models (NARMA). This means that RNNs have moving average components, therefore showing advantages over feedforward neural networks, similar to the advantages in which ARMA model possess over AR model (Connor et al., 1994). Hence, RNNs are well suited for time series that possess moving average components (Connor et al., 1994).

Most of real world applications require explicit treatment of **dynamics**. Feedforward RPHONN can only accommodate **dynamic** systems by including past inputs and target values in an augmented set of inputs. However, this kind of **dynamic** representation does not exploit a known feature of biological networks, that of internal feedback. DRPHONN, on the other hand, incorporates a **recurrent connection**, and as a consequence of this feedback, the network outputs depend not only on the initial values of external inputs, but also on the entire history of the system inputs. Hence, the introduction of recurrence feedback in the ordinary feedforward RPHONN is expected to improve the input-output mapping. This relates to the fact that the proposed DRPHONN has the capability of having a memory to solve the underlying task and exhibiting a rich **dynamic** behaviour.

The structure of the DRPHONN is constructed from a number of increasing order of Pi-Sigma units (refer to Figure 1) (Shin & Ghosh, 1991) with the addition of a feedback connection from the output layer to the input layer. The feedback connection feeds the activation of the output node to the summing nodes in each Pi-Sigma units, thus allowing each building block of Pi-Sigma unit to see the resulting output of the previous patterns. In contrast to RPHONN, the proposed DRPHONN, as shown in Figure 2 is provided with memories which give the network the ability of retaining information to be used later.

All the connection weights from the input layer to the first summing layer are learnable, while the rest are fixed to unity.

The rational of placing the **recurrent connection** from the output layer back to the input layer in the proposed DRPHONN is that instead of learning with complex and fully connected recurrent architectures, redundant connections should be eliminated in order to significantly increase the network's generalization capability. This architecture is similar to the Jordan recurrent network (Jordan, 1986). The feedforward part of Jordan network is a restricted case of a non-linear AR model, while the configuration with context units fed by the output layer is a restricted case of non-linear MA model (Beale & Jackson, 1990). From this, the proposed DRPHONN which has the feedback connection from the output layer to the input layer is seen to have an advantage over feedforward RPHONN in much the same way that ARMA models have advantages over the AR.

Suppose that M is the number of external inputs $U(n)$ to the network, and let $y(n-1)$ to be the output of the DRPHONN at previous time step. The overall input to the network are the concatenation of $U(n)$ and $y(n-1)$, and is referred to as $Z(n)$ where:

$$Z_i(n) = \begin{cases} U_i(n) & \text{if } 1 \leq i \leq M \\ y(n-1) & i = M+1 \end{cases} \tag{1}$$

The output of the k_{th} order DRPHONN is determined as follows:

$$y(n) = P\left(n \right)^k \sum_{i=1} i$$

$$P_i(n) = \prod_{j=1}^{i} \left(h_j(n) \right) \quad . \tag{2}$$

$$h_j(n) = \sum_{i=1}^{M+1} W_{ij} Z_i(n) + W_{jo}$$

where $\sigma(.)$ is a suitable nonlinear activation function, k is the number of Pi-Sigma units used, $P_i(n)$ is the output of each PSNN block, $h_j(n)$ is the net sum of the sigma unit in the corresponding PSNN block, W_{jo} is the bias, σ is the **sigmoid activation function**, and n is the current time step.

LEARNING ALGORITHM OF DRPHONN

The DRPHONN uses a constructive learning algorithm based on the asynchronous updating rule of the Pi-Sigma unit. The network adds a Pi-Sigma unit of increasing order to its structure when the relative different between the current and the previous errors is less than a predefined threshold value. DRPHONN follows the same training steps used in feedforward RPHONN, in addition to the Real Time Recurrent Learning algorithm (Williams & Zipser, 1989) for updating the weights of the Pi-Sigma unit in the network. A standard error measure used for training the network is the Sum Squared Error:

$$E(n) = \frac{1}{2} \sum e(n)^2 \tag{3}$$

The error between the target and forecast signal is determined as follows:

$$e(n) = d(n) - y(n) \tag{4}$$

where $d(n)$ is the target output at time n, $y(n)$ is the forecast output at time n.

At every time n, the weights are updated according to:

$$\Delta W_{kl}(n) = -\eta \left(\frac{\partial E(n)}{\partial W_{kl}} \right) \tag{5}$$

where η is the learning rate.

The value $\left(\frac{\partial E(n)}{\partial W_{kl}} \right)$ is determined as:

$$\frac{\partial E(n)}{\partial W_{kl}} = -e(n) \frac{\partial y(n)}{\partial W_{kl}} \tag{6}$$

$$\frac{\partial y(n)}{\partial W_{kl}} = \frac{\partial y(n)}{\partial P_i(n)} \frac{\partial P_i(n)}{\partial W_{kl}} \tag{7}$$

where

$$\frac{\partial y(n)}{\partial P_i(n)} = f' \left(\sum_{i=1}^{k} P_i(n) \right) \left(\prod_{\substack{j=1 \\ j \neq i}}^{i} h_j(n) \right) \tag{8}$$

and

$$\frac{\partial P_i(n)}{\partial W_{kl}} = \left(W_{ij} \frac{\partial y(n-1)}{W_{kl}} \right) + Z_i(n) \delta_{ik} \tag{9}$$

where δ_{ik} is the Krocnoker delta. Assume D as the **dynamic** system variable (the **state** of the ij^{th} neuron), where D is:

$$D_{ij}(n) = \frac{\partial y(n)}{\partial W_{kl}} \tag{10}$$

The **state** of a dynamical system is formally defined as a set of quantities that summarizes all the information about the past behaviour of the system that is needed to uniquely describe its future behaviour (Haykin, 1999). Substituting Equation (8) and (9) into (7) results in:

$$D_{ij}(n) = \frac{\partial y(n)}{\partial W_{kl}} = f'\left(\sum_{i=1}^{k} P_i(n)\right) \times \left(\prod_{\substack{j=1 \\ j \neq i}}^{i} h_j(n)\right)\left(W_{ij}D_{ij}(n-1) + Z_i(n)\delta_{ik}\right) \tag{11}$$

where $f'(.)$ is the first derivative of a nonlinear activation function.

For simplification, the initial values for $D_{ij}(n-1)=0$, and $Z_j(n-1)=0.5$. Then the weights updating rule is

$$\begin{aligned} "W_{ij}(n) &= \eta e(n)D_{ij}(n) \ + \ \alpha \Delta W_{ij}(n-1) \\ W_{ij}(n+1) &= W_{ij}(n) + "W_{ij}(n) \end{aligned} \tag{12}$$

where W_{ij} are **adjustable weights** and ΔW_{ij} are total of weight changes.

ISSUES OF STABILITY IN DRPHONN

While Recurrent Neural Networks have matured into a fundamental tool for solving many real world problems such as time series forecasting, approximating a dynamical system, forecasting a stream flow, string classification, character recognition, and system control, major difficulties for their application still remain. These are the known high numerical complexity of the training algorithm and the difficulties in assuring stability (Steil, 2005). In RNNs, the internal **state** evolves in time according to certain nonlinear **state** equations until it goes to **equilibrium**, or possibly other types of behaviour such as periodic or chaotic motion could occur (Atiya, 1988). However, one would be interested in having a steady and fixed output for every input applied to the network. Therefore, beginning in any initial condition, the **state** should ultimately go to a unique **equilibrium**. It is in fact that **equilibrium state** that determines the final output. The objective of the learning algorithm is to adjust the parameters of the network into small steps in order to move the unique **equilibrium state** in a way that will result finally in an output as close as possible to the required one. Since weight adjustment affects the evolution of **states** at every time steps during the network training, obtaining the error gradient is rather a complicated procedure (Atiya, 2000). This is due to the tendency of the network to become unstable.

One of the most useful properties of networks with **recurrent connection** is their ability to model the behaviour of arbitrary dynamical system. Hence, the existence of feedback in the proposed DRPHONN is expected to improve the performance of a given network. Despite the potential and capability of the DRPHONN which comprises the **recurrent connection**, the same problems of complexity and difficulty of training the network exist in the proposed DRPHONN, which are:

- The **states** of the processing elements, denoted by D_{ij} in Equation 10, affect both the output and the gradient. Therefore, calculating the gradients and updating the weights of a recurrent network is much more difficult.
- The network is more difficult to train than ordinary RPHONN. This relates to the fact that the training algorithm could become unstable which is the result of:
  - the error between the target and the output of the DRPHONN may not be monotonically decreasing,

   ◦   the gradient computation is more complicated,

   ◦   and the **convergence** time may be long.

In an attempt to overcome the stability and **convergence** problems in the proposed DRPHONN, the **convergence** of network is presented in the next section to ensure that the network posses a unique **equilibrium state**.

THE STABILITY CONDITION FOR DRPHONN

Based on the stability theorem for a general network proposed by (Atiya, 1988) and shown in Equation 13, any network that satisfies this theorem exhibits no other behaviour except going to a unique **equilibrium** for a given input:

$$\sum_{i=1}\sum_{j=1}w^2_{ij} < \frac{1}{\max(f')^2} \tag{13}$$

where w is the weight matrix and f' is the first derivative of a bounded and differentiable activation function.

From the given theorem, a unique fixed point is reached regardless of the initial condition. This means that for a given input, after a short transient period, the network will give a steady and fixed output, no matter what the initial network **state** was. In other words, beginning with any initial conditions, the **state** is to be attracted towards a unique **equilibrium**. In order to guarantee that the proposed DRPHONN shows a unique **equilibrium state**, a derivation of the stability **convergence** of the proposed network will be presented.

Let $y_1(t+1)$ and $y_2(t+1)$ be 2 outputs for the DRPHONN.

$$y_1(t+1) = f\left(\sum_{k=1}^{A}\prod_{L=1}^{k}h_{1L}(t+1)\right) \tag{14}$$

where f is a nonlinear transfer function.

$$y_2(t+1) = f\left(\sum_{k=1}^{A}\prod_{L=1}^{k}h_{2L}(t+1)\right) \tag{15}$$

$$h_{1L}(t+1) = \sum_{i=1}^{M}W_{Li}X_i + W_{L(M+1)}$$
$$+W_{L(M+2)}y_1(t)$$
$$= \alpha_L + \beta_L y_1(t) \tag{16}$$

with

$$\alpha_L = \sum_{i=1}^{M} W_{Li} X_i + W_{L(M+1)} \tag{17}$$

and

$$\beta_L = W_{L(M+2)} \tag{18}$$

while

$$h_{2L}(t+1) = \sum_{i=1}^{M} W_{Li} X_i + W_{L(M+1)}$$
$$+ W_{L(M+2)} y_2(t) \tag{19}$$
$$= \alpha_L + \beta_L y_2(t)$$

The aim is to get *J* approaching '0', which means that the 2 outputs of a given input are close. Let *J(t+1)* be:

$$J(t+1) = \left\| y_1(t+1) - y_2(t+1) \right\| \tag{20}$$

where $\| \ \|$ is the norm. Based on Mean Value Theorem (O'Connor & Robertson, 2000), which states that for a function *f(x)* which is continuous on the closed interval *[a,b]* and differentiable on the open interval *(a,b)*, there exists a value *c* on the interval *(a,b)* such that

$$f'(c) = \frac{f(b) - f(a)}{b - a} \tag{21}$$

where *f'* is the derivation of the function. Hence

$$f(b) - f(a) = f'(c) \bullet (b - a) \tag{22}$$

and

$$\left\| f(b) - f(a) \right\| = \left\| f'(c) \right\| \bullet \left\| b - a \right\| \tag{23}$$

which leads to

$$\left\| f(b) - f(a) \right\| \leq \max \left\| f'(c) \right\| \bullet \left\| b - a \right\| \tag{24}$$

substituting Equation (14) and (15) into Equation (20), results into

$$J(t+1) = \left\| f\left(\sum_{k=1}^{A} \prod_{L=1}^{k} h_{1L}(t+1) \right) - f\left(\sum_{k=1}^{A} \prod_{L=1}^{k} h_{2L} \ t+1) \right) \right\| \tag{25}$$

using Mean Value Theorem, leads to

$$\left\| f\left(\sum_{k=1}^{A}\prod_{L=1}^{k} h_{1L}(t+1) \right) - f\left(\sum_{k=1}^{A}\prod_{L=1}^{k} h_{2L}(t+1) \right) \right\|$$

$$\leq \max |f'| \bullet \left\| \sum_{k=1}^{A}\prod_{L=1}^{k} h_{1L}(t+1) - \sum_{k=1}^{A}\prod_{L=1}^{k} h_{2L}(t+1) \right\|$$

(26)

therefore, from Equation (25), Equation (26) becomes

$$J(t+1) \leq \max |f'| \bullet \left\| \sum_{k=1}^{A}\prod_{L=1}^{K} h_{1L}(t+1) - \sum_{k=1}^{A}\prod_{L=1}^{K} h_{2L}(t+1) \right\|$$

(27)

from Equation (14) & (16), let *g(y)* be

$$g(y) = \sum_{k=1}^{A}\prod_{L=1}^{K} (\alpha_L + \beta_L y)$$

$$= \sum_{k=1}^{A}\prod_{L=1}^{k} h_L(t+1)$$

(28)

hence

$$\left\| \sum_{k=1}^{A}\prod_{L=1}^{k} h_{1L}(t+1) - \sum_{k=1}^{A}\prod_{L=1}^{k} h_{2L}(t+1) \right\| = \left\| g(y_1(t)) - g(y_2(t)) \right\|$$

(29)

using the Mean Value Theorem again, leads to:

$$\left\| g(y_1(t)) - g(y_2(t)) \right\| \leq \max |g'| \bullet \left\| y_1(t) - y_2(t) \right\|$$

(30)

hence, from Equation (27),(29) & (30), results into:

$$J(t+1) \leq (\max |f'|) \bullet (\max |g'|) \bullet \left\| y_1(t) - y_2(t) \right\|$$

(31)

let δ be

$$\delta = (\max |f'|) \bullet (\max |g'|)$$

(32)

then

$$J(t+1) \leq \delta. \left\| y_1(t) - y_2(t) \right\|$$

(33)

from Equation (20), Equation (33) becomes

$$J(t+1) \leq \delta. J(t)$$

(34)

The aim is to get both *J(t+1)* and *J(t)* approaching very close to zero, and for large *(t),* and for any value of *(t)*. To achieve this, δ has to be very small value, which is less than 1. Hence, from Equation (32), when δ is < 1, leads into:

$$\left(\max\left|f'\right|\right) \bullet \left(\max\left|g'\right|\right) < 1 \tag{35}$$

from Equation (28), *g(y)* will be

$$g(y) = \sum_{k=1}^{A}\prod_{L=1}^{k}\left(\alpha_L + \beta_L y\right) \tag{36}$$

let *P(y)* be

$$P(y) = \prod_{L=1}^{k}\left(\alpha_L + \beta_L y\right) \tag{37}$$

then

$$\sum_{k=1}^{A}P(y) = \sum_{k=1}^{A}\prod_{L=1}^{k}\left(\alpha_L + \beta_L y\right) \tag{38}$$

therefore

$$g(y) = \sum_{k=1}^{A}P(y) \tag{39}$$

and

$$\left(g(y)\right)' = \sum_{k=1}^{A}P'(y) \tag{40}$$

from Equation (37)

$$\ln\left(P(y)\right) = \sum_{L=1}^{k}\ln\left(\alpha_L + \beta_L y\right) \tag{41}$$

and

$$\frac{P'(y)}{P(y)} = \sum_{L=1}^{k}\frac{\beta_L}{\left(\alpha_L + \beta_L y\right)} \tag{42}$$

hence

$$P'(y) = P(y).\sum_{L=1}^{k}\frac{\beta_L}{\left(\alpha_L + \beta_L y\right)} \tag{43}$$

substitute Equation (37) into Equation (43), having

$$P'(y) = \prod_{L=1}^{k}(\alpha_L + \beta_L y) \bullet \sum_{L=1}^{k} \frac{\beta_L}{(\alpha_L + \beta_L y)} \qquad (44)$$

then

$$P'(y) = \sum_{L=1}^{k}\beta_L \bullet \sum_{L=1}^{k}\frac{1}{(\alpha_L + \beta_L y)} \bullet \prod_{L=1}^{k}(\alpha_L + \beta_L y) \qquad (45)$$

$$P'(y) = \sum_{L=1}^{k}\beta_L \bullet \sum_{L=1}^{k}\prod_{\substack{S=1 \\ S \neq L}}^{k}(\alpha_S + \beta_S y) \qquad (46)$$

$$P'(y) = \sum_{L=1}^{k}\beta_L \bullet \prod_{\substack{S=1 \\ S \neq L}}^{k}(\alpha_S + \beta_S y) \qquad (47)$$

substituting Equation (47) into Equation (40), results into

$$(g(y))' = \sum_{k=1}^{A}\sum_{L=1}^{k}\beta_L \bullet \prod_{\substack{S=1 \\ S \neq L}}^{k}(\alpha_S + \beta_S y) \qquad (48)$$

and

$$\left|(g(y))'\right| = \left|\sum_{k=1}^{A}\sum_{L=1}^{k}\beta_L \bullet \prod_{\substack{S=1 \\ S \neq L}}^{k}(\alpha_S + \beta_S y)\right| \qquad (49)$$

therefore

$$\left|\sum_{k=1}^{A}\sum_{L=1}^{k}\beta_L \bullet \prod_{\substack{S=1 \\ S \neq L}}^{k}(\alpha_S + \beta_S y)\right|$$
$$= \left|\sum_{k=1}^{A}\sum_{L=1}^{k}\beta_L\right| \bullet \left|\prod_{\substack{S=1 \\ S \neq L}}^{k}(\alpha_S + \beta_S y)\right| \qquad (50)$$

hence

$$\left|\sum_{k=1}^{A}\sum_{L=1}^{k}\beta_L \bullet \prod_{\substack{S=1 \\ S \neq L}}^{k}(\alpha_S + \beta_S y)\right|$$
$$\leq \sum_{k=1}^{A}\sum_{L=1}^{k} |\beta_L| \bullet \prod_{\substack{S=1 \\ S \neq L}}^{k}(|\alpha_S| + |\beta_S y|) \qquad (51)$$

note that from Equation (17)

$$\alpha_L = \sum_{i=1}^{M} W_{Li} X_i + W_{L(M+1)} \tag{52}$$

therefore

$$|\alpha_L| = \sum_{m=1}^{M+1} |W_{Lm}| \tag{53}$$

note that from Equation (18) and Equation (51) results

$$\left| \sum_{k=1}^{A} \sum_{L=1}^{k} \beta_L \bullet \prod_{\substack{S=1 \\ S \neq L}}^{k} (\alpha_S + \beta_S y) \right|$$

$$\leq \sum_{k=1}^{A} \sum_{L=1}^{k} |W_{L(M+2)}| \bullet \prod_{\substack{S=1 \\ S \neq L}}^{k} \left(\sum_{m=1}^{M+1} |W_{Sm}| + |W_{S(M+2)}| \right) \tag{54}$$

hence

$$\left| \sum_{k=1}^{A} \sum_{L=1}^{k} \beta_L \bullet \prod_{\substack{S=1 \\ S \neq L}}^{k} (\alpha_S + \beta_S y) \right|$$

$$\leq \sum_{k=1}^{A} \sum_{L=1}^{k} |W_{L(M+2)}| \bullet \prod_{\substack{S=1 \\ S \neq L}}^{k} \sum_{m=1}^{M+2} |W_{Sm}| \tag{55}$$

therefore, from Equation (49) and (55) results into

$$\left| (g(y))' \right| = \sum_{k=1}^{A} \sum_{L=1}^{k} |W_{L(M+2)}| \bullet \prod_{\substack{S=1 \\ S \neq L}}^{k} \sum_{m=1}^{M+2} |W_{Sm}| \tag{56}$$

substituting Equation (56) into Equation (35), we get

$$(\max|f'|) \bullet \left(\max \left(\sum_{k=1}^{A} \sum_{L=1}^{k} |W_{L(M+2)}| \bullet \prod_{\substack{S=1 \\ S \neq L}}^{k} \sum_{m=1}^{M+2} |W_{Sm}| \right) \right) < 1 \tag{57}$$

therefore, the condition for DRPHONN to converge is described by

$$\left(\max \left(\sum_{k=1}^{A} \sum_{L=1}^{k} |W_{L(M+2)}| \bullet \prod_{\substack{S=1 \\ S \neq L}}^{k} \sum_{m=1}^{M+2} |W_{Sm}| \right) \right) < \frac{1}{(\max|f'|)} \tag{58}$$

This work guarantees the stability of DRPHONN for the **equilibrium** problem.

FUTURE TRENDS

The novel neural network model which is proposed and presented in this chapter can be viewed as starting points for future research direction, since the potential of DRPHONN, especially with respect to time series approximation, prediction and classification is by far not fully exploited yet. More research is needed with the use of DRPHONN to give a more general account of their abilities. Based on the currently ongoing research in the area of computer science and engineering, a continuation of this research work involving the use of *evolutionary computation* is suggested. It should be emphasized that DRPHONN is not without problem. The main intricacy when using the networks is to find the suitable parameters for successively adding a higher degree of Pi-Sigma unit in the networks. Training the networks can be a quite expensive procedure, as it is difficult to know the best combination of learning parameters used in the network. With respect to this deficiency which causing to a trial and error approach, it might be worthwhile to consider how Genetic Algorithm (GA) (Koza, 1992) can be used to automatically generating and finding suitable parameters for the networks. Evolutionary computation has been successfully used to automatically develop neural network structures, weights adaptation and learning parameter setting; rather than the user doing this task experimentally. However, research relating the use of HONNs and evolutionary computation remains largely unexplored. GA has proven to be capable at finding near optimal solutions for problems which have extremely large search spaces. In this way, GA searches promising areas of the solution space by evolving a population of rules that tends to become more adept at solving the problem in successive generations. By implementing a GA approach to the learning parameter selection, it is expected to an improvement in the training process and therefore leads to better performance of the networks.

CONCLUSION

In this chapter, the Dynamic Ridge Polynomial Higher Order Neural Network is presented as an extension of the ordinary feedforward Ridge Polynomial Higher Order Neural Network. In order to represent a **dynamic** system, the functionality and architecture of the feedforward RPHONN were extended by adding a feedback connection into the network. Subsequently, the stability and the **convergence** of the proposed network will be implemented to ensure having steady and fixed output. This superior property hold by the DRPHONN could promise many powerful applications in real world problems. Hence, it is anticipated that DRPHONN, can be used as an alternative or supplemental method for data approximation, prediction and classification, and thus justified the potential use of these models by practitioners. To conclude, DRPHONN is a promising intelligent computational technology that potentially can be a challenging tool for future research.

REFERENCES

Atiya, A. F. (1988). Learning on a general network. *In Proc. IEEE Conf. Neural Information Processing Systems*, 1987.

Atiya, A. F. (2000). New Results on Recurrent Network Training: Unifying the Algorithms and Accelerating Convergence. *IEEE Transactions on Neural Networks, 11*(3), 697–709. doi:10.1109/72.846741

Beale, R., & Jackson, T. (1990). *Neural Computing: An Introduction.* Bristol, UK: Hilger.

Chang, L. C., Chang, F. J., & Chiang, Y. M. (2004). A two-step-ahead recurrent neural network for stream-flow forecasting. *Hydrological Processes, 18*, 81–92. doi:10.1002/hyp.1313

Connor, J. T., Martin, R. D., & Atlas, L. E. (1994). Recurrent Neural Networks and Robust Time Series Prediction. *IEEE Transactions on Neural Networks, 5*(2), 240–254. doi:10.1109/72.279188

Giles, C. L., & Maxwell, T. (1987). Learning, invariance and generalization in high-order neural networks. *Applied Optics, 26*(23), 4972–4978. doi:10.1364/AO.26.004972

Haykin, S. (1999). *Neural Networks. A comprehensive foundation.* Second Edition, New Jersey: Prentice-Hall, Inc.

Jordan, M. I. (1986). *Serial order: A parallel distributed processing approach.* Institute for Cognitive Science report 8604, Institute for Cognitive Science, University of California, San Diego.

Kimura, M., & Nakano, R. (2000). Dynamical systems produced by recurrent neural networks. *Systems and Computers in Japan, 31*(4), 77–86. doi:10.1002/(SICI)1520-684X(200004)31:4<77::AID-SCJ8>3.0.CO;2-Y

Koza, J. R. (1992). *Genetic Programming: On the Programming of Computers by Means of Natural Selection.* Cambridge, MA: MIT Press

O'Connor, J. J., & Robertson, E. F. (2000). Paramesvara, MacTutor History of Mathematics archive. Retrieved (n.d.), from http://www.answers.com/topic/mean-value-theorem?cat=technology

Reyes, J. R., Yu, W., & Poznyak, A. S. (2000). Passivation and Control of Partially Known SISO Nonlinear Systems via Dynamic Neural Networks. *Mathematical Problems in Engineering, 6*, 61–83. doi:10.1155/S1024123X00001253

Shin, Y., & Ghosh, J. (1991). The Pi-Sigma Networks: An Efficient Higher-order Neural Network for Pattern Classification and Function Approximation. In . *Proceedings of International Joint Conference on Neural Networks, 1*, 13–18.

Shin, Y., & Ghosh, J. (1995). Ridge Polynomial Networks. *IEEE Transactions on Neural Networks, 6*(3), 610–622. doi:10.1109/72.377967

Steil, J. J. (2005). Stability of backpropagation-decorrelation efficient O(N) recurrent learning. In *ESANN'2005 proceedings - European Symposium on Artificial Neural Networks* (pp. 43-48). Belgium. Williams, R. J., & Zipser, D. (1989). A learning algorithm for continually running fully recurrent neural networks. *Neural Computation, 1*, 270–280.

Steil, J. J. (2006). Online stability of backpropagation-decorrelation recurrent learning. *Neurocomputing, 69*, 642–650. doi:10.1016/j.neucom.2005.12.012

Zhang, Y. Q., & Chan, L. W. (2000). Fourier recurrent Networks for Time series Prediction. In *Proceedings of International Conference on Neural Information Processing*, ICONIP 2000 (pp. 576-582). Taejon, Korea.

Section 3
Artificial Higher Order Neural Networks for Computer Engineering

Chapter 12

Fifty Years of Electronic Hardware Implementations of First and Higher Order Neural Networks

David R. Selviah
University College London, UK

Janti Shawash
University College London, UK

ABSTRACT

This chapter celebrates 50 years of first and higher order neural network (HONN) implementations in terms of the physical layout and structure of electronic hardware, which offers high speed, low latency, compact, low cost, low power, mass produced systems. Low latency is essential for practical applications in real time control for which software implementations running on CPUs are too slow. The literature review chapter traces the chronological development of electronic neural networks (ENN) discussing selected papers in detail from analog electronic hardware, through probabilistic RAM, generalizing RAM, custom silicon Very Large Scale Integrated (VLSI) circuit, Neuromorphic chips, pulse stream interconnected neurons to Application Specific Integrated circuits (ASICs) and Zero Instruction Set Chips (ZISCs). Reconfigurable Field Programmable Gate Arrays (FPGAs) are given particular attention as the most recent generation incorporate Digital Signal Processing (DSP) units to provide full System on Chip (SoC) capability offering the possibility of real-time, on-line and on-chip learning.

1. INTRODUCTION

Many researchers and developers of artificial first and higher order neural networks (HONNs) implement the artificial neural network (ANN) algorithms in software and run them on digital floating point central processing unit (CPU) personal computers (PCs), as the computers themselves are readily available and low cost for the computing power that they provide. Moreover, software has the convenience of flex-

DOI: 10.4018/978-1-61520-711-4.ch012

ibility; so they can be easily modified to suit a variety of applications. However, computers are bulky, heavy and lack easy portability. Another serious problem is their latency, which is the time taken for the input to be processed to give an output or the delay through the processing system. This is crucial for applications in real time control where speed is of importance.

The solution is to use dedicated parallel electronic hardware, which is either physically configured in the same way as the ANN with multiple interconnected simpler neuron processing elements or configured to perform the same mathematical functions as the ANN. Such hardware can be made low cost, small, low power, compact, and portable when mass-produced. The disadvantage of dedicated electronic hardware has been that the systems lack flexibility and so only perform the one task that they were designed for which is not convenient for experimenting with different ANN structures. However, relatively recently a new type of processor has been introduced known as the Field Programmable Gate Array (FPGA) which allows programmers to reconfigure the hardware connections within it between arrays of digital electronic logic gates and also, most recently, between arrays of digital signal processors (DSPs).

After the introduction, section 2 chronologically reviews 50 years of dedicated electronic hardware implementations of pattern recognition, artificial first and HONNs, and their training. Selected research papers are described in more depth while others are just described by their titles due to space constraints. Section 3 reviews the most recent electronic implementations of artificial first and HONNs on FPGAs and looks to the future with the promise of on-line and on-chip artificial first and HONN learning on FPGAs. The conclusion is given in section 4, acknowledgements in section 5 followed by extensive references to aid researchers in tracing the development of the subject.

2. CHRONOLOGICAL REVIEW OF ELECTRONIC HARDWARE IMPLEMENTATIONS OF ANNS AND HONNS

1950s

After several years studying biological neurons culminating in a paper in Nature on lateral inhibition and adaptation in the mammalian retina, Dr Wilfred K. Taylor published the first paper discussing how pattern recognition can be performed on analog electronic hardware (Taylor, 1959). His circuit diagrams show arrays of parallel differential amplifiers, which in those days were thermionic valves together with resistors. In (Taylor, 1959) he introduces the *maximum amplitude filter*, later called the Maxnet, which outputs the maximum value of several inputs. In (Taylor, 1959) he describes parallel processing machines for recognizing letters, numbers, and other simple patterns in various positions, orientations, having different contrast and with a noisy background.

1960s

More complex neuron models were introduced, such as the Adaptive Linear Neuron Element (ADALINE) and the Multi-Layer-Perceptron (MLP) (Widrow & Hoff, 1960), which provided solutions to problems of a higher degree of complexity. Herscher & Kelley, (1963) built an electronic model of a frog's retina. By 1963, pattern recognition systems had become adaptive to adjust to recognize new input patterns using on-line learning (Taylor, 1963).

Taylor, (1964) describes an analog computer, which simulates pattern recognition in the brain. Taylor, (1967) extends his earlier work to recognize photographs of faces. His learning machine had an input matrix of 100 photomultipliers, a middle layer of automatically adapting weight units composed of motor driven potentiometers, and 10 output units. The weights were originally set to zero. An external machine was used to provide training feedback when the system gave incorrect recognition. 105 presentations of each of 10 faces, in sequence were required in order to recognize them correctly. When a fault occurred in the system training was allowed to continue. Initially the performance degraded but then the system overcame the fault and after 250 presentations again always gave the correct recognition of all of the faces. This 1967 paper also mentions the case when the learning system gave no output which Taylor refers to as the "*the don't know condition*" which he treated as being an incorrect output during the training.

A second of the early pioneers who implemented ANNs on electronic hardware concentrating mainly on digital rather than analog hardware, was Professor Igor Aleksander. Aleksander introduces the first two of his three papers on Microcircuit learning nets for recognition of handwritten numerals using pattern feedback in (Aleksander & Albrow, 1968; Aleksander & Mamdani, 1968). Taylor, (1968b) describes parallel processing machines for recognizing letters, numbers, and other simple patterns in various positions, orientations, having different contrast and with a noisy background. Taylor, (1968b); Taylor, (1968a) discusses learning and training in pattern recognition machines.

1970s

Aleksander, (1970b); Aleksander & Fairhurst, (1970) reported on implementing ANNs on electronic hardware, learning of patterns in humans and Electronic Neural Networks (ENNs). Aleksander, (1970a) published his third paper on Microcircuit Learning Nets on Hamming distances. Fairhurst & Aleksander, (1971) discuss learning in ANNs on digital hardware. Muller & Taylor, (1973) began to refer to the system as *Neural Network* in their paper title. They compares biological neurons with electronic ones discussing integrating units and adaptive neurons. They also draw a distinction between pattern detection when a positive output is given for the match of an input and stored pattern and pattern discrimination when the signal generated from the match of the input pattern and one of the stored patterns is greater than that with any other stored pattern. They also discuss bipolar (positive and negative) pattern matching outputs. Taylor, (1973) comments that digital computers at that time had not demonstrated satisfactory pattern recognition performance despite their high processing speed while his earlier parallel analog processors could do so.

Taylor & Al-Kibasi, (1974) introduce the UCLM3 programmable pattern recognition machine. Taylor & Witkowsk, (1974) discuss electronic circuits for optical character pattern recognition. Muller & Taylor, (1976) note the importance of parallel processing in both the brain and ANNs. By then schematic diagrams of some of the biological NNs used in sensory pathways had been published and they were very similar to the circuits Taylor had designed in 1958-1963 10 to 15 years before. Wilson & Aleksander, (1977) begin to investigate pattern recognition using RAM-ROM arrays.

Taylor, (1978) patents a pattern recognition system, which performs inner products between an unknown input vector, and an array of reference stored vectors and then recognizes the input vector to be the stored reference vector having the largest inner product. W. K. Taylor's patent shows an architecture consisting of both clocked digital and analog circuit elements. Each input pattern (Fig. 1) is passed through a sensor giving an analog signal, is digitized in an analog-to-digital converter (ADC) and then reformed or multiplexed from parallel to serial, into the form of a vector having N bits using a clocked NAND gate, a latch flip-flop, counters and shift registers. The system initially learns by storing a set of M reference vectors, each in one of an array of M parallel shift registers. Each reference vectors has N bits. An unknown input vector of N bits length is also stored in another shift register. Then the unknown input vector is compared, *in parallel*, with each of the stored reference vectors. The input vector and set of reference vectors are all read out, under the control of clock pulses, from their shift registers, one element at a time. The element just read out of the input vector is compared simultaneously in parallel with the corresponding element in each of the reference vectors in an array of M comparators. The comparators are digital exclusive OR gates. The outputs of the M comparators are fed to an array of M integrators or accumulators to sum the result of the comparisons with each corresponding element in the vectors. Once all of the elements of the vectors have been compared, the magnitude of the signals in each of the M integrators or accumulators are compared with each other to find the maximum value and that indicates the vector having the closest match. The integrator or accumulator output signals can also be ranked according to magnitude using M flip-flops each connected to each integrator or accumulator.

1980s

Taylor & Ero, (1980) reported on a real time teaching and recognition system for robot vision. Lavie & Taylor, (1982) discuss errors that can occur in template matching optical pattern comparisons due to spatial quantization of the edges. They investigated this by considering the misalignment of one image compared to the template.

Taylor, Lavie, & Esatt, (1983) control a curvilinear snake arm with gripper-axis fiber-optic image processor feedback. In (Lavie & Taylor, 1983), a *real time* pattern recognition image processor was implemented using an 8085 microprocessor controlled by software for quality assurance automatic visual inspection of manufactured parts. Other researchers at the time were designing custom integrated circuits but at high cost. The system design appears to be an implementation of Taylor's earlier 1978 patent. The training involved the storage of image-processed edge extracted versions of known reference images, which downloaded to shift registers in operation. Instead of using another shift register for the input unknown image a RAM was used instead which enabled 4 rows of the image to be stored at the same time. As in Taylor's patent, the exclusive OR is calculated between the unknown input and stored reference images although in this design each reference image was compared to the input image in sequence. It was noted that a system could be constructed in which multiple arithmetic logic units could be used to compare all of the patterns in parallel in 20 ms although at the time this would have been a costly option. One of the problems experienced was the spatial quantization of the image to the pixel grid but it was found that this could be avoided by shifting two frames by one pixel and performing the AND logical operation between them. They also developed algorithms for putting the smallest rectangle around an object. The input image came from a CCD camera and was processed by bit-plane parallel processing with one image processing unit for each pixel in parallel, but this resulted in a costly system with slow processing speed so they chose to use a line scan camera instead. The gray-level input was digitized in an analog-to-digital converter (ADC) using 6, 7, and 8 bits giving 64, 128 and 256 gray-levels. For an image of 256×256 pixels at 8 bit gray-level resolution a 64 kbyte RAM was required into which one image could be written in 50 μs, i.e. 5.12×10^6 bytes/s. By feeding the input into a long fast shift register it could then be read in, in parallel, at a slower rate, to a parallel connected memory once the shift register is full in a form of pipeline processing. Schottky TTL hardware in the line scan mode

Figure 1. W. K Taylor's Patented Electronic Hardware Pattern Recognition Circuit (Adapted from (Taylor, 1978))

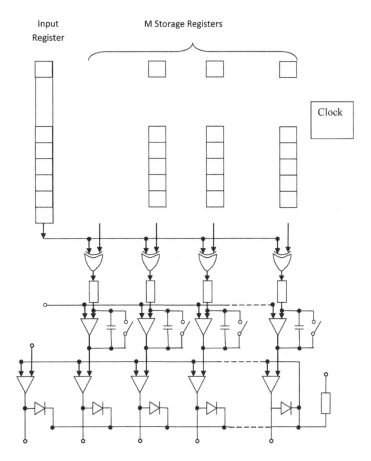

gave real time operation at the front end. Each frame could be acquired in 1/50 s. By storing 4 lines from the image scan camera into 4 rows in a RAM, image processing operations requiring arithmetic and logical calculations within a 4 × 4 template window could be performed such as edge detection and gradient direction detection. In addition, logical operations could be performed between any two image blocks consisting of 4 image rows. The pixel clock was extracted by an analog card from the clock in the standard composite video signal from the CCD camera. The analog magnitude of the signal in each pixel was digitized using a 6-bit flash ADC. Images from the ADC were sent to the RAM on a 6-bit sampled video bus. All other images were sent on an 8-bit parallel bus between the microcomputer, the frame processor, the magnitude and delay sections, and the storage. Fast 45 ns RAMs and 45 ns shift registers were used. The magnitudes of 6-bit signals from 4 or more pixels were compared to a threshold to yield a binary decision. The output was converted by a serial-to-parallel converter to an 8-bit byte and sent through the system bus. The frame processor performed 8-bit word logic operations on two 8 kbyte blocks of data within one frame time of 20 ms which was an order of magnitude improvement over standard microcomputer operation. The software was developed on a different external computer and when complete downloaded into the systems microcomputer.

Lee et al., (1986) discuss machine learning using a *higher order* correlation network. Grant & Sage, (1986) compared pattern recognition using matched filters and ANNs. Graf et al., (1986) AT&T Bell Laboratories, designed an ENN CMOS VLSI implementation of an ANN memory with 256 neurons on a single chip with both analog and digital VLSI technology using a custom fabrication process. The neurons were represented by amplifiers having inverting and non-inverting outputs to representing inhibitory and excitatory connections. Interconnections between neurons were via amorphous silicon resistors, which were trimmed by electron beam. Hopfield & Tank, (1986) reported a model for computing with neural circuits.

Giles & Maxwell, (1987) introduced *HONN*s for the first time with the motivation of converting the "Black box" design process into an "open box" model where each neuron maps variables to a function using optimal weights without the use of hidden layers. Alspector & Allen, (1987) introduces the Neuromorphic VLSI Learning System. Graf & de Vegvai, (1987); Hubbard et al., (1987) report a CMOS associative memory chip based on ANNs. Mackie, Graf, & Denker, (1987) discuss a microelectronic implementation of connectionist ANNs. Murray & Smith, (1987a); Murray & Smith, (1987b) discuss asynchronous signaling methods for VLSI neural systems. Sage, Thompson, & Withers, (1987) report an MNOS CCD ANN integrated circuit. Agranat & Yariv, (1987) describe a semiparallel CCD microelectronic implementation of ANNs. Tsividis, Y.P., & Anastassiou, (1987) describe switched capacitor ANNs. Carpenter & Grossberg, (1987) describe a highly parallel architecture for a self-organizing neural pattern recognition machine.

Murray & Smith, (1988) discuss asynchronous VLSI ANNs using pulse stream arithmetic. Murray, Smith, & Tarassenko, (1988) report fully programmable analog VLSI devices for implementation of an ANNs. Shoemaker, Lagnado, & Shimabukuro, (1988) discussed ANN implementation using floating gate MOS electronic devices. Allen, Mead, Faggin, & Cribble, (1988) discuss VLSI neuromorphic chips for orientation selective retinas. Faggin, Lynch, & Sukonick, (1988) patented an ENN. Lyon & Mead, (1988) discuss VLSI neuromorphic chips for artificial cochleas.

Selviah & Midwinter, (1989a); Selviah & Midwinter, (1989b); Selviah & Midwinter, (1989c); Selviah, Midwinter, Rivers, & Lung, (1989) extend the research of Grant 3 years earlier by introducing a proof that first order ANNs can be expressed equivalently as an array of inner product correlators or matched filters. The power of this approach is that it provides a conceptual framework which enables

1. An alternative direct hardware implementation in the form of arrays of correlators or matched filters in either electronic or optical technology
2. A clear understanding of the internal behavior of ANNs to be gained so that the effect of changing one weight by a certain amount can be assessed so abolishing the impenetrable "black box" nature of ANNs which deters analysts from using them
3. New ANNs and HONNS to be designed to suit a particular application or task
4. New training algorithms to be designed

demonstrated by the authors over subsequent years. Alspector, (1989) Bell Communications Research, Inc. is granted a patent for his Neuromorphic learning networks. Mead, (1989) published his book on VLSI ANNs. Intel (Holler, 1989) introduce an electrically trainable ANN (ETANN) (80170NB) with 10240 'floating gate' synapses for pattern recognition, which had a calculation rate of two billion weight multiplications per second. However, this performance was achieved at the cost of allowing errors introduced through reduced precision by operating at 7-bit accuracy multiplication. Hamilton, Murray, &

Tarassenko, (1989) report on programmable analog pulse-firing ANNs. Murray, Hamilton, Reekie, & Tarassenko, (1989) publish on Pulse-Stream Arithmetic in Programmable ANNs. Their asynchronous designs emitted pulses, as do biological neural systems. The presence or absence and rate of pulse firing of the neuron represent its state. The pulse-firing rate was multiplied by synaptic weights, which were stored on chip in digital memory, or in dynamic storage capacitors refreshed from off-chip digital RAM via a digital-to-analog converter. Clarkson, Gorse, & Taylor, (1989) began reporting research on digital electronic implementations of ANNs. Aleksander, (1989) discusses a canonical neural net based on logic nodes.

In W. K. Taylor's final paper (Mandanayake & Taylor, 1989) increase the speed of their 256×256 pixel image acquisition by using 8 bit parallel flash ADCs, which at a pixel sampling rate of 5-10 MHz had a latency of 200 ns. The parallel flash ADC consisted of 7000 digital gates over a 13 inch square of printed circuit board and took a month to design. They suggested that later it could be all incorporated into an ASIC. Their system again included gradient detection and thresholding but now over a larger 16×16 template window around each pixel. Pattern recognition could again be performed in the 20 ms frame time. Mandanayake et al., (1989) set a minimum threshold and rejected recognition signals below this to provide for the "don't know" state. They emphasized that the trained systems must be tested using images unlike those used for training to ensure that the system rejects them as not being members of the training pattern sets. They also discussed the tracking of recognized moving objects within the frame. They note that objects may appear in different locations, orientations (roll, pitch and yaw) and size and that these can also be recognized if the original known training images are also presented during training in a variety of orientations. To avoid the time for additional recordings of different orientations, a computer generated set of the original object in a series of orientations could be made instead for training. Variations in size can be accommodated by using a zoom lens or a size invariant transform or again multiple training examples of various sizes. They demonstrated recognition using photographs of faces, edge extracted typewritten characters and aircraft.

1990s

Aleksander, (1990) discusses ideal neurons for neural computers. Aleksander & Morton, (1991) describe a general neural unit for retrieving learned reference images at internal connections when distorted versions of the reference images are input to the external terminals. Halonen, Porra, Roska, & Chua, (1992) develop a programmable analog VLSI cellular ANN (CNN) chip. Tam et al., (1992) of Intel, describe a reconfigurable multi-chip analog neural network with recognition and back-propagation training.

Clarkson, Guan, Taylor, & Gorse, (1993) investigated the use of ANNs constructed from probabilistic random access memory pRAM electronic hardware. When these small highly non-linear ANNs were trained in the presence of noise, the network was shown to be able to generalize from the known training examples. Castro & Sweet, (1993) demonstrate character recognition and discuss the effects of radiation on the performance of the Intel Electrically Trainable ANN (ETANN) introduced in 1989. Castro, Tam, & Holler, (1993) of Intel describe an ANN with synaptic connections using floating gate non-volatile elements. Chua & Roska, (1993); Roska & Chua, (1993) describe cellular ANNs. Anguita, Pelayo, Prieto, & Ortega, (1993) report on analog CMOS cellular ANNs.

Grant, Taylor, & Houselander, (1994) described a fixed-weight Hamming binary neural classifier chip suitable for high-speed applications. Switched current-mode circuits were used to recognize the integers 0-9 in a single pass through the network. The circuit was fabricated in 2.4-μm N-well CMOS technology and operated at 10 MHz without error or instability. Macedo Filho, (1994) investigated the application of ANNs to microwave radar systems to classify radar signals. Pelka, Kalisz, & Szplet, (1996) trained an ANN on a CPU to control an FPGA time-to-digital converter. Bradshaw & Aleksander, (1996) improved the generalization ability of the N-tuple classifier using the effective VC dimension. The VC dimension predicts a worse generalization performance than is achieved in practice because an input Gaussian distribution gives a significantly lower effective VC dimension than the true VC dimension. As a result, a better generalization ability can be predicted without suffering from over-fitting. Browne & Aleksander, (1996) investigate when a network of partially connected neurons, which make state transitions with a controlled probability, operates better than a fully connected network of similar neurons. Stamos & Selviah, (1998) take their earlier correlator or matched filter array hardware model of first order ANNs and use the understanding it gives to design a novel feature enhancement and similarity suppression training algorithm, which enhances the unique features of the training patterns while suppressing their differences.

2000s

Gadea, Cerda, Ballester, & Mocholi, (2000) introduce on-line back propagation learning in which an ANN simultaneously operates and is trained using back error propagation by taking advantage of parallelism in the electronic hardware. Selviah & Stamos, (2002) use the understanding that their earlier correlator or matched filter array hardware model of first order ANNs to design a novel similarity suppression training algorithm which suppresses the differences between the training patterns resulting in an orthogonal basis set of patterns with maximum Hamming distance between them. Ortigosa et al., (2003) use ANNs to discern patterns in noisy data sets with real-time operation resulting in only 1% accuracy loss when compared to software. Yang & Paindavoine, (2003) compare RBF networks for real time face recognition implemented on field programmable gate array (FPGA), zero instruction set computer (ZISC) chips, and digital signal processor (DSP) and concluded that for their choice of chips and the way that they use them, the DSP gave best results and then the FPGA. Aleksander's final paper in the Electronic Engineering field (Lockwood & Aleksander, 2003) predicts the behavior of recursive probabilistic Generalizing Random Access Memory (G-RAM) neuron networks using combinatorial analysis. In earlier papers, Aleksander referred to similar neurons, as n-tuple, weightless or p-RAM systems and their recognition performance had been difficult to predict. The key to understanding their behavior was to consider their radius of retrievability in a vector space in which each known pattern is represented by a vector position. Distorted or noisy versions of the known reference pattern move the vector position to within a range from the original vector position. If the distance from the original vector position is more than the radius of retrievability then the pattern is not recognized; if less it is recognized. This radius can be found by using a set of random input patterns, which either converge, or do not. They found that increasing the set of training patterns reduces the radius of retrievability in a predictable manner. When distorted versions of the training patterns are input, the radius of retrievability is reduced to a value depending on the Hamming distance between members of the training set, in other words their correlation or inner product similarity. The G-RAMs have a generalization parameter, which determines the radius of retrievability in such a way that it is no longer dependent on the size or Hamming distance properties of the training set of patterns resulting in robust predictable behavior.

Lopez-Garcia, Moreno-Armendariz, Riera-Babures, Balsi, & Vilasis-Cardona, (2005) implement CNNs on an FPGA. Girones, Palero, Boluda, & Cortes, (2005) publish on on-line back propagation learning. Several types of electronic hardware were investigated for electronic implementations of ANNs: Application Specific Integrated Circuits (ASICs), enable optimized and power efficient Very Large Scale Integrated circuits (VLSI) chips to be realized to perform a specific task. ASICs can be redesigned to suit other tasks but at the expense of non-recurring engineering (NRE) costs (Zhang, Li, & Foo, 2006). Digital Signal Processing (DSP) boards can perform simple mathematical arithmetic: addition, subtraction, multiplication and division so that complex algorithms can be implemented in a serial form. FPGAs offer parallel operation and reconfigurabilty. Epitropakis, Plagianakos, & Vrahatis, (2006) investigated the training of Pi-Sigma HONNs using the distributed version of the Differential Evolution algorithm. They restricted the weights to have 6-bit integer values in the range [-32, 32] so that the network could be implemented more easily on electronic hardware. They found that the training was fast, stable, and reliable and led to good generalization ability of the HONN. Hardware implementation is used where reliability and predictability is needed (Chtourou, Chtourou, & Hammami, 2006).

Yunxi, (2007) investigated whether decision feedback equalizers (DFE) could be implemented as a multilayer ANN to compensate for dispersion and nonlinearity when signals at 10 Gb/s pass through 300 km of standard single mode optical fiber with the possibility of later implementing this in an FPGA. Garrigos, Martinez, Toledo, & Ferrandez, (2007) describe how to automate the implementation of ANNs on FPGAs. Maguire et al., (2007) provide a comprehensive review of the reported research on FPGA implementations of classical and spiking neural networks on FPGAs. Jung & Kim, (2007) implement real-time back propagation learning on an FPGA to control an ANN on a DSP. Selviah & Shawash, (2008) extended their hardware derived model of ANNs in terms of inner product correlators or matched filters, to instead use *outer product* correlators, which allowed them to design two new HONNs called the Generalized Correlation HONN (GCHONN) and the Correlation HONN (CHONN). This was demonstrated to predict financial time series better than currently available methods used by financial institutions. Other hardware derivatives include an ANN implementation on a Zero Instruction Set Chip (ZISC) manufactured by Recognetics Inc. (Recognetics, 2008), using many highly tuned multiply-add circuits. It has 1024 neurons, which operate in parallel. The input vector is 256 byte. Pattern recognition is performed in up to 10 µs on the Radial Basis Function or K-Nearest Neighbor (KNN) classifier ANN architecture after up to 10 µs learning time. By connecting several chips together via a parallel bus, the network size can be increased. It requires a 1.2 V power supply and consumes 500 mW at a clock speed of 15 MHz using 0.13 µm fabrication technology on a 8 mm × 8 mm die in a 100 pin package.

3. ANNS AND HONNS IMPLEMENTED ON FPGAS

Field Programmable Gate Arrays (FPGAs) were introduced in 1985 (Xilinx, 2008) offering the advantage over DSPs of parallel operation. Although FPGAs have not achieved the same levels of power efficiency, clock frequency and component density as custom designed ASICs, they do allow easy reprogrammability, fast development times, and reduced Non Recurring Engineering (NRE) costs, and are much faster than software implementations. FPGAs provide a System on Chip (SoC) capability in which arrays of logic gates, software or hardware CPU processor cores and, most recently, DSP units, can be interconnected and reconfigured to perform a task in real time with low latency, small area and power consumption (Chtourou et al., 2006).

Real time on-line training and on-chip training or run time reconfiguration (RTR) or self-reconfiguration ANNs on FPGAs has received a lot of interest growing approximately linearly from 1996 with over 90 papers published on the topic to date and with citations growing exponentially with time. Most of the papers deal with floating point calculations and the most popular FPGAs appear to be the Xilinx Virtex II, Virtex II PRO 2VP30, Virtex II XC2V2000-4ff896, with other FPGAs also used such as the Virtex H PRO XC2VP7, Alpha Delta Virtex-4LX160, Virtex XCV400, Virtex XCV600, Virtex 1000, Virtex XCV1000E, Xilinx SpartanII-300, CycloneII, IEEE-754, Altera RIPP10 reconfigurable board, 9 FLEX8K Celoxica RC100, and Celoxica RC203E development board. A range of ANNs have been investigated including multilayer perceptron (MNN), radial basis functions, wavelet transform networks, cellular ANNs (CNN), pulsed networks, Elman, Hopfield, B-Spline, Adaptive Logic Network (ALN), Probabilistic, General Regression and also the related field of fuzzy logic networks. A range of learning algorithms have also been implemented on-line including Back Error Propagation and its derivatives realized using difference methods, Reactive Tabu Search (RTS), Hebbian, Particle Swarm Optimization (PSO), Genetic Algorithms (GA), Stochastic Random Learning, Support Vector Machine, hybrid LNS, and Gradient Descent. The most popular demonstration is that of the exclusive OR (XOR). Applications include control of robot arms, an inverted pendulum, character recognition, sensor control, telecommunication problems such as channel equalization and packet routers, intrusion detection and active filtering systems, control systems that must compensate for unknown non-linear uncertainties, machine vision applications such as image processing, segmentation and recognition of video streams from a dynamic environment in real-time, high speed decision and classification, real-time power electronics and pattern recognition, discrimination and event classification for particle physics experiments, providing triggers for other hardware modules.

The powerful, high speed Xilinx Virtex-5 was introduced, which can be specified to include a number of Digital Signal Processors (DSPs) configured so that Multiply ACcumulate (MAC) operations occur at very high speeds. Already one paper has been published on implementation of ANNs on the Virtex-5. Shayani, Bentley, & Tyrrell, (2008) implemented an evolving and growing spiking digital ANN. They made use of the Piecewise-Linear Approximation of Quadratic Integrate and Fire (PLAQIF) soma model to realize a network of 161 neurons and 1610 synapses. Most recently the Xilinx Virtex–6 was introduced offering a possible increase in calculation speed by up to 10 times in the author's experience. The DSPs are fast but introduce the problem of their fixed point, limited precision. Most research on limited precision has focused on the effect on the operation of the network and not the training process on-chip (Stevenson, Winter, & Widrow, 1990). It was found that the operational phase of an ANN could tolerate lower precision than the learning phase, as sudden failure in learning occurred when the precision was reduced below a critical level. The most recent research on this topic on HONNs on FPGAs is reported in chapter 14 in this book by the same authors.

4. CONCLUSION

The chapter gives a chronological literature review of the first 50 years of electronic hardware implementations of artificial first and HONNs and their training from the earliest days on analog computers through to the most recent digital embedded FPGAs.

5. ACKNOWLEDGMENT

The authors thank their colleagues for useful discussions. The authors thank UCL for funding via an Overseas Research Scholarship and a Graduate School Scholarship for Janti Shawash.

6. REFERENCES

Agranat, A., & Yariv, A. (1987). Semiparallel Microelectronic Implementation of Neural Network Models Using CCD Technology. *Electronics Letters*, *23*(11), 580–581. doi:10.1049/el:19870416

Aleksander, I. (1970a). Microcircuit Learning Nets - Hamming-Distance Behaviour. *Electronics Letters*, *6*(5), 134–136. doi:10.1049/el:19700092

Aleksander, I. (1970b). Brain Cell to Microcircuit. *Electronics and Power*, *16*, 48.

Aleksander, I. (1989). Canonical Neural Nets Based on Logic Nodes. In *1st IEE International Conference on Artificial Neural Networks* (pp. 110-114).

Aleksander, I. (1990). Ideal Neurons for Neural Computers. In R. Eckmiller, G. Hartmann, & G. Hauske (Eds.), *ICNC 10th International Conference on Parallel Processing in Neural Systems and Computers* (pp. 225-228). Dusseldorf, Germany, 19th - 21st March

Aleksander, I., & Albrow, R. C. (1968). Microcircuit Learning Nets - Some Tests with Handwritten Numerals. *Electronics Letters*, *4*(19), 406–407. doi:10.1049/el:19680321

Aleksander, I., & Fairhurst, M. C. (1970). Pattern Learning in Humans and Electronic Learning Nets. *Electronics Letters*, *6*(16), 518–520. doi:10.1049/el:19700360

Aleksander, I., & Mamdani, E. H. (1968). Microcircuit Learning Nets - Improved Recognition by Means of Pattern Feedback. *Electronics Letters*, *4*(20), 425–426. doi:10.1049/el:19680333

Aleksander, I., & Morton, H. B. (1991). General Neural Unit - Retrieval Performance. *Electronics Letters*, *27*(19), 1776–1778. doi:10.1049/el:19911105

Allen, T., Mead, C., Faggin, F., & Cribble, G. (1988). An Orientation-Selective VLSI Retina. In *SPIE Conference on Visual Communications and Image Processing No. 3* (pp. 1040-1046). Bellingham, WA.

Alspector, J. (1989, October 17) *Neuromorphic learning networks*. Patent Number US 4874963.

Alspector, J., & Allen, T. B. (1987). A Neuromorphic VLSI Learning System. In *Advanced Research in VSLI: Standford Conference* (pp. 313-347).

Anguita, M., Pelayo, F. J., Prieto, A., & Ortega, J. (1993). Analog CMOS Implementation of a Discrete-Time CNN with Programmable Cloning Templates. *IEEE Transactions on Circuits and Systems II - Analog and Digital Signal Processing, 40*(3), 215-219.

Bradshaw, N. P., & Aleksander, I. (1996). Improving the generalisation of the N-tuple classifier using the effective VC dimension. *Electronics Letters*, *32*(20), 1904–1905. doi:10.1049/el:19961264

Browne, C., & Aleksander, I. (1996). Digital general neural units with controlled transition probabilities. *Electronics Letters, 32*(9), 824–825. doi:10.1049/el:19960565

Carpenter, G. A., & Grossberg, S. (1987). A massively parallel architecture for a self-organizing neural pattern recognition machine. *Computer Vision Graphics and Image Processing, 37*, 54–115. doi:10.1016/S0734-189X(87)80014-2

Castro, H. A., & Sweet, M. R. (1993). Radiation Exposure Effects on the Performance of an Electrically Trainable Artificial Neural Network (ETANN). *IEEE Transactions on Nuclear Science, 40*(6), 1575–1583. doi:10.1109/23.273503

Castro, H. A., Tam, S. M., & Holler, M. A. (1993). Implementation and Performance of an Analog Non-Volatile Neural Network. *Analog Integrated Circuits and Signal Processing, 4*, 97–113. doi:10.1007/BF01254862

Chtourou, S., Chtourou, M., & Hammami, O. (2006, July 16-21). Neural network based memory access prediction support for SoC dynamic reconfiguration. In *IEEE International Joint Conference on Neural Network* (pp. 2823-2829). Vancouver, Canada.

Chua, L. O., & Roska, T. (1993). The CNN Paradigm. *IEEE Transactions on Circuits and Systems. I, Fundamental Theory and Applications, 40*(3), 147–156. doi:10.1109/81.222795

Clarkson, T. G., Gorse, D., & Taylor, J. G. (1989). Hardware Realizable Models of Neural Processing. In *1st IEE International Conference on Artificial Neural Networks* (pp. 242-246).

Clarkson, T. G., Guan, Y., Taylor, J. G., & Gorse, D. (1993). Generalization in Probabilistic RAM Nets. *IEEE Transactions on Neural Networks, 4*(2), 360–363. doi:10.1109/72.207603

Epitropakis, M. G., Plagianakos, V. P., & Vrahatis, M. N. (2006, October). Integer weight higher-order neural network training using distributed differential evolution. In T. Simos & G. Maroulis (Eds.), *ICCMSE, Recent Progress in Computational Sciences and Engineering International Conference of Computational Methods in Science and Engineering,* (pp. -144). *Chania, Greece:* Brill Academic Publishers.

Faggin, F., & Lynch, G. & Sukonick, J. (1988, September 2) *Brain Emulation Circuit with Reduced Confusion.* Patent Number US 4,773,024.

Fairhurst, M. C., & Aleksander, I. (1971). Natural Pattern Clustering in Digital Learning Nets. *Electronics Letters, 7*(24), 724–726. doi:10.1049/el:19710497

Gadea, R., Cerda, J., Ballester, F., & Mocholi, A. (2000). Artificial neural network implementation on a single FPGA of a pipelined on-line backpropagation. In *ISSS 13th International Symposium on System Synthesis* (pp. 225-230).

Garrigos, J., Martinez, J. J., Toledo, J., & Ferrandez, J. M. (2007). HANNA: A tool for hardware prototyping and benchmarking of ANNs. In *Nature Inspired Problem-Solving Methods in Knowledge Engineering* (pp. 10-18).

Giles, C. L., & Maxwell, T. (1987). Learning, Invariance, and Generalization in High-Order Neural Networks. *Applied Optics, 26*(23), 4972–4978. doi:10.1364/AO.26.004972

Girones, R. G., Palero, R. C., Boluda, J. C., & Cortes, A. S. (2005). FPGA implementation of a pipelined on-line backpropagation. *Journal of VlSI Signal Processing Systems for Signal Image and Video Technology, 40*(2), 189–213. doi:10.1007/s11265-005-4961-3

Graf, H. P., & de Vegvai, P. (1987). A CMOS Associative Memory Chip Based on Neural Networks. In *IEEE International Conference on Solid State Circuits* (pp. 304-305). Piscataway, NJ

Graf, H. P., Jackel, L. D., Howard, R. E., Straughn, B., Denker, J. S., Hubbard, W., et al. (1986). VLSI Implementation of a Neural Network Memory with Several Hundreds of Neurons. In *AIP Conference on Neural Networks for Computing* (pp. 182-187).

Grant, D., Taylor, J., & Houselander, P. (1994). Design, Implementation and Evaluation of a High-Speed Integrated Hamming Neural Classifier. *IEEE Journal of Solid-State Circuits, 29*(9), 479–1157. doi:10.1109/4.309915

Grant, P. M., & Sage, J. P. (1986). A Comparison of Neural Network and Matched-Filter Processing for Detecting Lines in Images. In *Neural Networks for Computing* (pp. 194-200). American Institute of Physics.

Halonen, K., Porra, V., Roska, T., & Chua, L. (1992). Programmable Analog VLSI CNN Chip with Local Digital Logic. *International Journal of Circuit Theory and Applications, 20*(5), 573–582. doi:10.1002/cta.4490200510

Hamilton, A., Murray, A., & Tarassenko, L. (1989). Programmable analog pulse-firing neural networks. [San Francisco: Morgan Kaufmann.]. *Advances in Neural Information Processing Systems, 1*, 671–677.

Herscher, H. B., & Kelley, T. P. (1963). Functional electronic model of the frog retina. *IEEE Transactions on Military Electronics, MIL-7*(2), 98–103. doi:10.1109/TME.1963.4323057

Holler, M. (1989). An electrically trainable artificial neural network (ETANN) with 10240 'floating gate' synapses. In *International Joint Conf. Neural Networks* (pp. 191-196).

Hopfield, J. J., & Tank, D. W. (1986). Computing with Neural Circuits: A Model. *Science, 233*(4764), 625–633. doi:10.1126/science.3755256

Hubbard, W., Schwartz, D., Denker, J., Graf, H. P., Howard, R., Jackel, L., et al. (1987). Electronic Neural Networks. In *AIP Neural Networks for Computing, Snowbird, Utah, March* (pp. 227-234).

Jung, S., & Kim, S. S. (2007). Hardware implementation of a real-time neural network controller with a DSP and an FPGA for nonlinear systems. *IEEE Transactions on Industrial Electronics, 54*(1), 265–271. doi:10.1109/TIE.2006.888791

Lavie, D., & Taylor, W. K. (1982). Effects of Border Variations Due to Spatial Quantization on Binary-Image Template Matching. *Electronics Letters, 18*(10), 418–420. doi:10.1049/el:19820287

Lavie, D., & Taylor, W. K. (1983). A Microprocessor-Controlled Real-Time Image-Processor. *IEE Proceedings. Computers and Digital Techniques, 130*(5), 149–153.

Lee, Y. C., Doolen, G., Chen, H. H., Sun, G. Z., Maxwell, T., & Lee, H. Y. (1986). Machine Learning Using A Higher-Order Correlation Network. *Physica D. Nonlinear Phenomena, 22*(1-3), 276–306.

Lockwood, G. G., & Aleksander, I. (2003). Predicting the behavior of G-RAM networks. *Neural Networks, 16*(1), 91–100. doi:10.1016/S0893-6080(02)00220-4

Lopez-Garcia, J. C., Moreno-Armendariz, M. A., Riera-Babures, J., Balsi, M., & Vilasis-Cardona, X. (2005). Real time vision by FPGA implemented CNNs. In *European Conference on Circuit Theory and Design* (pp. 281-284).

Lyon, R. F., & Mead, C. (1988). An Analog Electronic Cochlea. *IEEE Transactions on Acoustics, Speech, and Signal Processing, 36*(7), 1119–1134. doi:10.1109/29.1639

Macedo Filho, A. D. (1994). Microwave neural network paradigms for radar signal clustering. In *MeleCON 7th Mediterranean Electrotechnical Conference* (pp. 471-474).

Mackie, W. S., Graf, H. P., & Denker, J. S. (1987). Microelectronic Implementation of Connectionist Neural Network Models. In *NIPS Conference on Neural Information Processing Systems* (pp. 515-523).

Maguire, L. P., McGinnity, T. M., Glackin, B., Ghani, A., Belatreche, A., & Harkin, J. (2007). Challenges for large-scale implementations of spiking neural networks on FPGAs. *Neurocomputing, 71*(1-3), 13–29. doi:10.1016/j.neucom.2006.11.029

Mandanayake, A., & Taylor, W. K. (1989). Specialised parallel hardware for flash recognition of windowed images in a television frame. In *3rd International Conference on Image Processing and its Applications, 18th-20th July* (pp. 501-505).

Mead, C. (1989). *Analog VLSI and Neural Systems*. Boston, MA: Addison-Wesley Longman Publishing Co. Inc.

Muller, F. J., & Taylor, W. K. (1973). Comparative Study of Electronic and Neural Networks Involved in Pattern-Recognition. *Journal of Theoretical Biology, 41*(1), 97–118. doi:10.1016/0022-5193(73)90191-4

Muller, F. J., & Taylor, W. K. (1976). Parallel Processing Model for Study of Possible Pattern-Recognition Mechanisms in Brain. *Pattern Recognition, 8*(1), 47–52. doi:10.1016/0031-3203(76)90028-5

Murray, A., Smith, A. V. W., & Tarassenko, L. (1988). Fully-Programmable Analogue VLSI Devices for the Implementation of Neural Networks. In W.R.Moore (Ed.), *VLSI for Artificial Intelligence* (pp. 236-244). Kluwer Academic Publishers.

Murray, A. F., Hamilton, A., Reekie, H. M., & Tarassenko, L. (1989). Pulse-Stream Arithmetic in Programmable Neural Networks. In *IEEE International Symposium on Circuits and Systems* (pp. 1210-1212).

Murray, A. F., & Smith, A. V. W. (1987a). A Novel Computational and Signalling Method for VLSI Neural Networks. In *European Conference on Solid State Circuits, Berlin* (pp. 19-22).

Murray, A. F., & Smith, A. V. W. (1987b). Asynchronous Arithmetic for VLSI Neural Systems. *Electronics Letters, 23*(12), 642–643. doi:10.1049/el:19870459

Murray, A. F., & Smith, A. V. W. (1988). Asynchronous VLSI Neural Networks using Pulse Stream Arithmetic. *IEEE Journal of Solid-State Circuits and Systems, 23*(3), 688–697. doi:10.1109/4.307

Ortigosa, E. M., Ortigosa, P. M., Canas, A., Ros, E., Agis, R., & Ortega, J. (2003). FPGA implementation of multi-layer perceptrons for speech recognition. In Cheung P.Y.K., Constantinides G.A., & DeSousa J.T. (Eds.), *FPL, 13th International Conference on Field-Programmable Logic and Applications, Lisbon, Portugal 1st - 3rd September* (pp. 1048-1052). Springer-Verlag.

Pelka, R., Kalisz, J., & Szplet, R. (1996). Nonlinearity correction of the integrated time-to-digital converter with direct coding. In *Conference on Precision Electromagnetic Measurements, Braunschweig, Germany* (pp. 548-549).

Recognetics (2008). *Bringing infinite intelligence to the application of pattern recognition, Recognetics.* Retrieved May 1, 2009, from http://www.recognetics.com/

Roska, T., & Chua, L. O. (1993). The CNN Universal Machine - An Analogic Array Computer. *IEEE Transactions on Circuits and Systems II - Analog and Digital Signal Processing, 40*(3), 163-173.

Sage, J. P., Thompson, K., & Withers, R. S. (1987). An artificial neural network integrated circuit base on MNOS/CCD principles. In *AIP Conference on Neural Networks for Computing, Snowbird, Utah* (pp. 381-385).

Selviah, D. R., & Midwinter, J. E. (1989a). Extension of the Hamming neural network to a multilayer architecture for optical implementation. In *1st IEE International Conference on Artificial Neural Networks* (pp. 280-283).

Selviah, D. R., & Midwinter, J. E. (1989b). Matched filter model for design of neural networks. In J. G. Taylor & C. L. T. Mannion (Eds.), *Institute of Physics conference New developments in neural computing* (pp. 141-148).

Selviah, D. R., & Midwinter, J. E. (1989c). Memory Capacity of a novel optical neural net architecture. In *ONERA-CERT Optics in Computing International Symposium* (pp. 195-201).

Selviah, D. R., Midwinter, J. E., Rivers, A. W., & Lung, K. W. (1989). Correlating matched filter model for analysis and optimisation of neural networks. *IEE Proceedings. Part F. Radar and Signal Processing, 136*(3), 143–148.

Selviah, D. R., & Shawash, J. (2008). Generalized Correlation Higher Order Neural Networks for Financial Time Series Prediction. Chapter 10, In M.Zhang (Ed.), *Artificial Higher Order Neural Networks for Artificial Higher Order Neural Networks for Economics and Business* (pp. 212-249).

Selviah, D. R., & Stamos, E. (2002). Similarity suppression algorithm for designing pattern discrimination filters. *Asian Journal of Physics, 11*(3), 367–389.

Shayani, H., Bentley, P. J., & Tyrrell, A. M. (2008). Hardware implementation of a bio-plausible neuron model for evolution and growth of spiking neural networks on FPGA. In D. Keymeulen, T. Arslan, M. Seuss, A. Stoica, A. T. Erdogan, & D. Merodio (Eds.), *AHS 3rd NASA/ESA Conference on Adaptive Hardware and Systems* (pp. 236-243).

Shoemaker, P., Lagnado, I., & Shimabukuro, R. (1988). Artificial Neural Network Implementation with Floating Gate MOS Devices. In *NSF and ONR Workshop on Hardware Implementation of Neuron Nets and Synapses* San Diego, CA.

Stamos, E., & Selviah, D. R. (1998). Feature enhancement and similarity suppression algorithm for noisy pattern recognition. In D. P. Casasent & T. H. Chao (Eds.), *Optical Pattern Recognition IX, Orlando* (pp. 182-189).

Stevenson, M., Winter, R., & Widrow, B. (1990). Sensitivity of feedforward neural networks to weight errors. *IEEE Transactions on Neural Networks, 1*(1), 71–80. doi:10.1109/72.80206

Tam, S., Holler, M., Brauch, J., Pine, A., Peterson, A., Anderson, S., et al. (1992). A reconfigurable multi-chip analog neural network: recognition and back-propagation training. In *IJCNN, International Joint Conference on Neural Networks, Baltimore, MD* (pp. 625-630).

Taylor, W. K. (1959). Pattern recognition by means of automatic analogue apparatus. *Proceedings of the Institution of Electrical Engineers, B 106*, 198-209.

Taylor, W. K. (1963). A pattern recognizing adaptive controller. In Butterworth (Ed.), *Automatic and Remote Control* (pp. 488-496).

Taylor, W. K. (1964). Cortico-Thalamic Organization and Memory. *Proceedings of the Royal Society of London. Series B. Biological Sciences, 159*(976), 466–478. doi:10.1098/rspb.1964.0014

Taylor, W. K. (1967). Machine Learning and Recognition of Faces. *Electronics Letters, 3*(9), 436–437. doi:10.1049/el:19670340

Taylor, W. K. (1968a). Machines That Learn. *Science Journal, 4*(10), 102–107.

Taylor, W. K. (1968b). Learning characteristics of a trainable pattern recognition machine. In *IEE Conference Publication* (pp. 238-249).

Taylor, W. K. (1973). Optical Texture Recognition. In *Institute of Physics Conference Series* (pp. 276-284).

Taylor, W. K. (1978) *Comparison apparatus, eg for use in character recognition*. Patent Number US 14,119,946.

Taylor, W. K., & Al-Kibasi, K. T. (1974). The UCLM3 programmable pattern recognition machine. *IEEE Conference Publication, 74CH0885-4C,* 341-246.

Taylor, W. K., & Ero, G. (1980). Real time teaching and recognition system for robot vision. *The Industrial Robot, 7*(2), 99–106.

Taylor, W. K., Lavie, D., & Esatt, I. I. (1983). A curvilinear snake arm with gripper-axis fiber-optic image processor feedback. *Robotica, 1*, 33–39. doi:10.1017/S0263574700001041

Taylor, W. K., & Witkowsk, J. J. (1974). Pattern-Recognition Circuits - Simple Programmable Circuits for Optical Character Recognition and Other Applications. *Wireless World, 80*(1465), 332–333.

Tsividis, Y. P., & Anastassiou, D. (1987). Switched-Capacitor Neural Networks. *Electronics Letters, 23*(18), 958–959. doi:10.1049/el:19870674

Widrow, B., & Hoff, M. E. (1960). Adaptive Switching Circuits. In *Institute of Radio Engineers, Western Electric Show and Convention* (pp. 96-104).

Wilson, M. J. D., & Aleksander, I. (1977). Pattern-Recognition Properties of RAM-ROM Arrays. *Electronics Letters*, *13*(9), 253–254. doi:10.1049/el:19770183

Xilinx (2008). Our History. *Xilinx*. Retrieved May 1, 2009, from http://www.xilinx.com/company/history.htm

Yang, F., & Paindavoine, M. (2003). Implementation of an RBF neural network on embedded systems: Real-time face tracking and identity verification. *IEEE Transactions on Neural Networks*, *14*(5), 1162–1175. doi:10.1109/TNN.2003.816035

Yunxi, L. (2007). Application of decision feedback equalisers based on multilayer neural network structures to compensate for optical fibre dispersion and nonlinearity. *IET Optoelectronics*, *14*(1), 169–174. doi:10.1049/iet-opt:20060097

Zhang, D., Li, H., & Foo, S. Y. (2006). A simplified FPGA implementation of neural network algorithms integrated with stochastic theory for power electronics applications. In *IECON 2005, 31st Annual Conference of IEEE Industrial Electronics Society* (pp. 1018-1023).

Chapter 13

Recurrent Higher Order Neural Network Control for Output Trajectory Tracking with Neural Observers and Constrained Inputs

Luis J. Ricalde
Universidad Autonoma de Yucatan, Mexico

Edgar N. Sanchez
CINVESTAV, Unidad Guadalajara, Mexico

Alma Y. Alanis
CUCEI, Universidad de Guadalajara, Mexico

ABSTRACT

This Chapter presents the design of an adaptive recurrent neural observer-controller scheme for non-linear systems whose model is assumed to be unknown and with constrained inputs. The control scheme is composed of a neural observer based on Recurrent High Order Neural Networks which builds the state vector of the unknown plant dynamics and a learning adaptation law for the neural network weights for both the observer and identifier. These laws are obtained via control Lyapunov functions. Then, a control law, which stabilizes the tracking error dynamics is developed using the Lyapunov and the inverse optimal control methodologies . Tracking error boundedness is established as a function of design parameters.

DOI: 10.4018/978-1-61520-711-4.ch013

1. INTRODUCTION

Over the past decade, adaptive neural control schemes have received an increasing attention for applications on nonlinear systems control. Mainly due to the seminal paper (Narendra & Parthasarathy, 1990), there has been continuously increasing interest in applying neural networks to identification and control of nonlinear systems. Lately, the use of recurrent neural networks is being developed, which allows more efficient modeling of the underlying dynamical systems (Poznyak et al.). Three representative books (Suykens et al., 1996), (Rovitahkis & Christodoulou, 2000) and (Poznyak et al., 2000) have reviewed the application of recurrent neural networks for nonlinear system identification and control. In particular, (Suykens et al., 1996) uses off-line learning, while (Rovitahkis & Christodoulou, 2000) analyzes adaptive identification and control by means of on-line learning, where stability of the closed-loop system is established based on the Lyapunov function method. In (Rovitahkis & Christodoulou, 2000), the trajectory tracking problem is reduced to a linear model following problem, with application to DC electric motors. In (Poznyak et al., 2000), analysis of Recurrent Neural Networks for identification, estimation and control are developed, with applications on chaos control, robotics and chemical processes. One recent publication (Sanchez et al., 2008), explores the application of Recurrent Higher Order Neural Networks (RHONN) for trajectory tracking control schemes using the Kalman filtering training with real time applications to electrical machines.

In many control applications, the process presents highly nonlinear behaviour, uncertainties, unknown disturbances and bounded inputs. All these phenomena are required to be considered for control analysis and synthesis. The problem of designing robust controllers for nonlinear systems with uncertainties, which guarantee stability and trajectory tracking, has received an increasing attention lately. The presence of constrained inputs limits the ability to compensate the effects of unmodeled dynamics and external disturbances. These effects impact on the loss of stability, undesired oscillations and other adverse effects. There are several results on linear control systems with input constrains, (Hu & Lin, 2001). For nonlinear systems, control with constrained inputs is restricted by requiring to know the system model. Some algorithms allow the presence of uncertainties satisfying the matching condition (El-Farra & Christofides, 2001). In (El-Farra & Christofides, 2001), a control law, based on the Sontag formula with constrained inputs, is developed and applied to a chemical reactor. To relax the restriction of requiring knowledge of the system model, identification via recurrent neural networks arises as a potential solution (Hokimyan, et. al., 2001). Most of the control algorithms for nonlinear systems use the assumption that all the states are available for measurement, which is a condition seldom satisfied. The nonlinear observers arise as a solution, and have received much attention lately. For linear unknown systems, the observer design has been widely investigated. For nonlinear systems, the results are too restrictive according to the nonlinearity and system structure. In (Marino, 1990), an adaptive observer for nonlinear systems is proposed, where the uncertainties are assumed to be linear and the nonlinearities are functions of the output. In (Kim, et al., 1996), a nonlinear observer based on neural networks is developed. The nonlinearities are not required to depend on the system output only, but having some restrictions on the structure of the dynamical system. Robust observers have a good performance even in presence of modelling erros and disturbance uncertainties, but their design process is too complex. Altough most of the approaches need the previous knowledge of the plant dynamics, recently, neural observers has emerged for unknown plant dynamics and have proven their hability of dealing with the presence of simultaneous external and internal uncertainties (Sanchez et al., 2007).

Figure 1. Recurrent neural control scheme

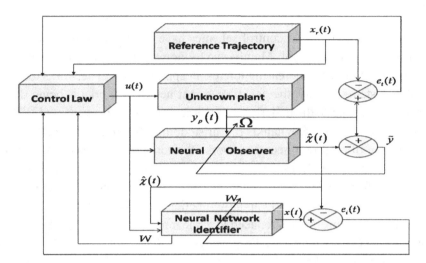

In this chapter, we extend our previous results (Sanchez & Ricalde, 2003), to nonlinear systems with less inputs than states. The output trajectory tracking problem with constrained inputs is solved with adaptive control scheme composed by a nonlinear observer based on recurrent high order neural networks, to estimate the full state information, a recurrent neural identifier, which is used to build an on-line model for the unknown plant, and a control law to force the unknown plant to track the output reference trajectory. The learning laws for the on-line adapted weights of the neural observer and identifier are developed based en Lyapunov analysis. The stability of the state estimation and identification errors are ensured via control Lyapunov functions. We demonstrate that the developed observer stabilizing law minimizes a meaningful cost functional related with the solution of a Hamilton-Jacobi-Bellman partial differential associated equation. To perform the stability analysis for trajectory tracking, we consider the overall system, including the neural observer, neural identifier and the unknown system, as shown in Figure 1. The control law is synthesized using the Lyapunov methodology and a modification of the Sontag control law for stabilizing systems with constrained inputs and uncertain terms. This control law explicitly depends on the input constraints. Boundedness of the tracking error is proven and an estimation of the closed loop stability region is given in order to determine the available bounds of the uncertainties and the desired tracking error. The proposed scheme is validated for the output trajectory tracking of a nonlinear oscillator.

The results have been satisfactory; the recurrent high order adaptive neural control scheme features the following advantages:

1. The neural identifier relaxes the condition of requiring knowledge of the system model, which is a common constraint in adaptive control. The recurrent neural network states converge to the real ones in a short time. Furthermore, its simple structure reduces the complexity for the trajectory tracking analysis. The on-line adaptability of the neural identifier provides the control scheme robustness to disturbances and parametric uncertainties.
2. The neural observer solves the problem of full state measurement required by the neural identifier. This neural observer had less restriction on its structure than other nonlinear observers. The main advantage is not requiring knowing the system dynamical model.

3. The modification of the Sontag's law, considers and depends explicitly of the input constraints. Since it does not cancel nonlinearities like feedback linearizing approaches, no control effort is wasted to cancel nonlinearities, possibly beneficial to the process. The Lyapunov analysis renders the stability region which depends on the input constraint and design parameters. Furthermore, the control law takes into account the modelling error, which is considered as a nonvanishing process uncertainty, an provides some degree of attenuation on the basis of the design parameters.

2. MATHEMATICAL PRELIMINARIES

2.1 Artificial Neural Networks

Artificial neural networks have become an useful tool for control engineering thanks to their applicability on modelling, state estimation and control of complex dynamic systems. Using neural networks, control algorithms can be developed to be robust to uncertainties and modelling errors.

Neural Networks consist of a number of interconnected processing elements or neurons. The way in which the neurons are interconnected determines its structure. For identification and control, the most used structures are:

Feedforward networks: In feedforward networks, the neurons are grouped into layers. Signals flow from the input to the output via unidirectional connections. The network exhibits high degree of connectivity, contains one or more hidden layers of neurons and the activation function of each neuron is smooth, generally a sigmoid function.

Recurrent networks: In a recurrent neural network, the outputs of the neuron are fed back to the same neuron or neurons in the preceding layers. Signals flow in forward and backward directions.

2.2 Recurrent Higher-Order Neural Networks

Artificial Recurrent Neural Networks are mostly based on the Hopfield model (Hopfield, 1984). These networks are considered as good candidates for nonlinear systems applications which deal with uncertainties and are attractive due to their easy implementation, relatively simple structure, robustness and the capacity to adjust their parameters on line.

In (Kosmatopoulos, et al. 1997), Recurrent Higher-Order Neural Networks (RHONN) are defined as

$$\dot{\chi}_i = -\alpha_i \chi_i + \sum_{k=1}^{L} \omega_{ik} \prod_{j \in I_k} y_j^{d_j(k)}, \qquad i = 1, ..., n \tag{1}$$

where χ_i is the ith neuron state, L is the number of higher-order connections, $\{I_1, I_2, ..., I_L\}$ is a collection of non-ordered subsets of $\{1, 2, ..., m + n\}$, $a_i > 0$, w_{ik} are the adjustable weights of the neural network, $d_j(k)$ are nonnegative integers, and y is a vector defined by $y = [y_1, ..., y_n, y_{n+1}, ..., y_{n+m}]^T = [S(\chi_1), ..., S(\chi_n), S(u_1), ..., S(u_m)]^T$

Figure 2. Recurrent higher-order neural network

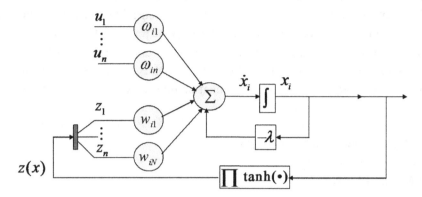

with $u = \left[u_1, u_2, ..., u_m\right]^T$ being the input to the neural network, and $S(\bullet)$ a smooth sigmoid function formulated by $S(\chi) = \dfrac{1}{1 + \exp(-\tau\chi)} + \zeta$. For the sigmoid function, τ is a positive constant and ζ is a small positive real number. Hence, $S(\chi) \in \left[\zeta, \zeta + 1\right]$. As can be seen, (1) allows the inclusion of higher-order terms.

By defining a vector

$$z\left(\chi, u\right) = \left[z_1\left(\chi, u\right)......, z_L\left(\chi, u\right)\right]^T = \left[\Pi_{j\varepsilon I_1} y_j^{d_j(1)}, ..., \Pi_{j\varepsilon I_L} y_j^{d_j(L)}\right]^T \qquad (1)$$

can be rewritten as

$$\dot{\chi}_i = -\alpha_i \chi_i + \sum_{k=1}^{L} \omega_{ik} z_k(\chi, u) \ , \qquad\qquad i = 1, ..., n$$
$$\dot{\chi}_i = -\alpha_i \chi_i + \omega_i z(\chi, u) \ , \qquad\qquad\qquad\qquad\qquad\qquad (2)$$

where $w_i = \left[w_{i,1}.....w_{i,L}\right]^T$. In this Chapter, terms as $y = \left[y_1, ...y_n, y_n + 1, ..., y_{n+m}\right]^T = \left[S\left(\chi_1\right), ..., S\left(\chi_n\right), u_1, ..., u_n\right]^T$ are considered. This means that the same number of inputs and states is used. We also assume that the RHONN is affine in the control, so that (2) can be rewritten as

$$\dot{\chi}_i = -\alpha_i \chi_i + \omega_i^T z(\chi) + \omega_{gi} u_i \ , \qquad (3)$$

Reformulating (3) in matrix form yields

$$\dot{\chi}_i = A\chi + Wz(\chi) + W_g u \qquad (4)$$

where $\chi \in \Re^n, W \in \Re^{n \times L}, W_g \in \Re^{n \times n}$, $z(x) \in \Re^L, u \in \Re^n$, and $A = -\lambda I \ \lambda > 0$.

For nonlinear identification applications, the term y_j in (1) can be either an external input or the identifier state of a neuron passed through the sigmoid function. Depending on the sigmoid function input, the RHONN can be classified as a Series-Parallel structure if $z(\cdot)=z(v)$, where v is an external input, or a Parallel one if $z(\cdot)=z(x)$, where x is the neural network state (Rovitahkis & Christodoulou, 2000). This terminology is standard in adaptive identification and control (Ioannou, 1996). The presented results can be extended to nonlinear systems with fewer inputs than states for the output tracking problem, where the full state measurement is not required, because neural observers are implemented.

2.3 Inverse Optimal Control

This section closely follows (Krstic & Deng, 1998) and (Sepulchre et al., 1997). As stated in (Sepulchre et al., 1997), optimal stabilization guarantees several desirable properties for the closed loop system, including stability margins. In a direct approach, we would have to solve a Hamilton-Jacobi-Bellman (HJB) associated equation, which is not an easy task. Besides, the robustness achieved is largely independent of the particular choice for functions $l(x)>0$ and $R(x)>0$ appearing in the cost functional. This fact is the motivation to pursue the development of design methods, which solve the inverse problem of optimal stabilization. The inverse optimal control approach is based on the concept of equivalence between input-to-state stability (ISS) and the solution of the H_∞ nonlinear control problem (Krstic & Deng, 1998). Using control Lyapunov functions (CLF), a stabilizing feedback is designed first and then shown to be optimal with respect to the cost functional

$$J = \int_0^\infty \left(l\left(x\right) + u^T R\left(x\right)u \right)dt \tag{5}$$

which imposes penalties on the error and the control input. The problem is inverse because the functions $l(x)$ and $R(x)$ are a posteriori determined for the stabilizing feedback, rather than a priory chosen for designing.

A stabilizing control law $u(x)$ solves an inverse optimal problem for the system

$$\dot{x} = f\left(x\right) + g\left(x\right)u \tag{6}$$

if it can be expressed as

$$u = -k\left(x\right) = -\frac{1}{2}R^{-1}\left(x\right)\left(L_g V\left(x\right)\right)^T, \quad R\left(x\right) = R^T\left(x\right) > 0 \tag{7}$$

where $V(x)$ is a positive semidefinite function, such that the negative semidefiniteness of

$$\dot{V} = L_f V\left(x\right) + L_g V\left(x\right)u$$
$$L_f V\left(x\right) = \frac{\partial V}{\partial x}f\left(x\right)$$
$$L_g V\left(x\right) = \frac{\partial V}{\partial x}g\left(x\right)$$

is achieved with the control $u = -\frac{1}{2}k(x)$. That is

$$\dot{V} = L_f V(x) - \frac{1}{2} L_g V(x) k(x) \leq 0 \qquad (8)$$

When the function *l(x)* is set to be

$$l(x) = -L_f V(x) + \frac{1}{2} L_g V(x) k(x) \geq 0 \qquad (9)$$

then $V(x)$ is a solution of the HJB equation

$$l(x) + L_f V(x) - \frac{1}{4}\left(L_g V(x)\right) R^{-1}(x)\left(L_g V(x)\right)^T = 0 \qquad (10)$$

This approach provides robust controllers, where robustness is obtained as a result of the control law optimality, which is independent of the cost functional.

3. RECURRENT HIGHER ORDER NEURAL OBSERVER (RHONO) DESIGN

3.1 Problem Formulation

Consider the single input - single output nonlinear system

$$\begin{aligned}
\dot{x} &= f(x) + bg(x)u(t) \\
y &= Cx \\
x, f &\in \Re^n, b \in \Re^n, g(x) \in \Re
\end{aligned} \qquad (11)$$

which is assumed to be observable. This constraint requires previous knowledge of the system structure. We assume that only part of the state is measurable. Let us consider that the system (11) can be modelled by the RHONN

$$\begin{aligned}
\dot{\chi} &= A\chi + \Omega^* z(y) + w_{per} + b\Omega_g^* z_g(y)u \\
y_{NN} &= Cx
\end{aligned} \qquad (12)$$

where the pair (A,C) is in observer canonical form and that there exist unknown but constant weights W^* such that the modelling error w_{per} is minimized. Consider the recurrent higher order neural observer (RHONO),

$$\begin{aligned}
\dot{\hat{\chi}} &= A\hat{\chi} + \Omega z(\hat{y}) + b\Omega_g z_g(y)u - bv(t) \\
\hat{y} &= C\hat{\chi}
\end{aligned} \qquad (13)$$

where the pair (A,C) is in observer canonical form. Assuming no modelling error for the RHONN, we define the observation error $\tilde{\chi} = \hat{\chi} - \chi$, whose dynamics is given by

$$\dot{\tilde{\chi}} = A\tilde{\chi} + \tilde{\Omega}z(y) + \Omega\phi_z(y) + b\tilde{\Omega}_g z_g(y)u + bv(t)$$
$$\tilde{y} = y - C\hat{\chi}$$
$$\tilde{\Omega} = \Omega^* - \Omega, \quad \tilde{\Omega}_g = \Omega_g^* - \Omega_g \tag{14}$$
$$\phi_z(y) = z(y) - z(\hat{y}) \le L_\phi \|\tilde{y}\|$$

The signal *v(t)*, which stabilizes the system (14), is determined via the Lyapunov methodology.

3.2 Stability Analysis for Neural Observer

Consider the Lyapunov function candidate

$$V = \frac{1}{2}\tilde{\chi}^T P\tilde{\chi} + \frac{1}{2\gamma}tr\left\{\tilde{\Omega}^T\tilde{\Omega}\right\} + \frac{1}{2\gamma_g}tr\left\{\tilde{\Omega}_g^T\tilde{\Omega}_g\right\} \tag{15}$$

where P is a positive definite symmetric matrix which solves the Ricatti equation, $A^T P + P^T A = -Q, \quad Pb = c^T, \quad \tilde{\chi}^T P = \frac{b^T}{\|b\|^2}\tilde{y}$ (for SISO systems), with Q a positive definite symmetric matrix.

The time derivative of (15) is given by

$$\dot{V} = \frac{1}{2}\tilde{\chi}^T PA\tilde{\chi} + \frac{1}{2}\tilde{\chi}^T P\bar{f} + \frac{1}{2}\tilde{\chi}^T Pbv(t) + \frac{1}{2}A^T\tilde{\chi}^T P\tilde{\chi} + \frac{1}{2}\bar{f}^T P\tilde{\chi} + \frac{1}{2}v(t)^T b^T P\tilde{\chi}$$
$$+ \frac{1}{\gamma}tr\left\{\dot{\tilde{\Omega}}^T\tilde{\Omega}\right\} + \frac{1}{\gamma_g}tr\left\{\dot{\tilde{\Omega}}_g^T\tilde{\Omega}_g\right\} \tag{16}$$
$$\bar{f} = \tilde{\Omega}z(y) + \Omega\phi_z(y) + b\tilde{\Omega}_g z_g(y)u$$

We simplify (16) as

$$\dot{V} \le -\frac{1}{2}\|Q\|\|\tilde{\chi}\|^2 + \tilde{\chi}^T P\tilde{\Omega}z(y) + \tilde{\chi}^T P\Omega\phi_z(y) + \tilde{\chi}^T Pb\tilde{\Omega}_g z_g(y,\hat{y})u$$
$$+ \tilde{y}v(t) + \frac{1}{\gamma}tr\left\{\dot{\tilde{\Omega}}^T\tilde{\Omega}\right\} + \frac{1}{\gamma_g}tr\left\{\dot{\tilde{\Omega}}_g^T\tilde{\Omega}_g\right\} \tag{17}$$

To this end, we now define the learning adaptation law

$$tr\left\{\dot{\tilde{\Omega}}^T\tilde{\Omega}\right\} = -\gamma\frac{b^T}{\|b\|^2}\tilde{y}\tilde{\Omega}z(y,\hat{y})$$
$$tr\left\{\dot{\tilde{\Omega}}_g^T\tilde{\Omega}_g\right\} = -\gamma_g\tilde{y}\tilde{\Omega}_g z_g(y,\hat{y})u \tag{18}$$

Replacing the learning law, we obtain

$$\dot{V} \le L_f V + \tilde{y}v(t)$$

$$L_f V = -\frac{1}{2}\|Q\|\|\tilde{\chi}\|^2 + \tilde{\chi}^T P\Omega\phi_z(y)\tilde{y}$$

$$\dot{V} \le -\frac{1}{2}\|Q\|\|\tilde{\chi}\|^2 + \frac{b^T}{\|b\|^2}\Omega\phi_z(y)\tilde{y} + \tilde{y}v(t)$$

Next, we consider the inequality

$$X^T Y + Y^T X \le X^T \Lambda X + Y^T \Lambda Y \tag{19}$$

which holds for all matrices $X,Y \in \Re^{n \times n}$, $\Lambda = \Lambda^T > 0$. Applying it to $b^T \Omega\phi_z(y)\tilde{y}$, with $\Lambda = I$, we obtain

$$\dot{V} \le -\frac{1}{2}\|Q\|\|\tilde{\chi}\|^2 + \left(\frac{1}{\|b\|^2} + \frac{1}{4}\|\Omega\|^2\right)\|\tilde{y}\|^2 + \tilde{y}v(t) \tag{20}$$

The asymptotic stability of the state estimation error is achieved if we select

$$v(t) = -\mu\left(\frac{1}{\|b\|^2} + \frac{1}{4}\|\Omega\|^2\right)\tilde{y} - \frac{b^T}{\|b\|^2}K\tilde{y} \tag{21}$$

where $\mu>1$ and K is selected such that *(A-KC)* is a Hurtwitz matrix.

Figure 3. Time evolution of Van Der Pol oscillator and neural observer

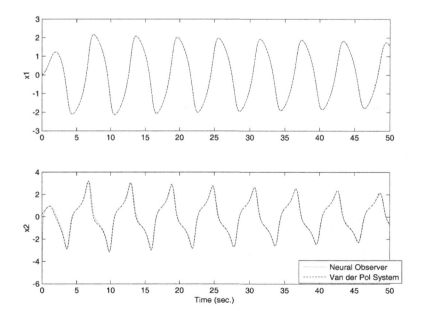

Figure 4. Time evolution for the estimation error

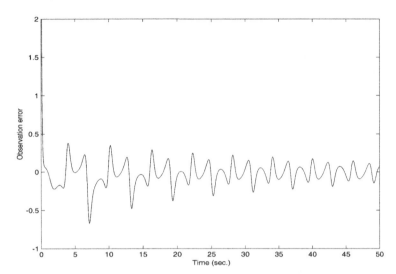

Then, the RHONO structure is given by

$$\dot{\hat{\chi}} = A\hat{\chi} + \Omega z\left(\hat{y}\right) + b\Omega_g z_g\left(y\right)u + \left(b\mu\left(\frac{1}{\|b\|^2} + \frac{1}{4}\|\Omega\|^2\right) + K\right)\tilde{y}$$

$$\hat{y} = C\hat{\chi} \tag{22}$$

In the next section, we proceed to analyze the optimality of (22).

3.4 Optimization with Respect to a Cost Functional

Once the observer stabilizing signal (21) is obtained, we proceed to analyze its optimality with respect to a cost functional, which considers the estimation error and the magnitude of the applied input *v(t)*.

Next, we prove that the control law (21) minimizes the meaningful cost functional given by

$$J\left(v\right) = \lim_{t\to\infty}\left\{2\beta_J V + \int_0^t\left(l\left(\tilde{\chi},\Omega\right) + v\left(t\right)^T R\left(\tilde{\chi},\Omega\right)v\left(t\right)\right)d\tau\right\} \tag{23}$$

where the Lyapunov function (23) solves the following Hamilton-Jacobi-Bellman family of partial derivative equations parameterized with $\beta_J > 0$

$$l\left(\tilde{\chi},\Omega\right) + 2\beta_J L_g V + \beta_J^2 L_g V R^{-1}\left(\tilde{\chi},\Omega\right)L_g V^T = 0 \tag{24}$$

Note that $2\beta V$ in (24) is bounded when t→∞, since by (20) and (21), V is a decreasing function and is bounded from below by *V(0)*. Therefore, lim*V(t)* exists and is finite.

In (Krstic & Deng, 1998), $l\left(\tilde{\chi},\Omega\right)$ is required to be positive definite and radial unbounded with respect to χ. Here, from (24) we have

Figure 5. Time evolution of Neural Observer weights

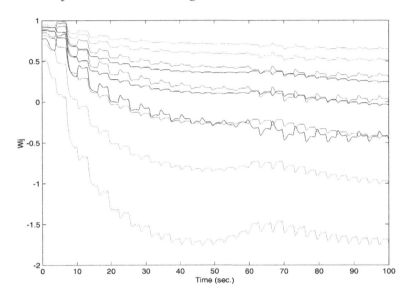

$$l\left(\tilde{\chi},\Omega\right) = -2\beta_{J}L_{g}V - \beta_{J}^{2}L_{g}VR^{-1}\left(\tilde{\chi},\Omega\right)L_{g}V^{T} \tag{25}$$

Substituting (25) into (23), with the learning adaptation law (18) and then applying (19) to the second term on the right side of $L_{f}V$, we have

$$l\left(\tilde{\chi},\Omega\right) \geq \frac{1}{2}\tilde{\chi}^{T}Q\tilde{\chi} + K\left\|\tilde{y}\right\|^{2} + \left(\mu-1\right)\left(\frac{1}{\left\|b\right\|^{2}} + \frac{1}{4}\left\|\Omega\right\|^{2}\right)\left\|\tilde{y}\right\|^{2} \tag{26}$$

Selecting $\mu > 1$, we ensure that $l\left(\tilde{\chi},\Omega\right)$ satisfies the condition of being positive definite and radial unbounded. Hence,(23) is a suitable cost functional.

The integral term in (23)can be written as

$$l\left(\tilde{\chi},\Omega\right) + v\left(t\right)^{T}R\left(\tilde{\chi},\Omega\right)v\left(t\right) = -2\beta_{J}L_{g}V + 2\beta_{J}^{2}L_{g}VR^{-1}\left(\tilde{\chi},\Omega\right)L_{g}V^{T} \tag{27}$$

The Lyapunov time derivative is defined as

$$\dot{V} = L_{f}V + L_{g}Vv\left(t\right) \tag{28}$$

and substituting (27) in(28), we obtain

$$\dot{V} = L_{f}V - L_{g}V\beta_{J}R^{-1}\left(\tilde{\chi},\Omega\right)L_{g}V^{T} \tag{29}$$

Then, multiplying V by $-2\beta_{J}$, we have

$$l\left(\tilde{\chi},\Omega\right) + v\left(t\right)^T R\left(\tilde{\chi},\Omega\right) v\left(t\right) = -2\beta_J \dot{V} \tag{30}$$

Replacing (30) in the cost functional (23), we obtain

$$
\begin{aligned}
J\left(v\right) &= \lim_{t\to\infty}\left\{2\beta_J V - 2\beta_J \int_0^t \dot{V} d\tau\right\} \\
&= \lim_{t\to\infty}\left\{2\beta_J V - 2\beta_J V\left(t\right) + 2\beta_J V\left(0\right)\right\} \\
&= 2\beta_J V\left(0\right)
\end{aligned}
$$

The cost functional optimal value is given by $J^* = 2\beta_J V\left(0\right)$. This is achieved by the stabilizing law (21). After all the state is estimated, the next step in this algorithm is to do the system identification and trajectory tracking analysis.

3.5 Simulation Results for Neural Observer

In this section, the neural observer is applied to the Van der Pol dynamical system.

$$
\begin{aligned}
\dot{x}_{p1} &= x_{p2} \\
\dot{x}_{p2} &= \left(0.5 - x_{p1}^{\;2}\right) x_{p2} - x_{p1} + 0.5\cos\left(1.1t\right)
\end{aligned}
$$

$$
\begin{aligned}
y &= x_{p1} \\
x_p\left(0\right) &= \begin{bmatrix} 0 & 0.25 \end{bmatrix}
\end{aligned}
\tag{31}
$$

In order to estimate the full state, we use the RHONO with the following parameters

$$
\begin{aligned}
z\left(y\right)_i &= \tanh^i\left(y\right), \quad i = 1,...,10, \quad \gamma = 470, \quad k = 0.65 \\
K &= \begin{bmatrix} 400 & 2600 \end{bmatrix}, \quad \hat{\chi}\left(0\right) = \begin{bmatrix} 0.5 & 0.5 \end{bmatrix}
\end{aligned}
$$

The results show that a good estimation performance for the state x_{p2} is achieved, as can be seen in Figure 3 to Figure 5. The estimation error can be made arbitrarily small by the inclusion of additional high order terms into the sigmoid function.

4. RECURRENT HIGHER ORDER NEURAL CONTROL

4.1 Nonlinear System Identification

Consider the unknown nonlinear plant with constrained inputs

$$\dot{x}_p = F_p\left(x_p, u\right) \triangleq f_p\left(x_p\right) + g_p\left(x_p\right) sat\left(u\right) \tag{32}$$

where $x_p, f_p \in \Re^n, g_p \in \Re^n, u \in \Re$ and

$$sat\left(u\right)_i = \begin{cases} u_{\max i} & \text{if } \left\|u_i\right\| > u_{\max i} \\ u_i & \text{if } u_{\min i} > \left\|u_i\right\| > u_{\max i} \\ u_{\min i} & \text{if } \left\|u_i\right\| < u_{\min i} \end{cases}$$

Taking into account that f_p is unknown, one can model (32) by a recurrent neural network as in (3). Hence we propose the following recurrent neural model for the unknown plant

$$\dot{x} = -\lambda x + Wz(x_p) + W_g z_g(x_p)sat\left(u\right) \tag{33}$$

where $\lambda > 0, x \in \Re^n, u \in \Re, W \in \Re^{n \times p}, W_g \in \Re^n, z\left(x_p\right) \in \Re$ x_p is the state to identify, x is the neural network state, and u is the applied input to the system. W, W_g are the neural network adapted weights, $z\left(x_p\right), z_g\left(x_p\right)$ are sigmoid functions.

Assumption 1. There exist unknown but constant weights W^*, W^*_g such that the plant is described, by the neural network plus a minimum bounded modelling error term w_{per}, i. e., each state x_p of the unknown dynamic system (32) satisfies

$$\dot{x}_p = -\lambda x_p + W^* z(x_p) + W^*_g z_g(x_p)sat\left(u\right) + w_{per}$$
$$w_{per} \leq w_b \in \Re^+ \tag{34}$$

where all the elements are as defined earlier.

Remark 1. The modelling error is defined as a mismatch between the system and the RHONN model with its optimal weight values. This mismatch is caused by an insufficient number of high order terms in the RHONN model. Though λ can be freely selected as long as it satisfies $\lambda>0$, greater values relative to x_p, can minimize the convergence time of the neural network output; but if it is too large, it can produce undesirable oscillations. It is recommended to adjust the values of λ via simulations.

In order to perform the stability analysis for the identification error dynamics and to obtain the neural network weights learning law, we assume no modelling error w_{per}. Though the assumption is seldom satisfied, the algorithm developed below is the base for the design of learning laws in presence of modelling errors, which are later mentioned.

Now, we proceed to analyze the error between the identifier (33) and the plant modelled by (34)

$$e_i = x_p - x \tag{35}$$

Taking its time derivative, and replacing $\dot{x}_p$ by (34) and $\dot{x}$ by (33), we obtain

$$\dot{e}_i = -\lambda x_p + W^* z\left(x_p\right) + W^*_g z_g\left(x\right)sat\left(u\right) - Ax - Wz\left(x_p\right) - W_g z\left(x_p\right)sat\left(u\right)$$
$$\dot{e}_i = Ae_i - \tilde{W}z\left(x_p\right) - \tilde{W}_g z\left(x_p\right)sat\left(u\right)$$
$$\tilde{W} = W - W^*, \quad \tilde{W}_g = W_g - W^*_g \tag{36}$$

Consider the Lyapunov function candidate

$$V = \frac{1}{2}\|e_i\|^2 + \frac{1}{2\gamma} tr\left\{\tilde{W}^T \tilde{W}\right\} + \frac{1}{2\gamma_g} tr\left\{\tilde{W}_g{}^T \tilde{W}_g\right\} \tag{37}$$

Differentiating (37), along the trajectories of (36), we obtain

$$\dot{V} = -\lambda\|e_i\|^2 - e_i{}^T \tilde{W} z\left(x_p\right) - e_i{}^T \tilde{W}_g z\left(x_p\right) sat\left(u\right) + \frac{1}{\gamma} tr\left\{\dot{\tilde{W}}^T \tilde{W}\right\} + \frac{1}{\gamma_g} tr\left\{\dot{\tilde{W}}_g{}^T \tilde{W}_g\right\} \tag{38}$$

We select the weight adaptation law as in (Rovitahkis & Christodoulou, 2000)

$$tr\left\{\dot{W}^T \tilde{W}\right\} = \gamma e_i{}^T \tilde{W} z\left(x_p\right)$$
$$tr\left\{\dot{W}_g{}^T \tilde{W}_g\right\} = \gamma_g e_i{}^T \tilde{W}_g z\left(x_p\right) sat\left(u\right) \tag{39}$$

Substituting the adaptation law in (38), gives

$$\dot{V} \le -\lambda\|e_i\|^2 \le 0 \quad \forall \lambda, e_i, \tilde{W} \ne 0 \tag{40}$$

However, the assumption of no modelling error, which is crucial to the development of the learning laws, is seldom satisfied. This is due to an insufficient number of high order terms for the neural network. In order to avoid parameter drift, the following robust learning law for the neural network weights, known as σ-modification, is proposed as in (Rovitahkis & Christodoulou, 2000):

$$\dot{W} = \begin{cases} -\gamma e_i z\left(x_{pj}\right) & \text{if } |w_{ij}| < w_m \\ -\gamma e_i z\left(x_{pj}\right) - \sigma\gamma w_{ij} & \text{if } |w_{ij}| \ge w_m \end{cases}$$
$$\dot{W}_g = \begin{cases} -\gamma_g e_i z\left(x_{pj}\right) u_i & \text{if } |w_{gi}| < w_{gm} \\ -\gamma_g e_i z\left(x_{pj}\right) ui - \sigma_g \gamma_g w_{gi} & \text{if } |w_{gi}| \ge w_{gm} \end{cases} \tag{41}$$

where σ, σ_g are a positive constants and w_m, w_{gm} are the upper bounds for the neural network weights. The terms σ, σ_g should be selected to have relatively large leakage terms $\sigma\gamma w_{ij}$ and $\sigma_g \gamma_g w_{gi}$; the estimation of these parameters depends on the upper bounds w_m, w_{gm} and the modelling error bound, for a detailed methodology see (Ioannou & Kokotovic, 1984) . By using the σ-modification, the neural networks weights are limited to balls of radius w_m and w_{gm}, to avoid numerical problems and the parameter drift that would impact on large control laws. For the control developed in this chapter, which explicitly depends on the value of W and W_g, the bounds w_m and w_{gm} can be selected via previous simulations as $w_m < w_M$ and $w_m < w_{gM}$ where w_g, w_{gM} are the largest non-drifting weights.

It can be shown that the robust learning law does not affect the stability of the identification error but improves it, making the Lyapunov function time derivative more negative. For a detailed demonstration, see (Rovitahkis & Christodoulou, 2000).

4.2 Trajectory Tracking Analysis

Consider the nonlinear system with constrained input (33), which we model by the neural network

$$\dot{x} = -\lambda x + W z\left(x_p\right) + w_{per} + W_g z_g\left(x_p\right) sat\left(u\right)$$
$$y = h\left(x\right)$$

(42)

where we assume that the modelling error is bounded. In the following, for simplicity, we will use u instead of *sat(u)*. We will design a robust controller that satisfies $|u| \leq u_{max}$ and guarantees boundedness of the tracking error between the plant and the reference signal generated by

$$\dot{x}_{ref} = f_{ref}\left(x_{ref}\right), \qquad x_{ref} \in \Re$$

(43)

The system (42) is converted in a partially linear system by the change of coordinates applied to the system output which we assume in this chapter is directly one of the states,

$$T\left(x\right) = \begin{bmatrix} \xi \\ \varsigma \end{bmatrix} = \begin{bmatrix} \xi_1 & \xi_2 & \cdots & \xi_r & \varsigma_r & \cdots & \varsigma_{n-r} \end{bmatrix}^T$$
$$= \begin{bmatrix} h\left(x\right) & L_f h\left(x\right) & \cdots & L_f^{r-1} h\left(x\right) & \psi_1\left(x\right) & \cdots & \psi_{n-r}\left(x\right) \end{bmatrix}^T$$

where r is the relative degree of (42), such that the system (42) is converted to

$$\dot{\xi}_1 = \xi_2$$
$$\vdots$$
$$\dot{\xi}_{r-1} = \xi_r$$
$$\dot{\xi}_r = L_f^r h\left(\psi^{-1}\left(\xi,\varsigma\right)\right) + L_w L_f^{r-1}\left(T^{-1}\left(\xi,\varsigma\right)\right) w_{per} + L_g L_f^{r-1} h\left(\psi^{-1}\left(\xi,\varsigma\right)\right) u$$
$$\dot{\varsigma}_1 = \Psi_1\left(\xi,\varsigma\right)$$
$$\vdots$$
$$\dot{\varsigma}_{n-r} = \Psi_{n-r}\left(\xi,\varsigma\right)$$
$$y = \xi_1$$

(44)

Now let us define $e_t^T = \begin{bmatrix} e_{t1}, e_{t2}, \ldots, e_{tr} \end{bmatrix}$ such that,

$$e_{t1} = \xi_1 - x_{ref}$$
$$e_{t2} = \dot{\xi}_1 - \dot{x}_{ref}$$
$$\vdots$$
$$e_{tr} = \xi_1^{r-1} - x_{ref}^{r-1}$$

From (44), we obtain the tracking error dynamic system

$$\dot{e}_{t1} = e_{t2}$$
$$\dot{e}_{t2} = e_{t3}$$
$$\vdots$$
$$\dot{e}_{tr} = L_f^r h\left(\psi^{-1}(\xi,\varsigma)\right) + L_w L_f^{-1}\left(T^{-1}(\xi,\varsigma)\right)w_{per} - x_{ref}^r + L_g L_f^{-1} h\left(\psi^{-1}(\xi,\varsigma)\right)u$$

$$\dot{e}_t = f_e(e_t) + w(e_t)w_{per} + g_e(e_t)u$$
$$f_e(e_t) = L_f^r h\left(\psi^{-1}(\xi,\varsigma)\right) - x_{ref}^r$$
$$w(e_t) = L_w L_f^{-1}\left(T^{-1}(\xi,\varsigma)\right)$$
$$g_e(e_t) = L_g L_f^{-1} h\left(\psi^{-1}(\xi,\varsigma)\right)$$

(45)

The tracking problem can be analyzed as a stabilization problem for the error dynamics (45).

4.3 Tracking Error Stabilization

To perform the stability analysis, we consider the overall system, including the neural observer, neural identifier and the unknown system, as shown in Figure 1. The following Lyapunov function is formulated:

$$V = \frac{1}{2}\tilde{\chi}^T P_o \tilde{\chi} + \frac{1}{2}\|e_i\|^2 + \frac{1}{2}e_t^T P e_t + \frac{1}{2\gamma}tr\left\{\tilde{W}^T W\right\} + \frac{1}{2\gamma_g}tr\left\{\tilde{W}_g^{\ T} W_g\right\}$$
$$+ \frac{1}{2\gamma}tr\left\{\tilde{\Omega}^T \tilde{\Omega}\right\} + \frac{1}{2\gamma_g}tr\left\{\tilde{\Omega}_g^{\ T}\tilde{\Omega}_g\right\}$$

(46)

where P_o is a positive definite symmetric matrix which solves the Ricatti equation,

$$A^T P_o + P_o^T A = -Q_o, \qquad P_o b = c^T$$

and P is a positive definite matrix which satisfies the Ricatti inequality

$$A^T P + P^T A - P b b^T P < 0$$

$$A = \begin{bmatrix} 0 & 1 & 0 & \cdots & 0 \\ 0 & 0 & 1 & \cdots & 0 \\ \vdots & \vdots & \vdots & \ddots & \vdots \\ 0 & 0 & 0 & \cdots & 1 \\ 0 & 0 & 0 & \cdots & 0 \end{bmatrix} \in \Re^{nxr}, b = \begin{bmatrix} 0 \\ 0 \\ \vdots \\ 0 \\ 1 \end{bmatrix} \in \Re^r, \quad P = \begin{bmatrix} c_p & 1 & \cdots & 1 \\ 1 & c_p & \cdots & 1 \\ \vdots & \vdots & \ddots & \vdots \\ 1 & 1 & \cdots & c_p \end{bmatrix}, \quad c_p \in R^+$$

Without loss of generality, we select P to solve

$$A^T P + P A - P b b^T P + I = 0$$

The time derivative of (46), along the trajectories of (45), is

$$\dot{V} = -\frac{1}{2}\tilde{\chi}^T Q \tilde{\chi} + \tilde{\chi}^T P\tilde{\Omega}z(y) + \tilde{\chi}^T P\tilde{\Omega}\phi_z(y) + \tilde{\chi}^T Pb\tilde{\Omega}_g z_g(y,\hat{y})u + \tilde{y}v(t)$$
$$+ \frac{1}{\gamma}tr\left\{\dot{\tilde{\Omega}}^T\tilde{\Omega}\right\} + \frac{1}{\gamma_g}tr\left\{\dot{\tilde{\Omega}}_g^{\ T}\tilde{\Omega}_g\right\} - \lambda\|e_i\|^2 + e_i^T\tilde{W}z(x_p) + e_i^T\tilde{W}_g z_g(x_p)u$$
$$+ L_{f_e}V + L_{we}Vw_{per} + L_{ge}Vu + \frac{1}{\gamma}tr\left\{\dot{\tilde{W}}^T W\right\} + \frac{1}{\gamma_g}tr\left\{\dot{\tilde{W}}_g^{\ T}W_g\right\}$$

(47)

Replacing the learning laws (18), (39) and the and the observer stabilizing signal (21) in (47) we obtain

$$\dot{V} = -\frac{1}{2}\|Q\|\|\tilde{x}\|^2 - \left(\frac{1}{\|b\|^2} + \frac{1}{4}\|\Omega\|^2\right)\|\tilde{y}\|^2 - \lambda\|e_t\|^2 + L_{f_e}V + L_{we}Vw_{per} + L_{ge}Vu \qquad (48)$$

Furthermore, we assume that the uncertain term $\left(L_w V\right)w_{per}$ is bounded by above as

$$\left(L_{we}V\right)w_{per} \le |e_t|w_b$$

In order to stabilize the tracking error dynamics, let us consider the following modification of the Sontag control law (El-Farra & Christofides, 2001; Sanchez & Ricalde, 2003),

$$\begin{aligned} u &= -\frac{1}{2}R^{-1}\left(e_t, W\right)L_g V \\ &= -\frac{L_{f_e} + \eta\sum_{k=1}^{q}w_{bk}\left|L_{wek}L_f^{r-1}h(x)\right|\left|2b^T Pe_t\right| + \sqrt{\left(L_{f_e}V + \eta w_b\left|L_{we}V\right|\right)^2 + \left(u_{max}L_g V\right)^4}}{\left(L_g V\right)^2\left[1 + \sqrt{1 + \left(u_{max}L_g V\right)^2}\right]}L_g V \end{aligned} \qquad (49)$$

where η is an adjustable parameter and under the conditions

$$L_f V + \eta w_b\left\|L_w V\right\| \le \left|L_g V u_{max}\right|$$

For the stability analysis, for simplicity we consider the case for $q=1$; for $q \ge 2$, the procedure is straightforward.

Replacing the control law (49) in (48) and taking into account the bound for $\left(L_w V\right)w_{per}$ we obtain

$$\begin{aligned} \dot{V} = &= -\lambda\|e_t\|^2 - \frac{\sqrt{\left(L_{f_e}V + \eta w_b\left|L_{we}V\right|\right)^2 + \left(u_{max}L_g V\right)^4}}{1 + \sqrt{1 + \left(u_{max}L_g V\right)^2}} + \frac{w_b\left|L_{we}L_f^{r-1}h(x)\right|\left|2b^T Pe_t\right|(1-\eta)}{\left[1 + \sqrt{1 + \left(u_{max}L_g V\right)^2}\right]} \\ &+ \frac{\left(L_{f_e}V + w_b\left|L_{we}V\right|\right)\sqrt{1 + \left(u_{max}L_g V\right)^2}}{\left[1 + \sqrt{1 + \left(u_{max}L_g V\right)^2}\right]} + |e_t|w_b \end{aligned} \qquad (50)$$

Now, we consider that the modelling error term is a disturbance which satisfies a growth bound of the form

$$\left|L_{we}L_f^{r-1}h(x)\right| \le \delta\left|2b^T Pe_t\right| + \mu$$

Substituting this bound in (50) we obtain

$$\begin{aligned} \dot{V} \le &-\lambda\|e_t\|^2 - (\eta-1)\frac{w_b\left(\left|\delta\left|2b^T Pe_t\right| + \mu\right|\right)\left|2b^T Pe_t\right|}{\left[1 + \sqrt{1 + \left(u_{max}L_g V\right)^2}\right]} + \frac{\left(L_{f_e}V + w_b\left|L_{we}V\right|\right)\sqrt{1 + \left(u_{max}L_g V\right)^2}}{\left[1 + \sqrt{1 + \left(u_{max}L_g V\right)^2}\right]} \\ &- \frac{\sqrt{\left(L_{f_e}V + \eta w_b\left|L_{we}V\right|\right)^2 + \left(u_{max}L_g V\right)^4}}{1 + \sqrt{1 + \left(u_{max}L_g V\right)^2}} + |e_t|w_b \end{aligned} \qquad (51)$$

Defining $\beta\left(\left|e_t\right|\right) = \dfrac{w_b\left(\left|\delta\left|2b^T Pe_t\right| + \mu\right|\right)\left|2b^T Pe_t\right|}{\left[1 + \sqrt{1 + \left(u_{max} L_g V\right)^2}\right]}$ we have

$$\dot{V} \leq -\lambda\left\|e_i\right\|^2 - (\eta - 1)\beta\left(\left|e_t\right|\right) + \left|e_t\right| w_b$$
$$+ \frac{\left(L_{fe} V + w_b \left|L_{we} V\right|\right)\sqrt{1 + \left(u_{max} L_g V\right)^2} - \sqrt{\left(L_{fe} V + \eta w_b \left|L_{we} V\right|\right)^2 + \left(u_{max} L_g V\right)^4}}{\left[1 + \sqrt{1 + \left(u_{max} L_g V\right)^2}\right]}$$

Now, to determine the sign of the last two terms, we consider two cases,

Case 1. $L_f V + \eta w_b \left|L_{w_e}\right| \leq 0$, substituting this inequality in (51) yields

$$\dot{V} \leq -\lambda\left(\left\|e_i\right\|^2 + \left\|e_t\right\|^2\right) - (\eta - 1)\beta\left(|e|\right) - \frac{\sqrt{\left(L_{fe} V + \eta w_b \left|L_{we} V\right|\right)^2 + \left(u_{max} L_g V\right)^4}}{1 + \sqrt{1 + \left(u_{max} L_g V\right)^2}} \tag{52}$$

Case 2. $0 < L_f V + \eta w_b \left|L_{w_e}\right| \leq u_{max}\left|L_g V\right|$. For this case, we consider the inequality

$$\left(L_f V + \eta w_b \left|L_{w_e} V\right|\right)^2 \leq \left(u_{max} L_g V\right)^2$$

Replacing this bound in (50), we obtain

$$\dot{V} \leq -\lambda\left(\left\|e_i\right\|^2 + \left\|e_t\right\|^2\right) + \left|e_t\right| w_b - (\eta - 1)\beta\left(\left|e_t\right|\right) + \frac{(1 - \eta)w_b \left|L_{we} V\right|\sqrt{1 + \left(u_{max} L_g V\right)^2}}{\left[1 + \sqrt{1 + \left(u_{max} L_g V\right)^2}\right]} \tag{53}$$

where we select η>1 such that the last terms on the right hand are strictly negative.

From (52) and (53), we deduce that exists a class *K* function α such that

$$\dot{V} \leq -\lambda\left(\left\|e_i\right\|^2 + \left\|e_t\right\|^2\right) - \alpha\left(\left|e_t\right|\right) + \left|e_t\right| w_b \tag{54}$$

Then, by an appropriate selection of the Higher Order terms we can make the modelling error small enough such that $\left|e_t\right| w_b \leq \dfrac{1}{2}\alpha\left(\left|e_t\right|\right)$ in order to obtain

$$\dot{V} \leq -\lambda\left(\left\|e_i\right\|^2 + \left\|e_t\right\|^2\right) - \frac{1}{2}\alpha\left(\left|e_i\right|, \left|e_t\right|\right) \tag{55}$$

Then, the designer can choose the parameter η in order to obtain a suitable tracking error. Since $\dot{V}$ is a semidefinite negative function, by the Barbalat's lemma (Khalil, 1996), we have

$$-\lambda\left(\left\|e_i\right\|^2 + \left\|e_t\right\|^2\right) - \alpha\left(\left|e_i\right|, \left|e_t\right|\right) + \beta\left(\left|e_t\right|\right) \to 0 \quad as\ t \to \infty$$

when $e_i \to 0,$ from the weight adaptation law, we have

$$\dot{w}_{ij} \to 0$$

then

$$\lim_{t \to \infty} W \to W_{\infty}$$
$$\lim_{t \to \infty} \tilde{W} \to \tilde{W}_{\infty}$$

where $W_{\infty}, \tilde{W}_{\infty}$ are constant values.

4.4 Inverse Optimality Analysis for Trajectory Tracking

Once the problem of defining the control law (49), which stabilizes (45), is solved, we can proceed to demonstrate that this control law minimizes a cost functional formulated as

$$J(v) = \lim_{t \to \infty} \left\{ 2V + \int_0^t \left(l(e_t, W, W_g) + u^T R(e_t, W, W_g) u(t) \right) d\tau \right\} \tag{56}$$

where the Lyapunov function (48) solves the associated Hamilton-Jacobi-Bellman partial derivative equations

$$l(e_t, W, W_g) + L_{fe} V - \frac{1}{4} L_{ge} V R^{-1}(e_t, W, W_g) L_g V^T + |L_{we} V| w_b = 0 \tag{57}$$

It is required $l(e_t, W, W_g)$ to be positive define and radially unbounded with respect to e_t; from (57) we have

$$l(e_t, W, W_g) = -L_{fe} V + \frac{1}{4} L_{ge} V R^{-1}(e_t, W, W_g) L_g V^T - |L_{we} V| w_b \tag{58}$$

Substituting $R^{-1}(e_t, W, W_g)$ into (58), taking into account that

$$L_{we} V = \frac{\partial V}{\partial e} w_{per} = L_{we} L_f^{r-1}(h(x)) w_{per}$$

we obtain after some algebraic manipulations

$$l(e_t, W, W_g) \geq \frac{-(L_{fe} V + w_b \|L_{we} V\|) - (L_{fe} V + \eta w_b \|L_{we} V\|)\sqrt{1 + (u_{max} L_{ge} V)^2}}{1 + \sqrt{1 + (u_{max} L_{ge} V)^2}}$$
$$+ \frac{\frac{1}{2}(L_{fe} V + \eta w_b \|L_{we} V\| |2b^T P e_t|) + \frac{1}{2}\sqrt{(L_{fe} V + \eta w_b \|L_{we} V\|)^2 + (u_{max} L_{ge} V)^4}}{1 + \sqrt{1 + (u_{max} L_{ge} V)^2}} \tag{59}$$

$$l(e_t, W, W_g) \geq \frac{(\eta |b^T P e_t| - 1) w_b \|L_{we} V\| - \frac{1}{2} L_{fe} V - (L_{fe} V + \|L_{we} V\| w_b)\sqrt{1 + (u_{max} L_{ge} V)^2}}{1 + \sqrt{1 + (u_{max} L_{ge} V)^2}}$$
$$+ \frac{\frac{1}{2}\sqrt{(L_{fe} V + \eta w_b \|L_{we} V\|)^2 + (u_{max} L_{ge} V)^4}}{1 + \sqrt{1 + (u_{max} L_{ge} V)^2}} \tag{60}$$

For Case 1, as in the previous section, where $L_{fe} V + \eta w_b \|L_{we} V\| \leq 0$, (60) is positive definite since

$$\left(\eta\left|b^T P e_t\right| - 1\right) w_b \left\|L_{we} V\right\| - \frac{1}{2} L_{fe} V > 0 \ .$$

For Case 2, where $0 < L_{fe} V + \eta w_b \left\|L_{we} V\right\| \le u_{max} \left\|L_{ge} V\right\|$ we have

$$l\left(e_t, W, W_g\right) = \eta \left\|L_{we} V\right\| w_b \frac{\left(\left\|b^T P e_t\right\| + \sqrt{1 + \left(u_{max} L_{ge} V\right)^2}\right)}{1 + \sqrt{1 + \left(u_{max} L_{ge} V\right)^2}}$$

$$- \frac{\frac{1}{2}\left(L_{fe} V + \eta w_b \left\|L_{we} V\right\|\right)\left(1 + \sqrt{1 + \left(u_{max} L_{ge} V\right)^2}\right)}{1 + \sqrt{1 + \left(u_{max} L_{ge} V\right)^2}} \tag{61}$$

For the region where $\left\|b^T P e_t\right\| \ge 1$, we proceed to rewrite (61) as

$$l\left(e_t, W, W_g\right) \ge -\left(L_{fe} V + \left\|L_{we} V\right\| w_b\right) + \frac{1}{2}\left(L_{fe} V + \eta w_b \left\|L_{we} V\right\|\right)$$

$$l\left(e_t, W, W_g\right) \ge \frac{1}{2}\left(\eta - 2\right) w_b \left\|L_{we} V\right\| - \frac{1}{2} L_{fe} V \tag{62}$$

Then, the designer should select χ such that from (62),

$$\left(\eta - 2\right) w_b \left\|L_{we} V\right\| - L_{fe} V > 0 \tag{63}$$

Then, $l\left(e_t, W, W_g\right)$ is positive definite and radially unbounded.
We rewrite (63) as

$$2\chi w_b \left\|e_t\right\| - 2 w_b \left\|e_t\right\| - L_{fe} V - \eta w_b \left\|e_t\right\| > 0$$

$$2\left(\eta - 1\right) w_b \left\|e_t\right\| - L_{fe} V - \eta w_b \left\|e_t\right\| > 0 \tag{64}$$

From $\left\|e_t\right\| u_{max} \left\|L_{ge} V\right\| - L_{fe} V - \eta w_b \left\|e_t\right\| \ge 0$ we have that (64) is satisfied selecting χ such that

$$\eta > \frac{u_{max}}{2 w_b} + 1$$

Then, by an appropriate selection of η we can satisfy (62). Hence, (56) is a suitable cost functional.

Now we proceed to prove that the control law (49) minimizes (56), replacing $R\left(e_t, W, W_g\right)$ in (56) we obtain

$$J(v) = \lim_{t \to \infty} \left\{ V + \int_0^t \left(l(e_t, W, W_g) + u^T R(e_t, W, W_g) u(t) \right) d\tau \right\}$$

$$= \lim_{t \to \infty} \left\{ V - \int_0^t \left[L_f V - \frac{1}{2} L_g V^T R^{-1}(e_t, W, W_g) L_g V + \|L_w V\| w_b \right] d\tau \right\}$$

$$= \lim_{t \to \infty} \left\{ V - \int_0^t \frac{\partial V}{\partial e} (f + gu + w_b) d\tau \right\}$$

$$= \lim_{t \to \infty} \left\{ V - \int_0^t \dot{V} d\tau \right\} = \lim_{t \to \infty} V(0) = V(0)$$

It is clear that the optimal value is

$$J^*(u) = V(0)$$

Then the obtained control law will ensure to have its optimal value when the trajectories evolve outside the region $\left\| b^T P e_t \right\| \geq 1$.

4.5 Simulation Results for the Observer-Controller Scheme

In this section, in order to demonstrate the applicability of the proposed adaptive control scheme with constrained inputs, the following example is tested. We consider a sinusoid reference tracking. We apply the proposed control scheme to the Van der Pol dynamical system defined as

$$\dot{x}_{p1} = x_{p2}$$
$$\dot{x}_{p2} = \left(0.5 - x_{p1}^2 \right) x_{p2} - x_{p1} + 0.5 \cos(1.1t)$$

$$y = x_{p1}$$
$$x_p(0) = \begin{bmatrix} 0 & 0.25 \end{bmatrix}$$

(65)

In order to estimate the full state, we use the RHONO with the following parameters

$$z(y)_i = \tanh^i(y), \quad i = 1, ..., 10, \quad \gamma = 470, \quad k = 0.65$$
$$K = \begin{bmatrix} 400 & 2600 \end{bmatrix}, \quad \hat{\chi}(0) = \begin{bmatrix} 0.5 & 0.5 \end{bmatrix}$$

We want this system output $y = x_{p_1}$ to track the following reference signal $x_r = 1.5 + \sin\left(\frac{t}{4}\right)$ for a maximum input $u_{max} = 5$. For simulations, the following recurrent neural network identifier is used:

$$\dot{x} = -\lambda x + W z(x_p) + b sat(u)$$
$$y(x) = x_1$$

(66)

with $\lambda = 15$, $b = \begin{bmatrix} 0 & 1 \end{bmatrix}^T$ and a eight order high order sigmoid vector defined as

Figure 6. Time evolution for the output of Van Der Pol oscillator

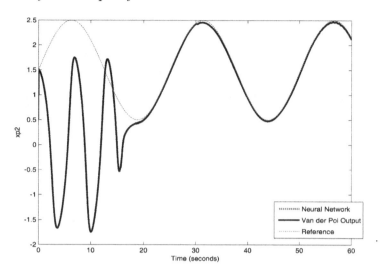

$$z\left(x_p\right) = \left[\tanh\left(x_{p1}\right) \quad \tanh\left(x_{p2}\right) \quad \tanh\left(x_{p1}\right)\tanh\left(x_{p2}\right)\right.$$
$$\tanh^2\left(x_{p1}\right) \quad \tanh^2\left(x_{p2}\right) \quad \tanh^2\left(x_{p1}\right)\tanh^2\left(x_{p2}\right)$$
$$\left.\tanh^3\left(x_{p1}\right) \quad \tanh^3\left(x_{p2}\right)\right]$$

To avoid parameter drift, we use the robust adaptation law (41) with $\gamma=250$, $w_{\mathrm{m}}=100$, $\sigma=50$. The coordinate change is set as

$$\left(\xi_1 \quad \xi_2\right) = \left(x_1 \quad -\lambda x_1 + \sum_{i=1}^{8} w_{1i} z_i\left(x_p\right)\right)$$

Figure 7. Time evolution of Van der Pol oscillator and neural observer outputs

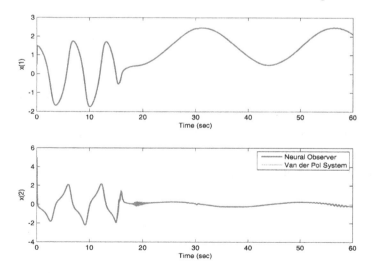

Figure 8. Applied input for trajectory tracking

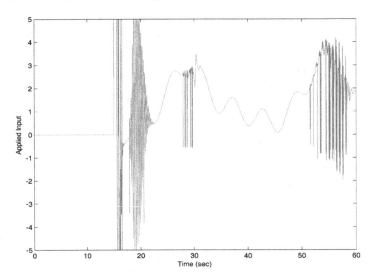

The tracking error is defined as $e_1 = \xi_1 - x_{r1}$, and the error system as

$$\dot{e}_1 = e_2$$
$$\dot{e}_2 = \dot{\xi}_2 - \ddot{x}_{r1}$$
$$= \lambda^2\left(e_1 + x_{r1}\right) - \lambda w_{per} - \lambda\sum_{i=1}^{8} w_{1i} z_i\left(x_p\right) + \sum_{i=1}^{8}\dot{w}_{1i} z_i\left(x_p\right) + \sum_{i=1}^{8} w_{1i}\dot{z}_i\left(x_p\right) - \ddot{x}_{r1}$$

where $\dot{w}_{1i}$ is obtained from (39).

For the Lyapunov function we select c=0.9. For the control law, we select $w_b = 0.2$, $\eta = 2$ and it is defined as

$$u = -\frac{L_{fe} + \eta w_b\left|L_{we} L_f^{r-1} h\left(x\right)\right|\left|2b^T Pe_i\right| + \sqrt{\left(L_{fe}V + \eta w_b\left|L_{we}V\right|\right)^2 + \left(u_{max} L_g V\right)^4}}{\left(L_g V\right)^2\left[1 + \sqrt{1 + \left(u_{max} L_g V\right)^2}\right]}L_g V$$

$$L_{fe}V = \left(e_1 + 0.9e_2\right)e_2 + \left(0.9e_1 + e_2\right)\dot{e}_2$$

$$L_{ge}V = \left(e_1 + 0.9e_2\right)\sum_{i=1}^{8} w_{1i}\frac{\partial z_i\left(x_{p1}, x_{p2}\right)}{\partial x_{p2}}\dot{x}_{p2}$$

$$L_{we}V = \left(0.9e_1 + e_2\right)\sum_{i=1}^{8} w_{1i}\frac{\partial z_i\left(x_{p1}, x_{p2}\right)}{\partial x_{p2}}\dot{x}_{p2}$$

Figure 6 displays the time evolution for the output of the plant compared to the reference trajectory. The control law is applied at *t=15 sec*. As can be seen, the control law achieves the desired tracking performance even in presence of uncertainties due to the modelling error and input constraints. The observer estimation is displayed in Figure 7. The results show that a good estimation performance of the state is achieved. The estimation error can be made arbitrarily small by the inclusion of more high order terms in the sigmoid function. The applied input is displayed in Figure 8.

Figure 9. Time evolution of the neural observer weights

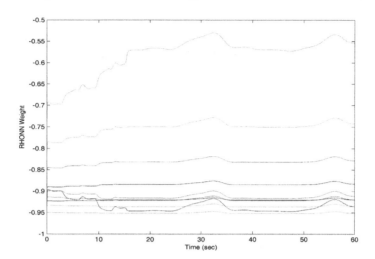

5. CONCLUSION

In this chapter it has been developed an adaptive recurrent neural observer-controller for nonlinear systems with uncertainties and unmodeled dynamics. The neural observer is composed of a Recurrent Higher Order Neural Network which builds and online model of the unknown plant and a learning adaptation law for the neural network weights, which ensures stability of the estimation error, is obtained via the Lyapunov methodology. We demonstrate that the developed observer stabilizing law is optimal related to a meaningful cost functional. A neural network identifier, is designed to build an on-line model of the unknown plant, which is the base to compute the time derivatives of the output. A control law for trajectory tracking with constrained inputs is developed using the Sontag law and the Lyapunov methodology which considers identification and tracking errors simultaneously. The results are validated via simulations for output trajectory tracking of the Van der Pol forced oscillator.

6. FUTURE TRENDS

Physical systems have yet to be analyzed for further applications. The potential applications of the present algorithm arise mainly for electromechanical systems, where the relative degree and structure of the system can be known, but where the process exhibits uncertainties, unmeasurable parameters and limited energy for the actuators.

On the other hand, further research is focussed to extend the adaptive control scheme for Multiple Inputs-Multiple Outputs systems. Even if the solution of this problem is straightforward from the algorithm provided in this Chapter, the structure of the recurrent neural network and its decoupling matrix has to be synthesized according to the relative degree of the unknown system.

ACKNOWLEDGMENT

The first author thanks the support of PROMEP and CONACYT Mexico, through Project FOMIX 66192. The third autor thanks the support of "CONACYT Fondo Institucional".

7. REFERENCES

El-Farra, N. H., & Christofides, P. D. (2001). Integrating robustness, optimality and constraints in control of nonlinear processes. *Chemical Engineering Science, 56*, 1841–1868. doi:10.1016/S0009-2509(00)00530-3

Hokimyan, N., Rysdyk, R., & Calise, A. (2001). Dynamic neural networks for output feedback control. *International Journal of Robust and Nonlinear Control, 11*, 23–39. doi:10.1002/1099-1239(200101)11:1<23::AID-RNC545>3.0.CO;2-N

Hopfield, J. (1984). Neurons with graded responses have collective computational properties like those of two state neurons. *Proceedings of the National Academy of Sciences of the United States of America, 81*, 3088–3092. doi:10.1073/pnas.81.10.3088

Hu, T., & Lin, Z. (2001), *Control Systems with Actuator Saturation: Analysis and Design.* Boston: Birkhäuser.

Ioannou, P., & Sun, J. (1996). *Robust Adaptive Control*, Prentice Hall, Upper Saddle River, NJ, USA.

Ioannou, P. A., & Kokotovic, P. V. (1984). Instability analysis and the improvement of robustness of adaptive control . *Automatica, 20*(5), 583–594. doi:10.1016/0005-1098(84)90009-8

Khalil, H. (1996). *Nonlinear Systems*, 2nd Ed., Upper Saddle River, NJ: Prentice Hall

Kim, Y. H., Lewis, F. L., & Abdallah, C. T. (1996, December). Nonlinear observer design using dynamic recurrent neural networks. In *Proceedings of the 35th Conference on Decision and Control*, Kobe, Japan.

Kosmatopoulos, E. B., Christodoulou, M. A., & Ioannou, P. A. (1997). Dynamical neural networks that ensure exponential identification error convergence . *Neural Networks, 10*(2), 299–314. doi:10.1016/S0893-6080(96)00060-3

Krstic, M., & Deng, H. (1998). *Stabilization of Nonlinear Uncertain Systems.* New York: Springer Verlag

Marino, R. (1990). Observers for single output nonlinear systems . *IEEE Transactions on Automatic Control, 35*, 1054–1058. doi:10.1109/9.58536

Rovitahkis, G. A., & Christodoulou, M. A. (2000), *Adaptive Control with Recurrent High-Order Neural Networks.* New York: Springer Verlag.

Sanchez, E. N., Alanis, A., & Loukianov, A. (2008), *Discrete-Time High Order Neural Control.* Berlin, Germany: Springer-Verlag

Sanchez, E. N., Alanis, A. Y., & Loukianov, A. G. (2007), Discrete-Time Recurrent High Order Neural Observer for Induction Motors, in *Foundations of Fuzzy Logic and Soft computing*, Melin, P., et al. (Ed.), Berlin Heidelberg, Germany: Springer-Verlag

Sanchez, E. N., & Ricalde, L. J. (2003). Chaos Control and Synchronization, with Input Saturation, via Recurrent Neural Networks. *Neural Networks*, *16*, 711–717. doi:10.1016/S0893-6080(03)00122-9

Sepulchre, R., Jankovic, M., & Kokotovic, P. V. (1997), *Constructive nonlinear control*. New York:Springer.

Chapter 14
Artificial Higher Order Neural Network Training on Limited Precision Processors

Janti Shawash
University College London, UK

David R. Selviah
University College London, UK

ABSTRACT

Previous research suggested Artificial Neural Network (ANN) operation in a limited precision environment was particularly sensitive to the precision and could not take place below a certain threshold level of precision. This study investigates by simulation the training of networks using Back Propagation (BP) and Levenberg-Marquardt algorithms in limited precision to achieve high overall calculation accuracy, using on-line training, a new type of Higher Order Neural Network (HONN) known as the Correlation HONN (CHONN), discrete XOR and continuous optical waveguide sidewall roughness datasets to find the precision at which the training and operation is feasible. The BP algorithm converged to a precision beyond which the performance did not improve. The results support previous findings in literature for ANN operation that discrete datasets require lower precision than continuous datasets. The importance of our findings is that they demonstrate the feasibility of on-line, real-time, low-latency training on limited precision electronic hardware such as Digital Signal Processors (DSPs) and Field Programmable Gate Arrays (FPGAs) to achieve high overall operational accuracy.

1. INTRODUCTION

There is a need for high speed, low latency (input to output delay), embedded computing for use in control systems for aircraft, vehicles, and robots, for example. Digital electronic hardware, such as Digital Signal Processors (DSPs) and Field Programmable Gate Arrays (FPGAs) can achieve this real-time, high speed, low latency operation but with the associated penalty of reduced precision. Indeed there is a trade-off of low latency and high precision. Artificial Neural Networks (ANNs) offer the possibility of

DOI: 10.4018/978-1-61520-711-4.ch014

giving low latency in a limited precision environment. The precision of individual parts of the calculation is reduced as low as possible to give low latency, but without sacrificing unduly, the best overall output error of the calculation performed on the full system. There have been many studies on the operation of ANNs on real-time, low precision electronic hardware (Jung & Kim, 2007; Sahin, Becerikli, & Yazici, 2006; Zhu & Sutton, 2003). It was found that the ANN output error depends on the number of hidden layers (Piche, 1995; Stevenson, Winter, & Widrow, 1990) so by reducing the size of the ANN simpler operating and learning algorithms and higher accuracy can be achieved. A number of researchers have found that they have to train ANNs offline on high precision floating point CPUs on PCs to preserve accuracy during training and then to truncate the final weights to obtain a lower precision and to download them into a limited precision environment such as on DSPs or FPGAs. The size of the ANN limits the learning offline in software as the time and memory requirements grow with ANN size. Parallel hardware processors significantly increase the speed (Lopez-Garcia, Moreno-Armendariz, Riera-Babures, Balsi, & Vilasis-Cardona, 2005; Maguire et al., 2007), but only if the area occupied by the ANN circuit is minimized. In real time hardware, the ANN size poses a more serious problem than in software running on a floating point CPU due to the more limited circuit resources such as memory.

(Dias, Antunes, Vieira, & Mota, 2006) demonstrated that it is possible to implement an on-line Levenberg-Marquardt (LM) training algorithm in software; the use of online learning, as opposed to batch learning, reduces the memory requirements and operation time. The ability to operate LM training online with reduced memory and operation complexity suggests that the LM algorithm may be ideally suited for implementation on real time reduced precision hardware where it has not been used. Therefore, we compare the LM online training with Back Propagation (BP) online training in a limited precision environment to find the lowest precision at which learning is feasible. Another way to reduce the size of an ANN is to use a Higher Order Neural Network (HONN) structure. So we investigate the implementation of the recently introduced Correlation HONN (CHONN) (Selviah & Shawash, 2008) and compare it with that of a first order ANN in a limited precision environment.

To our knowledge, no one has yet succeeded in training ANNs adequately in a very limited precision environment. It has been found that if training is performed in a limited precision environment the ANN converges correctly for high precision but below some threshold level of precision the training does not correctly converge. Moreover, to our knowledge no one has either trained nor even run or operated a HONN in a limited precision environment. We present the first demonstration of running and operating a HONN in a limited precision environment and show how to reduce the threshold precision which had earlier prevented training in very low precision environments and demonstrate for the first time training of both ANNs and HONNs in a very limited precision environment to achieve high overall calculation accuracy.

Section 2 describes HONNs and on-line learning algorithms. Section 3 details the experimental method, while sections 4, 5, and 6 present the simulations and the results. Discussions, conclusions, and acknowledgements are presented in sections 7 and 8, followed by references.

2. GENERALIZED CORRELATION HIGHER ORDER NEURAL NETWORKS

The ANN structure depends on the dimension of the input and output for the problem we are concerned with modeling. For example, when modeling a system that performs a one-step-ahead time series prediction with output, $\hat{y}$, the ANN has only one output neuron. The input data dimension is decided by criteria suggested in literature, it is recommend that a number of ANN with varying input dimensions are tested and benchmarked with regards to their performance against information criteria that takes into account both the performance and the number of parameters used for estimation (Fu, 1994; Smith, 1993; Walczak & Cerpa, 1999). In general, for time series prediction, ANNs with one input dimension, usually referred to as lag, make the model very simple; but on the other hand, lags of 10 or more samples are rarely used (Huang, Wang, Yu, Bao, & Wang, 2006).

There are many forms of information criteria, in this study we chose the Akaike Information Criterion (AIC). Information criteria are formulated to take into account the number of neurons making up the NN and its operational error. Masters (Masters, 1993) states that increasing the number of outputs of an ANN degrades its performance, which conforms with the information criteria mentioned earlier. This study examines ANN with only one hidden layer as research showed that one hidden layer consistently outperform a two hidden layer ANN in most applications (Walczak, 2001).

ANN applications expanded to take into account the highly complex non-linear data available in various systems, such as communications systems and economic data. In general, when the data complexity is increased, the ANN size needs to expand accordingly, with the possibility of reaching sizes that are impractical for ANN training even in software. One solution is to present the ANN with a function of the data, a function which exposes the interrelations that are difficult to capture using the hidden layer. These ANNs are sometimes referred to as functional-link networks (Masters, 1993).

HONNs provide a method to present the ANN with all of the possible high order interactions between the elements of the input vectors. For example, HONNs can easily model the exclusive OR function (XOR) as they can transform the input from a linearly inseparable space to a space where data can be classified more easily by simpler linear operators. HONN also proved to be a better way to store information (Giles & Maxwell, 1987; Lee et al., 1986; Personnaz, Guyon, & Dreyfus, 1987). HONNs were also successfully applied to financial prediction with an astonishing twofold improvement over ordinary ANNs in some cases (Fulcher, Zhang, & Xu, 2006).

Transforming input data for an ANN often dramatically speeds up training. Even though it increases the parameter count, the transformation helps reduce the ANN model dependence on the hidden layers; at times eliminating them by using outer products or tensor models (Pao, 1989). Selviah & Shawash (2008) (Selviah & Shawash, 2008) introduced the Generalized Correlation HONN that transforms input data by performing a localized correlation operation on the input data vector providing an enhancement in performance. A higher order functional link together with a feed through of the untransformed input data passes signals to the output through a single hidden layer as in equation (1) and Figure 1.

$$\hat{y} = \sum_{ii=1}^{m} W_{2,ii} \times F\left(b_1 + \sum_{i=1}^{n} W_{1,i} \times \begin{bmatrix} X_i \\ H(X_i) \end{bmatrix}\right) + b_2 \tag{1}$$

The higher order function is incorporated into the Neural Network as in Figure 1, where the higher order function is represented by a block resembling the Kronecker operator ($\otimes$). Let $\otimes$ be a higher-order function that produces a covariance matrix with the multiplicative interactions of all networks inputs of the second order which can be expressed by a Kronecker product which produces the Full Cross Product Higher Order Neural Network (FXPHONN).

Figure 1. Higher order neural network

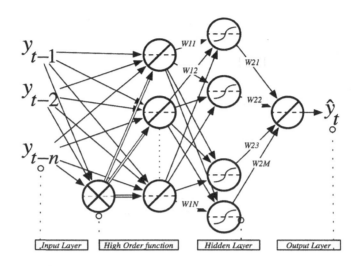

$$H\left(x_{i=1,\ldots,n}\right) = X \otimes X^T = \begin{bmatrix} x_1 \\ x_2 \\ \vdots \\ x_n \end{bmatrix} \times \begin{bmatrix} x_1 & x_2 & \cdots & x_n \end{bmatrix}$$

$$= \begin{bmatrix} x_1 x_1 & x_1 x_2 & \cdots & x_1 x_n \\ x_2 x_1 & x_2 x_2 & \ddots & \vdots \\ \vdots & \ddots & x_3 x_3 & \vdots \\ x_n x_1 & \cdots & \cdots & x_n x_n \end{bmatrix}$$

(2)

$$XPHONN = H_{i,j}, i : 1 \rightarrow n, j : i \rightarrow n$$

(3)

$$CHONN = \sum_{j=1}^{n} \sum_{i=j}^{n} H_{i,j}$$

(4)

We examine two types of HONN in this chapter based on equations (3) and (4).

By examining the characteristics of the resulting matrix $H(x)$, the full cross product (FXPHONN), we can exploit the symmetry in the result of the higher order interactions. The elements of the upper triangular section are selected, amounting to a total of $\dfrac{n+n^2}{2}$ elements of the resulting Kronecker matrix product covariance matrix we refer to as the Cross Products Higher-Order Network (XPHONN). Another type of input transform that leads to a more parsimonious model is the Correlation Higher Order Neural Network (CHONN) (Selviah & Shawash, 2008) which is the sum of the diagonal elements of the covariance matrix giving the inner product terms of the correlation and off-diagonal elements giving the outer product terms of the correlation. This increases the input dimension of the ANN by only n-elements. The significance of the reduction in the number of elements is shown in Figure 2, where it can be observed that the ordinary HONN incurs an exponential increase in the number of parameters

Figure 2. Number of inputs of HONNs compared to 3 layer ANN with 10 hidden neurons

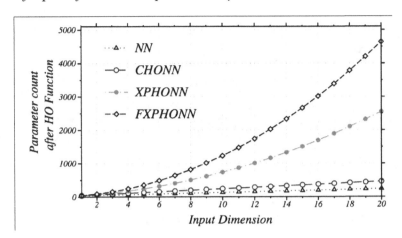

as the number of elements in the input vector increases; however the XPHONN reduces the number of higher order input parameters by half, while the modified CHONN has a linear relationship with increasing number of inputs. Compared to the CHONN at input dimension of 13, the ANN is has 54% less parameters, while the XPHONN and FXPHONN have 379% and 657% more parameters respectively. The representation of CHONN in (4) reduces the training strains associated with the inclusion of HONNs and hidden layers; the reduction of the number of neurons allows for better performance which is reflected in the estimated AIC.

Artificial Neural Network Training Algorithm Review

The training of ANNs aims to find a set of weights that give a global minimum in the error function surface where the optimal performance can be achieved. There are two methods to optimize a function, the deterministic and the probabilistic methods (Lee, 2007). In this study we consider two popular deterministic supervised learning methods (Lee, Choi, & Lee, 2004), the error Back-Propagation and the Levenberg-Marquardt algorithms (Marquardt, 1963; Press, Flannery, Teukolsky, & Vetterling, 1992). Since the error surface may be complex, convex and may have concave regions (Fu, 1994), it is more likely that the network settles into a local minimum than a global one when using a deterministic method.

This problem cannot be completely avoided in the deterministic training methods; however, it can be reduced in a number of ways. Firstly, early stopping (Haykin, 1999); where the data is split into three parts, training, validation and test sample sets; the training set is used to optimize the weights in the network, the validation set is used to stop the training when the validation error becomes less than a certain value with respect to the training error. Secondly, random selection of training, validation and test sets ameliorates the danger of training on data characterized by one set of a local type of data, thus giving a better generalization ability to the network (Kaastra & Boyd, 1996). Thirdly, local minima can be avoided by using randomly selected starting points for the weights being optimized (Masters, 1993), we use the Nguyen-Widrow initialization method (Nguyen & Widrow, 1990). Lastly, over-fitting can also be reduced by removing ANN complexity by reducing the number of elements in the ANN by estimating and selecting the best AIC with respect to lag and layer size. From our study of ANN properties in software, it was recommended to use the smallest network size which provides valid operation. The

Algorithm 1. Back propagation

	while $i <$ Max Iteration	
1.	$Net_{Hidden} = W_1 \times \begin{bmatrix} X_0 \\ 1 \end{bmatrix}$	*Output of first layer*
2.	$X_{Hidden} = f\left(Net_{Hidden}\right)$	*Output after hidden layer activation function*
3.	$Net_{Output} = W_2 \times \begin{bmatrix} X_{Hidden} \\ 1 \end{bmatrix}$	*Network output*
4.	$E = Target - Net_{output}$	*Error in output layer*
5.	$\Delta E_{out} = f'_{Linear}\left(X_{Hidden}\right) \cdot E$	*Output layer weight change according to output error vector*
6.	$\Delta W_2 = \Delta E_{out}$	
7.	$\Delta E_{Hidden} = W_2^T \times \Delta E_{out}$	*en layer weight change according to back propagation algorithm*
8.	$\Delta W_1 = f'_{Logistics}\left(X_{Hidden}\right) \cdot \Delta E_{Hidden}$	
9.	$W_{2_{new}} = a \times W_{2_{old}} + \left(1-a\right) \times \eta \times \Delta W_2 \cdot \begin{bmatrix} X_{Hidden} & 1 \end{bmatrix}^T$	*New hidden-output layer weights*
10.	$W_{1_{new}} = a \times W_{1_{old}} + \left(1-a\right) \times \eta \times \Delta W_1 \cdot \begin{bmatrix} X_0 & 1 \end{bmatrix}^T$	*New input-hidden layer weights*
Check if training conditions are still true, if yes: repeat, otherwise exit training		

same recommendations apply to hardware implementation to achieve the smallest circuit footprint and power efficiency (Marchiori & Warglien, 2008). The two learning methods are summarized in the following algorithms (1) and (2), where the stopping criteria (momentum, learning rates, and maximum training epoch number) are set to values used widely in literature.

3. EXPERIMENTAL METHOD

In order to investigate the effects of reduced precision on the learning process we followed algorithm (3) to convert from floating point operation to fixed point. The floating point learning algorithm is referred to as the Golden Algorithm and is used as the benchmark for comparing the effect of reduced precision ranging from 4 to 28 bits fixed-point representation (Zarrinkoub, 2006).

Data quantizers are used that transform the data into the limited precision domain by rounding and truncation in a manner similar to that of digital circuits. Quantizers were used before and after every operation presented in the network operation and learning modes (Algorithms 1 and 2). The precision of the quantizers were varied depending on the section and data path in the network operation and learning modes.

The best network structure was found in software using Matlab Neural Network Toolbox ver.6. The best structure was selected according to the AIC information criterion, where this parameter selects simplest and best performing ANN. Matlab, with the fixed-point toolbox ver.6, was chosen as the development environment. It allows for efficient prototyping and it provides the ability to incorporate fixed-point

Algorithm 2. Levenberg-Marquardt learning

	while $i <$ Max Iteration	
1.	$Net_{Hidden} = W_1 \times \begin{bmatrix} X_0 \\ 1 \end{bmatrix}$	*Output of first layer*
2.	$X_{Hidden} = f\left(Net_{Hidden}\right)$	*Output after hidden layer activation function*
3.	$Net_{Output} = W_2 \times \begin{bmatrix} X_{Hidden} \\ 1 \end{bmatrix}$	*Network output*
4.	$E = Target - Net_{output}$	*Error in output layer*
5.	$\theta = \begin{bmatrix} W_2 \\ W_1 \end{bmatrix}$	*Vector containing all weights and biases*
6.	$J\left(\theta\right) = \begin{bmatrix} f'_{Linear}\left(X_{Hidden}\right) \\ W_2 \times f'_{Logistics}\left(X_{Hidden}\right) \end{bmatrix}$	*Jacobian matrix*
7.	$\nabla J = J \times E$	*Error gradient*
8.	$H = J^T J$	*Hessian Matrix*
9.	$H = H + \lambda \times diag\left(H\right)$	*Updating Hessian matrix according to lambda*
10.	$\Delta\theta = H^{-1} \times \nabla J$	*Weight change according to LM*
11.	$\theta_{new} = \theta_{old} + \Delta\theta$	*New weight vector*
12.	$W_{2_{new}} = W_{2_{old}} + \theta_{new}\left(W_2\right)$	*New output layer weight matrix*
13.	$W_{1_{new}} = W_{1_{old}} + \theta_{new}\left(W_1\right)$	*New hidden layer weight matrix*
14.	*Updating* λ	
15.	$L = \Delta\theta^T \nabla J + \Delta\theta^T \Delta\theta\lambda_{old}$	*Calculating update conditions*
16.	$\lambda = \begin{Bmatrix} \lambda/2 & if & 2N\left(MSE - MSE_{new}\right) > 0.75L \\ 2\lambda & if & 2N\left(MSE - MSE_{new}\right) \le 0.25L \end{Bmatrix}$	*New lambda*
	Check if training conditions are still true, if yes: repeat, otherwise exit training	

Algorithm 3. Floating-point to fixed-point conversion workflow

1.	<u>*Golden Algorithm*</u> Our Reference Design which we seek to implement in hardware
2.	<u>*Floating Point Design Verification*</u> We need to validate our design before we continue with the conversion to hardware language
3.	<u>*Simulation of algorithm tradeoffs*</u> Explore design tradeoffs of functions that are impractical to implement in hardware
4.	<u>*Conversion to fixed-point*</u> Exploring a software implementation of fixed-point algorithmic behavior
5.	<u>*Simulation of fixed-point implementation tradeoffs*</u> Examine tradeoffs of word length variation, pipelining and loop unrolling if possible
6.	<u>*Generation of hardware code*</u> Automatic hardware code generation
7.	<u>*Validation and verification of design deployed on hardware*</u> Verification by analyzing test-bench performance

Box 1.

Sign bit	Range/Magnitude						.	Fraction/Resolution					
S	2^n	...	2^4	2^3	2^2	2^1	2^0 .	2^{-1}	2^{-2}	2^{-3}	2^{-4}	...	2^{-m}
Q			R				.			F			

functionality in signal processing algorithms with further functionality that can produce device specific targeted codes that can be ported onto a hardware circuit at a later stage for direct hardware implementation (Bhatt & McCain, 2005; Ou & Prasanna, 2004; Ou & Prasanna, 2005; Xilinx, 2008).

Fixed-Point Number Representation

Fixed point numbers are specified with a sign, range, and precision with a labeling convention $Q(R.F)$, where Q indicates whether the fixed-point number is signed, R shows the number of Binary Digits (bits) available in the integer bits, and F indicates the number of fractional bits.

The diagram above is an expansion of the $Q(R.F)$ format, where the R bits specify the maximum magnitude that the number can take, in powers of two while the F bit length specify the maximum accuracy which the number can have. Fixed-point numbers can reach 64 bits as in floating-point numbers, but the main difference is that when the mantissa is set, the location the fraction point indicates how many bits are assigned to R and F, and it cannot be changed dynamically, if not set correctly leading to overflow and underflow of number representation. $Q = R + F + 1$ *as* Q includes R, F, and a sign bit. Overflow occurs when dealing with numbers exceeding the allowable range in Q leading to serious problems in calculations. Underflow occurs from operations resulting in a value that is smaller than the smallest quantity which Q can represent.

For example if we want to represent the decimal signed number 2.65 in $Q(3.4)$, signed binary format, it would be [0010.1100]. However, if we want to represent the number 0.6 in 16 bit binary $Q(0.15)$ is 0.100110011001101 or 0.599969482 when converted back to decimal; this shows the effect of limiting the precision of fixed-point number representation resulting in a deviation from the original value with no ability to recover the original value, this referred to as underflow.

In the simulations in the next section, at low precision the fraction length can take negative values. For example, if we have a precision, Q of 4 bits, 1 sign bit, 4 Range bits, and -1 fraction bits $Q(4,-1)$.

This means that the number can take values with range $[-2^5, 2^5-2^1]$ with a resolution of 2^1.

A major drawback of limited precision operation is due to the multiply and accumulate (MAC) operations which form DSP algorithms. The multiplication and addition operations lead to a loss in numerical information if we do not allow for an increase in the precision of the fixed-point result of the MAC operation. For example, when multiplying two matrices of sizes *n*-by-*m* by *m*-by-*p*, it is required to process $n \times m \times p$ multiplication operations and $n \times m \times (m-1)$ additions (Press et al., 1992). When adding two fixed-point numbers, $Q_1(R.F)+Q_2(R.F)=Q_{res}(R+1.F)$, the result should accommodate another bit in its range to avoid overflows, having a penalty of increasing the precision by 1 bit per addition operation. While the multiplication of fixed-point numbers is as follows $Q_1(R.F)*Q_2(R.F)=Q_{res}(R_1+R_2+1.F_1+F_2)$, where the precision is doubled + 1.

This shows that the basic mathematical operations such as matrix multiplication, which occur at various stages in ANN operation, induce a loss of valuable information due to overflow when reducing the precision of such operations, thus, reducing the chance of reaching the optimal operational state of the network.

Learning Algorithms in Reduced Precision

In order to convert the learning algorithms into fixed-point, we need to find the correct quantizer levels $Q(R,F)$, by calculating the maximum/minimum levels that the floating-point algorithm reaches and we find these values by specifying a certain precision. This process is shown in algorithm (4).

4. SIMULATIONS

This section describes the way the simulations were structured in order to show the effect of reduced precision on network training algorithms. Matlab was used as our floating algorithm development environment and the fixed-point toolbox was used to convert the learning algorithms into fixed-point (reduced precision). The conversion from floating-point to fixed-point was applied to two learning algorithms BP, and LM. These two algorithms were implemented with precisions ranging from 4 to 28 bits and tested on two data sets: the XOR function and waveguide wall roughness measurements. These two functions were chosen as the data sets under consideration due to several factors; the XOR has discrete levels and the wall roughness is almost continuous, so they require different levels of quantization in order to operate and learn and both data sets are used in electronic engineering applications.

Algorithm 4. Finding quantizers that allow for the conversion from floating to fixed-point

1.	*Parameter Range Estimation* Recording the minimum and maximum value a parameter takes during the operation and learning phases in floating-point
2.	*Compute the maximum range the parameter takes* Range = ceil(log₂(Parameter)+1) *Ceil* is function that maps a number to the next largest integer.
3.	*Compute Fraction bits* Since Q = R+F+1, Fraction length = Q - R -1
4.	*Construct quantizers* Quantizers take the form of signed fixed-point numbers with *Range* and *Fractions* as defined in the previous two steps
5.	*Quantization of the data operation* Use the quantizers the limit to data operations to the fixed-point data type

Table 1. XOR function

A	0	1	0	1
B	0	0	1	1
C	0	1	1	0

Exclusive OR (XOR)

The XOR function was chosen as a demonstration as it is one of the functions that cannot be solved by linear models, ANNs without a hidden layer, or a single layer first order ANN. XOR input samples were generated by using a threshold function for 1000 values from a uniformly distributed pseudorandom number generator. The threshold function had a threshold level of 0.5.

During the Fixed-point training and operation data was split into two parts, training and testing. The networks structures were selected to (*IN-Hidden-Output*) where *IN*, the input dimension, depending on the estimation model used, the hidden layer has 4 neurons, and output dimension of 1.

The following table shows the maximum range which the data paths used during training with BP and LM displayed in different columns for clarity. The multiply and accumulate are given in algorithms (1) and (2) for these parameters. The table shows the minimum number of bits to take the maximum range into account, in order to prevent the algorithm from overflowing. Underflow is not considered in the table as some numbers require an infinite precision to represent, however underflow is reduced by increasing the overall precision.

Optical Waveguide Sidewall Roughness Estimation

There is a need to estimate the sidewall nano-roughness of multimode rectangular core optical waveguides for high bit rate short distance interconnects, as only small a region of the waveguide sidewall can be measured with an atomic force microscope (AFM) so estimation enables a larger region to be synthesized for modeling. Modeling allows us to investigate the coupling between bound modes and between bound and radiation modes which affect the equilibrium modal power distribution, cross-talk and loss (Papakonstantinou, James, & Selviah, 2009; Papakonstantinou, Selviah, Pitwon, & Milward, 2008).

Figure 3 (a) shows the first experimentally measured data of polymer optical waveguide sidewall roughness consisting of 10,000 samples taken every 20 nm. The data is non-stationary making it difficult for networks to model. Figure 3 (c) shows the histogram of the roughness measurements scaled by its standard deviation in order to compare it to the histogram in Figure 3 (d). Figure 3 (b) shows roughness measurements transformed into a stationary form by caluclating the differences of the logarithms of the non-stationary signal for adjacent points (Chatfield, 1989).

$$y_s = 100 \times \left[\log \left(y_{ns} \right) - \log \left(y_{ns-1} \right) \right] \tag{5}$$

Where, y_s is the stationary transformation of the non-stationary data represented by y_{ns}. This transformation operation is non-destructive, as no information is lost during this conversion, so the data can be converted back into the original non-stationary form when required. This transformation converts

Figure 3. (a) Waveguide sidewall roughness measurements with an accuracy of 6 significant figures. (b) Stationary transformed waveguide sidewall roughness. (c) Probability distribution function (PDF) of waveguide sidewall roughness. (d) PDF of stationary waveguide wall roughness

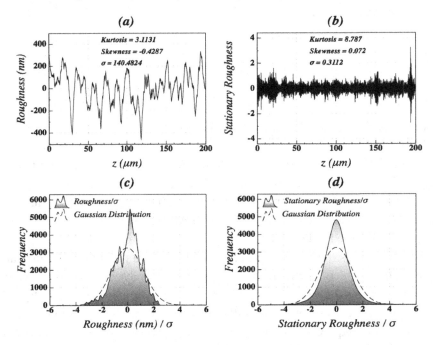

multiplicative (ratio) relationships in the data to simpler add (subtract) operations that simplify and improve network training (Masters, 1993). Haykin (Haykin, 1999) mentions that ANNs alone are insufficient to capture the dynamics of non-stationary systems. However, non-destructive data transformations can transform the data to a stationary form, thus alleviating this problem.

Figure 3 (c) and (d) show two PDFs of the non-stationary and stationary data with a common Gaussian distribution fit to the non-stationary data in both the figures to emphasize the effect of the data transformation and the way it converts the distribution of the non-stationary data into a form more similar to a Gaussian distribution.

We simulated various networks estimating wall roughness in software first to find the best for hardware implementation. All models were simulated with input dimension ranging from 1 to 9 input units, and hidden layers having 1 to 8 hidden neurons. To our knowledge there is no specific convention for choosing the correct ANN structure for use in limited precision, so we used the procedure given in Algorithm 4) choosing the best network models in software and converting these models into a format suitable for limited precision hardware.

Comparing Table 2 with Table 3, the ranges of the various stages have increased due to the nature of the roughness data set taking values close to a continuous function with a Gaussian distribution, while the XOR data had discrete values of 0 and 1.

Table 2. Minimum parameter range during training of the XOR function neural network models using two learning algorithms with three network types

Range	BP			Range	LM		
	ANN	CHONN	XPHONN		ANN	CHONN	XPHONN
X_0	1	1	1	X_0	1	1	1
W_1	2	2	2	W_1	3	2	2
W_2	2	2	1	W_2	2	1	2
Net_{Hidden}	3	2	3	Net_{Hidden}	4	1	4
X_{Hidden}	1	1	1	X_{Hidden}	1	1	1
Net_{Output}	2	2	1	Net_{Output}	1	1	1
δW_1	1	1	1	E	2	1	1
δW_2	2	2	1	J	1	1	1
ΔW_1	1	1	1	H	7	6	7
ΔW_2	2	2	1	∇J	5	4	4
				$\Delta\theta$	2	2	1

Figure-of-Merit Evaluation Criteria

The error provides a measure that reflects how much the operation of the network deviates from the ideal target performance. In the following equation, E is the error vector on a sample-by-sample basis, *n*, where *target* is the data we want to estimate and $\hat{y}$ is the output of ANN operation.

$$E_n = target_n - \hat{y}_n \tag{6}$$

The Mean Square Error (MSE) indicates the overall deviation in the following equation. N is the total number of samples under consideration.

$$MSE = \frac{1}{N}\sum_{n=1}^{N} E_n^2 \tag{7}$$

Even though the MSE shows the deviation of the ANN performance from the desired solution, it does not take into account the number of parameters that were used to reach the solution. So the AIC, (10), uses a function of the error vector called the log-likelihood function, (9), and the total number of weights represented by k, σ is the standard deviation of the error vector. In (10) an increase in k induces an increase/penalty in AIC. The main principle being that we need to make the network as simple as possible to provide better generalization ability (Haykin, 1999).

Table 3. Minimum parameter range during training for the estimation of waveguide sidewall roughness using two learning algorithms with three network types

	BP				LM		
Range	ANN	CHONN	XPHONN	Range	ANN	CHONN	XPHONN
X_0	3	4	4	X_0	3	4	4
W_1	2	2	2	W_1	3	3	3
W_2	2	2	1	W_2	*9*	*7*	*8*
Net_{Hidden}	*3*	*4*	*5*	Net_{Hidden}	2	2	2
X_{Hidden}	1	1	1	X_{Hidden}	1	1	1
Net_{Output}	2	2	2	Net_{Output}	1	1	1
δW_1	2	2	2	E	1	2	1
δW_2	2	3	3	J	4	5	4
ΔW_1	*2*	*4*	*4*	H	*21*	*22*	*19*
ΔW_2	2	3	3	∇J	*12*	*13*	*12*
				$\Delta\theta$	3	2	2

$$LLF = \frac{1}{2}\sum_{n=1}^{N}\left(\log\left(2\pi\sigma^2\right) + \frac{E_n^2}{\sigma^2}\right) \qquad (8)$$

$$AIC\left(k\right) = \frac{LLF}{N} + \frac{k}{N} \qquad (9)$$

The AIC was formulated for linear models. When applied to ANN estimation it showed inconsistencies in the search for optimum lag/input dimension (Oliveira & Meira, 2006). In order to distinguish the better performing models we use the *LLF* to select the model with better performance and *AIC* to take into account the penalty when increasing the number of parameters. We also use the Root Mean Square Error (RMSE) and Hit Rate (HR).

$$RMSE = \sqrt{\frac{1}{N}\sum_{n=1}^{N}E^2} \qquad (10)$$

The HR is useful when we want to see whether the directional changes of the predicted signal are similar to the directional changes of the target data under consideration.

$$HR = \frac{1}{N}\sum_{n=1}^{N}D_n$$
Where,
$$D_n = \begin{cases} 1 & , \quad \left(\hat{y} - y_{n-1}\right)\left(y_n - y_{n-1}\right) \\ 0 & , \qquad otherwise \end{cases} \qquad (11)$$

Table 4. XOR BP floating point estimation results of log-likelihood function (LLF) and Akaike Information Criteria (AIC) and the Root Mean Squared Error (RMSE) lower values indicate better performance

	LLF	AIC	RMSE
CHONN	**-8897.85423**	**-17.7657085**	**4.51E-09**
XPHONN	-7915.16279	-15.8043256	3.23E-08
ANN	-6737.17429	-13.4563486	3.40E-07
Linear	73.9634	0.7696	0.7083

5. XOR MODELING RESULTS

Table 4 shows the Linear and network evaluation criteria when BP training is preformed in floating point. The best performing models are in bold font. CHONN has the best LLF and AIC criteria. All networks models converge to a solution; the linear model is unable to capture the solution for the non-linear XOR function as expected.

Figure 4 shows the RMSE versus the number of BP training epochs for several levels of precision, Q for 3 networks. The best performing networks have lowest RMSE and are fastest in reaching this lowest error. ANN-BP convergence in Figure 4 (a) is very slow compared to graphs CHONN-BP convergence in (b) and XPHONN-BP convergence in (c). The CHONN-BP in graph (b) has the fastest initial convergence rate (epochs 3-30) compared to the other two networks with the same training method. Both CHONN and XPHONN convergence rates increase in later epochs. Based on these graphs inFigure 4, the new network CHONN is best for modeling the XOR when BP training in limited precision.

Figure 5. LM training error for several levels of precision, Q for XOR modeling

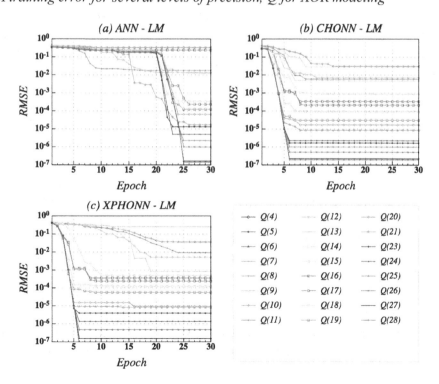

Figure 6. Networks output error after 55 epochs as a function of level of precision, Q for XOR modeling

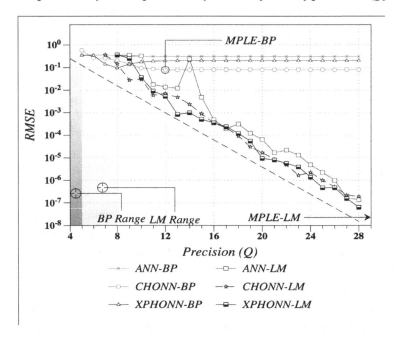

Figure 5 (a), (b), and (c) show that all networks reach lower RMSE values in a smaller number of epochs with the LM learning algorithm rather than the BP learning algorithm. In figures 5 (b) and (c) the HONNs converge after epoch 6 to high precision values (low RMSE), while ANNs require at least 23 epochs to achieve the same precision, incurring an almost 4 fold increase in convergence time. Higher levels of precision give progressively lower errors as seen in Figure 5.

The RMSE in the LM learning algorithm falls to very low values such as 10^{-7} due to the fixed-point nature of the number representation having two discrete levels at 0 or 1. As networks converge to the optimal solution, the values making up the error vector are rounded and truncated to 0, whereas the same parameters would leave small residuals in the error vector if operated in floating point. RMSE values lower than 10^{-6} can be considered as converged or optimal solutions with no need for further enhancement, as most learning algorithms use 10^{-6} as a training stopping criterion. The best choice for XOR modeling in reduced precision is either CHONN or XPHONN with LM training.

Figure 6 shows the RMSE for all networks for both learning algorithms as a function of precision level, Q after 55 epochs. The two shaded regions to the left of the figure indicate the region in which the minimum ranges shown in bold font in Table 2 make some of the quantizers operate with a fraction with negative power, i.e. shifting the fraction point to the left, leading to more severe levels of underflow. The CHONN gave the best error performance for BP training with the XPHONN second and the ANN worst. The CHONN and XPHONN vie for the lowest RMSE after LM training.

In BP learning, beyond a certain level of precision, increases in precision no longer lead to increases in RMSE. We refer to the point at which RMSE stops improving as the "Minimum Precision for Lowest Error" (MPLE). Setting the precision to the MPLE avoids increases in the design complexity and circuit size minimizing the overall latency. The MPLE for the XOR function under BP training is 12 bits. A further study needs to be done in order to determine the MPLE for LM training for XOR modeling, as the RMSE had not reached its floor before reaching the maximum precision of this study.

Table 5. Roughness LM trained floating point estimation results Log-likelihood function (LLF), Akaike Information Criteria (AIC), Root Mean Square Error (RMSE), lower values are better, Hit Rate (HR) -higher values are better

	LLF	AIC	RMSE	HR
CHONN	*-1923.5642*	*-0.1905*	0.019425	77.796
ANN	-1906.1974	-0.1896	0.019559	*77.802*
XPHONN	-1853.6991	-0.1799	**0.018712**	77.161

6. OPTICAL WAVEGUIDE SIDEWALL ROUGHNESS ESTIMATION RESULTS

This section presents the results of operating and training networks with an input dimension of 9, 1 hidden layer with 1 hidden node, estimating the next sample of the wall roughness. Floating point results are first presented followed by fixed-point simulations of the learning algorithms at different precisions. Table 5 shows that the CHONN is a better estimator than the ANN and XPHONN in floating point as indicated by bold italic format. Although XPHONN has better RMSE levels the other networks, best models are selected using the AIC criterion as mentioned previously.

Figure 7 shows that all of the algorithms reach the optimum performance after 30 epochs. ANN-BP Figure 7 (a) convergences faster than the CHONN and XPHONN in Figure 7 (b) and (c) respectively. HONN operations require higher precision in order to achieve similar performance levels to the ANN,

Figure 7. BP training error at several levels of precision, Q for estimating optical waveguide sidewall roughness

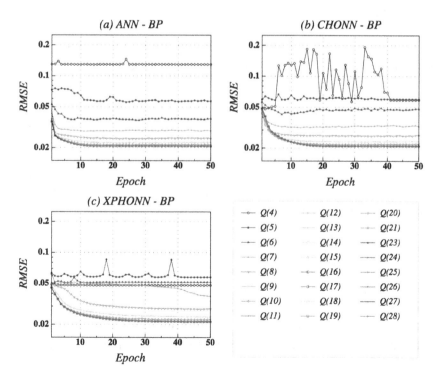

Figure 8. LM training error for several precisions, Q for estimating optical waveguide sidewall rough-ness

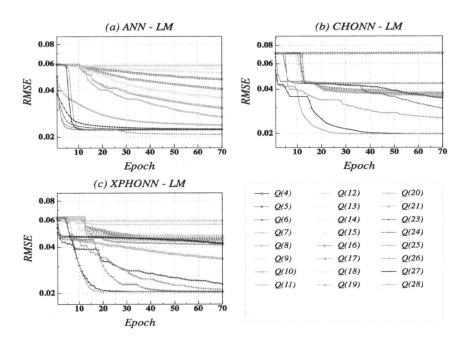

see Table 3. At epoch 10, the ANN is best for lowest RMSE then CHONN with the XPHONN having the worst error.

Figure 8 shows the LM training convergence curves for ANN in Figure 8 (a), CHONN in Figure 8 (b), and XPHONN in Figure 8 (c). After 10 epochs the ANN model had the fastest convergence compared to HONNs. The minimum range indicated in bold font in Table 3 leads to loss in fraction size due to higher range of high order interactions which in turn required higher precision to reach the optimum performance, these interactions led to information loss after MAC operations. CHONN and XPHONN models showed better performance in floating point.

Comparing graphs Figure 8 (b) and (c) the convergence of the CHONN is slower for the lowest RMSE than that of the XPHONN, due to the facts mentioned in the previous paragraph. As mentioned in section *Fixed-point number representation* the multiplication operation doubles the required precision and the range bits required an increase with every addition operation required by the CHONN.

Figure 9 shows the performance of all networks for both learning algorithms as a function of precision level for the waveguide sidewall roughness estimation. Figure 9 has two shaded regions that indicate the minimum required ranges as in Table 3. As in Figure 8, the effect of the HONN function leads to a deterioration of the estimating models for both learning algorithms less than a certain precision. The deviation between the HONNs and ANN performance almost disappears for precisions higher than 11 bits for BP training whereas the discrepancies increased for LM training as the number of MAC operations required by the algorithm increased. In the case of BP learning for more than 12 bits of precision the RMSE does not change so, MPLE-BP = 12 bits. The LM algorithm starts to converge to an optimal solution after 23 bit precision, having the best performance at 28 bits, so MPLE-LM > 28 bits. The dashed-and-dotted line in Figure 9 shows the performance in floating point RMSE = 0.0194. The fixed-

Figure 9. Output error after 70 epochs of BP and LM Training for several levels of precision for estimating optical waveguide sidewall roughness

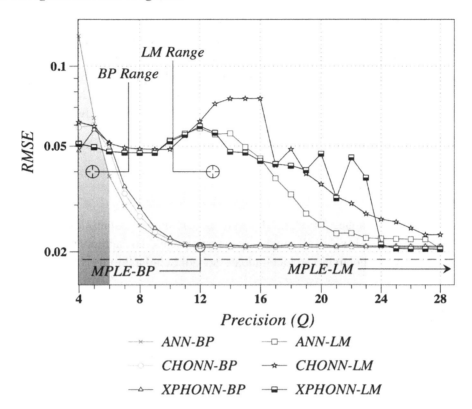

point RMSE reaches a minimum of 0.0204 when training the XPHONN using LM. The BP algorithm converges to a value that is always 0.0015 higher than the floating-point RMSE.

7. DISCUSSION AND CONCLUSION

Simulations were conducted to find the effect of a limited precision environment on learning algorithms used to train ANNs and HONNs. It was found that the learning algorithms required less precision when training on discrete data due to the limited levels this data takes and they required higher precision when dealing with almost-continuous functions. The BP algorithm reaches the "Minimum Precision for Lowest Error" (MPLE) at 12 bits for both the discrete and continuous functions under consideration, being the XOR function and optical waveguide sidewall roughness. The LM algorithm provided a significant enhancement to the discrete function modeling without requiring many range bits due to the discrete nature of the MAC operation it requires; however, the LM training algorithm required a significant increase in the precision in order to accommodate for the expansion of MAC operations within the learning algorithm. The MPLE for the LM algorithm was not established as greater precision levels greater than 28 are needed for it to reach its error floor. The minimum precision for minimum error was required to be 24 bits so only the 4 highest precisions could be studied.

The results of this study expand and support the findings of Piche and Stevenson (Piche, 1995; Stevenson et al., 1990) where it was shown that discrete functions require less precision than continuous functions during network operation and indicate a precision level MPLE beyond which no performance gain is achieved. This measure allows the hardware designer to make an efficient design in the least area possible enabling the hardware to reach the highest operational frequency at lowest power.

The study was made possible by using advanced high level languages such as Matlab ver.7.4 and Xilinx ISE ver.10 giving fast development time and model exploration with a high level of abstraction in algorithmic blocks for circuit and signal track operations on electronic hardware (Bhatt et al., 2005; Xilinx, 2008; Zarrinkoub, 2006).

8. ACKNOWLEDGMENT

The authors thank their colleagues for useful discussions, Dr I Papakonstantinou (UCL & CERN) for providing the optical waveguide sidewall roughness measurements. The authors thank UCL for funding via an Overseas Research Scholarship and a Graduate School Scholarship for J Shawash.

REFERENCES

Bhatt, T. M., & McCain, D. (2005). Matlab as a development environment for FPGA design. In *Proceedings of 42nd Design Automation Conference* (pp. 607-610).

Chatfield, C. (1989). *The Analysis of Time Series - An Introduction.* (4th ed.) London: Chapman & Hall.

Dias, F. M., Antunes, A., Vieira, J., & Mota, A. (2006). A sliding window solution for the on-line implementation of the Levenberg-Marquardt algorithm. *Engineering Applications of Artificial Intelligence, 19,* 1–7. doi:10.1016/j.engappai.2005.03.005

Fu, L. (1994). *Neural Networks in Computer Intelligence.* New York: McGraw-Hill.

Fulcher, J., Zhang, M., & Xu, S. (2006). Application of Higher-Order Neural Networks to Financial Time-Series Prediction. In *Artificial Neural Networks in Finance and Manufacturing* (pp. 80-108). Hershey, PA: Idea Group Publishing.

Giles, C. L., & Maxwell, T. (1987). Learning, Invariance, and Generalization in High-Order Neural Networks. *Applied Optics, 26*(23), 4972–4978. doi:10.1364/AO.26.004972

Haykin, S. (1999). *Neural Networks: A Comprehensive Foundation.* (2th ed.) New York: Prentice Hall.

Huang, W., Wang, S. Y., Yu, L., Bao, Y. K., & Wang, L. (2006). A new computational method of input selection for stock market forecasting with neural networks. In *Proceedings of Computational Science - ICCS 2006, Pt 4, 3994,* (308-315).

Jung, S., & Kim, S. S. (2007). Hardware implementation of a real-time neural network controller with a DSP and an FPGA for nonlinear systems. *IEEE Transactions on Industrial Electronics, 54*(1), 265–271. doi:10.1109/TIE.2006.888791

Kaastra, I., & Boyd, M. (1996). Designing a neural network for forecasting financial and economic time series. *Neurocomputing, 10*, 215–236. doi:10.1016/0925-2312(95)00039-9

Lee, D. W., Choi, H. J., & Lee, J. (2004). A regularized line search tunneling for efficient neural network learning. *Advances in Neural Networks - ISNN 2004, Pt 1, 3173*, (239-243).

Lee, J. (2007). A novel three-phase trajectory informed search methodology for global optimization. *Journal of Global Optimization, 38*, 61–77. doi:10.1007/s10898-006-9083-3

Lee, Y. C., Doolen, G., Chen, H. H., Sun, G. Z., Maxwell, T., & Lee, H. Y. (1986). Machine Learning using a Higher-Order Correlation Network. *Physica D. Nonlinear Phenomena, 22*(1-3), 276–306.

Lopez-Garcia, J. C., Moreno-Armendariz, M. A., Riera-Babures, J., Balsi, M., & Vilasis-Cardona, X. (2005). Real time vision by FPGA implemented CNNs. In *European Conference on Circuit Theory and Design* (pp. 281-284).

Maguire, L. P., McGinnity, T. M., Glackin, B., Ghani, A., Belatreche, A., & Harkin, J. (2007). Challenges for large-scale implementations of spiking neural networks on FPGAs. *Neurocomputing, 71*(1-3), 13–29. doi:10.1016/j.neucom.2006.11.029

Marchiori, D., & Warglien, M. (2008). Predicting human interactive learning by regret-driven neural networks. *Science, 319*, 1111–1113. doi:10.1126/science.1151185

Marquardt, D. W. (1963). An Algorithm for Least-Squares Estimation of Nonlinear Parameters. *Journal of the Society for Industrial and Applied Mathematics, 11*(2), 431–441. doi:10.1137/0111030

Masters, T. (1993). *Practical Neural Network Recipies in C++.* (1th ed.) New York: Morgan Kaufmann.

Nguyen, D., & Widrow, B. (1990). Improving the Learning Speed of 2-Layer Neural Networks by Choosing Initial Values of the Adaptive Weights. *IJCNN International Joint Conference on Neural Networks, 1-3*, C21-C26.

Oliveira, A. L. I., & Meira, S. R. L. (2006). Detecting novelties in time series through neural networks forecasting with robust confidence intervals. *Neurocomputing, 70*, 79–92. doi:10.1016/j.neucom.2006.05.008

Ou, J. Z., & Prasanna, V. K. (2004). PyGen: A MATLAB/Simulink based tool for synthesizing parameterized and energy efficient designs using FPGAs. In *FCCM'04 12th Annual IEEE Symposium on Field-Programmable Custom Computing Machines* (pp. 47-56).

Ou, J. Z., & Prasanna, V. K. (2005). MATLAB/Simulink Based Hardware/Software Co-Simulation for Designing Using FPGA Configured Soft Processors. In *Parallel and Distributed Processing Symposium* (pp. 148b).

Pao, Y. H. (1989). *Adaptive Pattern Recognition and Neural Networks.* Boston, MA:Addison Wesley.

Papakonstantinou, I., James, R., & Selviah, D. R. (2009). Radiation and Bound Mode Propagation in Rectangular Multimode Dielectric Channel Waveguides with Sidewall Roughness. *IEEE/OSA . Journal of Lightwave Technology, 27*(18), 4151–4163. doi:10.1109/JLT.2009.2022766

Papakonstantinou, I., Selviah, D. R., Pitwon, R. C. A., & Milward, D. (2008). Low-Cost, Precision, Self-Alignment Technique for Coupling Laser and Photodiode Arrays to Polymer Waveguide Arrays on Multilayer PCBs. *IEEE Transactions on Advanced Packaging, 31*(3), 502–511. doi:10.1109/TADVP.2008.924243

Personnaz, L., Guyon, I., & Dreyfus, G. (1987). High-Order Neural Networks: Information Storage without Errors. *Europhysics Letters, 4*, 863–867. doi:10.1209/0295-5075/4/8/001

Piche, S. W. (1995). The Selection of Weight Accuracies for Madalines. *IEEE Transactions on Neural Networks, 6*, 432–445. doi:10.1109/72.363478

Press, W. H., Flannery, B. P., Teukolsky, S. A., & Vetterling, W. T. (1992). *Numerical Recipes in C: The Art of Scientific Computing*. Cambridge, UK: Cambridge University Press.

Sahin, S., Becerikli, Y., & Yazici, S. (2006). Neural network implementation in hardware using FPGAs. In *NIP, Neural Information Processing* (pp. 1105-1112). Berlin: Springer Verlag.

Selviah, D. R., & Shawash, J. (2008). Generalized Correlation Higher Order Neural Networks for Financial Time Series Prediction. In M.Zhang (Ed.), *Artificial Higher Order Neural Networks for Artificial Higher Order Neural Networks for Economics and Business* (pp. 212-249). Hershey, PA: IGI Global.

Smith, M. (1993). *Neural Networks for Statistical Modeling*. New York: Van Nostrand Reinhold.

Stevenson, M., Winter, R., & Widrow, B. (1990). Sensitivity of feedforward neural networks to weight errors. *IEEE Transactions on Neural Networks, 1*(1), 71–80. doi:10.1109/72.80206

Walczak, S. (2001). An empirical analysis of data requirements for financial forecasting with neural networks. *Journal of Management Information Systems, 17*, 203–222.

Walczak, S., & Cerpa, N. (1999). Heuristic principles for the design of artificial neural networks. *Information and Software Technology, 41*, 107–117. doi:10.1016/S0950-5849(98)00116-5

Xilinx (2008). AccelDSP Synthesis Tool. Retrieved June, 2008, fromhttp://www.xilinx.com/tools/dsp.htm

Zarrinkoub, H. (2006). Fixed-point Signal Processing with Matlab and Simulink. www.mathworks.com, Retrieved May 25, 2008, from http://www.mathworks.com/webex/recordings/fixedpt_042006/fixedpt_042006.html

Zhu, J. H., & Sutton, P. (2003). FPGA implementations of neural networks - A survey of a decade of progress. In *Field-Programmable Logic and Applications* (pp. 1062-1066). Berlin/Heidelberg: Springer.

Chapter 15
Recurrent Higher Order Neural Observers for Anaerobic Processes

Edgar N. Sanchez
CINVESTAV, Unidad Guadalajara, Mexico

Diana A. Urrego
CINVESTAV, Unidad Guadalajara, Mexico

Alma Y. Alanis
Universidad de Guadalajara, Mexico

Salvador Carlos-Hernandez
CINVESTAV, Unidad Saltillo, México

ABSTRACT

In this chapter we propose the design of a discrete-time neural observer which requires no prior knowledge of the model of an anaerobic process, for estimate biomass, substrate and inorganic carbon which are variables difficult to measure and very important for anaerobic process control in a completely stirred tank reactor (CSTR) with biomass filter; this observer is based on a recurrent higher order neural network, trained with an extended Kalman filter based algorithm.

INTRODUCTION

Anaerobic digestion is a bioprocess developed in oxygen absence by different populations of bacteria; these micro-organisms degrade progressively complex organic molecules. One of the most important applications of this process is the wastewater treatment, and it is very efficient to treat substrates with high organic load; besides the treated water, this process produces biogas, which is mainly composed of methane and carbon dioxide and it is considered as an alternative energy. However, anaerobic digestion process is very sensitive to changes on operating conditions and parameters, such as hydraulic and organic overloads, pH, temperature, etc. Then, control strategies are required in order to guarantee an

DOI: 10.4018/978-1-61520-711-4.ch015

adequate operation of the process. Moreover, methane production, biomass growth and substrate degradation are good indicators of biological activity inside the reactor. These variables can be used for monitoring the process and to design control strategies. Some biogas sensors have been developed in order to measure methane production in bioprocesses. However, substrate and biomass measures are more restrictive. The existing biomass sensors are quite expensive, are designed from biological viewpoint and then, they are not reliable for control purposes. Besides, substrate measure is done off-line by chemical analysis and it requires at least two hours. Then, state observers are an interesting alternative in order to deal with this problematic. This chapter deals with the neural estimation of variables hard to measure in anaerobic process.

Nowadays, artificial neural networks are a useful tool for modelling, identification, state estimation and control of a wide variety of processes. Feedforward *neural networks* are a good option for simple dynamics; however, for complex nonlinear systems, higher order recurrent neural networks (RHONN) are a better alternative due to their excellent approximation capabilities, requiring fewer units (Rovithakis & Christodoulou, 2000). These kind of neural networks, compared to the first order ones, are more flexible and robust when faced with new and or noisy data patterns (Ghosh & Shin, 1992). Besides RHONN performed better than the multilayer first order ones using a small number of free parameters (Ghazali, Hussain & Merabti, 2006; Rovithakis & Christodoulou, 2000). Furthermore, different authors have demonstrated the feasibility and the advantages of using these architectures in applications for system identification and control (Ge, Zhang & Lee, 2004; Narendra & Parthasarathy, 1990; Rovithakis & Christodoulou, 2000; Sanchez & Ricalde, 2003; Yu & Li, 2004).

The best known training approach for recurrent neural networks (RNN) is the back propagation through time learning (Williams & Zipser, 1989). However, it is a first order gradient descent method and hence its learning speed could be very slow (Leunga & Chan, 2003). Recently, the *extended Kalman filter (EKF) based algorithms* has been introduced to train neural networks (Feldkamp, Prokhorov & Feldkamp, 2003), in order to improve the learning convergence (Leunga & Chan, 2003). The EKF training for neural networks, both feedforward and recurrent ones, has proven to be reliable and practical in many applications over the past fifteen years (Feldkamp, Prokhorov & Feldkamp, 2003; Haykin, 2001; Leunga & Chan, 2003; Williams & Zipser, 1989; Yu & Li, 2004).

On the other hand, many of the nonlinear control publications assume complete accessibility for the system state; this is not always possible (Poznyak, Sanchez & Yu, 2001). For this reason, nonlinear state estimation is a very important topic for nonlinear control (Poznyak, Sanchez & Yu, 2001). State estimation has been studied by many authors, who have obtained interesting results in different directions. Most of those results need the use of a special nonlinear transformation (Nicosia & Tornambe, 1989) or a linearization technique (Grover & Hwang, 1992; Krener & Isidori, 1983). Such approaches can be considered as a relatively simple method to construct nonlinear observers; however, they do not consider uncertainties (Li & Zhong, 2005; Liu, Wang & Liu, 2007; Wang, Ho & Liu, 2005). In practice, there exist external and internal uncertainties. Observers which have a good performance even in presence of model and disturbance uncertainties, are called robust; their design process is quite complex (Chen & Dunnigan, 2002; Coutinho & Pereira, 2005; Huang, Feng & Cao, 2008; Walcott & Zak, 1987). All the approaches mentioned above need the previous knowledge of the plant model, at least partially. Recently, other kind of observers has emerged: *neural observers* (Kim & Lewis, 1998; Levin & Narendra, 1996; Marino, 1990; Poznyak, Sanchez & Yu, 2001; Sanchez & Ricalde, 2003), for unknown plant dynamics. However (Kim & Lewis, 1998; Marino, 1990; Poznyak, Sanchez & Yu, 2001; Sanchez & Ricalde, 2003), are analyzed for continuous-time unknown nonlinear systems, besides for (Marino, 1990; Poznyak, Sanchez & Yu,

2001) no disturbances are considered. On the other hand the discrete-time case has not been studied at the same degree besides it is more suitable for real-time implementations. In (Levin & Narendra, 1996), the discrete time case is addressed without consider disturbances or any stability analysis. Then in this chapter we propose the use of a discrete-time neural observer for unknown discrete-time nonlinear systems, based on a RHONN trained on-line with an EKF-based algorithm, which is designed to operate under the presence of external disturbances and parametric uncertainties (Alanis, 2007).

This chapter is devoted to illustrate an interesting application of RHONN: the state observation in anaerobic wastewater treatment plants, which are complex biologic process with high non-linearity (Carlos-Hernandez, Beteau & Sanchez, 2006). A common problem in this kind of process is that the full state cannot be measured due to economical or technical constraints. This situation imposes interesting challenges in order to design observers and to select adequate sensors (Bastin & Dochain, 1990). Most of the techniques for design of nonlinear state estimator assume the complete knowledge of the system model, which is not always available; additionally, it is usually required to use special nonlinear transformations, which are not robust in presence of uncertainties. For this reason, the use of neural observers has emerged for estimation of process state whose mathematical model is unknown. The chapter is organized as follows. Next section describes the fundamentals of recurrent higher order neural networks: continuous and discrete time models, the Extended Kalman Filter as training algorithm and the design of neural observers. Section 2 is devoted to illustrate the application of neural observer to an anaerobic digestion for wastewater treatment, a process description is presented; after that, observers for estimate biomass, substrate and inorganic carbon are proposed. Finally, some relevant conclusions are stated.

1. RECURRENT HIGHER ORDER NEURAL NETWORKS

1.1. Continuous Time Model

In a continuous time *recurrent higher order neural network*, each neuron is represented by a differential equation as follows:

$$\dot{x}_i = -a_i x_i + b_i \sum_j w_{ij} y_j \tag{1.1}$$

where x_i stands for the i-th neuron, a_i, b_i are constants, w_{ij} is the synaptic weight relating the j-th input with the i-th neuron, y_j is an external input or the past state of neuron and it is defined by the next sigmoid function:

$$S(x) = \frac{\mu}{1 + e^{-\beta x}} + \varepsilon \tag{1.2}$$

where μ is the sigmoid bound, β is the sigmoid slope and ε is a positive real number which allow the sigmoid to be moved.

The equation (1.1) is the simplest structure since the input is a linear combination of the components y_j; however, this simplicity is a limitation when complex systems are considered (Poznyak, Sanchez & Yu, 2001). To enhance the neural network performance, RHONN are a good alternative, since they include not only linear combinations but also products, $y_j y_k$, allowing the neural network to be implemented as a higher order iterations structure. These RHONN are represented as.

$$\dot{x}_i = -a_i x_i + \sum_{k=1}^{L} w_{ik} \prod_{j \in I_k} y_j^{d_j(k)} \tag{1.3}$$

where x_i is the state of the i-th neuron, a_i are real coefficients, L is the number of *higher order connections*; $\{I_1, I_2 ..., I_L\}$ is a collection of non-ordered L subsets composed by $\{1, 2, ..., m+n\}$ elements, w_{ik} are the synaptic weights of the neural network, $d_j(k)$ are non negative integers, y is the input vector of each neuron and it is given by:

$$y = \begin{bmatrix} y_1 \\ y_2 \\ \vdots \\ y_n \\ y_{n+1} \\ \vdots \\ y_{n+m} \end{bmatrix} = \begin{bmatrix} S(x_1) \\ S(x_2) \\ \vdots \\ S(x_n) \\ u_1 \\ \vdots \\ u_m \end{bmatrix} \tag{1.4}$$

with $u = [u_1 \quad u_2 \quad \cdots \quad u_m]^T$, is the external input vector and the sigmoid function $S(\cdot)$ is defined as in (1.2).

To simplify (1.2), a z vector is introduced, which is defined as follows:

$$z = \begin{bmatrix} z_1 \\ z_2 \\ \vdots \\ z_L \end{bmatrix} = \begin{bmatrix} \prod_{j \in I_1} y_j^{d_j(1)} \\ \prod_{j \in I_2} y_j^{d_j(2)} \\ \vdots \\ \prod_{j \in I_L} y_j^{d_j(L)} \end{bmatrix} \tag{1.5}$$

The weight vector is rewritten as:

$$w_i = [w_{i1} \quad w_{i2} \quad \cdots \quad w_{iL}]^T \tag{1.6}$$

Replacing (1.5) and (1.6) in equation (1.2), next expression is obtained:

$$\dot{x}_i = -a_i x_i + w_i^T z(x, u) \tag{1.7}$$

where $a_i > 0, i = 1, 2, ..., n$; finally, the model for a RHONN in continuous time is defined by:

$$\dot{x} = Ax + W^T z(x, u) \tag{1.8}$$

where $x \in \mathbb{R}^n$, $W \in \mathbb{R}^{nxL}$ and $A \in \mathbb{R}^{nxn}$ is a diagonal matrix, with elements a_i in its diagonal.

Let consider the nonlinear system:

$$\dot{\chi} = F(\chi, u) \tag{1.9}$$

where $\chi \in \mathbb{R}^{n}$ is the system state, $u \in \mathbb{R}^{m}$ is the system input, and $F : \mathbb{R}^{n+m} \to \mathbb{R}^{n}$ is a vector field in a compact set $Y \in \mathbb{R}^{n+m}$. This is possible if only if the number of connections L is adequately selected.

Then this system (1.9) can be approximated by the RHONN (1.8), with the adequate connections L.

1.2. Discrete Time Model

The discrete time model *RHONN* has the same properties than the continuous one (Alanis, 2007; Ge, Zhang & Lee, 2004). From discretization of (1.7) the discrete model for a RHONN is obtained as:

$$x_{i}(k + 1) = w_{i}^{T} z(x(k), u(k)), \qquad i = 1, \dots, n \tag{1.10}$$

where $x_{i}(k)$ is the state of the i-th neuron, in the interaction k, w_{i} is the synaptic weight vector, these are adapted on-line; n represent the state dimension; $z(x(k), u(k))$ is defined as in (1.5); y is the input vector of each neuron and it is defined as in (1.4), and finally u stands the external input of the neural network, $S(\cdot)$ is a sigmoid function and it is defined as in (1.2). Figure 1 illustrates the structure of a discrete RHONN.

1.3. Extended Kalman Filter for Training RHONN

The well known Kalman filter is a set of mathematical equations formulated from a space state representation of a linear dynamic system; this approach supplies a recurrent solution to the optimal filtering problem (Grover & Hwang, 1992). That means, KF estimates linear system state with additive noise on the state and the outputs. Then, KF can be used as training method for *neural networks*. When it is done,

Figure 1. Discrete time RHONN scheme

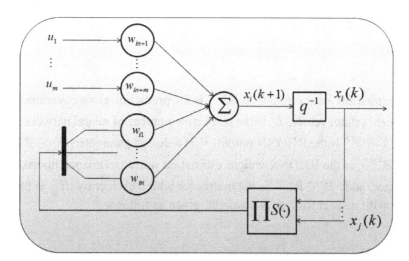

the synaptic *weights* and the output of the neural network are, respectively, the estimated state and the measurement used by the filter. It must be noted that the error between the output of the neural network and the system output can be considered as additive white noise. Besides, the weights estimation is done recursively: estimated weights updating is done from the previous weight and the current data, which implies that the storage of all the estimated weights is not necessary (Haykin, 2001; Leunga & Chan, 2003; Williams & Zipser, 1989; Yu & Li, 2004). For RHONN training, the *extended Kalman filter* is required since that kind of networks now constitutes nonlinear system. The training goal is to find the optimal weight values which minimize the predictions error. The *training* algorithm is described by

$$w(k+1) = w(k) + \eta K(k)[Y(k) - \hat{Y}(k)]$$
$$K(k) = P(k)H(k)[R(k) + H^T(k)P(k)H(k)]^{-1}$$
$$P(k+1) = P(k) - K(k)H^T(k)P(k) + Q(k) \qquad (1.11)$$

the vector w represents the synaptic *weights* of the neural network at the step k, η is design parameter, K is the Kalman gain matrix, Y is the plant output vector, $\hat{Y}$ is the NN output, P is the prediction error covariance, Q is the NN weight estimation noise covariance matrix, R is the error noise covariance. Finally H is the matrix for which each entry is the derivative of the each neural output with respect to each NN weight, given as follows:

$$H(k) = \left[\frac{\partial \hat{Y}_i(k)}{\partial w_j(k)} \right]^T \qquad i = 1,...,m \text{ y } j = 1,...,L \qquad (1.12)$$

The weight adaptation law can be computed either for all the weight or for each one separately. The generic equations for the second case are presented below:

$$w_i(k+1) = w_i(k) + \eta_i K_i(k)[Y(k) - \hat{Y}(k)]$$
$$K_i(k) = P_i(k)H_i(k)[R_i(k) + H_i^T(k)P_i(k)H_i(k)]^{-1} \qquad i = 1,...,n$$
$$P_i(k+1) = P_i(k) - K_i(k)H_i^T(k)P_i(k) + Q_i(k) \qquad (1.13)$$

with:

$$M_i(k) = [R_i(k) + H_i^T(k)P_i(k)H_i(k)]^{-1}$$
$$e(k) = Y(k) - \hat{Y}(k) \qquad (1.14)$$

where $e \in \mathbb{R}^p$ is the measurement error, $P_i \in \mathbb{R}^{L_i \times L_i}$ is the prediction error covariance matrix at step k, $w_i \in \mathbb{R}^{L_i}$ is the weight (state) vector, L_i is the respective number of neural network weights, $Y \in \mathbb{R}^p$, is the plant output, $\hat{Y} \in \mathbb{R}^p$ is the RHONN output, η is a design parameter, $K_i \in \mathbb{R}^{L_i \times m}$ is the Kalman gain matrix, $Q_i \in \mathbb{R}^{L_i \times L_i}$ is the RHONN weight estimation noise covariance matrix, $R_i \in \mathbb{R}^{p \times p}$ is the error noise covariance, and; $H_i \in \mathbb{R}^{L_i \times p}$ is the matrix for which each entry H_{pj} is the derivative of the p-th neural output with respect to j-th NN weight, given as follows:

$$H_{pj}(k) = \left[\frac{\partial \hat{Y}_p(k)}{\partial w_j(k)} \right]^T \qquad p = 1,...,m \ \text{y} \ j = 1,...,L \tag{1.15}$$

For the case where the NN output $\hat{Y}$ is a function of the state and of the external inputs, H is computed as:

$$\hat{Y}(k) = \varphi(x(k), u(k)) \tag{1.16}$$

Solving (1.16), the next equation is obtained:

$$\frac{\partial \hat{Y}(k)}{\partial w} = \frac{\partial \hat{Y}(k)}{\partial x(k)} \frac{\partial x(k)}{\partial w} \tag{1.17}$$

where x is the state of the i-th neuron, which is rewritten as follows:

$$x(k+1) = \psi(x(k), u(k), w(k)) \tag{1.18}$$

where $\psi(x(k), u(k), w(k))$ is a non-linear function of $x(k), u(k)$ and $w(k)$ which determines the transition of the neuron; with a sequence of recurrent derivatives it is possible to obtain a linearized dynamic system as:

$$\frac{\partial x(k+1)}{\partial w} = \frac{\partial \psi(x(k), u(k), w(k))}{\partial x(k)} \frac{\partial x(k)}{\partial w(k)} + \frac{\partial \psi(x(k), u(k), w(k))}{\partial w(k)} \tag{1.19}$$

Besides, it is important to remark that, usually, P_i and Q_i are initialized as diagonal matrices, with entries $P_i(0)$ and $Q_i(0)$ respectively. Additionally, $H_i(k)$, $K_i(k)$ and $P_i(k)$ for the EKF are bounded; for a detailed explanation of this fact see (Haykin, 2001).

1.4. Neural Identification

Identification is an experimental approach to determine unknown parameters of a process model, from measured variables: inputs, control variables, outputs, controlled variables and even disturbances if possible (Yu & Li, 2004).

Neural network are a good alternative to learning complex relationships from a data set; moreover, they have good intrinsic properties for on-line adaptability and for approximating dynamic behaviours. For these reasons, NN have been recognized as an important tool for modelling and identification of dynamic systems, especially when there exist non-linearities hard to determine (Alanis, 2007; Rovithakis & Christodoulou, 2000; Yu & Li, 2004). In this section, a methodology for dynamic systems identification based on RHONN is described.

Most of the dynamic systems can be represented by equations having the next structure:

$$\begin{aligned} \chi(k+1) &= F(\chi(k), u(k)) \\ Y(k) &= h(\chi(k)) \end{aligned} \tag{1.20}$$

where k is a sampled instant, $\chi \in \mathbb{R}^n$, $u \in \mathbb{R}^m$ and $Y \in \mathbb{R}^p$.

If functions F and h are unknown, then identification is required. The use by neural networks requires three main steps:

1. Selection of neural network inputs
2. Selection of neural network internal structure
3. Adjusting neural network parameters (synaptic weights) until to reach the required approximated error

There exist several neural network structures for identification; however, for systems with time variant parameters, only few of them are appropriated. The RHONN structures are able to adjust its parameters on-line and to approximate nonlinear functions (Alanis, 2007; Rovithakis & Christodoulou, 2000; Yu & Li, 2004). The set of adequate structures for based RHONN identification are shown below (Alanis, 2007; Rovithakis & Christodoulou, 2000; Yu & Li, 2004):

Parallel Model

$$x_i(k+1) = w_i^T z_i(x(k), u(k)), \quad i = 1, \dots, n \tag{1.21}$$

Series-Parallel Model

$$x_i(k+1) = w_i^T z_i(\chi(k), u(k)), \quad i = 1, \dots, n \tag{1.22}$$

Feedforward Model

$$x_i(k) = w_i^T z_i(u(k)), \quad i = 1, \dots, n \tag{1.23}$$

where x, is the NN state vector, χ is the process state vector and u is the NN input vector.

System (1.20) can be approximated by the next series-parallel discrete RHONN:

$$x_i(k+1) = w_i^{*T} z_i(\chi(k), u(k)) + \in_{z_i}, \quad i = 1, \dots, n \tag{1.24}$$

where x_i is the i-th NN state, χ is the process state vector, $\in_{z_i}$ is the approximation error; this error can be reduced by increasing the number of weights (*higher order connections*). It is that there exists an ideal weight vector w_i^*, such that $\left\| \in_{z_i} \right\|$ is minimal in a compact set $\Omega_{z_i} \subset \mathbb{R}^{L_i}$ (Alanis, 2007). Generally, it is supposed that this vector exists, is time-invariant and unknown.

1.5. Recurrent Higher Order Neural Network Observer (RHONNO)

In this section, we briefly present the development of the neural observer, proposed in (Alanis, 2007). We consider the state variable estimated of a discrete-time nonlinear system, which is assumed to be observable, given by

$$
\begin{aligned}
x(k+1) &= F(x(k), u(k)) + d(k) \\
Y(k) &= Cx(k)
\end{aligned}
\tag{1.25}
$$

where $x \in \mathbb{R}^n$ is the state vector of the system, $u \in \mathbb{R}^m$ is the input vector, $y \in \mathbb{R}^p$ is the output vector, $C \in \mathbb{R}^{p \times n}$ is a known output matrix, $d(k) \in \mathbb{R}^n$ is a disturbance vector and $F(\bullet)$ is a smooth vector field and $F_i(\bullet)$ its entries; hence (1.25) can be rewritten as:

$$
\begin{aligned}
x(k+1) &= [x_1(k)...x_i(k)...x_n(k)]^T \\
d(k) &= [d_1(k)...d_i(k)...d_n(k)]^T \\
x_i(k+1) &= F_i(x(k), u(k)) + d_i(k), \quad i = 1,...,n \\
Y(k) &= Cx(k)
\end{aligned}
\tag{1.26}
$$

For system (1.26), a Luenberger neural observer (RHONO) is proposed in (Alanis, 2007), with the following structure:

$$
\begin{aligned}
\hat{x}_i(k+1) &= w_i^T z_i(\hat{x}(k), u(k)) + L_i e(k), \quad i = 1,...,n \\
\hat{Y}(k) &= C\hat{x}(k)
\end{aligned}
\tag{1.27}
$$

with $L_i \in \mathbb{R}^p$, w_i and $z_i(\hat{x}(k), u(k))$ as in (1.5); the weight vectors are updated on-line with a decoupled EKF (1.13)-(1.15). The output error is defined by

$$
e(k) = Y(k) - \hat{Y}(k)
\tag{1.28}
$$

the state estimation error as

$$
\tilde{x}(k) = x(k) - \hat{x}(k)
\tag{1.29}
$$

and the weight estimation error as

$$
\tilde{w}_i(k) = w_i(k) - w_i^*
\tag{1.30}
$$

Then the dynamics of (1.27) can be expressed as:

$$
\begin{aligned}
\tilde{x}(k+1) &= x_i(k+1) - \hat{x}_i(k+1) \\
&= w_i^{*T} z_i(x(k), u(k)) + \in_{z_i} + d_i(k) \\
&\quad - w_i^T z_i(\hat{x}(k), u(k)) - L_i e(k) \\
&= \tilde{w}_i z_i(\hat{x}(k), u(k)) + \in_{z_i} + d_i(k) - L_i e(k)
\end{aligned}
\tag{1.31}
$$

Figure 2. Neural observation scheme

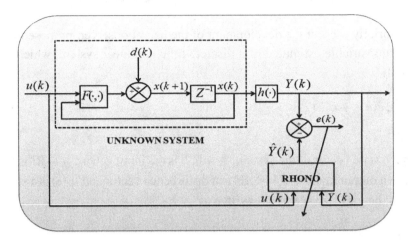

Considering (1.26) and (1.27)

$$e(k) = C\tilde{x}(k) \tag{1.32}$$

Then the error dynamics (1.29) can be rewritten as:

$$\tilde{x}(k+1) = \tilde{w}_i z_i(\hat{x}(k), u(k)) + \in'_{z_i} - L_i C\tilde{x}(k) \tag{1.33}$$

where $\in'_{z_i} = \in_{z_i} + d_i(k)$. On the other hand the dynamic of (1.30) is:

$$\tilde{w}_i(k+1) = w_i^* - w_i(k+1) = \tilde{w}_i(k) - \eta_i K_i(k)e(k) \tag{1.34}$$

For a detailed explanation of the design and proofs of the neural observer see (Alanis, 2007). Figure 2 displays the proposed observer scheme.

For more details with respect to design and proofs of the neural observer, see (Alanis, 2007).

2. APPLICATION TO ANAEROBIC DIGESTION

Anaerobic digestion is a biological complex process developed in oxygen absence. It is commonly used to treat wastewater with high organic load: the pollutants (substrate) are degraded by means of anaerobic microorganisms (biomass), producing a biogas mainly composed of methane (CH_4) and carbon dioxide (CO_2).

This process is very sensitive to operating conditions. Additionally, some variables are difficult to measure due to technical or economical constraints, i.e.: the substrate consumption measure is expensive, needs three hours and is done off-line. Biomass measure is still more restrictive because the existing sensors are designed from a biological approach, and are not adequate for automatic control. For this

Figure 3. Anaerobic digestion stages

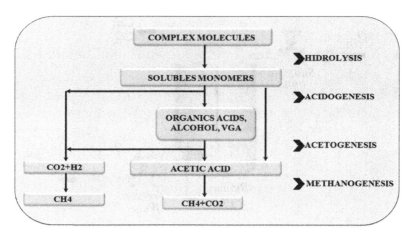

reason, a first step required for control analysis and design is to develop state observers in order to estimate unmeasured variables (Carlos-Hernandez, Beteau & Sanchez, 2006).

2.1. Process Description

The organic wastes are degraded in four successive stages (the products of one stage are the input for the next one): hydrolysis, aciodogenesis, acetogenesis and methanogenesis (Figure 3). Each one is developed by a different bacteria population and therefore presents different biological, physic-chemical and hydrodynamic phenomena (Carlos-Hernandez, Beteau & Sanchez, 2006).

The speed development of each stage is also different; the acidogenesis and acetogenesis are very fast stages; the hydrolysis is fast, and finally the methanogenesis is the slowest one and the most important for the process stability. In general, anaerobic digestion is very sensitive to variations in the operating conditions such as: pH, temperature, overload on substrate concentration, etc.

In this chapter a completely stirred tank reactor is considered. This kind of reactor is currently used in industrial processes because its hydrodynamic behaviour is relatively easy to model and to control. The substrate equivalent to glucose denoted by S_1, and the substrate equivalent to acetate denoted by S_2 is fed to the reactor with a flow rate Q_{in} (dilution rate $D_{in} = Q_{in} / V$ where V is the reactor volume), inorganic carbon IC and the cations presents in the reactor Z are fed at same flow. Into the reactor, the substrate is treated by the biomass and then, treated water is taken put at the same flow rate: $Q_{in} = Q_{out}$ .A biomass filter is used to improve substrate treatment: bacteria cannot go out of the reactor; hence, it avoids washout and enhances performances. In practice, the biomass is fixed in a solid support to get the biomass filter behavior. The model considers this condition in the biomass equations, where k_{d1}, k_{d2} is the death rate, which represent the biomass falling down of the support; which becomes inactive biomass (Carlos-Hernandez, Beteau & Sanchez, 2006).

2.2. Process Model

For modelling purposes, the organic components of the substrate considered in this chapter are classified as *equivalent glucose* (S_1) and *equivalent acetate* (S_2). The first one is assumed to model complex mol-

Figure 4. Completely stirred tank reactor with biomass filter

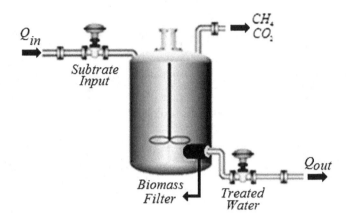

ecules, and the second one represents molecules which are transformed directly in acetic acid. Biomass is also classified in two types noted X_1 and X_2. X_1 represents the bacteria populations, which transform *equivalent glucose* substrates. and X_2 stands for bacteria degrading *equivalent acetate* substrates. This classification allows the process to be represented by only two stages: the methanogenesis, which is the limiting one (the most interesting for automatic control and energy approaches), and a preliminary stage (Angelidaki, Ellegaard & Ahring, 1998; Gentil, 1981). Such representation of anaerobic digestion is depicted on the functional scheme of Figure 5.

The physic-chemical phenomena (basic-acid equilibrium and mass conservation) are modelled by five algebraic equations:

$$
\begin{aligned}
HS + S^- - S_2 &= 0 \\
H^+ S^- - K_a HS &= 0 \\
H^+ B - K_b CO_{2d} &= 0 \\
B + CO_{2d} - IC &= 0 \\
B + S^- - Z &= 0
\end{aligned}
$$

(2.1)

Figure 5. Functional scheme of anaerobic digestion process

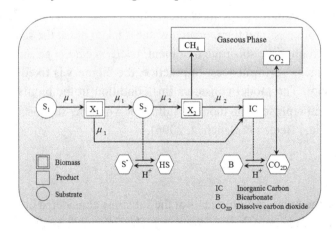

Ordinary differential equations are used to represent biomass growth, substrate transformations, inorganic carbon evolution (result of the biological phase) and cations which are biologically inert.

$$\frac{dX_1}{dt} = (\mu_1 - k_{d1})X_1$$

$$\frac{dS_1}{dt} = -R_6\mu_1 X_1 + D_{in}(S_{1in} - S_1)$$

$$\frac{dX_2}{dt} = (\mu_2 - k_{d2})X_2$$

$$\frac{dS_2}{dt} = -R_3\mu_2 X_2 + R_4\mu_1 X_1 + D_{in}(S_{2in} - S_2)$$

$$\frac{dIC}{dt} = R_2 R_3\mu_2 X_2 + R_5\mu_1 X_1 - \lambda R_1 R_3\mu_2 X_2 + D_{in}(IC_{in} - IC)$$

$$\frac{dZ}{dt} = D_{in}(Z_{in} - Z)$$

$$(2.2)$$

Finally, the gaseous phase considerate the process output and is represented by:

$$Y_{CH_4} = R_1 R_2\mu_2 X_2$$
$$Y_{CO_2} = \lambda R_3 R_2\mu_2 X_2$$

$$(2.3)$$

λ is computed as

$$\lambda = \frac{CO_{2D}}{P_t K_h - CO_{2D}}$$

$$(2.4)$$

where P_t is the atmospheric pressure, K_h is the Henry constant, with

$$CO_{2D} = \frac{H^+ IC}{K_b + H^+}$$

$$(2.5)$$

$$H^+ = 10^{-pH}$$

$$(2.6)$$

This model is used in order to validate the observer structure.

2.3. Neural Identification of Anaerobic Digestion

Anaerobic digestion identification requires a discrete model. For this reason, model (2.2) is discretized as follows:

$$
\begin{aligned}
X_1(k+1) &= X_1(k) + [(\mu_1(k) - k_{d1})X_1(k)]T \\
S_1(k+1) &= S_1(k) + [-R_6\mu_1(k)X_1(k) + D_{in}(k)(S_{1in}(k) - S_1(k))]T \\
X_2(k+1) &= X_2(k) + [(\mu_2(k) - k_{d2})X_2(k)]T \\
S_2(k+1) &= S_2(k) + [R_4\mu_1(k)X_1(k) - R_3\mu_2(k)X_2(k) + D_{in}(k)(S_{2in}(k) - S_2(k))]T \\
IC(k+1) &= IC(k) + [R_5\mu_1(k)X_1(k) + R_2 R_3\mu_2(k)X_2(k) - \lambda(k)R_1 R_3\mu_2(k)X_2(k) + \\
&\quad + D_{in}(k)(IC_{in}(k) - IC)(k)]T \\
Z(k+1) &= Z(k) + [D_{in}(k)(Z_{in}(k) - Z(k))]T
\end{aligned}
$$

$$(2.7)$$

Figure 6. Identification scheme for anaerobic digestion

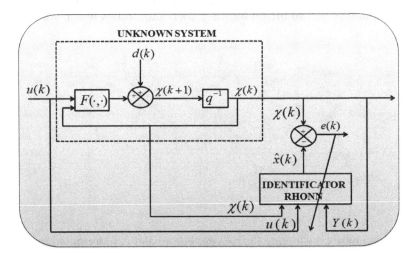

where T is the sampling time, selected as $T = 6\,\mathrm{min}$, since the dynamics of anaerobic digestion is very slow. The input vector is defined as:

$$u(k) = [D_{in}(k)\ IC_{in}(k)\ S_{2in}(k)] \tag{2.8}$$

It is assumed that all the process state are measurable, which mean that the output vector is equivalent to the state vector. Then, in (1.20) $h(\chi(k)) = C\chi(k)$, with $C = I$. A series-parallel RHONN structure (defined by 1.22) is used as approximation model and EKF (1.13) for training the NN. Figure 6 illustrates the identification scheme.

The next step is to modify the inputs $(D_{in}(k), IC_{in}(k))$ test enough to allow the process state to be excited. The objective is that the NN learn all the process dynamics. Figure 7-9 displays the input variables.

Figure 7. Dilution rate D_{in}

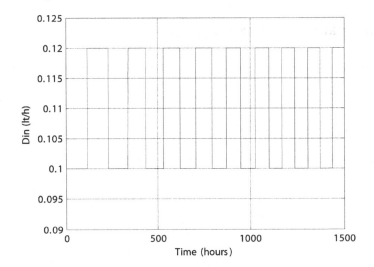

Figure 8. Inorganic carbon input IC_{in}

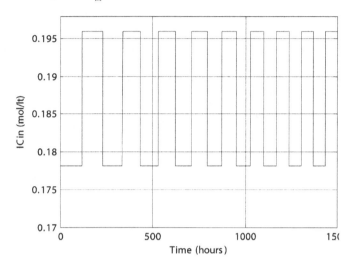

The structure of the *neural identifier* is given as:

$$\hat{X}_1(k+1) = w_{11}(k)S(X_1(k))$$
$$\hat{S}_1(k+1) = w_{21}(k)S(S_1(k)) + w_{22}(k)D_{in}(k)$$
$$\hat{X}_2(k+1) = w_{31}(k)S(X_2(k))$$
$$\hat{S}_2(k+1) = w_{41}(k)S(S_2(k)) + w_{42}(k)S(X_1(k)) + w_{43}(k)S(X_2(k)) + w_{44}(k)D_{in}(k)$$
$$I\hat{C}(k+1) = w_{51}(k)S(IC(k)) + w_{52}(k)S(X_2(k)) + w_{53}(k)S(X_1(k)) + w_{54}(k)D_{in}(k) +$$
$$+ w_{55}(k)IC_{in}(k)$$
$$\hat{Z}(k+1) = w_{61}(k)S(Z(k)) + w_{62}(k)D_{in}(k) + w_{63}(k)IC_{in}(k)$$

(2.9)

The NN output is:

Figure 9. Substrate input S_{2in}

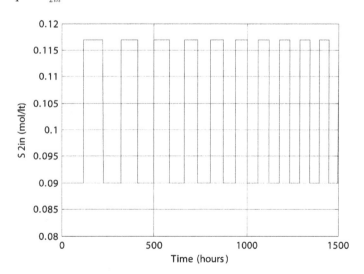

Figure 10. a) Time evolution of the biomass X_1 (solid line) and its estimated $\hat{X}_1$ (dashed line). b) Time evolution of the substrate S_1 (solid line) and its estimated $\hat{S}_1$ (dashed line)

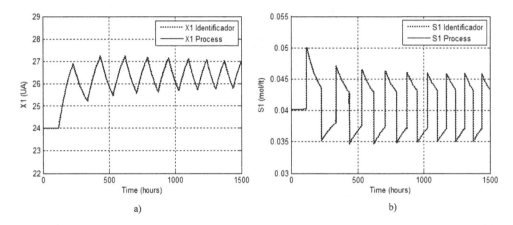

$$\hat{Y}(k) = \begin{bmatrix} \hat{X}_1(k) & \hat{S}_1(k) & \hat{X}_2(k) & \hat{S}_2(k) & I\hat{C}(k) & \hat{Z}(k) \end{bmatrix}^T \tag{2.10}$$

It is important to note that, the NN state $(\hat{X}_1, \hat{S}_1, \hat{X}_2, \hat{S}_2, I\hat{C}, \hat{Z})$, as well, the initial *weights* are initialized in a random way. The initial values of the covariance matrix for the EKF are selected experimentally. It is important to note a disadvantage of this kind of NN is, that there does not exist, to the best of our knowledgement, a methodology to determine its structure; then, it has to be selected experimentally. The best set of values is presented in Table 1.

The performance of the neural identification is illustrated on Figure 10-12.

As can be seen in these figures, the neural identification of anaerobic digestion is very well done; system variables are really close to their estimation. Moreover, effects due to the process inputs and disturbances changes are reduced in a fast way. Then, the RHONN structure can be used for state estimation in the anaerobic process.

Figure 11. a) Time evolution of the biomass X_2 (solid line) and its estimated $\hat{X}_2$ (dashed line). b) Time evolution of the substrate S_2 (solid line) and its estimated $\hat{S}_2$ (dashed line)

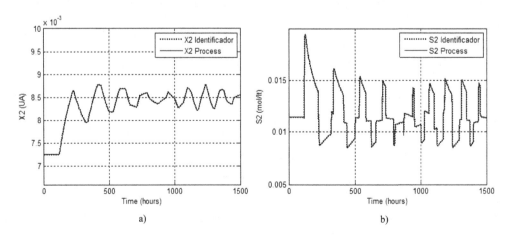

Table 1. Covariance matrices EFK for RHONN in the identification

$P_i(0)$	$Q_i(0)$	$R_i(0)$
$[P_1(0)]_{1\times1} = 1 \times 10^8$	$[Q_1(0)]_{1\times1} = 5 \times 10^5$	$[R_1(0)]_{1\times1} = 1 \times 10^4$
$[P_2(0)]_{2\times2} = diag\{1 \times 10^4\}$	$[Q_2(0)]_{2\times2} = diag\{5 \times 10^8\}$	$[R_2(0)]_{1\times1} = 5 \times 10^7$
$[P_3(0)]_{1\times1} = 1 \times 10^8$	$[Q_3(0)]_{1\times1} = 5 \times 10^3$	$[R_3(0)]_{1\times1} = 1 \times 10^4$
$[P_4(0)]_{4\times4} = diag\{4 \times 10^7\}$	$[Q_4(0)]_{4\times4} = diag\{1 \times 10^3\}$	$[R_4(0)]_{1\times1} = 1 \times 10^4$
$[P_5(0)]_{5\times5} = diag\{4 \times 10^4\}$	$[Q_5(0)]_{5\times5} = diag\{5 \times 10^8\}$	$[R_5(0)]_{1\times1} = 2 \times 10^4$
$[P_6(0)]_{3\times3} = diag\{1 \times 10^8\}$	$[Q_6(0)]_{3\times3} = diag\{5 \times 10^4\}$	$[R_6(0)]_{1\times1} = 2 \times 10^3$

2.4. Neural State Observer

For bioprocesses important problem is to measure the different variables. For anaerobic digestion there are specially two variables which are not easy to be measured, substrate and biomass. The first one is directly related to Demand Chemical Oxygen, which is determined off-line by chemical analysis requiring at least two hours. On the other hand, the existing biomass sensors are expensive and are designed from a biological viewpoint. These situations are not convenient for implementation efficient control strategies. To solve this measurement problem, it is required to develop state observers which allow variables hard to measure to be estimated form the available information.

Several observers have been proposed in order to estimate these variables: linear observers, asymptotic observer based on non-linear model, closed loop observer, interval observer, fuzzy observer. Each approach present advantages and disadvantages, such as difficulties synthesis, tune and to implement, and numerical instability due to ill conditioning of the process dynamics, estimation errors due to model uncertainties, etc.

Figure 12. a) Time evolution of the inorganic carbon IC (solid line) and its estimated $I\hat{C}$ (dashed line).
b) Time evolution of the cations Z (solid line) and its estimated $\hat{Z}$ (dashed line)

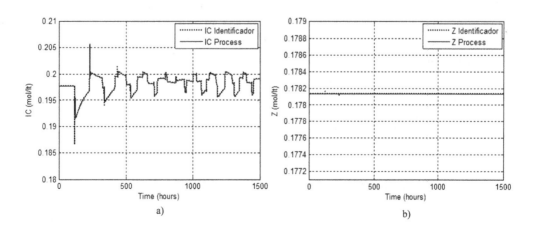

Figure 13. Neural observer scheme

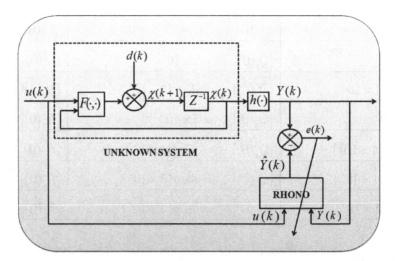

In this section, a discrete RHONNO for anaerobic digestion process is proposed. The objective is to estimate mainly biomass and substrate, they are good indicators of the biological activity in the reactors and are important variables for supervision and control purposes.

2.4.1. Neural Observers for Anaerobic Process

Anaerobic digestion has fast and slow dynamics. Usually, the main interest is focused in slow ones since they imposed the global dynamics of the process, additionally the slow stage is the most sensitive to variations on operating conditions. The associated state variables with slow stages are S_2 and X_2. IC is a product of the substrate degradation and even if it can be measured is advisable to estimate it. Cations are also present in the slow stage but they are biologically inert. Then, observer designed in this section is devoted to estimate biomass X_2 and substrate S_2. Figure 13 presents a schematic diagram of the neural observer.

2.4.2. RHONNO for Biomass X_2 Estimation.

This RHONNO for X_2 biomass is to estimate bacteria which degrade substrate *equivalent acetate*. A parallel representation is considered for the RHONNO and an on-line weights adaptation using EKF; additionally, it is supposed for this case S_2, IC and pH are available.

The *neural observer* structure is given by the next equation.

$$
\begin{aligned}
\hat{X}_2(k+1) = {} & w_1(k)S^{16}(\hat{X}_2(k))S^{12}(S_2(k))S^2(IC(k)) + w_2(k)(k)S^2(\hat{X}_2(k))S^4(S_2(k))S^2(IC(k)) \\
& + w_3(k)(k)S^{16}(\hat{X}_2(k))S^8(S_2(k))S^2(IC(k)) + w_4(k)(k)S^{16}(\hat{X}_2(k))S^{16}(S_2(k))S^2(IC(k)) \\
& + w_5(k)S^{18}(\hat{X}_2(k)) + w_6(k)S^{16}(\hat{X}_2(k))S^7(S_2(k))S^2(IC(k)) \\
& + w_7(k)S^{16}(\hat{X}_2(k))S^2(IC(k)) + w_8(k)S^{18}(\hat{X}_2(k))S^{13}(S_2(k))S^2(IC(k)) + Le(k)
\end{aligned}
\tag{2.11}
$$

where $L \in \mathbb{R}^{1 \times 2}$ is selected empirically: $L = \begin{bmatrix} 0.19 & 0.1 \end{bmatrix}$.

The NN outputs are represented by:

Figure 14. Input substrate S_{2in}

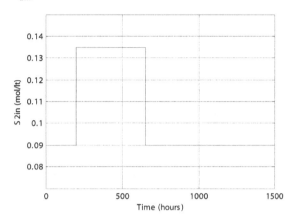

$$\hat{Y}_{CH_4} = R_1 R_2 \mu_2 \hat{X}_2$$
$$\hat{Y}_{CO_2} = \lambda R_2 R_3 \mu_2 \hat{X}_2$$

(2.12)

with λ as in (2.4).

Initialization is done as follows: the NN state X_2 is initialized randomly; covariance matrix is a unit matrix, $H(0) = 0$ since the NN outputs do not depend directly of weight vector as described in (1.17). In order to verify the observer performance, a disturbance is injected on the input substrate as shown in Figure 14. The amplitude of the square signal is 30% of the input substrate. It is assumed that the disturbance is not measured. The disturbance is injected at $t = 200h$ in order to assure an equilibrium point in the process, and it is stopped at $t = 650h$ to guarantee that the bacteria have reached the steady state. The obtained result from simulations is shown in Figure 15.

An exact estimation of biomass is done by the neural observer; moreover, there is not transient when the disturbance is incepted and taken out. This behaviour proves that the RHONN has learnt very fast the process complex dynamics. Additionally, in Figure 16 and 17 the observer outputs are compared with the process ones.

Different operating conditions are considered in order to verify the observer robustness. Disturbances on input inorganic carbon and dilution rate are incepted simultaneously at $t = 300h$ and taken out at $t = 750h$, as shown in Figure 18. Amplitude of these disturbances is 20% of the initial values for both variables. These inputs are measured variables which can be manipulated for control purposes. They are not included on the observer structure in order to illustrate its robustness. Figure 19 shows the obtained results considering these operating conditions.

The neural observer converges in a fast way to the process behaviour; the disturbances do not affect the variables estimation. Figure 20 and 21, displays the output comparison.

2.4.3. RHONNO for Substrate S_2 Estimation

To this end, a RHONNO for *equivalent acetate* substrate estimation is designed using a parallel representation and on-line weights adaptation. For this case, it is assumed that measure for X_2 and pH .are

Figure 15. Time evolution of the biomass X_2 (solid line) and its identification $\hat{X}_2$ (dashed line)

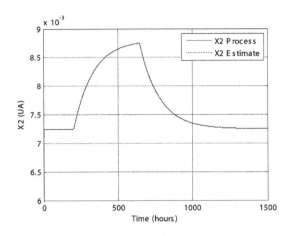

Figure 16. CH_4 model output (solid line) and neural network output (dashed line)

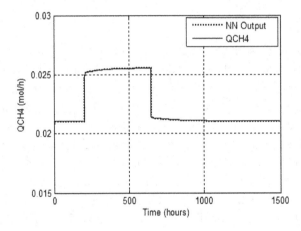

Figure 17. CO_2 model output (solid line) and neural network output (dashed line)

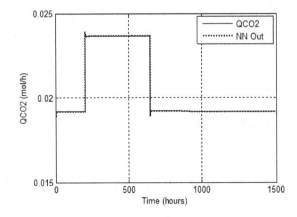

Figure 18. a) Dilution rate D_{in}. b) Inorganic carbon input IC_{in}

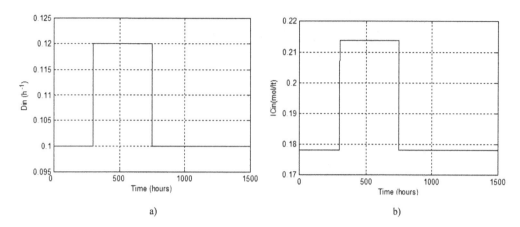

a)   b)

Figure 19. Time evolution of the biomass X_2 (solid line) and its estimate (dashed line)

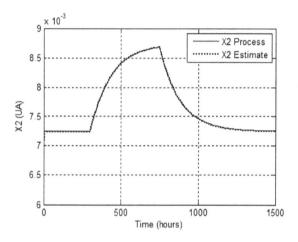

Figure 20. CH_4 model output (solid line) and neural network output (dashed line)

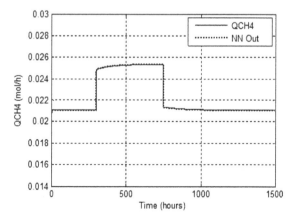

Figure 21. CO_2 model output (solid line) and neural network output (dashed line)

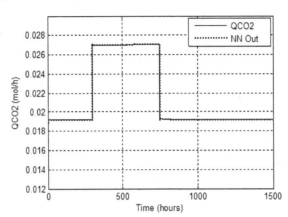

availables. The observer structure is presented below:

$$
\begin{aligned}
\hat{S}_2(k+1) &= w_1(k)\,S(\hat{S}_2(k)) + w_2(k)\,S^3(\hat{S}_2(k)) + w_3(k)\,S(\hat{S}_2(k))D_{in}(k) + \\
&\quad + w_4(k)D_{in}(k) + Le(k)
\end{aligned}
\tag{2.13}
$$

where $L \in \mathbb{R}^{1\times 2}$ is selected empirically: $L = \begin{bmatrix} 0.01 & 0.01 \end{bmatrix}$.

The NN outputs are:

$$
\begin{aligned}
\hat{Y}_{CH_4} &= R_1 R_2 \hat{\mu}_2 X_2 \\
\hat{Y}_{CO_2} &= \lambda R_2 R_3 \hat{\mu}_2 X_2
\end{aligned}
\tag{2.14}
$$

where λ is computed with (2.4).

For initialization, the RHONNO state is initialized with random values, the covariance matrix is set as a unit matrix, $H(0) = 0$.

In order to verify the *neural observer* performance, a disturbance is added to the input substrate as

Figure 22. Substrate input S_{2in}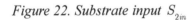

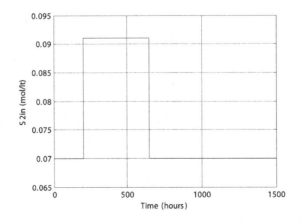

Figure 23. Time evolution of the substrate S_2 (solid line) and its estimate $\hat{S}_2$ (dashed line)

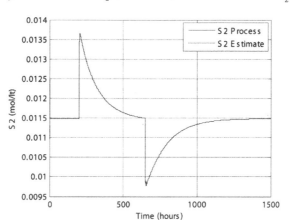

Figure 24. CH_4 model output (solid line) and neural network output (dashed line)

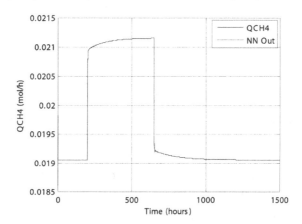

shown in Figure 22. The amplitude of the square signal is 30% of the input substrate. It is assumed that the disturbance is not measured. The disturbance is incepted at $t = 200h$ in order to assure an equilibrium point in the process, and it is taken out at $t = 650h$ to guarantee that the bacteria have reached the steady state. The obtained result from simulations is displayed in Figure 23.

An exact estimation of substrate is observed by the neural observer; moreover, there is not transient when the disturbance is incepted and taken out. Once again, this behaviour proves that the NN has learnt in a fast way the complex dynamic of the process. On the other hand, the observer outputs are compared with the process ones. The result of this comparison is shown in Figure 24 and 25.

2.4.4. RHONNO for Inorganic Carbon IC Estimation

The same representation as for X_2 and S_2 estimation is considered in this case. It is assumed that X_2, S_2 and pH measurements availables. The observer structure is:

$$\hat{IC}(k+1) = w_1(k)S(\hat{IC}(k)) + w_2(k)S(\hat{IC}(k))S^3(S_2(k))S^2(X_2(k))$$
$$+w_3(k)S(\hat{IC}(k))S(S_2(k))S(X_2(k)) + w_4(k)S^2(\hat{IC}(k)) + Le(k) \qquad (2.15)$$

Figure 25. CO_2 model output (solid line) and neural network output (dashed line)

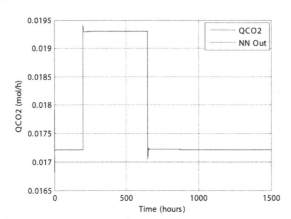

where $L \in \mathbb{R}^{1 \times 2}$ is selected empirically: $L = \begin{bmatrix} 1e-7 & 1e-4 \end{bmatrix}$.

The NN outputs are given by:

$$\hat{Y}_{CH_4} = R_1 R_2 \mu_2 X_2$$
$$\hat{Y}_{CO_2} = \hat{\lambda} R_2 R_3 \mu_2 X_2 \qquad (2.16)$$

where $\hat{\lambda}$ has the same form as in (2.4); however it is computed taking into account the estimated $\hat{IC}$ supplied by the RHONNO.

For initialization, the RHONNO state corresponding to IC is initialized with a random value near to the initial condition of the process variable, the covariance matrix is set as diagonal matrix $P(0) = 1.0051 \times 10^4$ and $Q(0) = 0.705$ finally, $H(0) = 0$.

In order to verify the observer performance, a disturbance is added to the input substrate as shown in Figure 26. The amplitude of the square signal is 30% of the input substrate; it is assumed that this disturbance is not measured. The disturbance is incepted at $t = 200h$ in order to assure an equilibrium

Figure 26. Substrate input S_{2in}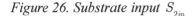

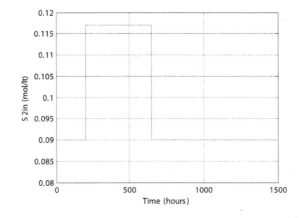

Figure 27. Time evolution inorganic carbon IC (solid line) and its estimation $I\hat{C}$ (dashed line)

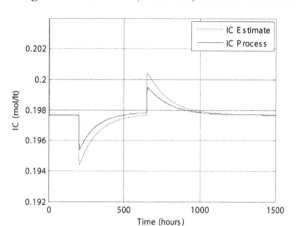

Figure 28. CH_4 model output (solid line) and neural network output (dashed line)

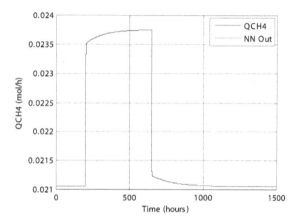

point in the process, and taken out at $t = 650h$ to guarantee that the bacteria have reached the steady state. The obtained result from simulations is shown in Figure 27.

As for previous cases, the observer outputs are compared with the process ones. The result of this comparison is shown in Figure 28 and 29.

The estimated variable converges to the real one; however, when a disturbance on the input substrate is considered there is a transient error. This error is eliminated when $t \to \infty$. The possible reason for this performance is because the inorganic carbon observer structure does not include the dynamics of biomass X_1.

2.4.5. RHONNO for Biomass X_2 and Substrate S_2 Estimation

The last application of RHONNO in this chapter is the simultaneous estimation of X_2 and S_2. In this case, it is assumed that there is an available measure for IC and pH. The observer structure is:

Figure 29. CO_2 model output (solid line) and neural network output (dashed line)

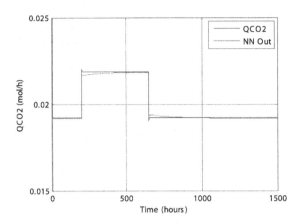

Figure 30. Substrate input S_{2in}

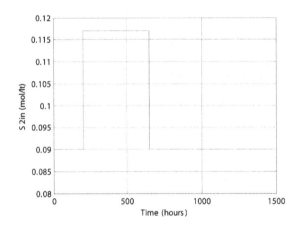

Figure 31. Time evolution of the biomass X_2 (solid line) and its estimate $\hat{X}_2$ (dashed line)

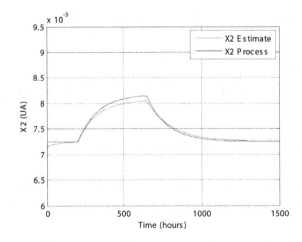

Figure 32. Time evolution of the substrate S_2 (solid line) and its estimate $\hat{S}_2$ (dashed line)

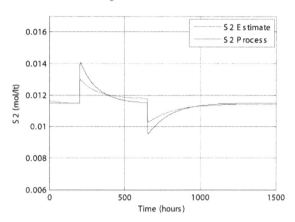

$$
\begin{aligned}
\hat{X}_2(k+1) &= w_{11}(k)\,S^{\,3}(\hat{S}_2(k)) + w_{21}(k)\,S(\hat{S}_2(k))S(\hat{X}_2(k)) + w_{31}(k)\,S(\hat{X}_2(k)) + \\
&\quad + w_{41}(k)\,S(\hat{X}_2(k)S(\hat{S}_2(k))D_e + w_{51}(k)\,S(D_e) \\
&\quad + w_{61}(k)\,S(\hat{S}_2(k))S^{\,5}(\hat{X}_2(k)) + L_1 e(k) \\
\hat{S}_2(k+1) &= w_{12}(k)\,S^{\,3}(\hat{X}_2(k)) + w_{22}(k)\,S^{\,2}(\hat{X}_2(k))S^{\,2}(\hat{S}_2(k)) + w_{32}(k)\,S^{\,2}(\hat{X}_2(k)) + \\
&\quad + w_{42}(k)\,S^{\,3}(\hat{X}_2(k)S^{\,5}(\hat{S}_2(k))D_e + w_{52}(k)\,S^{\,6}(\hat{X}_2(k))S^{\,3}(\hat{S}_2(k)) \\
&\quad + w_{62}(k)\,S^{\,2}(\hat{S}_2(k)) + L_2 e(k)
\end{aligned}
\tag{2.17}
$$

where $L_1, L_2 \in \mathbb{R}^{1\times 2}$, are selected empirically as:

$$
\begin{aligned}
L_1 &= \begin{bmatrix} 1e2 & 1e3 \end{bmatrix} \\
L_2 &= \begin{bmatrix} 1e7 & 1 \end{bmatrix}
\end{aligned}
$$

The RHONNO outputs are:

Figure 33. CH_4 model output (solid line) and neural network output (dashed line

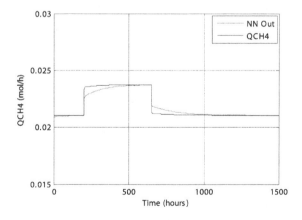

Table 2. Covariance matrices EFK for RHONN in the observation

$P_i(0)$	$Q_i(0)$	$R_i(0)$
$[P_1(0)]_{9\times9} = diag\{1\times10^{10}\}$	$[Q_1(0)]_{9\times9} = diag\{1.3\times10^{-2}\}$	$R_1(0) = \begin{bmatrix} 70 & 0 \\ 0 & 1500 \end{bmatrix}$
$[P_2(0)]_{6\times6} = diag\{7.9\times10^{4}\}$	$[Q_2(0)]_{6\times6} = diag\{1\times10^{-7}\}$	$R_2(0) = \begin{bmatrix} 850 & 0 \\ 0 & 80 \end{bmatrix}$

$$\hat{Y}_{CH_4} = R_1 R_2 \hat{\mu}_2 \hat{X}_2$$
$$\hat{Y}_{CO_2} = \lambda R_2 R_3 \hat{\mu}_2 \hat{X}_2$$

$$(2.18)$$

where λ is computed with (2.4).

For initialization, the RHONNO corresponding to X_2 and S_2 are initialized with a random value near to the initial condition of the process variables; the covariance matrix are set as diagonal matrix (see Table 2); finally, $H(0) = 0$.

In order to study the observer behaviour, a disturbance is incepted to on the input substrate as shown in Figure 30. The amplitude of the square signal is 30% of the input substrate; it is assumed that this disturbance is not measured. The disturbance is incepted at $t = 200h$ in order to assure an equilibrium point in the process, and it is taken out at $t = 650h$ to guarantee that the bacteria have reached the steady state. The obtained results from simulations are shown in Figure 31 and 32.

The observer convergence is clearly shown at the beginning of simulations. However, when a disturbance is incepted a small transient error appears in the biomass estimation, this error is eliminated in few hours, when the disturbance is taken out, a larger error is induced and it is not totally eliminated in $t \to \infty$. The error is present also for the substrate estimation and it is larger than the one for the biomass estimation. Nevertheless, it is important to remark that the qualitative estimation of two variables is well

Figure 34. CO_2 model output (solid line) and neural network output (dashed line)

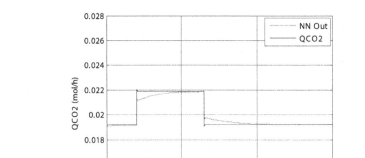

Figure 35. a) Dilution rate D_{in} b) Inorganic carbon input IC_{in}

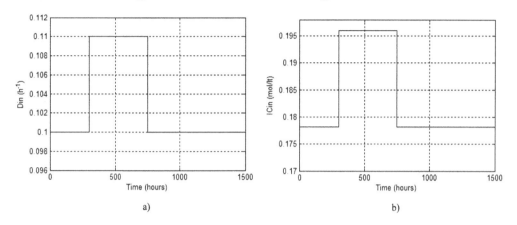

a)   b)

Figure 36. Time evolution of the biomass X_2 (solid line) and its estimate $\hat{X}_2$ (dashed line)

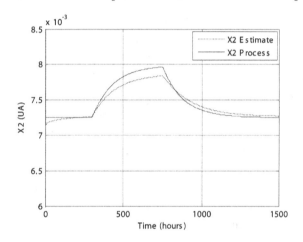

Figure 37. Time evolution of the substrate S_2 (solid line) and its estimate $\hat{S}_2$ (dashed line)

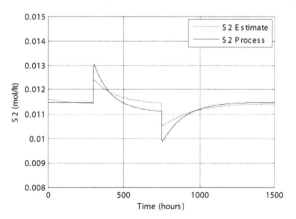

Figure 38. CH$_4$ model output (solid line) and neural network output (dashed line)

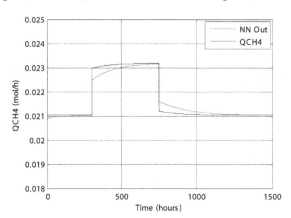

done by the neural observer, which means, the observer does not lose its properties to approximate the complex dynamics of anaerobic digestion, even in presence of changes on the operating conditions.

On Figure 33 and 34 a comparison between estimated outputs and process outputs is presented. A similar behaviour as for biomass and substrate estimation is obtained.

Different operating conditions are considered in order to verify the observer robustness. Disturbances on input inorganic carbon and dilution rate are incepted simultaneously at $t = 300h$ and taken out at $t = 750h$, as presented in Figure 2.33. Amplitude of these disturbances is 10% of the initial values for both variables. Inorganic carbon is not included on the observer structure; then, the disturbance on IC_{in} is considered as an external one. Figure 36 and 37 show the obtained results considering these operating conditions.

As for the previous cases, the observer convergence is shown at the beginning of simulations. When a disturbance is incepted (and taken out) a small transient error appears for the biomass and substrate estimation. This error is eliminated in $t \to \infty$.

On Figure 38 and 39, a comparison between estimated outputs and process outputs is presented. A similar behaviour as for biomass and substrate estimation is obtained.

Figure 39. CO$_2$ model output (solid line) and neural network output (dashed line)

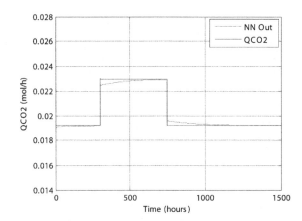

In general, it can be remarked that for all considered operating conditions the observer is able to approximate the process behaviour adequately. When a disturbance is incepted there is not oscillation or overshoot. This is an important advantage for control purposes since the estimated variables can be included in control strategies, since an adequate estimation is obtained by the neural observers proposed.

3. CONCLUSION

Recurrent Higher Order Neural Networks (RHONN) have been used as nonlinear systems estimators, its advantages, disadvantages and structures also have been presented; in addition the training algorithm with extended Kalman filter is also included. An identifier is developed using this kind of networks; it is applied to the anaerobic process were all the state are assumed to be measurable. A simulations, it is applied with the process model, the results obtained were exact, there is no transitory; in addition robustness is tested with disturbances for the effluent organic matter concentration and inorganic carbon and dilution rate inputs.

Finally neural observers are developed with a Luenberger structure, for the anaerobic process, when variables are not measured. The first observer designed is developed to estimate biomass (X_2); in this case the substrate (S_2) and the inorganic carbon (IC) are Assumed measurable, in addition the pH measurement is assumed available, it is true in the practice. The RHONNO weights vector is adjusted using an EKF to minimize the error between the neural network output and the process output. This observer is tested in simulation, with good results, illustrating its effectiveness and robustness in presence of disturbances on the substrate input and simultaneously on the inorganic carbon and dilution rate inputs. Additional observers are developed to estimate substrate (S_2) and inorganic carbon (IC), with the same assumptions that for the biomass observer; although for these observers good results are also obtained, the IC inorganic carbon observer presents a small approximation error.

Additionally, is developed an observer to estimate simultaneously biomass (X_2) and substrate (S_2), with inorganic carbon and pH measures are assumed availables. The results obtained are satisfactory. Furthermore, the proposed RHONNOs are robust in presence of disturbances.

FUTURE TRENDS

As future work the authors consider the real-time implementation of the proposed schemes, including control loop for the process.

ACKNOWLEDGMENT

The authors thank the support of CONACYT Mexico, through Project 57801Y. The authors also thank the useful comments of the anonymous reviewers, which help to improve this chapter.

REFERENCES

Alanís, A. Y. (2007). *Discrete-time Neural Control*. Ph. D. Disserattion, CINVESTAV Unidad Guadalajara, México.

Angelidaki, I., Ellegaard, L., & Ahring, B. K. (1998). A comprehensive model of anaerobic bioconversion of complex substrates to biogas. *Biotechnology and Bioengineering, 63*(3), 363–372. doi:10.1002/(SICI)1097-0290(19990505)63:3<363::AID-BIT13>3.0.CO;2-Z

Bastin, G., & Dochain, D. (1990). *On-line estimation and adaptive control of bioreactors*. Maryland Heights, USA: Elsevier.

Carlos-Hernandez, S., Beteau, J. F., & Sanchez, E. N. (2006, October). Design and real-time implementation of a TS fuzzy observer for anaerobic wastewater treatment plants. *IEEE International Symposium on Intelligent Control* (pp. 1252-1257), Munich, Germany.

Chen, F., & Dunnigan, M. W. (2002). Comparative study of a sliding-mode observer and Kalman filters for full state estimation in an induction machine. *Electric Power Applications . IEE Proceedings, 149*(1), 53–64.

Coutinho, D. F., & Pereira, L. P. F. A. (2005), A robust Luenberger-like observer for induction machines. In *Proceedings IEEE IECON*, North Carolina, USA.

Feldkamp, L. A., Prokhorov, D. V., & Feldkamp, T. M. (2003). Simple and conditioned adaptive behavior from Kalman filter trained recurrent networks. *Neural Networks, 16*(5-6), 683–689. doi:10.1016/S0893-6080(03)00127-8

Ge, S. S., Zhang, J., & Lee, T. H. (2004). Adaptive neural network control for a class of MIMO nonlinear systems with disturbances in discrete-time. *IEEE Transactions on Systems, Man and Cybernetics . Part B, 34*(4), 1630–1645.

Gentil, S. (1981). *Modélisation en ecologie: méthodologie et application aux ecosystèmes lacustres*. Ph. D. Dissertation (In French), Ecole des Sciences Physyques, France.

Ghazali, R., Hussain, A., & Merabti, M. (2006). Higher order neural networks and their applications to financial time series prediction. In *Proceedings of the IASTED Artificial Intelligence and Soft Computing*. Palma De Mallorca, Spain.

Ghosh, J., & Shin, Y. (1992). Efficient high-order neural networks for classification and function approximation. *International Journal of Neural Systems, 3*(4), 323–350. doi:10.1142/S0129065792000255

Grover, R., & Hwang, P. Y. C. (1992). *Introduction to Random Signals and Applied Kalman Filtering*. 2nd ed. NY: John Wiley and Sons

Haykin, S. (2001). *Kalman Filtering and Neural Networks. NY:* John Wiley and Sons.

Huang, H., Feng, G., & Cao, J. (2008). Robust state estimation for uncertain neural networks with time-varying delay. *IEEE Transactions on Neural Networks, 19*(8), 1329–1339. doi:10.1109/TNN.2008.2000206

Kim, Y. H., & Lewis, F. L. (1998). *High-Level Feedback Control with Neural Networks*. Singapore: World Scientific.

Krener, A. J., & Isidori, A. (1983). Linearization by output injection and nonlinear observers. *Systems & Control Letters*, *3*(1), 47–52. doi:10.1016/0167-6911(83)90037-3

Leunga, C., & Chan, L. (2003). Dual extended Kalman filtering in recurrent neural networks. *Neural Networks*, *16*(2), 223–239. doi:10.1016/S0893-6080(02)00230-7

Levin, A. U., & Narendra, K. S. (1996). Control of nonlinear dynamical systems using neural networks - part II: observability, identification and control. *IEEE Transactions on Neural Networks*, *7*(1), 30–42. doi:10.1109/72.478390

Li, J., & Zhong, Y. (2005). Comparison of three Kalman filters for speed estimation of induction machines. In *Proceedings of Industry Applications Conference* 2005, Hong Kong, China.

Liu, Y., Wang, Z., & Liu, X. (2007). Design of exponential state estimators for neural networks with mixed time delays. *Physics Letters. [Part A]*, *364*(5), 401–412. doi:10.1016/j.physleta.2006.12.018

Marino, R. (1990). Observers for single output nonlinear systems. *IEEE Transactions on Automatic Control*, *35*(9), 1054–1058. doi:10.1109/9.58536

Narendra, K. S., & Parthasarathy, K. (1990). Identification and control of dynamical systems using neural networks. *IEEE Transactions on Neural Networks*, *1*(1), 4–27. doi:10.1109/72.80202

Nicosia, S., & Tornambe, A. (1989). High-gain observers in the state and parameter estimation of robots having elastic joins. *Systems & Control Letters*, *13*(44), 331–337. doi:10.1016/0167-6911(89)90121-7

Poznyak, A. S., Sanchez, E. N., & Yu, W. (2001). *Differential Neural Networks for Robust Nonlinear Control*. Singapore: World Scientific

Rovithakis, G. A., & Christodoulou, M. A. (2000). *Adaptive Control with Recurrent High-Order Neural Networks*. New York: Springer Verlag

Sanchez, E. N., & Ricalde, L. J. (2003). Trajectory tracking via adaptive recurrent neural control with input saturation. In *Proceedings of International Joint Conference on Neural Networks* (pp. 359-364), Portland, OR.

Walcott, B. L., & Zak, S. H. (1987). State observation of nonlinear uncertain dynamical system. *IEEE Transactions on Automatic Control*, *32*(2), 166–170. doi:10.1109/TAC.1987.1104530

Wang, Z., Ho, D. W. C., & Liu, X. (2005). State estimation for delayed neural networks. *IEEE Transactions on Neural Networks*, *16*(1), 279–284. doi:10.1109/TNN.2004.841813

Williams, R. J., & Zipser, D. (1989). A learning algorithm for continually running fully recurrent neural networks. *Neural Computation*, *1*(2), 270–280. doi:10.1162/neco.1989.1.2.270

Yu, W., & Li, X. (2004). Nonlinear system identification using discrete-time recurrent neural networks with stable learning algorithms. *Information Sciences*, *158*(1), 131–147. doi:10.1016/j.ins.2003.08.002

Chapter 16
Electric Machines Excitation Control via Higher Order Neural Networks

Yannis L. Karnavas
Supreme Technological Educational Institution of Crete, Greece

ABSTRACT

This chapter is demonstrating a practical design of an intelligent type of controller using higher order neural network (HONN) concepts, for the excitation control of a practical power generating system. This type of controller is suitable for real time operation, and aims to improve the dynamic characteristics of the generating unit by acting properly on its original excitation system. The modeling of the power system under study consists of a synchronous generator connected via a transformer and a transmission line to an infinite bus. For comparison purposes and also for producing useful data in order for the demonstrating neural network controllers to be trained, digital simulations of the above system are performed using fuzzy logic control (FLC) techniques, which are based on previous work. Then, two neural network controllers are designed and applied by adopting the HONN architectures. The first one utilizes a single pi-sigma neural network (PSNN) and the significant advantages over the standard multi layered perceptron (MLP) are discussed. Secondly, an enhanced controller is designed, leading to a ridge polynomial neural network (RPNN) by combining multiple PSNNs if needed. Both controllers used, can be pre-trained rapidly from the corresponding FLC output signal and act as model dynamics capturers. The dynamic performances of the fuzzy logic controller (FLC) along with those of the two demonstrated controllers are presented by comparison using the well known integral square error criterion (ISE). The latter controllers, show excellent convergence properties and accuracy for function approximation. Typical transient responses of the system are shown for comparison in order to demonstrate the effectiveness of the designed controllers. The computer simulation results obtained show clearly that the performance of the developed controllers offers competitive damping effects on the synchronous generator's oscillations, with respect to the associated ones of the FLC, over a wider range of operating conditions, while their hardware implementation is apparently much easier and the computational time needed for real-time applications is drastically reduced.

DOI: 10.4018/978-1-61520-711-4.ch016

INTRODUCTION

The problem of electric power system dynamic stability has received growing attention over the last decades. The main reasons for this are the increasing size of generating units and the use of high-speed excitation systems. The effect of the high-speed excitation on dynamic stability is to add negative damping to the system thereby causing oscillations with weak damping. A design of such an excitation system should also be satisfactory for a wide range of operating conditions as well as for fault conditions. Practical methods for nonlinear control include an open-loop inverse model of the nonlinear plant dynamics and the use of feedback loops to cancel the plant nonlinearities. The approximation of a non-linear system with a linearized model yields to the application of adaptive control, where real-time measurements of the plant inputs are used, either to derive explicitly the plant model and design a controller based on this model (indirect adaptive control), or to directly modify the controller output (direct adaptive control). Typical studies concerning applications of modern algebraic and optimal control methods in excitation controller design using linear system models and output feedback have been presented before, (e.g. Papadopoulos, 1986; Papadopoulos, Smith & Tsourlis, 1989; Mao, Malik & Hope, 1990, Karnavas & Pantos, 2008).

The aim of this chapter is to investigate the use of HONNs as a replacement of an existing (designed previously) FLC, applied in the excitation part of a practical synchronous electric machine workbench system. The first type of the polynomial neural network used is called *pi-sigma network*. This network utilizes product cells as the output units to indirectly incorporate the capabilities of HONNs, while using a fewer number of weights and processing units. The motivation here is to develop a systematic type of controller which maintains the fast learning property of single-layer HONNs, while avoiding the exponential increase in the number of weights and processing units required. The network has a regular structure, exhibits much faster learning, and is amenable to the incremental addition of units to attain a desired level of complexity. If such an incremental addition of units takes place, then a *ridge polynomial network* (RPNN) is produced. The second controller described here refers to this kind of architecture. Simulation results show excellent convergence properties and accuracy for function approximation. Comparative results using a FLC output training data set are also provided to highlight the learning, and subsequently control, abilities of the proposed PSNN and RPNN controllers.

At first, digital simulations of the above system are performed with FLC controller based on previous works by the author under various disturbance conditions (Karnavas & Papadopoulos, 2000). Next, an effort is made on the design and simulation of the HONN controllers. The new results are compared with those of the FLC. The overall evaluation of the proposed PSNN and RPNN controllers is made through the ISE criterion.

The chapter is organized as follows, keeping in mind that throughout all Sections, a brief literature review will be reported accompanied by the relevant background and definitions. In the first Section, the electric power system under investigation (to which the associated controllers will be applied and evaluated) is discussed and the corresponding mathematical background is presented. A Section follows, referring to relevant work been done, where the philosophies of the conventional as well as of the intelligent controller design schemes are reviewed. Brief reviews of the main aspects of two modern intelligent control techniques (fuzzy, neural) are presented. For illustrations purposes, a fuzzy logic controller is also designed and applied to the aforementioned synchronous generator power system. Another Section follows which presents the polynomial neural network based controllers, where an explicit development of the PSNN and the RPNN type along with their learning rules and algorithms are demonstrated.

This effort is made to overcome the drawbacks of the previous methods. In the last Section some cases of study are being investigated and a comparison is made to show the relative goodness of the control strategies employed. The computer simulation results obtained over a number of simulations clearly illustrate that there are potential capabilities of this HONN approaches. From a practical point of view, the required computational time is reduced while the hardware implementation is much easier than i.e. a FLC. It is also demonstrated that the performance of the two developed controllers will offer competitive damping effects on the generator oscillations over a wider range of operating conditions, with the associated ones of the FLC design.

IMPORTANCE OF THE EXCITATION CONTROL PROBLEM

Transient stability is a fundamental property of power systems due to its evident impact on the performance of this kind of systems. Roughly speaking this property can be formulated as the ability of the synchronous generation units to preserve the system's behaviour around a given stable operating (equilibrium) point in spite of the presence of large disturbances and/or faults in the network (Willems, 1971). From a control perspective it is well known that transient stability improvement relies on the kind of the excitation controller used for the synchronous generation units (De Mello & Concordia, 1969). However, the design of these control devices is far to be obvious due (mainly) to the nonlinear and complex behaviour exhibited by power systems. Two currently accepted assumptions that simplify the excitation control design are: to consider a single generator connected to an infinite bus, i.e. a single machine infinite bus (SMIB) system and to approximate the actual dynamics of a synchronous generator by the classical third-order dynamic generator model (Pai, 1989).

Nevertheless, in spite of the aforementioned simplifications, finding a solution to the excitation control problem of SMIB systems still remains to be complicated due to the fact that the third-order representation is of a nonlinear nature, not all the machine state is available for measurement and the equilibrium point at which the generator operates (and that in its turn defines some of the model parameters) is not know. Fortunately, it is also possible to identify, in addition to the fact that mechanical speed is usually available for measurement in practical power systems, some conditions that alleviate at some extent the design procedure, e.g. it can be assumed that the mechanical power delivered to the generator is a known constant (Willems, 1971) and it has been recognized that in order to enhance transient stability power angle has to be one of the feedback variables (Guo et al., 2001).

Under the above-mentioned conditions, the design of the required controllers was initially studied from the theory of linear or linearized systems leading to the proposition of different (currently accepted as standard) solutions used in practice (IEEE Standard 425.1, 1992). However, it has been shown that the schemes obtained from this approach do not work properly under the new composition that the electric energy industry is witnessing (Kirschen et al., 2000). Hence, a topic that has attracted the attention is the proposition of new excitation control schemes that achieve the more stringent requirements imposed to the electric utility. Thus, it is possible to find designs based on feedback linearization (Chapman et al., 1993), singular perturbation (Sauer et al. 1998), Lyapunov stability (Machowski et al., 1998) and passivity ideas (Espinosa-Perez et al. 1997, Ortega et al., 1998). However, issues like stability analysis with output feedback and robustness against parameter uncertainty have not been completely clarified. Notwithstanding this lack of completeness in the proposed solutions, one of the approaches that has shown to be particularly interesting, due to the proposition of control schemes with a clear physical

Figure 1. Simplified representation of synchronous electric machine plus exciter supplying power to the electric utility system through an interconnection network

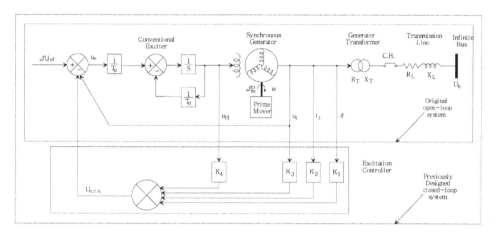

structure, is the so-called intelligent control. This kind of controllers can be roughly classified into damping injection and interconnection and damping assignment based controllers. Regarding the first kind, an intelligent dynamic damping injection controller could be proposed which enhances critical clearing times by feeding back the generator output (a nonlinear function of the machine state) and using an adaptation mechanism in order to deal with the uncertainty about the equilibrium point.

ELECTRIC MACHINE MODEL UNDER STUDY

The power system model to which the new PSNN and RPNN controllers' designs are applied consists of an 87.5kVA alternator-set model connected via a transformer and transmission line to an infinite bus, is taken from (Karnavas & Papadopoulos, 2000) and is shown here in Figure 1. The machine model was selected to have parameters broadly typical of those associated with larger machines. This approach can facilitate hardware changes as required and allows for practical tests to be carried out without disruptions in main generator sources. The main parameters for this machine are given in (Karnavas & Papadopoulos, 2000, 2002a, 2004), but for practical purposes are stated also in the Appendix A.

It is readily seen that the per-unit reactances are absolutely representative of turbogenerators in the range of 20-30MW used in the electric power industry.

Establishment of the Control Scheme

The linearized system equations can be expressed in the well known standard state-space differential form, i.e.

$$\dot{\mathbf{x}} = \mathbf{A}\mathbf{x} + \mathbf{B}\mathbf{u} \;,\; \mathbf{y} = \mathbf{C}\mathbf{x} \tag{1}$$

where $\mathbf{x} \in R^n$, $\mathbf{y} \in R^m$ and $\mathbf{u} \in R^p$ are the state, output and input vectors respectively, and $\mathbf{A}$, $\mathbf{B}$ and $\mathbf{C}$ are real constant system matrices of appropriate dimensions. The following system model designed in order to justify the most appropriate one and subsequently based on it for the development of the proposed HONN controller structures.

Non-Transformed Synchronous Machine Model

Based on (Karnavas & Papadopoulos, 2000) the non-transformed state-space model of the synchronous machine in the form of Eq. (1), is

$$\mathbf{x}^T = \begin{bmatrix} i_d & i_q & i_{fd} & i_{kd} & i_{kq} & \delta & \omega \end{bmatrix} \tag{2a}$$

$$\mathbf{u}^T = \begin{bmatrix} u_{fd} & P_m \end{bmatrix} \tag{2b}$$

where the explicit numerical values of **A** and **B** are based on the specific operating point given in Appendix A.

Transformed Synchronous Machine Model

The practical 7th-order transformed open-loop synchronous machine model, resulting from an appropriate transformation, is given by

$$\begin{bmatrix} \mathbf{x}' \end{bmatrix}^T = \begin{bmatrix} u_t & i_t & i_{fd} & i_{kd} & i_{kq} & \delta & \omega \end{bmatrix} \tag{3a}$$

$$\begin{bmatrix} \mathbf{u}' \end{bmatrix}^T = \mathbf{u}^T = \begin{bmatrix} u_{fd} & P_m \end{bmatrix} \tag{3b}$$

Case (a): 8th-order transformed open-loop synchronous machine model plus exciter model
The introduction of the 1st-order differential equation, describing the conventional exciter, to the above 7th-order model, yields the 8th-order transformed open-loop synchronous machine with conventional exciter model in the form of Eq.(1), i.e.

$$\begin{bmatrix} \mathbf{x}'' \end{bmatrix}^T = \begin{bmatrix} u_t & i_t & i_{fd} & i_{kd} & i_{kq} & \delta & \omega & u_{fd} \end{bmatrix} \tag{4a}$$

$$\begin{bmatrix} \mathbf{u}'' \end{bmatrix}^T = \begin{bmatrix} u_e \end{bmatrix} \tag{4b}$$

$$\begin{bmatrix} \mathbf{y}'' \end{bmatrix}^T = \begin{bmatrix} u_t & i_t & \delta & \omega \end{bmatrix} \tag{4c}$$

Eq. (4b) presupposes that the prime mover maintains P_m constant which is the usual assumption made for uncoupling the two control loops of the synchronous machine for carrying-out dynamic analysis based on small-input disturbances. Explicit matrices **A**" and **B**" of the system of Eqs. (4a) to (4c) are given in (Karnavas & Papadopoulos, 2000).

Case (b): 4ᵗʰ-order transformed open-loop synchronous machine model plus exciter model

Based on the output energy criterion, the 8ᵗʰ-order open-loop model was re-arranged in decreasing order of state variable participation in the output energy of the system, i.e.

$$\left[\mathbf{x}'''\right]^T = \begin{bmatrix} \delta & i_t & u_t & u_{fd} & \omega & i_{fd} & i_{kd} & i_{kq} \end{bmatrix} \tag{5a}$$

$$\left[\mathbf{u}'''\right]^T = \left[\mathbf{u}''\right] = \begin{bmatrix} u_e \end{bmatrix} \tag{5b}$$

$$\left[\mathbf{y}'''\right]^T = \begin{bmatrix} \delta & i_t & u_t & u_{fd} \end{bmatrix} \tag{5c}$$

The relevant system eigenvalue evaluation showed that the adequate reduced order open-loop model should be of 4ᵗʰ-order and in the form of Eq.(1) it becomes

$$\left[\mathbf{x_r}\right]^T = \begin{bmatrix} \delta & i_t & u_t & u_{fd} \end{bmatrix} \tag{6a}$$

$$\left[\mathbf{u_r}\right] = \left[\mathbf{u}''\right] = \begin{bmatrix} u_e \end{bmatrix} \tag{6b}$$

$$\left[\mathbf{y_r}\right]^T = \left[\mathbf{x_r}\right]^T \tag{6c}$$

where the relevant system matrices $\mathbf{A_r}$, $\mathbf{B_r}$ and $\mathbf{C_r}$ are also given in (Karnavas & Papadopoulos, 2000). By assuming zero initial conditions in the 8ᵗʰ-order model the corresponding initial conditions of the reduced order model are

$$\left[\mathbf{x_r}(0)\right]^T = \begin{bmatrix} 2.1457 & 0 & -0.7411 & 0 \end{bmatrix} \begin{bmatrix} u_e(0) \end{bmatrix}$$

Case (c): 8ᵗʰ-order transformed closed-loop model

With output feedback applied to the system of Eqs. (5a) to (5c) the following have been obtained: the gain output feedback vector **k**, i.e.

$$\mathbf{k}^T = \begin{bmatrix} -0.0219 & 0.0167 & -0.0412 & 0.4870 \end{bmatrix} \tag{7}$$

and the matrix $\overline{\mathbf{A}}''$ from the relationship:

$$\overline{\mathbf{A}}'' = \mathbf{A}'' - \mathbf{B}''\mathbf{k}^T \tag{8}$$

Case (d): 4ᵗʰ-order reduced closed-loop model

The associated reduced order model has given: the gain output feedback vector $\mathbf{k_r}$ as well as the new $\overline{\mathbf{A}}_r$ matrix

371

$$\mathbf{k}_r^T = \begin{bmatrix} -0.0056 & 0.0029 & 0.0037 & 1.327 \end{bmatrix} \tag{9}$$

$$\overline{\mathbf{A}}_r = \mathbf{A}_r - \mathbf{B}_r \mathbf{k}_r^T \tag{10}$$

Case (e): 8th-order transformed closed-loop model (with the controller of the reduced 4th-order closed-loop model)

The gain output feedback vector $\mathbf{k}_r$ of Eq. (9) along with the 8th-order transformed open-loop model defined by Eqs. (5a) to (5c) was used then, in order to design a new 8th-order closed-loop system model. The matrix of this model is obtained from the relationship:

$$\overline{\mathbf{A}}'^v = \mathbf{A}'' - \mathbf{B}'' \mathbf{k}_r^T \tag{11}$$

For the above five cases of system models the computed time responses of the output variables u_r, i_r, δ and u_{fd} for the small-input step change Δu_e=0.001pu are justified and the following conclusion derived:

The 8th-order transformed open-loop model is stable but does not necessarily possess satisfactory damping characteristics and sufficiently fast response. (*Case (a)*).

The outputs of the 4th-order reduced open-loop model follow quite well the corresponding outputs of the 8th-order open-loop model (*Case (b)*).

The dynamic stability characteristics of the reduced 4th-order closed-loop model are by far superior to those of the 8th-order transformed closed-loop model. (*Case (d)* far better than *Case (c)*). The degree of enhancement achieved in the dynamic stability characteristics in the *Case (e)* is practically the same as that achieved when the reduced 4th-order closed-loop system model was used.

Intelligent Techniques

Fuzzy Logic Control

Fuzzy logic control (Zadeh, 1965, Lee, 1990) essentially involves the derivation of a control law from heuristic an imprecise ("fuzzy") rules. While the mathematical models of the power system are available, they tend to be highly nonlinear and therefore the controller design becomes a highly formidable task. Fuzzy logic control has been applied for the design of power system stabilizers (Hassan, Malik, & Hope, 1991, Hiyama, 1989) and has been shown to give improved performance than conventional controllers.

Fuzzy approaches to intelligent control schemes treat situations where some of the defining relationships can be described by fuzzy sets and fuzzy relational equations (Ross, 1995, Hassan, Malik & Hope, 1991; Handschin et al., 1994; Djukanovic et al. 1997). Fuzzy logic controllers (FLCs) constitute knowledge-based systems that include fuzzy rules and fuzzy membership functions to incorporate human knowledge into their knowledge base. Some studies concerning applications in excitation controller design using fuzzy set theory have been developed before (e.g. Karnavas, Papadopoulos, 2002).

Figure 2 schematically depicts a typical closed-loop fuzzy control system. The reference signal and plant output, which are crisp values but non-fuzzy variables, must be fuzzified by a fuzzification

Figure 2. Block diagram of a typical closed-loop fuzzy control system

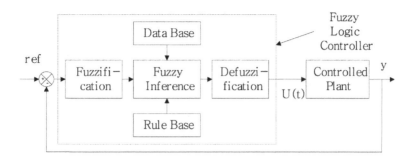

procedure. Similarly, the fact that the controlled plant can not directly respond to fuzzy logic controls accounts for why the fuzzy logic control signal generated by the fuzzy algorithm must be defuzzified by defuzzification before applied to control the plant. A rule base consists of a set of fuzzy rules. The data base contains membership functions of fuzzy subsets. A fuzzy rule may contain fuzzy variables, fuzzy subsets characterized by membership functions and a conditional statement. The fuzzy control algorithm consists of executing an ordered sequence of fuzzy rules by the concepts of fuzzy implication and the compositional rules of inference. Essentially, a FLC is a deterministic model-free, non-linear and robust controller.

The basic configuration of the designed FLC used here, comprises the four principal components: fuzzification interface, knowledge base, decision-making logic, and defuzzification interface (Figure 3). The input variables are defined as the deviation from a reference or setpoint value, called the error (e), and its first derivative, which in fuzzy control terms is usually called the *change in error* (ce). It is found that the use of a third input variable which is the terminal voltage difference (Δu_t) helps the FLC to display better performance. According to Figure 1 and Figure 3 the input variables are defined as:

$$
\begin{aligned}
e(t) &= \Delta U_{ref} - K_1\delta(t) - K_2 i_t(t) - K_3 u_t(t) - K_4 u_{fd}(t) \\
ce(t) &= \Delta e(t)/\Delta t = \left[e(t) - e(t-1)\right]/T_s \\
\Delta u_t(t) &= u_t(t) - u_t(t-1)
\end{aligned}
\tag{12}
$$

Figure 3. Structure of the designed fuzzy logic controller

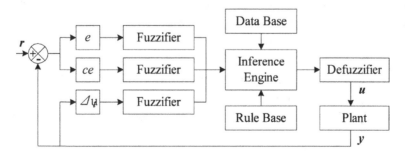

Figure 4. Membership functions of the (normalized) input fuzzy variables

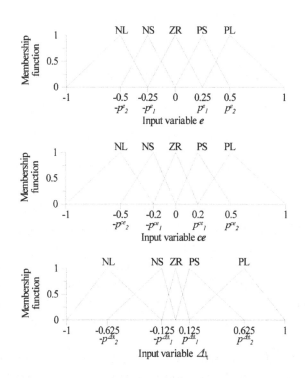

where T_s is the sampling time. The FLC output variable, which is the control input of the excitation system, is the field voltage u_{fd}.

Next, the fuzzy set values of the input and output fuzzy variables are specified. With respect to a robust realization five fuzzy sets are defined for each linguistic (input and output) variable. The fuzzy set values of the fuzzy variables are chosen as follows: NL (Negative Large), NS (Negative Small), ZR (Zero), PS (Positive Small), PL (Positive Large) for the input variables, and VL (Very Large), (L) Large, (NR) Normal, VS (Very Small), S (Small) for the output variable. The input fuzzy variables, with their respective fuzzy set values, are shown in Figure 4. To determine how to modify the control variable u_{fd} from the monitored fuzzy input variables, two fuzzy associative matrices (FAM) were established. The synthesized FAMs for the FLC are shown in Figure 5.

Neural Network Control

Many of the ANNs applications in control areas involve learning the control system dynamics and incorporating them, in some way to the overall system controller. The approaches differ in the methods used for such incorporation, the learning and adaptation of the ANN (Narendra, & Parthasarathy, 1990; Hu & Shao, 1992; Yamada, & Yabuta, 1992; Campolucci et al., 1996; Chen & Chang, 1996; Vecci, Piazza, & Uncini, 1998). One approach is to train the ANN off-line to learn the system dynamics and employ it as a feed-forward controller as shown in Figure 6a. In another approach the ANN is employed as a replacement for the plant dynamics evaluation inside the model-based control algorithm as shown in Figure 6b.

Figure 5. Fuzzy associative matrices for the output control variable u_{fd}

		ce				
		NL	NS	ZR	PS	PL
	NL	VL	VL	VL		
	NS	VL	L	L		
e	ZR	VL	L	NR	S	VS
	PS			S	S	VS
	PL			VS	VS	VS

Δu_t	NL	NS	ZR	PS	PL
u_{fd}	VL	L	NR	S	VS

Figure 6. (a) ANN as a feed-forward controller, (b) ANN as an adaptive controller

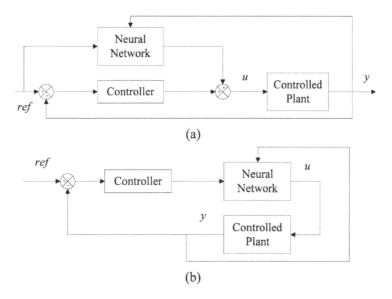

(a)

(b)

Furthermore, the function approximation capability of the network improves as the number of nodes in the hidden layer increases. In other words, a suitable network can always be found. For example, an extended result for learning conditional probability distributions was found by Allen and Taylor (1994). Here, two network layers are required in order to produce a smooth limit when the stochastic series being modeled becomes noise free. During learning, the outputs of a supervised neural network come to approximate the target values given the inputs in the training set. This ability may be useful in itself, but more often the purpose of using a neural net is to generalize - in other words, to have the network outputs approximate target values given inputs that are not in the training set. Generally speaking, there are three conditions that are typically necessary - although not sufficient - for good generalization.

The first necessary condition is that the network inputs contain sufficient information pertaining to the target, so that there exists a mathematical function relating correct outputs to inputs with the desired degree of accuracy (Caudill & Butler, 1990). The second necessary condition is that the function we are attempting to learn (relating inputs to desired outputs) be, in some sense, smooth (Devroye, Gyorfi, & Lugosi, 1996; Plotkin, 1993). In other words, small changes in inputs should produce small changes in outputs, at least most of the time. For continuous inputs and targets, function smoothness implies continuity and restrictions on the first derivative over most of the input space. Now some neural networks - including the HONN models - are able to learn discontinuities, provided the function consists of a finite number of continuous pieces. Conversely, very non-smooth functions (such as those produced by pseudorandom number generators and encryption algorithms) are not able to be generalized by standard neural networks. The third necessary condition for good generalization is that the training exemplars constitute a sufficiently large and representative subset ("sample" in statistics terminology) of the set of all cases we want to generalize to (the "population" in statistics terminology) (Wolpert, 1996a, 1996b). The importance of this condition is related to the fact that there are, generally speaking, two different types of generalization: interpolation and extrapolation. Interpolation applies to cases that are more or less surrounded by nearby training cases; everything else is extrapolation. In particular, cases that are outside the range of the training data require extrapolation. Cases inside large "holes" in the training data may also effectively require extrapolation. Interpolation can often be performed reliably, but extrapolation is notoriously unreliable. Hence, it is important to have sufficient training data to avoid the need for extrapolation. Methods for selecting good training sets are discussed in numerous statistical textbooks on sample surveys and experimental design (e.g., Diamond & Jeffries, 2001).

Despite the universal approximation capability of MLP/BP networks, their performance is limited when applied to high non-linear systems like the one examined here (synchronous generator excitation control) This is due in part to two limitations of feed-forward ANNs, namely: a) Their activation functions have fixed parameters only (e.g., sigmoid, radial-basis function, and so on), and b) They are capable of continuous function approximation only; MLPs are unable to handle discontinuous and/or piecewise-continuous functions.

Networks with adaptive activation functions seem to provide better fitting properties than classical architectures with fixed activation-function neurons. Vecci, Piazza, and Uncini (1998) studied the properties of a feed-forward neural network (FNN) which was able to adapt its activation function by varying the control points of a Catmull-Rom cubic spline. Their simulations confirmed that the special learning mechanism allows us to use the network's free parameters in a very effective way. In Chen and Chang (1996), real variables a (gain) and b (slope) in the generalized sigmoid activation function were adjusted during the learning process. They showed that from the perspective of static and dynamical system modeling, use of adaptive sigmoids (in other words, sigmoids with free parameters) leads to improved data modeling. Campolucci et al. (1996) built an adaptive activation function as a piecewise approximation with suitable cubic splines. This function had arbitrary shape and allowed the overall size of the neural network to be reduced, trading connection complexity against activation function complexity. Several other authors (Hu & Shao, 1992; Yamada & Yabuta, 1992) have also studied the properties of neural networks that utilize adaptive activation functions.

POLYNOMIAL NEURAL NETWORK CONTROLLERS

Higher Order Feedforward Networks vs Multi Layered Perceptrons

Neurons in an ordinary feedforward network is just a first order neuron, also called a "linear neuron" since it only uses a linear sum of its inputs for decision. This linearity, providing a hyperplane for decision limits the capability of the neuron to solve only linear discriminate problems (Guler & Sahin, 1994).

Since Minsky and Papert's results (1969), it is well known that usual feedforward neural networks with first-order units can implement only linear separability mappings. One possibility to drop this limitation is to use multilayer networks where so-called hidden units can combine the outputs of previous units and so give rise to nonlinear mappings (Hornik, Stinchcombe, & White, 1989). MLP is of type 1st order neural network which can effectively carry out inner products which are then weighted and summed before passing through the non-linear threshold function. The other way to overcome the restriction to linear maps is to introduce higher order units to model nonlinear dependences (Giles & Maxwell, 1987; Giles, Griffin, & Maxwell, 1998). It should be noted however that multi-layered perceptron (MLP) networks using the backpropagation learning rule (e.g. Rumelhart et. al, 1986; Lapedes & Farber, 1987; Refenes, 1994; Zhang & Fulcher, 1996; Zhang, Fulcher, & Scofield, 1997, Karnavas & Papadopoulos, 2002b) or its variants have been successfully applied to applications involving pattern classification, function approximation, time-series prediction as well as control schemes of power systems. Unfortunately, the training speeds for multi-layered networks are extremely slower than those for feed-forward networks being composed of a single layer of threshold logic units (TLU), and using the perceptron, ADALINE or Hebbian type learning rules (McClelland & Rumelhart, 1987). Moreover, these networks converge very slowly in typical situations dealing with complex and nonlinear problems, and do not scale well with problem size.

HONNs are type of feedforward neural networks which provide nonlinear decision boundaries, therefore offering a better classification capability than the linear neuron (Guler & Sahin, 1994). The nonlinearity is introduced into the HONNs by having multi-linear interactions between their inputs or neurons which enable them to expand the input space into higher dimensional space. This lead to an easy separation of nonlinear separability classes where linear separability is possible or a reduction in the dimension of the nonlinearity is achieved. For example, the XOR problem could not be solved with a network without a hidden layer or by a single layer of first-order units, as it is not linear separability. However the same problem is easily solved if the patterns are represented in three dimension in terms of an enhanced representation (Pao, 1989), by just using a single layer network with second-order terms.

The presence of higher order terms in HONNs allowing the multiplication activity in the networks. Multiplication is an arithmetic operation that, when used in neural networks, helps to increase their computational power (Schmitt, 2001). There are good reasons to explicitly apply multiplication in the network. For instance, empirical evidence is available and reported for the existence of exponential and logarithmic dendritic processes in biological neural systems, allowing multiplication and polynomial processing (Schmitt, 2001). Consequently, as argued in (Durbin & Rumelhart, 1990), in order to model biological neural networks, one should extend the standard MLP model with multiplicative or product units. Further, biological networks make use of non-linear activation components in the form of axo-axonic synapses performing pre-synaptic inhibition (Neville, Stonham, & Glover, 2000). The simplest way of modeling such synapses and introducing increased node complexity is to use multi-linear acti-vation, which is the node's activation is in 'higher order' nodes form (Rumelhart, Hinton, & Williams, 1986), resulting the use of non-linear activation components.

According to (Durbin & Rumelhart, 1989), there are various ways in which product units could be used in a network. One way is for a few of them to be made available as inputs to the network in addi-tion to the original raw inputs. Alternatively, they can be used as the output of the network itself. The other way of utilizing them is a whole hidden layer of product units, feeding into a subsequent layer of summing units. The attraction is rather in mixing both types of units; product unit and summing unit, so that product units are mainly used in a network where they occur together with summing units.

A major advantage of HONNs is that only one layer of trainable weights is needed to achieve nonlinear separability, unlike the typical MLP or feedforward networks (Park, Smith, & Mersereau, 2000). They are simple in their architecture and require fewer numbers of weights to learn the underlying equation when compared to ordinary feedforward networks, in order to deliver the same input-output mapping (Park et al., 2000; Leerink, Giles, Horne, & Jabri, 1995; Giles & Maxwell, 1987; Shin & Ghosh, 1995). Consequently, they can learn faster in view of the fact that each iteration of the training procedure takes less time (Cass & Radl, 1996). This makes them *suitable models for complex problem solving where the ability to retrain or adapt to the new data in real time is critical* (Pau & Phillips, 1995; Artyomov & Pecht, 2005). Moreover, higher order terms in HONNs can increase the information capacity of neural networks in comparison to neural networks that utilize summation units only. The larger capacity means that the same function or problem can be solved by network that has fewer units. As a result, the representational power of higher order terms can help solving complex problems with construction of significantly smaller network while maintaining fast learning capabilities (Leerink et al., 1995).

Although it is possible to implement any continuous function using two layers of such nodes as in the MLPs, the resources required in terms of hardware and time can be prohibited. Memory requirements are minimized, making the hardware requirements more feasible. The simpler characteristic of HONNs, which having a single layer of trainable weights, can offers a large saving of hardware in the implementation (Patra & Pal, 1995). HONNs are endowed with certain unique characteristics; stronger approximation property, faster convergence rate, greater storage capacity, and higher fault tolerance than lower order neural networks (Wang, Fang, & Liu, 2006). The networks have been considered as good candidates, due to their design flexibility for given geometric transforms, robustness to noisy and/or occluded inputs, inherent fast training ability, and nonlinearly separable (Park et al., 2000).

Two types of artificial HONNs; Pi-Sigma neural networks, and Ridge Polynomial neural networks are considered in this chapter. Each one of them employs the powerful capabilities of product units with some combinations with summing units. Their architectures are varied in the way the position where the product units or higher order terms are used in the networks. The Pi-Sigma neural networks utilizes the higher order terms at the output layer, as the output of the network itself. On the other hand, the Ridge Polynomial neural networks made the higher order terms available as the whole hidden layer of product units feeding into a subsequent layer of summing units. With different strength and capabilities, the structure and characteristic of these networks is elaborated and discussed below, as well as their training algorithms and applications used into.

HONNs have traditionally been characterized as those in which the input to a computational neuron is a weighted sum of the products of its inputs (Lee et al., 1986). Such neurons are sometimes called higher order processing units (HPUs) (Lippmann, 1989). It has been established that HONNs can successfully perform invariant pattern recognition (Psaltis, Park, & Hong, 1988; Reid, Spirkovska, & Ochoa, 1989; Wood & Shawe-Taylor, 1996). Giles and Maxwell (1987) showed that HONNs have impressive computational, storage, and learning capabilities. Redding, Kowalski and Downs (1993) proved that HONNs were at least as powerful as any other (similar order) feed-forward neural network (FNN). Kosmatopoulos et al. (1995) studied the approximation and learning properties of one class of recurrent HONNs and applied these architectures to the identification of dynamical systems. Thimm and Fiesler (1997) proposed a suitable initialization method for HONNs and compared this with FNN-weight initialization.

Higher order correlations among the input components can be used to construct a higher order network to yield a nonlinear discriminant function using only a single layer of cells (Lee & Maxwell, 1997).

Moreover, higher order correlations in the training data require more complex neuron activation functions (Barron, Gilstrap, & Shrier, 1987; Giles & Maxwell, 1987; Psaltis, Park, & Hong, 1988). The building block of such networks in the higher order processing unit (HPU), defined as a neural processing unit that includes higher order input correlations, and its output *y*, is given (Lippmann, 1989):

$$y = \sigma \left(\sum_j w_j x_j + \sum_{j,k} w_{jk} x_j x_k + \sum_{j,k,l} w_{jkl} x_j x_k x_l + \cdots \right) \tag{13}$$

where $\sigma(x)$ is a nonlinear function of input *x*, x_j is the jth component of *x*, and w_{jkl}... is an adjustable weight from product of inputs x_j, x_k, x_l... to the HPU. If the input is of dimension *N*, then a kth order HPU needs a total of

$$\sum_{i=0}^{k} \binom{N+i-1}{i} \tag{14}$$

weights if all products of up to $k \leq N$ components are to be incorporated (Minsky & Papert, 1969).

A single layer of HPU (SLHPU) network is one in which only one layer of mapping from input to output using HPUs is considered. The order of a SLHPU network is the highest order of any of the constituent HPUs. Thus output of the kth order SLHPU is a nonlinear function of up to the kth order polynomials. Since it does not have hidden units as in sigma-pi network, reliable single layer learning rules such as perceptron, ADALINE, or Hebbian type rules can be used. However, to accommodate all higher order correlations, the number of weights required increases combinatorially in the dimensionality of the inputs (Minsky & Papert, 1969). Limiting the order of the network leads to a reduction in the classification capability of the network.

There have been many approaches which maintain the powerful discrimination capability of higher order networks while reducing higher order terms. For example, sigma-pi networks use a hidden layer of higher order TLUs. A multi-layering strategy using sigma-pi units retains the full capability of a higher order network using a smaller number of weights and processing units, but its learning speed is slower due to layering. Another approach is to use *a priori* information to remove the terms which are irrelevant to the problem in a single layer of higher order TLUs (Reid et al. 1989b). However, since it is often difficult to find the properties of input pattern space *a priori*, this strategy has limited applications.

This is reminiscent of Rumelhart, Hinton, and Williams (1986) formulation of their so-called "sigma-pi" neurons, for which they show that the generalized Delta Rule (standard backpropagation) can be applied as readily as for simple additive neurons. Moreover, the increased computational load resulting from the large increase in network weights means that the complex input-output mappings, normally only achievable in multilayered networks, can now be realized in a single HONN layer (Zhang & Fulcher, 2004). In summary, HONN activation functions incorporate multiplicative terms. Now the output of a kth-order single-layer HONN neuron will be a nonlinear function comprising polynomials of up to k^{th}-order. Moreover, since no hidden layers are involved, both Hebbian and perceptron learning rules can be employed (Shin & Ghosh, 1991). Multiplicative interconnections within ANNs have been applied to many different problems, however their complexity usually limits their usefulness. Karayiannis and Venetsanopoulos (1993) made the observation that the performance of first-order ANNs can be improved, within bounds, by utilizing sophisticated learning algorithms. By contrast, HONNs can achieve superior performance even if the learning algorithm is based on the simpler outer-product rule. A different approach was taken by Redding, Kowalczy, and Downs (1993) and involved the development of a constructive HONN architecture that solved the binary mapping in polynomial time. Central to this process was the selection of the multiplicative nonlinearities as hidden nodes within the HONN, depending on their relevance to the pattern data of interest.

Pi-Sigma Network Architecture

Figure 7a shows the demonstrated PSNN controller for the present chapter. The input x is an N dimensional vector and x_k is the kth component of x. The inputs are weighted and fed to a layer of K linear summing units, where K is the desired order of the network. Let h_{ji} be the output of the jth summing unit for the ith output, y_i, then,

$$h_{ji} = \sum_k w_{kji} x_k + \theta_{ji} \ , \ \text{and} \quad y_i = \sigma\left(\prod_j h_{ji}\right) \tag{15}$$

where w_{kji} is an adjustable weight from input x_k to the jth summing unit of the ith output, and θ_{ji} is an adjustable threshold of the jth summing unit of the ith output. The $\sigma(x)$ denotes the nonlinear activation function, and is selected as the logistic function, $\sigma(x) = 1/(1 + e^{-x})$ for all the results reported in this chapter. Note that connections from summing units to an output have fixed weights. Thus there is no notion of hidden units in the network and fast learning rules can be used.

The basic idea behind this type of network is that we can represent the input of a Kth order processing unit by a product of K linear combinations of the input components (Shin & Ghosh, 1991). That is why this network is called pi-sigma instead of sigma-pi (Figure 7b). In the SLHPU representation, the polynomial is represented by summation of all partial products of input components up to order K, thereby leading to an exponential increase in the number of adjustable weights required, as indicated in Table 1.

Figure 7. (a) Proposed Pi-Sigma neural network (PSNN) controller architecture, (b) Standard MLFF neural network architecture

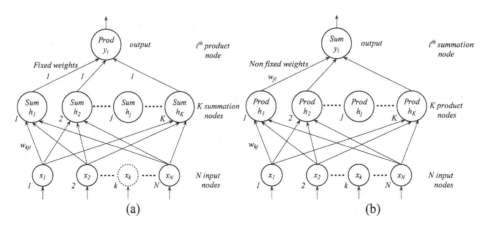

Table 1. Number of weights required for PSNN and SLHPU

Order of network	# of weights			
	Pi-Sigma		SLHPU	
	N=5	N=10	N=5	N=10
2	12	22	21	66
3	18	33	56	286
4	24	44	126	901

From the network topology point of view, this leads to an irregular structure. In the case of the PSNN, using an additional summing unit increases the network's order by 1 while preserving old connections and maintaining network topology.

Probabilistic Learning Rule Used in the PSNN

There are a total of $(N+1)K$ adjustable weights and thresholds for each output unit, since there are $N+1$ weights associated with each summing unit. The learning rule is a randomized version of the gradient descent procedure. Since the output y_i is a function of the product of all the h_{ji}'s, we do not have to adjust all the variable weights at each learning cycle. Instead, at each update step, we randomly select a summing unit and update the set of $N+1$ weights associated with its inputs based on a gradient descent approach. Let the mean square error (MSE) be

$$e^2 = \frac{1}{2}\sum_p \sum_i \left(d_i^p - y_i^p\right)^2 \tag{16}$$

where superscript p denotes the pth training pattern, d_i and y_i are the ith components of desired and actual outputs, respectively, and the summation is over all outputs and all training patterns. Applying gradient descent on this estimate of the MSE, we obtain the update rules for weights and threshold for each iteration step as

$$\Delta\theta_{li} = \eta\left(d_i - y_i\right)y_i' \prod_{j \neq l} h_{ji} \tag{17}$$

$$\Delta w_{kli} = \eta\left(d_i - y_i\right)y_i' \prod_{j \neq l} h_{ji} x_k = \Delta\theta_{li} x_k \tag{18}$$

where η is the scaling factor or the learning rate, and y_i' is the first derivative of the logistic function that is, $y_i' = \sigma'(x) = (1 - \sigma(x))\sigma(x)$. It is repeated that these updates are applied only to the set of weights and threshold corresponding to the lth summing unit which is chosen randomly at each step.

Ridge Polynomial Network Architecture

The PSNN provides only a constrained approximation of a power series. Because of this truncated approximation capability, the PSNN can not uniformly approximate all continuous multivariate functions that can be defined on a compact set. However, universal approximation can be attained by summing the outputs of several PSNN of different order. The resulting combined network of PSNN is called *ridge polynomial neural network*.

For $\mathbf{x}=(x_1, \ldots, x_d)^T$ and $\mathbf{w}=(w_1, \ldots, w_d)^T \in R^d$, the $\langle \mathbf{x}, \mathbf{w} \rangle$ is denoted as their inner product. For a given compact set $C \subset R^d$, all functions defined on C in the form of $f(\langle \mathbf{x}, \mathbf{w} \rangle)$, where f is a continuous function in one variable, are called ridge functions. A *ridge polynomial* is a ridge function that can be represented as

$$\sum_{i=0}^{n}\sum_{j=1}^{m} a_{ij} \left\langle \mathbf{x}, \mathbf{w}_{ij} \right\rangle^{i} \qquad (19)$$

for some $a_{ij} \in R$ and $\mathbf{w}_{ij} \in R^d$.

Let Π_k^d denote the set of all polynomials in R^d with degree $\leq k$. Then, for any polynomial $p(x)$ in Π_k^d, there exist $w_{ji} \in R$ and $\mathbf{w}_{ji} \in R^d$ such that,

$$p\left(x\right) = \sum_{j=1}^{N}\prod_{i=1}^{j}\left(\left\langle \mathbf{x}, \mathbf{w}_{ji} \right\rangle + w_{ji}\right) \qquad (20)$$

The original form of the theorem is more complicated that the one presented here. However, since we are concerned with the existence of a representation of multivariate polynomials in terms of ridge polynomials, a simpler statement is adopted. The detailed proof can be found in (Shin & Ghosh, 1992).

Figure 8 shows the generic network architecture of the RPNN using the PSNN as basic building blocks. Since, in general, there may not be much *a priori* information about the function to be approximated; it is difficult to choose an appropriate network size. On the other hand, an RPNN can be incrementally grown to meet a predefined error criterion.

Figure 8. Proposed ridge polynomial network (RPNN) controller architecture

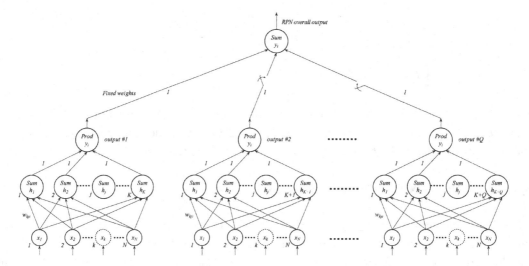

Incremental Learning Algorithm Used in the RPNN

Instead of limiting the activation functions to linear ones, we can use activation functions such as sigmoid or hyperbolic tangent. Thus, using fixed network architecture, an unknown function f in R^d can be approximated by the direct use of the RPNN model of degree up to k based on

$$f(x) \approx \sigma\left(\sum_{i=1}^{k} P_i(\mathbf{x})\right) \tag{21}$$

where

$$P_i(x) = \prod_{j=1}^{i}\left(\langle \mathbf{w}_j, \mathbf{x} \rangle + w_{j0}\right), \quad i = 1,\ldots,k \tag{22}$$

and $\sigma(.)$ is a suitable linear or nonlinear activation function, $w_j \in R^d$ and $w_{j0} \in R$ are determined by learning process. Since each P_i in Eq. (15) is obtainable as the output of a PSNN of degree i with linear output units, the learning algorithms for the PSNN can be used for the RPNN. Equipped with suitable error measure (e.g. MSE), every P_i is optimized by fixing other polynomials.

An incremental learning algorithm proceeds as follows. We denote k an algorithmic step at which P_k is added to the network with "predetermined" $P_0, \ldots, P_{k-1}$. That is, with $P_0 \equiv 0$, the function f is approximated by the RPNN at the kth step as,

$$f(x) \approx \sigma\left(\sum_{i=0}^{k-1} P_i(\mathbf{x}) + P_k(\mathbf{x})\right) \tag{23}$$

where the weights in $P_0, \ldots, P_{k-1}$ are frozen once the kth degree PSNN is added. This is equivalent to approximating $\sigma^{-1} \circ f(\mathbf{x}) - \sum_{i=0}^{k-1} P_i(\mathbf{x})$ with a kth degree PSNN, $P_k(\mathbf{x})$, with linear output units.

5. APPLICATION AND SIMULATION RESULTS

The designed new PSNN and RPNN controllers are applied to the power generating system of Figure 1 and several cases of interest have been investigated. Some of the cases studied, the results of which are shown here, are summarized in Table 2. For these cases of disturbance, the FLC model was also simulated under the same conditions in order to compare the results with the associated ones of the PSNN and RPNN controllers.

For Cases A through D the FLC input ($e(t)$, $ce(t)$, $\Delta u(t)$) and output (u_{fd}) signals was used to train the two proposed controllers. To show the capability of the learning algorithms used, the PSNN as well as the RPNN were not trained at all for the Case E and Case F, but the final weights of Case D were used instead. In the other Cases, the initial weights were randomly assigned values between -0.5 and 0.5 for all the PSNNs used. The learning rate was held constant for a PSNN but decreased by a factor of 1.7 if another PSNN was added. A new PSNN was added if the ratio of the difference between MSEs of the previous epoch and the current epoch and the MSE of the previous epoch was less than a threshold, ε_{th}. Since the dynamic range of the error between the desired output and the actual algorithm output becomes

Table 2. Disturbance cases applied to power system under study

Case No.	Δue (p.u.)	At time instant (sec)	Change in Δue (p.u.)	At time instant (sec)
A.	0.0010	0.0	-	-
B.	0.0010	0.0	0.002	4.0
C.	0.0020	0.0	-	-
D.	0.0020	0.0	0.002	4.0
E*	0.0015	0.0	0.002	4.0
F*	0.0005	0.0	0.004	4.0

(*) The weights that PSNN and RPNN use are from Case D.

smaller as learning proceeds, ε_{th} was decreased by a factor of 10 at each addition of a PSNN. In case of a RPNN used, the training started with a 3rd degree PSNN. The initial learning rate and ε_{th} were 0.8 and 0.0001 respectively. The learning was quite stable and the MSE decreased drastically when additional PSNNs were added.

Figure 9 and Figure 10 show the time responses of the generator's exciter field voltage (u_{fd}) and the generator's output voltage (u_t) -control variables- when FLC and PSNN are applied, whereas Figure 11 and Figure 12 show the corresponding responses when FLC and RPNN are applied for the disturbance cases of Table 2. From these figures it is clear that the PSNN and RPNN performance competes the associated one of the FLC. That proves the ability of the HONNs to capture the dynamics of the system they control (as can be seen from Figure 9 and Figure 11), not only for cases that they are trained for (i.e. Case A through D) but also for a much wider operating region (Case E and F).

Consequently, the relative improvement of the system's dynamics regarding the controlled variable (generator's terminal voltage) is readily seen in Figure 10 and Figure 12. Apparently, the developed controllers show very good convergence properties and accuracy for function approximation while their performance offers competitive damping effects on the generator oscillations, with respect to the

Figure 9. Time responses of field voltage (u_{fd}) when FLC and PSNN are applied. (a) through (f) are the corresponding cases of disturbance (Table 2)

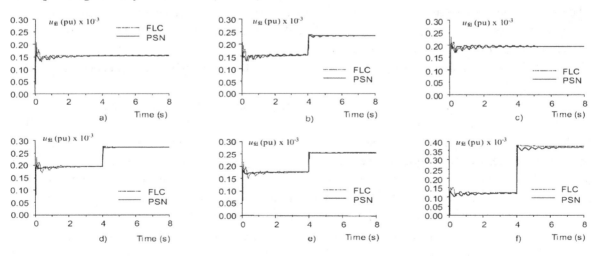

Figure 10. Time responses of terminal voltage (uₜ) when FLC and PSNN are applied. (a) through (f) are the corresponding cases of disturbance (Table 2)

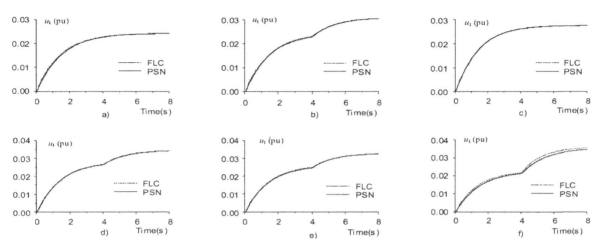

associated ones of the FLC. It is to be noted that the FLC and PSNN/RPNN controllers have quite the same characteristics due to the fact that the FLC was used to train the PSNN/RPNN ones. Moreover, the MSE for the Cases that the PSNN and RPNN are trained from the FLC input and output variables are shown in Figure 13.

From the latter figure, it can be seen that the RPNN (with one or two more PSNN blocks) can be trained quite faster and in a more stable manner than the single PSNN type. Finally, the integration-square-error-time (ISE) criterion of the following form is used to evaluate the quality performance of the relevant controller designs. The results derived through the whole set of simulation runs, are summarized in Table 3.

Figure 11. Time responses of ufd when FLC and RPNN are applied. (A) through (F) are the corresponding cases of disturbance (Table 2)

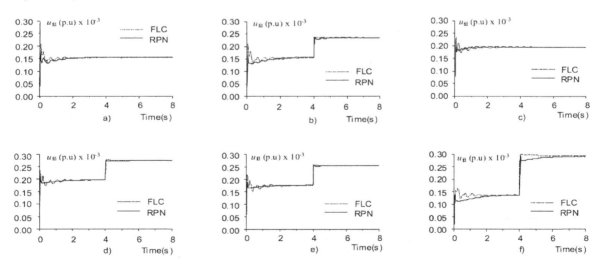

Figure 12. Time responses of terminal voltage (u$_t$) when FLC and RPNN are applied. (a) through (f) are the corresponding cases of disturbance (Table 2)

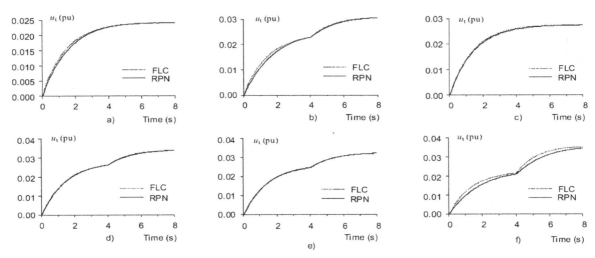

Figure 13. MSE for the PSNN and the RPNN training phases (Cases A through D)

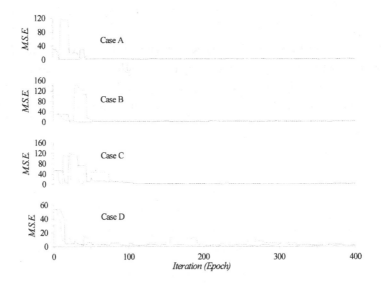

$$J = \int\limits_0^8 \left[u_{fd}\left(t\right) \right]^2 t dt \qquad (24)$$

CONCLUSION

In this chapter two implementations of excitation controllers for a synchronous electric machine using higher order neural networks were developed and presented. The designed controllers clearly demonstrate robust stability properties, since their training is based on a fuzzy sub-system which takes the actual

Table 3. Performance index (Eq. 24) of applied controllers

Case	FLC	PSNN	RPNN
A	0.1898	0.1870	0.1855
B	0.3128	0.3117	0.3065
C	0.3017	0.3009	0.3020
D	0.4499	0.4492	0.4464
E	0.3784	0.3802	0.3778
F	0.4231	0.4009	0.3939

operating conditions into consideration. The results obtained amply prove that the performance of the PSNN as well as the RPNN controllers are competitive with those obtained with the fuzzy logic excitation controller designs and techniques previously developed. The enhanced performance in the synchronous generator's excitation control using HONNs is due to the networks robustness caused by the reduced number of free parameters compared to the MLPs. The prudent representation of higher order terms in HONNs enables the networks to produce more precise output signals to the exciter part. A noteworthy advantage of RPNNs is the fact that there is no requirement to select the order of the networks as in PSNNs, or the number of hidden units as in MLPs. It is evident that certain intelligent control applications could increase the efficiency and subsequently make the operation of a power generating system more economic. It is emphasized that the hardware implementation for such kind of controllers is easier than FLC ones and the computational time needed for real-time applications is drastically reduced. A practical implementation on a microprocessor system could be used as an addition to the existing controllers of such power systems or as a substitute for an optimum control and supervision.

FUTURE RESEARCH

The main intricacy when using Ridge Polynomial neural networks is to find suitable parameters for successively adding a new Pi-Sigma unit in the network. Future research direction could involve the use of genetic algorithms or other search techniques (i.e. particle swarm optimization) to automatically generating and finding appropriate parameters used in the training of RPNNs. Another avenue for research will be the investigation on the use of recurrent links in the RPNNs. For example, there is a strong belief that a recurrent RPNN could be proven extremely significant since it will explore both the advantages of feedforward RPNN as well as the temporal dynamics induced by the recurrent connection. Electric machines excitation control using this recurrent RPNN may involve the construction of two separate components: (1) the "predictor" which is the feedforward part of the RPNN, and (2) a recurrent layer that provides the "temporal" signal context. The use of recurrent connection in the network may make the network well suited to produce even more effective control output signal. This is because of the recurrent network adherence to non-linearity as well as the subtle regularities found in these systems. Comparison with other recently developed (i.e. Alanis et. Al, 2008) types of neural networks for the same application, is judged necessary. Finally, the mail goal of this future effort will be established and justified in real time environment apart from the analytical -though necessary- computer simulations.

REFERENCES

Alanis, A. Y., Sanchez, E. N., & Loukianov, A. G. (2008). Discrete-Time Backstepping Synchronous Generator Stabilization Using a Neural Observer. In *Proceedings of the IFAC World Congress* (pp. 15897-15902). Seoúl, Korea.

Allen, D. W., & Taylor, J. G. (1994). Learning time series by neural networks. In M. Marinaro & P. Morasso (Eds.), *Proceedings of the International Conference on Neural Networks*, Sorrento, Italy (pp. 529-532). Berlin: Springer.

Artyomov, E., & Pecht, O. Y. (2005). Modified high-order neural network for invariant pattern recognition. *Pattern Recognition Letters*, *26*, 843–851. doi:10.1016/j.patrec.2004.09.029

Barron, R., Gilstrap, L., & Shrier, S. (1987). Polynomial and neural networks: Analogies and engineering applications. In [New York.]. *Proceedings of the International Conference on Neural Networks*, *2*, 431–439.

Bazanella, A., Silva, A. S., & Kokotovic, P. V. (1997), Lyapunov design of excitation control for synchronous machines. In *Proceedings of the 36th IEEE Conference on Decision and Control* (pp. 211–216). San Diego, CA

Campolucci, P., Capparelli, F., Guarnieri, S., Piazza, F., & Uncini, A. (1996). Neural networks with adaptive spline activation function. In *Proceedings of the IEEE MELECON'96 Conference* (pp. 1442-1445). Bari, Italy.

Cass, R., & Radl, B. (1996). Adaptive process optimization using functional-link networks and evolutionary algorithm. *Control Engineering Practice*, *4*(11), 1579–1584. doi:10.1016/0967-0661(96)00173-6

Caudill, M., & Butler, C. (1990). *Naturally intelligent systems*. Cambridge, MA: MIT Press.

Chapman, J. W., Ilic, M., King, C. A., Eng, L., & Kaufman, H. (1993). Stabilizing a multimachine power system via decentralized feedback linearizing excitation control. *IEEE Transactions on Power Systems*, *8*(1), 830–839. doi:10.1109/59.260921

Chen, C. T., & Chang, W. D. (1996). A feedforward neural network with function shape autotuning. *Neural Networks*, *9*(4), 627–641. doi:10.1016/0893-6080(96)00006-8

De Jong, K. (1980). Adaptive system design: a genetic approach . *IEEE Transactions on Systems, Man, and Cybernetics*, *SMC-10*(9), 1566–1574.

De Leon-Morales, J., Espinosa-Perez, G., & Macias-Cardoso, I. (2002). Observer-based control of a synchronous generator: a Hamiltonian approach. *International Journal of Electrical Power & Energy Systems*, *24*, 655–663. doi:10.1016/S0142-0615(01)00079-5

De León-Morales, J., Huerta-Guevara, O., Dugard, L., & Dion, J. M. 2003. Discrete-time nonlinear control scheme for synchronous generator, In *Proceedings of the IEEE Conference on Decision and Control 2003*, Maui, USA

De Mello, F. P., & Concordia, C. (1969). Concepts of synchronous machine stability as affected by excitation control. *IEEE Transactions on Power Apparatus and Systems, PAS-88*, 316–329. doi:10.1109/TPAS.1969.292452

Devroye, L., Gyorfi, L., & Lugosi, G. (1996). *A probabilistic theory of pattern recognition.* New York: Springer.

Diamond, I., & Jeffries, J. (2001). *Beginning statistics: An introduction for social sciences.* London: Sage Publications.

Djukanovic, M. B., Dobrijevic, D. M., Calovic, M. S., Novicevic, M., & Sobajic, D. J. (1997). Coordinated stabilizing control for the exciter and governor loops using fuzzy set theory and neural nets. *International Journal of Electrical Power & Energy Systems, 8*, 489–499. doi:10.1016/S0142-0615(97)00020-3

Durbin, R., & Rumelhart, D. E. (1990). Product units with trainable exponents and multilayer networks. In F. Fogelman Soulie, & J. Herault, (Eds.) *Neurocomputing: Algorithms, architecture and applications* (pp. 15-26). NATO ASI Series, vol. F68, New York:Springer-Verlag.

Espinosa-Perez, G., Godoy-Alcantar, M., & Guerrero-Ramırez, G. (1997). Passivity-based control of synchronous generators. In *Proceedings of the 1997 IEEE International Symposium on Industrial Electronics* (pp.SS101–SS106). Guimaraes, Portugal.

Fleming, P. J., & Fonseca, C. M. (1993). *Genetic algorithms in control systems engineering,* (Research Report No. 470), Sheffield, UK: University of Sheffield, Dept. of Automatic Control and Systems Engineering.

Giles, C. L., Griffin, R. D. & Maxwell, T. (1998). Encoding geometric invariances in HONN. *American Institute of Physics*, 310-309.

Giles, L., & Maxwell, T. (1987). Learning, invariance and generalisation in high-order neural networks. *Applied Optics, 26*(23), 4972–4978. doi:10.1364/AO.26.004972

Goldberg, D. E. (1989). *Genetic algorithms in search, optimization and machine learning.* Reading, MA: Addison-Wesley

Grefenstette, J. J. (1986). Optimization of control parameters for genetic algorithms. *IEEE Transactions on Systems, Man, and Cybernetics, 16*, 122–128. doi:10.1109/TSMC.1986.289288

Guler, M., & Sahin, E. (1994). A new higher order binary-input neural unit: Learning and generalizing effectively via using minimal number of monomials. *Third Turkish Symposium on Artificial Intelligence and Neural Networks Proceedings* (pp. 51-60). Middle East Technical University, Ankara, Turkey.

Guo, Y., Hill, D. J., & Wang, Y. (2001). Global transient stability and voltage regulation for power systems. *IEEE Transactions on Power Systems, 16*(4), 678–688. doi:10.1109/59.962413

Handschin, E., Hoffmann, W., Reyer, F., Stephanblome, Th., Schlucking, U., Westermann, D., & Ahmed, S. S. (1994). A new method of excitation control based on fuzzy set theory. *IEEE Transactions on Power Systems, 9*, 533–539. doi:10.1109/59.317569

Hassan, M. A., Malik, O. P., & Hope, G. S. (1991). A fuzzy logic based stabilizer for a synchronous machine. *IEEE Transactions on Energy Conversion, 6*(3), 407–413. doi:10.1109/60.84314

Hecht-Nielsen, R. (1987). Kolmogorov's mapping neural network existence theorem. In [New York: IEEE Press.]. *Proceedings of the International Conference on Neural Networks, 3*, 11–13.

Hiyama, T. (1989). Application of rule based stabilizer controller to electric power system, *IEE Proceedings . Part C, 136*(3), 175–181.

Holland, J. H. (1975). *Adaptation in Nature and Artificial Systems*. Ann Arbor, MI:University of Michigan Press.

Hornik, K. (1991). Approximation capabilities of multilayer feedforward networks. *Neural Networks, 4*, 251–257. doi:10.1016/0893-6080(91)90009-T

Hornik, K., Stinchcombe, M., & White, H. (1989). Multi-layer feedforward networks are universal approximators. *Neural Networks, 2*, 359–366. doi:10.1016/0893-6080(89)90020-8

Hu, Z., & Shao, H. (1992). The study of neural network adaptive control systems. *Control and Decision, 7*, 361–366.

IEEE Standards Board. (1992). IEEE recommended practice for excitation system models for power system stability analysis. *IEEE Standard, 425*, 1–1992.

Jagannathan, S. (2006). *Neural Network Control of Nonlinear Discrete-Time Systems*. Danvers, MA: CRC Press.

Karayiannis, N., & Venetsanopoulos, A. (1993). *Artificial neural networks: Learning algorithms, performance evaluation and applications*. Boston: Kluwer.

Karnavas, Y. L., & Pantos, S. (2008). Performance Evaluation of Neural Networks for μC Based Excitation Control of a Synchronous Generator, In *Proceedings of ICEM '08, the 18th International Conference on Electrical Machines*. CD Paper Ref. No. 437, Vilamura, Portugal

Karnavas, Y. L., & Papadopoulos, D. P. (2000). Excitation control of a power generating system based on fuzzy logic and neural networks. *European Transactions in Electrical Power, 10*(4), 233–241.

Karnavas, Y. L., & Papadopoulos, D. P. (2002, August 25-28). A genetic-fuzzy system for the excitation control of a synchronous machine. In *Proceedings of ICEM '02, the 15th International Conference in Electrical Machines*, CD paper Ref. No. 204, Bruges, Belgium

Karnavas, Y. L., & Papadopoulos, D. P. (2002). AGC for autonomous power station using combined intelligent techniques. *Int. J. Electr Pow Syst Res, 62*, 225–239. doi:10.1016/S0378-7796(02)00082-2

Karnavas, Y. L., & Papadopoulos, D. P. (2004). Excitation control of a synchronous machine using polynomial neural networks. *Journal of Electrical Engineering, 55*(7-8), 169–179.

Kirschen, D. S., Bacher, R., & Heydt, G. T. (2000). Special issue on the technology of power system competition. *Proceedings of the IEEE, 88*(2), 123–127. doi:10.1109/JPROC.2000.823993

Kosmatopoulos, E. B., Polycarpou, M. M., Christodoulou, M. A., & Ioannou, P. A. (1995). High-order neural network structures for identification of dynamical systems. *IEEE Transactions on Neural Networks, 6*(2), 422–431. doi:10.1109/72.363477

Lapedes, A. S., & Farber, R. (1987). Non-linear signal processing using neural networks: Prediction and system modelling. *Los Alamos National Laboratory* (Technical Report LA-UR-87).

Lee, C., & Maxwell, T. (1987). Learning, invariance, and generalization in high-order neural network. *Applied Optics*, *26*(23).

Lee, C. C. (1990). Fuzzy logic in control systems – Parts I and II . *IEEE Transactions on Systems, Man, and Cybernetics*, *20*(2), 404–435. doi:10.1109/21.52551

Lee, Y. C., Doolen, G., Chen, H., Sun, G., Maxwell, T., & Lee, H. (1986). Machine learning using a higher order correlation network. *Physica D. Nonlinear Phenomena*, *22*, 276–306.

Leerink, L. R., Giles, C. L., Horne, B. G., & Jabri, M. A. (1995). Learning with product units. In G. Tesaro, D. Touretzky, & T. Leen (Eds.), *Advances in Neural Information Processing Systems* (pp. 537-544). Cambridge, MA: MIT Press.

Lin, C. Y., & Hajela, P. (1992). Genetic algorithms in optimization problems with discrete and integer design variables . *Engineering Optimization*, *19*(4), 309–327. doi:10.1080/03052159208941234

Lippmann, R. P. (1989). Pattern classification using neural networks. *IEEE Communications Magazine*, *27*, 47–64. doi:10.1109/35.41401

Machowski, J., Bialek, J. W., Robak, S., & Bumby, J. R. (1998). Excitation control systems for use with synchronous generators. *IEE Proceedings. Generation, Transmission and Distribution*, *145*(5), 537–546. doi:10.1049/ip-gtd:19982182

Mao, H., Malik, O. P., Hope, G. S., & Fan, J. (1990). An adaptive generator excitation controller based on linear optimal control. *IEEE Transactions on Energy Conversion*, *EC-5*(4), 673–678.

McClelland, J., & Rumelhart, D. (1987). *Parallel Distributed Processing*. Cambridge, MA:The MIT Press.

Minsky, M., & Papert, S. (1969). *Perceptrons*. Cambridge, MA: The MIT Press.

Narendra, K. S., & Parthasarathy, K. (1990). Identification and control of dynamical systems using neural networks. *IEEE Transactions on Neural Networks*, *1*(1), 4–27. doi:10.1109/72.80202

Neville, R. S., Stonham, T. J., & Glover, R. J. (2000). Partially pre-calculated weights for the back-propagation learning regime and high accuracy function mapping using continuous input RAM-based sigma-pi nets. *Neural Networks*, *13*, 91–110. doi:10.1016/S0893-6080(99)00102-1

Ortega, R., Stankovic, A., & Stefanov, P. (1998). A passivation approach to power systems stabilization. In *Proceedings of the IFAC Symposium Nonlinear Control Systems Design*, Enschede, NL.

Pai, M. A. (1989). *Energy Function Analysis for Power System Stability*. Dordrecht The Netherlands: Kluwer Academic Publishers.

Pao, Y. H. (1989). *Adaptive pattern recognition and neural networks*. Addison-Wesley, USA.

Papadopoulos, D. P. (1986). Excitation control of turbogenerators with output feedback. *International Journal of Electrical Power & Energy Systems*, *8*, 176–181. doi:10.1016/0142-0615(86)90032-3

Papadopoulos, D. P., Smith, J. R., & Tsourlis, G. (1989). Excitation controller design of synchronous machine with output feedback using high and reduced order models. *Archiv fur Elektrotechnik, 72*, 415–426. doi:10.1007/BF01573760

Park, S., Smith, M. J. T., & Mersereau, R. M. (2000). Target recognition based on directional filter banks and higher order neural networks. *Digital Signal Processing, 10*, 297–308. doi:10.1006/dspr.2000.0376

Patra, J. C., & Pal, R. N. (1995). A functional link artificial neural network for adaptive channel equalization. *Signal Processing, 43*, 181–195. doi:10.1016/0165-1684(94)00152-P

Pau, Y. H., & Phillips, S. M. (1995). The Functional Link Net and learning optimal control. *Neurocomputing, 9*, 149–164. doi:10.1016/0925-2312(95)00066-F

Plotkin, H. (1993). *Darwin machines and the nature of knowledge.* Cambridge, MA: Harvard University Press.

Psaltis, D., Park, C., & Hong, J. (1988). Higher order associative memories and their optical implementations. *Neural Networks, 1*, 149–163. doi:10.1016/0893-6080(88)90017-2

Redding, N., Kowalczyk, A., & Downs, T. (1993). Constructive higher order network algorithm that is polynomial time. *Neural Networks, 6*, 997–1010. doi:10.1016/S0893-6080(09)80009-9

Refenes, A. N. (1994). *Neural networks in the capital markets.* Chichester, UK: Wiley.

Reid, M. B., et al. (1989) Rapid training of higher order neural networks for invariant pattern recognition. *In: Proc. of IJCNN*, Washington DC, *1*, 689-692.

Reid, M. B., Spirkovska, L., & Ochoa, E. (1989). Simultaneous position, scale, rotation invariant pattern classification using third-order neural networks. *International Journal of Neural Networks, 1*, 154–159.

Ross, T. J. (1995). *Fuzzy logic with engineering applications.* New York: McGraw Hill College Div.

Rumelhart, D., Hinton, G., & Williams, R. (1986). Learning internal representations by error propagation. In D. Rumelhart, & J. McClelland (Eds.), *Parallel distributed processing: Explorations in the microstructure of cognition, Volume 1 — Foundations.* Cambridge, MA: MIT Press.

Sauer, P. W., Ahmed-Zaid, S., & Kokotovic, P. V. (1998). An integral manifold approach to reduced order dynamic modeling of synchronous machines. *IEEE Transactions on Power Systems, 3*(1), 17–23. doi:10.1109/59.43175

Schmitt, M. (2001). On the complexity of computing and learning with multiplicative neural networks. *Neural Computation, 14*, 241–301. doi:10.1162/08997660252741121

Schultz, W. C., & Rideout, V. C. (1961). Control system performance measures: past, present and future *I.R.E. Transactions on Automatic Control, AC-6*(22), 22–35.

Shin, Y., & Ghosh, J. (1991). The Pi-Sigma Network: An efficient higher order neural network for pattern classification and function approximation. In *Proceedings of the International Joint Conference on Neural Networks* (pp. I: 13-18). Seattle, WA

Shin, Y., & Ghosh, J. (1992). Efficient higher order neural networks for function approximation and classification. *International Journal of Neural Systems, 3*(4), 323–350. doi:10.1142/S0129065792000255

Thimm, G., & Fiesler, E. (1997). High-order and multilayer perceptron initialization. *IEEE Transactions on Neural Networks, 8*(2), 349–359. doi:10.1109/72.557673

Vecci, L., Piazza, F., & Uncini, A. (1998). Learning and approximation capabilities of adaptive spline activation function neural networks. *Neural Networks, 11*, 259–270. doi:10.1016/S0893-6080(97)00118-4

Wang, Z., Fang, J., & Liu, X. (2006). Global stability of stochastic high-order neural networks with discrete and distributed delays. *Chaos, Solitons, and Fractals, 6*, 63.

Willems, J. L. (1971). Direct methods for transient stability studies in power systems analysis. *IEEE Transactions on Automatic Control, 16*(4), 332–341. doi:10.1109/TAC.1971.1099743

Wolpert, D. H. (1996a). The existence of a priori distinctions between learning algorithms. *Neural Computation, 8*, 1391–1420. doi:10.1162/neco.1996.8.7.1391

Wolpert, D. H. (1996b). The lack of a priori distinctions between learning algorithms. *Neural Computation, 8*, 1341–1390. doi:10.1162/neco.1996.8.7.1341

Wood, J., & Shawe-Taylor, J. (1996). A unifying framework for invariant pattern recognition. *Pattern Recognition Letters, 17*, 1415–1422. doi:10.1016/S0167-8655(96)00103-1

Wu, C. J., & Huang, C. H. (1997). A hybrid method for parameter tuning of PID Controllers. *Journal of the Franklin Institute, 334B*, 547–562. doi:10.1016/S0016-0032(96)00094-4

Yamada, T., & Yabuta, T. (1992). Remarks on a neural network controller which uses an auto-tuning method for nonlinear functions. In. *Proceedings of the International Joint Conference on Neural Networks, 2*, 775–780.

Yang, C., Ge, S. S., Chai, C. X. T., & Lee, T. H. (2008). Output Feedback NN Control for Two Classes of Discrete-Time Systems With Unknown Control Directions in a Unified Approach. *IEEE Transactions on Neural Networks, 19*(11), 1873–1886. doi:10.1109/TNN.2008.2003290

Zadeh, L. A. (1965). Fuzzy sets. *Information and Control, 8*, 338–353. doi:10.1016/S0019-9958(65)90241-X

Zhang, M., & Fulcher, J. (1996). Face recognition using artificial neural network group based adaptive tolerance (GAT) trees. *IEEE Transactions on Neural Networks, 7*(3), 555–567. doi:10.1109/72.501715

Zhang, M., & Fulcher, J. (2004). Higher order neural networks for satellite weather prediction. In J. Fulcher, & L. C. Jain (Eds.), *Applied intelligent systems: New directions* (pp. 17-57). Berlin: Springer.

Zhang, M., Fulcher, J., & Scofield, R. (1997). Rainfall estimation using artificial neural network group. *Neurocomputing, 16*(2), 97–115. doi:10.1016/S0925-2312(96)00022-7

APPENDIX A: PRINCIPAL SYSTEM DATA & MACHINE OPERATING POINT
Table 4.

Synchronous Machine	x_d	1.758 p.u.	R_a	0.0145 p.u.	
87.5kVA, 415V,	x_q	0.99 p.u.	R_{kd}	0.00422 p.u.	
4-pole	x_{fd}	1.761 p.u.	R_{kq}	0.0126 p.u.	
	x_{kd}	1.664 p.u.	R_{fd}	0.00268 p.u.	
	x_{kq}	0.955 p.u.	H	1.434 s	
	x_{md}	1.658 p.u.			
	x_{mq}	0.899 p.u.			
Conventional Exciter	K_e	1	T_e	0.472 s	
Transformer	R_T	0.0363 p.u.	X_T	0.0838 p.u.	
Transmission line	R_L	0.03744 p.u.	X_L	0.3903 p.u.	

P_t	Q_t	u_t	u_{fd}	δ	U_b
0.8 p.u.	0.84 p.u.	1.29 p.u.	0.0043 p.u.	0.56 rad	0.97 p.u.

APPENDIX B: LIST OF SYMBOLS

δ load angle

t time

i_{fd} field current

i_d, i_q stator currents in d and q axis circuits

i_t machine terminal current

u_{fd} field voltage

u_d, u_q stator voltages in d and q axis circuits

U_b busbar voltage

u_t machine terminal voltage

P_m generator-shaft mechanical power

R_a armature winding resistance

R_{kd}, R_{kq} damper winding resistances in d and q axes

R_{fd} field winding resistance

R_T, X_T transformer resistance and reactance

R_L, X_L transmission line resistance and reactance

i_{kd}, i_{kq} damper circuit currents in d and q axes

x_d, x_q

x_{kd}, x_{kq} damper winding reactances in d and q axes

x_{md}, x_{mq} magnetizing reactances in d and q axes

ω machine angular velocity (rotor speed)

K_e, T_e exciter gain and time constant

ΔU_{ref} incremental (step) voltage reference (input) change

$\underline{u}e$ excitation error

$u_{e.c.s.}$ excitation controller voltage signal

u output (defuzzified) value of the fuzzy controller

s Laplace operator

r plant reference operating set point

y plant output

X, **Y**, **U** state and output variable, and control vector of a model in state-space form

A, **B**, **C** system matrices of a dynamic model in state-space form

$[]^T$ transpose of a matrix/vector

e_t, ce_t error, change in error (at sampling instant t)

$\mu[R(x)]$ membership function value of fuzzy variable R for an input point x

J performance index

Section 4
Artificial Higher Order Neural Network Models and Applications

Chapter 17
Higher Order Neural Networks:
Fundamental Theory and Applications

Madan M. Gupta
University of Saskatchewan, Canada

Noriyasu Homma
Tohoku University, Japan

Zeng-Guang Hou
The Chinese Academy of Sciences, China

Ashu M. G. Solo
Maverick Technologies America Inc., USA

Ivo Bukovsky
Czech Technical University in Prague, Czech Republic

ABSTRACT

In this chapter, we provide fundamental principles of higher order neural units (HONUs) and higher order neural networks (HONNs). An essential core of HONNs can be found in higher order weighted combinations or correlations between the input variables. By using some typical examples, this chapter describes how and why higher order combinations or correlations can be effective.

1. INTRODUCTION

The human brain has more than 10 billion neurons, which have complicated interconnections, and these neurons constitute a large-scale signal processing and memory network. The mathematical study of a single neural model and its various extensions is the first step in the design of a complex neural network for solving a variety of problems in the fields of signal processing, pattern recognition, control of complex processes, neurovision systems, and other decision making processes. Neural network solutions for these problems can be directly used for computer science and engineering applications.

DOI: 10.4018/978-1-61520-711-4.ch017

A simple neural model is presented in Figure 1. In terms of information processing, an individual neuron with dendrites as multiple-input terminals and an axon as a single-output terminal may be considered a multiple-input/single-output (MISO) system. The processing functions of this MISO neural processor may be divided into the following four categories:

i.   **Dendrites:** They consist of a highly branching tree of fibers and act as input points to the main body of the neuron. On average, there are 10^3 to 10^4 dendrites per neuron, which form receptive surfaces for input signals to the neurons.
ii. **Synapse:** It is a storage area of past experience (knowledge base). It provides long-term memory (LTM) to the past accumulated experience. It receives information from sensors and other neurons and provides outputs through the axons.
iii. **Soma:** The neural cell body is called the *soma*. It is the large, round central neuronal body. It receives synaptic information and performs further processing of the information. Almost all logical functions of the neuron are carried out in the soma.
iv. **Axon:** The neural output line is called the *axon*. The output appears in the form of an action potential that is transmitted to other neurons for further processing.

The electrochemical activities at the synaptic junctions of neurons exhibit a complex behavior because each neuron makes hundreds of interconnections with other neurons. Each neuron acts as a parallel processor because it receives action potentials in parallel from the neighboring neurons and then transmits pulses in parallel to other neighboring synapses. In terms of information processing, the synapse also performs a crude pulse frequency-to-voltage conversion as shown in Figure 1.

1.1. Neural Mathematical Operations

In general, it can be argued that the role played by neurons in the brain reasoning processes is analogous to the role played by a logical switching element in a digital computer. However, this analogy is too simple. A neuron contains a sensitivity threshold, adjustable signal amplification or attenuation at each synapse and an internal structure that allows incoming nerve signals to be integrated over both space

Figure 1. A simple neural model as a multiple-input (dendrites) and single-output (axon) processor

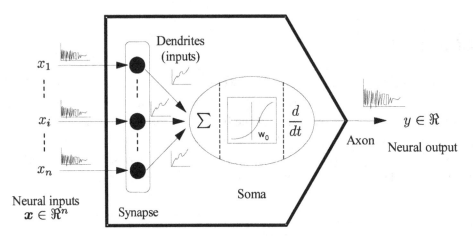

and time. From a mathematical point of view, it may be concluded that the processing of information within a neuron involves the following two distinct mathematical operations:

i.   **Synaptic operation:** The strength (weight) of the synapse is a representation of the storage of knowledge and thus the memory for previous knowledge. The synaptic operation assigns a relative weight (significance) to each incoming signal according to the past experience (knowledge) stored in the synapse.

ii. **Somatic operation:** The somatic operation provides various mathematical operations such as aggregation, thresholding, nonlinear activation, and dynamic processing to the synaptic inputs. If the weighted aggregation of the neural inputs exceeds a certain threshold, the soma will produce an output signal to its axon.

A simplified representation of the above neural operations for a typical neuron is shown in Figure 2. A biological neuron deals with some interesting mathematical mapping properties because of its nonlinear operations combined with a threshold in the soma. If neurons were only capable of carrying out linear operations, the complex human cognition and robustness of neural systems would disappear.

Observations from both experimental and mathematical analysis have indicated that neural cells can transmit reliable information if they are sufficiently redundant in numbers. However, in general, a biological neuron has an unpredictable mechanism for processing information. Therefore, it is postulated that the collective activity generated by large numbers of locally redundant neurons is more significant than the activity generated by a single neuron.

1.2. Synaptic Operation

As shown in Figure 2, let us consider a neural memory vector of accumulated past experiences $\mathbf{w} = [w_1, w_2, \ldots, w_n]^T \in \Re^n$, which is usually called synapse weights, and a neural input vector $\mathbf{x} = [x_1, x_2, \ldots, x_n]^T \in \Re^n$ as the current external stimuli. Through the comparison process between the neural memory $\mathbf{w}$ and the input $\mathbf{x}$, the neuron can calculate a similarity between the usual (memory base)

Figure 2. Simple model of a neuron showing (a) synaptic and (b) somatic operations

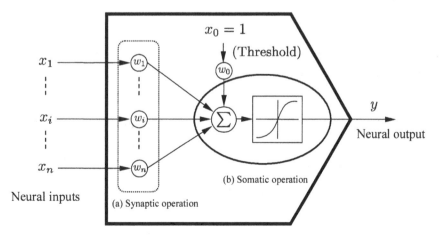

and current stimuli and thus know the current situation (Kobayashi, 2006). According to the similarity, the neuron can then derive its internal value as the membrane potential.

A similarity measure u can be calculated as an inner product of the neural memory vector $\mathbf{w}$ and the current input vector $\mathbf{x}$ given by

$$u = \mathbf{w} \cdot \mathbf{x} \left(= \mathbf{w}^T \mathbf{x}\right)$$

$$= w_1 x_1 + w_2 x_2 + \cdots + w_n x_n = \sum_{i=1}^{n} w_i x_i \tag{1}$$

The similarity implies the linear combination of the neural memory and the current input, or correlation between them. This idea can be traced back to the milestone model proposed by McCulloch and Pitts (1943).

As shown in Figure 3, the inner product can also be represented as

$$u = |\mathbf{w}| |\mathbf{x}| \cos\theta \tag{2}$$

where $|.|$ denotes the absolute value of the vector and θ is the angle between the vectors $\mathbf{w}$ and $\mathbf{x}$.

When a current input $\mathbf{x}$ points to the same or very similar direction of the neural memory $\mathbf{w}$, the similarity measure u becomes large and correlation between the memory $\mathbf{w}$ and the input $\mathbf{x}$ becomes positively strong due to $\cos\theta \approx 1$. If the input $\mathbf{x}$ points to the opposite or nearly opposite direction of the memory $\mathbf{w}$, the absolute value of the similarity measure $|u|$ also becomes large, but the negative correlation becomes strong because $\cos\theta \approx -1$. In these two cases, absolute values of the memory $\mathbf{w}$ and the input $\mathbf{x}$ also influence the similarity measure. The other particular case is that the input $\mathbf{x}$ and the memory $\mathbf{w}$ are orthogonal with each other. In this case, the similarity measure u becomes very small due to $\cos\theta \approx 0$. If the two vectors are strictly orthogonal, the similarity measure u is equal to 0. Thus, the similarity measure is independent of the absolute values of the memory $\mathbf{w}$ and the input $\mathbf{x}$.

The inner product indicates how much the directions of two vectors are similar to each other. Indeed, in the case of normalized vectors $\mathbf{w}$ and $\mathbf{x}$, i.e., $|\mathbf{w}| = |\mathbf{x}| = 1$, the similarity measure is nothing but $\cos\theta$:

$$u = |\mathbf{w}| |\mathbf{x}| \cos\theta = \cos\theta \equiv u_\theta \tag{3}$$

Figure 3. Inner product as a measure of similarity between a neural memory (past experience) $\mathbf{w}$ *and a neural input (current experience)* $\mathbf{x}$

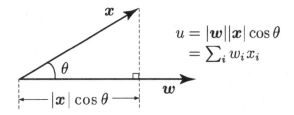

Note that the linear combination can be extended to higher order combinations as in the following section.

1.2.1. Higher Order Terms of Neural Inputs

In the linear combination given in eqn. (1), we considered a neural input vector consisting of only the first order terms of neural inputs in the polynomial. Naturally, we can extend the first order terms to the higher order terms of the neural inputs or any other nonlinear ones. To separate different classes of data with a nonlinear discriminant line, an HONN (Rumelhart et al., 1986a; Giles and Maxwell, 1987; Softky and Kammen, 1991; Xu et al., 1992; Taylor and Commbes, 1993; Homma and Gupta, 2002) is used. An HONN is composed of one or more HONUs.

Here let us consider the second order polynomial of the neural inputs. In this case, the extended neural input and memory vectors, $\mathbf{x}_a$ and $\mathbf{w}_a$, can be defined by

$$\mathbf{x}_a = [x_1, x_2, \ldots, x_n, x_1^2, x_1 x_2, \ldots, x_1 x_n, x_2^2, \ldots, x_{n-1} x_n, x_n^2]^T \tag{4}$$

$$\mathbf{w}_a = [w_{01}, w_{02}, \ldots, w_{0n}, w_{11}, w_{12}, \ldots, w_{1n}, w_{22}, \ldots, w_{(n-1)n}, w_{nn}]^T \tag{5}$$

Then the similarity measure can be given with the same notation

$$
\begin{aligned}
u_a &= \mathbf{w}_a \cdot \mathbf{x}_a = \mathbf{w}_a^T \mathbf{x}_a \\
&= w_1 x_1 + w_2 x_2 + \cdots + w_n x_n + w_{11} x_1^2 + w_{12} x_1 x_2 + \cdots + w_{1n} x_1 x_n \\
&\quad + w_{22} x_2^2 + \cdots + w_{(n-1)n} x_{n-1} x_n + w_{nn} x_n^2 \\
&= \sum_{i=1}^{n} w_i x_i + \sum_{i=1}^{n} \sum_{j=i}^{n} w_{ij} x_i x_j
\end{aligned}
\tag{6}
$$

The second order terms of $x_i x_j$ can be related to correlations between the two inputs x_i and x_j. That is, if the two inputs are statistically independent of each other, then the second order terms become 0 while absolute values of terms become large if there is a linear relation between them. The squared terms of neural inputs x_i^2 indicate the power of the inputs from the physical point of view.

Consequently, the similarity measure of general higher order terms can be defined as

$$u_a = \sum_{i=1}^{n} w_i x_i + \sum_{i=1}^{n} \sum_{j=i}^{n} w_{ij} x_i x_j + \cdots + \sum_{i_1=1}^{n} \sum_{i_2=i_1}^{n} \cdots \sum_{i_n=i_{n-1}}^{n} w_{i_1 i_2 \cdots i_n} x_{i_1} x_{i_2} \cdots x_{i_n} \tag{7}$$

1.3. Somatic Operation

Typical neural outputs are generated by a sigmoidal activation function of the similarity measure u of the inner product of neural memories (past experiences) and current inputs. In this case, the neural output y can be given as

$$y = \varphi(u) \in \Re^1 \tag{8}$$

where φ is a neural activation function. An example of the activation function can be defined as a so-called sigmoidal function given by

$$\varphi(x) = \frac{1}{1 + \exp(-x)} \qquad (9)$$

and shown in Figure 4.

Note that the activation function is not limited to the sigmoid one. However, this type of sigmoid function has been widely used in various fields. Here if the similarity u is large—that is, the current input $\mathbf{x}$ is similar to the corresponding neural memory $\mathbf{w}$—the neural output y is also large. On the other hand, if the similarity u is small, the neural output y is also small. This is a basic characteristic of biological neural activities. Note that the neural output is not proportional to the similarity u, but a nonlinear function of u with saturation characteristics. This nonlinearity might be a key mechanism to make the neural activities more complex as brains do.

1.4. Learning from Experiences

From the computational point of view, we have discussed how neurons, which are elemental computational units in the brain, produce outputs y as the results of neural information processing based on comparison of current external stimuli $\mathbf{x}$ with neural memories of past experiences $\mathbf{w}$. Consequently, the neural outputs y are strongly dependent on the neural memories $\mathbf{w}$. Thus, how neurons can memorize past experiences is crucial for neural information processing. Indeed, one of the most remarkable features of the human brain is its ability to adaptively learn in response to knowledge, experience, and environment. The basis of this learning appears to be a network of interconnected adaptive elements by means of which transformation between inputs and outputs is performed.

Learning can be defined as the acquisition of new information. In other words, learning is a process of memorizing new information. Adaptation implies that the element can change in a systematic manner and in so doing alter the transformation between input and output. In the brain, transmission within the neural system involves coded nerve impulses and other physical chemical processes that form reflections of sensory stimuli and incipient motor behavior.

Figure 4. A sigmoidal activation function

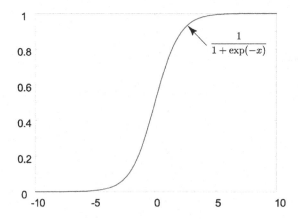

Many biological aspects are associated with such learning processes, including (Harston, 1990)

- Learning overlays hardwired connections
- Synaptic plasticity versus stability: a crucial design dilemma
- Synaptic modification providing a basis for observable organism behavior

Here, we have presented the basic foundation of neural networks starting from a basic introduction to the biological foundations, neural models, and learning properties inherent in neural networks. The rest of the chapter contains the following five sections:

In section 2, as the first step to understanding HONNs, we will develop a general matrix form of the second order neural units (SONUs) and the learning algorithm. Using the general form, it will be shown that, from the point of view of both the neural computing process and its learning algorithm, the widely used linear combination neural units described above are only a subset of the developed SONUs.

In section 3, we will conduct some simulation studies to support the theoretical development of second order neural networks (SONNs). The results will show how and why SONNs can be effective for many problems.

In section 4, HONUs and HONNs with a learning algorithm will be presented. Toward computer science and engineering applications, function approximation and time series analysis problems will be considered in section 5.

Concluding remarks and future research directions will be given in section 6.

2. SECOND ORDER NEURAL UNITS AND SECOND ORDER NEURAL NETWORKS

Neural networks, consisting of first order neurons which provide the neural output as a nonlinear function of the weighted linear combination of neural inputs, have been successfully used in various applications such as pattern recognition/classification, system identification, adaptive control, optimization, and signal processing (Sinha et al., 1999; Gupta et al., 2003; Narendra and Parthasarathy, 1990; Cichochi and Unbehauen, 1993).

The higher order combination of the inputs and weights will yield higher neural performance. However, one of the disadvantages encountered in the previous development of HONUs is the larger number of learning parameters (weights) required (Schmidt, 1993). To optimize the features space, a learning capability assessment method has been proposed by Villalobos and Merat (1995).

In this section, in order to reduce the number of parameters without loss of higher performance, an SONU is presented (Homma and Gupta, 2002). Using a general matrix form of the second order operation, the SONU provides the output as a nonlinear function of the weighted second order combination of input signals. Note that the matrix form can contribute to high speed computing, such as parallel and vector processing, which is essential for scientific and image processing.

Figure 5. An SONU defined by eqns. (10) and (11)

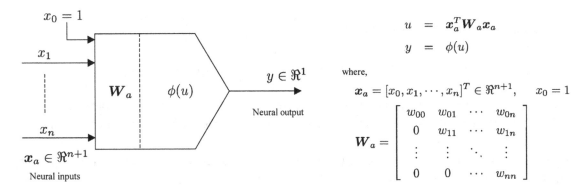

2.1. Formulation of the Second Order Neural Unit

An SONU with n-dimensional neural inputs, $\mathbf{x}(t) \in \Re^n$, and a single neural output, $y(t) \in \Re^1$ is developed in this section (Figure 5). Let $\mathbf{x}_a = [x_0, x_1, \ldots, x_n]^T \in \Re^{n+1}, x_0 = 1$, be an augmented neural input vector. Here a new second-order aggregating formulation is proposed by using an augmented weight matrix $\mathbf{W}_a(t) \in \Re^{(n+1)\times(n+1)}$ as

$$u = \mathbf{x}_a^T \mathbf{W}_a \mathbf{x}_a \tag{10}$$

Then the neural output, *y*, is given by a nonlinear function of the variable *u* as

$$y = \varphi(u) \in \Re^1 \tag{11}$$

Because both the weights w_{ij} and w_{ji}, $i, j \in \{0, 1, \ldots, n\}$ in the augmented weight matrix $\mathbf{W}_a$ yield the same second order term $x_i x_j$ (or $x_j x_i$), an upper triangular matrix or lower triangular matrix is sufficient to use. For instance, instead of separately determining values for w_{01} and w_{10}, both of which are weights for $x_0 x_1$, one can eliminate one of these weights and determine a value for either w_{01} or w_{10} that would be as much as both of these combined if they were computed separately. This saves time in the neural network's intensive procedure of computing weights. The same applies for other redundant weights. The equation for the discriminant line can be reexpressed as equal to transpose of the vector of neural inputs multiplied by the upper triangular matrix of neural weights multiplied by the vector of neural inputs again:

$$u = \mathbf{x}_a^T \mathbf{W}_a \mathbf{x}_a = \sum_{i=0}^n \sum_{j=i}^n w_{ij} x_i x_j, \quad x_0 = 1 \tag{12}$$

The number of elements, $\mathbf{W}_n$, in the matrix of neural weights with redundant elements is equal to $(n+1) * (n+1)$. To calculate the number of elements in the final matrix of neural weights with redundant elements eliminated, $\mathbf{W}_a$, first find the number of elements, which is $(n+1) * (n+1)$. Then subtract the number of diagonal elements in the matrix, which is $n+1$. Divide this by 2 and the result is the number of elements above or below the diagonal in the matrix. Then add back the number of diagonal elements in the matrix. Therefore, the number of elements in $\mathbf{W_a}$ with redundant elements eliminated is given as

$$\frac{(n+1)*(n+1)-(n+1)}{2}+(n+1)=\frac{n^2+3n+2}{2}$$

Note that the conventional first order weighted linear combination is only a special case of this second order matrix formulation. For example, the special weight matrix (row vector). $\mathbf{W_a} \equiv Row[w_{00}, w_{01}, \ldots, w_{0n}] \in \Re^{(n+1)\times(n+1)}$, can produce the equivalent weighted linear combination, $u = \sum_{j=0}^{n} w_{0j} x_j$. Therefore, the proposed neural model with the second order matrix operation is more general and, for this reason, it is called an SONU.

2.2. Learning Algorithm for Second Order Neural Units

Here learning algorithms are developed for SONUs. Let k denote the discrete time steps, $k = 1, 2, \ldots,$ and $y_d(k) \in \Re^1$ be the desired output signal corresponding to the neural input vector $\mathbf{x}(k) \in \Re^n$ at the k-th time step. A square error, $E(k)$, is defined by the error, $e(k) = y(k) - y_d(k)$ as

$$E(k) = \frac{1}{2}e(k)^2 \tag{13}$$

where $y(k)$ is the neural output corresponding to the neural input $\mathbf{x}(k)$ at the k-th time instant.

The purpose of the neural units is to minimize the error E by adapting the weight matrix $\mathbf{W_a}$ as

$$\mathbf{W_a}(k+1) = \mathbf{W_a}(k) + \Delta\mathbf{W_a}(k) \tag{14}$$

Here $\Delta\mathbf{W_a}(k)$ denotes the change in the weight matrix, which is defined as proportional to the gradient of the error function $E(k)$

$$\Delta\mathbf{W_a}(k) = -\eta\frac{\partial E(k)}{\partial\mathbf{W_a}(k)} \tag{15}$$

where $\eta > 0$ is a learning coefficient. Since the derivatives, $\partial E/\partial w_{ij}, i, j \in \{1, 2, \ldots, n\}$, are calculated by the chain rule as

$$\frac{\partial E(k)}{\partial w_{ij}(k)} = \frac{\partial E(k)}{\partial y(k)} \cdot \frac{\partial y(k)}{\partial u(k)} \cdot \frac{\partial u(k)}{\partial w_{ij}(k)}$$
$$= e(k)\varphi'(u(k))x_i(k)x_j(k) \tag{16}$$

or

$$\frac{\partial E(k)}{\partial\mathbf{W_a}(k)} = e(k)\varphi'(u(k))\mathbf{x_a}(k)\mathbf{x_a}^T(k) \tag{17}$$

The changes in the weight matrix are given by

$$\Delta \mathbf{W}_a(k) = -\eta e(k)\varphi'(u(k))\mathbf{x}_a(k)\mathbf{x}_a^T(k) \tag{18}$$

Here $\varphi'(u)$ is the slope of the nonlinear activation function used in eqn. (11). For activation functions such as sigmoidal function, $\varphi'(u) \geq 0$ and $\varphi'(u)$ can be regarded as a gain of the changes in weights. Then

$$\Delta \mathbf{W}_a(k) = -\gamma e(k)\mathbf{x}_a(k)\mathbf{x}_a^T(k) \tag{19}$$

where $\gamma = \eta\varphi'(u)$. Note that, taking the average of the changes for some input vectors, the changes in the weights, $\Delta w_{ij}(k)$, implies the correlation between the error $e(k)$ and the corresponding inputs term $x_i(k)x_j(k)$.

Therefore, conventional learning algorithms such as the backpropagation algorithm can easily be extended for multilayered neural network structures having the proposed SONUs.

3. PERFORMANCE ASSESSMENT OF SECOND ORDER NEURAL UNITS

To evaluate the learning and generalization abilities of the proposed general SONUs, the XOR classification problem is used. The XOR problem will provide a simple example of how well an SONU works for the nonlinear classification problem.

3.1. XOR Problem

Because the two-input XOR function is not linearly separable, it is one of the simplest logic functions that cannot be realized by a single linear combination neural unit. Therefore, it requires a multilayered neural network structure consisting of linear combination neural units.

Figure 6. Initial weights ($k = 0$), final weights, and the classification boundaries for the XOR problem

k	w_{00}	w_{01}	w_{02}	w_{11}	w_{12}	w_{22}	Boundaries
	(A hyperbolic boundary)						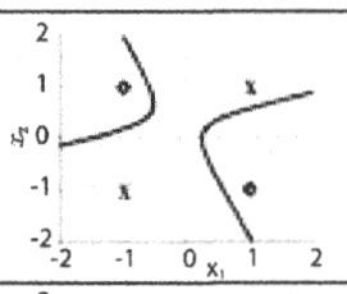
0	0.323	-0.870	-0.153	0.977	0.031	-0.332	
4	-0.177	0.630	0.347	0.477	-1.469	-0.832	
	(A hyperbolic boundary)						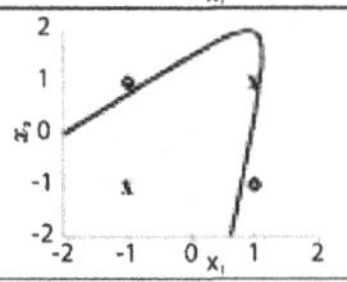
0	-0.773	0.818	0.748	0.793	-0.525	0.369	
4	-1.023	0.568	0.498	0.543	-0.775	0.119	
	(An elliptical boundary)						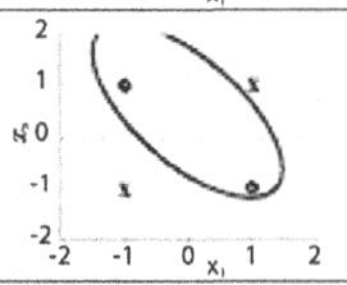
0	0.847	0.397	0.779	-0.996	-0.961	-0.803	
3	0.947	0.497	0.679	-0.896	-1.061	-0.703	

On the other hand, a single SONU can solve this XOR problem by using its general second order functions defined in eqn. (12). To implement the XOR function using a single SONU, the four learning patterns corresponding to the four combinations of two binary inputs $(x_1, x_2) \in \{(-1,-1),(-1,1),(1,-1),(1,1)\}$ and the desired output $y_d = x_1 \oplus x_2 \in \{-1,1\}$ were applied to the SONU.

For the XOR problem, the neural output, y, is defined by the signum function as $y = \varphi(u) = \text{sgn}(u)$. The correlation learning algorithm with a constant gain, $\gamma = 1$, in eqn. (19) was used in this case. The learning was terminated as soon as the error converged to 0. Because the SONU with the signum function classifies the neural input data by using the second order nonlinear function of the neural inputs $x_a^T W_a x_a$ as in eqn. (10), many nonlinear classification boundaries are possible such as a hyperbolic boundary and an elliptical boundary (Figure 6).

Note that the results of the classification boundary are dependent on the initial weights (Figure 6), and any classification boundary by the second order functions can be realized by a single SONU. This realization ability of the SONU is obviously superior to the linear combination neural unit, which cannot achieve such nonlinear classification using a single neural unit. At least three linear combination neural units in a layered structure are needed to solve the XOR problem.

Secondly, the number of parameters (weights) required for solving this problem can be reduced by using the SONU. In this simulation study, by using the upper triangular weight matrix, only six parameters including the threshold were required for the SONU whereas at least nine parameters were required for the layered structure with three linear combination neural units.

Each weight w_{ij} represents how the corresponding input correlation term $x_i x_j$ affects the neural output. If the absolute value of the weight is very small, then the effect of the corresponding input term on the output may also be very small. On the other hand, the corresponding term may be dominant or important if the absolute value of the weight is large compared to the other weights.

The weights in Figure 6 suggest that the absolute value of w_{12} is always large independent of the initial values and the largest except for only one case (middle row where it is still the second largest). The absolute value of w_{00} is the largest in one case (middle row) among three cases, but the smallest in one case (top row). The input term corresponding to the weight w_{00} is nothing but the bias. Note that the large $|w_{12}|$ implies a large contribution of the correlation term $x_1 x_2$ to the output and that the contribution of the term may be negative because $w_{12} < 0$. Indeed, the target XOR function can be defined as $y = -x_1 x_2$.

Consequently, if the target (unknown) function involves a higher order combination of the input variables, the ability of the higher order neural units can be superior to neural units that do not have necessary higher order input terms. Of course, this is only a discussion on the synaptic operation, and somatic operation may create higher order terms in the sense of Taylor expansion of the nonlinear activation functions. However, such higher order terms by somatic operation may be limited or indirect. Thus, the direct effect of the higher order terms is a reason why the higher order neural units can be effective for such problems that may involve the higher order terms of the input variables.

4. HIGHER ORDER NEURAL UNITS AND HIGHER ORDER NEURAL NETWORKS

To capture the higher order nonlinear properties of the input pattern space, extensive efforts have been made by Rumelhart et al. (1986), Giles and Maxwell (1987), Softky and Kammen (1991), Xu et al.

(1992), Taylor and Commbes (1993), and Homma and Gupta (2002) toward developing architectures of neurons that are capable of capturing not only the linear correlation between components of input patterns, but also the higher order correlation between components of input patterns. HONNs have proven to have good computational, storage, pattern recognition, and learning properties and are realizable in hardware (Taylor and Commbes, 1993). Regular polynomial networks that contain the higher order correlations of the input components satisfy the Stone-Weierstrass theorem that is a theoretical background of universal function approximators by means of neural networks (Gupta et al., 2003), but the number of weights required to accommodate all the higher order correlations increases exponentially with the number of the inputs. HONUs are the basic building block for such an HONN. For such an HONN as shown in Figure 7, the output is given by

$$y = \varphi(u) \tag{20}$$

$$u = w0 + \sum_{i_1}^{n} w_{i_1} x_{i_1} + \sum_{i_1, i_2}^{n} w_{i_1 i_2} x_{i_1} x_{i_2} + \cdots + \sum_{i_1, \ldots, i_N}^{n} w_{i_1 \cdots i_N} x_{i_1} \cdots x_{i_N} \tag{21}$$

where $\mathbf{x} = [x_1, x_2, \ldots, x_n]^T$ is a vector of neural inputs, y is an output, and $\varphi(.)$ is a strictly monotonic activation function such as a sigmoidal function whose inverse, $\varphi^{-1}(.)$, exists. The summation for the kth-order correlation is taken on a set $C(i_1 \cdots i_j), (1 \le j \le N)$, which is a set of the combinations of j indices $1 \le i_1 \cdots i_j \le n$ defined by

$$C(i_1 \cdots i_j) \equiv \{< i_1 \cdots i_j >: 1 \le i_1 \cdots i_j \le n, i_1 \le i_2 \le \cdots \le i_j\}, 1 \le j \le N$$

Figure 7. Block diagram of the HONU, eqns. (20) and (21)

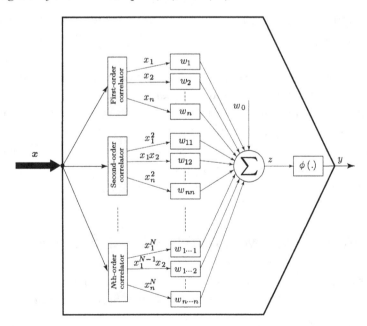

Also, the number of the *N*th-order correlation terms is given by

$$\binom{n+j-1}{j} = \frac{(n+j-1)!}{j!(n-1)!}, \qquad 1 \le j \le N$$

The introduction of the set $C(i_1 \cdots i_j)$ is to absorb the redundant terms due to the symmetry of the induced combinations. In fact, eqn. (21) is a truncated Taylor series with some adjustable coefficients. The *N*th-order neural unit needs a total of

$$\sum_{j=0}^{N} \binom{n+j-1}{j} = \sum_{j=0}^{N} \frac{(n+j-1)!}{j!(n-1)!}$$

weights including the basis of all of the products up to *N* components.

Example 1 In this example, we consider a case of the third order ($N = 3$) neural network with two neural inputs ($n = 2$). Here

$$C(i) = \{0, 1, 2\}$$

$$C(i_1 i_2) = \{11, 12, 22\}$$

$$C(i_1 i_2 i_3) = \{111, 112, 122, 222\}$$

and the network equation is

$$y = \varphi\left(w0 + w_1 x_1 + w_2 x_2 + w_{11} x_1^2 + w_{12} x_1 x_2 + w_{22} x_2^2 + w_{111} x_1^3 + w_{112} x_1^2 x_2 + w_{122} x_1 x_2^2 + w_{222} x_2^3\right)$$

The HONUs may be used in conventional feedforward neural network structures as hidden units to form HONNs. In this case, however, consideration of the higher correlation may improve the approximation and generalization capabilities of the neural networks. Typically, only SONNs are usually employed in practice to give a tolerable number of weights as discussed in sections 2 and 3. On the other hand, if the order of the HONU is high enough, eqns. (20) and (21) may be considered as a neural network with *n* inputs and a single output. This structure is capable of dealing with the problems of function approximation and pattern recognition.

To accomplish an approximation task for given input-output data $\{\mathbf{x}(k), y(k)\}$, the learning algorithm for the HONN can easily be developed on the basis of the gradient descent method. Assume that the error function is formulated as

$$E(k) = \frac{1}{2}[d(k) - y(k)]^2 = \frac{1}{2}e^2(k)$$

where $e(k) = d(k) - y(k)$, $d(k)$ is the desired output, and $y(k)$ is the output of the neural network. Minimization of the error function by a standard steepest descent technique yields the following set of learning equations:

$$w_0^{new} = w_0^{old} + \eta(d - y)\varphi'(u) \tag{22}$$

$$w_{ij}^{new} = w_{ij}^{old} + \eta(d - y)\varphi'(u)x_{i_1}x_{i_2}\cdots x_{i_j} \tag{23}$$

where $\varphi'(u) = d\varphi / du$. Like the backpropagation algorithm for a multilayered feedforward neural network (MFNN), a momentum version of the above is easily obtained.

Alternatively, because all the weights of the HONN appear linearly in eqn. (21), one may use the method for solving linear algebraic equations to carry out the preceding learning task if the number of patterns is finite. To do so, one has to introduce the following two augmented vectors

$$\mathbf{w} \equiv \left[w_0, w_1, \ldots, w_n, w_{11}, w_{12}, \ldots, w_{nn}, \ldots, w_{1\cdots1}, w_{2\cdots2}, \ldots, w_{n\cdots n} \right]^T$$

and

$$\mathbf{u}(\mathbf{x}) \equiv \left[x_0, x_1, \ldots, x_n, x_1^2, x_1 x_2, \ldots, x_n^2, \ldots, x_1^N, x_1^{N-1} x_2, \ldots, w_n^N \right]^T$$

where $x_0 \equiv 1$, so that the network equations, eqns. (20) and (21), may be rewritten in the following compact form:

$$y = \varphi(\mathbf{w}^T \mathbf{u}(\mathbf{x})) \tag{24}$$

For the given p pattern pairs $\{\mathbf{x}(k), d(k)\}$, ($1 \leq k \leq p$), define the following vectors and matrix

$$\mathbf{U} = \left[u^T(1), u^T(2), \ldots, u^T(p) \right]^T, \quad \mathbf{d} = \left[\varphi^{-1}(d(1)), \varphi^{-1}(d(2)), \ldots, \varphi^{-1}(d(p)) \right]^T$$

where $\mathbf{u}(k) = \mathbf{u}(\mathbf{x}(k)), 1 \leq k \leq p$. Then, the learning problem becomes one that finds a solution of the following linear algebraic equation

$$\mathbf{Uw} = \mathbf{d} \tag{25}$$

If the number of the weights is equal to the number of the data and the matrix $\mathbf{U}$ is nonsingular, then eqn. (25) has a unique solution

$$\mathbf{w} = \mathbf{U}^{-1}\mathbf{d}$$

A more interesting case occurs when the dimension of the weight vector $\mathbf{w}$ is less than the number of data p. Then the existence of the exact solution for the above linear equation is given by

Table 1. Truth table of XOR function $x_1 \oplus x_2 \oplus x_3$

Pattern	Input x_1	Input x_2	Input x_3	Output y
A	-1	-1	-1	-1
B	-1	-1	1	1
C	-1	1	-1	1
D	-1	1	1	-1
E	1	-1	-1	1
F	1	-1	1	-1
G	1	1	-1	-1
H	1	1	1	1

$$rank\left[\mathbf{U} \vdots \mathbf{d}\right] = rank\left[\mathbf{U}\right]$$

In case this condition is not satisfied, the pseudoinverse solution is usually an option and gives the best fit.

The following example shows how to use the HONN presented in this section to deal with pattern recognition problems that are also typical applications in computer science and engineering situations. It is of interest to show that solving such problems is equivalent to finding the decision surfaces in the pattern space such that the given data patterns are located on the surfaces.

Example 2 Consider a three-variable XOR function defined as

$$y = f(x_1, x_2, x_3) = (x_1 \oplus x_2) \oplus x_3 = x_1 \oplus (x_2 \oplus x_3) = (x_3 \oplus x_1) \oplus x_2 = x_1 \oplus x_2 \oplus x_3$$

The eight input pattern pairs and corresponding outputs are given in Table 1. This is a typical nonlinear pattern classification problem. A single linear neuron with a nonlinear activation function is unable to form a decision surface such that the patterns are separated in the pattern space. Our objective here is to find all the possible solutions using the third order neural network to realize the logic function.

A third order neural network is designed as

$$y = w_0 + w_1 x_1 + w_2 x_2 + w_3 x_3 + w_{12} x_1 x_2 + w_{13} x_1 x_3 + w_{23} x_2 x_3 + w_{123} x_1 x_2 x_3$$

where $x_1, x_2, x_3 \in \{-1, 1\}$ are the binary inputs, and the network contains eight weights. To implement the above mentioned logic XOR function, one may consider the solution of the following set of linear algebraic equations:

$$\begin{cases} w_0 - w_1 - w_2 - w_3 + w_{12} + w_{13} + w_{23} - w_{123} = -1 \\ w_0 - w_1 - w_2 + w_3 + w_{12} - w_{13} - w_{23} + w_{123} = 1 \\ w_0 - w_1 + w_2 - w_3 - w_{12} + w_{13} - w_{23} + w_{123} = 1 \\ w_0 - w_1 + w_2 + w_3 - w_{12} - w_{13} + w_{23} - w_{123} = -1 \\ w_0 + w_1 - w_2 - w_3 - w_{12} - w_{13} + w_{23} + w_{123} = 1 \\ w_0 + w_1 - w_2 + w_3 - w_{12} + w_{13} - w_{23} - w_{123} = -1 \\ w_0 + w_1 + w_2 - w_3 + w_{12} - w_{13} - w_{23} - w_{123} = -1 \\ w_0 + w_1 + w_2 + w_3 + w_{12} + w_{13} + w_{23} + w_{123} = 1 \end{cases}$$

The coefficient matrix U is given by

$$U = \begin{bmatrix} 1 & -1 & -1 & -1 & 1 & 1 & 1 & -1 \\ 1 & -1 & -1 & 1 & 1 & -1 & -1 & 1 \\ 1 & -1 & 1 & -1 & -1 & 1 & -1 & 1 \\ 1 & -1 & 1 & 1 & -1 & -1 & 1 & -1 \\ 1 & 1 & -1 & -1 & -1 & -1 & 1 & 1 \\ 1 & 1 & -1 & 1 & -1 & 1 & -1 & -1 \\ 1 & 1 & 1 & -1 & 1 & -1 & -1 & -1 \\ 1 & 1 & 1 & 1 & 1 & 1 & 1 & 1 \end{bmatrix}$$

which is nonsingular. The equations have a unique set of solutions:

$$w_0 = w_1 = w_2 = w_3 = w_{12} = w_{13} = w_{23} = 0, \quad w_{123} = 1$$

Therefore, the logic function is realized by the third order polynomial $y = x_1 x_2 x_3$. This solution is unique in terms of the third order polynomial.

Xu et al. (1992) as well as Taylor and Commbes (1993) also demonstrated that HONNs may be effectively applied to problems using a model of a curve, surface, or hypersurface to fit a given data set. This problem, called *nonlinear surface fitting*, is often encountered in many computer science and engineering applications. Some learning algorithms for solving such problems can be found in their papers. Moreover, if one assumes $\varphi(x) = x$ in the HONU, the weight exhibits linearity in the networks and the learning algorithms for the HONNs may be characterized as a linear least square (LS) procedure. Then the well-known local minimum problems existing in many nonlinear neural learning schemes may be avoided.

4.1. Modified Polynomial Neural Networks

4.1.1. Sigma-Pi Neural Networks

Note that an HONU contains all the linear and nonlinear correlation terms of the input components to the order n. A slightly generalized structure of the HONU is a polynomial network that includes weighted sums of products of selected input components with an appropriate power. Mathematically, the input-output transfer function of this network structure is given by

$$u_i = \prod_{j=1}^{n} x_j^{w_{ij}} \tag{26}$$

$$y = \varphi\left(\sum_{i=1}^{N} w_i u_i\right) \tag{27}$$

where $w_i, w_{ij} \in \Re$, N is the order of the network and u_i is the output of the *i*-th hidden unit. This type of feedforward network is called a *sigma-pi network* (Rumelhart et al. 1986). It is easy to show that this network satisfies the Stone-Weierstrass theorem if $\varphi(x)$ is a linear function. Moreover, a modified version of the sigma-pi network, as proposed by Hornik et al. (1989) and Cotter (1990), is

$$u_i = \prod_{j=1}^{n} \left(p\left(x_j\right)\right)^{w_{ij}} \tag{28}$$

$$y = \varphi\left(\sum_{i=1}^{N} w_i u_i\right) \tag{29}$$

where $w_i, w_{ij} \in \Re$ and $p\left(x_j\right)$ is a polynomial of x_j. It is easy to verify that this network satisfies the Stone-Weierstrass theorem, and thus, it can be an approximator for problems of functional approximations. The sigma-pi network defined in eqns. (26) and (27) is a special case of the above network while $p\left(x_j\right)$ is assumed to be a linear function of x_j. In fact, the weights w_{ij} in both the networks given in eqns. (26) and (28) may be restricted to integer or nonnegative integer values.

4.1.2. Ridge Polynomial Neural Networks

To obtain fast learning and powerful mapping capabilities, and to avoid the combinatorial increase in the number of weights of HONNs, some modified polynomial network structures have been introduced. One of these is the *pi-sigma network* (Shin and Ghosh, 1991), which is a regular higher order structure and involves a much smaller number of weights than sigma-pi networks. The mapping equation of a pi-sigma network can be represented as

$$u_i = \sum_{j=1}^{n} w_{ij} x_j + \theta_i \tag{30}$$

$$y = \varphi\left(\prod_{i=1}^{N} u_i\right) = \varphi\left(\prod_{i=1}^{N}\left[\sum_{j=1}^{n} w_{ij} x_j + \theta_i\right]\right) \tag{31}$$

The total number of weights for an *N*th-order pi-sigma network with *n* inputs is only $(n+1)N$. Compared with the sigma-pi network structure, the number of weights involved in this network is significantly reduced. Unfortunately, when $\varphi(x) = x$, the pi-sigma network does not match the conditions provided by the Stone-Weierstrass theorem because the linear subspace condition is not satisfied (Gupta et al., 2003). However, some studies have shown that it is a good network model for smooth functions (Shin and Ghosh, 1991).

To modify the structure of the above mentioned pi-sigma networks such that they satisfy the Stone-Weierstrass theorem, Shin and Ghosh (1991) suggested considering the *ridge polynomial neural network* (RPNN). For the vectors $\mathbf{w}_{ij} = \left[w_{ij1}, w_{ij2}, ..., w_{ijn} \right]^T$ and $\mathbf{x} = \left[x_1, x_2, ..., x_n \right]^T$ let

$$< \mathbf{x}, \mathbf{w}_{ij} >= \sum_{k=1}^{n} w_{ijk} x_k$$

which represents an inner product between the two vectors. A one-variable continuous function f of the form $< \mathbf{x}, \mathbf{w}_{ij} >$ is called a *ridge function*. A *ridge polynomial* is a ridge function that can be represented as

$$\sum_{i=0}^{N} \sum_{j=0}^{M} a_{ij} < \mathbf{x}, \mathbf{w}_{ij} >^i$$

for some $a_{ij} \in \Re$ and $\mathbf{w}_{ij} \in \Re^n$. The operation equation of a RPNN is expressed as

$$y = \varphi \left(\sum_{j=1}^{N} \prod_{i=1}^{n} \left(< \mathbf{x}, \mathbf{w}_{ij} > + \theta_{ji} \right) \right)$$

where $\varphi(x) = x$. The *denseness*, which is a fundamental concept for universal function approximators described in the Stone-Weierstrass theorem, of this network can be verified (Gupta et al., 2003).

The total number of weights involved in this structure is $N(N+1)(n+1)/2$. A comparison of the number of weights of the three types of polynomial network structures is given in Table 2. The results show that when the networks have the same higher-order terms, there are significantly less weights for a RPNN than for a sigma-pi network. This is a very attractive improvement offered by RPNNs.

Table 2. The number of weights in the polynomial networks

Order of network	Number of weights					
	Pi-sigma		RPNN		Sigma-pi	
N	n=5	n=10	n=5	n=10	n=5	n=10
2	12	22	18	33	21	66
3	18	33	36	66	56	286
4	24	44	60	110	126	1001

5. COMPUTER SCIENCE AND ENGINEERING APPLICATIONS

Function approximation problems are typical examples in many computer science and engineering situations. The capability to approximate nonlinear complex functions can be a basis of the complex pattern classification ability as well. Furthermore, the neural network approach with high approximation ability can be used for time series analysis by introducing time delay features into the neural network structure. Time series analysis or estimation is one of the most important problems in computer science and engineering applications. In this section, we will explain the function approximation ability of HONNs first. Neural network structures to represent time delay features will then be introduced for time series analysis.

5.1. Function Approximation Problem

For evaluating the function approximation ability of HONNs, an example was taken from Klassen et al. (1988). The task consists of learning a representation for an unknown, one-variable nonlinear function, $F(x)$, with the only available information being the 18 sample patterns (Villalobos and Merat, 1995).

For this function approximation problem, a two-layered neural network structure was composed of two SONUs in the first layer and a single SONU in the output layer (Figure 8). The nonlinear activation function of the SONUs in the first layer was defined by a bipolar sigmoidal function as $\varphi(u) = (1 - \exp(-u))/(1 + \exp(-u))$ but for the single output SONU, instead of the sigmoidal function, the linear function was used: $y = \varphi(u) = u$ The gradient learning algorithm with $\eta = 0.1$ was used for this problem.

The mapping function obtained by the SONU network after 10^7 learning iterations appears in Figure 9. In this case, the average square error taken over 18 patterns was 4.566E-6. The fact that the approximation accuracy shown in Figure 9 is extremely high is evidence of the high approximation ability of the SONN.

Figure 8. A two-layered neural network structure with two SONUs in the first layer and a single SONU in the output layer for the function approximation problem

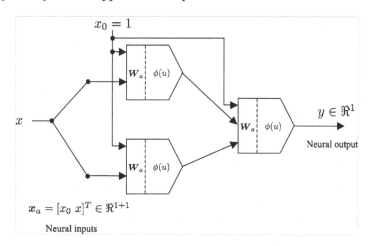

Figure 9. Training pairs and outputs estimated by the network with SONUs for the Klassen's function approximation problem (Klassen et al., 1988)

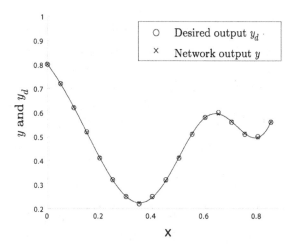

Five particular trigonometric functions, $\sin(\pi x)$, $\cos(\pi x)$, $\sin(2\pi x)$, $\cos(2\pi x)$ and $\sin(4\pi x)$, were used as special features of the extra neural inputs (Klassen et al., 1988). Also, it has been reported (Villalobos and Merat, 1995) that the term $\cos(\pi x)$ is not necessary to achieve a lower accuracy within the error tolerance 1.125E-4, but still four extra features were required.

On the other hand, in this study, the high approximation accuracy of the proposed SONU network was achieved by only two SONUs with the sigmoidal activation function in the first layer and a single SONU with the linear activation function in the output layer, and no special features were required for high accuracy. These are remarkable advantages of the proposed SONN structure.

5.2. Neural Network Structures with Time Delay Features

The so-called tapped delay line neural networks (TDLNNs) consist of MFNNs and some time delay operators as shown in Figure 10. Let $y(k) \in \Re$ be an internal state variable at the time instant k. The delayed states $y(k), y(k-1), ..., y(k-n)$ are used as inputs of a TDLNN. The various type of TDLNNs can be further defined on the basis of specified applications.

For time series analysis, the q-step prediction equations of the TDLNNs, as shown in Figure 10, can be given as follows:

$$y(k+q) = F(\mathbf{w}, y(k), ..., y(k-n), u(k)) \tag{32}$$

where $F(.)$ is a continuous and differentiable function that may be obtained from the operation of the MFNN. The input components of the neural networks are the time-delayed versions of the outputs of the networks. In this case, eqn. (32) represents a q-step-ahead nonlinear predictor. TDLNNs consisting of HONUs can further contribute to capture the complex nonlinear features by using the higher order combinations of inputs.

Figure 10. Tapped delay line neural networks (TDLNNs) for time series analysis

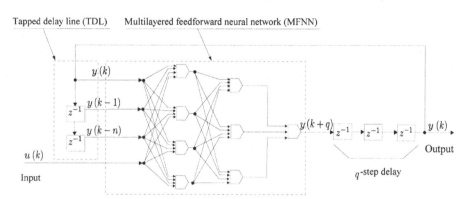

These neural network structures have the potential to represent a class of nonlinear input-output mappings of unknown nonlinear systems or communication channels without internal dynamics, and have been successfully applied to time series analysis (Matsuba, 2000). Because there are no state feedback connections in the network, the static backpropagation learning algorithm may be used to train the TDLNN so that the processes of system modeling or function approximation are carried out.

On the other hand, neural units with internal dynamics have been proposed (Gupta et al., 2003). Neural units with learning and adaptive capabilities discussed so far had only static input-output functional relationships. This implies, therefore, that for a given input pattern to such a static neural unit, an instantaneous output is obtained through a linear or nonlinear mapping procedure. Note that this is true even for TDLNNs in the neural unit level. However, a biological neuron not only contains a nonlinear mapping operation on the weighted sum of the input signals, but also has some dynamic processes such as the state signal feedback, time delays, hysteresis, and limit cycles. To emulate such a complex behavior, a number of dynamic or feedback neural units have been proposed relatively recently. As the basic building blocks of the dynamic feedback neural networks, these dynamic neural units may be used to construct a complex dynamic neural network structure through internal synaptic connections. To further use the higher order nonlinearity, the synaptic operation in HONUs can be incorporated into the dynamic neural units.

6. CONCLUDING REMARKS AND FUTURE RESEARCH DIRECTIONS

In this chapter, the basic foundation of neural networks, starting from a basic introduction to biological foundations, neural unit models, and learning properties, has been introduced. Then as the first step to understanding HONNs, a general SONU was developed. Simulation studies for both the pattern classification and function approximation problems demonstrated that the learning and generalization abilities of the proposed SONU and neural networks having SONUs are greatly superior to that of the widely used linear combination neural units and their networks. Indeed, from the point of view of both the neural computing process and its learning algorithm, it has been found that linear combination neural units widely used in multilayered neural networks are only a subset of the proposed SONUs. Some extensions of these concepts to radial basis function (RBF) networks, fuzzy neural networks, and dynamic neural units will be interesting future research projects.

There is certainly rapidly growing research interest in the field of HONNs. There are increasing complexities in applications not only in the fields of aerospace, process control, ocean exploration, manufacturing, and resource based industry, but also in computer science and engineering; this is the main issue of this book. This chapter deals with the theoretical foundations of HONNs and will help readers to develop or apply the methods to their own computer science and engineering problems. Most of the book deals with real computer science and engineering applications.

We hope that our efforts in this chapter will stimulate research interests, provide some new challenges to its readers, generate curiosity for learning more in the field, and arouse a desire to seek new theoretical tools and applications. We will consider our efforts successful if this chapter raises one's level of curiosity.

7. REFERENCES

Cichochi, A., & Unbehauen, R. (1993). *Neural Networks for Optimization and Signal Processing*. Chichester, UK: Wiley.

Cotter, N. (1990). The Stone-Weierstrass Theorem and Its Application to Neural Networks. *IEEE Transactions on Neural Networks, 1*(4), 290–295. doi:10.1109/72.80265

Giles, C. L., & Maxwell, T. (1987). Learning invariance, and generalization in higher-order networks. *Applied Optics, 26*, 4972–4978. doi:10.1364/AO.26.004972

Gupta, M. M., Jin, L., & Homma, N. (2003). *Static and Dynamic Neural Networks: From Fundamentals to Advanced Theory*. Hoboken, NJ: IEEE & Wiley.

Harston, C. T. (1990). The Neurological Basis for Neural Computation. In Maren, A. J., Harston, C. T., & Pap, R. M. (Eds.), *Handbook of Neural Computing Applications*, Vol. 1. (pp. 29-44). New York: Academic.

Homma, N., & Gupta, M. M. (2002). A general second order neural unit. *Bull. Coll. Med. Sci. Tohoku Univ., 11*(1), 1–6.

Hornik, K., Stinchcombe, M., & White, H. (1989). Multilayer Feedforward Networks Are Universal Approximators. *Neural Networks, 2*(5), 359–366. doi:10.1016/0893-6080(89)90020-8

Klassen, M., Pao, Y., & Chen, V. (1988). Characteristics of the functional link net: a higher order delta rule net. In Proceedings of IEEE 2nd Annual Int'l. Conf. Neural Networks.

Kobayashi, S. (2006). Sensation World Made by the Brain – Animals Do Not Have Sensors. Tokyo: Corona (in Japanese).

Matsuba, I. (2000). *Nonlinear time series analysis*. Tokyo: Asakura-syoten (in Japanese).

McCulloch, W. S., & Pitts, W. H. (1943). A logical calculus of the ideas imminent in nervous activity. *The Bulletin of Mathematical Biophysics, 5*, 115–133. doi:10.1007/BF02478259

Narendra, K., & Parthasarathy, K. (1990). Identification and control of dynamical systems using neural networks. *IEEE Transactions on Neural Networks, 1*, 4–27. doi:10.1109/72.80202

Pao, Y. H. (1989). *Adaptive Pattern Recognition and Neural Networks,* Reading, MA: Addison-Wesley.

Rumelhart, D. E., Hinton, G. E., & Williams, R. J. (1986). Learning Internal Representations by Error Propagation. In Rumelhart, D. E., & McClelland, J. L. (Eds.), *Parallel Distributed Processing: Explorations in the Microstructure of Cognition, Vol. 1* (pp. 318-362). Cambridge, MA: MIT Press.

Schmidt, W., & Davis, J. (1993). Pattern recognition properties of various feature spaces for higher order neural networks. *IEEE Transactions on Pattern Analysis and Machine Intelligence, 15,* 795–801. doi:10.1109/34.236250

Shin, Y., & Ghosh, J. (1991). The Pi-sigma Network: An Efficient Higher-order Neural Network for Pattern Classification and Function Approximation. In*Proceedings of. Int. Joint Conf. on Neural Networks* (pp. 13-18).

Sinha, N., Gupta, M. M., & Zadeh, L. (1999). Soft Computing and Intelligent Control Systems: Theory and Applications. New York: Academic.

Softky, R. W., & Kammen, D. M. (1991). Correlations in high dimensional or asymmetrical data sets: Hebbian neuronal processing. *Neural Networks, 4,* 337–347. doi:10.1016/0893-6080(91)90070-L

Taylor, J. G., & Commbes, S. (1993). Learning higher order correlations. *Neural Networks, 6,* 423–428. doi:10.1016/0893-6080(93)90009-L

Villalobos, L., & Merat, F. (1995). Learning capability assessment and feature space optimization for higher-order neural networks. *IEEE Transactions on Neural Networks, 6,* 267–272. doi:10.1109/72.363427

Xu, L., Oja, E., & Suen, C. Y. (1992). Modified hebbian learning for curve and surface fitting. *Neural Networks, 5,* 441–457. doi:10.1016/0893-6080(92)90006-5

ADDITIONAL READING

Amari, S. (1971). Characteristics of Randomly Connected Threshold-Element Networks and Network Systems. *Proceedings of the IEEE, 59*(1), 35–47. doi:10.1109/PROC.1971.8087

Amari, S. (1972). Characteristics of Random Nets of Analog Neuron - Like Elements. *IEEE Transactions on Systems, Man, and Cybernetics, 2,* 643–654. doi:10.1109/TSMC.1972.4309193

Amari, S. (1972). Learning Patterns and Pattern Sequences by Self-Organizing Nets of Threshold Elements. *IEEE Transactions on Computers, 21,* 1197–1206. doi:10.1109/T-C.1972.223477

Amari, S. (1977). A Mathematical Approach to Neural Systems. In J. Metzler (Ed.), *Systems Neuroscience* (pp. 67-118). New York: Academic.

Amari, S. (1977). Neural Theory of Association and Concept Formation. *Biological Cybernetics, 26,* 175–185. doi:10.1007/BF00365229

Amari, S. (1990). Mathematical Foundations of Neurocomputing. *Proceedings of the IEEE, 78*(9), 1443–1462. doi:10.1109/5.58324

Amit, D. J., Gutfreund, G., & Sompolinsky, H. (1985). Spin-Glass Model of Neural Networks. *Physical Review A., 32,* 1007–1018. doi:10.1103/PhysRevA.32.1007

Anagun, A. S., & Cin, I. (1998). A Neural-Network-Based Computer Access Security System for Multiple Users. In *Proceedings of 23rd Inter. Conf. Comput. Ind. Eng., Vol. 35* (pp. 351-354).

Anderson, J. A. (1983). Cognition and Psychological Computation with Neural Models. *IEEE Transactions on Systems, Man, and Cybernetics, 13,* 799–815.

Anninos, P. A., Beek, B., Csermel, T. J., Harth, E. E., & Pertile, G. (1970). Dynamics of Neural Structures. *Journal of Theoretical Biology, 26,* 121–148. doi:10.1016/S0022-5193(70)80036-4

Aoki, C., & Siekevltz, P. (1988). Plasticity in Brain Development. *Scientific American,* (Dec): 56–64.

Churchland, P. S., & Sejnowski, T. J. (1988). Perspectives on Cognitive Neuroscience. *Science, 242,* 741–745. doi:10.1126/science.3055294

Ding, M.-Z., & Yang, W.-M. (1997). Stability of Synchronous Chaos and On-Off Intermittency in Coupled Map Lattices. *Physical Review E: Statistical Physics, Plasmas, Fluids, and Related Interdisciplinary Topics, 56*(4), 4009–4016. doi:10.1103/PhysRevE.56.4009

Durbin, R. (1989). On the Correspondence Between Network Models and the Nervous System. In R. Durbin, C. Miall, & G. Mitchison (Eds.), *The Computing Neurons.* Reading, Mass.: Addison-Wesley.

Engel, K., Konig, P., Kreiter, A. K., & Singer, W. (1991). Interhemispheric Synchronization of Oscillatory Neuronal Responses in Cat Visual Cortex. *Science, 252,* 1177–1178. doi:10.1126/science.252.5009.1177

Ersu, E., & Tolle, H. (1984). A New Concept for Learning Control Inspired by Brain Theory. In *Proceedings of 9th World Congress IFAC* (pp. 245-250).

Forbus, K. D., & Gentner, D. (1983). Casual Reasoning About Quantities. In *Proceedings of 5th Annual Conf. of the Cognitive Science Society* (pp. 196-206).

Fujita, M. (1982). Adaptive Filter Model of the Cerebellum. *Biological Cybernetics, 45,* 195–206. doi:10.1007/BF00336192

Garliaskas, A., & Gupta, M. M. (1995). A Generalized Model of Synapse-Dendrite-Cell Body as a Complex Neuron. *World Congress on Neural Networks, Vol. 1* (pp. 304-307).

Gupta, M. M. (1988). Biological Basis for Computer Vision: Some Perspective. *SPW Conf. on Intelligent Robots and Computer Vision* (pp. 811-823).

Gupta, M. M., & Knopf, G. K. (1992). A Multitask Visual Information Processor with a Biologically Motivated Design. *J. Visual Communicat. Image Representation, 3*(3), 230–246. doi:10.1016/1047-3203(92)90020-T

Hiramoto, M., Hiromi, Y., Giniger, E., & Hotta, Y. (2000). The Drosophila Netrin Receptor Frazzled Guides Axons by Controlling Netrin Distribution. *Nature, 406*(6798), 886–888. doi:10.1038/35022571

Holmes, C. C., & Mallick, B. K. (1998). Bayesian Radial Basis Functions of Variable Dimension. *Neural Computation, 10*(5), 1217–1233. doi:10.1162/089976698300017421

Honma, N., Abe, K., Sato, M., & Takeda, H. (1998). Adaptive Evolution of Holon Networks by an Autonomous Decentralized Method. *Applied Mathematics and Computation, 9*(1), 43–61. doi:10.1016/S0096-3003(97)10008-X

Hopfield, J. (1990). Artificial Neural Networks are Coming. An Interview by W. Myers . *IEEE Expert*, (Apr): 3–6.

Joshi, A., Ramakrishman, N., Houstis, E. N., & Rice, J. R. (1997). On Neurobiological, Neurofuzzy, Machine Learning, and Statistical Pattern Recognition Techniques. *IEEE Transactions on Neural Networks*, 8.

Kaneko, K. (1994). Relevance of Dynamic Clustering to Biological Networks. *Physica D. Nonlinear Phenomena, 75*, 55–73. doi:10.1016/0167-2789(94)90274-7

Kaneko, K. (1997). Coupled Maps with Growth and Death: An Approach to Cell Differentiation. *Physica D. Nonlinear Phenomena, 103*, 505–527. doi:10.1016/S0167-2789(96)00282-5

Knopf, G. K., & Gupta, M. M. (1993). Dynamics of Antagonistic Neural Processing Elements. *International Journal of Neural Systems, 4*(3), 291–303. doi:10.1142/S0129065793000237

Kohara, K., Kitamura, A., Morishima, M., & Tsumoto, T. (2001). Activity-Dependent Transfer of Brain-Derived Neurotrophic Factor to Postsynaptic Neurons. *Science, 291*, 2419–2423. doi:10.1126/science.1057415

Kohonen, T. (1988). An Introduction to Neural Computing. *Neural Networks, 1*(1), 3–16. doi:10.1016/0893-6080(88)90020-2

Kohonen, T. (1990). The Self-Organizing Map. *Proceedings of the IEEE, 78*(9), 1464–1480. doi:10.1109/5.58325

Kohonen, T. (1991). Self-Organizing Maps: Optimization Approaches. In T. Kohonen, K. Makisara, O. Simula, & J. Kangas (Eds.), *Artificial Neural Networks* (pp. 981-990). Amsterdam, The Netherlands: Elsevier.

Kohonen, T. (1993). Things You Haven't Heard About The Self-Organizing Map. In *Proceedings of Inter. Conf. Neural Networks 1993* (pp. 1147-1156).

Kohonen, T. (1998). Self Organization of Very Large Document Collections: State of the Art. In *Proceedings of 8th Inter. Conf. Artificial Neural Networks, Vol. 1* (pp. 65-74).

LeCun, Y., Boser, B., & Solla, S. A. (1990). Optimal Brain Damage. In D. Touretzky (Ed.), *Advances in Neural Information Processing Systems, Vol. 2* (pp. 598-605). San Francisco:Morgan Kaufmann.

Lippmann, R. P. (1987). An Introduction to Computing with Neural Networks. IEEE *Acoustics . Speech and Signal Processing Magazine, 4*(2), 4–22.

Lovejoy, C. O. (1981). The Origin of Man. *Science, 211*, 341–350. doi:10.1126/science.211.4480.341

Maire, M. (2000). On the Convergence of Validity Interval Analysis. *IEEE Transactions on Neural Networks, 11*(3), 799–801. doi:10.1109/72.846751

Mantere, K., Parkkinen, J., Jaasketainen, T., & Gupta, M. M. (1993). Wilson-Cowan Neural Network Model in Image Processing. *Journal of Mathematical Imaging and Vision, 2*, 251–259. doi:10.1007/BF00118593

McCarthy, J., & Hayes, P. J. (1969). Some Philosophical Problems from the Standpoint of Artificial Intelligence. In Meltzer & Michie (Eds.), *Machine Intelligence, 4* (pp. 463-502). Edinburgh, UK: Edinburgh Univ. Press.

McCulloch, W. S., & Pitts, W. H. (1943). A Logical Calculus of the Ideas Imminent in Nervous Activity. *The Bulletin of Mathematical Biophysics, 5*, 115–133. doi:10.1007/BF02478259

McDermott, D. (1982). A Temporal Logic for Reasoning About Processes and Plans. *Cognitive Science, 6*, 101–155.

Melkonian, D. S. (1990). Mathematical Theory of Chemical Synaptic Transmission. *Biological Cybernetics, 62*, 539–548. doi:10.1007/BF00205116

Pecht, O. Y., & Gur, M. (1995). A Biologically-Inspired Improved MAXNET. *IEEE Transactions on Neural Networks, 6*, 757–759. doi:10.1109/72.377981

Petshe, T., & Dickinson, B. W. (1990). Trellis Codes, Receptive Fields, and Fault-Tolerance Self-Repairing Neural Networks. *IEEE Transactions on Neural Networks, 1*(2), 154–166. doi:10.1109/72.80228

Poggio, T., & Koch, C. (1987). Synapses that Compute Motion. *Scientific American*, (May): 46–52.

Rao, D. H., & Gupta, M. M. (1993). A Generic Neural Model Based on Excitatory - Inhibitory Neural Population. *IJCNN-93* (pp. 1393-1396).

Rosenblatt, F. (1958). The Perceptron: A Probabilistic Model for Information Storage and Organization in the Brain. *Psychological Review, 65*, 386–408. doi:10.1037/h0042519

Sandewall, E. (1989). Combining Logic and Differential Equations for Describing Real-World Systems. In *Proceedings of 1st Inter. Conf. on Principles of Knowledge Representation and Reasoning* (pp. 412-420). San Francisco: Morgan Kaufmann.

Setiono, R., & Liu, H. (1996). Symbolic Representation of Neural Networks. *Computer, 29*(3), 71–77. doi:10.1109/2.485895

Skarda, C. A., & Freeman, W. J. (1987). How Brains Make Chaos in Order to Make Sense of the World. *The Behavioral and Brain Sciences, 10*, 161–195.

Stevens, C. F. (1968). Synaptic Physiology. *Proceedings of the IEEE, 79*(9), 916–930. doi:10.1109/PROC.1968.6444

Wilson, H. R., & Cowan, J. D. (1972). Excitatory and Inhibitory Interactions in Localized Populations of Model Neurons. *Biophysical Journal, 12*, 1–24. doi:10.1016/S0006-3495(72)86068-5

Chapter 18

Identification of Nonlinear Systems Using a New Neuro-Fuzzy Dynamical System Definition Based on High Order Neural Network Function Approximators

Y.S. Boutalis
Democritus University of Thrace, Greece

M.A. Christodoulou
University of Crete, Greece

D.C. Theodoridis
Democritus University of Thrace, Greece

ABSTRACT

A new definition of adaptive dynamic fuzzy systems (ADFS) is presented in this chapter for the identification of unknown nonlinear dynamical systems. The proposed scheme uses the concept of adaptive fuzzy systems operating in conjunction with high order neural networks (HONN's). Since the plant is considered unknown, we first propose its approximation by a special form of an adaptive fuzzy system and in the sequel the fuzzy rules are approximated by appropriate HONN's. Thus the identification scheme leads up to a recurrent high order neural network, which however takes into account the fuzzy output partitions of the initial ADFS. Weight updating laws for the involved HONN's are provided, which guarantee that the identification error reaches zero exponentially fast. Simulations illustrate the potency of the method and comparisons on well known benchmarks are given.

DOI: 10.4018/978-1-61520-711-4.ch018

1. INTRODUCTION

Nonlinear dynamical systems can be represented by general nonlinear dynamical equations of the form

$$\dot{x} = f(x, u) \tag{1}$$

The mathematical description of the system is required, so that we are able to control it. Unfortunately, the exact mathematical model of the plant, especially when this is highly nonlinear and complex, is rarely known and thus appropriate identification schemes have to be applied which will provide us with an approximate model of the plant.

It has been established that neural networks and fuzzy inference systems are universal approximators (Hornik, Stinchcombe & White, 1989), (Wang, 1994), (Passino & Yurkovich, 1998), (Golea, Golea & Benmahammed, 2003), (Hojati & Gazor, 2002), that is, they can approximate any nonlinear function to any prescribed accuracy provided that sufficient hidden neurons and training data or fuzzy rules are available. Recently, the combination of these two different technologies has given rise to fuzzy neural or neuro fuzzy approaches, that are intended to capture the advantages of both fuzzy logic and neural networks. Numerous works have shown the viability of this approach for system modelling (Jang, 1993; Lin, 1995; Cho & Wang, 1996; Juang & Lin, 1998; Li & Mukaidono, 1995; Chui, 1994; Lin & Cunningham, 1995; Jang & Lin, 1998; Mitra & Hayashi, 2000).

The neural and fuzzy approaches are most of the time equivalent, differing between each other mainly in the structure of the approximator chosen. Indeed, in order to bridge the gap between the neural and fuzzy approaches several researchers introduce adaptive schemes using a class of parameterized functions that include both neural networks and fuzzy systems (Cho & Wang, 1996; Juang & Lin, 1998; Li & Mukaidono, 1995; Chui, 1994; Lin & Cunningham, 1995; Jang & Lin, 1998; Mitra & Hayashi, 2000). Regarding the approximator structure, linear in the parameters approximators are used in (Lin & Cunningham, 1995), (Chen, Lee & Chang, 1996), and nonlinear in (Spooner & Passino, 1996), (Narendra & Parthasarathy, 1990), (Polycarpou & Mears, 1998), (Lee & Teng, 2000), (Lina, Wang & Liub, 2004).

Recently (Kosmatopoulos & Christodoulou, 1996), (Christodoulou, Theodoridis & Boutalis, 2007), high order neural network function approximators (HONN's) have been proposed for the identification of nonlinear dynamical systems of the form (1), approximated by a fuzzy dynamical system. In this chapter HONN's are also used for the neuro fuzzy identification of unknown nonlinear dynamical systems. This approximation depends on the fact that fuzzy rules could be identified with the help of HONN's. The same rationale has been employed in (Theodoridis, Christodoulou & Boutalis, 2008), (Boutalis, Theodoridis & Christodoulou, 2009), where a neuro–fuzzy approach for the indirect control of unknown systems has been introduced.

In fuzzy or neuro-fuzzy approaches the identification phase usually consists of two categories: structure identification and parameter identification. Structure identification involves finding the main input variables out of all possible, specifying the membership functions, the partition of the input space and determining the number of fuzzy rules which is often based on a substantial amount of heuristic observation to express proper strategy's knowledge. Most of structure identification methods are based on data clustering, such as fuzzy C-means clustering (Chui, 1994), mountain clustering (Jang & Lin, 1998), and subtractive clustering (Mitra & Hayashi, 2000). These approaches require that all input-output data are ready before we start to identify the plant. So these structure identification approaches are off-line.

In the proposed approach structure identification is also made off-line based either on human expertise or on gathered data. However, the required a-priori information obtained by linguistic information or data is very limited. The only required information is an estimate of the centres of the output fuzzy membership functions. Information on the input variable membership functions and on the underlying fuzzy rules is not necessary because this is automatically estimated by the HONN's. This way the proposed method is less vulnerable to initial design assumptions. The parameter identification is then easily addressed by HONN's, based on the linguistic information regarding the structural identification of the output part and from the numerical data obtained from the actual system to be modelled. So, the parameters of identification model are updated on–line in such a way that the error between the actual system output and the model output reaches zero exponentially fast.

We consider that the nonlinear system is affine in the control and could be approximated with the help of two independent fuzzy subsystems. Every fuzzy subsystem is approximated from a family of HONNFs, each one being related with a group of fuzzy rules. Weight updating laws are given and we prove that when the structural identification is appropriate then the error converges very fast to zero.

The chapter is organized as follows. Section 2.1 presents preliminaries related to the concept of adaptive fuzzy systems (AFS) and the terminology used in the remaining chapter, while Section 2.2 gives a brief introduction about RHONN's and reports on the ability of HONN's to act as fuzzy rule approximators. The new neuro fuzzy representation of affine in the control dynamical systems is introduced in Section 2.3, while the adaptive parameter identification is presented in Section 2.4, where the associated weight adaptation laws are given. Finally, simulation results on the identification of well known benchmark problems are given in Section 2.5 and the performance of the proposed scheme is compared to another well known approach of the literature

2.1 Preliminaries

In this section we briefly present the notion of adaptive fuzzy systems and their conventional representation. We are also introducing the representation of fuzzy systems using the fuzzy rule indicator functions, which is used for the development of the proposed method.

2.1.1 Adaptive Fuzzy Systems

The performance, complexity, and adaptive law of an adaptive fuzzy system representation can be quite different depending upon the type of the fuzzy system (Mamdani or Takagi-Sugeno) (Mamdani, 1976), (Takagi & Sugeno, 1985). It also depends upon whether the representation is linear or nonlinear in its adjustable parameters. Adaptive fuzzy controllers depend also on the type of the adaptive fuzzy subsystems they use. Suppose that the adaptive fuzzy system is intended to approximate the nonlinear function $f(x)$. In the Mamdani type, linear in the parameters form, the following fuzzy logic representation is used (Wang, 1994), (Passino & Yurkovich, 1998):

$$f(x) = \sum_{l=1}^{M} \theta_l \xi_l(x) = \theta^T \xi(x) \tag{2}$$

where M is the number of fuzzy rules, $\theta = \left(\theta_1, ..., \theta_M\right)^T$, $\xi(x) = \left(\xi_1(x), ..., \xi_M(x)\right)^T$ and $\xi_l(x)$ is the fuzzy basis function defined by

$$\xi_l(x) = \frac{\prod_{i=1}^{n} \mu_{F_i^l}(x_i)}{\sum_{l=1}^{M} \prod_{i=1}^{n} \mu_{F_i^l}(x_i)} \tag{3}$$

θ_l are adjustable parameters, and $\mu_{F_i^l}$ are given membership functions of the input variables (can be Gaussian, triangular, or any other type of membership functions).

In Takagi-Sugeno formulation $f(x)$ is given by

$$f(x) = \sum_{l=1}^{M} g_l \xi_l(x) = \theta^T \xi(x) \tag{4}$$

Where $g_l(x) = a_{l,0} + a_{l,1} x_1 + ... + a_{l,n} x_n$, with $x_i, i = 1...n$ being the elements of vector x and $\xi_l(x)$ being defined in (3). According to (Passino & Yurkovich, 1998), (4) can also be written in the linear to the parameters form, where the adjustable parameters are all $a_{l,i}, l = 1...M, i = 1...n$.

From the above definitions it is apparent, in both Mamdani and Tagaki-Sugeno forms, that the success of the adaptive fuzzy system representations in approximating the nonlinear function $f(x)$ depends on the careful selection of the fuzzy partitions of input and output variables. Also, the selected type of the membership functions and the proper number of fuzzy rules contribute to the success of the adaptive fuzzy system. This way, any adaptive fuzzy or neuro-fuzzy approach following a linear in the adjustable parameters formulation becomes vulnerable to initial design assumptions related to the fuzzy partitions and the membership functions chosen. In this chapter this drawback is largely overcome by using the concept of rule indicator functions, which are in the sequel approximated by high order neural network approximators (HONN's). This way there is not any need for initial design assumptions related to the membership values and the fuzzy partitions of the if part.

2.1.2 The Concept of Fuzzy Dynamical Systems

Let us consider the system with input space $u \subset \Re^m$ and state – space $x \subset \Re^n$, with its i/o relation being governed by the following equation

$$z = f\left(x, u\right) \tag{5}$$

where $f(\cdot)$ is a continuous function and z, x, u are functions of time. In case the system is dynamic the above equation could be replaced by the following differential equation

$$\dot{x} = f\left(x, u\right) \tag{6}$$

By setting $y = \left[x, u\right]$, Eq. (5) may be rewritten as follows

$$z = f\left(y\right) \tag{7}$$

with $y \subset \Re^{m+n}$.

In case f in (7) is unknown we may wish to approximate it by using a fuzzy representation. In this case both y and z are initially replaced by fuzzy linguistic variables. Experts or data depended techniques may determine the form of the membership functions of the fuzzy variables and fuzzy rules will determine the fuzzy relations between y and u. Sensor input data, possibly noisy and imprecise measurements, enter the fuzzy system, are fuzzified, are processed by the fuzzy rules and the fuzzy implication engine and are in the sequel defuzzified to produce the estimated z (Wang, 1994), (Passino & Yurkovich, 1998). We assume here that a Mamdani type fuzzy system is used (Mamdani, 1976). This assumption together with the concept of indicator functions presented in section 2.1.3 permits the new neuro-fuzzy representation deployed in section 2.3.1. Fuzzy systems of Takagi-Sugeno type are not treated in this chapter.

Let now $\Omega^{l_1,l_2,\ldots,l_n}_{j_1,j_2,\ldots,j_{n+m}}$ be defined as the subset of (x,u) pairs, belonging to the $\left(j_1,j_2,\ldots,j_{n+m}\right)^{th}$ input fuzzy patch and pointing - through the vector field $f(\cdot)$ - to the subset of $z(k)$, which belong to the $\left(l_1,l_2,\ldots,l_n\right)^{th}$ output fuzzy patch. In other words, $\Omega^{l_1,l_2,\ldots,l_n}_{j_1,j_2,\ldots,j_{n+m}}$ contains input value pairs that are associated through a fuzzy rule with specific output values.

In the above notation, if $j_1 = l_1$ and $j_2 = l_2$ and ... and $j_n = l_n$, then these points participate to the definition of the same fuzzy rule. If $j_1 \neq l_1$ or $j_2 \neq l_2$ or ... or $j_n \neq l_n$, then these points define alternative fuzzy rules describing this transition. The influence of each fuzzy rule may be weighted up by its transition possibility estimated by the rule indicator function which will be defined in the following subsection.

Using the above definitions, we can see that the evolution of the dynamical system in Eq. (1) is described by fuzzy rules of the form

$$
R^{l_1,\ldots,l_n}_{j_1,\ldots,j_{n+m}} \Leftrightarrow \left\{
\begin{array}{l}
\quad IF \ \ y_1 \ is \ \tilde{y}_{1_{j_1}} \ AND \\
\quad y_{n+m} \ is \ \tilde{y}_{(n+m)_{j_{(n+m)}}} \\
THEN \ \text{at the next time-instant} \\
x_1 \ is \ \tilde{y}_{1_{l_1}} \ AND\ldots AND \ x_n \ is \ \tilde{y}_{n_{l_n}}
\end{array}
\right.
$$

where $\tilde{\bullet}$ denotes the fuzzy partition of variable $\tilde{\bullet}$ and y is partitioned into disjoint subsets $y_{j_1,j_2,\ldots,j_{n+m}}$ defined as follows

$$
y_{j_1,\ldots,j_{n+m}} := y_{1_{j_1}} \times \cdots \times y_{(n+m)_{j_{n+m}}}, j_i \in \{1,\ldots,k_i\}
$$

Consider now the next definitions.

Definition 1. A fuzzy dynamical system - (FDS) is a set of Fuzzy Rules of the form ($R^{l_1,\ldots,l_n}_{j_1,\ldots,j_{n+m}}$); the system in Eq. (1) is called the underlying dynamical system - (UDS) of the previously defined FDS. Alternatively, the system in Eq. (1) will be called a Generator of the FDS described by the rules ($R^{l_1,\ldots,l_n}_{j_1,\ldots,j_{n+m}}$).

Due to the linguistic description of the variables of the FDS it is not rare to have more than one systems of the form in Eq. (1) to be generators for the FDS that described by the rules ($R_{j_1,\dots,j_{n+m}}^{l_1,\dots,l_n}$). This fact justifies the next definition.

Definition 2. Consider the FDS ($R_{j_1,\dots,j_{n+m}}^{l_1,\dots,l_n}$). Then two systems of the form in Eq. (1) are called equivalent generators of the FDS ($R_{j_1,\dots,j_{n+m}}^{l_1,\dots,l_n}$) if they are both generators for the FDS ($R_{j_1,\dots,j_{n+m}}^{l_1,\dots,l_n}$).

2.1.3 Fuzzy System Description Using Rule Indicator Functions

In this subsection, we are briefly introducing the representation of fuzzy systems using the rule firing indicator functions (RFIF), or simply indicator functions (IF), which is used for the development of the proposed method.

According to the above notation the Indicator Function (IF) connected to $\Omega_{j_1,j_2,\dots,j_{n+m}}^{l_1,l_2,\dots,l_n}$ is defined as follows:

$$I_{j_1,j_2,\dots,j_{n+m}}^{l_1,l_2,\dots,l_n}\left(x,u\right) = \begin{cases} a & if \ \left(x,u\right) \in \Omega_{j_1,j_2,\dots,j_{n+m}}^{l_1,l_2,\dots,l_n} \\ 0 & otherwise \end{cases} \tag{8}$$

where a denotes the firing strength of the rule. According to standard fuzzy system description and fuzzy implication procedure (Passino & Yurkovich, 1998), this strength depends on the membership value of each x_i $i = 1,\dots,n$, u_j, $j = 1,\dots,m$ in the corresponding input membership functions denoted by the indices $j_1, j_2, \dots, j_{n+m}$. More specifically, $a = \min[\mu_{Fj_1}(x_1),\dots\mu_{Fj_n}(x_n),\mu_{Fj_{n+1}}(u_1),\dots\mu_{Fj_{m+n}}(u_m)]$

Define now the following system

$$z = \sum \bar{z}_{j_1,j_2,\dots,j_{n+m}}^{l_1,l_2,\dots,l_n} \times I_{j_1,j_2,\dots,j_{n+m}}^{l_1,l_2,\dots,l_n}\left(x,u\right) \tag{9}$$

Using concepts from standard defuzzification procedure (e.g. weighted average), $\bar{z}_{j_1,j_2,\dots,j_{n+m}}^{l_1,l_2,\dots,l_n} \in \Re^n$ is any constant vector consisting of the centres of the membership functions of each output variable z_i and $I_{j_1,j_2,\dots,j_{n+m}}^{l_1,l_2,\dots,l_n}\left(x,u\right)$ is the IF of (8) normalized by the sum of all IF participating in the summation of (9). Then, the system in (9) is a functional representation of the fuzzy system (FS).

It is obvious that Eq. (9) can be also valid for dynamic systems. In its dynamical form it becomes

$$\dot{x}(k) = \sum \bar{x}_{j_1,j_2,\dots,j_{n+m}}^{l_1,l_2,\dots,l_n} \times I_{j_1,j_2,\dots,j_{n+m}}^{l_1,l_2,\dots,l_n}\left(x,u\right) \tag{10}$$

Where $\bar{x}_{j_1,j_2,\dots,j_{n+m}}^{l_1,l_2,\dots,l_n} \in \Re^n$ be again any constant vector consisting of the centres of fuzzy partitions of every variable x_i and $I_{j_1,j_2,\dots,j_{n+m}}^{l_1,l_2,\dots,l_n}\left(x,u\right)$ is the normalized IF.

2.2 Recurrent High Order Neural Networks

In section 2.3 new adaptive neuro-fuzzy algorithms for identifying nonlinear systems are presented. The neural architecture used is that of the recurrent high order neural network (RHONN) form. Among the nice properties of RHONN's, we refer to the capability of approximating a large class of dynamical systems, their linear-in-the-weights property, and the fact that, under appropriate selection of the neural network sigmoidal functions, the regressor terms are strictly positive. These properties of RHONN's are appropriately combined in order to develop new adaptive laws. In this section RHONN's are briefly invoked. Also the use of HONN's as fuzzy rule approximators is presented.

2.2.1 Representation of RHONNs

Recurrent Neural Network (RNN) models (Kosmatopoulos & Christodoulou, 1994; Kosmatopoulos, Polycarpou, Christodoulou & Ioannou, 1995; Kosmatopoulos & Christodoulou, 1995; Rovithakis & Christodoulou, 2000) are characterized by a two - way connectivity between units. This distinguishes them from feed forward neural networks, where the output of one unit is connected only to units in the next layer. In the simple case, the state history of each unit or neuron is determined by a differential equation of the form

$$\dot{x}_i = a_i x_i + b_i \sum_j w_{ij} s_{f_j}(x) \tag{11}$$

where x_i is the state of the ith neuron, a_i, b_i are constants, w_{ij} is the synaptic weight connecting the jth input to the ith neuron, and s_{f_j} is the jth input to the above neuron. Each s_{f_j} is either an external input or the state of a neuron passed through a sigmoid nonlinearity.

In a recurrent second order neural network the total input to the neuron is not only a linear combination of the components s_{f_j}, but also of their products $s_{f_j} \cdot s_{f_k}$. Moreover, one can pursue along this line and include higher-order interactions represented by triplets $s_{f_j} \cdot s_{f_k} \cdot s_{f_l}$, quadruplets, e.t.c. This class of neural networks form is called a recurrent high-order neural network (RHONN).

Consider now a RHONN consisting of n neurons and m inputs. The state of each neuron is governed by a differential equation of the form

$$\dot{x}_i = a_i x_i + b_i \left[\sum_{p=1}^{L} w_{ip} \prod_{j \in I_p} s_j^{d_j(p)} \right] \tag{12}$$

where $\{I_1, I_2, ..., I_L\}$ is a collection of L not-ordered subsets of $\{1, 2, ..., m+n\}$, a_i, b_i are real coefficients, w_{ip} are the (adjustable) synaptic weights of the neural network, and $d_j(p)$ are non-negative integers. The state of the ith neuron is again represented by $\hat{x}_i$, and $s = [s_1, s_2, ..., s_{n+m}]^T$ is the vector consisting of inputs to each neuron, defined by

$$s = \begin{bmatrix} s_1 \\ \vdots \\ s_n \\ s_{n+1} \\ \vdots \\ s_{n+m} \end{bmatrix} = \begin{bmatrix} s(x_1) \\ \vdots \\ s(x_n) \\ s(u_{n+1}) \\ \vdots \\ s(u_{n+m}) \end{bmatrix} \tag{13}$$

where $u = \left[u_1, u_2, \ldots, u_m \right]^T$ is the external input vector to the network. The function $s(\cdot)$ is a monotone increasing, differentiable sigmoid function of the form

$$s(x) = \alpha \frac{1}{1 + e^{-bx}} - c$$

where α, b are positive real numbers and c is a real number. In the special case that $\alpha = b = 1$, $c = 0$, we obtain the logistic function, and by setting $\alpha = b = 2$, $c = 1$, we obtain the hyperbolic tangent function; these are the sigmoid activation functions most commonly used in neural network applications.

We now introduce the L-dimensional vector s_f, which is as

$$s_f = \begin{bmatrix} s_{f_1} \\ s_{f_2} \\ \vdots \\ s_{f_L} \end{bmatrix} = \begin{bmatrix} \prod_{j \in I_1} s_j^{d_j(1)} \\ \prod_{j \in I_2} s_j^{d_j(2)} \\ \vdots \\ \prod_{j \in I_L} s_j^{d_j(L)} \end{bmatrix} \tag{14}$$

and hence the RHONN model in Eq.(12) is rewritten as

$$\dot{x}_i = a_i x_i + b_i \left[\sum_{p=1}^{L} w_{ip} s_{f_p}(x) \right] \tag{15}$$

Moreover, if we define the adjustable parameter vector as $w_{f_i} = b_i \cdot \left[w_{i1} \ w_{i2} \ \cdots \ w_{iL} \right]^T$ than Eq.(12) - and hence Eq.(15) - becomes

$$\dot{x}_i = a_i x_i + w_{f_i} s_f(x) \tag{16}$$

The vectors w_{f_i} represent the adjustable weights of the network, while the coefficients a_i, $i = 1, \ldots, n$ are part of the underlying network architecture and are fixed during training. In order to guarantee that each neuron x_i is bounded - input bounded - state (BIBS) stable, we will assume that each $a_i < 0$.

The dynamic behaviour of the overall network is described by expressing Eq.(16) in vector notation as

$$\dot{x} = Ax + W_f s_f(x) \tag{17}$$

where $x = \left[x_1, x_2, \ldots, x_n \right]^T$ $W_f = \left[w_{f_1}, w_{f_2}, \ldots, w_{f_n} \right]^T \in R^{L \times n}$, and $A = diag\left[a_1, a_2, \ldots, a_n \right]$ is an $n \times n$ diagonal matrix. Since each $a_i < 0$, A is a stability matrix. Although it is not explicitly written, the vector s_f is a function of both the network state x_i and the external input u.

2.2.2 The HONN's as Fuzzy Rule Approximators

The main idea in presenting the main result of this section lies on the fact that functions of high order neurons are capable of approximating discontinuous functions; thus, we use high order neural network functions in order to approximate the indicator functions $I_{j_1,j_2,...,j_{n+m}}^{l_1,l_2,...,l_n}$. However, in order the approximation problem to make sense the space $y := x \times u$ must be compact. Thus, our first assumption is the following:

Assumption 1: $y := x \times u$ is a compact set.

Notice that since $y \subset \Re^{n+m}$, the above assumption is identical to the assumption that it is closed and bounded. Also, it is noted that even if y is not compact we may assume that there is a time instant T such that (x,u) remain in a compact subset of y for all $t < T$; that is if $y_T := \{(x,u) \in y, t < T\}$ we may replace assumption 1 by the following assumption.

Assumption 2: y_T is a compact set.

It is worth noticing, that while assumption 1 requires the system in Eq. (6) solutions to be bounded for all $u \in U_c$ and $x(0) \in X$, assumption 2 requires the system in Eq. (6) solutions to be bounded for a finite time period; thus, assumption 1 requires the system in Eq. (6) to be bounded input bounded state (BIBS) stable while assumption 2 is valid for systems that are not BIBS stable and, even more, for unstable systems and systems with finite escape times.

Based on the fact that functions of high order neurons are capable of approximating discontinuous functions (Kosmatopoulos & Christodoulou, 1996) and (Christodoulou, Theodoridis & Boutalis, 2007) we use high order neural network functions HONN's in order to approximate the IF $I_{j_1,j_2,...,j_{n+m}}^{l_1,l_2,...,l_n}$. A HONN is defined as:

$$N\left(x,u;w,L\right) = \sum_{hot=1}^{L} w_{hot} \prod_{j \in I_{hot}} \Phi_j^{d_j\left(hot\right)} \tag{18}$$

where $I_{hot} = \left\{I_1, I_2, ..., I_L\right\}$ (hot: high order terms) is a collection of L not-ordered subsets of $\left\{1,2,...,m+n\right\}$, $d_j\left(hot\right)$ are non-negative integers, Φ_j are sigmoid functions of the state or the input, which are the elements of the following vector

$$\Phi = \begin{bmatrix} \Phi_1 \\ \vdots \\ \Phi_n \\ \Phi_{n+1} \\ \vdots \\ \Phi_{m+n} \end{bmatrix} = \begin{bmatrix} s(x_1) \\ \vdots \\ s(x_n) \\ s(u_1) \\ \vdots \\ s(u_m) \end{bmatrix} \tag{19}$$

where $w := \begin{bmatrix} w_1 & \cdots & w_L \end{bmatrix}^T$ are the HONN weights. Eq. (18) can also be written

$$N\left(x, u; w, L\right) = \sum_{hot=1}^{L} w_{hot} S_{hot}\left(x, u\right) \tag{20}$$

where $S_{hot}\left(x, u\right)$ are high order terms of sigmoid functions of the state and/or input.

The next lemma (Kosmatopoulos & Christodoulou, 1996) states that a HONN of the form in Eq. (20) can approximate the indicator function $I^{l_1, l_2, \ldots, l_n}_{j_1, j_2, \ldots, j_{n+m}}$.

Lemma 1: Consider the indicator function $I^{l_1, l_2, \ldots, l_n}_{j_1, j_2, \ldots, j_{n+m}}$ and the family of the HONN's $N\left(x, u; w, L\right)$. Then for any $\varepsilon > 0$ there is a vector of weights $w^{j_1, \ldots, j_{n+m}; l_1, \ldots, l_n}$ and a number of $L^{j_1, \ldots, j_{n+m}; l_1, \ldots, l_n}$ high order connections such that

$$\sup_{(x,u) \in \overline{y}} \left\{ I^{l_1, l_2, \ldots, l_n}_{j_1, j_2, \ldots, j_{n+m}}\left(x, u\right) - N\left(x, u; w^{j_1, \ldots, j_{n+m}; l_1, \ldots, l_n}, L^{j_1, \ldots, j_{n+m}; l_1, \ldots, l_n}\right) \right\} < \varepsilon$$

where $\overline{y} \equiv y$ if assumption 1 is valid and $\overline{y_T} \equiv y$ if assumption 2 is valid.

Let us now keep $L^{j_1, \ldots, j_{n+m}; l_1, \ldots, l_n}$ constant, that is let us preselect the number of high order connections, and let us define the optimal weights of the HONNF with $L^{j_1, \ldots, j_{n+m}; l_1, \ldots, l_n}$ high order connections as follows

$$w^* := \arg \min_{w \in R^{j_1, \ldots, j_{n+m}; l_1, \ldots, l_n}} \times \sup_{(x,u) \in \overline{y}} \left\{ \left| I^{l_1, l_2, \ldots, l_n}_{j_1, j_2, \ldots, j_{n+m}}\left(x, u\right) - N\left(x, u; w, L^{j_1, \ldots, j_{n+m}; l_1, \ldots, l_n}\right) \right| \right\} < \varepsilon$$

and the modelling error as follows

$$\nu^{l_1, l_2, \ldots, l_n}_{j_1, j_2, \ldots, j_{n+m}}\left(x, u\right) = I^{l_1, l_2, \ldots, l_n}_{j_1, j_2, \ldots, j_{n+m}}\left(x, u\right) - N\left(x, u; w^{j_1, \ldots, j_{n+m}; l_1, \ldots, l_n}, L^{j_1, \ldots, j_{n+m}; l_1, \ldots, l_n}\right)$$

It is worth noticing that from Lemma 1, we have that $\displaystyle \sup_{(x,u) \in \overline{y}} \left| \nu^{l_1, l_2, \ldots, l_n}_{j_1, j_2, \ldots, j_{n+m}}\left(x, u\right) \right|$ can be made arbitrarily small by simply selecting appropriately the number of high order connections.

Using the approximation Lemma 1, it is natural to approximate system in Eq. (10) by the following dynamical system

$$\dot{z} = \sum \overline{x}^{l_1, l_2, \ldots, l_n}_{j_1, j_2, \ldots, j_{n+m}}\left(x, u\right) \times N\left(z, u; w^{j_1, \ldots, j_{n+m}; l_1, \ldots, l_n}, L^{j_1, \ldots, j_{n+m}; l_1, \ldots, l_n}\right)$$

Let now $x\left(x(0), u\right)$ denote the solution in Eq. (10) given that the initial state at $t = 0$ is equal to $x(0)$ and the input is u. Similarly we define $z\left(z(0), u\right)$. Also let

$$\nu\left(z, u\right) = \sum \left(\overline{x}^{l_1, l_2, \ldots, l_n}_{j_1, j_2, \ldots, j_{n+m}}\left(x, u\right) \times \nu\left(z, u\right) \right)$$

Then, it can be easily shown that

$$z\left(z(0), u\right) = x\left(x(0), u\right) + \nu\left(z, u\right) \tag{21}$$

Note now that from the approximation Lemma 1, and the definition of $\nu\left(z,u\right)$ we have that modelling error can be made arbitrarily small provided that $\left(z,u\right)$ remain in a compact set (for example $\overline{y}$).

Theorem 1: (Kosmatopoulos & Christodoulou, 1996), (Christodoulou, Theodoridis & Boutalis, 2007) Consider the FDS in (10) and suppose that system in Eq. (6) is its underlying system. Assume that either assumptions 1 or 2 hold. Also consider the RHONN in Eq. (17). Then, for any $\varepsilon > 0$ there exists a matrix W_f^* and a number L^* of high order connections such as $W_f = W_f^*$ is a generator for the FDS.

2.3 Problem Formulation and Proposed Neuro-Fuzzy Representation

This section gives the problem formulation and introduces the proposed neuro-fuzzy representation based on the concepts of HONN's and Indicator functions presented in the previous sections.

2.3.1 Problem Formulation

We consider affine in the control, nonlinear dynamical systems of the form

$$\dot{x} = f(x) + G(x) \cdot u \tag{22}$$

where the state $x \in \Re^n$ is assumed to be completely measured, the control u is in $\Re^m$, f is an unknown smooth vector field called the drift term and G is a matrix with columns the unknown smooth controlled vector fields g_i, $i = 1,\ldots,n$ and $G = \left[g_1, g_2, \ldots, g_n\right]$. The above class of continuous-time nonlinear systems are called affine, because in (22) the control input appears linear with respect to G. The main reason for considering this class of nonlinear systems is that most of the systems encountered in engineering, are by nature or design, affine. Furthermore, we note that non affine systems of the form given in (1) can be converted into affine, by passing the input through integrators, a procedure known as dynamic extension. The following mild assumptions are also imposed on (22), to guarantee the existence and uniqueness of solution for any finite initial condition and $u \in U$.

Assumption 3: Given a class U of admissible inputs, then for any $u \in U$ and any finite initial condition, the state trajectories are uniformly bounded for any finite $T > 0$. Meaning that we do not allow systems processing trajectories which escape at infinite, in finite time. Hence, $\left|x(T)\right| < \infty$.

Assumption 4: The vector fields f, g_i, $i = 1, 2,\ldots,n$ are continuous with respect to their arguments and satisfy a local Lipchitz condition so that the solution $x(t)$ of (22) is unique for any finite initial condition and $u \in U$.

2.3.2 Neuro-Fuzzy Representation

We are using an affine in the control fuzzy dynamical system, which approximates the system in (22) and uses two fuzzy subsystem blocks for the description of $f(x)$ and $G(x)$ as follows

$$\hat{f}_i(x) = a_i \hat{x}_i + \sum \left(\overline{x}_{f_i}\right)_{j_1,\ldots,j_n}^{l_1,\ldots,l_n} \times \left(I_{f_i}\right)_{j_1,\ldots,j_n}^{l_1,\ldots,l_n}(x) \tag{23}$$

$$\hat{g}_{ij}(x) = \sum (\overline{x}_{g_{ij}})_{j_1,\ldots,j_n}^{l_1,\ldots,l_n} \times \left(I_{g_{ij}}\right)_{j_1,\ldots,j_n}^{l_1,\ldots,l_n}(x) \tag{24}$$

Where $a_i < 0$ and the summation is carried out over the number of all available fuzzy rules, I_{f_i}, $I_{g_{ij}}$ are appropriate fuzzy rule indicator functions and the meaning of indices $\bullet_{j_1,\ldots,j_n}^{l_1,\ldots,l_n}$ has already been described in the previous section.

According to Lemma 1, every indicator function can be approximated with the help of a suitable HONN. Therefore, every I_{f_i}, $I_{g_{ij}}$ can be replaced with a corresponding HONN as follows

$$\hat{f}_i(x \mid W_f) = a_i \hat{x}_i + \sum \left(\overline{x}_{f_i}\right)_{j_1,\ldots,j_n}^{l_1,\ldots,l_n} \times \left(N_{f_i}\right)_{j_1,\ldots,j_n}^{l_1,\ldots,l_n}(x) \tag{25}$$

$$\tag{26}$$

$$\hat{g}_{ij}(x \mid W_g) = \sum (\overline{x}_{g_{ij}})_{j_1,\ldots,j_n}^{l_1,\ldots,l_n} \times \left(N_{g_{ij}}\right)_{j_1,\ldots,j_n}^{l_1,\ldots,l_n}(x) \tag{26}$$

where W_f, W_g are weights that results from adaptive laws which will discussed later, and N_{f_i}, $N_{g_{ij}}$ are appropriate HONN's.

So, the optimal approximation of $f(x)$ and $G(x)$ sub- functions of the dynamical system becomes

$$\hat{f}_i(x \mid W_f^*) = a_i \hat{x}_i + \sum \left(\overline{x}_{f_i}\right)_{j_1,\ldots,j_n}^{l_1,\ldots,l_n} \times \left(N_{f_i}^*\right)_{j_1,\ldots,j_n}^{l_1,\ldots,l_n}(x) \tag{27}$$

$$\hat{g}_{ij}(x \mid W_g^*) = \sum (\overline{x}_{g_{ij}})_{j_1,\ldots,j_n}^{l_1,\ldots,l_n} \times \left(N_{g_{ij}}^*\right)_{j_1,\ldots,j_n}^{l_1,\ldots,l_n}(x) \tag{28}$$

In order to simplify the model structure, since some rules result to the same output partition, we could replace the NN's associated to the rules having the same output with one NN and therefore the summations in (25), (26) are carried out over the number of the corresponding output partitions. Therefore, the affine in the control fuzzy dynamical system in (27), (28) is replaced by the following equivalent affine fuzzy-recurrent high order neural network (F-RHONN), which depends on the centres of the fuzzy output partitions $\overline{x}_{f_i}$ and $\overline{x}_{g_{ij}}$

$$\dot{\hat{x}}_i = a_i \hat{x}_i + \sum_{p=1}^{Npf} \left(\overline{x}_{f_i}\right) \times N_{f_i}(x) + \sum_{j=1}^{q} \left(\sum_{p=1}^{Npg_{ij}} \left(\overline{x}_{g_{ij}}\right) \times N_{g_i}(x)\right) \cdot u_j \tag{29}$$

Or in a more compact form

$$\dot{\hat{x}} = A\hat{x} + X_f W_f S_f(x) + X_g W_g S_g(x)u \tag{30}$$

Where X_f, X_g are matrices containing the centres of the partitions of every fuzzy output variable of $f(x)$ and $g(x)$ respectively, $S_f(x)$, $S_g(x)$ are matrices containing high order combinations of sigmoid functions of the state x and W_f, W_g are matrices containing respective neural weights according to (20) and (29). The dimensions and the contents of all the above matrices are chosen so that $X_f W_f S_f(x)$ is a $n \times 1$ vector and $X_g W_g S_g(x)$ is a $n \times n$ matrix. Without compromising the generality of the model we assume that the vector fields in (24) are such that the matrix G is diagonal. For notational simplicity we assume that all output fuzzy variables are partitioned to the same number, m, of partitions. Under these specifications X_f is a $n \times n \cdot m$ block diagonal matrix of the form $X_f = diag\left(X_{f_1}, X_{f_2}, \ldots, X_{f_n}\right)$ with each X_{f_i} being an m-dimensional raw vector of the form

$$X_{f_i} = \begin{bmatrix} \bar{x}^1_{f_i} & \bar{x}^2_{f_i} & \cdots & \bar{x}^m_{f_i} \end{bmatrix}$$

Or in a more detailed form

$$X_f = \begin{bmatrix} \bar{x}^1_{f_1} & \cdots & \bar{x}^m_{f_1} & 0 & \cdots & 0 & 0 & \cdots & 0 \\ 0 & \cdots & 0 & \bar{x}^1_{f_2} & \cdots & \bar{x}^m_{f_2} & 0 & \cdots & 0 \\ \vdots & \cdots & \vdots & \cdots & \vdots & \cdots & \vdots & \cdots & \vdots \\ 0 & \cdots & 0 & 0 & \cdots & 0 & \bar{x}^1_{f_n} & \cdots & \bar{x}^m_{f_n} \end{bmatrix}$$

where $\bar{x}^p_{f_i}$ with $p = 1, \ldots, m$ denotes the centre of the p-th partition of f_i. Also, $S_f(x) = \begin{bmatrix} s_1(x) & \cdots & s_k(x) \end{bmatrix}^T$ where each $s_i(x)$ is a high order combination of sigmoid functions of the state variables and W_f is a $n \cdot m \times k$ matrix with neural weights. W_f assumes the form $W_f = \begin{bmatrix} W_{f_1} & \cdots & W_{f_n} \end{bmatrix}^T$, where each W_{f_i} is a matrix $\begin{bmatrix} w^{pl}_{f_i} \end{bmatrix}_{m \times k}$. X_g is a $n \times n \cdot m$ block diagonal matrix $X_g = diag\left(X_{g_1}, X_{g_2}, \ldots, X_{g_n}\right)$ with each X_{g_i} being an m-dimensional raw vector of the form

$$X_{g_i} = \begin{bmatrix} \bar{x}^1_{g_i} & \bar{x}^2_{g_i} & \cdots & \bar{x}^m_{g_i} \end{bmatrix}$$

Or in a more detailed form

$$X_g = \begin{bmatrix} \bar{x}^1_{g_1} & \cdots & \bar{x}^m_{g_1} & 0 & \cdots & 0 & 0 & \cdots & 0 \\ 0 & \cdots & 0 & \bar{x}^1_{g_2} & \cdots & \bar{x}^m_{g_2} & 0 & \cdots & 0 \\ \vdots & \cdots & \vdots & \cdots & \vdots & \cdots & \vdots & \cdots & \vdots \\ 0 & \cdots & 0 & 0 & \cdots & 0 & \bar{x}^1_{g_n} & \cdots & \bar{x}^m_{g_n} \end{bmatrix}$$

where $\bar{x}^k_{g_i}$ denotes the centre of the k-th partition of g_{ii}. W_g is a $m \cdot n \times n$ block diagonal matrix $W_g = diag\left(W_{g_1}, W_{g_2}, \ldots, W_{g_n}\right)$, where each W_{g_i} is a column vector $\begin{bmatrix} w^p_{g_i} \end{bmatrix}_{m \times 1}$ of neural weights. Finally, $S_g(x)$ is a $n \times n$ diagonal matrix with each diagonal element $s_i(x)$ being a high order combination of sigmoid functions of the state variables.

According to the above definitions the configuration of the F-RHONN approximator is shown in Fig. (1). When the inputs are given into the fuzzy-neural network shown in Fig. (1), the output of layer IV gives indicator function outputs which activate the corresponding rules and are calculated by Eq. (18). At layer V, each node performs a fuzzy rule while layer VI gives the function output.

The approximator of indicator functions has four layers. At layer I, the input nodes represent input and state measurable variables. At layer II, the nodes represent the values of the sigmoidal functions. At

Figure 1. Overall scheme of the proposed adaptive neuro-fuzzy system

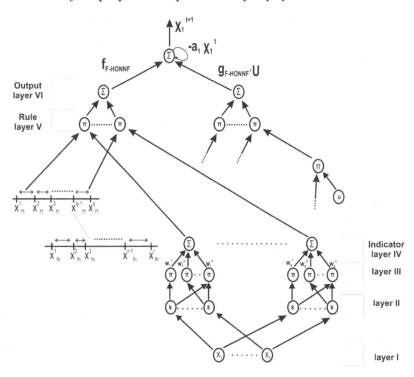

layer III, the nodes are the values of high order sigmoidal combinations. The links between layer III and layer IV are fully connected by the weighting factors $W_f = \begin{bmatrix} W_{f_1} & \cdots & W_{f_n} \end{bmatrix}^T$ the adjustable parameters. Finally, at layer IV the output represents the values of indicator functions.

It has to be mentioned here that the proposed neuro-fuzzy representation, finally given by (30), offers some advantages over other fuzzy or neural adaptive representations. Considering the proposed approach from the adaptive fuzzy system (AFS) point of view, the main advantage is that the proposed approach is much less vulnerable in initial AFS design assumptions because there is no need for a-priori information related to the IF part of the rules (type and centres of membership functions, number of rules). This information is replaced by the existence of HONN's. Considering the proposed approach from the NN point of view, the final representation of the dynamic equations is actually a combination of high order neural networks, each one being specialized in approximating a function related to a corresponding centre of output state membership function. This way, instead of having one large HONN trying to approximate 'everything' we have many, probably smaller, specialized HONN's. Conceptually, this strategy is expected to present better approximation results; this is also verified in the simulations section.

2.4 Adaptive Parameter Identification

We assume the existence of only parameter uncertainty, so, we can take into account that the actual system (15) can be modelled by the following neural form

$$\dot{x} = Ax + X_f W_f^* S_f(x) + X_g W_g^* S_g(x)u \tag{31}$$

Define now, the error between the identifier states and the real states as

$$e = \hat{x} - x \tag{32}$$

Then from (30) and (32) we obtain the error equation

$$\dot{e} = A e + X_f \tilde{W}_f S_f(x) + X_g \tilde{W}_g S_g(x) u \tag{33}$$

Where $\tilde{W}_f = W_f - W_f^*$ and $\tilde{W}_g = W_g - W_g^*$. Regarding the identification of W_f and W_g in (30) we are now able to state the following theorem.

Theorem 2:

Consider the identification scheme given by (33). The learning law

a) For the elements of W_{f_i}

$$\dot{w}_{f_i}^{pl}(x) = -\overline{x}_{f_i}^p p_i e_i s_l(x) \tag{34}$$

b) For the elements of W_{g_i}

$$\dot{w}_{g_i}^{p}(x) = -\overline{x}_{g_i}^p p_i e_i u_i s_i(x) \tag{35}$$

or equivalently $\dot{W}_{g_i}(x) = -\left(X_{g_i}\right)^T p_i e_i u_i s_i(x)$ with $i = 1,...,n$, $p = 1,...,m$ and $l = 1,...,k$ guarantees the following properties.

- $e, \hat{x}, \tilde{W}_f, \tilde{W}_g \in L_\infty$, $\quad e \in L_2$
- $\lim_{t \to \infty} e(t) = 0$, $\lim_{t \to \infty} \dot{\tilde{W}}_f(t) = 0$, $\lim_{t \to \infty} \dot{\tilde{W}}_g(t) = 0$

Proof: Consider the Lyapunov function candidate,

$$V\left(e, \tilde{W}_f, \tilde{W}_g\right) = \frac{1}{2} e^T P e + \frac{1}{2\gamma_1} tr\left\{\tilde{W}_f^T \tilde{W}_f\right\} + \frac{1}{2\gamma_2} tr\left\{\tilde{W}_g^T \tilde{W}_g\right\}$$

Where $P > 0$ is chosen to satisfy the Lyapunov equation

$$PA + A^T P = -I$$

Taking the derivative of the Lyapunov function candidate we get

$$\dot{V}\left(e, \tilde{W}_f, \tilde{W}_g\right) = \frac{1}{2} \dot{e}^T P e + \frac{1}{2} e^T P \dot{e}$$

$$+ \frac{1}{\gamma_1} tr\left\{\dot{\tilde{W}}_f^T \tilde{W}_f\right\} + \frac{1}{\gamma_2} tr\left\{\dot{\tilde{W}}_g^T \tilde{W}_g\right\}$$

which after substituting Eq. (33) becomes

$$\dot{V} = \frac{1}{2} e^T \left(A^T P + PA \right) e +$$

$$+ \left(\frac{1}{2} e^T P X_f \tilde{W}_f S_f + S_f^T \tilde{W}_f^T X_f^T P e \right)$$

$$+ \left(\frac{1}{2} e^T P X_g \tilde{W}_g S_g u + u^T S_g^T \tilde{W}_g^T X_g^T P e \right)$$

$$+ \frac{1}{\gamma_1} tr \left\{ \dot{\tilde{W}}_f^{\,T} \tilde{W}_f \right\} + \frac{1}{\gamma_2} tr \left\{ \dot{\tilde{W}}_g^{\,T} \tilde{W}_g \right\}$$

Now since $e^T P X_f \tilde{W}_f S_f$ and $e^T P X_g \tilde{W}_g S_g u$ are scalars, we have that

$$e^T P X_f \tilde{W}_f S_f = \left(S_f^T \tilde{W}_f^T X_f^T P e \right)^T$$

$$e^T P X_g \tilde{W}_g S_g u = \left(u^T S_g^T \tilde{W}_g^T X_g^T P e \right)^T$$

Therefore, $\dot{V}$ becomes

$$\dot{V} = -\frac{1}{2} e^T e + e^T P X_f \tilde{W}_f S_f + e^T P X_g \tilde{W}_g S_g u$$

$$+ \frac{1}{\gamma_1} tr \left\{ \dot{\tilde{W}}_f^{\,T} \tilde{W}_f \right\} + \frac{1}{\gamma_2} tr \left\{ \dot{\tilde{W}}_g^{\,T} \tilde{W}_g \right\}$$

In order to extract the adaptive law of the weights, we assume that

$$\frac{1}{\gamma_1} tr \left\{ \dot{\tilde{W}}_f^{\,T} \tilde{W}_f \right\} = -e^T P X_f \tilde{W}_f S_f$$

$$\frac{1}{\gamma_2} tr \left\{ \dot{\tilde{W}}_g^{\,T} \tilde{W}_g \right\} = -e^T P X_g \tilde{W}_g S_g u$$

Then, taking into account the form of W_f and W_g the above equations result in the element wise learning laws given in (34), (35). These laws can also be written in the following compact form

$$\dot{W}_f = -\gamma_1 X_f^T P e S_f^T \tag{36}$$

$$\dot{W}_g = -\gamma_2 X_g^T P E U S_g^T \tag{37}$$

Where E and U are diagonal matrices such that $E = diag\left(e_1, \ldots, e_n \right)$ and $U = diag\left(u_1, \ldots, u_n \right)$. Finally, the Lyapunov function candidate results in

$$\dot{V} = -\frac{1}{2} e^T e \leq 0$$

Since $\dot{V}$ is negative semi definite then we conclude that $V \in L_\infty$, which implies that e, $\hat{x}$, $\tilde{W}_f$, $\tilde{W}_g \in L_\infty$. Furthermore, $W_f = \tilde{W}_f + W_f^*$, $W_g = \tilde{W}_g + W_g^*$ are also bounded. Since V is a non-increasing function of time and bounded from below, the $\lim_{t\to\infty} V = V_\infty$ exists; therefore, by integrating $\dot{V}$ from 0 to ∞ we have

$$\int_0^\infty \|e\|^2 \, dt \le \left[V(0) - V_\infty\right] < \infty$$

which implies that $e \in L_2$.

Since $e \in L_2 \cap L_\infty$, using Barbalat's Lemma we conclude that $\lim_{t\to\infty} e(t) = 0$.

Now, using the bounded ness of u, S_f, S_g and the convergence of $e(t)$ to zero, we have that $\dot{\tilde{W}}_f$, $\dot{\tilde{W}}_g$ also converges to zero (Ioannou & Fidan, 2006).

2.5 Simulation Examples

Example 1: Comparison of function approximation abilities

Let f be the function to be approximated, which is described by the following equation

$$f(x_1, x_2) = \frac{g \sin x_1 - \dfrac{mlx_2^2 \cos x_1 \sin x_1}{m_C + m}}{l \left(\dfrac{4}{3} - \dfrac{m \cos^2 x_1}{m_C + m}\right)} \tag{38}$$

This function appear in the mathematical description of the well known inverted pendulum problem assuming dynamical equations of the following Brunovsky canonical form (Slotine & Li, 1997).

$$\begin{aligned} \dot{x}_1 &= x_2 \\ \dot{x}_2 &= f(x) + g(x) \cdot u \end{aligned} \tag{39}$$

In (38) $x_1 = \theta$ and $x_2 = \dot{\theta}$ are the angle from the vertical position and the angular velocity respectively. Also, $g = 9.8 \, m/s^2$ is the acceleration due to gravity, m_C is the mass of the cart, m is the mass of the pole, and l is the half-length of the pole. We choose $m_C = 1 \, kg$, $m = 0.1 \, kg$ and $l = 0.5 \, m$ in the following simulation.

It is our intention to compare the approximation abilities of the proposed neuro-fuzzy approach with Wang (Wang, 1994) adaptive fuzzy approach. To this end we assume that $f(x)$ can be approximated using Wang's approach and Eq. (2) or alternatively by the $X_f W_f S_f(x)$ term of Eq. (30) in the proposed approach. The weight updating laws are chosen to be: For the Wang approach ((Wang, 1994), page 115)

$$\dot{\theta}_f = -\gamma_1 e^T P b_C \xi(x) \tag{40}$$

where only the simplified approach, without parameter projection case was necessary to be used.

Figure 2. Approximation of the f function with Eq.(2)

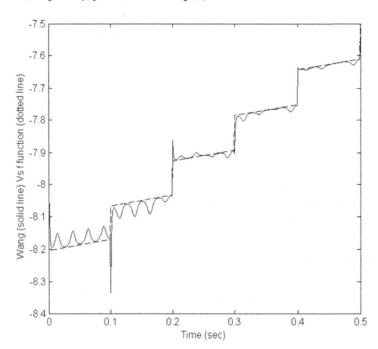

For the proposed approach we use the following adaptive law:

$$\dot{W}_f = -\gamma_1 X_f^T P e S_f^T \tag{41}$$

The experimental data were obtained as follows: Based on Wang's input variables limits and fuzzy partition we created an artificial stair-like signal shown in Fig. (2). Input variables x_1 and x_2 assume values in the interval $\left[-\pi / 6, \pi / 6\right]$.

Taking 5 samples from x_1 and 100 samples from x_2 we obtain 500 samples of $f(x_1, x_2)$ presenting the stair discontinuities when x_1 changes values. For the construction of ξ_i functions used in Eq. (2) and given in Eq. (3) we used the fuzzy membership partitions and the final rules characterizing $f(x_1, x_2)$ which comprises 25 fuzzy rules carefully chosen and given by Wang in (Wang, 1994), (page 129). Under these design specifications Eq. (2) assumes 25 adjustable weights.

In order our model to be equivalent with regard to adjustable parameters we have chosen 5 centres for the fuzzy output variables partition (-8, -4, 0, 4, 8) and 5 high order sigmoidal terms $\left(s(x_1), s(x_2), s(x_1) \cdot s(x_2), s^2(x_1), s^2(x_2)\right)$ in each HONNF. This configuration also assumes 25 adjustable weights. Terms $\gamma_1 P b_C$ in Eq. (33) and $\gamma_1 P$ (the updating learning rates) in Eq. (34) were chosen to have the same values. Fig. (2) shows the approximation abilities of (2) with the updating law of (40) while Fig. (3) shows the performance of the proposed approach with the updating law of (34).

The mean squared error (MSE) for Wang's approach was measured to be $6.24 \cdot 10^{-4}$, while for the proposed approach was $1.25 \cdot 10^{-5}$, demonstrating a significant (order of magnitude) increase in the approximation performance, although in our approach no a-priori information regarding the inputs were used.

Figure 3. Approximation of the f function with the proposed approach

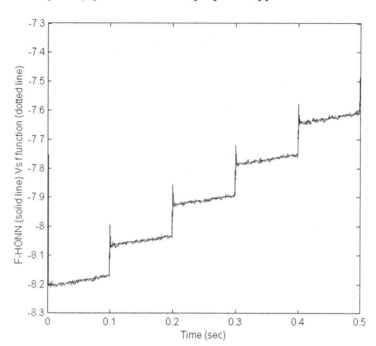

Example 2: Performance of the proposed F-RHONN scheme in approximating a time-varying dynamical model.

We assume the existence of only parametric uncertainty. Therefore we select an initial second order model of the form (31), where $A = diag(-8, -13)$, the number of fuzzy partitions appearing in X_f is 5, and the number of high order terms in $S_f(x)$ is also 5, assuming up to second order high order terms. In this case $S_f(x) = \begin{bmatrix} s(x_1) & s(x_2) & s(x_1)s(x_2) & s^2(x_1) & s^2(x_2) \end{bmatrix}^T$. The centres of the output partitions were arbitrarily selected and are given in the following matrix.

$$X_f = \begin{bmatrix} 0.0307 & -0.5857 & 0.6897 & -0.0921 & 0.9498 & 0 & 0 & 0 & 0 & 0 \\ 0 & 0 & 0 & 0 & 0 & 0.9848 & 0.7549 & 0.7989 & -0.8102 & -0.9731 \end{bmatrix}$$

Then, according to the definitions given in section 2.3.2 W_f^* is a 10x5 matrix of optimal weights. Similarly, the number of fuzzy partitions in X_g is 3 with

$$X_g = \begin{bmatrix} 148 & 149 & 150 & 0 & 0 & 0 \\ 0 & 0 & 0 & 42 & 43 & 44 \end{bmatrix}$$

and the number of high order terms in $S_g(x)$ is 2, assuming only first order terms. Therefore, W_g^* is a 6x2 matrix of optimal weights. The weights W_f^* and W_g^* are shown in tables 1 and 2 respectively. The parameters of the sigmoidal terms were selected to be $a_1 = 1$, $a_2 = 3$, $b_1 = b_2 = 1$ and $c_1 = c_2 = 0$. The inputs assume the persistently exciting form $u = 1 + 0.8\sin(3t)$. With a sampling time 10^{-3} sec and the time variable ranging between 0 and 9 seconds, this corresponds to 9000 samples of time varying inputs.

Table 1.

0.6669	0.7848	0.2271	0.3132	0.8488
0.1654	0.5776	0.3831	0.6733	0.0048
0.6068	0.5640	0.1076	0.9665	0.6119
0.0152	0.6603	0.8959	0.4103	0.1181
0.5613	0.3616	0.3845	0.4701	0.5335
0.3254	0.3147	0.2569	0.9380	0.0337
0.7551	0.6089	0.3899	0.6808	0.9781
0.7822	0.5819	0.8589	0.7045	0.9365
0.5822	0.4470	0.8773	0.8601	0.3356
0.5127	0.9641	0.3694	0.9679	0.7290

Table 2.

0.9993	0.6491
0.3032	0.5357
0.4929	0.6519
0.8544	0.6480
0.3693	0.1582
0.4829	0.2186

The weights of the initial ideal model change during the simulation every 1 second by multiplying the weights with a constant value (In this example the weights are multiplied by k =1,2,3 respectively every one second for the first three seconds and in the sequel are reduced back until they reach their initial values).

Since we assumed only parameter uncertainty, the F-RHONN approximator has the same structure with the ideal model given above but the optimal weights are unknown. Using the proposed weight adaptation algorithm ((34), (35)) with learning rates learning rates $\gamma_1 = 1$, $\gamma_2 = 5$ we monitor the performance of the F-RHONN approximator. The initial state values of the system were set to $\begin{bmatrix} 0.3 & 0.3 \end{bmatrix}$, while the initial state values of the F-RHONN approximator were set to $\begin{bmatrix} 20 & -5 \end{bmatrix}$. The initial weights for W_f and W_g of the approximator were set to zero. The evolution of system states as well as one of the weights and its estimation error is shown in figure 4. It can be observed that by following the proposed method the states of the approximator follow the states of the unknown system quite well, despite its changing behavior.

Example 3: Function approximation abilities of F-RHONN against RHONN's and Wang's approximations, using a well known benchmark.

Van der Pol oscillator is usually used as a simple benchmark problem for testing identification and control schemes. It's dynamical equations are given by

Figure 4. Two upper figures: States x_1, x_2 and their approximation. Third figure: Weight adaptation procedure for one representative weight ($W_g(1,2)$) and its ideal values. Last figure: weight estimation error of the same weight

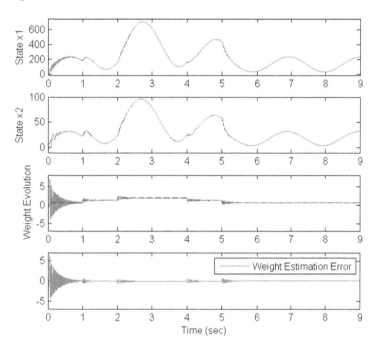

$$\dot{x}_1 = x_2$$
$$\dot{x}_2 = x_2 \cdot \left(a - x_1^2\right) \cdot b - x_1 + u \tag{42}$$

It is our intention to compare the approximation abilities of the proposed neuro-fuzzy approach with Wang (Wang, 1994) adaptive fuzzy approach and RHONN (Rovithakis & Christodoulou, 2000). Eq. (42) is similar with Eq. (22), so we assume that $f(x)$ and $g(x)$ can be approximated using Wang's approach and Eq. (3) or alternatively by the $X_f W_f S_f(x)$ and $X_g W_g S_g(x)$ term of Eq. (30) in the proposed approach, or WS and $W_1 S_1$ for RHONN approach (Rovithakis & Christodoulou, 2000), respectively. The weight updating laws are chosen to be: For the Wang approach ((Wang, 1994), page 115)

$$\dot{\theta}_f = -\gamma_1 e^T P b_c \xi(x) \tag{43}$$

$$\dot{\theta}_g = -\gamma_2 e^T P b_c \xi(x) u_c \tag{44}$$

where only the simplified approach, without parameter projection case was necessary to be used.

For the RHONN approach we use the adaptive laws, which are described in (Rovithakis & Christodoulou, 2000, page 37). For the proposed F-HONNF approach we use the following adaptive laws (Theodoridis, Christodoulou & Boutalis, 2008)

$$\dot{W}_f = -\gamma_1 X_f^T P e S_f^T \tag{45}$$

Figure 5. Evolution of variable x_1 for Wang, RHONN and F-RHONN approach

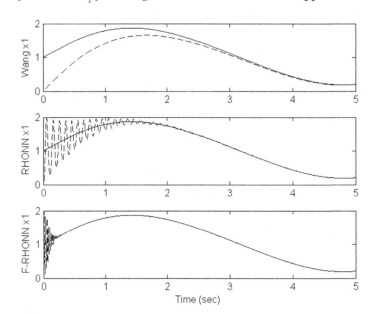

$$\dot{W}_g = -\gamma_2 X_g^T PEUS_g^T \tag{46}$$

Numerical training data were obtained by using Eqs. (42) with initial conditions $\begin{bmatrix} x_1(0) & x_2(0) \end{bmatrix} = \begin{bmatrix} 1 & 1 \end{bmatrix}$ and a persistently exciting input $u = 1 + 0.8\sin(0.001t)$.

The approximation of the dynamical equations using conventional fuzzy system approach requires a very large number of fuzzy rules for the approximation of the unknown functions. Choosing 40 or more membership functions for each variable x_i results in very accurate fuzzy representation. This representation requires 1600 rules, which in turn leads to a parameter explosion when using an adaptive scheme like that of Eq. (3) and consequently, it takes plenty of time for the simulations.

We are using the proposed approach with Eq. (30) to approximate Van der pol oscillator. The proposed Neuro-Fuzzy model was chosen to use 5 output partitions of f and 5 output partitions of g. The number of high order sigmoidal terms (HOST) used in HONNF's were chosen to be first 2 $\left(s(x_1), s(x_2)\right)$ and secondly 5 $\left(s(x_1), s(x_2), s(x_1) \cdot s(x_2), s^2(x_1), s^2(x_2)\right)$ for two different simulations with the same benchmark. Therefore, the number of adjustable weights is 20 or 50 respectively, which is a much smaller number to that used in the conventional fuzzy approach.

In order our model to be equivalent with regard to other parameters except the adjustable weights we have chosen terms $\gamma_1 Pb_C$ or $\gamma_2 Pb_C$ in Eqs. (43, 44) and $\gamma_1 P$ or $\gamma_2 P$ (the updating learning rate) in Eqs. (45, 46) to have the same values. Also, the RHONN model given from (Rovithakis & Christodoulou, 2000) is constructed with the same learning parameters and number of high order terms with these of F-RHONN approach. The parameters of the sigmoidal terms were chosen to be $a_1 = a_2 = 1$, $b_1 = b_2 = 1$ and $c_1 = c_2 = 0$. Fig. (5) and (6) shows the approximation of states x_1 and x_2 respectively when 5 HOST were used, while fig. (7) and (8) gives the respective evolution of errors e_1 and e_2.

Figure 6. Evolution of variable x_2 for Wang, RHONN and F-RHONN approach

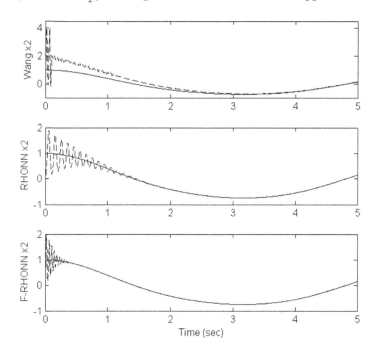

Figure 7. Approximation error e_1 of variable x_1 for Wang, RHONN and F-RHONN approach

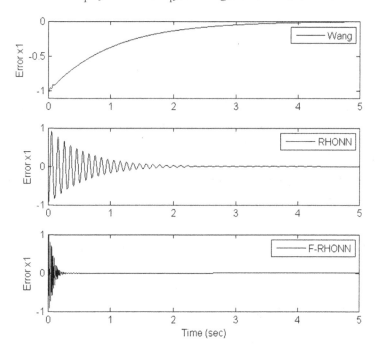

Figure 8. Approximation error e_2 for Wang, RHONN and F-RHONN approach

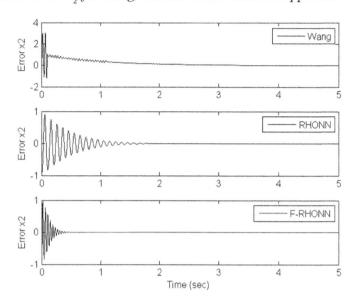

The mean squared error (MSE) for Wang's, RHONN and F-RONN approaches were measured and are shown in Tables 3 and 4, demonstrating a significant (order of magnitude) increase in the approximation performance, although no a-priori information regarding fuzzy partitions and membership functions of the inputs was used.

Conclusively, the comparison between Wang and F-RHONN leads to a huge superiority of F-RHONN regarding the number of adjustable parameters and the approximation abilities. With respect to the RHONN approach the proposed F-RHONN approach is also much better.

FUTURE TRENDS

The proposed identification scheme may find applications in various control schemes, where it can be used as the first, modelling part, of each scheme. Another issue that has not been considered so far, and may be an ambitious extension of the proposed approach is the simultaneous estimation of both the neural weights and the centres of the output membership functions, which are now considered given. In this case, the representation will become completely independent from initial expert opinions or pre-processing based on gathered past data.

Table 3. Comparison of Wang, RHONN and F-RHONN approaches for Van der pol oscillator with 2 HOST

	Wang	RHONN	F-RHONN
MSE x_1	0.1038	0.0303	0.0058
MSE x_2	0.1401	0.0259	0.0087

Table 4. Comparison of Wang, RHONN and F-RHONN approaches for Van der pol oscillator with 5 HOST

	Wang	RHONN	F-RHONN
MSE x_1	0.1038	0.0180	0.0013
MSE x_2	0.1401	0.0149	0.0018

CONCLUSION

The identification of unknown nonlinear dynamical systems using a new definition of Adaptive Fuzzy Systems (AFS) was presented in this chapter. The proposed scheme uses the concept of Adaptive Fuzzy Systems operating in conjunction with High Order Neural Network Functions (HONNFs). Under this scheme the identification is driven to a Fuzzy-Recurrent High Order Neural Network(F-RHONN), which takes into account the fuzzy output partitions of the initial AFS. The proposed scheme does not require a-priori expert's information on the number and type of input variable membership functions making it less vulnerable to initial design assumptions. Weight updating laws for the involved HONNFs are provided, which guarantee that the identification error reaches zero exponentially fast. Simulations illustrate the potency of the method by comparing its performance with this of conventional approaches.

REFERENCES

Boutalis, Y. S., Theodoridis, D. C., & Christodoulou, M. A. (2009). A new Neuro FDS definition for indirect adaptive control of unknown nonlinear systems using a method of parameter hopping. *IEEE Transactions on Neural Networks, 20*(4), 609–625. doi:10.1109/TNN.2008.2010772

Chen, B. S., Lee, C. H., & Chang, Y. C. (1996). Tracking design of uncertain nonlinear siso systems: Adaptive fuzzy approach. *IEEE transactions on Fuzzy Systems, 4*, 32–43. doi:10.1109/91.481843

Cho, K. B., & Wang, B. H. (1996). Radial basis function based adaptive fuzzy systems and their applications to system identification and prediction. *Fuzzy Sets and Systems, 83*, 325–339. doi:10.1016/0165-0114(95)00322-3

Christodoulou, M. A., Theodoridis, D. C., & Boutalis, Y. S. (2007). Building Optimal Fuzzy Dynamical Systems Description Based on Recurrent Neural Network Approximation. In Proceedings of *Int. Conf. of Networked Distributed Systems for Intelligent Sensing and Control* (pp. 386-393). Kalamata, Greece.

Chui, S. L. (1994). Fuzzy model identification based on cluster estimation. *Journal of Intelligent and Fuzzy Systems, 2*, 267–278. doi:10.1109/91.324806

Golea, N., Golea, A., & Benmahammed, K. (2003). Stable indirect fuzzy adaptive control. *IEEE Engineers Transactions on Fuzzy Systems, 137*, 353–366.

Hojati, M., & Gazor, S. (2002). Hybrid Adaptive Fuzzy Identification and Control of Nonlinear Systems. *IEEE transactions on Fuzzy Systems, 10*, 198–210. doi:10.1109/91.995121

Hornik, K., Stinchcombe, M., & White, H. (1989). Multilayer feed forward networks are universal approximators. *International Journal of Neural Networks, 2*, 359–366. doi:10.1016/0893-6080(89)90020-8

Ioannou, P., & Fidan, B. (2006). *Adaptive control tutorial.* SIAM: Advances in Design and Control Series.

Jang, C. F., & Lin, C. T. (1998). An online self-constructing neural fuzzy inference network and its applications. *IEEE transactions on Fuzzy Systems, 6*, 12–32. doi:10.1109/91.660805

Jang, J. S. R. (1993). ANFIS: Adaptive-network-based fuzzy inference system. *IEEE Transactions on Systems, Man, and Cybernetics, 23*, 665–684. doi:10.1109/21.256541

Juang, C. F., & Lin, C. T. (1998). An on-line self-constructing neural fuzzy inference network and its applications. *IEEE transactions on Fuzzy Systems, 6*, 12–32. doi:10.1109/91.660805

Kosmatopoulos, E. B., & Christodoulou, M. A. (1994). Stability, robustness, and approximation properties of gradient recurrent high order neural networks. *International Journal of Adaptive Control and Signal Processing, 8*, 393–406. doi:10.1002/acs.4480080408

Kosmatopoulos, E. B., & Christodoulou, M. A. (1995). Structural properties of gradient recurrent high-order neural networks. *IEEE Transactions on Circuits and Systems, 42*(9), 592–603. doi:10.1109/82.466645

Kosmatopoulos, E. B., & Christodoulou, M. A. (1996). Recurrent neural networks for approximation of fuzzy dynamical systems. *International Journal of Intelligent Control and Systems, 1*, 223–233. doi:10.1142/S0218796596000143

Kosmatopoulos, E. B., Polycarpou, M. M., Christodoulou, M. A., & Ioannou, P. A. (1995). High-order neural network structures for identification of dynamical systems. *IEEE on Neural Networks, 6*(2), 422–431. doi:10.1109/72.363477

Lee, C., & Teng, C. (2000). Identification and Control of Dynamic Systems Using Recurrent Fuzzy Neural Networks. *IEEE transactions on Fuzzy Systems, 8*, 349–366. doi:10.1109/91.868943

Li, R. P., & Mukaidono, M. (1995). A new approach to rule learning based on fusion of fuzzy logic and neural networks. *Institute of Electronics Information and Communication Engineers Transactions on Fuzzy Systems, 78*, 1509–1514.

Lin, C. T. (1995). A neural fuzzy control system with structure and parameter learning. *Fuzzy Sets and Systems, 70*, 183–212. doi:10.1016/0165-0114(94)00216-T

Lin, Y. H., & Cunningham, G. A. (1995). A new approach to fuzzy-neural system modelling. *IEEE transactions on Fuzzy Systems, 3*, 190–197. doi:10.1109/91.388173

Lina, T., Wang, C., & Liub, H. (2004). Observer-based indirect adaptive fuzzy-neural tracking control for nonlinear SISO systems using VSS and H_1 approaches. *Fuzzy Sets and Systems, 143*, 211–232. doi:10.1016/S0165-0114(03)00167-2

Mamdani, E. (1976). Advances in the linguistic synthesis of fuzzy controllers. *International Journal of Man-Machine Studies, 8*(6), 669–678. doi:10.1016/S0020-7373(76)80028-4

Mitra, S., & Hayashi, Y. (2000). Neuro-fuzzy rule generation: survey in soft computing framework. *IEEE Transactions on Neural Networks, 11*, 748–768. doi:10.1109/72.846746

Narendra, K. S., & Parthasarathy, K. (1990). Identification and control of dynamical systems using neural networks. *IEEE Transactions on Neural Networks, 1*, 4–27. doi:10.1109/72.80202

Passino, K. M., & Yurkovich, S. (1998). *Fuzzy Control*. Menlo Park, CA: Addison Wesley Longman.

Polycarpou, M. M., & Mears, M. J. (1998). Stable adaptive tracking of uncertain systems using nonlinearly parameterized online approximators. *International Journal of Control, 70*(3), 363–384. doi:10.1080/002071798222280

Rovithakis, G. A., & Christodoulou, M. A. (2000). *Adaptive Control with Recurrent High-Order Neural Networks: Theory and Industrial Applications*, in *Advances in Industrial Control* (M. A. Gribble and M.A. Johnson Eds), London: Springer Verlag.

Slotine, J. E., & Li, W. (1997). *It Applied Nonlinear Control*. Englewood Cliffs, NJ: Prentice-Hall.

Spooner, J. T., & Passino, K. M. (1996). Stable adaptive control using fuzzy systems and neural networks. *IEEE transactions on Fuzzy Systems, 4*, 339–359. doi:10.1109/91.531775

Takagi, T., & Sugeno, M. (1985). Fuzzy identification of systems and its applications to modelling and control. *IEEE Transactions on Systems, Man, and Cybernetics, 15*(1), 116–132.

Theodoridis, D. C., Christodoulou, M. A., & Boutalis, Y. S. (2008). Indirect Adaptive Neuro - Fuzzy Control Based On High Order Neural Network Function Approximators. In Proc. *16th Mediterranean Conference on Control and Automation - MED08* (pp. 386-393). Ajaccio, Corsica, France.

Wang, L. (1994). *Adaptive Fuzzy Systems and Control*. Englewood Cliffs, NJ: Prentice Hall.

Chapter 19
Neuro-Fuzzy Control Schemes Based on High Order Neural Network Function Approximators

D.C. Theodoridis
Democritus University of Thrace, Greece

M.A. Christodoulou
Technical University of Crete, Greece

Y.S. Boutalis
Democritus University of Thrace, Greece

ABSTRACT

The indirect or direct adaptive regulation of unknown nonlinear dynamical systems is considered in this chapter. Since the plant is considered unknown, we first propose its approximation by a special form of a fuzzy dynamical system (FDS) and in the sequel the fuzzy rules are approximated by appropriate high order neural networks (HONN's). The system is regulated to zero adaptively by providing weight updating laws for the involved HONN's, which guarantee that both the identification error and the system states reach zero exponentially fast. At the same time, all signals in the closed loop are kept bounded. The existence of the control signal is always assured by introducing a novel method of parameter hopping, which is incorporated in the weight updating laws. The indirect control scheme is developed for square systems (number of inputs equal to the number of states) as well as for systems in Brunovsky canonical form. The direct control scheme is developed for systems in square form. Simulations illustrate the potency of the method and comparisons with conventional approaches on benchmarking systems are given.

DOI: 10.4018/978-1-61520-711-4.ch019

2.1 INTRODUCTION

In this chapter, we design and analyse a class of adaptive control schemes based on fuzzy logic and high order neural networks referred to as fuzzy-recurrent high order neural networks (F-RHONN's).

Nonlinear dynamical systems can be represented by general nonlinear dynamical equations of the form

$$\dot{x} = f(x, u) \tag{1}$$

The mathematical description of the system is required, so that we are able to control it. Unfortunately, the exact mathematical model of the plant, especially when this is highly nonlinear and complex, is rarely known and thus appropriate identification schemes have to be applied which will provide us with an approximate model of the plant.

It has been established that neural networks and fuzzy inference systems are universal approximators (Hornik, Stinchcombe & White, 1989), (Wang, 1994), (Passino & Yurkovich, 1998), that is, they can approximate any nonlinear function to any prescribed accuracy provided that sufficient hidden neurons and training data or fuzzy rules are available. Recently, the combination of these two different technologies has given rise to fuzzy neural or neuro fuzzy approaches, that are intended to capture the advantages of both fuzzy logic and neural networks. Numerous works have shown the viability of this approach for system modelling (Jang, 1993; Lin, 1995; Cho & Wang, 1996; Juang & Lin, 1998; Li & Mukaidono, 1995; Chiu, 1994; Lin & Cunningham, 1995; Jang & Lin, 1998; Mitra & Hayashi, 2000).

The neural and fuzzy approaches are most of the time equivalent, differing between each other mainly in the structure of the approximator chosen. Indeed, in order to bridge the gap between the neural and fuzzy approaches several researchers introduce adaptive schemes using a class of parameterized functions that include both neural networks and fuzzy systems (Cho & Wang, 1996; Juang & Lin, 1998; Li & Mukaidono, 1995; Chiu, 1994; Lin & Cunningham, 1995; Jang & Lin, 1998; Mitra & Hayashi, 2000). Regarding the approximator structure, linear in the parameters approximators are used in (Lin & Cunningham, 1995), (Chen, Lee & Chang, 1996), and nonlinear in (Spooner & Passino, 1996), (Narendra & Parthasarathy, 1990), (Polycarpou & Mears, 1998).

Adaptive control theory has been an active area of research over the past years (Chen, Lee & Chang, 1996; Spooner & Passino, 1996; Narendra & Parthasarathy, 1990; Polycarpou & Mears, 1998; Rovithakis & Christodoulou, 1994; Golea, Golea & Benmahammed, 2003; Lina, Wang & Liub, 2004; Diao & Passino, 2002; Ordonez & Passino, 2001; Sbarbaro & Johansen, 2006; Hayakawa, Haddad, Hovakimyan & Chellaboina, 2005; Shuzhi & Thanh, 2007; Hovakimyan, Lavretsky, Bong & Calise, 2005; Ge & Jing, 2002; Lee & Teng, 2000; Hojati & Gazor, 2002; Nounou & Passino, 2005; Chen & Liu, 1994; Ioannou & Fidan, 2006; Rovithakis & Christodoulou, 2000; Spooner, Maggiore, Ordonez & Passino, 2002; Nounou & Passino, 2004; Park, Huh, Seo & Park, 2005; Leu, Wang & Lee, 2005; Bong & Calise, 2007; Yih, Wei & Tsu, 2005; Rovithakis & Christodoulou, 1995; Kosmatopoulos & Christodoulou, 1996; Christodoulou, Theodoridis & Boutalis, 2007; Theodoridis, Christodoulou & Boutalis, 2008; Boutalis, Theodoridis & Christodoulou, (2009); Theodoridis, Boutalis & Christodoulou, (in press); Theodoridis at al., (2009); Adetona, Sathananthan & Keel, 2002; Psillakis & Alexandridis, 2007; Leonhard, 1985; Slotine & Li, 1997; Antsaklis & Passino, 1993; Ordonez, Zumberge, Spooner & Passino, 1997; Maggiore & Passino, 2005; Lewis, Jagannathan & Yesildirek, 1999).

In the neuro or neuro fuzzy adaptive control two main approaches are followed. In the indirect adaptive control schemes (Chen, Lee & Chang, 1996; Spooner & Passino, 1996; Narendra & Parthasarathy, 1990; Polycarpou & Mears, 1998; Rovithakis & Christodoulou, 1994; Golea, Golea & Benmahammed, 2003; Theodoridis, Christodoulou & Boutalis, 2008; Boutalis, Theodoridis & Christodoulou, (2009); Lina, Wang & Liub, 2004), first the dynamics of the system are identified and then a control input is generated according to the certainty equivalence principle. In the direct adaptive control schemes (Diao & Passino, 2002; Ordonez & Passino, 2001; Sbarbaro & Johansen, 2006; Hayakawa, Haddad, Hovakimyan & Chellaboina, 2005; Shuzhi & Thanh, 2007; Hovakimyan, Lavretsky, Bong & Calise, 2005; Theodoridis, Boutalis & Christodoulou, 2009; Theodoridis at al., 2009) the controller is directly estimated and the control input is generated to guarantee stability without knowledge of the system dynamics. Also, many researchers focus on robust adaptive control that guarantees signal boundness in the presence of modelling errors and bounded disturbances (Ge & Jing, 2002). In (Lee & Teng, 2000) both direct and indirect approaches are presented, while in (Hojati & Gazor, 2002), (Nounou & Passino, 2005) a combined direct and indirect control scheme is used.

Recently (Kosmatopoulos & Christodoulou, 1996), (Christodoulou, Theodoridis & Boutalis, 2007), high order neural network function approximators (HONN's) have been proposed for the identification of nonlinear dynamical systems of the form (1), approximated by a Fuzzy Dynamical System. In this chapter HONN's are also used for the neuro fuzzy identification of unknown nonlinear dynamical systems. This approximation depends on the fact that fuzzy rules could be identified with the help of HONN's. The same rationale has been employed in (Theodoridis, Christodoulou & Boutalis, 2008; Boutalis, Theodoridis & Christodoulou, 2009), where a neuro – fuzzy approach for the indirect control of unknown systems has been introduced.

In this chapter HONN's are also used for the neuro fuzzy direct and indirect control of nonlinear dynamical systems. In the proposed approach the underlying fuzzy model is of Mamdani type. The structure identification is also made off-line based either on human expertise or on gathered data. However, the required a-priori information obtained by linguistic information or data is very limited. The only required information is an estimate of the centres of the output fuzzy membership functions. Information on the input variable membership functions and on the underlying fuzzy rules is not necessary because this is automatically estimated by the HONN's. This way the proposed method is less vulnerable to initial design assumptions. The parameter identification is then easily addressed by HONN's, based on the linguistic information regarding the structural identification of the output part and from the numerical data obtained from the actual system to be modelled.

We consider that the nonlinear system is affine in the control and could be approximated with the help of two independent fuzzy subsystems. Every fuzzy subsystem is approximated from a family of HONN's, each one being related with a group of fuzzy rules. Weight updating laws are given and we prove that when the structural identification is appropriate then the error converges very fast to zero.

The chapter is based on the work of the authors presented in (Theodoridis, Christodoulou & Boutalis, 2008; Boutalis, Theodoridis & Christodoulou, 2009; Theodoridis, Boutalis & Christodoulou, 2009; Theodoridis, Christodoulou and Boutalis, 2009). It is organized as follows. Section 2.2 presents the concept of indirect control for the new neuro-fuzzy representation of affine in the control dynamical systems with parametric uncertainties, introducing also a novel approach of parameter hopping, which assures the existence of control inputs. An alternative representation of the proposed F-RHONN model for systems in Brunovsky canonical form is presented in section 2.3, where the associated weight adaptation laws are given. In section 2.4 we introduce our method for the direct control of affine in the control dynamical systems following the same lines as in section 2.2. Finally, simulation results are given in Section 2.5 where the performance of the proposed scheme is tested and compared to another well known approach of the literature showing a significant superiority.

2.2 INDIRECT ADAPTIVE NEURO-FUZZY CONTROL

This section is devoted to the development of an indirect adaptive regulation technique (Theodoridis, Christodoulou & Boutalis, 2008; Boutalis, Theodoridis & Christodoulou, 2009), for controlling nonlinear dynamical systems with parametric uncertainties. The proposed technique is divided into two steps. In the first step, a neuro-fuzzy identification model of the unknown plant is constructed. Assuming only parameter uncertainty the parameters of the model are estimated based on system's operation data and on limited a-priori information regarding the fuzzy partitions of the involved variables. The adaptation algorithm guarantees that the error between the actual system states and its neuro-fuzzy approximation is approximately zero. In the second step, the controller receives information from the neuro-fuzzy system approximator and computes the required control input signal, which forces the system states to go to zero.

The successful completion of step one, implies that a reliable approximating model of the originally unknown nonlinear dynamical system has been obtained. The states of the approximator are used by the controller, where an appropriate state feedback is constructed to achieve asymptotic regulation of the output, while keeping bounded all signals in the closed loop.

The stability of the identification scheme plus convergence of the identification error to within a neighbourhood of zero is guaranteed with the aid of Lyapunov theory. The existence of the control signal is always assured by incorporating in the weight updating equations a novel method of parameter hopping.

As concerning the problem formulation we consider affine in the control, nonlinear dynamical systems of the form

$$\dot{x} = f(x) + G(x) \cdot u \tag{2}$$

where the state $x \in \Re^n$ is assumed to be completely measured, the control input u is a vector in $\Re^n$, f is an unknown smooth vector field called the drift term and G is a matrix with columns the unknown smooth controlled vector fields g_i, $i = 1, \ldots, n$ and $G = diag\left[g_1, g_2, \ldots, g_n \right]$.

The state regulation problem is known as our attempt to force the states to zero from an arbitrary initial value by applying appropriate feedback control to the plant input. However, the problem as it is stated above for the system (2), is very difficult or even impossible to be solved since the f, g are assumed to be completely unknown. To overcome this problem we assume that the unknown plant can be described by the following model arriving from a neuro-fuzzy representation described in (Boutalis, Theodoridis & Christodoulou, 2009) and (Boutalis, Theodoridis & Christodoulou, (2010)), where the weight values W_f^* and W_g^* are unknown.

$$\dot{x} = Ax + X_f W_f^* S_f(x) + X_g W_g^* S_g(x)u \tag{3}$$

The assumptions 3, 4 from (Boutalis, Theodoridis & Christodoulou, (2010)) are valid for this formulation. Thus, our attempt is to find a suitable control law, which under some restrictions will provide asymptotic regulation. Also, convergence of the regulation error to zero and boundedness of all signals in the closed-loop, has to be assured.

2.2.1 Parametric Uncertainty

We assume the existence of only parameter uncertainty. So, following the discussion and analysis of (Boutalis, Theodoridis & Christodoulou, 2009), an affine F-RHONN model of the form

$$\dot{\hat{x}} = A\hat{x} + X_f W_f S_f(x) + X_g W_g S_g(x)u \tag{4}$$

can be used to describe (2). In the above equation the approximated state variables $\hat{x} \in \Re^n$ and the control inputs $u \in \Re^n$. A is a $n \times n$ stable matrix which for simplicity can be taken to be diagonal, X_f is a $n \times n \cdot m$ block diagonal matrix of the form $X_f = diag\left(X_{f_1}, X_{f_2}, \ldots, X_{f_n}\right)$ with each X_{f_i} being an m-dimensional row vector of the form $X_{f_i} = \begin{bmatrix} \bar{x}_{f_i}^1 & \bar{x}_{f_i}^2 & \cdots & \bar{x}_{f_i}^m \end{bmatrix}$, where m is the number of fuzzy partitions. Also, W_f is a $n \cdot m \times k$ matrix with neural weights, where k is the number of high order terms and $S_f(x) = \begin{bmatrix} s_1(x) & \cdots & s_k(x) \end{bmatrix}^T$ is a k-dimensional column vector. Finally, X_g is a $n \times n \cdot m$ block diagonal matrix $X_g = diag\left(X_{g_1}, X_{g_2}, \ldots, X_{g_n}\right)$ with each X_{g_i} being an m-dimensional row vector of the form $X_{g_i} = \begin{bmatrix} \bar{x}_{g_i}^1 & \bar{x}_{g_i}^2 & \cdots & \bar{x}_{g_i}^m \end{bmatrix}$ W_g is a $n \cdot m \times n$ block diagonal matrix $W_g = diag\left(W_{g_1}, W_{g_2}, \ldots, W_{g_n}\right)$ with each W_{g_i} being a m-dimensional column vector. $S_g(x)$ is a $n \times n$ diagonal matrix with each diagonal element $s_i(x)$ being a high order combination of sigmoid functions of the state variables.

Define now the error between the identifier states and the real states as

$$e = \hat{x} - x \tag{5}$$

Then from (3) and (4) we obtain the error equation

$$\dot{e} = Ae + X_f \tilde{W}_f S_f(x) + X_g \tilde{W}_g S_g(x)u \tag{6}$$

Where $\tilde{W}_f = W_f - W_f^*$ and $\tilde{W}_g = W_g - W_g^*$.

Our objective is to find suitable control and learning laws to drive both e and $\hat{x}$ to zero exponentially fast, while all other signals in the closed loop remain bounded. Taking u to be equal to

$$u = -\left[X_g W_g S_g(x)\right]^{-1}\left(X_f W_f S_f(x)\right) \tag{7}$$

and substituting it into (4) we finally obtain

$$\dot{\hat{x}} = A\hat{x} \tag{8}$$

In the next theorem the weight updating laws are given, which can serve both the identification and the control objectives provided that the existence of $\left[X_g W_g S_g(x)\right]^{-1}$ is assured.

Theorem 1:

Consider the identification scheme given by (6). The learning law

a.   For the elements of W_{f_i}

$$\dot{w}_{f_i}^{pl}(x) = -\overline{x}_{f_i}^{p} p_i e_i s_l(x)$$ (9)

b.   For the elements of W_{g_i}

$$\dot{w}_{g_i}^{p}(x) = -\overline{x}_{g_i}^{p} p_i e_i u_i s_i(x)$$ (10)

or equivalently $\dot{W}_{g_i}(x) = -\left(X_{g_i}\right)^T p_i e_i u_i s_i(x)$ with $i = 1,\ldots,n$, $p = 1,\ldots,m$ and $l = 1,\ldots,k$ guarantees the following properties.

- $e, \hat{x}, \tilde{W}_f, \tilde{W}_g \in L_\infty$, $e, \hat{x} \in L_2$
- $\lim_{t \to \infty} e(t) = 0$, $\lim_{t \to \infty} x(t) = 0$, $\lim_{t \to \infty} \dot{\tilde{W}}_f(t) = 0$, $\lim_{t \to \infty} \dot{\tilde{W}}_g(t) = 0$

Proof: Consider the Lyapunov function candidate,

$$V\left(e,\hat{x},\tilde{W}_f,\tilde{W}_g\right) = \frac{1}{2} e^T Pe + \frac{1}{2}\hat{x}^T P\hat{x} + \frac{1}{2\gamma_1} tr\left\{\tilde{W}_f^T \tilde{W}_f\right\} + \frac{1}{2\gamma_2} tr\left\{\tilde{W}_g^T \tilde{W}_g\right\}$$

where $P > 0$ is chosen to satisfy the Lyapunov equation

$$PA + A^T P = -I$$

Taking the derivative of the Lyapunov function candidate we get

$$\dot{V}\left(e,\hat{x},\tilde{W}_f,\tilde{W}_g\right) = \frac{1}{2}\dot{e}^T Pe + \frac{1}{2}e^T P\dot{e} + \frac{1}{2}\dot{\hat{x}}^T P\hat{x} + \frac{1}{2}\hat{x}^T P\dot{\hat{x}} + \frac{1}{\gamma_1} tr\left\{\dot{\tilde{W}}_f^T \tilde{W}_f\right\} + \frac{1}{\gamma_2} tr\left\{\dot{\tilde{W}}_g^T \tilde{W}_g\right\}$$

which after substituting Eqs. (6) and (8) becomes

$$\dot{V} = \frac{1}{2}e^T\left(A^T P + PA\right)e + \frac{1}{2}\hat{x}^T\left(A^T P + PA\right)\hat{x} +$$

$$+\left(\frac{1}{2}e^T PX_f \tilde{W}_f S_f + S_f^T \tilde{W}_f^T X_f^T Pe\right)$$

$$+\left(\frac{1}{2}e^T PX_g \tilde{W}_g S_g u + u^T S_g^T \tilde{W}_g^T X_g^T Pe\right)$$

$$+\frac{1}{\gamma_1} tr\left\{\dot{\tilde{W}}_f^T \tilde{W}_f\right\} + \frac{1}{\gamma_2} tr\left\{\dot{\tilde{W}}_g^T \tilde{W}_g\right\}$$

Now since $e^T PX_f \tilde{W}_f S_f$ and $e^T PX_g \tilde{W}_g S_g u$ are scalars, we have that

$$e^T PX_f \tilde{W}_f S_f = \left(S_f^T \tilde{W}_f^T X_f^T Pe\right)^T$$

$$e^T P X_g \tilde{W}_g S_g u = \left(u^T S_g^T \tilde{W}_g^T X_g^T P e \right)^T$$

Therefore, $\dot{V}$ becomes

$$\dot{V} = -\frac{1}{2} e^T e - \frac{1}{2} \hat{x}^T \hat{x} + e^T P X_f \tilde{W}_f S_f + e^T P X_g \tilde{W}_g S_g u$$
$$+ \frac{1}{\gamma_1} tr \left\{ \dot{\tilde{W}}_f^T \tilde{W}_f \right\} + \frac{1}{\gamma_2} tr \left\{ \dot{\tilde{W}}_g^T \tilde{W}_g \right\}$$

Assuming that

$$\frac{1}{\gamma_1} tr \left\{ \dot{\tilde{W}}_f^T \tilde{W}_f \right\} = -e^T P X_f \tilde{W}_f S_f$$

$$\frac{1}{\gamma_2} tr \left\{ \dot{\tilde{W}}_g^T \tilde{W}_g \right\} = -e^T P X_g \tilde{W}_g S_g u$$

then, taking into account the form of W_f and W_g the above equations result in the element wise learning laws given in (9), (10). These laws can also be written in the following compact form

$$\dot{W}_f = -\gamma_1 X_f^T P e S_f^T \tag{11}$$

$$\dot{W}_g = -\gamma_2 X_g^T P E U S_g^T \tag{12}$$

Where E and U are diagonal matrices such that $E = diag\left(e_1, \ldots, e_n\right)$ and $U = diag\left(u_1, \ldots, u_n\right)$. Finally, the derivative of the Lyapunov function candidate becomes

$$\dot{V} = -\frac{1}{2} \|e\|^2 - \frac{1}{2} \|\hat{x}\|^2 \leq 0$$

Since $\dot{V}$ is negative semi definite then we conclude that $V \in L_\infty$, which implies that $e, \hat{x}, \tilde{W}_f, \tilde{W}_g \in L_\infty$. Furthermore, $W_f = \tilde{W}_f + W_f^*$, $W_g = \tilde{W}_g + W_g^*$ are also bounded. Since V is a non-increasing function of time and bounded from below, the $\lim_{t \to \infty} V = V_\infty$ exists; therefore, by integrating $\dot{V}$ from 0 to ∞ we have

$$\int_0^\infty \|e\|^2 \, dt + \int_0^\infty \|\hat{x}\|^2 \, dt \leq \left[V(0) - V_\infty \right] < \infty$$

which implies that $e, \hat{x} \in L_2$.

Since $e, \hat{x} \in L_2 \cap L_\infty$, using Barbalat's Lemma we conclude that $\lim_{t \to \infty} e(t) = 0$ and $\lim_{t \to \infty} \hat{x}(t) = 0$. Thus, from Eq. (5) we have $\lim_{t \to \infty} x(t) = 0$.

Now, using the boundedness of u, S_f, S_g, X_f, X_g and the convergence of $e(t)$ to zero, we have that $\dot{\tilde{W}}_f, \dot{\tilde{W}}_g$ also converges to zero (Ioannou & Fidan, 2006).

Remark 1: The control law (7) can be also extended to the following form

$$u = -\left[X_g W_g S_g(x)\right]^{-1} \cdot \left(X_f W_f S_f(x) + Kx\right) \tag{13}$$

where K is appropriate positive definite diagonal gain matrix. It can be easily verified that with this control law the negativity of the derivative of the Lyapunov function is further enhanced. Therefore, term Kx is actually acting as a robustifying term.

Proof: Indeed, by using the extended control law (13) the state estimate dynamics become

$$\dot{\hat{x}} = A\hat{x} - Kx \tag{14}$$

Then, using the weight updating laws given in theorem 1 and Eq. (14), the derivative of the Lyapunov function becomes

$$\dot{V} = -\frac{1}{2}\|e\|^2 - \frac{1}{2}\|\hat{x}\|^2 - xKP\hat{x} \Rightarrow$$

$$\Rightarrow \dot{V} = -\frac{1}{2}\|e\|^2 - \frac{1}{2}\|\hat{x}\|^2 - \hat{x}^T KP\hat{x} + e^T KP\hat{x} \Rightarrow$$

$$\Rightarrow \dot{V} \leq -\frac{1}{2}\|e\|^2 - \frac{1}{2}\|\hat{x}\|^2 - \lambda_{\min}(KP)\|\hat{x}\|^2 + \|e\|\|KP\|\|\hat{x}\| \Rightarrow$$

$$\Rightarrow \dot{V} \leq -\begin{bmatrix}\|e\| & \|\hat{x}\|\end{bmatrix} \cdot \begin{bmatrix} \dfrac{1}{2} & -\|KP\| \\ 0 & \dfrac{1}{2} + \lambda_{\min}(KP)\end{bmatrix} \cdot \begin{bmatrix}\|e\| \\ \|\hat{x}\|\end{bmatrix} < 0$$

The property of $\lambda_{\min}(KP)\|\hat{x}\|^2 \leq \hat{x}^T(KP)\hat{x} \leq \lambda_{\max}(KP)\|\hat{x}\|^2$, where $\lambda_{\min}(KP)$ and $\lambda_{\max}(KP)$ are the minimum and maximum eigenvalues of (KP) respectively, is valid when (KP) is a symmetric matrix with $(KP) \in \Re^{n \times n}$ and $(KP) \geq 0$, which is true according to the forms of K and P matrices.

2.2.2 Introduction to the Parameter Hopping

The weight updating laws presented previously are valid when the control law signal in (13) exists. Therefore, the existence of $\left[X_g W_g S_g(x)\right]^{-1}$ has to be assured. Since $S_g(x)$ is diagonal with its elements $s_i(x) \neq 0$ and X_g, W_g are block diagonal, the existence of the inverse is assured when $X_{g_i} \cdot W_{g_i} \neq 0, \forall\, i = 1, \ldots, n$. Therefore, W_g has to be confined such that $\left|X_{g_i} \cdot W_{g_i}\right| \geq \theta_i > 0$ with θ_i being a design parameter. In case the boundary defined by the above confinement is nonlinear the updating of W_g can be modified by using a projection algorithm (Ioannou & Fidan, 2006). However, in our case the boundary surface is linear and the direction of updating is normal to it because $\nabla\left|X_{g_i} \cdot W_{g_i}\right| = X_{g_i}$. Therefore, the projection of the updating vector on the boundary surface is of no use. Instead, using concepts from multidimensional vector geometry we modify the updating law such that, when the weight vector approaches (within a safe distance θ_i) the forbidden hyper-plane $X_{g_i} \cdot W_{g_i} = 0$ and the direction of updating is toward the forbidden hyper-plane, it introduces a *hopping* which drives the weights in the direction of the updating but on the other side of the space, where here the weight space is divided into two sides by the forbid-

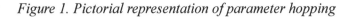

Figure 1. Pictorial representation of parameter hopping

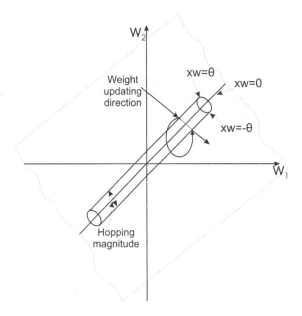

den hyper-plane. This procedure is depicted in Fig. 1, where a simplified 2-dimensional representation is given. Theorem 2 below introduces this *hopping* in the updating law.

Theorem 2: Consider the control scheme (6), (13), (14). The updating law:

a. For the elements of W_{f_i} given by (9)
b. For the elements of W_{g_i} given by the modified form

$$
\dot{W}_{g_i} = \begin{cases}
-\left(X_{g_i}\right)^T p_i e_i u_i s_i(x) & \begin{array}{l} if\ \left|X_{g_i} W_{g_i}\right| > \theta_i \\ or\ X_{g_i} W_{g_i} = \pm\theta_i \\ and\ X_{g_i} \dot{W}_{g_i} <> 0 \end{array} \\[3em]
-\left(X_{g_i}\right)^T p_i e_i u_i s_i(x) - \dfrac{2\left[X_{g_i} W_{g_i} \left(X_{g_i}\right)^T\right]}{tr\left\{\left(X_{g_i}\right)^T X_{g_i}\right\}} & \begin{array}{l} if\ 0 < X_{g_i} W_{g_i} < \theta_i \\ and\ X_{g_i} \dot{W}_{g_i} \geq 0 \\ or\ if -\theta_i < X_{g_i} W_{g_i} < 0 \\ and\ X_{g_i} \dot{W}_{g_i} \leq 0 \end{array}
\end{cases}
\tag{15}
$$

Proof: In order the properties of theorem 1 to be valid it suffices to show that by using the modified updating law for W_{g_i} the negative ness of the Lyapunov function is not compromised. Indeed the *if* part of the modified form of $\dot{W}_{g_i}$ is exactly the same with (10) and therefore according to theorem 1 the negative ness of V is in effect. The *if* part is used when the weights are at a certain distance (condition if $\left|X_{g_i} \cdot W_{g_i}\right| > \theta_i$) from the forbidden plane or at the safe limit (condition $\left|X_{g_i} \cdot W_{g_i}\right| = \theta_i$) but with the direction of updating moving the weights far from the forbidden plane (condition $X_{g_i} \dot{W}_{g_i} \leq 0$).

Figure 2. Vector explanation of parameter hopping

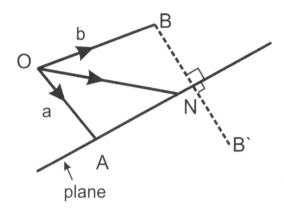

In the ***otherwise*** part of $\dot{W}_{g_i}$, term $-\dfrac{2\left(X_{g_i}W_{g_i}\left(X_{g_i}\right)^T\right)}{tr\left\{\left(X_{g_i}\right)^T X_{g_i}\right\}}$ determines the magnitude of weight *hopping*,

which as explained later and is depicted in Fig. 2 has to be two times the distance of the current weight vector to the forbidden hyper-plane. Therefore the ***existence*** of the control signal is assured because the weights never reach the forbidden plane. Regarding the ***negativity*** of $\dot{V}$ we proceed as follows.

Let that $W_{g_i}^*$ contains the initial values of W_{g_i} provided from the identification part such that $\left|X_{g_i}W_{g_i}^*\right| >> \theta_i$ and that $\tilde{W}_{g_i} = W_{g_i} - W_{g_i}^*$ Then, the weight hopping can be equivalently written with respect to $\tilde{W}_{g_i}$ as $\dfrac{-2\theta_i\tilde{W}_{g_i}}{\left\|\tilde{W}_{g_i}\right\|}$. Under this consideration the modified updating law is rewritten as

$$\dot{W}_{g_i} = -\left(X_{g_i}\right)^T p_i e_i u_i s_i(x) - \frac{2\theta_i\tilde{W}_{g_i}}{\left\|\tilde{W}_{g_i}\right\|}$$

With this updating law it can be easily verified that $\dot{V} \le -\dfrac{1}{2}\|e\|^2 - \dfrac{1}{2}\|\hat{x}\|^2 - \dfrac{H}{\gamma_2}$, with H being a positive constant expressed as $H = \dfrac{\sum 2\theta_i\left(\left(\tilde{W}_{g_i}\right)^T\tilde{W}_{g_i}\right)}{\left\|\tilde{W}_{g_i}\right\|} \ge 0$, where the summation includes all weight vectors

which require hopping. Therefore, the negativity of $\dot{V}$ is actually enhanced.

2.2.3 Vectorial Proof of Parameter Hopping

In selecting the terms involved in parameter hopping we start from the vector definition of a line, of a plane and the distance of a point to a plane. The equation of a line in vector form is given by $r = a + \lambda t$, where a is the position vector of a given point of the line, t is a vector in the direction of the line and λ is a real scalar. By giving different numbers to λ we get different points of the line each one represented by the corresponding position vector r. The vector equation of a plane can be defined by using one point of the plane and a vector normal to it. In this case $r \cdot n = a \cdot n = d$ is the equation of the plane, where a is the position vector of a given point on the plane, n is a vector normal to the plane and d is a scalar. When the plane passes through zero, then apparently $d = 0$. To determine the distance of a point B with position vector b from a given plane we consider Fig. 2 and combine the above definitions as follows. Line BN is perpendicular to the plane and is described by vector equation $r = b + \lambda n$, where n is the normal to the plane vector. However, point N also lies on the plane and in case the plane passes through zero

$$r \cdot n = 0 \Rightarrow \left(b + \lambda n\right) \cdot n = 0 \Rightarrow \lambda = \frac{-b \cdot n}{\left\|n\right\|}.$$

Apparently, if one wants to get the position vector of B' (the symmetrical of B in respect to the plane), this is given by

$$r = b - 2\frac{b \cdot n}{\left\|n\right\|}n.$$

In our problem $b = W_{g_i}$, our plane is described by the equation $X_{g_i} \cdot W_{g_i} = 0$ and as it has already been mentioned the normal to it is the vector X_{g_i}.

2.3 INDIRECT ADAPTIVE NEURO-FUZZY CONTROL FOR SYSTEMS IN BRUNOVSKY CANONICAL FORM

In the previous section, the neuro-fuzzy indirect control of unknown systems was presented, where the systems have a square form that is the number of inputs equals the number of states. In this section we present the application of the proposed neuro-fuzzy representation in systems that can be written in Brunovsky canonical form. Many real systems can be expressed in this form, including some popular control benchmarks.

As concerning the problem formulation, we consider nonlinear dynamical systems of the form

$$\dot{x} = A_c x + b_c \left[f(x) + g(x) \cdot u\right] \tag{16}$$

known as Brunovsky canonical form, where the state $x \in R^n$ is assumed to be completely measured, the control input $u \in R$ and $f, g \in R$ are functions of the state variable. Also,

$$A_c = \begin{bmatrix} 0 & 1 & 0 & \cdots & 0 \\ 0 & 0 & 1 & 0 & \vdots \\ \vdots & \vdots & 0 & \ddots & 0 \\ 0 & 0 & \vdots & 0 & 1 \\ 0 & 0 & \cdots & 0 & 0 \end{bmatrix} \text{ and } b_c = \begin{bmatrix} 0 & \cdots & 0 & 1 \end{bmatrix}^T$$

The state regulation problem is known as our attempt to force the state to zero from an arbitrary initial value by applying appropriate feedback control to the plant input. However, the problem as it is stated above for the system (16), is very difficult or even impossible to be solved if f, g are unknown. To overcome this problem we assume that the unknown plant can be described by the following model arriving from a neuro-fuzzy representation described below, where the weight values W_f^* and W_g^* are unknown.

$$\dot{x} = A_c x + b_c \left[X_f W_f^* S_f(x) + X_g W_g^* S_g(x) u \right] \tag{17}$$

The assumptions 3, 4 from (Boutalis, Theodoridis & Christodoulou, (in press)) are valid for this formulation. So, we have the following neuro-fuzzy representation for the proposed model.

2.3.1 Neuro-Fuzzy Representation of Brunovsky Canonical Form

We are using an affine in the control fuzzy dynamical system, which approximates the system in (16) and uses two fuzzy subsystem blocks for the description of $f(x)$ and $g(x)$ as follows

$$\hat{f}(x \mid W_f) = \sum \left(\overline{x}_f \right)^{l_n}_{j_1,\dots,j_n} \times \left(N_f \right)^{l_n}_{j_1,\dots,j_n} (x) \tag{18}$$

$$\hat{g}(x \mid W_g) = \sum \left(\overline{x}_g \right)^{l_n}_{j_1,\dots,j_n} \times \left(N_g \right)^{l_n}_{j_1,\dots,j_n} (x) \tag{19}$$

where the summation is carried out over the number of all available fuzzy rules and N_f, N_g are appropriate HONNFs.

The affine in the control fuzzy dynamical system in (16) using Eqs. (18), (19) is replaced by the following equivalent affine fuzzy - recurrent high order neural network (F-RHONN), which depends on the centres of the fuzzy output partitions $\overline{f}_l$ and $\overline{g}_l$

$$\dot{\hat{x}} = A_c \hat{x} + b_c \left[\sum_{p=1}^{Npf} \overline{x}_f^p \times N_{f_p}(x) + \left(\sum_{p=1}^{Npg} \overline{x}_g^p \times N_{g_p}(x) \right) \cdot u \right] \tag{20}$$

Or in a more compact form

$$\dot{\hat{x}} = A_c \hat{x} + b_c \left[X_f W_f S_f(x) + X_g W_g S_g(x) u \right] \tag{21}$$

Where X_f, X_g are row vectors containing the centres of the partitions of $f(x)$ and $g(x)$ respectively, $S_f(x)$, $S_g(x)$ are column vectors containing high order combinations of sigmoid functions of the state x and W_f, W_g are matrices containing respective neural weights according to (20). The dimensions and the contents of all the above matrices are chosen so that $X_f W_f S_f(x)$ is a 1×1 scalar and $X_g W_g S_g(x)$ is of the same form. For notational simplicity we also assume that $f(x)$ and $g(x)$ have the same number of fuzzy partitions. Under these specifications X_f is a $1 \times m$ row vector of the form

$$X_f = \begin{bmatrix} \overline{x}_f^1 & \overline{x}_f^2 & \cdots & \overline{x}_f^m \end{bmatrix}$$

where $\bar{x}_f^p$ denotes the centre or the p-th fuzzy partition of $f(x)$.

These centres can be determined manually or automatically with the help of a fuzzy c-means clustering algorithm as a part of the off-line structural identification procedure mentioned in the introduction.

Also, $S_f(x) = \left[s_1(x) \cdots s_k(x) \right]^T$, where each $s_l(x)$ with $l = 1, 2, ..., k$, is a high order combination of sigmoid functions of the state variables and W_f is a $m \times k$ matrix with neural weights. W_f can be also written as a collection of column vectors W_f^l, that is $W_f = \left[W_f^1 \; W_f^2 \cdots W_f^k \right]$. X_g is a $1 \times m$ row vector of the form

$$X_g = \left[\bar{x}_g^1 \quad \bar{x}_g^2 \quad \cdots \quad \bar{x}_g^m \right]$$

where $\bar{x}_g^p$ denotes the center or the p-th partition of $g(x)$. W_g, $S_g(x)$ have the same dimensions as W_f $S_f(x)$ respectively.

2.3.2 Identification and Adaptive Regulation

We assume the existence of only parameter uncertainty, so, we can take into account that the actual system (16) can be modelled by its approximation of Eq. (17). Our objective is to find suitable control and learning laws to drive both the approximation error e and states x to zero, while all other signals in the closed loop remain bounded. So, we take u to be equal to

$$u = -\frac{X_f W_f S_f(x) - k\hat{x}}{X_g W_g S_g(x)} \tag{22}$$

where k is a vector of the form $k = \left[-k_n \cdots -k_2 \; -k_1 \right] \in R^n$ such that all roots of the polynomial $h(s) = s^n + k_1 s^{n-1} + \cdots + k_n$ are in the open left half-plane.

After substituting Eq. (22), Eq. (21) becomes $\dot{\hat{x}} = A_c \hat{x} + b_c k \hat{x}$, or equivalently

$$\dot{\hat{x}} = \Lambda_c \hat{x} \tag{23}$$

Where $\Lambda_c = \begin{bmatrix} 0 & 1 & 0 & \cdots & 0 \\ 0 & 0 & 1 & 0 & \vdots \\ \vdots & \vdots & 0 & \ddots & 0 \\ 0 & 0 & \vdots & 0 & 1 \\ -k_n & -k_{n-1} & \cdots & -k_2 & -k_1 \end{bmatrix}$.

Also, the derivative of the approximation error becomes

$$\dot{e} = \dot{\hat{x}} - \dot{x} \tag{24}$$

Using Eqs. (17) and (21), Eq. (24) becomes

$$\dot{e} = \Lambda_c e - b_c ke + b_c \left[\tilde{f} + \tilde{g} \cdot u \right] \tag{25}$$

where $\tilde{f} = X_f \tilde{W}_f S_f(x)$ and $\tilde{g} = X_g \tilde{W}_g S_g(x)$. Also, $\tilde{W}_f = W_f - W_f^*$ and $\tilde{W}_g = W_g - W_g^*$.

In the next theorem the weight updating laws are given, which can serve the control objective provided that the updating of the weights of matrix W_g is performed so that the existence of $X_g W_g S_g(x)$ is assured.

Theorem 3:

Consider the identification scheme given by Eqs. (22), (23) and (25). The learning law

a.   For the elements of W_f

$$\dot{w}_f^{pl}(x) = -\gamma_1 \bar{x}_f^p b_c^T Pes_l(x) \tag{26}$$

b.   For the elements of W_g

$$\dot{w}_g^{pl}(x) = -\gamma_2 \bar{x}_g^p b_c^T Peus_l(x) \tag{27}$$

or equivalently $\dot{W}_g(x) = -\gamma_2 \left(X_g \right)^T b_c^T Peus_l(x)$ with $i = 1, \ldots, n$, $p = 1, \ldots, m$ and $l = 1, \ldots, k$ guarantees the following properties.

- $e, \hat{x}, \tilde{W}_f, \tilde{W}_g \in L_\infty$, $e, \hat{x} \in L_2$
- $\lim_{t \to \infty} e(t) = 0$, $\lim_{t \to \infty} x(t) = 0$, $\lim_{t \to \infty} \dot{\tilde{W}}_f(t) = 0$, $\lim_{t \to \infty} \dot{\tilde{W}}_g(t) = 0$

Proof: Consider the Lyapunov function candidate,

$$V\left(e, \hat{x}, \tilde{W}_f, \tilde{W}_g\right) = \frac{1}{2} e^T Pe + \frac{1}{2} \hat{x}^T P\hat{x} + \frac{1}{2\gamma_1} tr\left\{ \tilde{W}_f^T \tilde{W}_f \right\} + \frac{1}{2\gamma_2} tr\left\{ \tilde{W}_g^T \tilde{W}_g \right\}$$

Where $P > 0$ is chosen to satisfy the Lyapunov equation

$$P\Lambda_c + \Lambda_c^T P = -I$$

Taking the derivative of the Lyapunov function candidate we get

$$\dot{V} = \frac{1}{2} e^T \left(\Lambda_c^T P + P\Lambda_c \right) e + \frac{1}{2} \hat{x}^T \left(\Lambda_c^T P + P\Lambda_c \right) \hat{x} + e^T Pb_c X_f \tilde{W}_f S_f + e^T Pb_c X_g \tilde{W}_g S_g u + $$
$$+ \frac{1}{\gamma_1} tr\left\{ \dot{\tilde{W}}_f^T \tilde{W}_f \right\} + \frac{1}{\gamma_2} tr\left\{ \dot{\tilde{W}}_g^T \tilde{W}_g \right\}$$

when

$$tr\left\{ \dot{\tilde{W}}_f^T \tilde{W}_f \right\} = -\gamma_1 e^T Pb_c X_f \tilde{W}_f S_f$$

$$tr\left\{ \dot{\tilde{W}}_g^T \tilde{W}_g \right\} = -\gamma_2 e^T Pb_c X_g \tilde{W}_g S_g u$$

Then, taking into account the form of W_f and W_g the above equations result in the element wise learning laws given in (26), (27). These laws can also be written in the following compact form

$$\dot{W}_f = -\gamma_1 X_f^T b_c^T P e S_f^T \tag{28}$$

$$\dot{W}_g = -\gamma_2 X_g^T b_c^T P e u S_g^T \tag{29}$$

where e is a $n \times 1$ vector of the form $e = \begin{bmatrix} e_1, e_2, \ldots, e_n \end{bmatrix}^T$ and u is a scalar. Finally, the derivative of Lyapunov function candidate results

$$\dot{V} = -\frac{1}{2}\|e\|^2 - \frac{1}{2}\|\hat{x}\|^2 - e^T P b_c k e$$

$$\dot{V} = -\frac{1}{2}\|e\|^2 - \frac{1}{2}\|\hat{x}\|^2 + \|e\|^2 \|P b_c k\|$$

$$\dot{V} = -\begin{bmatrix} \|e\| & \|\hat{x}\| \end{bmatrix} \begin{bmatrix} \frac{1}{2} - \|P b_c k\| & 0 \\ 0 & \frac{1}{2} \end{bmatrix} \begin{bmatrix} \|e\| \\ \|\hat{x}\| \end{bmatrix} < 0$$

Using the above Lyapunov function candidate V and assuming that $\|P b_c k\| < \frac{1}{2}$ then we have proven that $\dot{V} \leq 0$. So, following the same lines of proof as in section 2.1 we have that all properties of theorem 3 are assured.

Theorem 4 below introduces the *hopping* in the updating law of weights.

Theorem 4: Consider the control scheme (22), (23), (25). The updating law:

a. For the elements of W_f given by (26)
b. For the elements of W_g given by the modified form

$$\dot{W}_{g_i} = \begin{cases} -\gamma_2 \left(X_g\right)^T b_c^T P e u s_i(x) & \begin{array}{l} if \left|X_g W_{g_i}\right| > \theta \\ or \ X_g W_{g_i} = \pm\theta \\ and \ X_g \dot{W}_{g_i} <> 0 \end{array} \\ -\gamma_2 \left(X_g\right)^T b_c^T P e u s_i(x) - \dfrac{2\left(X_g W_{g_i} \left(X_g\right)^T\right)}{tr\left\{\left(X_g\right)^T X_g\right\}} & \begin{array}{l} if \ 0 < X_g W_{g_i} < \theta \\ and \ X_g \dot{W}_{g_i} \geq 0 \\ or \ if - \theta < X_g W_{g_i} < 0 \\ and \ X_g \dot{W}_{g_i} \leq 0 \end{array} \end{cases}$$

The proof of theorem 4 is similar with that of theorem 2.

2.4 DIRECT ADAPTIVE NEURO-FUZZY CONTROL

This section is devoted to the development of direct adaptive neuro-fuzzy controller for affine in the control nonlinear dynamical systems (Theodoridis, Boutalis & Christodoulou, 2009). The fuzzy-recurrent high order neural networks are used as models of the unknown plant, practically transforming the original unknown system into a F-RHONN model which is of known structure, but contains a number of unknown constant value parameters, known as synaptic weights. The development leads to weight updating laws, which directly affect the control law without need of estimating the underlying model first. Actually, in the chosen representation the very parameters (weights) involved in the controller suffice for the description of the parameterized system model and this is an essential part in direct control schemes (see in (Ioannou & Fidan, 2006) for the relevant discussion). When the F-RHONN model matches the unknown plant, we provide a comprehensive and rigorous analysis of the stability properties of the closed loop system. Convergence of state to zero plus boundedness of all other signals in the closed loop is guaranteed without the need of parameter (weight) convergence, which is assured only if a sufficiency of excitation condition is satisfied.

2.4.1 Adaptive Regulation- Complete Matching

In this subsection we investigate the adaptive regulation problem with direct control, when the modelling error term is zero, or in other words, when we have complete model matching. Under this assumption the unknown system can be written as (3), where $x \in R^n$ is the system state vector, $u \in R^n$ are the control inputs, W_f^* is a $n \cdot m \times k$ matrix of synaptic weights, W_g^* is a $n \cdot m \times n$ block diagonal matrix and A is a $n \times n$ matrix with positive eigenvalues which for simplicity can be taken diagonal. Finally, X_f, X_g are $n \times n \cdot m$ block diagonal matrices, $S_f(x)$ is a k-dimensional vector and $S_g(x)$ is a $n \times n$ diagonal matrix with each diagonal element $s_i(x)$ being a high order combination of sigmoid functions of the state variables.

Let us take a function $h(x) : \Re^n \to \Re^+$ of class C^2 having the following form

$$h(x) = \frac{1}{2}|x|^2 = \frac{1}{2}x^T x \tag{30}$$

which involves the state variables.

The derivative of the above equation with respect to time and according to Eq. (3) is

$$\dot{h}(x) = \frac{\partial h^T}{\partial x}\frac{\partial x}{\partial t} = \frac{\partial h^T}{\partial x}\left[Ax + X_f W_f^* S_f(x) + X_g W_g^* S_g(x)u\right]$$

which is linear with respect to W_f^* and W_g^* and can be written as

$$\dot{h} - \frac{\partial h^T}{\partial x}Ax = \frac{\partial h^T}{\partial x}X_f W_f^* S_f(x) + \frac{\partial h^T}{\partial x}X_g W_g^* S_g(x)u \tag{31}$$

Define now, the e_{est} as

$$e_{est} = \frac{\partial h^T}{\partial x}X_f W_f S_f(x) + \frac{\partial h^T}{\partial x}X_g W_g S_g(x)u - \dot{h} + \frac{\partial h^T}{\partial x}Ax \tag{32}$$

After substituting Eq. (31), Eq. (32) becomes

$$e_{est} = \frac{\partial h^T}{\partial x} X_f \tilde{W}_f S_f(x) + \frac{\partial h^T}{\partial x} X_g \tilde{W}_g S_g(x) u \tag{33}$$

where W_f and W_g are estimates of W_f^* and W_g^* respectively, obtained by update laws which are to be designed in the sequel. This signal cannot be measured since $\dot{h}$ is unknown. To overcome this problem, we use the following filtered version of e_{est}

$$e_{est} = \dot{e}_f + \kappa e_f$$

and according to Eq. (32) we have that

$$\dot{e}_f + \kappa e_f = -\dot{h} + \frac{\partial h^T}{\partial x}\left[Ax + X_f W_f S_f(x) + X_g W_g S_g(x) u \right] \tag{34}$$

where κ is a strictly positive constant. To implement Eq. (34), we take

$$e_f = z - h \tag{35}$$

Employing Eq. (35), Eq. (34) can be written as

$$\dot{z} + \kappa z = \kappa h + \frac{\partial h^T}{\partial x}\left[Ax + X_f W_f S_f(x) + X_g W_g S_g(x) u \right] \tag{36}$$

with state $z \in \Re$. This method is referred to as error filtering. Furthermore, Eq. (36) substituting Eq. (30) becomes

$$\dot{z} + \kappa z = \kappa h - x^T Ax + x^T X_f W_f S_f(x) + x^T X_g W_g S_g(x) u \tag{37}$$

To continue, consider the Lyapunov-like function

$$L\left(e_f, \tilde{W}_f, \tilde{W}_g\right) = \frac{1}{2}e_f^2 + \frac{1}{2\gamma_1}tr\left\{\tilde{W}_f^T \tilde{W}_f\right\} + \frac{1}{2\gamma_2}tr\left\{\tilde{W}_g^T \tilde{W}_g\right\} \tag{38}$$

If we take the derivative of Eq. (32) with respect to time we obtain

$$\dot{L} = \dot{e}_f e_f + \frac{1}{\gamma_1}tr\left\{\dot{\tilde{W}}_{f_n}^T \tilde{W}_{f_n}\right\} + \frac{1}{\gamma_2}tr\left\{\dot{\tilde{W}}_{g_n}^T \tilde{W}_{g_n}\right\} \tag{39}$$

Employing Eq. (34), Eq. (39) becomes

$$\dot{L} = -\kappa e_f^2 + e_f\left[-\dot{h} + x^T Ax + x^T X_f W_f S_f(x) + e_f x^T X_g W_g S_g(x) u \right]$$
$$+ \frac{1}{\gamma_1}tr\left\{\dot{\tilde{W}}_f^T \tilde{W}_f\right\} + \frac{1}{\gamma_2}tr\left\{\dot{\tilde{W}}_g^T \tilde{W}_g\right\} \tag{40}$$

which together with Eq. (31) gives

$$\dot{L} = -\kappa e_f^2 + e_f x^T X_f \tilde{W}_f S_f(x) + e_f x^T X_g \tilde{W}_g S_g(x)u$$
$$+ \frac{1}{\gamma_1} tr\left\{\dot{W}_f^T \tilde{W}_f\right\} + \frac{1}{\gamma_2} tr\left\{\dot{W}_g^T \tilde{W}_g\right\} \tag{41}$$

Hence, if we choose

$$tr\left\{\dot{W}_f^T \tilde{W}_f\right\} = -\gamma_1 e_f^T x^T X_f \tilde{W}_f S_f(x) \tag{42}$$

and

$$tr\left\{\dot{W}_g^T \tilde{W}_g\right\} = -\gamma_2 e_f^T x^T X_g \tilde{W}_g S_g(x)u \tag{43}$$

$\dot{L}$ becomes

$$\dot{L} = -\kappa e_f^2 \leq 0 \tag{44}$$

which means that $\dot{L}$ is negative semi definite. It can be easily verified that Eqs. (42), (43) after making the appropriate operations, can be element wise written as

a.   For the elements of W_{f_i}

$$\dot{w}_{f_i}^{pl}(x) = -\gamma_1 e_f \overline{x}_{f_i}^p x_i s_l(x) \tag{45}$$

b.   For the elements of W_{g_i}

$$\dot{w}_{g_i}^{pl}(x) = -\gamma_2 e_f \overline{x}_{g_i}^p u_i s_i(x) \tag{46}$$

or equivalently $\dot{W}_{g_i}(x) = -\gamma_2 \left(X_{g_i}\right)^T e_f x_i u_i s_i(x)$ with $i = 1,...,n$, $p = 1,...,m$ and $l = 1,...,k$.
Equations (45) and (46) can be finally written in a compact form as

$$\dot{W}_f = -\gamma_1 e_f X_f^T x S_f^T(x) \tag{47}$$

$$\dot{W}_g = -\gamma_2 e_f X_g^T x_d U S_g^T(x) \tag{48}$$

where e_f is a scalar magnitude, x_d is a diagonal matrix such that $x_d = diag\left[x_1, x_2,...,x_n\right]$ and $U = diag\left[u_1, u_2,...,u_n\right]$.
Now we can prove the following lemma

Lemma 1: Consider the system

$$\dot{x} = Ax + X_f W_f^* S_f(x) + X_g W_g^* S_g(x)u$$

$$\dot{z} = -\kappa z + \kappa h + x^T A x + x^T X_f W_f S_f(x)$$
$$+ x^T X_g W_g S_g(x)u$$

$$e_f = z - h$$

$$h(x) = \frac{1}{2}|x|^2$$

The update laws (47) and (48) guarantee the following properties

- $e_f, |x|, \tilde{W}_f, \tilde{W}_g, z \in L_\infty$, $\quad |e_f| \in L_2$
- $\lim_{t\to\infty} e_f(t) = 0$, $\lim_{t\to\infty} \dot{W}_f(t) = 0$, $\lim_{t\to\infty} \dot{W}_g(t) = 0$

provided that $u \in L_\infty$.

Proof: From Eq. (44) we have that $L \in L_\infty$ which implies $e_f, \tilde{W}_f, \tilde{W}_g \in L_\infty$. Since $u \in L_\infty$ then $x \in L_\infty$, hence $h \in L_\infty$. Furthermore, $e_f = z - h$, hence $z \in L_\infty$. Since L is a monotone decreasing function of time and bounded from below, the $\lim_{t\to\infty} L(t) = L_\infty$ exists so by integrating $\dot{L}$ from 0 to ∞ we have $\int_0^\infty \|e_f\|^2 dt \leq \frac{1}{\kappa}|L(0) - L_\infty| < \infty$ which implies that $|e_f| \in L_2$. We also have that

$$\dot{e}_f = -\kappa e_f + x^T X_f \tilde{W}_f S_f(x) + x^T X_g \tilde{W}_g S_g(x)u$$

Hence, $\dot{e}_f \in L_\infty$ provided that $u \in L_\infty$. Having in mind that $e_f \in L_2 \cap L_\infty$ and $\dot{e}_f \in L_\infty$, applying Barbalat's Lemma (Ioannou & Fidan, 2006) we conclude that $\lim_{t\to\infty} e_f(t) = 0$. Now, using the bounded ness of $u, S_f(x), S_g(x), x$ and the convergence of $e_f(t)$ to zero, we have that $\dot{W}_f(t), \dot{W}_g(t)$ also converge to zero.

To proceed further, we observe that $\dot{h}$ can be written as

$$\dot{h} = x^T \left[Ax + X_f W_f S_f(x) + X_g W_g S_g(x)u \right]$$
$$- x^T X_f \tilde{W}_f S_f(x) - x^T X_g \tilde{W}_g S_g(x)u$$

Hence, if we choose the control input u to be

$$u = -\left[X_g W_g S_g(x) \right]^{-1} \cdot \left(X_f W_f S_f(x) \right) \tag{49}$$

then $\dot{h}$ becomes

$$\dot{h} = x^T A x - x^T X_f \tilde{W}_f S_f(x) - x^T X_g \tilde{W}_g S_g(x)u \tag{50}$$

Moreover, Eq. (50) can be written

$$\dot{h} \leq -\frac{c}{2}|x|^2 - \dot{e}_f - \kappa e_f \tag{51}$$

where $c = 2n\lambda_{\min}(A)$, with $\lambda_{\min}(A)$ denoting the minimum eigenvalue of matrix A. Observe that Eq. (51) is equivalent to

$$\dot{h} = -ch - \dot{e}_f - \kappa e_f \tag{52}$$

Furthermore, according to Eq. (35), Eq. (52) becomes

$$\dot{z} \le -cz + ce_f - \kappa e_f \le -cz + (c + \kappa)\left|e_f\right| \tag{53}$$

which as it will be seen later, can be used to prove that $x(t) \to 0$.

To assure the existence of the control law u in (49), the existence of $\left[X_g W_g S_g(x)\right]^{-1}$ has to be assured. This can be done by using the hopping technique already introduced in the previous sections. Theorem 5 below introduces this *hopping* in the weight updating law.

Theorem 5: Consider the control scheme described from equations (47), (48), (49) and (50). The updating law:

a.   For the elements of W_{f_i} given by (45)
b.   For the elements of W_{g_i} given by (46) modified according to the hopping method:

$$\dot{W}_{g_i} = \begin{cases} -\gamma_2\left(X_{g_i}\right)^T e_f x_i u_i s_i(x) & \begin{array}{l} \text{if } \left|X_{g_i} W_{g_i}\right| > \theta_i \\ \text{or } X_{g_i} W_{g_i} = \pm\theta_i \\ \text{and } X_{g_i}\dot{W}_{g_i} <> 0 \end{array} \\ -\gamma_2\left(X_{g_i}\right)^T e_f x_i u_i s_i(x) - \dfrac{2\left(X_{g_i} W_{g_i}\left(X_{g_i}\right)^T\right)}{tr\left\{\left(X_{g_i}\right)^T X_{g_i}\right\}} & \begin{array}{l} \text{if } 0 < X_{g_i} W_{g_i} < \theta_i \\ \text{and } X_{g_i}\dot{W}_{g_i} \ge 0 \\ \text{or if } -\theta_i < X_{g_i} W_{g_i} < 0 \\ \text{and } X_{g_i}\dot{W}_{g_i} \le 0 \end{array} \end{cases} \tag{54}$$

guarantees the properties of lemma 1 and assures the existence of the control signal, as have been shown in theorem 3.

The inclusion of weight hopping in the weights updating law guarantees that the control signal does not go to infinity. Apart from that, it is also of practical use to assure that $X_g W_g S_g(x)$ does not take even temporarily very large values because in this case the method may become algorithmically unstable driving at the same time the control signal to zero failing to control the system. To assure that this situation does not happen we have again to assure that $\left|X_{g_i} \cdot W_{g_i}\right| < \rho_i$ with ρ_i being again a design parameter determining an external limit for $X_{g_i} \cdot W_{g_i}$. Following the same lines of thought with the case of weight hopping introduced above we could again consider the forbidden hyper planes being defined by the equation $\left|X_{g_i} \cdot W_{g_i}\right| = \rho_i$. When the weight vector reaches one of the forbidden hyper planes $X_{g_i} \cdot W_{g_i} = \rho_i$ and the direction of updating is toward the forbidden hyper-plane, a new *hopping* is introduced which moves the weights to the other forbidden hyper-plane keeping however the direction of the updating intact. This procedure is depicted in Figure 3, in a simplified 2-dimensional representation.

Figure 3. Pictorial representation of inner and outer parameter hopping

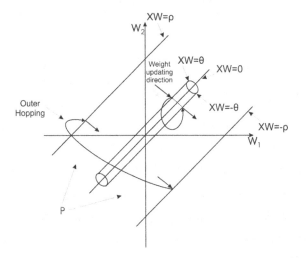

The magnitude of hopping is $-\dfrac{2\left(X_{g_i}W_{g_i}\left(X_{g_i}\right)^T\right)}{tr\left\{\left(X_{g_i}\right)^T X_{g_i}\right\}}$ being determined by following again the same

vectorial proof of section 2.1 and Figure 2. By performing *hopping* when $X_{g_i} \cdot W_{g_i}$ reaches either the inner or outer forbidden planes, $X_{g_i} \cdot W_{g_i}$ is confined to lie in space P defined by these hyper-planes. The weight updating law for W_{g_i} incorporating the two hopping conditions can now be expressed as

$$\dot{W}_{g_i} = \begin{cases} -\gamma_2\left(X_{g_i}\right)^T e_j x_i u_i s_i(x) & \begin{array}{l} if\ X_{g_i} \cdot W_{g_i} \in P\ or\ X_{g_i} \cdot W_{g_i} = \left(\pm\theta_i\ or\ \pm\rho_i\right) \\ and\ X_{g_i} \cdot \dot{W}_{g_i} <> 0\ or\ >< 0 \end{array} \\[2em] -\gamma_2\left(X_{g_i}\right)^T e_j x_i u_i s_i(x) - \dfrac{2\left(X_{g_i}W_{g_i}\left(X_{g_i}\right)^T\right)}{tr\left\{\left(X_{g_i}\right)^T X_{g_i}\right\}} & \begin{array}{l} if\ 0 < X_{g_i} \cdot W_{g_i} < \theta_i\ and\ X_{g_i} \cdot \dot{W}_{g_i} \geq 0 \\ or\ if\ -\theta_i < X_{g_i} \cdot W_{g_i} < 0\ and\ X_{g_i} \cdot \dot{W}_{g_i} < 0 \\ or\ if\ 0 < X_{g_i} \cdot W_{g_i} < -\rho_i\ and\ X_{g_i} \cdot \dot{W}_{g_i} \geq 0 \\ or\ if\ X_{g_i} \cdot W_{g_i} > \rho_i\ and\ X_{g_i} \cdot \dot{W}_{g_i} < 0 \end{array} \end{cases}$$

(55)

The following lemma presents the properties of the hopping algorithm in detail.

Lemma 2: The updating law (55) incorporating the two hopping conditions, can only make Lyapunov derivative more negative and in addition guarantee that $X_{g_i} \cdot W_{g_i} \in P$ for all $i = 1, 2, \ldots, n$, provided that $X_{g_i}(0) \cdot W_{g_i}(0) \in P$.

Proof: In order to prove that the hopping modification given by (55) can only make $\dot{L}$ more negative, we go with the following cases.

Case 1: Activation of first (inner) hopping condition $\left|X_{g_i} \cdot W_{g_i}\right| \leq \theta_i$

This case has already been examined in Theorem 5. $\dot{L}$ is augmented by the following quantity

$$\Re_a = -\frac{\Theta_{g,inner}}{\gamma_2} = -\sum \frac{2\theta_i\left(\left(W_{g_i}\right)^T W_{g_i}\right)}{\gamma_2\left\|W_{g_i}\right\|}$$

where the summation includes all weight vectors which require inner hopping. Obviously $\Re_a \leq 0$.

Case 2: Activation of second (outer) hopping condition $\left| X_{g_i} \cdot W_{g_i} \right| \geq \rho_i$

Following the same lines of proof as with Theorem 5 it is easy to conclude that in this case $\dot{L}$ is augmented by the following quantity

$$\Re_b = -\frac{\Theta_{g,outer}}{\gamma_2} = -\sum \frac{2\rho_i \left(\left(W_{g_i} \right)^T W_{g_i} \right)}{\gamma_2 \left\| W_{g_i} \right\|}$$

where the summation includes all weight vectors which require outer hopping. Obviously $\Re_b \leq 0$.

It is obvious that by following the procedure of inner or outer hopping, once the initial weights are such that $X_{g_i}(0) \cdot W_{g_i}(0) \in P$ then $X_{g_i} \cdot W_{g_i}$ will never leave P.

Lemma 3: Let η be a C^1 time function defined on $[0, T)$ where $0 \leq T \leq \infty$, satisfying

$$\dot{\eta} \leq -c\eta + a(t) + \beta(t),$$

where c is a strictly positive constant and $a(t)$, $\beta(t)$ are two positive time functions belonging to $L_2(0, T)$ that is

$$\int_0^T a^2(t)dt \leq M_1 < \infty,$$

and

$$\int_0^T \beta^2(t)dt \leq M_2 < \infty.$$

Under this assumption, $\eta(t)$ is upper bounded on $(0, T)$ and precisely

$$\eta(t) \leq e_f^{\frac{M_1}{c}} \left[\eta(0) + \sqrt{\frac{2}{c}} \sqrt{M_2} \right], \quad \forall t \in [0, T),$$

moreover, if T is infinite then

$$\lim_{t \to \infty} \sup \eta(t) \leq 0.$$

Observe that (53) with $\kappa = 1$ becomes

$$\dot{z} \leq -cz + (1+c)\left| e_f \right|, \tag{56}$$

however, from Lemma 1 we have that $\left| e_f \right| \in L_2$ so $(1 + c)\left| e_f \right| \in L_2$. Furthermore, observe that obviously T can be extended to be infinite. Hence, Lemma 3 can be applied in (56) with $M_1 = 0$ to obtain

$$\lim_{t \to \infty} \sup z(t) \le 0 . \tag{57}$$

Moreover, since $h = z - e_f$ and $h \ge 0$ we have $z(t) \ge e_f(t)$, or

$$-z(t) \le -e_f(t) \tag{58}$$

but from Lemma 1 we have

$$\lim_{t \to \infty} e_f(t) = 0 \tag{59}$$

Hence, (58) together with (57) and (59) prove

$$\lim_{t \to \infty} z(t) = 0 \tag{60}$$

Furthermore, since $h = z - e_f$, (59) and (60) yield

$$\lim_{t \to \infty} h\left(x\left(t \right) \right) = 0 ,$$

which by the definition of $h\left(x\left(t \right) \right)$ finally implies that

$$\lim_{t \to \infty} x\left(t \right) = 0 ,$$

therefore, we have proven the following theorem.

Theorem 6: The closed loop system

$$\dot{x} = Ax + X_f W_f^* S_f(x) + X_g W_g^* S_g(x)u$$

$$\dot{z} = -\kappa z + \kappa h + x^T Ax + x^T X_f W_f S_f(x)$$
$$\quad + x^T X_g W_g S_g(x)u$$

$$u = -\left[X_g W_g S_g(x) \right]^{-1} \cdot \left(X_f W_f S_f(x) \right)$$

$$e_f = z - h$$

$$h(x) = \frac{1}{2}\left| x \right|^2$$

$$\kappa = 1$$

together with update laws given by (45) and (55)guarantee that

$$\lim_{t \to \infty} x\left(t\right) = 0 \, .$$

From the aforementioned analysis it is obvious that different choices of $h(x)$ and κ, lead to different adaptive regulators. It is anticipated that appropriate selection of κ, could attenuate the effects of the uncertainties that may be present.

Remark 2: The control law (49) can be also extended to the following form

$$u = -\left[X_g W_g S_g(x)\right]^{-1} \cdot \left(X_f W_f S_f(x) + Kx\right) \tag{61}$$

where K is a positive definite diagonal matrix defined by the designer. It can be easily verified that with this control law $\dot{h}$ becomes

$$\dot{h} = -x^T \Lambda x - x^T X_f \tilde{W}_f S_f(x) - x^T X_g \tilde{W}_g S_g(x) u$$

where $\Lambda = A + K$ is a stable matrix. Therefore, c in (49) becomes $c = 2n\lambda_{\min}(\Lambda)$, with $\lambda_{\min}(\Lambda)$ denoting the minimum eigenvalue of the Λ matrix. Since $\lambda_{\min}(A) \le \lambda_{\min}(\Lambda)$ the proof of theorem 6 is still valid with the property of $\lim_{t \to \infty} x\left(t\right) = 0$ being actually enhanced. Therefore term Kx is actually acting as a robustifying term.

2.5 SIMULATION EXAMPLES

To demonstrate the potency of the proposed scheme we present simulation results. The full potential of the method is demonstrated in the simulation, where the proposed method is compared with the well known RHONN approach (Rovithakis & Christodoulou, 2000) in approximating and regulating a Dc Motor described by nonlinear equations. In this case both modelling approaches assume a generic affine in the control form. Also, the well known benchmark problem of controlling Duffing Forced Oscillator is considered and compared with alternative RHONN's (Rovithakis & Christodoulou, 2000), showing a much better performance. Due to the Brunovsky canonical form of the system the proposed method operates in a reduced model order, which although performing fairly well, does not permit to show off its full potential. Finally, the proposed method was implemented and used to regulate the Lorenz system.

Example 1: DC Motor Identification and Control

In this example we present simulations, where the proposed approach is applied to solve the problem of controlling the speed of a 1 KW DC motor with a normalized model described by the following dynamical equations (Leonhard, 1985)

$$T_a \frac{dI_a}{dt} = -I_a - \Phi\Omega + V_a$$
$$T_m \frac{d\Omega}{dt} = \Phi I_a - K_0 \Omega \tag{62}$$
$$T_f \frac{d\Phi}{dt} = -I_f + V_f$$

with $\Phi = \dfrac{aI_f}{1 + bI_f}$. The states are chosen to be the armature current, the angular speed and the stator flux $x = \begin{bmatrix} I_a & \Omega & \Phi \end{bmatrix}^T$. As control inputs the armature and the field voltages $u = \begin{bmatrix} V_a & V_f \end{bmatrix}^T$ are used. With this choice, we have

$$\begin{bmatrix} \dot{x}_1 \\ \dot{x}_2 \\ \dot{x}_3 \end{bmatrix} = \begin{bmatrix} -\dfrac{1}{T_a}x_1 - \dfrac{1}{T_a}x_2 x_3 \\ \dfrac{1}{T_m}x_1 x_3 - \dfrac{K_0}{T_m}x_2 \\ -\dfrac{1}{T_f}\dfrac{x_3}{a - bx_3} \end{bmatrix} + \begin{bmatrix} \dfrac{1}{T_a} & 0 \\ 0 & 0 \\ 0 & \dfrac{1}{T_f} \end{bmatrix} \cdot \begin{bmatrix} u_1 \\ u_2 \end{bmatrix} \tag{63}$$

which is of a nonlinear, affine in the control form.

The regulation problem of a DC motor is translated as follows: Find a state feedback to force the angular velocity and the armature current to go to zero, while the magnetic flux varies.

When Φ is considered constant, the above nonlinear 3rd order system can be linearized and reduced to a second order form having 2 states ($x_1 = I_a$ and $x_2 = \Omega$), with the value Φ being included as a constant parameter. Inspired by that, we first assume that the system is described, within a degree of accuracy, by a 2nd order ($n = 2$) nonlinear neuro-fuzzy system of the form (5), where $x_1 = I_a$ and $x_2 = \Omega$. Coefficients a_i in matrix A of (5) were chosen to be $a_i = -15$. The number of fuzzy partitions in X_f was chosen to be $m = 5$ and the range of $f_1 = \begin{bmatrix} -182.5667, 0 \end{bmatrix}$ $f_2 = \begin{bmatrix} -19.3627, 30.0566 \end{bmatrix}$. The depth of high order terms was $k = 2$ (only first order sigmoidal terms $s(x_1)$, $s(x_2)$ were used). The number of fuzzy partitions of each $\overline{x}_{g_i}$ in X_g is $m = 3$ and the range of $\overline{x}_{g_1}$ is $\begin{bmatrix} 148, 150 \end{bmatrix}$ and of $\overline{x}_{g_2}$ is $\begin{bmatrix} 42, 44 \end{bmatrix}$ The general form of sigmoid functions is given in (Boutalis, Theodoridis & Christodoulou, (in press)). The parameters of the sigmoidal that have been used in this simulation are $\alpha_1 = 0.4$, $\alpha_2 = 5$, $b_1 = b_2 = 1$ and $c_1 = c_2 = 0$. In the simulations carried out, the actual system is simulated by using the complete set of equations (63). The produced control law (7) is applied on this system, which in turn produces states x_1, x_2, which in the sequel are used for the computation of the estimation errors that are employed by the updating laws.

We simulated a 1KW DC motor with parameter values that can be seen in Table 1. Our two stage algorithm was applied.

Table 1. Parameter values for the DC motor

Parameter	Value
$1/T_a$	148.88 sec^{-1}
$1/T_m$	42.91 sec^{-1}
K_0/T_m	0.0129 sec^{-1}
T_f	31.88 sec
a	2.6
b	1.6

Figure 4. Evolution of error e_2 for F-RHONN and RHONN respectively. The error of RHONN is much larger

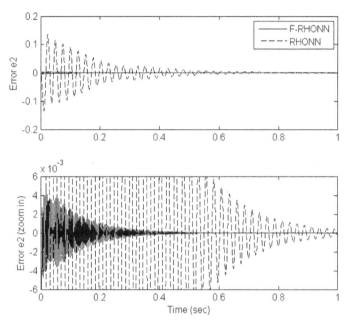

For comparison purposes we test the identification abilities of the proposed F-RHONN model against the conventional RHONN approximator presented in (Rovithakis & Christodoulou, 2000) using equivalent parameters regarding learning rate and number of high order terms used. Fig. 4 shows the performance of the proposed scheme (blue line) against the corresponding performance of RHONN (red line). In the embedded figure a detailed comparison between the two methods for the first iterations is presented, where the graph is adjusted to the scale of the lower error values (those of the F-RHONN model). The mean square error (MSE) was measured to be $5,87 \cdot 10^{-5}$ for the proposed scheme and $1,18 \cdot 10^{-2}$ for RHONN showing that the proposed scheme performs much better.

In the control phase, we assumed that the system variables have the initial values $\Omega = 0.1$, $I_a = 0.1$ $\Phi = 0.98$. The proposed feedback control law and the corresponding control law of (Rovithakis & Christodoulou, 2000) were applied, with the corresponding initial weight values resulted from the identification phase. Figure 5 give the evolution of the armature current, for F-RHONN and RHONN. As can be seen, both I_a converge to zero very fast as desired and the corresponding mean squared errors are 0.0013 and 0.0094 for x_2 (F-RHONN Vs RHONN approach), demonstrating a significant improvement when the proposed method is used.

Example 2: Indirect control of the well known benchmark 'Duffing Forced Oscillator'.

Its dynamical equations can assume the following Brunovsky canonical form (Slotine & Li, 1997)

$$\dot{x}_1 = x_2$$
$$\dot{x}_2 = -0.1x_2 - x_1^3 + u \tag{64}$$

Figure 5. Convergence of the armature current to zero from 0.1 initially

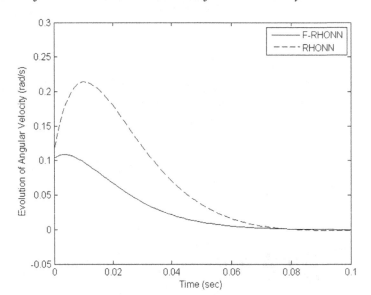

In the identification phase, we use the parameters $a_i = 15$ and the range of $f_1 = \left[-23.5667\,,\,10.0532\right]$ $f_2 = \left[-6.3627\,,\,5.0566\right]$ and $g_2 = \left[0.8\,,\,1.2\right]$. The input were chosen to be $u = 1 + 0.8\sin\left(0.001t\right)$ All initial values were set to zero.

The depth of high order terms was $k = 2$ (only first order sigmoidal terms $s(x_1)$, $s(x_2)$ were used).

It is our intention to compare the indirect control abilities of the proposed neuro-fuzzy approach with RHONN's (Rovithakis & Christodoulou, 2000) (page 35-39). We also, make the appropriate changes to RHONN's in order to be equivalent with F-RHONN 's (Brunovsky form) for comparison purposes.

For the proposed F-RHONN approach we use the adaptive and the control laws described by Theorem 4.

Numerical training data were obtained by using Eqs. (64) with initial conditions $\left[x_1(0)\quad x_2(0)\right] = \left[0.3\quad 0.4\right]$ and sampling time 10^{-3} sec.

Our neuro-fuzzy model was chosen to use 5 output partitions of f and 5 output partitions of g. The number of high order sigmoidal terms (HOST) used in HONN's (for F-RHONN and RHONN) were chosen to be 5 $\left(s(x_1), s(x_2), s(x_1) \cdot s(x_2), s^2(x_1), s^2(x_2)\right)$ for both benchmarks. Also, we have chosen the initial weights from the identification phase.

In order our model to be equivalent with RHONN's regarding other parameters we have chosen the updating learning rates to be $\gamma_1 = 0.01$ and $\gamma_2 = 0.1$. Also, the parameters of the sigmoidal terms were chosen such as $a_1 = 0.1$, $a_2 = 4$, $b_1 = b_2 = 1$ and $c_1 = c_2 = 0$. Finally, the constant values for Λ_c matrix were $k_1 = 4$ and $k_2 = 9$. Fig. (6) gives the evolution of state x_2, the evolution of error e_2 and control input u (with blue line for F-RHONN corresponding approach and red line for RHONN's).

As can be seen, x_2 converge to zero fast as desired and the corresponding mean squared errors are 0.0104 and 0.0186 for x_2 (F-RHONN Vs RHONN approaches), demonstrating a significant improvement when the proposed method is used.

Figure 6. Convergence of speed to zero from 0.3 (p.u) initially. Upper figure: Speed (state x_2), Middle figure: Error with respect to zero, Lower figure: Evolution of the control signals (RHONN-dotted, F-RHONN-solid lines)

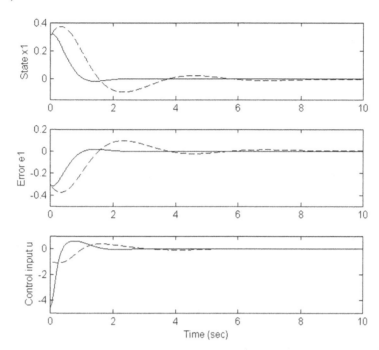

Example 4: Direct control of Lorenz system with parametric uncertainties.

The Lorenz system was derived to model the two-dimensional convection flow of a fluid layer heated from below and cooled from above. The model represents the Earth's atmosphere heated by the ground's absorption of sunlight and losing heat into space. It can be described by the following dynamical equations

$$
\begin{aligned}
\dot{x}_1 &= \sigma\left(x_2 - x_1\right) \\
\dot{x}_2 &= \rho x_1 - x_2 - x_1 x_3 \\
\dot{x}_3 &= -\beta x_3 + x_1 x_2
\end{aligned}
\tag{65}
$$

where x_1, x_2 and x_3 represent measures of fluid velocity, horizontal and vertical temperature variations, correspondingly. The parameters σ, ρ and β are positive and represent the Prandtl number, Rayleigh number and geometric factor, correspondingly. Selecting $\sigma = 10$, $\rho = 28$ and $\beta = \dfrac{8}{3}$ the system presents three unstable equilibrium points and the system trajectory wanders forever near a strange invariant set called strange attractor presenting thus a chaotic behaviour (Yeap & Ahmed, 1994).

However, the Lorenz system including control inputs can be expressed as (Yeap & Ahmed, 1994)

$$
\begin{aligned}
\dot{x}_1 &= \sigma\left(x_2 - x_1\right) + u_1 \\
\dot{x}_2 &= \rho x_1 - x_2 - x_1 x_3 + u_2 \\
\dot{x}_3 &= -\beta x_3 + x_1 x_2 + u_3
\end{aligned}
\tag{66}
$$

Figure 7. Convergence of states x_1, x_2 and x_3 to zero

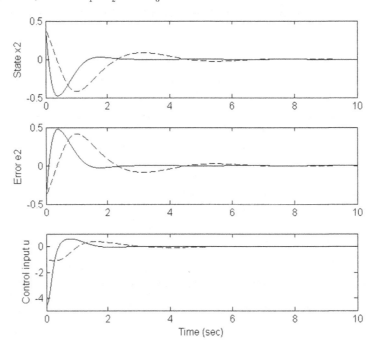

The control objective is to derive appropriate state feedback control law to regulate the system to one of its equilibrium, which is $(0,0,0)$. In particular, we consider that (66) has the following initial condition

$$x_0 = \left[-0.5, 0.8, 2\right]^T$$

The main parameters for the control law (61) and the learning laws (45), (55) are selected as

$$A = diag\left(-20, -10, -40\right) \text{ and } K = diag\left(21, 38, 40\right).$$

The parameters of the sigmoidal that have been used are $a_1 = a_2 = a_3 = 1$, $b_1 = b_2 = b_3 = 1$ and $c_1 = c_2 = c_3 = 0$.

In the sequel, we first assume that the system is described, within a degree of accuracy, by a neuro-fuzzy system of the form (37) with the number of states being $n = 3$, the number of fuzzy partitions being $m = 5$ and the depth of high order sigmoid terms $k = 9$. In this case $s_i(x)$ assume high order connection up to the second order.

Figure (7) shows the convergence of states x_1, x_2 and x_3 to zero exponentially fast.

FUTURE TRENDS

Future work will include the extension of the proposed algorithm to control systems in general MIMO non Brunovsky form, where the number of inputs is different than the number of states. Also, by using adaptive techniques for the calculation of fuzzy partitions of system states, this would give fully independence of any a-priori information related to the underlying fuzzy system.

CONCLUSION

Indirect and Direct adaptive control schemes were considered in this chapter, aiming at the regulation of non linear unknown plants. The approach is based on a new neuro-fuzzy dynamical systems definition, which uses the concept of adaptive fuzzy systems (AFS) operating in conjunction with high order neural networks (F-HONN's). Since the plant is considered unknown, we first propose its approximation by a special form of an affine in the control fuzzy dynamical system (FDS) and in the sequel the fuzzy rules are approximated by appropriate HONN's. Once the system is identified around an operation point is regulated to zero adaptively. The proposed scheme does not require a-priori expert's information on the number and type of input variable membership functions making it less vulnerable to initial design assumptions. Weight updating laws for the involved HONN's are provided, which guarantee that both the identification error and the system states reach zero exponentially fast, while keeping all signals in the closed-loop bounded. A method of parameter hopping assures the existence of the control signal and is incorporated in the weight updating law. Simulations illustrate the potency of the method by comparing its performance with this of established conventional approaches on benchmark problems.

REFERENCES

Adetona, O., Sathananthan, S., & Keel, L. H. (2002). Robust adaptive control of nonaffine nonlinear plants with small input signal changes. *IEEE Transactions on Neural Networks*, *15*(2), 408–416. doi:10.1109/TNN.2004.824423

Antsaklis, P. J., & Passino, K. M. (1993). *An Introduction to Intelligent and Autonomous Control*. Norwell, MA: Kluwer Academic Publishers.

Bong, J. Y., & Calise, A. J. (2007). Adaptive Control of a Class of Nonaffine Systems Using Neural Networks. *IEEE Transactions on Neural Networks*, *18*(4), 1149–1159. doi:10.1109/TNN.2007.899253

Boutalis, Y. S., Theodoridis, D. C., & Christodoulou, M. A. (2009). A new Neuro FDS definition for indirect adaptive control of unknown nonlinear systems using a method of parameter hopping. *IEEE Transactions on Neural Networks*, *20*(4), 609–625. doi:10.1109/TNN.2008.2010772

Boutalis, Y. S., Theodoridis, D. C., & Christodoulou, M. A. (2010). Identification of Nonlinear Systems Using a New Neuro-Fuzzy Dynamical System Definition Based on High Order Neural Network Function Approximators. *Chapter 18 in Artificial Higher Order Neural Networks for Computer Science and Engineering: Trends for Emerging Applications (M. Zhang Ed.)*. Pennsylvania: IGI Global.

Chen, B. S., Lee, C. H., & Chang, Y. C. (1996). Tracking design of uncertain nonlinear siso systems: Adaptive fuzzy approach. *IEEE transactions on Fuzzy Systems*, *4*, 32–43. doi:10.1109/91.481843

Chen, F. C., & Liu, C. C. (1994). Adaptively controlling nonlinear continuous-time systems using multilayer neural networks. *IEEE Transactions on Automatic Control*, *39*, 1306–1310. doi:10.1109/9.293202

Cho, K. B., & Wang, B. H. (1996). Radial basis function based adaptive fuzzy systems and their applications to system identification and prediction. *Fuzzy Sets and Systems*, *83*, 325–339. doi:10.1016/0165-0114(95)00322-3

Christodoulou, M. A., Theodoridis, D. C., & Boutalis, Y. S. (2007). Building Optimal Fuzzy Dynamical Systems Description Based on Recurrent Neural Network Approximation. In Proc. *Int. Conf. of Networked Distributed Systems for Intelligent Sensing and Control* (pp. 386-393). Kalamata, Greece.

Chui, S. L. (1994). Fuzzy model identification based on cluster estimation. *Journal of Intelligent and Fuzzy Systems*, *2*, 267–278. doi:10.1109/91.324806

Diao, Y., & Passino, K. M. (2002). Adaptive Neural/Fuzzy Control for Interpolated Nonlinear Systems. *IEEE transactions on Fuzzy Systems*, *10*(5), 583–595. doi:10.1109/TFUZZ.2002.803493

Ge, S. S., & Jing, W. (2002). Robust adaptive neural control for a class of perturbed strict feedback nonlinear systems. *IEEE Transactions on Neural Networks*, *13*(6), 1409–1419. doi:10.1109/TNN.2002.804306

Golea, N., Golea, A., & Benmahammed, K. (2003). Stable indirect fuzzy adaptive control. *Fuzzy Sets and Systems*, *137*, 353–366. doi:10.1016/S0165-0114(02)00279-8

Hayakawa, T., Haddad, W. M., Hovakimyan, N., & Chellaboina, V. (2005). Neural network adaptive control for nonlinear nonnegative dynamical systems. *IEEE Transactions on Neural Networks*, *16*(2), 399–413. doi:10.1109/TNN.2004.841791

Hojati, M., & Gazor, S. (2002). Hybrid Adaptive Fuzzy Identification and Control of Nonlinear Systems. *IEEE transactions on Fuzzy Systems*, *10*, 198–210. doi:10.1109/91.995121

Hornik, K., Stinchcombe, M., & White, H. (1989). Multilayer feed forward networks are universal approximators. *International Journal of Neural Networks*, *2*, 359–366. doi:10.1016/0893-6080(89)90020-8

Hovakimyan, N., Lavretsky, E., Bong, J. Y., & Calise, A. J. (2005). Coordinated decentralized adaptive output feedback control of interconnected systems. *IEEE Transactions on Neural Networks*, *16*(1), 185–194. doi:10.1109/TNN.2004.836198

Ioannou, P., & Fidan, B. (2006). *Adaptive control tutorial*. SIAM: Advances in Design and Control Series.

Jang, C. F., & Lin, C. T. (1998). An online self-constructing neural fuzzy inference network and its applications. *IEEE transactions on Fuzzy Systems*, *6*, 12–32. doi:10.1109/91.660805

Jang, J. S. R. (1993). ANFIS: Adaptive-network-based fuzzy inference system. *IEEE Transactions on Systems, Man, and Cybernetics*, *23*, 665–684. doi:10.1109/21.256541

Kosmatopoulos, E. B., & Christodoulou, M. A. (1996). Recurrent neural networks for approximation of fuzzy dynamical systems. *International Journal of Intelligent Control and Systems*, *1*, 223–233. doi:10.1142/S0218796596000143

Lee, C., & Teng, C. (2000). Identification and Control of Dynamic Systems Using Recurrent Fuzzy Neural Networks. *IEEE transactions on Fuzzy Systems*, *8*, 349–366. doi:10.1109/91.868943

Leonhard, W. (1985). *Control of Electrical Drives*. Springer-Verlag.

Leu, Y., Wang, W., & Lee, T. (2005). Observer-Based Direct Adaptive Fuzzy-Neural Control for Nonaffine Nonlinear Systems. *IEEE Transactions on Neural Networks*, *16*, 853–861. doi:10.1109/TNN.2005.849824

Lewis, F., Jagannathan, L. S., & Yesildirek, A. (1999). *Neural Network Control of Robot Manipulators and Nonlinear Systems*. Philadelphia, PA: Taylor and Fransis.

Li, R. P., & Mukaidono, M. (1995). A new approach to rule learning based on fusion of fuzzy logic and neural networks. *Institute of Electronics Information and Communication Engineers Transactions on Fuzzy Systems*, *78*, 1509–1514.

Lin, C. T. (1995). A neural fuzzy control system with structure and parameter learning. *Fuzzy Sets and Systems*, *70*, 183–212. doi:10.1016/0165-0114(94)00216-T

Lin, Y. H., & Cunningham, G. A. (1995). A new approach to fuzzy-neural system modelling. *IEEE Engineers Transactions on Fuzzy Systems*, *3*, 190–197. doi:10.1109/91.388173

Lina, T., Wang, C., & Liub, H. (2004). Observer-based indirect adaptive fuzzy-neural tracking control for nonlinear SISO systems using VSS and H_1 approaches. *Fuzzy Sets and Systems*, *143*, 211–232. doi:10.1016/S0165-0114(03)00167-2

Maggiore, M., & Passino, K. M. (2005). Output Feedback Tracking: A Separation Principle Approach. *IEEE Transactions on Automatic Control*, *50*(1), 111–117. doi:10.1109/TAC.2004.841126

Mitra, S., & Hayashi, Y. (2000). Neuro-fuzzy rule generation: survey in soft computing framework. *IEEE Transactions on Neural Networks*, *11*, 748–768. doi:10.1109/72.846746

Narendra, K. S., & Parthasarathy, K. (1990). Identification and control of dynamical systems using neural networks. *IEEE Transactions on Neural Networks*, *1*, 4–27. doi:10.1109/72.80202

Nounou, H. N., & Passino, K. M. (2004). Stable Auto-Tuning of Adaptive Fuzzy/Neural Controllers for Nonlinear Discrete-Time Systems. *IEEE transactions on Fuzzy Systems*, *12*(1), 70–83. doi:10.1109/TFUZZ.2003.822680

Nounou, H. N., & Passino, K. M. (2005). Stable Auto-Tuning of Hybrid Adaptive Fuzzy/Neural Controllers for Nonlinear Systems. *Engineering Applications of Artificial Intelligence*, *18*(3), 317–334. doi:10.1016/j.engappai.2004.09.005

Ordonez, R., & Passino, K. M. (2001). Adaptive Control for a Class of Nonlinear Systems with Time-Varying Structure. *IEEE Transactions on Automatic Control*, *46*(1), 152–155. doi:10.1109/9.898709

Ordonez, R., Zumberge, J., Spooner, J. T., & Passino, K. M. (1997). Adaptive Fuzzy Control: Experiments and Comparative Analyses. *IEEE transactions on Fuzzy Systems, 5*(2), 167–187. doi:10.1109/91.580793

Park, J. H., Huh, S. H., Seo, S. J., & Park, G. T. (2005). Direct adaptive controller for nonaffine nonlinear systems using self-structuring neural networks. *IEEE Transactions on Neural Networks, 16*(2), 414–422. doi:10.1109/TNN.2004.841786

Passino, K. M., & Yurkovich, S. (1998). *Fuzzy Control*. Menlo Park, CA: Addison Wesley Longman.

Polycarpou, M. M., & Mears, M. J. (1998). Stable adaptive tracking of uncertain systems using nonlinearly parameterized online approximators. *International Journal of Control, 70*(3), 363–384. doi:10.1080/002071798222280

Psillakis, H. E., & Alexandridis, A. T. (2007). NN-Based Adaptive Tracking Control of Uncertain Nonlinear Systems Disturbed by Unknown Covariance Noise. *IEEE Transactions on Neural Networks, 18*(6), 1830–1835. doi:10.1109/TNN.2007.901274

Rovithakis, G. A., & Christodoulou, M. A. (1994). Adaptive control of unknown plants using dynamical neural networks. *IEEE Transactions on Systems, Man, and Cybernetics, 24*, 400–412. doi:10.1109/21.278990

Rovithakis, G. A., & Christodoulou, M. A. (1995). Direct adaptive regulation of unknown nonlinear dynamical systems via dynamic neural networks. *IEEE Transactions on Systems, Man, and Cybernetics, 25*, 1578–1594. doi:10.1109/21.478444

Rovithakis, G. A., & Christodoulou, M. A. (2000). *Adaptive Control with Recurrent High Order Neural Networks (Theory and Industrial Applications), in Advances in Industrial Control*. (M.A. Grimble and M.A. Johnson Eds.), London: Springer Verlag.

Sbarbaro, D., & Johansen, T.A. (2006). Analysis of Artificial Neural Networks for Pattern-Based Adaptive Control. *IEEE Transactions on Neural Networks, 17*(5), 1184–1193. doi:10.1109/TNN.2006.879762

Shuzhi, S. G., & Thanh, T. H. (2007). Semiglobal ISpS Disturbance Attenuation With Output Tracking via Direct Adaptive Design. *IEEE Transactions on Neural Networks, 18*(4), 1129–1148. doi:10.1109/TNN.2007.899159

Slotine, J. E., & Li, W. (1997). *It Applied Nonlinear Control*. Englewood Cliffs, NJ: Prentice-Hall.

Spooner, J. T., Maggiore, M., Ordonez, R., & Passino, K. M. (2002). *Stable Adaptive Control and Estimation for Nonlinear Systems: Neural and Fuzzy Approximator Techniques*. NY: John Wiley and Sons.

Spooner, J. T., & Passino, K. M. (1996). Stable adaptive control using fuzzy systems and neural networks. *IEEE transactions on Fuzzy Systems, 4*, 339–359. doi:10.1109/91.531775

Theodoridis, D. C., Boutalis, Y. S., & Christodoulou, M. A. (2009). Direct Adaptive Control of Unknown Nonlinear Systems Using a new Neuro-Fuzzy Method Together with a Novel Approach of Parameter Hopping . *Kybernetica, 45*(3), 349–386.

Theodoridis, D. C., Christodoulou, M. A., & Boutalis, Y. S. (2008). Indirect Adaptive Neuro - Fuzzy Control Based On High Order Neural Network Function Approximators. In *Proc. 16th Mediterranean Conference on Control and Automation - MED08* (pp. 386-393). Ajaccio, Corsica, France.

Theodoridis, D. C., Christodoulou, M. A., & Boutalis, Y. S. (2009). Direct Adaptive Control of Unknown Nonlinear Systems with Robustness Analysis using a new Neuro-Fuzzy Representation and a Novel Approach of Parameter Hopping. In *17th Mediterranean Conference on Control and Automation - MED09* (pp. 558-563). Thessalonica, Greece.

Wang, L. (1994). *Adaptive Fuzzy Systems and Control*. Englewood Cliffs, NJ: Prentice Hall.

Yeap, T. H., & Ahmed, N. U. (1994). Feedback Control of Chaotic Systems. *Dynamics and Control, 4,* 97–114. doi:10.1007/BF02115741

Yih, G. L., Wei, Y. W., & Tsu, T. L. (2005). Observer-based direct adaptive fuzzy-neural control for nonaffine nonlinear systems. *IEEE Transactions on Neural Networks, 16*(4), 853–861. doi:10.1109/TNN.2005.849824

Chapter 20

Back–Stepping Control of Quadrotor:
A Dynamically Tuned Higher Order Like Neural Network Approach

Abhijit Das
The University of Texas at Arlington, USA

Frank Lewis
The University of Texas at Arlington, USA

Kamesh Subbarao
The University of Texas at Arlington, USA

ABSTRACT

The dynamics of a quadrotor is a simplified form of helicopter dynamics that exhibit the same basic problems of strong coupling, multi-input/multi-output design, and unknown nonlinearities. The Lagrangian model of a typical quadrotor that involves four inputs and six outputs results in an underactuated system. There are several design techniques are available for nonlinear control of mechanical underactuated system. One of the most popular among them is backstepping. Backstepping is a well known recursive procedure where underactuation characteristic of the system is resolved by defining 'desired' virtual control and virtual state variables. Virtual control variables is determined in each recursive step assuming the corresponding subsystem is Lyapunov stable and virtual states are typically the errors of actual and desired virtual control variables. The application of the backstepping even more interesting when a virtual control law is applied to a Lagrangian subsystem. The necessary information to select virtual control and state variables for these systems can be obtained through model identification methods. One of these methods includes Neural Network approximation to identify the unknown parameters of the system. The unknown parameters may include uncertain aerodynamic force and moment coefficients or unmodeled dynamics. These aerodynamic coefficients generally are the functions of higher order state polynomials. In this chapter we will discuss how we can implement linear in parameter first order neural network approximation methods to identify these unknown higher order state polynomials in every recursive step of the backstepping. Thus the first order neural network eventually estimates the higher

DOI: 10.4018/978-1-61520-711-4.ch020

order state polynomials which is in fact a higher order like neural net (HOLNN). Moreover, when these NN placed into a control loop, they become dynamic NN whose weights are tuned only. Due to the inherent characteristics of the quadrotor, the Lagrangian form for the position dynamics is bilinear in the controls, which is confronted using a bilinear inverse kinematics solution. The result is a controller of intuitively appealing structure having an outer kinematics loop for position control and an inner dynamics loop for attitude control. The stability of the control law is guaranteed by a Lyapunov proof. The control approach described in this chapter is robust since it explicitly deals with unmodeled state dependent disturbances without needing any prior knowledge of the same. A simulation study validates the results such as decoupling, tracking etc obtained in the paper.

1. INTRODUCTION

Nowadays helicopters are designed to operate with greater agility and rapid maneuvering, and are capable of work in degraded environments including wind gusts etc. Helicopter control often requires holding at a particular trimmed state, generally hover, as well as making changes of velocity and acceleration in a desired way (T. J. Koo & Sastry). The control of unmanned rotorcraft is also becoming more and more important due to their usefulness in rescue, surveillance, inspection, mapping etc. For these applications the ability of the rotorcraft to maneuver sharply and hover precisely is important.

Like fixed-wing aircraft control, rotorcraft control is also involved in controlling attitude pitch, yaw, and roll- and position, either separately or in a coupled way. But the main difference is that, due to the unique body structure of a rotorcraft, as well as the rotor dynamics, the attitude dynamics and position dynamics are strongly coupled. Therefore, it is very difficult to design a decoupled control law of good structure that stabilizes the faster and slower dynamics simultaneously. On the contrary, for a fixed wing aircraft it is easy to design decoupled standard control laws (B. L. Stevens & Lewis, 2003) with intuitively comprehensible performance. Controllers of good structure are needed for robustness, as well as to give some intuitive feel for the functioning of autopilots, Stability Augmentation System (SAS), and Control Augmentation System (CAS).

The dynamics of a quadrotor (A. Mokhtari, A. Benallegue, & Daachi, 2006; A. Mokhtari, A. Benallegue, & Orlov, 2006; P. Castillo, R. Lozano, & Dzul, 2005a; S. Bouabdallah, A. Noth, & Siegwart, 2004; T. Madani & Benallegue, 2006) are a simplified form of rotorcraft dynamics that exhibit the basic problems including underactuation, strong coupling, multi-input/multi-output design, and unknown nonlinearities. In the quadrotor, the movement is characterized by the resultant forces and moments of four independent rotors. Control design for a quadrotor is quite similar to a rotorcraft; therefore the quadrotor serves as a suitable, more tractable, case study for rotorcraft controls design. In view of the similarities between a quadrotor and a rotorcraft, control design for the quadrotor reveals corresponding approaches for rotorcraft control design. The 6-DOF airframe dynamics of a typical quadrotor involves force and moment dynamics in which the position dynamics often appear as kinematics. Backstepping control is one of the solutions to handle such coupled dynamic-kinematic systems.

There are many approaches such as (C. D. Yang & Liu, 2003; R. Enns & Si, 2000; R. Mahony & Hamel, 2005; V. Mistler, A. Benallegue, & M'Sirdi, 2001) etc. available which reveal different control techniques for rotorcraft models. Popular methods include input-output linearization and backstepping.

Often control design algorithms such as feedback linearization, model predictive control etc. are also used for rotorcraft UAV (A. J. Calise, B. S. Kim, J. Leitner, & Prasad, 1994; B. Bijnens, Q. P. Chu, G. M. Voorsluijs, & Mulder, 2005; H. J. Kim, D. H. Shim, & Sastry, 2002; P. Castillo, A. Dzul, & Lozano, 2004) has used dynamics inversion with neural networks to account for unknown dynamics and dynamic inversion errors. (E. Johnson & Kannan, May-June 2005) used innovative method known as pseudo-control hedging (PCH) with a single neural network employed for both inner and outer loops to account for unknown dynamics. (J. Farrell, M. Sharma, & Polycarpou, 2005) used backstepping with neural networks for unmanned air vehicle to tackle modeling errors and unmodeled dynamics caused during flight via adaptive function approximations. (S. Bouabdallah, et al., 2004) compares the performances of a PID controller with a LQ control law on a micro VTOL test bench. This chapter also discussed a good dynamic model, mechanical structure and sensors of the quadrotor. (T. Hamel, R. Mahony, R. Lozano, & Ostrowski, 2002) presented a Lagrangian dynamic model of X4-flyer with motor dynamics and gyroscopic effects included. (E. Altug, J. P. Ostrowski, & Mahony, 2002) presented different control architecture such as feedback linearization, backstepping etc based on visual feedback as the primary sensor. (M. Cheng & Huzmezan, 2003) presents dynamic modeling of a UAV Dragan flyer III and a H_∞ loop shaping flight controller as position control law. (I. D. Cowling, O. A. Yakimenko, J. F. Whidborne, & Cooke, 2007) presented quasioptimal trajectory planer with a LQR path following controller. (W. Guo & Horn, 2006) developed a simulation tool of a indoor flight capable quadrotor based on MEMS based sensors and rangefinders.

The estimation of aerodynamic coefficients for aerospace vehicles is remained in the region of interest for researchers in past decades. (Hess, 1993; Linse & Stengel, 1993; Raisinghani, Ghosh, & Kalra, 1998) etc showed how to implement the different neural nets to estimate aerodynamic coefficients (lateral and longitudinal).

Most work in quadrotor control that uses backstepping design such as (Mian & Daobo, 2008) or other control formulations like exact linearization are based on state-variable formulations. This results in the control laws that often require the evaluation of lie derivatives. (R. Mahony, T. Hamel, & Dzul, 1999) performs backstepping on Euler-Lagrange dynamics, but backstepping is performed on a bilinear product involving thrust input, which we avoid. In this chapter we apply backstepping to the coupled Lagrangian form (not the state-variable form) of the dynamics; this yields a structured controller with an attitude control inner loop and a position control outer loop. It is not straightforward to apply backstepping to the Lagrangian dynamics since the position subsystem (P. Castillo, et al., 2004) is bilinear in the control. This is confronted herein using an inverse kinematics solution (F. L. Lewis, C. T. Abdallah, & Dawson, 1993). To combat unknown nonlinearities we use neural networks (F. Lewis, S. Jagannathan, & Yesildirek, 1999; Y. H. Kim & Lewis, 1998) to estimate the nonlinear terms and aerodynamic forces and moments. Although the neural network used in this chapter is a first order one, but it estimates the higher order unknown state polynomials efficiently. More over the neural net used is a dynamic one as it uses the state dependent tuning rule. So structurally the neural net is not a higher order neural net (HONN), but functionally it appears as a dynamic HONN or more precisely one can say it is a higher order like neural net (HOLNN). The resulting controller has an appealing structure. Simulation results are shown to validate the control law discussed in this chapter.

2. BACKGROUND

2.a Boundedness of Dynamical Systems

Consider a dynamical system

$$\dot{s} = a(s, t) \tag{1}$$

with $s \in \Re^n$. A state s_e is an *equilibrium point* of the system if $a(s_e, t) = 0 \forall t \geq t_0$. If $s_0 = s_e$, so that the system starts out in the equilibrium state, then it will forever remain there. The equilibrium point s_e is said to be *uniformly ultimately bounded (UUB)* (Kailath, 1980) if there exists a compact set $S \subset \Re^n$ so that $\forall s_0 \in S \exists$ a bound B and a time $T(B, s_0)$ such that $\|s(t) - s_e\| \leq B \forall t \geq t_0 + T$.

2.b Lagrangian System

Newton's laws of motions are useful to examine forces in many dynamical systems. But, in some cases with larger dimension, it becomes too complicated to use Newton's law to study the forces, acceleration etc. Use of *Lagrangian* system in those cases simplifies the problem to a great extent. In contrast to Newton, Lagrange examined energy by using generalized coordinates.

Any set of independent quantities $q_1, q_2, \cdots \cdot q_n$ which completely define the position of the system with n degrees of freedom, are called generalized coordinates of the system, and the derivatives are called generalized velocities. Once a problem is described in Cartesian coordinates namely $x_1, x_2, \ldots, x_n$, the generalized coordinate systems can be described as $q_1 = q_1(x_1, x_2, \ldots, x_n), \ldots, q_n = q_n(x_1, x_2, \ldots, x_n)$. Inversely for a given generalized coordinates one can derive the Cartesian coordinates using inverse transformations. The generalized momentum in q_i can be defined as

$$p_i = \frac{\partial T}{\partial q_i} \tag{2}$$

where T is the kinetic energy in terms of the generalized coordinates. The Newtonian equation of motion

$$F = m\ddot{x} \tag{3}$$

where F, m and x are the force, mass and position in Cartesian coordinates. We rewrite (3) as

$$F = \dot{p} \tag{4}$$

But in generalized coordinates, Equations (3)-(4) does not work. Because, generalized force defined as Q is not just the time derivative of momentum p. If $V = V(q_1, q_2, \ldots, q_n)$ be the potential energy defined in terms of generalized coordinates then generalized force in terms of generalized coordinates can be defined as

$$Q_i = -\frac{\partial V}{\partial q_i} \qquad (5)$$

Thus in generalized coordinates, $\dot{p} \neq -\nabla V$ rather may be described as

$$\dot{p} = -\nabla V + \nabla T \qquad (6)$$

Now from Equations (2) and (6) give

$$\frac{d}{dt}\left(\frac{\partial T}{\partial \dot{q}_i}\right) - \left(\frac{\partial T}{\partial q_i}\right) = Q_i \qquad (7)$$

The equation (7) is known as Lagrange's equations of motions. In Section 3, we used this relation to derive the dynamics of a quadrotor.

2.c Backstepping Control

Consider a System given by

$$\dot{s} = a(s) + g(s)\nu \qquad (8)$$

$$\dot{\nu} = \delta \qquad (9)$$

Now, define

$$\nu = \rho(s), \rho(0) = 0 \qquad (10)$$

so that the origin of

$$\dot{s} = a(s) + g(s)\rho(s) \qquad (11)$$

is asymptotically stable. Also assume that there exist a Lyapunov function $V(s)$ which satisfy the following inequality (J.-J. E. Slotine & Li, 1991; Khalil, 1992, 2001)

$$\frac{\partial V}{\partial s}\left[a + g\rho\right] \leq -Q(s) \qquad (12)$$

where, $Q(s) > 0$. With the application of the control law given by (10), sub-system described in (8) is now given by

$$\dot{s} = \left[a(s) + g(s)\rho(s)\right] + \left[\nu - \rho(s)\right]g(s) \qquad (13)$$

Define,

$$O = \nu - \rho(s) \qquad (14)$$

So that,

$$\dot{s} = \left[a(s) + g(s)\rho(s)\right] + g(s)O$$
$$\dot{O} = \delta - \dot{\rho}(s) \tag{15}$$

From (15), it is seen that the control law $-\rho(s)$ designed for the subsystem (8) is *backstepped* by an integrator through the change of variable defined in (14). Note that $\dot{\rho}(s) = \dfrac{\partial \rho}{\partial s}\left[a + g\nu\right]$ is known. So we can reduce the new system (15) by defining $\alpha = \delta - \dot{\rho}(s)$ such that

$$\dot{s} = \left[a(s) + g(s)\rho(s)\right] + g(s)O$$
$$\dot{O} = \alpha \tag{16}$$

Now, one can notice that (16) has similar form of (8)-(9). But, subsystem (8) is Lyapunov stable at the origin. Now to consider the stability of the whole system define

$$V_l(s,\nu) = V(s) + \frac{1}{2}O^2 \tag{17}$$

Therefore it can be shown that for a suitable choice of $\alpha = -\dfrac{\partial V}{\partial s}g(s) - kO$ with $k > 0$

$$\dot{V}_l(s,\nu) \leq -Q(s) - kO^2 \tag{18}$$

Equation (18) proves that the overall system is asymptotically stable at origin.

2.d Neural Network and Function Approximation

Figure 1 shows a schematic diagram of two-layer Neural Network (NN) with n inputs and m outputs. Assuming the linear activation functions in the output layer one can write the output as (F. Lewis, et al., 1999)

$$p = W^T\sigma(V^T l) \tag{19}$$

where, V and W are the first and second layer weight matrices and $\sigma(\cdot)$ is defined as the activation function for first layer. Now if the first-layer weights and thresholds V in (19) are predetermined by some *a priori* method, then only the second-layer weights and thresholds W are to be determined to define the NN. Define, $\mu(l) \equiv \sigma(V^T l) \in \Re^L$ with L number of hidden first layer so that

$$p = W^T\mu(l) \tag{20}$$

This NN is *linear* in the parameter W.

The basic universal approximation result (K. Hornik, M. Stinchombe, & White, 1989) says that any smooth function $a(s)$ can be approximated arbitrary closely on a compact set using two-layer NN with

Figure 1. Two-layer neural network

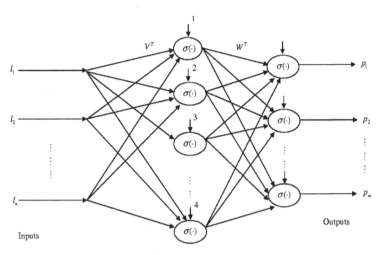

appropriate weights. If, $a(s): \Re^n \to \Re^m$ be a smooth function, then given a compact set $S \in \Re^n$ and a positive number ε_N, there exist a two-layer NN (20) such that

$$a(s) = W^T \mu(s) + \varepsilon \tag{21}$$

with $\|\varepsilon\| < \varepsilon_N \, \forall s \in S$ and for some large L. The term ε often known as the *NN function approximation error* and it is decreases as L increases.

Predetermination of V is sometimes become difficult. This problem is addressed by selecting the matrix V in (19) randomly. It is shown in (B. Igelnik & Pao, 1995) that, for random vector functional link (RVFL) nets, the resulting function $\mu(s) = \sigma(V^T s)$ is a basis, so that the RVFL NN has the universal approximation property. The NN described in (21) is a feed-forward NN. However it is shown subsequently that the weights in NN must be tuned online to achieve closed loop control stability and desired controller performance. The tuning functions are often nonlinear and contain higher order state variables. Therefore, in real applications the NN are in fact dynamically higher order.

2.e Higher Order Neural Net (HONN) and Higher Order Like Neural Net (HOLNN):

Higher order neural nets are the extension of the single layer neural net described in the previous section. Higher order generally describes any order of the neural net which is greater than one (Kosmatopoulos, Polycarpou, Christodoulou, & Ioannou, 1995). For example, the response of a second order neural net to the input pattern $L = \left[l_1, l_2, \ldots \ldots, l_{n_i} \right]$ is given by (Karayiannis, Venetsanopoulos, & Karayiannis, March 2004)

$$p_i = \text{sgn} \left(\sum_{j_1=1}^{n_i} \sum_{j_2=1}^{n_i} w_{i;j_1,j_2} l_{j_1} l_{j_2} \right) \tag{22}$$

where $w_{i;j_1,j_2}$ are the weights of the network. So we can see that in higher (second) order neural net, the network response depends on the weighted summation of the quadratic terms $l_{j_1} l_{j_2}$ for $1 \leq j_1, j_2 \leq n_i$. So the total input to the neuron is not only a linear combination of the components l_{j_i} but also their product $l_{j_1} l_{j_2}$. Like this, one can go further higher order interactions represented by $l_{j_1} l_{j_2} l_{j_3}$ ..... etc. This is the basic structure of a higher order neural network. Interestingly it can be shown that higher order neural network of any order can be trained by any of the learning algorithms developed for first order neural net.

In contrast to the HONN, the structure of *higher order like neural net* (HOLNN) is different in the sense that HOLNN has the basic structure of first order neural net

$$p_i = \text{sgn}\left(\sum_{j=1}^{n_i} w_{i,j} l_j\right) \tag{23}$$

Now, when this first order neural net is used in adaptive control loop simulation, then each time step the value of the weights $w_{i,j}$ can be derived from some weight tuning dynamics which involves different components of L and thus weights $w_{i,j} = w_{i,j}(l_1, l_2, ..., l_{n_i})$ are also the functions of different components of L. So if we look into the each time step of the dynamic simulation of the adaptive control involving first order neural network, the Equation (23) can be seen as

$$p_i = \text{sgn}\left(\sum_{j=1}^{n_i} w_{i,j}(L) l_j\right) \tag{24}$$

which more like the HONN response in (22). So (24) reveals the fact that a single layer neural net in the dynamic loop of adaptive control simulation involving dynamic weight tuning laws work similar to a higher order neural net. We will call it as *higher order like neural net* (HOLNN).

3. MODEL OF A QUADROTOR

Figure 2 shows a basic model of an unmanned quadrotor. The quadrotor has some basic advantage over the conventional helicopter (P. Castillo, et al., 2005a) in terms of simplicity of dynamics and control design. Given that the front and the rear motors rotate counter-clockwise while the other two rotate clockwise, gyroscopic effects and aerodynamic torques tend to cancel in trimmed flight. This four-rotor rotorcraft does not have a *swashplate*. In fact it does not need any blade pitch control. The collective input (or throttle input) is the sum of the thrusts of each motor (see Figure 2).

Pitch movement is obtained by increasing (reducing) the speed of the rear motor while reducing (increasing) the speed of the front motor. The roll movement is obtained similarly using the lateral motors. The yaw movement is obtained by increasing (decreasing) the speed of the front and rear motors while decreasing (increasing) the speed of the lateral motors.

In this subsection we will describe the basic state-space model of the quadrotor. The dynamics of the four rotors are relatively much faster than the main system and thus neglected in our case.

The generalized coordinates of the rotorcraft are $q = (x, y, z, \psi, \theta, \varphi)^T$ where (x, y, z) represents the relative position of the center of mass of the quadrotor with respect to an inertial frame I and (ψ, θ, φ)

Figure 2. Model of a typical quadrotor

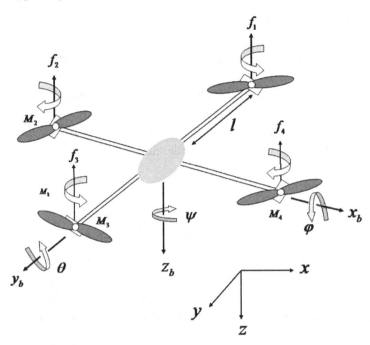

are the three Euler angles representing the orientation of the rotorcraft, namely yaw-pitch-roll of the vehicle. Let us assume that the transitional and rotational coordinates with respect to fixed inertial frame are in the form $\xi = (x, y, z)^T \in \Re^3$ and $\eta = (\psi, \theta, \varphi)^T \in \Re^3$. The body frame coordinates are $\xi_b = (x_b, y_b, z_b)^T \in \Re^3$. The force coming out from the ith rotor is denoted as f_i.

From Lagrangian formulation of conservation of energy for a rigid body,

$$L = \text{Kinetic Energy}\,(T) - \text{Potential Energy}\,(V) \tag{25}$$

where $T = \dfrac{m}{2}\dot{\xi}^T\dot{\xi} + \dfrac{1}{2}\omega^T I \omega$ ₍₂₆₎ and $V = mgz$ ₍₂₇₎ Again, $\omega = T_\eta \dot{\eta}$ ₍₂₈₎ where,

$$T_\eta = \begin{pmatrix} -\sin\theta & 0 & 1 \\ \cos\theta\sin\psi & \cos\psi & 0 \\ \cos\theta\cos\psi & -\sin\psi & 0 \end{pmatrix} \tag{29}$$

Define, $J = T_\eta^T I T_\eta$ ₍₃₀₎ and thus $T = \dfrac{m}{2}\dot{\xi}^T\dot{\xi} + \dfrac{1}{2}\dot{\eta}^T J \dot{\eta}$ ₍₃₁₎ $J(\eta) = J$ is often known as *auxiliary matrix* of the Lagrangian system.

Define, $q = (\xi, \eta)^T$. Now, rigid body dynamics of a typical quadrotor can be derived differentiating (25) so that,

$$\frac{d}{dt}\frac{\partial L}{\partial \dot{q}} - \frac{\partial L}{\partial q} = \begin{pmatrix} RF \\ \tau \end{pmatrix} \tag{32}$$

$$\text{Where, } R = \begin{bmatrix} c\varphi c\theta & s\varphi c\theta & -s\theta \\ c\varphi s\theta s\psi - s\varphi c\psi & s\varphi s\theta s\psi + c\varphi c\psi & c\theta s\varphi \\ c\phi s\theta c\psi + s\varphi s\psi & s\varphi s\theta s\psi - c\varphi s\psi & c\theta c\psi \end{bmatrix} \text{ and } F = \begin{bmatrix} 0 \\ 0 \\ f_1 + f_2 + f_3 + f_4 \end{bmatrix}. \text{ Matrix } R \text{ is}$$

often known as rotational matrix which is used to represent forces in inertial coordinates from body co-ordinates. From (32), after some algebraic manipulation we can write the following which also represent the final dynamic model of the rotorcraft (P. Castillo, R. Lozano, & Dzul, 2005b)

$$m\ddot{\xi} + \begin{pmatrix} 0 \\ 0 \\ mg \end{pmatrix} = F_R \tag{33}$$

$$J(\eta)\ddot{\eta} + \frac{d}{dt}\{J(\eta)\}\dot{\eta} - \frac{1}{2}\frac{\partial}{\partial\eta}(\dot{\eta}^T J(\eta)\dot{\eta}) = \tau \tag{34}$$

$$J(\eta)\ddot{\eta} + \frac{d}{dt}\{J(\eta)\}\dot{\eta} - \bar{C}(\eta,\dot{\eta}) = \tau \tag{35}$$

$$J(\eta)\ddot{\eta} + C(\eta,\dot{\eta}) = \tau \tag{36}$$

Where, $F_R = u \begin{pmatrix} -\sin\theta \\ \cos\theta\sin\varphi \\ \cos\theta\cos\varphi \end{pmatrix}$, $u = \sum_{i=1}^{4} f_i$, $\tau = \begin{pmatrix} \tau_\psi \\ \tau_\theta \\ \tau_\varphi \end{pmatrix}$ and I is the inertia matrix.

Remark: 1. The control distributions $\left(u, \tau^T\right)^T$ and the forces $\left(f_i = k_{\omega_i}\omega_i^2, i = 1...4\right)$ of the each rotor of the quadrotor is given by the following relation

$$\begin{pmatrix} u \\ \tau_\varphi \\ \tau_\theta \\ \tau_\psi \end{pmatrix} = \underbrace{\begin{bmatrix} 1 & 1 & 1 & 1 \\ -l & 0 & l & 0 \\ 0 & l & 0 & -l \\ c & -c & c & -c \end{bmatrix}}_{M} \underbrace{\begin{pmatrix} f_1 \\ f_2 \\ f_3 \\ f_4 \end{pmatrix}}_{f} = Mf \tag{37}$$

where l is the distance from the motors to the center of gravity, $\tau_{\varphi,\theta,\psi}$ is the couple produced by motor, and c is a constant known as force-to-moment scaling factor. So, if a required thrust and torque vector are given, one may solve for the rotor force using Eq. (37).

2. $C(\eta,\dot{\eta})$ is referred to as the coriolis term. From (34), $C(\eta,\dot{\eta})$ can be represented assuming the inertia matrix I for a typical quadrotor is symmetric.

$$C\left(\eta,\dot{\eta}\right) = \frac{d}{dt}J - \frac{1}{2}\frac{\partial}{\partial\eta}\left(\dot{\eta}^T J\left(\eta\right)\right)$$
$$= 2T_\eta^T I\dot{T}_\eta - \frac{1}{2}\frac{\partial}{\partial\eta}\left(\dot{\eta}^T J\left(\eta\right)\right) \tag{38}$$

3. It can be proved that $\left(\dfrac{d}{dt}J\left(\eta\right) - 2C\right)$ is skew-symmetric for proper choice of coordinate system for example given by (36). Note that for a quadrotor model inertia matrix I is constant but J is not a constant.

Now finally we obtain the coupled Lagrangian form of the dynamics

$$m\ddot{\xi} = u\begin{pmatrix} -\sin\theta \\ \cos\theta\sin\varphi \\ \cos\theta\cos\varphi \end{pmatrix} + \begin{pmatrix} 0 \\ 0 \\ -mg \end{pmatrix} \tag{39}$$

$$J\ddot{\eta} = -C\left(\eta,\dot{\eta}\right)\dot{\eta} + \tau \tag{40}$$

where, $u \in \Re$ and $\tau \in \Re^3$ are the control inputs. Thus, the system is a coupled Lagrangian form of underactuated system with six outputs and four inputs.

4. BACKSTEPPING CONTROL DESIGN FOR QUADROTOR

Backstepping control design is effective for a class of *underactuated* systems (I. Kanellakopoulos, P. V. Kokotovic, & Morse, 1991; Isidori, 1989; J.-J. E. Slotine & Li, 1991; Olfati-Saber, 2001; Vidyasagar, 1993). Many robot and aircraft control problems are included in the class of underactuated systems (F. L. Lewis, et al., 1993). Backstepping for the quadrotor has normally been applied to the state-variable form, which introduces unnecessary complications (e.g. lie derivatives). In this chapter we use backstepping control design for the Lagrangian quadrotor dynamics. This is complicated by the fact that Eq. (39) is bilinear in the controls.

Though the quadrotor as treated in the literature does not normally include aerodynamic forces and moments, we would like to include them here since such effects do occur in the helicopter dynamics. It is desired for the approach in this chapter to be applicable for straightforward extension to helicopter control design.

Rewriting the quadrotor dynamics to include unmodeled state dependent disturbances that includes aerodynamic forces and moments A_x, A_y, A_z, A_η yields the Lagrangian form

$$m\ddot{x} = -u\sin\theta + A_x$$
$$m\ddot{y} = u\cos\theta\sin\varphi + A_y \tag{41}$$
$$m\ddot{z} = u\cos\theta\cos\varphi - mg + A_z$$

$$J\begin{pmatrix} \ddot{\psi} \\ \ddot{\theta} \\ \ddot{\varphi} \end{pmatrix} = \begin{pmatrix} \tau_\psi \\ \tau_\theta \\ \tau_\varphi \end{pmatrix} - C\left(\eta,\dot{\eta}\right)\dot{\eta} + A_\eta \tag{42}$$

Figure 3. Control configuration

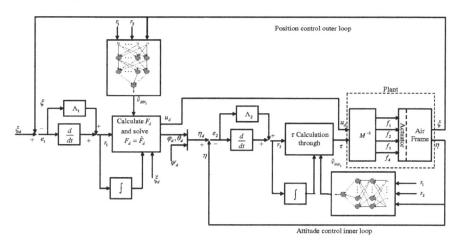

Now we will use backstepping to determine a control structure to make the position $\xi = \left(x, y, z\right)^T$ of the quadrotor to follow a desired trajectory $\left(x_d(t), y_d(t), z_d(t)\right)$. The end result is shown in Figure 3. To achieve this purpose, define the position tracking error $e_1(t)$ of the subsystem given by Eq. (41) and the sliding mode error $r_1(t)$ (Y. H. Kim & Lewis, 1998) as

$$e_1 = \left(x_d - x, y_d - y, z_d - z\right)^T = \xi_d - \xi \tag{43}$$

$$r_1 = \dot{e}_1 + \Lambda_1 e_1 \tag{44}$$

where, Λ_1 is a diagonal positive definite design parameter matrix. Common usage is to select Λ_1 diagonal with positive entries. Then, (44) is a stable system so that e_1 is bounded as long as the controller guarantees that the filtered error r_1 is bounded. In fact it is easy to show (F. Lewis, et al., 1999) that one has

$$\left\|e_1\right\| \le \frac{\left\|r_1\right\|}{\upsilon_{\min}(\Lambda_1)}, \left\|\dot{e}_1\right\| \le \left\|r_1\right\| \tag{45}$$

with $\upsilon_{\min}(\cdot)$ denotes the minimum singular value. Note that $\dot{e}_1 + \Lambda_1 e_1 = 0$ defines a stable sliding mode surface. The function of the controller to be designed is to force the system onto this surface by making r_1 small. The parameter Λ_1 is selected for a desired sliding mode response

$$e_1(t) = e_1^{-\Lambda_1 t} e_1(0) \tag{46}$$

We now focus on designing a controller to keep $\left\|r_1\right\|$ small. Then the error dynamics becomes

$$m\dot{r}_1 = m\ddot{e}_1 + m\Lambda_1 \dot{e}_1 \tag{47}$$

$$\Rightarrow m\dot{r}_1 = m\begin{bmatrix} \ddot{x}_d \\ \ddot{y}_d \\ \ddot{z}_d \end{bmatrix} - m\begin{bmatrix} \ddot{x} \\ \ddot{y} \\ \ddot{z} \end{bmatrix} + m\Lambda_1\left(r_1 - \Lambda_1 e_1\right) \tag{48}$$

$$m\dot{r}_1 = m\ddot{\xi}_d - \begin{pmatrix} -u\sin\theta \\ u\cos\theta\sin\varphi \\ u\cos\theta\cos\varphi \end{pmatrix} - \begin{pmatrix} 0 \\ 0 \\ -mg \end{pmatrix} - \begin{pmatrix} A_x \\ A_y \\ A_z \end{pmatrix} + m\Lambda_1(r_1 - \Lambda_1 e_1) \tag{49}$$

$$m\dot{r}_1 = m\ddot{\xi}_d + m\Lambda_1 r_1 - m\Lambda_1^2 e_1 - F_d - m_g - A_{xyz} \tag{50}$$

where, $F_d = \begin{pmatrix} -u\sin\theta \\ u\cos\theta\sin\varphi \\ u\cos\theta\cos\varphi \end{pmatrix}$, $A_{xyz} = \begin{pmatrix} A_x \\ A_y \\ A_z \end{pmatrix}$ and $m_g = \begin{pmatrix} 0 \\ 0 \\ -mg \end{pmatrix}$.

The ideal force F_d which stabilizes the tracking error r_1 is

$$\hat{F}_d = m\ddot{\xi}_d - m\Lambda_1^2 e_1 - m_g - \hat{A}_{xyz} + K_{r_1} r_1 + K_{i_1}\int_0^t r_1 dt' \tag{51}$$

where, $\hat{A}_{xyz}$ is an approximation of the aerodynamic function A_{xyz} and control gain matrices $K_{r_1} > 0, K_{i_1} > 0$ are diagonal.. Using Eq. (51) in Eq. (50) yields

$$m\dot{r}_1 = -\left(K_{r_1} - m\Lambda_1\right)r_1 - \tilde{A}_{xyz} - K_{i_1}\int_0^t r_1 dt' \tag{52}$$

where, $\tilde{A}_{xyz} = A_{xyz} - \hat{A}_{xyz}$ is the approximate error.

To generate the ideal force F_d in Eq. (51), would require the use of φ_d, θ_d and u_d given by the solution to

$$\begin{pmatrix} -u_d\sin\theta_d \\ u_d\cos\theta_d\sin\varphi_d \\ u_d\cos\theta_d\cos\varphi_d \end{pmatrix} = F_d \tag{53}$$

Thus, given F_d one may solve for φ_d, θ_d and u_d by the procedure to be given later in this chapter.

Now a NN is used to approximate A_{xyz} which is unknown. It can be shown from (K. Hornik, et al., 1989) that A_{xyz} can be approximated using a NN as

$$v_{NN_1} = -A_{xyz} \equiv W_1^T \mu_1\left(\chi_1\right) + \varepsilon_1 \tag{54}$$

where W_1 is the unknown ideal NN output weight matrix, $\chi_1 = \left(\xi, r_1, \eta, \dot{\eta}\right)^T$ is the input of the NN basis activation function $\mu_1(\cdot)$ which is used for NN approximation. The NN activation function $\mu_1(\cdot)$ should be chosen to capture any known nonlinearity present in the aerodynamics. ε_1 is the NN estimation error bounded by $\|\varepsilon_1\| < \varepsilon_{N_1}$ on a compact set. Note, one could use two-layer neural net which are *nonlinear in parameter* (NLIP). This technology has been described in (F. Lewis, et al., 1999). We use the linear-in-the-parameter NN in this chapter. Therefore

$$\hat{v}_{NN_1} = -\hat{A}_{xyz} = \hat{W}_1^T \mu_1\left(\chi_1\right) \tag{55}$$

with $\hat{W}_1$ the actual NN weights. It can be noted that $\hat{A}_{xyz}$ can be any higher order polynomial of states and thus we used the activation function $\mu_1(\cdot)$ as the function of higher order state polynomials. Thus the resultant neural net structure estimate A_{xyz} using dynamic state dependent tuning rule which is discussed later.

In Section 7 we will discuss how to tune $\hat{W}_1$ to provide stability and bounded sliding mode error $r_1(t)$. Thus

$$\hat{F}_d = m\ddot{\xi}_d - m\Lambda_1^2 e_1 - m_g + \hat{W}_1^T \mu_1\left(\chi_1\right) + K_{r_1} r_1 + K_{i_1} \int_0^t r_1 dt \tag{56}$$

Define,

$$-\tilde{A}_{xyz} = W_1^T \mu_1\left(\chi_1\right) - \hat{W}_1^T \mu_1\left(\chi_1\right) + \varepsilon_1 \equiv \tilde{W}_1^T \mu_1\left(\chi_1\right) + \varepsilon_1 \tag{57}$$

Now Eq. (52) becomes,

$$m\dot{r}_1 = -\left(K_{r_1} - m\Lambda_1\right) r_1 + \tilde{W}_1^T \mu_1\left(\chi_1\right) - K_{i_1} \int_0^t r_1 dt + \varepsilon_1 \tag{58}$$

By solving (53) as detailed in following section, the desired *pseudo-commands* φ_d, θ_d, u_d for the subsystem given by Eq. (41) are determined. Note that u_d is directly applied to the plant as input. Now, the second step of backstepping is performed. We select a control input τ for Eq. (42) to generate φ_d, θ_d Note that ψ_d does not appear in Eq. (41) and so can be selected as an independent desired reference input.
Define $\eta_d = \left(\varphi_d, \theta_d, \psi_d\right)^T$
Defining the tracking error $e_2(t)$ and the sliding mode error $r_2(t)$ as,

$$e_2 = \left(\psi_d - \psi, \theta_d - \theta, \varphi_d - \varphi\right)^T \tag{59}$$

$$r_2 = \dot{e}_2 + \Lambda_2 e_2 \tag{60}$$

where, Λ_2 is a diagonal positive definite design parameter matrix with similar characteristic of Λ_1 Then designing a controller to keep $\|r_2\|$ small will guarantee that $\|e_2\|$ and $\|\dot{e}_2\|$ are small.
Then error dynamics given by

$$J\dot{r}_2 = J\ddot{e}_2 + J\Lambda_2\dot{e}_2$$
$$= J\ddot{\eta}_d - \left\{\tau - C(\eta,\dot{\eta})\dot{\eta} + A_\eta\right\} + J\Lambda_2(r_2 - \Lambda_2 e_2) \tag{61}$$

Define,

$$\tilde{v}_{NN_2} = v_{NN_2} - \hat{v}_{NN_2}$$
$$= W_2^T\varphi_2(\chi_2) - \hat{W}_2^T\varphi_2(\chi_2) + \varepsilon_2$$
$$= \tilde{W}_2^T\varphi_2(\chi_2) + \varepsilon_2 \tag{62}$$

and from Eq. (60)

$$\dot{\eta} = -r_2 + \dot{\eta}_d + \Lambda_2 e_2 \tag{63}$$

Substituting $\dot{\eta}$ from Eq. (62) in Eq. (61) yields

$$J\dot{r}_2 = J\ddot{\eta}_d - \left\{\tau - C(\eta,\dot{\eta})(-r_2 + \dot{\eta}_d + \Lambda_2 e_2) + A_\eta\right\}$$
$$+ J\Lambda_2(r_2 - \Lambda_2 e_2) \tag{64}$$
$$J\dot{r}_2 = -\tau - C(\eta,\dot{\eta})r_2$$
$$+ \left\{J\ddot{\eta}_d - A_\eta + C(\eta,\dot{\eta})(\dot{\eta}_d + \Lambda_2 e_2) - J\Lambda_2^2 e_2\right\} + J\Lambda_2 r_2 \tag{65}$$

Now, a second NN is introduced to approximate $\left\{J\ddot{\eta}_d - A_\eta + C(\eta,\dot{\eta})(\dot{\eta}_d + \Lambda_2 e_2) - J\Lambda_2^2 e_2\right\}$ According-ing to (K. Hornik, et al., 1989), this can be approximated as

$$\left\{J\ddot{\eta}_d - A_\eta + C(\eta,\dot{\eta})(\dot{\eta}_d + \Lambda_2 e_2) - J\Lambda_2^2 e_2\right\}$$
$$= v_{NN_2} \equiv W_2^T\mu_2(\chi_2) + \varepsilon_2 \tag{66}$$

where W_2 is the unknown ideal NN weight matrix, $\mu_2(\cdot)$ is an another basis activation function based on higher order state polynomials. It is to be chosen to estimate the known nonlinearities present in the system. ε_2 is estimation error which is bounded by $\|\varepsilon_2\| \leq \varepsilon_{N_2}$ on a compact set with the input to the NN is selected as $\chi_2 = (\eta, r_1, r_2)^T$ and thus one can select

$$\hat{v}_{NN_2} \equiv \hat{W}_2^T\mu_2(\chi_2) \tag{67}$$

with $\hat{W}_2$ is the actual NN weights. Note that the second neural net is also estimating the higher order state polynomials using a dynamic state dependent tuning rule discussed later.

Define the control input τ as

$$\tau = \hat{v}_{NN_2} + K_{r_2}r_2 + K_{i_2}\int_0^t r_2 dt' \tag{68}$$

with $K_{r_2} > 0, K_{i_2} > 0$ are diagonal gain matrices. Then Eq. (65) reduces to the form,

$$J\dot{r}_2 = \tilde{v}_{NN_2} + J\Lambda_2 r_2 - C\left(\eta, \dot{\eta}\right)r_2 - K_{r_2}r_2 - K_{i_2}\int_0^t r_2 dt' \tag{69}$$

$$J\dot{r}_2 = \tilde{W}_2^T \mu_2\left(\chi_2\right)$$
$$- \left\{K_{r_2} + C\left(\eta, \dot{\eta}\right) - J\Lambda_2\right\}r_2 - K_{i_2}\int_0^t r_2 dt' + \varepsilon_2 \tag{70}$$

with the estimation error

$$\tilde{v}_{NN_2} = v_{NN_2} - \hat{v}_{NN_2}$$
$$= W_2^T \mu_2\left(\chi_2\right) - \hat{W}_2^T \mu_2\left(\chi_2\right) + \varepsilon_2 \tag{71}$$
$$= \tilde{W}_2^T \mu_2\left(\chi_2\right) + \varepsilon_2$$

5. SOLUTION AND FEASIBILITY OF CONTROL LAW

Here, we show how to confront the *bilinearity* in the control which appears in the position dynamics given by Eq. (41). We derive the final control law based on the assumption that F_d is feasible that is, it is possible to find out in the position dynamics some practical solution for u_d, φ_d and θ_d in Eq. (53). The solution based on *inverse kinematics* (F. L. Lewis, D. M. Dawson, & Abdallah, 2004) is given here. Inverse Kinematics is one of the popular methods in robotics used for finding the joint variables given a desired Cartesian position (I. Fantoni, A. Zavala, & Lozano, 2002). For the problem discussed above, one must find angular positions $\left(u_d, \varphi_d, \theta_d\right)$ for a given F_d in

$$\begin{pmatrix} -u_d \sin\theta_d \\ u_d \cos\theta_d \sin\varphi_d \\ u_d \cos\theta_d \cos\varphi_d \end{pmatrix} = F_d(t) \in R^3 \tag{72}$$

Define

$$a = u_d \sin\theta_d, b = u_d \cos\theta_d \tag{73}$$

Then

$$\begin{pmatrix} -a \\ b\sin\varphi_d \\ b\cos\varphi_d \end{pmatrix} = F_d(t) \equiv \begin{pmatrix} f_{x_d}(t) \\ f_{y_d}(t) \\ f_{z_d}(t) \end{pmatrix} \tag{74}$$

so that

$$a = -f_{x_d}(t) \tag{75}$$

And

$$b^2 \sin^2 \varphi_d + b^2 \cos^2 \varphi_d = f_{y_d}^2(t) + f_{z_d}^2(t) \tag{76}$$

$$\Rightarrow b = \sqrt{f_{y_d}^2(t) + f_{z_d}^2(t)} \tag{77}$$

From (74),

$$\left(u_d \sin\theta_d\right)^2 + \left(u_d \cos\theta_d\right)^2 = a^2 + b^2 \tag{78}$$

$$\Rightarrow u_d^2 = a^2 + b^2 \tag{79}$$

$$u_d = \sqrt{a^2 + b^2} \tag{80}$$

And

$$\tan\theta_d = \frac{a}{b} \tag{81}$$

$$\theta_d = \tan^{-1}\left(\frac{a}{b}\right) \tag{82}$$

Finally from Eq. (74)

$$\tan\varphi_d = \frac{f_{y_d}}{f_{z_d}} \tag{83}$$

$$\varphi_d = \tan^{-1}\left(\frac{f_{y_d}}{f_{z_d}}\right) \tag{84}$$

This procedure shows that Eq. (53) has a solution $\left(u_d, \theta_d, \varphi_d\right)$ for all F_d. We assume that $f_{z_d} \neq 0$ i.e. φ and ψ are not $90°$. Then $\left(u_d, \varphi_d, \theta_d\right)$ are given respectively by (80), (82) and (84).

6. STABILITY ANALYSIS AND NEURAL NETWORK TUNING

In the previous Section, the control law given by Eq. (68) is derived from desired attitude φ_d, θ_d and ψ_d where φ_d, θ_d is obtained from the solution of Eq. (53) and given by Eqs. (82), (84) respectively. The required u_d is given by (80) and ψ_d is an external command. The control structure is shown in Figure 3. There, one has an outer kinematics loop with inputs the desired positions (x_d, y_d, z_d), and an inner dynamics loop for attitude control. Note that, the desired command inputs are (x_d, y_d, z_d) as well as desired yaw ψ_d which are given as reference trajectory inputs.

Based on the *Lyapunov theory* the feasibility of the control law given by Eq. (68) is discussed in this section, and tuning laws are given for the NN weights to guarantee stability. The related background literature can be found in (F. Lewis, et al., 1999).

Assumption 6.1

a. Desired trajectory $q_d = \left(\xi_d^T \quad \eta_d^T \right)^T$ is bounded i.e. $\|q_d\| < q_B$ for some known bound q_B

b. Ideal NN weights W_1, W_2 are bounded, i.e. $\left\| \begin{matrix} W_1 \\ W_2 \end{matrix} \right\| < W_B$ for some known bound W_B

c. The auxiliary matrix can be upper bounded as $J(\eta) \leq J_M$ with $J_M \in \Re$ are some positive real constant.

Note that assumption a) always holds. Assumption b) holds on a compact set, and assumption c) holds since J is functions of $\sin(\cdot)$ and $\cos(\cdot)$ of $\left[\varphi \quad \theta \quad \psi \right]^T$.

Now follows the main result given by Theorem 5.1 which proves that r_1 and r_2 are Uniformly Ultimately Bounded (UUB) if the NN are properly tuned. According to the definition given by Eq. (44) of r_1 and Eq. (60) of r_2, this guarantees that e_1 and e_2 are UUB since

$$\|e_1\| \leq \|s + \Lambda_1\|^{-1} \|r_1\| \leq \left(\sigma_{\min}\left(\Lambda_1 \right) \right)^{-1} \|r_1\|$$
$$\|e_2\| \leq \|s + \Lambda_2\|^{-1} \|r_2\| \leq \left(\sigma_{\min}\left(\Lambda_2 \right) \right)^{-1} \|r_2\|$$

(85)

where $\sigma_{\min}\left(\Lambda_i \right)$ is the minimum eigenvalue of $\Lambda_i, i = 1, 2$.

Theorem 6.1 *Given the system as described in Eqs. (41) and (42) with a control architecture given by Eqs. (80), (68) and shown in Figure 3. Under the assumptions, suppose that*

$$\left[K_{r_1} - m\Lambda_1 \right] > 0, \left[K_{r_2} - J_M\Lambda_2 \right] > 0$$

and the state dependent NN weight tuning laws are given as

$$\left. \begin{matrix} \dot{\hat{W}}_1 = F_1 \mu_1 r_1^T - \kappa \|r\| F_1 \hat{W}_1 \\ \dot{\hat{W}}_2 = F_2 \mu_2 r_2^T - \kappa \|r\| F_2 \hat{W}_2 \end{matrix} \right\}$$

(86)

with proposed desired tuning parameter matrices $F_1 = F_1^T > 0, F_2 = F_2^T > 0$. *Then the errors* $r_1(t), r_2(t)$ and the NN weight estimation errors $\tilde{W}_1(t), \tilde{W}_2(t)$ are UUB with practical bounds given by Eq. (95) *and Eq. (97). Moreover the tracking errors* r_1, r_2 *can be made arbitrarily small with a suitable choice of design parameters* $K_{r_1}, K_{r_2}, \Lambda_1$ *and* Λ_2.

Proof:

Define, $r = \begin{bmatrix} r_1 \\ r_2 \end{bmatrix}, \hat{W} = \begin{pmatrix} \hat{W}_1 \\ \hat{W}_2 \end{pmatrix}, \mu_r = \begin{pmatrix} \mu_1 r_1^T \\ \mu_2 r_2^T \end{pmatrix}$ and $F = F^T = \begin{bmatrix} F_1 & 0 \\ 0 & F_2 \end{bmatrix} > 0, \kappa > 0$

Consider the following Lyapunov function candidate:

$$L = \frac{1}{2} r_1^T m r_1 + \frac{1}{2} r_2^T J r_2 + \frac{1}{2} \left[\int_0^t r_1^T dt' \right] K_{i_1} \left[\int_0^t r_1 \, dt' \right]$$
$$+ \frac{1}{2} \left[\int_0^t r_2^T dt' \right] K_{i_2} \left[\int_0^t r_2 \, dt' \right] + \frac{1}{2} tr \left\{ \tilde{W}^T F^{-1} \tilde{W} \right\} \tag{87}$$

Then,

$$\dot{L} = -r^T \begin{bmatrix} K_{r_1} - m\Lambda_1 & 0 \\ 0 & K_{r_2} - J\Lambda_2 \end{bmatrix} r + r^T \begin{bmatrix} \varepsilon_1 \\ \varepsilon_2 \end{bmatrix}$$
$$+ \frac{1}{2} r_2^T \dot{J} r_2 - r_2^T C r_2 + tr \left\{ \tilde{W}^T \left(F^{-1} \dot{\tilde{W}} + \mu_r \right) \right\} \tag{88}$$

Now let,

$$\dot{\hat{W}} = -F\mu_r + \kappa \|r\| F \hat{W} \tag{89}$$

Continuing with Eq. (87) using Eq. (89),

$$\dot{L} \leq -r^T K_v r + r^T \varepsilon_v + \frac{1}{2} r^T \left(\dot{J} - 2C \right) r$$
$$+ \kappa \|r\| tr \left\{ \tilde{W}^T \hat{W} \right\} \tag{90}$$

where

$$K_v = \begin{bmatrix} K_{r_1} - m\Lambda_1 & 0 \\ 0 & K_{r_2} - J_M \Lambda_2 \end{bmatrix}, \varepsilon_v = \begin{bmatrix} \varepsilon_1 \\ \varepsilon_2 \end{bmatrix} \tag{91}$$

The hypothesis guarantees $K_v > 0$. Therefore

$$\dot{L} \leq -r^T K_v r + r^T \varepsilon_v + \frac{1}{2} r^T \left(\dot{J} - 2C \right) r$$
$$+ \kappa \|r\| tr \left\{ \tilde{W}^T \left(W - \tilde{W} \right) \right\} \tag{92}$$

where, $\left(\dot{J} - 2C \right)$ is skew symmetric (F. L. Lewis, et al., 1993) and thus it can be shown that $r^T \left(\dot{J} - 2C \right) r = 0$. Since, $tr \left\{ \tilde{W}^T \left(W - \tilde{W} \right) \right\} \leq \|\tilde{W}\|_F \|W\|_F - \|\tilde{W}\|_F^2$ with $\|\cdot\|_F$ the *Frobenius* norm, there results

$$\dot{L} \leq - \left\| K_v \right\|_{\min} \left\| r \right\|^2 + \kappa \left\| r \right\| \left\{ \left\| \tilde{W} \right\|_F \left\| W \right\|_F - \left\| \tilde{W} \right\|_F^2 \right\} + \left\| \varepsilon_v \right\|_{\max} \left\| r \right\|$$

$$= - \left\| r \right\| \left\{ \left\| K_v \right\|_{\min} \left\| r \right\| + \kappa \left\{ \left\| \tilde{W} \right\|_F^2 - \left\| \tilde{W} \right\|_F \left\| W \right\|_F \right\} - \left\| \varepsilon_v \right\|_{\max} \right\} \tag{93}$$

where, $\left\| K_v \right\|_{\min}$ is the minimum possible norm of for different parameter values of K_v. Similarly, $\left\| \varepsilon_v \right\|_{\max}$ is the maximum possible vector norm of ε_v.

Now equation (93) can be rewritten as,

$$\dot{L} \leq - \left\| r \right\| \left\{ \kappa \left[\left\| \tilde{W} \right\|_F - \frac{\left\| W \right\|_F}{2} \right]^2 - \kappa \frac{\left\| W \right\|_F^2}{4} + \left\| K_v \right\|_{\min} \left\| r \right\| - \left\| \varepsilon_v \right\|_{\max} \right\} \tag{94}$$

If $\left\| W \right\|_F \leq W_B$ then, $\dot{L} \leq 0$ if and only if,

$$\left\| r \right\| > \frac{\kappa \dfrac{W_B^2}{4} + \left\| \varepsilon_v \right\|_{\max}}{\left\| K_v \right\|_{\min}} \equiv b_r \tag{95}$$

or from Eq. (93) we can write considering positive definiteness of K_v and

$$\kappa \left\| \tilde{W} \right\|_F \left\{ \left\| \tilde{W} \right\|_F - \left\| W \right\|_F \right\} - \left\| \varepsilon_v \right\|_{\max} > 0 \tag{96}$$

$$\left\| \tilde{W} \right\|_F > \frac{W_B}{2} + \sqrt{\left(\frac{W_B^2}{4} + \frac{\left\| \varepsilon_v \right\|_{\max}}{\kappa} \right)} \equiv b_w \tag{97}$$

Thus, $\dot{L}$ is negative outside a compact set. Selecting the gain K_v ensures that the compact set defined by $\left\| r \right\| \leq b_r$ is bounded, so that the approximation property holds throughout. This ensures UUB for $\left\| r \right\|$ and $\left\| \tilde{W} \right\|_F$ stated in Eqs. (95) and (97) respectively.

Remarks: The tuning law addressed in (86) is a function of state and is designed to make the closed loop system stable. Also the outputs of the neural nets ν_{NN_1} and ν_{NN_2} are designed to estimate higher order state polynomials which as a whole in turn give the flavor of a dynamic HONN as per its functionality is concerned.

7. EXAMPLE AND SIMULATIONS

In practice the NN's can be initialized with zero weights. Then, during the initialization, the PID controllers defined by (51) and (68) with NN's removed stabilize the closed loop system until the NN weights are being updated by the tuning law (89). An assumption on the initial tracking error magnitude is technically needed. For details see (F. Lewis, et al., 1999) in page 198.

7.a Rotorcraft Model

Simulation for a typical quadrotor is performed using the following parameters (SI unit):

$$M_1 = \begin{bmatrix} 1 & 0 & 0 \\ 0 & 1 & 0 \\ 0 & 0 & 1 \end{bmatrix}; \; I = diag(I_x, I_y, I_z) = \begin{bmatrix} 5 & 0 & 0 \\ 0 & 5 & 0 \\ 0 & 0 & 5 \end{bmatrix}; \; g = 9.81.$$

The centripetal/coriolis components are defined by (38) with the auxiliary matrix

$$J(\eta) = \begin{pmatrix} I_x s_\theta^2 + I_y c_\theta^2 s_\psi^2 + I_z c_\theta^2 c_\psi^2 & (I_y - I_z) c_\theta s_\psi c_\psi & -I_x s_\theta \\ (I_y - I_z) c_\theta c_\psi s_\psi & I_y c_\psi^2 + I_z s_\psi^2 & 0 \\ -I_x s_\theta & 0 & I_x \end{pmatrix} \tag{98}$$

The aerodynamic components are taken as representative functions as follows

$$A_{xyz} = \begin{pmatrix} \dot{x}^2 \dot{\varphi} \\ \dot{y}^2 \dot{\theta} \\ \dot{z}^2 \dot{\psi} \end{pmatrix}, A_\eta = \begin{pmatrix} \dot{x} \dot{\varphi}^2 \\ \dot{y} \dot{\theta}^2 \\ \dot{z} \dot{\psi}^2 \end{pmatrix} \tag{99}$$

The physical interpretation of A_{xyz}, A_η have been elaborated already. The terms introduced here are merely a representation of the unmodeled state dependent disturbances used in this particular study.

These terms are used in the simulation but are not required to implement the control law. In actual UAV, the aerodynamic forces and moments will be more complicated, but they are estimated by the NNs.

7.b Reference Trajectory Generation

As outlined in (Hogan, 1984; T. Flash & Hogan, 1985), a reference trajectory a reference trajectory is derived that minimizes the jerk (rate of change of acceleration) over the time horizon. The trajectory ensures that the velocities and accelerations at the end point are zero while meeting the position tracking objective. The following summarizes this approach. Select

$$\dot{x}_d(t) = a_{1_x} + 2a_{2_x} t + 3a_{3_x} t^2 + 4a_{4_x} t^3 + 5a_{5_x} t^4 \tag{100}$$

Differentiating again,

$$\ddot{x}_d(t) = 2a_{2_x} + 6a_{3_x} t + 12a_{4_x} t^2 + 20a_{5_x} t^3 \tag{101}$$

As we indicated before that initial and final velocities and accelerations are zero; so from Eqs. (100) and (101) we can conclude the following

$$\begin{bmatrix} d_x \\ 0 \\ 0 \end{bmatrix} = \begin{bmatrix} 1 & t_f & t_f^2 \\ 3 & 4t_f & 5t_f^2 \\ 6 & 12t_f & 20t_f^2 \end{bmatrix} \begin{bmatrix} a_{3_x} \\ a_{4_x} \\ a_{5_x} \end{bmatrix} \tag{102}$$

where, $d_x = \left(x_{d_f} - x_{d_0} \right) / t_f^3$. Now, solving for coefficients

$$\begin{bmatrix} a_{3_x} \\ a_{4_x} \\ a_{5_x} \end{bmatrix} = \begin{bmatrix} 1 & t_f & t_f^2 \\ 3 & 4t_f & 5t_f^2 \\ 6 & 12t_f & 20t_f^2 \end{bmatrix}^{-1} \begin{bmatrix} d_x \\ 0 \\ 0 \end{bmatrix} \tag{103}$$

Thus the desired trajectory for the x direction is given by

$$x_d(t) = x_{d_0} + a_{3_x} t^3 + a_{4_x} t^4 + a_{5_x} t^5 \tag{104}$$

Similarly, the reference trajectories for the y and z directions are gives by Eq. (105) and Eq. (106) respectively.

$$y_d(t) = y_{d_0} + a_{3_y} t^3 + a_{4_y} t^4 + a_{5_y} t^5 \tag{105}$$

$$z_d(t) = z_{d_0} + a_{3_z} t^3 + a_{4_z} t^4 + a_{5_z} t^5 \tag{106}$$

The beauty of this method lying in the fact that more demanding changes in position can be accommodated by varying the final time. That is acceleration/torque ratio can be controlled smoothly as per requirement. For example,

Figure 4. Example trajectory simulation for different final positions

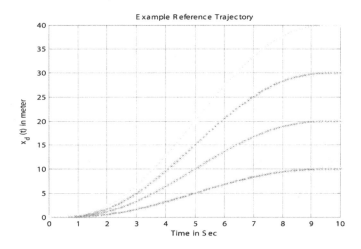

Let us assume at $t = 0$, $x_{d_0} = 0$ and at $t = 10$ sec, $x_{d_f} = 10$. Therefore $d_x = 0.01$ and the trajectory is given by Eq. (107) and shown in Figure 4 for various desired final positions.

$$x_d(t) = 0.1t^3 - 0.015t^4 + 0.0006t^5 \qquad (107)$$

7.c Neural Network Parameters

The number of NN neurons used in the simulation is 10. The simulation was done with 8 neurons and performance detoriated. On the other hand, a simulation using 12 neurons id not improve performance. Therefore, 10 neurons are selected. NN weight tuning gains are given by $F_1 = diag\left(5[1;1;1]\right)$; $F_2 = diag\left(5[1;1;1]\right)$; $\kappa_1 = 0.01; \kappa_2 = 0.01$.

The following cases are considered in the simulation to show the decoupling and good tracking property of the control law. In the all following cases we set the yaw angle to $\psi_d = 0$.

7.d Simulation

Case1: To Show Effectiveness in Following a Desired (Guided) Trajectory

Figure 5 describes the controlled motion of the quadrotor from its initial position $(0,0,0)$ to final position $(20,5,10)$ for a given time (40 seconds). The actual trajectories $x(t), y(t), z(t)$ match exactly their desired values $x_d(t), y_d(t), z_d(t)$ respectively nearly exactly. The errors along the three axes are also shown in the same figure. It can be seen that the tracking is almost perfect as well as the tracking errors are significantly small. Figure 6 describes the attitude of the quadrotor φ, θ along with their demands

Figure 5. Three position commands simultaneously

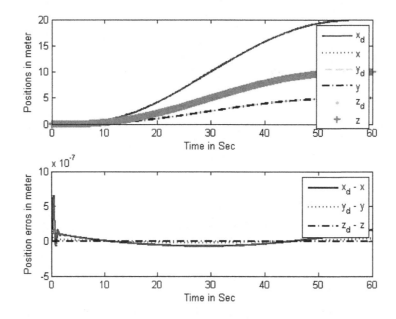

Figure 6. Resultant angular positions and errors

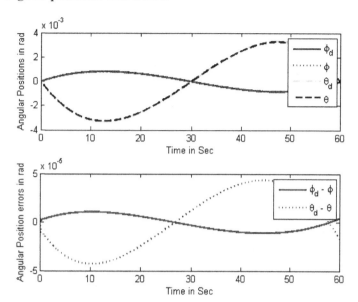

φ_d, θ_d and attitude errors in radian. Again the angles match their command values nearly perfectly. Figure 7 describes the control input requirement which is very much realizable. Note that as described before the control requirement for yaw angle is $\tau_\psi = 0$ and it is seen from Figure 7.

Case 2: To Show the Motion Decoupling in Response to Position Commands

Figure 8-9 illustrates the decoupling phenomenon of the control law. Figure 8 shows that $x(t)$ follows the command $x_d(t)$ nearly perfectly unlike $y(t)$ and $z(t)$ are held their initial values. Figure 9 shows

Figure 7. Input commands for Case I

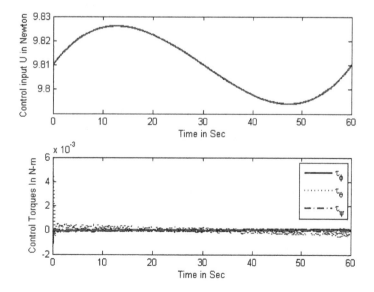

Figure 8. Plots of position and position tracking errors for x command only

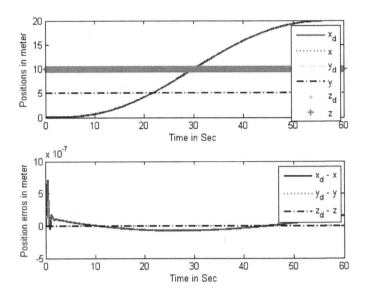

that the change in x does not make any influence on φ. The corresponding control inputs are also shown in Figure 10 and due to the full decoupling effect it is seen that τ_φ is almost zero.

The similar type of simulations are performed for y and z directional motions separately and similar plots are obtained showing excellent tracking.

Remarks: We conclude from the simulation results that NN backstepping controller gives satisfactory results for a wide range of nonlinearities. The resulting controller structure in Figure 3 yields excellent

Figure 9. Angular variations due to change in x

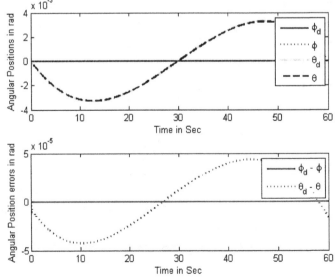

Figure 10. Input commands for variation in x (Case II)

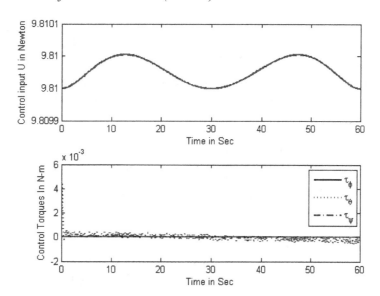

decoupling between command channels. The NN learns on-line to effectively compensate for the unknown aerodynamics forces and moments as well as the nonlinear terms $C(\eta,\dot{\eta})$.

8. CONCLUSION

A backstepping approach to design nonlinear controller for a quadrotor dynamics is discussed in this chapter. Using this approach, an intuitively structured controller was derived that has an outer kinematics position control loop and an inner dynamic attitude control loop. The dynamics of a quadrotor are a simplified form of helicopter dynamics that exhibits the basic problems including underactuation, strong coupling, multi-input/multi-output, and unknown nonlinearities. The force dynamics of the quadrotor is completely independent of the rotational dynamics except through the aerodynamic state dependent disturbances including aerodynamic coefficients. These unmodeled state dependent dynamics are estimated by higher order like neural net and thus yielding a robust control law. The simulation results shown at the end demonstrate the validity of the control law discussed in the paper.

ACKNOWLEDGMENT

The research work presented in this chapter is supported by NSF grant ECCS-0801330 and ARO grant W91NF-05-1-0314 and the Army National Automotive Center NAC.

REFERENCES

Altug, E., Ostrowski, J. P., & Mahony, R. (2002). *Control of a quadrotor helicopter using visual feedback.* Paper presented at the IEEE International Conference on Robotics and Automation, Washington, DC.

Bijnens, B., Chu, Q. P., Voorsluijs, G. M., & Mulder, J. A. (2005, 15 - 18 August 2005). *Adaptive feedback linearization flight control for a helicopter UAV.* Paper presented at the AIAA Guidance, Navigation, and Control Conference and Exhibit, San Francisco.

Bouabdallah, S., Noth, A., & Siegwart, R. (2004). *PID vs LQ control techniques applied to an indoor micro quadrotor.* Paper presented at the International Conference on Intelligent Robots and Systems.

Calise, A. J., Kim, B. S., Leitner, J., & Prasad, J. V. R. (1994). Helicopter adaptive flight control using neural networks. In *Proceedings of the 33rd Conference on Decision and Control*, Lake Buena Vista, FL.

Castillo, P., Dzul, A., & Lozano, R. (2004). Real-time Stabilization and Tracking of a Four-Rotor Mini Rotorcraft. *IEEE Transactions on Control Systems Technology, 12*, 510–516. doi:10.1109/TCST.2004.825052

Castillo, P., Lozano, R., & Dzul, A. (2005a). *Modelling and Control of Mini Flying* Machines. Berlin: Springer-Verlag.

Castillo, P., Lozano, R., & Dzul, A. (2005b). Stabilization of a Mini Rotorcraft Having Four Rotors. *IEEE Control Systems Magazine, 25*, 45–55. doi:10.1109/MCS.2005.1550152

Cheng, M., & Huzmezan, M. (2003, Aug. 11-14). *A combined MBPC/2 DOF hinf controller for quad rotor unmanned air vehicle.* Paper presented at the AIAA Atmospheric Flight Mechanics Conference and Exhibit, Austin, Texas, USA.

Cowling, I. D., Yakimenko, O. A., Whidborne, J. F., & Cooke, A. K. (2007, July 2-5). *A prototype of an autonomous controller for a quadrotor UAV.* Paper presented at the Proceedings of the European Control Conference, Kos, Greece.

Enns, R., & Si, J. (2000). *Helicopter flight control design using a learning control Approach1.* Paper presented at the Proceedings of the 39th Conference on Decision and Control, Sydney, Australia.

Fantoni, I., Zavala, A., & Lozano, R. (2002). *Global stabilization of a PVTOL aircraft with bounded thrust.* Paper presented at the Proceedings of the 41st Conference on Decision and Control, Las Vegas, NV.

Farrell, J., Sharma, M., & Polycarpou, M. (2005). Backstepping-Based Flight Control with Adaptive Function Approximation. *AIAA Journal of Guidance, Control and Dynamics, 28*.

Flash, T., & Hogan, N. (1985). The Coordination of Arm Movements: an Experimentally Confirmed Mathematical Model. *The Journal of Neuroscience, 5*, 1688–1703.

Guo, W., & Horn, J. (2006, Aug. 21-26). *Modeling and simulation for the development of a quad-rotor UAV capable of indoor flight.* Paper presented at the Modeling and Simulation Technologies Conference and Exhibit, Keystone, CO.

Hamel, T., Mahony, R., Lozano, R., & Ostrowski, J. (2002). *Dynamic modeling and configuration stabilization for an X4-flyer.* Paper presented at the IFAC 15th Triennial World Congress, Barcelona, Spain.

Hess, R. A. (1993). *On the use of backpropagation with feed forward neural networks for the aerodynamic estimation problem.* Paper presented at the AIAA paper 93-3638.

Hogan, N. (1984). Adaptive Control of Mechanical Impedance by Coactivation of Antagonist Muscles. *IEEE Transactions on Automatic Control, 29,* 681–690. doi:10.1109/TAC.1984.1103644

Hornik, K., Stinchombe, M., & White, H. (1989). Multilayer Feedforward Networks are Universal Approximations. *Neural Networks, 20,* 359–366. doi:10.1016/0893-6080(89)90020-8

Igelnik, B., & Pao, Y. H. (1995). Stochastic choice of basis functions in adaptive function approximation and the functional-link net. *IEEE Transactions on Neural Networks, 6*(6), 1320–1329. doi:10.1109/72.471375

Isidori, A. (1989). *Nonlinear Control Systems* (second ed.). Berlin: Springer-Verlag.

Johnson, E., & Kannan, S. (2005, May-June). Adaptive Trajectory Control for Autonomous Helicopters. *AIAA Journal of Guidance . Control and Dynamics, 28,* 524–538. doi:10.2514/1.6271

Kailath, T. (1980). *Linerar Systems.* New Jersey: Prentice Hall.

Kanellakopoulos, I., Kokotovic, P. V., & Morse, A. S. (1991). Systematic Design of Adaptive Controllers for Feedback Linearizable Systems. *IEEE Transactions on Automatic Control, 36,* 1241–1253. doi:10.1109/9.100933

Karayiannis, N. B., Venetsanopoulos, A. N., & Karayiannis, N. (March 2004). *Artificial neural networks: Learning Algorithms, Performance Evaluation, and Applications.* Berlin: Springer-Verlag.

Khalil, H. K. (1992). *Nonlinear Systems.* New York: Macmillan.

Khalil, H. K. (2001). *Nonlinear Systems* (3rd ed.)New Jersey: Prentice Hall.

Kim, H. J., Shim, D. H., & Sastry, S. (2002). *Nonlinear model predictive tracking control for rotorcraft-based unmanned aerial vehicles.* Paper presented at the Proceedings of the American Control Conference, Anchorage, AK.

Kim, Y. H., & Lewis, F. L. (1998). High Level Feedback Control with Neural Networks. *World Scientific, 21.*

Koo, T. J., & Sastry, S. *Output tracking control design of a helicopter model based on approximate linearization.* Paper presented at the Proceedings of the 37th Conference on Decision and Control, Tampa, FL.

Kosmatopoulos, E. B., Polycarpou, M. M., Christodoulou, M. A., & Ioannou, P. A. (1995). higher-Order Neural Network Structures for Identification of Dynamical Systems. *IEEE Transactions on Neural Networks, 6*(2), 422–431. doi:10.1109/72.363477

Lewis, F., Jagannathan, S., & Yesildirek, A. (1999). *Neural Network Control of Robot Manipulators and Nonlinear Systems.* London: Taylor and Francis.

Lewis, F. L., Abdallah, C. T., & Dawson, D. M. (1993). *Control of Robot Manipulators*. New York: Macmillan.

Lewis, F. L., Dawson, D. M., & Abdallah, C. T. (2004). *Robot Manipulator Control: Theory and Practices*. New York: Marcel Dekker Inc.

Linse, D. J., & Stengel, R. F. (1993). Identification of Aerodynamic Coefficients Using Computational Neural Networks. *Journal of Guidance, Control, and Dynamics*, *16*(6). doi:10.2514/3.21122

Madani, T., & Benallegue, A. (2006, Oct. 9-15). *Backstepping control for a quadrotor helicopter.* Paper presented at the Proceedings of the 2006 IEEE/RSJ International Conference on Intelligent Robots and Systems, Beijing, China.

Mahony, R., & Hamel, T. (2005). Robust Trajectory Tracking for a Scale Model Autonomous Helicopter. *Int. J. Robust Nonlinear Control, s, 14*, 1035–1059. New York: John Wiley & Son

Mahony, R., Hamel, T., & Dzul, A. (1999). *Hover control via lyapunov control for an autonomous model helicopter.* Paper presented at the Proceedings of the 38th Conference on Decision & Control, Phoenix, Arizona.

Mian, A. A., & Daobo, W. (2008). Modeling and Backstepping-based Nonlinear Control Strategy for a 6 DOF Quadrotor Helicopter. *Chinese Journal of Aeronautics*, *21*(3), 261–268. doi:10.1016/S1000-9361(08)60034-5

Mistler, V., Benallegue, A., & M'Sirdi, N. K. (2001). *Exact linearization and non-interacting control of a 4 rotors helicopter via dynamic feedback.* Paper presented at the 10th IEEE Int. Workshop on Robot-Human Interactive Communication, Paris.

Mokhtari, A., Benallegue, A., & Daachi, B. (2006). Robust Feedback Linearization and GH∞ Controller for a Quadrotor Unmanned Aerial Vehicle. *Journal of Electrical Engineering, 57.*

Mokhtari, A., Benallegue, A., & Orlov, Y. (2006). Exact linearization and sliding mode observer for a quadrotor unmanned aerial vehicle. *International Journal of Robotics and Automation*, *21*(1), 39–49. doi:10.2316/Journal.206.2006.1.206-2842

Olfati-Saber, R. (2001). Nonlinear Control of Underactuated Mechanical Systems with Application to Robotics and Aerospace Vehicles.

Raisinghani, S. C., Ghosh, A. K., & Kalra, P. K. (1998). Two new techniques for aircraft parameter estimation using neural networks. *Aeronautical Journal*, *102*, 25–29.

Slotine, J. J. E., & Li, W. (1991). *Applied Nonlinear Control*. New Jersey: Prentice Hall.

Stevens, B. L., & Lewis, F. L. (2003). *Aircraft Control and Simulation*. New York: Wiley and Sons.

Vidyasagar, M. (1993). *Nonlinear System Analysis*. New Jersey: Prentice Hall.

Yang, C. D., & Liu, W. H. (2003). *Nonlinear Hoo Decoupling hover control of helicopter with parameter uncertainties.* Paper presented at the Proceedings of the American Control Conference, Denver, CO.

APPENDIX

Nomenclature

i = subscript or superscript index

m = mass of quadrotor

I = inertia matrix

J = auxiliary matrix

x,y,z = position of quadrotor in inertial frame

φ = roll angle

θ = pitch angle

ψ = yaw angle

q,s = generalized state vector representation

ξ = position vector

η = attitude vector

ξ_d = desired position vector

η_d = desired attitude vector

g = gravity

f_i = force from the i'th motor

u = summation of four motor forces

ω_i = rotational speed of i'th motor

l = distance from motor to center of gravity

c = force-to-moment scaling factor

τ = torque vector

C = coriolis component

A_{xyz} = state dependent disturbances including aerodynamic nonlinearities

A_η = state dependent disturbances including aerodynamic nonlinearities

e_1,e_2 = tracking errors

r_1,r_2 = sliding mode errors

$\mu_i(\cdot)$ = basis function for NN approximation

W_i = ideal NN weights

F_d = desired ideal force

Λ_i = positive definite design matrix

F_i = positive definite design matrix

K_v = controller gain matrix

ε_v = NN tuning error vector

κ = design constant

Chapter 21
Artificial Tactile Sensing and Robotic Surgery Using Higher Order Neural Networks

Siamak Najarian
University of Technology, Iran

Sayyed Mohsen Hosseini
Amirkabir University of Technology, Iran

Mehdi Fallahnezhad
Amirkabir University of Technology (Tehran Polytechnic), Iran

ABSTRACT

In this chapter, a new medical instrument, namely, the Tactile Tumor Detector (TTD) able to simulate the sense of touch in clinical and surgical applications is introduced. All theoretical and experimental attempts for its construction are presented. Theoretical analyses are mostly based on finite element method (FEM), artificial neural networks (ANN), and higher order neural networks (HONN). The TTD is used for detecting abnormal masses in biological tissue, specifically for breast examinations. We also present a research work on ANN and HONN done on the theoretical results of the TTD to reduce the subjectivity of estimation in diagnosing tumor characteristics. We used HONN as a stronger open box intelligent unit than traditional black box neural networks (NN) for estimating the characteristics of tumor and tissue. The results show that by having an HONN model of our nonlinear input-output mapping, there are many advantages compared with ANN model, including faster running for new data, lesser RMS error and better fitting properties.

DOI: 10.4018/978-1-61520-711-4.ch021

INTRODUCTION

Tactile sensing is the process of determining physical properties and events through contact with objects in the world, and a tactile sensor is a device or system that can measure a given property of an object or contact event by physical contact between the sensor and the object. These properties include shape, location, size, temperature, roughness, softness, and so on.

In addition to surgical usages of the tactile sensing, physical examinations performing by physicians on the patient's body such as the detection of the presence of abnormal masses is the other application of tactile sensing. In this case, design and construction of a device mimicking the sense of touch and compensating the lack of skillfulness is necessary.

In this chapter, we introduce a medical instrument, namely, the TTD which can provide the surgeons with tactile information. All the theoretical analyses, mostly based on FEM, and experiments will be presented. Moreover, there is a specific work on ANN and HONN done on the theoretical results of the TTD. By performing this work, a consistent method employing systematic engineering approaches, such as FEM, ANN, and HONN, has been offered to reduce the subjectivity and individuality in clinical palpations.

BACKGROUND

Tactile sensors are utilized to sense a wide range of stimuli in various biomedical engineering and medical robotics applications, such as detection of the presence or absence of a grasped tissue/object or even mapping of a complete tactile image (Dargahi, 2001; Dargahi & Najarian, 2004a; Najarian *et al*, 2009). These sensors normally consist of an array of sensors (Fisch *et al*, 2003; Najarian *et al*, 2006).

In clinical practice, doctors routinely palpate the patients' body with the fingers and palm, especially for those diseases where a palpable nodule or lump in tissue is the most common symptom. Even if the nodule is detected via palpation, there is a lack of any precise measuring devices, so all that can be documented is the general location of the tumor within the tissue (Barman & Guha, 2006). In some patients, this technique has preference over some imaging techniques (Zeng *et al*, 1997). In consequence, many new breast examination techniques have been proposed, most of which are based on the difference between tissue stiffness and tumor stiffness (Kane *et al*, 1996). Artificial tactile sensing is a new method for obtaining the characteristics of a tumor in the soft tissue (Dargahi & Najarian, 2004b; Dargahi & Najarian, 2005). This includes detecting the presence or absence of a tumor or even mapping a complete tactile image (Bar-Cohen *et al*, 2000; Dargahi, 2002; Singh *et al*, 2003). Artificial palpation is another important application of tactile sensing.

It is known that elastography is a merger of several related fields of study: tissue elastic constant (biomechanics), tissue contrast differences, tissue motion by using imaging systems (X-ray, ultrasound and magnetic resonance imaging), and vibrating targets by using coherent radiation (laser, sonar and ultrasound) (Gao *et al*, 1996). In recent years, atomic force microscopy (AFM) has been successfully applied to local elasticity measurements especially in biological fields (Vinckier & Semenza, 1998). In addition to aforementioned methods, tactile sensing technology is another approach with which the measurement of soft tissue elasticity is possible. This technology tries to imitate the sense of touch which is of crucial importance in the field of minimally invasive surgery (MIS) and robotic surgery (Lee, 2000) examined the state-of-the-art of tactile sensing in its mechatronic aspects. Following this, another research team reviewed the tactile sensing technology for minimal access surgery (Eltaib & Hewit, 2003).

THE TACTILE TUMOR DETECTOR (TTD)

Detection of Tumors Using a Computational Tactile Sensing Approach

Materials and Methods

In each application of tactile sensing, physical contact between a tactile sensor and an object is very important. In fact, there are two important aspects, which have been the main motivations behind designing a variety of tactile sensors; the first is the type of application and the second is the type of object to be contacted (Son *et al*, 1996).

Definition of Problem

In many diagnostic tests, doctors examine the patient's body using the fingers and palm to obtain information on conditions inside the body. Such a diagnostic test can be used to detect breast tumors (clinical breast examination or CBE). The present study investigated the effects of an embedded object as a tumor on the surface of biological tissue.

Modeling, Simplifications and Assumptions

According to the physical standard for soft tissue simulation (Kerdoke *et al*, 2003), a cube with a stiffer object inside it was chosen as a simplified model of tissue and a cancerous tumor. In order to analyze the problem thoroughly, the following "Input Parameters' were defined:

1. Tissue loading (compression of the upper surface of the cube), l.
2. Tissue thickness, t.
3. Tumor diameter, d.
4. Tumor depth, h.
5. Stiffness ratio of tumor to tissue, Er.
6. Tumor shape, s.

The elastic modulus of the tissue was 5 kPa and the Poisson's ratios of the tissue and tumor were 0.49 and 0.3, respectively (Wellman & Howe, 1999). Since many biological tissues demonstrate non-linear mechanical properties, we chose different stiffness ratios by varying the value of the tumor stiffness (Dargahi & Najarian, 2005a).

Finite Element Modeling and Boundary Conditions

This problem was modeled and solved by the numerical method of FEM, using ANSYS software (Release 10.0). Considering the input parameter ranges shown in Table 1 and tumor shapes including sphere, oval, block and torus, we selected the width and length of the cube as 10 cm.

Procedure

The goal was to investigate the effects of an object embedded in biological tissue associated with the application of mechanical loading on the tissue. The stress distribution solution of FEM was called the "Tactile Image". Following this, a graph plotting the stress magnitude on a specific line, called the "Stress Graph', was extracted. A code with the general form ($s : l; t; d; h; Er$) was defined, showing the

Table 1. Ranges of input parameters

l (mm)	*t* (cm)	*d* (cm)	*h* (cm)	*Er*
3	4	0.5	1.5	10
4	5	1	2	20
5	6	1.5	2.5	30
6	7	2	3	40
7	8	2.5	3.5	50

value of each input parameter, and the code (sphere: l, 5 mm; t, 5 cm; d, 2 cm; h, 2.5 cm; Er, 30) was dedicated as that of the base model.

Results and Comparisons

According to the input parameters in Table 1 and the procedure of making new models, 24 cases were modeled and solved by the software and two specific results were extracted from each solution. They are as follows:

1. The stress distribution on the surface of the tissue, called the tactile image.
2. The stress graph, taken on a path defined by a straight line in the middle of the upper surface of the cube from the left to the right side.

The following results can be elicited from tactile images and stress graphs:

- Appearance of the effects of an embedded object on the surface in tactile images.
- Determining the tumor shape and size with respect to the stress distribution produced on the surface.
- Appearance of an overshoot in stress graphs. This overshoot of the graph, seen in all cases of Table 1, not only confirms the tumor's existence but also locates the exact position of the tumor.

A Medical Tactile Sensing Instrument for Detecting Embedded Objects with Specific Application for Breast Examination

Definition of the Problem

In many diagnostic tests, such as the breast mass examinations, doctors routinely examine the patient's body using the fingers and palm to get information on the conditions inside the body. The subject of this section is to investigate the presence of an abnormal object as a mass in the biological tissue with the help of tactile approach.

Numerical Method

Modeling, Simplifications and Assumptions

According to the physical standard for simulation of soft tissues (Kerdoke *et al*, 2003), the presence of the mass in the breast organ is simplified to a circle (as a mass) in a rectangle (as a tissue), and then according to the fingertip shape, a sensor with a convex surface at the point of contact is added to the model. In order to analyze the problem thoroughly, seven parameters called "Input Parameters" are defined. They are as follows:

1. Tissue loading (compression of the upper surface of the cube), l.
2. Tissue thickness, t.
3. Tumor diameter, d.
4. Tumor depth, h.
5. Stiffness ratio of tumor to tissue, Er.
6. Distance between the sensor center and tissue center, x.
7. Tumor shape, s.

Figure 2 shows the simplified model of the problem with input parameters.

The elastic modulus of the tissue and the Poisson's ratio of the tissue and mass are 5 kPa, 0.49, and 0.3, respectively (Wellman & Howe, 1999). Also, the sensor is supposed to be rigid.

Finite Element Modeling and Boundary Conditions

This problem is modeled and solved by the ANSYS software (Release 10.0). According to the size range of the mass diameter, usually between 5 to 25 mm for spherical masses (Galea, 2004), the length of the tissue was assumed 10 cm so that the tissue sides are far enough from the mass and have no effects on the stress distribution around the mass.

Figure 1. A typical stress graph

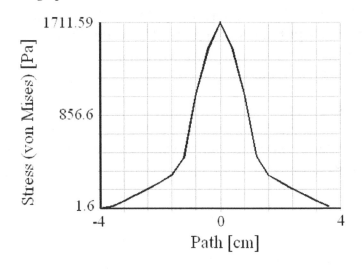

Figure 2. Simplified model of the problem with input parameter

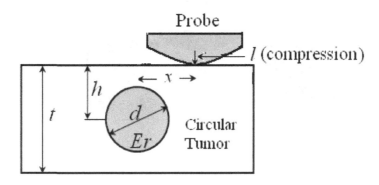

Procedure for Obtaining Numerical Results

The goal is to detect the presence of an abnormal object inside a simulated biological tissue associated with the application of a mechanical loading of a tactile sensor on the tissue surface. In order to investigate the problem, the tactile sensor scans the surface of the tissue and exerts a constant compression everywhere.

Numerical Results

To report the results, the model with the code "circle: l, 4 mm; t, 3 cm; d, 1 cm; h, 2 cm; Er, 30; x, 0 cm" was chosen, and then analyses of the tissue response versus the compression caused by the tactile sensor for different values of parameter x, were performed.

Figures 3(a) and 3(b) show the stress distribution for the two different sensor positions.

In Figure 3, it is shown that the stress distribution is appeared on the tissue surface. To analyze carefully what happens on the surface, a path is defined exactly on the upper surface of the rectangle and the stress taken on this path is depicted in a distinct graph called "Stress Graph". Figures 4(a) and 4(b) show the Stress Graphs related to Figures 3(a) and 3(b), respectively.

In these graphs, the location of the maximum stress coincides with the center of sensor. Figure 5 shows a number of different stress graphs obtained by changing the sensor position (input parameter x).

Experimental Method

Design and Construction of the Tactile Tumor Detector (TTD)

In order to validate the results obtained by the numerical analysis of the FEM, we built a system working according to Figure 6 showing the main components of a tactile sensing system and the flowchart of data circulation.

This instrument called "Tactile Tumor Detector (TTD)" consists of some elements to collect, process and display data. The main parts of this device are shown schematically in Figure 7.

Experimental Models

A type of gel is used to simulate the biological tissue to try the device on. The simulation of the cancerous masses is performed according to their being stiffer than the biological tissue. Additionally, some small and hard balls with different sizes are chosen to simulate masses.

Figure 3. (a) Stress distribution for the code "circle: l, 4 mm; t, 3 cm; d, 1 cm; h, 2 cm; Er, 30; x, 0 cm."
(b) Stress distribution for the code "circle: l, 4 mm; t, 3 cm; d, 1 cm; h, 2 cm; Er, 30; x, +2 cm"

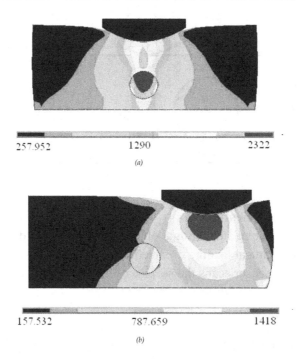

Experiments Procedure

Figure 8 shows the TTD. First, the tactile probe is held by the user, and then the surfaces of the simulated models are touched by the tactile probe on a straight line passing over the abnormal object.

Experiments Using Robot

Although it is possible to perform the experiments manually, these experiments usually accompany by the lack of applying uniform compression on the tissue surface. To eliminate that type of error (non-uniform compression), an industrial 6 DOF robot (MOTOMAN, Yaskawa, Japan) was programmed to perform the experiments in our lab. Therefore, the tactile probe was installed on the robot hand as the end effecter. Figure 9 shows the experimental setup with the robot.

The result of an experiment is shown in Figure 10. In this figure, the middle peak being higher than the others not only confirms the presence of an abnormal object in the model, but also small difference between the value of the maximum peak and that of the other peaks shows that the mass is placed far from the surface of contact.

Numerical and Experimental Results Comparisons

In order to compare the numerical and experimental results, the robot was trained to touch the surface of the model on a straight line passing over the abnormal object. In Figure 11, the operation of the TTD is compared with the operation of tactile sensor modeled by the computer software. The appearance of an overshoot coincides exactly with the mass location in Stress Graphs and it points out that the experimental results verify the numerical ones reasonably well.

Figure 4. (a) Stress graph for the code "circle: l, 4 mm; t, 3 cm; d, 1 cm; h, 2 cm; Er, 30; x, 0 cm."(b) Stress graph for the code "circle: l, 4 mm; t, 3 cm; d, 1 cm; h, 2 cm; Er, 30; x, +2 cm"

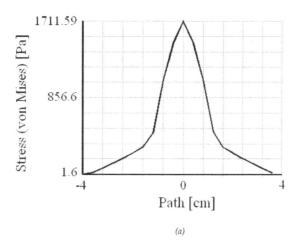

(a)

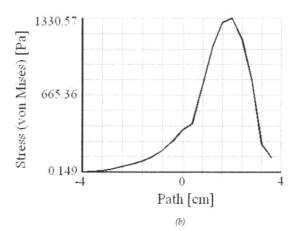

(b)

Application of a Hybrid Configuration of HONN for the Estimation of Tumor Characteristics in Biological Tissues

Motivation and Outline

In this section, following the results of the previous sections that demonstrated the existence of an alien object inside a typical tissue in a forward approach, we aim to introduce a method able to predict a number of detected tumor characteristics by employing efficient models of HONN in an inverse approach.

The results show that there is a non-linear correlation between the tumor characteristics and their effects on the extracted features. In this case, artificial FNNs based on single layer and Multilayer Perceptron (MLP) by employing the back propagation (BP) algorithm can be investigated. Although BPNs are recognized for their excellent performance in mathematical function approximation, nonlinear classification, pattern matching and pattern recognition, they have several limitations. They do not excel in

Figure 5. Variations of stress graphs by changing input parameter x

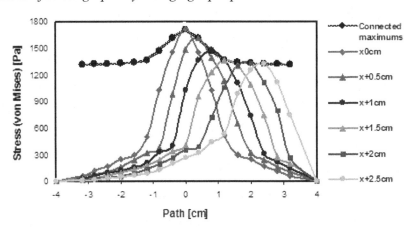

non-continues or non-smooth data mining and knowledge learning (Fulcher, 2006; Zhang, 2002) and also they cannot deal well with incomplete or noisy data (Dong, 2007; Peng, 2007; Wang, 2003). Single hidden layer FNNs cannot realize every nonlinear decision regions. FNNs by more hidden layers are well-known for their long time convergence, usually stuck in local minima rather than global and their more complex structure than the others. BPNs are acting like black box models and inasmuch as the number of hidden layers increases this black box become harder to understand.

HONNs have been applied widely in various research branches especially finance and economics, time series prediction (Fulcher et al, 2006; Ghazali et al, 2007; Hussain & Liatsis, 2008; Xu, 2008), clustering (Ramanathan & Guan, 2007), classification (Abdelbar, 1998), pattern recognition and mathematical function approximation (Artyomov & Yadid-Pecht, 2005; Foresti & Dolso, 2004; Rovithakis et al 2004; Tsai, in press; Wang & Lin, 1995; Zhang, 2008).Traditional NNs provide each network output as a nonlinear function of first order neurons. By combining inputs nonlinearly HONNs make a higher order correlation among inputs (Zurada, 1992). In contrast with BPNs, HONN successfully provides an efficient open-box model of nonlinear input-output mapping providing easier understanding of data mining. By leaving necessity of hidden layers, HONN structures become simpler than FNNs and initializing of learning parameters including weights will not be very difficult. HONNs perform better than Multilayer Perceptron FNNs using a small number of free parameters (Rovitakis & Chistodoulou, 2000) or at least when the order of HONN and FNN are the same. Additionally, HONN proved to be as powerful as any other FNN network (Redding et al, 1993).

Moreover, HONNs are most often faster in running than FNNs. Examples in implementation of two-input and three-input XOR function by using second order neural network (SONN) showed SONN is several times faster than FNN (Gupta *et al*, 2009; Zhang, 2008). Considering the mentioned limitations of ANNs and advantageous of HONNs, we are motivated to use HONNs to estimate a number of tissue and tumor characteristics in biological tissues.

Introduction to HONN Structures and Models
In recent years, many different types of HONN structures have been developed. Many different explanations of higher-order are given by different researchers. This includes neuron type (linear, power, multiplicative, sigmoid, etc.) and neuron activation function type (polynomial, sigmoid, cosine, sine,

Figure 6. Components of the artificial tactile sensing system

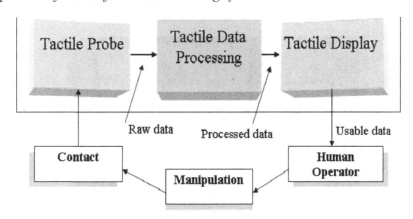

SINC, etc.) (Fulcher *et al*, 2006). The simplest structure is where the inputs of network in addition to the original inputs are some product of them (Lee et al 1986). A SONN that learned to distinguish between two objects was applied to handle classification problems by Reid et al (1989). HONN uses a higher correlation of input neurons for better fitting properties leading to a higher number of learning parameters (Kosmatopoulos et al, 1995). The greater the order used, the higher the number of parameters will be. Many efforts for decreasing the number of parameters (Shin & Ghosh, 1991; Shin & Ghosh, 1995) and non-fully connected HONNs (Spirkovska & Reid, 1990) in different areas have been done.

In summary, two major forms of HONN have been considered, sigma-pi network known as higher-order processing unit (HPU) or sigma-pi network and pi-sigma network (PSN). Higher order nets format as a higher-order processing unit (HPU) was first suggested by Lippmann (1989). Homma & Gupta (2002) developed a sigma-pi artificial second order neural unit (ASONU) without losing the higher performance. Shin & Ghosh (1991) have introduced an efficient HONN as a PSN model and they have studied several pattern classification and function approximation problems. They claimed that a generalization of PSN can approximate any measurable function. Recurrent PSN (RPSN) and converging

Figure 7. Schematic design of TTD

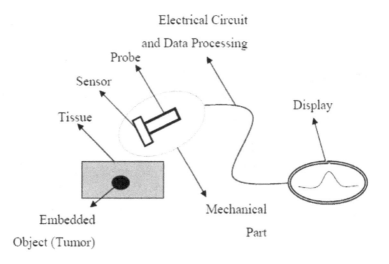

Figure 8. The TTD: A- tactile probe, B- electronic and data processor box, C- LCD display, D- power cable, E- USB to serial convertor cable, and F- monitor display

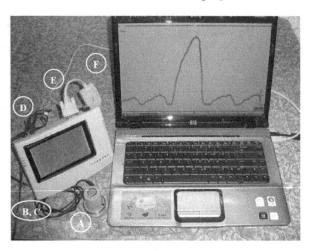

challenges are proposed and used in predicting the foreign currency exchange rates and the results are compared with feed-forward and other recurrent structures (Hussain & Liatsis; 2008). Nonetheless, PSN is not a universal approximator, a generalization of PSN is the Ridge Polynomial HONN (RPHONN) proposed by Shin & Ghosh (1995). Dynamic RPHONN is used in prediction of the exchange rate of different time series data (Ghazali et al; 2007).

Furthermore, activation function in some structure of HONNs is adaptive (sigmoid, sine, cosine, SINC, etc.) or even for better fitting specifications, model may have more than one activation function type (Xu, 2008). Chen et al (1996) introduces an adoptive sigmoid activation function and compares the results with traditional FNN for modeling the static and dynamic systems. Campolucci et al (1996) proposes an adaptive activation function as a spline piecewise approximation for reducing the size of NN. Zhang et al (2002) proposes N-dimensional neuron adoptive HONNs (NAHONNs) and discusses the learning algorithm and converging issues for being a universal approximator. Also, a discussion

Figure 9. Experimental setup with robot: A- robot, B- power supply, C- display, D- electronic board, E- serial port, F- robot gripper, G- tactile probe, H- simulated tissue and mass

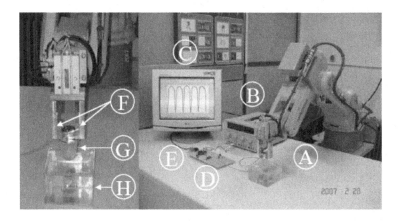

Figure 10. Tactile probe output after scanning the entire surface with robot

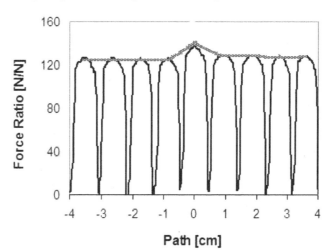

for NAHONN group (NAHONG) models is given by Zhang et al (2002). The experimental result has confirmed that NAHONG models provides superior approximation capabilities of gamma function to traditional fixed NN group model and normal neuron adoptive NN group model (Zhang et al, 1999). Xu (2008) applies the adoptive HONN models in business applications such as simulating and forecasting the total taxation revenues and the reserve bank of Australia assets.

Zhang (2008) introduces a general aspect of sigma-pi models in three structures named 1b, 1 and 0 models. Formulas (1), (2) and (3) show the presented models for a network including two features, x_1 and x_2, in every sample.

HONN Model 1b:

$$Z = \sum_{i,j=0}^{N} a_{ij}^{\ 0} \cdot \left\{ a_{ij}^{\ kx_1} \cdot f_i^{x_1} \left(a_i^{\ x_1} \cdot x_1 \right) \right\} \cdot \left\{ a_{ij}^{\ hx_2} \cdot f_j^{x_2} \left(a_j^{\ x_2} \cdot x_2 \right) \right\} \tag{1}$$

HONN Model 1:

Figure 11. Operational comparison between computational and robotic results

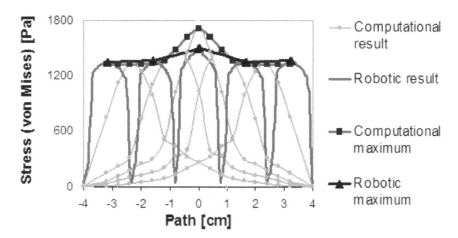

$$Z = \sum_{i,j=0}^{N} a_{ij}{}^{0} \cdot \left\{ f_i^{x_1} \left(a_i^{x_1} \cdot x_1 \right) \right\} \cdot \left\{ f_j^{x_2} \left(a_j^{x_2} \cdot x_2 \right) \right\} \qquad (2)$$

HONN Model 0:

$$Z = \sum_{i,j=0}^{N} a_{ij}{}^{0} \cdot \left\{ f_i^{x_1} \left(x_1 \right) \right\} \cdot \left\{ f_j^{x_2} \left(x_2 \right) \right\} \qquad (3)$$

Zhang (2008) also developed six different models while each model can be implemented in one of structures 1b, 1 and 0. In fact, by changing one of these six models to another, neuron activation function inside of the sigma symbol changes. They prove mathematically that the presented HONN models always converge and have better accuracy than SASNLIN. The six different models are organized as follows: PHONN, THONN, UCSHONN, SXSPHONN, SINCHONN, and SPHONN.

$$z_l = Y \times V = v_{j0} + \sum_{j=1}^{K} v_{jl} y_j \left(\overline{x} \right), Z = \left[z_1, ..., z_l, ..., z_L \right]$$

As Equations 1 and 2 demonstrate, the number of learning parameters in HONN model 1b and 1 is more than HONN model 0. As the order of model is getting higher, updating of the parameters will be more disastrous. Thus, in this study, we propose a two hidden-layered HONN including online updating orders of four high-order unit

Figure 12. HONN: model 0 and neuron activation function f(x)

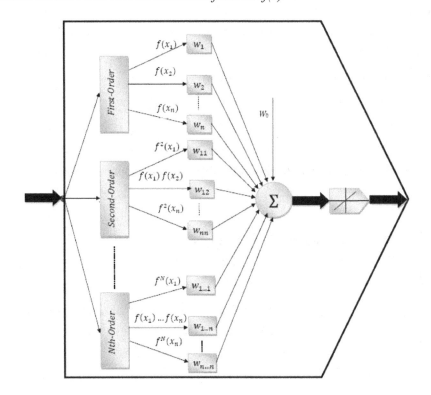

$$z_l = Y \times V = v_{j0} + \sum_{j=1}^{K} v_{jl} y_j \left(\overline{x} \right), \, Z = \left[z_1, ..., z_l, ..., z_L \right]$$

including PHONN, SPHONN, SINCHONN, THONN models implemented by HONN model 0 in the first layer and in the second layer linear, a combination of these high-order units are chosen. Figure 12 shows the structure of each high-order unit of our proposed hybrid HONN. In fact, like the prior works on using group models of neuron adoptive HONNs (Zhang et al, 1999; Zhang et al, 2002), we aim to use a group model of PHONN, SPHONN, SINCHONN, THONN implemented as model 0. Equations 4 and 5 are illustrating the mathematical overview of our proposed hybrid HONN.

$$z_l = Y \times V = v_{j0} + \sum_{j=1}^{K} v_{jl} y_j \left(\overline{x} \right), \, Z = \left[z_1, ..., z_l, ..., z_L \right]$$

$$y_j(\overline{x}) =$$

$$w_{j0}^{(1)} + \sum_{i_1=1}^{P} w_{j i_1}^{(1)} f_1\left(x_{i_1}\right) + \sum_{i_1=1}^{P}\sum_{i_2=i_1}^{P} w_{j i_1 i_2}^{(1)} f_1\left(x_{i_1}\right) f_1\left(x_{i_2}\right) + ... + \sum_{i_1=1}^{P} \cdot \cdot \sum_{i_{N_1}=i_{N_1-1}}^{P} w_{j i_1 \cdots i_{N_1}}^{(1)} f_1\left(x_{i_1}\right) \cdot f_1\left(x_{i_{N_1}}\right)$$

$$+ w_{j0}^{(2)} + \sum_{i_1=1}^{P} w_{j i_1}^{(2)} f_2\left(x_{i_1}\right) + \sum_{i_1=1}^{P}\sum_{i_2=i_1}^{P} w_{j i_1 i_2}^{(2)} f_2\left(x_{i_1}\right) f_2\left(x_{i_2}\right) + ... + \sum_{i_1=1}^{P} \cdot \cdot \sum_{i_{N_2}=i_{N_2-1}}^{P} w_{j i_1 \cdots i_{N_2}}^{(2)} f_2\left(x_{i_1}\right) \cdot f_2\left(x_{i_{N_2}}\right)$$

$$+ ...$$

$$+ w_{j0}^{(K)} + \sum_{i_1=1}^{P} w_{j i_1}^{(K)} f_K\left(x_{i_1}\right) + \sum_{i_1=1}^{P}\sum_{i_2=i_1}^{P} w_{j i_1 i_2}^{(K)} f_K\left(x_{i_1}\right) f_K\left(x_{i_2}\right) + ... + \sum_{i_1=1}^{P} \cdot \cdot \sum_{i_{N_K}=i_{N_K-1}}^{P} w_{j i_1 \cdots i_{N_K}}^{(K)} f_K\left(x_{i_1}\right) \cdot f_K\left(x_{i_{N_K}}\right)$$

$$z_l = Y \times V = v_{j0} + \sum_{j=1}^{K} v_{jl} y_j \left(\overline{x} \right), \, Z = \left[z_1, ..., z_l, ..., z_L \right] \tag{4}$$

$$z_l = Y \times V = v_{j0} + \sum_{j=1}^{K} v_{jl} y_j \left(\overline{x} \right), \, Z = \left[z_1, ..., z_l, ..., z_L \right] \tag{5}$$

where, L is the number of outputs (Bit number of output binary code), P is the number of input samples, K is the number of higher order units having the order greater than 0 and $N_1, N_2, ... N_K$ consecutively are optimum acquired order of higher order units 1, 2 to K.

The number of hidden neurons in the first layer is directly specifying by the order of high-order units. The second hidden layer of our proposed hybrid HONN is only a linear combination of the first hidden layer's output. As the features of output for each tumor/tissue parameter is one, so we set one hidden neuron for this layer.

The first layer weights subsequently update by Equation 6:

$$w_{j i_1 \cdots i_{N_k}}^{(k)}\left(t+1\right) = w_{j i_1 \cdots i_{N_k}}^{(k)}\left(t\right) - \eta \cdot \left(\partial E / \partial w_{j i_1 \cdots i_{N_k}}^{(k)} \right)$$

$$\frac{\partial E}{\partial w_{j i_1 \cdots i_{N_k}}^{(k)}} = \frac{\partial E}{\partial y_j} \cdot \frac{\partial y_j}{\partial w_{j i_1 \cdots i_{N_k}}^{(k)}} = \frac{\partial E}{\partial y_j} \cdot f_K\left(x_{i_1}\right) \cdots f_K\left(x_{i_{N_K}}\right)$$

$$\frac{\partial E}{\partial y_j} = \frac{\partial}{\partial y_j} \left[\frac{1}{2} \sum_{l=1}^{L} \left(d_l - z_l\right)^2 \right] = \sum_{l=1}^{L} \left(d_l - z_l\right) \frac{\partial}{\partial y_j}\left(Y \times V\right) = \sum_{l=1}^{L} \left(d_l - z_l\right) v_{jl} \tag{6}$$

where, t is training state, η is learning coefficient, E is error, W is weight matrix of first hidden layer and V is weight matrix of second hidden layer, L is the number of outputs (Bit number of output binary code), P is the number of input samples, K is the number of higher order units which have the order greater than 0 and N_1, N_2, ..., N_k consecutively are optimum acquired order of higher order units 1, 2 to K.

In the next sections, by using hybrid HONN presented above, we will probe the best fitted model of hybrid HONN over each tumor and tissue parameter. In addition, we will try to find out a best fitted model of multilayered back propagation feed-forward neural network (BPN/FNN) for each tumor and tissue parameter, and finally, we will compare FNN models with HONN models.

Definition of the Problem

As discussed in the previous sections, for simulation purposes, the physical examination process for the lumps in the breast was divided into two parts: first, the prediction of the tumor's existence; and second, the determination of the tumor's characteristics, such as diameter, depth and stiffness. The parameters are the ones we used earlier in the FEM method. These parameters are the input parameters of the forward models. Figure 1 shows a stress graph obtained in the forward solution. Although it is predicted that the results of the forward approach can show the existence of tumors, they do not provide the physicians with detailed information on the tumor characteristics. To this end, we propose the use of an inverse approach on forward results using HONN model and compare it with ANN results.

Materials and Methods

It would appear that HONNs are promising in providing better solutions for determining tumor characteristics inside the tissue. We employed NNs to determine the tumor characteristics, where stress graphs were the inputs of the network and the tumor characteristics were the desired outputs. The distinct features of the NN make this approach very useful in situations where the functional dependence between the inputs and outputs is not clear.

In this study, to train the network effectively, a feature extraction step had to be undertaken. It involves examining the data collected through the forward results. In selecting these features, we carefully examined all of the stress graphs obtained. To determine which features were most important in characterizing these data, we focused on the stress graphs to extract some features that best corresponded to the desired tumor characteristics: diameter (d), depth (h) and tumor/tissue stiffness ratio (Er). Five features extracted from the stress graphs were:

1. The maximum stress.
2. The stress value corresponding to one-fifth of the distance between the peak and the beginning of the stress graph.
3. The stress value corresponding to two-fifths of the distance between the peak and the beginning of the stress graph.
4. The stress at the beginning.
5. The transverse value (fatness or narrowness) of the stress graphs at 50% of the difference between the maximum stress and the stress at the beginning of the stress graphs. Figure 13 shows these features in a typical stress graph.

By using these five features, we have converted and reduced the total stress graphs into five more effective numbers, being the inputs of the NN. For example, Figure 14(a) shows stress graphs for different values of tumor diameter (d) when the other tumor characteristics are kept constant. It can be perceived from this figure that changing the tumor diameter causes the stress graph to change and, as a result, the extracted features are also altered. This situation also applies to tumor depth (h; see Figure

Figure 13. Extracted features in the stress graph

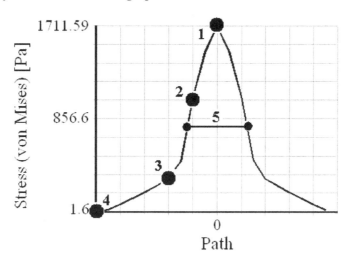

14(b)), tissue loading (*l*; see Figure 14(c)) and tissue thickness (*t*; see Figure 14(d)). Figure 14(e) shows the trivial changes of the extracted features by altering the tumor tissue stiffness ratio (*Er*).

Simulations and Results

In the supervised learning paradigm, a set of experimental pairs (forward analyses) of an input output mapping is needed to train the NN. In this work, we used 20 data samples obtained from the forward approach to train HONN and ANN. A data sample was a vector with five elements (numbers), being the extracted features of a stress graph. Therefore, 20 data samples meant that there were 20 vectors containing five extracted features of 20 stress graphs. These vectors were the inputs of our NN. In addition to different cases made by changing just one tumor parameter, we constructed models in which more tumor characteristics were altered. This helped the NN to have an expanded input space.

There was significant variation in the scales of the values of the input variables. These different scales of the inputs led to ill-conditioning of the problem (Sun *et al*, 2003). To avoid this problem, the input data were normalized using formula (4):

$$\bar{x}_i = \frac{x_i - mean\left(X_j\right)}{\sqrt{\text{var}\left(X_j\right)}}$$

$$mean\left(X_j\right) = \frac{\sum_{i=1}^{n} x_i}{n}$$

$$where :$$

$$X_j = \left[x_1, ..., x_i, ..., x_n\right] \tag{7}$$

Figure 14. Stress graphs for different values of: (a) tumor diameter; (b) tumor depth; (c) Tissue loading; (d) Tissue thickness; (e) stiffness ratio of tumor to tissue

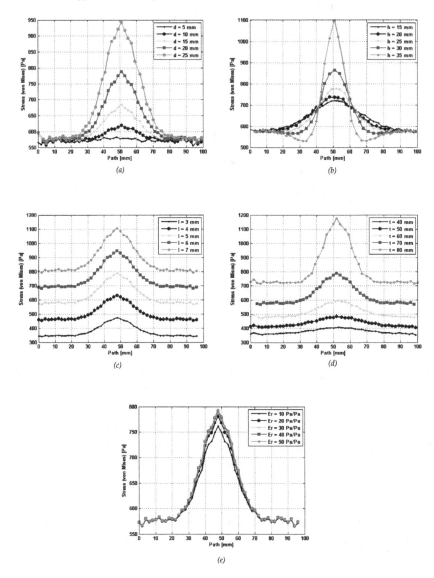

$\overline{x}_i$ is the normalized value, x_i is the original value of the variable, x_j is the set of value of feature j including x_i and n is the number of samples.

In the following part, we introduce our criteria for developing each one of the FNN and HONN models.

1. HONN Models for Tumor Parameter Estimation

To find the best model and order of each HONN model for each tumor-tissue parameter we used structure 0 written as formula (3) and combination of HONN models 1, 2, 5 and 6 which are PHONN,

Table 2. Best HONN model of each parameter

Tumor/Tissue parameter	l	t	d	h
PHONN	-	4	1	1
SPHONN - TANSIG	1	3	1	5
SPHONN - LOGSIG	4	5	1	5
SINCHONN	-	-	1	6
THONN	-	2	1	1

Table 3. Best FNN model of each parameter

Tumor/Tissue parameter		l	t	d	h	Er
No. of Hidden Layers		1	1	2	2	3
No. of Hidden Neurons	Hidden Layer 1	15	3	6	6	5
	Hidden Layer 2	-	-	8	3	5
	Hidden Layer 3	-	-	-	-	9

THONN, SINCHONN, and SPHONN, respectively. SPHONN can be implemented by both LOGSIG and TANSIG activation functions. We used all combination of the five models (1, 2, 5 and 6 with LOGSIG and TANSIG) and also used all orders from 0 to 8. By comparing all of these models (by changing just one model's order every time) we achieved the best HONN structure being the best fitted input-output mapping for each tumor and tissue parameter. Table 2 shows the best HONN model for each of tumor and tissue parameters.

2.   FNN Models for Tumor Parameter Estimation

There exist no analytical methods to determine the optimum number of hidden layers and optimum number of hidden neurons in each layer required for a specific problem (Su & Khorasani, 2001). For FNN, several rules of thumb to select the number of hidden neurons have been proposed by various researchers (Igelnik & Parikh, 2003). In this work, the comparative study showed that in the case of *Er* estimation, more hidden layer required than other parameters. For each FNN network, a combination of sigmoid activation functions and linear transfer function are used in the hidden and output layers, respectively. This combination has been shown to be sufficient to learn any types of mapping (Chen & Chen, 1995). Our investigations demonstrate that the TANSIG function produces better results than the LOGSIG function. So by changing the number of hidden layers (1 up to 3) and neuron numbers (1 up to 20) in every hidden layer we achieved the final FNN model being the best fitted for input-output mapping. Table 3 shows the acquired FNN models of each output parameter.

Levenberg-Marquardt Back-propagation (Hagan *et al*, 1996) was utilized for minimizing the error function in training both FNN and HONN networks. As discussed before, we use structure 0; therefore, the process learning of both FNN and HONN are same and somehow we can compare the running time by the number of epoch that best result occurred.

Comparisons of FNN Nonlinear Models and HONN Nonlinear Models

In this section, according to the result of previous section for finding the best nonlinear model of FNN and HONN, we compare the efficiency of models based on 2 specificities including Output Linear Regression (R^2) and root-mean square (RMS) of error. Also, as discussed before, as a result of our HONN approach, we can compare the training epoch number for investigation of convergence timing.

From statistics, linear regression with one independent variable represents a straight line and evaluate by regression coefficient R^2 given as formula (5):

where $\overline{y}$ is the mean value of output, y_i is ith output of network and $\hat{y}_i$ is the desired value. Also, to evaluate the precision of estimations, we calculated the root-mean square defined by formula (6):

$$R^2 = 1 - \frac{\sum_{i=1}^{n}\left(y_i - \hat{y}_i\right)^2}{\sum_{i=1}^{n}\left(y_i - \hat{y}\right)^2}$$

$$\overline{y} = \frac{1}{n}\sum_{i=1}^{n}y_i$$

(8)

$$Mean\ Squared\ Error(MSE) = \frac{1}{n}\sum_{i=1}^{n}\left(\hat{y}_i - y_i\right)^2$$

$$RMS = \sqrt{MSE} = \sqrt{\frac{1}{n}\sum_{i=1}^{n}\left(\hat{y}_i - y_i\right)^2}$$

(9)

The regression schematic of the NNs is illustrated in Figures 15, 16, 17 and 18, comparing the tumor characteristics calculated by the FNN and HONN with the desired values.

Figure 15(a) and 15(b) show the linear regression of tissue loading estimations calculated by FNN and HONN, respectively and present a comparison with the desired values. As can be seen in Figure 15(a) and 15(b), all points are located on or very close to the diagonal line and this verifies that the results obtained from ANN and HONN agreed well with the desired values. It is concluded that the value of regression for the HONN is better. Similarly, Figures 16, 17 and 18, respectively show the comparison of linear regression between FNN and HONN for tissue loading (l), tissue thickness (t), tumor diameter (d), and tumor depth (h). Detailed values of regression for validation data and all data (training and validation samples) are given in Figure 19 and 20 and Table 4. In all parameters regression value of HONN is closer to 1. Figure 19 shows the comparison of R^2 value of all tumor and tissue parameters for FNN and HONN. Figure 20 shows the comparison of R^2 value of validation samples of tumor and tissue parameters for FNN and HONN.

Experiment results show that the estimation of *Er* cannot be carried out by a FNN including two hidden layers. The result of regression for the best FNN included 2 hidden layers is shown in Figure 21(a). As we showed in Table 3, the complex network has 3 hidden layers including 5, 5 and 9 neurons, respectively in the first, second and third hidden layer. The result of regression for the best FNN included 3 hidden layers is shown in Figure 21(b). Each model can have an order 0 up to 8. In spite of this effort, there was not a good HONN model for estimating *Er*. As a result, comparative figures of FNN and HONN are not including HONN model for estimating *Er*.

Figure 15. Comparison of tissue loading estimation and desired values calculated by: (a) FNN; (b) HONN

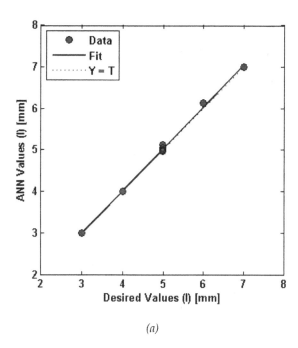

(a)

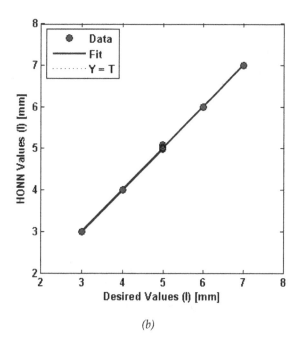

(b)

Figure 16. Comparison of tissue thickness estimation and desired values calculated by: (a) FNN; (b) HONN

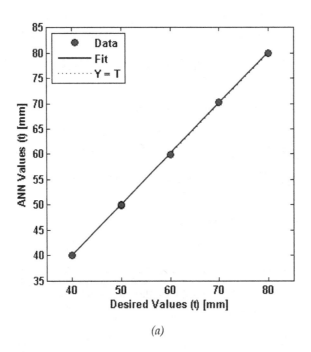

(a)

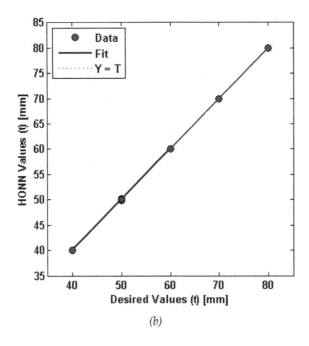

(b)

Figure 17. Comparison of tumor diameter estimation and desired values calculated by: (a) FNN; (b) HONN

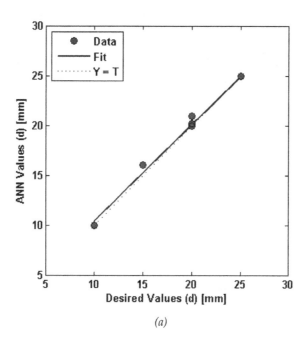

(a)

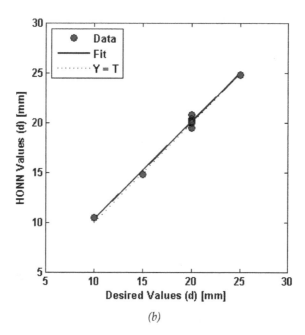

(b)

Figure 18. Comparison of tumor depth estimation and desired values calculated by: (a) FNN; (b) HONN

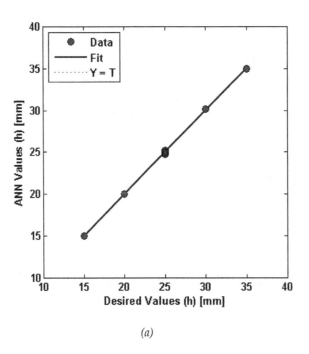

(a)

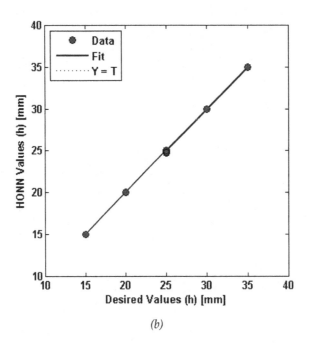

(b)

Figure 19. Comparison of linear regression (R2) between FNN and HONN for all samples (including training and validation samples)

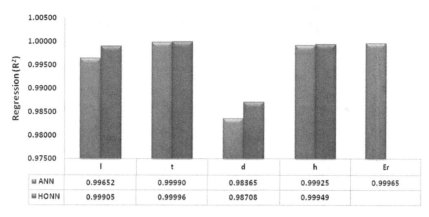

Figure 20. Comparison of linear regression (R²) between FNN and HONN for validation samples

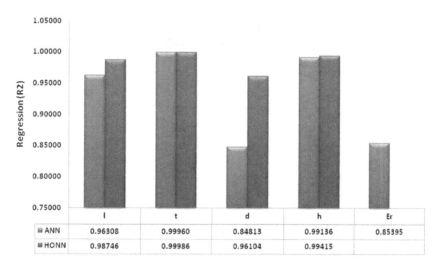

Table 4. Comparison of root-mean square (RMS), linear regression (R²) and epoch number between FNN and HONN

Tumor / Tissue parameter	Model	Epoch No.	Validation samples RMS	All samples RMS	Validation samples R²	All samples R²
Tissue loading (*l*)	FNN	100	0.007151	0.042282	0.96308	0.99652
	HONN	24	0.001902	0.021808	0.98746	0.99905
Tissue thickness (*t*)	FNN	17	0.026815	0.081886	0.99960	0.99990
	HONN	5	0.008652	0.049936	0.99986	0.99996
Tumor diameter (*d*)	FNN	96	0.452408	0.336307	0.84813	0.98365
	HONN	23	0.193201	0.301077	0.96104	0.98708
Tumor depth (*h*)	FNN	3197	0.037598	0.096951	0.99136	0.99925
	HONN	5	0.025111	0.079492	0.99415	0.99949
Tumor: Tissue Stiffness (*Er*)	FNN	59	0.070134	0.132447	0.85395	0.99965
	HONN	-	-	-	-	-

Figure 21. Linear regression (R²) for (a) the best two hidden layered FNN (R²=0.85669); (b) the best three hidden layered FNN (R²=0.99965)

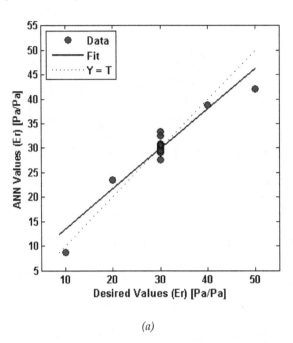

(a)

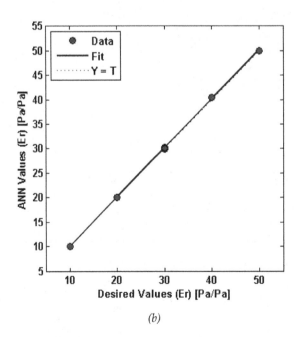

(b)

Figure 22. Comparison of root-mean square (RMS) between FNN and HONN for all samples (including training and validation samples)

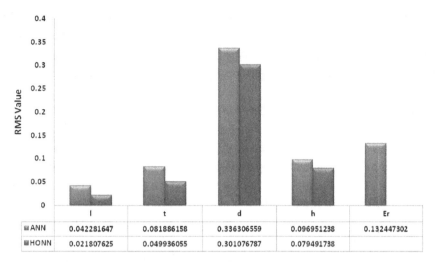

	l	t	d	h	Er
ANN	0.042281647	0.081886158	0.336306559	0.096951238	0.132447302
HONN	0.021807625	0.049936055	0.301076787	0.079491738	

Figure 23. Comparison of root-mean square (RMS) between FNN and HONN for validation samples

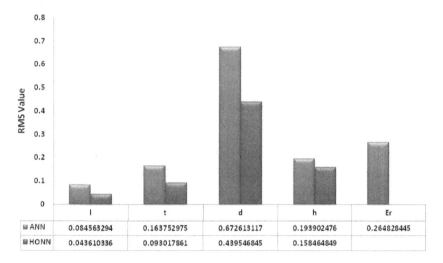

	l	t	d	h	Er
ANN	0.084563294	0.163752975	0.672613117	0.193902476	0.264828445
HONN	0.043610336	0.093017861	0.439546845	0.158464849	

We used formula (6) for calculating both RMS values of FNN and HONN. Figure 22 shows the RMS value of each FNN and HONN for all data samples including training and validation. Figure 23 shows RMS values for validation samples. Indeed, these figures demonstrate the better fitting properties of HONN models over the nonlinear mapping of stress graph and tissue/tumor parameters.

Finally, we present the detailed performance of each FNN and HONN model in Table 4. Table 4 shows convergence epoch number of ANN models and HONN models for each tumor-tissue parameter.

CONCLUSION

Determination of the effective parameters of artificial tactile sensing by using ANN, FEM, and HONN is proposed in this chapter. A significant and discriminating aspect of the theoretical studies on the TTD is the 3-D analysis of the tissue and tumor. This is because performing modeling in a 3-D mode is the only way to observe and examine the contours produced on the surface of the tissue that, in turn, are used to determine the shape of the tumor.

For estimation of the tumor/tissue characteristics we used HONNs instead of commonly used FNNs. As simulation results showed HONNs most often have better fitting specifications. By using one-hidden layered HONNs we were able to have an open box model of input-output mapping making outputs as a nonlinear function of inputs. In some tumor parameters (depth and diameter), using one hidden layered FNN could not suitably fit over the input-output mapping, so we were forced to use more complex FNN that increased the intelligibility of fitted model and also provided us with long time convergence. Instead, by using HONN and adding other functions and enhancing the function orders we were able to have a simply explainable function for our data mapping.

An important feature of the TTD is the benefits of the artificial tactile sensing approach for surgeons in their diagnostic procedures. The immediate application is that by the TTD a medical doctor can easily obtain adequate information about the presence of the mass without any kind of penetration into the patient's body.

REFERENCES

Artyomov, E., & Yadid-Pecht, O. (2005). Modified high-order neural network for invariant pattern recognition. *Pattern Recognition Letters*, *26*(6), 843–851. doi:10.1016/j.patrec.2004.09.029

Bar-Cohen, Y., Mavroidis, C., Bouzit, M., et al. (2000). Virtual reality robotic operation simulations using MEMICA haptic system. *International Conference for Smart systems and Robotics for Medicine and Space Applications*, Houston, TX, USA.

Barman, I., & Guha, S. K. (2006). Analysis of a new combined stretch and pressure sensor for internal nodule palpation. *Sensors and Actuators A*, *125*, 210–216. doi:10.1016/j.sna.2005.07.010

Campolucci, P., Capparelli, F., Guarnieri, S., Piazza, F., & Uncini, A. (1996). Neural networks with adaptive spline activation function. In [Bari, Italy.]. *Proceedings of IEEE MELECON*, *96*, 1442–1445.

Chen, C. T., & Chang, W. D. (1996). A feed-forward neural network with function shape autotuning. *Neural Networks*, *9*(4), 627–641. doi:10.1016/0893-6080(96)00006-8

Chen, T., & Chen, H. (1995). Universal approximation to non-linear operators by neural networks with arbitrary activation functions and its application to dynamical system. *IEEE Transactions on Neural Networks*, *6*(4), 911–917. doi:10.1109/72.392253

Dargahi, J. (2001). A study of the human hand as an ideal tactile sensor used in robotic and endoscopic applications. In *Proceedings of CSME International Conference*, (pp. 21–22). Montreal, Quebec.

Dargahi, J. (2002). An endoscopic and robotic tooth-like compliance and roughness tactile sensor. *Journal of Mechanical Design, 124*, 576–582. doi:10.1115/1.1471531

Dargahi, J., & Najarian, S. (2004a). Human tactile perception as a standard for artificial tactile sensing. A review. *International Journal of Medical Robotics and Computer Assisted Surgery, 1*(13), 23–35. doi:10.1002/rcs.3

Dargahi, J., & Najarian, S. (2004b). Analysis of a membrane type polymeric-based tactile sensor for biomedical and medical robotic applications. *Sensor. Mater, 16*(1), 25–41.

Dargahi, J., & Najarian, S. (2005a). Measurements and modeling of compliance using a novel multi sensor endoscopic grasper device. *Sensors Mater, 17*, 7–20.

Dargahi, J., & Najarian, S. (2005b). Advances in tactile sensors design/manufacturing and its impact on robotics application. A review. *The Industrial Robot, 32*(3), 268–281. doi:10.1108/01439910510593965

Dong, G., & Pei, J. (2007). *Sequence Data Mining (Advances in Database Systems).* New York: Springer.

Eltaib, M. E. H., & Hewit, J. R. (2003). Tactile sensing technology for minimal access surgery – a review . *Mechatronics, 13*, 1163–1177. doi:10.1016/S0957-4158(03)00048-5

Fearing, R. S., Moy, G., & Tan, E. (1997). Some basic issues in teletaction. In *Proceedings of IEEE International Conference Robotics and Automation*, (pp. 3093–3099). Albuquerque, NM.

Foresti, G. L., & Dolso, T. (2004). An adaptive high-order neural tree for pattern recognition, *IEEE Transactions on Systems, Manufacturing, and Cybernetics . Part B: Cybernetics, 34*(2), 988–996. doi:10.1109/TSMCB.2003.818538

Fulcher, J., Zhang, M., & Shuxiang, X. (2006). Application of higher-order nueral networks to financial time series prediction. In Kamruzzaman, J., Begg, R. K. & Sarker, R. A. (Eds.), *Artificial neural networks in finance and manufacturing* (pp. 80-108). Hershey, PA: Information Science Reference.

Fung, Y. C. (1993). *Biomechanics: Mechanical Properties of Living Tissues*, 2nd ed., New York: Springer Verlag.

Galea, A. M. (2004). *Mapping tactile imaging information: parameter estimation and deformable registration.* Cambridge, MA: Harvard University Dissertation.

Gao, L., Parker, K. J., Lerner, R. M., & Levinson, S. F. (1996). Imaging of the elastic properties of tissue – a review. *Ultrasound in Medicine & Biology, 22*(8), 959–977. doi:10.1016/S0301-5629(96)00120-2

Ghazali, R., Hussain, A. J., Al-jumeily, D., & Merabti, M. (2007). Dynamic Ridge Polynomial Neural Networks in Exchange Rates Time Series Forecasting. In B. Beliczynski, A. Dzielinski, M. Iwanowski, & B. Ribeiro, *Adaptive and Natural Computing Algorithms.* (pp. 123-132). Berlin, Germany: Springer.

Gupta, M. M., Homma, N., Hou, Z., Solo, A. M. G., & Goto, T. (2009). Fundamental theory of artificial higher order neural networks. In Zhang, M. (Ed.), *Artificial higher order neural networks for economics and business* (pp. 368-388). Hershey, PA: Information Science Reference.

Hagan, M. T., Demuth, H. B., & Beale, M. (1996). *Neural network design*. Boston: PWS Publishing Company.

Hibbeler, R. C. (2002). *Mechanics of Materials*, 5th ed. New Jersey: Prentice Hall Publishing Co.

Homma, N., & Gupta, M. M. (2002). A general second order neural unit. *Bull. Coll. Med. Sci. Tohoku Univ., 11*(1), 1–6.

Hussain, A., & Liatsis, P. (2008). A Novel Recurrent Polynomial Neural Network for Financial Time Series Prediction. In Z. M., *Higher Order Neural Networks for Economics and Business.* (pp. 190- 211). Hershey, PA: Idea Group Inc (IGI).

Igelnik, B., & Parikh, N. (2003). Komogorov's spline network. *IEEE Transactions on Neural Networks, 14*(4), 725–733. doi:10.1109/TNN.2003.813830

Kane, B. J., Cutkosky, M. R., & Kavacs, G. T. (1996). Compatible traction stress sensor for use in high resolution tactile imaging. *Sensors and Actuators A, 54*, 511–516. doi:10.1016/S0924-4247(95)01191-9

Kerdoke, A. E., Cotin, S. M., & Ottensmeyer, M. P. (2003). Truth cube: establishing physical standard for soft tissue simulation. *Medical Image Analysis, 7*, 283–291. doi:10.1016/S1361-8415(03)00008-2

Kosmatopoulos, E. B., Polycarpou, M. M., Christodoulou, M. A., & Ioannou, P. A. (1995). High-order neural network structures for identification of dynamical systems. *IEEE Transactions on Neural Networks, 6*, 422–431. doi:10.1109/72.363477

Lee, M. H. (2000). Tactile sensing: new directions, new challenges. *The International Journal of Robotics Research, 19*(7), 636–643.

Lee, Y. C., Doolen, G., Chen, H., Sun, G., Maxwell, T., Lee, H., & Giles, C. L. (1986). Machine learning using a higher order correlation network . *Physica D. Nonlinear Phenomena, 22*, 276–306.

Lippmann, R. P. (1989). Pattern classification using neural networks. *Communications Magazine, IEEE, 27*(11).

Melzer, H. H., Schurr, M. O., Kunert, W., Buess, G., Voges, U., & Meyer, J. U. (1993). Intelligent surgical instrument system. *Endoscopic Surgery and Allied Technologies, 1*(3), 165–170.

Najarian, S. Dargahi, J. & Changizi, M. A. (2006). A tactile probe with applications in biomedical robotics. In *Proceedings of the IEEE ISIE06 Automated Conference Submission System*, Montreal, Canada.

Najarian, S., Dargahi, J., & Abouie, A. (2009). Artificial Tactile Sensing in Biomedical Engineering. New York: *McGraw-Hill Publication Co.*

Peng, H., & Zhu, S. (2007). Handling of incomplete data sets using ICA and SOM in data mining . *Neural Computing & Applications, 16*(2), 167–172. doi:10.1007/s00521-006-0058-6

Redding, N., Kowalczyk, A., & Downs, T. (1993). Constructive high-order network algorithm that is polynomial time. *Neural Networks, 6*, 997–1010. doi:10.1016/S0893-6080(09)80009-9

Reid, M. B., Spirkovska, L., & Ochoa, E. (1989). Simultaneous position, scale, rotation invariant pattern classification using third-order neural networks. *Int. J. Neural Networks, 1,* 154–159.

Rovithakis, G. A., Chalkiadakis, I., & Zervakis, M. E. (2004). High-order neural network structure selection for function approximation applications using genetic algorithms, *IEEE Transactions on Systems, Manufacturing, and Cybernetics . Part B: Cybernetics, 34*(1), 150–158. doi:10.1109/TSMCB.2003.811767

Rovithakis, G. A., & Chistodoulou, M. A. (2000). Adaptive control with recurrent high-order neural networks. New York: Springer Verlag.

Shin, Y., & Ghosh, J. (1991). The Pi-Sigma Networks: An Efficient Higher-order Neural Network for Pattern Classification and Function Approximation In *Proceedings of International Joint Conference on Neural Networks, 1,* 13-18.

Shin, Y., & Ghosh, J. (1995). Ridge Polynomial Networks. *IEEE Transactions on Neural Networks, 6*(3), 610–622. doi:10.1109/72.377967

Singh, H., Dargahi, J., & Sedaghati, R. (2003) Experimental and finite element analysis of an endoscopic tooth-like tactile sensor. *2nd IEEE International Conference on Sensors,* Toronto, Canada.

Spirkovska, L. Reid, M. B. (1990). Connectivity strategies for higher-order neural networks applied topattern recognition. *International Joint Conference on Neural Network,* 21-26 vol.1.

Su, Z., & Khorasani, K. (2001). A neural network-based controller for a single-link flexible manipulator using the inverse dynamics approach. *IEEE Transactions on Industrial Electronics, 48*(6), 1074–1086. doi:10.1109/41.969386

Sun, Y., Peng, Y., Chen, Y., & Shukla, A. J. (2003). Application of artificial neural networks in the design of controlled release drug delivery systems. *Advanced Drug Delivery Reviews, 55,* 1201–1215. doi:10.1016/S0169-409X(03)00119-4

Tsai, H. (in press). Hybrid high order neural networks. *International Journal of Applied Soft Computing.*

Vinckier, A., & Semenza, G. (1998). Measuring elasticity of biological materials by atomic force microscopy. *FEBS Letters, 430*(1/2), 12–16. doi:10.1016/S0014-5793(98)00592-4

Wang, J. H., & Lin, J. H. (1995). Qualitative analysis of the BP composed of product units and summing units. *IEEE International Conference on Systems, Manufacturing and Cybernetics, 1,* 35–39.

Wang, S. H. (2003). Application of self-organizing maps for data mining with incomplete data sets . *Neural Computing & Applications, 12*(1), 42–48. doi:10.1007/s00521-003-0372-1

Wellman, P. S., & Howe, R. D. (1999). *The mechanical properties of breast tissue in compression* (Tech. Rep. No. 99003). Harvard BioRobotics Laboratory, Cambridge, MA.

Xu, S. (2008). Adaptive Higher Order Neural Network Models and Their Applications in Business. In M. Zhang (Ed.), *Artificial Higher Order Neural Networks for Economics and Business* (pp. 314-329). Hershey, PA: IGI Global.

Zeng, J., Wang, Y., Freedman, M. T., & Mum, S. K. (1997). Finger tracking for breast palpation quantification using color image features. *SPIE J Opt Eng, 36*(12), 3455–3461. doi:10.1117/1.601585

Zhang, M. (2008). Artificial Higher Order Neural Networks nonlinear models: SAS NLIN or HONNs? In M. Zhang (Ed.), *Artificial Higher Order Neural Networks for Economics and Business* (pp. 1-47). Herhsey, PA: IGI Global.

Zhang, M., Xu, S., & Fulcher, J. (2002). Neuron-adaptive higher order neural-network models for automated financial data modeling. *IEEE Transactions on Neural Networks, 13*(1).

Zhang, M., Xu, S., & Lu, B. (1999). Neuron-adaptive higher order neural-network group models. *International Joint Conference on Neural Networks*, 333-336.

Chapter 22

A Theoretical and Empirical Study of Functional Link Neural Networks (FLNNs) for Classification

Satchidananda Dehuri
Fakir Mohan University, India

Sung-Bae Cho
Yonsei University, Korea

ABSTRACT

In this chapter, the primary focus is on theoretical and empirical study of functional link neural networks (FLNNs) for classification. We present a hybrid Chebyshev functional link neural network (cFLNN) without hidden layer with evolvable particle swarm optimization (ePSO) for classification. The resulted classifier is then used for assigning proper class label to an unknown sample. The hybrid cFLNN is a type of feed-forward neural networks, which have the ability to transform the non-linear input space into higher dimensional space where linear separability is possible. In particular, the proposed hybrid cFLNN combines the best attribute of evolvable particle swarm optimization (ePSO), back-propagation learning (BP-Learning), and Chebyshev functional link neural networks (CFLNN). We have shown its effectiveness of classifying the unknown pattern using the datasets obtained from UCI repository. The computational results are then compared with other higher order neural networks (HONNs) like functional link neural network with a generic basis functions, Pi-Sigma neural network (PSNN), radial basis function neural network (RBFNN), and ridge polynomial neural network (RPNN).

INTRODUCTION

In recent years, neural networks, in particular higher order neural networks (Ghosh & Shin, 1992) have been widely used to classify non-linearly separable patterns and can be viewed as a problem of approximating an arbitrary decision boundary. In the sequel it can successfully distinguish the various

DOI: 10.4018/978-1-61520-711-4.ch022

classes in the feature space. In reality, the boundaries between classes are as a rule nonlinear. It is also known that using a number of hyperplanes can approximate any non-linear surface. Hence the problem of classification can be viewed as approximating the linear surfaces that can appropriately model the class boundaries while providing minimum number of misclassified data points. In other words, a classifier partitions the training candidate space X into class-labeled regions of C_i, $i=1,2,3,...,k$, where k is the number of classes such that $\bigcup_{i=1}^{k} C_i = X$, and $C_j \cap C_m = \varphi$ for j, $m=1(1)k$ and $j \neq m$ (if there is no fuzziness). The feature space is denoted as D. If D with four or more dimensions is partitioned linearly, the decision functions are called hyperplanes. Otherwise the decision functions are hypercubes. A general hyperplane can be represented as $H(x)=W.X^T=w_1.x_1+w_2.x_2+....+w_D.x_D+w_{D+1}$, where $W=[w_1, w_2,..., w_D, w_{D+1}]$ and $X=[x_1, x_2,..., x_D, 1]$ are called the weight and augmented feature vectors respectively.

Artificial neural networks have become one of the most acceptable soft computing tools for approximating the decision boundaries of a classification problem (Haykin, 1999; Mangasarian & Wild, 2008). This well-liked behavior stems from a number of reasons, including: their capability to capture nonlinear relationships between input-output of patterns; their biological plausibility, as compared to conventional statistical models (Fukunaga, 1990; Theodorodis & Koutroumbas, 1999); their potential for parallel implementations; their celebrated robustness and graceful degradation, etc. In fact, a multi-layer perceptron (MLP) with a suitable architecture is capable of approximating virtually any function of interest (Hornik, 1991). This does not mean that finding such a network is easy. On the contrary, problems, such as local minima trapping, saturation, weight interference, initial weight dependence, and over-fitting, make neural network training difficult.

An easy way to avoid these problems consists in removing the hidden layers. This may sound a little inconsiderate at first, since it is due to them that nonlinear input output relationships can be captured. Encouragingly enough, the removing procedure can be executed without giving up non-linearity, provided that the input layer is endowed with additional higher order units (Giles & Maxwell, 1987; Pao, 1989). This is the idea behind HONNs (Antyomov & Pecht, 2005) like functional link neural networks (FLNNs) (Misra & Dehuri, 2007), ridge polynomial neural networks (RPNN) (Shin & Ghosh, 1995; Shin & Ghosh, 1992a), recurrent high-order neural networks (RHONNs) (Kosmatopoulos, Polycarpou, Christodoulou & Ioannou, 1995; Kosmatopoulos & Christodoulou, 1997; Rovithakis & Christodoulou, 2000), and so on.

Furthermore, HONNs have been used in many applications such as image compression (Liatsis & Hussain, 1999), time series prediction (Tawfik & Liatsis, 1997), system identification (Mirea & Marcu, 2002), function approximation and pattern recognition (Shin & Ghosh, 1991; Shin & Ghosh, 1992b; Kaita, Tomita & Yamanaka, 2002). HONNs are simple in their architectures and require less number of weights to learn the underlying approximating polynomials. This potentially reduces the number of required training parameters. As a result, they can learn faster since each iteration of the training procedure takes less time. This makes them suitable for complex problem solving where the ability to retrain or adapt to new data in real time is critical. Currently, there have been many algorithms used to train the functional link neural networks, such as back-propagation learning algorithm, genetic algorithm (Goldberg, 1989), particle swarm optimization (Kennedy & Eberhart, 1995), and so on. However back-propagation (BP) learning algorithms have their own limitations, which are described below.

In the context of training FLNN, the mostly used algorithm is the BP learning algorithms (a brief survey on FLNN with various type of learning schemes are given in Table 3 of Section 2. Hence some inherent problems exist in BP learning algorithm are also frequently encountered in the use of this algorithm. Firstly, the BP learning algorithm will easily get trapped in local optima especially for those non-linearly separable classification problems. Second, the convergent speed of the BP learning is too slow even if the learning goal, a given termination error, can be achieved. In addition, the convergent behavior of the BP learning algorithm depends very much on the choices of initial values of the network connection weights as well as the parameters in the algorithm such as the learning rate and momentum. But we can advocate that if the search for the BP learning algorithms starts from the near optimum with a small tuning of the learning parameters, the searching results can be improved.

We can harness the supremacy of genetic algorithms and particle swarm optimization for training the FLNN to reduce the local optimality and speed up the convergence. But training using genetic algorithm has some limitations: in the training process it requires encoding and decoding operator which is commonly treated as a long standing barrier of neural networks researchers. The important problem of applying genetic algorithms to train neural networks may be unsatisfactory because recombination operators incur several problems, such as competing conventions (Schaffer, Whitley & Eshelman, 1992) and the epitasis effect (Davidor, 1990). For better performance and make the coding easier, real coded genetic algorithms (Eshelman & Schaffer, 1993; Muhlenbein & Schlierkamp, 1993) have been introduced. However, they generally employ random-based mutations, and hence still require lengthy local searches near local optima.

On the other hand PSO has some attractive properties. It retains previous useful information; whereas GA destroys the previous knowledge of the problems once the population changes. PSO encourages constructive cooperation and information sharing among particles, which enhances the search for a global optimal solution. Successful applications of PSO to some optimization problems such as function minimization (Schutte & Groenwold, 2005; Ali & Kaelo, 2008) and neural networks design (Yu, Wang & Xi, 2008; Da, & Ge, 2005), have demonstrated its potential. It is considered to be capable to reduce the ill effect of the BP learning algorithm of neural networks, because it does not require gradient and differentiable information.

Unlike the GA, the PSO algorithm has no complicated operators such as crossover and mutation. In the PSO algorithm, the potential solutions, called as particles, are obtained by flowing through the problem space by following the current optimum particles. Generally speaking, the PSO algorithm has a strong ability to find the most optimistic result, but it has a disadvantage of easily getting trap into a local optimum. After suitably modulating the parameters for the PSO algorithm, the rate of convergence can be speeded up and the ability to find the global optimistic result can be enhanced. The PSO algorithm search is based on the orientation by tracing *pbest* that is each particle's best position in its history, and tracing *gbest* that is all particles best position in their history, it can rapidly arrive around the global optimum. However, because the PSO algorithm has several parameters to be adjusted by empirical approach, if these parameters are not appropriately set, the search will become very slow near the global optimum. Hence to cope with this problem we suggested a novel evolvable PSO (ePSO) and back propagation (BP) algorithm as a learning method of Chebyshev functional link neural network (cFLNN) for fine-tuning the connection weights.

In this work we combined the best attributes of ePSO and BP learning algorithm for training the Chebyshev functional link neural network. In FLNN a set of Chebyshev orthogonal polynomial are used for expanding the feature values. Therefore, we referred it as cFLNN. The concept of Chebyshev functional link neural network is not new but its usage for approximation of decision boundary in classification problem is the art of this work. In addition training cFLNN using the combined effort of ePSO and BP learning algorithm is another contribution of this work. This hybrid model uses the ePSO for global search in the beginning stage, and then uses the BP learning algorithm to do local search around the global optimum *gbest*.

Chapter Outline: The remainder of this chapter is structured as follows. In Section 2 we have discussed a quick introduction to some of the important HONNs. Some of the recently proposed functional link artificial neural networks (FLNNs) are discussed in Section 3. Section 4 provides the details about the algorithm of hybrid cFLNN for classification. In Section 5 we have presented experimental results with a comparative study. Section 6 concludes the chapter with future research directions.

Higher-Order Neural Networks: A Quick Review

In this Section we will discuss a few of the recently proposed higher order neural networks as a principle of enhancing the understandability of the designed method and consequently for empirical comparative purpose.

Pi -Sigma Neural Networks

PSNNs belong to the class of higher order neural networks. The term *pi-sigma* comes from the fact that these networks use product of sums of input components as in higher order processing unit. PSNNs were first introduced by Shin and Ghosh (Shin & Ghosh, 1991). The primary motivation of PSNNs were to develop a systematic method for maintaining the fast learning property and powerful mapping capability while avoiding the combinatorial increase in the number of weights and processing units required. A PSNN is a feed forward network with a single hidden layer of linear cells that uses product units in the output layer. PSNNs have a highly regular structure and need a much smaller number of weights as compared to other single layer higher order networks. The presence of only one layer of adaptive weights results in fast training. The PSNNs are categorized into two types: analog pi-sigma neural networks (APSNNs) and the binary pi-sigma neural networks (BPSNNs). APSNN has been successfully used for function approximation and pattern classification, and a generalization of the APSNN is shown to have a universal approximation capability. The BPSNN is capable of realizing any Boolean function (Shin & Ghosh, 1991b). More details about the architecture and working principle of PSNN can found in (Shin & Ghosh, 1991). Some of the recent developments of PSNN are discussed below:

Based on (Shin & Ghosh, 1991) Hussain and Liatsis proposed a recurrent *pi-sigma* neural network for DPCM image coding (Hussain & Liatsis, 2002). The novelty of their method is the incorporation of a recurrent link from the output to the input layer. Xiong et al. (Xiong, et al., 2007) introduced a new method of training named *an online gradient algorithm with penalty for small weight update* to train the *pi-sigma* network. Iyoda et al. (Iyoda, et al., 2007) has extended the pi-sigma neural architecture named *pi$_i$-sigma neural network* for application in image compression and reconstruction. Hussain et al. (Hussain, et al., 2008) applied their proposed recurrent *pi-sigma* neural network for physical time series prediction to validate the robustness of the method. Nie and Deng (Nie & Deng, 2008) have proposed a hybrid genetic learning algorithms for *pi-sigma* neural network and proved that the method is converged to the global optima with a high probability.

Although significant progress has been made in both theory and application of pi-sigma neural networks but still its ability has not yet been explored in the domain of data mining. Therefore harnessing its power in classification task of data mining can be a challenging task in near future.

Ridge Polynomial Neural Networks (RPNNs)

RPNNs are a new class of higher-order feed-forward neural networks and were introduced by Shin and Ghosh (Shin & Ghosh, 1995). This network can approximate any multivariate continuous function on a compact set in multi-dimensional input space with any degree of accuracy. The RPNN is a special form of ridge polynomial. RPNN is a generalized neural architecture of *pi-sigma neural* network. It is constructed by embedding different degrees of PSNNs as the basic building blocks. Figure 1 shows a generic structure of the RPNN. Similar to the PSNNs, RPNNs have only a single layer of adaptive weights and they preserve all the advantages of PSNNs.

In general there may not be much a priori information about the decision functions/boundaries to be approximated and also it is very difficult to choose an appropriate network size. Thus, using fixed network architecture an unknown decision boundary f in R^D can be approximated by the direct use of the RPNN model of degree up to n based on

$$f(x) \approx s(\sum_{i=1}^{n} h_i(x)),$$ (1)

where $h_i(x) = \prod_{j=1}^{i}(xw_j^T + w_{j0}), i = 1, 2, ..., n,$ (2)and $s(.)$ is a suitable linear or non-linear activation function, $w_j \in R^{D1}$ and $w_{j0} \in R$ are determined by learning process. Since each h_i is obtainable as the output of a PSNN of degree i with linear output units, the learning algorithms for the PSNN can be used for the RPNN.

Tawfik and Liatsis (Tawfik & Liatsis, 1997) have tested the RPNN for one step prediction of the Lorenz attractor and solar spot time series. They proved that RPNN has a more regular structure and a superior performance in terms of speed and efficiency when compared to multi-layer perceptron (MLP). Voutriaridis, et al. (Voutriaridis, Boutalis & Mertzios, 2003) found that RPNN could give satisfactory results when used in function approximation and character recognition.

Radial Basis Function Neural Network

The RBFNN is a feed-forward neural network, which is used to solve several problems such as modeling, non-linear control, speech processing, and pattern classification (Li, Tian & Chen, 2008; Dybowski, 1998). The construction of a radial basis function network in its most basic form involves three layers, depicted in Figure 2, with input layer, one hidden layer and output layer.

The input layer does not process the information; it only distributes the input variables to the hidden layer. Each neuron on the hidden layer represents a radial function and the number of radial functions depends on the problem to be solved.

The mostly used radial basis function is the symmetrical Gaussian function illustrated in Figure 3. They are characterized by two parameters: the centroid represented c_j and the width represented by σ_j. The output from the jth Gaussian kernel for an input vector x_i can be estimated by the following equation:

$$\phi_j(x) = \exp(-(\|x_i - c_j\|^2 / \sigma_j^2)),$$ (3)

Figure 1. Ridge polynomial neural network

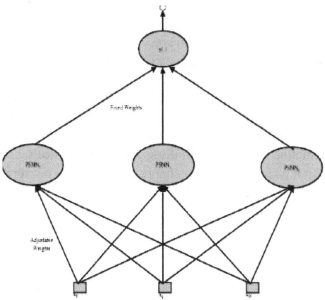

where $x_i = \{x_{i1}, x_{i2}, \ldots, x_{id}\}$ is the d-dimensional input vector, c_j is the centroid vector, and σ_j is the width of the radius, which determines the portion of the input space, where the jth kernel will have a non-significant zero response.

The parameters of the RBFNN in classification tasks are estimated by learning algorithms, and the main difficulty is the configuration of the hidden layer structure. A variety of approaches for training RBFNN has been developed, such as the combined GA and orthogonal least square algorithm (Chen, Wu & Luk, 1999), constructive methods (Leonardis & Bischof 1998), and pruning methods (Zhu, Cai & Liu, 1999). However, for the purpose of comparison we follow a state-of-the-art method, which is decoupled with two stages of training the RBFNN. The two-stage training is as follows. In the first stage only the input values are used for determining the centers and widths of the radial basis functions. The learning is unsupervised, here we used k-means for finding out the centers and then a nearest neighborhood is used to get the spread of the kernel.

The k-means clustering algorithm finds a set of cluster centers. Each cluster center is then associated with one of the kernels or nodes in the hidden layer. After the centers are established the width of each kernel is determined to cover the training points to allow a smooth fit of the desired network output. An appropriate width can be computed by equation (4) using the n_g-nearest neighbor heuristics for 2 nearest neighbor, i.e. $n_g = 2$.

$$\sigma_j = \sqrt{\frac{1}{n_g} \sum_{i=1}^{n_g} \left\| c_j - \mu_i \right\|^2}, \tag{4}$$

where μ_i is the n_g-nearest kernel centers of c_j, and c_j is the center of the jth kernel node.

Once the function parameters are fixed, the second stage of training will start with a supervised mode. With only using the target information we can determine the weights of the connection between hidden layer and output layer. As the neurons in the output layer contain linear activation functions,

Figure 2. Radial basis function neural network

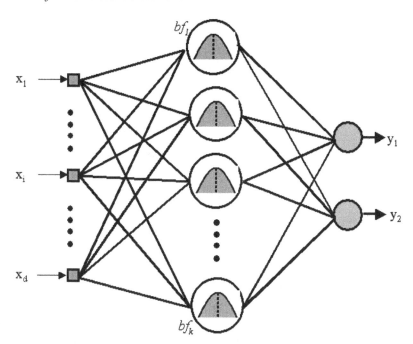

these weights can be calculated directly using matrix inversion (using singular value decomposition) and matrix multiplication.

Previous Work on FLNN

FLNNs are higher order neural networks without hidden units introduced by Klassen and Pao (Klasser & Pao, 1988) in 1988. Despite their linear nature, FLNNs can capture non-linear input-output relationships, provided that they are fed with an adequate set of polynomial inputs, or the functions might be a subset of a complete set of orthonormal basis functions spanning a n-dimensional representation space, which are constructed out of the original input attributes (Pao & Takefuji, 1992).

In contrast to the linear weighting of the input pattern produced by the linear links of artificial neural network, the functional link acts on an element of a pattern or on the entire pattern itself by generating a set of linearly independent functions, then evaluating these functions with the pattern as an argument. Thus class separability is possible in the enhanced feature space. Let us consider a two-dimensional input sample $x = [x_1, x_2]$. This sample has been mapped to a higher dimensional space by functional expansion using polynomials with certain degree. For example, two attributes yield six polynomials up to degree 2 (i.e. $(1, x_1, x_2, x_1^2, x_2^2, x_1.x_2)$. In general for a D-dimensional classification problem there are $((D+r)!)/(D!.r!)$ possible polynomials up to degree r. For most of the real life problems, this is too big number, even for degree 2, which obviously discourages us to achieving our goal. However, we can still resort to constructive and pruning algorithms in order to address this problem. In fact Sierra et al. (Sierra, Macias & Corbacho, 2001) has proposed a new algorithm for the evolution of functional link networks, which makes use of a standard GAs (Goldberg, 1989) to evolve near optimal linear architectures. Moreover, the complexity of the algorithm still needs to be investigated.

Figure 3. Symmetrical gaussian kernel function

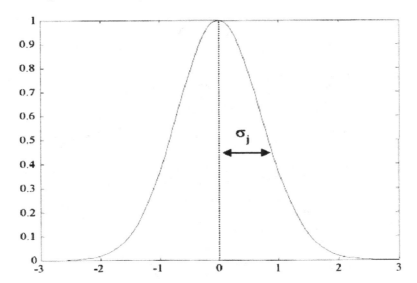

However, the dimensionality of many problems itself is very high and further increasing the dimensionality to a very large extent may not be an appropriate choice. So, it is advisable and also a new research direction to choose a small set of alternative functions, which can map the function to the desired extent with an output of significant improvement. FLNN with a trigonometric basis functions for classification, as proposed in (Misra & Dehuri, 2007) is obviously an example. Chebyshev FLNN is also another improvement in this direction; the detailed is discussed in Section 3.

Figure 4 shows the architecture of the FLNN of 2nd order. The output is computed as follows: $o=s(w_0+w_1.x_1+w_2.x_2+w_3.x_1^2+w_4.x_2^2+w_5.x_1.x_2)$, where s is a suitable activation function, w_0 is the threshold and w_i, $i=1(1)5$ are the weights to be trained.

Let us discuss some of the potential contributions in FLNNs and their success in variety of problems:

Haring, et al. (Haring & Kok, 1995) has proposed an algorithm that uses evolutionary computation (specifically genetic algorithm and genetic programming) for the determination of functional links (one based on polynomials and another based on expression tree) in neural network. Patra, et al. (Patra & Pal, 1995) has proposed a FLNN and applied to the problem of channel equalization in a digital communication channel.

Haring, et al. (Haring & et al, 1997) was presented a different ways to select and transform features using evolutionary computation and shows that this kind of selection of features is a special case of so called functional links.

Dash, et al. (Dash & et al, 1999) has proposed a FLNN with trigonometric basis functions to forecast the short-term electric load. Panagiotopoulos, et al. (Panagiotopoulos & et al, 1999) has reported better results by applying FLNN for planning in an interactive environment between two systems: the challenger and the responder. Patra, et al. (Patra & et al, 1999) has proposed a FLNN with back-propagation learning for identification of non-linear dynamic systems.

Patra, et al. (Patra & et al, 2000) has proposed a FLNN with three sets of basis functions such as Chebyshev, Legendre and power series to develop an intelligent model of the CPS involving less computational complexity. In the sequel, its implementation can be economical and robust.

In (Sierra, Macias & Corbacho, 2001) a genetic algorithm for selecting an appropriate number of polynomials as a functional input to the network has proposed by Sierra, et al. and applied to the classification problem.

A Chebyshev functional link artificial neural network has proposed by Patra, et al. (Patra & et al, 2002) for non-linear dynamic system identification. Sing et al. (Sing & Srivastava, 2002) has estimated the degree of insecurity in a power system with a set of orthonormal trigonometric basis functions.

In (Marcu & Koppen-Seliger, 2004) an evolutionary search of genetic type and multi-objective optimization such as accuracy and complexity of the FLNN in the Pareto sense is used to design a generalized FLNN with internal dynamics and applied to system identification.

Majhi, et al. (Majhi & et al, 2005) has applied FLNN for digital watermarking, their results shows that FLNN has better performance than other algorithms in this line. In (Abu-Mahfouz, 2005) has given a comparative performance of three artificial neural networks for the detection and classification of gear faults. They reported FLNN is comparatively better than others.

Misra and Dehuri (Misra & Dehuri, 2007) has proposed a FLNN for classification problem in data mining. Purwar, et al. (Purwar & et al, 2007) has proposed a Chebyshev functional link neural network for system identification of unknown dynamic non-linear discrete time systems. Weng, et al. (Weng & et al, 2007) has proposed a reduced decision feed-back Chebyshev functional link artificial neural networks (RDF-CFLANN) for channel equalization.

Two simple modified FLNNs are proposed by Krishnaiah, et al. (Krishnaiah & et al, 2008) for estimation of carrageenan concentration. In the first model a hidden layer is introduced and trained by EBP. In the second model, functional links are introduced to the neurons in the hidden layer and it is trained by EBP. In (Patra & et al, 2008) a FLNN with trigonometric polynomial functions are used in intelligent sensors for harsh environment that effectively linearizes the response characteristics, compensates for nonidealities and calibrates automatically. Dehuri et al.

(Dehuri & et al, 2008) has proposed a novel strategy for feature selection using genetic algorithm and then used as the input in FLANN for classification.

Figure 4. (a) Input Vector expansion model of a FLNN; and (b) architecture of FLNN with two input features and of 2nd order polynomial

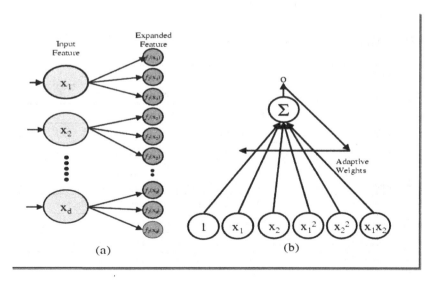

With this brief discussion on functional link artificial neural networks we can conclude that a very few applications has so far been made in classification task of data mining. Although theoretically this area is rich but application in classification is poor. Therefore, the proposed contribution can be another improvement in this direction.

Table 3 presents a summary of the development of functional link neural networks and their applications to various fields. For compact representation of the Table we used the denotations listed in Tables 1, and 2.

Hybrid Chebyshev FLNN

This section is divided into four Subsections. Subsection 4.1 discusses the Chebyshev functional link neural network and its importance. In Subsection 4.2 we give a novel learning algorithm based on PSO with evolvable inertia. In Subsection 4.3 the combined effort of ePSO and BP-learning is discussed. Finally, we summarize with a few computational steps of the hybrid cFLNN algorithm in Subsection 4.4.

Table 1. List of denotations (1)

Functional link neural network for classification task in data mining	FLANN
Finding functional links for neural networks by evolutionary computation	FFLAN
Planning with a functional neural network architecture	PFNN
Identification of non-linear dynamic systems using functional link artificial neural networks	IFLANN
Dynamic functional link neural networks genetically evolved applied to system identification	DFLANN
A functional link neural network for adaptive channel equalization	FLANNCE
Functional link neural network cascaded with Chebyshev orthogonal polynomial for non-linear channel equalization	COFLANN
Feature selection for neural networks through functional links found by evolutionary computation	FSFLNN
Genetic feature selection for optimal functional link neural network in classification	GFLANN
An improved scheme for digital watermarking using functional link artificial neural network	ISFLANN

Table 2. List of denotations (2)

Evolution of functional link networks	EFLN
Modelling of an intelligent pressure sensor using functional link artificial neural networks	IPSFLANN
Functional link neural networks-based intelligent sensors for harsh environments	HEFLANN
A functional link neural network for short term electric load forecasting	FLANNEL
Application of ultrasonic waves coupled with functional link neural network for estimation of carrageenan concentration	UFLANN
Degree of insecurity estimation in a power system using functional link neural network	PSFLANN
A comparative study of three artificial neural networks for the detection and classification of gear faults	CSFLANN
On-line system identification of complex systems using Chebyshev neural networks	OCFLANN
A channel equalizer using reduced decision feedback Chebyshev function link artificial neural networks	RDFCFLANN
Non-linear dynamic system identification using Chebyshev functional link artificial neural networks	DSICFLANN

Table 3. Summary of the FLNNs thus far developed

Method	Basis Function	Learning	Application	Authors
FFLAN	Polynomial	Pseudoinverse	Classification	Haring, et al., 1995
PFNN	Polynomial	-	Planning	Panagiotopoulos, et al. 1999
IFLANN	Trigonometric	BP	System Identification	Patra, et al., 1999
EFLN	Polynomial	GA+BP	Classification	Sierra, et al., 2001
DFLANN	Trigonometric	DBP	System Identification	Marcu, et al., 2004
FLANNCE	Trigonometric	BP	Channel Equalization	Patra, et al., 1995
COFLANN	Chebyshev	NLMS	Channel Equalization	Zhao, et al., 2008
FSFLNN	Trigonometric	BP	Classification	Haring, et al., 1997
IPSFLANN	Chebyshev, Legendre, Power Series	BP	Intelligent Pressure Sensor	Patra, et al., 2000
GFLANN	Trigonometric	BP	Classification	Dehuri, et al., 2008
FLANN	Trigonometric	BP	Classification	Misra, et al., 2007
ISFLANN	Trigonometric	BP	Digital Watermarking	Majhi, et al., 2005
HEFLANN	Trigonometric	BP	Intelligent Sensors	Patra, et al., 2008
FLANNEL	Trigonometric	BP	Electric Load Forecasting	Dash, et al., 1999
UFLANN	Polynomial	EBP	Carrageenan Concentration	Krishnaiah, et al., 2008
PSFLANN	Trigonometric	Adaptive	Insecurity Estimation	Sing, et al., 2002
CSFLANN	Sigmoidal	Adaptive	Classification	Abu-Mahfouz, et al., 2005
OCFLANN	Chebyshev	BP	System Identification	Purwar, et al., 2007
RDFCFLANN	Chebyshev	BP	Channel Equalization	Weng, et al., 2007
DSICFLANN	Chebyshev	BP	System Identification	Patra, et al., 2002

Chebyshev Functional Link Neural Network

It is well known that the non-linear approximation capacity of the Chebyshev orthogonal polynomial is very powerful by the approximation theory. Combining the characteristics of the FLNN and Chebyshev orthogonal polynomial the Chebyshev Functional Link Neural Network what we named as cFLNN is resulted. The proposed method utilizes the FLNN input-output pattern, the non-linear approximation capabilities of Chebyshev orthogonal polynomial and the evolvable particle swarm optimization (ePSO)-back-propagation learning scheme for classification.

The Chebyshev FLNN used in this chapter is a single layer neural network. The block diagram of the cFLNN is shown in Figure 5. The architecture consists of two parts, namely transformation part (i.e., from a low dimensional feature space to high-dimensional feature space) and learning part. The transformation deals with the input feature vector to the hidden layer by approximate transformable method. The transformation is the functional expansion (FE) of the input pattern comprising of a finite set of Chebyshev polynomial. As a result the Chebyshev polynomial basis can be viewed as a new input vector. The learning part uses the newly proposed ePSO-BP learning.

Alternatively, we can approximate a function by a polynomial of truncated power series. The power series expansion represents the function with a very small error near the point of expansion, but the error increases rapidly as we employ it at points farther away. The computational economy to be gained by

Figure 5. Structure of cFLNN

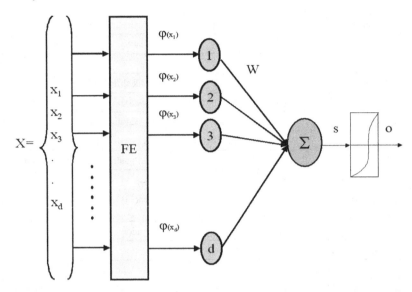

Chebyshev series increases when the power series is slowly convergent. Therefore, Chebyshev series are frequently used for approximations to functions and are much more efficient than other power series of the same degree. Among orthogonal polynomials, the Chebyshev polynomials convergence rapidly than expansion in other set of polynomials (Misra & Dehuri, 2007). Moreover, Chebyshev polynomials are easier to compute than trigonometric polynomials. With these interesting properties of Chebyshev polynomial motivated us to use Chebyshev FLNN for approximation of decision boundaries in the feature space.

The first few Chebyshev polynomials are given by $Ch_0(x)=1$, $Ch_1(x)=x$, and $Ch_2(x)=2x^2-1$. The higher order Chebyshev polynomials can be generated with the following recursive formulae:

$$\phi_1(x) = Ch_0(x) = 1,$$
$$\phi_2(x) = Ch_1(x) = x,$$
$$\dots\dots\dots\dots\dots\dots\dots\dots$$
$$\phi_n(x) = Ch_{n+1}(x) = 2xCh_n(x) - Ch_{n-1}(x).$$

For example, consider a two-dimensional input pattern $x=[x_1, x_2]^T$. An expanded pattern obtained by using Chebyshev functions is given by: $\varphi=[1, Ch_1(x_1), Ch_2(x_1),\dots; 1, Ch_1(x_2), Ch_2(x_2),\dots]^T$, where $Ch_i(x_j)$ is a Chebyshev polynomial, i the order of the polynomials chosen and $j=1,2$.

The following theorem can guide us the cohesiveness property of cFLNN with feed forward multi-layer perceptron (MLP).

Theorem: Assume a feed-forward MLP neural network with only one hidden layer and activation function of the output layer are all-linear. If all the activation functions of the hidden layer satisfy the Riemann integrable condition, then the feed-forward neural network can always be represented as a Chebyshev neural network. The detailed proof of the theorem can be obtained in (Lee & Jeng, 1998).

Evolvable Particle Swarm Optimization (ePSO)

Evolvable particle swarm optimization (ePSO) is an improvement over the PSO (Kennedy & Eberhart, 1995). PSO is a kind of stochastic algorithm to search for the best solution by simulating the movement and flocking of birds. The algorithm works by initializing a flock of birds randomly over the searching space, where every bird is called as a particle. These particles fly with a certain velocity and find the global best position after some iteration. At each iteration k, the ith particle is represented by a vector x_i^k in multidimensional space to characterize its position. The velocity v_i^k is used to characterize its velocity. Thus PSO maintains a set of positions:

$$S=\{x_1^k, x_2^k,...,x_N^k\},$$

and a set of corresponding velocities

$$V=\{v_1^k, v_2^k,....,v_N^k\}.$$

Initially, the iteration counter $k = 0$, and the positions x_i^0 and their corresponding velocities v_i^0 (i=1,2,...,N), are generated randomly from the search space Ω. Each particle changes its position x_i^k, per iteration. The new position x_i^{k+1} of the ith particle (i=1,2,..,N) is biased towards its best position p_i^k with best function value referred to as personal best or *pbest*, found by the particle so far, and the very best position p_g^k, referred to as the global best or *gbest*, found by its companions. The *gbest* is the best position in the set

$$P=\{p_1^k, p_2^k,...,p_N^k\}, \text{ where } p_i^0 = x_i^0, \forall i.$$

We can say a particle in S as good or bad depending on its personal best being a good or bad point in P. Consequently, we call the ith particle (j^{th} particle) in S the worst (the best) if p_i^k (p_j^k) is the least (best) fitted, with respect to function value in P. We denote the *pbest* of the worst particle and the best particle in S as p_h^k and p_g^k, respectively. Hence

$$p_g^k = \arg \underset{i\in\{1,2,..,N\}}{\min} f(p_i^k) \text{ and } p_h^k = \arg \underset{i\in\{1,2,...,N\}}{\max} f(p_i^k)$$

At each iteration k, the position x_i^k of the ith particle is updated by a velocity v_i^{k+1} which depends on three components: its current velocity v_i^k, the cognition term (i.e., the weighted difference vectors $(p_i^k - x_i^k)$) and the social term (i.e., the weighted difference vector $(p_g^k - x_i^k)$).

Specifically, the set S is updated for the next iteration using

$$x_i^{k+1} = x_i^k + v_i^{k+1}, \text{ where} \tag{5}$$

$$v_i^{k+1} = v_i^k + r_1.c_1.(p_i^k - x_i^k) + r_2.c_2.(p_g^k - x_i^k).$$

The parameters r_1 and r_2 are uniformly distributed random numbers in $[0,1]$ and c_1 and c_2, known as the cognitive and social parameters respectively, are popularly chosen to be $c_1 = c_2 = 2.0$ (Kennedy & Eberhart, 1999). Thus the values $r_1 c_1$ and $r_2 c_2$ introduce some stochastic weighting in the difference vectors $(p_i^k - x_i^k)$

and $(p_g^k - x_i^k)$, respectively. The set P is updated as the new positions x_i^{k+1} are created using the following rules with a minimization of the cost function: $p_i^{k+1} = x_i^{k+1}$ if $f(x_i^{k+1}) < f(p_i^k)$, otherwise $p_i^{k+1} = p_i^k$.

This process of updating the velocities v_i^k, positions x_i^k, *pbest* p_i^k and the *gbest* p_g^k is repeated until a user-defined stopping condition is met.

We now briefly present a number of improved versions of PSO and then show where our modified PSO can stand.

Shi and Eberhart (Shi & Eberhart, 1998) has done the first modification by introducing a constant inertia w, which controls how much a particle tends to follow its current directions compared to the memorized *pbest* p_i^k and the *gbest* p_g^k. Hence the velocity update is given by:

$$v_i^{k+1} = w.v_i^k + r_1.c_1.(p_i^k - x_i^k) + r_2.c_2.(p_g^k - x_i^k),$$ where the values of r_1 and r_2 are realized component-wise.

(6)

Again Shi and Eberhart (Shi & Eberhart, 1998) proposed a linearly varying inertia weight during the search. The inertia weight is linearly reduced during the search. This entails a more globally search during the initial stages and a more local search during the final stages. They also proposed a limitation of each particle's velocity to a specified maximum velocity v^{max}. The maximum velocity was calculated as a fraction τ ($0 < \tau \le 1$) of the distance between the bounds of the search space, i.e., $v^{max} = \tau.(x^u - x^l)$.

Fourie and Groenwold (Fourie & Groenwold, 2002) suggested a dynamic inertia weight and maximum velocity reduction. In this modification an inertia weight and maximum velocity are then reduced by fractions α and β respectively, if no improvement in p_g^k occur after a pre-specified number of iterations h, i.e.,

if $f(p_g^k) = f(p_g^{k-1})$ then $w_{k+1} = \alpha.w_k$ and $v_k^{max} = \beta.v_k^{max}$, where α and β are such that $0 < \alpha, \beta < 1$.

Clerc and Kennedy (Clerc & Kennedy, 2002) introduced another interesting modification to PSO in the form of a constriction coefficient χ, which controls all the three components in velocity update rule. This has an effect of reducing the velocity as the search progress. In this modification, the velocity update is given by

$$v_i^{k+1} = \chi(v_i^k + r_1.c_1.(p_i^k - x_i^k) + r_2.c_2.(p_g^k - x_i^k)),$$ where $\chi = 2/|2 - \varphi - \sqrt{\varphi^2 - 4\varphi}|$, $\varphi = c_1 + c_2 > 4$.

Da and Xiurun (Da & Ge, 2005), also modified PSO by introducing a temperature like control parameter as in the simulated annealing algorithm. Zhang, et al. (Zhang & et al, 2007) has modified the PSO by introducing a new inertia weight during the velocity update. Generally in the beginning stages of their algorithm, the inertial weight w, should be reduce rapidly, when around optimum the inertial weight w should be reduced slowly. They adopted the following rule:

$$w = \begin{cases} w_0 - \left(\frac{w_1}{MAXITER1}\right) \cdot k & if \quad 1 \le k \le MAXITER1 \\ (w_0 - w_1) \cdot e^{((MAXITER1 - k)/\nu)} & if \ MAXITER1 < k \le MAXITER, \end{cases}$$

where w_0 is the initial inertia weight, w_1 is the inertial weight of linear section ending, *MAXITER* is the total searching generations; *MAXITER1* is the used generations that inertia weight is reduced linearly, k is a variable whose range is [1, *MAXITER*]. By adjusting k, they are getting different ending values of inertial weight.

In this work, the inertial weight is evolved as a part of searching the optimal sets of weights. However, the evolution of inertial weight is restricted between an upper limit w^u and lower limits w^l. If it exceeds the boundary during the course of training the network then the following rule is adopted for restricting the value of w:

$$w = w^l + (c\_value/(3.w^u)).(w^u\text{-}w^l), \text{ where } c\_value \text{ is the exceeded value.} \tag{7}$$

In addition, the proposed method also uses the adaptive cognitive acceleration coefficient c_1 and the social acceleration coefficients c_2. c_1 has been allowed to decrease from its initial value of c_{1i} to c_{1f} while c_2 has been increased from c_{2i} to c_{2f} using the following equations as in (Ratnaweera, Halgamuge & Watson, 2004).

$$c_1^k = (c_{1f}\text{-}c_{1i}).(k/MAXITER) + c_{1i}, \text{ and} \tag{8}$$

$$c_2^k = (c_{2f}\text{-}c_{2i}).(k/MAXITER) + c_{2i}, \tag{9}$$

ePSO-BP Learning Algorithm

The ePSO-BP is an learning algorithm which combines the ePSO global searching capability with the BP algorithm local searching capability. Similar to the GA, the ePSO algorithm is a global algorithm, which has a strong ability to find global optimistic result, this ePSO algorithm, however, has a disadvantage that the search around global optimum is very slow. The BP algorithm, on the contrary, has a strong ability to find local optimistic result, but its ability to find the global optimistic result is weak. By combining the ePSO with the BP, a new algorithm referred to as ePSO-BP hybrid learning algorithm is formulated in this chapter. The fundamental idea for this hybrid algorithm is that at the beginning stage of searching for the optimum, the PSO is employed to accelerate the training speed. When the fitness function value has not changed for some generations, or value changed is smaller than a predefined number, the searching process is switched to gradient descending searching according to this heuristic knowledge. Similar to the ePSO algorithm, the ePSO-BP algorithm's searching process is also started from initializing a group of random particles. First, all the particles are updated according to the equation (5), until a new generation set of particles are generated, and then those new particles are used to search the global best *gbest* position in the solution space. Finally the BP algorithm is used to search around the global optimum. In this way, this hybrid algorithm may find an optimum more quickly. The procedure for this ePSO-BP algorithm can be summarized by the following computational steps:

1. Initialize the positions and velocities of a group of particles randomly in the range of [0, 1]. Initialize the cognitive and social acceleration initial and final coefficients (i.e., c_{1i}, c_{1f}, c_{2i}, and c_{2f}).
2. Evaluate each initialized particle's fitness value, and pbest is set as the positions of the current particles, while gbest is set as the best position of the initialized particles.
3. If the maximal iterative generations are arrived, go to Step 10, else, go to Step 4.
4. The best particle of the current particles is stored. The positions and velocities of all the particles are updated according to equation (5), and then a group of new particles are generated.
5. Adjust the value of c_1 and c_2 by using equation (8) and (9).

6. Evaluate each new particle's fitness value, and the worst particle is replaced by the stored best particle. If the ith particle's new position is better than pbest, pbest is set as the new position of the ith particle. If the best position of all new particles is better than gbest, then gbest is updated.
7. Adjust the inertia weights w according to equation (7) if it flies beyond the boundary of w.
8. If the current gbest is unchanged for 15 consecutive generations, then go to Step 9; else, go to Step 3.
9. Use the BP algorithm to search around gbest for some epochs, if the search result is better than gbest, output the current search result; or else, output gbest.
10. Output the global optimum gbest.

The parameter *w*, in the above ePSO-BP algorithm evolves simultaneously with the weights of the cFLNN during the course of training. The parameter *MAXITER1* generally adjusted to an appropriate value by many repeated experiments, then an adaptive gradient descending method is used to search around the global optimum *gbest*. The BP algorithm based on gradient descending has parameter called learning rate, which controls the convergence of the algorithm to an optimal local solution. In practical applications, users usually employed theoretical, empirical or heuristic methods to set a good value for this learning rate. In this chapter, we adopted the following strategy for learning rate:

$$\mu = k.e^{(-\nu*epoch)},$$
(10)

where μ is learning rate k, ν are constants, *epoch* is a variable that represents iterative times, through adjusting k and ν, we can control the reducing speed of learning rate.

ePSO-BP Learning Algorithm for cFLNN

Learning of a cFLNN may be considered as approximating or interpolating a continuous multivariate function $\varphi(X)$ by an approximating function $\varphi_W(X)$. In cFLNN architecture, a set of basis functions φ, and a fixed number of weight parameters W are used to represent $\varphi_W(X)$. With a specific choice of a set of basis functions φ, the problem is then to find the weight parameters W that provides the best possible approximation of φ on the set of input-output samples. This can be achieved by iteratively updating W. The interested reader about the detailed theory of FLNN can refer to (Misra & Dehuri, 2007).

Let k training patterns be applied to the FLNN and can be denoted by $<X_i, Y_i>$, i=1 (1) k and let the weight matrix be W. At the ith instant i=1 (1) k, the D-dimensional input pattern and the cFLNN output are given by $X_i=<x_{i1},x_{i2},...,x_{iD}>$, i=1(1)k and $\hat{Y_i} = [\hat{y_i}]$, respectively. Its corresponding target pattern is represented by $Y_i=[y_i]$, i=1(1)k. Hence $\forall i, X=[X_1, X_2,....., X_k]^T$. The augmented matrix of D-dimensional input pattern and the cFLNN output are given by:

$$<X:\hat{Y}> = \begin{pmatrix} x_{11} & x_{12} & \cdot & x_{1D} & : & \hat{y}_1 \\ x_{21} & x_{22} & \cdot & x_{2D} & : & \hat{y}_2 \\ \cdot & \cdot & \cdot & \cdot & : & \cdot \\ \cdot & \cdot & \cdot & \cdot & : & \cdot \\ x_{k1} & x_{k2} & \cdot & x_{kD} & : & \hat{y}_k \end{pmatrix}$$

As the dimension of the input pattern is increased from D to D' by a set of basis functions φ, given by $\varphi(X_i)=[Ch_1(x_{i1}), Ch_2(x_{i1}),..., Ch_1(x_{i2}), Ch_2(x_{i2}),...,Ch_1(x_{iD}), Ch_2(x_{iD}),...]$. The $k \times D'$ dimensional weight matrix is given by $W=[W_1, W_2,...,W_k]^T$, where W_i is the weight vector associated with the ith output and is given by $W_i=[w_{i1}, w_{i2}, w_{i3},...,w_{iD'}]$. The ith output of the cFLNN is given by $\hat{y}_i(t) = \rho(\sum_{j=1}^{D'} Ch_j(x_{ij}).w_{ij}), \forall i$

. The error associated with the ith output is given by $e_i(t) = y_i(t) - \hat{y}_i(t)$. Using the ePSO-BP learning, the weights of the cFLNN can be optimized. The high-level algorithms then can be summarized as follows:

Learning Algorithm

```
Input the set of given k training patterns.
Choose the set of orthonormal basis functions.
For i = 1: k
Expand the feature values using the choosen basis functions.
Calculated the weighted sum and then fed to the output node.
error= error + e(k).
End for
If the error is tolerable then stop otherwise go to 9.
Update the weights using ePSO-BP learning rules and go to step 3.
```

Empirical Study

This Section is divided into five subsections. Subsection 5.1 describe the datasets taken from UCI (Asuncion & Newman, 2007) repository of machine learning databases. The parameters required for the proposed method are given in Subsection 5.2. The performance of the hybrid cFLNN using some of the datasets especially considered by Sierra et al. (Sierra, Macias & Corbacho, 2001) compared with the model proposed by Sierra et al. in Subsection 5.3. In Subsection 5.4 the classification accuracy of hybrid cFLNN are compared with RBF, RPNN and PSNN model. Subsection 5.5 we compared the performance of hybrid cFLNN with FLNN proposed in (Misra & Dehuri, 2007) using the cost matrix analysis and then compared with the results obtained by Statlog project (Michie, Spiegelhalter & Taylor, 1994).

Description of the Datasets

The availability of results, with previous evolutionary and constructive algorithms (e.g. Sierra et al. (Sierra, Macias & Corbacho, 2001), Prechelt (Preshelt, 1994) has guided us the selection of the following varied datasets taken from the UCI repository of machine learning databases for the addressed neural network learning. Let us briefly discuss the datasets, used for our experimental setup.

IRIS Dataset: The dataset consists of d=4 features made on each of the 150 iris plants of class c=3 species. The three distinct species corresponds to three different classes such as Iris Setosa, Iris Versicolor and Iris Virginica. The problem is to classify each test point to its correct species based on the four measurements.

WINE Dataset: These data are the results of a chemical analysis of wines grown in the same region in Italy but derived from three different cultivars. The analysis determined the quantities of 13 constituents found in each of the three types of wines. The number of instances is 178 and it is distributed as 59 for class 1, 71 for class 2 and 48 for class 3. The number of attributes is 13 all are continuous in nature. There are no missing attributes.

PIMA Indians Diabetes Dataset: This dataset consists of d=8 numerical medical attributes and c=2 classes (tested positive or negative for diabetes). There are n=768 instances. Further, data set related to the diagnosis of diabetes in an Indian population that lives near the city of Phoenix, Arizona. All inputs are continuous. 65.1% samples are diabetes negatives.

BUPA Liver Disorders Dataset: This is related to the diagnosis of liver disorders and created by BUPA Medical Research, Ltd. It consists of 6 numerical attributes, 345 patterns and 2 classes.

Heart Disease Dataset: This is related to diagnoses of people with heart problems. It has 270 patterns, 6 attributes and 2 classes.

Cancer Dataset: In this dataset the task of classifier is to classify a tumor as either benign or malignant based on cell descriptions gathered by microscopic examinations. Input attributes are for instance the clump thickness, the uniformity of cell size and cell shape, the amount of marginal adhesion, and the frequency of bare nuclei. It is described by 9 inputs, 2 classes, and 699 samples. All inputs are continuous, 34.5% are belongs to the class of malignant.

Table 4 presents a summary of the main features of each database that has been used in this study.

Parameters

All the algorithms have some parameters that have to be provided by the user. The parameters for the proposed hybrid cFLNN are listed in Table 5. However, the parameters for other algorithms are set based on the suggestion. The parameters for EFLN were adopted as suggested in (Sierra, Macias & Corbacho, 2001). Similarly the parameters for FLNN, RPNN and PSNN were set as suggested in (Misra & Dehuri, 2007),(Shin & Ghosh, 1995), and (Shin & Ghosh, 1991) respectively. In the case of RBFNN we used

Table 4. Summary of the datasets

Dataset	Patterns	Attribute	Class	Patterns in Class 1	Patterns in Class 2	Patterns in Class 3
IRIS	150	4	3	50	50	50
WINE	178	13	3	71	59	48
PIMA	768	8	2	500	268	-
BUPA	345	6	2	145	200	-
HEART	270	13	2	150	120	-
CANCER	699	9	2	458	241	-

Table 5. Description of the parameters

Symbol	Purpose
N	Size of the swarm
w	Inertia weight
w^u	Upper limit of the inertia
w^l	Lower limit of the inertia
c_1	Cognitive Parameter
c_{1i}	Left boundary value of cognitive parameter
c_{1f}	Right boundary value of cognitive parameter
c_2	Social parameter
c_{2i}	Left boundary value of social parameter
c_{2f}	Right boundary value of social parameter
MAXITER	Maximum iterations for stopping an algorithm

k-means algorithm for finding out the centers and nearest neighbor algorithm for spread. The weight vector are optimized based on the standard least square method.

The values of the parameters used in this chapter are as follows: We set $N=20*d$, where d is the dimension of the problem under consideration. The upper limit (w^u) and lower limit (w^l) of the inertia are set to [0.2, 1.8]. Similarly the initial and final value of cognitive acceleration coefficients are set to $c_{1i}=2.5$ and $c_{1f}=0.5$. The initial and final value of social acceleration coefficients are set to $c_{2i}=0.5$ and $c_{2f}=2.5$. The maximum number of iteration is fixed to *MAXITER*=500.

In the case of BP-learning, the learning parameter μ and the momentum factor v in hybrid cFLNN were choosen after a several runs to obtain the best results. In the similar manner the functional expansion of the hybrid cFLNN was carried out.

Hybrid cFLNN vs EFLN

In this Subsection we will compare the results of hybrid cFLNN with the results of EFLN with polynomial basis functions of degree 1,2, and 3. The choice of the polynomial degree is obviously a key question in FLNN with polynomial basis functions. However, Sierra, et al. (Sierra, Macias & Corbacho, 2001) has given some guidance to optimize the polynomial degree that can best suit to the architecture.

Table 6. Possible number of expanded inputs of degrees one, two, and three

Dataset	Attribute	Degree 1	Degree 2	Degree 3
IRIS	4	5	15	35
WINE	13	14	105	560
PIMA	8	9	45	165
BUPA	6	7	28	84
HEART	13	14	105	560
CANCER	9	10	55	220

Table 7. Comparing results of cFLNN with EFLN for the cancer and PIMA dataset by considering the average training error (MTre), average validation error (MVe), and average test error (MTe)

Dataset	cFLNN			EFLN		
	Mtre	Mve	MTe	MTre	MVe	MTe
Cancer1	4.01	2.76	2.57	4.27	1.89	2.09
Cancer2	3.95	3.97	4.66	4.37	2.96	3.96
Cancer3	4.13	3.51	4.43	3.29	3.01	4.65
BUPA1	16.26	21.98	22.62	19.07	22.44	23.29
BUPA2	17.90	24.12	22.35	19.84	18.63	20.37
BUPA3	15.34	19.92	21.96	16.68	17.81	24.44

Considering degrees of the polynomial 1, 2 and 3 the possible number of expanded inputs of the above datasets is given in Table 6.

For the sake of convenience we report the results of the experiments conducted on CANCER and BUPA and then compared with the methods EFLN (Sierra, Macias & Corbacho, 2001). We partitioned both the datasets into three sets: training, validation and test sets. Both the networks are trained for 1500 epochs (it should be carefully examined) on the training set and the error on the validation set was measured after every 10 epochs. Training was stopped when a maximum of 1500 epochs had been trained. The test set performance was then computed for that state of the network, which had minimum validation set error during the training process. This method called early stopping is a good way to avoid overfitting of the network to the particular training examples used, which would reduce the generalization performance. The average error rate corresponding to cFLNN, and EFLN w.r.t. training, validation and testing of CANCER and BUPA datasets is shown in Table 7.

Hybrid cFLNN vs RBFNN, RPNN, and PSNN

Here we will discuss the comparative performance of hybrid cFLNN with RBFNN, RPNN and PSNN using three datasets IRIS, WINE, and PIMA. In this case the total set of samples are randomly divided into two equal folds. Each of these two folds are alternatively used either as a training set or as a test set.

Table 8. Performance of classifiers (HPTr: hit percentage in training subset; HPTe: hit percentage in test subset; cFLN: cFLNN)

Dataset	CFLN		PSNN		RBFNN		RPNN	
	HPTr	HPTe	HPTr	HPTe	HPTr	HPTe	HPTr	HPTe
IRIS	99.72	98.41	92.24	91.94	95.05	93.63	94.25	92.55
	99.57	98.87	94.45	93.37	94.56	92.98	96.91	94.07
WINE	98.08	96.15	84.27	80.90	84.27	82.02	91.30	89.28
	98.76	98.02	76.40	85.39	86.52	76.40	97.32	95.99
PIMA	80.26	78.96	78.12	74.47	78.13	74.48	76.49	74.90
	81.03	79.60	77.60	76.82	77.60	76.82	78.23	76.17

As the proposed learning method ePSO-BP learning is a stochastic algorithm so 10 independent runs were performed for every single fold. The results obtained, averaged over 10 runs and are presented in Table 8.

Upon a closer inspection we can found that cFLNN is exhibiting better performance at the time of testing in all the datasets.

Tables 9 and 10 presents the average performance for each dataset, measured in terms of each models hit percentage. To quantify how precise the accuracy rate is, we compute its confidence interval for a confidence level (α) of 95% and 98% respectively.

Similarly, the comparative performance of cFLNN with FLANN (Misra & Dehuri, 2007) is given in the Tables 11 and 12 w.r.t to the different confidence level (α) of 95% and 98% respectively.

Table 9. Comparing Average Performance of Classifiers based on the Confidence Level (α=95%)

Dataset	Folds	cFLNN	PSNN	RBFNN	RPNN
IRIS	Training	0.996±0.0136	0.933±0.0564	0.948±0.0502	0.956±0.0465
	Test	0.986±0.0262	0.927±0.0591	0.933±0.0566	0.933±0.0565
WINE	Training	0.984±0.0259	0.803±0.0286	0.854±0.0734	0.943±0.0481
	Test	0.971±0.0350	0.831±0.0778	0.792±0.0843	0.926±0.0542
PIMA	Training	0.806±0.0395	0.779±0.0415	0.779±0.0415	0.774±0.0419
	Test	0.793±0.0405	0.756±0.0429	0.756±0.0429	0.755±0.0430

Table 10. Comparing average performance of classifiers based on the confidence level (α=98%)

Dataset	Folds	cFLNN	PSNN	RBFNN	RPNN
IRIS	Training	0.996±0.0161	0.933±0.0671	0.948±0.0597	0.956±0.0553
	Test	0.986±0.0312	0.927±0.0702	0.933±0.0673	0.933±0.0672
WINE	Training	0.984±0.0308	0.803±0.0982	0.854±0.0872	0.943±0.0572
	Test	0.971±0.0416	0.831±0.0925	0.792±0.1002	0.926±0.0645
PIMA	Training	0.806±0.0470	0.779±0.0494	0.779±0.0494	0.774±0.0498
	Test	0.793±0.0482	0.756±0.0510	0.756±0.0510	0.755±0.0511

Table 11. Comparing average performance of cFLNN and FLANN based on the confidence level (α=95%)

Dataset	Folds	cFLNN	FLANN
IRIS	Training	0.996±0.0136	0.9866±0.0260
	Test	0.986±0.0262	0.9866±0.0260
WINE	Training	0.984±0.0259	0.9605±0.0405
	Test	0.971±0.0350	0.9550±0.0431
PIMA	Training	0.806±0.0395	0.7877±0.0409
	Test	0.793±0.0405	0.7812±0.0414

Performance of Hybrid cFLNN vs FLANN Based on Heart Data

In this subsection, we will explicitly examine the performance of the cFLNN model by considering the heart dataset with the use of the 9-fold cross validation methodology. The reason for using 9-fold cross validation is that to compare the performance with the performance of few of the representative algorithms considered in Statlog Project (Michie, Spiegelhalter & Taylor, 1994). In 9-fold cross validation we partition the database into nine subsets (heart1.dat, heart2.dat, ..., heart9.dat), where eight subsets are used for training and the remaining one is used for testing. The process is repeated nine times in such a way that each time a different subset of data is used for testing. Thus the dataset was randomly segmented into nine subsets with 30 elements each. Each subset contains about 56% of samples from class 1(without heart disease) and 44% of samples from class 2 (with heart disease).

The procedure makes use of a weight matrix, which is described in Table 13.

The purpose of such a matrix is to penalize wrongly classified samples based on the weight of the penalty of the class. In general, the weight of the penalty for class 2 samples that are classified as class 1 samples is w_1, while the weight of the penalty for class 1 records that are classified as class 2 samples is w_2. Therefore, the metric used for measuring the cost of the wrongly classifying patterns in the training and test dataset is given by equations (11) and (12).

$$C_{train} = (S_1 \times w_1 + S_2 \times w_2) / S_{train}, \tag{11}$$

$$C_{test} = (S_1 \times w_1 + S_2 \times w_2) / S_{test}, \tag{12}$$

where C_{train} is the cost of the training set; C_{test} is the cost of test set; S_1 and S_2 denote the patterns that are wrongly classified as belongs to class 1 and 2 respectively; S_{train} and S_{test} are the total number of training and test patterns respectively.

Table 12. Comparing average performance of cFLNN and FLANN based on the confidence level ($\alpha=98\%$)

Dataset	Folds	CFLNN	FLANN
IRIS	Training	0.996±0.0161	0.9866±0.0309
	Test	0.986±0.0312	0.9866±0.0309
WINE	Training	0.984±0.0308	0.9605±0.0481
	Test	0.971±0.0416	0.9550±0.0512
PIMA	Training	0.806±0.0470	0.7877±0.0486
	Test	0.793±0.0482	0.7812±0.0492

Table 13. Weight matrix of classes to penalize

Real Classification	Model Classification	
	Class 1	Class 2
Class 1	0	w_2
Class 2	w_1	0

Table 14. Heart disease classification performance of FLANN

Data Subset	Error in Training Set		Error in Test Set		C_{train}	C_{test}
	Class 1	Class 2	Class 1	Class 2		
Heart1	13/133	14/107	1/17	1/13	0.35	0.2
Heart2	14/133	12/107	2/17	1/13	0.31	0.23
Heart3	13/134	15/106	4/16	2/14	0.37	0.47
Heart4	13/133	10/107	1/17	4/13	0.26	0.7
Heart5	13/133	16/107	3/17	2/13	0.39	0.43
Heart6	13/134	14/106	6/16	0/14	0.35	0.2
Heart7	15/133	13/107	0/17	3/13	0.33	0.5
Heart8	18/133	17/107	1/17	0/13	0.43	0.03
Heart9	20/134	9/106	2/16	1/14	0.27	0.23
Mean					**0.34**	**0.33**

Table 14 presents the errors and costs of the training and test sets for the FLANN model with a weight value of $w_1=5$ and $w_2=1$.

Table 15 illustrates the performance of cFLNN based on the above definition of cost matrix. The errors in training and test set are explicitly given.

The classification results found by the cFLANN for the heart disease dataset were compared with the results found in the StatLog project (Michie, Spiegelhalter & Taylor, 1994). According to (Michie, Spiegelhalter & Taylor, 1994), comparison consists of calculating the average cost produced by the nine data subsets used for validation. Table 16 presents the average cost for the nine training and test subsets. The result of the cFLANN is highlighted in bold.

Table 15. Heart disease classification performance of cFLNN

Data Subset	Error in Training Set		Error in Test Set		C_{train}	C_{test}
	Class 1	Class 2	Class 1	Class 2		
Heart1	13/133	14/107	1/17	1/13	0.35	0.2
Heart2	13/133	12/107	1/17	2/13	0.30	0.36
Heart3	12/134	13/106	5/16	1/14	0.32	0.33
Heart4	13/133	10/107	4/17	1/13	0.26	0.30
Heart5	13/133	15/107	3/17	2/13	0.37	0.43
Heart6	13/134	12/106	5/16	1/14	0.30	0.30
Heart7	14/133	13/107	1/17	2/13	0.33	0.37
Heart8	16/133	16/107	0/17	2/13	0.40	0.33
Heart9	18/134	10/106	2/16	1/14	0.28	0.23
Mean					**0.32**	**0.31**

Table 16. Comparing classification performance of cFLNN and FLANN with some of the potential methods reported in statlog project using heart disease benchmark dataset

Methods	CFLNN	FLANN	HNFB⁻¹	Alloc80	Cal5	CART	Knn	LVQ	Ko-honen	C4.5
C_{test}	0.31	0.33	0.37	0.41	0.44	0.45	0.478	0.60	0.69	0.78
C_{train}	0.32	0.34	0.59	0.39	0.33	0.44	0	0.14	0.43	0.44

Conclusion and Research Directions

In this chapter, we developed a new hybrid higher order neural network (HONN). The hybrid model is constructed using the newly proposed ePSO-back propagation learning algorithm and functional link artificial neural network with the orthogonal Chebyshev polynomials. The model was designed for the task of classification in data mining. The method was experimentally tested on various benchmark datasets obtained from publicly available UCI repository. The performance of the proposed method demonstrated that the classification task is quite well in all the cases. Further, we compared this model with most of the popular and well-known higher order neural networks such as RPNN, RBFNN, EFLN, FLANN and SPNN. The comparative result of the developed model is showing a clear edge among RPNN, SPNN, and RBFNN. However, it is showing a competitive result with the previously proposed FLANN. Compared with EFLN, the proposed method has been shown to yield state-of-the-art recognition error rate for the classification problems such as CANCER and BUPA.

With this encouraging results of hybrid cFLANN our future research includes: (i) testing the proposed method on a more number of real life bench mark classification problems with highly non-linear boundaries; (ii) mapping the input features with other polynomials such as Legendre, Gaussian, Sigmoid, power series, etc for better approximation of the decision boundaries; (iii) the stability and convergence analysis of the proposed method; and (iv) the evolution of optimal FLANN using particle swarm optimization.

The hybrid cFLNN architecture, because of its simple architecture and computational efficiency may be conveniently employed in other tasks of data mining and knowledge discovery in databases (Ghosh, Dehuri & Ghosh, 2008; Kriegel & et al, 2007) such as clustering, feature selection, feature extraction, association rule mining, regression, and so on. The extra calculation generated by the higher order units can be eliminated, provided that these polynomial terms are stored in memory instead of being recalculated each time the hybrid cFLNN trained.

ACKNOWLEDGMENT

Authors would like to thank BK21 research program on Next Generation Mobile Software at Yonsei University, South Korea for their financial support.

REFERENCES

Abu-Mahfouz, I.-A. (2005). A comparative study of three artificial neural networks for the detection and classification of gear faults. *International Journal of General Systems, 34*(3), 261–277. doi:10.1080/03081070500065726

Ali, M. M., & Kaelo, P. (2008). Improved particle swarm algorithms for global optimization. *Applied Mathematics and Computation, 196*, 578–593. doi:10.1016/j.amc.2007.06.020

Antyomov, E., & Pecht, O. Y. (2005). Modified higher order neural network for invariant pattern recognition. *Pattern Recognition Letters, 26*, 843–851. doi:10.1016/j.patrec.2004.09.029

Asuncion, A., & Newman, D. J. (2007). UCI machine learning repository. Retrieved (n.d.)., from http://www.ics.uci.edu/~mlearn/MLRepository.html. *Irvine, CA: University of California, School of Information and Computer Science.*

Chen, S., Wu, Y., & Luk, B. L. (1999). Combined genetic algorithm optimization and regularized orthogonal least square learning for radial basis function networks. *IEEE Transactions on Neural Networks, 10*(5), 1239–1243. doi:10.1109/72.788663

Clerc, M., & Kennedy, J. (2002). The particle swarm explosion, stability and convergence in a multidimensional complex space. *IEEE Transactions on Evolutionary Computation, 6*(1), 58–73. doi:10.1109/4235.985692

Da, Y., & Ge, X. R. (2005). An improved PSO-based ANN with simulated annealing technique. *Neurocomputing, 63*, 527–533. doi:10.1016/j.neucom.2004.07.002

Dash, P. K. (1999). A functional link neural network for short term electric load forecasting. *Journal of Intelligent and Fuzzy Systems, 7*, 209–221.

Davidor, Y. (1990). Epitasis variance: suitability of a representation to genetic algorithms. *Complex Systems, 4*, 368–383.

Dehuri, S., et al. (2008). Genetic feature selection for optimal functional link neural network in classification. In C. Fyfe, et al. (Eds.) *IDEAL* (pp.156-163), LNCS, 5326.

Dybowski, R. (1998). Classification of incomplete feature vectors by radial basis function networks. *Pattern Recognition Letters, 19*, 1257–1264. doi:10.1016/S0167-8655(98)00096-8

Eshelman, L. J., & Schaffer, J. D. (1993). Real coded genetic algorithms and interval schemata. In: L. D. Whitley (Ed.) Foundation of Genetic Algorithms (pp.187-202). Sam Francisco: Morgan Kaufmann.

Forie, P. C., & Groenwold, A. A. (2002). The particle swarm optimization algorithm in size and shape optimization. *Structural and Multidisciplinary Optimization, 23*(4), 259–267. doi:10.1007/s00158-002-0188-0

Fukunaga, K. (1990). *Introduction to statistical pattern recognition.* New York: Academic Press.

Ghosh, A., Dehuri, S., & Ghosh, S. (2008). *Multi-objective Evolutionary Algorithms for Knowledge Discovery from Databases.* New York: Springer.

Ghosh, J., & Shin, Y. (1992). Efficient higher-order neural networks for classification and function approximation. *International Journal of Neural Systems*, *3*, 323–350. doi:10.1142/S0129065792000255

Giles, C. L., & Maxwell, T. (1987). Learning, invariance and generalization in higher-order neural networks. *Applied Optics*, *26*(23), 4972–4978. doi:10.1364/AO.26.004972

Goldberg, D. E. (1989). *Genetic algorithms in search, optimization and machine learning*. San Francisco: Morgan Kaufmann.

Haring., et al. (1997). Feature selection for neural networks through functional links found by evolutionary computation. In: Liu, X., et al. (Eds.) *Advances in Intelligent Data Analysis* (IDA-97)(pp.199-210), LNCS, 1280.

Haring, B., & Kok, J. N. (1995). Finding functional links for neural networks by evolutionary computation. In T. Van de Merckt, et al. (Eds.) BENELEARN'95, *Proceedings of the fifth Belgian-Dutch Conference on Machine Learning* (pp.71-78), Brussels, Belgium.

Haykin, S. (1999). *Neural networks: A comprehensive foundation*. Englewood Cliffs, NJ: Prentice Hall.

Hornik, K. (1991). Approximation capabilities of multi-layer feed-forward networks. *Neural Networks*, *4*(2), 251–257. doi:10.1016/0893-6080(91)90009-T

Hussain, A. J. (2008). Physical time series prediction using recurrent pi-sigma neural networks. *International Journal of Artificial Intelligence and Soft Computing*, *1*(1), 130–145. doi:10.1504/IJAISC.2008.021268

Hussain, A. J., & Liatsis, P. (2002). Recurrent pi-sigma networks for DPCM image coding. *Neurocomputing*, *55*, 363–382. doi:10.1016/S0925-2312(02)00629-X

Iyoda, E. M. (2007). Image compression and reconstruction using pi_t-sigma neural networks. *Soft Computing*, *11*, 53–61. doi:10.1007/s00500-006-0052-z

Kaita, T., Tomita, S., & Yamanaka, J. (2002). On a higher order neural network for distortion invariant pattern recognition. *Pattern Recognition Letters*, *23*, 977–984. doi:10.1016/S0167-8655(02)00028-4

Kennedy, J., & Eberhart, R. C. (1995). Particle swarm optimization. In: *Proceedings of the IEEE International Conference on Neural Networks*, Pisacataway, NJ, 1942-9148.

Kennedy, J., & Eberhart, R. C. (1999). The particle swarm: social adaptation in information processing systems. In: D. Corne, M. Dorigo, & F. Glover (Eds.) *New Ideas in Optimization* (pp.379-387), Cambridge, UK: McGraw-Hill.

Klasser, M. S., & Pao, Y. H. (1988). Characteristics of the functional link net: a higher order delta rule net. In *IEEE Proceedings of 2nd Annual International Conference on Neural Networks*, San Diago, CA, I, 507-513.

Kosmatopoulos, E. B., & Christodoulou, M. A. (1997). Techniques and applications of higher-order neural network systems in the identification of dynamical systems. In: Leondes, C. T. (Eds.) *Neural Network Systems Techniques and Applications*, New York: Academic Press.

Kosmatopoulos, E. B., Polycarpou, M. M., Christodoulou, M. A., & Ioannou, P. A. (1995). High-order neural network structures for identification of dynamical systems. *IEEE Transactions on Neural Networks*, *6*(2), 422–431. doi:10.1109/72.363477

Kriegel, H.-P. (2007). Future trends in data mining. *Data Mining and Knowledge Discovery*, *15*(1), 87–97. doi:10.1007/s10618-007-0067-9

Krishnaiah, D. (2008). Application of ultrasonic waves coupled with functional link neural network for estimation of carrageenan concentration. *International Journal of Physical Sciences*, *3*(4), 90–96.

Lee, T. T., & Jeng, J. T. (1998). The Chebyshev polynomial based unified model neural networks for function approximations. *IEEE Transactions on Systems Man and Cybernetics-Part B*, *28*, 925–935. doi:10.1109/3477.735405

Leonardis, A., & Bischof, H. (1998). An efficient MDL based construction of RBF networks. *Neural Networks*, *11*, 963–973. doi:10.1016/S0893-6080(98)00051-3

Li, M., Tian, J., & Chen, F. (2008). Improving multiclass pattern recognition with a co-evolutionary RBFNN. *Pattern Recognition Letters*, *29*, 392–406. doi:10.1016/j.patrec.2007.10.019

Liatsis, P., & Hussain, A. J. (1999). Non-linear one-dimensional DPCM image prediction using polynomial neural network. In [San Jose, California]. *Proceedings of SPIE Applications of Artificial Neural Networks in Image Processing IV*, *3647*, 58–68.

Majhi, B. (2005). An improved scheme for digital watermarking using functional link artificial neural network. *Journal of Computer Science*, *1*(2), 169–174. doi:10.3844/jcssp.2005.169.174

Mangasarian, O. L., & Wild, E. W. (2008). Non-linear knowledge based classification. *IEEE Transactions on Neural Networks*, *19*(10), 1826–1832. doi:10.1109/TNN.2008.2005188

Marcu, T., & Koppen-Seliger, B. (2004). Dynamic functional link neural networks genetically evolved applied to system identification. In *Proceedings of ESANN'2004*, Bruges (Belgium), 115-120.

Michie, D., Spiegelhalter, D. J., & Taylor, C. C. (1994). *Machine Learning, Neural and Statistical Classification*. West Sussex, UK: Ellis Horwood.

Mirea, L., & Marcu, T. (2002). System ident. using functional link neural networks with dynamic structure. *15th Trien. Wrld. Cong.*, Barcelona, Spain.

Misra, B. B., & Dehuri, S. (2007). Functional link neural network for classification task in data mining. *Journal of Computer Science*, *3*(12), 948–955. doi:10.3844/jcssp.2007.948.955

Muhlenbein, H., & Schlierkamp-Voosen, D. (1993). Predictive models for the breeder genetic algorithm I. Continuous parameters optimization. *Evolutionary Computation*, *1*(1), 24–49. doi:10.1162/evco.1993.1.1.25

Nie, Y., & Deng, W. (2008). A hybrid genetic learning algorithm for pi-sigma neural network and the analysis of its convergence. In *Proceedings of Fourth International Conference on Natural Computation (IEEE Press)*, 19-23.

Panagiotopoulos, D. A. (1999). Planning with a functional neural network architecture. *IEEE Transactions on Neural Networks, 10*(1), 115–127. doi:10.1109/72.737498

Pao, Y. H. (1989). *Adaptive pattern recognition and neural network*. Reading, MA: Addison-Wesley.

Pao, Y. H., & Takefuji, Y. (1992). Functional link net computing: theory, system, architecture and functionalities. *IEEE Computer*, 76-79.

Patra, J. C. (1999). Identification of non -linear dynamic systems using functional link artificial neural networks. *IEEE Transactions on Systems, Man, and Cybernetics. Part B, Cybernetics, 29*(2), 254–262. doi:10.1109/3477.752797

Patra, J. C. (2000). Modeling of an intelligent pressure sensor using functional link artificial neural networks. *ISA Transactions, 39*, 15–27. doi:10.1016/S0019-0578(99)00035-X

Patra, J. C. (2002). Non-linear dynamic system identification using Chebyshev functional link artificial neural networks. *IEEE Transactions on Systems, Man, and Cybernetics. Part B, Cybernetics, 32*(4), 505–511. doi:10.1109/TSMCB.2002.1018769

Patra, J. C. (2008). Functional link neural networks-based intelligent sensors for harsh environments. *Sensors and Transducers Journal, 90*, 209–220.

Patra, J. C., & Pal, N. R. (1995). A functional link neural network for adaptive channel equalization. *Signal Processing, 43*, 181–195. doi:10.1016/0165-1684(94)00152-P

Preshelt, L. (1994). Proben1-a set of neural network benchmark problems and benchmarking rules. *Technical Report 21/94,* Universitat Karlsruhe, Germany.

Purwar, S. (2007). On-line system identification of complex systems using Chebyshev neural networks. *Applied Soft Computing, 7*, 364–372. doi:10.1016/j.asoc.2005.08.001

Ratnaweera, A., Halgamuge, S. K., & Watson, H. C. (2004). Self-organizing hierarchical particle swarm optimizer with time varying acceleration coefficients. *IEEE Transactions on Evolutionary Computation, 8*(3), 240–255. doi:10.1109/TEVC.2004.826071

Rovithakis, G. A., & Christodoulou, M. A. (2000). Adaptive control with recurrent high-order neural networks (Theory and Industrial Applications). In: Grimble, M. A. & Johnson, M. A. (Eds.) *Advances in Industrial Control*, London: Springer Verlag.

Schaffer, J. D., Whitley, D., & Eshelman, L. J. (1992). Combinations of genetic algorithms and neural networks: A survey of the state of the art. In *Proceedings of International Workshop on Combinations of Genetic Algorithms and Neural Networks*, 1-37.

Schutte, J. F., & Groenwold, A. A. (2005). A study of global optimization using particle swarms. *Journal of Global Optimization, 31*(1), 93–108. doi:10.1007/s10898-003-6454-x

Shi, Y., & Eberhart, R. C. (1998). A modified particle swarm optimizer. In *Proceedings of the IEEE International Conference on Evolutionary Computation* (pp.69-73), Pisacataway, NJ: IEEE Press

Shi, Y., & Eberhart, R. C. (1998). Parameter selection in particle swarm optimization. *Evolutionary Programming VII* (pp.591-600), LNCS, 1447, Berlin, Germany: Springer.

Shin, Y., & Ghosh, J. (1991). The pi-sigma networks: an efficient higher order neural network for pattern classification and function approximation. In . *Proceedings of International Joint Conference on Neural Networks, I*, 13–18.

Shin, Y., & Ghosh, J. (1991b). Realization of Boolean functions using binary pi-sigma networks. In *Proceedings of Conference on Artificial Neural Networks in Engineering, St. Louis.*

Shin, Y., & Ghosh, J. (1992a). Approximation of multivariate functions using ridge polynomial networks. In . *Proceedings of International Joint Conference on Neural Networks, II*, 380–385.

Shin, Y., & Ghosh, J. (1992b): Computationally efficient invariant pattern recognition with higher order pi-sigma networks (Tech Report). *The University of Texas at Austin.*

Shin, Y., & Ghosh, J. (1995). Ridge polynomial networks. *IEEE Transactions on Neural Networks, 6*(2), 610–622. doi:10.1109/72.377967

Sierra, A., Macias, J. A., & Corbacho, F. (2001). Evolution of functional link networks. *IEEE Transactions on Evolutionary Computation, 5*(1), 54–65. doi:10.1109/4235.910465

Sing, S. N., & Srivastava, K. N. (2002). Degree of insecurity estimation in a power system using functional link neural network. *ETEP, 12*(5), 353–359.

Tawfik, H., & Liatsis, P. (1997). Prediction of non-linear time series using higher order neural networks. In *Proceedings of IWSSIP '97*, Poznan, Poland.

Theodorodis, S., & Koutroumbas, K. (1999). *Pattern recognition.* San Diego, USA: Academic Press

Voutriaridis, C., Boutalis, Y. S., & Mertzios, G. (2003). Ridge polynomial networks in pattern recognition. *4th EURASIP Conference Focused on Video/ Image Processing and Multimedia Communications*, Croatia, 519-524.

Weng, W.-D. (2007). A channel equalizer using reduced decision feedback Chebyshev function link artificial neural networks. *Information Sciences, 177*, 2642–2654. doi:10.1016/j.ins.2007.01.006

Xiong, Y. (2007). Training *pi-sigma* network by on-line gradient algorithm with penalty for small weight update. *Neural Computation, 19*, 3356–3368. doi:10.1162/neco.2007.19.12.3356

Yu, J., Wang, S., & Xi, L. (2008). Evolving artificial neural networks using an improved PSO and DPSO. *Neurocomputing, 71*, 1054–1060. doi:10.1016/j.neucom.2007.10.013

Zhang, J. R. (2007). A hybrid particle swarm optimization-back-propagation algorithm for feed-forward neural network training. *Applied Mathematics and Computation, 185*, 1026–1037. doi:10.1016/j.amc.2006.07.025

Zhao, H., & Zhang, J. (2008). Functional link neural network cascaded with Chebyshev orthogonal polynomial for non-linear channel equalization. *Signal Processing, 88*, 1946–1957. doi:10.1016/j.sigpro.2008.01.029

Zhu, Q., Cai, Y., & Liu, L. (1999). A global learning algorithm for a RBF network. *Neural Networks, 12*, 527–540. doi:10.1016/S0893-6080(98)00146-4

Compilation of References

Abdelbar, A. M. (1998). Achieving superior generalisation with a high order neural network. *Neural Computing & Applications*, 7(2), 141–146. doi:10.1007/BF01414166

Abdelbar, A. M., & Tagliarini, G. A. (1998, May 4-9). A hybrid Bayesian neural learning strategy applied to CONNECT-4. In *Proceeding of the IEEE World Congress on Computational Intelligence* (vol.1, pp.402 – 407).

Abu-Mahfouz, I.-A. (2005). A comparative study of three artificial neural networks for the detection and classification of gear faults. *International Journal of General Systems*, 34(3), 261–277. doi:10.1080/03081070500065726

Adetona, O., Sathananthan, S., & Keel, L. H. (2002). Robust adaptive control of nonaffine nonlinear plants with small input signal changes. *IEEE Transactions on Neural Networks*, 15(2), 408–416. doi:10.1109/TNN.2004.824423

Alanís, A. Y. (2007). *Discrete-time Neural Control*. Ph. D. Disserattion, CINVESTAV Unidad Guadalajara, México.

Alanis, A. Y., Sanchez, E. N., & Loukianov, A. G. (2006, July 16-21). Discrete- Time Recurrent Neural Induction Motor Control using Kalman Learning. In *Proceedings of International Joint Conference on Neural Networks* (pp.1993 – 2000).

Alanis, A. Y., Sanchez, E. N., & Loukianov, A. G. (2007). Discrete-Time Adaptive Backstepping Nonlinear Control via High-Order Neural Networks. *IEEE Transactions on Neural Networks*, 18(4), 1185–1195. doi:10.1109/TNN.2007.899170

Alanis, A. Y., Sanchez, E. N., & Loukianov, A. G. (2008). Discrete-Time Backstepping Synchronous Generator Stabilization Using a Neural Observer. In *Proceedings of the IFAC World Congress* (pp. 15897-15902). Seoúl, Korea.

Alba, E. (2002). Parallel evolutionary algorithms can achieve super-linear performance. *Information Processing Letters*, 82(1), 7–13. doi:10.1016/S0020-0190(01)00281-2

Alba, E., & Tomassini, M. (2002). Parallelism and evolutionary algorithms. *IEEE Transactions on Evolutionary Computation*, 6(5), 443–462. doi:10.1109/TEVC.2002.800880

Alba, E., & Troya, J. M. (1999). A survey of parallel distributed genetic algorithms. *Complex.*, 4(4), 31–52. doi:10.1002/(SICI)1099-0526(199903/04)4:4<31::AID-CPLX5>3.0.CO;2-4

Albert, A. (1972). *Regression and the Moore-Penrose Pseudoinverse*. New York: Academic Press.

Ali, M. M., & Kaelo, P. (2008). Improved particle swarm algorithms for global optimization. *Applied Mathematics and Computation*, 196, 578–593. doi:10.1016/j.amc.2007.06.020

Allen, D. W., & Taylor, J. G. (1994). Learning time series by neural networks. In M. Marinaro & P. Morasso (Eds.), *Proceedings of the International Conference on Neural Networks*, Sorrento, Italy (pp. 529-532). Berlin: Springer.

Al-Rawi, M. (2006). *Learning affine invariant pattern recognition using high-order Neural Networks*. International Conference on Artificial Intelligence and Machine Learning, (24-29.) Sharm El Sheikh, Egypt.

Al-Rawi, M., & Bisher, A. (2005). *An improved neural network builder that includes graphical networks and PI nodes. Human Computer Interaction.* (229-237), International Conference on Human Computer Interaction, Al-Zaytoona University, Amman, Jordan.

Altug, E., Ostrowski, J. P., & Mahony, R. (2002). *Control of a quadrotor helicopter using visual feedback.* Paper presented at the IEEE International Conference on Robotics and Automation, Washington, DC.

Amari, S. (1971). Characteristics of Randomly Connected Threshold-Element Networks and Network Systems. *Proceedings of the IEEE, 59*(1), 35–47. doi:10.1109/PROC.1971.8087

Amari, S. (1972). Characteristics of Random Nets of Analog Neuron - Like Elements. *IEEE Transactions on Systems, Man, and Cybernetics, 2,* 643–654. doi:10.1109/TSMC.1972.4309193

Amari, S. (1972). Learning Patterns and Pattern Sequences by Self-Organizing Nets of Threshold Elements. *IEEE Transactions on Computers, 21,* 1197–1206. doi:10.1109/T-C.1972.223477

Amari, S. (1977). A Mathematical Approach to Neural Systems. In J. Metzler (Ed.), *Systems Neuroscience* (pp. 67-118). New York: Academic.

Amari, S. (1977). Neural Theory of Association and Concept Formation. *Biological Cybernetics, 26,* 175–185. doi:10.1007/BF00365229

Amari, S. (1990). Mathematical Foundations of Neurocomputing. *Proceedings of the IEEE, 78*(9), 1443–1462. doi:10.1109/5.58324

Amit, D. J., Gutfreund, G., & Sompolinsky, H. (1985). Spin-Glass Model of Neural Networks. *Physical Review A., 32,* 1007–1018. doi:10.1103/PhysRevA.32.1007

An, Z. G., Mniszewski, S. M., Lee, Y. C., Papcun, G., & Doolen, G. D. (1988, March 14-18). HIERtalker: a default hierarchy of high order neural networks that learns to read English aloud. In *Proceedings of the Fourth Conference on Artificial Intelligence Applications* (pp.388).

An, Z. G., Mniszewski, S. M., Lee, Y. C., Papcun, G., & Doolen, G. D. (1988, July 24-27). HIERtalker: a default hierarchy of high order neural networks that learns to read English aloud. In. *Proceedings of IEEE International Conference on Neural Networks, 2,* 221–228. doi:10.1109/ICNN.1988.23932

Anagun, A. S., & Cin, I. (1998). A Neural-Network-Based Computer Access Security System for Multiple Users. In *Proceedings of 23rd Inter. Conf. Comput. Ind. Eng., Vol.* 35 (pp. 351-354).

Anand, R., Mehrotra, K., & Mohan, C. K. (1995). Efficient classification for multiclass problems using modular neural networks. *IEEE Transactions on Neural Networks, 6,* 117–123. doi:10.1109/72.363444

Anderson, J. A. (1983). Cognition and Psychological Computation with Neural Models. *IEEE Transactions on Systems, Man, and Cybernetics, 13,* 799–815.

Angelidaki, I., Ellegaard, L., & Ahring, B. K. (1998). A comprehensive model of anaerobic bioconversion of complex substrates to biogas. *Biotechnology and Bioengineering, 63*(3), 363–372. doi:10.1002/(SICI)1097-0290(19990505)63:3<363::AID-BIT13>3.0.CO;2-Z

Angeline, P. J. (1998). Evolutionary optimization versus particle swarm optimization: Philosophy and performance differences. In *EP '98: Proceedings of the 7th International Conference on Evolutionary Programming VII,* (pp. 601-610). London, UK: Springer-Verlag.

Anninos, P. A., Beek, B., Csermel, T. J., Harth, E. E., & Pertile, G. (1970). Dynamics of Neural Structures. *Journal of Theoretical Biology, 26,* 121–148. doi:10.1016/S0022-5193(70)80036-4

Antsaklis, P. J., & Passino, K. M. (1993). *An Introduction to Intelligent and Autonomous Control.* Norwell, MA: Kluwer Academic Publishers.

Antyomov, E., & Pecht, O. Y. (2005). Modified higher order neural network for invariant pattern recognition. *Pattern Recognition Letters, 26,* 843–851. doi:10.1016/j.patrec.2004.09.029

Aoki, C., & Siekevltz, P. (1988). Plasticity in Brain Development. *Scientific American,* (Dec): 56–64.

Armstrong, W. W., & Gecsei, J. (1979). Adaptation Algorithms for Binary Tree Networks. *IEEE Transactions on Systems, Man, and Cybernetics, 9*(5), 276–285. doi:10.1109/TSMC.1979.4310196

Artyomov, E., & Pecht, O. Y. (2005). Modified high-order neural network for invariant pattern recognition. *Pattern Recognition Letters, 26*, 843–851. doi:10.1016/j.patrec.2004.09.029

Ash, T. (1989). Dynamic node creation in backpropagation networks. *Connection Science, 1*(4), 365–375. doi:10.1080/09540098908915647

Asuncion, A., & Newman, D. J. (2007). UCI machine learning repository. Retrieved (n.d.)., from http://www.ics.uci.edu/~mlearn/MLRepository.html. *Irvine, CA: University of California, School of Information and Computer Science.*

Atiya, A. F. (1988). Learning on a general network. *In Proc. IEEE Conf. Neural Information Processing Systems*, 1987.

Atiya, A. F. (2000). New Results on Recurrent Network Training: Unifying the Algorithms and Accelerating Convergence. *IEEE Transactions on Neural Networks, 11*(3), 697–709. doi:10.1109/72.846741

Baeck, T., Fogel, D. B., & Michalewicz, Z. (Eds.). (1997). *Handbook of Evolutionary Computation.* Oxford, UK: Oxford University Press.

Baldi, P., & Venkatesh, S. S. (1993). Random interactions in higher order neural networks. *IEEE Transactions on Information Theory, 39*(1), 274–283. doi:10.1109/18.179374

Bar-Cohen, Y., Mavroidis, C., Bouzit, M., et al. (2000). Virtual reality robotic operation simulations using MEMICA haptic system. *International Conference for Smart systems and Robotics for Medicine and Space Applications*, Houston, TX, USA.

Barman, I., & Guha, S. K. (2006). Analysis of a new combined stretch and pressure sensor for internal nodule palpation. *Sensors and Actuators A, 125*, 210–216. doi:10.1016/j.sna.2005.07.010

Barron, A. R. (1994). Approximation and Estimation Bounds for Artificial Neural Networks. *Machine Learning, 14*, 115–133.

Barron, A. R., & Cover, T. M. (1991). Minimum complexity density estimation. *IEEE Transactions on Information Theory, 37*, 1034–1054. doi:10.1109/18.86996

Barron, R., Gilstrap, L., & Shrier, S. (1987). Polynomial and neural networks: Analogies and engineering applications. In [New York.]. *Proceedings of the International Conference on Neural Networks, 2*, 431–439.

Bastin, G., & Dochain, D. (1990). *On-line estimation and adaptive control of bioreactors.* Maryland Heights, USA: Elsevier.

Bayraktaroglu, I., Ogrenci, A. S., & Dundar, G. (1999). ANNSyS: an analog neural network synthesis system. *Neural Networks, 12*, 325–338. doi:10.1016/S0893-6080(98)00122-1

Bazanella, A., Silva, A. S., & Kokotovic, P. V. (1997), Lyapunov design of excitation control for synchronous machines. In *Proceedings of the 36th IEEE Conference on Decision and Control* (pp. 211–216). San Diego, CA

Beale, R., & Jackson, T. (1990). *Neural Computing: An Introduction.* Bristol, UK: Hilger.

Bhatt, T. M., & McCain, D. (2005). Matlab as a development environment for FPGA design. In *Proceedings of 42nd Design Automation Conference* (pp. 607–610).

Bigus, J. P. (1996). *Data Mining with Neural Networks.* New York: McGraw-Hill.

Bijnens, B., Chu, Q. P., Voorsluijs, G. M., & Mulder, J. A. (2005, 15 - 18 August 2005). *Adaptive feedback linearization flight control for a helicopter UAV.* Paper presented at the AIAA Guidance, Navigation, and Control Conference and Exhibit, San Francisco.

Bishop, C. M. (1995). *Neural Networks for Pattern Recognition.* Oxford, UK: Oxford Univ. Press.

Bishop, M. C. (2006). *Pattern Recognition and Machine Learning.* New York:Springer.

Bloch, G., Lauer, F., Colin, G., & Chamaillard, Y. (2008). Support vector regression from simulation data and few experimental samples. *Information Sciences, 178*(20), 3813–3827. doi:10.1016/j.ins.2008.05.016

Bong, J. Y., & Calise, A. J. (2007). Adaptive Control of a Class of Nonaffine Systems Using Neural Networks. *IEEE Transactions on Neural Networks, 18*(4), 1149–1159. doi:10.1109/TNN.2007.899253

Bouabdallah, S., Noth, A., & Siegwart, R. (2004). *PID vs LQ control techniques applied to an indoor micro quadrotor.* Paper presented at the International Conference on Intelligent Robots and Systems.

Boutalis, Y. S., Theodoridis, D. C., & Christodoulou, M. A. (2009). A new Neuro FDS definition for indirect adaptive control of unknown nonlinear systems using a method of parameter hopping. *IEEE Transactions on Neural Networks, 20*(4), 609–625. doi:10.1109/TNN.2008.2010772

Boutalis, Y. S., Theodoridis, D. C., & Christodoulou, M. A. (2010). Identification of Nonlinear Systems Using a New Neuro-Fuzzy Dynamical System Definition Based on High Order Neural Network Function Approximators. *Chapter 18 in Artificial Higher Order Neural Networks for Computer Science and Engineering: Trends for Emerging Applications (M. Zhang Ed.).*Pennsylvania: IGI Global.

Bouzerdoum, A. (1999, November 16-20). A new class of high-order neural networks with nonlinear decision boundaries. In. *Proceedings of International Conference on Neural Information Processing, 3*, 1004–1009.

Brachman, R. J., Khabaza, T., Kloesgen, W., Piatetsky-Shapiro, E., & Simoudis, E. (1996). Mining business databases. *Communications of the ACM, 39*(11), 42–48. doi:10.1145/240455.240468

Bramer, M. (2007). *Principles of Data Mining.* New York: Springer.

Branke, J. (1995). Evolutionary Algorithms for Neural Network Design and Training. In *Proceedings of the First Nordic Workshop on Genetic Algorithms and its Applications*, (pp. 145-163).

Browne, A., Hudson, B. D., Whitley, D. C., Ford, M. G., & Picton, P. (2004). Biological data mining with neural networks: implementation and application of a flexible decision tree extraction algorithm to genomic problem domains. *Neurocomputing, 57*, 275–293. doi:10.1016/j.neucom.2003.10.007

Brucoli, M., Carnimeo, L., & Grassi, G. (1997). Associative memory design using discrete-time second-order neural networks with local interconnections. *IEEE Transactions on Circuits and Systems. I, Fundamental Theory and Applications, 44*(2), 153–158. doi:10.1109/81.554334

Büker, U., & Nixdorf, N. (1998). Hybrid Object Models: Combining Symbolic and Subsymbolic Object Recognition Strategies In *Proceedings of SCI'98 / ISAS'98* (pp. 444-451).

Burshtein, D. (1998). Long-term attraction in higher order neural networks. *IEEE Transactions on Neural Networks, 9*(1), 42–50. doi:10.1109/72.655028

Butt, N. R., & Shafiq, M. (2006, April 22-23). Higher-Order Neural Network Based Root-Solving Controller for Adaptive Tracking of Stable Nonlinear Plants. In *Proceedings of IEEE International Conference on Engineering of Intelligent Systems* (pp.1 – 6).

Calise, A. J., Kim, B. S., Leitner, J., & Prasad, J. V. R. (1994). Helicopter adaptive flight control using neural networks. In *Proceedings of the 33rd Conference on Decision and Control*, Lake Buena Vista, FL.

Campolucci, P., Capparelli, F., Guarnieri, S., Piazza, F., & Uncini, A. (1996). Neural networks with adaptive spline activation function. In *Proceedings of the IEEE MELECON'96 Conference* (pp. 1442-1445). Bari, Italy.

Campolucci, P., Capparelli, F., Guarnieri, S., Piazza, F., & Uncini, A. (1996). Neural networks with adaptive spline activation function. In [Bari, Italy.]. *Proceedings of IEEE MELECON, 96*, 1442–1445.

Campos, J., Loukianov, A. G., & Sanchez, E. N. (2003, December 9-12). Synchronous motor VSS control using recurrent high order neural networks. In *Proceedings of 42nd IEEE Conference on Decision and Control* (vol. 4, pp.3894 – 3899)

Cantù-Paz, E. (1998). A survey of parallel genetic algorithms. *Calculateurs Paralèlèles. Réseaux et Systèmes Répartis, 10*(2), 141–171.

Cantù-Paz, E. (2000). *Efficient and Accurate Parallel Genetic Algorithms*. Norwell, MA: Kluwer Academic Publishers

Cao, L. J., Chua, K. S., Chong, W. K., Lee, H. P., & Gu, Q. M. (2003). A comparison of PCA, KPCA and ICA for dimensionality reduction in support vector machine. *Neurocomputing, 55*, 321–336. doi:10.1016/S0925-2312(03)00433-8

Carlos-Hernandez, S., Beteau, J. F., & Sanchez, E. N. (2006, October). Design and real-time implementation of a TS fuzzy observer for anaerobic wastewater treatment plants. *IEEE International Symposium on Intelligent Control* (pp. 1252-1257), Munich, Germany.

Carnell, A., & Richardson, D. (2007). Parallel computation in spiking neural nets. *Theoretical Computer Science, 386*(1-2), 57–72. doi:10.1016/j.tcs.2007.06.017

Cass, R., & Radl, B. (1996). Adaptive process optimization using functional-link networks and evolutionary algorithm. *Control Engineering Practice, 4*(11), 1579–1584. doi:10.1016/0967-0661(96)00173-6

Castillo, P., Dzul, A., & Lozano, R. (2004). Real-time Stabilization and Tracking of a Four-Rotor Mini Rotorcraft. *IEEE Transactions on Control Systems Technology, 12*, 510–516. doi:10.1109/TCST.2004.825052

Castillo, P., Lozano, R., & Dzul, A. (2005a). *Modelling and Control of Mini Flying Machines*. Berlin: Springer-Verlag.

Castillo, P., Lozano, R., & Dzul, A. (2005b). Stabilization of a Mini Rotorcraft Having Four Rotors. *IEEE Control Systems Magazine, 25*, 45–55. doi:10.1109/MCS.2005.1550152

Caudill, M., & Butler, C. (1990). *Naturally intelligent systems*. Cambridge, MA: MIT Press.

Chakraborty, U. K. (2008). *Advances in Differential Evolution*. Springer Publishing.

Chang, C., & Cheung, J. Y. (1992, June 7-11). Back-propagation algorithm in higher order neural network. In. *Proceedings of International Joint Conference on Neural Networks, 3*, 511–516.

Chang, C.-H., Lin, J.-L., & Cheung, J.-Y. (1993, March 28). Polynomial and standard higher order neural network. In. *Proceedings of IEEE International Conference on Neural Networks, 2*, 989–994. doi:10.1109/ICNN.1993.298692

Chang, L. C., Chang, F. J., & Chiang, Y. M. (2004). A two-step-ahead recurrent neural network for streamflow forecasting. *Hydrological Processes, 18*, 81–92. doi:10.1002/hyp.1313

Chapman, J. W., Ilic, M., King, C. A., Eng, L., & Kaufman, H. (1993). Stabilizing a multimachine power system via decentralized feedback linearizing excitation control. *IEEE Transactions on Power Systems, 8*(1), 830–839. doi:10.1109/59.260921

Chatfield, C. (1989). *The Analysis of Time Series - An Introduction*. (4th ed.) London: Chapman & Hall.

Chen, B. S., Lee, C. H., & Chang, Y. C. (1996). Tracking design of uncertain nonlinear siso systems: Adaptive fuzzy approach. *IEEE transactions on Fuzzy Systems, 4*, 32–43. doi:10.1109/91.481843

Chen, C. T., & Chang, W. D. (1996). A feedforward neural network with function shape autotuning. *Neural Networks, 9*(4), 627–641. doi:10.1016/0893-6080(96)00006-8

Chen, C., & Honavar, V. (1999). A Neural Network Architecture for Syntax Analysis. *IEEE Transactions on Neural Networks, 10*(1), 94–114. doi:10.1109/72.737497

Chen, F. C., & Liu, C. C. (1994). Adaptively controlling nonlinear continuous-time systems using multilayer neural networks. *IEEE Transactions on Automatic Control, 39*, 1306–1310. doi:10.1109/9.293202

Chen, F., & Dunnigan, M. W. (2002). Comparative study of a sliding-mode observer and Kalman filters for full state estimation in an induction machine. *Electric Power Applications. IEE Proceedings, 149*(1), 53–64.

Chen, L. (1982). Topological Structure in Visual Perception. *Science, 218,* 699. doi:10.1126/science.7134969

Chen, S., Wu, Y., & Luk, B. L. (1999). Combined genetic algorithm optimization and regularized orthogonal least square learning for radial basis function networks. *IEEE Transactions on Neural Networks, 10*(5), 1239–1243. doi:10.1109/72.788663

Chen, T., & Chen, H. (1995). Universal approximation to non-linear operators by neural networks with arbitrary activation functions and its application to dynamical system. *IEEE Transactions on Neural Networks, 6*(4), 911–917. doi:10.1109/72.392253

Cheng, M., & Huzmezan, M. (2003, Aug. 11-14). *A combined MBPC/2 DOF hinf controller for quad rotor unmanned air vehicle.* Paper presented at the AIAA Atmospheric Flight Mechanics Conference and Exhibit, Austin, Texas, USA.

Cho, K. B., & Wang, B. H. (1996). Radial basis function based adaptive fuzzy systems and their applications to system identification and prediction. *Fuzzy Sets and Systems, 83,* 325–339. doi:10.1016/0165-0114(95)00322-3

Christodoulou, M. A., & Iliopoulos, T. N. (2006, June). Neural Network Models for Prediction of Steady-State and Dynamic Behavior of MAPK Cascade. In *Proceedings of 14th Mediterranean Conference on Control and Automation* (pp.1 – 9).

Christodoulou, M. A., Theodoridis, D. C., & Boutalis, Y. S. (2007). Building Optimal Fuzzy Dynamical Systems Description Based on Recurrent Neural Network Approximation. In Proceedings of *Int. Conf. of Networked Distributed Systems for Intelligent Sensing and Control* (pp. 386-393). Kalamata, Greece.

Christodoulou, M., & Zarkogianni, D. (2006, June). Recurrent High Order Neural Networks for Identification of the EGFR Signaling Pathway. In *Proceedings of 2006. MED '06. 14th Mediterranean Conference on Control and Automation* (pp.1 – 6).

Chui, S. L. (1994). Fuzzy model identification based on cluster estimation. *Journal of Intelligent and Fuzzy Systems, 2,* 267–278. doi:10.1109/91.324806

Churchland, P. S., & Sejnowski, T. J. (1988). Perspectives on Cognitive Neuroscience. *Science, 242,* 741–745. doi:10.1126/science.3055294

Cichochi, A., & Unbehauen, R. (1993). *Neural Networks for Optimization and Signal Processing.* Chichester, UK: Wiley.

Cios, K. J., Pedrycz, W., Swiniarski, R. W., & Kurgan, L. A. (2007). *Data Mining: A Knowledge Discovery Approach.* New York: Springer.

Clark, J. (1995). Tracking, code recognition, and memory management with high-order neural networks. *Applications and Science of Artificial Neural Networks,* SPIE *2492,* 964-973.

Clerc, M. (2006). *Particle Swarm Optimization.* ISTE Publishing Company.

Clerc, M., & Kennedy, J. (2002). The particle swarm explosion, stability and convergence in a multidimensional complex space. *IEEE Transactions on Evolutionary Computation, 6*(1), 58–73. doi:10.1109/4235.985692

Comer, D. E., & Stevens, D. L. (1996). *Internetworking with TCP/IP vol III (2nd ed.): client-server programming and applications BSD socket version}.* Upper Saddle River, NJ: Prentice-Hall.

Connor, J. T., Martin, R. D., & Atlas, L. E. (1994). Recurrent Neural Networks and Robust Time Series Prediction. *IEEE Transactions on Neural Networks, 5*(2), 240–254. doi:10.1109/72.279188

Cooper, B. S. (1995, November 27). Higher order neural networks for combinatorial optimisation improving the scaling properties of the Hopfield network. In. *Proceedings of IEEE International Conference on Neural Networks, 4,* 1855–1860. doi:10.1109/ICNN.1995.488904

Corless, M. J., & Leitmann, G. (1981). Countinuous State Feedback Guaranteeing Uniform Ultimate Boundness for Uncertain Dynamic Systems. *IEEE Transactions on Automatic Control, 26*(7), 1139–1144. doi:10.1109/TAC.1981.1102785

Cotter, N. (1990). The Stone-Weierstrass Theorem and Its Application to Neural Networks. *IEEE Transactions on Neural Networks, 1*(4), 290–295. doi:10.1109/72.80265

Coutinho, D. F., & Pereira, L. P. F. A. (2005), A robust Luenberger-like observer for induction machines. In *Proceedings IEEE IECON*, North Carolina, USA.

Cowling, I. D., Yakimenko, O. A., Whidborne, J. F., & Cooke, A. K. (2007, July 2-5). *A prototype of an autonomous controller for a quadrotor UAV.* Paper presented at the Proceedings of the European Control Conference, Kos, Greece.

Cybenco, G. (1989). Approximations by supperpositions of a sigmoid function. *Mathematics of Control, Signals, and Systems, 2,* 303–314. doi:10.1007/BF02551274

Da, Y., & Ge, X. R. (2005). An improved PSO-based ANN with simulated annealing technique. *Neurocomputing, 63,* 527–533. doi:10.1016/j.neucom.2004.07.002

Dargahi, J. (2001). A study of the human hand as an ideal tactile sensor used in robotic and endoscopic applications. In *Proceedings of CSME International Conference,* (pp. 21–22). Montreal, Quebec.

Dargahi, J. (2002). An endoscopic and robotic tooth-like compliance and roughness tactile sensor. *Journal of Mechanical Design, 124,* 576–582. doi:10.1115/1.1471531

Dargahi, J., & Najarian, S. (2004a). Human tactile perception as a standard for artificial tactile sensing. A review. *International Journal of Medical Robotics and Computer Assisted Surgery, 1*(13), 23–35. doi:10.1002/rcs.3

Dargahi, J., & Najarian, S. (2004b). Analysis of a membrane type polymeric-based tactile sensor for biomedical and medical robotic applications. *Sensor. Mater, 16*(1), 25–41.

Dargahi, J., & Najarian, S. (2005a). Measurements and modeling of compliance using a novel multi sensor endoscopic grasper device. *Sensors Mater, 17,* 7–20.

Dargahi, J., & Najarian, S. (2005b). Advances in tactile sensors design/manufacturing and its impact on robotics application. A review. *The Industrial Robot, 32*(3), 268–281. doi:10.1108/01439910510593965

Dash, P. K. (1999). A functional link neural network for short term electric load forecasting. *Journal of Intelligent and Fuzzy Systems, 7,* 209–221.

Davidor, Y. (1990). Epitasis variance: suitability of a representation to genetic algorithms. *Complex Systems, 4,* 368–383.

De Jong, K. (1980). Adaptive system design: a genetic approach. *IEEE Transactions on Systems, Man, and Cybernetics, SMC-10*(9), 1566–1574.

De Leon-Morales, J., Espinosa-Perez, G., & Macias-Cardoso, I. (2002). Observer-based control of a synchronous generator: a Hamiltonian approach. *International Journal of Electrical Power & Energy Systems, 24,* 655–663. doi:10.1016/S0142-0615(01)00079-5

De León-Morales, J., Huerta-Guevara, O., Dugard, L., & Dion, J. M. 2003. Discrete-time nonlinear control scheme for synchronous generator, In *Proceedings of the IEEE Conference on Decision and Control 2003,* Maui, USA

De Mello, F. P., & Concordia, C. (1969). Concepts of synchronous machine stability as affected by excitation control. *IEEE Transactions on Power Apparatus and Systems, PAS-88,* 316–329. doi:10.1109/TPAS.1969.292452

Dehuri, S., et al. (2008). Genetic feature selection for optimal functional link neural network in classification. In C. Fyfe, et al. (Eds.) *IDEAL* (pp.156-163), LNCS, 5326.

Devroye, L., Gyorfi, L., & Lugosi, G. (1996). *A probabilistic theory of pattern recognition.* New York: Springer.

Diamantaras, K. I., & Kung, S. Y. (1996). *Principal Component Neural Networks: Theory and Applications.* Hoboken, NJ: John Wiley & Sons.Drezet, P. M. L., & Harrison, R. F. (2001). A new method for sparsity control in support vector classification and regression. *Pattern Recognition, 34,* 111–125.

Diamond, I., & Jeffries, J. (2001). *Beginning statistics: An introduction for social sciences.* London: Sage Publications.

Diao, Y., & Passino, K. M. (2002). Adaptive Neural/Fuzzy Control for Interpolated Nonlinear Systems. *IEEE transactions on Fuzzy Systems, 10*(5), 583–595. doi:10.1109/TFUZZ.2002.803493

Dias, F. M., Antunes, A., Vieira, J., & Mota, A. (2006). A sliding window solution for the on-line implementation of the Levenberg-Marquardt algorithm. *Engineering Applications of Artificial Intelligence, 19*, 1–7. doi:10.1016/j.engappai.2005.03.005

Ding, M.-Z., & Yang, W.-M. (1997). Stability of Synchronous Chaos and On-Off Intermittency in Coupled Map Lattices. *Physical Review E: Statistical Physics, Plasmas, Fluids, and Related Interdisciplinary Topics, 56*(4), 4009–4016. doi:10.1103/PhysRevE.56.4009

Djukanovic, M. B., Dobrijevic, D. M., Calovic, M. S., Novicevic, M., & Sobajic, D. J. (1997). Coordinated stabilizing control for the exciter and governor loops using fuzzy set theory and neural nets. *International Journal of Electrical Power & Energy Systems, 8*, 489–499. doi:10.1016/S0142-0615(97)00020-3

Dolenko, B. K., & Card, H. C. (1995). Tolerance to analog hardware of onchip learning in backpropagation networks. *IEEE Transactions on Neural Networks, 6*, 1045–1052. doi:10.1109/72.410349

Dong, G., & Pei, J. (2007). *Sequence Data Mining (Advances in Database Systems)*. New York: Springer.

Duda, R., Hart, P., & Strok, D. (2000). *Pattern classification*. 2nd Ed., New York: Wiley-Interscience.

Dundar, G., & Rose, K. (1995). The effects of quantization on multilayer neural networks. *IEEE Transactions on Neural Networks, 6*, 1446–1451. doi:10.1109/72.471364

Durbin, R. (1989). On the Correspondence Between Network Models and the Nervous System. In R. Durbin, C. Miall, & G. Mitchison (Eds.), *The Computing Neurons*. Reading, Mass.: Addison-Wesley.

Durbin, R., & Rumelhart, D. E. (1989). Product Units: A Computationally Powerful and Biologically Plausible Extension to Backpropagation Networks. *Neural Computation, 1*, 133–142. doi:10.1162/neco.1989.1.1.133

Durbin, R., & Rumelhart, D. E. (1990). Product units with trainable exponents and multilayer networks. In F. Fogelman Soulie, & J. Herault, (Eds.) *Neurocomputing: Algorithms, architecture and applications* (pp.

15-26). NATO ASI Series, vol. F68, New York: Springer-Verlag.

Dybowski, R. (1998). Classification of incomplete feature vectors by radial basis function networks. *Pattern Recognition Letters, 19*, 1257–1264. doi:10.1016/S0167-8655(98)00096-8

Eberhart, R. C., & Kennedy, J. (1995). A new optimizer using particle swarm theory. In *Proceedings of 6th Symposium on Micro Machine and Human Science*, (pp. 39-43). Nagoya, Japan.

Eberhart, R., Simpson, P., & Dobbins, R. (1996). *Computational intelligence PC tools*. San Diego, CA: Academic Press Professional

Egardt, P. (1979). *Stability of Adaptive Controllers*, Lecture Notes in Control and Information Sciences. Berlin, Germany: Springer-Verlag.

El-Farra, N. H., & Christofides, P. D. (2001). Integrating robustness, optimality and constraints in control of nonlinear processes. *Chemical Engineering Science, 56*, 1841–1868. doi:10.1016/S0009-2509(00)00530-3

Elman, J. (1990). Finding structure in time. *Cognitive Science, 14*, 179-211

Eltaib, M. E. H., & Hewit, J. R. (2003). Tactile sensing technology for minimal access surgery – a review. *Mechatronics, 13*, 1163–1177. doi:10.1016/S0957-4158(03)00048-5

Engel, K., Konig, P., Kreiter, A. K., & Singer, W. (1991). Interhemispheric Synchronization of Oscillatory Neuronal Responses in Cat Visual Cortex. *Science, 252*, 1177–1178. doi:10.1126/science.252.5009.1177

Enns, R., & Si, J. (2000). *Helicopter flight control design using a learning control Approach1*. Paper presented at the Proceedings of the 39th Conference on Decision and Control, Sydney, Australia.

Epitropakis, M. G., Plagianakos, V. P., & Vrahatis, M. N. (2006). Higher-order neural networks training using differential evolution. In *International Conference of Numerical Analysis and Applied Mathematics*, (pp. 376-379). Crete, Greece: Wiley-VCH.

Ersu, E., & Tolle, H. (1984). A New Concept for Learning Control Inspired by Brain Theory. In *Proceedings of 9ᵗʰ World Congress IFAC* (pp. 245-250).

Eshelman, L. J., & Schaffer, J. D. (1993). Real coded genetic algorithms and interval schemata. In: L. D. Whitley (Ed.) Foundation of Genetic Algorithms (pp.187-202). Sam Francisco: Morgan Kaufmann.

Espinosa-Perez, G., Godoy-Alcantar, M., & Guerrero-Ramırez, G. (1997). Passivity-based control of synchronous generators. In *Proceedings of the 1997 IEEE International Symposium on Industrial Electronics* (pp. SS101–SS106). Guimaraes, Portugal.

Estevez, P. A., & Okabe, Y. (1991, November 18-21). Training the piecewise linear-high order neural network through error back propagation. In [).Seattle, USA.]. *Proceedings of IEEE International Joint Conference on Neural Networks, 1*, 711–716. doi:10.1109/IJCNN.1991.170483

Fahlman, S., & Lebiere, C. (1990). The cascade-correlation learning architecture. In *Advances in Neural Information Processing Systems, 2*, 524-532, San Mateo, CA: Morgan Kaufmann.

Fantoni, I., Zavala, A., & Lozano, R. (2002). *Global stabilization of a PVTOL aircraft with bounded thrust.* Paper presented at the Proceedings of the 41st Conference on Decision and Control, Las Vegas, NV.

Farlow, S. J. (1984). *Self-Organizing Methods in Modeling: GMDH Type Algorithms. New York*: Marcel Dekker.

Farrell, J., Sharma, M., & Polycarpou, M. (2005). Backstepping-Based Flight Control with Adaptive Function Approximation. *AIAA Journal of Guidance, Control and Dynamics, 28.*

Fayyad, U. M., Piatetsky-Shapiro, G., Smyth, P., & Uthurusamy, R. (1996). *Advances in Knowledge Discovery and Data Mining.* Cambridge, MA: AAAI Press/The MIT Press.

Fearing, R. S., Moy, G., & Tan, E. (1997). Some basic issues in teletaction. In *Proceedings of IEEE International Conference Robotics and Automation,* (pp. 3093–3099). Albuquerque, NM.

Feldkamp, L. A., Prokhorov, D. V., & Feldkamp, T. M. (2003). Simple and conditioned adaptive behavior from Kalman filter trained recurrent networks. *Neural Networks, 16*(5-6), 683–689. doi:10.1016/S0893-6080(03)00127-8

Fiori, S. (2003). Closed-form expressions of some stochastic adapting equations for nonlinear adaptive activation function neurons. *Neural Computation, 15*(12), 2909–2929. doi:10.1162/089976603322518795

Flash, T., & Hogan, N. (1985). The Coordination of Arm Movements: an Experimentally Confirmed Mathematical Model. *The Journal of Neuroscience, 5*, 1688–1703.

Fleming, P. J., & Fonseca, C. M. (1993). *Genetic algorithms in control systems engineering,* (Research Report No. 470), Sheffield, UK: University of Sheffield, Dept. of Automatic Control and Systems Engineering.

Fogel, D. (1996). *Evolutionary Computation: Towards a New Philosophy of Machine Intelligence.* Piscataway, NJ: IEEE Press

Fogel, L. J., Owens, A. J., & Walsh, M. J. (1966). *Artificial intelligence through simulated evolution.* West Sussex, Uk: Wiley.

Foltyniewicz, R. (1995). Efficient high order neural network for rotation, translation and distance invariant recognition of gray scale images. Computer Analysis of Images and Patterns. *Lecture Notes in Computer Science, 970*, 424-431.

Forbus, K. D., & Gentner, D. (1983). Casual Reasoning About Quantities. In *Proceedings of 5ᵗʰ Annual Conf. of the Cognitive Science Society* (pp. 196-206).

Foresti, G. L., & Dolso, T. (2004). An adaptive high-order neural tree for pattern recognition, *IEEE Transactions on Systems, Manufacturing, and Cybernetics. Part B: Cybernetics, 34*(2), 988–996. doi:10.1109/TSMCB.2003.818538

Forie, P. C., & Groenwold, A. A. (2002). The particle swarm optimization algorithm in size and shape optimization. *Structural and Multidisciplinary Optimization, 23*(4), 259–267. doi:10.1007/s00158-002-0188-0

Forum, M. P. I. (1994). MPI: A message-passing interface standard. (Technical Report UT-CS-94-230).

Foster, I., & Kesselman, C. (1997). Globus: A meta-computing infrastructure toolkit. *The International Journal of Supercomputer Applications, 11*, 115–128. doi:10.1177/109434209701100205

Fu, L. (1994). *Neural Networks in Computer Intelligence.* New York: McGraw-Hill.

Fujita, M. (1982). Adaptive Filter Model of the Cerebellum. *Biological Cybernetics, 45*, 195–206. doi:10.1007/BF00336192

Fukunaga, K. (1990). *Introduction to statistical pattern recognition.* New York: Academic Press.

Fukushima, K., & Wake, N. (1991). Handwritten alpha-numeric character recognition by the Neocognition. *IEEE Transactions on Neural Networks, 2*(3), 355-365.

Fulcher, J., Zhang, M., & Shuxiang, X. (2006). Application of higher-order nueral networks to financial time series prediction. In Kamruzzaman, J., Begg, R. K. & Sarker, R. A. (Eds.), *Artificial neural networks in finance and manufacturing* (pp. 80-108). Hershey, PA: Information Science Reference.

Fulcher, J., Zhang, M., & Xu, S. (2006).Chapter V. Application of Higher-Order Neural Networks to Financial Time-Series Prediction, *Artificial Neural Networks in Finance and Manufacturing*, edited by Joarder Kamruzzaman, Rezaul Begg, and Ruhul Sarker. Hershey, PA: IGI Global.

Fung, Y. C. (1993). *Biomechanics: Mechanical Properties of Living Tissues*, 2nd ed., New York: Springer Verlag.

Gabriel, E., Fagg, G. E., Bosilca, G., Angskun, T., Dongarra, J. J., Squyres, J. M., et al. (2004). Open MPI: Goals, concept, and design of a next generation MPI implementation. In *Proceedings, 11th European PVM/MPI Users' Group Meeting*, (pp. 97-104). Budapest, Hungary.

Galea, A. M. (2004). *Mapping tactile imaging information: parameter estimation and deformable registration.* Cambridge, MA: Harvard University Dissertation.

Gao, L., Parker, K. J., Lerner, R. M., & Levinson, S. F. (1996). Imaging of the elastic properties of tissue – a review. *Ultrasound in Medicine & Biology, 22*(8), 959–977. doi:10.1016/S0301-5629(96)00120-2

Garcia-Osorio, C., & Fyfe, C. (2005). Regaining sparsity in kernel principal components. *Neurocomputing, 67,* 398–402. doi:10.1016/j.neucom.2004.10.115

Garliaskas, A., & Gupta, M. M. (1995). A Generalized Model of Synapse-Dendrite-Cell Body as a Complex Neuron. *World Congress on Neural Networks, Vol. 1* (pp. 304-307).

Ge, S. S., & Jing, W. (2002). Robust adaptive neural control for a class of perturbed strict feedback nonlinear systems. *IEEE Transactions on Neural Networks, 13*(6), 1409–1419. doi:10.1109/TNN.2002.804306

Ge, S. S., Zhang, J., & Lee, T. H. (2004). Adaptive neural network control for a class of MIMO nonlinear systems with disturbances in discrete-time. *IEEE Transactions on Systems, Man and Cybernetics. Part B, 34*(4), 1630–1645.

Ge, S. S., Zhang, J., & Lee, T. H. (2004). Adaptive neural network control for a class of MIMO nonlinear systems with disturbances in discrete-time. *IEEE Transactions on Systems, Man and Cybernetics. Part B, 34*(4), 1630–1645.

Gentil, S. (1981). *Modélisation en ecologie: méthodologie et application aux ecosystèmes lacustres.* Ph. D. Dissertation (In French), Ecole des Sciences Physyques, France.

Ghazali, R., Hussain, A. J., Al-jumeily, D., & Merabti, M. (2007). Dynamic Ridge Polynomial Neural Networks in Exchange Rates Time Series Forecasting. In B. Beliczynski, A. Dzielinski, M. Iwanowski, & B. Ribeiro, *Adaptive and Natural Computing Algorithms.* (pp. 123-132). Berlin, Germany: Springer.

Ghazali, R., Hussain, A., & Merabti, M. (2006). Higher order neural networks and their applications to financial time series prediction. In *Proceedings of the IASTED Artificial Intelligence and Soft Computing*. Palma De Mallorca, Spain.

Ghosh, A., Dehuri, S., & Ghosh, S. (2008). *Multi-objective Evolutionary Algorithms for Knowledge Discovery from Databases*. New York: Springer.

Ghosh, J., & Shin, T. (1992). Efficient higher-order neural networks for classification and function approximation. *International Journal of Neural Systems*, *3*(4), 323-350.

Giles, C. L., & Maxwell, T. (1987). Learning, Invariance, and Generalization in High-Order Neural Networks. *Applied Optics*, *26*(23), 4972–4978. doi:10.1364/AO.26.004972

Giles, C. L., Griffin, R. D. & Maxwell, T. (1998). Encoding geometric invariances in HONN. *American Institute of Physics*, 310-309.

Giles, C., Griffin, R., & Maxwell, T. (1988). Encoding geometric invariant in higher-order neural networks. In Anderson D (ed), *Neural Information Processing Systems* (pp.301-309), Proceedings of American Institute of Physics Conference..

Giles, C., Miller, C., Chen, D., Chen, H., Sun, G., & Lee, Y. (1992). Learning and extracting finite state automata with second-order recurrent neural networks. *Neural Computation*, *4*(3), 393–405. doi:10.1162/neco.1992.4.3.393

Giles, L., & Maxwell, T. (1987). Learning Invariance and Generalization in High-Order Neural Networks. *Applied Optics*, *26*(23), 4972–4978. doi:10.1364/AO.26.004972

Goldberg, D. (1989). *Genetic Algorithms in Search, Optimization, and Machine Learning*. Reading, MA: Addison Wesley

Golea, N., Golea, A., & Benmahammed, K. (2003). Stable indirect fuzzy adaptive control. *IEEE Engineers Transactions on Fuzzy Systems*, *137*, 353–366.

Gorges-Schleuter, M. (1991). Explicit parallelism of genetic algorithms through population structures. In *PPSN I: Proceedings of the 1st Workshop on Parallel Problem Solving from Nature*, (pp 150-159). London: Springer-Verlag.

Gori, M., & Maggini, M. (1996). Optimal convergence of on-Line backpropagation. *IEEE Transactions on Neural Networks*, *7*, 251–254. doi:10.1109/72.478415

Gorman, R. P., & Sejnowski, T. J. (1988). Analysis of hidden units in a layered network trained to classify sonar targets. *Neural Networks*, *1*, 75–89. doi:10.1016/0893-6080(88)90023-8

Goudreau, M., Giles, C., Chakradhar, S., & Chen, D. (1994). First-Order Versus Second-Order Single-Layer Recurrent Neural Networks. *IEEE Transactions on Neural Networks*, *5*(3), 511–513. doi:10.1109/72.286928

Grant, E., & Zhang, B. (1989). A neural net approach to supervised learning of pole placement. In *Proc. of 1989 IEEE Symposium on Intelligent Control*.

Grefenstette, J. J. (1986). Optimization of control parameters for genetic algorithms. *IEEE Transactions on Systems, Man, and Cybernetics*, *16*, 122–128. doi:10.1109/TSMC.1986.289288

Grover, R., & Hwang, P. Y. C. (1992). *Introduction to Random Signals and Applied Kalman Filtering*. 2nd ed. NY: John Wiley and Sons

Gruau, F., Ratajszczak, J., & Wiber, G. (1995). A Neural Compiler. *Theoretical Computer Science*, *141*(1-2), 1–52. doi:10.1016/0304-3975(94)00200-3

Guler, M., & Sahin, E. (1994). A new higher order binary-input neural unit: Learning and generalizing effectively via using minimal number of monomials. *Third Turkish Symposium on Artificial Intelligence and Neural Networks Proceedings* (pp. 51-60). Middle East Technical University, Ankara, Turkey.

Gulez, K., Mutoh, N., Harashima, F., Ohnishi, K., & Pastaci, H. (2000, October 22-28). Design of a HONN (high order neural network) by using a DSP based system for the performance increasing of an induction motor under changeable load. In *Proceedings of 26th Annual Conference of the IEEE on Industrial Electronics Society* (Vol. 4, pp. 2315 – 2320).

Guo, W., & Horn, J. (2006, Aug. 21-26). *Modeling and simulation for the development of a quad-rotor UAV capable of indoor flight.* Paper presented at the Modeling and Simulation Technologies Conference and Exhibit, Keystone, CO.

Guo, Y., Hill, D. J., & Wang, Y. (2001). Global transient stability and voltage regulation for power systems. *IEEE Transactions on Power Systems, 16*(4), 678–688. doi:10.1109/59.962413

Guoguang, H., Cao, Z., Zhu, P., & Ogura, H. (2003). Controlling chaos in a chaotic neural network. *Neural Networks, 16*(8), 1195–1200. doi:10.1016/S0893-6080(03)00055-8

Gupta, M. M. (1988). Biological Basis for Computer Vision: Some Perspective. *SPW Conf. on Intelligent Robots and Computer Vision* (pp. 811-823).

Gupta, M. M., & Knopf, G. K. (1992). A Multitask Visual Information Processor with a Biologically Motivated Design. *J. Visual Communicat. Image Representation, 3*(3), 230–246. doi:10.1016/1047-3203(92)90020-T

Gupta, M. M., Homma, N., Hou, Z., Solo, A. M. G., & Goto, T. (2009). Fundamental theory of artificial higher order neural networks. In Zhang, M. (Ed.), *Artificial higher order neural networks for economics and business* (pp. 368-388). Hershey, PA: Information Science Reference.

Gupta, M. M., Jin, L., & Homma, N. (2003). *Static and Dynamic Neural Networks: From Fundamentals to Advanced Theory.* Hoboken, NJ: IEEE & Wiley.

Gurney, K. N. (1992). Training Nets of Hardware Realizable Sigma-Pi Units. *Neural Networks, 5*(2), 289–303. doi:10.1016/S0893-6080(05)80027-9

Gustafson, S., & Burke, E. K. (2006). The speciating island model: an alternative parallel evolutionary algorithm. *Journal of Parallel and Distributed Computing, 66*(8), 1025–1036. doi:10.1016/j.jpdc.2006.04.017

Hadzic, I., & Kecman, V. (2000). Support vector machines trained by linear programming: theory and application in image compression and data classification. In *Prceedings*

of IEEE 5th Seminar on Neural Network Applications in Electrical Engineering

Hagan, M. T., Demuth, H. B., & Beale, M. (1996). *Neural network design.* Boston: PWS Publishing Company.

Hagan, M., & Menhaj, M. (1994). Training feed forward network with the Marquardt algorithm. *IEEE Transactions on Neural Networks, 5*(6), 989-993.

Hamel, T., Mahony, R., Lozano, R., & Ostrowski, J. (2002). *Dynamic modeling and configuration stabilization for an X4-flyer.* Paper presented at the IFAC 15th Triennial World Congress, Barcelona, Spain.

Han, J., & Kamber, M. (2006). *Data Mining: concepts and techniques,* Amsterdam; Boston: Elsevier.

Handschin, E., Hoffmann, W., Reyer, F., Stephanblome, Th., Schlucking, U., Westermann, D., & Ahmed, S. S. (1994). A new method of excitation control based on fuzzy set theory. *IEEE Transactions on Power Systems, 9,* 533–539. doi:10.1109/59.317569

Hansen, J. V., & Nelson, R. D. (2002). Data mining of time series using stacked generalizers. *Neurocomputing, 43,* 173–184. doi:10.1016/S0925-2312(00)00364-7

Hansen, N., & Ostermeier, A. (2001). Completely derandomized self-adaptation in evolution strategies. *Evolutionary Computation, 9*(2), 159–195. doi:10.1162/106365601750190398

Haring, B., & Kok, J. N. (1995). Finding functional links for neural networks by evolutionary computation. In T. Van de Merckt, et al. (Eds.) BENELEARN'95, *Proceedings of the fifth Belgian-Dutch Conference on Machine Learning* (pp.71-78), Brussels, Belgium.

Haring., et al. (1997). Feature selection for neural networks through functional links found by evolutionary computation. In: Liu, X., et al. (Eds.) *Advances in Intelligent Data Analysis* (IDA-97)(pp.199-210), LNCS, 1280.

Harston, C. T. (1990). The Neurological Basis for Neural Computation. In Maren, A. J., Harston, C. T., & Pap, R. M. (Eds.), *Handbook of Neural Computing Applications,* Vol. 1. (pp. 29-44). New York: Academic.

Hassan, M. A., Malik, O. P., & Hope, G. S. (1991). A fuzzy logic based stabilizer for a synchronous machine. *IEEE Transactions on Energy Conversion, 6*(3), 407–413. doi:10.1109/60.84314

Hayakawa, T., Haddad, W. M., Hovakimyan, N., & Chellaboina, V. (2005). Neural network adaptive control for nonlinear nonnegative dynamical systems. *IEEE Transactions on Neural Networks, 16*(2), 399–413. doi:10.1109/TNN.2004.841791

Haykin, S. (2001). *Kalman Filtering and Neural Networks. NY:* John Wiley and Sons.

He, J., & Yao, X. (2006). Analysis of scalable parallel evolutionary algorithms. In *CEC 2006: IEEE Congress on Evolutionary Computation*, (pp 120-127).

He, Z, & Siyal, M. (1999). Improvement on higher-order neural networks for invariant object recognition. *International Journal of Computer Vision, 10*(1), 49-55.

He, Z., & Siyal, M. Y. (1998). Recognition of transformed English letters with modified higher-order neural networks. *Electronics Letters, 34*(25), 2415–2416. doi:10.1049/el:19981654

Hecht-Nielsen, R. (1987). Kolmogorov's mapping neural network existence theorem. In [New York: IEEE Press.]. *Proceedings of the International Conference on Neural Networks, 3*, 11–13.

Hendler, J., & Dickens, L. (1991). Integrating Neural and Expert Reasoning: An Example. In *Proceedings of AISB-91*, Leeds. Cited in Wilson, 93.

Hess, R. A. (1993). *On the use of backpropagation with feed forward neural networks for the aerodynamic estimation problem.* Paper presented at the AIAA paper 93-3638.

Heywood, M., & Noakes, P. (1993, March 28). Simple addition to back-propagation learning for dynamic weight pruning, sparse network extraction and faster learning. In. *Proceedings of the IEEE International Conference on Neural Networks, 2*, 620–625. doi:10.1109/ICNN.1993.298546

Hibbeler, R. C. (2002). *Mechanics of Materials*, 5th ed. New Jersey: Prentice Hall Publishing Co.

Hidalgo, J. I., Lanchares, J., de Vega, F. F., & Lombraina, D. (2007). Is the island model fault tolerant? In *GECCO '07: Proceedings of the 2007 GECCO conference companion on Genetic and evolutionary computation*, (pp. 2737-2744), New York: ACM.

Hiramoto, M., Hiromi, Y., Giniger, E., & Hotta, Y. (2000). The Drosophila Netrin Receptor Frazzled Guides Axons by Controlling Netrin Distribution. *Nature, 406*(6798), 886–888. doi:10.1038/35022571

Hirose, Y., Yamashita, I. C., & Hijiya, S. (1991). Back-propagation algorithm which varies the number of hidden units. *Neural Networks, 4*.

Hiyama, T. (1989). Application of rule based stabilizer controller to electric power system, *IEE Proceedings. Part C, 136*(3), 175–181.

Ho, D. W. C., Liang, J. L., & Lam, J. (2006). Global exponential stability of impulsive high-order BAM neural networks with time-varying delays. *Neural Networks, 19*(10), 1581–1590. doi:10.1016/j.neunet.2006.02.006

Hogan, N. (1984). Adaptive Control of Mechanical Impedance by Coactivation of Antagonist Muscles. *IEEE Transactions on Automatic Control, 29*, 681–690. doi:10.1109/TAC.1984.1103644

Hohil, M. E., Liu, D., & Smith, S. H. (1999). Solving the n-bit parity problem using neural networks. *Neural Networks, 12*(9), 1321–1323. doi:10.1016/S0893-6080(99)00069-6

Hojati, M., & Gazor, S. (2002). Hybrid Adaptive Fuzzy Identification and Control of Nonlinear Systems. *IEEE transactions on Fuzzy Systems, 10*, 198–210. doi:10.1109/91.995121

Hojati, M., & Gazor, S. (2002). Hybrid Adaptive Fuzzy Identification and Control of Nonlinear Systems. *IEEE transactions on Fuzzy Systems, 10*, 198–210. doi:10.1109/91.995121

Hokimyan, N., Rysdyk, R., & Calise, A. (2001). Dynamic neural networks for output feedback control. *International Journal of Robust and Nonlinear Control, 11*, 23–39. doi:10.1002/1099-1239(200101)11:1<23::AID-RNC545>3.0.CO;2-N

Holland, J. H. (1975). *Adaptation in natural and artificial system*. Ann Arbor, MI:University of Michigan Press.

Hollis, P. W., & Paulos, J. J. (1990). Artificial neural networks using MOS analog multipliers. *IEEE Journal of Solid State Circuits, 25*, 849–855. doi:10.1109/4.102684

Holmes, C. C., & Mallick, B. K. (1998). Bayesian Radial Basis Functions of Variable Dimension. *Neural Computation, 10*(5), 1217–1233. doi:10.1162/089976698300017421

Holt, J. L., & Hwang, J.-N. (1993). Finite error precision analysis of neural network hardware implementations. *IEEE Transactions on Computers, 42*, 1380–1389.

Homma, N., & Gupta, M. M. (2002). A general second order neural unit. *Bull. Coll. Med. Sci. Tohoku Univ., 11*(1), 1–6.

Honma, N., Abe, K., Sato, M., & Takeda, H. (1998). Adaptive Evolution of Holon Networks by an Autonomous Decentralized Method. *Applied Mathematics and Computation, 9*(1), 43–61. doi:10.1016/S0096-3003(97)10008-X

Hopfield, J. (1984). Neurons with graded responses have collective computational properties like those of two state neurons. *Proceedings of the National Academy of Sciences of the United States of America, 81*, 3088–3092. doi:10.1073/pnas.81.10.3088

Hopfield, J. (1990). Artificial Neural Networks are Coming. An Interview by W. Myers. *IEEE Expert*, (Apr): 3–6.

Hornik, K. (1991). Approximation capabilities of multilayer feed-forward networks. *Neural Networks, 4*(2), 251–257. doi:10.1016/0893-6080(91)90009-T

Hornik, K., Stinchcombe, M., & White, H. (1989). Multilayer feed forward networks are universal approximators. *International Journal of Neural Networks, 2*, 359–366. doi:10.1016/0893-6080(89)90020-8

Hovakimyan, N., Lavretsky, E., Bong, J. Y., & Calise, A. J. (2005). Coordinated decentralized adaptive output feedback control of interconnected systems. *IEEE Transactions on Neural Networks, 16*(1), 185–194. doi:10.1109/TNN.2004.836198

Hu, Shengfa, & Yan, P. (1992). Level-by-Level learning for artificial neural groups. *ACTA Electronica SINICA, 20*(10), 39-43.

Hu, T., & Lin, Z. (2001), *Control Systems with Actuator Saturation: Analysis and Design*. Boston: Birkhäuser.

Hu, Z., & Shao, H. (1992). The study of neural network adaptive control systems. *Control and Decision, 7*, 361–366.

Huang, D. S., Ip, H. H. S., Law, K. C. K., & Chi, Z. (2005). Zeroing polynomials using modified constrained neural network approach. *IEEE Transactions on Neural Networks, 16*(3), 721–732. doi:10.1109/TNN.2005.844912

Huang, H., Feng, G., & Cao, J. (2008). Robust state estimation for uncertain neural networks with time-varying delay. *IEEE Transactions on Neural Networks, 19*(8), 1329–1339. doi:10.1109/TNN.2008.2000206

Huang, W., Wang, S. Y., Yu, L., Bao, Y. K., & Wang, L. (2006). A new computational method of input selection for stock market forecasting with neural networks. In *Proceedings of Computational Science - ICCS 2006, Pt 4, 3994*, (308-315).

Hughen, J., & Hollon, K. (1991). Millimeter wave radar stationary-target classification using a high-order neural network, *SPIE, 1469*, 341-350.

Hunt, K. J., & Sbarbaro, D. (1991). Neural Networks for Nonlinear Internal Model Control. *IEE Proceedings. Control Theory and Applications, 38*, 431–438.

Hussain, A. J. (2008). Physical time series prediction using recurrent pi-sigma neural networks. *International Journal of Artificial Intelligence and Soft Computing, 1*(1), 130–145. doi:10.1504/IJAISC.2008.021268

Hussain, A. J., & Liatsis, P. (2002). Recurrent pi-sigma networks for DPCM image coding. *Neurocomputing, 55*, 363–382. doi:10.1016/S0925-2312(02)00629-X

Hussain, A. J., Soraghan, J. J., & Durbani, T. S. (1997). A New Neural Network for Nonlinear Time-Series Modelling. *Neurovest Journal*, 16-26.

Hussain, A., & Liatsis, P. (2008). A Novel Recurrent Polynomial Neural Network for Financial Time Series

Prediction. In Z. M., *Higher Order Neural Networks for Economics and Business.* (pp. 190- 211).Hershey, PA: Idea Group Inc (IGI).

IEEE Standards Board. (1992). IEEE recommended practice for excitation system models for power system stability analysis. *IEEE Standard, 425,* 1–1992.

Igelnik, B., & Pao, Y. H. (1995). Stochastic choice of basis functions in adaptive function approximation and the functional-link net. *IEEE Transactions on Neural Networks, 6*(6), 1320–1329. doi:10.1109/72.471375

Igelnik, B., & Parikh, N. (2003). Komogorov's spline network. *IEEE Transactions on Neural Networks, 14*(4), 725–733. doi:10.1109/TNN.2003.813830

Inui, T., Tanabe, Y., & Onodera, Y. (1978). *Group Theory and Its Application in Physics.* Heidelberg, Germany:Springer-Verlag.

Ioannou, P. A., & Kokotovic, P. V. (1984). Instability analysis and the improvement of robustness of adaptive control. *Automatica, 20*(5), 583–594. doi:10.1016/0005-1098(84)90009-8

Ioannou, P. A., & Sun, J. (1996). *Robust Adaptive Control.* Upper Saddle River, NJ: Prentice-Hall, Inc.

Ioannou, P., & Fidan, B. (2006). *Adaptive control tutorial.* SIAM: Advances in Design and Control Series.

Isidori, A. (1989). *Nonlinear Control Systems* (second ed.). Berlin: Springer-Verlag.

Ismail, A., & Engelbrecht, A. P. (2000). Global optimization algorithms for training product unit neural networks. *In IJCNN 2000. Proceedings of the IEEE-INNS-ENNS International Joint Conference on, 1*(2), 132–137.

Iyoda, E. M. (2007). Image compression and reconstruction using pi_t-sigma neural networks. *Soft Computing, 11,* 53–61. doi:10.1007/s00500-006-0052-z

Iyoda, E., Nobuhara, H., & Hirota, K. (2003). A solution for the N-bit parity problem using a single translated multiplicative neuron. *Neural Processing Letters, 18*(3), 213-218.

Jacobs, R. A., & Jordan, M. I. (1993). Learning piece-wise control strategies in a modular neural network architecture. *IEEE Transactions on Systems, Man, and Cybernetics, 23,* 337–345. doi:10.1109/21.229447

Jagadeesan, A., Maxwell, G., & Macleod, C. (2005). Evolutionary algorithms for real-time artificial neural network training. *Lecture Notes in Computer Science, 3697,* 73–78.

Jagannathan, S. (2006). *Neural Network Control of Nonlinear Discrete-Time Systems.* Danvers, MA: CRC Press.

Jagannathan, S., & Lewis, F. L. (1996). Identification of nonlinear dynamical systems using multilayered neural networks. *Automatica, 32*(12), 1707–1712. doi:10.1016/S0005-1098(96)80007-0

Jang, C. F., & Lin, C. T. (1998). An online self-constructing neural fuzzy inference network and its applications. *IEEE transactions on Fuzzy Systems, 6,* 12–32. doi:10.1109/91.660805

Jang, J. S. R. (1993). ANFIS: Adaptive-network-based fuzzy inference system. *IEEE Transactions on Systems, Man, and Cybernetics, 23,* 665–684. doi:10.1109/21.256541

Jeffries, C. (1989, June 18-22). High order neural networks. In. *Proceedings of International Joint Conference on Neural Networks, 2,* 594. doi:10.1109/IJCNN.1989.118384

Jeffries, C. (1989, March 26-28). Dense memory with high order neural networks. In *Proceedings of Twenty-First Southeastern Symposium on System Theory* (pp.436 – 439).

Jiang, M., & Gielen, G. (2001). The effect of quantization on the Higher Order function neural networks. In *Proceedings of IEEE International Workshop on Neural Networks for Signal Processing* (pp.143-152). New York: IEEE Press.

Jiang, M., & Gielen, G. (2003). The Effects of Quantization on Multilayer Feedforward Neural Networks. *International Journal of Pattern Recognition and Artificial Intel-*

ligence, *17*, 637–661. doi:10.1142/S0218001403002514

Jiang, M., & Gielen, G. (2004). Backpropagation Analysis of the Limited Precision on Higher Order Function Neural Networks. In J. Wang, (Ed.), *Advances in Neural Networks - ISNN 2004: Part I, Lecture Notes in Computer Science: Vol. 3173,* (pp. 305-310). Heidelberg, Germany: Springer-Verlag.

Jiang, M., Gielen, G., & Xing, B. (2002). A Fast Learning Algorithms of Time-Delay Neural Networks. *Information Sciences, 148,* 27–39. doi:10.1016/S0020-0255(02)00273-6

Jiang, M., Gielen, G., & Zhang, B. (2003). Fast learning algorithms for feedforward neural networks. *Applied Intelligence, 18,* 37–54. doi:10.1023/A:1020922701312

Johnson, E., & Kannan, S. (2005, May-June). Adaptive Trajectory Control for Autonomous Helicopters. *AIAA Journal of Guidance. Control and Dynamics, 28,* 524–538. doi:10.2514/1.6271

Jordan, M. (1993). Hierarchical Mixtures of Experts and the EM Algorithm, In *Proc. 1993 Int. Joint Conf. Neural Networks* (pp. 1339-1344).

Jordan, M. I. (1986). *Serial order: A parallel distributed processing approach.* Institute for Cognitive Science report 8604, Institute for Cognitive Science, University of California, San Diego.

Joshi, A., Ramakrishman, N., Houstis, E. N., & Rice, J. R. (1997). On Neurobiological, Neurofuzzy, Machine Learning, and Statistical Pattern Recognition Techniques. *IEEE Transactions on Neural Networks, 8.*

Juang, C. F., & Lin, C. T. (1998). An on-line self-constructing neural fuzzy inference network and its applications. *IEEE transactions on Fuzzy Systems, 6,* 12–32. doi:10.1109/91.660805

Jung, S., & Kim, S. S. (2007). Hardware implementation of a real-time neural network controller with a DSP and an FPGA for nonlinear systems. *IEEE Transactions on Industrial Electronics, 54*(1), 265–271. doi:10.1109/TIE.2006.888791

Kaastra, I., & Boyd, M. (1996). Designing a neural network for forecasting financial and economic time

series. *Neurocomputing, 10,* 215–236. doi:10.1016/0925-2312(95)00039-9

Kailath, T. (1980). *Linerar Systems.* New Jersey: Prentice Hall.

Kaita, T., Tomita, S., & Yamanaka, J. (2002). On a higher order neural network for distortion invariant pattern recognition. *Pattern Recognition Letters, 23,* 977–984. doi:10.1016/S0167-8655(02)00028-4

Kane, B. J., Cutkosky, M. R., & Kavacs, G. T. (1996). Compatible traction stress sensor for use in high resolution tactile imaging. *Sensors and Actuators A, 54,* 511–516. doi:10.1016/S0924-4247(95)01191-9

Kaneko, K. (1994). Relevance of Dynamic Clustering to Biological Networks. *Physica D. Nonlinear Phenomena, 75,* 55–73. doi:10.1016/0167-2789(94)90274-7

Kaneko, K. (1997). Coupled Maps with Growth and Death: An Approach to Cell Differentiation. *Physica D. Nonlinear Phenomena, 103,* 505–527. doi:10.1016/S0167-2789(96)00282-5

Kanellakopoulos, I., Kokotovic, P. V., & Morse, A. S. (1991). Systematic Design of Adaptive Controllers for Feedback Linearizable Systems. *IEEE Transactions on Automatic Control, 36,* 1241–1253. doi:10.1109/9.100933

Karayiannis, N. B., & Venetsanopoulos, A. N. (1992). Fast learning algorithms for neural networks. *IEEE Transactions on Circuits and Systems-II: Analog and Digital Signal Processing, 39,* 453–474. doi:10.1109/82.160170

Karayiannis, N. B., Venetsanopoulos, A. N., & Karayiannis, N. (March 2004). *Artificial neural networks: Learning Algorithms, Performance Evaluation, and Applications.* Berlin: Springer-Verlag.

Kariniotakis, G. N., Stavrakakis, G. S., & Nogaret, E. F. (1996). Wind power forecasting using advanced neural networks models. *IEEE Transactions on Energy Conversion, 11*(4), 762–767. doi:10.1109/60.556376

Karnavas, Y. L., & Pantos, S. (2008). Performance Evaluation of Neural Networks for μC Based Excitation Control of a Synchronous Generator, In *Proceedings of ICEM '08, the 18th International Conference on Electrical Machines.* CD Paper Ref. No. 437, Vilamura, Portugal

Karnavas, Y. L., & Papadopoulos, D. P. (2000). Excitation control of a power generating system based on fuzzy logic and neural networks. *European Transactions in Electrical Power, 10*(4), 233–241.

Karnavas, Y. L., & Papadopoulos, D. P. (2002). AGC for autonomous power station using combined intelligent techniques. *Int. J. Electr Pow Syst Res, 62,* 225–239. doi:10.1016/S0378-7796(02)00082-2

Karnavas, Y. L., & Papadopoulos, D. P. (2002, August 25-28). A genetic-fuzzy system for the excitation control of a synchronous machine. In *Proceedings of ICEM '02, the 15th International Conference in Electrical Machines,* CD paper Ref. No. 204, Bruges, Belgium

Karnavas, Y. L., & Papadopoulos, D. P. (2004). Excitation control of a synchronous machine using polynomial neural networks. *Journal of Electrical Engineering, 55*(7-8), 169–179.

Kashefi, F. (1999). *Rapidly Training Device for Fiber Optic Neural Network.* Unpublished doctoral dissertation, University of Texas at Dallas.

Kennedy, J., & Eberhart, R. C. (1995). Particle swarm optimization. In *Proceedings IEEE International Conference on Neural Networks, IV,* (pp 1942-1948). Piscataway, NJ: IEEE Service Center.

Kennedy, J., & Eberhart, R. C. (1995). Particle swarm optimization. In: *Proceedings of the IEEE International Conference on Neural Networks,* Pisacataway, NJ, 1942-9148.

Kennedy, J., & Eberhart, R. C. (1999). The particle swarm: social adaptation in information processing systems. In: D. Corne, M. Dorigo, & F. Glover (Eds.) *New Ideas in Optimization* (pp.379-387), Cambridge, UK: McGraw-Hill.

Kerdoke, A. E., Cotin, S. M., & Ottensmeyer, M. P. (2003). Truth cube: establishing physical standard for soft tissue simulation. *Medical Image Analysis, 7,* 283–291. doi:10.1016/S1361-8415(03)00008-2

Khalil, H. (1996). *Nonlinear Systems,* 2nd Ed., Upper Saddle River, NJ: Prentice Hall

Khalil, H. K. (1992). *Nonlinear Systems.* New York: Macmillan.

Khalil, H. K. (2001). *Nonlinear Systems* (3rd ed.)New Jersey: Prentice Hall.

Kim, H. J., Shim, D. H., & Sastry, S. (2002). *Nonlinear model predictive tracking control for rotorcraft-based unmanned aerial vehicles.* Paper presented at the Proceedings of the American Control Conference, Anchorage, AK.

Kim, S. H., & Noh, H. J. (1997). Predictability of interest rates using data mining tools: a comparative analysis of Korea and the US. *Expert Systems with Applications, 13*(2), 85–95. doi:10.1016/S0957-4174(97)00010-9

Kim, Y. H., & Lewis, F. L. (1998). High Level Feedback Control with Neural Networks. *World Scientific, 21.*

Kim, Y. H., Lewis, F. L., & Abdallah, C. T. (1996). Nonlinear observer design using dynamic recurrent neural networks. *35th Conf. Decision Contr.*

Kim, Y. H., Lewis, F. L., & Abdallah, C. T. (1996, December). Nonlinear observer design using dynamic recurrent neural networks. In *Proceedings of the 35th Conference on Decision and Control,* Kobe, Japan.

Kimura, M., & Nakano, R. (2000). Dynamical systems produced by recurrent neural networks. *Systems and Computers in Japan, 31*(4), 77–86. doi:10.1002/(SICI)1520-684X(200004)31:4<77::AID-SCJ8>3.0.CO;2-Y

Kirby, M., & Sirovich, L. (1990). Application of the Karhunen-Loève procedure for the characterization of human faces. *IEEE Transactions on Pattern Analysis and Machine Intelligence, 12*(1), 103–108. doi:10.1109/34.41390

Kirschen, D. S., Bacher, R., & Heydt, G. T. (2000). Special issue on the technology of power system competition. *Proceedings of the IEEE, 88*(2), 123–127. doi:10.1109/JPROC.2000.823993

Klassen, M., Pao, Y., & Chen, V. (1988). Characteristics of the functional link net: a higher order delta rule net.

In Proceedings of IEEE 2nd Annual Int'l. Conf. Neural Networks.

Knopf, G. K., & Gupta, M. M. (1993). Dynamics of Antagonistic Neural Processing Elements. *International Journal of Neural Systems, 4*(3), 291–303. doi:10.1142/S0129065793000237

Knuth, D. (1997). *Fundamental Algorithms*. 3rd Ed. Reading, MA: Addison-Wesley.

Kobayashi, S. (2006). Sensation World Made by the Brain – Animals Do Not Have Sensors. Tokyo: Corona (in Japanese).

Kohara, K., Kitamura, A., Morishima, M., & Tsumoto, T. (2001). Activity-Dependent Transfer of Brain-Derived Neurotrophic Factor to Postsynaptic Neurons. *Science, 291*, 2419–2423. doi:10.1126/science.1057415

Kohonen, T. (1988). An Introduction to Neural Computing. *Neural Networks, 1*(1), 3–16. doi:10.1016/0893-6080(88)90020-2

Kohonen, T. (1990). The Self-Organizing Map. *Proceedings of the IEEE, 78*(9), 1464–1480. doi:10.1109/5.58325

Kohonen, T. (1991). Self-Organizing Maps: Optimization Approaches. In T. Kohonen, K. Makisara, O. Simula, & J. Kangas (Eds.), *Artificial Neural Networks* (pp. 981-990). Amsterdam, The Netherlands: Elsevier.

Kohonen, T. (1993). Things You Haven't Heard About The Self-Organizing Map. In *Proceedings of Inter. Conf. Neural Networks 1993* (pp. 1147-1156).

Kohonen, T. (1998). Self Organization of Very Large Document Collections: State of the Art. In *Proceedings of 8th Inter. Conf. Artificial Neural Networks, Vol. 1* (pp. 65-74).

Kohonen, T. (2000). *Self organizing networks*: 3rd edition. New York: Springer series in information sciences.

Kohonen, T., Kaski, S., Lagus, K., Salojarvi, J., Honkela, J., Paatero, V., & Saarela, A. (2000). Self organization of a massive document collection. *IEEE Transactions on Neural Networks, 11*, 574–585. doi:10.1109/72.846729

Koo, T. J., & Sastry, S. *Output tracking control design of a helicopter model based on approximate linearization.* Paper presented at the Proceedings of the 37th Conference on Decision and Control, Tampa, FL.

Kosmatopoulos, E. B., & Christodoulou, M. A. (1994). Filtering, prediction, and learning properties of ECE neural networks. *IEEE Transactions on Systems, Man, and Cybernetics, 24*(7), 971–981. doi:10.1109/21.297787

Kosmatopoulos, E. B., & Christodoulou, M. A. (1994). Stability, robustness, and approximation properties of gradient recurrent high order neural networks. *International Journal of Adaptive Control and Signal Processing, 8*, 393–406. doi:10.1002/acs.4480080408

Kosmatopoulos, E. B., & Christodoulou, M. A. (1995). Structural properties of gradient recurrent high-order neural networks. *IEEE Transactions on Circuits and Systems II: Analog and Digital Signal Processing, 42*(9), 592–603. doi:10.1109/82.466645

Kosmatopoulos, E. B., & Christodoulou, M. A. (1996). Recurrent neural networks for approximation of fuzzy dynamical systems. *International Journal of Intelligent Control and Systems, 1*, 223–233. doi:10.1142/S0218796596000143

Kosmatopoulos, E. B., & Christodoulou, M. A. (1997). High-order neural networks for the learning of robot contact surface shape. *IEEE Transactions on Robotics and Automation, 13*(3), 451–455. doi:10.1109/70.585906

Kosmatopoulos, E. B., & Christodoulou, M. A. (1997). Techniques and applications of higher-order neural network systems in the identification of dynamical systems. In: Leondes, C. T. (Eds.) *Neural Network Systems Techniques and Applications*, New York: Academic Press.

Kosmatopoulos, E. B., Christodoulou, M. A., & Ioannou, P. A. (1997). Dynamical neural networks that ensure exponential identification error convergence. *Neural Networks, 10*(2), 299–314. doi:10.1016/S0893-6080(96)00060-3

Kosmatopoulos, E. B., Ioannou, P. A., & Christodoulou, M. A. (1992, December 16-18). Identification of nonlinear systems using new dynamic neural network structures.

In *Proceedings of the 31st IEEE Conference on Decision and Control* (vol.1, pp. 20 – 25).

Kosmatopoulos, E. B., Polycarpou, M. M., Christodoulou, M. A., & Ioannou, P. A. (1995). High-Order Neural Network Structures for Identification of Dynamical Systems. *IEEE Transactions on Neural Networks*, 6(2), 442–431. doi:10.1109/72.363477

Koza, J. R. (1992). *Genetic Programming: On the Programming of Computers by Means of Natural Selection.* Cambridge, MA: MIT Press

Krener, A. J., & Isidori, A. (1983). Linearization by output injection and nonlinear observers. *Systems & Control Letters*, 3(1), 47–52. doi:10.1016/0167-6911(83)90037-3

Kriegel, H.-P. (2007). Future trends in data mining. *Data Mining and Knowledge Discovery*, 15(1), 87–97. doi:10.1007/s10618-007-0067-9

Krishnaiah, D. (2008). Application of ultrasonic waves coupled with functional link neural network for estimation of carrageenan concentration. *International Journal of Physical Sciences*, 3(4), 90–96.

Kroner, S. (1995). Adaptive averaging in higher order neural networks for invariant pattern recognition. In *Proceedings of the IEEE International Conference on Neural Networks* (Vol. Pp. 2438 - 24435)

Krstic, M., & Deng, H. (1998). *Stabilization of Nonlinear Uncertain Systems.* New York: Springer Verlag

Kulisch, U. (2002). *Advanced Arithmetic for the Digital Computer.* 1st Ed. New York: Springer;

Kuroe, Y. (2004, August 4-6). Learning and identifying finite state automata with recurrent high-order neural networks. In *Proceedings of SICE 2004 Annual Conference* (vol. 3, pp.2241 – 2246).

Kuroe, Y., Ikeda, H., & Mori, T. (1997, October 12-15). Identification of nonlinear dynamical systems by recurrent high-order neural networks. In. *Proceedings of IEEE International Conference on Systems, Man, and Cybernetics*, 1, 70–75.

Lange, T., Hodges, J., Fuenmayor, M., & Belyaev, L. (1989). Descartes: Development Environment for Simu-

lating Hybrid Connectionism Architectures, In *Proceedings of the 11ᵗʰ Annual Conference of the Cognitive Science Society,* Ann Arbor, MI. Cited in Wilson, 93.

Lapedes, A. S., & Farber, R. (1987). Non-linear signal processing using neural networks: Prediction and system modelling. *Los Alamos National Laboratory* (Technical Report LA-UR-87).

Law, A. M., & Kelton, W. D. (2000). *Simulation Modeling and Analysis.* New York: McGraw-Hill

LeCun, Y., Boser, B., & Solla, S. A. (1990). Optimal Brain Damage. In D. Touretzky (Ed.), *Advances in Neural Information Processing Systems, Vol. 2* (pp. 598-605). San Francisco:Morgan Kaufmann.

Lee Giles, C. (1987). Learning, Invariance and Generalization in Higher-Order Neural Networks. *Applied Optics*, 26(23), 4972–4978. doi:10.1364/AO.26.004972

Lee, C. C. (1990). Fuzzy logic in control systems – Parts I and II. *IEEE Transactions on Systems, Man, and Cybernetics*, 20(2), 404–435. doi:10.1109/21.52551

Lee, C., & Teng, C. (2000). Identification and Control of Dynamic Systems Using Recurrent Fuzzy Neural Networks. *IEEE transactions on Fuzzy Systems*, 8, 349–366. doi:10.1109/91.868943

Lee, D. W., Choi, H. J.; & Lee, J. (2004). A regularized line search tunneling for efficient neural network learning. *Advances in Neural Networks - ISNN 2004, Pt 1, 3173,* (239-243).

Lee, J. (2007). A novel three-phase trajectory informed search methodology for global optimization. *Journal of Global Optimization*, 38, 61–77. doi:10.1007/s10898-006-9083-3

Lee, K. C., & Ou, J. S. (2007). Radar target recognition by using linear discriminant algorithm on angular-diversity RCS. *Journal of Electromagnetic Waves and Applications*, 21(14), 2033–2048. doi:10.1163/156939307783152902

Lee, M. H. (2000). Tactile sensing: new directions, new challenges. *The International Journal of Robotics Research*, 19(7), 636–643.

Lee, M., Lee, S. Y., & Park, C. H. (1992). Neural controller of nonlinear dynamic systems using higher order neural networks. *Electronics Letters*, *28*(3), 276–277. doi:10.1049/el:19920170

Lee, T. T., & Jeng, J. T. (1998). The Chebyshev polynomial based unified model neural networks for function approximations. *IEEE Transactions on Systems Man and Cybernetics-Part B*, *28*, 925–935. doi:10.1109/3477.735405

Lee, Y. C., Doolen, G., Chen, H. H., Sun, G. Z., Maxwell, T., & Lee, H. Y. (1986). Machine Learning using a Higher-Order Correlation Network. *Physica D. Nonlinear Phenomena*, *22*(1-3), 276–306.

Lee, Y. C., Doolen, G., Chen, H., Sun, G., Maxwell, T., & Lee, H. (1986). Machine learning using a higher order correlation network. *Physica D. Nonlinear Phenomena*, *22*, 276–306.

Leerink, L. R., Giles, C. L., Horne, B. G., & Jabri, M. A. (1995). Learning with product units. In G. Tesaro, D. Touretzky, & T. Leen (Eds.), *Advances in Neural Information Processing Systems 7*, (pp 537-544). Cambridge, MA: MIT Press.

Leonardis, A., & Bischof, H. (1998). An efficient MDL based construction of RBF networks. *Neural Networks*, *11*, 963–973. doi:10.1016/S0893-6080(98)00051-3

Leonhard, W. (1985). *Control of Electrical Drives*. Springer-Verlag.

Leshno, M, Lin, V., & Ya, P., A., & Schocken, S. (1993). Multilayer feedforward networks with a nonpolynomial activation function can approximate any function. *Neural Networks*, *6*, 861–867. doi:10.1016/S0893-6080(05)80131-5

Leu, Y., Wang, W., & Lee, T. (2005). Observer-Based Direct Adaptive Fuzzy-Neural Control for Nonaffine Nonlinear Systems. *IEEE Transactions on Neural Networks*, *16*, 853–861. doi:10.1109/TNN.2005.849824

Leunga, C., & Chan, L. (2003). Dual extended Kalman filtering in recurrent neural networks. *Neural Networks*, *16*(2), 223–239. doi:10.1016/S0893-6080(02)00230-7

Levin, A. U., & Narendra, K. S. (1996). Control of nonlinear dynamical systems using neural networks - part II: observability, identification and control. *IEEE Transactions on Neural Networks*, *7*(1), 30–42. doi:10.1109/72.478390

Lewis, F. L., Abdallah, C. T., & Dawson, D. M. (1993). *Control of Robot Manipulators*. New York: Macmillan.

Lewis, F. L., Dawson, D. M., & Abdallah, C. T. (2004). *Robot Manipulator Control: Theory and Practices*. New York: Marcel Dekker Inc.

Lewis, F. L., Yesildirek, A., & Liu, K. (1996). Multilayer Neural-Net Robot Controller with Guaranteed Tracking Performance. *IEEE Transactions on Neural Networks*, *7*(2), 388–399. doi:10.1109/72.485674

Lewis, F., Jagannathan, L. S., & Yesildirek, A. (1999). *Neural Network Control of Robot Manipulators and Nonlinear Systems*. Philadelphia, PA: Taylor and Fransis.

Lewis, P., Goodman, O., & Miller, J. (1969). A pseudorandom number generator for the System 360. *IBM Systems Journal*, *8*(2), 136–145.

Li, D., Hirasawa, K., & Hu, J. (2003, August 4-6). A new strategy for constructing higher order neural networks with multiplication units. In *Proceedings of SICE 2003 Annual Conference* (Vol. 3, pp. 2342 – 2347).

Li, D., Hirasawa, K., Hu, J., & Murata, J. (2001). Universal Learning Networks with Multiplication Neurons and its Representation Ability. In *Proc. Int. Joint Conf. Neural Networks* (pp. 150-155).

Li, J., & Zhong, Y. (2005). Comparison of three Kalman filters for speed estimation of induction machines. In *Proceedings of Industry Applications Conference* 2005, Hong Kong, China.

Li, M., Tian, J., & Chen, F. (2008). Improving multiclass pattern recognition with a co-evolutionary RBFNN. *Pattern Recognition Letters*, *29*, 392–406. doi:10.1016/j.patrec.2007.10.019

Li, R. P., & Mukaidono, M. (1995). A new approach to rule learning based on fusion of fuzzy logic and neural networks. *Institute of Electronics Information and Communication Engineers Transactions on Fuzzy Systems, 78,* 1509–1514.

Li, W., Wang, Y., Li, W., Zhang, J., & Li, J. (1998, May 4-9). Sparselized higher-order neural network and its pruning algorithm. In *Proceedings of 1998 IEEE World Congress on Computational Intelligence* (Vol. 1, pp. 359 – 362).

Li, X., & Yu, W. (2004). Robust Adaptive Control Using Neural Networks and Projection, *Advances in Neural Networks -ISNN 2004, Srpinger-Verlgag. Lecture Notes in Computer Science, 3174,* 77–82.

Liatsis, P., & Hussain, A. J. (1999). Non-linear one-dimensional DPCM image prediction using polynomial neural network. In [San Jose, California]. *Proceedings of SPIE Applications of Artificial Neural Networks in Image Processing IV, 3647,* 58–68.

Liatsis, P., Wellstead, P. E., Zarrop, M. B., & Prendergast, T. (1994, August 24-26). A versatile visual inspection tool for the manufacturing process. In *Proceedings of the Third IEEE Conference on Control Applications* (vol.3, pp. 1505 – 1510).

Lin, C. T. (1995). A neural fuzzy control system with structure and parameter learning. *Fuzzy Sets and Systems, 70,* 183–212. doi:10.1016/0165-0114(94)00216-T

Lin, C. Y., & Hajela, P. (1992). Genetic algorithms in optimization problems with discrete and integer design variables. *Engineering Optimization, 19*(4), 309–327. doi:10.1080/03052159208941234

Lin, C., Wu, K., & Wang, J. (2005, October 10-12). Scale equalized higher-order neural networks. In *Proceedings of IEEE International Conference on Systems, Man and Cybernetics* (Vol. 1, pp. 816 – 821).

Lin, Y. H., & Cunningham, G. A. (1995). A new approach to fuzzy-neural system modelling. *IEEE transactions on Fuzzy Systems, 3,* 190–197. doi:10.1109/91.388173

Lina, T., Wang, C., & Liub, H. (2004). Observer-based indirect adaptive fuzzy-neural tracking control for nonlinear SISO systems using VSS and H_1 approaches.

Fuzzy Sets and Systems, 143, 211–232. doi:10.1016/S0165-0114(03)00167-2

Linhart, G., & Dorffner, G. (1992). A self-learning visual pattern explorer and recognizer using a higher order neural network. In. *Proceedings of International Joint Conference on Neural Networks, 3,* 705–710.

Linse, D. J., & Stengel, R. F. (1993). Identification of Aerodynamic Coefficients Using Computational Neural Networks. *Journal of Guidance, Control, and Dynamics, 16*(6). doi:10.2514/3.21122

Liou, R.-J., & Azimi-Sadjadi, M. R. (1993). Dim target detection using high order correlation method. *IEEE Transactions on Aerospace and Electronic Systems, 29*(3), 841–856. doi:10.1109/7.220935

Lippmann, R. P. (1987). An Introduction to Computing with Neural Networks. IEEE *Acoustics. Speech and Signal Processing Magazine, 4*(2), 4–22.

Lippmann, R. P. (1989). Pattern classification using neural networks. *IEEE Communications Magazine, 27,* 47–64. doi:10.1109/35.41401

Lisboa, P., & Perantonis, S. (1991). Invariant Pattern Recognition Using Third-Order Networks and Zernlike Moments. In []. Singapore.]. *Proceedings of the IEEE International Joint Conference on Neural Networks, II,* 1421–1425. doi:10.1109/IJCNN.1991.170599

Liu, Y., Wang, Z., & Liu, X. (2007). Design of exponential state estimators for neural networks with mixed time delays. *Physics Letters. [Part A], 364*(5), 401–412. doi:10.1016/j.physleta.2006.12.018

Lont, J. B., & Guggenbuhl, W. (1992). Analog CMOS implementation of a multiplayer perceptron with nonlinear synapses. *IEEE Transactions on Neural Networks, 3,* 457–465. doi:10.1109/72.129418

Lopez-Garcia, J. C., Moreno-Armendariz, M. A., Riera-Babures, J., Balsi, M., & Vilasis-Cardona, X. (2005). Real time vision by FPGA implemented CNNs. In *European Conference on Circuit Theory and Design* (pp. 281-284).

Lourenço, C. (2004). Attention-locked computation with chaotic neural nets. *International Journal of Bifurcation and Chaos in Applied Sciences and Engineering, 14*(2), 737–760. doi:10.1142/S0218127404009442

Lovejoy, C. O. (1981). The Origin of Man. *Science, 211*, 341–350. doi:10.1126/science.211.4480.341

Lu, Z., & Sun, J. (2008). Soft-constrained linear programming support vector regression for nonlinear black-box systems identification, In D. Vrakas and I. Vlahavas (Ed.), *Artificial Intelligence for Advanced Problem Solving Techniques* (pp. 137–146). Information Science Reference Publishing.

Lu, Z., & Sun, J. (2009). Non-Mercer Hybrid kernel for linear programming support vector regression in nonlinear systems identification. *Applied Soft Computing, 9*, 94–99. doi:10.1016/j.asoc.2008.03.007

Lu, Z., Shieh, L. S., & Chen, G. R. (2008). A new topology for artificial higher order neural networks: polynomial kernel networks, In M. Zhang (Ed.), *Artificial Higher Order Neural Networks for Economics and Business* (pp. 430–441). Information Science Reference Publishing.

Lu, Z., Sun, J., & Butts, K. R. (2009). Linear programming support vector regression with wavelet kernel: A new approach to nonlinear dynamical systems identification. *Mathematics and Computers in Simulation, 79*(7), 2051–2063. doi:10.1016/j.matcom.2008.10.011

Lumer, E. D. (1992). Selective attention to perceptual groups: the phase tracking mechanism. *International Journal of Neural Systems, 3*(1), 1–17. doi:10.1142/S0129065792000024

Machado, R. J. (1989, June 18-22). Handling knowledge in high order neural networks: the combinatorial neural model. In. *Proceedings of the International Joint Conference on Neural Networks, 2*, 582. doi:10.1109/IJCNN.1989.118339

Machowski, J., Bialek, J. W., Robak, S., & Bumby, J. R. (1998). Excitation control systems for use with synchronous generators. *IEE Proceedings. Generation, Transmission and Distribution, 145*(5), 537–546. doi:10.1049/ip-gtd:19982182

Madani, T., & Benallegue, A. (2006, Oct. 9-15). *Backstepping control for a quadrotor helicopter.* Paper presented at the Proceedings of the 2006 IEEE/RSJ International Conference on Intelligent Robots and Systems, Beijing, China.

Maggiore, M., & Passino, K. M. (2005). Output Feedback Tracking: A Separation Principle Approach. *IEEE Transactions on Automatic Control, 50*(1), 111–117. doi:10.1109/TAC.2004.841126

Magoulas, G. D., Plagianakos, V. P., & Vrahatis, M. N. (2004). Neural network-based colonoscopic diagnosis using on-line learning and differential evolution. *Applied Soft Computing, 4*, 369–379. doi:10.1016/j.asoc.2004.01.005

Magoulas, G. D., Vrahatis, M. N., & Androulakis, G. S. (1997). Effective backpropagation training with variable stepsize. *Neural Networks, 10*(1), 69–82. doi:10.1016/S0893-6080(96)00052-4

Maguire, L. P., McGinnity, T. M., Glackin, B., Ghani, A., Belatreche, A., & Harkin, J. (2007). Challenges for large-scale implementations of spiking neural networks on FPGAs. *Neurocomputing, 71*(1-3), 13–29. doi:10.1016/j.neucom.2006.11.029

Mahony, R., & Hamel, T. (2005). Robust Trajectory Tracking for a Scale Model Autonomous Helicopter. *Int. J. Robust Nonlinear Control, s, 14*, 1035–1059. New York: John Wiley & Son

Mahony, R., Hamel, T., & Dzul, A. (1999). *Hover control via lyapunov control for an autonomous model helicopter.* Paper presented at the Proceedings of the 38th Conference on Decision & Control, Phoenix, Arizona.

Maire, M. (2000). On the Convergence of Validity Interval Analysis. *IEEE Transactions on Neural Networks, 11*(3), 799–801. doi:10.1109/72.846751

Majhi, B. (2005). An improved scheme for digital watermarking using functional link artificial neural network. *Journal of Computer Science, 1*(2), 169–174. doi:10.3844/jcssp.2005.169.174

Malone, J., McGarry, K., Wermter, S., & Bowerman, C. (2006). Data mining using rule extraction from Kohonen self-organising maps. *Neural Computing & Applications, 15*(1), 9–17. doi:10.1007/s00521-005-0002-1

Mamdani, E. (1976). Advances in the linguistic synthesis of fuzzy controllers. *International Journal of Man-Machine Studies, 8*(6), 669–678. doi:10.1016/S0020-7373(76)80028-4

Mangasarian, O. L., & Wild, E. W. (2008). Non-linear knowledge based classification. *IEEE Transactions on Neural Networks, 19*(10), 1826–1832. doi:10.1109/TNN.2008.2005188

Mantere, K., Parkkinen, J., Jaasketainen, T., & Gupta, M. M. (1993). Wilson-Cowan Neural Network Model in Image Processing. *Journal of Mathematical Imaging and Vision, 2*, 251–259. doi:10.1007/BF00118593

Mao, H., Malik, O. P., Hope, G. S., & Fan, J. (1990). An adaptive generator excitation controller based on linear optimal control. *IEEE Transactions on Energy Conversion, EC-5*(4), 673–678.

Marchiori, D., & Warglien, M. (2008). Predicting human interactive learning by regret-driven neural networks. *Science, 319*, 1111–1113. doi:10.1126/science.1151185

Marco, G., & Marco, M. (1996). Optimal convergence of on-line backpropagation. *IEEE Transactions on Neural Networks, 7*, 251–254. doi:10.1109/72.478415

Marcu, T., & Koppen-Seliger, B. (2004). Dynamic functional link neural networks genetically evolved applied to system identification. In *Proceedings of ESANN'2004*, Bruges (Belgium), 115-120.

Marino, R. (1990). Observers for single output nonlinear systems. *IEEE Transactions on Automatic Control, 35*, 1054–1058. doi:10.1109/9.58536

Marquardt, D. W. (1963). An Algorithm for Least-Squares Estimation of Nonlinear Parameters. *Journal of the Society for Industrial and Applied Mathematics, 11*(2), 431–441. doi:10.1137/0111030

Masseglia, F., Poncelet, P., & Teisseire, M. (2007). Successes and New Directions in Data Mining. *Information Science Reference*. Hershey, PA: IGI Global.

Masters, T. (1993). *Practical Neural Network Recipies in C++*. (1th ed.) New York: Morgan Kaufmann.

Matsuba, I. (2000). *Nonlinear time series analysis.* Tokyo: Asakura-syoten (in Japanese).

Matsuoka, T., Hamada, H., & Nakatsu, R. (1989). Syllable Recognition Using Integrated Neural Networks In *Proceedings of Intl. Joint Conf.* [Washington D.C.]. *Neural Networks*, 251–258.

McCarthy, J., & Hayes, P. J. (1969). Some Philosophical Problems from the Standpoint of Artificial Intelligence. In Meltzer & Michie (Eds.), *Machine Intelligence, 4* (pp. 463-502). Edinburgh, UK: Edinburgh Univ. Press.

McClelland, J., & Rumelhart, D. (1987). *Parallel Distributed Processing.* Cambridge, MA:The MIT Press.

McCue, C. (2007). *Data Mining and Predictive Analysis: Intelligence Gathering and Crime Analysis.* Oxford, UK: Butterworth-Heinemann.

McCulloch, W. S., & Pitts, W. H. (1943). A logical calculus of the ideas imminent in nervous activity. *The Bulletin of Mathematical Biophysics, 5*, 115–133. doi:10.1007/BF02478259

McDermott, D. (1982). A Temporal Logic for Reasoning About Processes and Plans. *Cognitive Science, 6*, 101–155.

Mcmillan, C., Mozer, M., & Smolensky, P. (1992). Rule induction through integrated symbolic and subsymbolic processing. *Advances in Neural Information Processing Systems, 4*, 969–976.

Mekuz, N., Bauckhagea, C., & Tsotsos, J. K. (2009). Subspace manifold learning with sample weights. *Image and Vision Computing, 27*, 80–86. doi:10.1016/j.imavis.2006.10.007

Melkonian, D. S. (1990). Mathematical Theory of Chemical Synaptic Transmission. *Biological Cybernetics, 62*, 539–548. doi:10.1007/BF00205116

Melzer, H. H., Schurr, M. O., Kunert, W., Buess, G., Voges, U., & Meyer, J. U. (1993). Intelligent surgical instrument system. *Endoscopic Surgery and Allied Technologies, 1*(3), 165–170.

Mendes, R., Kennedy, J., & Neves, J. (2004). The fully informed particle swarm: simpler, maybe better. *Evolutionary Computation. IEEE Transactions on, 8*(3), 204–210.

Mian, A. A., & Daobo, W. (2008). Modeling and Backstepping-based Nonlinear Control Strategy for a 6 DOF Quadrotor Helicopter. *Chinese Journal of Aeronautics, 21*(3), 261–268. doi:10.1016/S1000-9361(08)60034-5

Michie, D., Spiegelhalter, D. J., & Taylor, C. C. (1994). *Machine Learning, Neural and Statistical Classification.* West Sussex, UK: Ellis Horwood.

Mika, S., Rätsch, G., Weston, J., Schölkopf, B., & Müller, K. R. (1999). Fisher discriminant analysis with kernel. In Y.H. Hu, J. Larsen, and S. Wilson, E. Douglas, (Eds.), *Neural Networks for Signal Processing,* (pp. 41–48). IEEE Press.

Milenkovic, S., Obradovic, Z., & Litovski, V. (1996). Annealing Based Dynamic Learning in Second-Order Neural Networks, (Technical Report), Department of Electronic Engineering, University of Nis, Yugoslavia.

Ming Zhang. (2008), *Artificial Higher Order Neural Networks for Economics and Business,* Christopher Newport University, USA.

Minsky, M. (1967). *Computation: Finite and Infinite Machines.* Upper Saddle River, NJ: Prentice Hall.

Minsky, M., & Papert, S. (1969). *Perceptrons.* Cambridge, MA, MIT Press.

Mirea, L., & Marcu, T. (2002). System ident. using functional link neural networks with dynamic structure. *15th Trien. Wrld. Cong.,* Barcelona, Spain.

Mishra, S. (2006). Neural-network-based adaptive UPFC for improving transient stability performance of power system. *IEEE Transactions on Neural Networks, 17*(2), 461–470. doi:10.1109/TNN.2006.871706

Misra, B. B., & Dehuri, S. (2007). Functional link neural network for classification task in data mining. *Journal of Computer Science, 3*(12), 948–955. doi:10.3844/jcssp.2007.948.955

Mistler, V., Benallegue, A., & M'Sirdi, N. K. (2001). *Exact linearization and non-interacting control of a 4 rotors helicopter via dynamic feedback.* Paper presented at the 10th IEEE Int. Workshop on Robot-Human Interactive Communication, Paris.

Mitra, S., & Hayashi, Y. (2000). Neuro-fuzzy rule generation: survey in soft computing framework. *IEEE Transactions on Neural Networks, 11,* 748–768. doi:10.1109/72.846746

Mitra, S., & Hayashi, Y. (2000). Neuro-fuzzy rule generation: survey in soft computing framework. *IEEE Transactions on Neural Networks, 11,* 748–768. doi:10.1109/72.846746

Miyajima, H., Yatsuki, S., & Kubota, J. (1995. November 27-December 1). Dynamical properties of neural networks with product connections. In *Proceedings of the IEEE International Conference on Neural Networks* (vol.6, pp. 3198 – 3203).

Mjalli, F. S., Al-Asheh, S., & Alfadala, H. E. (2007). Use of artificial neural network black-box modeling for the prediction of wastewater treatment plants performance. *Journal of Environmental Management, 83*(3), 329–338. doi:10.1016/j.jenvman.2006.03.004

Moerland, P., & Fiesler, E. (1997). Neural network adaptations to hardware implementations. In E. Fiesler & R. Beale (Eds), *Handbook of Neural Computation* (pp.1-13). Cambridge, MA: Institute of Physics publishing and Oxford University Publishing.

Mokhtari, A., Benallegue, A., & Daachi, B. (2006). Robust Feedback Linearization and GH∞ Controller for a Quadrotor Unmanned Aerial Vehicle. *Journal of Electrical Engineering, 57.*

Mokhtari, A., Benallegue, A., & Orlov, Y. (2006). Exact linearization and sliding mode observer for a quadrotor unmanned aerial vehicle. *International Journal of Robotics and Automation, 21*(1), 39–49. doi:10.2316/Journal.206.2006.1.206-2842

Moller, M. (1993). A scaled conjugate gradient algorithm for fast supervised learning. Neural Networks, 6(4), 525-533.

Montalvo, A. J., Gyurcsik, R. S., & Paulos, J. J. (1997). Toward a general purpose analog VLSI neural network with on-chip learning. *IEEE Transactions on Neural Networks*, 8, 413–423. doi:10.1109/72.557695

Moore, C. (1990). Unpredictability and Undecidability in Dynamical Systems. *Physical Review Letters*, *64*(20), 2354–2357. doi:10.1103/PhysRevLett.64.2354

Morad, A. H., & Yuan, B. Z. (1998, October 12-16). HONN approach for automatic model building and 3D object recognition. In *Proceedings of 1998 Fourth International Conference on Signal Processing* (vol.2, pp. 881 – 884).Naimark, M. A., & Stern, A. I. (1982). *Theory of Group Representations*. Berlin, Germany: Springer-Verlag.

Muhlenbein, H., & Schlierkamp-Voosen, D. (1993). Predictive models for the breeder genetic algorithm I. Continuous parameters optimization. *Evolutionary Computation*, *1*(1), 24–49. doi:10.1162/evco.1993.1.1.25

Munakata, T., Sinha, S., & Ditto, W. (2002). Chaos Computing: Implementations of Fundamental Logical Gates by Chaotic Elements. *IEEE Transactions on Circuits and Systems*, *49*(11), 1629–1633. doi:10.1109/TCSI.2002.804551

Murata, J., Nakazono, T., & Hirasawa, K. (1999). Neural Networks with Node Gates. In *Proc. 1999 Int. Conf. Electrical Engineering* (pp. 358-361).

Myint, H. M., Murata, J., Nakazono, T., & Hirasawa, K. (2000). Neural Networks with Node Gates. In *Proc. 9th IEEE Int. Workshop. Robot and Human Interface Communication* (pp. 253-257).

Najarian, S. Dargahi, J. & Changizi, M. A. (2006). A tactile probe with applications in biomedical robotics. In *Proceedings of the IEEE ISIE06 Automated Conference Submission System*, Montreal, Canada.

Najarian, S., Dargahi, J., & Abouie, A. (2009). Artificial Tactile Sensing in Biomedical Engineering. New York: *McGraw-Hill Publication Co.*

Narendra, K. S., & Parthasarathy, K. (1990). Identification and control for dynamic systems using neural networks. *IEEE Transactions on Neural Networks*, *1*(1), 4–27. doi:10.1109/72.80202

Nedjah, N., Alba, E., & de Macedo Mourelle, L. (2006). *Parallel Evolutionary Computations (Studies in Computational Intelligence)*. New York, &Secaucus, NJ. Springer-Verlag

Neto, J., & Costa, J. F. (1999). *Building Neural Net Software* (Tech. Rep. DI-99-05), Computer Science Department, University of Lisbon.

Neto, J., Costa, J. F., & Ferreira, A. (2000). Merging Sub-symbolic and Symbolic Computation, In H. Bothe and R. Rojas (eds). In*Proceedings of the Second International ICSC Symposium on Neural Computation* (pp.329-335).

Neto, J., Ferreira, A., & Coelho, H. (2006). On Computation over Chaos using Neural Networks Application to Blind Search and Random Number Generation. *Journal of Bifurcation and Chaos in Applied Sciences and Engineering*, *16*(1), 59–66. doi:10.1142/S0218127406014587

Neto, J., Siegelmann, H., & Costa, J. F. (2003). Symbolic Processing in Neural Networks. *Journal of the Brazilian Computer Society*, *8*(3), 58–70. doi:10.1590/S0104-65002003000100005

Neville, R. S., Stonham, T. J., & Glover, R. J. (2000). Partially pre-calculated weights for the backpropagation learning regime and high accuracy function mapping using continuous input RAM-based sigma-pi nets. *Neural Networks*, *13*, 91–110. doi:10.1016/S0893-6080(99)00102-1

Nguyen, D., & Widrow, B. (1990). Improving the Learning Speed of 2-Layer Neural Networks by Choosing Initial Values of the Adaptive Weights. *IJCNN International Joint Conference on Neural Networks*, *1-3*, C21-C26.

Nicosia, S., & Tornambe, A. (1989). High-Gain Observers in the State and Parameter Estimation of Robots Having Elastic Joins. *Systems & Control Letters*, *13*(2), 331–337. doi:10.1016/0167-6911(89)90121-7

Nie, Y., & Deng, W. (2008). A hybrid genetic learning algorithm for pi-sigma neural network and the analysis of its convergence. In *Proceedings of Fourth International Conference on Natural Computation (IEEE Press)*, 19-23.

Nounou, H. N., & Passino, K. M. (2004). Stable Auto-Tuning of Adaptive Fuzzy/Neural Controllers for Nonlinear Discrete-Time Systems. *IEEE transactions on Fuzzy Systems, 12*(1), 70–83. doi:10.1109/TFUZZ.2003.822680

Nounou, H. N., & Passino, K. M. (2005). Stable Auto-Tuning of Hybrid Adaptive Fuzzy/Neural Controllers for Nonlinear Systems. *Engineering Applications of Artificial Intelligence, 18*(3), 317–334. doi:10.1016/j.engappai.2004.09.005

O'Connor, J. J., & Robertson, E. F. (2000). Paramesvara, MacTutor History of Mathematics archive. Retrieved (n.d.), from http://www.answers.com/topic/mean-value-theorem?cat=technology

Olfati-Saber, R. (2001). Nonlinear Control of Underactuated Mechanical Systems with Application to Robotics and Aerospace Vehicles.

Oliveira, A. L. I., & Meira, S. R. L. (2006). Detecting novelties in time series through neural networks forecasting with robust confidence intervals. *Neurocomputing, 70*, 79–92. doi:10.1016/j.neucom.2006.05.008

Oppenheim, A. V., & Schaffer, R. W. (1975). *Digital signal processing*. Englewood Cliffs, NJ: Prentice-Hall, Inc.

Ordonez, R., & Passino, K. M. (2001). Adaptive Control for a Class of Nonlinear Systems with Time-Varying Structure. *IEEE Transactions on Automatic Control, 46*(1), 152–155. doi:10.1109/9.898709

Ordonez, R., Zumberge, J., Spooner, J. T., & Passino, K. M. (1997). Adaptive Fuzzy Control: Experiments and Comparative Analyses. *IEEE transactions on Fuzzy Systems, 5*(2), 167–187. doi:10.1109/91.580793

Ortega, R., Stankovic, A., & Stefanov, P. (1998). A passivation approach to power systems stabilization. In *Proceedings of the IFAC Symposium Nonlinear Control Systems Design*, Enschede, NL.

Osorio, A., & Poznyak, A. S. (1997). Robust Deterministic Filtering for Linear Uncertain Time Varing Systems, *America Control Conference*.

Osório, F., & Amy, B. (1999). INSS: A hybrid system for constructive machine learning. *Neurocomputing, 28*, 191–205. doi:10.1016/S0925-2312(98)00124-6

Ou, J. Z., & Prasanna, V. K. (2004). PyGen: A MATLAB/Simulink based tool for synthesizing parameterized and energy efficient designs using FPGAs. In *FCCM'04 12th Annual IEEE Symposium on Field-Programmable Custom Computing Machines* (pp. 47-56).

Ou, J. Z., & Prasanna, V. K. (2005). MATLAB/Simulink Based Hardware/Software Co-Simulation for Designing Using FPGA Configured Soft Processors. In *Parallel and Distributed Processing Symposium* (pp. 148b).

Pai, M. A. (1989). *Energy Function Analysis for Power System Stability*. Dordrecht The Netherlands: Kluwer Academic Publishers.

Pal, S. K., & Mitra, P. (2004). *Pattern recognition algorithms for data mining: scalability, knowledge discovery, and soft granular computing*, Boca Raton, FL: Chapman & Hall/CRC. UCI Machine Learning Repository. (n.d.). Retrieved January 21, 2009, from, http://archive.ics.uci.edu/ml/index.html

Panagiotopoulos, D. A. (1999). Planning with a functional neural network architecture. *IEEE Transactions on Neural Networks, 10*(1), 115–127. doi:10.1109/72.737498

Pao, Y. H. (1989). *Adaptive pattern recognition and neural networks*. Reading, MA: Addison-Wesley Publishing Company Inc.

Pao, Y. H., & Takefuji, Y. (1992). Functional link net computing: theory, system, architecture and functionalities. *IEEE Computer*, 76-79.

Papadopoulos, D. P. (1986). Excitation control of turbogenerators with output feedback. *International Journal of Electrical Power & Energy Systems, 8*, 176–181. doi:10.1016/0142-0615(86)90032-3

Papadopoulos, D. P., Smith, J. R., & Tsourlis, G. (1989). Excitation controller design of synchronous machine with output feedback using high and reduced order models. *Archiv fur Elektrotechnik, 72*, 415–426. doi:10.1007/BF01573760

Papakonstantinou, I., James, R., & Selviah, D. R. (2009). Radiation and Bound Mode Propagation in Rectangular Multimode Dielectric Channel Waveguides with Sidewall Roughness. *IEEE/OSA. Journal of Lightwave Technology, 27*(18), 4151–4163. doi:10.1109/JLT.2009.2022766

Papakonstantinou, I., Selviah, D. R., Pitwon, R. C. A., & Milward, D. (2008). Low-Cost, Precision, Self-Alignment Technique for Coupling Laser and Photodiode Arrays to Polymer Waveguide Arrays on Multilayer PCBs. *IEEE Transactions on Advanced Packaging, 31*(3), 502–511. doi:10.1109/TADVP.2008.924243

Park, J. H., Huh, S. H., Seo, S. J., & Park, G. T. (2005). Direct adaptive controller for nonaffine nonlinear systems using self-structuring neural networks. *IEEE Transactions on Neural Networks, 16*(2), 414–422. doi:10.1109/TNN.2004.841786

Park, S., Smith, M. J. T., & Mersereau, R. M. (2000). Target recognition based on directional filter banks and higher order neural networks. *Digital Signal Processing, 10*, 297–308. doi:10.1006/dspr.2000.0376

Parsopoulos, K. E., & Vrahatis, M. N. (2002). Recent approaches to global optimization problems through particle swarm optimization. *Natural Computing: an international journal, 1*(2-3), 235-306.

Parsopoulos, K. E., & Vrahatis, M. N. (2004). On the computation of all global minimizers through particle swarm optimization. *IEEE Transactions on Evolutionary Computation, 8*(3), 211–224. doi:10.1109/TEVC.2004.826076

Passino, K. M., & Yurkovich, S. (1998). *Fuzzy Control.* Menlo Park, CA: Addison Wesley Longman.

Patra, J. C. (1999). Identification of non -linear dynamic systems using functional link artificial neural networks. *IEEE Transactions on Systems, Man, and Cybernetics. Part B, Cybernetics, 29*(2), 254–262. doi:10.1109/3477.752797

Patra, J. C. (2000). Modeling of an intelligent pressure sensor using functional link artificial neural networks. *ISA Transactions, 39*, 15–27. doi:10.1016/S0019-0578(99)00035-X

Patra, J. C. (2002). Non-linear dynamic system identification using Chebyshev functional link artificial neural networks. *IEEE Transactions on Systems, Man, and Cybernetics. Part B, Cybernetics, 32*(4), 505–511. doi:10.1109/TSMCB.2002.1018769

Patra, J. C. (2008). Functional link neural networks-based intelligent sensors for harsh environments. *Sensors and Transducers Journal, 90*, 209–220.

Patra, J. C., & Pal, N. R. (1995). A functional link neural network for adaptive channel equalization. *Signal Processing, 43*, 181–195. doi:10.1016/0165-1684(94)00152-P

Pau, Y. H., & Phillips, S. M. (1995). The Functional Link Net and learning optimal control. *Neurocomputing, 9*, 149–164. doi:10.1016/0925-2312(95)00066-F

Pecht, O. Y., & Gur, M. (1995). A Biologically-Inspired Improved MAXNET. *IEEE Transactions on Neural Networks, 6*, 757–759. doi:10.1109/72.377981

Peng, H., & Zhu, S. (2007). Handling of incomplete data sets using ICA and SOM in data mining. *Neural Computing & Applications, 16*(2), 167–172. doi:10.1007/s00521-006-0058-6

Pentland, A., & Turk, M. (1989). Face Processing: Models for Recognition, In *Proceedings of SPIE - Intelligent Robots and Computer Vision VIII: Algorithms and Technology* (pp 20-35).

Perantonis, S. J., & Lisboa, P. J. G. (1992). Translation, rotation, and scale invariant pattern recognition by high-order neural networks and moment classifiers. *IEEE Transactions on Neural Networks, 3*(2), 241–251. doi:10.1109/72.125865

Perantonis, S., Ampazis, N., Varoufakis, S., & Antoniou, G. (1998). Constrained learning in neural networks: Application to stable factorization of 2-d polynomials. *Neural Processing Letters, 7*(1), 5–14. doi:10.1023/A:1009655902122

Personnaz, L., Guyon, I., & Dreyfus, G. (1987). High-Order Neural Networks: Information Storage without Errors. *Europhysics Letters, 4*, 863–867. doi:10.1209/0295-5075/4/8/001

Petshe, T., & Dickinson, B. W. (1990). Trellis Codes, Receptive Fields, and Fault-Tolerance Self-Repairing Neural Networks. *IEEE Transactions on Neural Networks*, *1*(2), 154–166. doi:10.1109/72.80228

Piche, S. W. (1995). The Selection of Weight Accuracies for Madalines. *IEEE Transactions on Neural Networks*, *6*, 432–445. doi:10.1109/72.363478

Plagianakos, V. P., & Vrahatis, M. N. (1999). Neural network training with constrained integer weights. In Angeline, P., Michalewicz, Z., Schoenauer, M., Yao, X., & Zalzala, A., (eds.), *Congress of Evolutionary Computation (CEC'99)*, (pp 2007-2013). Washington DC: IEEE Press.

Plagianakos, V. P., & Vrahatis, M. N. (2002). Parallel evolutionary training algorithms for 'hardware-friendly' neural networks. *Natural Computing*, *1*, 307–322. doi:10.1023/A:1016545907026

Plagianakos, V. P., Magoulas, G. D., & Vrahatis, M. N. (2005). Evolutionary training of hardware realizable multilayer perceptrons. *Neural Computing & Applications*, *15*, 33–40. doi:10.1007/s00521-005-0005-y

Plotkin, H. (1993). *Darwin machines and the nature of knowledge*. Cambridge, MA: Harvard University Press.

Poggio, T., & Koch, C. (1987). Synapses that Compute Motion. *Scientific American*, (May): 46–52.

Pollack, J. (1987). *On Connectionism Models of Natural Language Processing* (Ph.D. thesis), Computer Science Dept., Univ. of Illinois, Urbana.

Polycarpou, M. M., & Mears, M. J. (1998). Stable adaptive tracking of uncertain systems using non-linearly parameterized online approximators. *International Journal of Control*, *70*(3), 363–384. doi:10.1080/002071798222280

Poznyak, A. S., & Sanchez, E. N. (1995). Nonlinear system approximation by neural networks: error stability analysis. *Intelligent Automation and Soft Computing*, *1*(2), 247–258.

Poznyak, A. S., Sanchez, E. N., & Yu, W. (2001). *Differential Neural Networks for Robust Nonlinear Control*. Singapore: World Scientific

Poznyak, A. S., Yu, W., Sanchez, E. N., & Perez, J. P. (1999). Nonlinear Adaptive Trajectory Tracking Using Dynamic Neural Networks. *IEEE Transactions on Neural Networks*, *10*(5), 1402–1411. doi:10.1109/72.809085

Preshelt, L. (1994). Proben1-a set of neural network benchmark problems and benchmarking rules. *Technical Report 21/94*, Universitat Karlsruhe, Germany.

Press, W. H., Flannery, B. P., Teukolsky, S. A., & Vetterling, W. T. (1992). *Numerical Recipes in C: The Art of Scientific Computing*. Cambridge, UK: Cambridge University Press.

Price, K., Storn, R. M., & Lampinen, J. A. (2005). *Differential Evolution: A Practical Approach to Global Optimization (Natural Computing Series)}*. New York: Springer-Verlag

Psaltis, D., Park, C., & Hong, J. (1988). Higher order associative memories and their optical implementations. *Neural Networks*, *1*, 149–163. doi:10.1016/0893-6080(88)90017-2

Psillakis, H. E., & Alexandridis, A. T. (2007). NN-Based Adaptive Tracking Control of Uncertain Nonlinear Systems Disturbed by Unknown Covariance Noise. *IEEE Transactions on Neural Networks*, *18*(6), 1830–1835. doi:10.1109/TNN.2007.901274

Punch, W. (1998). How effective are multiple populations in genetic programming. In Koza, J. e. a., editor, *Proceedings of the Third Annual Conference on Genetic Programming* (pp 308-313). Madison, WI: Morgan Kaufmann.

Purwar, S. (2007). On-line system identification of complex systems using Chebyshev neural networks. *Applied Soft Computing*, *7*, 364–372. doi:10.1016/j.asoc.2005.08.001

Qi, H., & Zhang, M. (2001, July 15-19). Rainfall estimation using M-PHONN model. In *Proceedings of International Joint Conference on Neural Networks* (Vol., pp.1620 – 1624).

Raisinghani, S. C., Ghosh, A. K., & Kalra, P. K. (1998). Two new techniques for aircraft parameter estimation using neural networks. *Aeronautical Journal, 102,* 25–29.

Ramanathan, K., & Guan, S. U. (2007). Multiorder neurons for evolutionary higher-order clustering and growth. *Neural Computation, 19*(12), 3369–3391. doi:10.1162/neco.2007.19.12.3369

Randolph, T. R., & Smith, M. J. T. (2000, December 17-20). A new approach to object classification in binary images. In *Proceeding of the 7th IEEE International Conference on Electronics, Circuits and Systems* (vol.1, pp.307 – 310).

Rao, D. H., & Gupta, M. M. (1993). A Generic Neural Model Based on Excitatory - Inhibitory Neural Population. *IJCNN-93* (pp. 1393-1396).

Ratnaweera, A., Halgamuge, S. K., & Watson, H. C. (2004). Self-organizing hierarchical particle swarm optimizer with time varying acceleration coefficients. *IEEE Transactions on Evolutionary Computation, 8*(3), 240–255. doi:10.1109/TEVC.2004.826071

Rechenberg, I. (1994). Evolution strategy. In Zurada, J., Marks II, R., & Robinson, C., (eds). *Computational Intelligence: Imitating Life.* Piscataway, NJ: IEEE Press.

Redding, N. J., Kowalczyk, A., & Downs, T. (1993). Constructive Higher-Order Network Algorithm that is Polynomial in Time. *Neural Networks, 6,* 997–1010. doi:10.1016/S0893-6080(09)80009-9

Refenes, A. N. (1994). *Neural networks in the capital markets.* Chichester, UK: Wiley.

Reid, M. B., et al. (1989) Rapid training of higher order neural networks for invariant pattern recognition. *In: Proc. of IJCNN,* Washington DC, *1,* 689-692.

Reid, M. B., Spirkovska, L., & Ochoa, E. (1989). Simultaneous position, scale, rotation invariant pattern classification using third-order neural networks. *International Journal on Neural Networks, 1,* 154–159.

Reid, M. B., Spirkovska, L., & Ochoa, E. (1989, June 18-22). Rapid training of higher-order neural networks

for invariant pattern recognition. In *Proceedings of International Joint Conference on Neural Networks, 1,* 689–692. doi:10.1109/IJCNN.1989.118653

Reyes, J. R., Yu, W., & Poznyak, A. S. (2000). Passivation and Control of Partially Known SISO Nonlinear Systems via Dynamic Neural Networks. *Mathematical Problems in Engineering, 6,* 61–83. doi:10.1155/S1024123X00001253

Reyner, L. M., & Filippi, E. (1991). An analysis of the performance of silicon implementations of back-propagation algorithms for artificial neural networks. *IEEE Transactions on Computers, 40,* 1380–1389. doi:10.1109/12.106223

Ricalde, L. J., & Sanchez, E. N. (2005, July 31). Inverse optimal nonlinear recurrent high order neural observer. In. *Proceedings of IEEE International Joint Conference on Neural Networks, 1,* 361–365. doi:10.1109/IJCNN.2005.1555857

Riedmiller, M., & Braun, H. (1993). A direct adaptive method for faster backpropagation learning: the Rprop algorithm. In *Proceedings of the International Conference on Neural Networks,* San Francisco.

Riedmiller, M., & Braun, H. (1994). RPROP -- *Description and Implementation Details* (Technical Report). Universitat Karlsruhe.

Rivals, I., & Personnaz, L. (2000, May 23-26). *A statistical procedure for determining the optimal number of hidden neurons of a neural model,* Second International Symposium on Neural Computation (NC'2000), Berlin, Germany.

Rosenblatt, F. (1958). The Perceptron: A Probabilistic Model for Information Storage and Organization in the Brain. *Psychological Review, 65,* 386–408. doi:10.1037/h0042519

Rosipal, R., Girolami, M., Trejo, L. J., & Cichocki, A. (2001). Kernel PCA for Feature Extraction and De-Noising in Nonlinear Regression. *Neural Computing & Applications, 10,* 231–243. doi:10.1007/s521-001-8051-z

Ross, T. J. (1995). *Fuzzy logic with engineering applications.* New York: McGraw Hill College Div.

Rovitahkis, G. A., & Christodoulou, M. A. (2000), *Adaptive Control with Recurrent High-Order Neural Networks*. New York: Springer Verlag.

Rovithakis, G. (1999). Robustifying nonlinear systems using high-order neural network controllers. *IEEE Transactions on Automatic Control, 44*(1), 102-108.

Rovithakis, G. A. (1998, December 16-18). Reinforcing robustness using high order neural network controllers. In *Proceedings of the 37th IEEE Conference on Decision and Control* (vol.1, pp.1052 – 1057).

Rovithakis, G. A. (2000). Performance of a neural adaptive tracking controller for multi-input nonlinear dynamical systems in the presence of additive and multiplicative external disturbances. *IEEE Transactions on Systems, Man and Cybernetics. Part A, 30*(6), 720–730.

Rovithakis, G. A. (2000, July 17-19). Robustness of a neural controller in the presence of additive and multiplicative external perturbations. In *Proceedings of the 2000 IEEE International Symposium on Intelligent Control* (pp. 7 – 12).

Rovithakis, G. A., & Chistodoulou, M. A. (2000). Adaptive control with recurrent high-order neural networks. New York: Springer Verlag.

Rovithakis, G. A., & Christodoulou, M. A. (1994). Adaptive control of unknown plants using dynamical neural networks. *IEEE Transactions on Systems, Man, and Cybernetics, 24*, 400–412. doi:10.1109/21.278990

Rovithakis, G. A., & Christodoulou, M. A. (1995). Direct adaptive regulation of unknown nonlinear dynamical systems via dynamic neural networks. *IEEE Transactions on Systems, Man, and Cybernetics, 25*, 1578–1594. doi:10.1109/21.478444

Rovithakis, G. A., & Christodoulou, M. A. (2000). *Adaptive Control with Recurrent High -Order Neural Networks*. New York: Springer Verlag

Rovithakis, G. A., Chalkiadakis, I., & Zervakis, M. E. (2004). High-order neural network structure selection for function approximation applications using genetic algorithms. *IEEE Transactions on Systems, Man and Cybernetics. Part B, 34*(1), 150–158.

Rovithakis, G. A., Kosmatopoulos, E. B., & Christodoulou, M. A. (1993, October 17-20). Robust adaptive control of unknown plants using recurrent high order neural networks-application to mechanical systems. In *Proceedings of International Conference on Systems, Man and Cybernetics* (vol.4, pp. 57 – 62).

Rovithakis, G. A., Malamos, A. G., Varvarigon, T., & Christodoulou, M. A. (1998, December 16-18). Quality assurance in networks-a high order neural net approach. In *Proceedings of the 37th IEEE Conference on Decision and Control* (vol.2, pp.1599 – 1604).

Rovithakis, G. A., Maniadakis, M., & Zervakis, M. (2000, June 5-9). Artificial neural networks for feature extraction and classification of vascular tissue fluorescence spectrums. In *Proceedings. 2000 IEEE International Conference on Acoustics, Speech, and Signal Processing* (vol.6, pp.3454 – 3457).

Rovithakis, G., Chalkiadakis, I., & Zervakis, M. (2004). High-order neural network structure selection for function approximation applications using genetic algorithms. *IEEE Transactions Systems Man Cybernetics (B), 34*(1), 150-158.

Rovithakis, G., Gaganis, V., Perrakis, S., & Christodoulou, M. (1996, December 11-13). A recurrent neural network model to describe manufacturing cell dynamics. In *Proc. of the 35th IEEE Conf. on Decision and Control* (vol.2, pp.1728 – 1733).

Rovithakis, G., Maniadakis, M., & Zervakis, M. (2000, September 11-13). A genetically optimized artificial neural network structure for feature extraction and classification of vascular tissue fluorescence spectrums. In *Proceedings of Fifth IEEE International Workshop on Computer Architectures for Machine Perception* (pp.107 – 111).

Rumelhart, D. E., Hinton, G. E., & McClelland, J. L. (1986). A General Framework for Parallel Distributed Processing. In *Parallel Distributed Processing, Vol.1: Foundations* (pp. 45-76). Cambridge, MA: MIT Press.

Rumelhart, D. E., Hinton, G. E., & Williams, R. J. (1986). Learning representations by back-propagation errors. *Nature, 323*, 533–536. doi:10.1038/323533a0

Rumelhart, D. E., Hinton, G. E., & Williams, R. J. (1986). Learning Internal Representations by Error Propagation. In Rumelhart, D. E., & McClelland, J. L. (Eds.), *Parallel Distributed Processing: Explorations in the Microstructure of Cognition, Vol. 1* (pp. 318-362). Cambridge, MA: MIT Press.

Rumelhart, D. E., McClelland, J. L., & the PDP Research Group, editors (1987). *Parallel Distributed Processing - Vol. 1*. Cambridge, MA: The MIT Press.

Rumelhart, D., Hinton, G., & Williams, R. (1986). Learning internal representations by error propagation. In D. Rumelhart, & J. McClelland (Eds.), *Parallel distributed processing: Explorations in the microstructure of cognition, Volume 1 — Foundations*. Cambridge, MA: MIT Press.

Sahin, S., Becerikli, Y., & Yazici, S. (2006). Neural network implementation in hardware using FPGAs. In *NIP, Neural Information Processing* (pp. 1105-1112). Berlin: Springer Verlag.

Sakaue, S., Kohda, T., & Yamamoto, H. (1993). Reduction of required precision bits for back-propagation applied to pattern recognition. *IEEE Transactions on Neural Networks, 4*, 270–275. doi:10.1109/72.207614

Salem, G. J., & Young, T. Y. (1991, July 8-14). Interpreting line drawings with higher order neural networks. In []. Seattle, USA.]. *Proceedings of the International Joint Conference on Neural Networks, 1*, 713–721.

Sanchez, E. N., & Ricalde, L. J. (2003). Chaos Control and Synchronization, with Input Saturation, via Recurrent Neural Networks. *Neural Networks, 16*, 711–717. doi:10.1016/S0893-6080(03)00122-9

Sanchez, E. N., & Ricalde, L. J. (2003). Trajectory tracking via adaptive recurrent neural control with input saturation. In *Proceedings of International Joint Conference on Neural Networks* (pp. 359-364), Portland, OR.

Sanchez, E. N., Alanis, A. Y., & Loukianov, A. G. (2007), Discrete-Time Recurrent High Order Neural Observer for Induction Motors, in *Foundations of Fuzzy Logic and Soft computing*, Melin, P., et al. (Ed.), Berlin Heidelberg, Germany: Springer-Verlag

Sanchez, E. N., Alanis, A., & Loukianov, A. (2008), *Discrete-Time High Order Neural Control*. Berlin, Germany: Springer-Verlag

Sandewall, E. (1989). Combining Logic and Differential Equations for Describing Real-World Systems. In *Proceedings of 1st Inter. Conf. on Principles of Knowledge Representation and Reasoning* (pp. 412-420). San Francisco: Morgan Kaufmann.

Sanger, T. D. (1991). A Tree-Structured Adaptive Network for Function Approximation in High-Dimensional Spaces. *IEEE Transactions on Neural Networks, 2*(2), 285–293. doi:10.1109/72.80339

Sankar, A., & Mammone, R. J. (1993). Growing and pruning neural network tree network. *IEEE Transactions on Computers, 42*(3), 291–299. doi:10.1109/12.210172

Sauer, P. W., Ahmed-Zaid, S., & Kokotovic, P. V. (1998). An integral manifold approach to reduced order dynamic modeling of synchronous machines. *IEEE Transactions on Power Systems, 3*(1), 17–23. doi:10.1109/59.43175

Sbarbaro, D., & Johansen, T. A. (2006). Analysis of Artificial Neural Networks for Pattern-Based Adaptive Control. *IEEE Transactions on Neural Networks, 17*(5), 1184–1193. doi:10.1109/TNN.2006.879762

Schaffer, J. D., Whitley, D., & Eshelman, L. J. (1992). Combinations of genetic algorithms and neural networks: A survey of the state of the art. In *Proceedings of International Workshop on Combinations of Genetic Algorithms and Neural Networks*, 1-37.

Schmidt, W. A. C., & Davis, J. P. (1993). Pattern recognition properties of various feature spaces for higher order neural networks. *IEEE Transactions on Pattern Analysis and Machine Intelligence, 15*(8), 795–801. doi:10.1109/34.236250

Schmidt, W., & Davis, J. (1993). Pattern recognition properties of various feature spaces for higher order neural networks. *IEEE Transactions on Pattern Analysis and Machine Intelligence, 15*, 795–801. doi:10.1109/34.236250

Schmitt, M. (2001). On the complexity of computing and learning with multiplicative neural networks. *Neural Computation, 14*, 241–301. doi:10.1162/08997660252741121

Schölkopf, B., Burges, C. J. C., & Smola, A. J. (1998). Nonlinear component analysis as a kernel eigenvalue problem, *Neural Computation, 10*, 1299–1319. Schölkopf, B., & Smola, A. J. (2002). *Learning with Kernels: Support Vector Machines, Regularization, Optimization, and Beyond*. Cambridge, MA: MIT Press.

Schultz, W. C., & Rideout, V. C. (1961). Control system performance measures: past, present and future. *I.R.E. Transactions on Automatic Control, AC-6*(22), 22–35.

Schutte, J. F., & Groenwold, A. A. (2005). A study of global optimization using particle swarms. *Journal of Global Optimization, 31*(1), 93–108. doi:10.1007/s10898-003-6454-x

Scofield, R. A. (1987). The NESDIS operational convective precipitation estimation technique. *Monthly Weather Review, 115*, 1773–1792. doi:10.1175/1520-0493(1987)115<1773:TNOCPE>2.0.CO;2

Selviah, D. R., & Shawash, J. (2008). Generalized Correlation Higher Order Neural Networks for Financial Time Series Prediction. In M.Zhang (Ed.), *Artificial Higher Order Neural Networks for Artificial Higher Order Neural Networks for Economics and Business* (pp. 212-249). Hershey, PA: IGI Global.

Sepulchre, R., Jankovic, M., & Kokotovic, P. V. (1997), *Constructive nonlinear control*. New York:Springer.

Setiono, R. (2000). Extracting M-of-N Rules from Trained Neural Networks. *IEEE Transactions on Neural Networks, 11*(2), 512–519. doi:10.1109/72.839020

Setiono, R., & Liu, H. (1996). Symbolic Representation of Neural Networks. *Computer, 29*(3), 71–77. doi:10.1109/2.485895

Shepherd, G. (1994). *Neurobiology, 3rd ed.* Oxford, UK:Oxford University Press.

Shi, Y., & Eberhart, R. C. (1998). A modified particle swarm optimizer. In *Proceedings of the IEEE International Conference on Evolutionary Computation* (pp.69-73), Pisacataway, NJ: IEEE Press

Shi, Y., & Eberhart, R. C. (1998). Parameter selection in particle swarm optimization. *Evolutionary Programming VII* (pp.591-600), LNCS, 1447, Berlin, Germany: Springer.

Shima, T., Kimura, T., & Kamatani, Y. (1992). Neural chips with on-chip backpropagation and / or Hebbian learning. *IEEE Journal of Solid State Circuits, 27*, 1868–1876. doi:10.1109/4.173117

Shin, Y., & Ghosh, J. (1991). The Pi-sigma Network: An Efficient Higher-Order Neural Network for Pattern Classification and Function Approximation. In *Proc. Int. Joint Conf. Neural Networks* (pp. 13-18).

Shin, Y., & Ghosh, J. (1991b). Realization of boolean functions using binary pi-sigma networks. In Dagli, C. H., Kumara, S. R. T., & Shin, Y. C., (eds.), *Intelligent Engineering Systems through Artificial Neural Networks*, (pp 205-210). New York: ASME Press.

Shin, Y., & Ghosh, J. (1992). Efficient higher order neural networks for function approximation and classification. *International Journal of Neural Systems, 3*(4), 323–350. doi:10.1142/S0129065792000255

Shin, Y., & Ghosh, J. (1992a). Approximation of multivariate functions using ridge polynomial networks. In. *Proceedings of International Joint Conference on Neural Networks, II*, 380–385.

Shin, Y., & Ghosh, J. (1992b): Computationally efficient invariant pattern recognition with higher order pi-sigma networks (Tech Report). *The University of Texas at Austin*.

Shin, Y., & Ghosh, J. (1995). Ridge polynomial networks. *IEEE Transactions on Neural Networks, 6*(2), 610–622. doi:10.1109/72.377967

Shuzhi, S. G., & Thanh, T. H. (2007). Semiglobal ISpS Disturbance Attenuation With Output Tracking via Direct Adaptive Design. *IEEE Transactions on Neural Networks, 18*(4), 1129–1148. doi:10.1109/TNN.2007.899159

Siddiqi, A. A. (2005, August 16-18). Genetically evolving higher order neural networks by direct encoding method. In *Proceedings of Sixth International Conference on*

Computational Intelligence and Multimedia Applications (pp. 62 – 67).

Siegelmann, H. (1993). *Foundations of Recurrent Neural Networks* (Tech. Rep. DCS-TR-306), Department of Computer Science, Laboratory for Computer Science Research, The State University of New Jersey Rutgers.

Siegelmann, H. (1996). On NIL: The Software Constructor of Neural Networks. *Parallel Processing Letters*, *6*(4), 575–582. doi:10.1142/S0129626496000510

Siegelmann, H. (1999). *Neural Networks and Analog Computation: Beyond the Turing Limit*, Birkhäuser.

Siegelmann, H., & Sontag, E. (1994). Analog Computation via Neural Networks. *Theoretical Computer Science*, *131*, 331–360. doi:10.1016/0304-3975(94)90178-3

Siegelmann, H., & Sontag, E. (1995). On the Computational Power of Neural Nets. *Journal of Computer and System Sciences*, *50*(1), 132–150. doi:10.1006/jcss.1995.1013

Sierra, A., Macias, J. A., & Corbacho, F. (2001). Evolution of functional link networks. *IEEE Transactions on Evolutionary Computation*, *5*(1), 54–65. doi:10.1109/4235.910465

Sing, S. N., & Srivastava, K. N. (2002). Degree of insecurity estimation in a power system using functional link neural network. *ETEP*, *12*(5), 353–359.

Singh, H., Dargahi, J., & Sedaghati, R. (2003) Experimental and finite element analysis of an endoscopic tooth-like tactile sensor. *2nd IEEE International Conference on Sensors*, Toronto, Canada.

Sinha, N., Gupta, M. M., & Zadeh, L. (1999). Soft Computing and Intelligent Control Systems: Theory and Applications. New York: Academic.

Sinha, S., & Ditto, W. (1998). Computing with distributed chaos. *Physical Review E: Statistical Physics, Plasmas, Fluids, and Related Interdisciplinary Topics*, *60*(1), 363–377. doi:10.1103/PhysRevE.60.363

Skarda, C. A., & Freeman, W. J. (1987). How Brains Make Chaos in Order to Make Sense of the World. *The Behavioral and Brain Sciences*, *10*, 161–195.

Skolicki, Z. (2005). An analysis of island models in evolutionary computation. In *GECCO '05: In Proceedings of the 2005 workshops on Genetic and evolutionary computation*, (386-389). New York: ACM.

Skolicki, Z., & Jong, K. D. (2005). The influence of migration sizes and intervals on island models. In *GECCO '05: Proceedings of the 2005 conference on Genetic and evolutionary computation*, (pp 1295-1302). New York: ACM.

Slotine, J. E., & Li, W. (1997). *IT Applied Nonlinear Control*. Englewood Cliffs, NJ: Prentice-Hall.

Slotine, J. J. E., & Li, W. (1991). *Applied Nonlinear Control*. New Jersey: Prentice Hall.

Smith, M. (1993). *Neural Networks for Statistical Modeling*. New York: Van Nostrand Reinhold.

Smola, A. J., Mangasarian, O. L., & Schölkopf, B. (1999) *Sparse kernel feature analysis* (Technical Report 99-04), University of Wiscosin, Data Mining Institute, Madison.

Smola, A. J., Schölkopf, B., & Ratsch, G. (1999). *Linear programs for automatic accuracy control in regression*. In International Conference on Artificial Neural Networks, Berlin, Germany.

Softky, R. W., & Kammen, D. M. (1991). Correlations in high dimensional or asymmetrical data sets: Hebbian neuronal processing. *Neural Networks*, *4*, 337–347. doi:10.1016/0893-6080(91)90070-L

Spirkovska, L. Reid, M. B. (1990). Connectivity strategies for higher-order neural networks applied to pattern recognition. *International Joint Conference on Neural Network*, 21-26 vol.1.

Spirkovska, L., & Reid, M. (1993). Coarse-coded higher-order neural networks for PSRI object recognition. *IEEE Trans on Neural Networks*, *4*(2), 276 – 283.

Spirkovska, L., & Reid, M. B. (1990, November 6-9). An empirical comparison of ID3 and HONNs for distortion invariant object recognition. In *Proceedings of the 2nd International IEEE Conference on Tools for Artificial Intelligence* (pp. 577 – 582).

Spirkovska, L., & Reid, M. B. (1991, July 8-14). Coarse-coding applied to HONNs for PSRI object recognition. In []. Seattle, USA.]. *Proceedings of the International Joint Conference on Neural Networks, 2,* 931.

Spirkovska, L., & Reid, M. B. (1992). Robust position, scale, and rotation invariant object recognition using higher-order neural networks. *Pattern Recognition, 25*(9), 975–985. doi:10.1016/0031-3203(92)90062-N

Spirkovska, L., & Reid, M. B. (1994). Higher-order neural networks applied to 2D and 3D object recognition. *Machine Learning, 15*(2), 169–199.

Spooner, J. T., & Passino, K. M. (1996). Stable adaptive control using fuzzy systems and neural networks. *IEEE transactions on Fuzzy Systems, 4,* 339–359. doi:10.1109/91.531775

Spooner, J. T., Maggiore, M., Ordonez, R., & Passino, K. M. (2002). *Stable Adaptive Control and Estimation for Nonlinear Systems: Neural and Fuzzy Approximator Techniques.* NY: John Wiley and Sons.

Sprave, J. (1999). A unified model of non-panmictic population structures in evolutionary algorithms. In Angeline, P. J., Michalewicz, Z., Schoenauer, M., Yao, X., & Zalzala, A., (eds.), *Proceedings of the Congress on Evolutionary Computation, 2,* (pp 1384-1391). IEEE Press.

Starke, J., Kubota, N., & Fukuda, T. (1995, November 27). Combinatorial optimization with higher order neural networks-cost oriented competing processes in flexible manufacturing systems. In. *Proceedings of IEEE International Conference on Neural Networks, 5,* 2658–2663. doi:10.1109/ICNN.1995.487830

Steil, J. J. (2005). Stability of backpropagation-decorrelation efficient O(N) recurrent learning. In *ESANN'2005 proceedings - European Symposium on Artificial Neural Networks* (pp. 43-48). Belgium.Williams, R. J., & Zipser, D. (1989). A learning algorithm for continually running fully recurrent neural networks. *Neural Computation, 1,* 270–280.

Steil, J. J. (2006). Online stability of backpropagation-decorrelation recurrent learning. *Neurocomputing, 69,* 642–650. doi:10.1016/j.neucom.2005.12.012

Stevens, B. L., & Lewis, F. L. (2003). *Aircraft Control and Simulation.* New York: Wiley and Sons.

Stevens, C. F. (1968). Synaptic Physiology. *Proceedings of the IEEE, 79*(9), 916–930. doi:10.1109/PROC.1968.6444

Stevenson, M., Winter, R., & Widrow, B. (1990). Sensitivity of feedforward neural networks to weight errors. *IEEE Transactions on Neural Networks, 1*(1), 71–80. doi:10.1109/72.80206

Storn, R. (1999). System design by constraint adaptation and differential evolution. *IEEE Transactions on Evolutionary Computation, 3,* 22–34. doi:10.1109/4235.752918

Storn, R., & Price, K. (1997). Differential evolution - a simple and efficient adaptive scheme for global optimization over continuous spaces. *Journal of Global Optimization, 11,* 341–359. doi:10.1023/A:1008202821328

Su, Z., & Khorasani, K. (2001). A neural network-based controller for a single-link flexible manipulator using the inverse dynamics approach. *IEEE Transactions on Industrial Electronics, 48*(6), 1074–1086. doi:10.1109/41.969386

Sun, G., Chen, H., Lee, Y., & Giles, C. (1991). Turing equivalence of neural networks with second-order connections weights. In *Proceedings of International Joint Conference on Neural Networks.*

Sun, Y., Peng, Y., Chen, Y., & Shukla, A. J. (2003). Application of artificial neural networks in the design of controlled release drug delivery systems. *Advanced Drug Delivery Reviews, 55,* 1201–1215. doi:10.1016/S0169-409X(03)00119-4

Sunderam, V. S. (1990). PVM: a framework for parallel distributed computing. *Concurrency: Pract. Exper., 2*(4), 315–339. doi:10.1002/cpe.4330020404

Takagi, H., & Hayashi, I. (1991). NN-driven fuzzy reasoning. *International Journal of Approximate Reasoning, 5,* 191–212. doi:10.1016/0888-613X(91)90008-A

Takagi, T., & Sugeno, M. (1985). Fuzzy identification of systems and its applications to modelling and control.

IEEE Transactions on Systems, Man, and Cybernetics, 15(1), 116–132.

Tanaka, K., & Kumazawa, I. (1996, June 3-6). Learning regular languages via recurrent higher-order neural networks. In. *Proceedings of IEEE International Conference on Neural Networks, 2,* 1378–1383.

Tanese, R. (1987). Parallel genetic algorithms for a hypercube. In *Proceedings of the Second International Conference on Genetic Algorithms on Genetic algorithms and their application,* (pp 177-183). Mahwah, NJ: Lawrence Erlbaum Associates.

Tang, C. Z., & Kwan, H. K. (1993). Multilayer feedforward neural networks with single power-of-two weights. *IEEE Transactions on Signal Processing, 41,* 2724–2727. doi:10.1109/78.229903

Tasoulis, D. K., Pavlidis, N. G., Plagianakos, V. P., & Vrahatis, M. N. (2004). Parallel differential evolution. In *IEEE Congress on Evolutionary Computation (CEC 2004). 2,* (pp 2023-2029).

Tasoulis, D. K., Plagianakos, V. P., & Vrahatis, M. N. (2005). Clustering in evolutionary algorithms to efficiently compute simultaneously local and global minima. In *IEEE Congress on Evolutionary Computation (CEC 2005), 2,* (pp. 1847-1854).

Tawfik, H., & Liatsis, P. (1997). Prediction of non-linear time series using higher order neural networks. In *Proceedings of IWSSIP'97,* Poznan, Poland.

Taylor, J. G., & Commbes, S. (1993). Learning higher order correlations. *Neural Networks, 6,* 423–428. doi:10.1016/0893-6080(93)90009-L

Theodoridis, D. C., Boutalis, Y. S., & Christodoulou, M. A. (2009). Direct Adaptive Control of Unknown Nonlinear Systems Using a new Neuro-Fuzzy Method Together with a Novel Approach of Parameter Hopping. *Kybernetica, 45*(3), 349–386.

Theodoridis, D. C., Christodoulou, M. A., & Boutalis, Y. S. (2008). Indirect Adaptive Neuro - Fuzzy Control Based On High Order Neural Network Function Approximators. In Proc. *16th Mediterranean Conference*

on Control and Automation - MED08 (pp. 386-393). Ajaccio, Corsica, France.

Theodoridis, D. C., Christodoulou, M. A., & Boutalis, Y. S. (2009). Direct Adaptive Control of Unknown Nonlinear Systems with Robustness Analysis using a new Neuro-Fuzzy Representation and a Novel Approach of Parameter Hopping. In *17th Mediterranean Conference on Control and Automation - MED09* (pp. 558-563). Thessalonica, Greece.

Theodorodis, S., & Koutroumbas, K. (1999). *Pattern recognition.* San Diego, USA: Academic Press

Thimm, G. (1998). *Optimization of high order perceptrons.* A PhD dissertation, Signal processing laboratory of the Swiss federal institute of technology.

Thimm, G., & Fiesler, E. (1997). High-order and multilayer perceptron initialization. *IEEE Transactions on Neural Networks, 8*(2), 249-259.

Thrun, S. B. et.al. (1991). The MONK's problems: A performance comparison of different learning algorithms (Technical Report CS-91-197), Pittsburgh, PA.

Tsai, H. (in press). Hybrid high order neural networks. *International Journal of Applied Soft Computing.*

Tsao, T.-R. (1989, June 18-22). A group theory approach to neural network computing of 3D rigid motion. In *Proceedings of Intl. Joint Conf. Neural Networks. 2,* 275-280. Washington D.C.

Tseng, Y.-H., & Wu, J.-L. (1994, June 27-July1). Constant-time neural decoders for some BCH codes. In *Proceedings of IEEE International Symposium on Information Theory* (pp.343).

Ulam, S., & von Neumann, J. (1947). On combination of stochastic and deterministic processes [abstract]. *Bulletin of the American Mathematical Society, 53,* 1120.

van der Waerden, B. L. (1970). *Algebra. New York:* Frederick Ungar Publishing Co.

Vecci, L., Piazza, F., & Uncini, A. (1998). Learning and approximation capabilities of adaptive spline activation function neural networks. *Neural Networks, 11,* 259–270. doi:10.1016/S0893-6080(97)00118-4

Vidyasagar, M. (1993). *Nonlinear System Analysis*. New Jersey: Prentice Hall.

Vidyasagar, M. (1993, March 28). Convergence of higher-order neural networks with modified updating. In. *Proceedings of the IEEE International Conference on Neural Networks, 3*, 1379–1384. doi:10.1109/ICNN.1993.298758

Villalobos, L., & Merat, F. (1995). Learning capability assessment and feature space optimization for higher-order neural networks. *IEEE Transactions on Neural Networks, 6*, 267–272. doi:10.1109/72.363427

Vinckier, A., & Semenza, G. (1998). Measuring elasticity of biological materials by atomic force microscopy. *FEBS Letters, 430*(1/2), 12–16. doi:10.1016/S0014-5793(98)00592-4

von Neumann, J. (1951). Various techniques used in connection with random digits, In *von Neumann Collected Works* (pp. 768-770), Pergamon Press, Oxford.

Voutriaridis, C., Boutalis, Y. S., & Mertzios, B. G. (2003, July 2-5). Ridge polynomial networks in pattern recognition. In *Proceedings of 4th EURASIP Conference on Video/Image Processing and Multimedia Communications* (vol.2, pp.519 – 524).

Voutriaridis, C., Boutalis, Y. S., & Mertzios, G. (2003). Ridge polynomial networks in pattern recognition. *4th EURASIP Conference Focused on Video/ Image Processing and Multimedia Communications*, Croatia, 519-524.

Wagner, N. (1993). The logistic equation in random number generation. In *Proc. 13th Allerton Conference on Communications, Control, and Computing* (pp. 922-931). University of Illinois.

Walcott, B. L., & Zak, S. H. (1987). State observation of nonlinear uncertain dynamical system. *IEEE Transactions on Automatic Control, 32*(2), 166–170. doi:10.1109/TAC.1987.1104530

Walczak, S. (2001). An empirical analysis of data requirements for financial forecasting with neural networks. *Journal of Management Information Systems, 17*, 203–222.

Walczak, S., & Cerpa, N. (1999). Heuristic principles for the design of artificial neural networks. *Information and Software Technology, 41*, 107–117. doi:10.1016/S0950-5849(98)00116-5

Wan, L., & Sun, L. (1996, May 20-23). Automatic target recognition using higher order neural network. In *Proceedings of the IEEE 1996 National Aerospace and Electronics Conference* (Vol. 1, pp. 221 – 226).

Wang, J. H., & Lin, J. H. (1995). Qualitative analysis of the BP composed of product units and summing units. *IEEE International Conference on Systems, Manufacturing and Cybernetics, 1*, 35–39.

Wang, J., Sun, Y., & Chen, Q. (2003, November 2-5). Recognition of digital annotation with invariant HONN based on orthogonal Fourier-Mellin moments. In *Proceedings of 2003 International Conference on Machine Learning and Cybernetics* (Vol. 4, pp.2261 – 2264).

Wang, J., Wu, K., & Chang, F. (2004, November 8-10). Scale equalization higher-order neural networks. In *Proceedings of the 2004 IEEE International Conference on Information Reuse and Integration* (612 – 617).

Wang, L. (1994). *Adaptive Fuzzy Systems and Control*. Englewood Cliffs, NJ: Prentice Hall.

Wang, L. (1996). Suppressing chaos with hysteresis in a higher order neural network. *IEEE Transactions on Circuits and Systems II: Analog and Digital Signal Processing, 43*(12), 845–846. doi:10.1109/82.553405

Wang, S. H. (2003). Application of self-organising maps for data mining with incomplete data sets. *Neural Computing & Applications, 12*(1), 42–48. doi:10.1007/s00521-003-0372-1

Wang, Z., Fang, J., & Liu, X. (2006). Global stability of stochastic high-order neural networks with discrete and distributed delays. *Chaos, Solitons, and Fractals, 6*, 63.

Wang, Z., Ho, D. W. C., & Liu, X. (2005). State estimation for delayed neural networks. *IEEE Transactions on Neural Networks, 16*(1), 279–284. doi:10.1109/TNN.2004.841813

Wellman, P. S., & Howe, R. D. (1999). *The mechanical properties of breast tissue in compression* (Tech. Rep. No. 99003). Harvard BioRobotics Laboratory, Cambridge, MA.

Weng, W.-D. (2007). A channel equalizer using reduced decision feedback Chebyshev function link artificial neural networks. *Information Sciences, 177,* 2642–2654. doi:10.1016/j.ins.2007.01.006

Wessels, L. F. A., & Barnard, E. (1992). Avoiding false local minima by proper initialization of connections. *IEEE Transactions on Neural Networks, 3,* 899–905. doi:10.1109/72.165592

Weston, J., Gammerman, A., Stitson, M. O., Vapnik, V., Vovk, V., & Watkins, C. (1999). Support vector density estimation, In B. Schölkopf, C.J.C. Burges, A.J. Smola (Eds.), *Advances in Kernel Methods: Support Vector Learning,* (pp. 293–305). Cambridge, MA: MIT Press.

Willcox, C. R. (1991). Understanding hierarchical neural network behaviour: a renormalization group approach. *Journal of Physics. A. Mathematical Nuclear and General, 24,* 2655–2644. doi:10.1088/0305-4470/24/11/030

Willems, J. C. (1971). Least squares optimal control and algebraic Riccati equations. *IEEE Transactions on Automatic Control, 16*(6), 621–634. doi:10.1109/TAC.1971.1099831

Willems, J. L. (1971). Direct methods for transient stability studies in power systems analysis. *IEEE Transactions on Automatic Control, 16*(4), 332–341. doi:10.1109/TAC.1971.1099743

Williams, R. J., & Zipser, D. (1989). A learning algorithm for continually running fully recurrent neural networks. *Neural Computation, 1*(2), 270–280. doi:10.1162/neco.1989.1.2.270

Wilson, A., & Hendler, J. (1993). *Linking Symbolic and Subsymbolic Computing* (Tech. Rep.), Dept. of Computer Science, University of Maryland.

Wilson, H. R., & Cowan, J. D. (1972). Excitatory and Inhibitory Interactions in Localized Populations of Model Neurons. *Biophysical Journal, 12,* 1–24. doi:10.1016/S0006-3495(72)86068-5

Witten, I. H., & Frank, E. (2005). *Data mining: practical machine learning tools and techniques.* Amsterdam The Netherlands: Elsevier/Morgan Kaufman.

Wolpert, D. H. (1996a). The existence of a priori distinctions between learning algorithms. *Neural Computation, 8,* 1391–1420. doi:10.1162/neco.1996.8.7.1391

Wolpert, D. H. (1996b). The lack of a priori distinctions between learning algorithms. *Neural Computation, 8,* 1341–1390. doi:10.1162/neco.1996.8.7.1341

Wood, J., & Shawe-Taylor, J. (1996). A unifying framework for invariant pattern recognition. *Pattern Recognition Letters, 17,* 1415–1422. doi:10.1016/S0167-8655(96)00103-1

Woodhead, B. (2006, October 10). *Retailers Scour Loyalty Data.* Retrieved January 6, 2008, from, http://www.australianit.news.com.au/story/0,24897,20551538-15306,00.html

Woodhead, B. (2007). *Myer Plans Data Slice and Dice.* Retrieved October 2, 2007, from http://www.theaustralian.com.au/australian-it/myer-plans-data-slice-and-dice/story-e6frgamo-1111114546456

Wu, C. J., & Huang, C. H. (1997). A hybrid method for parameter tuning of PID Controllers. *Journal of the Franklin Institute, 334B,* 547–562. doi:10.1016/S0016-0032(96)00094-4

Wu, J., & Chang, J. (1993, October 25-29). Invariant pattern recognition using higher-order neural networks. In [].Nagoya, Japan.]. *Proceedings of International Joint Conference on Neural Networks, 2,* 1273–1276.

Xie, J., & Scofield, R. A. (1989). Satellite-derived rainfall estimates and propagation characteristics associated with mesoscal convective system (MCSs). *NAOO Technical Memorandum NESDIS, 25,* 1–49.

Xie, Y., & Jabri, M. A. (1992). Analysis of the effects of quantization in multilayer neural networks using a statistical model. *IEEE Transactions on Neural Networks, 3,* 334–338. doi:10.1109/72.125876

Xilinx (2008). AccelDSP Synthesis Tool. Retrieved June, 2008, from http://www.xilinx.com/tools/dsp.htm

Xiong, Y. (2007). Training *pi-sigma* network by on-line gradient algorithm with penalty for small weight update. *Neural Computation*, *19*, 3356–3368. doi:10.1162/neco.2007.19.12.3356

Xu, L., Oja, E., & Suen, C. Y. (1992). Modified hebbian learning for curve and surface fitting. *Neural Networks*, *5*, 441–457. doi:10.1016/0893-6080(92)90006-5

Xu, S. (2008). Adaptive Higher Order Neural Network Models and Their Applications in Business. In M. Zhang (Ed.), *Artificial Higher Order Neural Networks for Economics and Business* (pp. 314-329). Hershey, PA: IGI Global.

Xu, S., & Zhang, M. (2000, July). Justification of a Neuron-Adaptive Activation Function, In *Proceeding of IJCNN'2000 (CD-ROM), paper NN0162*. Como, Italy

Xu, S., & Zhang, M. (2002, November 18-22). An adaptive higher-order neural networks (AHONN) and its approximation capabilities. In *Proceedings of the 9th International Conference on Neural Information Processing* (Vol. 2, pp. 848 – 852).

Yamada, T., & Yabuta, T. (1992). Remarks on a neural network controller which uses an auto-tuning method for nonlinear functions. In *Proceedings of the International Joint Conference on Neural Networks*, *2*, 775–780.

Yamashita, T., Hirasawa, K., Hu, J., & Murata, J. (2002, November 18-22). Multi-branch structure of layered neural networks. In *Proceedings of the 9th International Conference on Neural Information Processing* (vol.1, pp.243 – 247).

Yang, C. D., & Liu, W. H. (2003). *Nonlinear Hoo Decoupling hover control of helicopter with parameter uncertainties*. Paper presented at the Proceedings of the American Control Conference, Denver, CO.

Yang, C., Ge, S. S., Chai, C. X. T., & Lee, T. H. (2008). Output Feedback NN Control for Two Classes of Discrete-Time Systems With Unknown Control Directions in a Unified Approach. *IEEE Transactions on Neural Networks*, *19*(11), 1873–1886. doi:10.1109/TNN.2008.2003290

Yang, H., & Guest, C. C. (1990, June 17-21). High order neural networks with reduced numbers of interconnection weights. In *Proceedings of the International Joint Conference on Neural Networks*, *3*, 281–286. doi:10.1109/IJCNN.1990.137857

Yang, X. (1990). Detection and classification of neural signals and identification of neural networks (synaptic connectivity). *Dissertation Abstracts International - B*, *50*(12), 5761.

Yatsuki, S., & Miyajima, H. (1997, June 9-12). Associative ability of higher order neural networks. In *Proceedings of International Conference on Neural Networks*, *2*, 1299–1304.

Yeap, T. H., & Ahmed, N. U. (1994). Feedback Control of Chaotic Systems. *Dynamics and Control*, *4*, 97–114. doi:10.1007/BF02115741

Yih, G. L., Wei, Y. W., & Tsu, T. L. (2005). Observer-based direct adaptive fuzzy-neural control for nonaffine nonlinear systems. *IEEE Transactions on Neural Networks*, *16*(4), 853–861. doi:10.1109/TNN.2005.849824

Yoon, S., & MacGregor, J. F. (2004). Principal-component analysis of multiscale data for process monitoring and fault diagnosis. *AIChE Journal. American Institute of Chemical Engineers*, *50*(11), 2891–2903. doi:10.1002/aic.10260

Young, S., & Downs, T. (1993). Generalisation in higher order neural networks. *Electronics Letters*, *29*(16), 1491–1493. doi:10.1049/el:19930996

Yu, D. L., & Gomm, J. B. (2002). Enhanced neural network modelling for a real multivariable chemical process. *Neural Computing & Applications*, *10*(4), 289–299. doi:10.1007/s005210200001

Yu, J., Wang, S., & Xi, L. (2008). Evolving artificial neural networks using an improved PSO and DPSO. *Neurocomputing*, *71*, 1054–1060. doi:10.1016/j.neucom.2007.10.013

Yu, S. J., & Liang, D. N. (1995, May 22-26). Neural network based approach for eigenstructure extraction. In *Proceedings of the IEEE 1995 National Aerospace and Electronics Conference* (vol.1, pp. 102 – 105).

Yu, W., & Li, X. (2001). Some New Results on System Identification with Dynamic Neural Networks. *IEEE Transactions on Neural Networks*, *12*(2), 412–417. doi:10.1109/72.914535

Yu, W., & Li, X. (2004). Nonlinear system identification using discrete-time recurrent neural networks with stable learning algorithms. *Information Sciences*, *158*(1), 131–147. doi:10.1016/j.ins.2003.08.002

Yu, W., & Poznyak, A. S. (1999). Indirect Adaptive Control via Parallel Dynamic Neural Networks. *IEE Proceedings. Control Theory and Applications*, *146*(1), 25–30. doi:10.1049/ip-cta:19990368

Zadeh, L. A. (1965). Fuzzy sets. *Information and Control*, *8*, 338–353. doi:10.1016/S0019-9958(65)90241-X

Zardoshti-Kermani, M., & Afshordi, A. (1995, November 27). Classification of chromosomes using higher-order neural networks. In. *Proceedings of IEEE International Conference on Neural Networks*, *5*, 2587–2591. doi:10.1109/ICNN.1995.487816

Zarrinkoub, H. (2006). Fixed-point Signal Processing with Matlab and Simulink. www.mathworks.com, Retrieved May 25, 2008, from http://www.mathworks.com/webex/recordings/fixedpt_042006/fixedpt_042006.html

Zeeman, E. C. (1962), The topology of the brain and visual perception. In M. K. Fork, Jr (eds.), *Topology of 3-manifolds and related Topics* (pp.240-256).Englewood Cliffs, NJ: Prentice-Hall, Inc.

Zeng, J., Wang, Y., Freedman, M. T., & Mum, S. K. (1997). Finger tracking for breast palpation quantification using color image features. *SPIE J Opt Eng*, *36*(12), 3455–3461. doi:10.1117/1.601585

Zhang, J. C., Zhang, M., & Fulcher, J. (1997, March 24-25). Financial simulation system using a higher order trigonometric polynomial neural network group model. In *Proceedings of the IEEE/IAFE 1997 Computational Intelligence for Financial Engineering (CIFEr)* (pp.189–194).

Zhang, J. R. (2007). A hybrid particle swarm optimization-back-propagation algorithm for feed-forward neural network training. *Applied Mathematics and Computation*, *185*, 1026–1037. doi:10.1016/j.amc.2006.07.025

Zhang, J., Ge, S. S., & Lee, T. H. (2005). Output feedback control of a class of discrete MIMO nonlinear systems with triangular form inputs. *IEEE Transactions on Neural Networks*, *16*(6), 1491–1503. doi:10.1109/TNN.2005.852242

Zhang, M. (2001, July 15-19). Financial data simulation using A-PHONN model. *In Proceedings of International Joint Conference on Neural Networks* (Volume 3, pp.1823 – 1827).

Zhang, M. (2008). Artificial Higher Order Neural Networks nonlinear models: SAS NLIN or HONNs? In M. Zhang (Ed.), *Artificial Higher Order Neural Networks for Economics and Business* (pp. 1-47). Herhsey, PA: IGI Global.

Zhang, M. (2009A). *Artificial Higher Order Neural Networks for Economics and Business*. Hershey, PA: IGI-Global.

Zhang, M. (2009C). Ultra High Frequency Trigonometric Higher Order Neural Networks, Book chapter in Ming Zhang (Editor), *Artificial Higher Order Neural Networks for Economics and Business* (pp. 133-163), Hershey, PA:IGI-Global.

Zhang, M. Xu. S., Lu, B. (1999, July 10-16). Neuron-adaptive higher order neural network group models. In *Proceedings of International Joint Conference on Neural Networks* (Vol. 1, pp. 333 - 336).

Zhang, M., & Bo Lu (2001, July 15-19). Financial data simulation using M-PHONN model. In *Proceedings of IJCNN '01. International Joint Conference on Neural Networks* (vol.3, pp.1828 – 1832).

Zhang, M., & Fulcher, J. (1996). Face recognition using artificial neural network group-based adaptive tolerance (GAT) trees. *IEEE Transactions on Neural Networks*, *7*(3), 555–567. doi:10.1109/72.501715

Zhang, M., & Fulcher, J. (1996, September 15-18). Neural network group models for financial data simulation. In *Proceedings of World Congress On Neural Networks* (pp. 910-913). San Diego, CA.

Zhang, M., & Fulcher, J. (2004). Higher order neural networks for satellite weather prediction. In J. Fulcher, & L. C. Jain (Eds.), *Applied intelligent systems: New directions* (pp. 17-57). Berlin: Springer.

Zhang, M., & Scofield, R. A. (1994). Artificial neural network techniques for estimating heavy convective rainfall and recognition cloud mergers from satellite data. *International Journal of Remote Sensing, 15*(16), 3241–3262. doi:10.1080/01431169408954324

Zhang, M., & Scofield, R. A. (2001, July 15-19). Rainfall estimation using A-PHONN model. In. *Proceedings of International Joint Conference on Neural Networks, 3*, 1583–1587.

Zhang, M., & Xu, S., 7 Fulcher, J. (2007). ANSER: an Adaptive-Neuron Artificial Neural Network System for Estimating Rainfall Using Satellite Data. *International Journal of Computers and Applications, 29*(3), 215–222. doi:10.2316/Journal.202.2007.3.202-1585

Zhang, M., Crowley, J., Dunstone, E., & Fulcher, J. (1993, October 14). Face Recognition, *Australia Patent*, No.PM1828.

Zhang, M., Fulcher, J., & Scofield, R. (1997). Rainfall estimation using artificial neural network group. *Neurocomputing, 16*(2), 97–115. doi:10.1016/S0925-2312(96)00022-7

Zhang, M., Murugesan, S., & Sadeghi, M. (1995, October 30 - November 3). Polynomial higher order neural network for economic data simulation. In *Proceedings of International Conference On Neural Information Processing* (pp. 493-496). Beijing, China.

Zhang, M., Xu, S., & Fulcher, J. (2002). Neuron-adaptive higher order neural-network models for automated financial data modeling. *IEEE Transactions on Neural Networks, 13*(1), 188–204. doi:10.1109/72.977302

Zhang, M., Xu, S., & Fulcher, J. (2007). ANSER: an Adaptive-Neuron artificial neural network System for

Estimating Rainfall using satellite data. *International Journal of Computers and Applications, 29*(3), 1–8. doi:10.2316/Journal.202.2007.3.202-1585

Zhang, M., Xu, S., & Lu, B. (1999). Neuron-adaptive higher order neural-network group models. *International Joint Conference on Neural Networks*, 333-336.

Zhang, M., Zhang, J. C., & Fulcher, J. (2000, April). Higher order neural network group models for data approximation. *International Journal of Neural Systems, 10*(2), 123–142.

Zhang, S. J., Jing, Z. L., & Li, J. X. (2004). Fast learning high-order neural networks for pattern recognition. *Electronics Letters, 40*(19), 1207–1208. doi:10.1049/el:20045550

Zhang, Y. Q., & Chan, L. W. (2000). Fourier recurrent Networks for Time series Prediction. In *Proceedings of International Conference on Neural Information Processing*, ICONIP 2000 (pp. 576-582). Taejon, Korea.

Zhao, H., & Zhang, J. (2008). Functional link neural network cascaded with Chebyshev orthogonal polynomial for non-linear channel equalization. *Signal Processing, 88*, 1946–1957. doi:10.1016/j.sigpro.2008.01.029

Zhou, X., Koch, M. W., & Roberts, M. W. (1991, July 14). Selective attention of high-order neural networks for invariant object recognition. In []. Seattle, USA.]. *Proceedings of International Joint Conference on Neural Networks, 2*, 9378.

Zhu, J. H., & Sutton, P. (2003). FPGA implementations of neural networks - A survey of a decade of progress. In *Field-Programmable Logic and Applications* (pp. 1062-1066). Berlin/Heidelberg: Springer.

Zhu, Q., Cai, Y., & Liu, L. (1999). A global learning algorithm for a RBF network. *Neural Networks, 12*, 527–540. doi:10.1016/S0893-6080(98)00146-4

Zomaya, A. Y. H. (1996). *Parallel and Distributed Computing Handbook*. New York: McGraw-Hill

Zurada, J. M. (1992). *Introduction to Artificial Neural Systems*. St. Paul MN:West Publishing Company.

About the Contributors

Ming Zhang was born in Shanghai, China. He received the M.S. degree in information processing and Ph.D. degree in the research area of computer vision from East China Normal University, Shanghai, China, in 1982 and 1989, respectively. He held Postdoctoral Fellowships in artificial neural networks with the Chinese Academy of the Sciences in 1989 and the USA National Research Council in 1991. He was a face recognition airport security system project manager and Ph.D. co-supervisor at the University of Wollongong, Australia in 1992. Since 1994, he was a lecturer at the Monash University, Australia, with a research area of artificial neural network financial information system. From 1995 to 1999, he was a senior lecturer and Ph.D. supervisor at the University of Western Sydney, Australia, with the research interest of artificial neural networks. He also held Senior Research Associate Fellowship in artificial neural networks with the USA National Research Council in 1999. He is currently a full Professor and graduate student supervisor in computer science at the Christopher Newport University, VA, USA. With more than 100 papers published, his current research includes artificial neural network models for face recognition, weather forecasting, financial data simulation, and management.

* * *

Alma Y. Alanis was born in Durango, Durango, Mexico, in 1980. She received the B. Sc degree from Instituto Tecnologico de Durango (ITD), Durango Campus, Durango, Durango, in 2002, the M.Sc. and the Ph.D. degrees in electrical engineering from the Advanced Studies and Research Center of the National Polytechnic Institute (CINVESTAV-IPN), Guadalajara Campus, Mexico, in 2004 and 2007, respectively. Since 2008 she has been with University of Guadalajara, where she is currently a Professor in the Department of Computer Science. She is also member of the Mexican National Research System (SNI-1). She has published papers in International Journals and Conferences. Her research interest centers on neural control, backstepping control, block control, chaos reproduction and their applications to electrical machines and power systems.

Kamal R, AlRawi was born in Ana, Anbar, Iraq in 1953. He Received the B.Sc. degree in physics from the University of Mosul, Mosul, Iraq in 1977, the M.Sc. degree in atmospheric science from the Oklahoma University, Norman, OK, USA in 1985, the Ph.D. degree in atmospheric physics (remote sensing) from University of Valladolid, Valladolid, Spain in 2000, and the Ph.D. degree in computer science (neural networks) from University Polytechnic of Madrid, Madrid, Spain in 2001. He is currently associate professor of computer science in the Faculty of Information Technology, Petra University, and Amman, Jordan. His research interests include the development, analysis, and application of neural networks. His major works on the Adaptive Resonance Theory (ART) neural networks, ART supervisions, and their application in the analysis of satellites' images and pattern recognitions. He was the director of the cultural relation office in Anbar University, and council member in two faculties.

Mohammed S. Al-Rawi received the B.S. degree from Baghdad University in 1989, the M.S. degree in Invariant Image Recognition- Physics department from Baghdad University in 1993, and the Ph.D. degree in Pattern Recognition and Intelligent systems from the Institute of Image Processing and Pattern Recognition, Shanghai Jiao- Tong University in 2002. He was a lecturer in the electronics and communications engineering department in Baghdad University from 1994 to 1998. Since September 2002 until2008 he was an assistant professor in the Computer Science department at the University of Jordan. He is currently a postdoctoral researcher at the IEETA, the University of Aveiro, Portugal working on image processing and pattern recognition issues related to functional magnetic resonance imaging researches. His research interests are in the field of pattern recognition, neural networks, genetic algorithms applications, and computer vision.

Yiannis Boutalis (M'86) received the diploma of Electrical Engineer in 1983 from Democritus University of Thrace (DUTH), Greece and the PhD degree in Electrical and Computer Engineering (topic Image Processing) in 1988 from the Computer Science Division of National Technical University of Athens, Greece. Since 1996, he serves as a faculty member, at the Department of Electrical and Computer Engineering, DUTH, Greece, where he is currently an Associate Professor and director of the Automatic Control Systems lab. Currently, he is also a Visiting Professor for research cooperation at Erlangen-Nuremberg University of Germany, chair of Automatic Control. He served as an assistant visiting professor at University of Thessaly, Greece, and as a visiting professor in Air Defence Academy of General Staff of air forces of Greece. He also served as a researcher in the Institute of Language and Speech Processing (ILSP), Greece, and as a managing director of the R&D SME Ideatech S.A, Greece, specializing in pattern recognition and signal processing applications. His current research interests are focused in the development of Computational Intelligence techniques with applications in Control, Pattern Recognition, Signal and Image Processing Problems.

Ivo Bukovsky graduated from Czech Technical University in Prague where he received his Ph.D. in the field of Control and System Engineering in 2007. He spent seven months working as a visiting researcher under supervision of Dr. M.M. Gupta at the Intelligent Systems Research Laboratory at the University of Saskatchewan within the frame of the NATO Science Fellowships Award in 2003. His Ph.D. thesis on nonconventional neural units and adaptive approach to evaluation of complex systems was recognized by the Verner von Siemens Excellence Award 2007. He is currently an assistant professor at the Czech Technical University in Prague and his major research interest is the development of new neural architectures and their applications to complex real dynamic systems.

Salvador Carlos-Hernandez, was born in Jilotepec, Mexico in 1976. He obtained the BSEE (major in Electronics) from the Instituto Tenológico de Toluca, Mexico, in 1999, and the MSEE (major in Control Systems) from Cinvestav, Guadalajara Campus, Mexico in 2001, and a Ph.D. degree in Control Systems from the Institut National Polytechnique de Grenoble, France in 2005. Since 2006 he is a Research Scientist at Cinvestav Saltillo, Mexico, in the Natural and Energetic Resources group. His research interests center in: a) applications of automatic control theory in energetic processes such as anaerobic wastewater treatment and gasification of solid fuels, b) study of raw materials of biological origin for energy generation. He has published papers in International Journals and Conferences.

Sung-Bae Cho received the Ph.D. degrees in computer science from KAIST (Korea Advanced Institute of Science and Technology), Taejeon, Korea, in 1993. He was an Invited Researcher of Human Information Processing Research Laboratories at ATR (Advanced Telecommunications Research) Institute, Kyoto, Japan from 1993 to 1995, and a Visiting Scholar at University of New South Wales, Canberra, Australia in 1998. He was also a Visiting Professor at University of British Columbia, Vancouver, Canada from 2005 to 2006. Since 1995, he has been a Professor in the Department of Computer Science, Yonsei University. His research interests include neural networks, pattern recognition, intelligent man-machine interfaces, evolutionary computation, and artificial life. He is a Senior Member of IEEE and a Member of the Korea Information Science Society, the IEEE Computer Society, the IEEE Systems, Man, and Cybernetics Society, and the Computational Intelligence Society.

Manolis Christodoulou (S'78–M'82–SM'89) was born in Kifissia, Greece, in 1955. He received the diploma degree (EE'78) from the National Technical University of Athens, Greece, the M.S. degree (EE'79) from the University of Maryland, College Park the engineer degree (EE'82) from the University of Southern California, Los Angeles, and the Ph.D. degree (EE'84) from the Democritus University, Thrace, Greece. He joined The Technical University of Crete, Greece in 1988, where he is currently a Professor of Control. He has been a Visiting Professor at Georgia Tech, Syracuse University, the University of Southern California, Tufts University, Victoria University and the Massachusetts Institute of Technology. He has authored and co-authored more than 200 journal articles, book chapters, books, and conference publications in the areas of control theory and applications, robotics, factory automation, computer integrated manufacturing in engineering, neural networks for dynamic system identification and control, in the use of robots for minimally invasive surgeries and recently in systems biology. Dr. Christodoulou is the organizer of various conferences and sessions of IEEE and IFAC and guest editor in various special issues of International Journals. He is managing and cooperating on various research projects in Greece, in the European Union and in collaboration with the United States. He has held many administrative positions such as the Vice Presidency of the Technical University of Crete, as Chairman of the office of Sponsored research and as a member of the board of governors of the University of Peloponnese. He is a member of the Technical Chamber of Greece. He has been active in the IEEE CS society as the founder and first Chairman of the IEEE Control Systems Society Greek Chapter, which received the 1997 Best Chapter of the Year Award and as the founder of the IEEE Mediterranean Conference on Control and Automation, which became an annual event. Dr Christodoulou received the MCA Founders award in 2005. He is a member of the board of governors of the Mediterranean Control Association since 1993.

Abhijit Das is a PhD student at Automation and Robotics Research Institute (ARRI), The University of Texas at Arlington. He obtained his Bachelor's and Master's degree from The Bengal Engineering and Science University, Shibpur and Indian Institute of Technology at Kharagpur respectively. During his Masters, he worked in several Defense projects funded by Defense Research and Development Organization, India. After his masters he directly joined ARRI as a graduate research assistant to pursue his PhD. His current research interest includes nonlinear adaptive control and neural networks, robust control and networked control. He is the author of two journal papers, several conference papers and two book chapters. He is a student member of IEEE and life time member of System Society of India.

Satchidananda Dehuri is a Reader in P.G. Department of Information and Communication Technology, Fakir Mohan University, Vyasa Vihar, Balasore, Orissa. He received his M.Sc. degree in Mathematics from Sambalpur University, Orissa in 1998, and the M.Tech. and Ph.D. degrees in Computer Science from Utkal University, Vani Vihar, Orissa in 2001 and 2006, respectively. He completed his Post Doctoral Research in Soft Computing Laboratory, Yonsei University, Seoul, Korea under the BOYSCAST Fellowship Program of DST, Govt. of India. He was at the Center for Theoretical Studies, Indian Institute of Technology Kharagpur as a Visiting Scholar in 2002. During May-June 2006 he was a Visiting Scientist at the Center for Soft Computing Research, Indian Statistical Institute, Kolkata. His research interests include Evolutionary Computation, Neural Networks, Pattern Recognition, Data Warehousing and Mining, Object Oriented Programming and its Applications and Bioinformatics. He has already published about 65 research papers in reputed journals and referred conferences, has published two text books for undergraduate students and edited one book, and is acting as an editorial member of various journals. He chaired the sessions of various International Conferences.

Michael G. Epitropakis received his Diploma in Mathematics form the Department of Mathematics, University of Patras, Greece in 2004. He received his M.Sc. degree in 2008 from the interdepartmental program "Mathematics of Computers and Decision Making", an association of Department of Mathematics and Computer Engineering and Informatics Department, at University of Patras, Greece. He is currently a Ph.D. candidate. His research interests include evolutionary algorithms, differential evolution, neural networks, parallel and distributed computations, intelligent optimization, and real-world problem solving. Mr. Epitropakis is a Student Member of the IEEE Computational Intelligence Society, the ACM, and the University of Patras Artificial Intelligence Research Center (UPAIRC).

Mehdi Fallahnezhad was born in Karaj, Iran in December 1982. He received his B.Sc. degree in Electronics Engineering from Sharif University of Technology, Tehran, Iran. He is currently working toward the M.Sc. degree in Biomedical Engineering at Bioelectronics Department of Amirkabir University of Technology (Tehran Polytechnic). He is also a member of Biomedical Instrumentation and Signal Processing Laboratory, Amirkabir University of technology (Tehran Polytechnic). His current research interests include wireless ECG, telecardiology, de-noising and heart-failure detection. He has also worked on several pattern classification and forecasting time-series benchmarks.

Rozaida Ghazali received her B.Sc. (Hons) degree in Computer Science from Universiti Sains Malaysia, and M.Sc. degree in Computer Science from Universiti Teknologi Malaysia. She obtained her Ph.D. degree in Higher Order Neural Networks for Financial Time series Prediction at Liverpool John Moores University, UK. She is currently a teaching staff at Faculty of Information technology and Multimedia, Universiti Tun Hussein Onn Malaysia (UTHM). Her research area includes neural networks, data mining, financial time series prediction, data analysis, physical time series forecasting, and fuzzy logic.

G. E. Gielen received the Ph.D. degree in Electrical Engineering from the Katholieke Universiteit Leuven, Belgium, in 1990. Currently he is a professor at the Department of Electrical Engineering at this university. He is the author or co-author of more than 200 published papers in journals and conference proceedings. His research interests include the design and particularly the computer-aided design of analog and mixed-signal integrated circuits, signal processing and neural networks. Dr. Gielen serves regularly on the program committees of international conferences and on the editorial board of international journals. He is a Fellow of IEEE, a member of the Board of Governors as well as a Distinguished Lecturer of the IEEE Circuits and Systems Society. He was the 1997 Laureate of the Belgian Royal Academy of Sciences, Literature and Arts in the category of engineering sciences, and he received the 1995 Best Paper Award of the John Wiley international journal on Circuit Theory.

Madan M. Gupta is a professor emeritus in the Department of Mechanical Engineering and director of the Intelligent Systems Research Laboratory at University of Saskatchewan. Dr. Gupta's current research interests are in the areas of neuro-vision systems, neuro-control systems, integration of fuzzy-neural systems, neuronal morphology of biological vision systems, intelligent and cognitive robotic systems, cognitive information, new paradigms in information processing, and chaos in neural systems. He is also developing new architectures of computational neural networks and computational fuzzy neural networks for application to advanced robotics, aerospace, medical, and industrial systems. His interest also lies in signal and image processing with applications to medical systems. Dr. Gupta has authored or coauthored over 900 published research papers. He coauthored the seminal book *Static and Dynamic Neural Networks: From Fundamentals to Advanced Theory.* Dr. Gupta previously coauthored *Introduction to Fuzzy Arithmetic: Theory and Applications,* the first book on fuzzy arithmetic, and *Fuzzy Mathematical Models in Engineering and Management Science.* Both of these books had Japanese translations. Also, Dr. Gupta edited 19 books in the fields of adaptive control systems, fuzzy computing, neurocomputing, neuro-vision systems, and neuro-control systems. Dr. Gupta was elected fellow of the Institute of Electrical and Electronics Engineers (IEEE) for his contributions to the theory of fuzzy sets and adaptive control systems and for the advancement of the diagnosis of cardiovascular disease. He was elected fellow of the International Society for Optical Engineering (SPIE) for his contributions to the field of neurocontrol and neuro-fuzzy systems. He was elected fellow of the International Fuzzy Systems Association (IFSA) for his contributions to fuzzy-neural systems. In 1991, Dr. Gupta was corecipient of the Institute of Electrical Engineering Kelvin Premium. In 1998, Dr. Gupta received the Kaufmann Prize Gold Medal for research in the field of fuzzy logic. He has been elected as a visiting professor and a special advisor in the area of high technology to the European Centre for Peace and Development (ECPD), University for Peace, which was established by the United Nations. Dr. Gupta received B.E. (Hons.) and M.E. degrees in electronics-communications engineering from the Birla Engineering College (now the Birla Institute of Technology & Science), Pilani, India, in 1961 and 1962, respectively. He received his Ph.D. degree from the University of Warwick, United Kingdom, in 1967 in adaptive control systems. In 1998, for his extensive contributions in neuro-control, neuro-vision, and fuzzy-neural systems, Dr. Gupta received an earned doctor of science (D.Sc.) degree from the University of Saskatchewan.

Noriyasu Homma received a BA, MA, and PhD in electrical and communication engineering from Tohoku University, Japan, in 1990, 1992, and 1995, respectively. From 1995 to 1998, he was a lecturer at the Tohoku University, Japan. He is currently an associate professor of the Cyberscience Center at the Tohoku University. From 2000 to 2001, he was a visiting professor at the Intelligent Systems Research Laboratory, University of Saskatchewan, Canada. His current research interests include neural networks, complex and chaotic systems, soft-computing, cognitive sciences, medical systems and brain sciences. He has published over 90 papers, and co-authored 1 book and 5 chapters in 5 research books in these fields. Currently, he is an Associate Editor of the Journal of Intelligent and Fuzzy Systems, and an Editorial Board Member of the International Journal of Engineering Business Management, and International Journal of Artificial Life and Robotics.

Sayyed Mohsen Hosseini received his B.Sc. degree in Mechanical Engineering from Islamic Azad University of Mashhad, Iran in 2004 and finished his M.Sc. in Biomedical Engineering at Amirkabir University of Technology (Tehran Polytechnic), Iran in 2007. He is a member of the National Foundation of Elites in Iran and he is the winner of *Invention, Innovation, Novelty and Scientific Hypothesis Award* of the 14th. Razi Medical Sciences Research Festival as the Young Researcher in Iran. In 2009, he joined to the Orthopaedic Biomechanics group of the Biomedical Engineering Department of Eindhoven University of Technology (TU/e), the Netherlands for doing his Ph.D.

Zeng-Guang Hou received the B.E. and M.E. degrees in electrical engineering from Yanshan University (formerly North-East Heavy Machinery Institute), Qinhuangdao, China, in 1991 and 1993, respectively, and the Ph.D. degree in electrical engineering from Beijing Institute of Technology, Beijing, China, in 1997. From May 1997 to June 1999, he was a Postdoctoral Research Fellow at the Laboratory of Systems and Control, Institute of Systems Science, Chinese Academy of Sciences, Beijing. He was a Research Assistant at the Hong Kong Polytechnic University, Hong Kong SAR, China, from May 2000 to January 2001. From July 1999 to May 2004, he was an Associate Professor at the Institute of Automation, Chinese Academy of Sciences, and has been a Full Professor since June 2004. From September 2003 to October 2004, he was a Visiting Professor at the Intelligent Systems Research Laboratory, College of Engineering, University of Saskatchewan, Saskatoon, SK, Canada. His current research interests include neural networks, optimization algorithms, robotics, and intelligent control systems. Currently, he is an Associate Editor of the IEEE Transactions on Neural Networks, and an Editorial Board Member of the International Journal of Intelligent Systems Technologies and Applications, Journal of Intelligent and Fuzzy Systems, and International Journal of Cognitive Informatics and Natural Intelligence.

Abir Jaafar Hussain is a full time Senior Lecturer at the School of Computer and Mathematical Sciences at Liverpool John Moores University, UK. Her main research interests are neural networks, signal prediction, telecommunication fraud detection and image processing. She completed her BSc degree at the Department of Electronic and Electrical Engineering at Salford University, UK. She then joined the control systems centre at the University of Manchester, UK (UMIST) to complete her MSc degree in Control and Information Technology. Then she pursued a PhD research project at the Control Systems Centre at UMIST. In November 2001 Dr. Abir Hussain joined the Distributed Multimedia Systems (DMS) at Liverpool John Moores University, UK as a full-time Senior Lecturer.

Minghu Jiang received the Ph.D. degree in Signal and Information Processing from Beijing Jiaotong University in 1998. From May 1998 till April 2000 he worked as a postdoctoral at the State Key Lab of Intelligent Technology & Systems, at Tsinghua University, Beijing, China. Then he became an associate professor and faculty member of Computer Science, Cognitive Science and Computational Linguistics at Tsinghua University, Beijing, China. From Dec. 2000 till Dec. 2001 he was a postdoctoral researcher in the Department of Electrical Engineering of the Katholieke Universiteit Leuven, Belgium. Currently, he is a professor of Tsinghua University, Beijing. He is the author or co-author of more than 120 published papers in journals and conference proceedings. His research interests include neural networks for signal processing, pattern recognition and artificial intelligence, natural language processing.

Yannis L. Karnavas was born in Volos, Hellas in 1969. He received the Diploma and the Ph.D. in Electrical & Computer Engineering, both from the Dept. of Electrical & Computer Engineering of Democritus University of Thrace, Xanthi, Hellas, in 1994 and 2002 respectively. Currently, he is with the Lab. of Electrical Machines and Installations, Dept. of Electrical Engineering, School of Technological Applications, Technological Educational Institution of Crete, where he is a full time Assistant Professor. He is also a Chartered Electrical Engineer and he carries out technical studies. His research interests mainly include operation and control of electric machines and power systems as well as applications of artificial intelligence techniques to them. He serves as an Associate Editor in 2 International Journals, as an Editorial Board Member in 3 International Journals, as an International Program Committee Member of 15 International Conferences, and also as a Member of 6 IASTED Technical Committees. He has served as a Conference Reviewer in more than 60 International Conferences. He is a member of IEEE, PES (Power Engineering Society), NNC (Neural Network Council), RAS (Robotics and Automation Society), TEE (Technical Chamber of Hellas), ΠΣΔΜΗΕ (National Board of Electrical and Mechanical Engineers), EETN (Greek Artificial Intelligence Society) and EΠY (Greek Computer Society).

Lewis L. Lewis, Fellow IEEE, Fellow IFAC, Fellow U.K. Institute of Measurement & Control, PE Texas, U.K. Chartered Engineer, is Distinguished Scholar Professor and Moncrief-O'Donnell Chair at University of Texas at Arlington's Automation & Robotics Research Institute. He obtained the Bachelor's Degree in Physics/EE and the MSEE at Rice University, the MS in Aeronautical Engineering from Univ. W. Florida, and the Ph.D. at Ga. Tech. He works in feedback control, intelligent systems, and sensor networks. He is author of 6 U.S. patents, 209 journal papers, 328 conference papers, 12 books, 41 chapters, and 11 journal special issues. He received the Fulbright Research Award, NSF Research Initiation Grant, ASEE *Terman Award*, and Int. Neural Network Soc. *Gabor Award* 2008. Received Outstanding Service Award from Dallas IEEE Section, selected as Engineer of the year by Ft. Worth IEEE Section. Listed in Ft. Worth Business Press Top 200 Leaders in Manufacturing. He was appointed to the NAE Committee on Space Station in 1995. He is an elected Guest Consulting Professor at both South China University of Technology and Shanghai Jiao Tong University. Founding Member of the Board of Governors of the Mediterranean Control Association. Helped win the IEEE Control Systems Society Best Chapter Award (as Founding Chairman of DFW Chapter), the National Sigma Xi Award for Outstanding Chapter (as President of UTA Chapter), and the US SBA Tibbets Award in 1996 (as Director of ARRI's SBIR Program).

Zhao Lu received his M.S. degree in the major of Control Theory and Engineering from Nankai University, Tianjin, China, in 2000, and his Ph.D. degree in Electrical Engineering from University of Houston, USA, in 2004. From 2004 to 2006, he has been working as a post-doctoral research fellow in the Department of Electrical and Computer Engineering at Wayne State University, Detroit, USA, and the Department of Naval Architecture and Marine Engineering at University of Michigan, Ann Arbor, USA, respectively. Since 2007, he has joined the faculty of the Department of Electrical Engineering at Tuskegee University, Tuskegee, USA. His research interests mainly include nonlinear control theory, machine learning, and pattern recognition.

Junichi Murata received the Master of Engineering and the Doctor of Engineering degrees in 1983 and 1986, respectively, from Kyushu University, Japan. He then became a Research Associate at Kyushu University, and now is an Associate Professor at Department of Electrical Engineering, Kyushu University. In the meantime, he stayed at the University of Reading, the United Kingdom as a Senior

Visiting Research Fellow. He has been working on artificial neural networks, reinforcement learning and multi-agent systems and their applications to modeling and control of engineering and social systems. His latest research interests include interactive multi-objective optimization as well. Dr. Murata is a member of IEEE, SICE, ISCIE and IEEJ.

Siamak Najarian has completed his Ph.D. in Biomedical Engineering at Oxford University, England and had a pos-doc position at the same university for one year. Prof. Najarian serves as the Full-Professor and Dean of Faculty of Biomedical Engineering at Amirkabir University of Technology (Tehran Polytechnic). His research interests are the applications of artificial tactile sensing (especially in robotic surgery) and design of artificial organs. He is the author and translator of 24 books in the field of biomedical engineering, 8 of which are written in English. Prof. Najarian has published more than 150 international journal and conference papers in the field of biomedical engineering.

Nazri Mohd Nawi received his B.S. degree in Computer Science from University of Science Malaysia (USM), Penang, Malaysia. His M.Sc. degree in computer science was received from University of Technology Malaysia (UTM), Skudai, Johor, Malaysia. He received his Ph.D degree in Mechanical Engineering department, Swansea University, Wales Swansea. He is currently a lecturer in Software Engineering Department at Universiti Tun Hussein Onn Malaysia (UTHM). His research interests are in optimisation, data mining techniques and neural networks.

João Pedro Neto has a university degree in Computer Science (1993) and a Master degree in Machine Learning (1995) at the New University of Lisbon. He achieved his Ph.D. in Neural Networks and Theory of Computation (2002) at the University of Lisbon, focusing in the connections between classical Theory of Computation and the field of Neural Computation to integrate symbolic and sub-symbolic computations into a homogeneous neural net architecture. He also investigates in the subject of Multiagent systems. He published a book about programming and algorithms (in Java), three books about recreational mathematics and abstract games and had several contributions with Portuguese national newspapers and magazines in the subject of the history of mathematics and ancient board games.

Vassilis P. Plagianakos was born in Athens, Greece, in 1973. He received the Bachelor's and Ph.D. degrees in Mathematics from the University of Patras, Greece, in 1996 and 2003, respectively. From 1996 to 2006, he had been a Research Assistant with the Computational Intelligence Lab, Department of Mathematics, and University of Patras and participated in several research projects funded by public and private organizations. From 1998 to 2005 he has worked in Greek industry as network and systems engineer. He has been a visiting Lecturer at three Greek Universities and Postdoctoral Fellow in the Department of Mathematics, University of Patras (2004-2006). He is currently an Assistant Professor at the Department of Computer Science and Biomedical Informatics, University of Central Greece, Greece (2008-). His research interests are in the areas of neural networks and machine learning, applications in pattern recognition, intelligent decision making, evolutionary and genetic algorithms, parallel and distributed computations, bioinformatics, clustering, intelligent optimization, and real-world problem solving. He is co-author of more than 20 journal publications and 60 conference papers. His published work has received more than 200 citations. Dr. Plagianakos is a Member of the IEEE Neural Networks Society, the ACM, and the University of Patras Artificial Intelligence Research Center (UPAIRC).

Luis J. Ricalde was born in 1975, in Merida, Yucatan, Mexico. He received the Mechanical Engineer Degree, from Instituto Tecnologico de Merida, Yucatan, Mexico in 1999, the MSEE major in Automatic Control and the PhD in Automatic Control from CINVESTAV-IPN (Advanced Studies and Research Center of the National Polytechnic Institute), Guadalajara, Mexico, in 2001 and 2005. He was a professor of the graduate program in Electronics and Mechatronics Engineering of the Universidad Autonoma de Guadalajara (UAG) Jalisco, Mexico, from 2005 to 2006. Since 2007, he has been with Universidad Autonoma de Yucatan (UADY), Merida, Mexico as Professor of Mechatronics Engineering graduate program. His research interest centers in neural network control, adaptive nonlinear control, constrained inputs nonlinear control and wind energy generation systems. He was granted with the Arturo Rosenblueth's Award in 2005 and is member of the Mexican National Research System (SNI-C). He has published several technical papers, and served as reviewer for different international journals and conferences.

Edgar N. Sanchez was born in 1949, in Sardinata, Colombia, South America. He obtained the BSEE, major in Power Systems, from Universidad Industrial de Santander (UIS), Bucaramanga, Colombia in 1971, the MSEE from CINVESTAV-IPN (Advanced Studies and Research Center of the National Polytechnic Institute), major in Automatic Control, Mexico City, Mexico, in 1974 and the Docteur Ingenieur degree in Automatic Control from Institut Nationale Polytechnique de Grenoble, France in 1980. In 1971, 1972, 1975 and 1976, he worked for different Electrical Engineering consulting companies in Bogota, Colombia. In 1974 he was professor of Electrical Engineering Department of UIS, Colombia. From January 1981 to November 1990, he worked as a researcher at the Electrical Research Institute, Cuernavaca, Mexico. He was a professor of the graduate program in Electrical Engineering of the Universidad Autonoma de Nuevo Leon (UANL), Monterrey, Mexico, from December 1990 to December 1996. Since January 1997, he has been with CINVESTAV-IPN, Guadalajara Campus, Mexico, as a Professor of Electrical Engineering graduate programs. His research interest center in Neural Networks and Fuzzy Logic as applied to Automatic Control systems. He has been advisor of 6 Ph. D. thesis and 33 M. Sc Thesis.

David R. Selviah studied Physics and Theoretical Physics at Trinity College, Cambridge University, UK specializing in mathematical modeling. After developing Surface Acoustic Wave (SAW) correlators and filters for real time pattern detection, recognition, and discrimination at Plessey, Caswell, and Oxford University, UK, he joined the Department of Electronic and Electrical Engineering, UCL in 1987. He has over 150 publications, patents, invited talks, and book chapters, in areas including real time hardware implementations of first and higher order (HONNs), pattern recognition, and discrimination. He is technical leader of £1.3 million EPSRC IeMRC Flagship project on Optical waveguide Printed Circuit Boards (OPCBs) with 3 universities and 8 companies, and of TSB Fast Track Digital Art Capture Project with 8 universities and art galleries. David is on the organizing committee of the IEEE Annual Workshop on Interconnections within High Speed Digital Systems and is co-chairman of the IEEE International Symposium on Photonic Packaging.

Janti Shawash achieved his Bachelors Honors degree in Electronic Engineering at the Princess Sumaya University for Technology in Amman, Jordan. He was ranked top (in the top 1%), in his final project "Image Processing Using Nonlinear Two-Dimensional Spatial Filters". Thereafter, he studied for an MSc in Technologies for Broadband Communications at Department of Electronic and Electrical Engineering, UCL and carried out a project on "Real Time Image Processing Techniques using Graphical Processing Units." He was awarded the MSc degree and began his PhD studies in October 2006, after being awarded an Overseas Research Scholarship and a UCL Graduate School Scholarship. He has already published a chapter on Higher Order Neural Networks and has programmed Artificial Higher Order Neural Networks on the most recent FPGAs for several years.

Leang-San Shieh received his B.S. degree from the National Taiwan University, Taiwan in 1958, and his M.S. and Ph.D. degrees from the University of Houston, Houston, Texas, in 1968 and 1970, respectively, all in electrical engineering. He is a Professor in the Department of Electrical and Computer Engineering and the Director of the Computer and Systems Engineering. He was the recipient of more than 10 College Outstanding Teacher Awards, the 1973 and 1997 College Teaching Excellence Awards, the 1988 College Senior Faculty Research Excellence Award, the 2003-2004 Fluor Daniel Faculty Excellence Award, the highest award given in the College, and the 2009 College of Engineering Career Teaching Award, from the Cullen College of Engineering, University of Houston. In addition, he was the recipient of the 1976 University Teaching Excellence Award and the 2001-2002 El Paso Faculty Achievement Award in Teaching and Scholarship from the University of Houston.

Ashu M. G. Solo is an electrical and computer engineer, mathematician, progressive political writer, and entrepreneur. His primary research interests are in math and intelligent systems theory and applications as well as public policy. Solo has over 150 publications in these and other fields. He co-developed some of the best published methods for maintaining power flow in and multiobjective optimization of radial power distribution system operations using intelligent systems. He has served on 98 international program committees for 94 research conferences and 4 research multiconferences. Solo has won a Distinguished Service Award and two Achievement Awards from research conferences. Solo is the principal of Maverick Technologies America Inc. He previously worked in nine different research and development labs in universities and industry. Solo served honorably as an infantry officer and platoon commander understudy in the Cdn. Army Reserve.

Gangbing Song is the founding Director of the Smart Materials and Structures Laboratory and a Professor of Mechanical Engineering at the University of Houston. Dr. Song is a recipient of the NSF CAREER grant in 2001. Dr. Song received his Ph.D. and MS degrees from the Department of Mechanical Engineering at Columbia University in the City of New York in 1995 and 1991, respectively. Dr. Song received his B.S. degree in 1989 from Zhejing University, P.R.China. He has expertise in smart materials and structures, structural vibration control, and structural health monitoring and damage detection. He has developed two new courses in smart materials and published more than 190 papers, including 72 peer reviewed journal articles. Dr. Song is also a co-inventor of a US patent. He has received research funding in smart materials and related research from NSF, NASA, OSGC (Ohio Space Grant Consortium), OAI (Ohio Aerospace Institute), ODoT (Ohio Department of Transportation), TSGC (Texas Space Grant Consortium), UTMB (University of Texas Medical Branch), HP, OptiSolar, and Cameron.

Kamesh Subbarao, Assistant Professor at University of Texas at Arlington's Mechanical and Aerospace Engineering department. He obtained the Bachelor's and Masters' degrees in Aerospace Engineering from the Indian Institute of Technology, Kanpur and the Indian Institute of Science, Bangalore respectively. He got his PhD at Texas A & M, also in Aerospace Engineering. He was employed at the Defense R & D Labs, Hyderabad and the Aeronautical Development Agency, Bangalore after his MS. After his PhD, he worked at The MathWorks Inc., Natick, MA as applications developer for the Control & System Identification toolboxes group. He works in feedback control, intelligent systems, distributed parameter systems, optimization, astrodynamics and sensor networks. He is author of several journal and conference papers. He is the university representative for the Texas Space Grants Consortium and is a member of AIAA's Guidance, Navigation and Control Technical Committee.

Dimitrios C. Theodoridis, was born in Solingen (Germany) in 1974. He received a diploma in Physics and a M.Sc. degree in Electrical Physics (Radioelectrology) from the Aristotle University of Thessaloniki (AUTH) in 1997 and 1999 respectively. He is currently a Ph.D. candidate at the Democritus University of Thrace (DUTH). Since 2005 he serves as a lecturer in the Department of Industrial Informatics in the Technological Educational Institute of Kavala. His main research interests lay in the field of fuzzy neural networks, applications to electric drive systems, fuzzy logic control, adaptive control, neural networks, intelligent control and nonlinear control systems.

Diana A. Urrego, was born in Bogota, Colombia in 1979. She obtained her BSEE (major in Control Systems) from National University of Colombia in 2006, and MSEE (major in Control Systems) from CINVESTAV, Guadalajara Campus, Mexico in 2008. She is a Ph D student at CINVESTAV, Guadalajara campus. She has published papers in different international conferences.

Michael N. Vrahatis received his PhD in Computational Mathematics (1982) from the University of Patras, Greece. His work includes topological degree theory, systems of nonlinear equations, numerical and intelligent optimisation, data mining and unsupervised clustering as well as computational and swarm intelligence. He is a Professor of Computational Mathematics in the University of Patras, since 2000 and serves as Director of the Computational Intelligence Laboratory of the same Department (since 2004). He has participated in the organisation of over 60 conferences serving at several positions, and participated in over 190 conferences, congresses and advanced schools as a speaker (participant as well as invited) or observer. Additionally, he is the (co-)author of over 300 publications that have been cited by researchers over 3350 times (co-authors citations excluded). He is/was a member of the editorial board of the journals "Annals of Mathematics, Computing & Teleinformatics (since 2003)", "International Journal of Computational Intelligence (2004-2005)", "International Journal of Signal Processing (2004-2005)", "Journal of Computational and Applied Mathematics (Special Issue Editor (2008))", "The Open Medical Informatics Journal (since 2008)", "International Journal of Bio-Inspired Computation (IJBIC) (since 2008)", "Applied Numerical Mathematics (Special Issue Editor (2009))", "International Journal on Information Technologies and Security (since 2009)".

Lin Wang received Bachelor & Master degrees in Dept of Biology, Shandong Teacher University, China, 1986 and 1989, respectively. 1989- 1995 worked as a lecturer in Dept of Biochemistry, Shandong Education University, China; 1995-1998, Researcher in histology & embryology, Medicine College, Shandong University, China; 1998-2000 worked as a lecturer of bio-chemistry, School of Life Science, Tsinghua University, Beijing, China; 2001-2004, Ph.D AG Molekularbiologie, Klinik für Innere Medizin II, Friedrich-Schiller-Universität Jena, Germany. Currently she is an associate professor at School of Electronics & Engineering, Beijing University of Post and Telecommunication, Beijing; her research interests include biomedicine, biotechnology and bioinformatics. About 50 published papers in international journals and conferences.

Shuxiang Xu won from the Australian government a scholarship (Overseas Postdraguate Research Award) to research a PhD at the University of Western Sydney, Sydney, Australia in 1996, and was awarded a PhD in Computing by this university in 2000. He received a M.Sc in Applied Mathematics and a B.Sc. in Mathematics in 1989 and1996, respectively, from the University of Electronic Science and Technology of China, Chengdu, China. His current interests include the theory and applications of Artificial Neural Networks, Genetic Algorithms, Data Mining, and Pattern Recognition. He is currently a lecturer at the School of Computing, University of Tasmania, Tasmania, Australia.

Wen Yu received the B.S. degree in electrical engineering from Tsinghua University, Beijing, China in 1990 and the M.S. and Ph.D. degrees, both in Electrical Engineering, from Northeastern University, Shenyang, China, in 1992 and 1995, respectively. From 1995 to 1996, he served as a Lecturer at the Department of Automatic Control, Northeastern University. In 1996, he joined CINVESTAV-IPN, México, where he is currently a Professor at the Departamento de Control Automático. He also held a research position with the Instituto Mexicano del Petróleo, from December 2002 to November 2003. Since October 2006, he has been a senior visiting research fellow at Queen's University Belfast. He also held a visiting professorship at Northeastern. He serves as an Associate Editor of Neurocomputing and the International Journal of Modelling, Identification and Control. He is a member of the Mexican Academy of Science.

Index